SOCIAL PSYCHOLOGY

THIRD EDITION

ELLIOT ARONSON
UNIVERSITY OF CALIFORNIA, SANTA CRUZ

TIMOTHY D. WILSON
UNIVERSITY OF VIRGINIA

ROBIN M. AKERT
WELLESLEY COLLEGE

An imprint of Addison Wesley Longman, Inc.

New York • Reading, Massachusetts • Menlo Park, California
Harlow, England • Don Mills, Ontario • Sydney
Mexico City • Madrid • Amsterdam

Acquisitions Editor: Eric Stano
Development Editor: Michael Kimball
Development Manager: Lisa Pinto
Marketing Manager: Anne Wise
Supplements Editor: Cyndy Taylor
Project Coordination, Text Design, Art Studio, and Electronic Page Makeup:
  Thompson Steele Production Services, Inc.
Cover Design Manager: Nancy Danahy
Cover Designer: Joel Zimmerman
Cover Illustration: Original art © by Diana Org/SuperStock, Inc.; derivative by
  Joel Zimmerman
Full Service Production Manager: Eric Jorgensen
Photo Researcher: Julie Tesser
Print Buyer: Denise Sandler
Printer and Binder: World Color
Cover Printer: The Lehigh Press, Inc.

Library of Congress Cataloging-in-Publication Data

Aronson, Elliot.
  Social Psychology / Elliot Aronson, Timothy D. Wilson, Robin M. Akert.--3rd ed.
    p.   cm.
  Includes bibliographical references and indexes.
  ISBN 0-321-02435-4 (alk. paper)
  1. Social psychology.   I. Wilson, Timothy D.   II. Akert, Robin M.
  III. Title.
  HM251.A794   1998
  302--dc21   98-20751
                                                                 CIP

Please visit our website at http://longman.awl.com

ISBN 0-321-02435-4

12345678910-WCT-01009998

To my family, Vera, Hal, Neal, Julie, and Joshua Aronson

—E.A.

To my family, Deirdre Smith, Christopher and Leigh Wilson

—T.D.W.

To my mentor, colleague, and friend, Dane Archer

—R.M.A.

BRIEF CONTENTS

Detailed Contents

Chapter 1 Introduction to Social Psychology 2

Chapter 2 Methodology: How Social Psychologists Do Research 30

CHAPTER 3   SOCIAL COGNITION: HOW WE THINK ABOUT THE SOCIAL WORLD 64

CHAPTER 4   SOCIAL PERCEPTION: HOW WE COME TO UNDERSTAND OTHER PEOPLE 104

◀ CHAPTER 5   SELF-KNOWLEDGE: HOW WE COME TO UNDERSTAND OURSELVES 148

Chapter 6 Self-Justification and the Need to Maintain Self-Esteem 188

CHAPTER 7   ATTITUDES AND ATTITUDE CHANGE: INFLUENCING THOUGHTS AND FEELINGS 234

CHAPTER 8   CONFORMITY: INFLUENCING BEHAVIOR 278

Chapter 9   Group Processes: Influence in Social Groups 326

Chapter 10   Interpersonal Attraction: From First Impressions to Close Relationships 370

CHAPTER 11   PROSOCIAL BEHAVIOR: WHY DO PEOPLE HELP? 416

CHAPTER 12   AGGRESSION: WHY WE HURT OTHER PEOPLE 454

Chapter 13   Prejudice: Causes and Cures 494

SOCIAL PSYCHOLOGY IN ACTION 1
SOCIAL PSYCHOLOGY AND HEALTH 546

SOCIAL PSYCHOLOGY IN ACTION 2
SOCIAL PSYCHOLOGY AND THE ENVIRONMENT 578

PREFACE

When we began writing this book, our one, overriding goal was to capture the excitement of social psychology. We have been pleased to hear, in many kind letters and E-mail messages from professors and students, that we succeeded. One of our favorites was from a student who said that the book was so interesting that she always saved it for last, to reward herself for finishing her other work. With that one student, at least, we succeeded in making our book an enjoyable, fascinating story, not a dry report of facts and figures.

There is always room for improvement, however, and our goal in this, the third edition, is to make the field of social psychology an even better read. When we teach the course, there is nothing more gratifying than seeing the sleepy students in the back row sit up with interest and say, "Wow, I didn't know that! Now *that's* interesting." We hope that students who read our book will have that very same reaction.

Social psychology comes alive for students when they understand the whole context of the field: how theories inspire research, why research is performed as it is, how further research triggers yet new avenues of study. We are confident that we have conveyed our own fascination with the research process in a down-to-earth, meaningful way and have presented the results of the scientific process in terms of the everyday experience of the reader. However, we did not want to "water down" our presentation of the field. In a world where human behavior can be endlessly surprising and where research results can be quite counterintuitive, it is important to prepare students by providing a firm foundation on which to build their understanding of this challenging discipline. Here, in more detail, is how we present a rigorous, scientific approach to social psychology in a way that engages and fascinates most students.

A Storytelling Approach

Social psychology is full of good stories, such as how the Kitty Genovese murder prompted research on bystander intervention, how the Holocaust inspired investigations into obedience to authority, and how

reactions to the marriage of the Crown Prince of Japan to Masako Owada, a career diplomat, illustrates cultural differences in the self-concept. By placing research in a real-world context, we make the material more familiar, understandable, and memorable.

Opening Vignettes

Each chapter begins with a real-life vignette that epitomizes the concepts to come. We refer to this event at several points in the chapter to illustrate to students the relevance of the material they are learning. Examples of the opening vignettes include descriptions of a national program called "Earning for Learning," in which children are paid $2 for every book they read (Chapter 5, *Self-Understanding*); a television network called Channel One that broadcasts news—and commercials—in many schools (Chapter 7, *Attitudes and Attitude Change*); the crash of Air Florida Flight 90 in Washington D.C., in which survivors were rescued by complete strangers (Chapter 11, *Prosocial Behavior*); and a real-life murder trial in which an innocent man was sentenced to death because of faulty eyewitness testimony (Social Psychology in Action 3: *Social Psychology and the Law*). To illustrate more specifically the way in which the opening vignettes are tied to social psychological principles, here are a couple of examples in more detail:

- In 1994, after ending an office romance, a woman threw a bag of her lover's letters, cards, and poems into a dumpster. A homeless man, searching through the dumpster for something to sell, stopped to read the letters and became quite curious as to how two people who had been so in love could now be apart. He found the phone number of the woman's lover on a piece of stationery and decided to give him a call and find out. "I would have called you sooner," he told the former boyfriend, "but this was the first quarter I was given today." (DeMarco, 1994). What would possess a man who was down on his luck—no home, no money, no food—to spend his only quarter on a phone call to a complete stranger? As we say at the beginning of Chapter 4 on *Social Perception*, it was an endless fascination that we all share about why people do what they do, which leads nicely into a discussion of research on social perception and attribution.

- Chapter 6 on *Self-Justification and the Need to Maintain Self-Esteem* begins with an intriguing tale from the recent mass suicide of the Heaven's Gate cult in California. The members of this cult believed that in the wake of the Hale-Bopp comet there was a large spaceship that would carry them off to a new incarnation. Several weeks before the mass suicide, a few members of the cult purchased a high-powered telescope so that they could glimpse the spaceship that was to be their salvation. They had no trouble finding the comet, but were disappointed when they did not see a spaceship in its wake. How did they deal with the dissonance this must have caused? We answer this question with a discussion of dissonance theory and other modern approaches to self-esteem maintenance. (In case you are wondering about what happened, needless to say, the members of the cult did not reduce dissonance by abandoning their beliefs about existence of the spaceship; they had invested too much time, energy and commitment for that. Rather, they assumed that the telescope must be defective and demanded their money back.)

"Mini" Stories in Each Chapter

Our storytelling approach is not limited to these opening vignettes. There are several "mini" stories woven into each chapter that illustrate specific concepts and make the material come alive. They each follow a similar format: First, we describe an example of a real-life phenomenon that is designed to pique students' interest. These stories are taken from current events, literature, and our own lives. Second, we describe an experiment that attempts to explain the phenomenon. This experiment is typically described in some detail, because we believe that students should learn not only the major theories in social psychology, but also understand and appreciate the methods used to test those theories. We often invite the students to pretend that they were participants in the experiment, to give them a better feel for what it was like and what it was found. Here are a few examples of our "mini" stories (by thumbing through the book, you will come across many others):

- In Chapter 4 on *Social Perception*, we introduce the concept of the fundamental attribution error by discussing the public reaction to the death of Diana, Princess of Wales. Immediately after Diana's death, Queen Elizabeth was openly and strongly criticized by the British people and the media for her lack of grief and for remaining in Scotland at Balmoral Castle during the week preceding the funeral. The public and the media made a dispositional attribution about the Queen's behavior, namely that she was uncaring and unmoved about Diana's death. The Queen offered a different explanation, namely that staying in seclusion in Scotland was the best thing for her grieving grandsons.

- In Chapter 6 on *Self-Justification and the Need to Maintain Self-Esteem* we discuss a phenomenon called the Ben Franklin Effect. Franklin was disturbed by the animosity of a fellow politician in the Pennsylvania state legislature and was determined to win him over. Rather than showering him with favors and affection, Franklin did quite the opposite: He asked the legislator to do favors for him. Those of you familiar with Jecker and Landy's (1969) classic dissonance study will see the wisdom in Franklin's approach: We often come to like the people we do favors for as a way of reducing dissonance. We use Ben Franklin's maneuver as an introduction to the Jecker and Landy study, as well as to modern studies by Leippe and Eisenstadt and Gail Williamson and her colleagues.

- In Chapter 8 on *Conformity*, we discuss normative social influence and the effect that it has had recently in Japanese public schools. "Bullying," in which a class (or even the whole student body) alternates between harassing and shunning one student because he or she is different in some way, has become a problem. The result of this treatment in a highly cohesive, group-oriented culture is profound: Twelve teenage victims of bullying killed themselves in one year.

- In Chapter 12 on *Aggression*, we present an interesting historical observation: For hundreds of years, the Iroquois Indians lived a peaceful existence, rarely, if ever, engaging in aggressive behavior. All of this changed in the seventeenth century, when the newly arrived Europeans brought the Iroquois into direct competition with their neighbors, the Hurons. Within a short time, the Iroquois developed into fierce warriors. What does this say about the causes of aggression and its roots in culture? This story leads into a discussion of research by Richard Nisbett and Dov Cohen and their colleagues on the cultural and economic roots of violence.

Social Psychological Methods: Another Good Story

It might seem that a storytelling approach would obscure the scientific basis of social psychology. Quite to the contrary, we believe that part of what makes the story so interesting is explaining to students how to test hypotheses scientifically. In recent years, the trend has been for textbooks to include only short sections on research methodology and to provide only brief descriptions of the findings of individual studies. In this book, we integrate the science and methodology of the field into our story, as follows:

Separate Chapter on Methodology

Unlike virtually all other texts, we devote an entire chapter to methodology (Chapter 2). "But wait," you might say, "How can you maintain students' interest and attention with an entire chapter on such dry material?" The answer is by integrating this material into our storytelling approach. Even the "dry" topic of methodology can come alive by telling it like a story. We begin the chapter on methodology with examples of two pressing, real-world problems related to violence and aggression: Does pornography promote violence against women? Why don't bystanders intervene more to help victims of violence? We then use actual research studies on these questions to illustrate the three major scientific methods (observational research, correlational research, and experimental research). Rather than a dry, recitation of methodological principles, the scientific method unfolds like a story with a "hook" (What are the causes of real-world aggression and apathy toward violence?) and a moral (such interesting, real-world questions can be addressed scientifically). Reactions to this chapter in the previous editions of our book have been very positive.

Detailed Descriptions of Individual Studies

We describe many, prototypical studies in more detail than most texts. We discuss how a study was set up, what the research participants perceived and did, how the research design derives from theoretical issues, and how the findings offer support for the initial hypotheses. As we mentioned earlier, we often ask the reader to pretend that he or she was a participant, in order to understand the study from the participants' point of view. Whenever pertinent, we've also included anecdotal information about how a study was done or came to be; these brief stories allow the reader to see the hitherto hidden world of creating research. See, for example, the description of Aronson's jigsaw puzzle technique in Chapter 13 (pp. 540–544).

Emphasis on Both Classic and Modern Research

As you will see from flipping through the book, we include a large number of data figures detailing the results of individual experiments. The field of social psychology is expanding rapidly and exciting new work is being done in all subareas of the discipline. In the third edition, we have added a great deal of new material, describing dozens of major studies done within the past few years. All told, we have added almost 1,000 new references, most from the 1990s. Thus, the book includes a thorough coverage of up-to-date, cutting-edge research.

In emphasizing what is new, many texts have a tendency to ignore what is old. We have striven to strike a balance between current, up-to-date research findings and classic research in social psychology. Some older studies deserve their status as classics (e.g., early work in dissonance, conformity, and attribution) and are important cornerstones of the discipline. We showcase many of the classics as well as covering cutting-edge, modern research. For example, unlike several current texts, we present detailed descriptions of the Schachter and Singer (1962) study on misattribution of emotion (Chapter 5), the Festinger and Carlsmith (1959) dissonance study (Chapter 6), and the Asch (1956) conformity studies (Chapter 8). To illustrate to students how research on the classics has been updated, we follow a discussion of the classics with modern approaches to these same topics, such as research on culture, self, and emotion (e.g., Fiske, Kitayama, Markus, & Nisbett, 1998, in Chapter 5); recent research on self-esteem maintenance in Chapter 6 (e.g., Steele's self-affirmation theory and Higgins's self-discrepancy theory), as well as recent research on the process of dissonance reduction in different cultures (e.g., Sakai, 1998; Stone,

Wiegand, Cooper, & Aronson, 1997; Viswesvaran & Deshpande, 1996); and research on minority influence in Chapter 8 (e.g., Wood, Lundgren, Ouellette, Busceme, & Blackstone, 1994). This way, students see the continuity and depth of the field, rather than viewing it only as a mass of studies published in the past few years.

Significant Changes to the Third Edition

To illustrate more concretely how the third edition has been updated, here is a sampling of new research that is covered:

- Chapter 2, *Methodology: How Social Psychologists Do Research:* More than 40 new references have been added to this chapter, including updated information on the effects of pornography on sexual aggression. The essential story line has remained unchanged, but the examples and references have been substantially updated.

- Chapter 3, *Social Cognition: How We Think about the Social World:* This chapter includes more than 75 new references to research on social cognition, most of them from the past few years. A number of new studies are showcased, such as Victoria Medvec, Scott Madey, and Tom Gilovich's (1995) study of counterfactual reasoning in Olympic athletes. The opening vignette has been replaced and parts of the chapter have been reorganized, such as the section on automatic versus controlled thinking.

- Chapter 4, *Social Perception: How We Come to Understand Other People:* This chapter includes over 90 new references, almost all from the 1990s. We have added new cultural research on nonverbal communication and attributional style and have expanded the discussion of research on two-step attributional processing and self-serving attribution.

- Chapter 5, *Self-Knowledge: How We Come to Understand Ourselves:* We have added more than 90 new references to this chapter, most from the past few years. We have added new sections on the "Function of the Self" and "Gender Differences in the Definition of Self." Other sections have been updated. For example, a recent controversy has erupted over the question of whether rewards can undermine intrinsic motivation. Though it would be tedious for stu-

dents to present all of the detailed issues involved in this debate, we do represent the recent views of the leading researchers in this area, including Mark Lepper, Ed Deci, and Judy Harackiewicz.

- Chapter 6, *Self-Justification and the Need to Maintain Self-Esteem:* Cognitive dissonance theory is enjoying a comeback in social psychology; increasingly, researchers are returning to basic questions about the nature of dissonance and how it is reduced. In this chapter we cover the most recent research on this question, including studies by J. Aronson, Blanton, and Cooper (1995); Beauvois and Rainis (1993); Elliot and Devine (1994); Fried and E. Aronson (1995); Gibbons, Eggleston, and Benthin (1997); Leippe and Eisenstadt (1997); Sakai (1998); and Stone, Weigand, Cooper, and E. Aronson (1997). The general issue of self-esteem maintenance is also a very active area of research, and this chapter includes up-to-date information on Higgin's self-discrepancy theory, Gollwitzer and Wicklund's self-completion theory, Tesser's self-evaluation maintenance theory, Steele's self-affirmation theory, and Swann's self-verification theory.

- Chapter 7, *Attitudes and Attitude Change: Influencing Thoughts and Feelings:* We include over 50 new references in this chapter to up-to-date, cutting-edge studies on attitudes. For example, we discuss Tesser's (1993) work on the heritability of attitudes and recent work on the effectiveness of advertising, including subliminal advertising (e.g., Pratkanis, Eskenazi, & Greenwald, 1994; Trappey, 1996). We include an updated account of Ajzen's theory of planned behavior (Ajzen, 1996).

- Chapter 8, *Conformity: Influencing Behavior:* This chapter includes over 90 new references. There is expanded coverage of a number of topics, such as normative social influence in everyday life (especially as it affects women's body image) and social impact theory (e.g., how it explains the likelihood that gay men and heterosexual college students will refrain from risky, AIDS-related sexual behavior).

- Chapter 9, *Group Processes: Influence in Social Groups:* We have included over 50 new references in this chapter, most of them from the past few years. Recent work by the leaders in the area of groups is discussed, such as Jim Davis, Norb Kerr, John Levine, and Richard Moreland, and

Garold Stasser. We have added a new section on social dilemmas with a discussion of recent research in this area.

- Chapter 10, *Interpersonal Attraction: From First Impressions to Close Relationships:* This chapter has been substantially revised with the addition of over 120 new references. In addition to covering the classic causes of attraction, such as similarity and propinquity, there is an expanded coverage of new approaches to close relationships, such as relationship dialectics. In addition, there is expanded coverage of research on the determinants of people's perceptions of beauty in the human face (e.g., Langlois & Roggman, 1994), cultural stereotypes of beauty, and cultural definitions of love.

- Chapter 11, *Prosocial Behavior: Why Do People Help?:* We have updated this chapter considerably and added a new section on culture and prosocial behavior. We present a thorough, balanced description of the evolutionary approach to prosocial behavior and an updated account of the question of whether there is any such thing as "pure" empathy.

- Chapter 12, *Aggression: Why We Hurt Other People:* We have made a great many changes in this chapter. In addition to a thorough updating of the existing research on causes and cures of aggression, we have expanded our discussion to include some of the recent work on teaching inner city kids social and problem-solving skills as a way of diminishing aggressive behavior (e.g., Ester, 1995). We have also expanded our discussion of empathy as a way of reducing aggression and have included some recent research on this topic coming from European and Japanese studies. We have also included some recent research on interventions aimed at trying to reduce bullying among school children in Europe (e.g., Olweus, 1997).

- Chapter 13, *Prejudice: Causes and Cures:* Is there any truth to the stereotype that women are more nurturant than men or is it simply a stereotype? Recent work by Janet Swim, Alice Eagly, and others sheds considerable light on this issue. Likewise, in discussing these apparent gender differences (for example that women appear to be more nurturant than men and that men appear to be more assertive than women), we highlighted the ongoing debate between those who feel that such apparent differences are cultural

(Deaux & LaFrance, 1998) and those who feel there may be an evolutionary basis for these differences (Buss, 1995, 1996; Buss & Kenrick, 1998; Buss & Schmitt, 1993). We have also added to our discussion of the minimal group phenomenon as well as to the nature of stereotypes. In addition, we have revisited the issue of whether or not there are genetic differences in intelligence as a function of race (*The Bell Curve,* Herrnstein & Murray, 1995), in the light of recent research by Claude Steele and his colleagues on stereotype threat. We have also updated our discussion of cures for prejudice (e.g., Aronson & Patnoe, 1996).

- *Social Psychology in Action 1: Health:* We have expanded and revised this applied unit considerably. There are new sections on self-efficacy and the effects of framing health messages in various ways. The sections on stress and social support have been expanded and updated. All told, more than 50 new references to recent work have been added.

- *Social Psychology in Action 2: The Environment:* We have replaced the opening vignette in this applied unit and included a new section on how to get people to recycle. Recent research on energy conservation is also showcased. As in all of the chapters, many new references are included, most from the 1990s.

- *Social Psychology in Action 3: The Law:* We have updated and expanded this applied unit considerably. The chapter now has a major new heading entitled "Why Do People Obey the Law?" with sections on whether severe penalties deter crimes (including the death penalty) and on procedural justice. We also include new sections on whether eyewitness memory can be improved and on the effects of jury size. Other sections have been revised and updated. More than 50 new references are included.

Integrated Coverage of Culture and Gender

To understand behavior in a social context, we must consider such influences as culture and gender. Rather than adding a chapter on these important topics, we discuss them in every chapter, as they apply to the topic at hand. In many places, we discuss the wonderful diversity of humankind, by presenting research on the differences between people of different cultures, races, or genders. We also discuss the commonalties people share, by illustrating the applicability of many phenomena across cultures and genders. Here are examples of our coverage of research on culture and gender:

- Chapter 1, *Introduction:* The issue of universality versus the cultural relativity of social psychological principles is introduced.
- Chapter 2, *Methodology:* The issue of how to generalize the results of studies across different types of people is discussed, in the section on external validity. In addition, we include a section on cross-cultural research methods.
- Chapter 3, *Social Cognition:* The opening vignette to this chapter concerns gender differences and achievement in middle-school and high school, raising the question of whether these differences are due to the expectations about gender held by teachers and parents. The vignette serves as an introduction to classic and modern research on expectation effects. There is also a section on the cultural determinants of schemas that discusses classic work by Bartlett.
- Chapter 4, *Social Perception:* This chapter includes a good deal of material on culture and gender, including a discussion of the universality of facial expressions of emotion; cultural differences in other channels of nonverbal communication, such as eye contact, gaze, and personal space; gender differences in nonverbal communication (including a discussion of Eagly's social role theory); cultural variation in implicit personality theories; and cultural differences in attribution processes.
- Chapter 5, *Self-Knowledge:* This chapter includes a major section on cultural differences in the definition of self that discusses research by Markus, Kitayama, Triandis, and others. There is a new section on gender differences in the definition of the self, discussing research by Cross and Madson (1997) and Deaux and LaFrance (1997). We also discuss cultural differences in impression management.
- Chapter 6, *Self-Justification:* This chapter includes a new section on cultural differences in dissonance and dissonance reduction that discusses recent research on dissonance in non-Western cultures.
- Chapter 7, *Attitudes and Attitude Change:* This chapter includes a section on culture and the basis

of attitudes, including the discussion of an experiment by Han and Shavitt (1994) that examined the effectiveness of different kinds of advertisements in Korea and the United States. In the context of a discussion of the effects of advertising, we discuss the way in which the media can transmit cultural stereotypes about race and gender.

- Chapter 8, *Conformity:* This chapter includes a discussion of the role of normative social influence in creating and maintaining cultural standards of beauty. We also discuss gender and cultural differences in conformity and a recent meta-analysis by Bond and Smith (1996) comparing conformity on the Asch line task in 17 countries.
- Chapter 9, *Group Processes:* We discuss research on gender and culture at several points in this chapter, including gender and cultural differences in social loafing, gender differences in leadership styles, and Brown's culture-value theory of group polarization. In addition, we discuss social roles and gender and include a student exercise in which students are asked to deliberately violate a gender role and keep a journal of people's responses to them.
- Chapter 10, *Interpersonal Attraction:* The role of culture comes up at several points in this chapter, including sections on cultural standards of beauty, cultural differences in the "what is beautiful is good" stereotype (Wheeler & Kim, 1997), and cultural differences in close relationships. We also discuss gender differences in the effects of physical attractiveness on liking and in reactions to the dissolution of relationships.
- Chapter 11, *Prosocial Behavior:* In this chapter we include a section on gender differences in prosocial behavior, including a discussion of meta-analyses by Eagly and Crowley (1986) and more recent work by McGuire (1994). We also include a new section on cultural differences in prosocial behavior.
- Chapter 12, *Aggression:* There is a major section in this chapter on cultural differences in aggression, including a discussion of recent research by Richard Nisbett and Dov Cohen, and of differences in homicide rates in different countries. We also discuss research on gender differences in aggression and the effects of violent pornography on violence against women.
- Chapter 13, *Prejudice:* An integral part of any discussion of prejudice is sex role stereotyping.

We have expanded our discussion of gender stereotypes, including a discussion of work by Alice Eagly, Kay Deaux, and Janet Swim. Issues about ingroups and outgroups and ways of reducing prejudice, are also an integral part of this chapter.

- *Social Psychology in Action* units on Health, the Environment, and Law: These chapters include numerous discussions relevant to culture and gender, such as a discussion of research on stereotype threat by Claude Steele and his colleagues, including studies on achievement in minority groups and men versus women. We also include a discussion of research on cultural differences in social support and in the Type A personality, a new discussion of the relationship between racism and stress, and a discussion of cultural differences in how density and crowding are perceived.

The Evolutionary Approach

In recent years, social psychologists have become increasingly interested in an evolutionary perspective on many aspects of social behavior. Once again, our approach is to integrate this perspective into those parts of chapters where it is relevant, rather than devoting a separate chapter to this topic. We present what we believe is a balanced approach, discussing evolutionary psychology as well as alternatives to it. Here are examples of places in which we discuss the evolutionary approach:

- Chapter 4, *Social Perception:* We discuss the question of whether some facial expressions are universal, including Darwin's view that they are.
- Chapter 10, *Interpersonal Attraction:* We present the evolutionary perspective on gender differences in romantic attraction and on why people fall in love.
- Chapter 11, *Prosocial Behavior:* Evolutionary psychology is presented as one of the major theories of why humans engage in prosocial behavior. We present evidence for and against this perspective and contrast it to other approaches, such as social exchange theory.
- Chapter 12, *Aggression:* We include a section on whether aggression is inborn or learned, including a discussion of an evolutionary explanation of aggressive behavior.

- Chapter 13, *Prejudice:* We have included a new discussion of research by David Buss on gender differences in nurturance.

Social Psychology: The Applied Side

One of the best ways to capture students' interest is to point out the real-world significance of the material they are studying. From the vignette that opens each chapter and runs throughout it to the discussions of historical events, current affairs, and our own lives that are embedded in the story line, the narrative is highlighted by real, familiar examples. Applications are an integral part of social psychology, however, and deserve their own treatment. In addition to an integrated coverage of applied topics in the body of the text, we include additional coverage in two ways.

Try It! Student Exercises

A new feature in the third edition is a series of Try It! exercises in which students are invited to apply the concepts they are learning to their everyday life. There are three such exercises in each chapter. They include detailed instructions about how to attempt to replicate actual social psychological experiments, such as Milgram's (1963) lost letter technique in Chapter 11, and Reno and colleagues' (1993) study on norms and littering in the Social Psychology in Action: *The Environment* unit. Other Try It! exercises reproduce self report scales and invite the students to fill them out to see where they stand on these measures. Examples include the Singelis's (1994) measure of people's interdependent and independent views of themselves in Chapter 5, and the Need for Cognition Scale in Chapter 7. Still others are quizzes that illustrate social psychological concepts, such as a Reasoning Quiz in Chapter 3 that illustrates judgmental heuristics, or demonstrations that explain how to use a particular concept in a student's everyday life, such as an exercise in Chapter 9 that instructs students to violate a sex role norm and observe the consequences. The format of, and the time frame required for, each of these exercises varies. You might want to flip through the book to look at other examples in more detail.

Try It! exercises are not only in the text itself, but they are built into the web site as well. Those concepts that have a related Try It! exercise on the web site are highlighted in the text with an icon 🐾. The web site also includes newspaper clips on current events that are relevant to social psychological concepts, practice tests for each chapter of the book, downloadable PowerPoint slides, and links to other sites. You can use Try It! exercises as class activities or as homework.

We believe that the Try It! exercises will generate a lot of interest in students and will make social psychological concepts more memorable and engaging.

Social Psychology in Action Units

You will note from the Table of Contents that there are three chapters devoted to applied topics in social psychology: One on health, one on the environment, and one on law. Each has the subtitle of *Social Psychology in Action.* You might wonder why these chapters have a different name and numbering system than the other chapters. The reason is that they are designed to be free-floating units that can be assigned at virtually any point in the text. Although we do occasionally refer to earlier chapters in these units, they are designed to be independent units that could fit into many different points of a course in social psychology.

In talking with many professors who teach social psychology, we have been struck by how differently they present applied material. Some prefer to assign these chapters at the end of the course, after they have covered the major concepts, theories, and research findings. Others prefer to integrate the applied chapters with the more theoretical material when relevant. Our applied units are designed to be used in either way. In fact, there are several ways in which the chapters in our book could be assigned. On the next page are some sample outlines that instructors have used successfully with our book. We are sure there are others; we intend these as a guide to illustrate the flexibility of the order in which the chapters and applied units can be assigned.

Organization of the Third Edition

We have seen a lot of syllabi from social psychology courses and spoken with many colleagues who teach the course, and have been impressed by the different ways in which the course can be taught. To accommodate the diverse ways in which instructors may choose to present topics, we have tried to create a sensible yet flexible organization.

Each chapter of *Social Psychology* is self-contained in terms of topics and concepts. Consequently, instructors can assign the chapters in any order they please; concepts are always explained in clear terms so that students won't have to have read earlier chapters in order to grasp the meanings of later ones. Further, as mentioned earlier, the three Psychology in Action units can be integrated into the course at several points or assigned at the end of the course. Two examples of course syllabi that work well are shown on the next page. There are many other possibilities as well; these two are offered as examples only.

Ancillary Package

A really good textbook should become part of the classroom experience, supporting and augmenting the professor's vision for his or her class. *Social Psychology* offers a number of supplements that will enrich both the professor's presentation of social psychology and the student's understanding of it.

Instructor's Supplements

- Video. A video is available that contains a series of clips that can be used as lecture openers or discussion lead-ins. Some of these clips are from classic psychology films. Others are from documentaries that are excellent illustrations of social psychological concepts. In still other clips, each of the authors of the text discusses some of his or her research. A Video Guide accompanies the video that discusses the principles covered in each clip, providing discussion questions for students, and listing relevant references.
- Color Transparencies of 50 figures and tables from the text.
- Instructor's Manual and Resource Kit by Elisa Wurf of Green Mountain College. Includes lecture ideas, teaching tips, suggested readings, chapter outlines, student projects and research assignments, Try It! exercises, critical thinking topics and discussion questions, and a media resource guide.
- Test Bank by Marti Hope Gonzales of the University of Minnesota. Each question in this 2,000 question test bank is referenced to parent text page number, topic, and skill level. The test bank is also available to adopters in Windows and in Macintosh computerized format. Our test generation TestGen software program allows professors to customize exams from Test Bank items, add new questions, or a combination of both TestGen and TestGen Mac.

Student Supplements

- Student Study Guide by Kathy Demitrakis of the Alburquerque Technical Vocational Institute contains chapter overviews, learning objectives and outlines, study questions, key terms, and practice tests.
- Web site (http://longman.awl.com/aronson) that includes additional Try It! exercises, updates on current events that are relevant to social psychological concepts, practice tests for each chapter, downloadable PowerPoint slides, and links to other sites. For example, we include abstracts to newspaper articles that are relevant to topics discussed in each of the chapters. These frequently updated articles can be used in several ways in the classroom. Professors can use the current events as examples in their lectures, or they can be the subject of in-class discussions or student research papers. The Try It! exercises that can be found on the web site are called out with an icon in the margins of the text 📖.
- *Psychology Is Social: Readings and Conversations in Social Psychology,* 4th edition, edited by

Edward Krupat of the Massachusetts College of Pharmacy and Allied Health Sciences. In its fourth edition, this reader exposes students to a wide spectrum of research and opinion, including articles by and interviews with highly acclaimed social psychologists. The selections, edited to maximize student comprehension, range from new to classic, popular to technical, and single study to review, and provide a glimpse into the minds of those who have shaped key areas of study in the field of social psychology.

- *How to Think Like a Social Scientist* by Thomas F. Pettigrew of the University of Santa Cruz. With examples drawn from the behavioral sciences, this inexpensive primer fosters critical thinking about psychology and the social sciences. It encourages readers to consider the nature of theory, comparisons and control, cause and change, sampling and selection, varying levels of analysis, and systems thinking in the social sciences.
- *Thinking Critically About Research on Sex and Gender,* Second Edition by Paula J. Caplan of Brown University and Jeremy B. Caplan of

Brandeis University. This supplement encourages students to evaluate the massive and diverse research that has appeared on this subject in recent decades. After demonstrating that much of the existing research is not as well-established as one would think, the book provides readers with the critical tools necessary to assess the huge body of literature and to draw realistic and constructive conclusions.

- *Influence: Science and Practice,* Third Edition by Robert B. Cialdini of Arizona State University. This fascinating bestseller draws on evidence from research and the working world of influence professionals to examine the psychology of compliance. Focus is on the six basic psychological principles directing human behavior—reciprocation, consistency, social validation, liking, authority, and scarcity. This is a read not to be missed!

Acknowledgments

Elliot Aronson is delighted to acknowledge the general contributions of his best friend (who also happens to be his wife), Vera Aronson. Vera, as usual, provided a great deal of inspiration for his ideas and acted as the sounding board for and supportive critic of many of his semiformed notions, helping to mold them into more sensible analyses. He would also like to thank his son, Joshua Aronson, a brilliant young social psychologist in his own right, for the many stimulating conversations that contributed mightily to the final version of this book. For this, the third edition, Linda Tropp provided invaluable specific research assistance.

Tim Wilson would like to thank his graduate mentor, Richard E. Nisbett, who nurtured his interest in the field and showed him the continuity between social psychological research and everyday life. He thanks his graduate students, David Centerbar, Michelle Damiani, Samuel Lindsey, Jay Meyers, Nicole Shelton, and Thalia Wheatley who helped keep him a well-balanced professor—a researcher as well as a teacher and author. He thanks his parents, Elizabeth and Geoffrey Wilson, for their overall support. Most of all, he thanks his wife, Deirdre Smith, and his children, Christopher and Leigh, for their love, patience, and understanding, even when the hour was late and the computer was still on.

Robin Akert would like to thank her students and colleagues at Wellesley College for their support and encouragement. In particular, she is beholden to

Professors Patricia Berman, Nancy Genero, Jonathan Cheek, and Alison Bibbins. Their advice, feedback, and senses of humor were invaluable. She is deeply grateful to her family, Michaela and Wayne Akert, and Linda and Jerry Wuichet; their inexhaustible enthusiasm and boundless support have sustained her on this project as on all the ones before it. Once again she thanks C. Issak for authorial inspiration. Finally, no words can express her gratitude and indebtedness to Dane Archer, mentor, colleague, and friend, who opened the world of social psychology to her and who has been her guide ever since.

No book can be written and published without the help of a great many people working with the authors behind the scenes, and our book is no exception. First, we would like to thank the many colleagues who read one or more chapters of previous editions of the book.

Reviewers of Past Editions

Jeffrey B. Adams, Saint Michael's College
John R. Aiello, Rutgers University
Charles A. Alexander, Rock Valley College
Art Aron, State University of New York at Stony Brook
Joan W. Baily, Jersey City State College
Norma Baker, Belmont University
William A. Barnard, University of Northern Colorado
Susan E. Beers, Sweet Briar College
Leonard Berkowitz, University of Wisconsin–Madison
Thomas Blass, University of Maryland, Baltimore County
C. George Boeree, Shippensburg University
Lisa M. Bohon, California State University, Sacramento
Peter J. Brady, Clark State Community College
Kelly A. Brennan, University of Texas at Austin
Richard W. Brislin, East-West Center of the University of Hawaii
Thomas P. Cafferty, University of South Carolina–Columbia
Melissa A. Cahoon, Wright State University
Nicholas Christenfeld, University of California at San Diego
Margaret S. Clark, Carnegie Mellon University
Susan D. Clayton, Allegheny College
Brian M. Cohen, University of Texas at San Antonio
Steven G. Cole, Texas Christian University

Eric J. Cooley, Western Oregon State College
Diana Cordova, Yale University
Keith E. Davis, University of South Carolina–Columbia
Steve Duck, University of Iowa
Karen G. Duffy, State University of New York at Geneseo
Steve L. Ellyson, Youngstown State University
Susan Fiske, University of Massachusetts, Amherst
Robin Franck, Southwestern College
William Rick Fry, Youngstown State University
Frederick X. Gibbons, Iowa State University
Cynthia Gilliland, Louisiana State University
Genaro Gonzalez, University of Texas
Beverly Gray, Youngstown State University
Judith Harackiewicz, University of Wisconsin–Madison
Vicki S. Helgeson, Carnegie Mellon University
Tracy B. Henley, Mississippi State University
Ed Hirt, Indiana University
David E. Hyatt, University of Wisconsin–Oshkosh
James D. Johnson, University of North Carolina–Wilmington
Lee Jussim, Rutgers University
Fredrick Koenig, Tulane University
Alan J. Lambert, Washington University
G. Daniel Lassiter, Ohio University
Joann M. Montepare, Tufts University
Richard Moreland, University of Pittsburgh
Carrie Nance, Stetson University
Todd D. Nelson, Michigan State University
W. Gerrod Parrott, Georgetown University
M. Susan Rowley, Champlain College
Connie Schick, Bloomsburg University
Richard C. Sherman, Miami University of Ohio
Randolph A. Smith, Ouachita Baptist University
Linda Solomon, Marymount Manhattan College
Jakob Steinberg, Fairleigh Dickinson University
T. Gale Thompson, Bethany College
Gary L. Wells, Iowa State University
Paul L. Wienir, Western Michigan University
Kipling D. Williams, University of Toledo
William H. Zachry, University of Tennessee-Martin

Reviewers of the Third Edition

Gordon Bear, Ramapo College
Frank Calabrese, Community College of Philadelphia
Michael Caruso, University of Toledo
Jack Cohen, Camden County College

Eric Cooley, Western Oregon State University
Jack Croxton, State University of New York, at Fredonia
Dorothee Dietrich, Hamline University
Susann Doyle, Gainesville College
Valerie Eastman, Drury College
Tami Eggleston, McKendree College
Alan Feingold, Yale University
Phil Finney, Southeast Missouri State University
William Rick Fry, Youngstown University
Gordon Hammerle, Adrian College
Vicki Helgeson, Carnegie Mellon University
Joyce Hemphill, Cazenovia College
Marita Inglehart, University of Michigan
Carl Kallgren, Penn State Erie, Behrend College
Bill Klein, Colby College
Emmett Lampkin, Kirkwook Community College
Patricia Laser, Bucks County Community College
G. Daniel Lassiter, Ohio University
John Malarkey, Wilmington College
Andrew Manion, St. Mary's University of Minnesota
Elaine Nocks, Furman University
Cheri Parks, Colorado Christian University
David Peterson, Mount Senario College
Connie Schick, Bloomsburg University
Janice Steil, Adelphi University
David Trafimow, New Mexico State
Mike Witmer, Skagit Valley College

We also thank the expert editorial staff of Addison Wesley Longman, especially our dedicated and persistent acquisitions editor, Eric Stano, and our developmental editor, Michael Kimball. We'd also like to thank the staff at Thompson Steele for their ongoing design and production services. Finally, we thank Mary Falcon, but for whom we never would have begun this project.

Thank you for inviting us into your classroom. We welcome your suggestions, and we would be delighted to hear your comments about this book.

Elliot Aronson
elliot@cats.ucsc.edu

Tim Wilson
tdw@virginia.edu

Robin Akert
rakert@wellesley.edu

ABOUT THE AUTHORS

ELLIOT ARONSON

When I was a kid, we were the only Jewish family in a virulently anti-Semitic neighborhood. I had to go to Hebrew school every day, late in the afternoon. Being the only youngster in my neighborhood going to Hebrew school made me an easy target for some of the older neighborhood toughs. On my way home from Hebrew school, after dark, I was frequently waylaid and roughed up by roving gangs shouting anti-Semitic epithets.

I have a vivid memory of sitting on a curb after one of these beatings, nursing a bloody nose or a split lip, feeling very sorry for myself and wondering

how these kids could hate me so much when they didn't even know me. I thought about whether those kids were taught to hate Jews or whether, somehow, they were born that way. I wondered if their hatred could be changed if they got to know me better, would they hate me less? I speculated about my own character. What would I have done if the shoe were on the other foot that is, if I were bigger and stronger than they, would I be capable of beating them up for no good reason?

I didn't realize it at the time, of course, but eventually I discovered that these were profound questions. And some 30 years later, as an experimental social psychologist, I had the great good fortune to be in a position to answer some of those questions and to invent techniques to reduce the kind of prejudice that had claimed me as a victim.

Elliot Aronson graduated from Brandeis University (where he worked with Abraham Maslow) and received his Ph.D. from Stanford University, working under the guidance of Leon Festinger. He has done pioneering research in the areas of social influence, persuasion, prejudice reduction, and AIDS prevention. Aronson has written or edited 15 books, including The Social Animal, The Handbook of Social Psychology, Age of Propaganda, The Jigsaw Classroom, *and* Methods of Research in Social Psychology. *He is among the world's most honored social psychologists, having received major national and international awards for the quality of his teaching, for his experimental research, for his books, and for his contributions to the betterment of society. He has served as president of the Society of Personality and Social Psychology and president of the Western Psychological Association. In 1992, he was elected to the American Academy of Arts and Sciences. He is currently a research professor of psychology at the University of California at Santa Cruz.*

TIM WILSON

One day, when I was eight, a couple of older kids rode up on their bikes to share some big news: They had discovered an abandoned house down a country road. "It's really neat," they said. "We broke a window and nobody cared!"

My friend and I hopped onto our bikes to investigate. We had no trouble finding the house—there it was, sitting off by itself, with a big, jagged hole in a first-floor window. We got off of our bikes and looked around. My friend found

a baseball-sized rock lying on the ground and threw a perfect strike through another first-floor window. There was something terribly exciting about the smash-and-tingle of shattering glass, especially when we knew there was nothing wrong with what we were doing. After all, the house was abandoned, wasn't it? We broke nearly every window in the house and then climbed through one of the first-floor windows to look around.

It was then that we realized something was terribly wrong. The house certainly did not look abandoned. There were pictures on the wall, nice furniture, books in shelves. We went home feeling frightened and confused. We soon learned that the house was not abandoned: It was the residence of an elderly couple who were away on vacation. Eventually my parents discovered what we had done and paid a substantial sum to repair the windows.

For years, I pondered this incident: Why did I do such a terrible thing? Was I a bad kid? I didn't think so, and neither did my parents. How, then, could a good kid do such a bad thing? Even though the neighborhood kids said the house was abandoned, why couldn't my friend and I see the clear signs that someone lived there? How crucial was it that my friend was there and threw the first rock? Though I didn't know it at the time, these reflections touched on several classic social psychological issues, such as whether only bad people do bad things, whether the social situation can be powerful enough to make good people do bad things, and the way in which our expectations about an event can make it difficult to see it as it really is. Fortunately, my career as a vandal ended with this one incident. It did, however, mark the beginning of my fascination with basic questions about how people understand themselves and the social world—questions I continue to investigate to this day.

Tim Wilson did his undergraduate work at Williams and Hampshire colleges and received his Ph.D. from the University of Michigan under the guidance of Richard E. Nisbett. Currently a professor of psychology at the University of Virginia, he has published numerous articles in the areas of introspection, judgment, and attitude change. His research has received the support of the National Science Foundation and the National Institute for Mental Health. He has been a member of the Executive Board of the Society for Experimental Social Psychology, a member of the Social and Groups Processes Review Committee at the National Institute of Mental Health, and a member of the editorial boards of several professional journals.

Robin Akert

One fall day, when I was about 16, I was walking with a friend along the shore of the San Francisco Bay. Deep in conversation, I glanced over my shoulder and saw a sailboat capsize. I pointed it out to my friend, who took only a perfunctory interest and went on talking. However, I kept watching as we walked, and I realized that the two sailors were in the water, clinging to the capsized boat. Again I said something to my friend, who replied, "Oh, they'll get it upright, don't worry."

But I *was* worried. Was this an emergency? My friend didn't think so. And I was no sailor; I knew nothing about boats. But I kept thinking, "That water is really cold. They can't stay in that water too long." I remember feeling very confused and unsure.  What should I do? Should I do anything? Did they really need help?

We were near a restaurant with a big window overlooking the bay, and I decided to go in and see if anyone had done anything about the boat. Lots of people were watching but not doing anything. This confused me too. Very meekly, I asked the bartender to call for some kind of help. He just shrugged. I went back to the window and watched the two small figures in the water. Why was everyone so unconcerned? Was I crazy?

Years later, I reflected on how hard it was for me to do what I did next: I demanded that the bartender let me use his phone. In those days before "911," it was lucky that I knew there was a Coast Guard station on the bay, and I asked the operator for the number. I was relieved to hear the Guardsman take my message very seriously.

It had been an emergency. I watched as the Coast Guard cutter sped across the bay and pulled the two sailors out of the water. Maybe I saved their lives that day. What really stuck with me over the years was how other people behaved and how it made me feel. The other bystanders seemed unconcerned and did nothing to help. Their reactions made me doubt myself and made it harder for me to decide to take action. When I later studied social psychology in college, I realized that on the shore of the San Francisco Bay that day, I had experienced the "bystander effect" fully: The presence of other, apparently unconcerned bystanders had made it difficult for me to decide if the situation was an emergency and whether it was my responsibility to help.

Robin M. Akert graduated summa cum laude from the University of California at Santa Cruz, where she majored in psychology and sociology. She received her Ph.D. in experimental social psychology from Princeton University. She is currently a professor of psychology at Wellesley College, where she was awarded the Pinanski Prize for Excellence in Teaching. She publishes primarily in the area of nonverbal communication and is the coauthor of the forthcoming book Interpretation and Awareness: Verbal and Nonverbal Factors in Person Perception.

SPECIAL TIPS FOR STUDENTS

There is then creative reading as well as creative writing.
—Ralph Waldo Emerson, 1837

I am a kind of burr; I shall stick.
—William Shakespeare, 1604

These two quotes, taken together, sum up everything you need to know to be a proficient student: Be an active, creative consumer of information and make sure it sticks! How do you accomplish these two feats? Actually it's not difficult at all. Like everything else in life, it just takes some work—some clever, well-planned, purposeful work. Here are some suggestions about how to do it.

Get to Know the Textbook

Believe it or not, in writing this book we thought very carefully about the organization and structure of each chapter. Things are the way they appear for a reason, and that reason is to help you learn the material in the best way possible. Here are some tips on what to look for in each chapter.

Key terms are in boldface type in the text so that you'll notice them. We define the terms in the text, and that definition appears again in the margin. These marginal definitions are there to help you out if later in the chapter you forget what something means. The marginal definitions are quick and easy to find. You can also look up key terms in the alphabetical Glossary at the end of this textbook.

Make sure you notice the headings and subheadings. The headings are the skeleton that holds a chapter together. They link together like vertebrae. If you ever feel lost, look back to the last heading and the headings before that one—this will give you the "big picture" of where the chapter is going. It should also help you see the connections between sections.

The summary at the end of each chapter is a succinct, shorthand presentation of the chapter information, with the key terms set in boldface. You should read it and make sure there are no surprises when you do so. If anything in the summary doesn't

ring a bell, go back to the chapter and reread that section. Most importantly, remember that the summary is purposefully brief, whereas your understanding of the material should be full and complete. Use the summary as a study aid before your exams. When you read it over, everything should be familiar and you should have that wonderful feeling of knowing more than is in the summary (in which case you are ready to take the exam).

At the end of each chapter, we list pertinent books or articles that we think are particularly good. These recommended readings are excellent resources for any papers you may be writing for your course. They are the first place to start in a bibliographic search for further information on the topic of your paper. As is always the case with literature searches, they will lead you to still other references. At the end of each chapter, we also list a few novels and movies that poignantly portray themes from that chapter.

Make sure you do the Try It! exercises. They will make concepts from social psychology concrete and help you see how they can be applied to your own life. Some of the Try It! exercises replicate social psychology experiments. Other Try It! exercises reproduce self-report scales so you can see where you stand in relation to other people. Still other Try It! exercises are short quizzes that illustrate social psychological concepts.

Visit our Web site at <http://longman.awl.com/aronson>. You will be able to do more Try It! exercises, read summaries of current events from newspapers that relate to social psychology, take interactive practice tests, and link to other sites.

Just Say No to the Couch Potato Within

Because social psychology is about everyday life, you might lull yourself into believing that the material is all common sense. Don't be fooled. The material is more complicated than it might seem. Therefore, we want to emphasize that the best way to learn it is to work with it in an active, not passive, fashion. You can't just read a chapter once and expect it to stick with you. You have to go over the material, wrestle with it, make your own connections to it, question it, and think about it. Actively working with material makes it memorable; it makes it your own. Since it's a safe bet that someone is going to ask you about this material later and you're going to have to pull it out of memory, do what you can to get it into memory now. Here are some techniques to use:

- Go ahead and be bold—use a highlighter! Go crazy—write in the margins! If you underline, highlight, circle, or draw little hieroglyphics next to important points, you will remember them better. We recall taking exams in college where we not only remembered the material but could actually see in our minds the textbook page it was written on and the little squiggles and stars we'd drawn in the margin.

- Read the textbook chapter before the applicable class lecture, not afterward. This way, you'll get more out of the lecture, which will introduce new material. The chapter will give you the big picture, as well as a lot of detail. The lecture will enhance that information and help you put it all together. If you don't read the chapter first, you may not understand some of the points made in the lecture or realize that they are important.

- Here's a good way to study material: Write out a difficult concept or a study (or say it out loud to yourself) in your own words, without looking at the book or your notes. Can you do it? How good was your version? Did you omit anything important? Did you get stuck at some point, unable to remember what comes next? If so, you now know that you need to go over that information in more detail. You can also study with someone else, describing theories and studies to each other and seeing if you're making sense.

- If you have trouble remembering the results of an important study, try drawing your own version of a graph of the findings (you can use our data graphs for an idea of how to proceed). If all the various points in a theory are confusing you,

try drawing your own flowchart of how it works. You will probably find that you remember the research results much better in pictorial form than in words and that the theory isn't so confusing (or missing a critical part) if you've outlined it. Draw information a few times and it will stay with you.

- Remember, the more you work with the material—the better you will learn and remember it. Write it in your own words, talk about it, explain it to others, or draw visual representations of it.

- Last but not least, remember that this material is a lot of fun. You haven't even started reading the book yet, but we think you're going to like it. In particular, you'll see how much social psychology has to tell you about your real, everyday life. As this course progresses, you might want to remind yourself to observe the events of your daily life with new eyes, the eyes of a social psychologist, and try to apply what you are learning to the behavior of your friends, acquaintances, strangers, and, yes, even yourself. Make sure you use the Try It! exercises and visit the Web site. You will find out how much social psychology can help us understand our lives. When you read newspapers or magazines or watch the nightly news, think about what social psychology has to say about such events and behaviors we believe you will find that your understanding of daily life is richer. If you notice a newspaper or magazine article that you think is an especially good example of social psychology "in action," please send it to us, with a full reference to where you found it and on what page. If we decide to use it in the next edition of this book, we'll list your name in the Acknowledgments.

We suspect that ten years from now, you may not remember all the facts, theories, and names you learn now. Although we hope you will remember some of them, our main goal is for you to take with you into your future a great many of the broad social psychological concepts presented herein. If you open yourself to social psychology's magic, we believe it will enrich the way you look at the world and the way you live in it.

SOCIAL PSYCHOLOGY

CHAPTER 1

INTRODUCTION TO SOCIAL PSYCHOLOGY

*t*he task of the psychologist is to try to understand and predict human behavior. Different kinds of psychologists go about this in different ways, and in this book we will attempt to show you how social psychologists do it. Let's begin with a few examples of human behavior. Some of these might seem important; others might seem trivial; one or two might seem frightening. To a social psychologist, all of them are interesting. Our hope is that, by the time you finish reading this book, you will find all of these examples as fascinating as we do. As you read these examples, try to think about how you would explain why what happened, happened.

1. In the predawn hours of June 1981, the residents of a trendy neighborhood in Los Angeles heard desperate cries for help coming from a yellow house. "Please don't kill me!" screamed one woman. Other neighbors reported hearing tortured screams and cries for mercy. And yet, not one neighbor bothered to investigate or help in any way. No one even called the police. One woman, who lived two houses away, went out onto her balcony when she heard the screams, but went back into her house without doing anything. Twelve hours later, an acquaintance arrived at the yellow house, and discovered that four people had been brutally murdered. A fifth person was critically wounded, and spent those 12 hours lying in a bedroom, bleeding from her wounds, waiting in vain for just one neighbor to lift their finger and dial the police (*New York Times*, July 3, 1981).

■ When people view violence on the street, why are most reluctant to help or even to dial 911?

Why do you think the neighbors failed to do anything after hearing the cries for help? Stop and think for a moment: What kinds of people are these neighbors? Would you like to have them as friends? If you had a small child, would you hire one of these neighbors as a baby-sitter?

2. A few years ago, Sally, a student of ours told us about the following incident. Several months after the presidential election, Sally was watching TV with a few of her acquaintances. On the tube, President Clinton was making an important policy speech. This was the first time Sally had listened really carefully to one of Clinton's substantive speeches. She was very favorably impressed by his homey, down-to-earth quality; she felt he was smart, honest, sincere, and compassionate. As soon as the speech was over, her friend Melinda said, "Boy, what a phony—I wouldn't trust that guy with my dirty laundry—I can't believe he's running our country. No wonder they call him Slick Willie!" The others quickly chimed in, voicing their agreement. Sally felt uncomfortable, and was frankly puzzled. Finally, she mumbled, "Yeah, I guess he did come off as a bit insincere."

What do you suppose was going on in Sally's mind? Did she actually come to see President Clinton in a new light, or was she simply trying to go along in order to get along?

3. We have a friend whom we will call Oscar. Oscar is a middle-aged executive with a computer software company. As a student, Oscar had attended a large state university in the Midwest, where he was a member of a fraternity we will call Delta Nu. He remembers having gone through a severe and somewhat scary hazing ritual in order to become a member but believes it was well worth it. Although he had been terribly frightened by the hazing, he loved his fraternity brothers and was proud to be a member of Delta Nu—easily the best of all fraternities. A few years ago, his son, Sam, was about to enroll in the same university; naturally, Oscar urged Sam to pledge Delta Nu: "It's a great fraternity—always attracts a wonderful bunch of fellows. You'll really love it." Sam did in fact pledge Delta Nu and was accepted. Oscar was relieved to learn that Sam was not

■ Although attorneys do their best to convince a jury, in the end the verdict will depend on how the individual jurors construe the evidence.

required to undergo a severe initiation in order to become a member; times had changed, and hazing was now forbidden. When Sam came home for Christmas break, Oscar asked him how he liked the fraternity. "It's all right, I guess," he said, "but most of my friends are outside the fraternity." Oscar was astonished.

How is it that Oscar had been so enamored of his fraternity brothers and Sam wasn't? Had the standards of old Delta Nu slipped? Was the fraternity now admitting a less desirable group of young men than in Oscar's day? Or was it just one of those inexplicable things? What do you think?

4. In the mid-1970s, several hundred members of the Peoples Temple, a California-based religious cult, emigrated to Guyana under the guidance of their leader, the Reverend Jim Jones. Their aim was to form a model interracial community, called Jonestown, based on "love, hard work, and spiritual enlightenment." In November 1978, Congressman Leo Ryan of California flew to Jonestown to investigate reports that some of the members were being held against their will. He visited the commune and found that several residents wanted to return with him to the United States. Reverend Jones agreed they could leave, but as Ryan was boarding a plane, he and several other members of his party were shot and killed by a member of the Peoples Temple, apparently on Jones's orders. On hearing that several members of Ryan's party had escaped, Jones grew despondent and began to speak over the public address system about the beauty of dying and the certainty that everyone would meet again in another place. The residents lined up in a pavilion in front of a vat containing a mixture of Kool-Aid and cyanide. According to a survivor, almost all of the residents drank willingly of the deadly solution. At least 80 babies and infants were given the poison by their parents, who then drank it themselves. More than 800 people died, including Reverend Jones.

How is it that people can agree to kill themselves and their own children? Were they crazy? Were they under some kind of hypnotic spell? How would you explain it?

We now have several questions about human social behavior—questions we find fascinating: Why did the Los Angeles residents ignore the screams coming from the yellow house when, by dialing 911, or by shouting out the window, they might have averted a tragedy? Why did Sally change her opinion about the sincerity of President Clinton and bring it into line with her acquaintances' opinion? Why did Oscar like his frat brothers so much more than Sam did? And how could large numbers of people be induced to kill their own children and themselves in Jonestown? In this chapter, we will consider what these examples have in common and why they are of interest to us. We will also put forth some reasonable explanations based upon social psychological research.   ◻

What Is Social Psychology?

> We are by all odds the most persistently and obsessively social of all species, more dependent on each other than the famous social insects, and really, when you look at us, infinitely more imaginative and deft at social living.
>
> –Lewis Thomas

Social Psychology
the scientific study of the way in which people's thoughts, feelings, and behaviors are influenced by the real or imagined presence of other people

At the very heart of social psychology is the phenomenon of social influence: We are all influenced by other people. When we think of social influence, the kinds of examples that readily come to mind are direct attempts at persuasion, whereby one person deliberately tries to change another person's behavior. This is what happens in an advertising campaign, when creative individuals employ sophisticated techniques to persuade us to buy a particular brand of toothpaste or, during an election campaign, when similar techniques are used to get us to vote for a particular political candidate. Direct attempts at persuasion also occur when our friends try to get us to do something we don't really want to do ("Come on, have another beer—everyone is doing it") or when the school-yard bully uses force or threats to get smaller kids to part with their lunch money or homework.

These direct social influence attempts form a major part of social psychology and will be discussed in our chapters on conformity, attitudes, and group processes. To the social psychologist, however, social influence is broader than attempts by one person to change another person's behavior. For one thing, social influence extends beyond behavior—it includes our thoughts and feelings as well as our overt acts. In addition, social influence takes on many forms other than deliberate attempts at persuasion. We are often influenced merely by the presence of other people. Moreover, even when we are not in the physical presence of other people, we are still influenced by them. Thus, in a sense we carry our mothers, fathers, friends, and teachers around with us, as we attempt to make decisions that would make them proud of us.

On a still subtler level, each of us is immersed in a social and cultural context. Social psychologists are interested in studying how and why our thoughts, feelings, and behaviors are shaped by the entire social environment. Taking all of these factors into account, we can define **social psychology** as the scientific study of the way in which people's thoughts, feelings, and behaviors are influenced by the real or imagined presence of other people (Allport, 1985). Of particular inter-

//

Explicit and Implicit Values

Make a list of the explicit and implicit beliefs and values of your parents and close relatives. Now make a list of the explicit and implicit values of some of your favorite professors and some of your closest college friends. Make note of the

similarities and differences in your two lists. How do these differences affect you? Do you find yourself rejecting one set of values in favor of the other? Are you trying to make a compromise between the two? Are you attempting to form a whole new set of values that are your own?

//

est to social psychologists is what happens in the mind of an individual when various influences come into conflict with one another, as is frequently the case when young people go off to college and find themselves torn between the beliefs and values they learned at home and the beliefs and values their professors or peers are expressing.

Other disciplines, like anthropology and sociology, are also interested in how people are influenced by their social environment. Social psychology is distinct, however, primarily because it is concerned not so much with social situations in any objective sense, but rather with how people are influenced by their interpretation, or **construal,** of their social environment. To understand how people are influenced by their social world, social psychologists believe it is more important to understand how they perceive, comprehend, and interpret the social world than it is to understand the objective properties of the social world itself (Lewin, 1943).

Construal
the way in which people perceive, comprehend, and interpret the social world

An example will clarify. Imagine that Jason is a shy high school student who admires Debbie from afar. Suppose that, as a budding social psychologist, you have the job of predicting whether or not Jason will ask Debbie to the senior prom. One way you might do this is to observe Debbie's objective behavior toward Jason. Does she pay attention to him and smile a lot? If so, the casual observer might decide that Jason will ask her out. As a social psychologist, however, you are more interested in viewing Debbie's behavior through Jason's eyes—that is, in seeing how Jason interprets Debbie's behavior. If she smiles at him, does Jason construe her behavior as mere politeness, the kind of politeness she would extend to any of the dozens of nerds and losers in the senior class? Or does he view her smile as an encouraging sign, one that inspires him to gather the courage to ask her out? If she ignores him, does Jason figure that she's playing "hard to get"? Or does he take it as a sign that she's not interested in dating him? To predict Jason's behavior, it is not enough to know the details of Debbie's behavior; it is imperative to know how Jason interprets Debbie's behavior.

Given the importance placed on the way people interpret the social world, social psychologists pay special attention to the origins of these interpretations. For example, when construing their environment, are most people concerned with making an interpretation that places them in the most positive light (e.g., Jason believing "Debbie is going to the prom with Eric because she is trying to make me jealous") or with making the most accurate interpretation, even if it is unflattering (e.g., "Painful as it may be, I must admit that Debbie would rather go to the prom with a sea slug than with me")? A great deal of research in social psychology has addressed these and other determinants of people's thoughts and behaviors. We will expand on these determinants later in this chapter.

Needless to say, the importance of construals extends far beyond the saga of Jason and Debbie. Consider an additional, rather prominent example: In a murder trial like that involving O. J. Simpson, the prosecution may present evidence concerning DNA and hair and fiber samples it believes will have a decisive impact on the verdict. But no matter how powerful the evidence might be, the final verdict will always hinge on precisely how each member of the jury construes that evidence—and these construals may rest on a variety of events and perceptions that may or may not bear objective relevance to the matter at hand. For instance: During cross-examination, did a key witness hesitate for a moment before answering, suggesting to some jurors that she might not be certain of her data? Or did some jurors consider the witness too remote, too arrogant, too certain of herself?

Another distinctive feature of social psychology is that it is an experimentally based science that tests its assumptions, guesses, and ideas about human social behavior empirically and systematically, rather than by relying on folk wisdom, common sense, the opinions and insights of philosophers, novelists, political pundits, grandmothers, and others wise in the ways of human beings. As you will see, doing systematic experiments in social psychology presents a great many challenges—primarily because we are attempting to predict the behavior of highly sophisticated organisms in a variety of complex situations. As scientists, our goal is to find objective answers to a wide array of important questions: What are the factors that cause aggression? How might we reduce prejudice? What variables cause two people to like or love each other? Why do certain kinds of political advertisements work better than others? The specific ways in which experimental social psychologists meet these challenges will be illustrated throughout this book and discussed in detail in Chapter 2.

We will spend most of this introductory chapter expanding on the issues raised in the above paragraphs—of what social psychology is and how it is distinct from other, related disciplines. A good place to begin is with what social psychology is not.

Some Alternative Ways of Understanding Social Influence

Let's take another look at the examples at the beginning of this chapter. Why did people behave the way they did? One way to answer this question might be simply to ask them. For example, we could question the residents in Los Angeles about why they didn't call the police; we could ask Sally why she changed her opinion of Bill Clinton. The problem with this approach is that people are not always aware of the origins of their own responses (Nisbett & Wilson, 1977). It is unlikely that the neighbors know exactly why they went back to sleep without calling the police or that Sally knows why she changed her mind about the president.

Folk Wisdom

Journalists, social critics, and novelists might have a great many interesting things to say about these situations. Such commentary is generally referred to as folk wisdom or common sense. For example, the mass suicide at Jonestown received considerable media attention; explanations for the event ranged from the (unfounded) assumption that Reverend Jones employed hypnotism and drugs to weaken the resistance of his followers, to suspicion that the people who were attracted to his cult must have been disturbed, self-destructive individuals in the

■ Why would any reasonable person blindly follow someone claiming to be Jesus Christ, give up personal freedoms, allow the leader to have sex with her 10-year-old daughter, and dictate which personal relationships will continue? While it may be easy to dismiss the followers of a cult leader like David Koresh as foolish, such oversimplifications and denial of the power of social influence can lead us to blame the victims.

first place. Such speculations, because they underestimate the power of the situation, are almost certainly incorrect—or, at the very least, oversimplified.

Unfortunately, because so-called common sense frequently turns out to be wrong or oversimplified, we tend not to learn from previous incidents. Jonestown was probably the first mass suicide involving Americans, but it wasn't the last. A few years ago in Waco, Texas, the followers of cult leader David Koresh barricaded themselves into a fortress-like compound to avoid arrest for the possession if illegal firearms and, when surrounded, apparently set fire to their own buildings resulting in the death of 86 people, including several children. Still more recently, 39 members of an obscure cult called Heaven's Gate committed group suicide at a luxury estate in Rancho Santa Fe, California. The existing evidence makes it clear that the cult members died willingly and peacefully, believing that a huge alien spaceship, following closely behind the Hale-Bopp Comet, would pick up their souls and carry them into space (Purdum, 1997).

In the aftermath of both the Waco conflagration and the Heaven's Gate tragedy, the general population was just as confused as it had been following the Jonestown suicides. It is difficult for most people to grasp just how powerful a cult can be in affecting the hearts and minds of relatively normal people. Accordingly, as was the case following the Jonestown suicides, the general population—including the U.S. Congress—was eager to find someone to blame. After the Heaven's Gate tragedy, many were quick to blame the victims themselves—accusing them of stupidity or suffering from mental illness. But subsequent evidence indicated that they were mentally healthy and, for the most part, uncommonly bright and well-educated. Following the Waco tragedy, many observers focused blame on the impatience of the FBI, the poor judgment of Attorney General Janet Reno, or the inadequate leadership of President Clinton. Fixing blame may make us feel better by resolving our confusion but it is no substitute for understanding the complexities of the situations that produced those events.

Don't get us wrong. We are not opposed to folk wisdom. Far from it. We are convinced that a great deal can be learned about social behavior from journalists, social critics, and novelists—and in this book we quote from all these sources. There is, however, at least one problem with full reliance on such sources: More often than not, they disagree with one another, and there is no easy way of determining which of them is correct. Consider what folk wisdom has to say about the factors that influence how much we like other people: On the one hand, we know that "birds of a feather flock together," and, with a little effort, each of us could come up with lots of examples where indeed we liked and hung around with people who shared our backgrounds and interests. But then again, folk wisdom also tells us that "opposites attract," and, if we tried, we could also come up with examples where people with different backgrounds and interests did attract us. Which is it?

Similarly, are we to believe that "out of sight is out of mind" or that "absence makes the heart grow fonder," that "haste makes waste" or that "he who hesitates is lost"? And who is to say whether the Jonestown massacre occurred because (a) Reverend Jones succeeded in attracting the kinds of people who were psychologically depressed to begin with; (b) only people with self-destructive tendencies join cults; (c) Jones was such a powerful, messianic, charismatic figure that virtually anyone—even strong, non-depressed individuals like you or us—would have succumbed to his influence; (d) people cut off from society are particularly vulnerable to social influence; (e) all of the above; or (f) none of the above?

Philosophy

Throughout the history of humankind, philosophy has been, and continues to be, a major source of insight about human nature. Indeed, the creativity and analytical thinking of philosophers are a major part of the foundation of contemporary psychology. This has more than mere historical significance. During this decade alone, psychologists have utilized current philosophical thinking in an attempt to gain greater understanding of such important issues as the nature of consciousness (e.g., Dennett, 1991) and how people form beliefs about the social world (e.g., Gilbert, 1991). Sometimes, however, even great thinkers find themselves in disagreement with one another; when this occurs, how is one to know who is right? Are there some situations where philosopher A might be right and other conditions where philosopher B might be right? How would you determine this?

We social psychologists address many of the same questions that philosophers address, but we attempt to look at these questions scientifically. Just as a physicist performs experiments to test hypotheses about the nature of the physical world, the social psychologist performs experiments to test hypotheses about the nature of the social world. The major reason we have conflicting philosophical positions (just as we have conflicting folk aphorisms) is that the world is a complicated place. Small differences in the situation might not be easily discernible; yet these small differences might produce very different effects. For example, in 1663, the great Dutch philosopher, Benedict Spinoza, came out with a highly original insight about love. He wrote that if we love someone whom we formerly hated, that love will be greater than if hatred had not preceded it.

Spinoza's proposition is beautifully worked out. His logic is impeccable. But how can we be sure that it holds up? Does it always hold? What are the conditions under which it does or doesn't hold? These are empirical questions for the social psychologist (Aronson, 1995; Aronson & Linder, 1965).

To elaborate on this point, let us return for a moment to our earlier discussion about the kinds of people we like and the relationship between absence and liking. We would suggest that, almost certainly, there are some conditions under which birds of a feather do flock together and other conditions under which opposites do attract; similarly, there are some conditions under which absence does make the heart grow fonder and others under which out of sight does mean out of mind. So both can be true. That statement helps—but is it good enough? Not really, for if you really want to understand human behavior, knowing that both *can* be true is not sufficient. One of the tasks of the social psychologist is to design experiments sophisticated enough to demonstrate the specific situations under which one or the other applies. This enriches our understanding of human nature and allows us to make accurate predictions once we know the key aspects of the prevailing situation. In Chapter 2, we will discuss the scientific methods social psychologists use in more detail.

Social Psychology Compared to Other Social Sciences

Social psychology's focus on social behavior is shared by several other disciplines in the social sciences, including sociology, economics, and political science. Each of these disciplines is concerned with the influence of social and societal factors on human behavior. There are important differences, however, between social psychology and the other social sciences, most notably in their level of analysis. Social psychology is a branch of psychology, and as such is rooted in an interest in individual human beings, with an emphasis on the psychological processes going on in their hearts and minds. For the social psychologist, the level of analysis is the individual in the context of a social situation. For example, to understand why people intentionally hurt one another, the social psychologist focuses on the specific psychological processes that trigger aggression in specific situations. To what extent is aggression preceded by a state of frustration? Is frustration necessary? If people are feeling frustrated, under what conditions will they vent their frustration with an overt, aggressive act? What factors might preclude an aggressive response by a frustrated individual? Besides frustration, what other factors might cause aggression? We will address these questions in Chapter 12.

Other social sciences are more concerned with broad societal, economic, political, and historical factors that influence events in a given society. Sociology, for example, is concerned with such topics as social class, social structure, and social institutions. It goes without saying that, because society is made up of collections of people, some overlap is bound to exist between the domains of sociology and those of social psychology. The major difference is this: Sociology, rather than focusing on the psychology of the individual, tends toward a more macro focus—that of society at large. Although sociologists, like social psychologists, are interested in aggressive behavior, sociologists are more likely to be concerned with why a particular society produces different levels and types of aggression in its members. Why, for example, is the murder rate in the United States so much higher than in Canada? Within the United States, why is the murder rate higher in some social classes than in others? How do changes in society relate to changes in aggressive behavior?

The difference between social psychology and other social sciences in level of analysis reflects another difference between the disciplines—namely, in what they are trying to explain. The goal of social psychology is to identify universal properties of human nature that make everyone—regardless of social class or culture—susceptible to social influence. The laws governing the relationship between frustration and aggression, for example, are hypothesized to be true of most people in most places, not just members of one social class, age-group, or race. Social psychology is a young science that, until recently, has developed mostly in the United States; thus, many of its findings have not yet been tested in other cultures to see if they are indeed universal. Nonetheless, our goal as social psychologists is to come up with such laws. And increasingly, as methods and theories developed by American social psychologists are adopted by European, Asian, African, Middle Eastern, and South American social psychologists, we are learning more about the extent to which these laws are universal. This type of cultural expansion is extremely valuable because it sharpens theories, either by demonstrating their universality or by leading us to discover additional variables whose incorporation will ultimately help us make more accurate predictions of human social behavior. We will encounter several examples of such cross-cultural research in subsequent chapters.

Social Psychology Compared to Personality Psychology

Like social psychology, some other areas of psychology focus on studying individuals and why they do what they do. Paramount among these is personality psychology. Let's discuss how social psychology and personality psychology differ in their approach and concerns.

If you are like most people, when you read the examples presented at the beginning of this chapter and began to think about how those events might have come about, your first thoughts were about the strengths, weaknesses, flaws, and quirks of the personalities of the individuals involved. When people behave in interesting or unusual ways, it is natural to try to pinpoint what aspects of their personalities led them to respond as they did. Why did the Los Angeles residents fail to call the police when they heard the cries for help? Most of us tend to assume that they possessed some personality flaw or quirk that made them reluctant to respond.

What might these be? Some people are leaders and others are followers; some people are bold and others are timid; some people are public-spirited and others are selfish. Think back: How did you answer the question about whether you would want any of these people as a friend or a baby-sitter?

When trying to find explanations of social behavior, personality psychologists generally focus their attention on **individual differences**—the aspects of people's personalities that make them different from other people. For example, to explain why the people at Jonestown ended their own lives and those of their children by drinking poison, it seems natural to point to their personalities. Perhaps they were all "conformist types" or weak-willed; maybe they were even psychotic. An understanding of personality psychology increases our understanding of human behavior, but social psychologists are convinced that explaining behavior primarily in terms of personality factors can be superficial because it leads to a serious underestimation of the role played by a powerful source of human behavior—social influence. Remember that it was not just a handful of people who committed suicide at Jonestown but almost 100 percent of the people in the village. While it is conceivable that they were all psychotic, this is highly improb-

Individual Differences the aspects of people's personalities that make them different from other people

Table 1.1

Social psychology compared to related disciplines.		
Sociology	**Social Psychology**	**Personality Psychology**
Provides general laws and theories about societies, not individuals.	Studies the psychological processes people have in common with one another that make them susceptible to social influence.	Studies the characteristics that make individuals unique and different from one another.

able. If we want a deeper, richer, more thorough explanation of this tragic event, we need to understand what kind of power and influence a charismatic figure like Jim Jones possesses, the nature of the impact of living in a closed society—cut off from other points of view, and a myriad of other factors that might have contributed to that tragic outcome (see Table 1.1).

These two different approaches can best be illustrated by focusing on a couple of mundane examples. Consider my friend Rosa. She is the wife of one of my colleagues and I see her frequently at faculty cocktail parties. At these cocktail parties, she generally looks rather uncomfortable. She usually stands off by herself and, when approached, has very little to say. Some people regard her as shy; others regard her as aloof, standoffish, even arrogant. It is easy to see why. But I have been a dinner guest at Rosa's home; and in that situation, she is charming, gracious, vivacious, a good listener, and an interesting conversationalist. So which is it? Is Rosa a shy person, an arrogant person, or a charming and gracious person? Will the real Rosa please stand up? It's the wrong question; the real Rosa is both and neither. All of us are capable of both shy and gracious behavior. A much more interesting question is: What factors are different in these two social situations that have such a profound effect on her (our) behavior? That is a social psychological question.

This is an important issue so we'll give you one more example. Suppose you stop at a roadside restaurant for a cup of coffee and a piece of pie. The waitress comes over to take your order, but you are having a hard time deciding which kind of pie to order. While you are hesitating, the waitress impatiently taps her pen against her order book, rolls her eyes toward the ceiling, scowls at you, and finally snaps, "Hey, I haven't got all day, you know!"

What do you conclude about this event? When faced with such a situation, most people would conclude that the waitress is a nasty or unpleasant person; consequently, they would be reluctant to enter that particular restaurant again—especially when *that* nasty person was on duty. That would certainly be understandable.

But suppose we were to tell you that the waitress is a single parent and was kept awake all night by the moaning of her youngest child, who has a painful terminal illness; that her car broke down on her way to work and she has no idea where she will find the money to have it repaired; that when she finally arrived at the restaurant, she learned that her co-worker was too drunk to work, requiring her to cover twice the usual number of tables; and that the short-order cook keeps screaming at her because she is not picking up the orders fast enough to please him. Given all that information, you might want to revise your judgment and conclude that she is not necessarily a nasty person—just an ordinary person under enormous stress.

The important fact remains that, in the absence of obvious situational information, when trying to account for a person's behavior in a complex situation, the overwhelming majority of people will jump to the conclusion that the behavior was caused by the personality of the individual involved. And this fact—that we often fail to take the situation into account—is important to a social psychologist, for it has a profound impact on how human beings relate to one another.

In sum, social psychology is located between its closest intellectual cousins, sociology and personality psychology. Social psychology shares an interest in situational and societal influences on behavior with sociology, but focuses more on the psychological makeup of individuals that renders people susceptible to social influence. Social psychology shares with personality psychology an emphasis on the psychology of the individual, but rather than focusing on what makes people different from one another, it emphasizes the psychological processes shared by most people that make them susceptible to social influence.

*T*he Power of Social Influence

Fundamental Attribution Error
the tendency to overestimate the extent to which people's behavior is due to internal, dispositional factors and to underestimate the role of situational factors

When trying to convince people that their behavior is greatly influenced by the social environment, the social psychologist is up against a formidable barrier: the inclination we all have for explaining people's behavior in terms of their personalities (e.g., the case of the waitress discussed above). This barrier is known as the **fundamental attribution error**—the tendency to explain our own and other people's behavior entirely in terms of personality traits, thereby underestimating the power of social influence.

If you are like most people, when you first encounter examples of social behavior your initial tendency will be to explain that behavior in terms of the personalities of the people involved—to overlook the power of social influence. Accordingly, we want to ask you a small favor: while reading this book, please

Try It

Social Situations and Behavior

1. Think about one of your friends or acquaintances whom you regard as a shy person. For a moment, try not to think about him or her as "a shy person," but rather as someone who has difficulty relating to people in some situations but not in others.

2. Make a list of the social situations which you think are most likely to bring out your friend's shy behavior.

3. Make a list of the social situations that might bring forth more outgoing behaviors on his/her part. (For example, if someone showed a real interest in one of your friend's favorite hobbies or topics of conversation, it might bring out behaviors that could be classified as charming or vivacious.)

4. Try to create a social environment in which this would be accomplished. Pay close attention to the effect that it has on your friend's behavior.

try to suspend judgment for a short time and consider the possibility that to understand why people do what they do, it is important to look closely at the nature of the social situation.

Underestimating the Power of Social Influence

When we underestimate the power of social influence, it tends to give us a feeling of false security. For example, when trying to explain why people do repugnant or bizarre things, such as the people of Jonestown, Waco, or Heaven's Gate taking their own lives or killing their own children, it is tempting and, in a strange way, comforting to write off the victims as flawed human beings. Doing so gives the rest of us the feeling that it could never happen to us. Ironically, this, in turn, increases our personal vulnerability to possibly destructive social influence by lulling us into lowering our guard. Moreover, by failing to fully appreciate the power of the situation, we tend to oversimplify complex situations; oversimplification decreases our understanding of the causes of a great deal of human behavior. Among other things, this oversimplification can lead us to blame the victim in situations where the individual was overpowered by social forces too difficult for most of us to resist—as in the Jonestown tragedy.

Here is an example of the kind of oversimplification we are talking about. Imagine a situation in which people are playing a two-person game wherein each player must choose one of two strategies: They can play competitively, where they try to win as much money as possible and make sure their partner loses as much as possible, or they can play cooperatively, where they try to make sure both they and their partner win some money. We will discuss the details of this game in Chapter 9. For now, it is important to note that there are only two basic strategies people can use when playing the game—competitive or cooperative. Now think about some of your friends. How do you think they would play this game?

Few people find this question hard to answer; we all have a feeling for the relative competitiveness of our friends. "Well," you might say, "I am certain that my friend Calvin, who is a cutthroat business major, would play this game more competitively than my friend Anna, who is a really caring, loving person." That is, we think of our friends' personalities and answer accordingly. We usually do not think much about the nature of the social situation when making our predictions.

But how accurate are such predictions? Should we think about the social situation? To find out, Lee Ross and Steven Samuels (1993) conducted the following experiment. First, they chose a group of students at Stanford University who were considered by the resident assistants in their dorm to be either especially cooperative or especially competitive. The researchers did this by describing the game to the resident assistants and asking them to think of students in their dormitories who would be most likely to adopt the competitive or cooperative strategy. As expected, the resident assistants had no trouble thinking of students who fit each category.

Next, Ross and Samuels invited these students to play the game in a psychology experiment. There was one added twist: The researchers varied a seemingly minor aspect of the social situation—namely, what the game was called. They told half the participants that the name of the game was the Wall Street Game and half that it was the Community Game. Everything else about the game was identical. Thus, people who were judged as either competitive or cooperative played a game that was called either the Wall Street or the Community Game, resulting in four conditions.

The head monkey at Paris puts on a traveller's cap, and all the monkeys in America do the same.
–Henry David Thoreau,
Walden, 1854

■ Is this person temporarily down on his luck or is he lazy or an addictive personality? How would this affect whether or not you give him money?

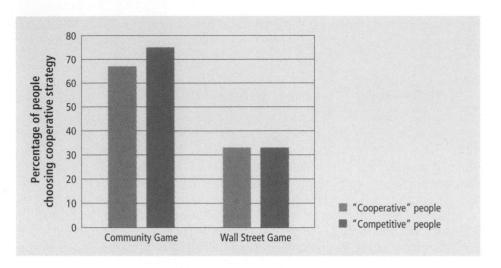

■ **FIGURE 1.1   What influences how cooperative people will be—their personalities or the nature of the social situation?**   Ross and Samuels (1993) found that college students' personalities, as rated by the resident assistants in their dormitories, did not determine how cooperative or competitive they were in a laboratory game. The name of the game—whether it was called the Wall Street Game or the Community Game—did, however, make a tremendous difference. Such seemingly minor aspects of the social situation can have powerful effects on people's behavior, overwhelming the differences in their personalities. (Adapted from Ross & Samuels, 1993)

Again, most of us go through life assuming that what really counts is an individual's personality—not something so trivial as what a game is called. Some people seem competitive by nature and would thus relish the opportunity to go head to head with a fellow student. Others seem much more cooperative and would thus achieve the most satisfaction by making sure no one lost too much money and no one's feelings were hurt. Right? Not so fast! As seen in Figure 1.1, even so trivial an aspect of the situation as the name of the game made a tremendous difference in how people behaved. When it was called the Wall Street Game, approximately two-thirds of the people responded competitively, whereas when it was called the Community Game, only a third of the people responded competitively. The name of the game conveyed strong social norms about what kind of behavior was appropriate in this situation, and, as we will see in Chapter 7, social norms can shape people's behaviors in powerful ways.

In this situation, a student's personality made no measurable difference in how he or she behaved. The students labeled "competitive" were no more likely to adopt the competitive strategy than those who were labeled "cooperative." This pattern of results is one we will encounter frequently in this book: Seemingly minor aspects of the social situation can have powerful effects, overwhelming the differences in people's personalities (Ross & Ward, 1996). This is not to say that personality differences do not exist or are unimportant; they do exist and frequently are of great importance. But we have learned that social and environmental situations are so powerful that they have dramatic effects on almost everyone. This is the domain of the social psychologist.

The Subjectivity of the Social Situation

We have argued that the social situation often has profound effects on human behavior. But what exactly do we mean by the social situation? One strategy for defining it would be to specify the objective properties of the situation, such as how rewarding it is to people, and then document the behaviors that follow from these objective properties.

This was the approach taken by **behaviorism**, a school of psychology maintaining that, to understand human behavior, one need only consider the reinforcing properties of the environment—that is, how positive and negative events in the environment are associated with specific behaviors. For example, dogs come when they are called because they have learned that compliance is followed by positive reinforcement (e.g., food or fondling); children will memorize their multiplication tables more quickly if you praise them, smile at them, and paste a gold star on their forehead following correct answers. Psychologists in this tradition, such as John Watson (1924) and B. F. Skinner (1938), suggested that all behavior could be understood by examining the rewards and punishments in the organism's environment and that there was no need to study such subjective states as thinking and feeling. Thus, to understand the behavior of the Los Angeles residents who ignored their neighbor's predawn cries for help, a behaviorist would analyze the situation to see what specific, objective factors were inhibiting any attempts to help. What were the objective rewards and punishments implicit in taking a specific course of action? What were the rewards and punishments implicit in sitting still and doing nothing?

Behaviorists chose not to deal with issues like cognition, thinking, and feeling, because they considered these concepts too vague and mentalistic and not sufficiently anchored to observable behavior. Elegant in its simplicity, the behavioristic approach can account for a great deal of behavior. But because behaviorism does not deal with cognition, thinking, and feeling—phenomena vital to the human social experience—this approach has proven inadequate for a complete understanding of the social world. We have learned that social behavior cannot fully be understood by confining our observations to the physical properties of a situation. Instead, it is important to look at the situation from the viewpoint of the people in it, to see how they construe the world around them (Griffin & Ross, 1991; Ross & Nisbett, 1991). For example, if a person approaches us, slaps us on the back, and asks us how we are feeling, is that rewarding or not? On the surface, it might seem like a reward, but it is, in actuality, a complex situation that depends on our thoughts and feelings. We might construe the meaning differently, depending on whether the question is asked by a close friend of ours who is deeply concerned that we might be working too hard, a casual acquaintance simply passing the time of day, or an automobile salesperson intending to sell us a used car—even if the question is worded the same and asked in the same tone of voice. In responding to the salesperson's question, it is unlikely that we will begin a detailed description of the pains we've been having in our kidney.

This emphasis on construal has its roots in an approach called **Gestalt psychology**. Initially proposed as a theory of how people perceive the physical word, Gestalt psychology holds that we should study the subjective way in which an object appears in people's minds (the gestalt, or whole), rather than the way in which the objective, physical attributes of the object combine. For example, one

Behaviorism
a school of psychology maintaining that to understand human behavior, one need only consider the reinforcing properties of the environment—that is, how positive and negative events in the environment are associated with specific behaviors

Gestalt Psychology
a school of psychology stressing the importance of studying the subjective way in which an object appears in people's minds, rather than the objective, physical attributes of the object

way to try to understand how people perceive a painting would be to break it down into its individual elements, such as the exact amounts of primary colors applied to the different parts of the canvas, the types of brush strokes used to apply the colors, and the different geometric shapes they form, and to attempt to determine how these elements are combined by the perceiver to form an overall image of the painting. According to Gestalt psychologists, however, it is impossible to understand the way in which an object is perceived simply by studying these building blocks of perception. The whole is different from the sum of its parts. One must focus on the phenomenology of the perceiver—that is, on how an object appears to people—instead of on the individual elements of the objective stimulus.

The Gestalt approach was formulated in Germany in the first part of this century by Kurt Koffka, Wolfgang Kohler, Max Wertheimer, and their students and colleagues. In the late 1930s, several of these psychologists immigrated to the United States to escape the Nazi regime and subsequently had such a major influence on American psychology that one astute observer remarked, "If I were required to name the one person who has had the greatest impact on the field, it would have to be Adolf Hitler" (Cartwright, 1979, p. 84).

Among these was Kurt Lewin, generally considered to be the founding father of modern experimental social psychology. As a young German-Jewish professor, Lewin directly experienced the intolerance for cultural diversity rampant in that country in the 1930s. This experience not only had a major impact on his own thinking but, once he came to America, helped shape American social psychology and directed it toward a deep and abiding interest in the exploration of causes and cures of prejudice and ethnic stereotyping.

As a theorist, Lewin took the bold step of applying Gestalt principles beyond the perception of objects to social perception—how people perceive other people and their motives, intentions, and behaviors. Lewin was the first scientist to fully realize the importance of taking the perspective of the people in any social situation to see how they construe (e.g., perceive, interpret, distort) this social environment. Social psychologists soon began to focus on the importance of considering subjective situations (how they are construed by people). These early social psychologists and their key statements are presented on the following pages.

Such construals can be rather simple, as in the example of the question "How are you feeling?" discussed earlier. Other construals might appear simple but are, in reality, remarkably complex. For example, suppose Maria gives Shawn a kiss on the cheek at the end of their first date. How will Shawn respond to the kiss? We would say that it depends on how he construes the situation: Does he interpret it as a first step—a sign of awakening romantic interest on Maria's part? Or does he see it as an aloof, sisterly expression—a signal that Maria wants to be friends but nothing more? Or does he see it as a sign that Maria is interested in him but wants things to go slow in their developing relationship?

Were Shawn to misconstrue the situation, he might commit a serious blunder; he might turn his back on what could have been the love of his life—or he might express passion inappropriately. In either case, we believe that the best strategy for understanding Shawn's reaction would be to find a way to determine Shawn's construal of Maria's behavior, rather than to dissect the objective nature of the kiss itself (its length, degree of pressure, etc.). But how are these construals formed? Stay tuned.

Where Construals Come From: Basic Human Motives

How will Shawn determine why Maria kissed him? If it is true that subjective and not objective situations influence people, then we need to understand how people arrive at their subjective impressions of the world. What are people trying to accomplish when they interpret the social world? Again, we could address this question from the perspective of people's personalities. What is it about Shawn, including his upbringing, family background, and unique experiences, that makes him view the world the way he does? As we have seen, such a focus on individual differences in people's personalities, while valuable, misses what is usually of far greater importance: the effects of the social situation on people. To understand these effects, we need to understand the fundamental laws of human nature, common to all, that explain why we construe the social world the way we do.

We human beings are complex organisms; at a given moment, myriad intersecting motives underlie our thoughts and behaviors. Over the years, social psychologists have found that two of these motives are of primary importance: the need to be as accurate as possible and the need to feel good about ourselves.

As we go through life, there are times when each of these motives pulls us in the same direction. Often, however, we find ourselves in situations where these two motives tug us in opposite directions—where to perceive the world accurately requires us to face up to the fact that we have behaved foolishly or immorally.

Fritz Heider—"Generally, a person reacts to what he thinks the other person is perceiving, feeling, and thinking, in addition to what the other person may be doing." (1958)

Leon Festinger—"The way I have always thought about it is that if the empirical world looks complicated, if people seem to react in bewilderingly different ways to similar forces, and if I cannot see the operation of universal underlying dynamics, then that is my fault. I have asked the wrong questions; I have, at a theoretical level, sliced up the world incorrectly. The underlying dynamics are there, and I have to find the theoretical apparatus that will enable me to reveal these uniformities."

Kurt Lewin—"If an individual sits in a room trusting that the ceiling will not come down, should only his 'subjective probability' be taken into account for predicting behavior or should we also consider the 'objective probability' of the ceiling's coming down as determined by engineers? To my mind, only the first has to be taken into account." (1943)

Leon Festinger, one of social psychology's most innovative theorists, was quick to realize that it is precisely when these two motives tug an individual in opposite directions that we can gain our most valuable insights into the workings of the human heart and mind. An example will clarify. Imagine you are the president of the United States and your country is engaged in a difficult and costly war in Southeast Asia. You have poured hundreds of billions of dollars into that war, and it has consumed tens of thousands of American lives as well as a great many more lives of innocent Vietnamese civilians. The war seems to be at a stalemate; no end is in sight. You frequently wake up in the middle of the night bathed in the cold sweat of conflict: On the one hand, you deplore all the carnage that is going on; on the other hand, you don't want to go down in history as the first American president to lose a war.

Some of your advisers tell you that they can see the light at the end of the tunnel—that if you intensify the bombing, the enemy will soon capitulate and the war will be over. This would be a great outcome for you; not only will you have succeeded in achieving your military and political aims, but history will consider you to have been a hero. Other advisers, however, believe that intensifying the bombing will result only in strengthening the enemy's resolve; they advise you to sue for peace (McNamara, 1995).

Which advisers are you likely to believe? As we shall see in Chapter 6, President Lyndon Johnson was faced with exactly this dilemma. Not surprisingly, he chose to believe those advisers who suggested that he escalate the war, for if he could succeed in winning the war he would justify his prior behavior as commander in chief, whereas if he withdrew from Vietnam he not only would go down in history as the first president to lose a war, but also would have to justify the fact that all those lives and all that money had been spent in vain. This advice, however, proved to be erroneous. Increasing the bombing served only to strengthen the enemy's resolve, thereby needlessly prolonging the war. As this example illustrates, the need for self-justification can fly in the face of the need to be accurate—and can have catastrophic consequences.

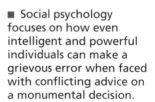

■ Social psychology focuses on how even intelligent and powerful individuals can make a grievous error when faced with conflicting advice on a monumental decision.

The Self-Esteem Approach: The Desire to Feel Good About Ourselves

Most people have a strong need to maintain reasonably high **self-esteem**—that is, to see themselves as good, competent, and decent (Aronson, 1992; Aronson, 1998; Baumeister, 1993; Blaine & Crocker, 1993; Harter, 1993; Kunda, 1990; Pyszczynski et al., 1995; Stone, 1998; Thibodeau & Aronson, 1992; Tice, 1993). The reason people view the world the way they do can often be traced to this underlying need to maintain a favorable image of themselves. Given the choice between distorting the world in order to feel good about themselves and representing the world accurately, people often take the first option.

Self-Esteem
people's evaluations of their own self-worth—that is, the extent to which they view themselves as good, competent, and decent

Justifying Past Behavior

Suppose a couple gets divorced after ten years of a marriage made difficult by the husband's irrational jealousy. Suppose the husband blames the breakup of his marriage on the fact that his ex-wife was not sufficiently responsive or attentive to his needs, rather than admitting the truth: that his jealousy and over possessiveness drove her away. His interpretation serves some purpose, in that it makes him feel better about himself—it is very difficult to own up to major deficiencies in ourselves, even when the cost is seeing the world inaccurately. The consequence of this distortion, of course, is that it decreases the probability of learning from experience; that is, in his next marriage the husband is likely to run into the same problems.

We do not mean to imply that people totally distort reality, denying the existence of all information that reflects badly on them; such extreme behavior is rare outside of mental institutions. Yet it is often possible for normal people like you and us to put a slightly different spin on the existing facts, one that puts us in the best possible light. Consider Roger; everybody knows someone like Roger. He's the guy whose shoes are almost always untied and who frequently has coffee stains on the front of his shirt or mustard stains around his lips. Most observers might consider Roger to be a slob, but Roger might see himself as casual and noncompulsive. Or, if Heather is playing basketball and has missed six or seven easy lay-ups in succession, her teammates might consider her to be untalented and might begin to think twice about passing the ball to her; on the other hand, Heather might simply feel that she hasn't yet gotten into her rhythm.

The fact that people distort their interpretation of reality so that they might feel better about themselves is not surprising, even to the most casual observer of human behavior. The ways in which this motive operates, however, are often startling—and shed a great deal of light on behavior that would otherwise be mystifying.

Suffering and Self-Justification

Let's go back to one of our early scenarios: the case of Oscar and his son, Sam. Why was Sam less enamored of his fraternity brothers than Oscar had been when he was in college? You will recall that Oscar was quick to form the hypothesis that perhaps his fraternity was not attracting the kinds of wonderful people who were there when he was in college. This might be true. But we would assert that a far more compelling possibility involves the hazing itself. Specifically, we would contend that a major factor that increased Oscar's liking for his fraternity brothers was the unpleasant hazing ritual he underwent, a ritual Sam was able to avoid. That sounds a little strange. Why would something so unpleasant cause Oscar to like his fraternity? Didn't behavioristic psychology teach us that rewards, not punishments, make us like things associated with them? Quite so. But as we indicated earlier, in recent years social psychologists have discovered that this formulation is far too simple to account for human thinking and motivation. Unlike rats and pigeons, human beings have a need to justify their past behavior, and this need leads them to thoughts, feelings, and behaviors that don't always fit into the neat categories of the behaviorist.

Here's how it works. If Oscar goes through a severe hazing in order to become a member of the fraternity but later discovers unpleasant things about his fraternity brothers, he will feel like a fool: "Why did I go through all that pain and embarrassment in order to live in a house with a bunch of jerks? Only a moron would do a thing like that." In order to avoid feeling like a fool, he will try to justify his decision to undergo the hazing by distorting his interpretation of his fraternity experience. That is, he will try to put a positive spin on his experiences.

Suppose that, having gone through all that hazing, Oscar moves into the fraternity house and begins to experience things that, to an outside observer, are not very positive: The fraternity dues make a significant dent in Oscar's budget; the frequent parties are mindless and take a toll on the amount of studying he can do, and consequently his grades begin to suffer; most of the meals served in the house are only a small step up from dog chow. While an unmotivated observer—someone who didn't go through the hazing—might consider these experiences to be extremely negative, Oscar is motivated to see them differently; indeed, he considers them to be a small price to pay for the sense of brotherhood he feels toward his fraternity brothers. He focuses on the good parts of living in the fraternity, and he distorts or dismisses the bad parts as inconsequential. The result of all this self-justification is bound to make Oscar more kindly disposed toward the fraternity than Sam was, because Sam, not having gone through the hazing, had no need to justify his behavior and thus no need to see his fraternity experiences in a positive light. The end result? Oscar loved his fraternity; Sam did not.

Does this sound far-fetched? How do we know that the people in the fraternity were not objectively nicer when Oscar was a member than when Sam was a member? In a series of well-controlled laboratory experiments, social psychologists have investigated the phenomenon of hazing, holding constant everything in the situation—including the precise behavior of the fraternity members—except for the severity of the hazing students underwent in order to become members. These experiments demonstrated conclusively that the more unpleasant the procedure the participants underwent to get into a group, the better they liked the group—even though, objectively, the group members were the same people, behaving in the same manner (Aronson & Mills, 1959; Gerald & Mathewson, 1966). This phenomenon will be discussed more thoroughly in Chapter 6. The important points to remember here are that (a) human beings are motivated to maintain a positive picture of themselves, in part by justifying their past behavior, and (b) under certain specifiable conditions, this leads them to do things that at first glance might seem surprising or paradoxical—for example, to prefer those people and things for whom they have suffered to those people and things they associate with easiness and pleasure.

Again, we want to emphasize that the results of this research tradition should not be taken to mean that behaviorist theories are dead wrong; those theories ex-

■ Our desire to maintain self-esteem can have surprising consequences. Does undergoing a dangerous or embarrassing fraternity hazing increase or decrease people's liking for the fraternity? Social psychological research demonstrates that when people volunteer to undergo a painful or embarrassing initiation in order to join a group, they need to justify the experience to avoid feeling foolish. One way they do this is to decide that the initiation was worth it, because the group is so wonderful.

plain some behavior very well (e.g., see our discussion in Chapter 10 of the research on social exchange theory). In our view, however, behavioristic approaches are inadequate to account for a huge subset of important attitudes and behaviors. This will become much clearer as you read on; in future chapters, we will try to specify the precise conditions under which one or the other set of principles is more likely to apply.

The Social Cognition Approach: The Need to Be Accurate

As mentioned earlier, even when people are bending the facts to cast themselves in as favorable a light as they can, they do not completely distort reality. It would not be very adaptive to live in a fantasy world, believing that the car speeding toward us as we step off the curb is really a mirage, or that our future spouse will be Denzel Washington or Kim Basinger, as soon as he or she gets done making movies and arrives at our doorstep. In fact, human beings are quite skilled at thinking, contemplating, and deducing. One of the major hallmarks of being human is the ability to reason. As a species, we have highly developed logical and computational abilities that are truly amazing. In our lifetime alone, we have witnessed such extraordinary cognitive achievements as the invention and development of computers, the exploration of outer space, and the conquering of many human diseases.

Moreover, on a more common (but perhaps more important) level, it is impossible to observe the cognitive development of a child without being awestruck. Just think of the vast gains in knowledge and reasoning that occur in the first few years of life. In a relatively short time, we see our child transform from a squirming, helpless newborn, who can do little but eat, cry, and sleep, into a sophisticated, garrulous four-year-old, who can utter complex sentences, hatch diabolic plots to frustrate a younger sibling, and evoke consternation (and pride) in parents.

Social Cognition

Given the amazing cognitive abilities of our species, it makes sense that social psychologists, when formulating theories of social behavior, would take into consideration the way in which human beings think about the world. We call this the cognitive approach to social psychology, or **social cognition** (Fiske & Taylor, 1991; Markus & Zajonc, 1985, 1998; Nisbett & Ross, 1980). Those researchers who attempt to understand social behavior from the perspective of social cognition begin with the assumption that all people try to view the world as accurately as possible. Accordingly, human beings are viewed by researchers as amateur sleuths who are doing their best to understand and predict their social world.

But this is by no means as easy or as straightforward as it may seem. We human beings frequently run into problems because we almost never know all the facts we need in order to make the most accurate judgment of a given situation. Whether it is a relatively simple decision, like which breakfast cereal is the best combination of healthfulness and tastiness, or a slightly more complex decision, like our desire to buy the best car we can for under $18,000, or a much more complex decision, like choosing a marriage partner who will make us deliriously happy for the rest of our lives, it is almost never easy to gather all the relevant facts in advance. Moreover, we make countless decisions every day; even if there was a way to gather all the facts for each decision, we simply lack the time or the stamina to do so.

Does this sound a bit overblown? Aren't most decisions fairly easy? Let's take a closer look. We will begin by asking you a simple question: Which breakfast cereal is better for you, Lucky Charms or 100% Natural from Quaker? If you are like most of our students, you answered "100% Natural from Quaker." After all, everybody knows that Lucky Charms is a kid's cereal, full of sugar and cute little marshmallows. Besides, there is a picture of a leprechaun on the box, for goodness' sake. And 100% Natural has a picture of raw wheat on the box, the box is the color of natural wheat (light tan), and doesn't natural mean "good for you"?

Social Cognition
how people think about themselves and the social world; more specifically, how people select, interpret, remember, and use social information

■ Which of these cereals is better for you? The answer may surprise you (see the discussion in the text to find out). Even when we are trying to make accurate judgments about the social world, we often make mistakes.

If that is the way you reasoned, you have, understandably, fallen into a common cognitive trap—you have generalized from the cover to the product. A careful reading of the ingredients (in small print on the package) will inform you that, although Lucky Charms has a bit more sugar in it than 100% Natural, the latter contains far more fat—so much so that the respected journal *Consumer Reports* has judged it to be less healthful than Lucky Charms. Things are not always what they appear to be; thus, coming up with an accurate picture of the social world is not always easy.

Expectations About the Social World

To add to the difficulty, sometimes our expectations about the social world get in the way of perceiving it accurately. Our expectations can even change the nature of the social world. Imagine, for example, that you are an elementary school teacher dedicated to improving the lives of your students as best you can. You are aware at the beginning of the academic year how each student performed on standardized intelligence tests. Early in your career, you were pretty sure, but not *entirely* sure that these tests could gauge each child's true potential. But after several years of teaching, you have gradually become certain that these tests are accurate. Why the change? Almost without fail, you have come to see that the kids who got high scores on these tests are the ones who did the best in your classroom, and the kids who got low scores performed poorly in class.

This scenario doesn't sound all that surprising, except for one key fact: You might be very wrong about the validity of the intelligence tests. It might be that the tests weren't very accurate but that you unintentionally treated the kids with high scores and the kids with low scores differently, making it look like the tests were accurate. This is exactly what Robert Rosenthal and Lenore Jacobson (1968) found in their investigation of a phenomenon called the *self-fulfilling prophecy.* They first entered elementary school classrooms and administered a test. They then informed each teacher that, according to the test, a few specific students were bloomers—that is, they were about to take off and perform extremely well. In actuality, the test showed no such thing; the children labeled as bloomers were chosen by drawing names out of a hat and thus were no different, on average, from any of the other kids. Lo and behold, on returning to the classroom at the end of the school year, Rosenthal and Jacobson found that the bloomers were performing extremely well. The mere fact that the teachers were led to expect these students to do well caused a reliable improvement in their performance. This striking phenomenon is no fluke; it has been replicated a number of times in a wide variety of schools (Rosenthal, 1995).

How did it come about? Though this outcome seems almost magical, it is imbedded in an important aspect of human nature. If you were one of those teachers and were led to expect two or three specific students to perform well, you would be more likely to treat those students in special ways—such as paying more attention to them, listening to them with more respect, calling on them more frequently, encouraging them, and trying to teach them more difficult material. This in turn would almost certainly make these students feel happier, more respected, more motivated, and smarter, and—voilà—a self-fulfilling prophecy. Thus, even when we are trying to perceive the social world as accurately as we can, there are many ways in which we can go wrong, ending up with the wrong impressions. We will see why—and the conditions under which social perception is accurate—in Chapters 3 and 4.

Other Motives

We want to reiterate what we stated earlier: The two major sources of construals we have emphasized here—the need to maintain a positive view of ourselves (the self-esteem approach) and the need to view the world accurately (the social cognition approach)—are the most important of our social motives, but they are certainly not the only motives influencing people's thoughts and behaviors. As noted earlier, we human beings are complex organisms, and under various conditions a variety of motives influence what we think, feel, and do. Biological drives such as hunger and thirst, of course, can be powerful motivators, especially under circumstances of extreme deprivation. At a more psychological level, we can be motivated by fear or by the promise of love, favors, and other rewards involving social exchange. These motives will be discussed at length in Chapters 10 and 11.

Still another significant motive is the need for control. Research has shown that people need to feel they exert some control over their environment (Langer, 1975; Seligman, 1975; Taylor, 1989; Thompson, 1981). When people experience a loss of control, such that they believe they have little or no influence over whether good or bad things happen to them, there are a number of important consequences; we will discuss these further along in this book.

Social Psychology and Social Problems

To recapitulate, social psychology can be defined as the scientific study of social influence. Social influence can best be understood by examining the basic human motives that produce the subjective views people form about their environment. It might have occurred to you to ask why we want to understand social influence in the first place. Who cares? And what difference does it make whether a behavior has its roots in the desire to be accurate or in the desire to bolster our self-esteem?

There are several answers to these questions. The most basic answer is simple: We are curious. Social psychologists are fascinated by human social behavior and want to understand it on the deepest possible level. In a sense, all of us are social psychologists. We all live in a social environment, and we all are more than mildly curious about such issues as how we become influenced, how we influence others, and why we fall in love with some people, dislike others, and are indifferent to still others.

Many social psychologists have another reason for studying the causes of social behavior—namely, to contribute to the solution of social problems. From the very beginnings of our young science, social psychologists have been keenly interested in such social problems as the reduction of hostility and prejudice and the increase of altruism and generosity. Contemporary social psychologists have continued this tradition and have broadened the issues of concern to include such endeavors as inducing people to conserve natural resources like water and energy (Dickerson et al., 1992), educating people to practice safer sex in order to reduce the spread of AIDS (Aronson, 1997, 1998; Stone et al., 1994), understanding the relationship between viewing violence on television and the violent behavior of television-watchers (Eron et al., 1996), developing effective negotiation strategies for the reduction of international conflict (Kelman, 1997), finding ways to reduce racial prejudice (Aronson & Patnoe, 1997), and helping people adjust to life changes like the entry to college or the death of a loved one (Harris, 1986).

> "Understanding does not cure evil, but it is a definite help, inasmuch as one can cope with a comprehensible darkness.
>
> —Carl Jung

■ Among the many kinds of relevant issues social psychologists investigate are these: (a) Does watching violence on TV produce violent behavior in youngsters? (b) Does cooperation reduce prejudice? (c) Are celebrity endorsements effective in selling a product?

The ability to understand and explain complex and dysfunctional social behavior brings with it the challenge to change it. For example, when our government began to take the AIDS epidemic seriously, it mounted an advertising campaign that seemed intent on frightening people into practicing safer sex. This seems consistent with common sense: If you want people to do something they wouldn't ordinarily do, why not scare the daylights out of them?

This is certainly not a stupid idea. As we shall see in subsequent chapters, there are many dysfunctional acts (e.g., cigarette smoking, drunk driving) for which the induction of fear can and does motivate people to take rational, appropriate action to preserve their health (Levy-Leboyer, 1988; Wilson, Purdon, and Wallston, 1988). But based on years of systematic research on persuasion, social psychologists were quick to realize that, in the specific situation of AIDS, arousing fear would almost certainly not produce the desired effect for most people. The weight of the research evidence suggests that, where sexual behavior is involved, the situation becomes infinitely more murky. Specifically, most people do not want to be thinking about dying or contracting a painful illness while they are getting ready to have sex. Such thoughts can, to say the least, interfere with the romantic aspect of the situation. Moreover, most people do not enjoy using condoms, because they feel that interrupting the sexual act to put on a condom tends to destroy the mood. Given these considerations, when people have been exposed to frightening messages, instead of engaging in rational problem-solving behavior most tend to reduce that fear by engaging in denial ("It can't happen to me," "Surely none of my friends have AIDS," etc.).

The astute reader will see that the process of denial stems not from the desire to be accurate but from the desire to maintain one's self esteem. That is, if people can succeed in convincing themselves that their sexual partners do not have AIDS, then they can continue to enjoy unprotected sex while maintaining a reasonably good picture of themselves as a rational person. By understanding the conditions under which self-esteem maintenance prevails, social psychologists have been able to contribute important insights to AIDS education and prevention, as we shall see (Aronson, 1997; Aronson, Fried, & Stone, 1991; Stone et al., 1994).

Throughout this book, we will examine many similar examples of the applications of social psychology. Likewise, throughout this book we will also discuss some of the underlying human motives and the characteristics of the social situation that produce significant social behaviors, with the assumption that, if we are interested in changing our own or other people's behavior, we must first know something about these fundamental causes. Although most of the studies discussed in these chapters are concerned with such fundamental causes, in the process they also address critical social problems, including the effects of the mass media on attitudes and behavior (Chapter 7), violence and aggression (Chapter 12), and prejudice (Chapter 13). For the benefit of the interested reader, we have also included three separate "modules" centering on the application of social psychology to contemporary issues involving health, the environment, and law. These are briefer and less detailed than regular chapters; the instructor may assign them at any time during the semester or may decide not to assign them at all, allowing that decision to depend on the curiosity of the individual student.

Summary

People are constantly being influenced by other people. **Social psychology** is defined as the scientific study of the way in which people's thoughts, feelings, and behaviors are influenced by the real or imagined presence of other people. Social influence is often powerful, usually outweighing and frequently overwhelming **individual differences** in people's personalities as determinants of human behavior. To appreciate this fact, we must try to avoid making the **fundamental attribution error**—the tendency to explain our own and others' behavior entirely in terms of personality traits, thus underestimating the power of social influence.

To appreciate the power of social influence, we must understand how people form **construals** of their social environment. We are not computer-like organisms who respond directly and mechanically to environmental stimuli; rather, we are complex human beings who perceive, think about, and sometimes distort information from our environment. By emphasizing the way in which people construe the social world, social psychology has its roots more in the tradition of **Gestalt psychology** than in that of **behaviorism.**

Although human behavior is complex and nonmechanical, it is not unfathomable. A person's construals of the world are rooted primarily in two fundamental motives: the desire to maintain **self-esteem** and the desire to form an accurate picture of oneself and the social world (the **social cognition** approach). Accordingly, to understand how we are influenced by our social environments we must understand the processes by which we do the perceiving, thinking, and distorting. Two major concepts in social psychology can thus be stated succinctly: (a) Social influence has a powerful impact on people, and (b) to understand the power of social influence, we must examine the motives that determine how people construe the social environment.

We also discussed another important point about social psychology: It is an empirical science.

Social psychologists attempt to find answers to key questions about social influence by designing and conducting research, rather than by relying on common sense or the wisdom of the ages. In Chapter 2, we will discuss the scientific methods social psychologists use when conducting such research.

If You Are Interested

Aron, A., & Aron, E. (1992). *The heart of social psychology.* Lexington, MA: Lexington Books. A highly readable look behind the scenes at how eminent social psychologists view their discipline.

Festinger, L. (Ed.). (1980). *Retrospections on social psychology.* New York: Oxford University Press. A collection of articles by many of the most eminent scientists in the field of social psychology. Even though this book is almost two decades old, it remains an excellent source of articles about the origins of the field and its current research trends.

Fiske, S., & Taylor, S. (1991). *Social cognition.* New York: McGraw-Hill. Everything you always wanted to know about the topic of social cognition—and more. Scholarly, thorough, and well-written by two of the leading figures in the area.

Jones, E. E. (1998). Major developments in social psychology during the past six decades. In D. Gilbert, S. Fiske, & G. Lindzey (Eds.), *The handbook of social psychol-* ogy. (4th ed., Vol. 1, 1998). New York: McGraw-Hill. A thorough treatment of the history of social psychology from a leading researcher in the field. This chapter discusses the roots of the field, plots the changes in its emphases and trends, and details its intellectual history.

Ross, L., & Nisbett, R. E. (1991). *The person and the situation: Perspectives of social psychology.* New York: McGraw-Hill. An entertaining, insightful look at many of the ideas presented in this chapter, including the importance of considering people's construals of social situations and the ways in which those construals are often more powerful determinants of people's behavior than their personalities are.

Taylor, S. (1998). Conceptualizations of the social being. In D. Gilbert, S. Fiske, & G. Lindzey (Eds.), *The handbook of social psychology* (4th ed., Vol. 1, 1998). New York: McGraw-Hill. A scholarly analysis of the different theoretical approaches to understanding human social behavior.

CHAPTER 2

METHODOLOGY: HOW SOCIAL PSYCHOLOGISTS DO RESEARCH

n 1985, the attorney general of the United States, Edwin Meese III, convened a commission to address an important question: Does exposure to pornography increase the likelihood that people will commit sexual violence? This group, which became known as the Meese Commission, concluded that pornography is a cause of rape and other violent crimes. Many social critics have agreed with this conclusion (e.g., Russell, 1997). For example, Catharine MacKinnon (1993) described horrendous crimes being committed by Serbs against Croatian and Muslim women, including rape, torture, and murder, and pointed to pornography as one of the causes: "Pornography is the perfect preparation—motivator and instruction manual in one—for the sexual atrocities ordered in this genocide" (p. 28).

However, several other experts were quick to disagree with the conclusions of the Meese Commission, claiming that its findings were based more on political and moral concerns than on solid scientific evidence (Vance, 1986; Strossen, 1997). In fact, the commission's conclusions were the opposite of those of the 1970 Presidential Commission on Obscenity and Pornography, which reported that pornography did not contribute significantly to sexual violence. This is an extremely important question to answer, given the increasing availability of sexually explicit material, such as on the internet. But as with many other issues, different experts have different opinions. How can we decide who is right? A national news magazine often polls its readers about various psychological questions, such as the effects of pornography. Is this a case where majority opinion rules, or is there a more scientific way to determine the answers?

In addition to addressing important questions about the causes of violent behavior, we also need to find ways of stopping violence once it occurs. If you happen to witness someone being attacked by another person you might not intervene directly, out of fear for your own safety. Most of us assume that we would help in some way, though, such as by calling the police. It is because of this very assumption that people were so shocked by an incident that occurred in the early 1960s, in the Queens section of New York City. A woman named Kitty Genovese was attacked while walking to her car and brutally murdered in the alley of an apartment complex. The attack lasted 45 minutes. No fewer than 38 of the apartment residents admitted later that they had rushed to their windows after hearing Genovese's screams for help. However, not one of the bystanders attempted in any way to help her—none of them even bothered to telephone the police. As you might imagine, the Kitty Genovese murder received a

■ This is the area where Kitty Genovese was attacked, in full view of her neighbors. Why didn't anyone call the police?

great deal of publicity. Reporters, commentators, and pundits of all kinds came forward with their personal theories about why the bystanders had done nothing. The most popular explanation was that there is something dehumanizing about living in a metropolis that inevitably leads to apathy, indifference to human suffering, and lack of caring. The blame was laid on New York and New Yorkers; the general belief was that this kind of thing would not have happened in a small town, where people care more about each other (Rosenthal, 1964). Was big-city life the cause of the bystanders' behavior? Or was there some other explanation? Again, how can we find out?

Social Psychology: An Empirical Science

A fundamental principle of social psychology is that many social problems, like the causes of and reactions to violence, can be studied empirically (Aronson, Wilson, & Brewer, 1998; Kenny, Kashy, & Bolger, 1998; Judd & McClelland, 1998). As mentioned in Chapter 1, it is insufficient to rely on personal beliefs, folk wisdom, hope, or magazine polls when answering questions about human behavior. Many personal observations are astute and accurate reflections of social reality, whereas others are far off the mark. To tell the difference, our observations must be translated into hypotheses that can be tested scientifically. In the case of pornography, respected experts disagree as to its effects, and scientific investigations are the true arbiters of such disputes.

Because we will describe the results of many empirical studies in this book, it is important to discuss how social psychological research is done. We begin with a warning: The results of some of the experiments you encounter will seem obvious, because the topic of social psychology is something with which we are all intimately familiar—social behavior and social influence. Note that this fact separates social psychology from other sciences. When you read about an experiment in particle physics, it is unlikely that the results will connect with your personal experiences and have a ring of familiarity. We don't know about you, but we have never thought, "Wow! That experiment on quarks was just like what happened to me while I was waiting for the bus yesterday," or "My grandmother always told me to watch out for quarks, positrons, and antimatter." When reading about the results of a study on helping behavior or aggression, however, it is quite common to think, "Aw, come on, I could have predicted that. That's the same thing that happened to me last Friday."

The thing to remember is that such findings appear obvious only in retrospect because most examples of human behavior seem to make sense and to have been easily predictable (Fischhoff, 1975; Hertwig, Gigerenzer, & Hoffrage, 1997; Nario & Branscombe, 1995; Roese & Olson, 1996). Given that many folk sayings are contradictory, the opposite finding of an experiment might have seemed just as obvious. The trick is to predict what will happen in an experiment before you know how it turned out. To illustrate what we mean when we say that not all obvious findings are easy to predict in advance, take the Try It! quiz on page 34. Each answer is based on well-established social psychological research. In our

//   *Try It !*

Social Psychology Quiz

Take a moment to answer the questions below, each of which is based on social psychological research. Though the correct answers may seem obvious in retrospect, many are hard to guess in advance.

1. Suppose an authority figure asks college students to administer near-lethal electric shocks to another student who has not harmed them in any way. What percentage of these students will agree to do it?

2. If you give children a reward for doing something they already enjoy doing, they will subsequently like that activity (a) more, (b) the same, or (c) less.

3. Who do you think would be happiest with their choice of a consumer product, such as an art poster? (a) people who spend several minutes thinking about why they like or dislike each poster; (b) people who choose a poster without analyzing the reasons for their feelings.

4. Repeated exposure to a stimulus, such as a person, a song, or a painting, will make you like it (a) more, (b) the same, or (c) less.

5. You ask an acquaintance to do you a favor—for example, to lend you $10—and he or she agrees. As a result of doing you this favor, the person will probably like you (a) more, (b) the same, or (c) less.

6. True or false: It is most adaptive and beneficial to people's mental health to have a realistic view of the future, an accurate appraisal of their own abilities and traits, and an accurate view of how much control they have over their lives.

7. In the United States, female college students tend not to do as well on math tests as males do. Under which of the following circumstances will women do as well as men? (a) When they are told that there are no gender differences on a test, (b) when they are told that women tend to do better on a difficult math test, because under these circumstances, they rise to the challenge, or (c) when they are told that men outperform women under almost all circumstances.

8. Which kind of advertising is most effective? (a) subliminal messages implanted in advertisements, or (b) normal, everyday advertising, such as TV ads for pain killers or laundry detergents.

9. In public settings, (a) women touch men more, (b) men touch women more, or (c) there is no difference—men and women touch each other equally.

10. Which things in their past do people regret the most? (a) actions they performed that they wish they had not, (b) actions they did not perform that they wish they had, or (c) it depends on how long ago the events occurred.

ANSWERS

1. In studies conducted by Stanley Milgram (1974), up to 65 percent of participants administered what they thought were near-lethal shocks to another subject. (In fact, no real shocks were administered.)

2. (c) Rewarding people for doing something they enjoy will typically make them like that activity less in the future (e.g., Lepper, Greene, & Nisbett, 1973; Lepper, 1995, 1996).

3. (b) Wilson et al. (1993) found that people who did not analyze their feelings were the most satisfied with their choice of posters when contacted a few weeks later (see also Wilson, LaFleur, & Lindsey, in press).

4. (a) Under most circumstances, repeated exposure increases liking for a stimulus (Zajonc, 1968).

5. (a) More (Jecker & Landy, 1969).

6. False (Taylor & Brown, 1988, 1994).

7. (a) Research by Spencer, Steele, and Quinn (1997) found that when women think there are sex differences on a test they do worse, because of the fear that they might confirm a negative stereotype about their gender—the fear of *stereotype threat*. When women were told that there were no gender differences in performance on the test, they did as well as men.

8. (b) There is no evidence that subliminal messages in advertising have any effect, whereas there is substantial evidence that normal, everyday advertising is quite effective (Abraham & Lodish, 1990; Chaiken, Wood, & Eagly, 1996; Liebert & Spratkin, 1988; Moore, 1982; Weir, 1984; Wilson, Houston, & Meyers, in press).

9. (b) Men touch women more than vice versa (Henley, 1977).

10. (c) Gilovich and Medvec have found that in the short run, people regret acts of commission (things they did that they wish they hadn't) more than acts of omission (things they didn't do that they wish they had). In the long run, however, people come to regret acts of omission more than acts of commission (Gilovich & Medvec, 1995; Gilovich, Medvec, & Chen, 1995).

//

experience as teachers, we have found that few of our students get all the answers correct. Findings that seem obvious in retrospect may not be so easy to predict in advance.

Social psychology is an empirical science, with a well-developed set of methods to answer questions about social behavior, such as the ones about violence with which we began this chapter. These methods are of three types: the observational method, the correlational method, and the experimental method. Any of these methods could be used to explore a specific research question; each is a powerful tool in some ways and a weak tool in others. Part of the creativity in conducting social psychological research involves choosing the right method, maximizing its strengths, and minimizing its weaknesses.

In this chapter, we will discuss these methods in detail. We, the authors of this book, are not primarily textbook writers—we are social scientists who have done a great deal of experimental research in social psychology. As such, we will try to provide you with an understanding of both the joy and the difficulty of doing research. The joy comes in unraveling the clues about the causes of interesting and important social behaviors, just as a sleuth gradually unmasks the culprit in a murder mystery. Each of us finds it exhilarating that we have the tools to provide definitive answers to questions philosophers have debated for centuries. At the same time, as seasoned researchers, we have learned to temper this exhilaration with a heavy dose of humility, for the practical and ethical constraints involved in creating and conducting social psychological research are formidable.

Formulating Hypotheses and Theories

Research begins with a hunch, or hypothesis, that the researcher wants to test. Thus, a good place to begin is with the origin of these hypotheses. There is a lore in science that brilliant insights come all of a sudden, as when Archimedes shouted "Eureka! I have found it!" when the solution to a problem flashed into his mind. Though such insights do sometimes occur suddenly, science is a cumulative process, and people often generate hypotheses from previous theories and research.

Inspiration from Previous Theories and Research

Many studies stem from a researcher's dissatisfaction with existing theories and explanations. After reading other people's work, a researcher might believe that he or she has a better way of explaining people's behavior (e.g., why they fail to help in an emergency). In the 1950s, for example, Leon Festinger was dissatisfied with the ability of a major theory of the day, behaviorism, to explain attitude change. He formulated a new approach—dissonance theory—that made specific predictions about when and how people would change their attitudes. As we will see in an upcoming chapter, other researchers were dissatisfied with Festinger's explanation of the results he obtained, and so they conducted further research to test other possible explanations. Social psychologists, like scientists in other disciplines, engage in a continual process of theory refinement: A theory is developed; specific hypotheses derived from that theory are tested; based on the results obtained, the theory is revised and new hypotheses are formulated.

Hypotheses Based on Personal Observations

Theory is not the only way to derive a new hypothesis in social psychology. Researchers often observe a phenomenon in everyday life that they find curious and interesting. The researchers then construct a theory about why this phenomenon occurred and design a study to see if they are right.

Consider the murder of Kitty Genovese that we discussed earlier. As we saw, most people blamed her neighbors' failure to intervene on the apathy, indifference, and callousness that big-city life breeds. Two social psychologists who taught at universities in New York, however, had a different idea. Bibb Latané and John Darley got to talking one day about the Genovese murder. Here is how Latané describes it: "One evening after [a] downtown cocktail party, John Darley . . . came back with me to my 12th Street apartment for a drink. Our common complaint was the distressing tendency of acquaintances, on finding that we called ourselves social psychologists, to ask why New Yorkers were so apathetic" (Latané, 1987, p. 78). Instead of focusing on "what was wrong with New Yorkers," Latané and Darley thought it would be more interesting and more important to examine the social situation in which Genovese's neighbors found themselves: "We came up with the insight that perhaps what made the Genovese case so fascinating was itself what made it happen—namely, that not just one or two, but thirty-eight people had watched and done nothing" (Latané, 1987, p. 78).

The researchers had the hunch that, paradoxically, the more people who witness an emergency, the less likely it is that any given individual will intervene. Genovese's neighbors might have assumed that someone else had called the police, a phenomenon Latané and Darley (1968) referred to as the *diffusion of responsibility*. Perhaps the bystanders would have been more likely to help had each thought he or she alone was witnessing the murder.

Once a researcher has a hypothesis, whether it comes from a theory, previous research, or an observation of everyday life, how can he or she tell if it is true? How could Latané and Darley tell whether the number of eyewitnesses in fact affects people's likelihood of helping a victim? In science, idle speculation will not do; the researcher must collect data to test his or her hypothesis. Let's look at how the observational method, the correlational method, and the experimental method are used to explore research hypotheses such as Latané and Darley's. These methods are summarized in Table 2.1.

Table 2.1

A summary of research methods.	
Method	**Questions Answered**
1. Observational	Description: What is the nature of the phenomenon?
2. Correlational	Prediction: From knowing X, can we predict Y?
3. Experimental	Causality: Is variable X a cause of variable Y?

The Observational Method: Describing Social Behavior

As its name implies, the **observational method** is the technique whereby a researcher observes people and systematically records measurements of their behavior. It goes without saying that observation is not the exclusive province of social scientists; it is practiced with great success by writers, filmmakers, and journalists interested in a particular social problem or the manner in which an institution works. For example, both Frederick Wiseman and Susan Sheehan spent a considerable amount of time in mental hospitals—not as patients but as observers—Wiseman (1967) recording his observations in a documentary film and Sheehan (1982) in writing. These works had a powerful impact and have been responsible for changing many people's views about the role of mental hospitals in our society.

In social psychology, the observers are trained social scientists who set out to answer questions about a particular social phenomenon by observing and coding it according to a prearranged set of criteria. This method varies according to the degree to which the observer actively participates in the scene. At one extreme, the observer neither participates nor intervenes in any way; instead, the observer is unobtrusive and tries to blend in with the scenery as much as possible. For example, a researcher interested in children's social behavior might stand outside a playground fence to observe children at play. In this case, the observer would be systematically looking for particular behaviors, such as aggression, cooperation, leadership, or assertiveness. These social behaviors are concretely defined before the observation begins. For instance, cooperation might be defined as a child sharing a toy with another or interacting with others to achieve a goal. The observer then notes when these behaviors occur and makes the appropriate check marks under the type of cooperation observed. If the researcher were interested in

> **Observational Method**
> the technique whereby a researcher observes people and systematically records measurements of their behavior

THE FAR SIDE   By GARY LARSON

PRIMATE STUDIES

"For crying out loud, gentlemen! That's us! Someone's installed the one-way mirror in backward!"

■ The hazards of the observational method.

exploring possible sex and age differences in social behavior, he or she would also note the child's gender and age.

Some situations, by their very nature, require **participant observation.** Participant observation is a form of the observational method whereby the observer interacts with the people being observed, but tries not to alter the situation in any way. For example, several years ago a group of people in the Midwest predicted that the world would come to an end in a violent cataclysm on a specific date. They also announced that they would be rescued in time by a spaceship that would land in their leader's backyard. Assuming that the end of the world was not imminent, Leon Festinger and his colleagues thought it would be interesting to observe this group closely and chronicle how they reacted when their beliefs and prophecy were disconfirmed (Festinger, Riecken, & Schachter, 1956). However, unlike the case of observing children at play, the researchers couldn't stand outside the fence and unobtrusively observe the subtleties of the group members' behavior. In order to monitor the hour-to-hour conversations of this group, the social psychologists found it necessary to join the group and pretend they too believed the world was about to end (see Chapter 6 for a description of Festinger and his colleagues' findings). Similarly, Raphael Ezekiel (1995) attended the meetings of neo-Nazi groups and the Klu Klux Klan in order to gain insights into the nature of such extremist groups. Whereas he did not join these groups, he did interact with and interview many of the group members.

Archival Analysis

Participant Observation
a form of the observational method whereby the observer interacts with the people being observed, but tries not to alter the situation in any way

Archival Analysis
a form of the observational method, whereby the researcher examines the accumulated documents, or archives, of a culture (e.g., diaries, novels, magazines, and newspapers)

Interjudge Reliability
the level of agreement between two or more people who independently observe and code a set of data; by showing that two or more judges independently come up with the same observations, researchers ensure that the observations are not the subjective, distorted impressions of one individual

Another form of the observational method is **archival analysis,** whereby the researcher examines the accumulated documents, or archives, of a culture (Simonton, in press). For example, diaries, novels, suicide notes, popular music lyrics, television shows, movies, magazine and newspaper articles, and advertising all tell us a great deal about how a society views itself. Much like our earlier example, specific, well-defined categories are created and then applied to the archival source. **Interjudge reliability,** which is the level of agreement between two or more people who independently observe and code a set of data, is assessed. By showing that two or more judges independently come up with the same observations, researchers ensure that the observations are not the subjective, distorted impressions of one individual. For example, the content analysis of magazine advertisements should not reflect the subjective opinion of one individual, but should be an objective, scientific rating of what is actually in the source document, agreed on by anyone who analyzes the advertisements. (Interjudge reliability is important to establish in other forms of the observational method as well, such as the earlier example of observing children on a playground.)

Archival analysis is a powerful form of observational research because it allows a unique look at the values and interests of a culture. Think back to the question of the relationship between pornography and violence. One problem with addressing this question is in defining what pornography is. Most of us have come across sexually explicit material at one time or another—for example, the centerfold photographs in magazines like *Playboy.* Does this constitute pornography? What about nudity in the movies, or newspaper ads for lingerie that show scantily clad models? For decades, the nation as a whole has been struggling to define pornography; as Supreme Court Justice Potter Stewart put it, "I know it when I see it," but describing its exact content is not easy. What is being portrayed in American "adults-only" literature and photographs?

Archival analysis is a good tool for answering this question, for it enables researchers to describe the content of documents present in the culture—in this case, the photographs and fictional stories that represent currently available pornography in the marketplace. Don Smith (1976) was one of the first researchers to examine the content of pornography, specifically in adults-only fiction paperback books. He purposefully chose for his study locations that were far from the pornography centers of the country (e.g., cities in Nebraska and Tennessee), because he wanted to study the type of pornography that is typically and widely available. For the same reason, he studied books sold at newsstands and regular bookstores, and not those sold at special adults-only bookstores. His method involved choosing every fifth paperback on the shelves at one store in each of eight cities across five states. His content analysis covered many variables, such as how much sex was in the book, what kinds of sex occurred, and what the plots or themes were.

Smith (1976) found that the typical character in these books was young, single, white, physically attractive, and heterosexual. His data strikingly indicated that "the world of pornography is a male's world" (p. 21). Compared to the depictions of women, males' physical characteristics were given little attention; women's bodies were described in minute detail. The most disturbing finding of his study was that almost one-third of all the sex episodes coded in the books involved the use of force (physical, mental, or blackmail) by a male to make a female engage in unwanted sex. Thus, aggression against women was a major theme in these pornographic stories (Cowan & Campbell, 1994).

A second archival analysis, this time focusing on photographs, also found evidence of sexual violence against women. Park Dietz and Barbara Evans (1982) classified the cover photographs of magazines in adults-only bookstores in the pornography district of Forty-Second Street in New York City. They randomly selected four stores in this area and coded all the magazines that had one or more women on the cover. Their categories reflected the specific sexual acts depicted, the clothes and physical appearance of the women, and so forth. Whereas two

■ Archival studies have found that women and men are portrayed differently in our society. To learn more about these differences, see the Try It! exercise on p. 41.

■ Many people believe that pornography is a cause of sexual violence against women. How could this hypothesis be tested scientifically? Which research method would you use?

people engaged in sexual activity was the most common type of cover photograph (37.3 percent of all covers), the second most common type portrayed bondage and domination (17.2 percent of covers), wherein a woman was shown bound with ropes, handcuffs, chains, shackles, constrictive garments, or other material.

Observational research, in the form of archival analysis, can tell us a great deal about society's values and beliefs. The prevalence in pornography of sexual violence against women suggests that these images and stories appeal to many readers (Dietz & Evans, 1982; Lowry, Love, & Kirby, 1981). These disturbing results lead us inexorably to frightening questions: Is pornography associated with sexually violent crimes against women that occur in our society? Do reading and looking at pornography cause some men to commit violent sexual acts? To answer these questions, research methods other than archival analysis must be used. Later in this chapter, we will see how the correlational method and the experimental method have been used to investigate these important questions about sexual violence against women.

Limits of the Observational Method

The observational method is a good one if the researcher's goal is to provide a description of social behavior. This method has some significant drawbacks, however. First, certain kinds of behavior are difficult to observe because they occur only rarely or only in private. For example, had Latané and Darley chosen the observational method to study the effects of the number of bystanders on people's willingness to help a victim, we might still be waiting for an answer. In order to determine how witnesses react to a violent crime, the researchers would have had to linger on street corners throughout the city, wait patiently for assaults to occur, and then keep careful track of the responses of any and all bystanders. Obviously, they would have had to wait a very long time before an assault hap-

//

Archival Analysis

Try doing your own archival analysis to see how women and men are portrayed in the media. Choose 3–4 magazines that differ in their topic and audience; for example, a news magazine, a "women's" magazine such as *Glamour,* a "men's" magazine such as *GQ,* and a literary magazine such as the *New Yorker.* In each magazine, open the pages randomly until you find an advertisement that has at least one picture of a person in it. Repeat so that you look at 2–3 such ads in each magazine.

Make a note of how much of the image is devoted to the person's face and whether the person in the ad is a woman or a man. Specifically, place the picture of each person into one of these categories: (a) You can see the person's entire body; (b) you can see the person from the waist up, or (c) you can see primarily the head and face. Did you find any differences in the way women and men are portrayed? If so, why do you think this is? When you are done, read the section below to see how actual research of this sort turned out.

Dane Archer, Bonita Iritani, Debra Kimes, and Michael Barrios (1983) and Robin Akert, Judy Chen, and Abigail Panter (1991) performed an archival analysis of portrait art and news and advertising photographs in print and television media. They coded the photographs according to the amount of the images that was devoted to the person's face. Their results indicated that across five centuries, across cultures, and across different forms of media, men are visually presented in a more close-up style (focusing on the head and face), whereas women are visually presented in a more long-shot style (focusing on the body). These researchers interpret their findings as indicating a subtle form of sex-role stereotyping: Men are being portrayed in a stronger style that emphasizes their intellectual achievements, whereas women are being portrayed in a weaker style that emphasizes their total physical appearance.

//

pened to occur in their presence, and they would have found it difficult to gather data while a real-life emergency occurred at their feet.

Instead, Latané and Darley might have used the archival analysis version of the observational method—for example, by examining newspaper accounts of violent crimes and noting the number of bystanders and how many offered assistance to the victim. Yet here too, the researchers would have quickly run into problems: Did each journalist mention how many bystanders were present? Was the number accurate? Were all forms of assistance noted in the newspaper article? Clearly, these are messy data. As is always the case with archival analysis, the researcher is at the mercy of the original compiler of the material; the journalists had different aims when they wrote their articles and may not have included all the information researchers would later need.

Another limitation of the observational method is that it is confined to one particular group of people, one particular setting, and one particular type of activity—one doomsaying group in the Midwest, or one type of pornography. This can be a problem if the goal is to generalize from what is observed to different populations, settings, and activities. For example, in contrast to archival studies such as Dietz and Parks (1982), other studies have found that the depiction of violence and aggression in pornography is relatively rare (Garcia & Milano, 1990; Scott & Cuvelier, 1993). This may be due to the fact that Dietz and Park looked at "hard-core" pornography sold in adult bookstores in New York City, whereas the other studies looked at "softer" pornography in certain magazines and videos available at video rental stores. Which study best reflects the amount of violence in American pornography in general? It is difficult to tell.

The Correlational Method: Predicting Social Behavior

Social scientists usually want to do more than describe social behavior. A goal of social science is to understand relationships between variables and to be able to predict when different kinds of social behavior will occur. For example, what is the relationship between the amount of pornography people see and their likelihood of engaging in sexually violent acts? Is there a relationship between the amount of violence children see on television and their aggressiveness? To answer such questions, researchers frequently use a different approach—the correlational method.

Correlational Method
the technique whereby two or more variables are systematically measured and the relationship between them (i.e., how much one can be predicted from the other) is assessed

The **correlational method** is the technique whereby two variables are systematically measured and the relationship between them—how much you can predict one from the other—is assessed. In correlational research, people's behavior and attitudes can be measured in a variety of ways. Just as with the observational method researchers sometimes make direct observations of people's behavior. For example, using the correlational method researchers might be interested in testing the relationship between children's aggressive behavior and how much violent television they watch. They too might observe children on the playground, but here the goal is to assess the relationship, or correlation, between the children's aggressiveness and other factors, like TV viewing habits, that the researchers also measure.

Surveys

Researchers often want to judge the relationship between variables that are difficult to observe, such as how often they engage in safer sex. When the variables of interest cannot easily be observed, researchers rely on surveys, on which people are questioned about their beliefs, attitudes, and behaviors. The researcher looks at the relationship between the questions asked on the survey, such as whether people who know a lot about how AIDS is transmitted are more likely than other people to engage in safer sex.

Correlation Coefficient
a statistical technique that assesses how well you can predict one variable from another; e.g., how well you can predict people's weight from their height

Researchers look at such relationships by calculating the **correlation coefficient,** which is a statistic that assesses how well you can predict one from another; e.g., how well you can predict people's weight from their height. A positive correlation means that increases in the value of one variable are associated with increases in the value of the other variable. Height and weight are positively correlated; the taller people are, the more they tend to weigh. A negative correlation means that increases in the value of one variable are associated with decreases in the value of the other. If height and weight were negatively correlated in human beings, we would look very peculiar—short people, such as children, would look like penguins, whereas tall people, like NBA basketball players, would be all skin and bones! It is also possible, of course, for two variables to be completely uncorrelated, so that a researcher cannot predict one variable from the other.

Correlation coefficients are expressed as numbers that can range from –1.00 to +1.00. A correlation of 1.00 means that two variables are perfectly correlated in a positive direction; thus, by knowing people's standing on one variable, the researcher can predict exactly where they stand on the other variable. In everyday life, of course, perfect correlations are rare. For example, one study found that the correlation between height and weight was .47, in a sample of men ages 18 to 24 (Freedman, Pisani, Purves, & Adhikari, 1991). This means that, on average, the taller people were heavier than the shorter people, but there were exceptions. A correlation of −1.00 means that two variables are perfectly correlated in a negative direction, whereas a correlation of zero means that two variables are not correlated.

Surveys have many advantages, not the least of which is the ability to sample representative segments of the population. Answers to a survey are useful only if they reflect the responses of people in general—not just the sample of people actually tested. Survey researchers go to great lengths to ensure that the people they sample are typical. They select samples that are representative of the population on a number of characteristics important to a given research question (e.g., age, educational background, religion, gender, income level). They also make sure to use a **random selection** of people from the population at large, which is a way of ensuring that a sample of people is representative of a population, by giving everyone in the population an equal chance of being selected for the sample. As long as the sample is selected randomly, we can assume that the responses are a reasonable match to those of the population as a whole.

There are some famous cases whereby people tried to generalize from samples that were not randomly selected—to their peril. In the fall of 1936, a weekly magazine called the *Literary Digest* conducted a large survey asking people who they planned to vote for in the upcoming presidential election. The magazine obtained the names and addresses of its sample from telephone directories and automobile registration lists. The results of its survey of 2 million people indicated that the Republican candidate, Alf Landon, would win by a landslide. Of course, you know that there never was a President Landon; instead, Franklin Delano Roosevelt won every state in the Union but two. What went wrong with the *Literary Digest*'s poll? In the depths of the Great Depression, many people could not afford telephones or cars. Those who could afford these items were, by definition, doing well financially, were frequently Republican, and overwhelmingly favored Alf Landon. However, the majority of the voters were poor—and overwhelmingly supported the Democratic candidate, Roosevelt. By using a list of names that excluded the less affluent members of the population, the *Literary Digest* created a nonrepresentative sample. (The *Literary Digest* never recovered from this methodological disaster and went out of business shortly after publishing its poll.)

Modern surveys and political polls are not immune from such sampling errors. During the 1984 presidential race, polls conducted by Ronald Reagan's campaign staff found that Reagan had a comfortable lead over Walter Mondale, except when the polls were conducted on Friday nights. After an initial panic, they figured out that because Democrats tend to be poorer than Republicans, they were less likely to be out at the movies or out to eat on Friday nights and thus were more likely to be at home when the pollsters called (*Newsweek*, September 28, 1992). Despite such notable glitches, or perhaps because of them, surveys have improved enormously over the years and can now accurately detect correlations between many interesting social variables.

Another potential problem with survey data is the accuracy of the responses. Straightforward questions—regarding what people think about an issue or what they typically do—are relatively easy to answer. But, asking survey participants to predict how they might behave in some hypothetical situation or to explain why they behaved as they did in the past is an invitation to inaccuracy (Schuman & Kalton, 1985; Schwarz, Groves, & Schuman, 1998). Often people simply don't know the answer—but they think they do. Richard Nisbett and Tim Wilson (1977) demonstrated this "telling more than you can know" phenomenon in a number of studies in which people often made inaccurate reports about why they

Random Selection
a way of ensuring that a sample of people is representative of a population, by giving everyone in the population an equal chance of being selected for the sample

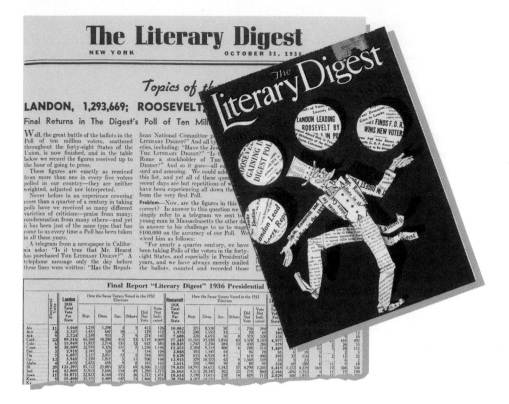

■ The importance of random selection in surveys. In 1936, the *Literary Digest* conducted one of the first political polls. They randomly selected names from telephone directories and automobile registration lists and asked people for whom they planned to vote in the presidential election: Alf Landon or Franklin Roosevelt. As seen here, the poll indicated that Landon would win by a landslide. He didn't, of course; Roosevelt carried virtually every state in the union. What went wrong with this poll?

responded the way they did. Their reports about the causes of their responses pertained more to their theories and beliefs about what should have influenced them than to what actually influenced them. (We discuss these studies at greater length in Chapter 5.) Finally, survey researchers have to be careful that they do not influence people's responses by the way they phrase the question (Hippler, Schwarz, & Sudman, 1987).

Limits of the Correlational Method: Correlation Does Not Equal Causation

The major shortcoming of the correlational method is that it tells us only that two variables are related, whereas the goal of the social psychologist is to identify the causes of social behavior. We want to be able to say that A causes B, not just that A is related to, or correlated with, B.

If a researcher finds that there is a correlation between two variables, it means that there are three possible causal relationships between these variables. For example, researchers have found a correlation between the amount of violent television children watch and how aggressive they are (Eron, 1982). One explanation of this correlation is that watching TV violence causes kids to become more violent themselves. It is equally probable, however, that the reverse is true: that kids who are violent to begin with are more likely to watch violent TV. Or there might be no causal relationship between these two variables; instead, both TV watching and violent behavior could be caused by a third variable, such as having neglectful parents who do not pay much attention to their kids. (In Chapter 12, we will present experimental evidence that supports one of these causal relationships.) When we use the correlational method, it is wrong to jump to the conclusion that one variable is causing the other to occur. Correlation does not prove causation.

Unfortunately, one of the most common methodological errors in the social sciences is to forget this adage. Consider, for example, the report of a resident of Los Angeles, following a severe earthquake that rocked Southern California:

> A lot of people probably think that in one way or another they caused the earthquake, but I'm here to tell you that I'm the one who really did it. At seven-forty-two this morning, I pressed the button that raises the door of my garage, and all hell broke loose. The first thing I said to myself was "I've got to get this thing fixed." (*New Yorker,* October 19, 1987)

While this account is clearly tongue-in-cheek, it underscores a trap that is very easy to fall into: concluding that if two variables are correlated, one must have caused the other. Other examples of this error are not nearly so comical or inconsequential, such as the conclusions drawn from a study of birth control methods and sexually transmitted diseases (STDs) in women (Rosenberg, Davidson, Chen, Judson, & Douglas, 1992). The researchers examined the records of women who had visited a clinic for STDs, noting which method of birth control they used and whether they had STDs. Surprisingly, the researchers found that women who relied on condoms had significantly more STDs than women who used diaphragms or contraceptive sponges. This result was widely reported in the popular press, with the conclusion that the use of diaphragms and sponges caused a lower incidence of disease. Some reporters urged women whose partners used condoms to switch to other methods.

Can you see the problem with this conclusion? The fact that the incidence of disease was correlated with the type of contraception women used is open to a number of causal interpretations. Perhaps the women who used sponges and

■ A recent study found a correlation between the type of birth control women used and their likelihood of getting a sexually transmitted disease (STD). Surprisingly, women who relied on condoms were more likely to have an STD than women who used diaphragms or contraceptive sponges. Does this mean that the use of condoms caused the increase in STDs? Not necessarily—correlation does not prove causation. (See the text for some alternative explanations of this research finding.)

Try It !

Correlation Does Not Equal Causation Quiz

It can be rather difficult to remember that correlation does not allow us to make causal inferences, especially when a correlation suggests a particularly compelling cause. It is easy to forget that there are alternative explanations for the obtained correlation; for example, other variables could be causing both of the observed variables to occur. For each of the following examples, think about why the correlation was found. Even if it seems obvious which variable was causing the other, are there alternative explanations?

Correlation Does Not Equal Causation Quiz

1. Recently, a politician extolled the virtues of the Boy and Girl Scouts organizations. In his salute to the Scouts, the politician mentioned that few teenagers convicted of street crimes had been members of the Scouts. In other words, he was positing a negative correlation between activity in Scouting and frequency of criminal behavior. Why might this be?

2. A research study found that having a pet in childhood is correlated with a reduced likelihood of becoming a juvenile delinquent in adolescence. Why is this?

3. A recent study of soldiers stationed on army bases found that the number of tattoos a soldier had is correlated positively with becoming involved in a motorcycle accident. Why?

4. Officials in the Reagan administration took credit for a reduction in the crime rate, because the crime rate went down after Reagan took office. That is, there was a negative correlation between the onset of the Reagan administration and the crime rate. What are some alternative explanations for this correlation?

5. Recently, it was reported that a correlation exists between people's tendency to eat breakfast in the morning and how long they live, such that people who skip breakfast die younger. Does eating Wheaties lead to a long life?

6. A few years ago, newspaper headlines announced, "Coffee suspected as a cause of heart attacks." Medical studies had found a correlation between the amount of coffee people drank and their likelihood of having a heart attack. Are there any alternative explanations?

(continued on next page)

diaphragms had sex with fewer partners. (In fact, condom users were more likely to have had sex with multiple partners in the previous month.) Perhaps the partners of women who relied on condoms were more likely to have STDs than the partners of women who used sponges and diaphragms. There is simply no way of knowing. Thus, the conclusion that any of the three types of birth control was the cause of protection against STDs cannot be drawn from this correlational study.

As another example of the difficulty of inferring causality from correlational designs, let's return to the question of whether pornography causes aggressive sexual acts against women, such as rape. To address this question, Larry Baron and Murray Straus (1984) examined the relationship between the amount of pornography sold in different states and the number of rapes reported in those states. To measure the amount of pornography, they chose eight sexually explicit magazines (e.g., *Playboy, Hustler, Chic*) and gathered data on how many issues were sold in 1979 in each state. They compared this information to the incidence of rape in each state, using the FBI *Uniform Crime Reports* publication. (Since rape is an underreported crime, these data are undoubtedly conservative estimates of the actual number of rapes committed.)

///

(continued)

7. A positive correlation exists between the viscosity of asphalt in city playgrounds and the crime rate. How can this be? When asphalt becomes viscous (softer), is some chemical released that drives potential criminals wild? When the crime rate goes up, do people flock to the playgrounds, such that the pounding of feet increases the viscosity of the asphalt? What explains this correlation?

8. A news magazine recently reported that the more time fathers spend with their children, the less likely they are to sexually abuse them. Why might this be?

ANSWERS

1. The politician ignored possible third variables that could cause both Scout membership and crime, such as socioeconomic class. Traditionally, Scouting has been most popular in small towns and suburbs among middle-class youngsters; it has never been very attractive or even available to youths growing up in densely populated, urban, high-crime areas.

2. Families who can afford or are willing to have a pet might differ in any number of ways from families who neither can afford nor are willing to have one.

3. Did tattoos cause motorcycle accidents? Or, for that matter, did motorcycle accidents cause tattoos? The researchers suggested that a third (unmeasured) variable was in fact the cause of both: A tendency to take risks and to be involved in flamboyant personal displays led to tattooing one's body and to driving a motorcycle recklessly.

4. By chance, the size of the cohort in the population that is most likely to commit crimes—teenagers—went down when Reagan took office.

5. Not necessarily. People who do not eat breakfast might differ from people who do in any number of ways that influence longevity—for example, in how obese they are, in how hard-driving and high-strung they are, or even in how late they sleep in the morning.

6. Coffee drinkers may be more likely to engage in other behaviors that put them at risk, such as smoking cigarettes or not exercising regularly.

7. Both the viscosity of asphalt and the crime rate go up when the temperature is high—for example, on a hot summer day or night.

8. The news magazine concluded that spending time with one's child reduces the urge to engage in sexual abuse (Adler, 1997). Can you think of alternative explanations? Perhaps child abuse leads to less time with children, due to feelings of guilt or fear of being caught. Or perhaps there is a third variable, such as an antisocial personality, that contributes to child abuse and less time spent with one's child.

///

The researchers' data revealed a positive correlation of .63 between pornography readership and rape. (Probability theory indicates that there is only 1 chance in 1,000 that a correlation of this size would occur by chance.) In addition, the researchers found that the amount of pornography sold was not as highly correlated with nonsexual violent crimes. Thus, they ruled out the possible explanation that pornography leads to more violent crimes in general, and not just to sexually violent crimes.

As suggestive as these findings are, they do not establish that pornography was a cause of rape. Can you think of alternative explanations for this correlation? Baron and Straus (1984) took pains to acknowledge that causality was not proved in their study. As they noted, the findings could reflect differences between states in a hypermasculine culture pattern that led men both to purchase more pornographic magazines and to commit rape (Harris, 1994).

Latané and Darley also might have used the correlational method to determine if the number of bystanders affects helping behavior. They might have surveyed victims and bystanders of crimes and then correlated the total number of bystanders at each crime scene with the number of bystanders who helped or tried to help the victims. Let's say that a negative correlation was found in these data: The greater the number of bystanders, the less likely it was that any one of them intervened. Would this be evidence that the number of bystanders caused helping behavior to occur or not? Unfortunately, no. Any number of unknown third variables could be causing both the number of bystanders and the rate of helping to occur. For example, the seriousness of the emergency could be such a third variable, in that serious, frightening emergencies, as compared to minor mishaps, tend to draw large numbers of bystanders and make people less likely to intervene. Other examples of the difficulty of inferring causality from correlational studies are shown in Try It! on page 46.

The Experimental Method: Answering Causal Questions

Experimental Method
the method in which the researcher randomly assigns participants to different conditions and ensures that these conditions are identical except for the independent variable (the one thought to have a causal effect on people's responses)

The only way to determine causal relationships is with the **experimental method**, whereby the researcher systematically orchestrates the event so that people experience it in one way (e.g., they witness an emergency along with other bystanders) or another way (e.g., they witness the same emergency but are the sole bystander). The experimental method is the method of choice in most social psychological research, because it allows the experimenter to make causal inferences. The observational method is extremely useful in helping us describe social behavior; the correlational method is extremely useful in helping us understand what aspects of social behavior are related. However, only a properly executed experiment allows us to make cause-and-effect statements. For this reason, the experimental method is the crown jewel of social psychological research design.

The experimental method always involves a direct intervention on the part of the researcher. By carefully changing only one aspect of the situation (e.g., group size), the researcher can see whether this aspect is the cause of the behavior in question (e.g., whether people help in an emergency). Sound simple? Actually, it isn't. Stop and think for a moment how you might stage such an experiment to test Latané and Darley's hypothesis about the effects of group size. A moment's reflection will reveal that some rather severe practical and ethical difficulties are involved. What kind of emergency should be used? Ideally (from a scientific perspective), it should be as true to the Genovese case as possible. Accordingly, you would want to stage a murder that passersby could witness. In one condition, you could stage the murder so that only a few onlookers were present; in another condition, you could stage it so that a great many onlookers were present.

Clearly, there are some glaring ethical problems with this scenario. No scientist in his or her right mind would stage a murder for unsuspecting bystanders. But how can we arrange a realistic situation that is upsetting enough to be similar to the Genovese case without it being too upsetting? In addition, how can we ensure that each bystander experiences the same emergency except for the variable whose effect we want to test—in this case, the number of bystanders?

Let's see how Latané and Darley (1968) dealt with these problems. Imagine you were a participant in their experiment. You arrive at the scheduled time and find yourself in a long corridor with doors to several small cubicles. An experimenter greets you and takes you into one of the cubicles, mentioning that five other students, seated in the other cubicles, will be participating with you. The experimenter leaves after giving you a pair of headphones with an attached microphone. You put on the headphones, and soon you hear the experimenter explaining to everyone that he is interested in learning about the kinds of personal problems college students experience. To ensure that people will discuss their

> *T*heory is a good thing but a good experiment lasts forever.
> —Peter Leonidovich Kapista

problems openly, he explains, each participant will remain anonymous; each will stay in his or her separate room and communicate with the others only via the intercom system. Further, the experimenter says, he will not be listening to the discussion, so that people will feel freer to be open and honest. Finally, the experimenter asks that participants take turns presenting their problems, each speaking for two minutes, after which each person will comment on what the others said. To make sure this procedure is followed, he says, only one person's microphone will be turned on at a time.

The group discussion then begins. You listen as the first participant admits he has found it difficult to adjust to college. With some embarrassment, he mentions that he sometimes has seizures, especially when under stress. When his two minutes are up, you hear the other four participants discuss their problems, after which it is your turn. When you have finished, it is the first person's turn to speak again. To your astonishment, after he makes a few further comments, he begins to experience one of the seizures he mentioned earlier:

> I—er—um—I think I—I need—er—if—if could—er—er—somebody er—er—er—er—er—er—er—give me a little—er—give me a little help here because—er—I—er—I'm—er—er—h—h—having a—a—a real problem—er—right now and I—er—if somebody could help me out it would—it would—er—er s—s—sure be—sure be good . . . because—er—there—er—er—a cause I—er—I—uh—I've got a—a one of the—er—sei—er—things coming on and—and—and I could really—er—use some help so if somebody would—er—give me a little h—help—uh—er—er—er—er c—could somebody—er—er—help—er—uh—uh—uh (choking sounds) . . . I'm gonna die—er—er—I'm . . . gonna die—er—help—er—er—seizure—er (chokes, then quiet). (Darley & Latané, 1968, p. 379)

Stop and think for a moment: What would you have done in this situation? If you were like most of the participants in the actual study, you would have remained in your cubicle, listening to your fellow student having a seizure, and done nothing about it. Does this surprise you? Latané and Darley kept track of the number of people who left their cubicle to find the victim or the experimenter before the end of the victim's seizure. Only 31 percent of the participants sought help in this way. Fully 69 percent of the students remained in their cubicles and did nothing—just as Kitty Genovese's neighbors had failed to offer assistance in any way.

Does this finding prove that the failure to help was due to the number of people who witnessed the seizure? How do we know that it wasn't due to some other factor? Here is the major advantage of the experimental method: We know because Latané and Darley included two other conditions in their experiment. In these conditions, the procedure was identical to that described above, with one crucial difference: The size of the discussion group was smaller, meaning that fewer people were witnesses to the seizure. In one condition, the participants were told that there were three other people in the discussion group besides themselves (the victim plus two others). In another condition, participants were told that there was only one other person in their discussion group (namely, the victim). In this latter condition, each participant believed he or she was the only one who could hear the seizure.

Independent and Dependent Variables

The number of people witnessing the emergency was the **independent variable** in the Latané and Darley study, which is the variable a researcher changes or varies

Independent Variable
the variable a researcher changes or varies to see if it has an effect on some other variable

Independent Variable	Dependent Variable
The variable that is hypothesized to influence the dependent variable. Participants are treated identically except for this variable.	The response that is hypothesized to depend on the independent variable. All participants are measured on this variable.

Example: Darley and Latané (1968)	
The number of bystanders	**How many subjects helped?**
Participant + Victim	85%
Participant + Victim + Two others	62%
Participant + Victim + Four others	31%

■ **FIGURE 2.1**
Independent and dependent variables in experimental research.

Dependent Variable
the variable a researcher measures to see if it is influenced by the independent variable; the researcher hypothesizes that the dependent variable will depend on the level of the independent variable

to see if it has an effect on some other variable. The **dependent variable** is the variable a researcher measures to see if it is influenced by the independent variable; the researcher hypothesizes that the dependent variable will be influenced by the level of the independent variable. That is, the dependent variable is hypothesized to depend on the independent variable (see Figure 2.1). Latané and Darley found that their independent variable—the number of bystanders—did have an effect on the dependent variable—whether they tried to help. When the participants believed that four other people were witnesses to the seizure, only 31 percent offered assistance. When the participants believed that only two other people were aware of the seizure, the amount of helping behavior increased to 62 percent of the participants. When the participants believed that they were the only person listening to the seizure, nearly everyone helped (85 percent of the participants).

These results indicate that the number of bystanders strongly influences the rate of helping, but it does not mean that the size of the group is the only cause of people's decision to help. After all, when there were four bystanders, a third of the participants still helped; conversely, when participants thought they were the only witness, some of them failed to help. Obviously, other factors influence helping behavior—the bystanders' personalities, their prior experience with emergencies, and so on. Nonetheless, Latané and Darley succeeded in identifying one important determinant of whether people help—the number of bystanders that people think are present.

Internal Validity in Experiments

How can we be sure that the differences in help across conditions in the Latané and Darley (1968) seizure study were due to the different numbers of bystanders who witnessed the emergency? Could this effect have been caused by some other aspect of the situation? Again, this is the beauty of the experimental method: We can be sure of the causal connection between the number of bystanders and helping, because Latané and Darley made sure that everything about the situation was the same in the different conditions except the independent variable, the number of bystanders. Keeping everything the same but the independent variable is referred to as *internal validity* in an experiment (we'll provide a more formal definition of this term shortly). Latané and Darley were careful to maintain high internal validity by making sure that everyone witnessed the same emergency. They prerecorded the supposed other participants and the victim and played their voices over the intercom system.

The astute reader will have noticed, however, that there was a key difference between the conditions of the Latané and Darley experiment other than the number of bystanders: different people participated in the different conditions. Maybe the observed differences in helping were due to characteristics of the participants instead of the independent variable. The people in the sole witness condition might have differed in any number of ways from their counterparts in the other conditions, making them more likely to help. Maybe they were more likely to have had loving parents, to know something about epilepsy, or to have experience helping in emergencies. Were any of these possibilities true, it would be difficult to conclude that it was the number of bystanders, rather than something about the participants' backgrounds, that led to differences in helping.

Fortunately, there is a technique that allows experimenters to minimize differences among participants as the cause of the results: **random assignment to condition**. This is the process whereby all participants have an equal chance of taking part in any condition of an experiment; through random assignment, researchers can be relatively certain that differences in the participants' personalities or backgrounds are distributed evenly across conditions. Because Latané and Darley's participants were randomly assigned to the conditions of their experiment, it is very unlikely that the ones who knew the most about epilepsy all ended up in one condition. Knowledge about epilepsy should be randomly (i.e., roughly evenly) dispersed across the three experimental conditions. This powerful technique is the most important part of the experimental method.

However, even with random assignment there is always the (very small) possibility that different characteristics of people did not distribute themselves evenly across conditions. For example, if we randomly divide a group of 40 people into two groups, it is possible that those who know the most about epilepsy will by chance end up more in one group than the other—just as it is possible to get more heads than tails when you flip a coin 40 times. This is a possibility we take seriously in experimental science. The analyses of our data come with a **probability level (*p*-value)**, which is a number, calculated with statistical techniques, that tells researchers how likely it is that the results of their experiment occurred by chance and not because of the independent variable. The convention in science, including social psychology, is to consider results significant if the probability level is less than 5 in 100 that the results might be due to chance factors, and not the independent variables studied. For example, if we flipped a coin 40 times and got 40 heads, we would probably assume that this was very unlikely to have occurred by chance and that there was something wrong with the coin (we might check the other side to make sure it wasn't one of those trick coins with heads on both sides!). Similarly, if the results in two conditions of an experiment differ significantly from what we would expect by chance, we assume that the difference was caused by the independent variable (e.g., the number of bystanders present

Random Assignment to Condition the process whereby all participants have an equal chance of taking part in any condition of an experiment; through random assignment, researchers can be relatively certain that differences in the participants' personalities or backgrounds are distributed evenly across conditions

Probability Level (*p*-value) a number, calculated with statistical techniques, that tells researchers how likely it is that the results of their experiment occurred by chance and not because of the independent variable(s); the convention in science, including social psychology, is to consider results significant if the probability level is less than 5 in 100 that the results might be due to chance factors and not the independent variables studied

during the emergency). The *p*-value tells us how confident we can be that the difference was due to chance rather than the independent variable.

To summarize, the key to a good experiment is to maintain high **internal validity,** which we can now define as making sure that the independent variable, and only the independent variable, influences the dependent variable; this is accomplished by controlling all extraneous variables and by randomly assigning people to different experimental conditions (Campbell & Stanley, 1967). When internal validity is high, the experimenter is in a position to judge whether the independent variable causes the dependent variable. This is the hallmark of the experimental method that sets it apart from the observational and correlational methods: Only the experimental method can answer causal questions, such as whether exposure to pornography causes men to commit sexually violent acts. In Chapter 12 we will discuss some experiments that attempted to answer this question, by randomly assigning people to watch pornographic or non-pornographic films (the independent variable) and measuring the extent to which people acted aggressively toward women (the dependent variable). Obviously, such experiments are not easy to do and great care must be taken to treat people ethically. The advantage of such experiments, however, cannot be underestimated—the ability to assess causality.

External Validity in Experiments

For all the advantages of the experimental method, there are some drawbacks. By virtue of gaining enough control over the situation so as to randomly assign people to conditions and rule out the effects of extraneous variables, the situation can become somewhat artificial and distant from real life. For example, one could argue that Latané and Darley went far astray from the original inspiration for their study, the Kitty Genovese murder. What does witnessing a seizure while participating in a laboratory experiment in a college building have to do with a brutal murder in Queens? How often in everyday life do we have discussions with other people through an intercom system? Did the fact that the participants knew they were in a psychology experiment influence their behavior?

These are important questions that concern **external validity,** which is the extent to which the results of a study can be generalized to other situations and other people. Note that two kinds of generalizability are at issue: (a) the extent to which we can generalize from the situation constructed by an experimenter to real-life situations (generalizability across *situations*), and (b) the extent to which we can generalize from the people who participated in the experiment to people in general (generalizability across *people*).

Generalizability Across Situations

A possible criticism of research in social psychology is that it is often conducted in artificial situations that cannot be generalized to real life. To address this problem, social psychologists attempt to increase the generalizability of their results by making their studies as realistic as possible. But it is important to note that there are different ways in which an experiment can be realistic. By one definition—the similarity of an experimental situation to events that occur frequently in everyday life—it is clear that many experiments are decidedly unreal. In many experiments, people are placed in situations they would rarely, if ever, encounter in everyday life, such as occurred in Latané and Darley's group discussion of personal problems over an intercom system. We can refer to the extent to which an

---

Internal Validity
making sure that nothing else besides the independent variable can affect the dependent variable; this is accomplished by controlling all extraneous variables and by randomly assigning people to different experimental conditions

External Validity
the extent to which the results of a study can be generalized to other situations and to other people

experiment is similar to real-life situations as the **mundane realism** (Aronson & Carlsmith, 1968) of the experiment.

A more important kind of realism is **psychological realism,** which is the extent to which the psychological processes triggered in an experiment are similar to psychological processes that occur in everyday life (Aronson, Wilson, & Brewer, 1998). Even though Latané and Darley staged an emergency that in significant ways was unlike ones encountered in everyday life, was it psychologically similar to real-life emergencies? Were the same psychological processes triggered? Did the participants have the same types of perceptions and thoughts, make the same types of decisions, and choose the same types of behaviors that they would in a real-life situation? If so, then the study is high in psychological realism and the results are generalizable to everyday life.

Making an experiment realistic, both mundanely and psychologically, is no easy task. It is, perhaps, where the creative talents of researchers come most into play. For example, the simplest way to study bystander intervention would be to say to people, "Look, we are interested in how people react to emergencies, so at some point during this study we are going to stage an accident, and then we'll see how you respond." We think you will agree, however, that such a procedure would be very low in psychological realism and mundane realism. In everyday life, we do not know when emergencies are going to occur, we do not have time to plan our responses to them, and we do not think a researcher is observing our reactions to them. Thus, the situation itself and the kinds of psychological processes triggered would differ widely from those of a real emergency.

Further, as discussed earlier, people don't always know why they do what they do or even what they will do until it happens. Thus, describing an experimental situation to participants and then asking them to respond normally will produce responses that are, at best, suspect. For example, after describing the Latané and Darley seizure experiment to our students, we often ask them to predict how they would respond, just as we asked you earlier. Invariably, almost all of our students think they would have helped the victim, even when they know that in the condition where the group size was six, most people did not help. Unfortunately, we cannot depend on people's predictions about what they would do in a hypothetical situation; we can only find out what people will really do when we construct a situation that triggers the same psychological processes as occur in the real world.

To make a study psychologically real, it is often necessary to tell the participants a **cover story**—a description of the purpose of the study that is different from its true purpose. You might have wondered why Latané and Darley told people that the purpose of the experiment was to study the personal problems of college students. It certainly would have been simpler to tell participants that the point of the study was to see how they would react to emergencies. However, this revealing comment would have considerably reduced the study's psychological realism, making it difficult to generalize the results to people's reactions to emergencies in everyday life. Psychological realism is heightened if people find themselves engrossed in a real event.

Generalizability Across People

Recall that social psychologists study the way in which people in general are susceptible to social influence. Latané and Darley's experiment documented an interesting, unexpected example of social influence, whereby the mere knowledge that

Mundane Realism
the extent to which an experiment is similar to real-life situations

Psychological Realism
the extent to which the psychological processes triggered in an experiment are similar to psychological processes that occur in everyday life; psychological realism can be high in an experiment, even if mundane realism is low

Cover Story
a description of the purpose of a study, given to participants, that is different from its true purpose; cover stories are used to maintain psychological realism

others were present inhibited helping behavior. But what have we learned about people in general? The participants in their study were 52 male and female students at New York University, who received course credit for participating in the experiment. It is reasonable to ask whether the same results would have been found had a different population been used. Would the number of bystanders have influenced helping behavior had the participants been middle-aged blue-collar workers instead of college students? Midwesterners instead of New Yorkers? Japanese instead of American?

The only way to be certain that the results of an experiment represent the behavior of a particular population is to ensure that the participants are randomly selected from that population. Ideally, samples in experiments should be randomly selected, just as they are in surveys. Unfortunately, it is impractical and expensive to select random samples for social psychology experiments. It is difficult enough to convince a random sample of Americans to agree to answer a few questions over the telephone as part of a political poll, and such polls can cost thousands of dollars to conduct. Imagine the difficulty Latané and Darley would have had convincing a random sample of Americans to board a plane to New York to take part in their study, not to mention the cost of such an endeavor. Even trying to gather a random sample of students at New York University would not have been easy, given that each person contacted would have had to agree to take time out of his or her busy schedule to spend an hour in Latané and Darley's laboratory.

Of course, concerns about practicality and expense are not good excuses for doing poor science. More importantly, given the goal of social psychology it is unnecessary to select random samples for every experiment performed. As noted in Chapter 1, social psychologists attempt to identify basic psychological processes that make people susceptible to social influence. If we accept the premise that there are fundamental psychological processes shared by all people in all places, and that it is these processes that are being studied in social psychology experiments, then it becomes relatively unimportant to select participants from every corner of the earth. Many social psychologists assume that the processes they study—such as the diffusion of responsibility caused by the presence of others in an emergency—are basic components of human nature, common to New Yorkers, Midwesterners, and Japanese alike.

Replications

Suppose a researcher claims that her study is high in psychological realism, that it has thus captured psychological functioning as it occurs in everyday life, and that it doesn't matter that only college sophomores at one university participated, because these psychological processes are universal. Should we take her word for it?

Replication
repeating a study, often with different subject populations or in different settings

Not necessarily. The ultimate test of an experiment's external validity is **replication**—conducting the study over again, often with different subject populations or in different settings. Do we think that Latané and Darley found the results they did only because their participants knew they were in a psychology experiment? Then we should try to replicate their study in an experiment conducted outside of the laboratory. Do we think their results are limited to only certain kinds of emergencies? Then we should try to replicate it with an emergency different from an epileptic seizure. Do we think that only New Yorkers would be so unhelpful? Then we should try to replicate it with southerners, Californians, or Germans.

■ Some psychological processes are common to all people whereas some differ across age, gender, and culture. To see if the results of an experiment are generalized to other groups of people, the study must be replicated with diverse populations.

Only with such replications can we be certain about how generalizable the results are.

Often, when many studies on one problem are conducted, the results are somewhat variable. Several studies might find an effect of the number of bystanders on helping behavior, for example, whereas a few do not. How can we make sense out of this? Does the number of bystanders make a difference or not? Fortunately, there is a statistical technique called **meta analysis** that averages the results of two or more studies to see if the effect of an independent variable is reliable. Earlier we discussed p-levels, which tell us the probability that the findings of one study are due to chance or to the independent variable. A meta analysis essentially does the same thing, except that it averages across the results of many different studies. If, say, an independent variable is found to have an effect in only one of 20 studies, the meta analysis will tell us that that one study was probably an exception and that, on average, the independent variable is not influencing the dependent variable. If an independent variable is having an effect in most of the studies, the meta analysis is likely to tell us that, on average, it does influence the dependent variable.

Virtually all findings we will discuss in this book have been replicated in a number of different settings, with different populations, thus demonstrating that they are reliable phenomena that are not limited to the laboratory or to college sophomores. For example, Anderson and Bushman (1997) recently compared laboratory studies on the causes of aggression with studies conducted in the real world. They found a substantial amount of agreement in the findings of the two types of studies, such as the finding that violence in the media causes aggressive behavior. Similarly, Latané and Darley's original findings have been replicated in numerous studies. Increasing the number of bystanders has been found to inhibit

Meta Analysis
a statistical technique that averages the results of two or more studies to see if the effect of an independent variable is reliable

helping behavior with many kinds of people, including children, college students, and future ministers (Darley & Batson, 1973; Latané & Nida, 1981); in both small towns and large cities (Latané & Dabbs, 1975); in a variety of settings, such as psychology laboratories, city streets, and subway trains (Harrison & Wells, 1991; Latané & Darley, 1970; Piliavin, Dovidio, Gaertner, & Clark, 1981; Piliavin & Piliavin, 1972); and with a variety of types of emergencies, such as seizures, potential fires, fights, and accidents (Latané & Darley, 1968; Shotland & Straw, 1976; Staub, 1974), as well as with less serious events, such as having a flat tire (Hurley & Allen, 1974). Many of these replications have been conducted in real-life settings (e.g., on a subway train) where people could not possibly have known an experiment was being conducted. We will frequently point out similar replications of the major findings we discuss in this book.

Cross-Cultural Research

As noted in Chapter 1, experimental social psychology began primarily as an American discipline; thus, one limit on the generalizability of the results is that most research in the field has been conducted by Americans with American participants. More and more social psychological experiments are being performed in other cultures, however, and this activity will enrich our understanding of the external validity of many findings. Cross-cultural research has two main goals. The first is to try to demonstrate that a particular psychological process or law is universal, in that it operates the same way in all human beings. This type of research emphasizes what we as human beings have in common, regardless of our backgrounds and culture. For example, Charles Darwin (1872) argued that there is a basic set of human emotions (e.g., anger, happiness) that are expressed and understood throughout the world. Although a lively controversy has arisen as to whether Darwin was right (Russell, 1994), a lot of subsequent research has shown that people in different cultures express emotions on their faces in the same way, even in remote cultures having no contact with the rest of the world (Ekman, 1994; Izard, 1994; Ekman & Friesen, 1971). As another example, the effects of bystanders on helping behavior have been replicated in at least one other country (Israel; Schwartz & Gottlieb, 1976).

Clearly, however, the diversity of our backgrounds shapes our lives in interesting ways. The second goal of cross-cultural research is to explore the differences between us, by examining how culture influences basic social psychological processes (Fiske, Markus, Kitayama, & Nisbett, 1998; Moghaddam, Taylor, & Wright, 1993). Some findings in social psychology are culture-dependent, as we will see at many points throughout this book. In Chapter 5, for example, we will see that there are cultural differences in the very way people define themselves. Many Western cultures tend to emphasize individualism and independence, whereas many Asian cultures emphasize collectivism and interdependence (Markus & Kitayama, 1991, 1994; Triandis, 1989). In Chapter 12, we will see that people's cultural and economic backgrounds have intriguing effects on how aggressive they are (Cohen, Nisbett, Bowdle, & Schwarz, 1996; Nisbett, 1993; Nisbett & Cohen, 1996).

We do not have the space to discuss how to conduct cross-cultural research and the many nuances involved (see Leung & Vijver, 1996). Suffice it to say that it is not a simple matter of traveling to another culture, translating materials into the local language, and replicating a study there. Researchers have to be very careful that they are not imposing their own viewpoints and definitions, learned

Doonesbury

BY GARRY TRUDEAU

■ As more and more social psychological studies are conducted in diverse cultures, interesting cultural differences are being documented.

from their culture, onto another culture with which they are unfamiliar. They also have to be sure that their independent and dependent variables are understood in the same way in different cultures (Bond, 1988; Lonner & Berry, 1986).

Suppose, for example, that you wanted to replicate the Latané and Darley (1968) seizure experiment in another culture. Clearly, you could not conduct the exact same experiment somewhere else. The tape-recorded discussion of college life used by Latané and Darley (1968) was specific to the lives of New York University students in the 1960s and could not be used elsewhere. What about more subtle aspects of the study, such as the way people viewed the person who had the seizure? There is considerable variation across cultures in how people define whether another person is a member of their social group, and this factor can be an important determinant of how they behave toward that person (Gudykunst, 1988; Triandis, 1989). If people in one culture view the victim as a member of their social group, whereas people in another culture view the victim as a member of a rival social group, you might find very different results in the two cultures—not because the psychological processes of helping behavior are different but because people interpreted the situation differently. It can be quite daunting to conduct a study that is interpreted and perceived similarly in dissimilar cultures. Most cross-cultural researchers are sensitive to these issues, and as more and more cross-cultural research is conducted carefully, we will be able to determine which social psychological processes are universal and which are culture-bound.

The Basic Dilemma of the Social Psychologist

One of the best ways to increase external validity is by conducting **field experiments.** In a field experiment, people's behavior is studied outside of the laboratory, in its natural setting. In contrast to systematic observation or the correlational method, however, the researcher controls the occurrence of an independent variable (e.g., group size) to see what effect it has on a dependent variable (e.g., helping behavior) and randomly assigns people to the different conditions. Thus, a field experiment is identical in design to a laboratory experiment except that it is conducted in a real-life setting, rather than in the relatively artificial laboratory setting. The participants in a field experiment are unaware that the events they

field experiments
experiments conducted in natural settings, rather than in the laboratory

experience are in fact an experiment. The external validity of such an experiment is high, since, after all, it is taking place in the real world, with real people who are more diverse than a typical college student sample.

Many such field studies have been conducted in social psychology. For example, Latané and Darley (1970) tested their hypothesis about group size and bystander intervention in a convenience store outside of New York City. Two "robbers" (with full knowledge and permission of the cashier and manager of the store) waited until there were either one or two other customers at the checkout counter. Then they asked the cashier to name the most expensive beer the store carried. The cashier answered the question and then said he would have to check in the back to see how much of that brand was in stock. While the cashier was gone, the robbers picked up a case of beer in the front of the store, declared that "They'll never miss this," put the beer in their car, and drove off.

Given that the robbers were rather burly fellows, no one attempted to intervene directly to stop the theft. The question was, when the cashier returned, how many people would help by telling him that a theft had just occurred? The number of bystanders had the same inhibiting effect on helping behavior as in the laboratory seizure study: Significantly fewer people reported the theft when there was another witness/customer in the store than when they were alone.

It might have occurred to you to ask why laboratory studies are conducted at all, since field experiments are obviously so much better in terms of external validity. Why not dispense with laboratory studies and do all research in the field? Indeed, it seems to us that the perfect experiment in social psychology would be one that was conducted in a field setting, with a sample randomly selected from a population of interest, and with extremely high internal validity (all extraneous variables controlled; people randomly assigned to the conditions). Sounds good, doesn't it? The only problem is that it is very difficult to satisfy all these conditions in one study—making such studies virtually impossible to conduct.

There is almost always a trade-off between internal and external validity—that is, between (a) having enough control over the situation to ensure that no extraneous variables are influencing the results and randomly assigning people to condition, and (b) making sure that the results can be generalized to everyday life. Control is best exerted in a laboratory setting, but the laboratory may be unlike real life. Real life can best be captured by doing a field experiment, but it is very difficult to control all extraneous variables in such studies. For example, the astute reader will have noticed that Latané and Darley's (1970) beer theft study was unlike laboratory experiments in an important respect: People could not be randomly assigned to the alone or in pairs conditions. Were this the only study Latané and Darley had performed, we could not be certain whether the kinds of people who prefer to shop alone, as compared to the kinds of people who prefer to shop with a friend, differ in ways that might influence helping behavior. By randomly assigning people to conditions in their laboratory studies, Latané and Darley were able to rule out such alternative explanations.

The trade-off between internal and external validity has been referred to as the basic dilemma of the social psychologist (Aronson & Carlsmith, 1968). The way to resolve this dilemma is to not try to do it all in a single experiment. Most social psychologists opt first for internal validity, conducting laboratory experiments in which people are randomly assigned to different conditions and all extraneous variables are controlled; here there is little ambiguity about what is causing what. Other social psychologists prefer external validity to control, conducting most of their research in field studies. And many social psychologists do both. Taken together, both types of studies meet the requirements of our perfect experiment. Through replication, a given research question can thus be studied with maximal internal and external validity.

Basic versus Applied Research

Now that we have discussed the three major research methodologies in social psychology, there are two remaining issues about research we need to address. First, you might have wondered how people decide which specific topic to study. Why would a social psychologist decide to study helping behavior, cognitive dissonance theory, or the effects of pornography on aggression? Is he or she simply curious? Or does the social psychologist have a specific purpose in mind, such as trying to reduce sexual violence?

In general, we can distinguish between two types of research, each having a different purpose. The goal in **basic research** is to find the best answer to the question of why people behave the way they do, purely for reasons of intellectual curiosity. No direct attempt is made to solve a specific social or psychological problem. In contrast, the goal in **applied research** is to solve a particular social problem; building a theory of behavior is usually secondary to solving the specific problem, such as alleviating racism, reducing sexual violence, and stemming the spread of AIDS.

The difference between basic and applied research is easily illustrated by examples from other sciences. Some biology researchers, for example, are concerned primarily with fundamental theoretical issues, such as the role DNA plays in the transmission of genetic information, without an immediate concern with how these issues can be applied to everyday problems. Other biology researchers are concerned primarily with applied issues, such as how to develop a strain of rice that has more protein and is more resistant to disease, in order to help solve problems of world hunger.

In most sciences, however, the distinction between basic and applied research is fuzzy. Even though many researchers label themselves as either basic or applied scientists, it is clear that the endeavors of one group are not independent of those of the other group. There are countless examples of advances in basic science that at the time had no known applied value but later proved to be the key to solving a significant applied problem. Basic research on DNA and genetics has led to a technology that enables researchers to create new strains of bacteria, with several important real-world applications in medicine and environmental control. For example, genetically engineered bacteria are now used in oil spills to help break up and disperse the oil. The same is true in social psychology. As we will see later in this book, for instance, basic research with dogs, rats, and fish on the effects of feeling in control of one's environment has led to the development of techniques to improve the health of elderly nursing home residents (Langer & Rodin, 1976; Richter, 1957; Schulz, 1976; Seligman, 1975).

Most social psychologists would agree that in order to solve a specific social problem, it is vital to have a good understanding of the psychological processes responsible for it. Kurt Lewin (1951), one of the founders of social psychology, coined a phrase that has become a motto for the field: "There is nothing so practical as a good theory." He meant that to solve such difficult social problems as urban violence or racial prejudice, one must first understand the underlying psychological dynamics of human nature and social interaction. In the beginning of

Basic Research
studies that are designed to find the best answer to the question of why people behave the way they do and that are conducted purely for reasons of intellectual curiosity

Applied Research
studies designed specifically to solve a particular social problem; building a theory of behavior is usually secondary to solving the specific problem

There is nothing so practical as a good theory.
—Kurt Lewin, 1951

social psychology as a discipline, differences emerged in the extent to which researchers focused directly on solving a social problem versus studying basic aspects of human nature. Lewin's own research group fell into these two camps. This dichotomy is present in the field today, with some social psychologists doing basic research primarily in laboratory settings and others doing applied research primarily in field settings.

This book reflects the first school of social psychologists, those concerned mainly with basic theoretical issues. The subject matter of social psychology, however, is such that even when the goal is to discover the psychological processes underlying social behavior, the findings often have clear applied implications. Thus, throughout this book we will see many examples of research that have direct applications. We also include at the end of the book three "Social Psychology in Action" units that discuss how social psychology has been applied to important social problems.

Ethical Issues in Social Psychology

Last but not least, it is important to discuss ethical issues that arise in research in social psychology. In their quest to create realistic, engaging situations, social psychologists frequently face an ethical dilemma. On the one hand, for obvious scientific reasons we want our experiments to resemble the real world as much as possible and to be as sound and well controlled as we can make them. On the other hand, we want to avoid causing our participants undue and unnecessary stress, discomfort, or unpleasantness. These two goals often conflict as the researcher goes about his or her business of creating and conducting experiments.

Researchers are concerned about the health and welfare of the individuals participating in their experiments. Researchers are also in the process of discovering important information about human social behavior—such as bystander intervention, prejudice, conformity, aggression, and obedience to authority. Many of these discoveries are bound to be of benefit to society. Indeed, given the fact that social psychologists have developed powerful tools to investigate such issues scientifically, many scholars feel it would be immoral not to conduct these experiments. However, in order to gain insight into such critical issues, researchers must create vivid events that are involving for the participants. Some of these events, by their very nature, are likely to produce a degree of discomfort in the participants. Thus, what is required for good science and what is required for ethical science can be contradictory. The dilemma cannot be resolved by making pious claims that no participant ever experiences any kind of discomfort in an experiment or by insisting that all is fair in science and forging blindly ahead. Clearly, some middle ground is called for.

Informed Consent
the procedure whereby the nature of the experiment is explained to participants before it begins and their consent to participate in the experiment is obtained

The dilemma would be less problematic if researchers could obtain **informed consent** from their participants prior to their participation. Informed consent is the procedure whereby the researcher explains the nature of the experiment to participants before it begins and asks for their consent to participate. If the experimenter fully describes to participants the kinds of experiences they are about to undergo and asks them if they are willing to participate, then the ethical dilemma is resolved. In many social psychology experiments, this sort of description is feasible—and where it is feasible, it is done. In other kinds of experiments,

---

ETHICAL PRINCIPLES OF PSYCHOLOGISTS IN THE CONDUCT OF RESEARCH

1. Psychologists must take steps to avoid harming their research participants.

2. When planning research, psychologists must evaluate its ethical acceptability. Because individual researchers might not be objective judges of the ethical acceptability of their studies, they should seek ethical advice from others, including Institutional Review Boards. (Institutional Review Boards are a group of scientists and nonscientists who judge whether the risks to participants outweigh the potential gains of the research.)

3. As much as possible, the researcher should describe the procedures to participants before they take part in a study, and obtain informed consent from participants that documents their agreement to take part in the study as it was described to them.

4. Deception may be used only if there are no other viable means of testing a hypothesis and only if an Institutional Review Board rules that it does not put participants at undue risk. After the study, participants must be provided with a full description and explanation of all procedures, in a post-experimental interview called the debriefing.

5. All participants must be informed that they are free to withdraw from a study at any point.

6. All information obtained from individual participants must be held in strict confidence, unless the consent of the participant is obtained to make it public.

■ **FIGURE 2.2   Procedures for the protection of participants in psychological research.**
(Adapted from *Ethical principles of psychologists in the conduct of research,* American Psychological Association, 1992)

however, it is impossible. Suppose Latané and Darley had told their participants that a seizure was about to be staged, that it wouldn't be a real emergency, and that the hypothesis stated they should offer help. As we saw earlier, such a procedure would be bad science. In this kind of experiment, it's essential that the participant experience contrived events as if they were real; this is called a deception experiment. **Deception** in social psychological research involves misleading participants about the true purpose of a study or the events that transpire. (It is important to note that not all research in social psychology involves deception.)

Over the years, a number of guidelines have been developed to deal with these dilemmas about the ethics of experiments and to ensure that the dignity and safety of research participants are protected. For example, the American Psychological Association has published a list of ethical principles that govern all research in psychology; these ethical guidelines are summarized in Figure 2.2. In addition, all research conducted by psychologists must be reviewed by an Institutional Review Board, or ethics committee. Any aspect of the experimental procedure that this committee judges to be stressful or upsetting must be changed or deleted before the study can be conducted. When deception is used, the post-experimental interview, called the debriefing session, is crucial and must occur. **Debriefing** is the process of explaining to the participants, at the end of the experiment, the purpose of the study and exactly what transpired. If any participants experienced discomfort, the researchers attempt to undo and alleviate it. Finally, the debriefing session provides an opportunity to inform the participants about the goals and purpose of the research, thereby serving an important educational function. The best researchers question their participants carefully and listen to what they say, regardless of whether or not deception was used in the experiment. (For a detailed description of how debriefing interviews should be conducted, see Aronson, Ellsworth, Carlsmith, & Gonzales, 1990.)

Deception
the procedure whereby participants are misled about the true purpose of a study or the events that will actually transpire

Debriefing
the process of explaining to the participants, at the end of the experiment, the purpose of the study and exactly what transpired

THE FAR SIDE   By GARY LARSON

■ It is unlikely that an Institutional Review Board would have approved this study.

In our experience, virtually all participants understand and appreciate the need for deception, as long as the time is taken in the postexperimental debriefing session to go over the purpose of the research and to explain why alternative procedures could not be used. Several investigators have gone a step further and assessed the impact on people of participating in deception studies (e.g., Christensen, 1988; Finney, 1987; Gerdes, 1979). These studies have consistently found that people do not object to the kinds of mild discomfort and deceptions typically used in social psychological research. In fact, some studies have found that most people who participated in deception experiments said they had learned more and enjoyed the experiments more than those who participated in nondeception experiments did (Smith & Richardson, 1983). For example, Latané and Darley (1970) reported that during their debriefing, the participants said that the deception was necessary and that they were willing to participate in similar studies in the future—even though they had experienced some stress and conflict during the study.

We do not mean to imply that all deception is beneficial. Nonetheless, if mild deception is used and time is spent after the study discussing the deception with participants and explaining why it was necessary, the evidence is that people will not be adversely affected.

Summary

The goal of social psychology is to answer questions about social behavior scientifically. The principal research designs used are the observational, correlational, and experimental methods. Each has its strengths and weaknesses and is most appropriate for certain research questions. Each method causes the researcher to make a different type of statement about his or her findings.

The **observational method** primarily fulfills a descriptive function; it allows a researcher to observe and describe a social phenomenon, with the objectivity of the researcher's observations tested through **interjudge reliability**. Two forms of the observational method are **participant observation,** whereby the researcher interacts with the people being observed, and **archival analysis,** whereby the researcher examines the accumulated documents or archives of a culture. The **correlational method** allows the researcher to determine if two or more variables are related—that is, whether one can be predicted from the other. The **correlation coefficient** is a statistical technique that reveals the extent to which one variable can be predicted from another. Correlations are often calculated from survey data, in which there is **random selection** of a sample from a larger population. This ensures that the responses of the sample are representative of those of the population. The major drawback of the correlational method is that it cannot determine causality. It is not possible to determine from a correlation whether A causes B, B causes A, or some other variable causes both A and B.

For this reason, the **experimental method** is the preferred design in social psychology; it alone allows the researcher to infer the presence of causality. Experiments can be conducted in the laboratory or in the field; **field experiments** are those conducted in natural settings. In experiments, researchers vary the level of an **independent variable,** which is the one hypothesized to have a causal effect on behavior. The **dependent variable** is the measured variable that is hypothesized to be caused or influenced by the independent variable. The researcher makes sure that participants are treated identically except for the independent variable and randomly assigns people to the experimental conditions. **Random assignment to condition,** the hallmark of true experimental design, minimizes the possibility that different types of people are unevenly distributed across conditions. A **probability level** (*p*-value) is calculated, telling the researcher how likely it is that the results are due to chance versus the independent variable.

Experiments are designed to be as high as possible in **internal validity** (making sure that nothing else besides the independent variables is influencing the results) and in **external validity** (making sure that the results can be generalized across people and situations). **Mundane realism** reflects the extent to which the experimental setting is similar to real-life settings. **Psychological realism** reflects the extent to which the experiment involves psychological responses like those occurring in real life. The best test of external validity is **replication**—repeating the experiment in different settings with different people, to see if the results are the same. A statistical technique called **meta analysis** allows researchers to see how reliable the effects of an independent variable are over many replications.

Researchers engage in both **basic research** and **applied research.** While the line between these is often blurred, basic research aims to gain understanding of human social behavior, without trying specifically to solve a particular problem, whereas applied research aims to solve a specific problem, often one with social policy implications. Finally, a major concern in social psychological research is the ethical treatment of participants. The American Psychological Association's guidelines are followed carefully and include such procedures as obtaining **informed consent,** the ability to leave the experiment at any time, ensured anonymity and confidentiality, and **debriefing** following an experiment, particularly if **deception** (involving a **cover story** about the supposed purpose of the study or the independent or dependent variables) has been used.

If You Are Interested

Aron, A., & Aron, E. N. (1990). *The heart of social psychology* (2nd ed.). Lexington, MA: Heath. A behind-the-scenes look at how social psychologists conduct research, based on interviews with leading researchers.

Aronson, E., Ellsworth, P., Carlsmith, J. M., & Gonzales, M. (1990). *Methods of research in social psychology* (2nd ed.). New York: Random House. An entertaining, thorough treatment of how to conduct social psychological research.

Aronson, E., Wilson, T. D., & Brewer, M. (1998). Experimental methods. In D. Gilbert, S. Fiske, & G. Lindzey (Eds.), *The handbook of social psychology* (4th ed., Vol 1, pp. 99–142). New York: McGraw-Hill. An expanded discussion of many of the issues discussed in this chapter, for those considering social psychology as a profession.

Ghostbusters (1984). At the beginning of this movie there is a scene in which Bill Murray, playing a psychologist, conducts an experiment on ESP. It is an amusing illustration of how not to do experimental research.

Rosenthal, R., & Rosnow, R. L. (1991). *Essentials of behavioral research: Methods and data analysis* (2nd ed.). New York: McGraw-Hill. A detailed guide to methodology and statistical analyses, for professionals and the advanced student.

CHAPTER 3

SOCIAL COGNITION: HOW WE THINK ABOUT THE SOCIAL WORLD

New York, Sunday, May 11, 1997: In a stunning defeat, Gary Kasparov, the reigning chess champion of the world, lost to an unranked challenger. Kasparov resigned after only 19 moves, conceding defeat in the sixth and decisive game of the match. Amazingly, this was the first time Kasparov had lost a match in his professional career. Even more amazingly, he lost not to a fellow human being, but to an IBM computer named Deep Blue, housed in two imposing black boxes, each 6 feet 5 inches tall. For the first time in our history, a machine went head-to-head (or chip-to-head, as it were) with one of the smartest members of our species and came out the victor. One commentator, upon hearing the news, said that he felt "a twinge of IQ loss and an increase in hairiness" (Dunn, 1997).

Computers, of course, have already outdone us in many ways. They guide spaceships to Mars, solve difficult mathematical problems, and balance our checkbooks to the penny. There was, however, something especially unsettling about Deep Blue's defeat of Gary Kasparov. Chess is considered to be one of the most difficult challenges to the human mind,

■ Gary Kasparov, the best chess player in the world, lost a match to an IBM computer named Big Blue in May of 1997. Whereas humans may not be as good at chess as computers, we are far better at social thinking—the ability to think about and understand ourselves and other people.

requiring incredible insight, concentration, and creativity. Is it possible that we humans are no longer the smartest things on the planet?

Actually, we still are. As startling as Deep Blue's victory was, people are still far better than computers at some very important kinds of thought. We refer to people's skills as social thinkers—the ability to understand and think about other people. It is one thing for a computer to figure out that bishop to f6 is an excellent chess move, but quite another to figure out what people are like.

Imagine, for example, that Deep Blue was with you during your first week of college. As you meet each new acquaintance, a computer operator scans a photograph of that person into the computer and types in everything he or she says. (The computer operator would be needed because computers are especially bad at understanding human language and recognizing faces; Pinker, 1994). At the end of the week, both you and the computer make several ratings of each of the people you met, such as what kind of people they were, how much they liked you, and how much they liked each other. Although such an experiment has never been done, we have no doubt that you would be far superior to the computer at making these kinds of social judgments.

Suppose that when you are introduced to your new roommate, Cindy, she says, "Nice to meet you!" with genuine warmth and enthusiasm. She seems really nice and you can tell that you're going to hit it off with her. Later that day you meet Jason, who just happens to be your ex-boyfriend's cousin. You and your ex-boyfriend are not on the best of terms and Jason knows all the gory details. After being introduced he, too, says, "Nice to meet you." He sounds enthusiastic but you can tell he doesn't really mean it; after exchanging a few niceties he excuses himself and quickly leaves the room.

Although it might seem easy to interpret these simple interactions and figure out that things are going to go better with Cindy than Jason, think about the vast amount of knowledge you used to figure this out. You know a lot about romantic relationships, what happens when they end, how long you should chat with someone when you first meet them before excusing yourself, what your ex-boyfriend told you about Jason, what you've heard about Cindy, and so on. You combined this vast amount of social knowledge rapidly and expertly to make judgments about Cindy and Jason. It would be very hard to provide the computer with all of this knowledge. Even if we could, it would be very hard to write a program that would tell the computer how to use this knowledge to figure out that Jason's "nice to meet you" meant something very different from Cindy's. Maybe Deep Blue is good at chess, but as of now, at least, there is no computer that can come anywhere close to matching our accomplishments as social thinkers.

In this chapter we will explore **social cognition**, which is the way in which people think about themselves and the social world—how they select, interpret, remember, and use social information to make judgments and decisions. Now that we've illustrated how good we are at this kind of thinking—better than the most powerful of computers—we need to point out that we are not perfect. True, we are able to make complex judgments about people at lightning speed. But we occasionally make mistakes and sometimes these mistakes are costly. Maybe we were wrong about Cindy and Jason—Cindy might turn out to be a disaster as a roommate whereas Jason might end up being one of our best friends. (For example, maybe he seemed unfriendly because he picked up on *our* nervousness and distrust.) In this chapter we will see how sophisticated we are as social thinkers, as well as see the kinds of mistakes we are prone to make.

To understand how people think about the social world, we will first consider the procedures, rules, and strategies they use. It is often impossible to consider the overwhelming amount of information we have about the people

> "It is the mind which creates the world about us, and even though we stand side by side in the same meadow, my eyes will never see what is beheld by yours.
> —George Gissing,
> *The Private Papers of Henry Ryecroft*, 1903

Social Cognition
how people think about themselves and the social world; more specifically, how people select, interpret, remember, and use social information to make judgments and decisions

around us. Consequently, people rely on a variety of mental shortcuts that serve them well. As we will see, people are quite practical, adopting different procedures and rules according to their goals and needs in that situation. Even so, human reasoning is not perfect, and in the last section we will consider ways of improving the way people think.   ☐

People as Everyday Theorists: Schemas and Their Influence

The first shortcut we will consider is the use of theories about what people and things are like. Scientists develop many theories and hypotheses about their specialty, be it the behavior of subatomic particles or of witnesses to an emergency. All of us, in our everyday lives, also develop theories that help us understand ourselves and the social world. These theories, called **schemas**, are mental structures people use to organize their knowledge around themes or topics (Bartlett, 1932; Markus, 1977; Taylor & Crocker, 1981).

We have schemas about many things—other people, ourselves, social roles (e.g., what a librarian or an engineer is like), and specific events (e.g., what usually happens when people eat a meal in a restaurant). In each case, our schemas contain our basic knowledge and impressions. For example, our schema about the members of the Animal House fraternity might be that they're loud, obnoxious partyers with a propensity for projectile vomiting. Schemas profoundly affect what information we notice, think about, and later remember (Kerr & Stanfel, 1993; Trafimow & Schneider, 1994; Trafimow & Wyer, 1993; von Hippel, Jonides, Hilton, & Narayan, 1993). If you see a member of the Animal House acting in a calm, polite, and studious manner, this information will be inconsistent with your schema and under most circumstances you will forget it, ignore it, or fail to even notice it. Thus, schemas act as filters, straining out information that is contradictory to or inconsistent with the prevailing theme (Fiske, 1993; Higgins & Bargh, 1987; Olson, Roese, & Zanna, 1996; Stangor & McMillan, 1992).

Sometimes, of course, a fact can be so inconsistent with a schema that we cannot ignore or forget it. If we encounter a member of the Animal House who is actively campaigning to raise the drinking age to 25 and prefers poetry readings to raucous parties, he is such a glaring exception to our schema that he will stick in our minds—particularly if we spend time pondering how he could ever have ended up in the same house as his party-loving brothers (Burgoon, 1993; Hastie, 1980; Stangor & McMillan, 1992). In most cases, however, we are likely to notice and think about the behavior of the Animal House frat members that fits our preconceptions about them. In this way, our schemas become stronger and more resistant to change over time. For example, Claudia Cohen (1981) showed people a videotape of a woman engaged in various activities and identified her as either a librarian or a waitress. When later asked to recall scenes from the video, the participants more accurately recalled information that was consistent with the occupational label, such as the fact that the librarian had been listening to classical music.

In addition, human memory is reconstructive. We don't remember exactly what occurred in a given setting, as if our minds were a film camera recording the

Schemas
mental structures people use to organize their knowledge about the social world around themes or subjects; schemas affect what information we notice, think about, and remember

❝Theory helps us to bear our ignorance of facts.
   —George Santayana,
   The Sense of Beauty, 1896

■ "Beam me up, Scotty." Did the characters in the original *Star Trek* television series ever speak this line?

precise images and sounds. Instead, we remember some information that was there (particularly information our schema leads us to notice and pay attention to) and we remember other information that was never there but that we have unknowingly added later (Darley & Akert, 1991; Markus & Zajonc, 1985). For example, if you ask people what is the most famous line of dialogue in the classic Humphrey Bogart and Ingrid Bergman movie *Casablanca,* they will probably say, "Play it again, Sam." Similarly, if you ask them what is one of the most famous lines from the original (1966–69) *Star Trek* television series, they will probably say, "Beam me up, Scotty."

Here is a piece of trivia that might surprise you: Both of these lines of dialogue are reconstructions—the characters in the movie and the television series never said them. Not surprisingly, memory reconstructions tend to be consistent with our schema. For example, in Cohen's (1981) librarian/waitress study, participants misremembered what beverage the librarian had been drinking in the videotape. They reconstructed the scene in memory so that she was drinking wine, not beer, because that fit their schema of what a librarian would drink. As we will discuss in Chapter 13, the very way in which our schemas operate makes prejudiced attitudes highly resistant to change.

The Function of Schemas: Why Do We Have Them?

If schemas can sometimes make us misperceive the world, why do we have them? Think, for a moment, what it would be like to have no schemas about the social world. What if everything you encountered was inexplicable, confusing, and unlike anything else you'd ever known? Tragically, this is what happens to people who suffer from a neurological disorder called Korsakov's syndrome. They lose the ability to form new memories and must approach every situation as if they were encountering it for the first time—even if they have actually encountered it many times before. This can be so unsettling—even terrifying—that some people with Korsakov's syndrome go to great lengths to try to impose meaning on their experiences. The neurologist Oliver Sacks gives the following description of a Korsakov patient named Mr. Thompson:

> He remembered nothing for more than a few seconds. He was continually disoriented. Abysses of amnesia continually opened beneath him, but he would bridge them, nimbly, by fluent confabulations and fictions of all kinds. For him they were not fictions, but how he suddenly saw, or interpreted, the world. Its radical flux and incoherence could not be tolerated, acknowledged, for an instant—there was, instead, this strange, delirious, quasi-coherence, as Mr. Thompson, with his ceaseless, unconscious, quick-fire inventions, continually improvised a world around him . . . *for such a patient must literally make himself (and his world) up every moment.* (Sacks, 1987, pp. 109–110; emphasis in original)

In short, it is so important to us to have continuity, to relate new experiences to our past schemas, that people who lose this ability invent schemas where none exist.

Schemas are particularly important when we encounter information that can be interpreted in a number of ways, because they provide us with a way of reducing this ambiguity. Consider a classic study by Harold Kelley (1950) in which students in different sections of a college economics class were told that a guest lecturer would be filling in that day. In order to create a schema about what the guest lecturer would be like, Kelley told the students that the economics department was interested in how different classes reacted to different instructors and that the students would thus receive a brief biographical note about the instructor before he arrived. The note contained information about the instructor's age, background, and teaching experience. It also gave one of two descriptions of his personality. One version said, "People who know him consider him to be a rather cold person, industrious, critical, practical, and determined." The other version was identical, except that the phrase "a rather cold person" was replaced with "a very warm person." The students were randomly given one of these personality descriptions.

The guest lecturer then conducted a class discussion for 20 minutes, after which the students rated their impressions of him. How humorous was he? How sociable? How considerate? Given that there was some ambiguity in this situation—after all, the students had seen the instructor for only a brief time—Kelley hypothesized that they would use the schema provided by the biographical note to fill in the blanks. This hypothesis was confirmed: The students who expected the instructor to be warm gave him significantly higher ratings than the students who expected him to be cold, even though all the students had observed the same teacher behaving in the same way. Students who expected the instructor to be warm were also more likely to ask him questions and to participate in the class discussion. Think for a minute if this has ever happened to you. Has what you've known about a professor prior to the first day of class affected your impressions of him or her? Did you find, oddly enough, that the professor acted just as you'd expected? Next time, ask a classmate who had a different expectation about the professor what he or she thought. See if the two of you have different perceptions of the instructor based on the different schemas you were using.

Of course, people are not totally blind to what is actually out there in the world. Sometimes what we see is relatively unambiguous and we do not need to

■ People who know him consider him to be a very warm person, industrious, critical, practical, and determined.

■ People who know him consider him to be a rather cold person, industrious, critical, practical, and determined.

use our schemas to help us interpret it. For example, in one of the classes in which Kelley conducted his study, the guest instructor happened to be unambiguously self-confident, even cocky. Given that cockiness is a relatively unambiguous trait, the students did not need to rely on their expectations to fill in the blanks. They rated the instructor as being immodest in both the warm and cold conditions. However, when they rated this instructor's sense of humor, which was less clear-cut, the students relied on their schemas: The students in the warm condition thought he was more humorous than the students in the cold condition did. Thus, the more ambiguous information is, the more we use schemas to fill in the blanks.

It is important to note that there is nothing wrong with what Kelley's students did. As long as people have reason to believe their schemas are accurate, it is perfectly reasonable to use them to resolve ambiguity. If a suspicious-looking character comes up to you in a dark alley and says "Take out your wallet," your schema about such encounters tells you the person wants to steal your money, not admire pictures of your family. This schema helps you avert a serious and perhaps deadly misunderstanding. If you bring to mind the wrong schema you can get yourself into hot water—not many muggers want to ooh and ah over your pictures of Aunt Martha and Uncle Julio.

> "I know that often I would not see a thing unless I thought of it first.
>
> –Norman Maclean,
> *A River Runs Through It*

Cultural Determinants of Schemas

Have you ever met someone from another culture and been amazed at what she or he noticed and remembered about your country? Tim Wilson relates an experience he had when he was a teenager: One Sunday a guest from Iran came to his house for dinner. This man, Mr. Khetabdari, was visiting the United States for the first time and had arrived only a few days before. When he visited the Wilson house, Tim was idly watching a football game on television. As Mr. Khetabdari took off his coat and was introduced to the family, he glanced at the TV and re-acted with horror to the sight of the men in weird outfits slamming into each other and throwing each other to the ground. "Oh, what are they doing?" he asked. "Why are these people hurting each other?" Mr. Khetabdari knew nothing about football and could not imagine why these groups of large, overgrown men were chasing each other while wearing strange clothes and hats. Or why Tim and his family were watching them do it. American football was so foreign to Mr. Khetabdari's schemas of the world that he was quite horrified by the game on television.

Clearly, an important source of our schemas is the culture in which we grow up. In Chapter 5, we will see that, across cultures, there are fundamental differences in people's schemas about themselves and the social world, with some interesting consequences. For now, we point out that the schemas our culture teaches us have a large influence on what we notice and remember about the world. Frederic Bartlett (1932), for example, noted that different cultures have schemas about different things, depending on what is important to that culture. These schemas influence what people in different cultures are likely to remember.

To illustrate the relationship between culture, schemas, and memory, Bartlett interviewed a Scottish settler and a local Bantu herdsman in Swaziland, a small country in southeast Africa. Both men had been present at a complicated cattle transaction that had transpired a year earlier. The Scottish man had little memory about the details of the transaction; he had to consult his records to remember how many cattle were bought and sold and for how much. The Bantu man, when asked, promptly recited from memory every detail of the transaction, including from whom each ox and cow had been bought, the color of each ox and cow, and the price of each transaction. The Bantu people's memory for cattle is so good that they do not bother to brand them; if a cow happens to wander away and get mixed up with a neighbor's herd, the owner simply goes over and takes it back—having no trouble distinguishing his cow from the dozens of others.

Perhaps the Bantu simply have better memories overall. Bartlett (1932) argues convincingly, however, that their memories are no better than the memories of people in other cultures. Each of us has a superb memory, he suggests, in the areas that are important to us, areas for which we thus have well-developed schemas. Cattle are a central part of the Bantu economy and culture, and thus the Bantu have well-developed schemas about cattle. To a person who grew up in a different culture, one cow might look like any other. This person undoubtedly has well-developed schemas about and an excellent memory for things that are quite foreign to the Bantu, such as transactions on the New York Stock Exchange, foreign movies, or, for that matter, American football.

Schemas Can Distort What We See and Remember

As we have seen, schemas are very useful tools that help us remember what is important to us. They have some drawbacks, however. Sometimes we distort the evidence so that it will be consistent with our schemas, making it difficult for any truly inconsistent information to register. A classic demonstration of such distortion was performed by Al Hastorf and Hadley Cantril (1954). They showed a film of a football contest between Dartmouth and Princeton to students from both schools and asked them to record the number of infractions committed by each team. The game had been a particularly rough one, generating heated protests on both campuses; each school blamed the other for the injuries that had occurred. Hastorf and Cantril conjectured that one reason for this difference of opinion was that the students from the two universities noticed different things in the same game, due to their partisanship. This hypothesis was confirmed: The Princeton students who watched the film saw more in-

■ People view reality through schema-tinted glasses. Students from Princeton and Dartmouth watched the same film of a rough football game between the two schools. The Princeton students saw more penalties committed by the Dartmouth team, whereas the Dartmouth students saw more penalties committed by the Princeton team.

fractions committed by Dartmouth than Princeton, whereas the Dartmouth students saw just the reverse. It is important to note that the students were perfectly sincere about their perceptions—they really saw two different realities in the same film.

There is a tendency for us to view the world in yes-or-no terms, wherein our own side is the hero and the other side is the villain. Interestingly, this biased view can make partisans think that most other people are interpreting reality incorrectly. For example, what would have happened had the Princeton and Dartmouth students seen a balanced, neutral newscast reporting that both football teams had exhibited rough, unsportsmanlike behavior? Each side would think the newscast was biased against their school, because it did not present the extreme view they "knew" to be the truth. Vallone, Ross, and Lepper (1985) demonstrated this **hostile media phenomenon**, whereby opposing partisan groups both perceive neutral, balanced media presentations as hostile to their side, because the media have not presented the facts in the one-sided fashion the partisans "know" to be true. They showed news broadcasts about conflicts in the Middle East (reporting the massacre of civilians in refugee camps in Lebanon in 1982) to students who were either pro-Arab or pro-Israel. As expected, each group believed the newscasts were biased in favor of the other side (Giner-Sorolla & Chaiken, 1994).

The participants in the Hastorf and Cantril (1954) and Vallone and colleagues (1985) studies were highly involved in the issues and had a substantial investment in viewing their side as the good guys. It is likely that they were motivated to see things in a way that confirmed their view of the world. For example, when the Princeton students saw one of their own players commit a questionable act, they were likely to interpret it as a rough but sportsmanlike play that was well within the rules, due to their investment in the belief that their school was blameless. The students from Dartmouth were likely to interpret the same act as a

Hostile Media Phenomenon
the finding that opposing partisan groups both perceive neutral, balanced media presentations as hostile to their side, because the media have not presented the facts in the one-sided fashion the partisans "know" to be true

ruthless, unsportsmanlike attempt to injure one of their players, so that they could maintain the view that their side was blameless. People often interpret the world in a way that is consistent with their self-esteem. One need only attend a few sessions of divorce court to witness this kind of distortion, whereby two people give conflicting accounts, each swearing that his or her version of reality is true.

There are, however, conditions under which people will interpret the facts as consistent with their schemas and expectations even when they have relatively little investment in the issues. Consider research on what is called the **primacy effect**, which occurs when our first impression of another person influences our later impressions of him or her. The primacy effect occurs because people form schemas on the basis of the first information they receive, and these schemas then influence the interpretation of later information. That is, people often cling to their first impression, and later information that contradicts it is ignored, discounted, or reinterpreted. Whereas there are circumstances under which recency effects occur—whereby information received last has the greatest impact—such effects appear to be the exception.

This dominance of first impressions was demonstrated in a simple, elegant experiment by Ned Jones and colleagues (Jones, Rock, Shaver, Goethals, & Ward, 1968). Participants watched a male student trying to solve 30 multiple-choice analogy questions that were said to be of equal difficulty. The student always solved half the items correctly. The only difference was that in one condition, he started off very well, getting most of the first items right, and then began to do poorly, getting most of the last items wrong. In the other condition, this sequence was reversed: He got most of the first items wrong and then got most of the last ones right. After observing the student, the participants were asked to judge his intelligence and to recall how many items he had solved correctly.

As predicted, the participants were strong theorists who distorted the data to fit their first impressions. Those who observed the student start off well thought he was more intelligent and recalled that he had solved a higher number of items on the test than those who saw him start off poorly. Remember, in both cases the student solved 15 of the 30 items, all of which were of equal difficulty. Even so, the participants exhibited a strong primacy effect: What they saw first dominated their impressions, leading them to discount (and indeed to misrepresent) what came later (see Figure 3.1). Why? It seems unlikely that participants in this study

---

Primacy Effect
the process whereby our first impression of another person influences our later impressions of him or her

---

■ **FIGURE 3.1   The primacy of first impressions.** People observed a student's work on 30 test questions and then recalled how many he answered correctly. Those who saw him get most of the first ones right overestimated the total number whereas those who saw him get most of the first ones wrong underestimated the total number (in both cases, he got 15 out of 30 correct). (Adapted from Jones et al., 1968)

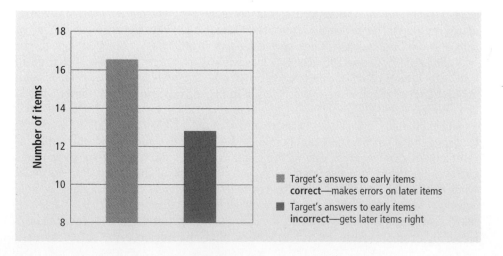

distorted reality in order to feel better about themselves. The participants were judging another student, one who was a stranger to them and whom they would probably never see again. It appears that people's schemas, once formed, take on a life of their own, influencing how new information is viewed, regardless of whether people have an investment in what they see.

Schemas Can Persist Even After They Are Discredited

There is another way in which schemas can take on a life of their own: They persist even after the evidence for them has been completely debunked. Sometimes we hear something about an issue or another person that later turns out not to be true. For example, a jury might hear something in the courtroom about a defendant that is untrue or labeled as inadmissible evidence and be told by the judge to disregard that information. The problem is that, due to the way schemas operate, our beliefs can persist even after the evidence for them proves to be false.

To illustrate this point, imagine you were a participant in a study by Lee Ross, Mark Lepper, and Michael Hubbard (1975). You are given a stack of cards containing both real and fictitious suicide notes. Your job is to guess which ones are real, supposedly to study the effects of physiological processes during decision making. After each guess, the experimenter tells you whether you are right or wrong. As the experiment progresses, you find out that you are pretty good at this task. In fact, you guess right on 24 of the 25 cards, which is much better than the average performance of 16 correct.

At this point, the experimenter tells you that the study is over and explains that it was actually concerned with the effects of success and failure on physiological responses. You learn that the feedback you received was bogus; that is, you had been randomly assigned to a condition in which the experimenter said you were correct on 24 of the cards, regardless of how well you actually did. The experimenter then gives you a final questionnaire, which asks you how many answers you think you really got correct and how many times you think you would guess correctly on a second, equally difficult test with new cards. What would you say? Now pretend you were in the other condition of the study. Here everything is identical, except you are told that you got only 10 of the 25 answers correct, which is much worse than average. How would you respond to the questionnaire, once you found out that the feedback was bogus?

Depending on which condition you were in, you would have formed a schema that you were either very good or very poor at the task. What happens when the evidence for this schema is discredited? Ross and colleagues (1975) went to some pains to make sure the participants believed the feedback had been randomly determined and had nothing to do with their actual performance. Even though the participants believed this, those who had received the "success" feedback still thought they had gotten more of the items correct and would do better on a second test than people who had received the "failure" feedback did. In addition, when asked how they would do on a new test, success participants said they would do better than failure participants did (see Figure 3.2).

This result is called the **perseverance effect**, because people's beliefs persevered even after the original evidence for them was discredited. When people received the feedback, they explained to themselves why they were doing so well or so poorly, bringing to mind evidence from their past that was consistent with their performance (e.g., "I am really very perceptive. After all, last week I was the

Perseverance Effect
the finding that people's beliefs about themselves and the social world persist even after the evidence supporting these beliefs is discredited

■ **FIGURE 3.2   The perseverance effect.** People were told they had done very well (success feedback) or very poorly (failure feedback) on a test of their social sensitivity. They were then told that the feedback was bogus and had nothing to do with their actual performance. People's impressions that they were good or bad at the task persevered, even after learning that the feedback was bogus. (Adapted from Ross, Lepper, & Hubbard, 1975)

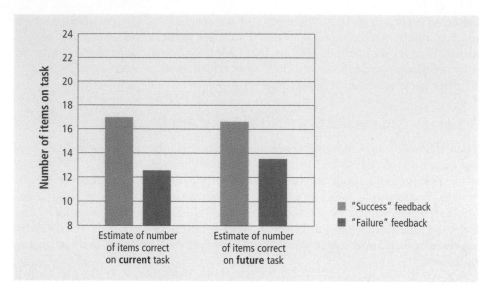

only one who realized that Jennifer was depressed" or "Well, I'm not so good at this stuff; my friends always say I'm the last to know"). Even after learning that the feedback was false, these thoughts were still fresh in people's minds, making them think they were particularly good or bad at the task (Anderson, 1995; Anderson & Sechler, 1986).

Making Our Schemas Come True: The Self-Fulfilling Prophecy

We have seen that when people encounter new evidence or have old evidence discredited, they tend not to revise their schemas as much as we might expect. People are not always passive recipients of information, however—they often act on their schemas and in doing so can change the extent to which these schemas are supported or contradicted. In fact, people can inadvertently make their schemas come true by the way they treat people. This is called a **self-fulfilling prophecy,** which occurs when people have an expectation about what another person is like, which influences how they act toward that person, which in turn causes that person to behave consistently with people's original expectations—making the expectations come true. Figure 3.3 illustrates this sad, self-perpetuating cycle of a self-fulfilling prophecy.

Self-Fulfilling Prophecy
the case whereby people (a) have an expectation about what another person is like, which (b) influences how they act toward that person, which (c) causes that person to behave consistently with people's original expectations

Self-fulfilling prophecies can have some frightening consequences. Consider these facts: In elementary schools in the United States, girls outperform boys on standardized tests of reading, writing, social studies, and math. By the middle school years, however, girls start to fall behind, and by high school, boys do better than girls on most kinds of standardized tests (Hedges & Nowell, 1995). On the Scholastic Aptitude Test (SAT), used by many colleges to select students, males outscore females by 50 points on the math section and 10 points on the verbal section (Sadker & Sadker, 1994). Although some people have argued that male and female brains process information differently (Geary, 1996; Kimura, 1987; Witelson, 1992), it is unlikely that differences in academic performance can be explained solely by any such biological differences (Bonora & Huteau, 1991; Chipman, 1996; Emanuelson & Fischbein, 1986; Feingold, 1996; Ghiselin, 1996; Hyde, 1997).

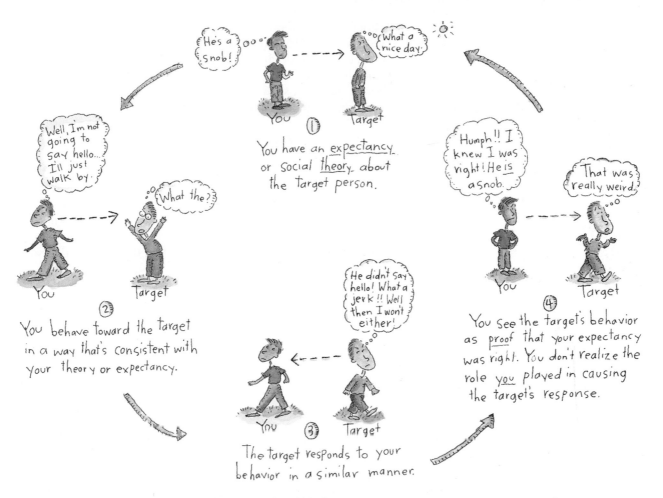

■ **FIGURE 3.3   The self-fulfilling prophecy: A sad cycle in four acts.**

Why do girls do worse than boys academically? Consider these pieces of the puzzle: If you ask teachers which of their current students are most academically gifted, or who their most outstanding students have been over the years, an embarrassing truth leaks out—most of the students they mention are male. Many teachers, even if they are women themselves, believe that males are brighter and more likely to succeed academically than females (Jussim & Eccles, 1992). Parents hold similar beliefs about the talents of their children, as do adolescents about their own talents (Parsons, Kaczala, & Meece, 1982; Yee & Eccles, 1988).

Is it possible that girls do worse academically because of a self-fulfilling prophecy? Are teachers and parents treating males and females differently, in ways that make their expectations about gender and academic performance come true? First, let's be very clear: No one is suggesting that teachers or parents deliberately treat girls in ways that inhibit their performance. Schemas are powerful things, however, and it may be that teachers and parents unintentionally behave in ways that make their expectations about girls come true.

Here's an example given by Myra and David Sadker (1994), who have spent years observing the ways in which teachers treat boys versus girls. A fifth-grade teacher is explaining a difficult problem to her students and asks one of the girls

> **P**rophecy is the most gratuitous form of error.
> —George Eliot (Mary Ann Evans Cross), 1871

to hold the math book so that everyone can see the problem. She then does something interesting: She turns her back to the girls (who are seated on her right) and explains the problem to the boys (who are seated on her left). Although she occasionally turns to the girls to read an example from the book, she directs virtually all of her attention to the boys, such that the girls can see only the back of her head. "The girl holding the math book had become a prop," note Sadker and Sadker (1994). "The teacher . . . had unwittingly transformed the girls into spectators, an audience for the boys" (p. 3). The Sadkers document many such cases of teachers treating boys more favorably than girls.

Such anecdotes, while interesting, certainly do not prove that self-fulfilling prophecies are at work in our schools. It is necessary to conduct controlled studies in which teacher's expectations are controlled experimentally. Robert Rosenthal and Lenore Jacobson (1968) did so in an elementary school, in what has become one of the most famous studies in social psychology. They administered an IQ test to all of the students in the school and told the teachers that some of the students had scored so well that they were sure to "bloom" academically in the upcoming year. In fact, this was not necessarily true: The students identified as "bloomers" were chosen randomly by the researchers. As we discussed in Chapter 2, the use of random assignment means that, on average, the students designated as bloomers were no smarter or more likely to bloom than any of the other kids. The only way in which these students differed from their peers was in the minds of the teachers (neither the students nor their parents were told anything about the results of the test).

After creating the expectations in the teachers that some of the kids would do especially well, Rosenthal and Jacobson waited to see what would happen. They observed the classroom dynamics periodically over the school year, and at the end of the year they tested all of the children again with an actual IQ test. Did the prophecy come true? Indeed it did—the students in each class who had been labeled as bloomers showed significantly higher gains in their IQ scores than the other students did (see Figure 3.4). The teachers' expectations had become reality.

■ **FIGURE 3.4 The self-fulfilling prophecy: Percentage of first- and second-graders who improved on an IQ test over the course of the school year.** Those whom the teachers expected to do well actually improved more than the other students. (Adapted from Rosenthal & Jacobson, 1968)

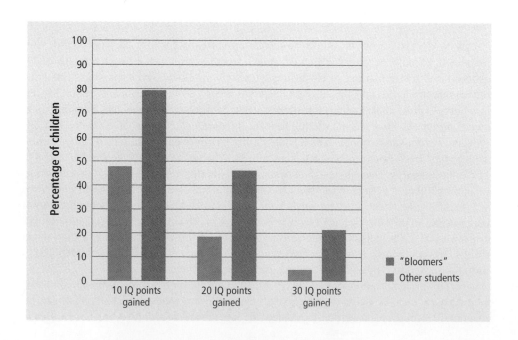

Rosenthal and Jacobson's findings have since been replicated in a number of both experimental and correlational studies (Babad, 1993; Blanck, 1993; Bratesani, Weinstein, & Marshall, 1984; Jussim, 1989, 1991; Madon, Jussim, & Eccles, 1997).

It is important to note that the teachers did not callously decide to direct their limited time and resources to the bloomers. Most teachers are incredibly dedicated and would be horrified to learn that they treated some students in a more advantageous manner than others. Interestingly, the teachers in the Rosenthal and Jacobson study reported that they spent slightly less time with the students who were labeled as bloomers. In subsequent studies, however, teachers have been found to treat bloomers (the students they expect to do better) differently in four general ways: (a) They create a warmer emotional climate for bloomers, giving them more personal attention, encouragement, and support; (b) they give bloomers more material to learn and material that is more difficult; (c) they give bloomers more and better feedback on their work; and (d) they give bloomers more opportunities to respond in class and give them longer to respond (Brophy, 1983; Jussim, 1986; Rosenthal, 1994; Snyder, 1984).

Many other studies have reinforced the idea that self-fulfilling prophecies are not the result of a deliberate attempt by people to confirm their schemas; rather, they occur inadvertently and unconsciously. Even when people try to treat others in an evenhanded, unbiased manner, their expectations can creep in and change their behavior, which in turn changes the behavior of the person with whom they are interacting (Darley & Gross, 1983). In fact, when people are distracted and can't concentrate on what people are like as an individual, they are even more likely to act in accord with their expectations. Monica Harris and Rebecca Perkins (1995) found a greater self-fulfilling prophecy when people were distracted by having to remember an 8-digit number than when people were not distracted. Presumably the distracted participants found it even more difficult to treat people like individuals and easier to rely on their expectations about what people would be like.

Remember the teacher who taught math more to the boys than the girls in her class? It is interesting to note that her behavior was being videotaped, with her knowledge and cooperation, for a segment of the NBC television program *Dateline* on sexism in the schools. One would assume, then, that she was trying very hard not to treat the girls any differently from how she treated the boys. Nonetheless, she did, which suggests how difficult it can be to recognize that we are acting in accord with our expectations.

Self-fulfilling prophecies are not limited to the way teachers treat students. Each of us has all sorts of schemas about what other people are like, and whenever we act on these schemas in a way that makes the schema come true a self-fulfilling prophecy results (Darley & Fazio, 1980). Self-fulfilling prophecies have been found among diverse populations, with diverse expectations, including college students' schemas about what a potential dating partner is like, mothers' schemas about what premature babies are like, supervisors' expectations about the performance of assembly-line workers, judges' expectations about the guilt of a defendant, and physicians' expectations about their patients' health (Blanck, 1993; Eden & Zuk, 1995; Friedman, 1993; King, 1971; Snyder & Swann, 1978; Stern & Hildebrandt, 1986).

A distressing implication of research on the self-fulfilling prophecy is that our schemas may be resistant to change because we see a good deal of false evidence that confirms them. Suppose a teacher has the schema that boys possess innate

Try It !

Avoiding Self-Fulfilling Prophecies

Examine some of your own schemas and expectations about social groups, especially groups you don't particularly like. These might be members of a particular race or ethnic group, of a rival fraternity, of a political party, or people with a particular sexual orientation. Why don't you like members of this group? "Well," you might think, "one reason is that whenever I interact with African Americans [substitute whites, Jews, gentiles, gays, straights, Sigma Chis, Democrats, Republicans, or any other social group], they seem cold and unfriendly." And you might be right. Perhaps they do respond to you in a cold and unfriendly fashion. Not, however, because they are this way by nature but because they are responding to the way you have treated them.

Try this exercise to counteract the self-fulfilling prophecy: Find someone who is a member of a group you dislike and strike up a conversation with him or her. For example, sit next to this person in one of your classes or go up to him or her at a party. Try to imagine that this individual is the friendliest, kindest, sweetest person you have ever met. Be as warm and charming as you can be. Don't go overboard—if, after never speaking to this person, you suddenly act like Mr. or Ms. Congeniality, you might arouse suspicion. The trick is to act as if you expect him or her to be extremely pleasant and friendly.

Observe this person's reactions. Are you surprised by how friendly he or she responded to you? People you thought were inherently cold and unfriendly will probably behave in a warm and friendly manner themselves, in response to the way you have treated them. If this doesn't work on your first encounter with the person, try it again on one or two occasions. In all likelihood, you will find that friendliness really does breed friendliness (see Chapter 10).

ability that makes them superior in math to girls. "But Mr. Jones," we might say, "how can you hold such a belief? There are plenty of girls who do very well in math." Mr. Jones would probably be unconvinced, because he would have data to support his schema. "In my classes over the years," he might note, "nearly three times as many boys as girls have excelled at math." His error lies not with his characterization of the evidence but in his failure to realize his role in producing it. Robert Merton referred to this process as a "reign of error," whereby people can "cite the actual course of events as proof that [they were] right from the very beginning" (1948, p. 195). See Try It! above for a way to overcome your own self-fulfilling prophecies.

To summarize, we have seen that the amount of information with which we are faced every day is so vast that we have to reduce it to a manageable size. In addition, much of this information is ambiguous or difficult to decipher. One way we deal with these problems is by relying on schemas, which help us reduce the amount of information we need to take in and help us interpret ambiguous information. We turn now to other, more specific mental shortcuts that people use.

Mental Strategies and Shortcuts

How did you decide which colleges to apply to? One strategy would be to investigate thoroughly every one of the more than 2,000 colleges and universities in the United States. You could have read every catalog from cover to cover, visited every campus, and interviewed as many faculty members, deans, and students as you could find. Getting tired yet? Such a strategy would, of course, be prohibitively time-consuming and costly. Instead of considering every college and university, most high school students narrow down their choice to a small number of options and find out what they can about these schools.

This example is like many decisions and judgments we make in everyday life. When deciding which job to accept, what car to purchase, or whom to marry, we usually do not conduct a thorough search of every option ("OK, it's time for me to get married; I think I'll consult the Census lists of unmarried adults in my town and begin my interviews tomorrow"). Instead, we use mental strategies and shortcuts that make the decisions easier, allowing us to get on with our lives without turning every decision into a major research project. These shortcuts do not always lead to the best decision. For example, if you had exhaustively studied all 2,000 colleges in the United States, maybe you would have found one that you liked better than the one where you are now. Mental shortcuts are efficient, however, and usually lead to good decisions in a reasonable amount of time (Gigerenzer & Goldstein, 1996; Nisbett & Ross, 1980).

What shortcuts do people use? One, as we have already seen, is to use schemas to understand new situations. Rather than starting from scratch when examining our options, we often apply our previous knowledge and schemas. We have many such schemas, about everything from colleges and universities (e.g., what Ivy League colleges and big, midwestern universities are like) to other people (e.g., teachers' beliefs about the abilities of boys versus girls). When making specific kinds of judgments and decisions, however, we do not always have a ready-made schema to apply. Other times there are too many schemas that could apply, and it is not clear which one to use. What do we do?

At times like this, people often use mental shortcuts called **judgmental heuristics**. The word *heuristic* comes from the Greek word meaning "to discover"; in the field of social cognition, heuristics refer to the mental shortcuts people use to make judgments quickly and efficiently. Before discussing these heuristics, we should note that they do not guarantee that people will make accurate inferences about the world. Sometimes heuristics are inadequate for the job at hand or are misapplied, leading to faulty judgments. In fact, a good deal of research in social cognition has focused on just such mistakes in reasoning; we will document many such mental errors in this chapter, such as the case of teachers who mistakenly believed that boys were smarter than girls. As we discuss the mental strategies that sometimes lead to errors, however, it is important to keep in mind that people use heuristics for a reason: Most of the time, they are highly functional and serve us well.

Judgmental Heuristics
mental shortcuts people use to make judgments quickly and efficiently

How Easily Does It Come to Mind? The Availability Heuristic

Suppose you are sitting in a restaurant with several friends one night when it becomes clear that the waiter made a mistake with one of the orders. Your friend Alphonse ordered the Veggie Burger with onion rings but instead got the Veggie Burger with fries. "Oh, well," he says, "I'll just eat the fries." This starts a discussion of whether he should have sent back his order, and some of the gang accuses Alphonse of being unassertive. He turns to you and asks, "Do you think I'm an unassertive person?" How would you answer this question?

One way, as we have seen, would be to call on a ready-made schema that provides the answer. If you know Alphonse well and have already formed a picture of how assertive he is, you can recite your answer easily and quickly: "Don't worry, Alphonse, if I had to deal with a used-car salesman, you'd be the first person I'd call." Suppose, though, that you've never really thought about how assertive Alphonse is and have to think about your answer. In these situations, we often rely on how easily different examples come to mind. If it is easy to think of times Alphonse acted assertively (e.g., "that time he stopped someone from butting in line in front of him at the movies"), you will conclude that Alphonse is a pretty assertive guy. If it is easier to think of times Alphonse acted unassertively (e.g., "that time he let a phone solicitor talk him into buying a Veg-O-Matic for $29.99"), you will conclude that he is pretty unassertive.

Availability Heuristic
a mental rule of thumb whereby people base a judgment on the ease with which they can bring something to mind

This mental rule of thumb is called the **availability heuristic**, which is basing a judgment on the ease with which you can bring something to mind (Manis, Shedler, Jonides, & Nelson, 1993; Rothman & Hardin, 1997; Schwarz et al., 1991; Tversky & Kahneman, 1973; Wänke, Schwarz, & Bless, 1995). There are many situations in which the availability heuristic is a good strategy to use. If you can easily bring to mind several times when Alphonse stood up for his rights, he probably is an assertive person; if you can easily bring to mind several times when he was timid or meek, he probably is not. The trouble with the availability heuristic is that sometimes what is easiest to bring to mind is not typical of the overall picture, leading to faulty conclusions.

Consider the case of medical diagnosis. It might seem like it is a relatively straightforward matter for a doctor to observe your symptoms and figure out what disease, if any, you have. Sometimes, though, medical symptoms are quite ambiguous and might be a sign of several different disorders. Do doctors use the availability heuristic, whereby they are more likely to consider diagnoses that come to mind easily? Several studies of medical diagnoses suggest that the answer is yes (Eraker & Politser, 1988; Fox, 1980; Schiffmann, Cohen, Nowik, & Selinger, 1978; Travis, Phillippi, & Tonn, 1989; Weber, Bockenholt, Hilton, & Wallace, 1993).

Consider Dr. Robert Marion's diagnosis of Nicole, a bright, sweet, nine-year-old patient who came to his office one day. Nicole was normal in every way, except that once or twice a year she had strange, neurological attacks, characterized by disorientation, insomnia, slurred words, and strange mewing sounds. Nicole

■ Physicians have been found to use the availability heuristic when making diagnoses. Their diagnoses are influenced by how easily they can bring to mind different diseases.

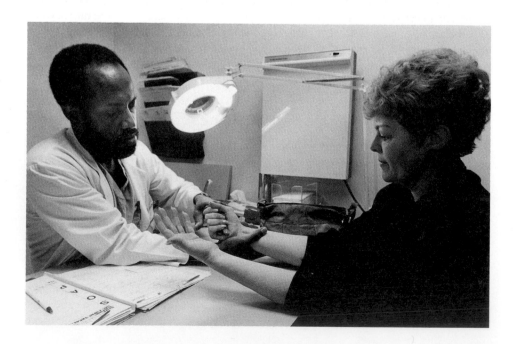

had been hospitalized three times, had seen over a dozen specialists, and had undergone many diagnostic tests, including CT scans, brain-wave tests, and virtually every blood test there is. The doctors were stumped; they could not figure out what was wrong with her. Within minutes of seeing her, however, Dr. Marion correctly diagnosed her problem as a rare, inherited blood disorder called acute intermittent poryphria (AIP). The blood chemistry of people with this disorder often gets out of synch, causing a variety of neurological symptoms. It can be controlled with a careful diet and by avoiding certain medications.

How did Dr. Marion diagnose Nicole's disorder so quickly, when so many other doctors failed to do so? Dr. Marion had just finished writing a book on the genetic diseases of historical figures, including a chapter on King George III of England, who, you guessed it—suffered from AIP. "I didn't make the diagnosis because I'm a brilliant diagnostician or because I'm a sensitive listener," reports Dr. Marion. "I succeeded where others failed because [Nicole] and I happened to run into each other in exactly the right place, at exactly the right time" (Marion, 1995, p. 40).

In other words, Dr. Marion used the availability heuristic. AIP happened to be available in Dr. Marion's memory, making the diagnosis easy. Though this was a happy outcome of the use of the availability heuristic, it is easy to see how it can go wrong. As Dr. Marion says, "Doctors are just like everyone else. We go to the movies, watch TV, read newspapers and novels. If we happen to see a patient who has symptoms of a rare disease that was featured on the previous night's 'Movie of the Week,' we're more likely to consider that condition when making a diagnosis" (Marion, 1995, p. 40). That's all well and good if your disease happens to be the topic of last night's movie. It's not so good if your disease doesn't happen to be available in your doctor's memory, as was the case with the twelve doctors Nicole had seen previously.

Do people use the availability heuristic to make judgments about themselves? It might seem like we have well-developed ideas about our own personalities, such as how assertive we are. Often, however, people do not have firm schemas about their own traits (Markus, 1977) and thus might make judgments about themselves based on how easily they can bring to mind examples of their own behavior. To see if this is the case, Norbert Schwarz and his colleagues (1991) performed a clever experiment in which they altered how easy it was for people to bring to mind examples of their own past behaviors. In one condition, they asked people to think of 6 times they had acted assertively. Most people found this to be pretty easy; examples came to mind quickly. In another condition, the researchers asked people to think of 12 times they had acted assertively. This was much more difficult; people had to try very hard to think of this many examples. All participants were then asked to rate how assertive they thought they really were.

The question was, did people use the availability heuristic (the ease with which they could bring examples to mind) to infer how assertive they were? As seen on the left-hand side of Figure 3.5, they did. People asked to think of 6 examples rated themselves as relatively assertive, because it was easy to think of this many examples ("Hey, this is easy—I guess I'm a pretty assertive person"). People asked to think of 12 examples rated themselves as relatively unassertive, because it was difficult to think of this many examples ("Hm, this is hard—I must not be a very assertive person"). Other people were asked to think of 6 or 12 times they had acted *un*assertively and similar results were found—those asked to think of 6 examples rated themselves as relatively unassertive (see the right-hand side of Figure 3.5). In short, people use the availability heuristic—the ease with which

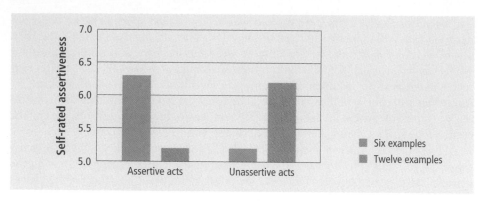

■ **FIGURE 3.5   Availability and how assertive we think we are.**   People asked to think of 6 times they behaved assertively found it easy to do so and thus concluded that they were pretty assertive people. People asked to think of 12 times they behaved assertively found it difficult to think of so many examples and thus concluded they were not very assertive people (see the left-hand side of the graph). Similar results were found among people asked to think of 6 or 12 times they behaved unassertively (see the right-hand side of the graph). These results show that people often base their judgments on availability, or how easily they can bring information to mind. (Adapted from Schwarz et al., 1991)

they can bring examples to mind—when making judgments about themselves and other people.

Mentally Undoing the Past: Counterfactual Reasoning

The ease with which we can think of examples of our own behaviors, then, influences the kind of person we think we are. The ease with which we can reconstruct the past has also been found to be important in our judgments about ourselves and others. People often engage in **counterfactual thinking**: mentally changing some aspect of the past as a way of imagining what might have been (Gilovich & Medvec, 1995; Johnson, 1986; Kahneman & Miller, 1986; Markman, Gavanski, Sherman, & McMullen, 1995; Kahneman & Tversky, 1982; Roese, 1997; Roese & Olson, 1997; Sherman & McConnell, 1995). "If only I hadn't fallen asleep while studying the night before the test," you might think, "I would have gotten a better grade." The ease with which people can mentally undo the past—that is, how easy it is to think of alternative outcomes—can have a large impact on the way in which they explain the past and how they feel about it.

Suppose you learn, for example, about a businesswoman who always took the same plane to Chicago on Monday mornings. Tragically, one day the plane crashed and the woman was killed. Given that taking this plane was a regular part of her routine, it is difficult to imagine how she could have avoided this fate. Suppose, however, you learn that one Monday the woman missed her plane by 60 seconds and thus took the next flight to Chicago. Tragically, this plane crashed and she was killed. In this example, it is easy to mentally undo the outcome: "If only she hadn't gotten that phone call right before she left home; if only she hadn't gotten stuck in traffic on the way to the airport; if, if, if . . ." Even though the outcome is the same in both cases—she perished in a plane crash, through no fault of her own—the second case, in which she barely missed her regular flight, seems much more tragic, because it is easier to "undo" through counterfactual thinking (Miller, Turnbull, & McFarland, 1990).

Counterfactual Thinking
mentally changing some aspect of the past as a way of imagining what might have been

"Look in my face; my name is Might-have been; I am also called No-more, Too-late, Farewell.
—Dante Gabrielle Rossetti

As you can see, counterfactual thoughts that are available in memory have a big influence on people's emotional reactions to events. The easier it is to mentally "undo" an outcome, the stronger the emotional reaction to it (Landman, 1993; Niedenthal, Tangney, & Gavanski, 1994). Christopher Davis, Darrin Lehman, Camille Wortman, Roxane Silver, and Suzanne Thompson (1995), for example, interviewed people who had suffered the loss of a spouse or child. As expected, the more people imagined ways in which the tragedy could have been averted, by mentally "undoing" the circumstances preceding it, the more distress they reported (Branscombe, Owen, Garstka, & Coleman, 1996; Davis & Lehman, 1995).

Counterfactual reasoning can lead to some paradoxical effects on our emotions. For example, who do you think would be happiest: an Olympic athlete who won a silver medal (came in second) or an Olympic athlete who won a bronze medal (came in third)? Though it might seem like the athlete who performed better (the silver medal winner) would be happier, that is not what Victoria Medvec, Scott Madey, and Tom Gilovich (1995) predicted. They reasoned that the silver winner medal should feel worse, because he or she could more easily imagine having won the event, and would thus engage in more counterfactual reasoning. To see if they were right, they analyzed videotapes of the 1992 Olympics. Both immediately after their event and while they received their medals, silver medal winners appeared less happy than bronze medal winners. And, during interviews with reporters, silver medal winners engaged in more counterfactual reasoning, by saying things like, "I almost pulled it off; it's too bad . . ." The moral seems to be, if you're not going to win, it's better to lose by a lot.

When are people most likely to engage in counterfactual reasoning? The above example suggests the answer—when something bad happens to us and it was a close call (Roese, 1997; Roese & Olson, 1997; Sanna & Turley, 1996). If something good happens to us, we seldom ruminate about how things could have turned out differently. If something bad happens to us but we lost by a lot, we don't spend much time "mentally undoing" the outcome. It's when the event is negative and it was a close call, such as finishing second in the Olympics in a

■ Who do you think would be happier: the silver or bronze medalist in an Olympic event? Research by Medvec, Madey, and Gilovich (1995) suggests that bronze medalists are happier because it is harder for them to engage in counterfactual reasoning—imagining ways in which they could have won the event.

photo finish, that we are most likely to engage in counterfactual reasoning and feel badly as a result.

How Similar Is A to B? The Representativeness Heuristic

People use another mental shortcut when trying to categorize something: They judge how similar it is to their idea of the typical case. Suppose, for example, that you attend a state university in New York. At the student union one day, you meet a student named Brian. Brian has blond hair and a dark tan, seems to be very mellow, and likes to go to the beach. What state do you think Brian is from? Because Brian seems similar to many people's stereotype of what Californians are like, you might guess California, or at least seriously entertain this possibility. If so, you would be using the **representativeness heuristic**, which is a mental shortcut whereby people classify something according to how similar it is to a typical case, such as how similar Brian is to your conception of Californians (Dawes, 1998; Garb, 1996; Kahneman & Tversky, 1973; Hamm, 1996; Lupfer & Layman, 1996; Moore, Smith, & Gonzalez, 1997; Thomsen & Borgida, 1996; Tversky & Kahneman, 1974).

Categorizing things according to representativeness is often a perfectly reasonable thing to do. If we did not use the representativeness heuristic, how else would we decide where Brian comes from? Should we just randomly choose a state, without making any attempt to judge his similarity to our conception of students from New York State versus out-of-state students? Actually, there is another source of information we might use. If we knew nothing about Brian, it would be wise to guess that he was from New York State, because at state universities there are more in-state than out-of-state students. If we guessed New York State, we would be using what is called **base rate information**, or information about the relative frequency of members of different categories in the population (e.g., the percentage of students at New York state universities who are from New York).

What do people do when they have both base rate information (e.g., knowing that there are more New Yorkers than Californians at a university) and contradictory information about the person in question (e.g., knowing that Brian is blond and mellow and likes to hang out at the beach)? Kahneman and Tversky (1973) found that people do not use base rate information sufficiently, paying most attention to how representative the information about the specific person is of the general category (e.g., Californians). While this is not a bad strategy if the information about the person is very reliable, it can get us into trouble when the information is flimsy. Given that the base rate of Californians attending state universities in New York is low, you would need to have very good evidence that this person was a Californian before ignoring the base rate and guessing that he is one of the few exceptions. And given that it is not that unusual to find people from eastern states who have blond hair, are laid-back, and like to go to the beach, you would be wise not to ignore the base rate in this instance.

We don't mean to imply that people totally ignore base rate information (Koehler, 1993, 1996). Baseball managers consider the overall likelihood of left-handed batters getting a hit off of left-handed pitchers when deciding who to send up as a pinch hitter, and birdwatchers consider the prevalence of different species of birds in their area when identifying individual birds ("that probably wasn't a bay-breasted warbler because they've never been seen in this area"). The point is that people often focus too much on individual characteristics of what

Representativeness Heuristic
a mental shortcut whereby people classify something according to how similar it is to a typical case

Base Rate Information
information about the frequency of members of different categories in the population

they observe ("But it did seem to have a chestnut-colored throat; hm, maybe it was a bay-breasted warbler") and too little on the base rates.

People's overreliance on the representativeness heuristic can cause problems. Throughout history, for example, people have assumed that the cure for a disease must resemble (be representative of) the symptoms of the disease, even when this isn't the case. At one time, consuming the lungs of a fox was thought to be a cure for asthma, because foxes have a strong respiratory system (Mill, 1974). Such a reliance on representativeness may even impede the discovery of the actual cause of a disease. Around the turn of the century, an editorial in a Washington newspaper denounced the foolhardy use of federal funds on ridiculous, far-fetched ideas about the causes of yellow fever, such as the absurd idea of one Walter Reed that yellow fever was caused by, of all things, a mosquito (Nisbett & Ross, 1980).

Taking Things at Face Value: The Anchoring and Adjustment Heuristic

Suppose you are trying to quit smoking and are sitting around with a group of friends who also smoke. "How likely am I to get cancer anyway?" you say, reaching for a cigarette. "I bet that not all that many people end up with lung cancer. In fact, of all the students at our university, I wonder how many will get cancer in their lifetimes?" One of your friends throws out a number. "I don't know," he says. "I'd guess maybe 4,500." Would your friend's response influence your answer to the question? It would if you use the **anchoring and adjustment heuristic** (Tversky & Kahneman, 1974), a mental shortcut whereby people use a number or value as a starting point and then adjust their answer away from this anchor. You might begin by saying, "Hm, 4,500—that sounds high; I'd say it's a little lower than that."

Like all the other mental shortcuts we have considered, the anchoring and adjustment heuristic is a good strategy under many circumstances. If you have no idea what the answer is but your friend is a medical resident specializing in oncology, it is wise to stick pretty close to his or her answer. But like the other heuristics, this one can get us into trouble. The problem with anchoring and adjustment is that people sometimes use completely arbitrary values as starting points and then stick too close to these values. For example, Tim Wilson, Chris Houston, Kate Etling, and Nancy Brekke (1996) asked college students to copy several words or numbers, supposedly as part of a study of handwriting analysis. In one condition, people copied several pages of numbers, all of which happened to be around 4,500. In the other condition, people copied down words, such as "sofa." Then, as part of what was supposedly an unrelated study, everyone was asked how many students at their university would get cancer in the next 40 years. Those who copied down numbers gave much higher estimates (average answer = 3,145) than people who copied words did (average answer = 1,645). Similar anchoring effects have been found in many other studies (e.g., Allison & Beggan, 1994; Cadinu & Rothbart, 1996; Chapman & Bornstein, 1996; Cervone & Peake, 1986; Czaczkes & Ganzach, 1996; Ganzach, 1996; Jacowitz & Kahneman, 1995; Quattrone, Lawrence, Finkel, & Andrus, 1984; Slovic & Lichtenstein, 1971; Strack & Musssweiler, 1997; Tversky & Kahneman, 1974).

The examples of anchoring and adjustment we have seen so far have concerned numerical judgments. This process, however, occurs with many other kinds of judgments as well. When we form judgments about the world, we often

Anchoring and Adjustment Heuristic
a mental shortcut that involves using a number or value as a starting point, and then adjusting one's answer away from this anchor; people often do not adjust their answer sufficiently

Biased Sampling
making generalizations
from samples of
information that are
known to be biased

allow our personal experiences and observations to anchor our impressions, even when we know our experiences are unusual. Suppose, for example, that you go to a popular restaurant that all your friends rave about. As luck would have it, the waiter is rude and your entree is burned. You know your experience is atypical; after all, your friends have had great meals at this restaurant. Nonetheless, your experiences are likely to anchor your impression of the restaurant, making you reluctant to return. When generalizing from a sample of information we know to be biased (e.g., one meal in a restaurant) to the population of information (e.g., all meals in that restaurant), we are engaging in a process called **biased sampling**—making generalizations from samples of information that we know are biased.

Even when we know that a piece of information is biased or atypical, it can be hard to ignore it completely. We all know that reporters, television producers, and authors seldom present information that is typical; their job is to present what is unusual, interesting, and attention-grabbing, not what is average. (Imagine that a reporter said, "Leading the news tonight: Barbara Kowalski did not have a car accident on her way to the office, and Jerome Smith had an average day driving his city bus up and down Main Street.") Nonetheless, we seem to find it hard to avoid making generalizations from what we see.

For example, Ruth Hamill, Tim Wilson, and Richard Nisbett (1980) asked people to read a story about a welfare mother whose life was irresponsible and bleak. They told some participants that this woman was typical of people on welfare and others that she was very atypical of people on welfare. Not surprisingly, the participants who thought she was typical became more negative in their attitudes toward all welfare recipients (see Figure 3.6). More surprisingly, people who thought she was atypical also became more negative toward all welfare recipients. This is another example of the anchoring and adjustment heuristic. People have a starting point, or an anchor ("this welfare recipient is irresponsible and undeserving"), from which they should adjust their judgment

■ Biased sampling: How would you feel about the entire state of New Jersey if you visited only one of these locations? People have been found to generalize from small samples of information, even when they know that these samples are biased (not typical).

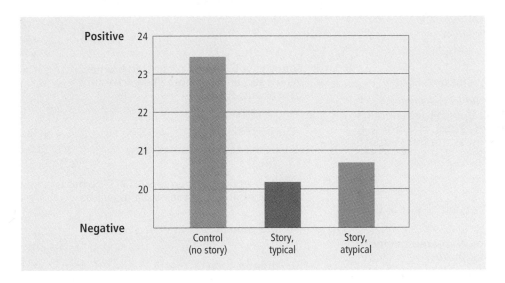

■ **FIGURE 3.6   Attitudes toward welfare recipients.** People who read a story about one unlikable welfare recipient had more negative attitudes toward welfare recipients in general, regardless of whether they believed she was typical or atypical. (Adapted from Hamill, Wilson, & Nisbett, 1980)

("but she is not at all typical, thus I shouldn't generalize from her to welfare recipients in general"). As with many other kinds of anchoring effects, however, people do not adjust sufficiently and are influenced too much by their initial judgment.

To summarize, we have discussed two general types of strategies used by the social thinker: schemas and judgmental heuristics. There is a close relationship between these two types of cognitive processing. Schemas are organized bits of knowledge about people and situations, like books in a mental library. When making judgments about the social world, however, it is not always clear which schema is most appropriate to use. The particular schema that is used and how this schema operates depend on the judgmental heuristics we have just considered. The availability heuristic refers to judgments based on the ease with which something can be brought to mind, which, in our library analogy, would refer to how easily a book can be brought up from the stacks. If we're wondering how assertive we are and the easiest "books" to find are examples of assertiveness, we infer we are pretty assertive people. The more a person or situation is representative of a particular schema (the more similar the contents of the book are to the situation we are in), the more likely we are to use it. Once we call up a particular schema, it anchors our judgments. We use it as a starting point to interpret a situation, and we find it difficult to adjust away from this schema (once a book has been retrieved, we apply it to the judgment at hand and it is hard to completely forget it and send it back to the stacks, replacing it with another book). Now that you have learned about some of the ways in which people reason, try the quiz in Try It! on page 90.

The Flexible Social Thinker

So far, our portrayal of the social thinker has not been entirely flattering. True enough, people often use heuristics to their advantage and apply schemas effortlessly and efficiently. We have seen many examples, however, of times when these

> My thinking is first and last and always for the sake of doing.
> —William James,
> *The Principles of Psychology,* 1890

///   *Try It* **!**

Reasoning Quiz

Answer each of the following questions:

1. Consider the letter "R" in the English language. Do you think that this letter occurs more often as the *first* letter of words (e.g., "rope") or more often as the third letter of words (e.g., "park")?

   A. the first letter

   B. the third letter

   C. about equally often as the first as the third letter

2. Which of these do you think causes more fatalities in the United States?

   A. accidental death

   B. death from strokes

   C. they cause about the same number of deaths

3. Suppose you flipped a fair coin 6 times. Which sequence is more likely to occur? (H = heads, T = tails)

   A. HTTHTH

   B. HHHTTT

   C. both sequences are equally likely

4. After observing the sequence TTTTT, what is the probability that the next flip will be heads?

   A. less than .5

   B. .5

   C. greater than .5

ANSWERS

1. The correct answer is (b), the third letter. Tversky and Kahneman (1974) found that most people thought that the answer was (a), the first letter. Why do people make this mistake? Because, say Tversky and Kahneman, they find it easier to think of examples of words that begin with "R.". By using the availability heuristic, they assumed that the ease with which they could bring examples to mind meant that such words were more common.

2. The correct answer is (b). Slovic, Fischhoff, and Lichtenstein (1976) found that most people think that (a) is correct (accidental deaths). Why did people make this error? Again, it's the availability heuristic: Accidental deaths are more likely to reported by the media, thus people find it easier to bring to mind examples of such deaths than deaths from strokes.

3. The correct answer is (c). Both outcomes are equally likely, given that the outcomes of coin flips are random events. Tversky and Kahneman (1974) argue that due to the representativeness heuristic, people expect a sequence of random events to "look" random. That is, they expect events to be representative of their conception of randomness. Thus, many people choose HTTHTH, because this sequence is more representative of people's idea of randomness than HHHTTT. In fact, the chance that either sequence will occur is 1 out of 2^6 times, or 1/64. As another illustration of this point, if you were to buy a lottery ticket with four numbers, would you rather have the number 6957 or 1111? Many people prefer the former number, because it seems more "random" and thus more likely to be picked. In fact, both numbers have a 1/1,000 chance of being picked.

4. The correct answer is (b). Many people choose (c), because they think that after five tails in a row, heads is more likely "to even things out." This is called the gambler's fallacy, which is the belief that prior random events (e.g., five tails in a row) has an influence on subsequent random events. Assuming the coin is fair, prior tosses have no influence on future ones. Tversky and Kahneman (1974) suggest that the gambler's fallacy is due in part to the representativeness heuristic: Five tails and one head seems more representative of a chance outcome than six tails in a row.

///

Cognitive Misers
the idea that people are so limited in their ability to think and make inferences that they take mental shortcuts whenever they can

strategies lead to mistakes and errors in reasoning. People often let their schemas do the talking even in the face of contradictory information and make rash generalizations from atypical experiences. Sometimes these shortcomings in human inference have very unfortunate consequences, as in the case of teachers' expectations about gender differences leading to lower performance among girls. Findings such as these have led some to characterize people as **cognitive misers,** persons who are so limited in their ability to think and make inferences that they take mental shortcuts whenever they can (Taylor, 1981).

But can it really be the case that our thought processes are so flawed? After all, most of us make it through the day quite well, without stumbling too badly.

Some people argue that social psychologists exaggerate the extent to which human reasoning is flawed, and a new view of the social thinker is emerging: people as **motivated tacticians,** those who have a large arsenal of mental rules and strategies and who choose wisely among these strategies, depending on their particular needs and goals (Fiske, 1993; Fiske & Taylor, 1991). A good deal of recent research has suggested that people are flexible thinkers: When little is at stake, they may be "miserly" in the sense that they rely on mental shortcuts that are good enough to get by, but when faced with more important decisions, people choose different and more effective strategies. Further, when people are concerned that their judgments might be biased, they take steps to correct them (Wegener & Petty, 1997; Wilson & Brekke, 1994). Consider a college professor who is grading her students' term papers. She might be concerned that she will be influenced by how well students did on a previous paper or by how much she likes the students. To avoid these potential biases she grades the papers without looking at who wrote them, so that she can be sure that she is grading the papers solely on their merits.

Several studies have examined the question of whether people change the way they reason when the stakes are high. In many cases, they do, as we will now see.

Motivated Tacticians
the idea that people have a large arsenal of mental rules and strategies, and choose wisely among these strategies depending on their particular needs and goals

The Motivated Social Thinker

It may have struck you that in some experiments we have discussed, people have been asked to make judgments that are of little importance to them. In the Jones and colleagues (1968) study on primacy effects, for example, people watched another student work on a test and judged how intelligent he was (see Figure 3.1). The student was not anyone they would see again (or even meet in person); thus, people might not have bothered to make the more effortful, accurate inferences of which they were capable. This point is illustrated by several studies showing that when more consequential tasks are used, people do make more complex and accurate inferences (Borgida & Howard-Pitney, 1983; Chaiken, Liberman, & Eagly, 1989; Hilton & Darley, 1991; Fiske, 1993; Kruglanski, 1989; Kruglanski & Webster, 1996; Martin, Seta, & Crelia, 1990; Strack & Hannover, 1996). For example, Allan Harkness, Kenneth DeBono, and Eugene Borgida (1985) gave female participants information about a person named Tom Ferguson, whom they had never met. The participants learned how interested Tom was in dating each of several women and learned several things about these women, such as how good a sense of humor they had. They were asked to judge the relationship between the qualities of the women (e.g., their sense of humor) and Tom's willingness to date them. As with many other studies that have examined people's ability to judge such relationships, Harkness and colleagues (1985) found that the participants used simple strategies that, while not totally wrong, were not particularly accurate.

Unless, that is, they were highly motivated to make careful judgments. Some of the participants thought that they were taking part in a dating study and that they themselves would be dating Tom for several weeks. Now that the women cared more about what Tom liked and disliked in a dating partner, they used more complex mental strategies and made judgments that were more accurate. In general, people have been found to be flexible thinkers, able to choose, at least to some extent, from a variety of mental strategies. When the stakes are high, people use more sophisticated strategies than when the stakes are low, make more accurate judgments, and are more likely to notice facts that conflict with their prior schemas (Chaiken, 1987; Dunn & Wilson, 1990; Fiske, 1993; Flink & Park, 1991; Hastie, 1980; Kruglanski, 1989; Neuberg, in press; Petty & Cacioppo, 1986; Stangor & McMillan, 1992; Tetlock, 1992; Trope & Lieberman, 1996).

We do not mean to imply that with a little motivation people become perfect reasoners. We will see several examples in later chapters whereby people make erroneous judgments about the social world, in spite of their best efforts and intentions. The world is a complex place and even when motivation is high, we can make mistakes in characterizing it. Brett Pelham and Efrat Neter (1995), for example, found that motivating people made their judgments more accurate on relatively simple tasks, but actually made their judgments worse on complex tasks. When we are really motivated to do well but the problem is difficult, we might try so hard that we get tense and confused, thereby doing worse than if we were more relaxed and cared less about doing well (Arkes, 1991).

Further, even when people are motivated to fix judgments that they think might be biased, they might not know how to do so or even correct their judgments too much. Human judgment is not like a car engine, where it is pretty easy to tell when it breaks down and to figure out how to fix it. It is often hard to know exactly how we formed a judgment, whether it is biased, and how much, if at all, we should correct it (Nisbett & Wilson, 1977; Martin, 1986; Schwarz & Bless, 1992; Wegener & Petty, 1997; Wilson & Brekke, 1994). Nonetheless, it is often true that the more motivated people are to form unbiased judgments, the greater the likelihood that they will do so.

Automatic versus Controlled Thinking

People's level of motivation is a key determinant of whether they engage in what is called automatic versus controlled thinking. Think back to what it was like to learn a new skill, such as riding a bicycle or using in-line skates. The first time you rode a two-wheeler, you probably felt awkward and ungainly as you wobbled across the pavement, and you may have paid for your inexperience with a skinned elbow or knee. You were probably concentrating on what you were doing with your feet, knees, and hands, and it seemed like you would never figure it out. Once you became an experienced rider, however, your actions became automatic, in the sense that you no longer had to think about what you were doing.

Just as our actions can become automatic, so too can the way we think (Bargh, 1994, 1996; Wegner & Bargh, 1998). The more practice we have in thinking in a certain way, the more automatic that kind of thinking becomes, to the point where we can do it unconsciously, with no effort. **Automatic processing** can be defined as thinking that is nonconscious, unintentional, involuntary, and effortless. Though different kinds of automatic thinking meet these criteria to varying degrees (Bargh, 1989), for our purposes we can define automaticity as thinking that satisfies all or most of these criteria.

Automatic processing is difficult to describe, precisely because it occurs outside of awareness and is thus unfamiliar to us. Actually, we have already described some examples of this type of thinking—namely, using schemas to understand the social world. Human beings are programmed to categorize the world quickly and efficiently. When we enter a classroom, we do not see a bunch of objects that have platforms parallel to the floor connected to four legs, with another flat surface at a right angle, that we then mentally assemble to figure out what they are. Instead of having to pause and think "Let's see. Oh, yes, those are chairs," we quickly, unconsciously, and effortlessly categorize the objects into our

Automatic Processing
thinking that is nonconscious, unintentional, involuntary, and effortless

■ Thinking can become automatic, in that it can occur quickly and nonconsciously. For example, we quickly and effortlessly categorize things we see without even intending to do so. Automatic thinking allows us to do two things at the same time, such as painting a fence and talking on the telephone.

"chair" schema. The fact that we do this automatically allows us to use our conscious minds for other, more important purposes ("What's going to be on the quiz today?" or "Should I strike up a conversation with that cute guy in the third row?"). Similarly, when we encounter other people we categorize them effortlessly into prior schemas. Doing so saves time and effort.

As with all of the strategies and properties of social cognition we have considered, however, efficiency comes with a cost. If we automatically categorize a thing or person incorrectly, we can get into trouble. Imagine the embarrassment of a friend of ours who drove up to a fancy restaurant and, noticing the sign that said there was valet parking, gave his keys to a young Hispanic man standing by the door. It turned out that the man was not the parking attendant but another customer about to enter the restaurant. Or think back to our example of teachers and the self-fulfilling prophecy. One reason people's expectations can be so consequential is that they operate automatically, without intention, making it difficult for people to know when they are acting on these expectations. We pigeonhole people quickly, such that our schemas based on race, gender, age, or physical attractiveness are invoked automatically (Devine, 1989; Fiske, 1989). This is one reason stereotypes are so difficult to overcome—they often operate without our knowing it.

Clearly, not all thinking is automatic; like Rodin's statue of the thinker, sometimes we pause and think deeply about ourselves and the social world. This kind of thinking is called **controlled processing**, which is defined as thinking that is conscious, intentional, voluntary, and effortful. An example of controlled processing is the kind of conscious musing people often engage in: "I wonder what's for lunch today?" or "When will the authors get on with it and finish this chapter?" You can "turn on" or "turn off" this type of thinking at will, and you are fully aware of what you are thinking.

One purpose of controlled thinking is to provide a check and balance for automatic processing. Just as an airline captain can turn off the automatic pilot and take control of the plane when trouble occurs, our controlled thinking takes over when unusual events occur. Unlike automatic processing, however, controlled thinking requires motivation and effort. We have to want to do it, and we have to

Controlled Processing
thinking that is conscious, intentional, voluntary, and effortful

have the time and energy to devote to it. Thus, when the stakes are low and we do not particularly care about the accuracy of a decision or judgment, we often let our automatic thinking do the job, without bothering to check or correct it. If we are idly watching television after a long day, for example, we might be judging the people we see on the tube rather mindlessly, without thinking too much about it. As we will discuss in Chapter 13, such mindless processing often means that we stereotype people without thinking too much about it. People must make the effort to engage in controlled processing in order to counteract stereotypes that come to mind automatically.

Automatic Believing, Controlled Unbelieving

There are other interesting ways in which controlled processing acts as a check and balance for automatic processing. As we saw earlier, when people use the anchoring and adjustment heuristic they use starting points in their judgments and fail to adjust sufficiently from these points. One explanation for this process is that we automatically use whatever we encounter as a starting point, without even fully realizing that we are doing so, and then attempt to adjust from this starting point with controlled processing. This characterization of human judgment was made by the philosopher Benedict Spinoza three centuries ago: When people initially see, hear, or learn something, they take it at face value and assume it is true. Only after accepting the veracity of a fact do people go back and decide whether it might be false. Although other philosophers (e.g., René Descartes) have disagreed, recent research by Daniel Gilbert and his colleagues shows that Spinoza was right (Gilbert, 1991, 1993, 1998; Krull & Dill, 1996).

Gilbert argues that people are programmed to believe automatically everything they hear and see. This automatic, "seeing is believing" process is built into human beings, he suggests, because pretty much everything people hear and see *is* true. If we had to stop and deliberate about the truthfulness of everything we encountered, life would be difficult indeed ("Let's see, it looks like a car careening toward me down the street, but maybe it's really an illusion . . . CRASH!"). Occasionally, however, what we see or hear is not true; thus, we need a check and balance system to be able to "unaccept" what we have initially believed. When we hear a candidate for governor say, "If elected, I will lower your taxes, balance the budget, reduce crime, and wash your car every Sunday afternoon," we initially believe what we hear, argues Gilbert (1991), but the "unacceptance" part of the process quickly kicks in, making us doubt the truth of what we've just heard ("Now wait just a minute . . ."). The process is depicted in Figure 3.7.

■ **FIGURE 3.7   Gilbert's theory of automatic believing.**   According to Gilbert (1991), people initially believe everything they hear and see. They then assess whether or not what they heard or saw is really true and "unaccept" it if necessary. The second and third parts of the process, in which people assess and unaccept information, take time and effort. If people are tired or preoccupied these parts of the process are difficult to execute, increasing the likelihood that people will believe false information. (Adapted from Gilbert, 1991)

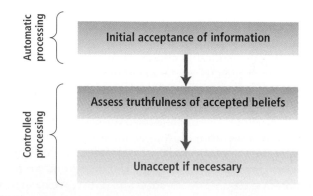

The interesting thing about this process is that the initial acceptance part occurs automatically, which, as we have seen, means that it occurs nonconsciously and without effort or intention. The assessment and unacceptance part of the process is the product of controlled processing, however, which means that people have to have the energy and motivation to do it. If people are preoccupied, tired, or unmotivated, the acceptance part of the process will operate unchecked, and this can lead to the acceptance of falsehoods.

Consider the following experiment conducted by Gilbert, Tafarodi, and Malone (1993). They asked participants to read crime reports on a computer screen and then to recommend prison sentences for the people who had committed the crimes. They told participants that some of the statements in the reports were false, because there had been a mixup and these statements actually were from other, unrelated crime reports. These statements were printed in red on the computer screen, whereas all of the true statements were printed in black. As it happened, the false statements made the crime seem worse in one condition (e.g., one said that the criminal threatened to sexually assault a clerk). In another condition, the false statements made the crime seem less severe (e.g., one said that the criminal was ashamed of what he had done). After reading the reports, people were asked to recommend a prison sentence for the criminal from 0 to 20 years.

Imagine you were in this study. As you read the reports, you occasionally see one of the false statements printed in red. Although these statements make the crime seem more or less severe, you know they're false and so you don't let them influence the sentence you recommend. This is exactly what happened in some conditions of the study: People who got false extenuating statements recommended about the same sentence as people who got false exacerbating statements (see the left-hand side of Figure 3.8). According to Gilbert, people initially believed the false statements but then rapidly "unaccepted" them, such that these statements had no effect on their recommendations.

■ **FIGURE 3.8   Cognitive load and the ability to unaccept false statements.**   People read false information about a criminal that was either extenuating (making his crime seem less severe) or exacerbating (making his crime seem worse). When people were not under cognitive load—they had the time to consider and reject this information— the false information had little influence on the sentence they recommended for the criminal. When people were under cognitive load—they had to push a button whenever certain numbers appeared on the computer screen—they had difficulty rejecting the false information. For example, as seen on the right-hand side of the graph, people in the cognitive load condition who heard the exacerbating information recommended much higher sentences, even though they knew the exacerbating information was false. (Adapted from Gilbert et al., 1993)

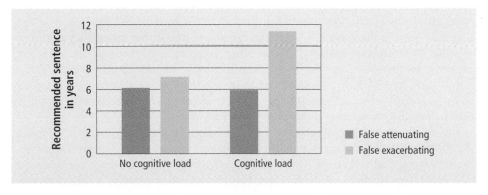

How can we tell for sure? These results alone do not show that people went through the process of acceptance and unacceptance. Recall that the second stage, unacceptance, is said to be a more deliberate, controlled process that requires mental effort. If so, then reducing people's ability to concentrate should interrupt this process, allowing automatic acceptance to operate unchecked. To test this hypothesis, Gilbert et al. (1993) gave some participants a second task to do while they were reading the crime reports, thereby increasing their "cognitive load." Similar to an emergency weather bulletin, a string of numbers crawled across the television screen underneath the crime report, and people had to push a button whenever the number 5 appeared in this string of numbers—while reading the crime reports aloud. The number task was designed to reduce people's ability to engage in much controlled processing, thereby disrupting the unacceptance stage of the process. The premise was that this should cause people to recommend longer sentences when the false statements suggested the crime was more severe and shorter sentences when the false statements suggested the crime was less severe, because people would have difficulty unaccepting the false statements. As seen on the right-hand side of Figure 3.8, this is generally what happened.

In everyday life, of course, we are rarely asked to search for digits on a television screen while performing another task. It is not uncommon, however, to encounter false or misleading information (e.g., extreme claims made in advertisements) while we are preoccupied with some other task (e.g., making sure our three-year-old does not pour her juice on her baby brother). It is under these conditions that people's defenses are down and they are most susceptible to believing false things.

Ironic Processing and Thought Suppression

Thought Suppression
the attempt to avoid thinking about something we would just as soon forget

There is another interesting consequence of being preoccupied and unable to engage in much controlled processing: It reduces our ability to engage in **thought suppression**—the attempt to avoid thinking about something we would just as soon forget, such as a lost love, an unpleasant encounter with one's boss, or a delectable piece of cheesecake in the refrigerator. According to Daniel Wegner (1992, 1994), successful thought suppression depends on the interaction of two processes, one relatively automatic and the other relatively controlled. The first, automatic part of the system, called the monitoring process, searches for evidence that the unwanted thought is about to intrude upon consciousness. Once the unwanted thought is detected, the second, more controlled part of the system, called the operating process, comes into play. This is the effortful, conscious attempt to distract oneself by finding something else to think about. These two processes operate in tandem, like two parents conspiring to keep their kids away from junk-food outlets at a mall. One parent's job, akin to the monitoring process, is to keep a watch out for the food joints and let the other one know when they are in the vicinity ("McDonald's alert!"). The other parent's job, akin to the operating process, is then to divert the kids' attention away from the food places ("Hey, kids—look at the picture of Barney in that store"). This system works pretty well as long as each process (parent) does its job, one ever alert for intrusions and the other diverting these intrusions from consciousness.

What happens, though, when the controlled, operating process is unable to do its job because the person is tired or preoccupied? The monitoring process continues to find instances of the unwanted thought, which then intrude upon consciousness unchecked by the conscious, controlled system. Consequently, a

The Amazing Pendulum

Make a pendulum by tying a small weight to the end of a 20-inch piece of string or fishing line (a large nut or bolt works well). Then, draw a large plus sign on a piece of paper. Each of the two lines should be about four inches long. The point of this exercise is to hold the pendulum over the middle of the plus sign, keeping it as steady as possible.

Specifically, hold the string in your dominant hand, about 12 inches up from the weight. Wrap the rest of the string around your index finger. Then hold the weight about an inch over the paper as steady as you can. *Make absolutely sure that the weight does not move side to side.* That is, make sure it does not move parallel to the horizontal line on the page. Do this for 30 seconds and have a friend keep track of how many times the pendulum moved side to side and how many times it moved up and down. How did you do?

Now try it again, with one additional instruction: While you are holding the pendulum and trying to make sure that it does not move sideways, count backwards from 1000 by threes in your head. Again, have a friend count the number of times the pendulum moved sideways and how many times it moved up and down. How did you do this time?

This is a version of an experiment by Daniel Wegner, Matthew Ansfield, and Daniel Pilloff (in press) on the mental control of action. Just as it can be difficult to suppress a thought, it can be difficult to suppress movements. The same processes are involved; a monitoring process that looks for examples of what is being suppressed (e.g., sideways movements of the pendulum) and an operating process that attempts to avoid the undesired state (e.g., by making sure that the pendulum doesn't move sideways). The operating process requires more mental effort, so if people are distracted, it does not work very well. The consequence? The monitoring process operates unchecked, creating the very state the person is trying to avoid.

You can probably figure out the prediction for the pendulum test. It should be especially hard to keep the pendulum from moving side to side when you are counting backwards by threes, because here the operating process is unable to correct for sideways movements that the monitoring process detects. In the Wegner and colleagues study (in press), participants moved the pendulum sideways an average of 3.1 times when they had to count backwards by threes, whereas they moved it sideways an average of only 2.2 times when they did not have to count backward by threes.

state of hyperaccessibility exists, whereby the unwanted thought occurs with high frequency. If the parent whose job it is to distract the children stops doing his or her job, for example, the kids will become even more aware that fast-food joints are in the vicinity, because they will keep hearing the other parent point them out.

To illustrate this process, Daniel Wegner, Ralph Erber, and Robert Bowman (1995) asked people to try not to make sexist responses when completing sentences during a laboratory task. If people had a lot of time to respond they were able to suppress sexist responses, because their monitoring and operating processes worked together: One looked for sexist answers and the other suppressed these answers. Another group, however, was instructed not to be sexist and asked to respond immediately. Under these conditions, the operating process did not have time to suppress. The automatic monitoring process that searched for sexist thoughts found many examples and people reported them at a high rate, unchecked by the operating process. Consequently, people in this condition gave the highest number of sexist responses of all. The irony is that, when it is most important to people not to express prejudiced thoughts (e.g., you are on guard not to make any jokes about short people, because your four-foot-eight

■ Sometimes we try our best not to think about something, such as fattening foods when we are on a diet. According to research by Daniel Wegner (1994), trying not to think about something can backfire. Particularly when we are under cognitive load, trying to suppress a thought can make that thought come to mind all the more.

boss is standing next to you), if you are tired or preoccupied—that is, under cognitive load—these thoughts are especially likely to spill out unchecked. The Try It! exercise on page 97 shows what happens when you are trying your hardest not to do something.

A Portrayal of Social Judgment

By now we have seen two rather different portraits of the social thinker: Cognitive misers, who take mental shortcuts whenever they can, and motivated tacticians, who choose wisely from an arsenal of mental strategies. Exactly how accurate is social thinking anyway?

A problem in answering this question is defining what a "correct" inference is. Are people at fault for not making inferences in the same way as trained logicians? Should we aspire to be like the IBM Deep Blue computer, processing information rationally at all times, devoid of any feeling or emotion? Who is the final judge of human thought? These are thorny philosophical issues that cannot be done justice here. (See Cohen, 1981; Gigerenzer, 1993; Gigerenzer & Goldstein, 1996; Kahneman & Tversky, 1983; Nisbett & Ross, 1980; Stich, 1990, for an in-depth discussion of these issues.) We offer what in our view is the best resolution of the debate about how good people are as social thinkers.

We believe that the best portrait of the social thinker lies in between the analogies of people as cognitive misers and motivated tacticians. First, it is clear that research in the "cognitive miser" tradition has exaggerated the shortcomings of human thought. When people are motivated to make careful inferences and have the time and capacity to think, they often think in quite sophisticated ways. No one has yet been able to construct a computer that comes close to matching the power of the human brain. As we saw earlier, Deep Blue may have defeated Gary Kasparov, but no computer can match people as social thinkers. Second, there is plenty of room for improvement in human thought. The shortcomings of social thinking we have documented can be quite consequential (Gilovich, 1991; Nisbett & Ross, 1980; Quattrone, 1982; Slusher & Anderson, 1989). For exam-

> The greatest of all faults, I should say, is to become conscious of none.
> —Thomas Carlyle

ple, in Chapter 13 we will see that racial prejudice can, in part, be traced back to faulty reasoning processes. The treacherous operation of self-fulfilling prophecies, whereby teachers make their false beliefs come true by the way they treat their students, is another example. One of us has gone so far as to use the term *mental contamination* to describe the kinds of biases in our thinking that are pervasive in everyday life (Wilson & Brekke, 1994). Given the evidence that human thinking can sometimes go very wrong, we do not believe that the "motivated tactician" analogy is quite right. People as "flawed scientists" is a better metaphor. This captures the idea that people are often brilliant thinkers, attempting to discover the nature of the social world in a logical, scientific way. It also captures the idea that people are not perfect scientists. We are often blind to truths that don't fit our schemas and sometimes treat others in ways that make our schemas come true—something that good scientists would never do.

> "Modest doubt is called the beacon of the wise.
> —William Shakespeare

Teaching Reasoning Skills

Given that human reasoning is sometimes flawed and can have unpleasant and even tragic consequences, it is important to consider how these mistakes can be corrected. Is it possible to teach people to make better inferences, thereby avoiding some of the mistakes we have discussed in this chapter? If so, what is the best way to do it? Educators, philosophers, and psychologists have debated this question for decades, and recently some fascinating experiments have provided encouraging answers.

One approach is to make people a little more humble about their reasoning abilities. Often we have greater confidence in our judgments than we should (Lichtenstein, Fischhoff, & Phillips, 1982; Plous, 1995; Vallone, Griffin, Lin, & Ross, 1990). Teachers, for example, sometimes have greater confidence in their beliefs about the abilities of boys versus girls than is warranted. Anyone trying to improve human inference is thus up against an **overconfidence barrier**. Many people seem to think that their reasoning processes are just fine the way they are and hence that there is no need for any remedial action. One approach, then, might be to address this overconfidence directly, getting people to consider the possibility that they might be wrong. This tack was taken by Lord, Lepper, and Preston (1984), who found that when they asked people to consider the opposite point of view to their own, people realized there were other ways to construe the world than their own way and were less likely to make errors in their judgments (see also Anderson, Lepper, & Ross, 1980; Anderson & Sechler, 1986; Koriat, Lichtenstein, & Fischhoff, 1980; Plous, 1995).

Overconfidence Barrier the finding that people usually have too much confidence in the accuracy of their judgments; people's judgments are usually not as correct as they think they are

Another approach is to teach people directly some basic statistical and methodological principles about how to reason correctly, with the hope they will apply these principles in their everyday lives. Many of these principles are already taught in courses in statistics and research design, such as the idea that if you want to generalize from a sample of information (e.g., a group of welfare mothers) to a population (e.g., all welfare mothers), you must have a large, unbiased sample. Do people who take such courses apply these principles in their everyday lives? Are they less likely to make the kinds of mistakes we have discussed in this chapter? A number of recent studies have provided encouraging answers to these questions, showing that people's reasoning processes can be improved by college statistics courses, graduate training in research design, and even brief, one-time lessons (Agnoli, 1991; Cheng, Holyoak, Nisbett, & Oliver, 1986; Crandall & Greenfield, 1986; Fong, Krantz, & Nisbett, 1986; Nisbett, Fong, Lehman, &

> "The sign of a first-rate intelligence is the ability to hold two opposed ideas at the same time.
> —F. Scott Fitzgerald

PEOPLE'S REASONING ABILITIES

1.   The city of Middleopolis has had an unpopular police chief for a year and a half. He is a political appointee who is a crony of the mayor and he had little previous experience in police administration when he was appointed. The mayor has recently defended the chief in public, announcing that in the time since he took office, crime rates decreased by 12 percent. Which of the following pieces of evidence would most deflate the mayor's claim that his chief is competent? (a) The crime rates of the two cities closest to Middleopolis in location and size have decreased by 18 percent in the same period. (b) An independent survey of the citizens of Middleopolis shows that 40 percent more crime is reported by respondents in the survey than is reported in police records. (c) Common sense indicates that there is little a police chief can do to lower crime rates. These are for the most part due to social and economic conditions beyond the control of officials. (d) The police chief has been discovered to have business contacts with people who are known to be involved in organized crime.

2.   After the first two weeks of the major league baseball season, newspapers begin to print the top ten batting averages. Typically, after two weeks, the leading batter has an average of about .450. Yet no batter in major league history has ever averaged .450 at the end of a season. Why do you think this is? (a) a player's high average at the beginning of the season may be just a lucky fluke. (b) A batter who has such a hot streak at the beginning of the season is under a lot of stress to maintain his performance record. Such stress adversely affects his playing. (c) Pitchers tend to get better over the course of the season, as they get more in shape. As pitchers improve, they are more likely to strike out batters, so batters' averages go down. (d) When a batter is known to be hitting for a high average, pitchers bear down more when they pitch to him. (e) When a batter is known to be hitting for a high average, he stops getting good pitches to hit. Instead, pitchers "play the corners" of the plate because they don't mind walking him.

Questions taken from Lehman, D. R., Lempert, R. O., & Nisbett, R. E. (1988). The effects of graduate training on reasoning: Formal discipline and thinking about everyday-life events. *American Psychologist, 43,* 431–442, p. 442.

ANSWERS

1. (a) This question assesses methodological reasoning, namely the recognition that there are several reasons why crime has gone down other than actions taken by the police chief, and that a better "test" of the major's claim is to compare the crime rate in Middleopolis with other, similar cities.
2. (a) This question assesses statistical reasoning, namely the recognition that large samples of information are more likely to reflect true scores and abilities than small samples of information. For example, if you flip a fair coin four times it is not unusual to get all heads or all tails, but if you flip the coin 1000 times it is extremely unlikely that you will get all heads or all tails. Applied to this example, this statistical principle says that when baseball players have a small number of at bats it is not unusual to see very high (or very low) averages just by chance. By the end of the season, however, when baseball players have hundreds of at bats, it is very unlikely that they will have a very high average just by luck.

FIGURE 3.9 Sample questions from the test of people's reasoning abilities. (Adapted from Lehman, Lempert, & Nisbett, 1988)

Cheng, 1987; Nisbett, Krantz, Jepson, & Kunda, 1983; Schaller, Asp, Rosell, & Heim, 1996).

Richard Nisbett, Geoffrey Fong, Darrin Lehman, and Patricia Cheng (1987), for example, examined how different kinds of graduate training influenced people's reasoning on everyday problems involving statistical and methodological reasoning—that is, the kind of reasoning we have considered in this chapter, such as people's understanding of how to generalize from small samples of information (see Figure 3.9 for sample questions). The researchers predicted that students in psychology and medicine would do better on the statistical reasoning problems

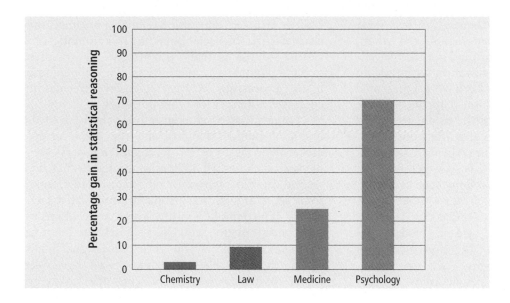

■ **FIGURE 3.10**
Performance on a test of statistical reasoning abilities by graduate students in different disciplines. After two years of graduate study, students in psychology and medicine showed more improvement on statistical reasoning problems than students in law and chemistry did. (Adapted from Nisbett et al., 1987)

than students in law and chemistry would, because graduate programs in psychology and medicine include more training in statistics than programs in the other two disciplines do.

As seen in Figure 3.10, after two years of graduate work, students in psychology and medicine improved on the statistical reasoning problems more than students in law and chemistry did. The improvement among the psychology graduate students was particularly impressive. Interestingly, the students in the different disciplines performed equally well on sample items from the Graduate Record Exam, suggesting that they did not differ in overall intelligence. Instead, the different kinds of training they had received appeared to influence how accurately and logically they reasoned on everyday problems (Nisbett, Fong, Lehman, & Cheng, 1987). Thus, there are grounds for being optimistic about people's ability to overcome the kinds of mistakes we have documented in this chapter. And you don't have to go to graduate school to do it. Sometimes it helps simply to consider the opposite, as participants in the Lord and colleagues (1984) study did. Beyond this, formal training in statistics helps, at both the graduate and undergraduate levels. So, if you were dreading taking a college statistics course, take heart: It might not only satisfy a requirement for your major but improve your reasoning as well!

Summary

Social cognition is the study of how people select, interpret, and use information to make judgments and decisions. People have developed several strategies and rules to help them understand the social world. **Schemas** are cognitive structures that organize information around themes or subjects. Schemas have a powerful effect on what information we notice, think about, and remember. Relying on schemas is adaptive and functional up to a point, but people can be overzealous theorists. For example, sometimes we persevere in our beliefs even when they're disproved, as shown in research on the **perseverance effect**. At times, we distort information so that it fits our schemas; for example, the **primacy effect** shows how our first impression of a person causes us to interpret his or her subsequent behavior in a schema-consistent manner. Because schemas can bias what we see, a **hostile media phenomenon** can result, whereby opposing partisan groups both perceive a neutral, balanced media presentation as hostile to their side. Inasmuch as the media have not presented the facts in the one-sided fashion partisans perceive to be true, each group believes the media are biased against them. Finally, schemas also affect our behavior—we act on the basis of our schemas. The most fascinating example of this is the **self-fulfilling prophecy**, wherein our schemas come true by unconsciously treating others in such a way that makes them act consistently with our schemas.

In addition to schemas, we use **judgmental heuristics** to help us deal with the large amount of social information with which we are faced. Heuristics are rules of thumb people follow in order to make judgments quickly and efficiently. The **availability heuristic**, the ease with which we can think of something, has a strong effect on how we view the world. One example of the influence of availability is **counterfactual thinking**—that is, mentally changing some aspect of the past as a way of imagining what might have been. The ease with which people can bring to mind alternative scenarios is an example of the use of the availability heuristic, and it can influence people's emotional reactions to events. The **representativeness heuristic** helps us decide how similar one thing is to another; we use it to classify people or situations on the basis of their similarity to a typical case. When using this heuristic, we have a tendency to ignore **base rate information**—the prior probability that something or someone belongs in that classification. People also rely on the **anchoring and adjustment heuristic**, wherein an initial piece of information acts as an anchor, or starting point, for subsequent thoughts on the topic. One example of anchoring and adjustment is **biased sampling**, whereby people make generalizations from samples of information they know are biased or atypical. Whereas all three heuristics are useful, they can also

lead to incorrect conclusions. Finally, an important characteristic of social thinking is **automatic processing**—thinking that is nonconscious, unintentional, involuntary, and effortless. Engaging in automatic processing is very efficient, freeing up cognitive resources for other purposes.

Some social psychologists have emphasized the limits of human thinking and the errors people make, referring to people as **cognitive misers**—people with such limited abilities to think that they take mental shortcuts whenever they can. More recently, some have argued that people are **motivated tacticians**—skilled thinkers with a large arsenal of mental rules and strategies, who choose wisely among these strategies, depending on their needs and goals. Consistent with this latter view, people have been found to make fewer errors when the stakes are high—that is, when it is more important to them to be accurate. In addition, people often engage in **controlled processing**—thinking that is conscious, intentional, voluntary, and effortful—to counteract the negative effects of automatic processing. When people are unmotivated or preoccupied, however, controlled processing is difficult to do. In such cases, people are more likely to accept false information and to have difficulty engaging in **thought suppression**: the attempt to avoid thinking about something they would just as soon forget.

Perhaps the best metaphor of the social thinker is that people are like flawed scientists—brilliant thinkers who often blind themselves to truths that don't fit their theories and who sometimes treat others in ways that make those theories come true. Though people often use strategies effectively, there is room for improvement in social thinking. For one thing, people are up against an **overconfidence barrier**, whereby they are too confident in the accuracy of their judgments. Fortunately, recent research has indicated that some of the shortcomings of human reasoning can be improved, particularly by training in statistics.

If You Are Interested

Dostoevsky, Fyodor (1945). *Notes from Underground*. A classic discourse on the role of consciousness in human thinking and feeling.

Fiske, S. T., & Taylor, S. E. (1991). *Social cognition* (2nd

ed.). New York: McGraw-Hill. An encyclopedic review of the literature on social cognition by two experts in the field.

Gilovich, T. (1991). *How we know what isn't so: The*

fallibility of human reason in everyday life. New York: Free Press. An entertaining overview of the many ways in which mental shortcuts can get us into trouble.

Kahneman, D., Slovic, P., & Tversky, A. (1982). *Judgment under uncertainty: Heuristics and biases.* New York: Cambridge University Press. A classic collection of chapters by researchers in the area of human inference.

Nisbett, R. E., & Ross, L. (1980). *Human inference: Strategies and shortcomings of human judgment.* Englewood Cliffs, NJ: Prentice Hall. A lively, poignant review of mental shortcuts and biases in human reasoning by the people who discovered many of them.

Plous, S. (1993). *The psychology of judgment and decision making.* New York: McGraw-Hill. An interesting review of how people form judgments and make decisions, one that expands upon many of the strategies and heuristics we have discussed.

Stand and Deliver (1987). A tough math teacher in an inner-city school challenges his students to do well in calculus. Based on a true story, the teacher expects the students to do well—and they do. An interesting portrayal of the power of social expectations.

Tootsie (1982). An unemployed, male, New York actor finally lands a role on a popular soap opera—as a woman. An amusing, poignant look at the expectations we have about each other based on gender.

CHAPTER 4

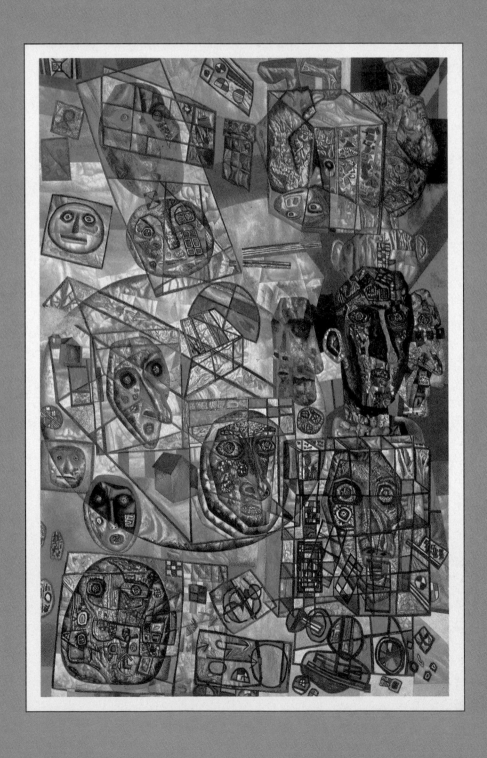

SOCIAL PERCEPTION: HOW WE COME TO UNDERSTAND OTHER PEOPLE

s you have no doubt noticed, other people are not easy to figure out. Why are they the way they are? Why do they do what they do? The frequency and urgency with which we pose these questions are demonstrated in this touching story, sent in by a reader to the *New York Times*:

> After ending an office romance, a female friend of mine threw a bag full of her former paramour's love letters, cards, and poems into an outside dumpster. The following day he called and wanted to know why she would throw out his letters. She was stunned. He explained that a homeless person going through the garbage read the correspondence and called the number found on a piece of stationery. The homeless man was curious as to why two people who seemed so in love could now be apart. "I would have called you sooner," he told the former boyfriend, "but this was the first quarter I was given today." (DeMarco, 1994)

The homeless man was down on his luck—no home, no money, reduced to rifling through garbage cans—and yet that endless fascination with the human condition still asserted itself. He needed to know why the couple broke up. He even spent his only quarter to find out.

We all have a fundamental fascination with explaining other people's behavior. But the reasons for why others behave as they do are usually hidden from us. All we have to go on is observable behavior: what people do, what they say, their facial expressions, gestures, and tone of voice. Unfortunately, we don't have the ability to read other people's minds—we can't know, truly and completely, who they are and what they mean. Instead, we rely on our impressions and theories, putting them together as well as we can, hoping they will lead to reasonably accurate and useful conclusions.

Why do we expend so much time and energy trying to explain the behavior of others? Because doing so helps us understand and predict our social world (Heider, 1958; Kelley, 1967). In this chapter, we will discuss **social perception**—the study of how we form impressions of other people and how we make inferences about them. One important source of information that we use is people's nonverbal behavior, such as their facial expressions, body movements, and tone of voice.   ☐

Social Perception
the study of how we form impressions of and make inferences about other people

*N*onverbal Behavior

What do we know about people when we first meet them? We know what we can see and hear, and even though we know we should not judge a book by its cover, this kind of easily observable information is critical to our first impressions. Physical characteristics such as people's attractiveness and facial configuration (e.g., a "baby face") influence others' judgments of them (Berry & McArthur, 1986; Hatfield & Sprecher, 1986; McArthur, 1990; Zebrowitz, 1997; Zebrowitz & Montepare, 1992). We also pay a great deal of attention to what people say. After all, our most noteworthy accomplishment as a species is the development of verbal language.

But people's words are not the full story. There is a rich source of information about people other than their words—the ways they communicate nonverbally (Ambady & Rosenthal, 1992, 1993; DePaulo & Friedman, 1998; Gifford, 1991, 1994). **Nonverbal communication** refers to a large body of research on how people communicate, intentionally or unintentionally, without words. Facial expressions, tone of voice, gestures, body positions and movement, the use of touch, and eye gaze are the most frequently used and diagnostic channels of nonverbal communication (Henley, 1977; Knapp & Hall, 1997). Even in a setting where you might think the verbal channel is paramount—a courtroom—various forms of nonverbal communication can prove so powerful and disruptive that a judge is forced to "outlaw" them. For instance, in February 1995 Judge Lance Ito publicly reprimanded all persons attending the trial of O. J. Simpson for displaying their emotions and reactions to courtroom events. Judge Ito said, "Let me remind you that any reactions, gestures . . . facial expressions . . . made during these court sessions, especially when the jury is here, those activities are inappropriate and will result in your expulsion" ("Gestures," 1995, p. 3).

Nonverbal Communication
the way in which people communicate, intentionally or unintentionally, without words; nonverbal cues include facial expressions, tone of voice, gestures, body position and movement, the use of touch, and eye gaze

How does nonverbal communication work? Nonverbal cues serve many functions in communication. The primary uses of nonverbal behavior are (a) *expressing emotion* (your eyes narrow, your eyebrows lower, you stare intensely, your mouth is set in a thin, straight line—you're angry), (b) *conveying attitudes* (e.g., "I like you"—smiles, extended eye contact—or "I don't like you"—eyes averted, flat tone of voice, body turned away), (c) *communicating one's personality traits* ("I'm outgoing"—broad gestures, changes in inflection when speaking, an energetic tone of voice), and (d) *facilitating verbal communication* (you lower your voice and look away as you finish your sentence so that your conversational partner knows you are done and it is his or her turn to speak)(Argyle, 1975).

In addition, some nonverbal cues repeat or complement the spoken message, as when you smile while saying "I'm so happy for you!" Others actually contradict the spoken words. Communicating sarcasm is the classic example of verbal-nonverbal contradiction. Think about how you'd say "I'm so happy for you" sarcastically. (You could use your tone of voice, stressing the word *so* with an ironic twist, or you could roll your eyes as you speak, a sign of sarcasm in North American culture.) Nonverbal cues can also substitute for the verbal message. Hand gestures such as flashing the "OK" sign or drawing a finger across your throat convey clear messages without any words at all (Ekman, 1965).

Nonverbal forms of communication have typically been studied individually, in their separate "channels" (e.g., eye gaze or gestures), even though in everyday life nonverbal cues of many kinds occur all at the same time in a quite dazzling orchestration of information (Archer & Akert, 1980, 1984, 1998). Let's focus on a few of these channels and then turn to how we interpret the full symphony of nonverbal information as it naturally occurs.

> An eye can threaten like a loaded and leveled gun, or can insult like hissing or kicking; or, in its altered mood, by beams of kindness, it can make the heart dance with joy.
>
> –Ralph Waldo Emerson,
> *The Conduct of Life*, 1860

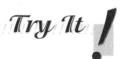

Using Your Voice as a Nonverbal Cue

Even though the words you say are full of information, the *way* you say them gives your listener even more of an idea of what you mean. You can take a perfectly straightforward sentence like "I don't know her," and give it many different meanings, depending on how you say it. Try saying that sentence out loud so that it communicates each of the emotions listed below. Experiment with the pitch of your voice (e.g., high or low), the speed with which you speak, the loudness or softness of your voice, and whether you stress some words and not others.

"I don't know her."

◆ you're angry
◆ you're being sarcastic
◆ you're scared
◆ you're surprised
◆ you're disgusted
◆ you're very happy

Now, try this exercise with a friend. Turn your back to your friend as you say each sentence; you want your friend to have to rely on your voice as the only cue, without help from any facial expressions you might make. How well does he or she guess the emotions you are expressing? Have your friend try the exercise too—can you understand his or her nonverbal cues of the voice? If you don't always correctly identify each other's voices, discuss what was missing or confusing about the voice. In this way, you'll be able to figure out, for example, what a "disgusted" voice sounds like as compared to an "angry" or "scared" voice.

Facial Expressions of Emotion

Without doubt, the crown jewel of nonverbal communication is the facial expressions channel. This aspect of communication has the longest history of research, beginning with Charles Darwin's (1872) book *The Expression of the Emotions in Man and Animals;* its primacy is due to the exquisite communicativeness of the human face (Kappas, 1997; McHugo & Smith, 1996). Look at the photographs on the next page; we bet you can figure out the meaning of these expressions with very little effort.

Darwin's research on facial expressions has had a major impact on the field in many areas; we will focus on his belief that the primary emotions conveyed by the face are universal—all human beings everywhere **encode** or express these emotions in the same way, and all human beings can **decode** or interpret them with equal accuracy. Darwin's (1872) interest in evolution led him to believe that nonverbal forms of communication were "species-specific" and not "culture-specific." He stated that facial expressions were vestiges of once-useful physiological reactions—for example, if early hominids ate something that tasted terrible, they would have wrinkled their noses in displeasure (from the bad smell) and expelled the food from their mouths. Note that the photograph on the next page showing the disgusted expression demonstrates this sort of reaction. Darwin (1872) states that such facial expressions then acquired evolutionary significance; being able to communicate such emotional states (e.g., the feeling of disgust, not for food but for another person or a situation) had survival value for the developing species (Hansen & Hansen, 1988; Izard, 1994; McArthur & Baron, 1983). Was Darwin right? Are facial expressions of emotion universal?

The answer is yes, for the six major emotional expressions: anger, happiness, surprise, fear, disgust, and sadness. For example, in a particularly well-designed study, Paul Ekman and Walter Friesen (1971) traveled to New Guinea, where they studied the decoding ability of the South Fore, a preliterate tribe that had had no contact with Western civilization. They told the Fore people brief stories with emotional content and then showed them photographs of American men and women expressing the six emotions; the Fore's job was to match the facial expressions of emotion to the stories. They were as accurate as Western subjects had been. The researchers then asked the Fore people to demonstrate, while being photographed, facial expressions that would match the stories they were told. These photographs, when later shown to American research participants, were also decoded accurately. Thus, there is considerable evidence that the ability to interpret at least the six major emotions is cross-cultural—part of being human and not a product of people's cultural experience (Biehl et al., 1997; Buck, 1984; Ekman, 1993, 1994; Ekman, Friesen, & Ellsworth, 1982a, 1982b; Ekman et al., 1987; Izard, 1969, 1977, 1994).

Besides the six major emotions, are there other emotional states that are communicated with distinctive and readily identifiable facial expressions? Current research is exploring just this question for emotions such as anxiety, contempt, and embarrassment (Ekman, O'Sullivan, & Matsumoto, 1991a, 1991b; Harrigan & O'Connell, 1996; Marcus, Wilson, & Miller, 1996; Miller & Marcus, 1996). For example, recent research by Dacher Keltner (1995) suggests that embarrassment has a distinctive nonverbal display as tested in his sample of Caucasian and African American undergraduates (Keltner & Buswell, 1996). Keltner's (1995) research participants were asked to perform difficult tasks that often made them feel lacking in ability or poise, all the while receiving explicit feedback from the

Encode
to express or emit nonverbal behavior, such as smiling or patting someone on the back

Decode
to interpret the meaning of the nonverbal behavior other people express, such as deciding that a pat on the back was an expression of condescension and not kindness

> "W hen the eyes say one thing, and the tongue another, a practiced man relies on the language of the first.
> —Ralph Waldo Emerson,
> *The Conduct of Life,* 1860

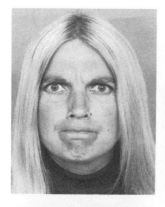

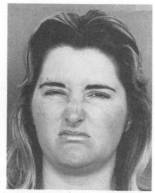
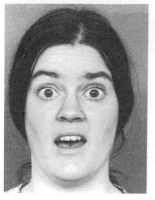

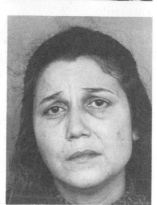

■ These photographs depict facial expressions of the six major emotions. Can you guess the emotion expressed on each face? (Adapted from Ekman & Friesen, 1975)

Answers: (clockwise, beginning with upper-left photo): Anger, fear, disgust, sadness, happiness, and surprise.

experimenter on how they were doing. Needless to say, they often felt embarrassed (as well as other emotions, e.g., amused). Keltner carefully coded photographs of the various expressions on their faces during the tasks, and he later asked other research participants to decode them. Keltner (1995) concluded that a distinctive expression of embarrassment existed, composed of turning the head away, looking down, shifting the gaze to the side, evincing a controlled smile (e.g., with the lips pressed), and sometimes, touching the face with one's hand—all lasting about four to five seconds in a typical instance. The photograph on this page illustrates this prototypical "embarrassed" nonverbal response. Further research will tell us whether this is a universal expression of embarrassment or one that is found only in American (or Western) society.

While there is ample proof that the six major emotions are expressed the same way by people all over the world, culture does play a role as to when and how people display emotions on their faces. Paul Ekman and his colleagues (Ekman & Friesen, 1969; Ekman & Davidson, 1994) note that **display rules** are particular to each culture and dictate what kind of emotional expression people are supposed to show. For example, American cultural norms discourage emotional displays in men, such as grief or crying, but allow the facial display of such emotions in women. In Japan, traditional cultural rules dictate that women should not exhibit a wide, uninhibited smile (Ramsey, 1981); Japanese women will often hide their wide smiles behind their hands, while Western women are allowed—indeed encouraged—to smile broadly and often (Henley, 1977). In fact, the cultural display rules that govern Japanese nonverbal expression are surprisingly different from Western ones. Japanese norms lead people to cover up

■ This man is expressing all of the nonverbal cues of embarrassment. He has turned his head away, looked down and to the side, smiled with pressed lips, and touched his face.

Display Rules
culturally determined rules about which nonverbal behaviors are appropriate to display

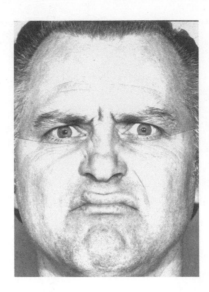 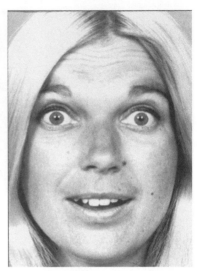

■ Often people express more than one emotion at the same time. Can you tell which emotions these people are expressing? The answers are printed below. (Adapted from Ekman & Friesen, 1975)

Answers: The man is expressing a blend of anger and disgust. The woman is expressing a blend of surprise and happiness.

negative facial expressions with smiles and laughter and to display fewer facial expressions in general than is true in the West (Friesen, 1972; Gudykunst, Ting-Toomey, & Nishida, 1996; Morsbach, 1973; Leathers, 1997; Richmond & McCroskey, 1995). This is undoubtedly what lies behind the Western stereotype that Asians are "inscrutable" and "hard to read."

A final note about decoding facial expressions accurately: This situation is more complicated than it appears, because people frequently display **affect blends** (Ekman & Friesen, 1975), wherein one part of their face is registering one emotion and another part is registering a different emotion. Take a look at the photographs on this page and see if you can tell which two emotions are being expressed in each face. In the photograph on the left, we see a blend of anger (the eye and eyebrow region) and disgust (the nose and mouth region). (It may help to cover half of the photograph with your hand to see each emotional expression clearly.) This is the sort of expression you might display if a person told you something that was both horrible and inappropriate—you'd be disgusted with the content and angry that the person told you.

Affect Blends
a facial expression where one part of the face is registering one emotion and another part of the face is registering a different emotion

Other Channels of Nonverbal Communication

There are, of course, other channels of nonverbal communication. Eye contact and gaze are particularly powerful nonverbal cues. Members of American culture become suspicious when a person doesn't "look them in the eye" while speaking, and they find talking to someone who is wearing dark sunglasses quite disconcerting. However, as you can see in Figure 4.1, in other parts of the world direct eye gaze is considered invasive or disrespectful. Another form of nonverbal communication is how people use personal space. Imagine you are talking to a person who stands too close to you (or too far away); these deviations from "normal" spacing will affect your impressions of him or her. Cultures vary greatly in what is considered normative use of personal space (Hall, 1969). For example, most Americans like to have a bubble of open space, a few feet in radius, surrounding them; in comparison, in some other cultures, strangers will think nothing of standing right next to each other, to the point of touching.

CULTURAL DIFFERENCES IN NONVERBAL COMMUNICATION

Many forms of nonverbal behavior are specific to a given culture. For example, the photographs on page 113 demonstrate French gestures that are understandable in France but meaningless in the United States. Not only do some of the nonverbal behaviors of one culture mean nothing in another, the same nonverbal behavior can exist in two cultures, but have very different meanings in each. Such nonverbal differences can lead to misunderstanding when people from different societies interact. Some of these cultural differences are listed below.

Eye contact and gaze

In American culture, direct eye contact is valued; a person who won't "look you in the eye" is perceived as being evasive or even as lying. However, in many parts of the world, direct eye contact is considered disrespectful, especially with superiors. For example, in Nigeria, Puerto Rico, and Thailand, children are taught not to make direct eye contact with their teachers and other adults. Cherokee, Navajo, and Hopi Native Americans use minimal eye contact as well. Japanese use far less direct eye contact than Americans. In contrast, Arabs use a great deal of eye contact, with a gaze that would be considered piercing by people from some other cultures.

Personal space and touching

Societies vary in whether they are high-contact cultures, where people stand close to each other and touch frequently, or low-contact cultures, where people maintain more interpersonal space and touch less often. High-contact cultures include Middle Eastern countries, South American countries, and Southern European countries. Low-contact cultures include North American countries, Northern European countries, Asian countries, Pakistan, and Native American peoples. Cultures also differ in how appropriate they consider same-sex touching among friends. For example, in Korea and Egypt, men and women hold hands, link arms, or walk hip to hip with their same-sex friends, and these nonverbal behaviors carry no sexual connotation. In the United States, such behavior is much less common, particularly between male friends.

Hand and head gestures

The "OK" sign: The OK sign is formed by making a circle with your thumb and index finger, with your three other fingers extended upward. In the United States, this means "OK." However, in Japan, this hand gesture means "money." In France, it means "zero"; in Mexico, it means "sex." In Ethiopia, it means "homosexuality." Finally, in some South American countries, like Brazil, it is an obscene gesture, carrying the same meaning as the American "flipping the bird" sign, where the middle finger is the only one extended.

The "thumb up" gesture: In the United States, raising one thumb upward with the rest of the fingers in the fist means "OK." Several European countries have a similar meaning for this gesture; for example, in France it means "excellent!". However, in Japan, the same gesture means "boyfriend," while in Iran and Sardinia, it is an obscene gesture.

The "hand-purse" gesture: This gesture is formed by straightening the fingers and thumb of one hand and bringing them together so the tips touch, pointing upwards. This gesture has no clear meaning in American culture. However, in Italy, it means "What are you trying to say?"; in Spain, it means "good"; in Tunisia, it means "Slow down"; and in Malta, it means "You may seem good, but you are really bad."

Nodding the head: In the United States, nodding one's head up and down means "yes" and shaking it from side to side means "no." However, in some parts of Africa and India, the opposite is true: nodding up and down means "no," and shaking from side to side means "yes." To complicate this situation even more, in Korea, shaking one's head from side to side means "I don't know" (which in the United States is communicated by a shrug of the shoulders). Finally, Bulgarians indicate disagreement by throwing their heads back and then returning them to an upright position—which is frequently mistaken by Americans as meaning agreement.

■ **FIGURE 4.1   Cultural Differences in Nonverbal Communication.**   Based on Archer (1991, 1997a, 1997b); Gudykunst, Ting-Toomey, & Nishida (1996); Knapp & Hall (1997); Leathers (1997); Richmond & McCroskey (1995).

■ Cambodians in downtown Phnom Penh watch a television broadcast of the trial of Pol Pot, the leader of the Khmer Rouge, a Cambodian revolutionary group which was responsible for the murder of over one million civilians during the country's civil war in the mid-1970's. The Cambodians' facial expressions show emotions like anger and surprise (the two children in the foreground) as well as affect blends of surprise with fear or anger (the adults around them).

Emblems
nonverbal gestures that have well-understood definitions within a given culture; they usually have direct verbal translations, such as the "OK" sign

Gestures of the hands and arms are also a fascinating means of communication. We are very adept at understanding certain gestures, such as the "OK" sign, in which one forms a circle with the thumb and forefinger and the rest of the fingers curve above the circle, and "flipping the bird," in which one bends all the fingers down at the first knuckle except the longest, middle finger. Gestures like these, for which there are clear, well-understood definitions, are called **emblems** (Ekman & Friesen, 1975; Archer, 1997b). The important point about emblems is that they are not universal; each culture has devised its own emblems, and these need not be understandable to people from other cultures (see Figure 4.1). Thus, "flipping the bird" will be a clear communicative sign of an obscenity in American society, whereas in some parts of Europe you'd need to make a quick gesture with a cupped hand under your chin to convey the same message. President Bush once used the "V for Victory" sign (where two fingers form a V shape) but he did it backwards—the palm of his hand was facing him instead of the audience. Unfortunately, he flashed this gesture to a large crowd in Australia—and in Australia, this emblem is the equivalent of "flipping the bird" (Archer, 1997b)! The photos on page 113 illustrate some French emblems that are different from our American emblems.

Multichannel Nonverbal Communication

Except for certain specific situations (e.g., talking on the telephone), everyday life is made up of social interaction in a multichannel nonverbal sense (Archer & Akert, 1998; Rosenthal et al., 1979). Typically, many nonverbal cues are available to us when we talk to or observe other people. How do we use this information? And how accurately do we use it?

In order to study multichannel nonverbal decoding, Dane Archer and Robin Akert (1991, 1998) have constructed a nonverbal communication decoding task that closely mirrors real-life interpretative situations. The Social Interpretations Task (SIT) videotape is composed of 20 scenes of naturally occurring nonverbal

La barbe! Rasoir!: How dull. "Beard! Razor!" acquired the meaning "boring" in the nineteenth century.

Mon oeil!: "My eye!" You can't fool me!

Il est bourré!: He's stuffed; he's potted; he's drunk.

■ These photographs depict French nonverbal emblems. The gestures are clearly understood in France. However, because emblems are culturally determined, an American would find it difficult or impossible to understand these gestures. (Adapted from Wylie, 1977)

behavior (Archer & Akert, 1977a, 1977b, 1980, 1984). Real people, not actors, are seen and heard having real conversations, not scripted ones. The scenes last a minute or so, giving the viewer a slice of a real interaction. Following each scene, the viewer is asked a question about the people in the scene or their relationship to each other. For example, in one scene two women are seen playing with a baby. The viewer is asked, "Which woman is the mother of the baby?" A clear criterion for accuracy exists for each of the scenes; one of the women really is the mother of the baby. However, neither of the women states this fact out loud; nor did the women realize this would be the interpretative question paired with their scene.

In order to get this and the other scenes right, the viewer must pay attention to and interpret the nonverbal behavior of the people in the scenes. Archer and Akert (1998) found that 64 percent of the more than 1,400 people tested were able to decode this scene accurately, far above the chance level of accuracy of 33 percent. People reported using several different channels of nonverbal communication to help them choose the right answer to this scene. For example, they compared the tone of voice of the real mother when talking to the baby to the other woman's tone of voice; they noted the body position and posture of the non-mother as she held the baby, as well as the way she held the baby; they relied on eye contact cues, especially the baby's eye contact with the mother versus the non-mother; and they focused on the way the mother touched the baby versus the non-mother's touch.

Further research with the SIT videotape has shown that the important, or diagnostic, nonverbal information is actually diffused throughout each scene (Archer & Akert, 1980, 1998). In other words, it is not typically the case that only one significant clue signals the right answer. Instead, useful nonverbal information is present across many channels in each scene. This makes the decoder's job easier: If you fail to notice the eye gaze behavior, you may notice the tone of voice or the unusual gesture and still arrive at an accurate judgment. Research has also shown that some people are particularly talented at decoding nonverbal

1. Which of these two women is the mother of the baby?
a. The woman on the left.
b. the woman on the right.
c. neither woman.

2. Are these two people: a. Friends who have known each other for at least six months? b. Acquaintances who have had several conversations? c. Strangers who have never talked before?

3. All three of these men claim to have won the poker game. Who really won the game? a. The man on the left; b. The man in the center; c. The man on the right.

■ The above photographs provide examples of the Social Interpretations Task. The answers are printed below. (Adapted from Archer & Akert, 1977)

Answers: 1-b; 2-c; 3-c.

cues accurately, while others are dismally poor at this task. Robin Akert and Abigail Panter have explored various personality traits to see if these predict who the good decoders are; for example, there is some evidence that extraverts are more accurate decoders of nonverbal cues on a SIT-like task than introverts are (Akert & Panter, 1986).

Gender Differences in Nonverbal Communication

It may have occurred to you to wonder whether one sex is better than the other at understanding nonverbal communication. Who is better at decoding nonverbal cues—men or women? And who is better at encoding nonverbal information? A large number of studies have found that women are better at both decoding and encoding (Hall, 1979, 1984; Rosenthal & DePaulo, 1979).

As with most rules, however, there is an exception: Though women are superior to men at deciphering someone's nonverbal cues when that person is telling the truth, they lose their superiority when the person is lying (DePaulo, Epstein & Wyer, 1993). Robert Rosenthal and Bella DePaulo (1979) found that women were more likely to take deceptive communications at face value, believing the lie, while men were more likely to pick up on the nonverbal cues and correctly conclude the individual was lying. Given that women are generally superior decoders, why do they lose their advantage when faced with deceptive communications? Rosenthal and DePaulo (1979) suggest that it is because women are more polite than men. While women have the ability to decode nonverbal cues of lying, they tend to turn off this skill when faced with deception, in order to be polite to the speaker.

This interpretation fits nicely with a theory of sex differences offered by Alice Eagly (1987). According to Eagly's **social-role theory**, in most societies there is a division of labor on the basis of gender. Typically, women are more likely than men to hold certain familial and occupational roles, such as being the primary caregiver to children. According to Eagly, this division of labor has two important consequences. First, gender-role expectations arise, wherein members of the society expect men and women to have attributes consistent with their role. Because of the social roles they occupy, women are expected to be more nurturing, friendly, expressive, and sensitive—and so they are. Second, men and women develop different sets of skills and attitudes, based on their gender roles. Because of their position in many societies, it is more important for women to learn skills such as sensitivity and communication. In addition, because women are less powerful in many societies and are less likely to occupy roles of higher status, it is more important for women to learn to be accommodating and polite (Deaux & Major, 1987; Henley, 1977). According to Eagly (1987), gender-role expectations and sex-typed skills combine to produce sex differences in social behavior, such as the differences in nonverbal behavior we just discussed.

One way to test this theory would be to examine sex differences in cultures that have different gender-role expectations and sex-typed skills. If women are more polite in reading nonverbal cues because of the social roles they occupy in society, then this tendency to be polite should be especially strong in those cultures where women are most oppressed. This is exactly what Judith Hall (1979) found in her cross-cultural study of nonverbal behavior. First, she classified each of 11 countries as to the level of oppression of women, based on such statistics as the number of women who go to college and the prevalence of women's groups in each country. She then examined how likely women in each country were to show the "politeness pattern" when reading other people's nonverbal behaviors—that is, to focus on nonverbal cues that convey what people want others to see and to ignore nonverbal cues that "leak" people's true feelings. Sure enough, the tendency of women to be nonverbally polite in this manner was especially strong in those cultures where women are most oppressed.

To summarize, we can learn quite a lot about people from their nonverbal behavior, including their attitudes, emotions, and personality traits. Nonverbal behavior gives us many bits of information, "data," as it were, that we then use to construct our overall impressions or theories about people. What is someone really like? What caused her to act as she did? In the next sections, we turn to the cognitive processes people use to form impressions of others.

Implicit Personality Theories: Filling in the Blanks

As we saw in Chapter 3, when people are unsure about the nature of the social world, they use their schemas to fill in the gaps. An excellent example of this use of schemas is the way in which we form impressions of other people. If we know someone is kind, we use an important type of schema called an **implicit personality theory** to determine what else the person is like. These theories consist of our ideas about what kinds of personality traits go together (Anderson & Sedikides, 1990; Sedikides & Anderson, 1994; Sherman & Klein, 1994; Schneider, 1973). If

Social-Role Theory the theory that sex differences in social behavior are due to society's division of labor between the sexes; this division leads to differences in gender-role expectations and sex-typed skills, both of which are responsible for differences in men's and women's social behavior

Implicit Personality Theory a type of schema people use to group various kinds of personality traits together; for example, many people believe that if someone is kind, he or she is generous as well

a person is kind, our implicit personality theory tells us he or she is probably generous as well; if a person is stingy, we believe he or she is probably irritable too.

These implicit theories about personality serve the same function as any schema: As "cognitive misers," we can extrapolate from a small to a much larger amount of information (Fiske & Taylor, 1991; Markus & Zajonc, 1985). In this case, we can use just a few observations of a person as a starting point and then, using our schema, create a much fuller understanding of what that person is like (Kim & Rosenberg, 1980). This way, we can form impressions quickly, without having to spend weeks with people to figure out what they are like.

Implicit personality theories are interesting in that there are shared components to them—many of us have very similar theories—and there is also room for idiosyncratic variation—we have some theories that are different (Hamilton, 1970; Kuusinen, 1969; Pedersen, 1965). These social theories are developed over time and with experience. Not surprisingly, they often have a strong cultural component: In a given society, most people will share some implicit personality theories because these are cultural beliefs passed on in that society (Anderson, 1995; Vonk, 1995). For example, research on implicit personality theories of Americans indicates that if people are perceived to be "helpful," they are also believed to be "sincere"; if they are thought to be "practical," then they are also "cautious" (Rosenberg, Nelson, & Vivekananthan, 1968). A strong implicit personality theory in this culture involves physical attractiveness. We presume that "what is beautiful is good"—that people with physical beauty will also have a whole host of other wonderful qualities (Dion, Berscheid, & Walster, 1972; Eagly, et al., 1991; Jackson, Hunter, & Hodge, 1995).

Cultural variation in implicit personality theories was demonstrated in an intriguing study by Curt Hoffman, Ivy Lau, and David Johnson (1986). They noted that different cultures have different ideas about personality types—that is, the kinds of people for whom there are simple, agreed-on verbal labels. For example, in Western cultures we agree that there is a kind of person who has an artistic personality: This is a person who is creative, intense, and temperamental and who has an unconventional lifestyle. The Chinese, however, do not have a schema or implicit personality theory for an artistic type. There are no labels in the Chinese language to describe someone with this collection of traits. Granted, there are words in Chinese to describe the individual characteristics of such people, such as the word for creative, but there are no labels like "an artistic

> *O*thers are to us like the "characters" in fiction, external and incorrigible; the surprises they give us turn out in the end to have been predictable—unexpected variations on the theme of being themselves.
> —Mary McCarthy

■ Implicit personality theories differ from culture to culture. Westerners assume there is an artistic type of person—someone who is creative, intense, temperamental, and unconventional (for example, the artist Andy Warhol, on the left). The Chinese have no such implicit personality theory. The Chinese have a category of a *shi gú* person—someone who is worldly, devoted to his or her family, socially skillful, and somewhat reserved. Westerners do not have this implicit personality theory.

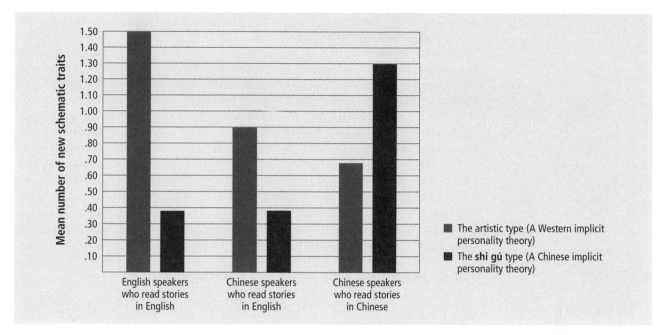

■ **FIGURE 4.2   Implicit personality theories: How our culture and language shape our impressions of other people.**   People formed an impression of other people that was consistent with the implicit personality theory contained in their language. For example, when Chinese-English bilinguals read stories about people in English, they were likely to form impressions consistent with a Western implicit theory, the artistic personality. When Chinese-English bilinguals read the same stories in Chinese, they were likely to form impressions consistent with a Chinese implicit theory, the *shi gú* personality. (Adapted from Hoffman, Lau, & Johnson, 1986)

type" or "a bohemian" that describe the whole constellation of traits implied by the English term. Similarly, in China there are categories of personality that do not exist in Western cultures. For example, a *shi gú* person is someone who is worldly, devoted to his or her family, socially skillful, and somewhat reserved.

Hoffman and colleagues (1986) hypothesized that these cultural implicit personality theories influence the way people form impressions of others. To test this hypothesis, they wrote stories that described a person behaving like an artistic type of person or *shi gú* type of person, without using those labels to describe the person. These stories were written in both English and Chinese. The English versions were given to a group of native English speakers who did not speak any other language and to a group of Chinese-English bilinguals. Another group of Chinese-English bilinguals received the versions written in Chinese.

If people were using their cultural theories to understand the stories they read, what would we expect to happen? One measure of the use of theories (or schemas) is the tendency to fill in the blanks—that is, to believe that information fitting the schema was observed when in fact it was not. Hoffman and colleagues (1986) asked the participants to write down their impressions of the characters in the stories; they then looked to see whether the participants listed traits that were not used in the stories but did fit the artistic or *shi gú* personality type. For example, "unreliable" was not mentioned in the "artistic personality type" story but is consistent with that implicit personality theory.

As seen in Figure 4.2, when the native English speakers read about the characters in English, they were much more likely to form an impression that was consistent with the artistic type than with the *shi gú* type. Similarly, when the Chinese-English bilinguals read the descriptions of the characters in English, they too formed an impression that was consistent with the artistic type but not with the *shi gú* type, because English provides a convenient label for the artistic type. In comparison, Chinese-English bilinguals who read the descriptions in Chinese showed the opposite pattern of results. Their impression of the *shi gú* character was more consistent with the schema than their impression of the artist was, because the Chinese language provides a convenient label or implicit personality theory for this kind of person. These results are consistent with a well-known argument by Whorf (1956) that the language people speak influences the way they think about the world. Characters described identically were perceived differently by the bilingual research participants, depending on the language (and therefore the implicit personality theory) that was used. Thus, one's culture and one's language produce widely shared implicit personality theories, and these theories can influence the kinds of impressions people form of each other.

Using Mental Shortcuts When Forming Impressions

Sometimes it is unclear which theory or trait applies to someone we meet. People's behavior can be ambiguous, making it difficult to decide what kind of person they are. Imagine, for example, that you are riding on a city bus and a man gets on and sits beside you. You can't help but notice that he's acting a little strangely. He mutters incoherently to himself, stares at everyone on the bus, and repeatedly rubs his face with one hand. How would you make sense out of his behavior? You have many implicit personality theories, and more than one could explain his ambiguous behavior. What dictates your choice?

The Role of Accessibility and Priming in Person Perception

Accessibility
the ease with which different thoughts and ideas can be brought to mind; an idea that is accessible is already on our minds or can easily be brought to mind

Recent research indicates that your impression of the man on the bus can be affected by the **accessibility** of trait categories, defined as the extent to which thoughts, ideas, and traits are at the forefront of our minds and are therefore likely to be used when we are making judgments about the social world (Higgins, 1996; Wyer & Srull, 1989).

Traits become accessible two ways. First, some traits can be chronically accessible due to past experience (Dijksterhuis & van Knippenberg, 1996; Higgins & Brendl, 1995; Rudman & Borgida, 1995). For example, if there is a history of alcoholism in your family, traits describing an alcoholic are likely to be very accessible to you, increasing the likelihood that these traits will come to mind when you are thinking about the behavior of the man on the bus. If someone you know suffers from mental illness, however, then thoughts about how the mentally ill behave are more likely to be accessible than thoughts about alcoholics are, leading you to interpret the man's behavior very differently.

Second, several studies have shown that traits can also become accessible for more arbitrary reasons (Bargh, 1990, 1996; Higgins & Bargh, 1987). Whatever we happen to have been thinking or doing prior to encountering an event can prime a trait, making it more accessible and thus more likely to be used to interpret that event. Suppose, for example, that right before the man on the bus sat down, you were reading Ken Kesey's *One Flew over the Cuckoo's Nest*, a novel about patients in a mental hospital. Given that thoughts about mental patients were accessible in your mind, you would probably assume that the man's strange behavior was due to mental illness. If, on the other hand, thoughts about alcoholism were fresh in your mind—for example, you had just looked out the window and seen an alcoholic leaning against a building drinking a bottle of wine—you would probably assume the man on the bus had had a few too many (see Figure 4.3). These are examples of **priming**, whereby a recent experience, such as reading Kesey's novel, increases the accessibility of certain traits, such as those describing the mentally ill, making it more likely that these traits will be used to interpret a new event—such as the behavior of the man on the bus—even though this new event is completely unrelated to the one that originally primed the traits.

Tory Higgins, Stephen Rholes, and Carl Jones (1977) illustrated this priming effect in the following experiment. Research participants were told that they would take part in two unrelated studies. The first was a perception study, where they would be asked to identify different colors while at the same time memorizing a list of words. The second was a reading comprehension study, where they would be asked to read a paragraph about someone named Donald and then give

Priming
the process by which recent experiences increase a trait's accessibility

■ **FIGURE 4.3   How we interpret an ambiguous situation: The role of accessibility and priming.**

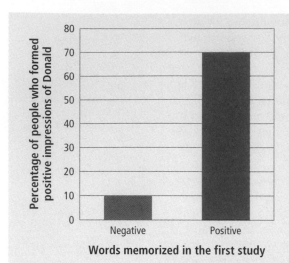

Description of Donald

Donald spent a great deal of time in his search of what he liked to call excitement. He had already climbed Mt. McKinley, shot the Colorado rapids in a kayak, driven in a demolition derby, and piloted a jet-powered boat—without knowing very much about boats. He had risked injury, and even death, a number of times. Now he was in search of new excitement. He was thinking, perhaps, he would do some skydiving or maybe cross the Atlantic in a sailboat. By the way he acted one could readily guess that Donald was well aware of his ability to do many things well. Other than business engagements, Donald's contacts with people were rather limited. He felt he didn't really need to rely on anyone. Once Donald made up his mind to do something it was as good as done no matter how long it might take or how difficult the going might be. Only rarely did he change his mind even when it might well have been better if he had.

■ **FIGURE 4.4 Priming and accessibility.** People read the above paragraph about Donald and formed an impression of him. In a prior study, some people had memorized words that could be used to interpret Donald in a negative way (e.g., *reckless, conceited*), while others had memorized words that could be used to interpret Donald in a positive way (e.g., *adventurous, self-confident*). As seen in the graph, those who had memorized the negative words formed a much more negative impression of Donald than those who had memorized the positive words. (Adapted from Higgins, Rholes, & Jones, 1977)

> **A**ll thought is a feat of association: having what's in front of you bring up something in your mind that you almost didn't know you knew.
>
> —Robert Frost, interview, *Writers at Work: Second Series*, 1963

their impressions of him. This paragraph is shown in Figure 4.4. Take a moment to read it. What do you think of Donald?

You might have noticed that many of Donald's actions are ambiguous, interpretable in either a positive or a negative manner. Take the fact that he piloted a boat without knowing much about it and wants to sail across the Atlantic. It is possible to put a positive spin on these acts, deciding that Donald has an admirable sense of adventure. It's just as easy, however, to put a negative spin on these acts, assuming that Donald is a rather reckless and foolhardy individual.

How did the participants interpret Donald's behavior? Higgins and his colleagues (1977) found, as expected, that it depended on whether positive or negative traits were primed and accessible. In the first study, the researchers divided people into two groups and gave them different words to memorize. People who had first memorized the words *adventurous, self-confident, independent,* and *persistent* later formed positive impressions of Donald, viewing him as a likable man who enjoyed new challenges. People who had first memorized *reckless, conceited, aloof,* and *stubborn* later formed negative impressions of Donald, viewing him as a stuck-up person who took needlessly dangerous chances.

We should note that it was not just memorizing any positive or negative words that influenced people's impressions of Donald. In other conditions, research participants memorized words that were also positive or negative, such as *neat* or *disrespectful*. However, these traits did not influence their impressions of Donald, because the words did not apply to Donald's actions. Thus, thoughts have to be both accessible and applicable before they will act as primes, exerting an influence on our impressions of the social world.

Causal Attribution: Answering the "Why" Question

We have seen that when we observe other people, we have a rich source of information—their nonverbal behavior—on which to base our impressions. From their nonverbal behavior, we can also make guesses about people's personalities, such as how friendly or outgoing they are. And once we get this far, we use our implicit personality theories to fill in the blanks: If a person is friendly, he or she must be sincere as well.

However, nonverbal behavior is not a fail-safe indicator of what a person is really thinking or feeling. If you encounter an acquaintance and she says "It's great to see you!" with enthusiastic nonverbal cues, does she really mean it? Perhaps she is acting more thrilled than she really feels, out of politeness. Perhaps she is outright lying and really can't stand you. The point is that even though nonverbal communication is sometimes easy to decode, there is still substantial ambiguity as to what a person's behavior really means (DePaulo, 1992; DePaulo, Stone, & Lassiter, 1985; Schneider, Hastorf, & Ellsworth, 1979).

To answer the "why" question, we need to go beyond the information given, inferring, from what we observe, what people are really like and what motivates them to act as they do. How we go about answering these questions is the focus of **attribution theory**, the study of how we infer the causes of other people's behavior.

The Nature of the Attributional Process

Fritz Heider (1958) is frequently referred to as the father of attribution theory. His influential book defined the field of social perception, and his legacy is still very much evident in current research (Gilbert, 1998). Heider (1958) discussed what he called "naive" or "commonsense" psychology. In his view, people were like amateur scientists, trying to understand other people's behavior by piecing together information until they arrived at a reasonable explanation or cause. Heider (1958) was intrigued by what seemed reasonable to people and by how they arrived at their conclusions.

One of Heider's (1958) most valuable contributions is a simple dichotomy: When trying to decide why people behave as they do—for example, why a father has just yelled at his son—we can make one of two attributions. We can make an **internal attribution**, deciding that the cause of the father's behavior was something about him—his disposition, personality, attitudes, or character—an explanation that assigns the causality of his behavior internally. For example, we might decide that the father has poor parenting skills and disciplines his child in inappropriate ways. Conversely, we can make an **external attribution**, deciding that the cause of his behavior was something about the situation—such as the fact that his son had just stepped into the street without looking—an explanation that assigns the causality of his behavior externally (i.e., it was the child's actions that triggered the father's behavior, not something distinctive about the father's personality, attitudes, or character).

Notice that our impression of the father will be very different depending on the type of attribution we make. If we make an internal attribution, we'll have a negative impression of him. If we make an external attribution, we won't learn much about him—after all, most parents would have done the same thing if they were in that situation and their child had just disobeyed them by stepping into the street. Quite a difference!

> "In the beginning was not the word, not the deed, not the silly serpent. In the beginning was *why?* Why did she pluck the apple? Was she bored? Was she inquisitive? Was she paid? Did Adam put her up to it? If not, who did?
> —John le Carré,
> *The Russia House,* 1989

Attribution Theory
a description of the way in which people explain the causes of their own and other people's behavior

Internal Attribution
the inference that a person is behaving in a certain way because of something about him or her, such as the person's attitudes, character, or personality

External Attribution
the inference that a person is behaving a certain way because of something about the situation he or she is in; the assumption is that most people would respond the same way in that situation

Another of Heider's (1958) important contributions was his discussion of our preference for internal attributions over external ones. While either type of attribution is always possible, Heider (1958) noted that we tend to see the causes of a person's behavior as residing in that person. We are perceptually focused on people—they are who we notice—and the situation, which is often hard to see and hard to describe, can be overlooked (Bargh, 1994; Carlston & Skowronski, 1994; Fletcher, Reeder, & Bull, 1990; Newman & Uleman, 1993; Pittman & D'Agostino, 1985; Uleman & Moskowitz, 1994).

Correspondent Inference Theory: From Acts to Dispositions

Correspondent Inference Theory
the theory that we make internal attributions about a person when there are (a) few noncommon effects of his or her behavior and (b) the behavior is unexpected

This observation of Heider's, that internal attributions are particularly attractive to perceivers, is the starting point for one of the basic theories of how people make attributions—correspondent inference theory (Jones & Davis, 1965). Edward Jones and Keith Davis developed **correspondent inference theory** to describe the process by which we arrive at an internal attribution: how we infer dispositions, or internal personality characteristics, from corresponding behaviors or actions (Jones, 1990; Jones & Davis, 1965; Jones & McGillis, 1976). Suppose, for example, we learn that Karen has accepted a job in an advertising agency in New York City. Why? Did Karen accept the job because she is interested in advertising? Because she wants to live in New York? Because the job pays well? Correspondent inference theory is concerned with how we narrow down these possibilities to a specific conclusion about why Karen did what she did.

The Role of Noncommon Effects in Correspondent Inference Theory

The main way we make internal attributions, according to the theory, is by comparing what people could accomplish by the behavior they chose to perform with what they could have accomplished with alternative actions (comparing the effects of the different choices, in the words of the theory). For example, to determine why Karen accepted the advertising job, we would consider what Karen accomplished by accepting this job, compared to what she could have accomplished by making a different choice. An internal attribution is easier to the extent that there are few **noncommon effects** of these different choices—that is, if by accepting the job in New York Karen could accomplish only one or two things that she could not accomplish by accepting other jobs.

Noncommon Effects
effects produced by a particular course of action that could not be produced by alternative courses of action

For instance, suppose we knew that when Karen accepted the advertising job, she turned down an offer to teach history in a rural high school in Wyoming. Here it would be hard to know why she chose the advertising job, because by taking this job she could accomplish so many things that she could not accomplish by accepting the teaching job—starting a career in advertising, living in a large city, earning more money (see Figure 4.5). In this situation, there would be many noncommon (or unique) effects of the two options. Suppose, however, we knew that Karen had narrowed down her choices to two options: (a) a job with the Hook 'Em Agency, which specializes in cigarette ads, and (b) a job with the Help 'Em Agency, which specializes in public service ads. Suppose, further, that we knew the two jobs paid the same and had the same opportunities for advancement. If we learn that Karen accepted the job at the Help 'Em Agency, we would be more confident about why Karen made the choice she did, because there is only one noncommon effect between the two options: their areas of specialization. Clearly, Karen must have wanted to work on public service ads more than cigarette ads.

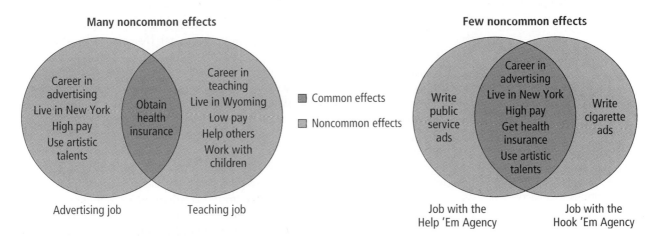

Many noncommon effects

Career in advertising
Live in New York
High pay
Use artistic talents

Obtain health insurance

Career in teaching
Live in Wyoming
Low pay
Help others
Work with children

Advertising job   Teaching job

■ Common effects
□ Noncommon effects

Few noncommon effects

Write public service ads

Career in advertising
Live in New York
High pay
Get health insurance
Use artistic talents

Write cigarette ads

Job with the Help 'Em Agency   Job with the Hook 'Em Agency

■ **FIGURE 4.5 The role of noncommon effects.**   When people can accomplish many things by one action that they cannot accomplish by an alternative action, it can be difficult to tell why they did what they did (see left side of figure). When there are few noncommon effects—when people can accomplish very few things by one action that they cannot accomplish by the other action—it is easier to make an internal attribution for why they did what they did (see right side of figure).

The Role of Expectations in Correspondent Inference Theory

Think back to our example about Karen. Suppose we know she was deciding between two jobs that were nearly identical, except that one paid $50,000 a year and the other paid $10,000 a year. Since there is only one noncommon effect—the amount of pay—we should be able to make a confident, internal attribution about Karen once we know which job she chooses. But can we? What if Karen chooses the $50,000 job over the $10,000 job? Have we really learned anything about Karen? Not really; everyone would take the high-paying job over the low-paying one if everything else was equal. Thus, a person's behavior may be uninformative even when it involves one noncommon effect, because the behavior is what we'd expect everyone to do (Jones, 1990). We learn more about people when the noncommon effects are something that not everyone would have chosen to accomplish. If Karen chose the $10,000 job instead of the $50,000 job,

■ We learn more about people when they behave in unexpected ways than when they behave in expected ways. Here, President Bill Clinton and Russian President Boris Yeltsin act decidedly "unpresidential"!

this action would be so unexpected—and so unlike what most people would do—that we would feel we'd learned something about her (for example, she has no sense when it comes to the value of money.)

Two different types of expectations come into play here: category-based expectancies and target-based expectancies (Jones & McGillis, 1976; Weisz & Jones, 1993). **Category-based expectancies** refer to expectations about people based on groups to which they belong. For example, you might be surprised to learn that Mick Jagger graduated from the London School of Economics, a very prestigious institution, for this is not the typical background or behavior of a rock-and-roll star. **Target-based expectancies** refer to how you expect a particular person to behave, based on his or her past actions. For example, many people were very surprised when, in 1995, former President George Bush publically withdrew his membership in the National Rifle Association, a group that he had supported and that had supported him in the past. In both examples, you would make a correspondent inference—the assumption that Mick Jagger's and George Bush's behaviors match their dispositions.

In sum, making attributions, according to correspondent inference theory, is kind of like being a detective. When we try to deduce why someone behaved the way he or she did, the culprits are the various things the person might have been trying to accomplish (the effects of his or her actions). We reduce the number of possibilities by examining what the person could have accomplished by behaving in some alternative manner (Jones, 1990; Newtson, 1974). We also take into account how much we expected people to do what they did, for unexpected actions are much more diagnostic of what someone is really like than expected actions are.

The Covariation Model: Internal versus External Attributions

Harold Kelley (1967) took a somewhat different approach when he developed his theory of attribution. Whereas Jones and Davis (1965) focused on the information people use to make a dispositional (internal) attribution, Kelley (1967) focused on the first step in the process of social perception—how people decide whether to make an internal or an external attribution. Another difference between the two theories is that correspondent inference theory applies to a single observation of a behavior (e.g., your friend refuses to lend you his car), whereas Kelley's (1967) **covariation model** applies to multiple instances of behavior, occurring across time and across different situations (e.g., Did your friend refuse to lend you his car in the past? Does he lend it to other people? Does he dislike lending you other possessions of his?).

Kelley (like Heider before him) assumes that when we are in the process of forming an attribution, we gather information, or data, that will help us reach a judgment. The data we use, according to Kelley, are how a person's behavior covaries across time, place, different actors, and different targets of the behavior. By discovering covariation in people's behavior (e.g., your friend refuses to lend you his car; he agrees to lend it to others), you are able to reach a judgment about what caused their behavior.

When we are forming an attribution, what kinds of information do we examine for covariation? Kelley (1967) states there are three important types of information: *consensus*, *distinctiveness*, and *consistency*. Let's describe these three through an example: You are working at your part-time job in a clothing store and you observe your boss yelling at another employee, Hannah, telling her in no uncertain terms that she's an idiot. Without any conscious effort on your part,

---

Category-Based Expectancies
expectations about people based on the groups to which they belong, such as expecting someone to love going to parties because he or she belongs to a party-loving fraternity or sorority

Target-Based Expectancies
expectations about a person based on his or her past actions, such as expecting someone to go to the beach on vacation because he or she has always gone to the beach in the past

Covariation Model
a theory which states that in order to form an attribution about what caused a person's behavior, we systematically note the pattern between the presence (or absence) of possible causal factors and whether or not the behavior occurs

you pose that attributional question: "Why is the boss yelling at Hannah and being so critical—is it something about the boss, or is it something about the situation that surrounds and affects him?"

Now let's look at how Kelley's (1967) model of covariation assessment answers this question. **Consensus information** refers to how other people behave toward the same stimulus—in this case, Hannah. Do other people at work also yell at Hannah and criticize her? **Distinctiveness information** refers to how the actor (the person whose behavior we are trying to explain) responds to other stimuli. Does the boss yell at and demean other employees in the store? **Consistency information** refers to the frequency with which the observed behavior between the same actor and the same stimulus occurs across time and circumstances. Does the boss yell at and criticize Hannah regularly and frequently, whether the store is busy with customers or empty?

According to Kelley's theory, when these three sources of information combine into one of two distinct patterns, a clear attribution can be made. People are most likely to make an *internal attribution* (deciding the behavior was due to something about the boss) when the consensus and distinctiveness of the act are low but its consistency is high (Figure 4.6). We would be pretty confident that the boss yelled at Hannah because he is a mean and vindictive person if we knew that no one else yells at Hannah, that the boss yells at other employees, and that the boss yells at Hannah every chance he gets. People are likely to make an *external attribution* (in this case, about Hannah) if consensus, distinctiveness, and consistency are all high. Finally, when consistency is low we cannot make a clear internal or external attribution and so resort to a special kind of external or *situational*

Consensus Information information about the extent to which other people behave the same way toward the same stimulus as the actor does

Distinctiveness Information information about the extent to which one particular actor behaves in the same way to different stimuli

Consistency Information information about the extent to which the behavior between one actor and one stimulus is the same across time and circumstances

■ **FIGURE 4.6 The covariation model.** Why did the Boss yell at his employee Hannah? To decide whether a behavior was caused by internal, or dispositional factors, or external, or situational factors, people use consensus, distinctiveness, and consistency information.

Why did the Boss yell at his employee, Hannah?			
People are likely to make an *internal attribution*—it was something about the Boss—if they see this behavior as	*low* in consensus: the Boss is the only person working in the store who yells at Hannah	*low* in distinctiveness: the Boss yells at all the employees	*high* in consistency: the Boss yells at Hannah almost every time he sees her
People are likely to make an *external attribution*—it was something about Hannah—if they see this behavior as	*high* in consensus: all of the employees yell at Hannah too	*high* in distinctiveness: the Boss doesn't yell at any of the other employees	*high* in consistency: the Boss yells at Hannah almost every time he sees her
People are likely to think it was something peculiar about the particular circumstances in which the Boss yelled at Hannah if they see this behavior as	*low or high* in consensus	*low or high* in distinctiveness	*low* in consistency: this is the first time that the Boss has yelled at Hannah

// *Try It* !

Listen as People Make Attributions

Forming attributions is a major part of daily life—note the Ann Landers column on page 135! You can watch the attribution process in action too. All it takes is a group of friends and an interesting topic to discuss. Perhaps one of your friends is telling you about something that happened to her that day, or perhaps your group is discussing another person whom everybody knows. As they talk, pay very close attention to what they say. They will be trying to figure out why the person being discussed did what she did or said what he said. In other words, they will be making attributions. Your job is to try to keep track of their comments and label the attributional strategies they are using.

In particular, do they make internal attributions, about a person's character or personality, or do they make situational attributions, about all the other events and variables that make up a person's life? Do your friends seem to prefer one type of attribution over the other? If their interpretation is dispositional, what happens when you suggest another possible interpretation, one that is situational? Do they agree or disagree with you? What kinds of information do they offer as "proof" that their attribution is right?

Observing people when they are making attributions in real conversations will show you just how common and powerful this type of thinking is when people are trying to understand each other.

//

attribution, one that assumes something unusual or peculiar is going on in these circumstances—for example, the boss just received very upsetting news and lost his temper with the first person he saw.

Both correspondent inference theory and the covariation model assume that people make causal attributions in a rational, logical fashion. People observe the clues, such as the distinctiveness of the act, and then draw a logical inference about why the person did what he or she did. Several studies have confirmed that people often do make attributions the way that Jones and Davis's (1965) and Kelley's (1967) models say they should (Fosterling, 1989; Gilbert, 1998; Hazelwood & Olson, 1986; Hewstone & Jaspars, 1987; Major, 1980; Ruble & Feldman, 1976; Zuckerman, 1978)—with one exception. In research studies, people don't use consensus information as much as Kelley's theory predicted; they rely more on consistency and distinctiveness information when forming attributions (McArthur, 1972; Wright, Luus, & Christie, 1990).

To summarize, correspondent inference theory and the covariation model portray people as master detectives, deducing the causes of behavior as systematically and logically as Sherlock Holmes would. However, as we see in Chapters 3 and 6, people sometimes aren't that accurate or rational when forming judgments about others. Sometimes they distort information to satisfy their need for high self-esteem (see Chapter 6). Other times they use mental shortcuts that, while often helpful, can lead to inaccurate judgments (see Chapter 3). Unfortunately, the attributions we make are sometimes just plain wrong. In the next section, we will discuss some specific errors or biases that plague the attribution process. One shortcut is very common, at least in Western cultures: The idea that people do what they do because of the kind of people they are, not because of the situation they are in. This has been termed the fundamental attribution error.

The Fundamental Attribution Error: People as Personality Psychologists

In the early morning of August 31, 1997 Diana, Princess of Wales, died in a car accident in Paris. The world-wide reaction was immediate—disbelief, horror, and unmitigated sorrow. Nowhere was the public response stronger than in her own country of Great Britain. Bouquets of flowers were left in memorial at Buckingham Palace and at her home, Kensington Palace—so many flowers that they covered acres of grounds. People waited in line for over 12 hours just so they could pay their respects and share their feelings of loss in special remembrance books. But what was most striking was the way the British people and the media turned against the royal family. During that week, the royal family had remained in seclusion in Scotland at Balmoral Castle. The British people and the media accused Queen Elizabeth and Charles, Prince of Wales, of being aloof and uncaring about the Princess' death, in marked contrast to their own reaction of deep and very public grieving. The major newspapers openly criticized the Queen (an unheard of event in Britain), running headlines like "Where is our Queen?," "Your people are suffering, speak to us, Ma'am," and "Show us you care" (Hoge, 1997).

The British public had made a strong and negative dispositional attribution about the Queen's absence and silence during that week: She was a cold, uncaring woman who had never liked Diana and wasn't as upset by her death as they were.

■ Immediately after the death of Diana, Princess of Wales, the Queen of England was openly and strongly criticized by the British people and the media for her lack of grief. Stung by this criticism; the royal family took the the unprecedented step of responding to public criticism; the Queen had stayed in seclusion in Scotland because this was the best thing to do for her grieving grandsons. It appears that the British people and press had made the fundamental attribution error, thinking the Queen's behavior was due to her disposition instead of the situation. In this photograph, the royal family has returned to London in response to the criticism; Prince Charles and the Princes William and Harry mingled with Londoners and paid their respects at the public memorial of flower bouquets.

Stung by this criticism and antagonism on the part of the people, the Queen's press secretary released a statement, saying "The Royal family have been hurt by suggestions that they are indifferent to the country's sorrow at the tragic death of the Princess of Wales" (Hoge, 1997; p. A1). Queen Elizabeth then conducted her first-ever, unscheduled television statement to the British people, assuring them that she was grieving too. Why had she remained behind closed doors in Scotland? The Palace offered a situational explanation: "Prince William and Prince Henry [Diana's sons] themselves want to be with their father and grandparents at this time in the quiet haven of Balmoral. As their grandmother, the Queen is helping the Princes to come to terms with their loss" (Hoge, 1997; p. A1). Thus, the Queen had been absent from London not because she is a remote, aloof individual who didn't care about Princess Diana's death (a dispositional attribution); she chose to stay at Balmoral because her grieving grandsons needed her and needed to be in a secluded setting, where the media could not intrude (a situational attribution) (Hoge, 1997; Lyall, 1997).

The pervasive, fundamental theory or schema most of us have about human behavior is that people do what they do because of the kind of people they are, not because of the situation they are in. When thinking this way, we are more like personality psychologists, who see behavior as stemming from internal dispositions and traits, than social psychologists, who focus on the impact of social situations on behavior. This bias toward being personality psychologists is so pervasive that social psychologist Lee Ross (1977) termed it the **fundamental attribution error** (Heider, 1958; Jones, 1990; Ross & Nisbett, 1991).

There have been many empirical demonstrations of the tendency to see people's behavior as a reflection of their dispositions and beliefs, rather than as influenced by the situation (Allison et al., 1993; Miller, Ashton, & Mishal, 1990). Edward Jones and Victor Harris (1967), for example, asked college students to read an essay written by a fellow student that either supported or opposed Fidel Castro's rule in Cuba and then to guess how the author of the essay really felt about Castro (see Figure 4.7). In one condition, the researchers told the students that the author freely chose which position to take in the essay, thereby making it easy to guess how he really felt. If he chose to write in favor of Castro, then

Fundamental Attribution Error
the tendency to overestimate the extent to which people's behavior is due to internal, dispositional factors, and to underestimate the role of situational factors

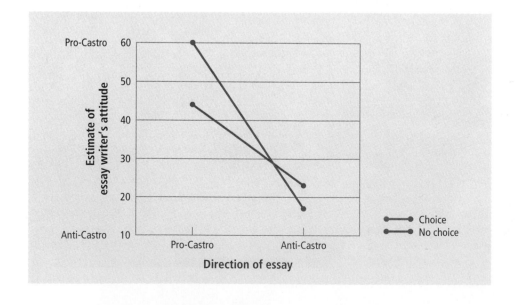

■ **FIGURE 4.7 The fundamental attribution error.** Even when people knew that the author's choice of an essay topic was externally caused (i.e., in the no-choice condition), they assumed that what he wrote reflected how he really felt about Castro. That is, they made an internal attribution from his behavior. (Adapted from Jones & Harris, 1967)

clearly he must indeed be sympathetic to Castro. In another condition, however, the students learned that the author did not have any choice about which position to take—he had been assigned the position as a participant in a debate. Logically, if we know someone could not choose the topic, we should not assume the writer believes what he or she wrote. Yet the participants in this study, and in the dozens of others like it, assumed that the author really believed what he wrote, even when they knew he could not choose which position to take. As seen in Figure 4.7, people moderated their guesses a little bit—there was not as much difference in people's estimates of the author's attitude in the pro-Castro and anti-Castro conditions—but they still assumed that the content of the essay reflected the author's true feelings.

Why is the tendency to explain behavior in terms of people's dispositions called the fundamental attribution error? It is not always wrong to make an internal attribution; clearly, people often do what they do because of the kind of people they are. However, there is ample evidence that social situations can have a large impact on behavior; indeed, the major lesson of social psychology is that these influences can be extremely powerful. The point of the fundamental attribution error is that people tend to underestimate these influences when explaining other people's behavior. Even when a situational constraint on behavior is obvious, as in the Jones and Harris (1967) experiment, people persist in making internal attributions (Lord et al., 1997; Newman, 1996; Ross, 1977; Ross, Amabile, & Steinmetz, 1977; Ross & Nisbett, 1991).

The Role of Perceptual Salience in the Fundamental Attribution Error

Why do people commit the fundamental attribution error? One reason is that when we try to explain someone's behavior, our focus of attention is usually on the person, not on the surrounding situation (Heider, 1958; Jones & Nisbett, 1971). In fact, as Daniel Gilbert and Patrick Malone (1995) have pointed out, the situational causes of another person's behavior are practically invisible to us. If we don't know what happened to a person earlier in the day (e.g., she received an F on her midterm), we can't use that situational information to help us understand her current behavior. Even when we know "her situation," we still don't know how she interprets it—for example, the F may not have upset her, because she's planning to drop the course anyway. If we don't know the meaning of the situation for her, we can't accurately judge its effects on her behavior. Thus, information about the situational causes of behavior is frequently unavailable to us and/or difficult to interpret accurately (Gilbert & Malone, 1995).

What information does that leave us? While the situation may be close to invisible, the individual is extremely perceptually prominent—people are what our eyes and ears notice. And as Heider (1958) pointed out, what we notice seems to be the reasonable and logical cause of the observed behavior.

Several studies have confirmed the importance of perceptual salience—in particular, an elegant one by Shelley Taylor and Susan Fiske (1975). In this study, two male students engaged in a "get acquainted" conversation. (They were actually both accomplices of the experimenters and were following a specific script during their conversation.) At each session, six actual research participants also took part. They sat in assigned seats, surrounding the two conversationalists (see Figure 4.8). Two of them sat on each side of the actors; they had a clear, profile view of both individuals. Two observers sat behind each actor; they could see the back of one actor's head but the face of the other. Thus, who was visually

> Be not swept off your feet by the vividness of the impression, but say "Impression, wait for me a little. Let me see what you are and what you represent."
> —Epictetus, *Discourses*

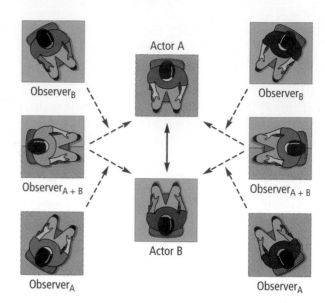

■ **FIGURE 4.8 Manipulating perceptual salience.** This is the seating arrangement for two actors and the six research participants in the Taylor and Fiske study. Participants rated each actor's impact on the conversation. Researchers found that people rated the actor they could see most clearly as having the largest role in the conversation. (Adapted from Taylor and Fiske, 1975)

salient—that is, who the participants could see the best—was cleverly manipulated in this study.

After the conversation, the research participants were asked questions about the two men—for example, who had taken the lead in the conversation and who had chosen the topics to be discussed? As you can see in Figure 4.9, the person whom they could see the best was the person who they thought had the most impact on the conversation. Even though all the observers heard the same conversation, those who were facing student A thought he had taken the lead and chosen the topics, whereas those who were facing student B thought he had taken the lead and chosen the topics. In comparison, those who could see both students equally well thought both were equally influential. **Perceptual salience,** or our visual point of view, helps explain why the fundamental attribution error is so widespread. We focus our attention more on people than on the surrounding situation because the situation is so hard to see or know; we underestimate (or even forget about) the influence of the situation when we are explaining human behavior. But this is only part of the story. Why should the simple fact that we are focused on a person make us exaggerate the extent to which that person is the cause of his or her actions?

The culprit is one of the mental shortcuts we discussed in Chapter 3; the *anchoring/adjustment heuristic.* We saw several examples in which people began with a reference point when making a judgment and then did not adjust sufficiently away from this point. The fundamental attribution error is another byproduct of this shortcut. When making attributions, people use the focus of their attention as a starting point. For example, when we hear someone argue strongly in favor of Castro's regime in Cuba, our first inclination is to explain this in dispositional terms: "This person must hold radical political views." We realize this explanation might not be the whole story, however. We might think, "On the other hand, I know he was assigned this position as part of a debate," and adjust our attributions more toward a situational explanation. However, the problem is that people often don't adjust their judgments enough. In the Jones and Harris (1967) experiment, participants who knew the essay writer did not have a

Perceptual Salience
information that is the focus of people's attention; people tend to overestimate the causal role of perceptually salient information

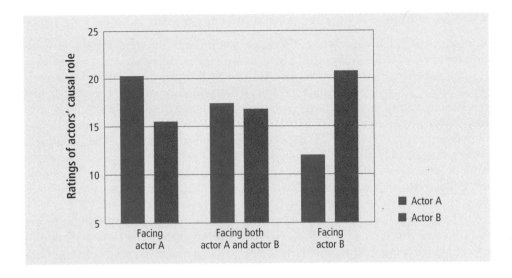

■ **FIGURE 4.9 The effects of perceptual salience.** These are the ratings of each actor's causal role in the conversation. People thought that the actor they could see the best had the most impact on the conversation. (Adapted from Taylor & Fiske, 1975)

choice of topics nevertheless thought he believed what he had written, at least to some extent. They adjusted insufficiently from their anchor, the position advocated in the essay.

In sum, people go through a **two-step process** when they make attributions (Gilbert, 1989, 1991, 1993; Krull, 1993). They begin by making an internal attribution, assuming that a person's behavior was due to something about him or her. They then attempt to adjust this attribution by taking into account the situation the person was in. As we have seen, people often do not make enough of an adjustment in this second step. An interesting implication of this fact is that if people are distracted or preoccupied when explaining someone's behavior, they might not get to the second step, thereby making an even more extreme internal attribution. Why? Because the initial step (making the internal attribution) occurs quickly and spontaneously, whereas the second step (adjusting for the situation) requires more effort and conscious attention.

Daniel Gilbert and colleagues have performed several experiments that support this view. Subjects in his studies are asked to explain why someone did what he or she did, but are distracted by having to do something else at the same time, such as remembering an eight-digit number. These subjects make even more extreme internal attributions than subjects who are not distracted because they are unable to mentally adjust their initial impression that the person's behavior emanated solely from within him or her, uninfluenced by the situation (Gilbert & Osborne, 1989; Gilbert, Pelham, & Krull, 1988).

Thus, perceivers who are distracted or cognitively "busy" will be more likely to commit the fundamental attribution error because they stop at the first step—making a dispositional attribution—and they don't proceed to the second, more effortful step—checking for possible situational explanations. However, perceivers will engage in this second step of attributional processing if they consciously slow down and think carefully before they reach a judgment; if they are motivated to reach as accurate a judgment as possible; or if they are suspicious about the behavior of the target person, for example, believing that he or she is lying or has ulterior motives (Burger, 1991; Fein, 1996; Hilton, Fein, & Miller, 1993; Webster, 1993).

Two-Step Process of Attribution
when people analyze another person's behavior, they typically make an internal attribution automatically (the first step in the process); they may then consciously choose to engage in the effortful, second step in the process, where they think about possible situational reasons for the behavior; after engaging in the second step, they may adjust their original internal attribution to take into account situational factors

The Role of Culture in the Fundamental Attribution Error

Recent research has suggested a second reason for why the fundamental attribution error occurs: Western culture, which emphasizes individual freedom and autonomy, socializes us to prefer dispositional attributions over situational ones (Dix, 1993; Rholes, Newman, & Ruble, 1990). In comparison, collectivist (often Eastern) cultures emphasize group membership, interdependence, and conformity to group norms (Fletcher & Ward, 1988; Markus & Kitayama, 1991; Newman, 1991; Triandis, 1990; Zebrowitz-McArthur, 1988). These cultural values suggest that people would be socialized to prefer situational dispositions over dispositional ones. As a result of this very different socialization, do people in collectivist cultures make fewer fundamental attribution errors than Westerners do?

To find out, Joan Miller (1984) asked people of two cultures—Hindus living in India and Americans living in the United States—to think of various examples of behaviors performed by their friends and to explain why those behaviors occurred. Consistent with what we've said so far, the American participants preferred dispositional explanations for the behaviors. They were more likely to say that the causes of their friends' behaviors were the kind of people they were, rather than the situation or context in which the behaviors occurred. In contrast, Hindu participants preferred situational explanations for their friends' behaviors (Miller, 1984).

"But," you might be thinking, "perhaps the Americans and Hindus generated different kinds of examples. Perhaps the Hindus thought of behaviors that really were more situationally caused, whereas the Americans thought of behaviors that really were more dispositionally caused." To test this alternative hypothesis, Miller (1984) took some of the behaviors generated by the Hindu participants and gave them to Americans to explain. The difference in internal and external attributions was again observed: Americans preferred dispositional causes for the behaviors that the Hindus had thought were situationally caused.

The cultural explanation of the fundamental attribution error received further support from a clever study that compared newspaper articles in Chinese- and English-language newspapers. Michael Morris and Kaiping Peng (1994) targeted two very similar crimes, both mass murders, one committed by a Chinese graduate student in Iowa, and one committed by a Caucasian postal worker in Michigan. The researchers coded all the news articles about the two crimes that appeared in the *New York Times* and the *World Journal,* a Chinese-language U.S. newspaper. As you can see in Figure 4.10, journalists writing in English made significantly more dispositional attributions about both mass murderers than journalists writing in Chinese did. For example, American reporters described one murderer as a "darkly disturbed man" with a "sinister edge" to his personality. Chinese reporters, when describing the same murderer, emphasized more situational causes, such as "not getting along with his advisor" and his "isolation from the Chinese community."

Thus, people in Western cultures appear to be more like personality psychologists, viewing behavior in dispositional terms. When making attributions about others, the initial, automatic, and effortless attribution tends to be dispositional. Only if they are motivated to think more deeply will they come up with situational explanations. In contrast, people in Eastern cultures seem to be more like social psychologists, viewing behavior in situational terms. Their initial, auto-

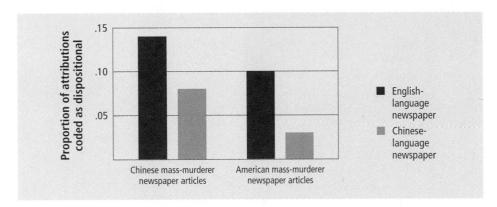

■ FIGURE 4.10   The role of culture in the fundamental attribution error.   Newspaper articles about two murderers, appearing in English- and Chinese-language newspapers, were coded for the types of attributions made. Journalists writing in English made significantly more dispositional attributions about both the Chinese and Anglo-American murderer than did journalists writing in Chinese. (Source: Adapted from Morris & Peng, 1994)

matic, and effortless attribution tends to be situational, and again, only if they are motivated to engage in more cognitive work will they come up with possible dispositional attributions (Krull, 1993).

A recent and elegant study shows just these effects in action. Fiona Lee, Mark Hallahan, and Thaddeus Herzog (1996) compared the attributions made in newspaper articles in the United States and Hong Kong. Consistent with prior research, they hypothesized that articles in U.S. papers would explain events more dispositionally, while articles in Hong Kong papers would explain the same events more situationally. However, they also compared two different types of articles—editorials and sports stories. First, they hypothesized that writing editorials would require more cognitive effort than writing sports stories, for the following reasons: As compared to sports writers, editorial writers deal with more uncertain and ambiguous topics; their topics are open to many alternative points of view; and they are directly and personally responsible for their ideas. Second, because editorials are particularly effortful to write, the researchers hypothesized that the second step in the *two-step process of attribution* was more likely to occur for editorial writers than for sports writers. Thus, the initial tendency to write dispositionally in the U.S. and situationally in Hong Kong should decrease for editorials, as U.S. writers make the effort to think of situational causes and Hong Kong writers make the effort to think of dispositional causes.

As you can see in Figure 4.11, this is just what Fiona Lee and her colleagues (1996) found. The straightforward sports articles showed the effect of a culture bias: U.S. writers made more dispositional attributions about events in soccer games, and Hong Kong writers made more situational attributions about events in their soccer games. However, when it came to the more cognitively effortful editorial articles, writers in both countries engaged in the second step of attribution formation. They corrected their initial tendency (for U.S. writers, to be dispositional; for Hong Kong writers, to be situational), and included the opposite type of attribution as well. U.S. editorial writers became less dispositional and Hong Kong writers became less situational. Thus, culture does appear to play a role in whether perceivers are overly dispositional (the fundamental attribution error) or

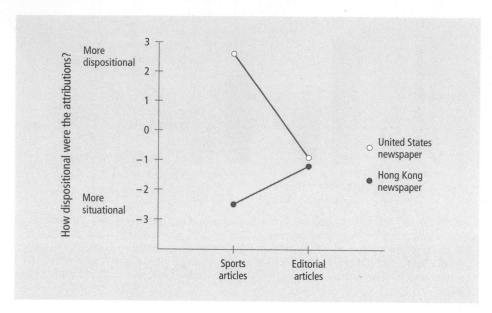

■ **FIGURE 4.11** **Culture and the two-step process of making attributions.** Two types of newspaper articles, editorials and sports stories, were coded for dispositional and situational attributions in U.S. and Hong Kong newspapers. Sports stories, the less cognitively effortful of the two types to write, showed the culture bias: U.S. sports articles contained more dispositional attributions and Hong Kong sports articles contained more situational attributions. In comparison, editorial articles showed a very different pattern. By engaging in the second step of processing, both U.S. and Hong Kong writers corrected their tendency to use one type of attribution more than the other. As a result, attributions in editorial articles showed a mix of situational and dispositional attributions in both countries. (Adapted from Lee, Hallahan, & Herzog, 1996)

overly situational. However, cognitive effort can bring these extreme attributions to a more moderate, mixed level—and this second stage of processing occurs cross-culturally.

The Actor/Observer Difference

An interesting twist on the fundamental attribution error is that it does not apply to our attributions about ourselves to the same extent that it applies to our attributions about other people. While we tend to see others' behavior as dispositionally caused (the fundamental attribution error), we are less likely to rely so extensively on dispositional attributions when we are explaining our own behavior. Instead, we frequently make situational attributions about why we did what we did. Thus, an interesting attributional dilemma is created: The same action can trigger dispositional attributions in people observing the action and situational attributions in the person performing the action. This is called the **actor/observer difference** (Frank & Gilovich, 1989; Herzog, 1994; Johnson & Boyd, 1995; Jones & Nisbett, 1972; Nisbett et al., 1973; Robins, Spranca, & Mendelsohn, 1996). The letter to Ann Landers on the next page is an interesting demonstration of the actor/observer difference. The writer is very aware of the external forces that are affecting her life and shaping her behavior. Ann Landers, however, will have none of it. Ann responds with a strong, internal attribution—the woman herself, not

Actor/Observer Difference
the tendency to see other people's behavior as dispositionally caused, while focusing more on the role of situational factors when explaining one's own behavior

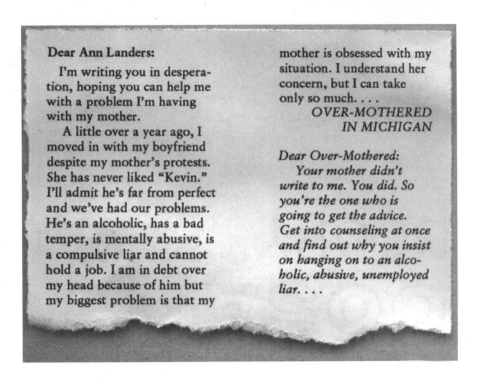

Dear Ann Landers:

I'm writing you in desperation, hoping you can help me with a problem I'm having with my mother.

A little over a year ago, I moved in with my boyfriend despite my mother's protests. She has never liked "Kevin." I'll admit he's far from perfect and we've had our problems. He's an alcoholic, has a bad temper, is mentally abusive, is a compulsive liar and cannot hold a job. I am in debt over my head because of him but my biggest problem is that my mother is obsessed with my situation. I understand her concern, but I can take only so much. . . .
OVER-MOTHERED
IN MICHIGAN

Dear Over-Mothered:
Your mother didn't write to me. You did. So you're the one who is going to get the advice. Get into counseling at once and find out why you insist on hanging on to an alcoholic, abusive, unemployed liar. . . .

■ The letter and its response depict actor/observer differences in attribution. Schoeneman and Rubanowitz (1985) examined letters to the "Dear Ann Landers" and "Dear Abby" advice columns and found strong evidence for actor/observer differences. The letter writers tended to attribute their problems to external factors (e.g., this letter writer says her biggest problem is her mother), whereas the advice columnists tended to make dispositional attributions to the letter writers (e.g., "Get into counseling at once"). (From the *Boston Globe,* September 10, 1991)

her situation, is the cause of her problems. As you might guess, the actor/observer difference can lead to some striking disagreements between people. Why, at times, do the attributions made by actors and observers diverge so sharply?

Perceptual Salience Revisited

One reason for such divergence is our old friend perceptual salience (Jones & Nisbett, 1972). As we said earlier, just as we notice other people's behavior more than their situation, so too do we notice our own situation more than our own behavior. None of us is so egotistic or self-centered that we walk through life holding up a full-length mirror in order to observe ourselves constantly. We are looking outward; what is perceptually salient to us is other people, objects, and the events that unfold. We don't (and can't) pay as much attention to ourselves. Thus, when the actor and the observer think about what caused a given behavior, they are swayed by the information that is most salient and noticeable to them: the actor for the observer and the situation for the actor.

Michael Storms (1973) conducted a fascinating experiment that demonstrates the role of perceptual salience in both the fundamental attribution error and the actor/observer difference. In a design reminiscent of the Taylor and Fiske (1975) study presented earlier, Storms (1973) seated groups of four research participants in a special way (see Figure 4.12). Two of them were going to chat with each other (actor A and actor B), and two of them would observe this conversation, focusing on one of the conversationalists (observer of A and observer of B). In addition, two video cameras were present; one filmed actor A's face, and the other filmed actor B's face.

Following the conversation, the four participants were asked to make attributions about themselves (for actors) or about the actor they were watching (for observers). For example, they were asked to what extent the actor's behavior was

> **R**esemblances are the shadows of differences. Different people see different similarities and similar differences.
> –Vladimir Nabokov,
> *Pale Fire,* 1962

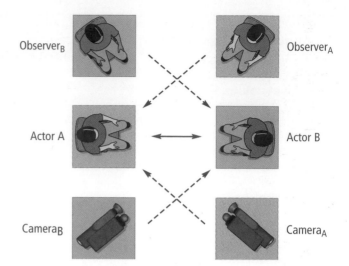

■ **FIGURE 4.12   Seating arrangements in the Storms study.**   People's behavior was videotaped, so that some of them could view it later from a different perspective. (Adapted from Storms, 1973)

due to personal characteristics or to characteristics of the situation (the topic of conversation, the behavior of the conversational partner, etc.). Storms (1973) found that the observers attributed more dispositional characteristics to the actor they were watching (demonstrating the fundamental attribution error as in the Taylor & Fiske, 1975, study), whereas the actors made more situational attributions about the same behavior—their own (see the left-hand side of Figure 4.13).

In a particularly elegant addition to the study's design, Storms (1973) showed the videotapes to some of the participants before they made their ratings. Some of them saw on tape what they had experienced live—actor A saw a tape of actor B's face, and actor B saw the videotape of actor A's face; observer A saw a tape of actor A, and observer B saw a tape of actor B. When asked to make causal attributions, these participants showed the same actor/observer difference as before, although the actors made even stronger situational attributions about themselves when they had the chance to sit back and observe their situation again (see middle of Figure 4.13).

■ **FIGURE 4.13   Effects of perceptual salience (visual orientation) on actors' and observers' attributions.** When people got to see their own or another person's behavior from a new orientation (see right-hand side of figure), they made attributions very different from those of people who did not see the behavior from a new orientation (see middle and left-hand side of figure). (Adapted from Storms, 1973)

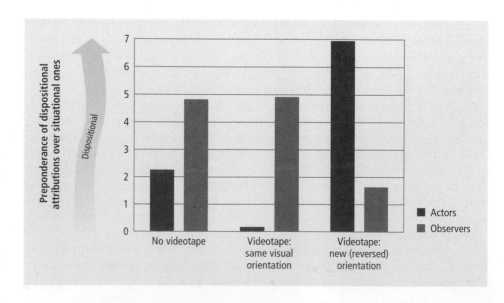

Another group of participants was placed in the most interesting position of all. After the conversation, they saw a videotape that had the opposite visual orientation to the one they had experienced in real life. Actor A and actor B each saw their own face; observer A saw the videotape of actor B, and observer B saw the tape of actor A. Now the object of perceptual salience was completely reversed. How did these participants assign causality? As can be seen on the far right of Figure 4.13, this change in perceptual salience erased the typical actor/observer difference. After looking at themselves, actors made more dispositional attributions. After looking at their actor's (the conversational partner's) situation, observers made more situational attributions about their actor.

The Role of Information Availability in the Actor/Observer Difference

The actor/observer difference occurs for another reason as well. Actors have more information about themselves than observers do (Jones & Nisbett, 1972; Greenwald & Banaji, 1989; Malle & Knobe, 1997). Actors know how they've behaved over the years; they know what happened to them that morning. They are far more aware than observers are of both the similarities and the differences in their behavior across time and across situations. In Kelley's (1967) terms, actors have far more consistency and distinctiveness information about themselves than observers do. For example, if you are behaving in a quiet, shy fashion at a party, an observer is likely to make a dispositional attribution about you—"Gee, that person is quite an introvert." In fact, you may know that this is not your typical way of responding to a party setting. Perhaps you are shy only at parties where you don't know anyone, or you might be tired, or depressed by some recent bad news. Thus, it is not surprising that actors' self-attributions often reflect situational factors, because they know more about how their behavior varies from one situation to the next than do most observers, who see them in limited contexts.

So far, our discussion of the mental shortcuts people use when making attributions has covered the role of priming, accessibility, perceptual salience, information availability, and culture. But what about a person's needs, desires, hopes, and fears—do these more emotional factors also create biases in our attributions? Are you motivated to see the world in certain ways because these views make you feel better, about both yourself and life in general? The answer is yes. The shortcuts we will discuss below have a *motivational basis;* they are attributions that protect our self-esteem and our belief that the world is a safe and just place.

Self-Serving Attributions

Imagine that Bill goes to his chemistry class one day with some apprehension because he will find out how he did on the midterm. The professor gives him his exam. Bill turns it over. He sees that he has received an A. What will Bill think is the reason for why he got such a good grade? It probably will come as no surprise that people tend to take personal credit for their successes, but explain away their failures as due to external events that were outside their control. Thus, Bill is likely to think that his success was due to him—he's good at chemistry and just plain smart.

How can we explain this departure from the typical actor/observer pattern of attributions? The answer is that when people's self-esteem is threatened, they often make **self-serving attributions**. Simply put, these attributions refer to our tendency to take credit for our successes (by making internal attributions) but to

Self-Serving Attributions explanations for one's successes that credit internal, dispositional factors and explanations for one's failures that blame external, situational factors

■ An interesting arena for studying self-serving attributions is sports. We can conjecture about what kind of attributions were made by Houston Comet Tammy Jackson (23) and New York Liberty's Vickie Johnson (55) and Kym Hampton (34) after the Comets won the first WBNA championship game.

blame others (or the situation) for our failures (Miller & Ross, 1975). Many studies have shown that people make internal attributions when they do well on a task but make external attributions when they do poorly (Carver, DeGregorio, & Gillis, 1980; Davis & Stephan, 1980; Elig & Frieze, 1979; McAllister, 1996; Whitley & Frieze, 1985).

A particularly interesting arena for studying self-serving attributions is professional sports. For example, Richard Lau and Dan Russell (1980) examined the explanations made by professional athletes and coaches for why their team won or lost a game. When explaining their victories, the athletes and coaches overwhelmingly pointed to aspects of their own teams or players; in fact, 80 percent of the attributions for wins were to such internal factors. When explaining why the New York Yankees defeated the Los Angeles Dodgers in game 4 of the 1977 World Series, Yankees' manager Billy Martin attributed it to a player on his team: "Piniella has done it all" (Lau & Russell, 1980). Losses were more likely to be attributed to things external to one's own team. For example, members of the Dodgers attributed their loss not to their inferior ability or poor play but instead to bad luck or the superior play of the Yankees. In the words of Tommy Lasorda, the Dodgers' manager, "It took a great team to beat us, and the Yankees definitely are a great team" (Lau & Russell, 1980).

Who is more likely to make self-serving attributions? Scott Roesch and James Amirkham (1997) explored this idea, also within the realm of sports. They wondered if a player's skill, experience, and type of sport (team sports versus solo sports like tennis) affected the type of attribution he or she made about a sports outcome. The researchers found that less experienced athletes were more likely to make self-serving attributions than experienced ones. Experienced athletes realize that losses sometimes are their fault and that wins are not always due to them. Highly skilled athletes made more self-serving attributions than those with lower ability. The highly talented athlete believes success is due to his or her prowess while failure, an unusual (and upsetting) outcome, is due to teammates or other circumstances of the game. Finally, athletes in solo sports made more self-serving attributions than those in team sports. Solo athletes know that winning and losing rests on their shoulders.

Why do people make self-serving attributions? As pointed out in our discussion of cognitive dissonance theory in Chapter 6, people try to maintain their self-esteem whenever possible, even if that means distorting reality by changing a cognition. Here we see a specific attributional strategy that can be used to maintain or raise self-esteem—just locate "causality" where it does you the most good (Brown & Rogers, 1991; Greenberg, Pyszczynski, & Solomon, 1982; Ickes & Layden, 1978; Miller & Ross, 1975; Snyder & Higgins, 1988).

A second reason has to do with how we present ourselves to other people (Goffman, 1959). We want people to think well of us and to admire us. Telling others that our poor performance was due to some external cause is such a self-presentational strategy—in fact, we sometimes call it "making excuses"! (Greenberg et al., 1982; Tetlock, 1981; Weary & Arkin, 1981).

A third reason people make self-serving attributions has to do with our earlier discussion about the kind of information that is available to people. Let's imagine the attributional process of another student in the chemistry class, Dexter, who did poorly on the midterm. Dexter knows that he studied very hard for the midterm, that he typically does well on chemistry tests, and that in general he is a very good student. The D on the chemistry midterm comes as a surprise. The most logical attribution Dexter can make is that the test was unfair—the D grade wasn't due to a lack of ability or effort on his part. The professor, however, knows that some students did well on the test; thus, given the information that is available to the professor, it is logical for him or her to conclude that Dexter, and not the fact that it was a difficult test, was responsible for the poor grade (Miller & Ross, 1975; Nisbett & Ross, 1980).

People also alter their attributions to deal with other kinds of threats to their self-esteem. One of the hardest things to understand in life is the occurrence of

Try It!

Self-Serving Attributions in the Sports Pages

Do athletes and coaches tend to take credit for their wins but make excuses for their losses? Find out for yourself the next time you read the sports section of the newspaper or watch television interviews after a game. Analyze the sports figures' comments to see what kinds of attributions they make about the cause of their performance. Is the pattern a self-serving one?

For example, after a win, does the athlete make internal attributions like "We won because of excellent teamwork; our defensive line really held today," or "My serve was totally on"? After a loss, does the athlete make external attributions like "All the injuries we've had this season have really hurt us," or "That line judge made every call against me"? According to the research, these self-serving attributions should occur more often than the opposite pattern, for example, where a winner says, "We won because the other team played so badly it was like they were dead" (external), or where a loser says, "I played terribly today. I stunk" (internal).

Next, see if you can find examples that fit Roesch & Amirkham's (1997) research. Are self-serving attributions more common among solo-sport athletes than team-sport athletes? Do the athlete "stars" make more self-serving attributions than their less talented colleagues?

Finally, think about the three reasons we list for why people make self-serving attributions (maintaining self-esteem, presenting yourself positively to others, and personal knowledge about your past performances). When a sports figure makes a self-serving attribution, which one of these three motives do you think is at work? For example, if Michael Jordan attributes his team's loss to factors outside of himself, do you think he is protecting his self-esteem, trying to look good in front of others, or making the most logical attribution he can given his experience (i.e., he's so talented, most team losses aren't his fault!)?

Defensive Attributions
explanations for behavior that avoid feelings of vulnerability and mortality

Unrealistic Optimism
a form of defensive attribution wherein people think that good things are more likely to happen to them than to their peers and that bad things are less likely to happen to them than to their peers

Belief in a Just World
a form of defensive attribution wherein people assume that bad things happen to bad people and that good things happen to good people

tragic events, such as rapes, terminal diseases, and fatal accidents. Even when they happen to strangers we have never met, they can be upsetting. They remind us that if such tragedies can happen to someone else, they can happen to us. Of all the kinds of self-knowledge that we have, the knowledge that we are mortal and that bad things can happen to us is perhaps the hardest to accept (Greenberg, Pyszczynski, & Solomon, 1986; Greening & Chandler, 1997). We thus take steps to deny this fact. One way we do so is by making **defensive attributions**, which are explanations for behavior that defend us from feelings of vulnerability and mortality.

One form of defensive attribution is **unrealistic optimism,** where people believe good things are more likely to happen to them than to others, and bad things are less likely to happen to them than to others (Harris, 1996; Heine & Lehman, 1995; Klein, 1996; Regan, Snyder, & Kassin, 1995; Weinstein & Klein, 1996). Suppose we asked you to estimate how likely it is that each of the following will happen to you, compared to how likely it is that they will happen to other students at your college or university—owning your own home, liking your postgraduate job, living past age 80, having a drinking problem, getting divorced, and being unable to have children. When Neil Weinstein (1980) asked college students these and similar questions, he found that people were too optimistic. Virtually everyone thought that the good things were more likely to happen to them than to their peers and that the bad things were less likely to happen to them than to their peers.

Unrealistic optimism undoubtedly explains what lies behind the popularity of "extreme sports"—athletic activities that take place under very dangerous conditions where the chance of death is definitely present. How can these athletes take such risks? Wendy Middleton and her colleagues (Middleton, Harris, & Surman, 1996) interviewed British bungee jumpers right before they jumped. (To bungee, one ties a high-strength cord around one ankle and then leaps off a very high tower or bridge, free falling, and then bouncing at the end of the tether.) The researchers found strong support for unrealistic optimism among the jumpers: Each jumper perceived his or her own risk of injury to be less than that of the typical jumper. Thus, being overly optimistic is one way people try to protect themselves from unpleasant feelings of mortality.

Sometimes, of course, it's hard to deny that bad things happen in life. We have only to pick up a newspaper to see that people suffer terrible misfortunes every day. How do we deal with these unsettling reminders that bad things happen? One way is by explaining them, to make it seem like they could never happen to us. We do so by believing that bad things happen only to bad people. Melvin Lerner (1980) has called this a **belief in a just world**—the assumption that people get what they deserve and deserve what they get. Because most of us view ourselves as decent, good human beings, then surely bad things won't happen to us (Lipkus, Dalbert, & Siegler, 1996).

The "just world" belief has some sad and even tragic consequences. For example, suppose a female student on your campus was the victim of a date rape by a male fellow student. How do you think you and your friends would react? Would you wonder if she'd done something to trigger the rape? Was she acting suggestively earlier in the evening? Had she invited the man into her room?

Research by Elaine Walster (1966) and others has focused on such attributions, which these investigators call "blaming the victim" (e.g., Burger, 1981; Lerner & Miller, 1978; Stormo, Lang, & Stritzke, 1997). In several experiments, they have found that the victims of crimes or accidents are often seen as causing

■ Research has shown that participants in "extreme sports," like bungee jumping, are unrealistically optimistic, believing that their chances for injury are less than those of other jumpers. This cartoon suggests that some drivers may feel the same way about big city parking.

their fate. For example, not only do people tend to believe that rape victims are to blame for the rape (Bell, Kuriloff, & Lottes, 1994; Burt, 1980), but battered wives are often seen as responsible for their abusive husbands' behavior (Summers & Feldman, 1984). By using this attributional bias, the perceiver does not have to acknowledge that there is a certain randomness in life, that an accident or criminal may be waiting just around the corner for an innocent person—like oneself. The belief in a just world keeps anxious thoughts about one's own safety at bay.

Thus, the belief in a just world is a defensive attribution that helps people maintain their vision of life as safe, orderly, and predictable. Is there a cultural component to it as well? Adrian Furnham (1993) argues that in a society where most people tend to believe the world is a just place, economic and social inequities are considered "fair." In such societies, people believe that the poor and disadvantaged have less because they deserve less. Thus, the just world attribution can be used to explain and justify injustice. Preliminary research suggests that there is cross-cultural variation in the extent to which people use just world attributions, and that this defensive attribution is more prevalent in cultures where there are extremes of wealth and poverty (Dalbert & Yamauchi, 1994; Furnham, 1993; Furnham & Procter, 1989). For example, research participants in India and South Africa received higher scores on the just world belief scale than did participants in the United States, Australia, Hong Kong, and Zimbabwe, who had scores in the middle of the scale. The lowest scoring groups in the sample—those who believed the least in a just world—were the British and Israelis (Furnham, 1993).

How Accurate Are Our Attributions and Impressions?

When we make attributions, our goal is to be able to understand other people and predict what they will do. It is obviously to our advantage to make attributions that are as accurate as possible. But how accurate are we? The answer, in a nutshell, is that under many circumstances we are not very accurate, especially

> Things are seldom as they seem, skim milk masquerades as cream.
> —W.S. Gilbert,
> *H.M.S. Pinafore,* 1878

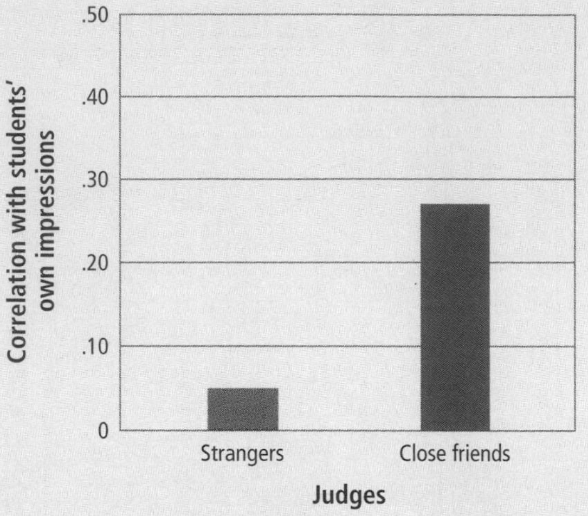

■ **FIGURE 4.14 How accurate are our impressions of other people's personalities?** Strangers watched a videotape of a student and then rated his or her personality. The strangers' impressions corresponded very poorly to the student's impressions of his or her own personality. There was more agreement between a close friend's impressions of the student and the student's own impressions. (Adapted from Funder & Colvin, 1988)

compared to how accurate we *think* we are. For example, research has found that first impressions, the quick, attributional snapshots we form when we first meet someone, are not very accurate (DePaulo et al., 1987; Funder & Colvin, 1988). However, our impressions of others do become more accurate the more we get to know them (Wegener & Petty, 1995). For example, David Funder and C. Randall Colvin (1988) compared the personality ratings that strangers gave to students they had observed for five minutes, to ratings that close friends gave to the same students. As seen in Figure 4.14, the friends made more accurate assessments of the students than the strangers did.

It is not particularly earthshaking to conclude that the longer we know someone, the better we know that person. However, there are two interesting twists to this statement. First, in the Funder and Colvin (1988) study, the accuracy rate for close friends was not that high. As you can see in Figure 4.14, the correlation between the friends' impressions and the students' own impressions of their personalities was only .27; you'll recall from Chapter 2 that a perfect correlation is 1.00. Second, people are not as accurate as they think they are. David Dunning and colleagues (1990) found that while college roommates were fairly accurate at predicting each other's behavior, they were also overconfident, believing their predictions to be more correct than they were. Whether we are thinking about close friends or strangers, why do we make attributional mistakes?

Why Are Our Impressions of Others Sometimes Wrong?

Our impressions are sometimes wrong because of the mental shortcuts we use when forming social judgments. The first culprit is our familiar friend, the fundamental attribution error. People are too ready to attribute others' actions to their personalities rather than to the situation. For example, suppose you meet Andrea at a party and she is acting in an outgoing, sociable manner. If you are like most people, you will conclude that Andrea is outgoing and sociable. How accurate are you likely to be?

Not too accurate, if it is the social situation that is causing her to act extraverted. Maybe Andrea really isn't, as a rule, outgoing or sociable. In fact, she may be rather shy and reserved, but happens to be in a situation where most people act sociably—a fun party. Our conclusion that she is outgoing will be wrong, due to the fundamental attribution error: overestimating the extent to which Andrea's behavior reflects the way she always acts, rather than something about the situation.

We don't mean to imply that people are always wrong when making dispositional attributions. Even if people underestimate the power of social situations, their impressions can still be correct because of the fact that actors' dispositions cause them to gravitate to certain situations and to avoid others. Suppose Andrea really is an outgoing person who chooses to attend parties on a frequent basis and work in a job that requires a great deal of interaction and social contact. In this case, it is not so much the situation that is affecting her behavior as it is her disposition that is choosing her situations (Gilbert & Malone, 1995; Snyder & Ickes, 1985). In cases such as these, it really doesn't matter whether we say Andrea is outgoing because of the situation or her disposition, because both are true—her outgoing disposition caused her to be in a situation that encouraged her to act in an outgoing manner. Nonetheless, situations can be very powerful and sometimes override people's dispositions, and to the extent that we fail to take the situation into account, we will form inaccurate impressions.

Another reason our impressions can be wrong concerns our use of schemas. As we have seen, people use implicit personality theories to fill in the gaps in their knowledge about other people and use schemas or theories to decide why other people do what they do. Thus, our impressions are only as accurate as our theories. While many of our theories are likely to be correct, there are some dramatic illustrations of how they can lead us astray.

For example, consider what happened to David Rosenhan (1973). He and several other researchers went to the admissions departments of local mental hospitals and pretended they had been hearing voices. All were admitted to the hospitals, most with the diagnosis of schizophrenia. Despite the fact that from then on, they all behaved in a perfectly normal manner, the psychiatric staff continued to treat them as if they were mentally ill. Not one of the researchers was identified as a fake by the staff, and all were kept in the hospitals for several days. (One person had to spend more than seven weeks in the hospital before being released.) Interestingly, the staff interpreted behavior that was perfectly normal as confirmation of their schema. For example, all of the fake patients kept diaries during their hospitalization, and the staff viewed this "engaging in writing behavior" as an indication that they were psychologically disturbed.

Why Does It Seem Like Our Impressions Are Accurate?

Why does it seem like our impressions are accurate, when, as we have just reviewed, these impressions are often wrong? We can point to three reasons. First, we often see people in a limited number of situations and thus never have the opportunity to see that our impressions are wrong. For example, you probably interact with your social psychology professor only in an academic setting. Let's say you have formed attributions about her—she is stern and unyielding and not likely to give extensions on papers. Because you don't know her in other situations, you don't realize that she is also kind and fun-loving, a permissive parent, and a giving friend. In fact, her behavior in your class is due to some bad experiences she has had with students and is not a reflection of her overall personality. Thus, you have committed the fundamental attribution error. But does it really matter? Your dispositional attribution may be overly harsh and, in a broad sense, inaccurate, but you are right about her behavior in the classroom, and that is what is most important and useful for you (Ross & Nisbett, 1991; Swann, 1984). In the narrow sphere where it matters, your attribution is accurate. However, you may never realize the wider inaccuracy of your attribution unless you happen to observe your professor in a completely different situation and see that she acts quite differently there.

Second, we will not realize that our impressions are wrong if we make them come true. This is the case with self-fulfilling prophecies, which we discussed in Chapter 3. Even if an initial impression is incorrect, we often make it come true by the way we treat a person. For example, suppose you ran into your social psychology professor at the mall and gave her a curt, unfriendly "Hello," because after all, she is a stern person who wouldn't give you an extension on your last paper. Your unfriendly greeting will probably cause your professor to respond in a less friendly manner than she normally would, thereby confirming your (in this case, inaccurate) impression of her.

Third, we might not realize we are wrong if a lot of people agree on what someone is like—even when everyone is wrong. David Kenny and colleagues have found that different observers often reach the same conclusion about what a person is like after a very brief time (Albright et al., 1997; Kenny, 1991; Kenny et al., 1992, 1994). This is particularly true for traits like extraversion, in the sense that these traits translate into observable behaviors, such as how much a person talks or how animated she or he is. Thus, when everyone agrees with us that Sonya is extraverted but Barry is not, we feel confident that our impressions are correct—even if they are not.

In order to improve the accuracy of your attributions and impressions, remember that the fundamental attribution error and self-fulfilling prophecies exist, and try to counteract these biases. For example, the next time you hear about the victim of a crime or accident, stop yourself from immediately attributing responsibility to him or her. The world is not always a just place; bad things do happen to good people. Watch out for the other kinds of biases we have discussed as well, such as relying too much on implicit personality theories or falling prey to the actor/observer difference.

Now that we've delivered the sermon, let's cut to the chase. Yes, we are quite accurate perceivers of other people. We do very well indeed most of the time. We are adept at reading and interpreting nonverbal forms of communication; in fact, most of us are actually better at this than we realize. We become more accurate at perceiving others as we get to know them better, and since most of our truly important social interactions involve people we know well, this is good news. In short, we are capable of making both blindingly accurate assessments of people and horrific attributional mistakes—it's up to you to determine the difference in your life.

Summary

Social perception is the study of how people form impressions and make inferences about other people. People constantly form such impressions because doing so helps them understand and predict their social worlds.

One source of information people use is the nonverbal behavior of others. **Nonverbal communication** is used to **encode** or express emotion, convey attitudes, communicate personality traits, and facilitate and regulate verbal speech. Many studies show that people can accurately **decode** subtle nonverbal cues. For example, the six major facial expressions of emotion are perceived accurately around the world. Sometimes, facial expressions are **affect blends**, where one part of the face registers one emotion and another part of the face registers another. Facial expressions can vary according to culturally determined **display rules**. These rules dictate which expressions are appropriate to display. **Emblems**—nonverbal gestures that have specific meanings—are also culturally determined. In general, women are better at understanding and conveying emotion nonverbally. One exception, though, is that women are less accurate at detecting deception when observing nonverbal behavior. According to the **social-role theory** of sex differences, this may be because in many societies women have learned different skills, one of which is to be polite in social interactions, overlooking the fact that someone is lying.

Often it is difficult to tell how someone feels, or what kind of person he or she is, solely from the person's nonverbal behavior. As a result, we go beyond the information given in people's behavior, making inferences about their feelings, traits, and motives. One way we do this is to rely on an **implicit personality theory** to fill in the blanks. Such a theory is composed of our general notions about which personality traits go together in one person. When people's behavior is ambiguous and we cannot rely on an implicit personality theory, our attributions about them may be affected by **priming**, a process whereby recent experiences increase a trait's **accessibility** or ready availability in our minds.

According to **attribution theory**, we try to determine why people do what they do, in order to uncover the feelings and traits that are behind their actions. **Correspondent inference theory** focuses on how we make **internal attributions**, or how we infer dispositions from corresponding behavior. We do so by observing how many **noncommon effects** are produced by a person's behavior and how much the behavior is inconsistent with our **category-based expectancies** and **target-based expectancies**. The **covariation model**, another theory of attribution, focuses on observations of behavior across time, place, different actors, and different targets of the behavior and examines how the perceiver chooses either an **internal** or an **external attribution.** We make such choices by using **consensus, distinctiveness**, and **consistency** information.

People also use various mental shortcuts when making attributions, including the use of schemas and theories. One common shortcut is the **fundamental attribution error**, which is the tendency to overestimate the extent to which people do what they do because of internal, dispositional factors. A reason for this error is that a person's behavior often has greater **perceptual salience** than the surrounding situation does. **Culture** also plays a role; people from Western cultures are more likely to engage in the fundamental attribution error than people from Eastern cultures. The **two-step process of attribution** indicates that the initial, automatic attribution about another person's behavior tends to be dispositional, but it can be corrected at the second step with conscious and effortful thinking, bringing to mind possible situational explanations. The **actor/observer difference** is a qualification of the fundamental attribution error: We are more likely to commit this error when explaining other people's behavior than when explaining our own behavior. The actor/observer effect occurs because **perceptual saliency** and **information availability** differ for the actor and the observer.

People's attributions are also influenced by their personal needs. **Self-serving attributions** occur when people make internal attributions for their successes and external attributions for their failures. **Defensive attributions** help people avoid feelings of mortality. One type of defensive attribution is **unrealistic optimism** about the future, whereby we think that good things are more likely to happen to us than to other people, and bad things are less likely to happen to us than to others. Another type of defensive attribution is the **belief in a just world**, whereby we believe that bad things happen to bad people and good things happen to good people.

Not surprisingly, the more we get to know someone, the more accurate we are. Even when judging people we know well, however, the shortcuts we use sometimes lead to mistaken impressions. For example, we tend to make more dispositional attributions about other people than are warranted. Often, however, we do not realize our impressions are wrong, because we see people in limited situations and because the way we treat people causes them to behave the way we expect them to (the self-fulfilling prophecy).

If You Are Interested

Dorris, Michael. *A Yellow Raft in Blue Water*. New York: Warner Books, 1988. Three generations of women—a daughter, a mother, and a grandmother—tell the stories of their lives on a Native American reservation, and in the telling, indicate how they have both understood and misunderstood each other.

Fiske, S. T., & Taylor, S. E. (1991). *Social cognition* (2nd ed.). New York: McGraw-Hill. A recent, encyclopedic review of the literature on social perception by two experts in the field.

Higgins, E. T. (1996). Knowledge application: Accessibility, applicability, and salience. In E. T. Higgins and A. R. Kruglanski (Eds.), *Social psychology: Handbook of basic principles*. New York: Guilford: pp. 133–168.

Jones, E. E. (1990). *Interpersonal perception*. New York: Freeman. An up-to-date review of social perception (with an emphasis on attribution theory) by one of the pioneers in the field.

McArthur, L. Z. (1990). *Social perception*. Pacific Grove, CA: Brooks/Cole. A general review of social perception and impression formation.

Rashomon: A classic film set in medieval Japan, directed by Akira Kurosawa, and winner of the Academy Award for Best Foreign Film. A violent murder and rape occurs. In an exploration of truth, lies, and attributions, four people tell their own, very different versions of what happened.

Ross, L., & Nisbett, R. E. (1991). *The person and the situation: Perspectives of social psychology*. New York: McGraw-Hill. A lively, in-depth discussion of many of the aspects of social perception we have discussed, such as the fundamental attribution error.

Simpson, Mona. *Anywhere But Here*. New York: Vintage Books, 1988. A novel both comic and tragic, telling the story of a young girl and her mother, their confused, destructive, but often hilarious relationship, their relentless quest for the American dream, and how they make sense out of their lives and each other.

CHAPTER 5

SELF-KNOWLEDGE: HOW WE COME TO UNDERSTAND OURSELVES

There is one thing, and only one in the whole universe which we know more about than we could learn from external observation. That one thing is [ourselves]. We have, so to speak, inside information; we are in the know. —C. S. Lewis, 1960

We are unknown, we knowers, ourselves to ourselves; this has its own good reason. We have never searched for ourselves—how should it then come to pass, that we should ever find ourselves? —Friedrich Nietzsche, 1918

top for a moment and think about how you feel right now. Are you happy or sad? Tired or energetic? Calm or irritated? Questions like these are usually pretty easy to answer; as C. S. Lewis says, we are "in the know" about ourselves. Few of us, however, would claim to know ourselves perfectly. Sometimes our thoughts and feelings are a confused jumble of contradictory reactions. And even if we know how we feel, it is not always clear why we feel that way. A lot about ourselves is inscrutable and difficult to determine, as Nietzsche implies.

How do we gain self-knowledge? According to social psychologists, it is not a simple matter of looking inward.

Because it is often difficult to know exactly how we feel or why we are doing what we are doing, we look outward to the social environment for clues. This is why self-knowledge is a key social psychological topic: Our views of ourselves are shaped by the world around us. We learn a great deal by observing how people treat us and how we treat others.

Let's turn this question around for a moment: Not only do other people influence our self-views; we influence their self-views. The way in which we do so can have important consequences. Suppose, for example, that you are an elementary school teacher and want your students to develop a love of reading. In this case, you are deliberately trying to influence how your students view themselves—you want them to look in the mirror and see someone who loves books. How might you go about accomplishing this? If you are like many teachers and educators, you might arrive at the following solution: Reward the kids for reading. Maybe that will get them to love books.

Teachers have always rewarded kids with a smile or a pat on the head, of course, but recently they have used more powerful incentives. In some school districts, a national chain of pizza restaurants offers second-graders a certificate for a free pizza for every 22 books they read. A few years ago, Mel Steely, a professor at West Georgia College, decided to offer underprivileged children an even more lucrative reward. He started a program called Earning by Learning, in which low-income children were offered $2 for every book they read. The program was financed in part by a friend of Steely's, House Speaker Newt Gingrich, who donated some of his speaking fees to the program. The

■ Many programs try to get children to read more by rewarding them. Do such rewards influence a child's self-concept? Do they increase or decrease a child's love of reading?

program has since been expanded to several cities, including Chicago, Denver, and Houston (Alford, 1995; Buzbee, 1995; Callahan, 1996; Kiernan, 1995).

Supporters of programs like these argue that kids are better off reading than watching television or playing video games and that whatever it takes to get them to read is well worth it. There is no doubt that rewards are powerful motivators and that pizzas and money will get kids to read more. One of the oldest and most fundamental psychological principles is that behavior followed by rewards will increase in frequency. Whether it be a rat pressing a bar in order to obtain a food pellet or a child reading to get a free pizza, rewards can change behavior.

But people are not rats and we have to consider the effects of rewards on what's inside—people's thoughts about themselves, their self-concept, their motivation to read in the future. Does getting money for reading, for example, change people's ideas about why they are reading? The danger of reward programs such as Earning for Learning is that the kids will begin to think they are reading to earn money, not because they find reading to be an enjoyable activity in its own right. Well-intentioned efforts to reward children might actually reduce their enjoyment of the activity by encouraging them to think they are doing it for the money (or the pizzas). When the reward programs end and money or pizzas are no longer forthcoming, children may actually read less than they did before. In this chapter, on the self and self-knowledge, we will see why.   ☐

*T*he Nature of the Self

Who are you? How did you come to be this person you call "myself"? The founder of American psychology, William James (1842–1910), described the basic duality of our perception of self. First, the self is composed of our thoughts and beliefs about ourselves, or what James (1890) called the "known," or, more simply, the "me." Second, the self is also the active processor of information, the "knower," or "I." In modern terms, we refer to the known aspect of the self as the **self-concept**, which is the contents of the self (our knowledge about who we are) and to the knower aspect as **self-awareness**, which is the act of thinking about ourselves. These two aspects of the self combine to create a coherent sense of identity: Your self is both a book (full of fascinating contents collected over time) and the reader of that book (who at any moment can access a specific chapter or add a new one). In this chapter we will consider both aspects of the self—the nature of the self-concept and how we come to know ourselves through self-awareness.

A good place to begin is with the question of whether we are the only species with a sense of self. Some fascinating studies by Gordon Gallup (1977; 1993; 1994; Gallup & Suarez, 1986) suggest that we are not alone in this regard. Gallup placed a mirror in an animal's cage until it became familiar with it. The

Self-Concept
the contents of the self; that is, our knowledge about who we are

Self-Awareness
the act of thinking about ourselves

■ Research by Gordon Gallup (1977) has found that some apes (chimpanzees and orangutans) have a sense of self, whereas other mammals do not.

animal was then briefly anesthetized and an odorless red dye was painted on its brow or ear. What happens when the animal wakes up and looks in the mirror? Chimpanzees and orangutans immediately touch the area of their heads that contain the red spot. Gorillas and many species of monkeys, on the other hand, do not seem to recognize that the image in the mirror is themselves. They rarely touch the red spot and, unlike chimps and orangutans, are no more likely to touch it when the mirror is present than when the mirror is absent. These studies indicate that chimps and orangutans have a rudimentary self-concept. They realize that the image in the mirror is themselves and not another ape, and recognize that they look different from how they looked before (Gallup et al., in press; Povinelli, 1993, 1994; Sedikides & Skowronski, 1997).

What about humans? When we are toddlers we seem to have a similar, rudimentary self-concept. Researchers have used a variation of the red dye test with humans and found that self-recognition develops at around two years of age (Bertenthal & Fischer, 1978; Lewis, 1986; Povinelli, Landau, & Perilloux, 1996). Lewis and Brooks (1978), for example, found that 75 percent of 21- to 25-month-old infants touched their rouged noses, while only 25 percent of the 9- to 12-month-old infants did so.

As we grow older, this rudimentary self-concept, of course, becomes more complex. Psychologists have studied how people's self-concept changes from childhood to adulthood, by asking people of different ages to answer the simple question "Who am I?" Typically, a child's self-concept is concrete, with references to clear-cut, easily observable characteristics like age, sex, neighborhood, and hobbies. In a study by Montemayor and Eisen (1977), for example, a 9-year-old answered the "Who am I?" question this way: "I have brown eyes. I have brown hair. I have brown eyebrows. . . . I'm a boy. I have an uncle that is almost 7 feet tall" (Montemayor & Eisen, 1977, p. 317). As we mature, we place less emphasis on physical characteristics and more emphasis on psychological states (e.g., our thoughts and feelings) and on considerations of how other people judge us (Hart & Damon, 1986; Livesley & Bromley, 1973; Montemayor & Eisen, 1977). Consider this twelfth-grade high school student's answer to the "Who am I" question:

> I am a human being. . . . I am a moody person. I am an indecisive person. I am an ambitious person. I am a very curious person. I am not an individual. I am a loner. I am an American (God help me). I am a Democrat. I am a liberal person. I am a radical. I am a conservative. I am a pseudoliberal. I am an atheist. I am not a classifiable person (i.e., I don't want to be). (Montemayor & Eisen, 1977, p. 318)

As you can see, this person has moved considerably beyond descriptions of her hobbies and physical appearance.

The Function of the Self

Why do human adults have such a multifaceted, complex definition of self? In all likelihood a sense of "me" serves some basic adaptive functions (Baumeister, 1998; Cross & Madson, 1997; Graziano, Jensen-Campbell, & Finch, 1997; Higgins, 1996; Mischel, Cantor, & Feldman, 1996; Sedikides & Skowronski, 1997). Researchers have pointed to three important functions served by the self. First, it has a *managerial function,* informing us of our relationship to the physical and social world, organizing our behavior, and planning for the future. We appear to be the only species, for example, who can imagine events that have not yet occurred and engage in long-term planning. Second, the self has an *organizational function,* acting as an extremely important schema that helps us interpret and recall information about ourselves and the social world (Dunning & Hayes, 1996; Kihlstrom & Klein, 1994; Markus, 1977; Markus, Smith, & Moreland, 1985; Symons & Johnson, 1997). As discussed in Chapter 3, a schema is mental structure people have to organize their knowledge about the social world around themes or subjects. One of our most important schemas is the self-concept; the information we notice, think about, and remember is organized around our view of ourselves. Third, the self has an *emotional function,* helping to determine our emotional responses (Campbell, 1990; Higgins, 1987; Markus & Nurius, 1986; Pelham, 1991). Tory Higgins (1987) suggests that we frequently think about how our sense of who we truly our (our actual self) compares to who we want to be (our ideal self) and who we think we should be (our ought self). When we feel that our actual self falls short of our ideal self, we feel depressed; when we feel that our actual self falls short of our ought self, we feel agitated.

Of course, just because the self serves these basic adaptive functions does not mean that everyone defines him or herself in exactly the same way. As we will now see, the way in which people define themselves can vary a lot in different cultures, even though these different self-concepts serve the same functions (managerial, organizational, emotional).

Cultural Differences in the Definition of Self

In June, 1993, Masako Owada, a 29-year-old Japanese woman, married Crown Prince Naruhito of Japan. Masako was a very bright career diplomat in the foreign ministry, educated at Harvard and Oxford. She spoke five languages and was on the fast track to a prestigious diplomatic career. Her decision to marry the prince surprised some observers, because it meant she would have to give up her career. Indeed, she gave up any semblance of an independent life, becoming subservient to the prince and the rest of the royal family and spending much of her time participating in rigid royal ceremonies. Her primary role was to produce a male heir to the royal throne.

■ People had very different reactions to Masako Owada's decision to give up her promising career to marry Crown Prince Naruhito of Japan, due in part to cultural differences in the importance of independence versus interdependence.

Independent View of the Self
a way of defining oneself in terms of one's own internal thoughts, feelings, and actions, and not in terms of the thoughts, feelings, and actions of other people

Interdependent View of the Self
a way of defining oneself in terms of one's relationships to other people; recognizing that one's behavior is often determined by the thoughts, feelings, and actions of others

> The squeaky wheel gets the grease.
> —American proverb

> The nail that stands out gets pounded down.
> —Japanese proverb

How do you feel about Masako's decision to marry the prince? Your answer may say something about the nature of your self-concept and the culture in which you grew up. In many Western cultures people have an **independent view of the self,** which is a way of defining oneself in terms of one's own internal thoughts, feelings, and actions, and not in terms of the thoughts, feelings, and actions of others (Cross, 1995; Fiske, Markus, Kitayama, & Nisbett, 1998; Kitayama & Markus, 1994; Markus & Kitayama, 1991, 1994; Markus, Kitayama, & Heiman, 1996; Tafarodi & Swann, 1996; Trafimow, Triandis, & Goto, 1991; Triandis, 1989, 1995). Westerners learn to define themselves as quite separate from other people and to value independence and uniqueness. Consequently, many Western observers were mystified by Masako's decision to marry the crown prince. They assumed she was coerced into the marriage by a backward, sexist society that did not properly value her worth as an individual with an independent life of her own.

In contrast, many Asian and other non-Western cultures have an **interdependent view of the self,** which is a way of defining oneself in terms of one's relationships to other people and recognizing that one's behavior is often determined by the thoughts, feelings, and actions of others. Connectedness and interdependence between people is valued, whereas independence and uniqueness are frowned upon. For example, when asked to complete sentences beginning with "I am . . . ," people from Asian cultures are more likely to refer to social groups, such as one's family or religious group, than people from Western cultures are (Bochner, 1994; Triandis, 1989). To many Japanese and other Asians, Masako's decision to give up her career was not at all surprising and was a positive, natural consequence of her view of herself as connected and obligated to others, such as her family and the royal family. What is viewed as positive and normal behavior by one culture might be viewed very differently by another.

Recently, Ted Singelis (1994) developed a questionnaire that measures the extent to which people view themselves as interdependent or independent. Sample items from this scale are given in Try It! on page 155. Singelis (1994) gave the questionnaire to students at the University of Hawaii at Manoa and found that Asian Americans agreed more with the interdependence than the independence items, whereas Caucasian Americans agreed more with the independence than the interdependence items.

We do not mean to imply that every member of a Western culture has an independent view of the self and that every member of an Asian culture has an interdependent view of the self. Within cultures, there are differences in the self-concept, and these differences are likely to increase as contact between cultures increases. It is interesting to note, for example, that Masako's decision to marry the prince was unpopular among at least some young Japanese women, who felt that her choice was not a positive sign of interdependence but a betrayal to the feminist cause in Japan (Sanger, 1993).

Nonetheless, the differences between the Western and Eastern sense of self is real and has interesting consequences for communication between the cultures. Indeed, the differences in the sense of self are so fundamental that it is very difficult for people with independent selves to appreciate what it is like to have an interdependent self, and vice versa. Western readers might find it difficult to appreciate the Asian sense of interdependence; similarly, many Japanese find it difficult to comprehend that Americans could possibly know who they are separate from the social groups to which they belong. After giving a lecture on the Western view of the self to a group of Japanese students, one psychologist reported that the students "sighed deeply and said at the end, 'Could this really be true?' " (Kitayama

Try It

A Measure of Independence and Interdependence

		strongly disagree						strongly agree
1. My happiness depends on the happiness of those around me.		1	2	3	4	5	6	7
2. I will sacrifice my self-interest for the benefit of the group I am in.		1	2	3	4	5	6	7
3. It is important to me to respect decisions made by the group.		1	2	3	4	5	6	7
4. If my brother or sister fails, I feel responsible.		1	2	3	4	5	6	7
5. Even when I strongly disagree with group members, I avoid an argument		1	2	3	4	5	6	7
6. I am comfortable with being singled out for praise or rewards.		1	2	3	4	5	6	7
7. Being able to take care of myself is a primary concern for me.		1	2	3	4	5	6	7
8. I prefer to be direct and forthright when dealing with people I've just met.		1	2	3	4	5	6	7
9. I enjoy being unique and different from others in many respects.		1	2	3	4	5	6	7
10. My personal identity, independent of others, is very important to me.		1	2	3	4	5	6	7

Note: These questions are taken from a scale developed by Singelis (1994) to measure the strength of a people's interdependence and independent views of themselves. The actual scale consists of 12 items that measure interdependence and 12 items that measure independence. We have reproduced five of each type of item here: The first five are designed to measure interdependence and the last five are designed to measure independence. Singelis (1994) found that Asian Americans agreed more with the interdependence than the independence items, whereas, Caucasian Americans agreed more with independence than the interdependence items. (Adapted from Singelis, 1994)

& Markus, 1994, p. 18). To paraphrase William Shakespeare, in Western society the self is the measure of all things. But, however natural we consider this conception of the self to be, it is important to remember that it is only a construction and not an inherent reality.

Gender Differences in the Definition of Self

Susan Cross and Laura Madson (1997) have recently suggested that there is a parallel between cultural differences in the self-concept and gender differences in the self-concept. They argue that in the United States, women are more likely to have an interdependent view of themselves, whereas men are more likely to have an independent view of themselves. They point out that starting in early childhood, American girls are more likely to develop intimate friendships, cooperate with others, and focus their attention on social relationships. Boys are more likely to engage in competitive activities and focus on dominance over others (Maccoby, 1990). Cross and Madson (1997) suggest that these differences persist into adulthood, such that women define themselves more in relation to other people, whereas men define themselves more as independent of others.

Research on gender differences is controversial, and we should be clear about what researchers are saying here. First, Cross and Madson (1997) are not arguing that women in the United States have the exact same sense of self as people living in Asia. Second, they acknowledge that men desire intimate relationships as much as women do. Nonetheless there are differences in the kinds of relationships each sex desires and the way in which they manage these relationships. Women focus more on intimacy and cooperation with a small number of close others, whereas men focus more on power and status with a larger number of others (Baumeister & Sommer, 1997). Further, when with their friends, women are more likely to discuss personal topics and disclose their emotions than men are (Caldwell & Peplau, 1982; Davidson & Duberman, 1982). It is important not to overemphasize sex differences such as these; as Kay Deaux and Marianne LaFrance (1998) point out, doing so stresses opposites rather than the vast overlap in the psychological makeup of women and men. Nevertheless, there do appear to be differences in the way women and men define themselves in the United States, with women having more of an interdependent sense of self than men.

To summarize, the self-concept serves basic adaptive functions common to all cultures (e.g., the managerial function). There are also interesting differences across cultures and between women and men in how people define themselves. But how do people learn who they are in the first place? How did you discover those things that make you uniquely *you?* For the remainder of this chapter we will discuss how people gain self-knowledge. It turns out that there are some basic motives that govern how people view themselves (Banaji & Prentice, 1994; Baumeister, 1998; Sedikides & Strube, 1997). People want accurate self-knowledge (self-assessment), they want confirmations of what they already believe (self-verification), and they want positive feedback (self-enhancement). The emphasis on these motives differs from culture to culture and, within cultures, at different points of the life cycle (Heine & Lehman, 1997; Kitayama & Karasawa, 1997; Kitayana, Markus, Matsumoto, & Norasakkunkit, 1997; Strough, Berg, & Sansone, 1996). Nonetheless, most psychologists agree that the motives are fundamental and common to all people. In the remainder of this chapter we will discuss self-assessment, or the ways in which people attempt to gain accurate knowledge about themselves. We will discuss the other self-motives in Chapter 6.

Knowing Ourselves through Introspection

When we told you we were going to describe the sources of information you use to construct a self-concept, you may have thought, "Good grief! I don't need a social psychology textbook to tell me that! It's not exactly a surprise; I just think about myself. No big deal." In other words, you rely on **introspection**, where you look inward and examine the "inside information" that you, and you alone, have about your thoughts, feelings, and motives. And indeed, you do find some answers when you introspect. But there are two interesting things about introspection: (a) People do not rely on this source of information as often as you might think—surprisingly, people spend very little time thinking about themselves—and (b) even when people do introspect, the reasons for their feelings and behavior can be hidden from conscious awareness. In short, self-scrutiny isn't all it's cracked up to be, and if this were our only source of knowledge about ourselves, we would be in trouble.

How often do people think about themselves? To find out, Mihaly Csikszentmihalyi and Thomas Figurski (1982) asked 107 employees, who ranged in age from 19 to 63 and worked at five different companies, to wear beepers for one week. The beepers went off at random intervals between 7:30 A.M. and 10:30 P.M., for a total of seven to nine times a day. At the sound of the beeper, the par-

Introspection
the process whereby people look inward and examine their own thoughts, feelings, and motives

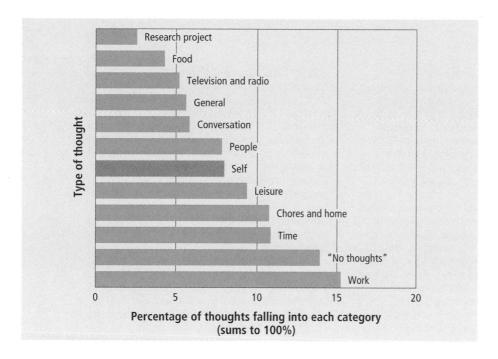

■ **FIGURE 5.1** **"What are you thinking about?"** For a week, people wore beepers that went off at random intervals several times a day. Each time the beepers went off, people described what they had just been thinking about. Thoughts about the self were surprisingly infrequent. (Adapted from Csikszentmihalyi & Figurksi, 1982)

ticipants answered a series of questions about their activities, thoughts, and moods at that time. The responses were content-analyzed into categories, including thoughts about oneself (e.g., "How lazy I've been all day," "It hurts," or "Why did I get this fat?"). As you can see in Figure 5.1, people thought about themselves surprisingly little. Only 8 percent of the total thoughts recorded were about the self; more often, the participants thought about work, chores, and time. In fact, the response of "no thoughts" was more frequent than that of thoughts about the self. Thus, while we certainly engage in introspection at times, it is not a frequent cognitive activity. Mundane thoughts about everyday life, and indeed thoughts about other people and our conversations with them, account for the vast majority of our daily thoughts (see Figure 5.1). Try It! on page 158 describes how to measure what you think about on a typical day.

> **"** Introspection is difficult and fallible . . . [t]he difficulty is simply that of all observation of whatever kind.
> —William James, 1890

Focusing on the Self: Self-Awareness Theory

When we are thinking about ourselves, what happens? What are the consequences of turning the spotlight of consciousness on ourselves, instead of focusing our attention on the world around us? As we just saw, we do not focus on ourselves very often. Sometimes, however, we encounter something in the environment that triggers self-awareness, such as knowing that people are watching us, hearing our tape-recorded voices, seeing ourselves on videotape, or staring at ourselves in a mirror. For example, if you are watching a home video taken by a friend with her new camcorder and you are the featured attraction, you will be in a state of self-awareness; you become the focus of your attention.

According to **self-awareness theory,** when we focus our attention on ourselves we evaluate and compare our current behavior against our internal standards and values (Carver & Scheier, 1981; Duval & Wicklund, 1972; Wicklund, 1975; Wicklund & Frey, 1980). In short, we become self-conscious, in the sense that we become objective, judgmental observers of ourselves. Let's say that you

Self-Awareness Theory the idea that when people focus their attention on themselves, they evaluate and compare their behavior to their internal standards and values

// *Try It* !

What's on Your Mind?

This exercise, based on the Csikszentmihalyi and Figurski (1982) study described in the text, is designed to assess the kinds of things you think about on a typical day. The idea is to sample your thoughts at random intervals over the next few days. The best way to do this is to use a watch with an alarm. Each morning, ask a friend to set the alarm for a time that day, without telling you what the time is. Be sure to carry a pad and pencil with you. When the alarm goes off, write down the answer to this question: "What were you thinking about when you were beeped?" If you don't have a watch with an alarm, then simply write down what you were thinking about at different times each day (e.g., two hours after you wake up on one day, an hour before going to bed on another).

After you have done this for several days, read over your thoughts and count how many of them were about yourself. Csikszentmihalyi and Figurski (1982) classified a thought as about the self if it was primarily about some emotional or physical state (examples were, "How relaxed I

was," "Why did I get this fat?", and "How lazy I have been all day.").

As seen in Figure 5.1, Csikszentmihalyi and Figurski (1982) found that a surprisingly small percentage of people's thoughts were about themselves (only 8 percent). Did you find the same thing? Other things to look for are the quality of your thoughts about yourself. In the Csikszentmihalyi and Figurski (1982) study, people's thoughts about themselves tended to be unpleasant. This is consistent with self-awareness theory, which says that when we focus on ourselves, we often think about how we fall short of our morals and standards.

You might also take note of the way in which you thought about yourself. Susan Nolen-Hoeksema has focused on a particular kind of self-thought called rumination, defined as focusing on and questioning one's feelings. Her findings: People who ruminate a lot tend to be more depressed, and women tend to ruminate more than men (Lyubomirsky & Nolen-Hoeksema, 1993; Nolen-Hoeksema, 1990).

//

> "But as I looked into the mirror, I screamed, and my heart shuddered: for I saw not myself but the mocking, leering, face of a devil.
>
> –Friedrich Nietzsche, *Thus Spake Zarathustra*

believe it is important for you to be honest with your friends. One day, while conversing with a friend, you lie to him. In the midst of this conversation, you catch sight of yourself in a large mirror. How do you think you will feel?

According to Shelley Duval and Robert Wicklund (1972), seeing yourself will make you aware of the disparity between your behavior and your moral standards. If you can change your behavior to match your internal guidelines (e.g., say something particularly nice to your friend or admit you lied and ask for forgiveness), you will do so. If you feel you can't change your behavior, then being in a state of self-awareness will be very uncomfortable, for you will be confronted with disagreeable feedback about yourself. In this situation, you will stop being self-aware as quickly as possible (e.g., by turning so that your back is to the mirror or by saying good-bye to your friend and leaving the room). Figure 5.2 illustrates this process—how self-awareness makes us conscious of our internal standards and directs our subsequent behavior.

This dissatisfaction with ourselves can be painful. Jane Bybee and her colleagues, for example, found that the more people thought about their ideal selves—the kind of person they most wanted to be—the more anxious and angry they felt (Bybee, Luthar, Zigler, & Merisca, 1997; Higgins, 1987). Because it can be unpleasant, people are often motivated to avoid self-awareness, by engaging in such mundane, distracting activities as watching television or reading a book. Sometimes, however, people go even further in their attempt to escape the self. Roy Baumeister (1991) has pointed out that such diverse activities as alcohol abuse, binge eating, sexual masochism, and suicide have one thing in common:

■ **FIGURE 5.2   Self-awareness theory: The consequences of self-focused attention.**
When people focus on themselves they compare their behavior to their internal standards. (Adapted from Carver and Scheier, 1981)

All are effective ways of turning off the internal spotlight on oneself. Getting drunk, for example, is one way of avoiding negative thoughts about oneself (at least temporarily). Suicide, of course, is the ultimate way of ending self-scrutiny. The fact that people regularly engage in such dangerous behaviors, despite their risks, is an indication of how aversive self-focus can be (Hull, 1981; Hull & Young, 1983; Hull, Young, & Jouriles, 1986).

Not all means of escaping the self, however, are so damaging. Baumeister (1991) points out that many forms of religious expression and spirituality are also an effective means of avoiding self-focus. Further, self-focus is not always aversive. If you have just achieved a life goal or experienced a major success, then focusing on yourself can be pleasant indeed, because it highlights your successes (Greenberg & Musham, 1981).

Self-focus can also be a way of keeping you out of trouble, by reminding you of your sense of right and wrong. For example, several studies have found that when people are self-aware (e.g., in front of a mirror), they are more likely to follow their moral standards, such as avoiding the temptation to cheat on a test (Beaman, Klentz, Diener, & Svanum, 1979; Diener & Wallbom, 1976; Gibbons, 1978).

> **I** swear to you . . . that to be overly conscious is a sickness, a real, thorough sickness.
> —Dostoevsky,
> *Notes from Underground*

Try It !

A Measure of Private Self-Consciousness

Answer the following questions as honestly and accurately as possible on a scale from 1 to 5, where:

> 1 = extremely *un*characteristic (not at all like me)
>
> 2 = somewhat *un*characteristic
>
> 3 = neither characteristic nor uncharacteristic
>
> 4 = somewhat characteristic
>
> 5 = extremely characteristic (very much like me)

1. I'm always trying to figure myself out.   _____
2. Generally, I'm not very aware of myself.   _____
3. I reflect about myself a lot.   _____
4. I'm often the subject of my own fantasies.   _____
5. I never scrutinize myself.   _____
6. I'm generally attentive to my inner feelings.   _____
7. I'm constantly examining my motives.   _____
8. I sometimes have the feeling that I'm off somewhere watching myself.   _____
9. I'm alert to changes in my mood.   _____
10. I'm aware of the way my mind works when I work through a problem.   _____

As noted in the text, everyone is self-aware at times, such as when they are in front of a mirror. People differ, however, in how frequently they focus their attention on themselves when on their own. The questions above are taken from a scale developed by Fenigstein, Scheier, and Buss (1975) to measure private self-consciousness, which is the consistent tendency to be self-aware. Here's how to score it: First, reverse your answers to Questions 2 and 5. If you answered "1" to these questions change it to a "5," if you answered "2" change it to a "4," and so on. Then, add your ratings for all 10 questions. The higher your score, the more likely you are to focus your attention on yourself. Fenigstein et al. (1975) found that the average score was 26 in a sample of college students. (Adapted from Fenigstein et al., 1975)

To summarize, self-awareness is particularly aversive when it reminds people of their shortcomings, and under these circumstances (e.g., right after failing a test) people try to avoid it. Other times, however—such as when that little devil is on your shoulder pushing you into temptation—a dose of self-awareness is not such a bad thing, because it makes us more aware of our morals and ideals. How self-aware do you tend to be? See Try It! above to find out.

Judging Why We Feel the Way We Do: Telling More Than We Can Know

Another kind of self-knowledge is more difficult to obtain, even when we are self-aware and introspect to our heart's content—knowing why we feel the way we do. Imagine trying to decide why you love someone. Being in love typically makes you feel giddy, euphoric, and preoccupied; in fact, the ancient Greeks thought love was a sickness. But why do you feel this way? Exactly what is it about your sweetheart that made you fall in love? Most of us would be tongue-tied when trying to answer this question. We know it is something about our loved one's looks, personality, values, and background. But precisely what? How can we possibly verbalize the special chemistry that exists between two people? A friend of ours once claimed he was in love with a woman because she played the saxophone. Was this really the only reason? Or even an important one? The heart works in such mysterious ways that it is difficult to tell.

Unfortunately, it's not just love that is difficult to explain. Many of our basic mental processes occur outside of awareness (Kihlstrom, 1987; Mandler, 1975; Neisser, 1976). This is not to say that we are thinkers without a clue—we are aware of the final result of our thought processes (e.g., that we are in love) but often unaware of the cognitive processing that led to the result. It's as if the magician pulled a rabbit out of a hat: You see the rabbit, but you don't know how it got there. How do we deal with this rabbit problem? Whereas we often don't know why we feel a certain way, it seems we are always able to come up with an explanation. We are the proud owners of the most powerful brain to evolve on this planet, and we certainly put it to use. Unfortunately, it didn't come with an owner's manual. Thus, introspection may not lead us to the true causes of our feelings and behavior, but we'll manage to convince ourselves that it did.

Richard Nisbett and Tim Wilson explored this phenomenon, or how we tell more than we know (Nisbett & Ross, 1980; Nisbett & Wilson, 1977; Wilson, 1985; 1994; Wilson & Stone, 1985). For example, Tim Wilson, Pat Laser, and Julie Stone (1982) asked college students to keep journals of their daily moods every day for five weeks. The students also kept track of things that might predict

> *I* have often wished I had time to cultivate modesty . . . But I am too busy thinking about myself.
> –Dame Edith Sitwell

■ The people on the couch look awfully smug; they must like what they see when they are self-aware.

"Steer clear of that group. They're all terribly self-aware."

their daily moods, such as the weather and how much sleep they had gotten the night before. At the end of the five weeks the students estimated how much their mood was related to these other variables, such as their sleep habits. An analysis of the actual data showed that in many cases people were wrong about what predicted their mood. For example, most people believed that the amount of sleep they got predicted how good a mood they were in the next day, when in fact this wasn't true: Amount of sleep was unrelated to people's moods. The participants had introspected and found or generated some logical-sounding theories that in fact weren't always right (Bargh & Pietromonaco, 1982; Kihlstrom, 1987; Jacoby, Lindsay, & Toth, 1992; Niedenthal & Kitayama, 1994).

Causal Theories
theories about the causes of one's own feelings and behaviors; often we learn such theories from our culture (e.g., "absence makes the heart grow fonder")

What these participants had relied on, at least in part, were their **causal theories**. People have many theories about what influences their feelings and behavior (e.g., "My mood should be affected by how much sleep I got last night") and often use these theories to help them explain why they feel the way they do (e.g., "I am in a bad mood; I bet the fact that I got only six hours of sleep last night has a lot to do with it"). We learn many of these theories from the culture in which we grow up, such as the idea that absence makes the heart grow fonder, that people are in bad moods on Mondays, or that people who have been divorced are a poor choice for a successful second marriage. The only problem is that, as discussed in Chapter 3, our schemas and theories are not always correct and thus can lead to incorrect judgments about the causes of our actions.

Consider this example of causal theories in action from the researchers who have studied them: One night, Nisbett and Wilson were meeting in an office at the University of Michigan. They were trying to think of ways to test the hypothesis that introspection often can't tell us why we feel the way we do and that we rely on causal theories when trying to uncover the reasons for our feelings, judgments, and actions. Brilliant insights were not forthcoming, and the researchers were frustrated by their lack of progress. Then they realized that a source of their frustration (or so they thought) was the annoying whine of a vacuum cleaner that a custodial worker was operating right outside their office. Because it took them a while to realize that the noise of the vacuum was disrupting their meeting, they experienced what seemed like an inspiration—maybe distracting background noises are more bothersome than people think. Maybe this was an example of the very kind of stimulus they were looking for—one that would influence people's judgments but, because their causal theories did not adequately cover this possibility, would be overlooked when people explained their behavior.

> We can never, even by the strictest examination, get completely behind the secret springs of action.
>
> —Immanuel Kant

Nisbett and Wilson (1977) designed a study to test this possibility (after shutting the door). They asked people to rate how interesting a documentary film was. In one condition, a construction worker (actually, Dick Nisbett) ran a power saw right outside the door to the room in which the film was shown. The irritating burst of noise began about a minute into the film. It continued intermittently until Tim Wilson, the experimenter, went to the door and shouted to the worker to please stop sawing until the film was over. The participants rated how much they enjoyed the film, and then the experimenter asked them to indicate whether the noise had influenced their evaluations. To see if the noise really did have an effect, Nisbett and Wilson included a control condition in which other participants viewed the film without any distracting noise. The hypothesis was that the noise would lower people's evaluation of the film but that people would not realize the noise was responsible for the negative evaluation.

As it happened, this hypothesis was completely wrong. The participants who watched the film with the annoying background noise did not like it any less than

■ People are not always correct about the causes of their feelings and judgments. People in a study by Nisbett and Wilson (1977) reported that a distracting noise lowered their enjoyment of a film, when in fact the noise had no detectable effect on their enjoyment.

those who saw the film without the distracting noise did (in fact, they liked the film slightly more). When the participants were asked how much the noise had influenced their ratings, however, their hypothesis agreed with Nisbett and Wilson's. Even though the noise had no detectable effect on people's ratings, most people reported that it had lowered their ratings of the film. In this case, both the participants and the researchers had the same causal theory, but the theory wasn't true—at least, not when it came to watching a documentary while hearing construction noise.

In further studies, other factors that seem like they should not influence people's judgments—that is, factors that are not part of people's causal theories—actually did have an effect. For example, in one study people evaluated the quality of items of clothing, such as pantyhose, in a shopping mall (Nisbett & Wilson, 1977). Much to the surprise of the researchers, the position of the items on the display table had a large effect on people's preferences. The more to the right an item was, the more people liked it. The researchers knew that it was the position and not something distinctive about the different pairs of pantyhose that influenced people's judgments, because in fact all four pairs were identical. However, the participants were completely in the dark about this effect of position on their judgments. Such an odd reason for their choice of pantyhose was not evident when they introspected about the reasons for their choice.

We do not mean to imply that people rely solely on their causal theories when introspecting about the reasons for their feelings and behaviors. In addition to culturally learned causal theories, we have a great deal of information about ourselves, such as how we have responded in the past and what we happen to have been thinking about before making a choice (Gavanski & Hoffman, 1987; Wilson & Stone, 1985). The fact remains, however, that introspecting about our past actions and current thoughts does not always yield the right answer about why we feel the way we do.

The Consequences of Introspecting about Reasons

Not only is it difficult to uncover all of our reasons by introspecting; it may not always be a good idea to try to do so. Have you ever, when faced with a difficult decision, spent time reflecting about why you felt the way you did about each alternative? Perhaps when you decided where to go to college, you were faced with two or more attractive alternatives and had trouble making up your mind. Maybe you couldn't decide which courses to take this year. In situations like these, people sometimes analyze the alternatives very carefully, maybe even making a list of the pluses and minuses of each choice. Benjamin Franklin argued that this is the best way to proceed:

> My way is to divide half a sheet of paper by a line into two columns, writing over the one Pro, and over the other Con. Then, during three or four days consideration, I put down under the different heads short hints of the different motives, that at different times occur to me, for or against each measure . . . When each [reason] is thus considered, separately and comparatively, and the whole lies before me, I think I can judge better, and am less likely to make a rash step. (Quoted in Goodman, 1945, p. 746)

Tim Wilson has found, however, that analyzing the reasons for our feelings is not always the best strategy and in fact can make matters worse (Wilson, Dunn, Kraft, & Lisle, 1989; Wilson & Hodges, 1992; Wilson, Hodges, & LaFleur, 1995; Wilson & LaFleur, 1995). Because it is difficult to know exactly why we feel the way we do about something, we bring to mind reasons that sound plausible and come to mind easily. The reasons that sound plausible, however, may not be the correct reasons. Even worse, we might convince ourselves that these reasons are correct, thereby changing our minds about how we feel to match our reasons.

Suppose, for example, that we asked you to take out a piece of paper and write down exactly why you feel the way you do about a romantic partner. When people list reasons in this manner, they often change their attitudes toward their partners, at least temporarily (Wilson, Dunn, Bybee, Hyman, & Rotondo, 1984; Wilson & Kraft, 1993). Why? It is difficult to know exactly why we love someone; thus, we latch onto reasons that sound good and that happen to be on our minds. In Wilson's studies, the reasons people report are such things as how well they communicate with their dating partner and how similar they are to him or her in their interests and backgrounds. Whereas these reasons may often be correct, people probably overlook other reasons that are not so easy to verbalize, such as the "special chemistry" that can exist between two people.

The trouble comes when the reasons that are accessible in people's memories and are easy to verbalize imply a different attitude from the one people had before. Suppose, for instance, that things are going well between you and your dating partner but you have trouble verbalizing exactly why this is so. What comes to mind is the fact that you have rather different backgrounds and interests. "We really don't have much in common," you might say. "I guess this relationship doesn't have much of a future." Consequently, you are likely to change your mind about how you feel, resulting in **reasons-generated attitude change**, which is attitude change resulting from thinking about the reasons for your attitudes; you assume that your attitudes match the reasons that are plausible and easy to generate. Researchers have found just this sequence of events in a number of studies

Reasons-Generated Attitude Change
attitude change resulting from thinking about the reasons for one's attitudes; people assume their attitudes match the reasons that are plausible and easy to verbalize

(e.g., Levine, Halberstadt, & Goldstone, 1996; Wilson, Hodges, & LaFleur, 1995; Wilson & Kraft, 1993).

It's difficult to know, of course, which attitude is the right one—the positive feelings you had before analyzing reasons or the more negative ones you have afterward. Wilson and his colleagues have found, however, that the attitudes people express immediately after analyzing reasons should not be trusted too much. When people make decisions based on these attitudes, they come to regret what they have chosen (Wilson, Lisle, Schooler, Hodges, Klaaren, & LaFleur, 1993). Why? The determinants of your feelings that are hard to verbalize (e.g., that "something special" your sweetheart has) do not go away and are likely to shape your feelings in the future. Thus, if you focus only on the reasons that are easy to verbalize (e.g., the fact that you and your sweetheart have different backgrounds), you might behave in ways—such as breaking up with your sweetheart—that you later regret. Several studies, for example, have found that the attitudes people express after analyzing their reasons do not predict their future attitudes and behavior very well (Halberstadt & Levine, 1997; Millar & Tesser, 1986; Reifman, Larrick, Crandall, & Fein, 1996; Wilson et al., 1984; Wilson & LaFleur, 1995).

Knowing Ourselves through Observations of Our Own Behavior

As we have seen, it is often difficult to know exactly why we feel the way we do, and it can be dangerous to think too much about our reasons. If introspection has its limits, how else might we find out what sort of person we are and what our attitudes are? We turn now to another source of self-knowledge—observations of our own behavior.

Inferring Who We Are from How We Behave: Self-Perception Theory

If you aren't sure how you feel about something, there is another way you can find out: Observe your own behavior. If you want to know whether you like country music, for example, you might think, "Well, I always listen to the country music station on my car radio," concluding that you like country tunes. It might seem a little strange to say that you find out how you feel by observing what you do, but according to Daryl Bem (1972), such observations are an important source of self-knowledge.

Bem's (1972) **self-perception theory** argues that when our attitudes and feelings are uncertain or ambiguous, we infer these states by observing our behavior and the situation in which it occurs. Let's consider each part of this theory: First, we infer our inner feelings from our behavior only when we are not sure how we feel. If you've always known that you are a country music lover, then you do not need to observe your behavior to figure this out (Andersen, 1984; Andersen & Ross, 1984). Maybe, though, your feelings are murky; you've never really thought about how much you like country music. If so, you are especially likely to use your behavior as a guide to how you feel (Chaiken & Baldwin, 1981; Kunda, Fong, Sanitioso, & Reber, 1993; Wood, 1982).

> I've always written poems . . . I never know what I think until I read it in one of my poems.
> –Virginia Hamilton Adair, 1995

Self-Perception Theory the theory that when our attitudes and feelings are uncertain or ambiguous, we infer these states by observing our behavior and the situation in which it occurs

DENNIS THE MENACE

© 1991 North American Syndicate

"MOM, WHAT DO I FEEL LIKE DOING?"

■ According to self-perception theory, people often do not know their own feelings and motives and must infer them from observing their behavior.

Second, people judge whether their behavior really reflects how they feel or whether it was the situation that made them act that way. If you freely choose to listen to the country station—no one makes you do it—you are especially likely to conclude that you listen to that station because you love country music. If it is your spouse and not you who always tunes in the country station, you are unlikely to conclude that you listen to country music in your car because you love it.

Sound familiar? In Chapter 4 we discussed attribution theory—the way in which people infer someone else's attitudes and feelings by observing that person's behavior. Bem argues that people use the same attributional principles to infer their own attitudes and feelings. For example, if you were trying to decide whether a friend likes country music, you would observe her behavior and explain why she behaved that way. You might notice, for example, that your friend is always listening to country music in the absence of any situational pressures or constraints—no one makes her play those Garth Brooks CDs. You would make an internal attribution for her behavior and conclude that she loves those Nashville tunes. Bem's self-perception theory says we infer our own feelings in the same way: We observe our behavior and make an attribution about why we behaved that way. A large number of studies have supported Bem's theory, as we will now see (Fazio, 1987; Wilson, 1990).

Being Rewarded Too Much: The Overjustification Effect

According to self-perception theory, when people realize their behavior is caused by an external factor, they do not assume it reflects their internal feelings. This is pretty logical; if you know the only reason you are waiting on tables over the summer is that the pay is good, you will not assume you are doing it because you just love standing on your feet all day. In other words, after looking at your behavior and the situation, you will make an external attribution ("I'm doing it for the money") and not an internal attribution ("I love doing this so much that I would do it for free"). The problem is that when external causes for our behavior are conspicuous, we go overboard, discounting the extent to which internal factors played a role. **Discounting** occurs when people underestimate the effects of one cause of their behavior because another cause is conspicuous (Kelley, 1972; Nisbett & Valins, 1972). This process of discounting has important implications for a major area of life—our motivation to engage in activities and our subsequent interest in and enjoyment of those activities.

Let's say you love to play the piano. You spend many hours happily practicing, simply enjoying the act of making music and the feeling that you are getting better. We would say that your interest in playing the piano stems from **intrinsic motivation**, which is the desire to engage in an activity because you enjoy it or find it interesting, not because of external rewards or pressures (Cordova & Lepper, 1996; Deci, Eghrari, Patrick, & Leone, 1994; Deci & Flaste, 1995; Deci & Ryan, 1985; Harackiewicz & Elliot, 1993, in press; Harackiewicz, Manderlink, & Sansone, 1992; Hirt, Melton, McDonald, & Harackiewicz, 1996; Pittman & Heller, 1987; Sansone & Harackiewicz, 1996). Your reasons for engaging in the activity have to do with you—the enjoyment and pleasure you feel when playing the piano. In other words, playing the piano is play, not work. According to Mihaly Csikszentmihalyi (1975, 1988), intrinsically motivated behavior creates an optimal experience called *flow*. When in a state of flow, the individual centers his or her attention on the task, blocks out other stimuli, and concentrates intently. The individual feels competent and is unconcerned about how well he or she is doing; feedback about performance is clear and unambiguous. Finally, the individual experiences a lack of self-awareness. Think about some recent activity of yours that you really enjoyed; you were probably experiencing this state of flow, as with our example of the piano player.

Now let's say your parents get the brilliant idea of rewarding you with money for playing the piano. They figure that this will make you practice even harder. After all, rewards work, don't they? However, your parents have now added an extrinsic reason for you to play the piano. Your playing, hitherto stemming from intrinsic motivation, now stems from **extrinsic motivation** as well, which is the desire to engage in an activity because of external rewards or pressures, not because you enjoy the task or find it interesting. Unfortunately, extrinsic rewards can undermine intrinsic motivation. Whereas before you played the piano because you loved it, now you're playing it so that you'll get the reward. What was once play is now work. The sad outcome is that replacing intrinsic motivation with extrinsic motivation makes people lose interest in the activity they initially enjoyed. This result is called the **overjustification effect**, whereby people view their behavior as caused by compelling extrinsic reasons (e.g., a reward), making them underestimate the extent to which their behavior was caused by intrinsic reasons (e.g., Deci & Ryan, 1985; Harackiewicz, 1979; Kohn, 1993; Lepper, 1995; Lepper & Greene, 1978; Lepper, Keavney, & Drake, 1996; Ryan & Deci, 1996; Tang & Hall, 1995).

Sound familiar? The danger of programs such as Earning by Learning, described at the beginning of this chapter, now become clear: Giving children money or pizzas to read books may backfire by lowering their intrinsic interest in reading. During the programs, children might well read more, in order to get the rewards. No one doubts that rewards are powerful motivators and can change what people do. It's the changes that occur inside people's heads that are often overlooked. Once the programs end, children might actually be less likely to read than they were before the programs began. Why? They might think, "I was reading to get money. Now that there is nothing in it for me, why should I read? I think I'll play a video game."

Discounting
underestimating the effects of one cause of our behavior because another cause is conspicuous

Intrinsic Motivation
the desire to engage in an activity because we enjoy it or find it interesting, not because of external rewards or pressures

Extrinsic Motivation
the desire to engage in an activity because of external rewards or pressures, not because we enjoy the task or find it interesting

Overjustification Effect
the case whereby people view their behavior as caused by compelling extrinsic reasons, making them underestimate the extent to which their behavior was caused by intrinsic reasons

■ Making children read for external reasons can lead to an overjustification effect, whereby they infer that they have no intrinsic interest in reading.

The overjustification effect has been found in dozens of laboratory and field experiments, with several kinds of rewards, activities, and age-groups. For example, David Greene, Betty Sternberg, and Mark Lepper (1976) conducted the following study with fourth- and fifth-grade students. The teachers introduced four new math games to the students, and during a 13-day baseline period they simply noted how long each child played with each math game. As seen in the first panel of Figure 5.3, the children had some intrinsic interest in the math games initially, in that they played with them for several minutes during this baseline period. For the next several days, a reward program was introduced, whereby the children could earn credits toward certificates and trophies by playing with the math games. The more time they spent playing with the games, the more credits they could earn. As seen in the middle panel of Figure 5.3 this program was effective in increasing the amount of time the kids spent on the math games, showing that the rewards were an effective motivator.

The key question, however, is what happened after the program was terminated and the kids could no longer earn rewards for playing with the games? According to the overjustification hypothesis, the children should conclude that they were playing with the math games only to earn prizes, thereby undermining any intrinsic interest they had at the outset; as a result, when the rewards were taken away, the children should spend significantly less time with the games than they had during the baseline period (e.g., "I can't earn prizes playing with these games anymore—why play with them at all?"). This is exactly what happened, as

■ **FIGURE 5.3   The over-justification effect.** During the initial baseline phase, researchers measured how much time elementary school children played with math games. During the reward program, they rewarded the children with prizes for playing the games. When the rewards were taken away (during the follow-up), the children played with the games even less than they had during the baseline phase, indicating that the rewards had lowered their intrinsic interest in the games. (Adapted from Greene, Sternberg, & Lepper, 1976)

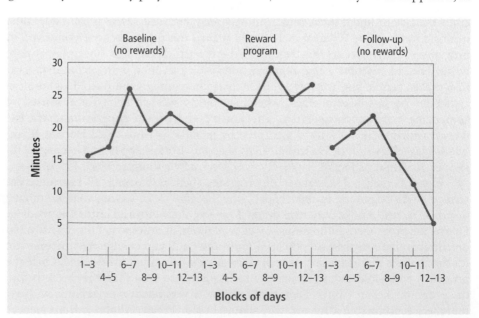

seen in the right-hand panel of Figure 5.3. After the reward program ended, the children spent significantly less time with the math games than they had initially, before the rewards were introduced. (The researchers determined, by comparing these results to those of a control condition, that it was the rewards that made people like the games less, and not the fact that everyone became bored with the games as time went by.) In short, the rewards destroyed the children's intrinsic interest in the games, such that by the end of the study they were hardly playing with the games at all.

The results of overjustification studies are distressing, given the wide use of rewards and incentives by parents, educators, and employers. In the workplace, for example, people sometimes find themselves doing things they used to do for the pure joy of it but for which they are now getting paid. Consider basketball great Bill Russell's description of how becoming a professional affected his love for the game:

> I remember that the game lost some of its magical qualities for me once I thought seriously about playing for a living. This first happened in 1955, in my junior year, after USF [the University of San Francisco] won the NCAA national championship. As a result, all through my senior year at USF I played with the idea of turning professional, and things began to change. Whenever I walked on the court I began to calculate how this particular game might affect my future. Thoughts of money and prestige crept into my head. Over the years the professional game would turn more and more into a business. (Russell & Branch, 1979, p. 98)

What can we do to protect intrinsic motivation from the slings and arrows of our society's reward system? Fortunately, there is room for some optimism, as recent research has identified conditions under which overjustification effects can be avoided. First, rewards will undermine interest only if interest was high initially (Calder & Staw, 1975; Tang & Hall, 1995). If you think a task is excruciatingly boring, rewards obviously can't reduce your interest any further. Similarly, if a child has no interest whatsoever in reading, then getting him or her to read by offering free pizzas is not a bad idea, because there is no initial interest to undermine. The danger arises when a child already likes to read, because then offering free pizzas is likely to convince the child that he or she is reading to earn pizzas, not because reading is interesting in its own right.

Second, the type of reward makes a difference. So far, we have discussed **task-contingent rewards,** meaning that people get them only for doing a task, regardless of how well they do it. Sometimes **performance-contingent rewards** are used, whereby the reward depends on how well people perform the task. For example, grades are performance-contingent, because you get a high reward (an A) only if you do well in the class. This type of reward is less likely to decrease interest in a task—and may even increase interest—because it conveys the message that you are good at the task (Deci & Ryan, 1985; Sansone & Harackiewicz, 1997; Tang & Hall, 1995). Thus, rather than giving kids a reward for playing with math games regardless of how well they do (task-contingent), it is better to reward them for doing well at math. Even performance-contingent rewards must be used with care, however, because they too can backfire. Though people like the positive feedback these rewards convey, they do not like the tension and apprehension that come with being evaluated (Harackiewicz, 1989; Harackiewicz, Manderlink, & Sansone, 1984). The trick is to convey positive feedback without making people feel nervous and apprehensive about being evaluated.

■ "I remember that the game lost some of its magical qualities for me once I thought seriously about playing for a living." —Basketball great Bill Russell

Task-Contingent Rewards
rewards that are given for performing a task, regardless of how well we do that task

Performance-Contingent Rewards
rewards that are based on how well we perform a task

Avoiding the Overjustification Effect

Another hopeful sign is that children can be taught to avoid the damaging effects of rewards. Because rewards can never be eliminated from our society, Beth Hennessey and her colleagues focused on ways of helping children to operate within the system—that is, to maintain their intrinsic motivation even with rewards dangled all around them (Hennessey, Amabile, & Martinage, 1989; Hennessey & Zbikowski, 1993). They showed children a videotape in which a boy and girl noted that getting rewards was nice but that the real reason they did things, such as their schoolwork, was because of how much they enjoyed these activities. Did this videotape "immunize" the kids against the negative effects of rewards? To find out, the children came back the next day and took part in what they thought was another study. The researchers asked the kids to make up stories to accompany a series of pictures and offered half of them a reward for doing so.

Previous studies had found that when people are rewarded for activities such as these they lose interest and produce stories that are low in creativity (Amabile, Hennessey, & Grossman, 1986). Among the kids who did not see the videotape, the same thing happened here: The reward, looming before them, lessened their intrinsic motivation for what is typically an enjoyable task, and they produced stories that were less creative than those produced by the nonrewarded children (see the left-hand side of Figure 5.4). What about the kids who had watched the videotape? As seen in the right-hand side of Figure 5.4, the reward had little effect on the creativity of their stories (in fact, the kids who were rewarded made up stories that were slightly more creative than did those who were not rewarded). The information they learned in the video seems to have kept them focused on their intrinsic interest in the task, thereby "short-circuiting" the negative effects of rewards. This research suggests an encouraging solution to the dilemma posed by our society's use of rewards: Your intrinsic interest in an activity, as well as your creativity when engaged in that activity, can be maintained in the face of rewards, if you try to ignore the reward and remind yourself of how much you enjoy doing the task for its own sake.

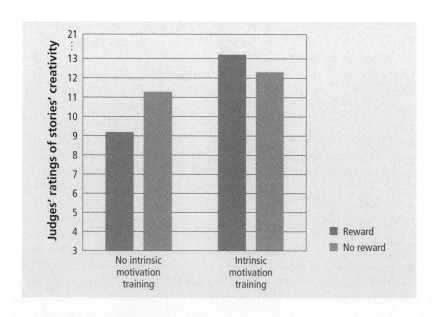

■ **FIGURE 5.4 Avoiding the overjustification effect.** As seen on the left-hand side of the graph, children who were rewarded told stories that were less creative, demonstrating the standard overjustification effect. As seen on the right-hand side of the graph, children who were immunized—by watching a videotape that stressed the importance of intrinsic motivation—did not demonstrate the overjustification effect. That is, when they received a reward, they still wrote creative stories. (Adapted from Hennessey & Zbikowski, 1991)

Understanding Our Emotions: The Two-Factor Theory of Emotion

We have just seen that people often use observations of their behavior to determine what they think and what kind of person they are. You may have wondered whether the same is true of other kinds of views of yourself. For example, what about your emotions, such as how happy, angry, or afraid you feel at any given time—how do you know which emotion you are experiencing? Think about a time you felt angry—how did you know you felt that way? This question probably sounds kind of silly; it seems like we just know how we feel, without having to think about it or, as self-perception theory suggests, observing our behavior to see how we feel.

Though it may seem like we just know how we feel, the experience of emotion is not as simple as it appears. Stanley Schachter (1964) proposed a theory of emotion that says we infer what our emotions are in the same way that we infer what kind of person we are or how interested we are in math games—by observing our behavior and then explaining why we are behaving that way. The only difference is in the kind of behavior we observe. Schachter says we observe our internal behaviors—namely, how physiologically aroused we feel. If we feel aroused, we then try to figure out what is causing this arousal. For example, let's say your heart is pounding and your body feels tense. Is it because you just saw your professor—the one from whom you got a paper extension because supposedly you had to go to your grandmother's funeral that day—or is it because you just saw the person standing next to the professor—the one on whom you have the most amazing crush in the universe? Are you feeling unholy fear or stomach-churning love?

Schachter's theory is called the **two-factor theory of emotion**, because understanding our emotional states requires two steps: First, we must experience physiological arousal, and second, we must seek an appropriate explanation or label for it. Because our physical states are difficult to label on their own, we use information in the situation to help us make an attribution about why we feel aroused. Figure 5.5 illustrates the two-factor theory of emotion.

Stanley Schachter and Jerome Singer (1962) conducted an experiment to test this provocative theory; imagine you were a participant. When you arrive, the experimenter tells you he is studying the effects of a vitamin compound called Suproxin on people's vision. After a physician injects you with a small amount of Suproxin, the experimenter asks you to wait while the drug takes effect. He introduces you to another participant, who, he says, has also been given some Suproxin. The experimenter gives each of you a questionnaire to fill out, saying he will return in a little while to give you the vision tests. You look at the questionnaire and notice it contains some highly personal and insulting questions. For example, one question asks, "With how many men (other than your father) has your mother had extramarital relationships?" (Schachter & Singer, 1962, p. 385). The other participant reacts angrily to these offensive questions, becoming more and more furious, until he finally tears up his questionnaire, throws it on the floor, and stomps out of the room. How do you think you would feel? Would you feel angry as well?

As you have no doubt gathered, the real purpose of this experiment was not to test people's vision. The researchers set up a situation where the two crucial variables—arousal and an emotional explanation for that arousal—would be present or absent and then observed which, if any, emotions people experienced.

Two-Factor Theory of Emotion
the idea that emotional experience is the result of a two-step self-perception process in which people first experience physiological arousal and then seek an appropriate explanation for it

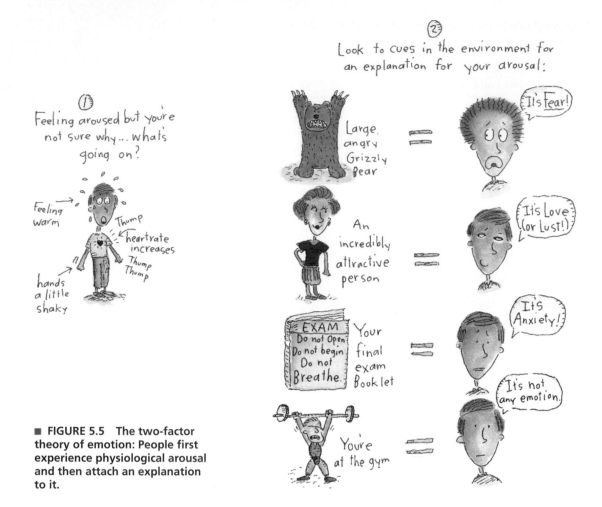

■ **FIGURE 5.5 The two-factor theory of emotion: People first experience physiological arousal and then attach an explanation to it.**

The participants did not really receive an injection of a vitamin compound. Instead, the arousal variable was manipulated in the following way: Some participants received epinephrine, a drug that causes arousal (body temperature and heart and breathing rates increase), and the other half received a placebo that had no physiological effects at all.

Imagine how you would have felt had you received the epinephrine: As you read the insulting questionnaire, you begin to feel aroused. (Remember, the experimenter didn't tell you the drug was epinephrine and so you don't realize that it's the drug that's making you aroused.) The other participant—who was actually an accomplice of the experimenter—reacts with rage. You are likely to infer that you are feeling flushed and aroused because you too are angry. You have met the conditions Schachter (1964) argues are necessary to experience an emotion—you are aroused, and you have sought out and found a reasonable explanation for your arousal in the situation that surrounds you. Thus, you become furious. This is indeed what happened—participants who had been given epinephrine reacted much more angrily than participants who had been given the placebo did.

A fascinating implication of Schachter's theory is that people's emotions are somewhat arbitrary, depending on what the most plausible explanation for their arousal happens to be. Schachter and Singer (1962) demonstrated this idea in two ways. First, they showed that they could prevent people from becoming angry by providing a nonemotional explanation for why they felt aroused. They did this by informing some of the people who received epinephrine that the drug would increase their heart rate, make their face feel warm and flushed, and cause their hands to shake slightly. When people actually began to feel this way, they inferred that it was not because they were angry but because the drug was taking effect. As a result, these participants did not react angrily to the questionnaire.

Even more impressively, Schachter and Singer showed that they could make participants experience a very different emotion by changing the most plausible explanation for their arousal. In other conditions, participants did not receive the insulting questionnaire and the accomplice did not respond angrily. Instead, the accomplice acted in a euphoric, devil-may-care fashion, playing basketball with rolled-up pieces of paper, making paper airplanes, and playing with a Hula-Hoop he found in the corner. How did the real participants respond? If they had received epinephrine but had not been told of its effects, they inferred that they must be feeling happy and euphoric and often joined the accomplice's impromptu games.

The Schachter and Singer (1962) experiment has become one of the most famous studies in social psychology, because it shows that emotions can be the result of a self-perception process whereby people look for the most plausible explanation for their arousal. Sometimes the most plausible explanation is not the right explanation, and so people end up experiencing a mistaken emotion. The people who became angry or euphoric in the Schachter and Singer (1962) study did so because they felt aroused and thought this arousal was due to the obnoxious questionnaire or to the infectious, happy-go-lucky behavior of the accomplice. The real cause of their arousal, the epinephrine, was hidden from them; all they had to go on were situational cues to explain their behavior.

Finding the Wrong Cause: Misattribution of Arousal

To what extent do the results found by Schachter and Singer (1962) generalize to everyday life? Do people form mistaken emotions in the same way as participants in that study did? In everyday life, one might argue, people usually know why they are aroused. If a mugger points a gun at us and says "Stick 'em up!", we feel aroused and correctly label this arousal as fear. If our heart is thumping while we walk on a deserted moonlit beach with the man or woman of our dreams, we correctly label this arousal as love or sexual attraction.

Many everyday situations, however, present more than one plausible cause for our arousal, and it is difficult to identify how much of the arousal is due to one source versus another. Imagine that you go to see a scary movie with an extremely attractive date. As you are sitting there, you notice that your heart is thumping and you are a little short of breath. Is this because you are wildly attracted to your date, or because the movie is terrifying you? It is unlikely that you could say, "Fifty-seven percent of my arousal is due to the fact that my date is gorgeous, 32 percent is due to the scary movie, and 11 percent is due to indigestion from all the popcorn I ate." Because of this difficulty in pinpointing the precise causes of our arousal, we sometimes form mistaken emotions. You might think that most of your arousal is a sign of attraction to your date, when in fact a lot of it is due to the movie (or maybe even indigestion).

In recent years, many studies have demonstrated the occurrence of such **misattribution of arousal,** whereby people make mistaken inferences about what is causing them to feel the way they do (Ross & Olson, 1981; Schachter, 1977; Storms & McCaul, 1976; Storms & Nisbett, 1970; Valins, 1966; Zillmann,

> "I could feel all the excitement of losing the big fish going through the transformer and coming out as anger at my brother-in-law.
> —Norman Maclean,
> *A River Runs Through It*

Misattribution of Arousal
the process whereby people make mistaken inferences about what is causing them to feel the way they do

■ Misattribution. When people are aroused for one reason, such as occurs when they cross a scary bridge, they often attribute this arousal to the wrong source—such as attraction to the person they are with.

1978). Consider, for example, an intriguing field experiment by Donald Dutton and Arthur Aron (1974). Imagine you were one of the participants, who were all men. You are visiting a park in British Columbia. An attractive young woman approaches you and asks if you could fill out a questionnaire for her, as part of a psychology project on the effects of scenic attractions on people's creativity. You decide to help her out. After you complete the questionnaire, the woman thanks you and says she would be happy to explain her study in more detail when she has more time. She tears off a corner of the questionnaire, writes down her name and phone number, and tells you to give her a call if you want to talk with her some more. How attracted do you think you would be to this woman? Would you telephone her and ask for a date?

This is a hard question to answer. Undoubtedly, it depends on whether you are dating someone else, how busy you are, and so on. It might also depend, however, on how you interpret any bodily symptoms you are experiencing. If you are aroused for some extraneous reason, you might mistakenly think some of the arousal is the result of attraction to the young woman. To test this idea, Dutton and Aron (1974) had the woman (a confederate) approach males in the park under two very different circumstances. Again, imagine you were a participant. As you are walking in the park, you come to the edge of a deep canyon. Spanning the canyon is a narrow, 450-foot-long suspension bridge made of wooden planks attached to wire cables. You decide to walk across it. As you do, you have to stoop to hold onto the handrails, which are very low. When you get a little way across, the wind picks up and causes the bridge to sway from side to side. You feel like you are about to tumble over the edge, and you hold on for dear life. Then you make the mistake of looking down. You see nothing but a sheer 200-foot drop to a rocky, raging river. You become more than a little aroused—your heart is thumping, you breathe rapidly, and you begin to perspire. At this point, the attractive woman approaches and asks you to fill out her questionnaire. How attracted do you feel toward her?

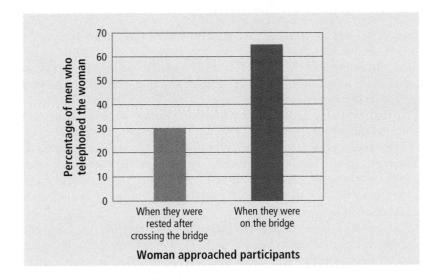

■ **FIGURE 5.6   Misattribution of arousal.**   When a woman approached men on a scary bridge and asked them to fill out a questionnaire, a high percentage of them were attracted to her and called her for a date. When the same woman approached men after they had crossed the bridge and were rested, relatively few called her for a date. (Adapted from Dutton & Aron, 1974)

Think about this for a moment, and now imagine that the woman approaches you under different circumstances. You make it across the bridge, and you have been resting awhile on a bench in the park. You have had a chance to calm down—your heart is no longer pounding against your chest, and your breathing rate has returned to normal. You are peaceably admiring the scenery when the woman asks you to fill out her questionnaire. How attracted do you feel toward her now? The prediction from Schachter's two-factor theory is clear: If you are on the bridge, you will be considerably aroused and will mistakenly think some of this arousal is the result of attraction to the beautiful woman. This is exactly what happened in the actual experiment. A large proportion of the men approached on the bridge telephoned the woman later to ask her for a date, whereas relatively few of the men approached on the bench telephoned the woman (see Figure 5.6). The moral is this: If you encounter an attractive man or woman and your heart is going thump-thump, think carefully about why you are aroused—you might fall in love for the wrong reasons!

Interpreting the Social World: Cognitive Appraisal Theories of Emotion

Though a great many studies have confirmed the idea that people can misattribute the cause of their arousal, ending up with a mistaken or exaggerated emotion (e.g., Sinclair, Hoffman, Mark, Martin, & Pickering, 1994), it has become clear that explaining why we are aroused is not the only way in which we determine our emotions. Sometimes our emotions result from an interpretation of a situation in the absence of any arousal. Suppose, for example, that your best friend tells you she was just admitted to the top medical school in the country. What emotion will you feel? A central idea of **cognitive appraisal theories of emotion** is that it depends on the way in which you interpret or explain this event, in the absence of any physiological arousal (Ellsworth, 1994; Frijda, 1986; Lazarus, 1995; Omdahl, 1995; Ortony, Clore, & Collins, 1988; Roseman, Antoniou, & Jose, 1996; Scherer, 1988). Two kinds of appraisals are especially important: (a) your view of whether the event has good or bad implications for you, and (b) your view of what caused the event.

Cognitive Appraisal Theories of Emotion theories holding that emotions result from people's interpretations and explanations of events, even in the absence of any physiological arousal

Virtually any event can be viewed in many different ways and people's emotional reaction will depend on whether they put a positive or negative spin on the event. If your life dream is to be a doctor but you haven't gotten into medical school yet, then you might feel threatened by your friend's success. Rather than feeling good about her acceptance to medical school, you might feel resentful and angry, due to your interpretation of her success as a threat to your own. Otherwise, you will probably interpret her success in quite positive terms and bask in her reflected glory (Tesser, 1988). The emotion people experience also depends on how they explain the cause of the event. If you think you contributed to your friend's success (she wouldn't have made it through that tough physics course without your help), you will probably feel pride; if you think she did it entirely on her own, you will probably feel admiration (assuming, of course, that you don't feel threatened by her success).

Cognitive appraisals are very much like one of the two factors in Schachter's two-factor theory—the part whereby people try to explain the causes of an event and their reactions to it (see the right-hand side of Figure 5.5). The main difference between Schachter's theory and cognitive appraisal theories concerns the role of arousal. According to cognitive appraisal theories, arousal does not always come first; the cognitive appraisals alone are a sufficient cause of emotional reactions. The two theories are not incompatible, however. When people are aroused and not certain where this arousal comes from, the way in which they explain the arousal determines their emotional reaction (Schachter's two-factor theory). When people are not aroused, the way in which they interpret and explain what happens to them determines their emotional reaction (cognitive appraisal theories). Both theories agree that one way people learn about themselves is by observing events—including their own behavior—and trying to explain those events.

Knowing Ourselves through Self-Schemas

People can thus learn a great deal about themselves through introspection and observations of their own behavior. What do people do with all of this information once they have it? Not surprisingly, we organize our self-knowledge in much the same way that we organize our knowledge about the external world—into schemas.

In Chapter 3, we noted that people use schemas—knowledge structures about a person, topic, or object—to understand the social world. We do not have a random, helter-skelter collection of thoughts about the world; we organize our knowledge into schemas, which help us understand and interpret new experiences. It should come as no surprise that we form **self-schemas** as well, the organized knowledge structures about ourselves, based on our past experiences, that help us understand, explain, and predict our own behavior (Andersen & Cyranowski, 1994; Cantor & Kihlstrom, 1987; Deaux, 1993; Dunning & Hayes, 1996; Linville & Carlston, 1994; Markus, 1977; Markus & Nurius, 1986; Malle & Horowitz, 1995). Thus, we do not have a random, helter-skelter collection of thoughts about ourselves either: We organize our self-views into coherent schemas, which influence how we interpret new things that happen to us. Suppose, for example, that you lose a close tennis match to your best friend. How will you react? In part, the answer depends on the nature of your self-schemas. If you define yourself as competitive and athletic, you are likely to feel bad and

Self-Schemas
organized knowledge structures about ourselves, based on our past experiences, that help us understand, explain, and predict our own behavior

want a rematch as soon as possible; whereas if you define yourself as cooperative and nurturing, losing the match won't be such a big deal.

As children develop, their shallow, concrete self-concept progresses to a unique, complex one, based on the formation of increasingly sophisticated self-schemas. One line of research, conducted by William McGuire and his colleagues, suggests that people develop self-schemas for the aspects of self that make them distinct from other people (McGuire & McGuire, 1981; McGuire, McGuire, Child, & Fujioka, 1978; McGuire & Padawer-Singer, 1976). Thus, red-haired children are more likely to mention their hair color when asked to describe themselves, since this physical trait sets them apart from most other people. Similarly, an African American child in a predominantly white school is more likely to mention his or her ethnicity than the white children are, because this aspect of the individual is distinct in this setting.

Autobiographical Memory

Self-schemas also help us organize our pasts, by influencing our **autobiographical memories**, which are memories about our own past thoughts, feelings, and behaviors. Whereas these memories define us, it is also the case that we define our memories. It is certainly not possible to remember everything that has happened in our lives or to remember it perfectly. Distortions, fabrications, and outright forgetting occur over time; as Anthony Greenwald (1980) has pointed out, if historians revised and distorted history to the same extent that we do with our own lives, they'd lose their jobs! Such distortion and revision of autobiographical memory are often not accidental—we rewrite our history. How? Just as self-schemas help us organize new information about ourselves, so too do they help us organize memories about our past actions. If being independent is part of your self-schema but being competitive is not, you will probably remember more times when you acted independently than competitively (Akert, 1993; Bahrick, Hall, & Berger, 1996; Markus, 1977; Thompson, Skowronski, Larsen, & Betz, 1996).

What about our memories for our past feelings and attitudes—do our theories and schemas color these memories as well? Michael Ross and his colleagues have found that the answer is yes (Conway & Ross, 1984; Ross, 1989; Ross & McFarland, 1988). People have many theories about the stability of their feelings. Some feelings, like our moods or how happy we are in a new romantic relationship, are expected to fluctuate over time. Other feelings, like our attitudes about social issues (e.g., the death penalty), are expected to be relatively stable—people assume that the way they feel now is how they felt in the past. Interestingly, Ross has found that these theories are not always correct, leading to distortions in memory. For example, attitudes toward social issues sometimes do change, but because people's theories are that these attitudes remain stable, they underestimate the amount of change that occurs. "I've always been against the death penalty," we might think, underestimating the extent to which our attitude has evolved over the years.

Recovered Memories: Real or Imagined?

Research by Ross and others, then, suggests that our memories can be reconstructive, whereby we invent our pasts in ways that were never so. Much of the research in this area, however, has concerned relatively benign memories, such as people's recollections about their past attitudes. What about much more important and jarring memories, such as the sudden recollection that one was sexually

> The sense of our own personal identity . . . is exactly like any of our other perceptions of sameness among phenomena.
>   —William James, 1910

Autobiographical Memories
memories about one's own past thoughts, feelings, and behaviors

> Herein lies a difficulty in any autobiographical sketch. . . . It is a story of oneself in the past, read in light of one's present self. There is much supplementary inference—wherein "must have been" masquerades as "was so."
>   —Lloyd Morgan

Recovered Memories recollections of a past event, such as sexual abuse, that had been forgotten or repressed; a great deal of controversy surrounds the accuracy of such memories

abused as a child? These are called **recovered memories**, which are recollections of a past event, such as sexual abuse, that had been forgotten or repressed. In recent years there has been a great deal of controversy over the accuracy of such memories (Pezdek & Banks, 1996; Pope, 1996).

For example, in 1988 in Olympia, Washington, Paul Ingram was accused of sexual abuse, satanic rituals, and murder by his daughters, who claimed to have suddenly recalled these events years after they occurred. The police could find no evidence for the crimes and Ingram initially denied that they had ever occurred. He eventually became convinced that he too must have repressed his past behavior and that he must have committed the crimes, even though he could not remember having done so. According to experts who have studied this case, Ingram's daughters genuinely believed the abuse and killing occurred, but they were in fact wrong. What they thought they remembered were actually false memories (Wright, 1994).

The question of the accuracy of recovered memories has become extremely controversial. On one side are writers such as Ellen Bass and Laura Davis (1994), who claim that it is not uncommon for women who were sexually abused to repress these traumas, so that they have absolutely no memory of them. The abuse and its subsequent repression, according to this view, are responsible for many psychological problems, such as depression and eating disorders. Later in life, often with the help of a psychotherapist, these events can be "recovered" and brought back into memory. On the other side of the controversy are academic psychologists and others, who argue that the accuracy of recovered memories cannot be accepted on faith (e.g., Loftus & Ketcham, 1994; Ofshe & Waters,

■ In Olympia, Washington, in 1988, Paul Ingram was accused by his daughters of sexual abuse, satanic rituals, and murder. His daughters claimed to have suddenly recalled these events years after they occurred. According to experts who studied the case, Ingram's daughters genuinely believed the abuse and killing occurred, but in fact they were wrong: What they thought they remembered were actually false memories. Ingram eventually became convinced that he too must have repressed his past behavior and that he must have committed the crimes. Due to his "confession," he is currently serving a prison sentence.

1994; Schacter, 1995, 1996; Wegner, Quillan, & Houston, in press). These writers acknowledge that sexual abuse and other childhood traumas are a terrible problem and are more common than we would like to think. They further agree that claims of sexual abuse should be taken extremely seriously and investigated fully and that, when sufficient evidence of guilt exists, the person responsible for the abuse should be prosecuted.

But here's the problem: What is "sufficient evidence"? Is it enough that someone remembers, years later, that she or he has been abused, in the absence of any other evidence of abuse? According to many researchers, the answer is no, because of what is called the **false memory syndrome**: People can recall a past traumatic experience that is objectively false but that they believe is true (Kihlstrom, 1996, 1997). There is evidence that people can acquire vivid memories of events that never occurred, especially if another person—such as a psychotherapist—suggests that the events occurred (Johnson & Raye, 1981; Loftus, 1993; for other evidence on the reconstructive nature of memory, see the section on eyewitness testimony in "Social Psychology in Action 3: Social Psychology and the Law"). In addition to numerous laboratory demonstrations of false memories, there is evidence from everyday life that memories of abuse can be incorrect. Often these memories are contradicted by objective evidence (e.g., no evidence of satanic murders can be found); sometimes people who suddenly acquire such memories decide later that the events never occurred; and sometimes the memories are so bizarre (e.g., that people were abducted by aliens) as to strain credulity. Unfortunately, some psychotherapists do not sufficiently consider that, by suggesting past abuse, they may be implanting false memories rather than helping clients remember real events.

This is not to say, however, that all recovered memories are inaccurate. Although scientific evidence for repression and recovery—the idea that something can be forgotten for years and then recalled with great accuracy—is sparse, there may be instances in which people do suddenly remember traumatic events that really did occur. Thus, any claim of abuse should be taken with the utmost seriousness. Unfortunately, it is very difficult to distinguish the accurate memories from the false ones, in the absence of any corroborating evidence. Thus, claims of abuse cannot be taken on faith, especially if they are the result of suggestions from other people.

False Memory Syndrome a memory of a past traumatic experience that is objectively false but that people believe occurred

Knowing Ourselves through Social Interaction

So far, we have seen that people learn about themselves through introspection and observations of their own behavior and that they organize this information into self-schemas. As important as these sources of self-knowledge are, there is still something missing. We are not solitary seekers of self-knowledge but social beings who often see ourselves through the eyes of other people. In fact, much of what we learn about ourselves can be influenced by others. James (1890) stressed the importance of social relationships in our definition of self, noting that we can have different "selves" that develop in response to different social situations. For example, when one of us is at the stable, training her horse and chatting with other riders and stablehands, she presents a different aspect of herself than when she is at a national psychology conference with her colleagues. Her "barn self" is more colloquial, less intellectual; she alters her vocabulary and topics of conversation (Knowles & Sibicky, 1990). Not only do we present ourselves differently to different people, but how they view us shapes our self-definition. It's as if other people hold up a mirror and reflect their image of you back at you to see.

The Looking-Glass Self

The idea that we see ourselves through the eyes of other people and incorporate their views into our self-concept is called the **looking-glass self** (Cooley, 1902; Mead, 1934). The ability to look at ourselves through other people's eyes is crucial to developing a sense of self, because it allows us to understand that we may see the world differently from how others do. If we cannot see ourselves through the eyes of other people, our own image will be a blur, because we have no social looking glass in which to view ourselves. Remember the mirror and red dye test we discussed earlier, used to determine if animals and young children have a self-concept? You'll recall that children 9 to 12 months of age do not react to their red nose when they see it in a mirror, whereas 2-year-olds do. The younger children do not understand that this image is themselves. Why? One reason is that children at 1 year of age have far less experience with social interaction than 2-year-olds do.

Experiments conducted with great apes have indicated that social contact is indeed crucial to the development of a self-concept. For example, Gordon Gallup (1977) compared the behavior of chimpanzees raised in normal, family groupings with that of chimps who were raised alone, in complete social isolation. Both types of chimps were painted with the red dye, as described earlier, and placed alone in a room without a mirror. The frequency with which they touched their marked but unseen browridge and ear was noted; these are the pretest data shown in Figure 5.7. Then a mirror was brought into the room. Now the chimps could see themselves and their new "cosmetics." The socially experienced chimps showed the typical response of great apes (and human beings)—they immediately used their mirrored image to explore the red areas of their heads. However, the socially isolated chimps did not react to their reflections at all—they did not recognize themselves in the mirror (see Figure 5.7). In primates as well as human beings, social interaction is crucial for developing a sense of self.

■ **FIGURE 5.7   Effects of social isolation on the development of the self-concept.**   When in front of a mirror, chimps raised in social isolation touched the red-dyed parts of their bodies much less than chimps raised in social groups did. (Adapted from Gallup, 1977)

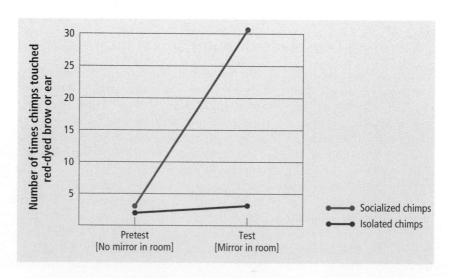

Social Comparison Theory

We also come to know ourselves by comparison to other people (Brown, 1990; Collins, 1996; Helgeson & Mickelson, 1995; Kruglanski & Mayseless, 1990; McFarland & Miller, 1994; Niedenthal & Beike, 1997; Suls & Wills, 1991; Wheeler, Martin, & Suls, 1997; Wood, 1989, 1996). If you are trying to determine your feelings, traits, and abilities, other people and their feelings, traits, and abilities are a valuable source of information. Suppose, for example, we gave you a test that measured your social sensitivity, or how aware you are of other people's problems. The test involves reading excerpts from autobiographies and guessing the nature of the authors' personal problems, if any. After you've taken the test, we tell you that you achieved a score of 35. What have you learned about yourself? Not much, because you don't know what a score of 35 means. Is it a good score or a bad score? Suppose we told you that the test is scored on a scale from 0 to 50. Now what have you learned? A little more than you knew before, perhaps, because you know that although you did not achieve a perfect score, you did score above the middle of the scale. This is still pretty uninformative, though, without knowing how other people did on the test. If we told you that everyone else in your class scored between 0 and 20, you would probably say, "Wow—I really am a extremely sensitive person!" On the other hand, you might feel differently if we told you that everyone else scored between 45 and 50.

This example illustrates Leon Festinger's (1954) **social comparison theory**, which holds that people learn about their own abilities and attitudes by comparing themselves to other people. The theory revolves around two important questions (Goethals, 1986; Latané, 1966): (a) When do you engage in social comparison, and (b) with whom do you choose to compare yourself? The answer to the first question is that you socially compare when there is no objective standard for you to measure yourself against and when you experience some uncertainty about yourself in a particular area (Suls & Fletcher, 1983; Suls & Miller, 1977). That is, when you're not sure how well you're doing or what exactly you're feeling, you'll observe other people and compare yourself to them.

As to the second question—With whom should you compare yourself?—recent research by Daniel Gilbert and his colleagues reveals a surprising answer (Gilbert, Giesler, & Morris, 1995). People's initial impulse, they argue, is to compare themselves with anyone who is around. This initial comparison occurs quickly and automatically (see our discussion of automatic judgment in Chapter 3). After a quick assessment of how our performance compares to others', however, we then decide how appropriate that comparison is—realizing that not all comparisons are equally informative.

Suppose, for example, you are wondering about your artistic ability. Is it most appropriate to compare yourself to Picasso, your 4-year-old sister, or your fellow students in a drawing class? Not surprisingly, people find it most informative to compare themselves to others who are similar to them on the important attribute, or dimension (Goethals & Darley, 1977; Miller, 1982; Wheeler, Koestner, & Driver, 1982). Observing the ability of your classmates in drawing class will give you an idea of how artistically talented you are. Comparing yourself to Picasso is aiming too high; you'll only become discouraged if, as a beginner, you compare yourself to one of the great artists of the twentieth century.

Sometimes people engage in **upward social comparison**, whereby they compare themselves to people who are better than they are on a particular trait. One reason to look upward is that we can determine what excellence, or the best,

Social Comparison Theory
the idea that we learn about our own abilities and attitudes by comparing ourselves to other people

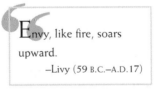

Envy, like fire, soars upward.
—Livy (59 B.C.–A.D. 17)

Upward Social Comparison
the process whereby we compare ourselves to people who are better than we are on a particular trait or ability

■ This man has engaged in too much upward social comparison.

"Of course you're going to be depressed if you keep comparing yourself with successful people."

> There is little satisfaction in the contemplation of heaven for oneself if one cannot simultaneously contemplate the horrors of hell for others.
> —P. D. James,
> *The Children of Men,* 1992

Downward Social Comparison
the process whereby we compare ourselves to people who are worse than we on a particular trait or ability

really is. In terms of self-knowledge, however, it is often more useful to compare ourselves to someone who is similar to us (Thornton & Arrowood, 1966; Wheeler et al., 1982; Zanna, Goethals, & Hill, 1975). Comparing your artistic talent to that of your little sister is aiming too low; her fingerpainting and scribbles tell you little about your abilities. It is better to compare yourself to your classmates in the drawing class, if your goal is to assess your own abilities.

However, constructing an accurate image of ourselves is only one reason that we engage in social comparison (Helgeson & Mickelson, 1995). When we are trying to assess our standing on a trait that is very important to us, we also use social comparison in order to boost our egos. Is it very important to you to believe that you are a fabulous artist-in-the-making? Then compare yourself to your little sister—you have her beat! This use of **downward social comparison**—comparing yourself to people who are worse than you on a particular trait or ability—is a self-protective, self-enhancing strategy (Aspinwall & Taylor, 1993; Pyszczynski, Greenberg, & LaPrelle, 1985; Reis, Gerrard, & Gibbons, 1993; Wheeler & Kunitate, 1992). If you compare yourself to people who are less smart, talented, or sick than you are, you'll feel very good about yourself. For example, Joanne Wood, Shelley Taylor, and Rosemary Lichtman (1985) found evidence of downward comparison in interviews with cancer patients. The vast majority of patients spontaneously compared themselves to other cancer patients who were more ill than they were, presumably as a way of making them feel more optimistic about the course of their own disease.

In sum, to whom we compare ourselves depends on the nature of our goals. When we want an accurate assessment of our abilities and opinions, we compare ourselves to people who are similar to us. When we want information about what we can strive toward, we make upward social comparisons. Finally, when our goal is self-enhancement, we compare ourselves to those who are less fortunate; such downward comparisons make us look better by comparison.

Impression Management: All the World's a Stage

Now that you've come to know yourself, what do you do with all that knowledge? Being a member of a highly social species, you present yourself to others. You have many aspects to your self-concept; you can be many selves. Thus, a basic aspect of your social existence is **self-presentation**, whereby you present who you are (or who you want people to believe you are) through your words, nonverbal behavior, and actions (Arkin & Shepperd, 1990; DePaulo, 1992; Goffman, 1959; Leary, 1995; Nail, Van Leeuwen, & Powell, 1996; Schlenker, 1980; Schlenker, Britt, & Pennington, 1996; Schlenker, Dlugolecki, & Doherty, 1994; Tedeschi, 1981). However, self-presentation is not always a simple, straightforward process; there are times when you want people to form a particular impression of you. At these times, you engage in **impression management**, consciously or unconsciously orchestrating a carefully designed presentation of self that will create a certain impression, one that fits your goals or needs in a social interaction (Goffman, 1959; Schlenker, 1980; Schlenker & Weigold, 1992).

The concepts of self-presentation and impression management were eloquently discussed by Erving Goffman (1955, 1959, 1967, 1971). His theory of social interaction was based on a dramaturgical model, which uses the theater as a metaphor for social life. On the stage, the actors present certain aspects of self (or their roles) to each other; Goffman says that in everyday life, we do the same thing in our social interactions. Further, just as in the theater, real life is made up of backstage and frontstage areas. Frontstage is when you're "on," when you are actively presenting a particular self to others so as to create or maintain a certain impression in their eyes. Thoroughly cleaning your room, apartment, or house before company arrives (and saying, "Oh, it's nothing," when they compliment you on how lovely it looks) is preparing for and being on frontstage. In contrast, backstage is when you are not actively managing or creating a particular impression. We become uncomfortable when people invade our backstage areas, for we are, by definition, unprepared. Witness how annoying and embarrassing it is when people you'd like to impress drop by to visit you unannounced and your place is a slovenly pigsty and you are looking your grungiest!

It is undoubtedly true that people in all cultures are concerned with impression management. The form in which this takes place, however, differs considerably from culture to culture. Earlier, we mentioned that people in Asian cultures tend to have a more interdependent view of themselves than people in Western cultures do. One consequence of this identity is that "saving face," or avoiding public embarrassment, is extremely important in Asian cultures. In Japan, for example, it is very important that people have the "right" guests at their weddings and enough mourners at the funerals of their loved ones—so important, in fact, that if guests or mourners are unavailable, you can go to a local "convenience agency" and rent some. These agencies (or *benriya*) keep a staff of employees ready to pretend that they are your closest friends. A woman named Hiroko, for example, was concerned that not enough guests would attend her second wedding. No problem—she simply hired some. She rented six guests, including a man

Self-Presentation
the attempt to present who we are, or who we want people to believe we are, through our words, nonverbal behaviors, and actions

Impression Management
our conscious or unconscious orchestration of a carefully designed presentation of self so as to create a certain impression that fits our goals or needs in a social interaction

> Keep up appearances whatever you do.
> —Charles Dickens, 1843

> To succeed in the world, we do everything we can to appear successful.
> —La Rochefoucauld, 1678

■ Impression management in action: In the 1970s, David Duke was a leader in the Ku Klux Klan; in 1991, he ran for governor of Louisiana as a mainstream conservative Republican. A remarkable change occurred in Duke's presentation of self during this time. Besides undergoing facial cosmetic surgery to improve his appearance, he claimed during his campaign that he no longer supported Nazi ideology or the Ku Klux Klan.

to pose as her boss, at a cost of $1,500. Her "boss" even delivered a flattering speech about her at the wedding (Jordan & Sullivan, 1995).

People from Western cultures are likely to chuckle at what to them seems like impression management taken to absurd lengths. Sometimes, however, Westerners also go to great lengths to influence what others think of them. Consider this disturbing example of impression management from the 1991 gubernatorial campaign in Louisiana. David Duke, who for most of his adult life had been a white supremacist and anti-Semite and who in 1989 had sold Nazi literature from his legislative office, was running for governor as a mainstream conservative Republican (Duke, 1991, p. 1). A remarkable change had occurred in Duke's presentation of self (see the photos on this page). Besides having undergone facial cosmetic surgery to improve his appearance, he claimed during the campaign that he no longer supported Nazi ideology or the Ku Klux Klan, of which he had been the leader (or Grand Wizard) in the 1970s. However, his campaign rhetoric was correctly perceived by many Louisiana voters as the same racist message disguised in new clothes, and he was defeated by the Democratic candidate, Edwin Edwards (Eisenman, 1994).

Most of us, of course, do not go to quite these lengths to manage the impressions we convey. All of us, however, attempt to manage our impressions to some extent. Ned Jones and Thane Pittman (1982) have described several strategic self-presentational techniques that people use in everyday life. One strategy is **ingratiation**, whereby you flatter, praise, and generally make yourself likable to another, often higher-status person (Jones & Wortman, 1973; Gordon, 1996). One can ingratiate through compliments, by agreeing with another's ideas, by commiserating and offering sympathy, and so on. If your professor's 3-year-old

Ingratiation
the process whereby people flatter, praise, and generally try to make themselves likable to another, often higher-status person

spits on you and kicks you in the shin and you say "Oh, what an adorable child!" you are probably ingratiating. Ingratiation is a powerful technique, since we all enjoy having someone be nice to us—which is what the ingratiator is good at. However, such a ploy can backfire if the recipient of your ingratiation figures out what you're doing (Jones, 1964; Kauffman & Steiner, 1968).

Another self-presentational strategy, and the one that has attracted the most research attention, is **self-handicapping**. This is the case in which people create obstacles and excuses for themselves, so that if they do poorly on a task, they have a ready-made excuse. Doing poorly or failing at a task is damaging to your self-esteem. In fact, just doing less well than you expected or than you have in the past can be upsetting, even if it is a good performance. How can you deal with this disappointment attributionally? Self-handicapping is the rather surprising solution: You can set up excuses, before the fact, just in case you do poorly (Arkin & Baumgardner, 1985; Jones & Berglas, 1978).

Let's say it's the night before the final exam in one of your courses. It's a difficult course, required for your major, and one in which you'd like to do well. A sensible strategy would be to eat a good dinner, study for a while, and then go to bed early and get a good night's sleep. The self-handicapping strategy would be to pull an all-nighter, do some heavy partying, then wandering into the exam the next morning bleary-eyed and muddle-headed. If you don't do well on the exam, you have an excuse. In other words, you have an external attribution to offer to others to explain your performance, one that deflects the potential negative, internal attribution they might otherwise make (that you're not smart). And if you do ace the exam, well, all the better—you did it under adverse conditions (no sleep), which suggests that you are especially smart and talented.

There are two major ways in which people self-handicap. In its most extreme form, people create obstacles that reduce the likelihood they will succeed on a task, so that if they do fail they can blame it on these obstacles rather than on their lack of ability. The obstacles people have been found to use include drugs, alcohol, reduced effort on the task, and failure to prepare for an important event (Berglas & Jones, 1978; Deppe & Harackiewicz, 1996; Greenberg, 1983; Higgins & Harris, 1988; Koditz & Arkin, 1982; Rhodewalt & Davison, 1984; Tice & Baumeister, 1990).

The second type of self-handicapping is less extreme. People do not create obstacles to success but do devise ready-made excuses in case they fail (Baumgardner, Lake, & Arkin, 1985; Greenberg, Pyszczynski, & Paisley, 1984; Hirt, Deppe, & Gordon, 1991; Snyder, Smith, Augelli, & Ingram, 1985). Thus, we might not go so far as to pull an all-nighter the night before an important exam, but we might complain that we are not feeling well. People have been found to arm themselves with all kinds of excuses, such as blaming their shyness, test anxiety, bad moods, physical symptoms, and adverse events from their pasts. One problem with preparing ourselves with excuses in advance, however, is that we may come to believe these excuses and thus exert less effort on the task. Whereas self-handicapping may prevent unflattering attributions for our failures, it often has the adverse effect of causing the poor performance that is so feared. It can also lead to negative evaluations from others. Fred Rhodewalt and his colleagues found that when students offered excuses for why they would do poorly on a task, other students inferred that they had low ability and that their performance was not up to par (Rhodewalt, Sanbonmatsu, Tschanz, Feick, & Waller, 1995).

Self-Handicapping
creating obstacles and excuses for ourselves, so that if we do poorly on a task, we have ready-made excuses

Summary

In this chapter, we have explored the nature of the self, the function of the self, and how people come to know themselves. The **self-concept** is the contents of the self, namely our perception of our own thoughts, beliefs, and personality traits. **Self-awareness** refers to the act of thinking about ourselves. Whereas primates have a rudimentary self-concept, the human sense of self is uniquely complex and multifaceted. The self-concept serves three important functions: managerial (regulating our actions and planning for the future); organizational (acting as a schema that influences what we notice, think, and remember); and emotional (determining how we feel by assessing how our actual self compares to our ideal and ought selves). These functions of the self may well serve a survival function and are probably basic to all humans.

There are, however, interesting cross-cultural and gender differences in the self-concept. In many Western cultures, people have an **independent view of the self**, whereby they define themselves mainly in terms of their own thoughts, feelings, and actions. In many Asian cultures, people have an **interdependent view of the self**, whereby they define themselves primarily in terms of their relationships with other people. Recent evidence suggests that in the United States, women are more interdependent than men, defining themselves more in relation to other people and close intimate relationships.

There are four basic ways in which we come to know ourselves: through (1) **introspection**, (2) observations of our own behavior, (3) self-schemas, and (4) social interaction. Research on **self-awareness theory** has found that introspecting about ourselves can be unpleasant, because it focuses our attention on how we fall short of our internal standards. A benefit of self-focus is that it can make us more aware of our own feelings and traits. Thinking about why we feel the way we do, however, is more difficult. Many studies show that people's judgments about the reasons for their feelings and actions are often incorrect, in part because people rely on **causal theories** when explaining their behavior. Further, the act of thinking about reasons can cause **reasons-generated attitude change**, convincing us that our feelings match the reasons that happen to come to mind.

Self-perception theory holds that we come to know ourselves through observations of our own be-havior, just as an outsider would. This occurs in particular when our internal states are unclear and there appears to be no external reason for our behavior. One interesting application of self-perception theory is the **overjustification effect**, which is the **discounting** of our **intrinsic motivation** for a task, as a result of inferring that we are engaging in the task because of **extrinsic motivation**. That is, rewards and other kinds of external influences can undermine our intrinsic interest; an activity we once liked seems like work instead of play. The overjustification effect is especially likely to occur when **task-contingent rewards** are used. These rewards are given for completing a task, regardless of people's level of performance. **Performance-contingent rewards** are based on how well people perform a task. These rewards are less likely to decrease interest in a task and may even increase interest, if they convey the message that people are competent without making them feel nervous and apprehensive about being evaluated. Another example of self-perception is the **two-factor theory of emotion**, whereby we determine our emotions by observing how aroused we are and making inferences about the causes of that arousal. **Misattribution of arousal** can occur, whereby people attribute their arousal to the wrong source. Attributions about arousal are not the only source of emotions; **cognitive appraisal theories of emotion** argue that emotions can also result from our interpretations and explanations of events in the absence of any physiological arousal.

People also organize information about themselves into **self-schemas**, which are knowledge structures about the self that help people understand, explain, and predict their own behavior. Self-schemas also help us organize our pasts, by influencing what we remember about ourselves, or our **autobiographical memories**. There is evidence that our memories can be reconstructive, whereby we view the past not as it really was but in ways that are consistent with our current theories and schemas. A great deal of controversy exists over the validity of **recovered memories**, or the sudden recollection of an event, such as sexual abuse, that had been forgotten or repressed. Though recovered memories may be true in some instances, they can also be the result of a **false memory syndrome**, whereby people come to believe that memory is true when it actually is not. False memories are especially likely to occur when another person suggests to us that an event really occurred.

Another way we come to know ourselves is through social interaction. By interacting with other people, we develop a **looking-glass self**, whereby we determine who we are based on others' perceptions of us. We also know ourselves through comparison with others. **Social comparison theory** states that we will compare ourselves to others when we are unsure of our standing on some attribute and there is no objective criterion we can use. Typically, we choose to compare ourselves to similar others, for this is most diagnostic. **Upward social comparison**, comparing ourselves to those who are superior on the relevant attribute, can help define what the standard of excellence is. **Downward social comparison**, comparing ourselves to those who are inferior on the relevant attribute, can make us feel better about our current plight.

Once we know ourselves, we often attempt to manage the self we present to others through the processes of **self-presentation** and **impression management**. Social life is much like the theater, where we present selves (or roles) to others. Two self-presentational strategies are **ingratiation** and **self-handicapping**. Self-handicapping involves lining up a behavior, trait, or situational event before a performance so that we can later use it as an excuse if we don't do well. One problem with preparing ourselves with excuses in advance, however, is that we may come to believe these excuses and thus exert less effort on the task. Whereas self-handicapping may prevent unflattering attributions for our failures, it often has the adverse effect of causing the poor performance that is so feared.

If You Are Interested

Baumeister, R. F. (1991). *Escaping the self: Alcoholism, spirituality, masochism, and other flights from the burden of selfhood.* New York: Basic Books. An intriguing look at the many different ways in which people try to escape too much self-focus.

Deci, E. L., & Flaste, R. (1995). *Why we do what we do: The dynamics of personal autonomy.* New York: G. P. Putnam's Sons. A discussion of intrinsic motivation and autonomy relevant to the discussion of overjustification in this chapter.

Fiske, S. T., & Taylor, S. E. (1991). *Social cognition* (2nd ed.). New York: McGraw-Hill. An encyclopedic review of the literature on social cognition by two experts in the field. Includes a chapter on social cognition and the self that covers in greater detail some of the same material we discussed in this chapter.

Hoop Dreams (1994). A documentary about two high school basketball stars from Chicago. In terms of research on the self and overjustification effects, it is fascinating to see what happens to these two players' love for the game as they are rewarded more and more for playing basketball.

Kitayama, S., & Markus, H. R. (Eds.) (1994). *Emotion and culture: Empirical investigations of mutual influence.* Washington, D.C.: American Psychological Association Press. A collection of chapters on culture and emotion by top researchers in the area. The topics include how emotions are experienced within a cultural context, the role of language in culture and emotion, and the relation between culture, emotion, and morality.

Mann, Thomas (1932). *The Magic Mountain.* This novel was reportedly the inspiration for Stanley Schachter's two-factor theory of emotion. While Hans Castorp is at a tuberculosis sanatorium high in the Swiss Alps, he experiences feelings of arousal and shortness of breath, due to the thin air. He interprets these feelings as signs of love for Clauvida Chauchat.

Proust, Marcel (1934). *Remembrance of Things Past.* This classic novel is full of insights about how people gain self-knowledge.

Schlenker, B. R. (1980). *Impression management: The self-concept, social identity, and interpersonal relations.* Monterey, CA: Brooks/Cole. A classic look at research on impression management and self-presentation.

Tan, Amy (1989). *The Joy Luck Club.* A poignant novel about identity and growth within conflicting cultural contexts.

The Return of Martin Guerre (1984). A film about a young husband who disappears and then returns to his wife years later. But is it the same man or an imposter? The film raises interesting questions about the continuity of one's identity and how that identity is perceived by others. A 1993 remake of the film, starring Jodie Foster and Richard Gere, was called *Sommersby*.

SELF-JUSTIFICATION AND THE NEED TO MAINTAIN SELF-ESTEEM

On March 26, 1997, 39 people were found dead at a luxury estate in Rancho Santa Fe, California—participants in a mass suicide . They were all members of an obscure cult called Heaven's Gate founded by Marshall Herff Applewhite, a former college professor. Each body was laid out neatly, feet clad in brand new black Nikes, face covered with a purple shroud. The cult members died willingly and peacefully—and didn't really consider it suicide. They left behind detailed videotapes describing their beliefs and intentions: They believed the Hale-Bopp Comet, at the time clearly visible in the western sky, was their ticket to a new life in paradise. They were convinced that, in the wake of the Hale-Bopp Comet, there was a gigantic spaceship whose mission was to carry them off to a new incarnation. To be picked up by the spaceship, they first needed to rid themselves of their current "containers." That is, they needed to leave their own bodies by ending their lives. Needless to say, there was no spaceship following behind the comet.

Several weeks before the mass suicide, when Hale-Bopp was still too distant to be seen with the naked eye, a few members of the cult walked into a specialty store and purchased a very expensive high-powered telescope. They wanted to get a clearer view of the comet and the spaceship they believed was traveling behind it. A few days later, they made their way back to the store, returned the telescope, and politely asked for their money back. When the store manager asked them if they had problems with the scope, the reply was: "Well, gosh, we found the comet, but we can't find anything following it" (Ferris, 1997). Although the store manager tried to convince them that there was nothing wrong with the telescope and that there was nothing following the comet, they remained unconvinced. Their attitude was clear and, given their premise, their logic was impeccable: (a) We know an alien spaceship is following behind the Hale-Bopp comet, and (b) If an expensive telescope failed to reveal that spaceship, then (c) there must be something wrong with the telescope.

Their logic might strike you as strange, irrational, or stupid. But we hasten to add that, generally speaking, the members of the Heaven's Gate cult were not stupid, not irrational, not crazy. How do we know this? For one thing, neighbors who knew them considered them to be pleasant, smart, reasonable people. Moreover, they were expert at computers and the internet and earned their living by setting up highly innovative web pages. Clients who worked closely with them were impressed—describing them as unusually bright, talented, and creative. What is the process by which intelligent, sane people can succumb to such fantastic thinking and self-destructive behavior? We will attempt to explain their actions near the end of this chapter. For now, we will simply state that their behavior is not unfathomable—it is simply an extreme example of a normal human tendency—our tendency to justify our actions.   ☐

The Need to Justify Our Actions

During the past half-century, social psychologists have discovered that one of the most powerful determinants of human behavior stems from our need to preserve a stable, positive self concept; that is, to maintain a relatively favorable view of ourselves, particularly when we encounter evidence that contradicts our typically rosy self-image (Aronson, 1969, 1992, 1998; Baumeister, 1993; Cooper, 1998; Devine, 1998; Harmon-Jones, 1998; Leippe & Eisenstadt, 1998; Wicklund & Brehm, 1998). Most of us want to believe that we are reasonable, decent folks who make wise decisions, do not behave immorally, and have integrity. In short, we want to believe that we do not do stupid, cruel, or absurd things. But as we go through life, we encounter a great many challenges to this belief. The topic of this chapter is how human beings deal with those challenges.

> When the heart speaks, the mind finds it indecent to object.
> —Milan Kundera, 1989

© Peanuts. Reprinted by permission of United Features Syndicate, Inc.

■ Once we have committed a lot of time or energy to a cause, it is nearly impossible to convince us that the cause is unworthy.

The Theory of Cognitive Dissonance

Most of us have a need to see ourselves as reasonable, moral, and smart. When we are confronted with information implying we may have behaved in ways that are irrational, immoral, or stupid we will experience a good deal of discomfort. We will call the feeling of discomfort caused by performing an action that is discrepant from one's customary (typically positive) conception of oneself **cognitive dissonance.** A half-century of research has demonstrated that cognitive dissonance is a major motivator of human thought and behavior. Leon Festinger was the first to investigate the precise workings of this powerful phenomenon and elaborated his findings into what is arguably social psychology's most important and most provocative theory—the theory of cognitive dissonance (Festinger, 1957). Historically, it is worth noting that initially social psychologists believed that that dissonance could be caused by *any* two discrepant cognitions (Festinger, 1957; Festinger & Aronson, 1960; Brehm & Cohen, 1962; Wicklund & Brehm, 1976). But subsequent research made it clear that not all cognitive inconsistencies are equally upsetting. Rather, as indicated above, we discovered that dissonance is most powerful and most upsetting when people behave in ways that threaten their image of themselves. This is upsetting precisely because it forces us to confront the discrepancy between who we think we are and how we have behaved (Aronson, 1968, 1969, 1992, 1998; Aronson et al., 1974; Greenwald & Ronis, 1978; Thibodeau & Aronson, 1992; Harmon-Jones & Mills, 1998). Generally speaking, then, cognitive dissonance most often occurs whenever we do something that tends to make us feel absurd, stupid, or immoral—as defined by our

Cognitive Dissonance
a drive or feeling of discomfort, originally defined as being caused by holding two or more inconsistent cognitions and subsequently defined as being caused by performing an action that is discrepant from one's customary, typically positive self-conception

own standards of reasonableness, intelligence, and morality. Cognitive dissonance always produces discomfort and therefore motivates a person to try to reduce the discomfort, in much the same way as hunger and thirst produce discomfort that motivates a person to eat or drink. But unlike satisfying hunger or thirst by eating or drinking, the ways of reducing dissonance are not simple; rather, they often lead to fascinating changes in the way we think about the world and the way we behave. As you will see, many of these behaviors are powerful and nonobvious. How can an individual reduce dissonance? There are three basic ways:

- By changing our behavior to bring it in line with the dissonant cognition
- By attempting to justify our behavior through changing one of the dissonant cognitions
- By attempting to justify our behavior by adding new cognitions (see Figure 6.1.)

To illustrate, let's look at an absurd piece of behavior that millions of people engage in several times a day—smoking cigarettes. Suppose you are a smoker. You are likely to experience dissonance, because it is absurd to engage in behavior that stands a good chance of producing a painful, early death. How can you reduce this dissonance? The most direct way is to change your behavior—to give up smoking. Your behavior would then be consistent with your knowledge of the link between smoking and cancer. While many people have succeeded in doing just that, it's not easy—many have tried to quit and failed. What do these people

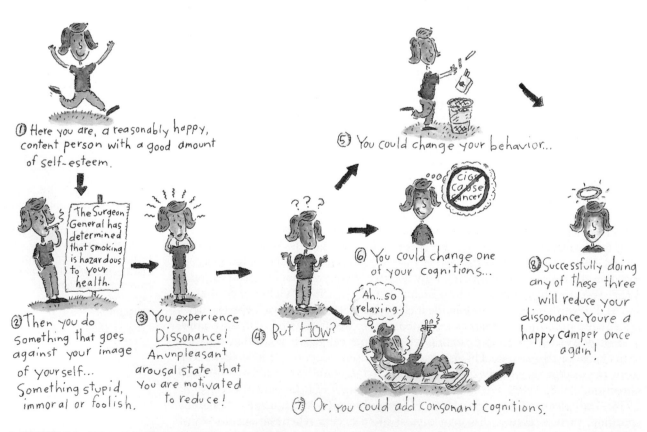

■ FIGURE 6.1   How we reduce cognitive dissonance.

do? It would be erroneous to assume that they simply swallow hard and prepare to die. They don't. Instead, they try to reduce their dissonance in a different way—namely, by convincing themselves that smoking isn't as bad as they thought. Thus, Rick Gibbons and his colleagues (1997) recently found that heavy smokers who attended a smoking cessation clinic, quit smoking for a while and then relapsed into heavy smoking again, actually succeeded in lowering their perception of the dangers of smoking.

Smokers can come up with pretty creative ways to justify their smoking; for example, some might try to convince themselves that the data linking cigarette smoking to cancer are inconclusive. Others will try to add new cognitions—for example, the erroneous belief that filters trap most of the harmful chemicals and thus reduce the threat of cancer. Some will add a cognition that allows them to focus on the vivid exception: "Look at old Sam Carouthers—he's 97 years old and he's been smoking a pack a day since he was 12. That proves it's not always bad for you." Still others will add the cognition that smoking is an extremely enjoyable activity, one for which it is worth risking cancer. Others may even succeed in convincing themselves that, all things considered, smoking is worthwhile because it relaxes them, reduces nervous tension, and so on.

These justifications may sound silly to the nonsmoker. That is precisely our point. People experiencing dissonance will often go to extreme lengths to reduce it. We did not make up the examples of denial, distortion, and justification listed above; they are based on actual examples generated by people who have tried and failed to quit smoking. Similar justifications have been generated by people who try and fail to lose weight, who refuse to practice safer sex, or who receive unwelcome information about their health (Aronson, 1997; Croyle & Jemmott, 1990; Goleman, 1982; Kassarjian & Cohen, 1965; Leishman, 1988). To escape from dissonance, people will engage in quite extraordinary rationalizing. Occasionally these illusions can be helpful; for example, Shelley Taylor and her colleagues have demonstrated that those who harbor unrealistically positive illusions about surviving a terminal illness, like AIDS, live longer than those who are more "realistic" (Taylor, 1989; Taylor & Armour, 1996; Taylor & Gollwitzer, 1995). Far more often (as in the case of smoking) these illusions are destructive.

Rational Behavior versus Rationalizing Behavior

Most people proudly believe that human beings are rational animals—and, to a large extent, they are right. But as the above examples illustrate, the need to maintain our self-esteem produces thinking that is not always rational; rather, it is rational*izing*. People who are in the midst of reducing dissonance are so involved with convincing themselves that they are right that they frequently end up behaving irrationally and maladaptively. In the case of cigarette smoking, the end result could be tragic.

To demonstrate the irrationality of dissonance-reducing behavior, Edward E. Jones and Rika Kohler (1959) performed a simple experiment in a southern town in the late 1950s, before desegregation was widely accepted. First, they selected individuals who were deeply committed to a position on the issue of racial segregation—some of the participants were in favor of segregation, and others were opposed to it. Next, the researchers presented these individuals with a series of arguments on both sides of the issue. Some of the arguments, on each side, were plausible, and others, on each side, were rather silly. The question was, which of the arguments would people remember best?

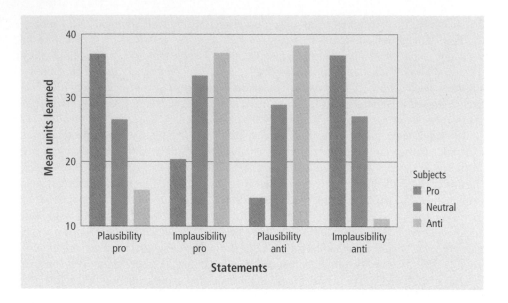

■ **FIGURE 6.2 The effects of plausibility on the learning of controversial statements.** People tend to remember plausible arguments that support their position and implausible arguments that support the opposing position. To remember either implausible arguments that support your position or plausible arguments that support the opposing position would arouse dissonance. (Adapted from Jones & Kohler, 1959)

If Jones and Kohler's (1959) participants were behaving in a purely rational manner, we would expect them to remember the plausible arguments best and the implausible arguments least—regardless of which side they were on. After all, why would anyone want to remember implausible arguments? What does dissonance theory predict? A silly argument in favor of one's own position arouses some dissonance, because it raises doubts about the wisdom of that position or the intelligence of the people who agree with it. Likewise, a sensible argument on the other side of the issue also arouses some dissonance, because it raises the possibility that the other side might be closer to the truth than the person had thought. Because these arguments arouse dissonance, one tries not to think about them; that is, one might not learn them very well, or one might simply forget about them. This is exactly what Jones and Kohler found. The participants in their experiment did not remember in a rational or functional manner. They tended to remember the plausible arguments agreeing with their own position and the implausible arguments agreeing with the opposing position. Subsequent research has yielded similar results on a wide variety of issues, from whether or not the death penalty deters people from committing murder, to the risks of contracting AIDS through heterosexual contact (e.g., Biek, Wood, & Chaiken, 1996; Edwards & Smith, 1996; Lord, Ross, & Lepper, 1979; Vallone, Ross, & Lepper, 1985). All of this research indicates that we human beings do not process information in an unbiased manner. Rather, we distort it in a way that fits our preconceived notions. The major results of the Jones and Kohler experiment are presented in Figure 6.2.

This process probably accounts for the fact that, on issues like politics and religion, people who are deeply committed to a view different from our own will almost never come to see things our way (the proper way!), no matter how powerful and balanced our arguments might be.

Decisions, Decisions, Decisions

Every time we make a decision we experience dissonance. How come? Let's take a close look at the process. Suppose you are about to buy a new car. After looking around, you are torn between a van and a sub-compact. There are various ad-

// *Try It* !

Justifying Decisions

The distinguished news show, *Meet the Press*, usually focuses on a current, controversial political issue. The typical format of the show is that articulate people, representing both sides of the issue, present their views in a forceful and articulate manner. Look at *TV Guide* to see what

issue is going to be debated next week. In advance, poll two or three of your friends or family members to ascertain their feelings about the issue. Try to get them to watch the show that week. Discuss their feelings about the issue and their feelings about the debaters after watching the show.

//

vantages and disadvantages to each: The van would be convenient; you can haul things in it, sleep in it during long trips and it has plenty of power, but it gets poor mileage and is not easy to park. The sub-compact is a lot less roomy, and you are concerned about its safety, but it is less expensive to buy and operate, it is a lot zippier to drive, and you've heard it has a pretty good repair record. My guess is that, before you make the decision, you will seek as much information as you can. Chances are you will read *Consumer Reports* to find out what this expert, unbiased source has to say. Perhaps you'll confer with friends who own a van or a sub-compact. You'll probably visit the automobile dealers to test-drive the vehicles to see how each one feels. All of this predecision behavior is perfectly rational. Let us assume you make a decision—you buy the sub-compact.

What happens after the decision? We predict that your behavior will change in a specific way: You will begin to think more and more about the number of miles to the gallon as though it were the most important thing in the world. Simultaneously you will almost certainly downplay the importance of the fact that you can't sleep in your sub-compact. Similarly, your mind will skim lightly over the fact that driving your new car can be particularly hazardous in a collision. How does this happen?

Distorting Our Likes and Dislikes

In any decision, whether it is between two cars, two colleges, or two potential lovers, the chosen alternative is seldom entirely positive, and the rejected alternative is seldom entirely negative. So, while making the decision, you have your doubts. After the decision, your cognition that you are a smart person is dissonant with all of the negative things about the car, college, or lover you chose; that cognition is also dissonant with all of the positive aspects of the car, college, or lover you rejected. We call this **postdecision dissonance.** Cognitive dissonance theory predicts that, in order to feel better about the decision, you will do some mental work to try to reduce the dissonance. What kind of work? An early experiment by Jack Brehm (1956) is illustrative. Brehm posed as a representative of a consumer testing service and asked women to rate the attractiveness and desirability of several kinds of appliances, such as toasters and electric coffeemakers. Each woman was told that, as a reward for having participated in the survey, she could have one of the appliances as a gift. She was given a choice between two of the products she had rated as being equally attractive. After she made her decision, her appliance was wrapped up and given to her. Twenty minutes later, each woman was asked to re-rate all the products. Brehm found that after receiving

Postdecision Dissonance
dissonance that is inevitably aroused after a person makes a decision; in this situation, dissonance is typically reduced by enhancing the attractiveness of the chosen alternative and devaluing the rejected alternatives

the appliance of their choice, the women rated its attractiveness somewhat higher than they had done the first time. Not only that, but they drastically lowered their rating of the appliance they might have chosen but decided to reject.

In other words, following a decision, to reduce dissonance, we change the way we feel about the chosen and unchosen alternatives—cognitively spreading them apart in our own minds in order to make ourselves feel better about the choice we made.

The Permanence of the Decision

It stands to reason that the more important the decision, the greater the dissonance. Deciding which car to buy is clearly more important than deciding between a toaster and a coffeemaker; deciding which person to marry is clearly more important than deciding which car to buy. Decisions also vary in terms of how permanent they are—that is, how difficult they are to revoke. It is usually a lot easier to go back to the car dealership and trade in your new car for another one than it is to extricate yourself from an unhappy marriage. The more permanent and less revocable the decision, the greater the need to reduce dissonance.

An excellent place to investigate the significance of irrevocability is the racetrack. Experienced bettors typically spend a great deal of time poring over the "dope sheets," trying to decide which horse to put their money on. When they make a decision, they head for the betting windows. While they are standing in line, they have already made their decision, but, we would hypothesize, because it is still revocable they have no urge to reduce dissonance. However, once they get to the window and place their bet—even if it's for only $2—it is absolutely irrevocable. Thirty seconds later, one cannot go back and tell the nice person behind the window that one has had a change of mind. Therefore, if irrevocability is an important factor, one would expect greater dissonance reduction among bettors a few minutes after placing the bet than a few minutes before placing the bet.

In a simple but clever experiment, Knox and Inkster (1968) intercepted people who were on their way to place $2 bets and asked them how certain they were their horses would win. The investigators also intercepted other bettors just as they were

■ Once an individual makes a final and irrevocable decision, he or she has a greater need to reduce dissonance. For example, at the racetrack, once we've placed our bet, our certainty is greater than it is immediately before we've placed our bet.

■ Car salespeople frequently use a high-pressure technique whereby they make the customer feel as if he or she had entered into an irrevocable agreement.

leaving the $2 window, after having placed their bets, and asked them the same question. Almost invariably, people who had already placed their bets gave their horses a much better chance of winning than those who had yet to place their bets did. Since only a few minutes separated one group from another, nothing real had occurred to increase the probability of winning; the only thing that had changed was the finality of the decision—and thus the dissonance it produced.

The irrevocability of a decision always increases dissonance and the motivation to reduce it. Because of this, unscrupulous salespeople have developed techniques for creating the illusion that irrevocability exists. One such technique, called **lowballing**, is a successful ploy used by some car salespeople. The social psychologist Robert Cialdini temporarily joined the sales force of an automobile dealership to observe this technique closely. Here's how it works: You enter an automobile showroom, intent on buying a particular car. Having already priced it at several dealerships, you know you can purchase it for about $18,000. You are approached by a personable, middle-aged man who tells you he can sell you one for $17,679. Excited by the bargain, you agree to the deal and, at the salesperson's request, write out a check for the down payment so that he can take it to the sales manager as proof you are a serious customer.

Meanwhile, you rub your hands in glee as you imagine yourself driving home in your shiny new bargain. But alas, ten minutes later the salesperson returns, looking forlorn. He tells you that, in his zeal to give you a good deal, he made an error in calculation and the sales manager caught it. The price of the car actually comes to $18,178. You are disappointed. Moreover, you are pretty sure you can get it a bit cheaper elsewhere. The decision to buy is not irrevocable. And yet in this situation, research by Cialdini and his colleagues (1978) suggests that far more people will go ahead with the deal than if the original asking price had been $18,178, even though the reason for purchasing the car from this particular dealer—the bargain price—no longer exists. How come?

There are at least three reasons that lowballing works. First, while the customer's decision to buy is certainly reversible, a commitment of sorts does exist, due to the act of signing a check for a down payment. This creates the illusion of

Lowballing
an unscrupulous strategy whereby a salesperson induces a customer to agree to purchase a product at a very low cost, subsequently claims it was an error, and then raises the price; frequently the customer will agree to make the purchase at the inflated price

irrevocability, even though, if the car buyer really thought about it, he or she would quickly realize it is a nonbinding contract. However, in the razzle-dazzle world of high-pressure sales, even temporary illusion can have powerful consequences. Second, this commitment triggered the anticipation of an exciting event: driving out with a new car. To have had the anticipated event thwarted (by not going ahead with the deal) would have produced dissonance and disappointment. Third, although the final price is substantially higher than the customer thought it would be, it is probably only slightly higher than the price at another dealership. Under these circumstances, the customer in effect says, "Oh, what the heck. I'm already here, I've already filled out the forms, I've already written out the check—why wait?" Thus, by using dissonance reduction and the illusion of irrevocability, high-pressure salespeople increase the probability that you will decide to buy their product at their price.

The Decision to Behave Immorally

Needless to say, life is made up of more than just decisions about cars, appliances, and racehorses. Often our decisions involve moral and ethical issues. When is it permissible to lie to a friend, and when is it not? When is an act stealing, and when is it borrowing? Resolving moral dilemmas is a particularly interesting area in which to study dissonance because of the powerful implications for one's self-esteem. Even more interesting is the fact that dissonance reduction following a difficult moral decision can cause people to behave either more or less ethically in the future.

Take the issue of cheating on an exam. Suppose you are a college sophomore taking the final exam in a physics course. Ever since you can remember, you have wanted to be a surgeon, and you know that your admission to medical school will depend heavily on how well you do in this physics course. The key question on the exam involves some material you know fairly well, but because so much is riding on this exam, you experience acute anxiety and draw a blank. The minutes tick away. You become increasingly anxious. You simply cannot think. You look up and notice that you happen to be sitting behind the smartest person in the class. You glance at her paper and discover that she is just completing her answer to the crucial question. You know you could easily read her answer if you chose to. Time is running out. What do you do? Your conscience tells you it's wrong to cheat—and yet if you don't cheat, you are certain to get a poor grade. And if you get a poor grade, there goes medical school. You wrestle with your conscience.

Regardless of whether or not you decide to cheat, you are doomed to experience the kind of threat to your self-esteem that arouses dissonance. If you cheat, your cognition "I am a decent, moral person" is dissonant with your cognition "I have just committed an immoral act." If you decide to resist temptation, your cognition "I want to become a surgeon" is dissonant with your cognition "I could have acted in such a way that would have ensured a good grade and admission to medical school, but I chose not to. Wow, was that stupid!"

In this situation, some students would decide to cheat; others would decide not to cheat. What happens to the students' attitudes about cheating after their decision? Suppose that after a difficult struggle, you decide to cheat. How do you reduce the dissonance? According to dissonance theory, it is likely that you would try to justify the action by finding a way to minimize the negative aspects of the action you chose. In this instance, an efficient path of dissonance reduction would entail a change in your attitude about cheating. In short, you will adopt a more lenient attitude toward cheating, convincing yourself that it is a victimless crime that doesn't hurt anybody, that everybody does it and so it's not really that bad.

Suppose, on the other hand, that after a difficult struggle you decide not to cheat. How would you reduce your dissonance? Once again, you could change your attitude about the morality of the act—but this time in the opposite direction. That is, in order to justify giving up a good grade, you must convince yourself that cheating is a heinous sin, that it's one of the lowest things a person can do, and that cheaters should be rooted out and severely punished.

What has come about is not merely a rationalization of your own behavior but an actual change in your system of values; individuals faced with this kind of choice will undergo either a softening or a hardening of their attitudes toward cheating on exams, depending on whether or not they decided to cheat. The interesting and important thing to remember is that two people acting in the two different ways described above could have started out with almost identical attitudes toward cheating. Their decisions might have been a hair's breadth apart— one came within an inch of cheating but decided to resist, while the other came within an inch of resisting but decided to cheat. Once they made their decisions, however, their attitudes toward cheating will diverge sharply as a consequence of their actions.

These speculations were put to the test by Judson Mills (1958) in an experiment he performed in an elementary school. Mills first measured the attitudes of sixth-graders toward cheating. He then had them participate in a competitive exam, with prizes being offered to the winners. The situation was arranged so that it was almost impossible to win without cheating. Mills made it easy for the children to cheat and created the illusion that they could not be detected. Under these conditions, as one might expect, some of the students cheated and others did not. The next day, the sixth-graders were again asked to indicate how they felt about cheating. Those children who had cheated became more lenient toward cheating, and those who had resisted the temptation to cheat adopted a harsher attitude toward cheating.

Classic experiments conducted in the laboratory often inspire contemporary research in the real world. A case in point: While conducting research among mid-level business executives in India, Chockalingam Visweswaran and Satish Deshpande (1996) came up with some interesting data pertinent to Mills's results. These investigators reasoned that those executives who were in the process of making a decision about whether or not to behave ethically were in a vulnerable state: On the one hand, they wanted to behave ethically; on the other hand, they were undoubtedly concerned lest they might need to behave unethically in order to succeed. The investigators found that those executives who had substantial reason to believe that managerial success could only be achieved through unethical behavior experienced far greater dissonance (in the form of job dissatisfaction) than those who were given no reason to believe this. Our guess is that if the investigators had returned a year or two later, they would have found a reduction in dissonance in this group; that is, as with Mills's subjects, most of those who behaved unethically would have found a way to justify that behavior after the fact.

The Justification of Effort

Most people are willing to put out a lot of effort in order to get something they really want. For example, if there's a particular job you want, you are likely to go

■ Going through a lot of effort to become a marine will increase the recruits' feelings of cohesiveness and their pride in the corps.

the extra mile in order to get it. This might involve shopping for appropriate clothing, studying extra hard to meet entrance requirements, passing a battery of difficult exams, or putting up with a series of stressful interviews.

Let's turn that proposition inside out. Suppose you expend a great deal of effort in order to get into a particular club and it turns out to be a totally worthless organization, consisting of boring, pompous people engaged in trivial activities. You would feel pretty foolish, wouldn't you? A sensible person doesn't work hard in order to gain something trivial. Such a circumstance would produce a fair amount of dissonance; your cognition that you are a sensible, adept human being is dissonant with your cognition that you worked hard to get into a worthless club. How would you reduce this dissonance? How would you justify your behavior? You might start by finding a way to convince yourself that the club and the people in it are nicer, more interesting, and more worthwhile than they appeared to be at first glance. How can one turn boring people into interesting people and a trivial club into a worthwhile one? Easy. Even the most boring people and trivial clubs have some redeeming qualities. Activities and behaviors are open to a variety of interpretations; if we are motivated to see the best in people and things, we will tend to interpret these ambiguities in a positive manner. We call this the **justification of effort**—the tendency for individuals to increase their liking for something they have worked hard to attain.

Justification of Effort
the tendency for individuals to increase their liking for something they have worked hard to attain

In a now classic experiment, Elliot Aronson and Judson Mills (1959) explored the link between effort and dissonance reduction. In their experiment, college students volunteered to join a group that would be meeting regularly to discuss various aspects of the psychology of sex. In order to be admitted to the group, they volunteered to go through a screening procedure. For one-third of the participants, the procedure was an extremely effortful and unpleasant one; for one-third it was only very mildly unpleasant; one-third were admitted to the group without undergoing any screening procedure.

Each participant was then allowed to listen in on a discussion being conducted by the members of the group they would be joining. Although they were led to believe that the discussion was a live, ongoing one, what they actually

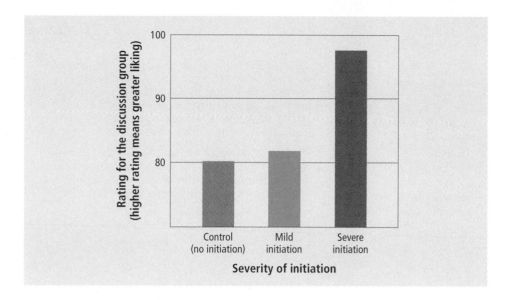

heard was a prerecorded tape. The taped discussion was arranged so that it was as dull and bombastic as possible. After the discussion was over, each participant was asked to rate it in terms of how much they liked it, how interesting it was, how intelligent the participants were, and so forth. The major findings are shown in Figure 6.3.

The results supported the predictions: Those participants who underwent little or no effort to get into the group did not enjoy the discussion very much. They were able to see it for what it was—a dull and boring waste of time. They regretted that they had agreed to participate. Those participants who went through a severe initiation, however, succeeded in convincing themselves that the same discussion, while not as scintillating as they had hoped, was dotted with interesting and provocative tidbits and therefore, in the main, was a worthwhile experience. In short, they justified their effortful initiation process by interpreting all the ambiguous aspects of the group discussion in the most positive manner possible (similar results were obtained by Gerard and Mathewson, 1966, and by Cooper, 1980).

It should be clear that we are not suggesting that most people enjoy effortful, unpleasant experiences—they do not. Nor are we suggesting that people enjoy things that are merely associated with unpleasant experiences. They do not. What we are asserting is that, if a person agrees to go through a difficult or an unpleasant experience in order to attain some goal or object, that goal or object becomes more attractive. Thus, if you were walking to the discussion group and a passing car splashed mud all over you, you would not like that group any better. However, if you volunteered to jump into a mud puddle in order to be admitted to a group that turned out to be trivial and boring, you would like the group better.

The Psychology of Insufficient Justification

When we were little, we were taught never to tell a lie. Indeed, our elementary school history courses were full of mythical stories (disguised as truths) like that of George Washington and the cherry tree, apparently aimed at convincing us that we had better be truthful if we aspired to the presidency. Alas, the world is a complicated place. There may be some people in the world who have never told a

Try It !

Justifying Actions

Think about something that you have gone after in the past that necessitated your going through a lot of trouble or effort. Perhaps you waited for several hours in a long line to get tickets to a concert; perhaps you knowingly sat in your car through an incredible traffic jam because it was the only way you could visit a close friend.

1. Specifically, list the things you had to go through in order to attain your goal.

2. Do you think you might have tried to justify all that effort? Did you find yourself exaggerating the good things about the goal and minimizing any negative aspects of the goal? List some of the ways you might have exaggerated the value of the goal.

3. The next time you find yourself in that kind of situation, you might want to monitor your actions and cognitions carefully to see if there is any self-justification involved.

---

lie, but most of us have yet to meet one. At times, most of us feel that, for good reason, we need to be less than perfectly truthful. One such reason involves something else that we were taught—namely, to be kind to one another. Occasionally, in order to be kind to someone, we find it necessary to tell a lie.

For example, suppose you walk into your friend Sam's house and notice an atrocious painting on the wall. You look at it, and it's so bad that you think it's a joke. You are about to burst into raucous laughter when Sam says, with considerable pleasure and excitement, "Do you like it? It cost a great deal. It's by a relatively unknown local artist named Carol Smear; I think she's very talented, so I went into hock to buy it from her. Don't you think it's beautiful?"

How do you respond? You hesitate. Chances are you go through something like the following thought process: "Sam seems so happy and excited. Why should I rain on his parade? If I were to tell him my true feelings, I would almost certainly cause him distress. He obviously likes the painting and paid a great deal for it. Telling him my honest opinion might make him annoyed with me or might make him feel he made a terrible mistake. Either way, it will be unpleasant. Even if I end up convincing Sam that it's a piece of garbage, he can't take it back. What's the sense in telling him the truth?"

So you tell Sam that you like the painting very much. Do you experience much dissonance? We doubt it. There are a great many thoughts that are consonant with having told this lie, as outlined in your reasoning in the above paragraph. In effect, your cognition that it is important not to cause pain to people you like provides ample **external justification** for having told a harmless lie.

Counter-Attitudinal Advocacy

What happens if you say something you don't really believe and there is no ample external justification for doing so? That is, what if your friend Sam was fabulously wealthy and bought paintings constantly? What if he sincerely needed to know your opinion of this purchase? What if in the past you'd told him he's bought a veritable eyesore and your friendship survived? Now the external justifications for lying to Sam about the painting are minimal. If you still refrain from giving your true opinion (saying instead, "Gee, Sam, uh, it's . . . interesting"), you will experience dissonance. When you can't find external justification for your be-

External Justification
a person's reason or explanation for his or her dissonant behavior that resides outside the individual (e.g., in order to receive a large reward or avoid a severe punishment)

havior, you will attempt to find **internal justification**—you will try to reduce dissonance by changing something about yourself (e.g., your attitude or behavior). How can you do this? You might begin looking for positive aspects of the painting—some evidence of creativity or sophistication that might have escaped you previously. If you look hard enough, you will probably find something. Within a short time, your attitude toward the painting will have moved in the direction of the statement you made—and that is how saying becomes believing. This phenomenon is generally referred to as **counter-attitudinal advocacy,** a process that occurs when a person states an opinion or attitude that runs counter to his or her private belief or attitude. When this is accomplished with a minimum of external justification, it results in a change in the individual's private attitude in the direction of the public statement.

This proposition was first tested in a ground-breaking experiment by Leon Festinger and J. Merrill Carlsmith (1959). In this experiment, college students were induced to spend an hour performing a series of excruciatingly boring and repetitive tasks. The experimenter then told them that the purpose of the study was to determine whether or not people would perform better if they had been informed in advance that the tasks were interesting. They were each informed that they had been randomly assigned to the control condition—that is, they had not been told anything in advance. However, he explained, the next participant, a young woman who was just arriving in the anteroom, was going to be in the experimental condition. The researcher said that he needed to convince her that the task was going to be interesting and enjoyable. Since it was much more convincing if a fellow student rather than the experimenter delivered this message, would the participant do so? Thus, with his request the experimenter induced the participants to lie about the task to another student .

Half of the students were offered $20 for telling the lie (a large external justification), while the others were offered only $1 for telling the lie (a very small external justification). After the experiment was over, an interviewer asked the lie-tellers how much they had enjoyed the tasks they had performed earlier in the experiment. The results validated the hypothesis: Those students who had been paid $20 for lying—that is, for saying the tasks had been enjoyable—rated the activities as the dull and boring experiences they were. But those who were paid only $1 for saying the task was enjoyable rated the task as significantly more enjoyable. In other words, people who had received an abundance of external justification for lying told the lie but didn't believe it, whereas those who told the lie without a great deal of external justification succeeded in convincing themselves that what they said was closer to the truth.

One might ask whether this phenomenon works when important attitudes are involved. Can you induce a person to change an attitude about things that matter? Subsequent research has shown that the Festinger-Carlsmith paradigm has wide ramifications in areas of great significance. Consider an experiment by A. R. Cohen (1962), for example. Cohen was a social psychologist at Yale University during a turbulent period, when the city police were often descending on the campus to control the overly exuberant behavior of the Yale students. Occasionally the police reacted with gleeful and excessive force. After one such altercation, Cohen visited a Yale dormitory, indicating he worked for a well-known research institute. He told the students that there were two sides to every issue and that the institute was interested in looking at both sides of the police-student issue. He then asked the students to write forceful essays supporting the behavior of the police. Moreover, he told them he was able to offer them an in-

Internal Justification
the reduction of dissonance by changing something about oneself (e.g., one's attitude or behavior)

Counter-Attitudinal Advocacy
the process that occurs when a person states an opinion or attitude that runs counter to his or her private belief or attitude

centive for writing the essay. Depending on the condition to which the students were assigned, he offered them 50 cents, $1, $5, or $10. (None of the students was aware of what the others were being offered.) After the students wrote their essays, Cohen assessed their real attitude toward the actions of the city police.

The results were clear: The smaller the incentive, the more favorable people became toward the city police. In other words, when the students were given a great deal of external justification for writing the essay, they did not need to convince themselves that they really believed what they had written. However, when they were faced with the fact that they had written positive things about the police for 50 cents or $1, they needed to convince themselves that there may have been some truth in what they had written.

In a similar experiment, Elizabeth Nel, Robert Helmreich, and Elliot Aronson (1969) approached college students who initially believed that marijuana was harmful, and induced them to compose and recite a videotaped speech favoring its use and legalization. Some were offered large incentives; others were offered small incentives. Again, the findings were clear: The smaller the incentive, the greater the softening of the attitude toward the use and legalization of marijuana.

In many of these experiments, people behaved without integrity (told a lie) in a manner that also might have harmed another person. For example, if you believe that marijuana is harmful and you tell someone that it is harmless, you might be doing that person a great deal of harm. Accordingly, it is reasonable to raise the following question: Is lying enough? Is harming another person a necessary condition for dissonance, or is dissonance produced simply by behaving without integrity—even if no harm results? A recent experiment by Eddie Harmon-Jones and his colleagues makes it clear that behaving without integrity, in and of itself, produces dissonance (Harmon-Jones et al., 1996). In their experiment, people who drank an awful-tasting beverage—and then volunteered to say that it tasted good, actually came to believe that it tasted good (compared to the rating of a control group). The way they "said" it tasted good was to write their false opinion down on a small slip of paper—which they then immediately crumpled up and threw away. Thus, although their lie could not possibly harm anyone, the act of lying produced changes in belief aimed at softening the dissonance and restoring a sense of integrity.

■ Under specific conditions, saying is believing.

Counter-Attitudinal Advocacy and Race Relations

How might the laboratory experiments on counter-attitudinal advocacy be applied directly to important societal problems? Let's look at race relations and racial prejudice—surely one of our nation's most important and enduring problems. Would it be possible to get people to endorse a policy favoring a minority group—and then see if their attitudes become more favorable toward that group? You bet! In an important set of experiments, Mike Leippe and Donna Eisenstadt (1994, 1998) induced white college students to write a counter-attitudinal essay publicly endorsing a controversial proposal at their university—to double the amount of funds available for academic scholarships for African American students. Because the total amount of funds were limited, this meant cutting by half the amount of scholarship funds available to white students. As you might imagine, this was a highly dissonant situation. How might they reduce dissonance? The best way would be to convince themselves that they really believed deeply in that policy. Moreover, it is reasonable to suggest that dissonance reduction might generalize beyond the specific policy—that is, the theory would predict that their general attitude toward African Americans would become more favorable and much more supportive. And that is exactly what Leippe and Eisenstadt found.

Hypocrisy and AIDS Prevention

In recent years, this aspect of dissonance theory has also been applied to another important societal issue—the prevention of the spread of AIDS. As you know, since it first made its presence known in the early 1980s, AIDS has become an epidemic of epic proportions. Hundreds of millions of dollars have been spent on AIDS information and prevention campaigns in the mass media. While these campaigns have been somewhat effective in conveying information, they have not been nearly so successful in preventing people from engaging in risky sexual behavior. For example, although college students are aware of AIDS as a serious problem, a surprisingly small percentage use condoms every time they have sex. The reason seems to be that condoms are inconvenient, unromantic, and remind people of disease—the last thing they want to be thinking about when getting ready to make love. Rather, as researchers have consistently discovered, people have a strong tendency to experience denial where sexual behavior is involved—in this case, to believe that while AIDS is a problem for most people, they themselves are not at risk. If the mass media have been ineffective, is there anything else that can be done?

In the past several years, Elliot Aronson and his students (Aronson, Fried, & Stone, 1991; Stone, Aronson, Crain, Winslow, & Fried, 1994) have had considerable success at convincing people to use condoms by employing a variation of the counter-attitudinal advocacy paradigm. They asked college students to compose a speech describing the dangers of AIDS and advocating the use of condoms every single time a person has sex. In one condition, the students merely composed the arguments. In another condition, the students composed the arguments and then recited them in front of a video camera, after being informed that the resulting videotape would be played to an audience of high school students. In addition, half the students in each condition were made mindful of their own failure to use condoms by making a list of the circumstances in which they had found it particularly difficult, awkward, or impossible to use them.

Essentially, then, the participants in one condition—those who made a video for high school students after having been made mindful of their own failure to use condoms—were in a state of high dissonance. This was caused by their being made aware of their own hypocrisy; they were fully aware of the fact that they were preaching behavior to high school students that they themselves were not practicing. In order to remove the hypocrisy and maintain their self-esteem, they would need to start practicing what they were preaching. And that is exactly what Aronson and his colleagues found: Each student was given the opportunity to purchase condoms very cheaply. The results demonstrated that the students in the hypocrisy condition were far more likely to buy condoms than students in any of the other conditions. Figure 6.4 illustrates the results of this experiment. A follow-up telephone interview several months after the experiment demonstrated that the effects were long-lasting: People in the hypocrisy condition reported far greater use of condoms than those in the control conditions.

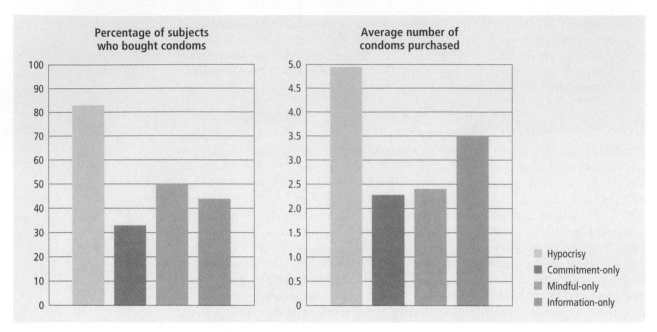

■ **FIGURE 6.4   People who are made mindful of their hypocrisy begin to practice what they preach.**   (Adapted from Stone, Aronson, Crain, Winslow, & Fried, 1993)

Insufficient Punishment

Another form of insufficient justification is insufficient punishment. Complex societies run, in part, on punishment or the threat of punishment. As members of society, we constantly find ourselves in situations where those who are charged with the duty of maintaining law and order are threatening to punish us if we do not comply with their rules and regulations. For example, while cruising down the highway at 75 miles an hour, we know that if we get caught, we will end up paying a substantial fine. If it happens often, we will lose our license. So we learn to obey the speed limit when patrol cars are in the vicinity. By the same token, youngsters in school know that if they cheat on an exam and get caught, they could be humiliated by the teacher and severely punished. So they learn not to cheat while the teacher is in the room watching them. But does harsh punishment teach adults to *want* to obey the speed limit? Does it teach youngsters to value honest behavior? We don't think so. Rather, we believe that all it teaches us is to try to avoid getting caught.

Let's look at bullying behavior. It is extremely difficult to persuade children that it's not right or enjoyable to beat up smaller children. But theoretically, it is conceivable that under certain conditions they will persuade themselves that such behavior is unenjoyable. Imagine that you are the parent of a 6-year-old boy who often beats up his 4-year-old brother. You've tried to reason with him, but to no avail. Thus, in order to make him a nicer person (and in order to preserve the health and welfare of his little brother), you begin to punish him for his aggressiveness. As a parent, you have at your disposal a number of possible punishments, ranging from the extremely mild (a stern look) to the extremely severe (a hard spanking, forcing the child to stand in the corner for two hours, and depriving him of TV privileges for a month). The more severe the threat, the greater the likelihood the youngster will cease and desist—while you are watching him. But he may very well hit his brother again as soon as you are out of sight. In short, just as most drivers learn to be vigilant of the Highway Patrol while speeding, your 6-year-old has not lost his enjoyment of bullying his little brother; he has merely learned not to do it while you are around to punish him. Suppose that you threaten him with a mild punishment. In either case—under threat of severe punishment or of mild punishment—the child experiences dissonance. He is aware that he is not beating up his little brother, and he is also aware that he would like to beat him up. When he has the urge to hit his brother and doesn't, he implicitly asks himself, "How come I'm not beating up my little brother?" Under severe threat, he has a convincing answer in the form of a sufficient external justification: "I'm not beating him up because if I do, my parents are going to really punish me." This serves to reduce the dissonance.

The child in the mild threat situation experiences dissonance too. But when he asks himself, "How come I'm not beating up my little brother?" he doesn't have a very convincing answer, because the threat is so mild that it does not provide a superabundance of justification. In short, this is **insufficient punishment.** The child is refraining from doing something he wants to do, and while he does have a modicum of justification for not doing it, he lacks complete justification. In this situation, he continues to experience dissonance. Therefore, the child must find another way to justify the fact that he is not aggressing against his kid brother.

The less severe you make the threat, the less external justification there is; the less external justification, the greater the need for internal justification. The child can reduce his dissonance by convincing himself that he doesn't really want to beat up his brother. In time, he can go further in his quest for internal justification and decide that beating up little kids is not fun. Allowing children the leeway to construct their own internal justification enables them to develop a permanent set of values.

Thus far, this has all been speculative. Will threats of mild punishment for performing any behavior diminish the attractiveness of that behavior to a greater extent than severe threats will? This proposition was first investigated by Elliot Aronson and J. Merrill Carlsmith (1963) in an experiment with preschoolers.

In this experiment, because the researchers were dealing with very young children, ethical concerns precluded their trying to affect important values, like those concerning aggressive behavior. Instead, they attempted to change something that was of no great importance to society but was of great importance to the children—their preference for different kinds of toys. The experimenter first asked each child to rate the attractiveness of several toys. He then pointed to a toy that the child considered to be among the most attractive and told the child that he or she was not allowed to play with it. Half the children were threatened with mild punishment if they disobeyed; the other half were threatened with severe punishment. The experimenter then left the room for several minutes to provide the children with the time and opportunity to play with the other toys and to resist the temptation of playing with the forbidden toy. None of the children played with the forbidden toy.

The experimenter returned to the room and asked each child to rate how much he or she liked each of the toys. Initially, all of the children had wanted to play with the forbidden toy. During the temptation period, all of them had refrained from playing with it. Clearly, this disparity means that dissonance was aroused in the children. How did they respond? The children who had received a severe threat had ample justification for their restraint. They knew why they hadn't played with

Insufficient Punishment
the dissonance aroused when individuals lack sufficient external justification for having resisted a desired activity or object, usually resulting in individuals devaluing the forbidden activity or object

■ How can we induce this child to give up playing with an attractive toy?

the attractive toy, and they thus had no reason to change their attitude about the toy. These children continued to rate the forbidden toy as highly desirable; indeed, some even found it more desirable than they had before the threat.

But what about the others? Lacking an abundance of external justification for refraining from playing with the toy, the children in the mild threat condition needed an internal justification to reduce their dissonance. They succeeded in convincing themselves that the reason they hadn't played with the toy was that they didn't really like it. They rated the forbidden toy as less attractive than they had at the beginning of the experiment. What we have here is a clear example of self-justification leading to self-persuasion in the behavior of very young children. The implications for child rearing are fascinating.

The Permanence of Self-Persuasion

Let's say you've attended a lecture on the evils of cheating. It might have a temporary effect on your attitudes toward cheating. But if a week or two later you found yourself in a highly tempting situation, your recent change in attitude would probably lack the staying power to act as a deterrent. Social psychologists know that mere lectures do not usually result in permanent or long-lasting attitude change. In contrast, suppose you went through the kind of situation experienced by the children in Judson Mills's (1958) experiment on cheating, discussed earlier in this chapter. Here we would expect the attitude change to be far more deep-seated and permanent. Those children who were tempted to cheat but resisted the temptation came to believe that cheating is a dastardly thing to do, not because someone told them so, but because they persuaded themselves of this belief as a means of justifying the fact that, by not cheating, they had given up an attractive prize.

The long-lasting effects of attitudes generated by **self-persuasion** and self-justification have been clearly demonstrated in a number of contexts. To take one

Self-Persuasion
a long-lasting form of attitude change that results from attempts at self-justification

dramatic example, Jonathan Freedman (1965) performed a replication of Aronson and Carlsmith's (1963) forbidden toy experiment. In Freedman's version of the experiment, the forbidden toy was an attractive battery-powered robot; all the children in the experiment were eager to play with it. But Freedman forbade them from doing so, indicating that they could play with the other toys—which were pallid by comparison—if they wanted to. Just as in the original experiment, Freedman issued either a mild threat or a severe threat for breaking the rule. Just as in the original experiment, all of the children obeyed the rule. Freedman then left the school and never returned.

Now here is the interesting part. Several weeks later, a young woman came to the school, ostensibly to administer some paper-and-pencil tests to the children. In actuality, she was working for Freedman; however, the children were totally unaware that her presence was in any way related to Freedman, the toys, or the threats that had occurred several weeks earlier. Coincidentally, she was administering her tests in the same room Freedman had used for his experiment—the room where the same toys were casually scattered about. After administering the test, she asked the children to wait for her while she went to the next room to score the test. She then casually suggested that the scoring might take a while and that—how lucky!—someone had left some toys around and the children could play with any of them they wanted to.

The results were striking: The overwhelming majority of the children whom Freedman had mildly threatened several weeks earlier decided, on their own, not to play with the robot; they played with the pallid toys instead. On the other hand, the great majority of the children who had been severely threatened did in fact play with the robot now that they had the opportunity to do so. Specifically, 78 percent of the children in the severe threat condition played with the toy, while only 33 percent of the children in the mild threat condition did so. Thus, a single mild threat was still very effective several weeks later, while a severe threat was not.

Again, the power of this phenomenon rests on the fact that the reason the children didn't play with the toy was not that some adult told them the toy was undesirable; such admonitions would not have persisted for very long after the admonishing adult had left the premises. The reason the mild threat persisted for at least several weeks was that the children were motivated to convince themselves the toy was undesirable. The results of Freedman's experiment are presented in Figure 6.5.

What Do We Mean by "Insufficient Justification"?

The term *insufficient external justification* needs clarification. In one sense, it is sufficient—sufficient to produce the behavior. For example, the students in Festinger and Carlsmith's (1959) experiment did agree to lie about how interesting it was to perform the boring job. The experimenter's request was just sufficient to get them to do the behavior, but it wasn't sufficient, later, for them to explain to themselves how they could have done such a mean thing to another student. After all, nobody had held a gun to their heads; they agreed, of their own free will, to lie—at least, that's how these participants saw it.

In fact, this situation, like many others in life, is characterized by the "illusion of freedom." We think we're free to choose our response, but powerful social norms and rules often dictate what we will actually do. How could these participants say no to a politely worded, fairly innocuous request from an authority figure? The cards were stacked—indeed, close to 100 percent of participants in

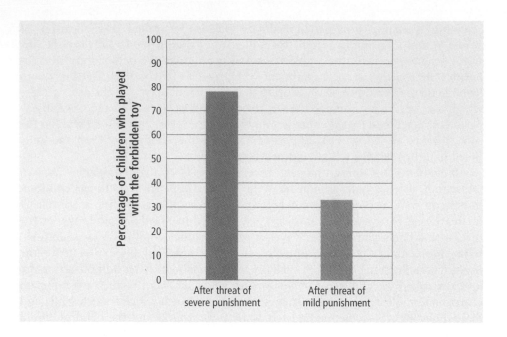

■ **FIGURE 6.5** Several weeks afterward, children who had received a threat of mild punishment were far less likely to play with the forbidden toy than children who had received a threat of severe punishment. Those given a mild threat had to provide their own justification by devaluing the attractiveness of the toy. (Adapted from Freedman, 1965)

these types of studies agree to the experimenter's request; basically, no one says no. So how much real choice could there be? Yet the participants don't perceive the inherent restraints on their ability to truly choose between saying yes or no to the request. Later, when thinking about why they lied to an innocent person, they don't blame it on the experimenter and his or her request; they see it as their personal choice. The best way to maintain their self-esteem is to decide that the task was sort of fun and interesting after all; hence, it wasn't such a lie.

Thus, while we like to think of ourselves as fully rational creatures, we frequently find ourselves doing things without entirely thinking them through—saying yes when we wanted to say no. Indeed, the irony is that precisely because we like to believe that we are rational, sensible, and moral creatures, we are vulnerable to dissonance-induced self-persuasion.

It Isn't Just Rewards or Punishments

As we have seen, a sizable reward or a severe punishment is an effective way of providing external justification for an action. Accordingly, if you want a person to do something or to refrain from doing something only once, the best strategy would be to promise a large reward or threaten a severe punishment. But if you want a person to develop a deep-seated attitude, the smaller the reward or punishment that will induce momentary compliance, the greater will be the eventual attitude change and therefore the more permanent the effect. Large rewards and severe punishments, because they are strong external justifications, are consonant with compliance and thus prevent attitude change.

We should note that this phenomenon is not limited to tangible rewards and punishments; justifications can come in more subtle packages as well. Take friendship, for example. We like our friends; we trust our friends; we do favors for our friends. Suppose you are at a formal dinner party at the home of a close friend. Your friend is passing around a rather strange-looking appetizer. It's not quite a potato chip, but it looks like it's been fried. "What is it?" you ask warily.

"Oh, it's a fried grasshopper; I'd really like you to try it," your friend answers. Because she's a good friend and you don't want to cause her any discomfort or embarrassment in front of the other guests, you gingerly pick one out of the bowl, place it in your mouth, chew it up, and swallow it. How much do you think you will like this new snack food?

Keep that in mind for a moment as we expand the example. Suppose you are a dinner guest at the home of a person you don't like very much, and he hands you, as an appetizer, a fried grasshopper and tells you that he'd really like you to try it. In much the same way, you put it in your mouth, chew it up, and swallow it.

Now the crucial question: In which of these two situations will you like the taste of the grasshopper better? Common sense might suggest that the grasshopper would taste better when recommended by a friend. But think about it for a moment; which condition involves less external justification? Common sense notwithstanding, dissonance theory makes the opposite prediction. In the first case, when you ask yourself "How come I ate that disgusting insect?" you have ample justification: You ate it because your good friend asked you to. In the second case, you lack this kind of justification for having eaten the grasshopper. Therefore, you must add some justification of your own; namely, you must convince yourself that it was tastier than you would have imagined, that as a matter of fact, it was quite good—"I'm thinking of laying in a supply myself."

While this may seem a rather bizarre example of dissonance-reducing behavior, it's not as far-fetched as you might think. Indeed, Philip Zimbardo and his colleagues (1965) conducted an experiment directly analogous to our example. In this experiment, army reservists were asked to eat fried grasshoppers as part of a research project on survival foods. Reservists who ate grasshoppers at the request of a stern, unpleasant officer increased their liking for grasshoppers far more than those who ate grasshoppers at the request of a well-liked, pleasant officer. Those who complied with the unfriendly officer's request had little external justification for their actions. As a result, they adopted more positive attitudes toward eating grasshoppers in order to justify their otherwise strange and dissonance-arousing behavior.

The Aftermath of Good and Bad Deeds

Whenever we act either kindly or cruelly toward a person, we never quite feel the same way about that person again.

The Ben Franklin Effect

It is obvious that when we like people, we tend to treat them well, speak kindly to them, do them favors, and smile at them with warmth and joy. If we don't like them, we treat them less kindly, avoid them, say bad things about them, and perhaps even go out of our way to snub them. But what happens when we do a person a favor? In particular, what happens when we are subtly induced to do a favor for a person we do not like—will we like them more? Or less? Dissonance theory predicts that we will like that person more after doing him or her the favor. Think about it. Can you see why? You might want to jot down your answer in the margin.

This phenomenon was not discovered by dissonance theorists; in fact, it has been a part of folk wisdom in several cultures for a very long time. For example, the great Russian novelist Leo Tolstoy wrote about it in 1869 (see quote in margin). And more than 100 years prior to Tolstoy's observation, Benjamin Franklin

> We do not love people so much for the good they have done us as for the good we have done them.
>
> —Leo Tolstoy

■ Without realizing it, Ben Franklin may have been the first dissonance theorist.

confessed to having utilized this bit of folk wisdom as a political strategy. While serving as a member of the Pennsylvania state legislature, Franklin was disturbed by the political opposition and apparent animosity of a fellow legislator. So he set out to win him over.

> I did not . . . aim at gaining his favour by paying any servile respect to him but, after some time, took this other method. Having heard that he had in his library a certain very scarce and curious book I wrote a note to him expressing my desire of perusing that book and requesting he would do me the favour of lending it to me for a few days. He sent it immediately and I returned it in about a week with another note expressing strongly my sense of the favour. When we next met in the House he spoke to me (which he had never done before), and with great civility; and he ever after manifested a readiness to serve me on all occasions, so that we became great friends and our friendship continued to his death. This is another instance of the truth of an old maxim I had learned, which says, "He that has once done you a kindness will be more ready to do you another than he whom you yourself have obliged." (*The Autobiography of Benjamin Franklin*, edited by J. Bigelow, pp. 216–217).

Benjamin Franklin was clearly pleased with the success of his blatantly manipulative strategy. But, as striking as this anecdote might be, as rigorous scientists, we should not be fully convinced by it. There is no way to be certain whether Franklin's success was due to this particular gambit or simply to his general, all-around charm. In order to be certain, it is important to design and conduct an experiment that controls for such things as charm. Such a study was conducted by Jon Jecker and David Landy (1969), more than 240 years after Franklin's more casual experiment. In the Jecker and Landy experiment, students participated in an intellectual contest that enabled them to win a substantial sum of money. After the experiment was over, one-third of the participants were approached by the experimenter, who explained that he was using his own funds for the experiment and was running short, which meant he might be forced to close down the experiment prematurely. He asked, "As a special favor to me, would you mind returning the money you won?" The same request was made to a different group of subjects—except this time, not by the experimenter but by the departmental secretary, who asked them if they would return

Try It!

Good Deeds

When you walk down a city street and view people sitting on the sidewalk, panhandling, or pushing their possessions around in a shopping cart, how do you feel about them? Think about it for a few moments and write down a list of your feelings. If you are like most college students, your list will reflect some mixed feelings. That is, most college students feel some compassion mixed with the feeling that they are a nuisance; that, if they really tried, they could get their lives together. Consider doing volunteer work at a shelter for the homeless—serving food, for example. After a few sessions, pay close attention to your feelings. Do you notice any changes?

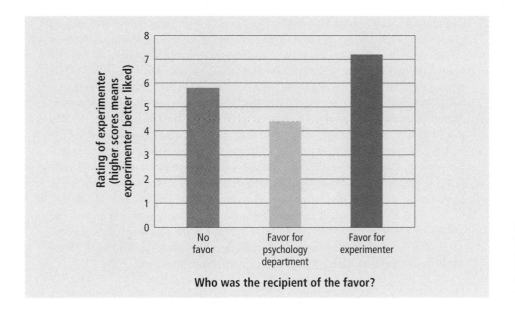

■ **FIGURE 6.6** If we have done someone a favor, we are more likely to feel more positively toward that person. (Adapted from Jecker & Landy, 1969)

the money as a special favor to the (impersonal) psychology department's research fund, which was running low. The remaining participants were not asked to return their winnings at all. Finally, all of the participants were asked to fill out a questionnaire that included an opportunity to rate the experimenter. Those participants who had been cajoled into doing a special favor for the experimenter found him the most attractive; i.e., after they did him a favor, they convinced themselves he was a wonderful, deserving fellow. The others thought he was a pretty nice guy but not anywhere near as wonderful as the people who had been asked to do him a favor. Figure 6.6 shows the results of this experiment.

Recall the experiment by Mike Leippe and Donna Eisenstadt discussed on page 204, in which white students became more favorable in their general attitudes toward African Americans after having made a public commitment favoring preferential treatment for African American students. Can you see how "the Ben Franklin effect" might apply here—how this act of helping might have contributed to their change in attitudes?

Suppose you find yourself in a situation where you have an opportunity to lend a helping hand to an acquaintance but, because you are in a hurry or because it is inconvenient, you decline to help that person. How do you think this act of omission might affect your feelings for this person? This is precisely the kind of situation investigated by Gail Williamson and her colleagues (Williamson, Clark, Pegalis, & Behan, 1996). As you might expect, this refusal led to a decline in the attractiveness of the acquaintance. This was an act of omission. But suppose you actually did harm to another person. What do you suppose might happen then? We will discuss that in the following section.

How We Come to Hate Our Victims

Several years ago, during the height of the war in Vietnam, one of us (Elliot Aronson) hired a young man to help him paint his house. Here are Elliot's reminiscences:

The painter was a gentle and sweet-natured person who had graduated from high school, joined the army, and fought in Vietnam. After leaving the army, he took up housepainting and was a good and reliable craftsman and an honest business-man. I enjoyed working with him. One day while we were taking a coffee break, we began to discuss the war and the intense opposition to it, especially at the lo-cal university. It soon became apparent that he and I were in sharp disagreement on this issue. He felt that the American intervention was reasonable and just and would "make the world safe for democracy." I argued that it was a terribly dirty war, that we were killing, maiming, and napalming thousands of innocent peo-ple—old people, women, children—people who had no interest in war or poli-tics. He looked at me for a long time; then he smiled sweetly and said, "Hell, Doc, those aren't people; those are Vietnamese! They're gooks." He said it matter-of-factly, without obvious rancor or vehemence. I was astonished and chilled by his response. I wondered how it could be that this apparently good-natured, sane, and gentle young man could develop that kind of attitude. How could he dismiss an entire national group from the human race?

Over the next several days, as we continued our dialogue I got to know more about him. It turned out that during the war he had participated in actions in which Vietnamese civilians had been killed. What gradually emerged was that initially he had been wracked by guilt—and it dawned on me that he might have developed this attitude toward the Vietnamese people as a way of assuaging his guilt. That is, if he could convince himself that the Vietnamese were not fully hu-man, it would make him feel less awful about having hurt them, and it would re-duce the dissonance between his actions and his self-concept as a decent person.

It goes without saying that these speculations about the causes of the house-painter's attitude are far from conclusive. While it is conceivable that he dero-gated the Vietnamese people as a way of reducing dissonance, the situation is complex; for example, he might always have had a negative and prejudiced atti-tude toward the Vietnamese, and this might have made it easier for him to behave brutally toward them. To be certain that the justification of cruelty can occur in

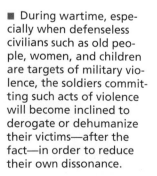

■ During wartime, espe-cially when defenseless civilians such as old peo-ple, women, and children are targets of military vio-lence, the soldiers commit-ting such acts of violence will become inclined to derogate or dehumanize their victims—after the fact—in order to reduce their own dissonance.

such situations, it is essential for the social psychologist to temporarily step back from the helter-skelter of the real world and test the proposition in the more controlled setting of the experimental laboratory.

Ideally, if we want to measure attitude change as a result of dissonant cognitions, we should know what the attitudes were before the dissonance-arousing behavior occurred. Such a situation was produced in an early experiment performed by Keith Davis and Edward E. Jones (1960). Each student's participation consisted of watching a young man being interviewed and then, on the basis of this observation, providing him with an analysis of his shortcomings as a human being. Specifically, the participants were told to tell the young man (a confederate) that they believed him to be a shallow, untrustworthy, boring person. The participants succeeded in convincing themselves they didn't like the victim of their cruelty—after the fact. In short, after saying things they knew were certain to hurt him, they convinced themselves that he deserved it. They found him less attractive than they had prior to saying the hurtful things to him.

Let us return to our housepainter example. Suppose for a moment that all the people he killed and injured in Vietnam had been fully armed enemy soldiers, instead of a sizable number of noncombatants. Do you think he would have experienced as much dissonance? We think it is unlikely. When engaged in combat with an enemy soldier, it is a "you or me" situation; if the housepainter had not killed the enemy soldier, the enemy soldier might have killed him. Thus, while hurting or killing another person is probably never taken lightly, it is not nearly so heavy a burden as it would be if the victim was an unarmed civilian—a child, a woman, an old person.

These speculations are supported by the results of an experiment by Ellen Berscheid and her colleagues (Berscheid, Boye, & Walster, 1968). In this study, college students volunteered for an experiment in which each of them administered a (supposedly) painful electric shock to a fellow student. As one might expect, these students derogated their victim as a result of having administered the shock to him or her. However, half of the students were told there would be a turnabout: The other student would be given the opportunity to retaliate against them at a later time. Those who were led to believe their victim would be able to retaliate later did not derogate the victim. In short, because the victim was going to be able to even the score, there was very little dissonance, and therefore the harm-doers had no need to belittle their victim in order to convince themselves that he or she deserved it.

The results of these laboratory experiments lend credence to our speculations about the behavior of the housepainter; the results suggest that during a war, military personnel have a greater need to derogate civilian victims (because these individuals can't retaliate) than military victims. Moreover, several years after Elliot's encounter with the housepainter, a similar set of events emerged during the court-martial of Lieutenant William Calley for his role in the slaughter of innocent civilians at My Lai in Vietnam. In a long and detailed testimony, Lieutenant Calley's psychiatrist made it clear that the lieutenant had come to regard the Vietnamese people as less than human.

As we have seen, systematic research in this area demonstrates that people do not perform acts of cruelty and come out unscathed. We can never be completely certain of how the housepainter, Lieutenant Calley, and thousands of other American military personnel came to regard the Vietnamese as subhuman, but it seems reasonable to assume that when people are engaged in a war where a great number of innocent people are being killed, they might try to derogate the victims

> There's nothing people can't contrive to praise or condemn and find justification for doing so.
> —Molière, *The Misanthrope*

■ Dehumanizing their victims provides aggressors with justification for brutal acts that feeds into a horrifying, endless chain of escalating violence against their victims.

in order to justify their complicity. They might poke fun at them, refer to them as "gooks," and dehumanize them. Ironically, success at dehumanizing the victim virtually guarantees a continuation or even an escalation of the cruelty. It becomes easier to hurt and kill subhumans than to hurt and kill fellow human beings. Thus, reducing dissonance in this way has sobering future consequences: It increases the likelihood that the atrocities people are willing to commit will become greater and greater through an endless chain of violence followed by self-justification (in the form of dehumanizing the victim), followed by greater violence and still more intense dehumanization. In this manner, unbelievable acts of human cruelty—such as the Nazi "Final Solution" that led to the murder of 6 million European Jews—can occur. Unfortunately, atrocities are not a thing of the past but are as recent as today's newspaper.

The Evidence for Motivational Arousal

The theory of cognitive dissonance is largely a motivational theory; in other words, the theorists maintain that discomfort and arousal are what drives the engine, what motivates the individual to change his or her attitude or behavior. How do we know this is in fact the case? Is there any independent evidence indicating that people who experience cognitive dissonance are in a state of discomfort or arousal? Recently, Patricia Devine has developed a paper-and-pencil instrument designed to measure this kind of arousal directly (Devine, 1998; Elliot & Devine, 1994). She finds that when people are put in a dissonance-arousing situation, they do, indeed, report feeling more agitated and more uncomfortable than people in the control condition.

Some striking behavioral evidence for the motivating qualities of dissonance has been provided by several investigators (e.g., Zanna & Cooper, 1974; Fried & Aronson, 1995). In the Zanna and Cooper study, participants were given a placebo pill. Some were told that the pill would arouse them and make them feel tense. Others were told that the pill would make them feel calm and relaxed. Participants in the control condition were told that the pill would not affect them

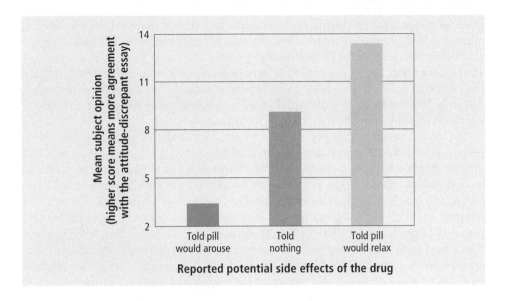

■ **FIGURE 6.7   If subjects can misattribute the arousal associated with the dissonance, they do not show the typical attitude change following a counter-attitudinal essay. This is strong support for the notion that dissonance causes physiological arousal.** (Adapted from Zanna & Cooper, 1974)

in any way. After ingesting the pill, each person voluntarily wrote a counterattitudinal essay, thus creating dissonance.

As you know, dissonance theory predicts that such participants will change their attitudes, bringing them in line with their essays in order to reduce their uncomfortable arousal state, only if they actually feel aroused. However, if some of the participants think the arousal they are experiencing is due to the pill, they won't need to alter their attitudes to feel better about themselves. At the opposite end of the spectrum, if some of the participants think they should be feeling relaxed due to the pill, any arousal they experience should be very salient to them and they should change their attitudes a great deal. Thus, the theory predicts that attitude change will come or go across conditions, depending on whether the arousal due to dissonance is masked by an alternative explanation ("Oh, right—I took a pill that's supposed to make me feel tense; that's why I'm feeling this way") or magnified by an alternative explanation ("Oh no—I took a pill that's supposed to make me feel relaxed and I feel tense").

And that is exactly what Zanna and Cooper found. Participants in the control condition underwent considerable attitude change, as would be expected in a typical dissonance experiment. Participants in the aroused condition, however, did not change their attitudes—they attributed their discomfort to the pill, not their counterattitudinal essay. Finally, participants in the relaxed condition changed their attitudes even more than the control participants did. They inferred that writing the counterattitudinal essay had made them very tense, since they were feeling aroused despite a relaxing drug. Thus, they inferred that their behavior was very inconsistent with their perception of themselves as decent and reasonable people, and they changed their attitude to bring it into line with their essay contents. These data are illustrated in Figure 6.7.

New Directions of Research on Self-Justification

Throughout this chapter, we've indicated that human beings generally have a need to see themselves as intelligent, sensible, and decent folks who behave with integrity. Indeed, what triggers the attitude change and distortion that can take place in the process of dissonance reduction is precisely the need people have to maintain this picture of themselves. At first glance, much of the behavior described in this chapter may seem startling—people coming to dislike others more after doing them harm; people liking others more after doing them a favor; people believing a lie they've told only if there is little or no reward for telling it. These behaviors would be difficult for us to understand if it weren't for the insights provided by the theory of cognitive dissonance.

In recent years, social psychologists have explored this basic premise—that people have a fundamental need to maintain a stable, positive sense of self—in greater depth and in new contexts. For example, most dissonance experiments have involved behavior that in some way falls short of people's standards of competence or morality, such as working hard for something of questionable value or lying to someone for no good reason. The work of E. Tory Higgins and his colleagues (Higgins, 1987, 1989, 1996; Higgins, Klein, & Strauman, 1987) is also concerned with understanding how such violations of personal standards influence people's emotional and motivational states. In particular, these researchers have taken a close look at the nature of the emotional distress that occurs when we perceive ourselves as not measuring up to our ideals and standards. It thus offers some support for the notion that dissonance involves specific patterns of psychological discomfort, in addition to physiological arousal.

Self-Discrepancy Theory

Self-discrepancy theory holds that people are motivated to maintain a sense of consistency among their various beliefs and perceptions about themselves. In particular, the theory posits that we become distressed when our sense of who we truly are—our actual self—is discrepant from our personal standards or desired self-conceptions. For Higgins and his colleagues, these standards are reflected most clearly in the various beliefs we hold about the type of person we aspire to be—our *ideal* self—and the type of person we believe we should be—or our *ought* self. Comparing our actual self with our ideal and ought selves provides us with an important means of self-evaluation. We make judgments about our abilities, our personal attributes, our behavior, and the extent to which we are adhering to our goals.

What happens when we become aware that we have failed to measure up to our standards? Like dissonance theory, self-discrepancy theory also predicts that this blow to our self-esteem will generate psychological distress, along with the motivation to reduce the inconsistency associated with the self-discrepancy. Engaging in various forms of self-justification allows us to narrow the gap that sometimes exists between who we are, as implied by our self-discrepant actions, and who we aspire to be.

To illustrate, consider the predicament of Sarah, a first-year college student who has always had very high academic standards. In terms of self-discrepancy theory, academic competence is a central component of her ideal self. Moreover, she's become accustomed to living up to these high standards over the years: With only a modest level of effort, it was pretty much a breeze in high school to earn A's in most subjects and B's in the others. In her first semester at a competitive, prestigious college, however, Sarah has discovered those A's much harder to come by. It seems that the courses she has enrolled in are far more rigorous and demanding than she had anticipated. As a matter of fact, in her introductory chemistry course—a prerequisite for her major—she barely managed to earn a C. Given this scenario, how is Sarah likely to experience this discrepancy between her ideal and actual selves?

To begin with, we might imagine that the threat to her self-concept as a high achiever would almost certainly generate fairly strong levels of emotional discomfort—for example, disappointment in herself and perhaps an unaccustomed sense of uncertainty regarding her abilities. Self-discrepancy research supports this view. In a series of studies, Higgins and his colleagues (Higgins, 1989; Higgins, Bond, Klein, & Strauman, 1988) have found that when people are made mindful of a discrepancy between their actual and ideal selves, they tend to experience a pattern of feelings involving dejection, sadness, dissatisfaction, and other depression-related emotions.

On the other hand, what if Sarah had encountered a self-discrepancy involving her ought self—that is, not the ideal self she aspired to but the "should" self she felt obligated to uphold? Imagine that being a top-notch student was not enormously significant to Sarah as a means of satisfying her own ideal self-aspirations. Instead, suppose that her parents had always held this standard as highly important and that Sarah, out of respect for them, was very responsive to their expectations regarding academic excellence. How, then, would Sarah experience this discrepancy between her actual and ought selves, in the face of a mediocre performance in her first semester at college? Higgins and his colleagues have found that, unlike the case of actual-ideal self-discrepancy described above, a different pattern of emotions would tend to occur. Specifically, their research indicates that Sarah would be likely to experience fear, worry, tension, and other anxiety-related emotions.

Coping with Self-Discrepancy

How might Sarah attempt to cope with the dissonance arousal and negative feelings generated by either of these two forms of self-discrepancy? According to the theory, self-discrepancies not only produce emotional discomfort but also provoke strivings to minimize the gap between the actual and the ideal or ought selves. As discussed throughout this chapter, self-justifying thoughts and behaviors provide a ready means of restoring a positive self-concept when it has been threatened by a self-discrepant experience. For example, recall the predicament of subjects in Festinger and Carlsmith's (1959) classic study who, for a paltry $1, told a "fellow student" that a tedious experimental task was actually quite fascinating. We could well imagine that the ideal or ought selves of these subjects included the notion of behaving with honesty and integrity. As a result, the act of lying would have produced a discrepancy between their actual selves and their standards. How did they reduce the dissonance associated with this self-discrepancy? By minimizing the extent of their dishonesty—that is, by expressing greater liking for the boring task.

In Sarah's case, reducing dissonance might involve construing her lackluster academic performance in a manner that protects her long-standing belief in herself as an excellent student. In fact, in several experiments undergraduate students who received a failing grade on an exam reacted in precisely this way: Failing students blamed their poor performance on the alleged unfairness of the test, rather than attributing it to personal factors such as poor ability or insufficient effort. In other words, when confronted with a discrepancy between their actual and desired selves, they reduced the discrepancy by eschewing personal responsibility for their dismal performance (Arkin & Maruyama, 1979; Davis & Stephan, 1980). Similarly, Sarah might convince herself that the grading was unfair, that her chemistry instructor was totally inept, or in some other way interpret her mediocre performance in the most positive light possible. Of course, as we've noted repeatedly in this chapter, self-justification—while a self-protective strategy in the short run—might not be the most adaptive approach Sarah could adopt in coming to terms with dissonance arousal. Rather, she would undoubtedly benefit far more from reassessing her situation—concluding, perhaps, that maintaining her high academic standards might require greater effort than she was accustomed to exerting in the past, when her courses were less challenging.

Self-Completion Theory

Robert Wicklund and Peter Gollwitzer have investigated how the need for self-maintenance plays itself out in the realm of social relationships (Gollwitzer & Wicklund, 1985; Wicklund & Gollwitzer, 1982; Brunstein & Gollwitzer, 1996). Specifically, their work on self-completion theory indicates that when people experience a threat to a valued aspect of their self-concept, or identity, they become highly motivated to seek some sort of social recognition of that identity. Once achieved, this acknowledgment allows people to restore their valued self-conceptions—thereby serving as a means of reducing dissonance and maintaining the self.

Imagine, for example, that you are an aspiring poet. You think your work has a good deal of promise, and one of your poems has already been published in a small, regional poetry journal. Bolstered by this success, you have recently sent out a new batch of poems to a more prestigious journal with a larger circulation. You are also committed to developing your talents further, and so you sign up for a writing course offered by an up-and-coming poet whose work you greatly admire. As you're leaving the house on your way to the first class, you stop off at your mailbox to pick up the mail. Sorting through it, you discover a letter from the poetry journal to which you've submitted your work. With great excitement, you rip open the letter. To your dismay, however, you find an impersonal form letter from the editor informing you that your poems have been deemed unacceptable for publication in the journal. Disappointed and annoyed, you tear up the letter, get into your car, and proceed to your writing class. After the classroom has filled, the instructor asks everyone to take out the samples of their work they had been asked to bring to the first meeting. She then announces that most of the class time will be spent listening to student poetry but that, given the unexpectedly large size of the group, only a few students will have the opportunity to read at the first meeting. She then asks for volunteers to read their work to the class.

Given the recent blow to your cherished identity as a poet, how do you think you would react to the instructor's request? Would you shrink back into your chair and let the others grab for the spotlight? Probably not. Rather, research on self-completion theory strongly suggests that even before the instructor had finished her sentence, your hand would have shot up into the air, vigorously vying for an opportunity to have your poems heard by the rest of the class. Why would this be the case? According to Wicklund and Gollwitzer, when we experience a threat to an identity to which we are committed, we become highly motivated to restore that aspect of our self-concept through social recognition. We tend to look for ways to signal to others that we do in fact have a credible, legitimate claim to a particular identity that has been challenged. Through such self-symbolizing activities—in this case, reading poems to a group of strangers—we are able to reduce the dissonance stemming from the threat to our valued notions of self.

In an experiment very similar to this hypothetical scenario, subjects who were committed to their identities as promising dancers wrote essays about their training in dance (Gollwitzer, 1986). Half the subjects were asked to describe the worst dance instructor they had ever trained with; the other half wrote essays about their most gifted instructor. In the former condition, then, subjects were made uncomfortably aware of an aspect of their training that undermined their identities as dancers (having a poor instructor), whereas in the latter condition subjects were asked to recall an aspect of their background that supported their identities as dancers (having a great instructor). Later, in an entirely different setting, all of the subjects were invited to participate in a dance concert and were given an opportunity to select a date for their performance. As self-completion theory predicts, dancers whose identities had been threatened—those who had recently been asked to recall an inadequate aspect of their training—expressed the desire to perform in public nearly two weeks earlier than subjects whose self-concepts as dancers had not been challenged. Similar results have been found in research involving medical students whose identities as aspiring physicians were threatened (Gollwitzer, 1986), as well as individuals who were made to feel inadequate about their identities as athletes (Gollwitzer & Wicklund, 1985). Compared to subjects whose self-concepts had not been called into question, threatened subjects were especially eager to engage in self-symbolizing activities that bolstered their claim to an identity that had recently been challenged.

Self-Evaluation Maintenance Theory

Most dissonance research concerns how our self-image is threatened by our own behavior, such as acting contrary to our attitudes or making a difficult decision. Abraham Tesser and his colleagues have explored how other people's behavior can threaten our self-concept in ways that have important implications for our interpersonal relationships (Tesser, 1988; Tesser, Martin, & Mendolia, 1995; Beach et al., 1996).

Suppose you consider yourself to be a good cook—in fact, the best cook of all your friends and acquaintances. You love nothing better than playing with a recipe, adding your own creative touches, until—voilà—you have a delectable new creation. Then you move to another town, make new friends, and, alas, your favorite new friend turns out to be a superb cook, far better than you. How does that make you feel? We suspect you will agree that you might feel more than a little uneasy about the fact that your friend outdoes you in your area of expertise.

Now consider a slightly different scenario. Suppose your new best friend is, instead of a superb cook, a very talented artist. Are you likely to experience any discomfort in this situation? Undoubtedly not; in fact, you are likely to bask in the reflected glory of your friend's success. "Guess what?" you will probably tell everyone. "My new friend has sold some of her paintings in the most exclusive New York galleries."

The difference between these two scenarios is that in the first one, your friend is superior at an attribute that is important to you and may even be a central part of how you define yourself. We all have abilities and traits that we treasure—we are especially proud of being good cooks, talented artists, gifted musicians, or inventive scientists. Whatever our most treasured ability, if we encounter someone who is better at it than we are, there is likely to be trouble—trouble of the dissonance variety. It is difficult to be proud of our ability to cook if our closest friend is a far better chef than we are.

This is the basic premise of Tesser's (1988) **self-evaluation maintenance theory:** One's self-concept can be threatened by another individual's behavior; the level of the threat is determined by both the closeness of the other individual and the personal relevance of the behavior. As seen in Figure 6.8, there is no problem if a close friend outperforms us on a task that is not that relevant to us. In fact, we feel even

Self-Evaluation Maintenance Theory
the theory that one's self-concept can be threatened by another individual's behavior and that the level of threat is determined by both the closeness of the other individual and the personal relevance of the behavior

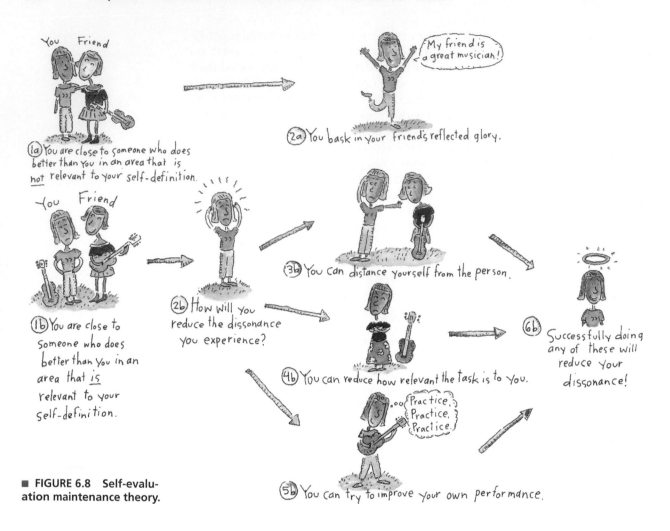

You   Friend

My friend is a great musician!

(1a) You are close to someone who does better than you in an area that is not relevant to your self-definition.

(2a) You bask in your friend's reflected glory.

You   Friend

(1b) You are close to someone who does better than you in an area that is relevant to your self-definition.

(2b) How will you reduce the dissonance you experience?

(3b) You can distance yourself from the person.

(4b) You can reduce how relevant the task is to you.

Practice, Practice, Practice.

(5b) You can try to improve your own performance.

(6b) Successfully doing any of these will reduce your dissonance!

■ **FIGURE 6.8   Self-evaluation maintenance theory.**

better about ourselves. Dissonance occurs when a close friend outperforms us on a task that is relevant to our self-definition.

The Reduction of Dissonance

We can try to change any one of the three components that produced this dissonance. First, we can distance ourselves from the person who outperforms us, deciding that he or she is not such a close friend after all. Pleban and Tesser (1981) tested this possibility by having college students compete against another student, who was actually an accomplice of the experimenter, on general knowledge questions. They rigged it so that in some conditions, the questions were on topics that were highly relevant to people's self-definitions and the accomplice got many more of the questions correct. Just as predicted, this was the condition in which people distanced themselves the most from the accomplice, saying they would not want to work with him again. It is too dissonance-producing to be close to someone who is better than we in our treasured areas of expertise (Wegner, 1986).

A second way to reduce such threats to our self-esteem is to change how relevant the task is to our self-definition. If our new friend is a far better cook than we are, we might lose interest in cooking, deciding that auto mechanics is really our thing. To test this prediction, Tesser and Paulus (1983) gave people feedback about how well they and another student had done on a test of a newly discovered ability, cognitive-perceptual integration. When people learned that the other student was similar to them (high closeness) and had done better on the test, they were especially likely to say that this ability was not very important to them—just as the theory predicts.

Finally, people can deal with self-esteem threats by changing the third component in the equation—their performance relative to the other person's. If our new best friend is a superb cook, we can reduce the dissonance by trying to make ourselves an even better cook. This won't work, however, if we are already performing to the best of our abilities. If so, we can take a more diabolic route, wherein we try to undermine our friend's performance so that it is not as good as ours. If our friend asks for a recipe, we might leave out a critical ingredient so that his or her salmon en brioche is not nearly as good as ours.

Why Might We Help a Stranger More Than a Friend?

Are people really so mean-spirited that they try to sabotage their friends' performances? Surely not always; there are many examples of times when we are extremely generous and helpful toward our friends. If our self-esteem is on the line, however, there is evidence that we are not as helpful as we would like to think. Tesser and Smith (1980) asked students to play a game of "Password®," wherein one person gave clues to another to guess a word, and to do so with both a friend and a stranger. The students could choose to give clues that were helpful, making it easy for the other player to guess the word, or obscure, making it hard for the other player to guess the word. The researchers set it up so that people first performed rather poorly themselves and then had the opportunity to help the other players by giving them easy or difficult clues. The question was, who would they help more—the strangers or their friends?

By now, you can probably see what self-evaluation maintenance theory predicts. If the task is not self-relevant to people, they should want their friends to do especially well, so that they can bask in the reflected glory. If the task is self-relevant, however, it would be threatening to people's self-esteem to have their friends outperform them. So they might make it difficult for their friends, by giving them especially hard clues. This is exactly what Tesser and Smith found. They made the task self-relevant for some participants, by telling them that performance on the game was highly correlated with their intelligence and leadership skills. Under these conditions, people gave more difficult clues to their friends than to the strangers, because they did not want their friends to shine on a task that was highly important to them. When the task was not self-relevant, people gave more difficult clues to the strangers than to their friends (see Figure 6.9).

In sum, research on self-evaluation maintenance theory has shown that threats to our self-concept have fascinating implications for our interpersonal relationships. Though much of the research has been with college students in laboratory settings, the theory has been confirmed in field and archival studies as well. Tesser (1980), for example, examined biographies of male scientists, noting how close these scientists were to their fathers. As the theory predicts, when the scientists' field of expertise was the same as their fathers', they had a more distant and strained relationship with their fathers. Similarly, the greatest amount of friction

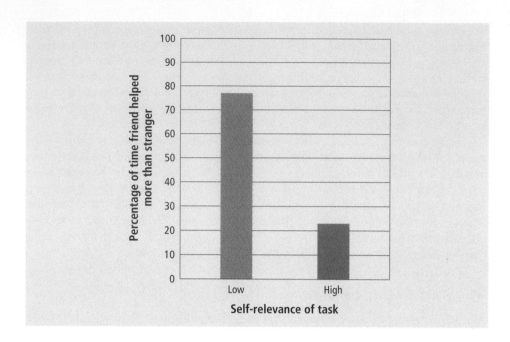

■ **FIGURE 6.9** People are more inclined to be helpful to a friend if the friend's success does not pose a threat to their own self-esteem. (Adapted from Tesser & Smith, 1980)

between siblings was found to occur when the siblings were close in age and one sibling was significantly better on key dimensions, such as popularity or intelligence. When performance and relevance are high, it can be difficult to avoid conflicts with family members. Consider how the novelist Norman Maclean (1983) describes his relationship with his brother in the story "A River Runs Through It": "One of the earliest things brothers try to find out is how they differ from each other. . . . Undoubtedly, our differences would not have seemed so great if we had not been such a close family."

Self-Affirmation Theory

As we have seen, people will go to great lengths to maintain a good image of themselves, by changing their attitudes, their behavior, or their relationships with other people. In each case, people try to restore a sense of integrity by warding off a specific threat to their self-concept. If we smoke cigarettes, we try to deal with the specific threat to our health by quitting or by convincing ourselves that smoking is not really bad for our health. Sometimes, however, threats to our self-concept can be so strong and difficult to avoid that the normal means of reducing dissonance do not work. It can be difficult to stop smoking, as millions of people have discovered. It is also difficult to ignore all the evidence indicating that smoking is bad for us and might even kill us. So what can we do? Are smokers doomed to wallow in a constant state of dissonance? **Self-affirmation theory** suggests that people will reduce the impact of a dissonance-arousing threat to their self-concept by focusing on and affirming their competence on some dimension unrelated to the threat.

Research by Claude Steele and his colleagues (Steele, 1988; Aronson, Cohen, & Nail, 1998) shows how self-affirmation comes about. "Yes, it's true that I smoke," you might say, "but I am a great cook" (or a terrific poet, or a wonderful friend, or a promising scientist). Self-affirmation occurs when our self-esteem

Self-Affirmation Theory
a theory suggesting that people will reduce the impact of a dissonance-arousing threat to their self-concept by focusing on and affirming their competence on some dimension unrelated to the threat

is threatened; if possible, we will attempt to reduce the dissonance by reminding ourselves of some irrelevant aspect of our self-concept that we cherish, as a way of feeling good about ourselves in spite of some stupid or immoral action we have just committed.

In a series of clever experiments, Steele and his colleagues demonstrated that if, prior to the onset of dissonance, you provide people with an opportunity for self-affirmation, they will often grab it (Steele, 1988; Steele, Hoppe, & Gonzales, 1986; Steele & Liu, 1981). For example, Steele, Hoppe, and Gonzales (1986) performed a replication of Jack Brehm's (1956) classic experiment on post-decision dissonance reduction. They asked students to rank-order ten record albums, ostensibly as part of a marketing survey. As a reward, the students were then told that they could keep either their fifth- or sixth-ranked album. Ten minutes after making their choice, they were asked to rate the albums again. You will recall that in Brehm's experiment, after selecting one of the kitchen appliances the participants spread apart their ratings of the appliances, rating the one they had chosen much higher than the one they had rejected. In this manner, they convinced themselves that they had made a smart decision. And that is exactly what the students did in this experiment, as well.

But Steele and his colleagues built an additional set of conditions into their experiment. Half of the students were science majors, and half were business majors. Half of the science majors and half of the business majors were asked to put on a white lab coat while participating in the experiment. Why the lab coat? As you know, a lab coat is associated with the idea of science. Steele and his colleagues suspected that the lab coat would serve a "self-affirmation function" for the science majors but not for the business majors. The results supported their predictions. Whether or not they were wearing a lab coat, business majors reduced dissonance just as the people in Brehm's (1956) experiment did: After their choice, they increased their evaluation of the chosen album and decreased their evaluation of the one they had rejected. Similarly, in the absence of a lab coat, science majors reduced their dissonance in the same way. However, science majors who were wearing the lab coat resisted the temptation to distort their perceptions; the lab coat reminded these students that they were promising scientists and thereby short-circuited the need to reduce dissonance by changing their attitudes toward the albums. In effect, they said, "I might have made a dumb choice in record albums, but I can live with that because I have other things going for me; at least I'm a promising scientist!" A simplified version of these findings is presented in Figure 6.10.

As you can see, self-affirmation is a rather indirect way of reducing dissonance in the sense that the individual does not deal directly with the cause of the dissonance. We would argue that because self-affirmation is less direct, it is also less complete and less efficient than dealing directly with the dissonant cognitions. That is, instead of changing our behavior to bring it in line with our beliefs or changing our beliefs in order to bring them in line with our behavior, we are simply adding a positive cognition about ourselves that makes us feel a bit better—but it doesn't really deal with the source of the dissonance. In short, although we have comforted ourselves, the fact still remains that we may have done a stupid or immoral thing.

Here's something to think about. Suppose you committed a stupid or immoral act. Let's say that you betrayed a friend by blabbing about something private that he had confided to you. What do you think you might do? Suppose, *after the fact*, you were given the opportunity either to change your behavior in a

■ **FIGURE 6.10**
Dissonance and self-affirmation. People who were allowed the opportunity to affirm their values (science majors wearing lab coats) were able to avoid the pressures to reduce dissonance by increasing the attractiveness of the chosen album. (Adapted from Steele, Hoppe, & Gonzales, 1986)

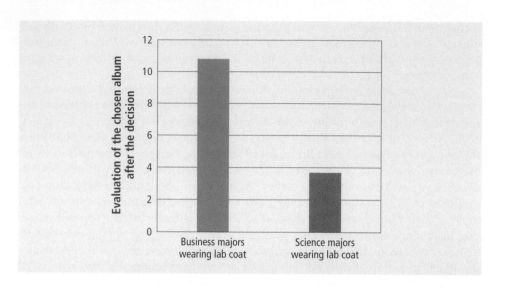

way that dealt directly with the action you had taken or to affirm some unrelated aspect of your self-concept. Which path do you think you would follow?

In a recent series of experiments, Jeff Stone and his colleagues asked that very question. They placed students in a situation where they were experiencing dissonance and had clear options; they could have gone in either direction. Their results showed that when given their choice, the overwhelming majority of participants chose the more direct and clearer path—they changed their behavior (Stone, Wiegand, Cooper, & E. Aronson, 1997; for related research, see also J. Aronson, Blanton, Hart, & Cooper, 1995; Blanton, J. Aronson et al., 1997).

Self-Justification versus Self-Maintenance: The Role of Negative Self-Beliefs

We have said repeatedly that people will typically experience dissonance whenever their self-concepts are threatened. The astute reader may have noticed that this prediction becomes tricky when applied to people who have a poor opinion of themselves. To illustrate, let's reconsider our example of smokers who continue to smoke, knowing full well that smoking is a great danger to their health. As we've noted, smokers are likely to experience high levels of dissonance because knowingly jeopardizing one's health is inconsistent with maintaining a positive self-concept. Note, however, that this conclusion rests on an important premise: It assumes that the smoker in question has a favorable self-image, one that would be inconsistent with foolish behavior. But what if we're dealing with smokers who have negative self-concepts, who already think of themselves as fairly incompetent and thus thoroughly capable of engaging in an absurdly self-destructive habit? In this case, dissonance reduction would not be required as a means of self-maintenance, since there is no need to reestablish a positive sense of self that is not present to begin with. While such individuals would almost certainly experience a blow to their self-esteem, the stability of their self-concepts would not be threatened by smoking, as would be the case for smokers who think highly of themselves.

It turns out that the vast majority of dissonance experiments have been conducted among college student populations who are known to have fairly high levels of self-esteem. For such individuals, acting in a foolish, immoral, or absurd manner not only is threatening to their self-esteem but also calls into question the stability of their self-conceptions. As a result, self-justification works in the service of self-maintenance: By reducing dissonance, people with favorable self-images are able to restore a positive sense of self as well as a consistent, stable sense of self.

Research that has taken self-esteem into account reveals that, in some instances, individuals with negative self-concepts do not engage in the kinds of self-justifying behaviors that are typical of people with relatively high self-esteem. For example, an experiment by David Glass (1964) involved subjects who were induced to deliver what they believed to be painful electric shocks to an innocent "fellow student," who was actually a confederate of the experimenter. Before doing so, however, subjects were given bogus feedback on a personality test, designed to temporarily lower or raise their self-esteem. In one condition, the test results were esteem-enhancing, depicting subjects as compassionate, highly mature, and otherwise virtuous individuals. For other subjects, however, the feedback described them as fairly self-centered, insensitive to others' feelings, and so forth. Glass found that, after "shocking" the confederate, the two groups of subjects did not react in the same way to this potentially dissonance-arousing situation. Specifically, subjects in the high self-esteem condition reduced dissonance by justifying their immoral behavior. They rated the "fellow student," whom they believed they had injured, as less attractive, less likable, and so forth. In contrast, subjects whose self-esteem had been temporarily lowered did not show this tendency to derogate the "victim." Why was this the case? For low self-esteem subjects, acting immorally was apparently consistent with their self-concepts. As a result, they had no need to derogate the "fellow student" as a means of restoring their self-concepts. Instead, they maintained their unfavorable self-concepts. High self-esteem subjects, on the other hand, engaged in self-justification in order to protect their threatened self-concepts as good and decent people.

Self-Verification versus Self-Enhancement

William Swann and his colleagues have explored this tendency we have to preserve our customary self-beliefs, even when those beliefs are unfavorable (Swann, 1990, 1996; Swann & Hill, 1982; Swann & Pelham, 1988; Swann & Schroeder, 1995; Giesler, Josephs, & Swann, 1996). Swann calls this **self-verification theory**—suggesting that people have a need to seek confirmation of their self-concept whether the self-concept is positive or negative; in some circumstances, this tendency can conflict with the desire to uphold a favorable view of oneself. For example, consider Patrick, who has always thought of himself as a lousy writer with poor verbal skills. One day he is working on a term paper with a friend, who remarks that she thinks his paper is skillfully crafted, beautifully written, and superbly articulate. How will Patrick feel? He should feel pleased and gratified, we might predict, because the friend's praise gives Patrick's self-esteem a boost.

On the other hand, Patrick's friend has given him feedback that challenges a long-standing view of himself as a poor writer, and he might be motivated to maintain this negative view. Why? For two reasons. First, like dissonance theory (Aronson, 1968, 1969), self-verification theory also rests on the basic premise that it is unsettling and confusing to have our views of ourselves disconfirmed; if we changed our self-concept every time we encountered someone with a different

Self-Verification Theory
a theory suggesting that people have a need to seek confirmation of their self-concept, whether the self-concept is positive or negative; in some circumstances, this tendency can conflict with the desire to uphold a favorable view of oneself

opinion of us, it would be impossible to maintain a coherent, consistent self-concept. Second, self-verification theory holds that interacting with people who view us differently from the way we view ourselves can be embarrassing. People who don't know us might have unrealistic expectations, and we might be embarrassed when they find out that we are not as smart or as artistic or as creative as they think we are. Better to let them know our faults at the outset.

In short, when people with negative self-views receive positive feedback, opposing needs go head to head—the desire to feel good about themselves by believing the positive feedback (self-enhancement needs) versus the desire to maintain a consistent, coherent picture of themselves and avoid the embarrassment of being found out (self-verification needs). Which needs win out?

Throughout this chapter, we have been telling you that human beings have a powerful need to feel good about themselves—in short, that the need for **self-justification** is a major determinant of our attitudes and behaviors. We now have to qualify this statement. Along with the Glass (1964) experiment described above, several studies suggest that when the two motives are in conflict, our need to maintain a stable self-concept under certain conditions overpowers our compelling desire to view ourselves in a positive light (Aronson & Carlsmith, 1962; Brock et al., 1965; Marecek & Mettee, 1972; Swann, 1990). For example, Swann and his colleagues have found that people prefer to remain in close relationships with those friends, roommates, and romantic partners whose evaluations of their abilities are consistent with their own (sometimes negative) self-evaluations (Swann, Hixon, & De La Ronde, 1992; Swann & Pelham, 1988). In other words, people prefer to be close to someone whose evaluations of them are not more positive than their self-concept. In a close relationship, most people find it better to be known than to be overrated.

The need to self-verify, however, appears to dominate our behavior only under a limited set of circumstances. First, people generally strive to uphold their negative self-beliefs only when they are highly certain of those beliefs (Maracek & Mettee, 1972; Swann & Ely, 1984; Swann & Pelham, 1988). Thus, if Patrick had been less thoroughly convinced of his poor talents as a writer, he almost certainly would have been more receptive to his friend's praise. Second, if the consequences of being improperly evaluated are not too great—for example, if our contact with these individuals is rare so that it is unlikely they will discover we are not who we appear to be—then even people with negative views prefer positive feedback (Aronson, 1992). Finally, if people feel there is nothing they can do to improve their abilities, then they generally prefer positive feedback to accurate feedback. Why remind ourselves that we are terrible if there is nothing we can do about it? If, however, people feel that a negative self-attribute can be changed with a little work, they prefer accurate feedback, because this information can help them figure out what they need to do to get better (Steele, Spencer, & Josephs, 1992).

Dissonance Reduction and Culture

Dissonance effects have been shown to exist in almost every part of the world (e.g., Beauvois & Joule, 1997, 1998; Beauvois & Rainis, 1993; Viswesvaran & Deshpande, 1996). But it does not always take the same form. Harry Triandis (1995) has argued that in less individualistic societies than ours, dissonance-reducing behavior might be less prevalent—at least on the surface—than behavior

Self-Justification
the tendency to justify one's actions in order to maintain one's self-esteem

" The mind is a strange machine which can combine the materials offered to it in the most astonishing ways.
    —Bertrand Russell,
    The Conquest of Happiness, 1930

that promotes group harmony rather than individual consistency. In a similar vein, Gui-Young Hong (1992) argues that dissonance-reducing behavior may be less extreme in Japan than it is in the Western world because the Japanese culture considers an individual's acceptance of inconsistency to be a sign of maturity and broad-mindedness. This reasoning received some support from a recent experiment by Steven Heine and Darrin Lehman (1997) who found that Japanese natives were less likely to engage in self-justification following a decision than were Canadians.

On the other hand, it may simply be that self-justification takes place in less individualistic societies but is triggered in more communal ways. In a striking set of experiments, Japanese social psychologist Haruki Sakai (1998) investigated dissonance reduction behavior in Japan by combining his interest in dissonance with his expert knowledge of Japanese community orientation. In a nutshell, what Sakai found was that in Japan, not only does a person reduce dissonance after saying that a boring task is interesting and enjoyable (as in the classic Festinger and Carlsmith experiment), but in addition, if a person merely observes someone he knows and likes saying that a boring task is interesting and enjoyable, that will cause *the observer* to experience dissonance. Consequently, in that situation, the observers' attitudes change. In short, the observers bring their evaluation more in line with the lie their *friend* has told!

Avoiding the Rationalization Trap

Dissonance-reducing behavior is ego-defensive behavior. It can be useful because it keeps our egos from being continually battered; it provides us with a feeling of stability and high self-esteem. But as we have seen, dissonance-reducing behavior can be dangerous as well. The tendency to justify our past behavior can lead us into an escalation of rationalizations that can be disastrous. We call this the **rationalization trap:** The potential for dissonance reduction to produce a succession of self-justifications that ultimately result in a chain of stupid or irrational actions. The irony, of course, is that in order to avoid thinking of ourselves as stupid or immoral, we set the stage for increasing our acts of stupidity or immorality.

Rationalization Trap
the potential for dissonance reduction to produce a succession of self-justifications that ultimately result in a chain of stupid or immoral actions

Learning from Our Mistakes

If we human beings were to spend all of our time and energy defending our egos, we would never learn from our mistakes. Instead, we would sweep our mistakes under the rug or, worse still, would try to turn them into virtues. If we did not learn from our mistakes, we would get stuck within the confines of our narrow minds and never grow or change. As we have seen throughout this chapter, the process of dissonance reduction perpetuates error and can lead to tragedy. For example, people who hurt others can derogate their victims to the point where their actions not only seem just but might even become heroic in their own eyes (we will elaborate on this phenomenon in our chapters on aggression and prejudice). Similarly, we have seen how people who say something they don't really believe will come to believe the statement—and some of those beliefs might be tragically erroneous. The memoirs of some of our most beleaguered former presidents are full of the kind of self-serving, self-justifying statements that can best be summarized as "If I had it all to do over again, I would not change anything important" (Johnson, 1971; Nixon, 1990; Reagan, 1990).

An interesting and more complex example of this phenomenon can be found in the memoirs of Robert McNamara (1995), who was secretary of defense and one of Lyndon Johnson's principal military advisers during the Vietnam War. In a painful revelation, McNamara admits he came to the realization that the war was unwinnable in 1967—several years prior to our eventual withdrawal from Vietnam. But he chose to remain silent on this issue after leaving office—while the war raged on, wasting several thousand additional American lives as well as countless Vietnamese lives. Most knowledgeable analysts believe that to have been a tragic and catastrophic error, arguing that if he had spoken out publicly, it could have shortened the war and saved thousands of lives. In his book, McNamara makes a spirited but unconvincing attempt to justify his public silence out of some sort of personal and professional loyalty to his commander in chief.

In order to learn from our mistakes, it would be helpful to learn to tolerate dissonance long enough to examine the situation critically and dispassionately. We then stand a chance of breaking out of the cycle of action, followed by self-justification, followed by more intense action. For example, suppose Mary has acted unkindly toward a fellow student. In order to learn from that experience, she must be able to resist the need to derogate her victim. Ideally, it would be effective if she were able to stay with the dissonance long enough to say, "OK, I blew it; I did a cruel thing. But that doesn't necessarily make me a cruel person. Let me think about why I did it."

We are well aware that this is easier said than done. But a clue as to how such behavior might come about is contained in some of the research on self-affirmation that we discussed previously (Steele, 1988). Suppose that, immediately after Mary acted cruelly but before she had an opportunity to derogate her victim, she was reminded of the fact that she had recently donated several pints of blood to the Red Cross to be used by earthquake victims, or that she had recently gotten a high score on her physics exam. This self-affirmation would be likely to provide her with the ability to resist engaging in typical dissonance-reducing behavior. In effect, Mary might be able to say, "It's true—I just did a cruel thing. But I am also capable of some really fine, intelligent, and generous behavior."

Indeed, self-affirmation can serve as a cognitive buffer, protecting a person from caving in to temptation and committing a cruel or immoral act. This was demonstrated in an early experiment on cheating (Aronson & Mettee, 1968). In this experiment, college students were first given a personality test and then given false feedback that was either positive (aimed at temporarily raising self-esteem) or negative (aimed at temporarily lowering self-esteem), or they received no information at all. Immediately afterward, they played a game of cards in which, to win a large pot, they could easily cheat without getting caught. The results were striking. Students in the high self-esteem condition were able to resist the temptation to cheat to a far greater extent than the students in the other conditions were. In short, a temporary boost in self-esteem served to inoculate these students against cheating, because the anticipation of doing something immoral was more dissonant than it would have been otherwise. Thus, when they were put in a tempting situation, they were able to say to themselves, "Terrific people like me don't cheat." And they didn't (see also Spencer, Josephs, & Steele, 1993; Steele, Spencer, & Lynch, 1993). We find these results encouraging. They suggest a viable way of reversing the rationalization trap.

Heaven's Gate Revisited

At the beginning of this chapter, we raised a vital question regarding the followers of Marshall Herff Applewhite of Heaven's Gate. Similar questions were raised in Chapter 1 about the followers of the Reverend Jim Jones and those of David Koresh in Waco, Texas. How could intelligent people allow themselves to be led into what, to the overwhelming majority of us, is obviously senseless and tragic behavior—resulting in mass suicide? Needless to say, the situation is a complex one; there were many factors operating, including the charismatic, persuasive power of each of these leaders, the existence of a great deal of social support for the views of the group (from other members of the group), and the relative isolation of each group from dissenting views—producing a closed system—a little like living in a roomful of mirrors.

In addition to these factors, we are convinced that one of the single-most powerful forces common to all of these groups was the existence of a great deal of cognitive dissonance within the minds of each of the participants. You know from reading this chapter, that when individuals make an important decision and invest heavily in that decision (in terms of time, effort, sacrifice, and commitment), this results in a strong need to justify those actions and that investment. The more they give up and the harder they work, the greater will be the need to convince themselves that their views are correct; indeed, they may even begin to feel sorry for those who do not share their beliefs. The members of the Heaven's Gate cult sacrificed a great deal for their beliefs: They abandoned their friends and families, turned their backs on their professions, relinquished their money and possessions, moved to another part of the world, worked hard and long for the particular cause they believed in—thus increasing their commitment to the belief. Those of us who have studied the theory of cognitive dissonance were not surprised to learn that the Heaven's Gate people, having bought a telescope that failed to reveal a spaceship that wasn't there, concluded that the telescope was faulty. To have believed otherwise would have created too much dissonance to bear. That they went on to abandon their "containers," believing that they were moving on to a higher incarnation, although tragic and bizarre, is not unfathomable. It is simply an extreme manifestation of a process that we have seen in operation over and over again throughout this chapter.

Summary

One of the most powerful determinants of human behavior is the need to justify our actions so that we might maintain a high level of self-esteem. In this chapter, we have seen that this need has intriguing consequences for people's attitudes and behaviors. According to **cognitive dissonance** theory, people experience discomfort (dissonance) whenever they are confronted with cognitions about some aspect of their behavior that is inconsistent with their **self-concept**. People are motivated to reduce this dissonance by either changing their behavior or justifying their past behavior, bringing it into line with a positive view of themselves. The resulting change in attitude stems from a process of **self-persuasion**.

Dissonance inevitably occurs after important decisions (**postdecision dissonance**), because the thought that "I chose alternative X" is inconsistent with the thought that "I might have been a lot better off with alternative Y." People reduce this dissonance by increasing their liking for the chosen alternative and decreasing their liking for the negative alternative. Unscrupulous salespeople have been known to take advantage of this human tendency through the utilization of a strategy called **lowballing,** which creates the illusion in the customer's mind that a commitment has been made to purchase the product, when in fact no such commitment exists.

Dissonance also occurs after people choose to exert a lot of effort to attain something boring or onerous. A **justification of effort** occurs, whereby people increase their liking for what they attained.

A third source of dissonance occurs when people commit foolish, immoral, or absurd acts for **insufficient punishment.** For example, when people say something against their attitudes (**counterattitudinal advocacy**) for low **external justification,** they find an **internal justification** for their behavior, coming to believe what they said. Similarly, if people avoid doing something desirable for insufficient punishment, they will come to believe that the activity wasn't really all that desirable. And if people find themselves doing someone a favor for insufficient justification, they assume that they did so because the person is likable. The flip side of this kind of dissonance reduction has sinister effects: If people find themselves acting cruelly toward someone for insufficient justification, they will derogate the victim, assuming he or she must have deserved it. Finally, consistent with the idea that dissonance is an uncomfortable state people are motivated to reduce, there is evidence that dissonance is accompanied by physiological arousal.

In recent years, social psychologists have expanded dissonance theory into fascinating new directions researching the idea that people are motivated to maintain their self-esteem. **Self-evaluation maintenance theory** argues that dissonance is produced in interpersonal relationships, whenever someone close to us outperforms us on a task that is highly relevant to our self-definition. People can reduce this dissonance by distancing themselves from the person, improving their performance, lowering the other person's performance, or reducing the relevance of the task. **Self-affirmation theory** argues that people are very flexible at dealing with threats to their self-esteem. When dissonance cannot be reduced by dealing with a specific threat, people can feel better about themselves by affirming themselves in some other area. Research on **self-verification theory** suggests that the need to bolster our self-esteem sometimes conflicts with the need to verify our self-views. When people with negative self-views are concerned that other people will discover they are not who they appear to be, and when they think it's possible to change and improve the less desirable side of themselves, they will prefer feedback that confirms their low opinion of themselves to feedback that is self-enhancing.

The problem with reducing dissonance in ways that make us feel better about ourselves (self-justification) is that it can result in a **rationalization trap,** whereby we set the stage for acts of increasing stupidity or immorality. As suggested by self-affirmation theory, we can avoid this trap by reminding ourselves that we are good and decent people, so that we do not have to justify and rationalize every stupid or immoral act we perform.

If You Are Interested

Aronson, E. (1998). Dissonance, Hypocrisy, and the Self-Concept. In E. Harmon-Jones, & J. S. Mills (Eds.), *Cognitive dissonance theory: Revival with revisions and controversies.* Washington, DC: American Psychological Association Press. Bringing Festinger's original theory up to date—with special reference to the role of self-esteem and the self-concept.

Aronson, E. (1992). The return of the repressed: Dissonance theory makes a comeback. *Psychological Inquiry, 3,* 303–311. A brief, but penetrating discussion of the conceptual linkage between the theory of cognitive dissonance and recent developments in cognitive psychology.

Aronson, E. (1997). The theory of cognitive dissonance: The evolution and vicissitudes of an idea. In C. McGarty & S. A. Haslam (Eds.), *The message of social psychology: Perspectives on mind in society.* Blackwell Publishers, Inc., Oxford, England, pp. 20–35. A readable account, tracing the development and evolution of the theory in the context of general social psychology.

Festinger, L. (1957). *A theory of cognitive dissonance.* Evanston, IL: Row, Peterson. The original presentation of dissonance theory. A classic in social psychology—clear, concise, and engagingly written.

Harmon-Jones, E. & Mills, J. S. (Eds.) (1998). *Cognitive dissonance theory: Revival with revisions and contro-*

versies. Washington, DC: American Psychological Association Press.

Swann, W. B. Jr., & Schroeder, D. G. (1995). The search for beauty and truth: A framework for understanding reactions to evaluations. *Personality and Social Psychology Bulletin, 21,* 1307–1318.

Wicklund, R., & Brehm, J. (1976). *Perspectives on cognitive dissonance.* Hillsdale, NJ: Earlbaum. A scholarly, readable presentation of dissonance theory some two decades after its inception. Contains a description of much of the early research as well as some of the more important conceptual modifications of the theory.

Films and Videos. There are a great many films (available on video) that illustrate the workings of dissonance. Among the best is *Remains of the Day,* adapted from Ishiguru's classic novel, this stunning 1993 film explores self-justification from the perspective of a proper British butler, played by Sir Anthony Hopkins. Shying away from friendship and romance, the butler rationalizes his lonely lifestyle by reasserting his belief that such intimacy is improper for a man in his position—and is worth it because of the worthiness of the gentleman in whose service he is employed.

CHAPTER 7

ATTITUDES AND ATTITUDE CHANGE: INFLUENCING THOUGHTS AND FEELINGS

How many times, in a given day, does someone attempt to change your attitudes? Be sure to count every advertisement you see or hear, because advertising is nothing less than an attempt to change your attitude toward a consumer product, be it a brand of laundry detergent, a type of automobile, or a political candidate. Don't forget to include ads you get in the mail, calls from telemarketers, and signs you see on the sides of buses, as well as those ever-present television commercials. How many did you come up with? You might be surprised at the answer, for on average Americans encounter 300 to 400 advertisements per day (Asker & Myers, 1987; Pratkanis & Aronson, 1991).

As if this were not enough, advertisers are ever on the lookout for new ways of reaching consumers. Entire cable television channels are now devoted to pitching products, either through "home shopping networks" or "infomercials" designed to look like regular television programs. The World Wide Web has opened a new frontier for advertisers that did not exist until a few years ago. Two brothers in Maryland

235

found a novel way of advertising to a captive audience: They started a business that places advertisements on the inside door of stalls in public restrooms ("Brothers flush with excitement," *The Daily Progress,* Aug. 31, 1997).

Yet advertisers are still not satisfied. We can only imagine the conversation that must have occurred a few years ago between marketers trying to find new inroads for advertising. Maybe it went something like this:

> Marketer 1: *You know, one of our best audiences is teenagers. They see an awful lot of ads on television.*
>
> Marketer 2: *Yeah, but doggone it, kids are out of reach for several hours a day— when they're in school. That's so unfair; if only we could figure out a way of reaching them during school hours.*
>
> Marketer 1: *Wait a minute—maybe you're on to something. Why don't we show kids advertisements in their classrooms?*
>
> Marketer 2: *Are you crazy? How are we going to show them ads during their English or math class? Teachers and principals would never stand for it.*
>
> Marketer 1: *I think I've got a way . . .*

Sound far-fetched? In 1990, "Channel One" was launched as a special news program broadcast via satellite to American schools. Whittle Communications offered hundreds of schools free video equipment if they agreed to show the 12-minute, daily news broadcasts to their students. The show consists of 10 minutes of news and 2 minutes of advertising. By 1992, nearly 40 percent of America's teenagers in school were watching Channel One—more than twice as many as watch popular television programs (Flynn, 1997; McGowan, 1993). Many companies jumped at the chance to pitch their products to captive audiences of teenagers, and by 1992 Whittle Communications was earning $100 million a year in advertising income.

This might sound pretty harmless. After all, schools get much-needed equipment and kids see only a couple of advertisements a day. What are two more ads, on top of the hundreds people see already? One troubling finding is that advertisements shown in schools are especially powerful because students believe that the schools endorse the advertised products (Toch, 1992). And as seen later in this chapter, there is evidence that advertising in general can be quite effective at shaping and changing people's attitudes.

How do advertisements try to change people's attitudes? Some go straight for the gut with the intent of manipulating your emotions, not your thoughts or

beliefs. Many advertisements for perfume, soft drinks, and jeans, for example, tell you absolutely nothing about the product but try to associate it with good feelings—often sexual feelings. Other kinds of ads, such as those for mutual funds, CD players, or coffeemakers, downplay emotions and instead throw lots of facts and figures at you. Often the same product can be advertised in either way. Consider the ad for the Dodge Caravan on this page. The ad is packed with facts and figures about cupholders, cubbyholes, and cargo room. At least for us, it evokes very little emotion. Compare it to other car ads you've seen that are just the opposite: They try hard to elicit feelings of freedom, autonomy, and sexual prowess. Meanwhile, they tell you very little about the car.

Which type of ad works better? There seems to be little doubt that sex (and other emotions) sells. But surely facts and figures can be persuasive as well. More than likely, people's attitudes can be influenced in either way. Under some conditions, people are swayed by a logical consideration of the facts; under other conditions, people are swayed by appeals to their fears, hopes, and desires. What are these conditions? Exactly what is an attitude, and how is it changed? These questions, which are some of the oldest in social psychology, are the subject of this chapter.

The Nature and Origin of Attitudes

Attitude
evaluations of people, objects, and ideas

Most social psychologists define an **attitude** as evaluations of people, objects, and ideas (Eagly & Chaiken, 1993, 1998; Olson & Zanna, 1993; Petty, Wegener, & Fabrigar, 1997; Petty & Wegener, 1998). Attitudes are evaluative in that they consist of a positive or negative reaction to something. People are not neutral observers of the world but constant evaluators of what they see (Bargh, Chaiken, Raymond, & Hymes, 1996; Hermans, De Houwer, & Eelen, 1994; De Houwer, Hermans, & Eelen, 1996; Fazio, Sanbonmatsu, Powell, & Kardes, 1986). It would be very odd to hear someone say, "My feelings toward anchovies, snakes, chocolate cake, and my roommate are completely neutral."

We can elaborate further on our definition of an attitude by stating more precisely what we mean by an "evaluation." Attitudes are made up of different components, or parts (Breckler, 1984; Crites, Fabrigar, & Petty, 1994; Eagly, Mladinic, & Otto, 1994; Haddock, Zanna, & Esses, 1993; McGuire, 1985; Rosselli, Skelly, & Mackie, 1995; Tesser & Martin, 1996). Specifically, attitudes are made up of an affective component, consisting of your emotional reactions toward the attitude object (e.g., another person or a social issue), a cognitive component, consisting of your thoughts and beliefs about the attitude object, and a behavioral component, consisting of your actions or observable behavior toward the attitude object.

For example, consider your attitude toward a particular model of car. First, there is your affective reaction, or the emotions and feelings the car triggers. These feelings might be a sense of excitement and aesthetic pleasure when you see the car, or feelings of anger and resentment (e.g., if you are a U.S. autoworker examining a new foreign-made model). Second, there is your cognitive reaction, or the beliefs you hold about the car's attributes. These might include your thoughts about the car's gas mileage, safety, steering and handling, and roominess. Third, there is your behavioral reaction, or how you act in regard to this type of car. For example, going to the dealership to test-drive the car and actually purchasing it are behaviors related to your attitude.

> "We never desire passionately what we desire through reason alone."
>
> —La Rochefoucauld, *Maxims*, 1678

Where Do Attitudes Come From?

Abraham Tesser (1993) suggests a provocative answer to the question of where attitudes come from: Some attitudes, at least, are linked to our genes. Evidence for this surprising conclusion comes from the fact that identical twins share more attitudes than fraternal twins, even when the identical twins were raised in different homes and never knew each other. One study, for example, found that identical twins had more similar attitudes toward such things as the death penalty and jazz than fraternal twins did (Martin et al., 1986). Now, we should be careful how to interpret this evidence. No one is arguing that there are specific genes that determine our attitudes; it is highly unlikely, for example, that there is a "jazz-loving" gene that determines your music preferences. It appears, though, that some attitudes are an indirect function of our genetic makeup. Tesser (1993) suggests that attitudes are related to things like our temperament and personality, which are directly related to our genes. People may have inherited a temperament and personality from their parents that made them predisposed to like jazz more than rock-and-roll.

Even if there is a genetic component, our social experiences clearly play a large role in shaping our attitudes. Social psychologists have focused primarily on the way in which attitudes are created by people's cognitive, affective, and behavioral experiences. One important finding is that not all attitudes are created equally. Whereas attitudes have affective, cognitive, and behavioral components, any given attitude can be based more on one type of experience than another (Zanna & Rempel, 1988).

Cognitively Based Attitudes

Sometimes our attitudes are based primarily on a perusal of the relevant facts, such as the objective merits of an automobile. How many miles to the gallon does it get? Does it have an air bag? To the extent that people's evaluation is based primarily on people's beliefs about the properties of an attitude object, we say it is a **cognitively based attitude**. The function of such an attitude is "object appraisal," meaning that we classify objects according to the rewards and punishments they can provide (Katz, 1960; Smith, Bruner, & White, 1956). In other words, the purpose of this kind of attitude is to classify the pluses and minuses of an object so that we can quickly tell whether it is worth our while to have anything to do with it. Consider your attitude toward a utilitarian object like a vacuum cleaner. Your attitude is likely to be based on your beliefs about the objective merits of particular brands, such as how well they vacuum up dirt and how much they cost—not on how sexy they make you feel.

Affectively Based Attitudes

An attitude based more on emotions and values than on an objective appraisal of pluses and minuses is called an **affectively based attitude** (Breckler & Wiggins, 1989; Zanna & Rempel, 1988). Sometimes we simply like a certain brand of car, regardless of how many miles to the gallon it gets or whether it has an air bag. Occasionally we even feel very positively about something—such as another person—in spite of having negative beliefs (see the quote in the margin from Smokey Robinson's song, "You've Really Got a Hold on Me").

As a guide to which attitudes are likely to be affectively based, consider the topics that etiquette manuals suggest should not be discussed at a dinner party: politics, sex, and religion. People seem to vote more with their hearts than their minds, for example, caring more about how they feel about a candidate than their beliefs about his or her specific policies (Abelson, Kinder, Peters, & Fiske, 1982; Granberg & Brown, 1989). In fact, Wattenberg (1987) estimates that one-third of the electorate knows virtually nothing about specific politicians but nonetheless has strong feelings about them!

If affectively based attitudes do not come from an examination of the facts, where do they come from? They have a variety of sources. First, they can stem from people's values, such as their basic religious and moral beliefs. People's feelings about such issues as abortion, the death penalty, and premarital sex are often based more on their values than on a cold examination of the facts. The function of such attitudes is not so much to paint an accurate picture of the world as to express and validate one's basic value system (Katz, 1960; Maio & Olson, 1995; Schwartz, 1992; Smith, Bruner, & White, 1956; Snyder & DeBono, 1989).

Other affectively based attitudes can be the result of a sensory reaction, such as liking the taste of chocolate (despite how many calories it has!), or an aesthetic reaction, such as admiring a painting or the lines and color of a car. Still others

Cognitively Based Attitude an attitude based primarily on people's beliefs about the properties of an attitude object

Affectively Based Attitude an attitude based more on people's feelings and values than on their beliefs about the nature of an attitude object

That is the way we are made; we don't reason; where we feel, we just feel.
—Mark Twain, *A Connecticut Yankee in King Arthur's Court*

I don't like you, but I love you.
Seems that I'm always, thinking of you.
You treat me badly, I love you madly.
You've really got a hold on me.
—Smokey Robinson

■ Some attitudes are based more on emotions and values than on facts and figures. Attitudes towards abortion may be such a case.

Classical Conditioning
the case whereby a stimulus that elicits an emotional response is repeatedly experienced along with a neutral stimulus that does not, until the neutral stimulus takes on the emotional properties of the first stimulus

can be the result of conditioning. **Classical conditioning** is the case in which a stimulus that elicits an emotional response is repeatedly experienced along with a neutral stimulus that does not, until the neutral stimulus takes on the emotional properties of the first stimulus. For example, suppose that when you were a child you experienced feelings of warmth and love when you visited your grandmother. Suppose also that there was always a faint smell of mothballs in the air at your grandmother's house. Eventually, the smell of mothballs themselves will trigger the emotions you experienced during your visits, through the process of classical conditioning (Cacioppo, Marshall-Goodell, Tassinary, & Petty, 1992; De Houwer, Baeyens, & Eelen, 1994; Gorn, 1982; Groenland & Schoormans, 1994; Stuart, Shimp, & Engle, 1987).

Operant Conditioning
the case whereby behaviors that people freely choose to perform increase or decrease in frequency, depending on whether they are followed by positive reinforcement or punishment

In **operant conditioning**, behaviors that we freely choose to perform increase or decrease in frequency, depending on whether they are followed by positive reinforcement or punishment. How does this apply to attitudes? Imagine that a 4-year-old white girl goes to the playground with her father and chooses to play with an African American girl. Her father expresses strong disapproval, telling her, "We don't play with that kind of child." It won't take long before the child associates interacting with minorities with punishment, thereby adopting her father's racist attitudes. Attitudes can take on a positive or negative affect through either classical or operant conditioning, as shown in Figure 7.1 (Cacioppo et al., 1992; Kuykendall & Keating, 1990).

Although affectively based attitudes can have varied sources, we can group them into one family, because they have certain key features in common: (a) They do not result from a rational examination of the issues; (b) they are not governed by logic (e.g., persuasive arguments about the issues seldom change an affectively

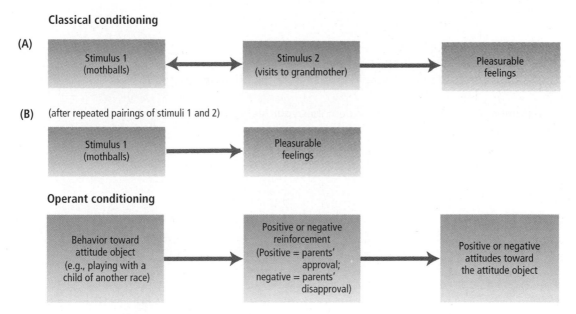

Classical conditioning

(A)

Stimulus 1 (mothballs) ←→ Stimulus 2 (visits to grandmother) → Pleasurable feelings

(B) (after repeated pairings of stimuli 1 and 2)

Stimulus 1 (mothballs) → Pleasurable feelings

Operant conditioning

Behavior toward attitude object (e.g., playing with a child of another race) → Positive or negative reinforcement (Positive = parents' approval; negative = parents' disapproval) → Positive or negative attitudes toward the attitude object

■ **FIGURE 7.1   Classical and operant conditioning of attitudes.**   Affectively based attitudes can result from either classical or instrumental conditioning.

based attitude); and (c) they are often linked to people's values, so that trying to change them challenges those values (Katz, 1960; Smith et al., 1956). How can we tell if an attitude is more affectively or cognitively based? See Try It! on page 242 for one way of measuring the bases of people's attitudes.

Behaviorally Based Attitudes

Just as an attitude can be based primarily on cognition or affect, so too can it be based primarily on behavior. A **behaviorally based attitude** is one based on observations of how you behave toward an attitude object. This may seem a little odd—how do we know how to behave if we don't already know how we feel? According to Daryl Bem's (1972) *self-perception theory*, under certain circumstances people don't know how they feel until they see how they behave. For example, suppose you asked a friend how much she enjoys exercising. If she replies, "Well, I guess I like it, because I always seem to be going for a run or heading over to the gym to work out," we would say she has a behaviorally based attitude. Her attitude is based more on an observation of her behavior than on her cognitions or affect.

As noted in Chapter 5, people infer their attitudes from their behavior only under certain conditions. First, their initial attitude has to be weak or ambiguous. If your friend already has a strong attitude toward exercising, she does not have to observe her behavior to infer how she feels about it. Second, people infer their attitudes from their behavior only when there are no other plausible explanations for their behavior. If your friend believes she exercises to lose weight or because her doctor has ordered her to, she is unlikely to assume that she runs and works out because she enjoys it. (See Chapter 5 for a more detailed description of self-perception theory.)

Behaviorally Based Attitude
an attitude based on observations of how one behaves toward an attitude object

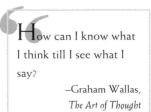

"How can I know what I think till I see what I say?
—Graham Wallas, *The Art of Thought*

// *Try It* !

Affective and Cognitive Bases of Attitudes

Fill out this questionnaire to see how psychologists measure the affective and cognitive components of attitudes.

1. Circle the number on each scale that best describes **your feelings** toward *snakes:*

hateful	−3	−2	−1	0	1	2	3	love
sad	−3	−2	−1	0	1	2	3	delighted
annoyed	−3	−2	−1	0	1	2	3	happy
tense	−3	−2	−1	0	1	2	3	calm
bored	−3	−2	−1	0	1	2	3	excited
angry	−3	−2	−1	0	1	2	3	relaxed
disgusted	−3	−2	−1	0	1	2	3	acceptance
sorrow	−3	−2	−1	0	1	2	3	joy

2. Please circle the number on each scale that best describes the **traits or characteristics** of *snakes:*

useless	−3	−2	−1	0	1	2	3	useful
foolish	−3	−2	−1	0	1	2	3	wise
unsafe	−3	−2	−1	0	1	2	3	safe
harmful	−3	−2	−1	0	1	2	3	beneficial
worthless	−3	−2	−1	0	1	2	3	valuable
imperfect	−3	−2	−1	0	1	2	3	perfect
unhealthy	−3	−2	−1	0	1	2	3	wholesome

Instructions: Answer each of the above questions. Then, sum each of your responses to Question 1 and each of your responses to Question 2.

These scales were developed by Crites, Fabrigar, and Petty (1994) to measure the affective and cognitive components of attitudes. Question 1 measures the affective component of your attitude toward snakes; you were asked to rate your feelings on such scales as "hateful/love". Question 2 measures the cognitive component of attitudes; you were asked to rate your beliefs about the characteristics of snakes on such scales as "worthless/valuable". Most people's attitudes toward snakes are more affectively than cognitively based. If this was true of you, your total score for Question 1 should depart more from zero (in a negative direction, for most people) than your total score for Question 2.

Now go back and fill out the scales again, but substitute "vacuum cleaners" for "snakes." Most people's attitudes toward a utilitarian object such as a vacuum cleaner are more cognitively than affectively based. If this was true of you, your total score for Question 2 should depart more from zero than your total score for Question 1.

//

Attitude Strength and Accessibility

Not only do attitudes differ in their affective, cognitive, or behavioral origins; they also differ in their strength (Fazio, 1995; Petty & Krosnick, 1995; Pomerantz, Chaiken, & Tordesillas, 1995). This probably does not come as a surprise; for most of us, our attitude toward the current price of rutabagas is weaker, and held with less conviction, than our religious views or our feelings toward a loved one. What determines attitude strength? There are a number of views. Tesser (1993) suggests that the key is how much an attitude is linked to our genes;

the more heritable an attitude is, the stronger it will be. Others argue that the key is how important the attitude is to us or how knowledgeable we are about the topic (Krosnick & Abelson, 1991; Wood, 1982; Wood, Rhodes, & Biek, 1995). There is consensus, however, on two important points: First, that a good way to measure attitude strength is by seeing how accessible it is in memory, and second, that the stronger an attitude, the more resistant to change it is.

Consider this example: In a moment, we are going to give you the name of an object. When we do, simply think about that object for a few seconds. Ready? Here is the object: a mountain bike. Did positive or negative feelings come to mind immediately, or did you think about a mountain bike without much feeling? These questions concern **attitude accessibility,** which Russ Fazio (1989, 1990, 1995) defines as the strength of the association between an object and an evaluation of it. If an attitude is highly accessible, then your attitude comes to mind whenever you encounter the object. For example, if your attitude toward mountain bikes is highly accessible, then as soon as you read the words, feelings of liking or disliking were triggered. If an attitude is relatively inaccessible, then feelings of liking or disliking came to mind more slowly.

Why is the strength of an attitude, as measured by its accessibility, important? For one thing, as we will see toward the end of this chapter, it determines how likely people are to behave consistently with their attitude. Accessibility also influences how easily people change their attitudes. In general, the more accessible an attitude is—the more quickly it comes to mind—the harder that attitude is to change (Houston & Fazio, 1989). Thus, if your attitude toward mountain bikes came to mind quickly, it would be difficult for someone to change your mind about how you feel.

Attitude Accessibility the strength of the association between an object and a person's evaluation of that object; accessibility is measured by the speed with which people can report how they feel about an issue or object

Attitude Change

Attitudes do sometimes change. In America, for example, the popularity of the president often seems to rise and dip with surprising speed. Consider people's attitudes toward George Bush when he was president. In 1991, just after the Gulf

■ When you looked at this picture, how quickly did your attitude toward mountain bikes come to mind? The faster your attitude came to mind the more accessible and resistant to change it is.

War, nearly 90 percent of Americans approved of President Bush's performance. A mere one year later, as the country entered an economic recession, fewer than half of those polled approved of his performance. And in the presidential election of 1992, President Bush received only 38 percent of the vote.

When attitudes change, they often do so in response to social influence. Our attitudes toward everything from a presidential candidate to a brand of laundry detergent can be influenced by what other people do or say. This is why attitudes are of such interest to social psychologists—even something as personal and internal as an attitude is a highly social phenomenon, influenced by the imagined or actual behavior of other people. The entire premise of advertising, for example, is that your attitudes toward consumer products can be influenced by hearing someone say that new and improved Scrubadub detergent cleans clothes the best or by seeing a sexy model wearing a particular brand of jeans. Let's take a look at the conditions under which attitudes are most likely to change.

Changing Attitudes by Changing Behavior: Cognitive Dissonance Theory Revisited

We have already discussed one way that attitudes change—when people behave inconsistently with their attitudes and cannot find external justification for their behavior. We refer, of course, to *cognitive dissonance theory.* As we discussed in Chapter 6, people experience dissonance when they do something that threatens their image of themselves as decent, kind, and honest, particularly if there is no way they can explain away this behavior as due to external circumstances.

Consider an example we gave in Chapter 6. You walk into your friend Sam's house and notice an atrocious painting on the wall. You are about to burst into raucous laughter when Sam says, with a great deal of pleasure and excitement, "Do you like it? It's by a relatively unknown artist named Carol Smear; I think she is very talented, so I went into hock to buy it. Don't you think it's beautiful?"

How do you respond? You hesitate, your mind racing. "Sam seems so happy and excited. Why should I rain on his parade? If I tell him my honest opinion, I'll hurt his feelings; he might get mad. I might make him feel that he made a terrible mistake. Anyway, he can't take it back. What's the sense in telling him the truth?" So you tell Sam that you like the painting very much. Do you experience much dissonance? We doubt it. There are a great many thoughts that are consonant with having told this lie, as outlined in your reasoning in the above sentences. For example, your cognition that it is important not to cause pain to people you like provides *external justification* for having told a harmless lie.

But what happens if you say something you don't really believe and there is no ample external justification for doing so? What if your friend Sam was fabulously wealthy and bought paintings constantly? In addition, what if you were a noted art historian whose opinion Sam valued? What if, in the past, you'd told him he'd bought a hideous eyesore and your friendship had survived? Now the external justifications for lying to Sam about the painting are minimal. If you still refrain from giving your true opinion (saying instead, "Gee, Sam, it's, uh . . . interesting"), you will experience dissonance.

When you can't find external justification for your behavior, you will attempt to find *internal justification*—by bringing the two cognitions (your attitude and your behavior) closer together. How do you do this? You begin looking for positive aspects of the painting—some evidence of creativity or sophistication that might have escaped you previously. Chances are that if you look hard enough,

> **❝**By persuading others, we convince ourselves
>
> —Junius, 1769

you will find something. Within a short time, your attitude toward the painting will have moved in the direction of the positive statement you have made, and that is how "saying is believing." This phenomenon is generally referred to as *counter-attitudinal advocacy*, a process by which individuals are induced to state publicly an opinion or attitude that runs counter to their own private attitudes. When this is accomplished with a minimum of external justification, it results in a change in the individual's private attitude in the direction of the public statement.

As we saw in Chapter 6, there is substantial evidence that counter-attitudinal advocacy is a powerful way to change someone's attitudes. If you wanted to change a friend's attitude toward smoking, you might succeed by getting him or her to give an antismoking speech, under conditions of low external justification. But what if your goal was to change attitudes on a mass scale? Suppose you were hired by the American Cancer Society to come up with an antismoking campaign that could be used nationwide. Though dissonance techniques are powerful, they are very difficult to carry out on a mass scale (e.g., it would be hard to have all American smokers make antismoking speeches under just the right conditions of low external justification). In order to change as many people's attitudes as possible, you would have to resort to other techniques of attitude change. You probably would construct some sort of **persuasive communication**, which is a communication such as a speech or television advertisement that advocates a particular side of an issue. How should you construct your message so that it would really change people's attitudes?

Persuasive Communication communication (e.g., a speech or television ad) advocating a particular side of an issue

Persuasive Communications and Attitude Change

Suppose the American Cancer Society has given you a five-figure budget to develop your advertising campaign. You have a lot of decisions ahead of you. Should you pack your public service announcement with facts and figures? Or should you take a more emotional approach, including frightening visual images of diseased lungs in your message? Should you hire a famous movie star to deliver your message, or

■ To sell a product, it is good to have a credible, trustworthy person endorse it. In this ad, Andre Agasse endorses a tennis shirt.

"Of the modes of persuasion furnished by the spoken word there are three kinds. The first kind depends on the personal character of the speaker; the second on putting the audience into a certain frame of mind; the third on the proof, or apparent proof, provided by the words of the speech itself.

—Aristotle, *Rhetoric*

a Nobel Prize-winning medical researcher? Should you take a friendly tone and acknowledge that it is hard to quit smoking, or should you take a hard line and tell smokers to (as the Nike ads put it) "just do it"? You can see the point—it's not easy to figure out how to construct a truly persuasive communication.

Luckily, social psychologists have conducted many studies over the past 50 years on what makes a persuasive communication effective, beginning with Carl Hovland and his colleagues (Hovland, Janis, & Kelley, 1953). Drawing on their experiences during World War II, when they worked for the U.S. armed forces to increase the morale of U.S. soldiers (Stouffer et al., 1949), Hovland and his colleagues conducted many experiments on the conditions under which people are most likely to be influenced by persuasive communications. In essence, they studied "who says what to whom," looking at the *source of the communication* (e.g., how expert or attractive the speaker is), *the communication itself* (e.g., the quality of the arguments; whether the speaker presents both sides of the issue), and *the nature of the audience* (e.g., which kinds of appeals work with hostile versus friendly audiences). Because these researchers were at Yale University, this approach to the study of persuasive communications is known as the **Yale Attitude Change approach.**

This approach yielded a great deal of useful information on how people change their attitudes in response to persuasive communications; some of this information is summarized in Figure 7.2. As the research mounted, however, a problem became apparent: Many aspects of persuasive communications turned out to be important, but it was not clear which were more important than others—that is, when one factor should be emphasized over another.

For example, let's return to that job you have with the American Cancer Society—they want to see their ad next month! If you were to read the many Yale Attitude Change studies, you might find lots of useful information about who should say what to whom in order to construct a persuasive communication. However, you might also find yourself saying, "Gee, there's an awful lot of information here, and I'm not sure where I should place the most emphasis: Should I worry most about who delivers the ads? Or should I worry more about the content of the message itself?"

Yale Attitude Change Approach
the study of the conditions under which people are most likely to change their attitudes in response to persuasive messages; researchers in this tradition focus on "who said what to whom"—that is, on the source of the communication, the nature of the communication, and the nature of the audience

The Central and Peripheral Routes to Persuasion

If you asked these questions, you would be in good company. Some well-known attitude researchers have wondered the same thing: When is it best to stress factors central to the communication—such as the strength of the arguments—and when is it best to stress factors peripheral to the logic of the arguments—such as the credibility or attractiveness of the person delivering the speech? This question has been answered by two influential theories of persuasive communication: Shelly Chaiken's *heuristic-systematic persuasion model* (Chaiken, 1987; Chaiken, Liberman, & Eagly, 1989; Chaiken, Wood, & Eagly, 1996) and Richard Petty and John Cacioppo's *elaboration likelihood model* (Petty & Cacioppo, 1986; Petty & Wegener, 1998). These theories specify when people will be influenced by what the speech says (i.e., the logic of the arguments) and when they will be influenced by more superficial characteristics (e.g., who gives the speech or how long it is). The theories have much in common; to avoid confusion, we will discuss here the ideas in the terminology of the **elaboration likelihood model,** and will return later to some of the specifics of the heuristic-systematic persuasion model.

Elaboration Likelihood Model
the theory that there are two ways in which persuasive communications can cause attitude change; the central route occurs when people are motivated and have the ability to pay attention to the arguments in the communication, and the peripheral route occurs when people do not pay attention to the arguments but are instead swayed by surface characteristics (e.g., who gave the speech)

THE YALE ATTITUDE CHANGE APPROACH

The effectiveness of persuasive communications depends on *who says what to whom.*

Who: The Source of the Communication

- Credible speakers (e.g., those with obvious expertise) persuade people more than speakers lacking in credibility (Hovland & Weiss, 1951; Petty, Wegener, & Fabrigar, 1997).
- Attractive speakers (whether due to physical or personality attributes) persuade people more than unattractive speakers do (Eagly & Chaiken, 1975; Petty, Wegener, & Fabrigar, 1997).

What: The Nature of the Communication

- People are more persuaded by messages that do not seem to be designed to influence them (Petty & Cacioppo, 1986; Walster & Festinger, 1962).
- Is it best to present a one-sided communication (one that presents only arguments favoring your position) or a two-sided communication (one that presents arguments for and against your position)? In general, two-sided messages work better, if you are sure to refute the arguments on the other side (Allen, 1991; Allen et al., 1990; Crowley & Hoyer, 1994; Lumsdaine & Janis, 1953).
- Is it best to give your speech before or after someone arguing for the other side? If the speeches are to be given back to back and there will be a delay before people have to make up their minds, it is best to go first. Under these conditions, there is likely to be a *primacy effect,* wherein people are more influenced by what they hear first. If there is a delay between the speeches and people will make up their minds right after hearing the second one, it is best to go last. Under these conditions, there is likely to be a *recency effect,* wherein people remember the second speech better than the first one (Haugtvedt & Wegener, 1994; Miller & Campbell, 1959).

To Whom: The Nature of the Audience

- An audience that is distracted during the persuasive communication will often be persuaded more than one that is not (Festinger & Maccoby, 1964; Petty & Cacioppo, 1986).
- People low in intelligence tend to be more influenceable than people high in intelligence, and people with moderate self-esteem tend to be more influenceable than people with low or high self-esteem (Rhodes & Wood, 1992)
- People are particularly susceptible to attitude change during the impressionable ages of 18 to 25. Beyond those ages, people's attitudes are more stable and resistant to change (Krosnick & Alwin, 1989; Sears, 1981).

■ **FIGURE 7.2   The Yale Attitude Change Approach**

Both theories state that, under certain conditions, people are motivated to pay attention to the facts in a communication, thus they will be most persuaded when these facts are logically compelling. That is, sometimes people elaborate on what they hear, carefully thinking about and processing the content of the communication. Petty and Cacioppo (1986) call this the **central route to persuasion.** Under other conditions, people are not motivated to pay attention to the facts; instead, they notice only the surface characteristics of the message, such as how long it is and who is delivering it. Here people will not be swayed by the logic of the arguments, because they are not paying close attention to what the communicator says. Instead, they are persuaded if the surface characteristics of the message—such as the fact that it is long or is delivered by an expert or attractive communicator—make it seem like a reasonable one. Petty and Cacioppo (1986) call

Central Route to Persuasion
the case whereby people elaborate on a persuasive communication, listening carefully to and thinking about the arguments; this occurs when people have both the ability and the motivation to listen carefully to a communication

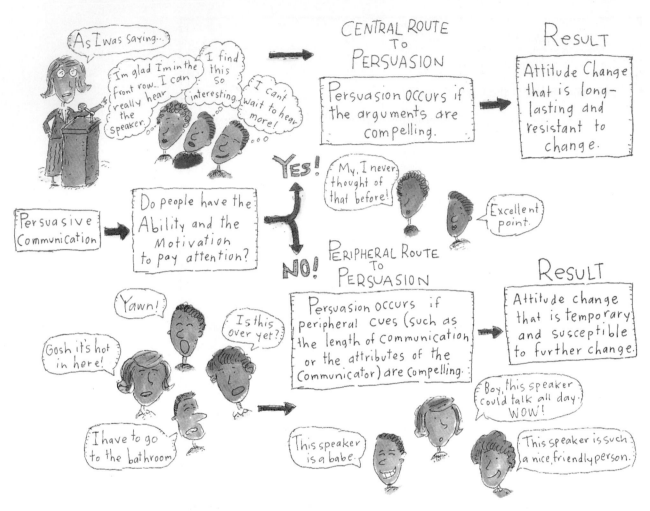

■ **FIGURE 7.3** The elaboration likelihood model describes how people change their attitudes when they hear persuasive communications.

this the **peripheral route to persuasion,** because people are swayed by things peripheral to the message itself.

What are the conditions under which people take the central versus the peripheral route to persuasion? The key, according to Richard Petty, John Cacioppo, and Shelly Chaiken, is whether people have the motivation and ability to pay attention to the facts. To the extent that people are truly interested in the topic and thus motivated to pay close attention to the arguments, they are more likely to take the central route. Similarly, if people have the ability to pay attention—for example, if nothing is distracting them—they are more likely to take the central route (see Figure 7.3).

The Motivation to Pay Attention to the Arguments

One determinant of whether people are motivated to pay attention to a communication is the personal relevance of the topic, namely the extent to which a topic has important consequences for a person's well-being. For example, consider the issue of whether Social Security benefits should be reduced. How personally relevant is this to you? If you are a 72-year-old whose sole income is from Social Security, this issue is obviously extremely relevant; if you are a 20-year-old from a well-to-do family, the issue has little personal relevance.

The more personally relevant an issue is, the more willing people are to pay attention to the arguments in a speech, and thus the more likely people are to take the central route to persuasion. Richard Petty, John Cacioppo, and Rachel Goldman (1981) demonstrated this point by asking college students to listen to a speech arguing that all college seniors should be required to pass a comprehensive exam in their major before they graduate. Half of the participants were told that their university was currently giving serious thought to requiring comprehensive exams; thus, for these participants the issue was personally relevant. For the other half, the issue was of the "hohum" variety—the students were told that their university was considering requiring the exams but not for ten years.

The researchers then introduced two variables that might influence whether people would agree with the speech. The first was the strength of the arguments presented. Half the participants heard arguments that were strong and persuasive (e.g., "The quality of undergraduate teaching has improved at schools with the exams"), whereas the others heard arguments that were weak and unpersuasive (e.g., "The risk of failing the exam is a challenge most students would welcome"). The second was a peripheral cue, namely the prestige of the speaker. Half the participants were told that the author was an eminent professor at Princeton University, whereas the others were told that the author was a high school student.

Thus, when deciding how much to agree with the position advocated by the speaker, the participants could use one or both of these different kinds of information. They could listen carefully to the arguments and scrutinize how convincing they were, or they could simply go by who said them (i.e., how prestigious the source was). As predicted by the elaboration likelihood model, the way in which people were persuaded depended on the personal relevance of the issue. The left-hand panel of Figure 7.4 shows what happened when the issue was highly relevant to the listeners. These students were very much influenced by the quality of the arguments (i.e., persuasion occurred via the central route). Those who heard strong arguments agreed much more with the speech than those who heard weak arguments did. They were decidedly unimpressed by who presented the arguments (the Princeton professor or the high school student). A good argument was a good argument, even if it was written by someone who lacked prestige.

What happens when a topic is of low relevance? As seen in the right-hand panel of Figure 7.4, what mattered was not the strength of the arguments but who the speaker was. Those who heard the strong arguments agreed with the speech only slightly more than those who heard the weak arguments, whereas those who heard the Princeton professor were much more swayed than those who heard the high school student.

This finding reflects a general rule: When an issue is personally relevant, people will pay attention to the arguments in a speech and will be persuaded to the extent that the arguments are sound—the "proof" of the speech, in Aristotle's words. When an issue is of low personal relevance, people will not pay as close attention to the arguments. Instead, they will take a mental shortcut, following such peripheral rules as "Prestigious speakers can be trusted" or "Length implies strong arguments" (Chaiken, 1987; Chaiken & Maheswaran, 1994; Howard, 1997; Petty & Cacioppo, 1986; Petty & Wegener, 1998).

In addition to the personal relevance of a topic, people's motivation to pay attention to a speech depends on their personality. Some people enjoy thinking

> "The ability to kill or capture a man is a relatively simple task compared with changing his mind.
> —Richard Cohen, *Washington Post,* February 28, 1991

> "I'm not convinced by proofs but signs.
> —Coventry Patmore

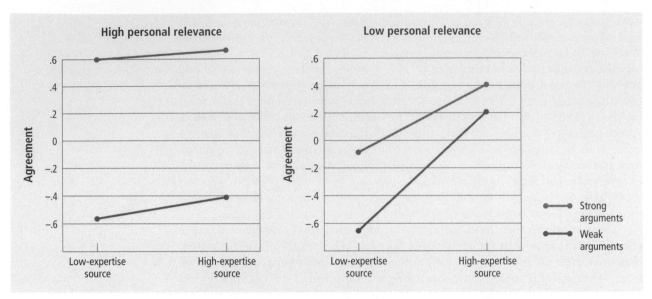

■ **FIGURE 7.4**   **Effects of personal relevance on type of attitude change.**   The higher the number, the more people agreed with the persuasive communication—namely, that their university should adopt comprehensive exams. *Left panel:* When the issue was highly relevant, people were swayed by the quality of the arguments more than the expertise of the speaker. This is the central route to persuasion. *Right panel:* When the issue was low in relevance, people were swayed by the expertise of the speaker more than the quality of the arguments. This is the peripheral route to persuasion. (Adapted from Petty & Cacioppo, 1986, based on a study by Petty, Cacioppo, & Goldman, 1981)

Need for Cognition
a personality variable reflecting the extent to which people engage in and enjoy effortful cognitive activities

things through more than others do; they are said to be high in the **need for cognition** (Cacioppo, Petty, Feinstein, & Jarvis, 1996). This is a personality variable that reflects the extent to which people engage in and enjoy effortful cognitive activities. People high in the need for cognition are more likely to form their attitudes by paying close attention to relevant arguments (i.e., via the central route), whereas people low in the need for cognition are more likely to rely on peripheral cues, such as how attractive or credible a speaker is. Try it! on page 251 can show you how high you are in the need for cognition.

The Ability to Pay Attention to the Arguments

Sometimes it is difficult to pay attention to a speech, even if we want to. Maybe we're tired; maybe we're distracted by an annoying construction noise outside the window; maybe the issue is too complex and hard to evaluate. Under such circumstances, people are unable to pay close attention to the arguments and thus are swayed more by peripheral cues (Festinger & Maccoby, 1964; Petty & Brock, 1981; Petty, Wells, & Brock, 1976). For example, a few years ago an exchange of letters appeared in Ann Landers's advice column about whether drugs such as cocaine and marijuana should be legalized. Readers from across the country wrote in with all sorts of compelling arguments on both sides of the issue, and it was difficult to figure out which arguments had the most merit. One reader resolved this dilemma by relying less on the content of the arguments than on the prestige and expertise of the source of the arguments. The reader noted that several eminent people have supported the legalization of drugs, including a Princeton pro-

Try It **!**

The Need for Cognition

Instructions: For each of the statements below, please indicate to what extent the statement is characteristic of you. Please use the following scale:

1 = extremely uncharacteristic of you (not at all like you)
2 = somewhat uncharacteristic
3 = uncertain
4 = somewhat characteristic
5 = extremely characteristic of you (very much like you)

1. I would prefer complex to simple problems. _____

2. I like to have the responsibility of handling a situation that requires a lot of thinking. _____

3. Thinking is not my idea of fun. _____

4. I would rather do something that requires little thought than something that is sure to challenge my thinking abilities. _____

5. I try to anticipate and avoid situations where there is a likely chance I will have to think in depth about something. _____

6. I find satisfaction in deliberating hard and for long hours. _____

7. I only think as hard as I have to. _____

8. I prefer to think about small, daily projects to long-term ones. _____

9. I like tasks that require little thought once I've learned them. _____

10. The idea of relying on thought to make my way to the top appeals to me. _____

11. I really enjoy a task that involves coming up with new solutions to problems. _____

12. Learning new ways to think doesn't excite me very much. _____

13. I prefer my life to be filled with puzzles that I must solve. _____

14. The notion of thinking abstractly is appealing to me. _____

15. I would prefer a task that is intellectual, difficult, and important to one that is somewhat important but does not require much thought. _____

16. I feel relief rather than satisfaction after completing a task that required a lot of mental effort. _____

17. It's enough for me that something gets the job done; I don't care how or why it works. _____

18. I usually end up deliberating about issues even when they do not affect me personally. _____

This scale measures the *need for cognition,* which is a personality variable reflecting the extent to which people engage in and enjoy effortful cognitive activities (Cacioppo et al., 1996). As noted in the text, people high in the need for cognition are more likely to form their attitudes by paying close attention to relevant arguments (i.e., via the central route), whereas people low in the need for cognition are more likely to rely on peripheral cues, such as how attractive or credible a speaker is. Here are some other findings: People who are high in the need for cognition are slightly higher in verbal intelligence, but no higher in abstract reasoning (Cacioppo et al., 1996). There are no gender differences in need for cognition (Cacioppo et al., 1996).

Scoring: First, reverse your responses to items 3, 4, 5, 7, 8, 9, 12, 16, and 17. Do so as follows: If you gave a 1 to these questions, change it to a 5; if you gave a 2, change it to a 4; if you gave a 3, leave it the same; if you gave a 4, change it to a 2; if you gave a 5, change it to a 1. Then, add up your answers to all 18 questions.

fessor who wrote in the prestigious publication *Science;* the economist Milton Friedman; Kurt Schmoke, the former mayor of Baltimore; columnist William F. Buckley; and former Secretary of State George Schultz. The reader decided to support legalization as well, not because of the strength of pro-legalization arguments he or she had read, but because that's the way several experts felt—a clear case of the peripheral route to persuasion.

Thus, if you are worried that your message is rather weak, you might consider distracting your audience—maybe by arranging for some construction noise just outside the room in which you are speaking. If your arguments are strong and convincing, however, make sure you have your audience's full attention, so that they can listen to (and be swayed by) your arguments.

How to Achieve Long-Lasting Attitude Change

Now that you know a persuasive communication can change people's attitudes in either of two ways—via the central or the peripheral route—you may be wondering what difference it makes. Does it really matter whether it was the logic of the arguments or the expertise of the source that changed students' minds about comprehensive exams in the Petty and colleagues (1981) study? Given the bottom line—they changed their attitudes—why should any of us care how they got to that point?

If we are interested in creating long-lasting attitude change, then we should care a lot. People who base their attitudes on a careful analysis of the arguments will be more likely to maintain this attitude over time, more likely to behave consistently with this attitude, and more resistant to counterpersuasion than people who base their attitudes on peripheral cues (Chaiken, 1980; Mackie, 1987; Petty, Haugvedt, & Smith, 1995; Petty & Wegener, 1998). For example, Shelly Chaiken (1980) conducted an experiment in which people changed their attitudes either by analyzing the logic of the arguments or by using peripheral cues. She accomplished this in the same way Petty, Cacioppo, and Goldman (1981) did—namely, by making the issue relevant to the former group but not to the latter. Chaiken telephoned the research participants ten days later to see if their attitude change had persisted. As predicted, people were more likely to have maintained their new attitude if they had formed it by analyzing the strength of the arguments in the communication—that is, if their attitude change had occurred via the central route.

Emotion and Attitude Change

If you are trying to create long-lasting attitude change, you should thus construct strong arguments and then get people to scrutinize and think about those arguments so that change occurs via the central route. Sounds pretty straightforward, doesn't it? You now know how to construct your ad for the American Cancer Society and will soon be able to pick up your check for your efforts. Right? Well, this approach can work, but there's a problem: Before people will consider your carefully constructed arguments, you will first have to get their attention. If you are going to show your antismoking ad on television, for example, how can you be sure people will watch the ad when it comes on, instead of changing the channel or heading for the refrigerator? One way is to grab people's attention by playing to their emotions. As we saw earlier, many advertisements do not simply present facts and figures—they go for the gut, evoking such feelings as fear, lust, or a general, fuzzy feeling of warmth and sentimentality. Does this approach work?

As it turns out, there are several ways in which emotions can influence attitude change.

Emotion Influences the Route to Persuasion

One interesting consequence of playing to people's emotions is that doing so can determine whether they pay close attention to the arguments in a speech (the central route) or take mental shortcuts (the peripheral route). For example, suppose things are really going your way one day, and you're feeling great. You pick up a copy of the student newspaper and glance at an editorial, written by the president of the student council, about a proposed increase in student fees. Are you likely to pore over every word in the editorial and carefully analyze the merits of each and every argument? Or will you give it a cursory glance and think, "Hey, whatever she says is cool with me." What if you are feeling kind of sad that day? Will you read the editorial carefully, or just take the author's word for it?

It turns out that when people are in good moods, they want to continue feeling that way; thus, they avoid activities—such as going to the effort to read an article about an unpleasant topic—that are likely to spoil their moods (Isen, 1987; Wegener & Petty, 1996). Thus, if you are feeling great, you are likely to glance at the newspaper editorial and take the author's word for it, without going to the effort to think carefully about all of her arguments—in short, to take the peripheral route to persuasion. But if you are in a sad or a neutral mood, you are more likely to take the central route, analyzing each argument in detail.

To illustrate this point, let's consider a study by Herbert Bless, Gerd Bohner, Norbert Schwarz, and Fritz Strack (1990), who put college students in temporarily good or bad moods by having them write about happy or sad events in their lives. Then, as part of what was supposedly another study, the researchers asked people to listen to a speech arguing that student fees at their university should be

■ How do people's moods influence the way in which their attitudes change? People who are in good moods often do not want to pay close attention to the content of persuasive communications, and thus change their attitudes via the peripheral route.

■ **FIGURE 7.5 Effects of mood on attitude change.** People in a sad mood paid attention to a speech, and thus were more convinced when the arguments were strong (see left-hand side of figure). People in a happy mood paid less attention to the speech, and thus were equally convinced by weak and strong arguments (see right-hand side of figure). (Adapted from Bless, Bohner, Schwarz, & Strack, 1990)

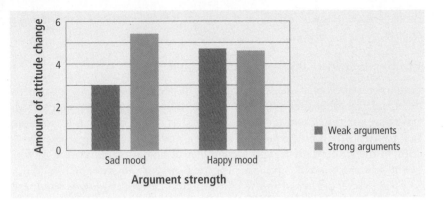

increased. In one condition the speech contained strong, well-reasoned arguments, whereas in another condition the speech contained weak, poorly reasoned arguments. The results were clear: People in a sad mood paid close attention to the arguments and thus changed their attitudes when the arguments were strong but not when the arguments were weak (see left-hand side of Figure 7.5). People in a good mood paid relatively little attention to the strength of the arguments. They seemed to take the speaker's word for it regardless of how strong the arguments were, and thus they were no more convinced when the arguments were strong than when the arguments were weak (see right-hand side of Figure 7.5). Other studies have shown that people in good moods are more likely to rely on peripheral cues, such as agreeing with speakers who are experts (Sinclair, Mark, & Clore, 1994; Worth & Mackie, 1987). This is especially likely to be true if people think that paying attention to the message will ruin their good mood (Wegener, Petty, & Smith, 1995).

Fear-Arousing Communications

In the study by Bless and colleagues (1990), people who were sad analyzed the message more carefully. What about other kinds of bad moods, such as being anxious, agitated, or afraid—what effect does this have on attitude change? By far the most research has examined the effects of fear on attitude change. Scaring people is one of the most common techniques for trying to change attitudes. When we asked you earlier how you would get people's attention when presenting your antismoking ad, it might have crossed your mind to use a **fear-arousing communication,** which is a persuasive message that attempts to change people's attitudes by arousing their fears. Public service ads often take this approach by trying to scare people into practicing safer sex, wearing their seatbelts, and staying away from drugs.

Do fear-arousing communications work? The answer lies in the extent to which fear influences people's ability to pay attention to and process the arguments in a message. If a moderate amount of fear is created and people believe that listening to the message will teach them how to reduce this fear, then they will be motivated to analyze the message carefully, changing their attitudes via the central route (Petty, 1995; Rogers, 1983). Consider a study by Howard Leventhal and his colleagues (Leventhal, Watts, & Pagano, 1967), who showed a group of smokers a graphic film depicting lung cancer and gave them pamphlets with specific instructions about how to quit smoking. As seen in the top line in

Fear-Arousing Communications persuasive messages that attempt to change people's attitudes by arousing their fears

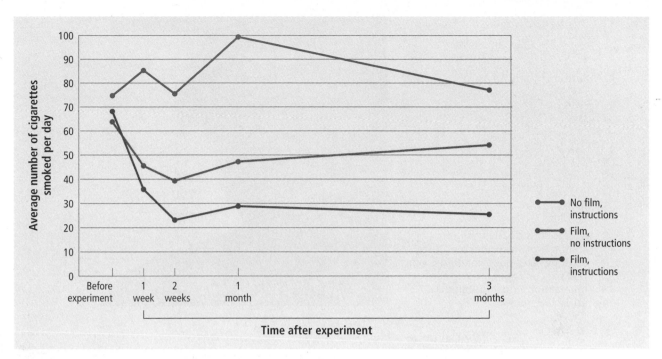

■ **FIGURE 7.6   Effects of fear appeals on attitude change.**   People were shown a scary film about the effects of smoking, instructions about how to stop smoking, or both. Those who were shown both reduced the number of cigarettes they smoked the most. (Adapted from Leventhal, Watts, & Pagano, 1967)

Figure 7.6, the members of this group reduced their smoking significantly more than people who were shown only the film or only the pamphlet. Why? Seeing the film made people scared, and giving them the pamphlet reassured them that there was a way to reduce this fear—by following the instructions on how to quit. Seeing only the pamphlet didn't work very well, because little fear was motivating people to read it carefully. Seeing only the film didn't work very well either, because people are likely to tune out a message that raises fear but does not give information about how to reduce it. This may explain why some attempts to frighten people into changing their attitudes and behaviors have not been very successful: They succeed in scaring people but do not provide specific recommendations for people to follow so that they can reduce their fear (Becker & Josephs, 1988; DeJong & Winsten, 1989; Job, 1988; Soames, 1988).

Fear-arousing appeals will also fail if they are too strong, such that people feel very threatened. If people are scared to death, they will become defensive, will deny the importance of the threat, and will be unable to think rationally about the issue (Baron, Inman, Kao, & Logan, 1992; Janis & Feshbach, 1953; Jepson & Chaiken, 1990; Liberman & Chaiken, 1992). So, if you have decided to arouse people's fear in your ad for the American Cancer Society, keep these points in mind: First, try to create enough fear to motivate people to pay attention to your arguments but not so much fear that people will tune out or distort what you say. Second, include some specific recommendations about how to stop smoking, so that people will be reassured that paying close attention to your arguments will help them reduce their fear.

HEROIN LETS YOU ESCAPE.

"After awhile, you're not
doing heroin to get high.
You're just sick, and you need it
to get normal."

Stacy, ex-entrepreneur, HIV-positive

■ This ad is clearly trying to scare people into changing their attitudes and behavior. Based on research on fear-arousing communications, do you think this ad would work?

Emotions as a Heuristic

Heuristic-Systematic Model of Persuasion
the theory that there are two ways in which persuasive communications can cause attitude change; people either systematically process the merits of the arguments or use mental shortcuts (heuristics), such as "Experts are always right"

Another way in which emotions can cause attitude change is by acting as a signal for how we feel about an issue. According to Shelly Chaiken's (1987) **heuristic-systematic model of persuasion,** when people take the peripheral route to persuasion they often use heuristics. Recall that in Chapter 3 we defined heuristics as mental shortcuts people use to make judgments quickly and efficiently; in the present context, a heuristic can be viewed as a simple decision rule people use to decide what their attitude is, without having to spend a lot of time analyzing every little fact about the matter. Examples of such heuristics are "Experts are always right" and "Length equals strength" (i.e., long messages are more persuasive than short ones).

Interestingly, our emotions and moods can themselves act as a heuristic to determine our attitudes. When trying to decide what our attitude is about something, we often rely on the "How do I feel about it?" heuristic (Forgas, 1995; Schwarz & Clore, 1988). If we feel good, we must have a positive attitude; if we feel bad, it's thumbs down. Now this probably sounds like a pretty good rule to follow, and, like most heuristics, it is—most of the time. Suppose you're at a Ford dealership checking out the new Taurus and are trying to decide if you prefer it to the Toyota Corolla. If you use the "How do I feel about it?" heuristic, you do a quick check of your feelings and emotions. If you feel great while you're sitting in the driver's seat of the new Taurus, you decide that you like it a lot.

The only problem is that sometimes it is difficult to tell where our feelings come from. Is it really the Taurus that made you feel great, or is it something completely unrelated to the Taurus? Maybe you were in a really good mood to begin with, or maybe on the way to the dealership you heard your favorite song on the radio. The problem with the "How do I feel about it" heuristic is that we can make mistakes about what is causing our mood. Sound familiar? In Chapter 5 we talked about *misattribution,* which is what happens when we think our feelings are coming from one source when they are really coming from another source. If people misattribute a prior good mood to something they are considering buying, they might get into trouble. Once they get the new car home, they might discover that the thrill is gone. From the point of view of advertisers, the goal is to create good feelings while they present their product (e.g., by playing appealing music or showing pleasant images), in the hope that people will attribute at least some of those feelings to the product the advertisers are trying to sell.

Emotion and Different Types of Attitudes

So far, we have been talking about the way in which persuasive communications and emotions influence attitude change in general. A question we have not considered is whether the success of different attitude change techniques depends on the type of attitude we are trying to change. As we saw earlier not all attitudes are created equally; some are based more on beliefs about the attitude object (cognitively based attitudes) whereas others are based more on emotions and values (affectively based attitudes). Several studies have shown that it is best to fight fire with fire: If an attitude is cognitively based, try to change it with rational arguments; if it is affectively based, try to change it with affect (Edwards, 1990; Edwards & von Hippel, 1995; Shavitt, 1989; Snyder & DeBono, 1989).

Sharon Shavitt (1990) has demonstrated this point in a study of the effectiveness of different kinds of advertisements. Some ads, she notes, stress the objective merits of a product, such as an ad for an air conditioner or a vacuum cleaner that discusses its price, efficiency, and reliability. Other ads stress emotions and values, such as ones for perfume or designer jeans that try to associate their brands with sex, beauty, and youthfulness, rather than saying anything about the objective qualities of the product. Which kind of ad is most effective?

To find out, Shavitt gave people different kinds of advertisements for different kinds of consumer products. Some of the items were ones Shavitt called utilitarian products, such as air conditioners and coffee. People's attitudes toward such products tend to be based on an appraisal of the utilitarian aspects of the products (e.g., how energy-efficient an air conditioner is), and thus are cognitively based. The other items were ones Shavitt called social identity products, such as perfume and greeting cards. People's attitudes toward these types of products are based more on their values and concerns about their social identity, and so are more affectively based.

As seen in Figure 7.7, people reacted most favorably to the ads that matched the type of attitude they had. If people's attitudes were cognitively based (e.g., toward air conditioners or coffee), then the ads that focused on the utilitarian aspects of these products, such as the features of the air conditioner, were most successful. If people's attitudes were more affectively based (e.g., toward perfume or greeting cards), then the ads that focused on values and social identity concerns were most successful. The graph displayed in Figure 7.7 shows the number of favorable thoughts people had in response to the different kinds of ads. Similar results were found on a measure of how much people intended to buy the products. Thus, if you ever get a job in advertising, the moral is to know what type of attitude most people have toward your product and then tailor your advertising accordingly.

> It is useless to attempt to reason a man out of a thing he was never reasoned into.
> —Jonathan Swift

Culture and Different Types of Attitudes

Shavitt (1990) found that people have different kinds of attitudes toward different kinds of consumer products (e.g., air conditioners versus perfume). Is it possible that there are differences across cultures in the kinds of attitudes people have toward the same products? As we discussed in Chapter 5, there are differences in people's self-concept across cultures; maybe these differences influence the kinds

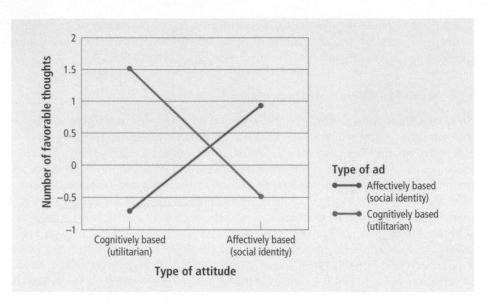

■ **FIGURE 7.7   Effects of affective and cognitive information on affectively and cognitively based attitudes.**   When people had cognitively based attitudes (e.g., toward air conditioners and coffee), then cognitively based advertisements that stressed the utilitarian aspects of the products worked best. When people had more affectively based attitudes (e.g., toward perfume and greeting cards), then affectively based advertisements that stressed values and social identity worked best. (The higher the number, the more favorable thoughts people listed about the products after reading the advertisements.) (Adapted from Shavitt, 1990)

of attitudes people have and thus how those attitudes change. Recall that Western cultures tend to stress independence and individualism, whereas many Asian cultures stress interdependence and collectivism.

Sang-pil Han and Sharon Shavitt (1994) reasoned that these differences in self-concept might also reflect differences in the kinds of attitudes people have toward consumer products. Perhaps people in Western cultures base their attitudes more on concerns about individuality and self-improvement, whereas people in Asian cultures base their attitudes more on concerns about their standing in their social group, such as their families. If so, then advertisements that stress individuality and self-improvement might work better in Western cultures, whereas advertisements that stress one's social group might work better in Asian cultures. To test their hypothesis, Han and Shavitt (1994) created ads for the same product that stressed independence (e.g., an ad for shoes said, "It's easy when you have the right shoes") or interdependence (e.g., "The shoes for your family") and showed them to both Americans and Koreans. Americans were persuaded most by the ads stressing independence; Koreans were persuaded most by the ads stressing interdependence. The researchers also analyzed actual magazine advertisements in the United States and Korea and found that these ads were in fact different: American ads tended to emphasize individuality, self-improvement, and benefits of the product for the individual consumer, whereas Korean ads tended to emphasize the family, concerns about others, and benefits for one's social group. In general, then, advertisements work best if they are tailored to the kind of attitude they are trying to change.

■ This advertisement focuses on individuality and self-improvement, namely how the product can benefit the individual who buys it. Han and Shavitt (1994) found that such ads are typical in the United States. In Korea, however, ads tend to focus more on interdependence, namely how the product can benefit one's social group, such as the family.

How to Make People Resistant to Attitude Change

By now, you are no doubt getting nervous (and not just because the chapter hasn't ended yet): With all these clever methods to change your attitudes, are you ever safe from persuasive communications? Indeed you are, or at least you can be, if you use some strategies of your own. Here's how to make sure all of those persuasive messages that bombard you don't turn you into a quivering mass of constantly changing opinion.

Attitude Inoculation

One approach is to get people to consider the arguments for and against their attitude before someone attacks it. The more people have thought about pro and con arguments beforehand, the better they can ward off attempts to change their minds using logical arguments. If people have not thought much about the issue—that is, if they formed their attitude via the peripheral route—they are particularly susceptible to an attack on that attitude using logical appeals.

William McGuire (1964) demonstrated this fact by using what he called **attitude inoculation.** This is the process of making people immune to attempts to change their attitudes by exposing them to small doses of arguments against their position. Having considered the arguments beforehand, people should thus be relatively immune to the effects of the communication, just as exposing people to a small amount of a virus can inoculate them against exposure to the full-blown viral disease.

In one study, for example, McGuire "inoculated" people by giving them brief arguments against cultural truisms, or beliefs that most members of a society believe uncritically, such as the idea that we should brush our teeth after every meal. Two days later, people came back and read a much stronger attack on the truism, one that contained a series of logical arguments about why brushing your teeth too frequently is a bad idea. The people who had been inoculated against these arguments were much less likely to change their attitudes than a control group

Attitude Inoculation
the process of making people immune to attempts to change their attitudes by initially exposing them to small doses of the arguments against their position

> "The chief effect of talk on any subject is to strengthen one's own opinions and, in fact, one never knows exactly what he does believe until he is warmed into conviction by the heat of the attack and defense.
>
> —Charles Dudley Warner,
> *Backlog Studies*, 1873

who had not been. Why? Those inoculated with weak arguments had the opportunity to think about why these arguments were unfounded and therefore were in a better position to contradict the stronger attack they heard two days later. The control group, never having considered why people should or should not brush their teeth frequently, was particularly susceptible to the strong communication arguing that they should not.

As we have seen, many attacks on our attitudes consist not of logical arguments but of appeals to our emotions. Is there some way of warding off this kind of opinion change, just as we can ward off the effects of logical appeals? This is an important question, because many critical changes in attitudes and behaviors occur not in response to logic but via more emotional appeals. Consider the way in which many adolescents begin to smoke, drink, or take drugs. Often they do so in response to pressure from their peers, at an age when they are particularly susceptible to such pressure. For example, one study found that the best predictor of whether an adolescent smokes marijuana is whether he or she has a friend who does so (Yamaguchi & Kandel, 1984).

Think about how this occurs. It is not as if peers present a set of logical arguments ("Hey, Jake—did you know that recent studies show that moderate drinking may have health benefits?"). Instead, peer pressure is linked more to people's values and emotions, playing on their fear of rejection and their desire for freedom and autonomy. In adolescence, peers become an important source of social approval—perhaps the most important—and can dispense powerful rewards for holding certain attitudes or behaving in certain ways, such as using drugs or engaging in unprotected sex. What is needed is a technique that will make young people more resistant to attitude change attempts via peer pressure, so that they will be less likely to engage in dangerous behaviors.

One possibility is to extend the logic of McGuire's (1964) inoculation approach to more affectively based persuasion techniques, such as peer pressure. That is, besides inoculating people with doses of logical arguments that they might hear, we could also inoculate them with samples of the kinds of appeals to their emotions that they might encounter. Consider Jake, a 13-year-old who is hanging out with some classmates, many of whom are smoking cigarettes. The

■ Peer pressure can be very persuasive because it appeals to people's emotions—to their desire to be liked and accepted. Young people may learn to resist persuasion via peer pressure if they are inoculated against it.

classmates begin to make fun of Jake for not smoking, calling him a wimp and a mama's boy. One of them even lights a cigarette and holds it in front of Jake, daring him to take a puff. Many 13-year-olds, faced with such pressure, would cave in. But suppose we immunized Jake to such social pressures by exposing him to mild versions of them and showing him ways to combat these pressures. We might have him role-play a situation where a friend calls him a chicken for not smoking a cigarette and teach him to respond by saying, "I'd be more of a chicken if I smoked it just to impress you." Would this help him to resist the more powerful pressures exerted by his classmates?

Several programs designed to prevent smoking in adolescents suggest that it would. For example, McAlister and his colleagues (1980) used a role-playing technique with seventh-graders, very much like the one described above. The researchers found that these students were significantly less likely to smoke three years after the study, compared to a control group that had not participated in the program. This result is encouraging and has been replicated in similar programs designed to reduce smoking (Chassin, Presson, & Sherman, 1990; Falck & Craig, 1988; Killen, 1985).

We should point out that it is sometimes difficult to determine precisely why programs such as these are effective. They usually involve several interventions, making it difficult to tell which of the interventions was most responsible for the program's success. For example, the McAlister and colleagues (1980) prevention program was multifaceted. In addition to the role-playing procedure to inoculate people against peer pressure, the participants made public commitments not to use tobacco, and they created antismoking skits and slogans (for which they received prizes). Thus, though the results are promising, it will take further research to illuminate which of these activities was most responsible for the success of the program.

When Persuasion Attempts Boomerang: Reactance Theory

It is important not to use too heavy a hand when trying to immunize people against assaults on their attitudes. Suppose you want to make sure that your child never smokes. "Might as well err on the side of giving too strong a message," you might think, absolutely forbidding your child to even look at a pack of cigarettes. "What's the harm?" you figure. "At least this way, my child will get the point about how serious a matter this is."

Actually, there is harm to administering strong prohibitions—the stronger they are, the more likely they will boomerang, causing an *increase* in interest in the prohibited activity. According to **reactance theory** (Brehm, 1966; Brehm & Brehm, 1981), people do not like to feel that their freedom to do or think whatever they want is being threatened. When they feel that their freedom is threatened, an unpleasant state of reactance is aroused, and people can reduce this reactance by performing the threatened behavior (e.g., smoking).

For example, James Pennebaker and Deborah Sanders (1976) placed one of two signs in the bathrooms on a college campus, in an attempt to get people to stop writing graffiti on the walls of restrooms. One sign read, "Do not write on these walls under any circumstances." The other gave a milder prohibition: "Please don't write on these walls." The researchers returned two weeks later and observed how much graffiti had been written since they posted the signs. As they predicted, significantly more people wrote graffiti in the bathrooms with the "Do not write . . ." sign than with the "Please don't write . . ." sign. Similarly, people

> A companion's words of persuasion are effective.
>
> –Homer

Reactance Theory
the idea that when people feel their freedom to perform a certain behavior is threatened, an unpleasant state of reactance is aroused; people can reduce this reactance by performing the threatened behavior

who receive strong admonitions against smoking, taking drugs, or getting their nose pierced become more likely to perform these behaviors, in order to restore their sense of personal freedom and choice (Bushman & Stack, 1996; Dowd, Hughes, Brockbank, Halpain, Seibel, & Seibel, 1988; Graybar, Antonuccio, Boutilier, & Varble, 1989).

When Will Attitudes Predict Behavior?

Now that we have seen how attitudes change, it is important to discuss the consequences of this change. Attitude change is a significant topic in part because of the relationship between attitudes and people's actual behavior. Many people bank on the fact that people act consistently with their attitudes. Advertisers assume that changing people's attitudes toward their products will result in increased sales and politicians assume that positive feelings toward a candidate will result in a vote for that candidate on Election Day. Sounds pretty straightforward, right?

Actually, the relationship between attitudes and behavior is not so straightforward, as indicated by a classic study by Richard LaPiere (1934). In the early 1930s, LaPiere embarked on a cross-country sightseeing trip with a young Chinese couple. Because prejudice against Asians was commonplace in the United States at this time, he was apprehensive about how his Chinese friends would be treated. At each hotel, campground, and restaurant they entered, LaPiere worried that his friends would confront anti-Asian prejudice and that they would be refused service. Much to his surprise, this almost never happened. Of the 251 establishments he and his friends visited, only one refused to serve them.

Struck by this apparent lack of prejudice, LaPiere decided to explore people's attitudes toward Asians in a different way. After his trip, he wrote a letter to each establishment he and his friends had visited, asking if it would serve a Chinese visitor. Of the many establishments who replied, only one said it would. More than 90 percent said they definitely would not; the rest said they were undecided. People's attitudes—as expressed in their response to LaPiere's written inquiry— were in stark contrast to their actual behavior toward LaPiere's Chinese friends.

LaPiere's study was not, of course, a controlled experiment. As LaPiere acknowledged, there are several reasons why his results may not show an inconsistency between people's attitudes and behavior. For example, he had no way of knowing whether the proprietors who answered his letter were the same people who had served him and his friends. Further, people's attitudes may have changed in the months that passed between the time they served the Chinese couple and the time they received the letter. Nonetheless, the lack of correspondence between people's attitudes and what they actually did was so striking that we might question our earlier assumption that behavior routinely follows from attitudes. This is especially the case in light of research performed after LaPiere's study. Allan Wicker (1969) reviewed dozens of more methodologically sound studies and reached the same conclusion: People's attitudes are poor predictors of their behavior.

But how can this be? Does a person's attitude toward Asians or political candidates really tell us nothing about how he or she will behave? How can we reconcile the LaPiere findings—and other studies like it—with the obvious notion that many times people do act in accord with their attitudes? Fortunately, in recent years social psychologists have learned a great deal about when and how attitudes will predict behavior. It is now clear that Wicker's (1969) conclusions

> "We give advice but we do not influence people's conduct.
>
> –La Rouchefoucauld,
> *Maxims*, 1678

■ It is commonly assumed that people's attitudes (e.g., toward a social issue) determine their behavior (e.g., signing a petition supporting that issue). This is not always true, however. If the behavior is spontaneous, it depends on how accessible people's attitudes are. If the behavior is deliberative, it depends on their behavioral intentions.

about attitude-behavior consistency were too pessimistic. Attitudes do predict behavior but only under certain specifiable conditions (DeBono & Snyder, 1995; Zanna & Fazio, 1982). One key factor is knowing whether the behavior we are trying to predict is spontaneous or is deliberative and planned (Fazio, 1990).

Predicting Spontaneous Behaviors

Sometimes we act spontaneously, giving little forethought to what we are about to do. When LaPiere and his Chinese friends entered a restaurant, the manager did not have a lot of time to reflect on whether to serve them; he or she had to make a snap decision. Similarly, when someone approaches us at a shopping mall and asks us to sign a petition in favor of a change in the local zoning laws, we usually don't stop to deliberate for ten minutes but instead decide whether to sign the petition on the spot.

Attitudes will predict spontaneous behaviors only when they are highly accessible to people (Fazio, 1990, 1995; Kallgren & Wood, 1986). As you will recall, accessibility refers to the strength of the association between an object and your attitude toward that object. When accessibility is high, your attitude comes to mind whenever you see the object. When accessibility is low, your attitude comes to mind more slowly. It follows that highly accessible attitudes will be more likely to predict spontaneous behaviors, because people are more likely to be thinking about their attitude when they are called on to act.

Russell Fazio, Martha Powell, and Carol Williams (1989) demonstrated the role of accessibility in a study of people's attitudes and behaviors toward consumer items. People first rated their attitudes toward several products, such as different brands of gum and candy bars. The accessibility of these attitudes was assessed by measuring how long it took people to respond to the attitude questions. People's actual behavior was measured by placing ten of the products on a table (in two rows of five) and telling people they could choose five of them to take home as a reward for being in the study. To what extent did people's attitude toward the products determine which ones they chose?

As predicted, it depended on the accessibility of their attitudes. Attitude-behavior consistency was high among people with accessible attitudes and relatively low among people with inaccessible attitudes. That is, people acted in accord with their attitudes only if their attitudes came quickly to mind when they were making their choice. What about people with inaccessible attitudes—what determined which products they chose? Interestingly, they were more influenced by an arbitrary aspect of the situation—which products happened to be in the first row on the table in front of them. The closer an item was, the more likely they were to choose it. This is consistent with the idea that when attitudes are inaccessible, people are more influenced by situational variables—in this case, how noticeable and within reach the products were.

Predicting Deliberative Behaviors

Sometimes behavior is not spontaneous but deliberative and planned. Most of us give a good deal of thought about where to go to college, whether to accept a new job, or where to spend our vacation. Under these conditions, the immediate accessibility of our attitude is not as important. Given enough time to think about an issue, even people with inaccessible attitudes can bring to mind how they feel. It is only when we have to decide how to act on the spot—without time to think it over—that accessibility matters (Eagly & Chaiken, 1993; Fazio, 1990).

Theory of Planned Behavior
a theory holding that the best predictors of a person's planned, deliberate behaviors are the person's attitudes toward specific behaviors, subjective norms, and perceived behavioral control

The best-known theory of how attitudes predict deliberative behaviors is Icek Ajzen and Martin Fishbein's **theory of planned behavior** (Ajzen, 1985, 1996; Ajzen & Fishbein, 1980; Fishbein & Ajzen, 1975). According to this theory, when people have time to contemplate how they are going to behave, the best predictor of their behavior is their intention, which is in turn determined by three things: their attitudes toward the specific behavior, their subjective norms, and their perceived behavioral control (see Figure 7.8). Let's consider each of these three things in turn. First, specific attitudes: What is important here is not people's general attitude about something but their specific attitude toward the behavior they are considering. According to the theory of planned behavior, only specific attitudes toward the behavior in question can be expected to predict that behavior.

For example, in a study of married women's use of birth control pills, Andrew Davidson and James Jaccard (1979) demonstrated that attitudes toward specific behaviors are better predictors of people's actions than more general attitudes are. A sample of women were asked a series of attitude questions, ranging from the general (their attitude toward birth control) to the specific (their attitude toward using birth control pills during the next two years; see Table 7.1). Two

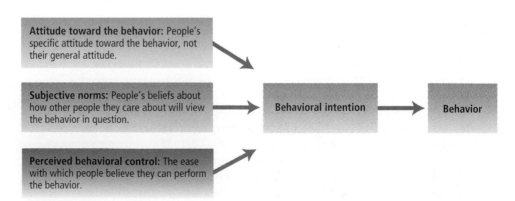

■ **FIGURE 7.8   The theory of planned behavior.**   According to this theory, the best predictor of people's planned, deliberative behaviors are their behavioral intentions. The best predictors of their intentions are their attitudes toward the specific behavior, their subjective norms, and their perceived behavioral control of the behavior. (Adapted from Ajzen, 1985)

Table 7.1

Specific attitudes are better predictors of behavior.

Different groups of women were asked about their attitudes toward birth control. The more specific the question, the better it predicted their actual use of birth control. *Note:* If a correlation is close to 0, it means that there is no relationship between the two variables. The closer the correlation is to 1, the stronger the relationship between attitudes and behavior. (Adapted from Davidson & Jaccard, 1979)

Attitude Measure	Attitude-Behavior Correlation
Attitude toward birth control	.08
Attitude toward birth control pills	.32
Attitude toward using birth control pills	.53
Attitude toward using birth control pills during the next two years	.57

years later, they were asked whether they had used birth control pills at any time since the last interview. As seen in Table 7.1, the women's general attitude toward birth control did not predict their use of birth control at all. This general attitude did not take into account other factors that could have influenced their decision, such as the women's concern about the long-term effects of the pill and their attitude toward other forms of birth control. The more specific the question was about the act of using birth control pills, the better this attitude predicted their actual behavior.

This may be one reason LaPiere (1934) found such inconsistency between people's attitudes and behaviors in his study. His question to the proprietors—whether they would serve "members of the Chinese race"—was stated very generally. Had he asked a much more specific question—such as whether they would serve an educated, well-dressed, well-to-do Chinese couple accompanied by a white American college professor—they might have given an answer that was more in line with their behavior.

In addition to measuring attitudes toward the behavior, we also need to measure people's **subjective norms**—their beliefs about how those they care about will view the behavior in question (see Figure 7.8). To predict someone's intentions, knowing these beliefs can be as important as knowing her or his attitudes. For example, suppose we want to predict whether Kristen intends to go to a heavy-metal concert and we know that she has a negative attitude toward this behavior—she can't stand heavy-metal music. We would probably say she won't go. Suppose we also know, though, that Kristen's best friend, Malcolm, really wants her to go. Knowing this subjective norm—her belief about how a close friend views her behavior—we might make a different prediction.

Finally, as seen in Figure 7.8, people's intentions are influenced by perceived behavioral control, which is the ease with which people believe they can perform the behavior. If people think it is difficult to perform the behavior, such as remembering to use condoms when having sex, then they will not form a strong intention to do so. If people think it is easy to perform the behavior, such as

> "If actions are to yield all the results they are capable of, there must be a certain consistency between them and one's intentions.
> —La Rochefoucauld, *Maxims,* 1678

Subjective Norms
people's beliefs about how those they care about will view the behavior in question

remembering to buy milk on the way home from work, they are more likely to form a strong intention to do so. A considerable amount of research supports the idea that asking people about these determinants of their intentions—attitudes toward specific behaviors, subjective norms, and perceived behavioral control—increases the ability to predict their planned, deliberative behaviors, such as the decision of what job to accept, whether to wear a seatbelt, whether to check oneself for disease, and whether to use condoms when having sex (Cochran, Mays, Ciarletta, Caruso, & Mallon, 1992; Reinecke, Schmidt, & Ajzen, 1996; Sheppard, Hartwick, & Warshaw, 1988; Stasson & Fishbein, 1990; Steffen, 1990; Trafimow, 1996; Trafimow & Finlay, 1996).

The Power of Advertising

We began this chapter with a discussion of daily assaults on our attitudes by advertisers. The world of advertising is rich with examples of the principles of attitude and behavior change we have been discussing. But is there evidence that advertising really works? Most of the research we have discussed was conducted in the laboratory with college students. What about changes in attitudes and behavior out there in the real world? If we see an ad campaign for Scrubadub detergent, are we really more likely to buy Scrubadub when we go to the store? Or are companies wasting the billions of dollars a year they are spending on advertising?

A curious thing about advertising is that most people think it works on everyone but themselves (Wilson & Brekke, 1994). A typical comment is, "Sure, it influences most people, but not me. Seeing those ads for Scrubadub doesn't influence me at all." Contrary to such beliefs, substantial evidence indicates that advertising works; when a product is advertised sales tend to increase (Abraham & Lodish, 1990; Liebert & Sprafkin, 1988; Ryan, 1991; Wells, 1997). The best evidence that advertising works comes from studies using what are called *split cable market tests*. Here, advertisers work in conjunction with cable television companies and grocery stores, showing a target commercial to a randomly selected group of people. They keep track of what people buy by giving potential consumers special ID cards that are scanned at checkout counters; thus, they can tell whether people who saw the commercial for Scrubadub actually buy more Scrubadub—the best measure of advertising effectiveness.

Magid Abraham and Leonard Lodish (1990) have conducted more than 300 split cable market tests. Their findings indicate that advertising does work, particularly for new products (Lodish et al., 1995). About 60 percent of the advertisements for new products led to an increase in sales, compared to 46 percent of the advertisements for established brands. When an ad was effective, how much did it increase sales? The difference in sales between people who saw an effective ad for a new product and those who did not averaged 21 percent. Although this figure might seem modest, it translates into millions of dollars when applied to a national advertising campaign. Further, these effective ads worked quickly, increasing sales substantially within the first six months they were shown.

How Advertising Works

How does advertising work, and which types of ads work the best? The answer to this question follows from our earlier discussion of attitude change. By way of review, advertisers should consider the kind of attitude they are trying to change.

> "You can tell the ideals of a nation by its advertisements.
> —George Norman Douglas,
> *South Wind*

If they are trying to change an affectively based attitude, then, as we have seen, it is best to fight emotions with emotions. Many advertisements take the emotional approach—for example, ads for different brands of soft drinks. Given that different brands of colas are not all that different, many people do not base their purchasing decisions on the objective qualities of the different brands. Consequently, soda advertisements do not stress facts and figures. As noted by one advertising executive, "The thing about soda commercials is that they actually have nothing to say" ("The Battle for Your Brain," *Consumer Reports*, August 1991, p. 521). Instead of presenting facts, soda ads play to people's emotions, trying to associate feelings of excitement, youth, energy, and sexual attractiveness with their brand.

If people's attitudes are more cognitively based, then we need to ask an additional question: How personally relevant is the issue? Does it have important consequences for people's everyday lives, or is it a remote issue that does not directly affect them? Consider, for example, the problem of heartburn. This is not a topic that evokes strong emotions and values in most people. Thus, it is more cognitively based. To people who suffer from frequent heartburn, however, it clearly is of direct personal relevance. In this case, the best way to change people's attitudes is to use logical, fact-based arguments—convince people that your product will reduce heartburn the best, and people will buy it (Chaiken, 1987; Petty & Cacioppo, 1986).

What if you are dealing with a cognitively based attitude that is not of direct personal relevance to people? Here you have a problem, because people are unlikely to pay close attention to your advertisement. You might succeed in changing their attitudes via the peripheral route, such as having attractive movie stars endorse your product. The problem here, as we have seen, is that attitude change triggered by simple peripheral cues is not long-lasting (Chaiken, 1987; Petty & Cacioppo, 1986). Thus, if you have a product that does not engage people's emotions and is not of direct relevance to people's everyday lives, you are in trouble.

But don't despair. The trick is to *make* your product personally relevant. Let's take a look at some actual ad campaigns to see how this is done. Consider the case of Gerald Lambert, who, in the early part of this century, inherited a company that made a surgical antiseptic used to treat throat infections—Listerine. Seeking a wider market for his product, Lambert decided to promote it as a mouthwash. The only problem was that no one at the time used a mouthwash or even knew what one was. And so, having invented the cure, Lambert invented the disease. Look at the ad on the next page, which appeared in countless magazines over the years.

Even though today we would find this ad incredibly sexist, at the time most Americans did not find it offensive. Instead, the ad successfully played on people's fears about social rejection and failure. The phrase "She was often a bridesmaid but never a bride" became one of the most famous in the history of advertising. In a few cleverly chosen, manipulative words, it succeeded in making a problem—*halitosis*—personally relevant to millions of people. Listerine became a best-selling product that has since earned a fortune. Incidentally, you might think halitosis is the official term of the American Medical Association for bad breath. In fact, it is nothing more than a fancy, medical-sounding term invented by Gerald Lambert and his advertising team to sound like a dreadful disease that we must avoid at all costs—by going to the nearest drugstore and stocking up on mouthwash.

■ Advertisers often try to make people's attitudes more affectively based. Whereas most people base their attitudes toward vacuum cleaners on their beliefs about how well they suck up dirt, this ad attempts to get people to base their attitude on style and color—more affective concerns.

■ This ad is one of the most famous in the history of advertising. Although today it is easy to see how sexist and offensive it is, when it appeared in 1936 it succeeded in making a problem (bad breath) personally relevant by playing to people's fears and insecurities about personal relationships. Can you think of any contemporary ads that try to raise similar fears?

> **P**rofits can be obtained either by producing what consumers want or by making consumers want what is actually produced.
>
> —Henry Simons

Gerald Lambert's success at playing to people's fears and sense of shame was not lost on other advertisers. Similar ads have been designed to create new markets for many new products, most having to do with personal hygiene or health: underarm deodorants, deodorant soaps, vitamin supplements, oat bran, fish oil, and more. These campaigns work by convincing people they have problems of great personal relevance and that the advertised product can solve these problems.

Many advertisements also try to make people's attitudes more affectively based by associating the product with important emotions and values (see our earlier discussion of classical conditioning). Consider, for example, advertisements for long-distance telephone service. This topic does not, for most of us,

"How about one of those sunny old grandpas who make things look honest?"

Drawing by Hamilton © 1984 New Yorker Magazine, Inc.

■ Advertising agencies are masters at linking emotional images and words to products.

evoke deep-rooted emotional feelings—until, that is, we see an ad where a man calls his long-lost brother to tell him he loves and misses him, or an ad where a man calls his mother to tell her he has just bought her a plane ticket so that she can come visit him. There is nothing logically compelling about these ads. After all, there is no reason to believe using AT&T service will magically make you closer to your family than using MCI or Sprint. However, by associating positive emotions with a product, an advertiser can turn a bland product into one that evokes feelings of nostalgia, love, warmth, and general goodwill.

Subliminal Advertising: A New Form of Mind Control?

We cannot leave the topic of advertising without discussing one of its most controversial topics—the use of **subliminal messages,** defined as words or pictures that, while not consciously perceived, supposedly influence people's judgments, attitudes, and behaviors. A majority of the public believe that these messages can shape their attitudes and behaviors, even though they do not know the messages have entered their minds (Zanot, Pincus, & Lamp, 1983). Given the near-hysterical claims that have been made about subliminal advertising, it is important to discuss whether it really works.

> **Subliminal Messages** words or pictures that are not consciously perceived but that supposedly influence people's judgments, attitudes, and behaviors

In the late 1950s, James Vicary convinced a movie theater in New Jersey to try a novel approach to selling drinks and popcorn. Imagine you happened to go to the theater that day to see *Picnic,* a popular movie at the time. Unbeknownst to you or the other patrons, you see more than the movie. Messages are flashed on the screen at speeds so quick that they are not consciously perceived, messages that urge you to "drink Coca-Cola" and "eat popcorn." Vicary claimed that these messages registered in the audience members' unconscious minds and caused them to develop a sudden hankering for a soda and a box of popcorn. Coca-Cola sales at the concession counter increased by 18 percent, he said, whereas popcorn sales increased by 58 percent.

When Vicary revealed what he had done, the public reaction was swift. Journalists blasted Vicary's sneaky attempt to boost sales. Minds have been "broken and entered," decried the *New Yorker* (1957, p. 33), and the *Nation* called

PEOPLE HAVE BEEN TRYING TO FIND THE BREASTS IN THESE ICE CUBES SINCE 1957.

The advertising industry is sometimes charged with sneaking seductive little pictures into ads.
Supposedly, these pictures can get you to buy a product without your even seeing them.
Consider the photograph above. According to some people, there's a pair of female breasts

hidden in the patterns of light refracted by the ice cubes.
Well, if you really searched you probably *could* see the breasts. For that matter, you could also see Millard Fillmore, a stuffed pork chop and a 1946 Dodge.
The point is that so-called "subliminal advertising" simply

doesn't exist. Overactive imaginations, however, most certainly do.
So if anyone claims to see breasts in that drink up there, they aren't in the ice cubes.
They're in the eye of the beholder.
ADVERTISING
ANOTHER WORD FOR FREEDOM OF CHOICE.
American Association of Advertising Agencies

■ There is no scientific evidence that implanting sexual images in advertising boosts sales of the product. The public is very aware of this subliminal technique, however—so much so that some advertisers have begun to poke fun at subliminal messages in their ads.

> "In the field of marketing . . . the trend toward selling [has] reached something of a nadir with the unveiling of so called subliminal projection. That is the technique designed to flash messages past our conscious guard.
>
> —Vance Packard, 1958

it "the most alarming and outrageous discovery since Mr. Gatling invented his [machine] gun" ("Diddling the Subconscious," 1957, p. 206). The Federal Communications Commission banned the use of subliminal messages on radio and television, fearing a kind of mind control like that described in George Orwell's novel *1984*. This was hardly, however, the last attempt to influence people with subliminal messages. According to Wilson Bryan Key (1973, 1989), who has written several best-selling books on hidden persuasion techniques, advertisers routinely implant sexual messages in print advertisements, such as the word *sex* in the ice cubes of an ad for gin, and male and female genitalia in everything from pats of butter to the icing in an ad for cake mix. Key (1973) argues that these images are not consciously perceived but put people in a good mood and make them pay more attention to the advertisement.

Subliminal messages are not just visual; they can be auditory as well. In the past decade, a large market has arisen for audiotapes containing subliminal messages to help people lose weight, stop smoking, improve their study habits, raise their self-esteem, and even shave a few strokes off their golf scores. In 1990, sales of subliminal self-help tapes were estimated to be $50 million (*Newsweek*, July 30, 1990). But are subliminal messages effective? Do they really make us more likely to buy consumer products, or help us to lose weight and stop smoking?

Debunking the Claims about Subliminal Advertising

It is important to note that few of the proponents of subliminal advertising have conducted controlled studies to back up their claims. James Vicary did not have a control group who saw the same movie on the same day but with no subliminal messages about Coca-Cola and popcorn. In fact, Vicary reportedly later admitted that he had made up his claims to boost business (Weir, 1984). Similarly, Wilson

Bryan Key did not conduct controlled studies comparing the impact of ads containing hidden sexual messages with the impact of the same ads containing no such messages. Fortunately, many controlled studies of subliminal perception have been conducted, allowing us to evaluate the sometimes hysterical claims that are made.

Simply stated, there is no evidence that the types of subliminal messages used in everyday life have any influence on people's behavior. Hidden commands to eat popcorn do not cause people to line up at the concession stand in greater numbers than they would normally do, and the subliminal commands on self-help tapes do not (unfortunately!) help us to quit smoking or lose a few pounds (Brannon & Brock, 1994; Merikle, 1988; Moore, 1982, 1992, 1995; Pratkanis, 1992; Pratkanis, Eskenazi, & Greenwald, 1994; Theus, 1994; Trappey, 1996). Anthony Greenwald and his colleagues (1991), for example, performed a careful test of the effectiveness of subliminal self-help tapes. Half the participants listened to tapes that, according to the manufacturer, contained subliminal messages designed to improve memory (e.g., "My ability to remember and recall is increasing daily"), whereas the others listened to tapes that had subliminal messages designed to raise self-esteem (e.g., "I have high self-worth and high self-esteem"). Neither of the tapes had any effect on people's memory or self-esteem. It would be nice if we could all improve ourselves simply by listening to music with subliminal messages, but alas, this study (and others) shows that subliminal tapes are no better at magically solving our problems than patent medicines or visits to an astrologist.

Interestingly, research participants in the Greenwald study *thought* the subliminal tapes were working, even though they were not. The researchers were a little devious, in that they correctly informed half the participants about which tape they listened to, but misinformed the others (i.e., half the people who got the memory tape were told it was designed to improve their memories, whereas the other half were told it was designed to improve their self-esteem). Those who thought they had listened to the memory tape believed their memories had improved, even if they had really heard the self-esteem tape. And people who thought they had listened to the self-esteem tape believed their self-esteem had improved, even if they had heard the memory tape. This finding explains why subliminal tapes are a $50 million business: Even though the tapes don't work, people think they do.

Evidence for Subliminal Influence in the Lab

When we said that subliminal messages are ineffective, you may have noticed a qualification: They do not work when used in everyday life. There *is* some evidence for such effects in carefully controlled laboratory studies. For example, Sheila Murphy and Robert Zajonc (1993) showed participants a series of Chinese ideographs (characters used in the Chinese written language) and asked them to rate how much they liked the appearance of each one. Unbeknownst to the participants, the Chinese characters were preceded by another picture—a human face expressing happiness, a human face expressing anger, or a polygon conveying no emotion. These pictures were flashed for only four milliseconds, which is too fast for people to perceive consciously. Nonetheless, as seen in Figure 7.9, these subliminal flashes influenced people's evaluations of the Chinese ideographs. People liked the ideographs the most when they were preceded by a happy face, second most when they were preceded by an unemotional polygon,

| Shown for 4 milliseconds | → | Shown for 2 seconds | → | Ratings of how much people liked the Chinese ideograph* |

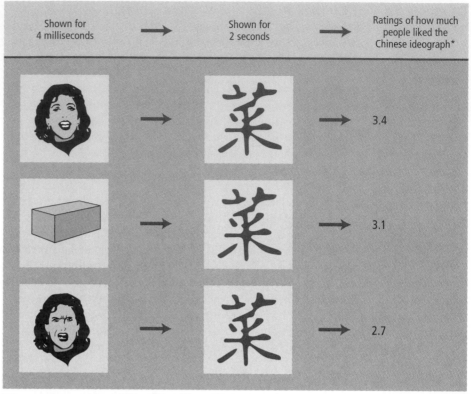

* On a scale that ranged from 1 ("did not like at all") to 5 ("liked quite a bit")

■ **FIGURE 7.9 Effects of subliminal exposure to faces on liking Chinese ideographs.** There is evidence from carefully controlled laboratory studies that subliminal exposures to words and faces can influence people's judgments and attitudes. In this study, people were shown pictures of Chinese ideographs (characters used in the Chinese written language) for two seconds, and asked how much they liked the appearance of each one. Unbeknownst to the participants, the ideographs were preceded by quick flashes of happy faces (top panel), unemotional polygons (middle panel), or angry faces (bottom panel). These flashes of pictures influenced how much people liked the ideographs, even though they could not be perceived consciously. All of the successful demonstrations of subliminal messages, however, have been done under carefully controlled laboratory conditions that would be difficult to duplicate in everyday life. Further, there is no evidence that subliminal messages can be used to get people to do things they prefer not to do. (Adapted from Murphy & Zajonc, 1993)

and least when they were preceded by an angry face—even though people didn't know that these faces or polygraph had been flashed. Several other researchers have found similar effects of pictures or words flashed at subliminal levels (e.g., Baldwin, Carrell, & Lopez 1990; Bargh & Pietromonaco, 1982; Bornstein, Leone, & Galley, 1987; Bornstein & Pittman, 1992).

It is frightening to think that our behavior can be influenced by information we do not even know we have seen. Before a new wave of hysteria about mind control begins, however, we should mention some key qualifications. All of the successful demonstrations of subliminal stimuli have been conducted under carefully controlled laboratory conditions that are difficult to reproduce in everyday life. To get subliminal effects, researchers have to make sure that the

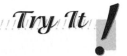

Advertising and Mind Control

Here is an exercise on people's beliefs about the power of advertising that you can try on your friends.

Ask about 10 friends the following questions—preferably friends who have not had a course in social psychology! See how accurate their beliefs are about the effects of different kinds of advertising.

1. Do you think that you are influenced by subliminal messages in advertising? (Define subliminal messages for your friends as words or pictures that are not consciously perceived but that supposedly influence people's judgments, attitudes, and behaviors.)

2. Do you think that you are influenced by everyday advertisements that you perceive consciously, such as television ads for laundry detergent and pain killers?

3. Suppose you had a choice to listen to one of two speeches that argued against a position you believe in, such as whether marijuana should be legalized. In Speech A, a person presents several arguments against your position. In Speech B, all of the arguments are presented subliminally—you will not perceive anything consciously. Which speech would you rather listen to, A or B?

Tally the results in the table below:

Question 1	Question 2	Question 3
Yes:	Yes:	Yes:
No:	No:	No:

See if your results match those of actual studies:

Question 1: Wilson, Gilbert, and Wheatley (in press) found that 80 percent of college students preferred not to receive a subliminal message because it might influence them in an undesirable way.

Question 2: Wilson et al. (in press) found that only 28 percent of college students preferred not to receive a regular, everyday TV ad because it might influence them in an undesirable way.

Question 3: When Wilson, Houston, & Meyers (in press) asked college students to choose to listen to the type of speech they thought would influence them the least, 69 percent chose the regular speech and 31 percent chose the subliminal speech. Ironically, it was the regular speech that changed people's minds the most.

Show off your knowledge to your friends. Ask them why they are more wary of subliminal messages than everyday advertising, when it is everyday advertising and not subliminal messages that changes people's minds. Why do *you* think that people are most afraid of the kinds of ads that are least effective? What does this say about people's awareness of their own thought processes?

illumination of the room is just right, that people are seated just the right distance from a viewing screen, and that nothing else is occurring to distract them as the subliminal stimuli are flashed. Further, even in the laboratory there is no evidence that subliminal messages can get people to act counter to their wishes, values, or personalities (Neuberg, 1988). These messages might have subtle influences on people's liking for an ambiguous stimulus (e.g., a Chinese ideograph), but they cannot override people's wishes and desires, making them march off to the supermarket to buy products they don't want or vote for candidates they despise.

Ironically, the hoopla surrounding subliminal messages has obscured a significant fact about advertising: Ads are *more* powerful when we can consciously perceive them. As we have seen, there is ample evidence that the ads we encounter in everyday life and perceive consciously can have substantial effects on our behavior—even though they do not contain subliminal messages. It is interesting that people fear subliminal advertising more than regular advertising, when it is regular advertising that is more powerful (Wilson, Houston, & Meyers, in press). Try It! on page 273 will help you see whether this is true of people you know.

Further, it is important to acknowledge that regular advertising influences more than just our consumer behavior. Advertisements transmit cultural stereotypes in their words and images, subtly linking a product with a desired image (e.g., Marlboro ads linking cigarettes with the rugged, macho Marlboro Man; beer ads linking beer consumption with sex). Advertisements can also reinforce and perpetuate stereotypical ways of thinking about social groups. Until recently, ads almost always showed groups of whites (token individuals of color are now mixed into the group), couples who are heterosexual, families that are traditional (with a mom, dad, and two kids of each gender), and so on. You would think that divorced families, the elderly, people of color, lesbians and gay men, the physically disabled, and others just didn't exist. Gender stereotypes are particularly pervasive in advertising imagery. Men are doers; women are observers. Erving Goffman (1976), in his book *Gender Advertisements*, offers fascinating examples of how the models in ads are typically posed so that their nonverbal behavior (e.g., their gestures, body position, facial expressions, and eye gaze) is powerful, nonemotional, and active if they are male, and passive, submissive, and highly expressive if they are female.

Even more disturbing is the trend in some ads, such as those used for Newport cigarettes or "Guess?®" clothing, that links the product with sexual hostility and violence (Leo, 1991). For example, a series of Newport cigarette ads depicted women who were being pulled by a horse collar, were about to be slammed with a pair of cymbals, or were carried off on a pole like a dead animal. The violence toward women shown in such ads is in no way subliminal; such obvious and overt images are much more powerful than anything hidden in ice cubes or cake icing. Thus, even if effects of subliminal messages in advertisements are eventually documented, those effects are unlikely to be any stronger, or any harder to resist, than the effects of more overt, consciously perceived kinds of advertising (Wilson & Brekke, 1994).

Summary

An **attitude** is a person's enduring evaluation of people, objects, and ideas. All attitudes have affective, cognitive, and behavioral components. Attitudes can be based more on one component than another. A **cognitively based attitude** is based mostly on people's beliefs about the properties of the attitude object. An **affectively based attitude** is based more on people's emotions and values; it can be created through **classical conditioning** or **operant conditioning**. A **behaviorally based attitude** is based on people's actions toward the attitude object. For example, research on *self-perception theory* shows that when people's attitudes are weak or unclear, they infer how they feel by observing how they behave. Behaviorally based attitudes are likely to be high in **attitude accessibility**, or the strength of the association between an object and the person's attitude toward that object.

Attitudes can be changed in a number of ways. As shown by research on *cognitive dissonance theory*, attitudes change when people engage in *counterattitudinal advocacy* for low *external justification*. When this occurs, people find *internal justification* for their behavior, bringing their attitudes in line with their behavior.

Another way attitudes change is when people receive a **persuasive communication**. According to the **Yale Attitude Change approach**, the persuasiveness of a communication depends on aspects of the communicator, or source of the message; aspects of the message itself (e.g., its content), and aspects of the audience. The **elaboration likelihood model** specifies when people are persuaded more by the strength of the arguments in the communication and when they are persuaded more by surface characteristics, such as the attractiveness of the speaker. People will take the **central route to persuasion** when they have both the motivation and the ability to pay close attention to the arguments. This is likely to occur when the topic of the communication is high in personal relevance or when people are high in the **need for cognition**. People will take the **peripheral route to persuasion** when they either do not want to or cannot pay close attention to the arguments. Under these conditions, they are persuaded by such peripheral cues as the attractiveness of the speaker or the length of the speech. Attitude change is longer-lasting and more resistant to attack when it occurs via the central route.

Emotions influence attitude change in a number of ways. People in positive moods are less likely to analyze a message carefully than people in negative moods are. **Fear-arousing communications** can cause lasting attitude change if a moderate amount of fear is aroused and people believe they will be reassured by the content of the message. Consistent with the **heuristic-systematic model of persuasion**, emotions can also be used as heuristics to gauge one's attitude; if people feel good in the presence of an object, they often infer that they like it, even if those good feelings were caused by something else. Finally, the effectiveness of persuasive communications also depends on the type of attitude people have. Appeals to emotion and social identity work best if the attitude is based on emotion and social identity.

It is possible to make people resistant to attacks on their attitudes. **Attitude inoculation** is the technique whereby people are exposed to small doses of arguments against their position, making it easier for them to refute these arguments when they hear them later. This approach may also inoculate people against attacks that play on their emotions and values, if people are first given small doses of these kinds of attacks. Attempts to manage people's attitudes, however, should not be used with too heavy a hand. Strongly prohibiting people from engaging in certain behaviors can actually cause an increase in liking for that activity. According to **reactance theory**, people experience an unpleasant state called reactance when their freedom of choice is threatened. One way people can reduce reactance is to perform the behavior that was threatened.

One reason that it is important to understand attitude change is that attitudes are presumed to influence behavior. The relation between attitudes and behavior, however, is not as straightforward as once thought. We need to distinguish between behaviors that are spontaneous versus those that are more planned and deliberative. Attitudes predict spontaneous behaviors only when they are relatively accessible. When attitudes are inaccessible, behavior is more likely to be influenced by situational and social factors. The **theory of planned behavior** specifies how we can predict people's planned and deliberative behaviors. Here it is necessary to know people's attitudes toward the specific act in question, their **subjective norms** (people's beliefs about how others view the behavior in question), and how much people believe they can control the behavior. Knowing these three things allows us to predict people's behavioral intentions, which are highly correlated with their planned behaviors.

We concluded with a discussion of advertising and why it works. Advertising has been found to be quite effective, as indicated by split cable market tests. It is most effective when the ad is tailored to the kind of attitude people have and when the product is made to appear to be personally relevant to people. One kind of advertising that has caused public concern is the use of words or pictures that are supposedly perceived unconsciously—that is, **subliminal messages**. Despite people's fears, this type of advertising has not been shown to influence consumer behavior. Under controlled laboratory conditions, subliminal messages can have subtle effects on people's preferences, but there is no evidence that subliminal messages have been used successfully in real-world marketing campaigns. Unfortunately, the use of such messages in self-help tapes is also ineffective.

If You Are Interested

Ajzen, I. (1988). *Attitudes, personality, and behavior.* Chicago, IL: Dorsey Press. An in-depth discussion of the relationship between attitudes and behaviors, with an emphasis on the theory of reasoned action.

Burgess, Anthony (1963). *A Clockwork Orange.* A nightmarish look at the future filled with out-of-control adolescents and harrowing techniques of mind control.

Eagly, A., & Chaiken, S. (1993). *The psychology of attitudes.* Fort Worth, TX: Harcourt Brace Jovanovich. An extremely thorough and insightful look at current social psychological research on attitudes.

Huxley, Aldous (1946). *Brave New World.* A classic portrayal of mind control in a futuristic society. It is interesting to draw parallels between Huxley's view of the future and modern techniques of attitude change.

Petty, R. E., & Cacioppo, J. T. (1986). *Communication and persuasion: Central and peripheral routes to attitude change.* New York: Springer-Verlag. A comprehensive discussion of the elaboration likelihood model of attitude change.

Pratkanis, A. R., & Aronson, E. (1991). *Age of propaganda: The everyday use and abuse of persuasion.* New York: Freeman. An engaging account of how our attitudes are shaped by the mass media.

The War Room (1994). A behind-the-scenes documentary of President Clinton's campaign in 1992. The film is an interesting portrayal of the day-to-day attempt to influence public opinion in a modern, presidential campaign.

Triumph of the Will (1934). A film commissioned by Adolph Hitler to disseminate Nazi propaganda. It is interesting to view this film in the light of research on attitude change and persuasion, to see how the film tries to change people's attitudes.

CHAPTER 8

CONFORMITY: INFLUENCING BEHAVIOR

n the late 1960s, Jim Jones founded a church in northern California, the Peoples Temple, preaching racial tolerance and acceptance. In 1977, following the publication of an unfavorable magazine article about the church, Jones and his congregation immigrated to an isolated jungle in Guyana. There they constructed "Jonestown." Over the years, Jones had become a messiahlike figure to his followers. He demanded and received total loyalty, devotion, and obedience. Interviews with defectors from the church indicated that Jones had also implemented strong punishments, from public humiliation to severe beatings, for any adult or child who disagreed with him.

In November 1978, California congressman Leo Ryan flew to Jonestown and investigated charges that church members were being held there against their will. As Ryan and his entourage boarded their plane to leave, Temple gunmen ambushed them and killed five, including Congressman Ryan. While these murders were occurring, Jones gathered the community together and told them that their enemies were everywhere and that the time had come to commit "revolutionary suicide." While his most trusted followers armed themselves and stood guard, others passed out cyanide-laced "Kool-Aid®." Jones instructed parents to first give the poison to their children and then drink it themselves. A few people tried to argue with Jones against the mass suicide but were shouted down by the rest of the congregation. When authorities reached the scene, they found the members of the congregation dead, lying in each other's arms. More than 800 people died that day by their own hand (Osherow, 1988).

The world was shocked and horrified by the events at Jonestown. How could people so mindlessly follow such a leader, conforming to his wishes and obeying his orders to the extent that they killed their children and committed suicide? Sadly, we saw history repeat itself in 1997, when the members of the Heaven's Gate cult committed mass suicide in Rancho Santa Fe, California. Eighteen men and 21 women, ranging in age from 26 to 72, followed the instructions of their leader, Marshall Herff Applewhite, on how to kill themselves: They took a large dose of phenobarbital, drank some vodka, and then tied plastic bags over their heads. Applewhite killed himself as well. As we discussed in Chapter 6, the Heaven's Gate cult believed they would be transported to outer space by extraterrestrials once they permanently left behind their "containers"— their bodies. The cult prerecorded many videotaped messages, where they indicated that they were eagerly looking forward to death and to their ultimate "release" from human form to a more perfect existence as aliens (Gleick, 1997; Hedges, 1997).

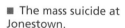
■ The mass suicide at Jonestown.

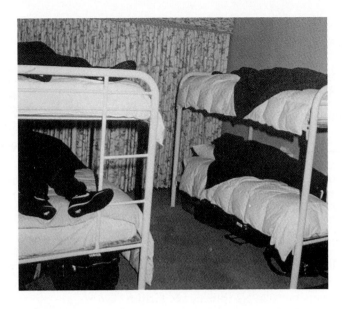

■ The mass suicide at the Heaven's Gate compound.

It is clear that Jim Jones and Marshall Applewhite had created very strong bonds of conformity and obedience among their followers, so strong that members killed themselves because their leaders said they should. How could such tragic conformity occur at Jonestown and the Heaven's Gate compound? Under what conditions and for what reasons do people fall under the influence of others?   □

Conformity: When and Why

Think for a moment about the word **conformity**, which we can define as a change in behavior due to the real or imagined influence of others (Kiesler & Kiesler, 1969). Which one of the two quotations on the right do you find more appealing? Which one best describes your immediate reaction to the word?

We wouldn't be surprised if you preferred the second quotation. American culture stresses the importance of not conforming (Hofstede, 1986; Markus, Kitayama, & Heiman, 1996). We think of ourselves as a nation of rugged individualists, people who think for themselves, who stand up for the underdog, who go against the tide for what they think is right. This cultural self-image has been shaped by the manner in which our nation was founded, by our system of government, and by our society's historical experience with Western expansion—the "taming" of the Wild West (Turner, 1932).

American mythology has celebrated the rugged individualist in many ways. For example, one of the longest-running and most successful advertising campaigns in American history is the "Marlboro Man." Since 1955, the photograph of a cowboy alone on the range has been an archetypal image. It has also sold a lot of cigarettes. People who have never seen a horse, let alone the American West, have responded for more than 40 years to this simple, evocative image.

Conformity
a change in behavior due to the real or imagined influence of other people

> Do as most do, and [people] will speak well of thee.
>
> —Thomas Fuller

> It were not best that we should all think alike; it is difference of opinion that makes horse races.
>
> —Mark Twain

■ American culture values independence and autonomy, not conformity. In this cartoon, the people with the picket signs reflect this view. However, the truth is, we frequently conform to other's behavior and attitudes. For example, the demonstrator on the right is there because all his friends are.

> To swallow and follow, whether old doctrine or new propaganda, is a weakness still dominating the human mind.
> —Charlotte Perkins Gilman

Clearly, it tells us something about ourselves that we want and like to hear: that we make up our own minds; that we're not spineless, weak conformists; that we're not puppets but players (Buehler & Griffin, 1994).

But are we, in fact, nonconforming creatures? Are the decisions we make always based on what we think, or do we sometimes use other people's behavior to help us decide what to do? The mass suicide at Jonestown suggests that people sometimes conform in extreme and surprising ways—even when making such a fundamental decision as whether or not to take their own lives. But, you might argue, this is an unusual case; surely most people do not conform to this extent. Perhaps the followers of Jim Jones and Marshall Applewhite were disturbed people who were somehow predisposed to do what a charismatic leader told them to do. There is, however, another, more chilling possibility: Maybe most of us would have acted the same way, had we been exposed to the same, long-standing conformity pressures as the members of Heaven's Gate and the residents of Jonestown. According to this view, almost anyone would have conformed had she or he been put in these same extreme situations.

If this statement is true, we should be able to find other situations in which people, put under strong social pressures, conform to surprising degrees. Unfortunately, we do not have to look very far to find such instances. Consider the case of the My Lai massacre in Vietnam. On the morning of March 16, 1968, in the midst of the Vietnam War, a company of American soldiers boarded helicopters that would take them to the village of My Lai. The soldiers were very apprehensive, because they had never been in combat before and the village was rumored to be occupied by the Forty-Eighth Vietcong Battalion, one of the most feared units of the enemy. One of the helicopter pilots radioed that he saw Vietcong soldiers below, and so the American soldiers jumped off the helicopters, with rifles firing. They soon realized the pilot was wrong—there were no enemy soldiers. Instead, the Americans found several villagers, all women, children, and elderly men, cooking their breakfast over small fires. Inexplicably, the leader of the platoon, Lieutenant William Calley, ordered one of the soldiers to kill the villagers. Other soldiers began firing too, and the carnage spread. The Americans rounded up and systematically murdered all the villagers of My Lai. They shoved women and children into a ravine and shot them; they threw hand grenades into huts filled with cowering villagers. Though no one knows the exact number of deaths, the estimates range from 450 to 500 Vietnamese civilians (Hersch, 1970; *Time*, 1969).

■ Under strong social pressure, individuals will conform to the group, even when this means doing something immoral. During the Vietnam War, American soldiers massacred several hundred Vietnamese civilians—old men, women and children—in the village of My Lai. This award-winning photograph of some of the victims chilled the nation. Why did the soldiers commit this atrocity? As you read this chapter, you will see how the social influence pressures of conformity and obedience can cause decent people to do indecent acts.

The examples we have seen so far are all cases of "bad" conformity; human beings lost their lives as a result of people doing what others did. However, despite the American emphasis on rugged individualism, it is not always best to be a nonconformer. Would you rather be thought of as a team player or as someone who never cooperates? Conformity is not simply "good" or "bad" in and of itself. Rather than labeling conformity as good or bad, the social psychologist is interested in why people conform. Knowing why and when people are influenced by others will help us understand if a given act of conformity in our own lives is wise or foolish.

Some of the people at Jonestown and My Lai probably conformed because they did not know what to do in a confusing or unusual situation; the behavior of the people around them served as a cue as to how to respond, and so they decided to act in a similar manner. Other people probably conformed because they did not wish to be ridiculed or punished for being different from everybody else; they chose to act the way the group expected them to so that they wouldn't be rejected or thought less of by group members. Let's see how each of these reasons for conforming operates.

Informational Social Influence: The Need to Know What's "Right"

One of the important things we get from interacting with other people is information. You won't be surprised to hear that sometimes people don't know what to do in a situation or even what is happening. Unfortunately, life, unlike our

"It's always best on these
occasions to do what the
mob do." "But suppose
there are two mobs?"
suggested Mr. Snodgrass.
"Shout with the largest,"
replied Mr. Pickwick.
—Charles Dickens,
Pickwick Papers

**Informational Social
Influence**
the influence of other
people that leads us to
conform because we see
them as a source of
information to guide our
behavior; we conform
because we believe that
others' interpretation of an
ambiguous situation is
more correct than ours and
will help us choose an
appropriate course of
action

clothing, does not come with little labels attached, telling us what is going on and how we should respond. Instead, the social world is frequently ambiguous and ill-defined.

For example, how should you address your psychology professor—as Dr. Berman, Professor Berman, Ms. Berman, or Patricia? How should you vote in the upcoming college referendum that would raise your tuition in order to increase student services? What combination of physical features best describes a beautiful woman or a handsome man? Is the scream you just heard coming from a person joking with friends or from the victim of a mugging?

In these and many other everyday situations, we feel uncertain about what to think or how to act. We simply don't know enough to make a good or accurate choice. Luckily, we have a powerful and useful source of knowledge available to us—the behavior of other people. Asking others what they think or watching what they do helps us reach a definition of the situation (Kelley, 1955; Thomas, 1928). When we subsequently act like everyone else, we are conforming, but not because we are weak, spineless individuals with no self-reliance. Instead, the influence of other people leads us to conform because we see them as a source of information to guide our behavior. We conform because we believe that others' interpretation of an ambiguous situation is more accurate than ours, and will help us choose an appropriate course of action. This is called **informational social influence** (Cialdini, 1993; Cialdini, Kallgren, & Reno, 1991; Cialdini & Trost, 1998; Deutsch & Gerard, 1955; Reno, Cialdini, & Kallgren, 1993; Stiff, 1994).

As an illustration of how other people can be a source of information, imagine you are a participant in the following experiment by Muzafer Sherif (1936). In the first phase of the study, you are seated alone in a dark room and asked to focus your attention on a dot of light 15 feet away. The experimenter asks you to estimate in inches how far the light moves. You stare earnestly at the light, and yes, it moves a little. You say, "About two inches," though it is not easy to tell exactly. The light disappears and then comes back; you are asked to judge again. The light seems to move a little more, and you say, "Four inches." After several of these trials, the light seems to move about the same amount each time—about two to four inches.

Now, the interesting thing about this task is that the light was not actually moving at all. It looked like it was moving, because of a visual illusion called the *autokinetic effect.* If you stare at a bright light in a uniformly dark environment (e.g., a star on a dark night), the light will appear to waver back and forth. This occurs because you have no stable reference point to anchor the position of the light. The distance that the light appears to move varies from person to person but becomes consistent for each person over time. In Sherif's (1936) experiment, the subjects all arrived at their own, stable estimate during the first phase of the study, but these estimates differed from person to person. Some people thought the light was moving only an inch or so, whereas others thought it was moving as much as ten inches.

Sherif chose to use the autokinetic effect because he wanted a situation that would be ambiguous—where the correct definition of the situation would be unclear to his participants. In the second phase of the experiment, a few days later, the participants were paired with two other people, each of whom had had the same prior experience alone with the light. Now the situation became a truly social one, as all three made their judgments out loud. Remember, the autokinetic effect is experienced differently by different people; some see a lot of movement,

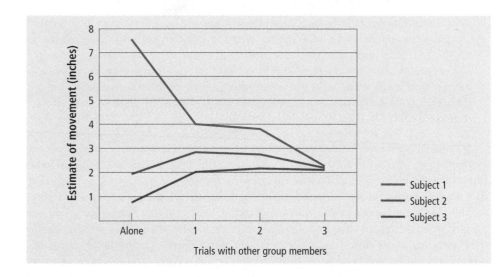

■ **FIGURE 8.1 One group's judgments in Sherif's (1936) autokinetic studies.** People estimated how far a point of light appeared to move in a dark room. When they saw the light by themselves, their estimates varied widely. When they were brought together in groups and heard other people announce their estimates, people conformed to the group's estimate of how much the light moved. (Adapted from Sherif, 1936)

some not much at all. After hearing their partners give judgments that were different from their own, what did people do?

Over the course of several trials, people reached a common estimate, and each member of the group conformed to that estimate. These results indicate that people were using each other as a source of information, coming to believe that the group estimate was the correct one (see Figure 8.1). An important feature of informational social influence is that it can lead to **private acceptance,** where people conform to the behavior of others because they genuinely believe that these other people are right.

It might seem equally plausible that people publicly conformed to the group but privately maintained the belief that the light was moving only a small amount. For example, maybe someone privately believed that the light was moving ten inches but announced that it had moved three inches, the group estimate, to avoid looking silly or foolish. This would be a case of **public compliance,** where a person conforms publicly without necessarily believing in what the group is saying or doing. Sherif casted doubt on this interpretation, however, by asking people to judge the lights once more by themselves, after participating in groups. Even though they no longer had to worry about looking silly in front of other participants, they continued to give the answer the group had given earlier. One study even found that people still conformed to the group estimate when they participated by themselves a year later (Rohrer, Baron, Hoffman, & Swander, 1954). These results suggest that people were relying on each other to define reality and came to privately accept the group estimate.

In everyday life, of course, we are rarely asked to judge how much a stationary light is moving. It is thus important to note that there are many everyday situations in which we rely on other people to help us define what is going on. Think about the first time you were at the symphony or ballet. You knew that applause was going to figure in sometime, but exactly when? What about standing ovations, or shouting "Encore!"? No doubt, you looked to others in the audience to help you interpret the appropriate way of showing approval in this quite formal setting. That the audience's behavior can be affected through conformity is not unknown in the performing arts. Davies (1988) describes the use of the claque (hired applause) in early nineteenth-century opera:

Private Acceptance
conforming to other people's behavior out of a genuine belief that what they are doing or saying is right

Public Compliance
conforming to other people's behavior publicly, without necessarily believing in what we are doing or saying

> An opera audience must contain people who know the work intimately. Nobody will dare to applaud if they don't know where, and when, and why. They might make an embarrassing mistake [and] look foolish. . . . [A] claque is a small body of experts . . . you must have your *bisseurs* who call out loud for encores; your *rieurs* who laugh at the right places . . . your *pleureurs* who sob when sobs are needed. . . . And all of this must be carefully organized—yes, orchestrated—by the *capo di claque*. (Davies, 1988, pp. 390–391)

Using other people to define social reality can also have a large impact on our emotions, as we saw in Chapter 5 (Schachter, 1959; Schachter & Singer, 1962). For example, you might be feeling quite calm about your upcoming midterm until you run into a group of acquaintances from the class, all of whom are extremely tense and stressed out about the exam. After talking with them, you feel a little disturbed too—are you being too complacent about this test? "Maybe they're right," you think. Like the research participants in Sherif's experiment, you may find yourself relying on other people to help you reach a definition of the situation: "Maybe I'm being way too calm about this midterm . . . I'd better study some more tonight."

Conversions and Crises

Informational social influence is certainly a part of everyday life. But this form of social influence also impinges on us in far more dramatic ways. For example, it comes into play when people experience a *conversion*—a sudden shift in the meaning of their lives based on new knowledge they have received from a group (Berger, 1963; Berger & Luckmann, 1967). People may experience conversion to a religion, to a political ideology, or to any one of the many cults that have arisen over recent decades. Often before the conversion experience, the individual feels indecisive and confused, dissatisfied with his or her life, and even despairing. On meeting members of the new group, the individual is exposed to a whole new definition of the situation, radically different from the one he or she knew before. These new beliefs are perceived by the individual to be more powerful and useful than his or her former convictions; conversion involves the individual conforming to the belief system of the new reference group. The individuals who joined the Heaven's Gate cult experienced such a conversion; they were searching for greater meaning in their lives and Marshall Applewhite's teachings seemed to them to provide the "answer."

In another example, Arthur Koestler (1959), a former Communist, describes his conversion to communism in the 1930s:

> To say that one had "seen the light" is a poor description of the mental rapture which only the convert knows (regardless of what faith he has been converted to). . . . [T]he whole universe falls into a pattern like the stray pieces of a jigsaw puzzle assembled by magic at one stroke. There is now an answer to every question; doubts and conflicts are a matter of the tortured past. (p. 19)

Another dramatic form of informational social influence occurs during crises. Here an individual is confronted with a frightening, potentially dangerous situation to which he or she is ill-equipped to respond (Killian, 1964). The person may have no idea of what is really happening or what he or she should do. When one's personal safety is involved, the need for information is acute   and the behavior of others is very informative.

Consider what happened on Halloween Night in 1938. Orson Welles, the gifted actor and film director, and the Mercury Theater broadcast a radio play based loosely on H. G. Wells's science fiction fantasy *War of the Worlds*. (Remember, this was the era before television; radio was a source of entertainment, with music, comedy, and drama programs, and the only source for fast-breaking news.) That night, Welles and his fellow actors put on a radio drama of cataclysm—the invasion of Earth by hostile Martians—that was so realistic and effective that at least a million American listeners became frightened and several thousand were panic-stricken (Cantril, 1940).

Why were so many Americans convinced that what they heard was a real news report of an actual invasion by aliens? One reason is that the play parodied existing radio news shows very well, and many listeners missed the beginning of the broadcast (when it was clearly labeled as a play) because they had been listening to the nation's number-one-rated show, *Charlie McCarthy*, on another station. Another culprit, however, was informational social influence. Many people were listening with friends and family and naturally turned to each other, out of uncertainty, to see whether they should believe what they heard. Seeing looks of concern and worry on their loved ones' faces added to the panic people were beginning to feel. "We all kissed one another and felt we would all die," reported one listener (Cantril, 1940, p. 95).

In addition, many frightened listeners misinterpreted actual events so that they fit the news on the radio program: "We looked out the window and Wyoming Avenue was black with cars. People were rushing away, I figured," or "No cars came down my street. Traffic is jammed on account of the roads being destroyed, I thought" (Cantril, 1940, p. 93). When a situation is highly ambiguous and people begin to believe they know what is happening, they will even reinterpret potentially disconfirming evidence so that it fits their definition of the situation.

> "Ninety-nine percent of the people in the world are fools and the rest of us are in great danger of contagion.
> —Thornton Wilder

New York Times

Copyright, 1938, by The New York Times Company.

NEW YORK

Radio Listeners in Panic, Taking War Drama as Fact

Many Flee Homes to Escape 'Gas Raid From Mars'—Phone Calls Swamp Police at Broadcast of Wells Fantasy

A wave of mass hysteria seized thousands of radio listeners throughout the nation between 8:15 and 9:30 o'clock last night when a broadcast of a dramatization of H. G. Wells's fantasy, "The War of the Worlds," led thousands to believe that an interplanetary conflict had started with invading Martians spreading wide death and destruction ... Jersey ... York ... ... on Page Four ...

and radio stations here and in other cities of the United States and Canada seeking advice on protective measures against the raids.

The program was produced by Mr. Welles and the Mercury Theatre on the Air over station WABC and the Columbia Broadcasting System's coast-to-coast network, from 8 to 9 o'clock.

■ The *New York Times* headlined the *War of the Worlds* incident. Partly because of informational social influences, many listeners believed that a fictional radio broadcast about an invasion by Martians was true.

Contagion
the rapid transmission of emotions or behaviors through a crowd

Gustav LeBon (1895) was the first researcher to document how emotions and behavior can rapidly spread through a crowd, seemingly out of control—an effect he called **contagion** (Gump & Kulick, 1997; Hatfield, Cacioppo, & Rapson, 1993; Jones & Jones, 1995). As we have learned, any time an individual is faced with a truly ambiguous situation, he or she will most likely rely on the interpretation of others. Unfortunately, in a truly ambiguous and confusing situation, other people may be no more knowledgeable or accurate than we are.

When Informational Conformity Backfires

The *War of the Worlds* incident reminds us that using other people as a source of information can be dangerous. If other people are misinformed, we will adopt their mistakes and misinterpretations. Depending on others to help us reach a definition of the situation can sometimes lead to an inaccurate definition indeed.

Mass Psychogenic Illness
the occurrence, in a group of people, of similar physical symptoms with no known physical cause

An example of extreme and misdirected informational social influence is **mass psychogenic illness** (Colligan, Pennebaker, & Murphy, 1982), the occurrence of similar physical symptoms, with no known physical cause, in a group of people. This form of contagion usually begins with just one person or a few people reporting physical symptoms; typically, these people are experiencing some kind of stress in their lives. Other people around them construct what seems to be a reasonable explanation for their illness. This explanation, a new definition of the situation, spreads, and more people begin to think that they too have symptoms. As the number of afflicted people grows, both the physical symptoms and their supposed explanation become more credible and thus more widespread (Kerckhoff & Back, 1968).

Several social psychologists have studied naturally occurring cases of mass psychogenic illness (e.g., Colligan & Murphy, 1979; Kerckhoff & Back, 1968; Schuler & Parenton, 1943; Singer, Baum, Baum, & Thew, 1982; Stahl & Lebedun, 1974). Donald Johnson (1945) examined a particularly fascinating case, that of the "phantom anesthetist" of Mattoon, Illinois. Here is Johnson's (1945) description of the panic:

> The story of the "phantom anesthetist" begins in Mattoon, Illinois, on the first night of September, 1944, when a woman reported to the police that someone had opened her bedroom window and sprayed her with a sickish sweet-smelling gas which partially paralyzed her legs and made her feel ill. Soon other cases with similar symptoms were reported, and the police organized a full-scale effort to catch the elusive "gasser." Some of the Mattoon citizens armed themselves with shotguns and sat on their doorsteps to wait for him; some even claimed that they caught a glimpse of him and heard him pumping his spray gun. As the number of cases increased—as many as seven in one night—and the facilities of the local police seemed inadequate to the size of the task, the state police . . . were called in, and scientific crime detection experts went to work, analyzing stray rags for gaseous chemicals and checking the records of patients recently released from state institutions. Before long the "phantom anesthetist" of Mattoon had appeared in newspapers all over the United States. . . . After ten days of such excitement, when all the victims had recovered and no substantial clues had been found, the police began to talk of "imagination" and some of the newspapers ran columns on "mass hysteria"; the episode of the "phantom anesthetist" was over. (p. 175)

Herald ·CHICAGO· **American**

AN AMERICAN ◁ PAPER ▷ FOR   THE ◁ AMERICAN ▷ PEOPLE

VOL. XLV NO. 17 ... 8   SATURDAY—SEPTEMBER 9—1944   In Two Sections, Also Color Comics and Magazine   41

Mattoon Principal Gassed

BY GLADYS ERICKSON,
Chicago Herald-American Staff Correspondent.

MATTOON, Ill., Sept. 9.—Miss Frances Smith, principal of the Mattoon grade school, revealed today that she, her sister and their mother were four-time victims of the madman who sprays a nerve gas wherever he goes.

Miss Smith, her sister, Maxine Smith, live at ... Their lips ... the sickening ... ists so far ha ... analyze.

Despite the ... Smith family sa ... authorities for s ... ing, they said, ...

not come again and fearing they would be adding to the hysteria among the town's 18,000 people

REPORTER A VICTIM.

The man appeared again last night — at another home — and some 70 persons who went to the scene felt the effect of the nerve gas. Among the 70 was this reporter.

Like the others milling about on Dewitt av., locale of the latest appearance of the long-fingered maniac, I reeled as I stepped into the cloying, paralyzing cloud that blanketed most of the street.

Three other persons were with me. They, too, stepped back from their sudden con... with the gas. Mrs N ... of Mattoon, ... me, almost ... s and com...eeling.

Maniac's Terror-Gas Traps Girl Reporter

Continued from First Page. Others said ... threat it gave me. Smelling it ... they felt the same. ...vers on ... man woul...

jerked up the blind. The eyes ... conflict of ... of the man blazed into hers for ... a moment, then, she said later ...rch and ...ss, repug... ...te ran fro refreshing. My lips ... I was light-headed. I ould not shake the feeling of unreality, the sense of lurking

Continued on Page 2. Column 3.

■ The "phantom anesthetist" of Mattoon, Illinois is an example of mass psychogenic illness. A woman told police that someone had gassed her bedroom window one night. Soon, many Mattoon residents claimed they too had been gassed; the State Police were eventually called in to handle the investigation. In fact, there was no psychopathic "gasser" on the loose. It was 1944 and people were feeling stress due to World War II. When they heard about the phantom anesthetist, informational social influence supplied them with a "cause" for their vague physical symptoms of stress—they had been "gassed" in the middle of the night by a madman.

How did the contagion spread? How did some people come to believe that their physical ailments were symptoms of a bizarre attack? Johnson (1945) determined that informational social influence had occurred primarily via newspaper articles. Few of the victims knew each other, and so they had not spread the information interpersonally. Instead, blaring headlines and sensationalist articles in the town newspapers were the means by which a new definition of the situation was communicated.

What is particularly interesting about modern cases of mass psychogenic illness (as well as other peculiar forms of conformity) is the powerful role that the mass media play in their dissemination. Through television, radio, newspapers, and magazines, information is spread quickly and efficiently to all segments of the population. While in the Middle Ages it took 200 years for the "dancing manias" (a kind of psychogenic illness) to crisscross Europe (Sirois, 1982), today it takes only minutes for most of the inhabitants of the planet to learn about a strange or even bizarre event. Luckily, the mass media also have the power to quickly squelch these uprisings of contagion by introducing more logical explanations for ambiguous events.

When Will People Conform to Informational Social Influence?

Let's review the situations that are the most likely to produce conformity because of informational social influence.

When the Situation Is Ambiguous

This is the most crucial variable for determining if people use each other as a source of information. When you are unsure of the correct response, the appropriate behavior, or the right idea, you will be most open to influence from others. The more uncertain you are, the more you will rely on others (Allen, 1965; Baron, Vandello, & Brunsman, 1996; Tesser, Campbell & Mickler, 1983). The situations we discussed at the beginning of this chapter were ambiguous ones for the people involved. While the conformity that occurred at Jonestown and My Lai was horrible and tragic in its consequences, informational social influence was at work. At Jonestown, for example, Reverend Jones had achieved such power that people allowed him to define reality for them. Over time, the residents of Jonestown came to entirely believe whatever Jones told them; they had no independent definition of the situation in any area of their lives. They believed him when he said that their situation was hopeless and that their enemies were closing in on them. They believed him when he said that suicide was the correct course of action. Instances of mind control or "brainwashing" can actually be extreme cases of informational social influence.

When the Situation Is a Crisis

Another variable also promotes the use of others as a source of information and often co-occurs with ambiguous situations. When the situation is a crisis, we usually do not have time to stop and think about exactly which course of action we should take. We need to act, and act now. If we feel scared and panicky, and are uncertain what to do, it is only natural for us to look and see how other people are responding—and to do likewise. Unfortunately, the people we imitate may also feel scared and panicky and not be behaving rationally.

■ 8,000 pumpkins meet the Eiffel Towel. Halloween is a popular holiday in the United States; in the last few years, retailers have increased the "hype" surrounding the holiday because it increases sales of their merchandise during a traditionally slow sales period—October. While the holiday is based on ancient British and Irish traditions surrounding "all Hollows' Eve," Halloween as we know it is a completely American phenomenon. Until October of 1997, that is, when "Olaween" was introduced to the French public by French retailers. Why? The French economy is in bad shape—a crisis—and French retailers needed to come up with an idea that would get people to buy merchandise. Informational social influence led them to borrow the Halloween concept from America, and informational social influence is how the French are literally learning what this holiday is about. As of Halloween 97, they have no idea what "treek au treeting" is, but we bet by Halloween 98, they will know about that custom too (Cohen, 1997).

The soldiers at My Lai, for example, expected to experience combat for the first time and were undoubtedly scared and on edge. Further, it was not easy to tell who the enemy was. In the Vietnam War, Vietnamese civilians who were sympathizers of the Vietcong were known to have laid mines in the path of U.S. soldiers, fired guns from hidden locations, and thrown or planted grenades. In a guerrilla war like Vietnam, it was often difficult to tell if civilians were in fact civilians or combatants, allies or enemies. Thus, when one or two soldiers began firing on the villagers in My Lai, it is perhaps not surprising that others followed suit, believing this to be the proper course of action. Had the soldiers not been in a crisis situation and instead had more time to think about their actions, perhaps the tragedy would have been avoided.

When Other People Are Experts

Typically, the more expertise or knowledge a person has, the more valuable he or she will be as a guide in an ambiguous situation (Allison, 1992; Bickman, 1974; Cialdini & Trost, 1998). For example, a passenger who sees smoke coming out of an airplane engine will probably look around for the flight attendants to check their reaction; they have more expertise than the vacationer in the next seat. However, experts are not always reliable sources of information. Imagine the fear felt by the young man who was listening to the *War of the Worlds*, called his local police department for an explanation—and discovered that the police too

Try It !

Informational Social Influence and Emergencies

One of the most interesting examples of informational social influence in action, is the behavior of bystanders in emergencies. An emergency is by definition a crisis situation. In many respects, it is an ambiguous situation as well; sometimes there are "experts" present (but sometimes there aren't). In an emergency, the bystander is thinking: What's happening? Is help needed? What should I do? What's everybody else doing?

As you'll recall from the story told by Robin Akert in the Preface (see page xxxi), trying to decide if an emergency is really happening and if your help is really needed can be very difficult. Bystanders often rely on informational social influence to help them figure out what to do. Other people's behavior is a source of important information in an unusual situation; unfortunately, as we saw in the story in the Preface, if other people are acting like nothing is wrong, you could be misled by their behavior and interpret the situation as a nonemergency too. In that case, informational social influence has backfired.

In order to explore informational social influence, gather some stories about people's reactions to emergencies when they were bystanders (not victims). Think about your own experiences, and ask your friends to tell you about emergencies they have been in. As you recollect your own experience, or talk to your friends about their experiences, note how informational social influence played a role:

1. How did you (and your friends) decide an emergency was really occurring? Did you glance at other passersby, and watch their response? Did you talk to other people to help you figure out what was going on?

2. Once you decided it was an emergency, how did you decide what to do? Did you do what other people were doing; did you show (or tell) them what to do?

3. Were there any experts present, people who knew more about the situation or how to offer assistance? Did you do what the experts told you to do? If you were in the role of expert (or were at least knowlegeable) at the scene of the emergency, did people follow your lead?

The issues raised by these questions are all examples of informational social influence in action.

thought the events described on the radio were actually happening. (In the Try It! on page 291, you can explore how the informational social influence variables of ambiguity, crisis, and expertise have operated in your life and your friend's lives.)

Resisting Informational Social Influence

As we have seen, relying on others to help us define what is happening can be an excellent idea or it can be a tragedy in the making. How can we tell when other people are a good source of information and when we should resist other people's definition of a situation?

First, it is important to remember that it *is* possible to resist illegitimate or inaccurate informational social influence. In all of our examples, some people resisted conforming to what they perceived to be incorrect information. At My Lai, not all the soldiers took part in the atrocity. One sergeant said he'd been ordered to "destroy the village," but he simply refused to follow the orders. Another soldier, watching as the others fired on civilians, purposefully shot himself in the foot so that he would have an excuse to be evacuated from the killing scene. One helicopter pilot, looking down on the grisly sight, landed and scooped up 15 Vietnamese children and ferried them off to safety deep in the forest. Thus, some soldiers rejected the behavior of others as a correct definition of what they should do. Instead, they relied on what they knew was right and moral; they refused to take part in the massacre of innocent people.

Similarly, during the *War of the Worlds* broadcast, not all of the listeners panicked (Cantril, 1940). Some engaged in rational problem solving; they checked other stations on the radio dial and discovered that no other station was broadcasting the same news. Instead of relying on others and being caught up in the contagion and mass panic, they searched for and found information on their own.

One reason that the decision about whether to conform is so important is that it influences how people define reality. If you decide to accept other people's definition of the situation, you will come to see the world as they do. If you decide to reject other people's definition of the situation, you will come to see the world very differently from the way they do. This basic fact was demonstrated in an interesting study by Roger Buehler and Dale Griffin (1994), who asked students to read newspaper reports of a real, highly controversial incident in which an African American teenager driving a stolen car was shot and killed by white police officers. Many of the details of the situation were ambiguous, such as how much the youth had threatened the officers and how much the officers feared for their lives.

Buehler and Griffin first asked participants how they interpreted the situation: How fast was the victim's car going? Was the victim trying to ram the police car? Did he realize that his pursuers were the police? What were the police officers thinking and feeling? Each participant was then told that other participants had agreed with the statement that the police were 75 percent responsible and the victim 25 percent responsible. After indicating whether they agreed with this assessment, the participants were asked how they interpreted the situation. The question was, did people's interpretation of the situation change, depending on whether they agreed with other people's assessments?

The first result of interest was that not everyone conformed to other people's views. In fact, only 32 percent of the participants agreed that the police were 75 percent responsible for the incident. Thus, as we have discussed, it is possible to resist informational influence. Did people's decision about whether to conform influence their definition of the situation? The answer is yes: People who agreed

> "Yes, we must, indeed, all hang together or, most assuredly, we shall all hang separately."
> —Benjamin Franklin to John Hancock, at the signing of the Declaration of Independence

WHAT LEMMINGS BELIEVE

■ When informational influence backfires: Lemmings are small, furry rodents. Occasionally, a colony will commit mass suicide as a means of population control. This cartoon is suggesting that lemmings' conformity is not a form of normative social influence (e.g., the fear of being rejected by the other lemmings), but a form of informational social influence. The lemmings in the lead have convinced the others that they can all fly. Unfortunately, the leaders are wrong.

with others that the police were responsible changed their interpretations to be consistent with the group; they now believed that the victim had not threatened the police and that police were not in fear of their lives. What about the people who did not conform? Interestingly, they also changed their interpretations, but in the opposite direction—they now believed that the victim's car was about to ram the police and that the police were in fear for their lives. In short, people changed their interpretations of reality to bolster their decision about whether to agree with the majority opinion.

Your decision as to whether to conform to informational influence, then, will affect not only your behavior but also your interpretation of reality. It is thus important to consider carefully whether other people's reaction to a situation is any more legitimate than your own. Do other people know any more about what is going on than you do? Is there an expert handy, someone who should know more? Do the actions of other people or experts seem sensible? If you behave the way they do, will it go against your common sense, or against your internal moral compass that tells you what is right and wrong? By knowing how informational social influence works in daily life, you are in a better position to know when it is useful and when it is not.

Normative Social Influence: The Need to Be Accepted

In Rio de Janeiro, Brazil, teenage boys and girls engage in a highly dangerous, reckless game: They "surf" on the tops of trains, standing with arms outstretched as the trains speed along. Despite the fact that an average of 150 teenagers die each year from this activity and 400 more are injured by falling off the trains or hitting the 3,000-volt electric cable, the surfing continues (Arnett, 1995). In the United States, one teenager died and two more were critically injured when they responded to a dare to reenact a scene from the movie *The Program*. Like the movie's protagonist, they lay down in the middle of a highway at night. Unlike the movie's protagonist, they were run over (Hinds, 1993).

Why do these adolescents engage in such risky behavior? Why does anyone follow the group's lead when the resulting behavior is less than sensible and may even be dangerous? We doubt that the Brazilian or American teenagers risked their lives due to informational conformity—it is difficult to argue that a boy or girl staring at a train would say, "Gee, I don't know what to do. I guess standing on top of a train going 60 miles an hour makes a lot of sense; everybody else is doing it." This example tells us that there is another reason for why we conform, besides the need for information: We also conform so that we will be liked and accepted by other people. We conform to the group's **social norms,** which are implicit (and sometimes explicit) rules for acceptable behaviors, values, and beliefs (Miller & Prentice, 1996; Deutsch & Gerard, 1955; Kelley, 1955). Groups have certain expectations about how the group members should behave, and members in good standing conform to these rules. Members who do not are perceived as different, difficult, and eventually deviant. Deviant members can be ridiculed, punished, or even rejected by other group members (Levine, 1989; Miller & Anderson, 1979; Schachter, 1951; Kruglanski & Webster, 1991).

For example, "bullying" is becoming a problem in Japanese public schools. A whole class (even the entire school) will turn against one student because he or she is different in some way. The students will alternate between harrassing the individual and completely shunning him or her. The result of this treatment in a highly cohesive, group-oriented culture is profound and tragic: 12 teenage victims of bullying killed themselves in one year (Jordan, 1996).

We human beings are by nature a social species. Few of us could live happily as hermits, never seeing or talking to another person. Through interactions with others, we receive emotional support, affection, and love, and we partake of enjoyable experiences. Other people are extraordinarily important to our sense of well-being. Research on individuals who have been isolated for long amounts of time indicates that being deprived of human contact is stressful and traumatic (Baumeister & Leary, 1995; Curtiss, 1977; Schachter, 1959; Zubek, 1969).

Given this fundamental human need for social companionship, it is not surprising that we often conform in order to be accepted by others. Conformity for normative reasons occurs in those situations where we do what other people are doing not because we are using them as a source of information but because we won't attract attention, be made fun of, get into trouble, or be rejected. Thus, **normative social influence** occurs when the influence of other people leads us to conform in order to be liked and accepted by them. This type of conformity results in public compliance with the group's beliefs and behaviors, but not necessarily in private acceptance of the group's beliefs and behaviors (Allison, 1992; Cialdini et al., 1990, 1991; Cialdini & Trost, 1998; Deutsch & Gerard, 1955; Opp, 1982; Reno, Cialdini, & Kallgren, 1993; Sorrels & Kelley, 1984).

You probably don't find it too surprising that people sometimes conform in order to be liked and accepted by others. After all, if the group is important to us and it is a matter of wearing the right kind of clothing or using the hip slang words, why not go along? But when it comes to more important kinds of behaviors, such as hurting another person, surely we will resist such conformity pressures. And surely we won't conform when we are certain of what the correct way of behaving is and the pressures are coming from a group that we don't care all that much about. Or will we?

Social Norms

the implicit or explicit rules a group has for the acceptable behaviors, values, and beliefs of its members

Normative Social Influence

the influence of other people that leads us to conform in order to be liked and accepted by them; this type of conformity results in public compliance with the group's beliefs and behaviors, but not necessarily with private acceptance of the group's beliefs and behaviors

Conformity and Social Approval: The Asch Line Judgment Studies

To find out, Solomon Asch (1951, 1956) conducted a series of classic studies exploring the parameters of normative social influence. Asch initiated this program of research because he believed that there are limits to how much people will conform. Naturally, people conformed in the Sherif studies, he reasoned, given that the situation was highly ambiguous—trying to guess how much a light was moving. Asch believed, however, that when a situation was completely unambiguous, people would act like rational, objective problem-solvers. When the group said or did something that contradicted an obvious truth, surely people would reject social pressures and decide for themselves what was going on.

To test his hypothesis, Asch conducted the following study. Had you been a participant, you would have been told that this was an experiment on perceptual judgment and that you would be taking part with seven other students. Here's the scenario: The experimenter shows everyone two cards, one with a single line on it, the other with three lines labeled 1, 2, and 3. He asks each of you to judge and then announce aloud which of the three lines on the second card is closest in length to the line on the first card (see Figure 8.2).

It is crystal-clear that the correct answer is the second line. Not surprisingly, each participant says, "Line 2." Your turn comes next to last, and of course you say, "Line 2" as well. The last participant concurs. The experimenter then presents a new set of cards and asks the group to again make their judgments and announce them out loud. Again, the answer is obvious, and everyone gives the correct answer. At this point, you are probably thinking to yourself, "What a boring experiment! How many times will we have to judge these silly lines? I wonder what they're serving for dinner in the dining hall tonight."

As your mind starts to wander, something surprising happens. The experimenter presents the third set of lines, and again the answer is obvious—line 3 is clearly the closest in length to the target line. But the first participant announces that the correct answer is line 1! "Geez, this guy must be so bored that he fell asleep," you think. Then the second person announces that he also believes that line 1 is the correct answer. The third, fourth, fifth, and sixth participants concur; then it is your turn to judge. By now startled, you are probably looking at the lines very closely to see if you missed something. But no, line 3 is clearly the correct answer. What will you do? Will you bravely blurt out, "Line 3," or will you go along with the group and give the obviously incorrect answer, "Line 1"?

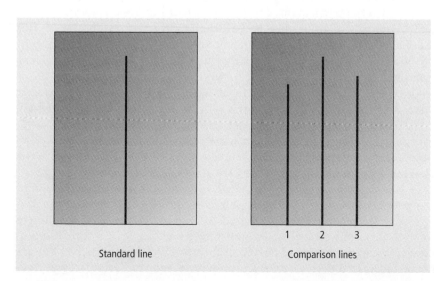

Standard line

1 2 3
Comparison lines

■ **FIGURE 8.2 The judgment task in Asch's line studies.** In a study of normative social influence, participants judged which of the three comparison lines on the right was closest in length to the standard line on the left. The correct answer was obvious (as it is here). However, members of the group (actually confederates) said the wrong answer out loud. Now the participant was in a dilemma: Should he say the right answer and go against the whole group, or should he conform to their behavior and give the obviously wrong answer? (Adapted from Asch, 1956).

■ Participants in an Asch line study. The real participant is seated in the middle. He is surrounded by experimenter's accomplices who have just given the wrong answer on the line task.

> ❝It isn't difficult to keep alive, friends—just don't make trouble—or if you must make trouble, make the sort of trouble that's expected.
>
> –Robert Bolt,
> *A Man for All Seasons*, 1962

As you can see, Asch set up a situation to see if people would conform even when the right answer was cut-and-dried. The other participants were actually accomplices of the experimenter, instructed to give the wrong answer on 12 of the 18 trials. Contrary to what Asch thought would happen, a surprising amount of conformity occurred: Seventy-six percent of the participants conformed on at least one trial. On average, people conformed on about a third of the 12 trials on which the accomplices gave the incorrect answer (see Figure 8.3).

Why did people conform so much of the time? One possibility is that people genuinely had a hard time with the task and thus assumed that other people were better judges of the length of lines than they were. If so, this would be another case of informational social influence, as we saw in the Sherif study. This interpretation doesn't make much sense, however, because the correct answers were obvious—so much so that when people in a control group made the judgments by themselves, they were accurate over 99 percent of the time. Instead, normative pressures came into play. Even though the other participants were strangers, the fear of being the lone dissenter was very strong, causing people to conform, at least occasionally. One participant, for example, had this to say about why he conformed: "Here was a group; they had a definite idea; my idea disagreed; this might arouse anger. . . . I was standing out as a sore thumb. . . . I didn't want particularly to make a fool of myself. . . . I felt I was definitely right . . . [but] they might think I was peculiar" (Asch, 1955, p. 46).

These are classic normative reasons for conforming: People know that what they are doing is wrong but go along anyway so as not to feel peculiar or look like a fool. These reasons illustrate an important fact about normative pressures: In contrast to informational social influence, normative pressures usually result in public compliance without private acceptance—that is, people go along with the group even if they do not believe in what they are doing or think it is wrong.

What is especially surprising about Asch's results is that people were concerned about looking foolish in front of complete strangers. It is not as if the participants were in danger of being ostracized by a group that was important to them. Nor was there any risk of open punishment or disapproval for failing to conform, or of losing the esteem of people they really cared about, such as friends and family members. Yet decades of research indicate that conformity for norma-

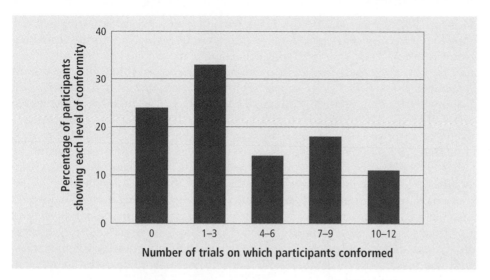

■ **FIGURE 8.3   Results of the Asch line judgment study.**   Participants in the Asch line study showed a surprisingly high level of conformity, given how obvious it was that the group was wrong in their judgments. Seventy-six percent of the participants conformed on at least one trial; only 24 percent of participants never conformed at all (see bar labelled zero). Most participants conformed on 1 to 3 of the 12 trials where the group gave the wrong answer. However, a sizeable number of participants conformed to the group's response nearly every time it gave the wrong answer (see the two bars on the right). (Adapted from Asch, 1957)

tive reasons can occur simply because we do not want to risk social disapproval, even from complete strangers we will never see again (Crutchfield, 1955; Tanford & Penrod, 1984). As Moscovici (1985, p. 349) comments, the Asch studies are "one of the most dramatic illustrations of conformity, of blindly going along with the group, even when the individual realizes that by doing so he turns his back on reality and truth."

Asch (1957) did a variation of his study that demonstrates the power of social disapproval in shaping a person's behavior. The confederates gave the wrong answer 12 out of 18 times, as before, but this time the participants wrote their answers on a piece of paper, instead of saying them out loud. Now people did not have to worry about what the group thought of them, because the group would never find out what their answers were. Conformity dropped dramatically, occurring on an average of only 1.5 of the 12 trials (Insko et al., 1985; Nail, 1986).

Normative social influence most closely reflects the negative stereotype of conformity we referred to earlier. At times, conforming for normative reasons can be spineless and weak; it can have negative consequences. Even in a dangerous situation, like that faced by the Brazilian teenagers, you might go ahead and conform because normative social pressures can be difficult to resist. The desire to be accepted is part of human nature, but it can have tragic consequences.

The Consequences of Resisting Normative Social Influence

One way to observe the power of normative social pressures is to see what happens when people manage to resist them. If a person refuses to do as the group asks and thereby violates its norms, what happens (Arnold & Greenberg, 1980; Kruglanski & Webster, 1991; Levine, 1980, 1989; Milgram & Sabini, 1978;

> "Customs do not concern themselves with right or wrong or reason. But they have to be obeyed; one reasons all around them until [one] is tired, but [one] must not transgress them, it is sternly forbidden.
> —Mark Twain

Mullen, 1991; Tata et al., 1996)? Think for a moment about the norms that operate in your group of friends. Some friends have an egalitarian norm for making group decisions. For example, when choosing a movie such groups will make sure that everyone gets to state a preference; the choice is then discussed until agreement is reached on one movie. Think about what would happen if, in a group with this kind of norm, you stated at the outset that you only wanted to see *Rebel Without a Cause* and weren't going with them otherwise. Your friends would be surprised by your behavior; they would also be annoyed with you or even angry. If you continued to disregard the friendship norms of the group by failing to conform to them, two things would most likely occur. First, the group members would attempt to bring you "back into the fold," chiefly through increased communication with you. Teasing comments and long discussions would ensue as your friends tried to figure out why you were acting so strangely and also tried to get you to conform to their expectations (Garfinkle, 1967). If these discussions didn't work, your friends would most likely curtail communication with you (Festinger & Thibaut, 1951; Gerard, 1953). At this point, in effect you would have been rejected.

This process of monitoring, convincing, and eventually rejecting the deviant was demonstrated by the jury of the famous Los Angeles riot trial, in which two black assailants were tried for beating a white truck driver, Reginald Denny. The jury told the judge that they wanted one of the jurors removed. The jury forewoman wrote, "On behalf of the 11 jurors, we are in agreement that Juror No. 373 cannot comprehend anything that we've been trying to accomplish. We tried patiently to talk and work with her, all to no avail!... She doesn't use common sense. Lastly, just when we've made progress in final decisions, she is totally oblivious to what we've discussed and decided" (Mydans, 1993, p. A16).

Stanley Schachter (1951) demonstrated how the group responds to an individual who ignores their normative influence. He asked groups of college students to read and discuss a case history of "Johnny Rocco," a juvenile delinquent. Most of the students took a middle-of-the-road position about the case, believing that Rocco should receive a judicious mixture of love and discipline. Unbeknownst to the participants, however, Schachter had planted an accomplice in the group, who was instructed to disagree with the group's recommendations. He consistently argued that Rocco should receive the harshest amount of punishment, regardless of what the other group members argued.

How was the deviant treated? He received the most comments and questions from the real participants throughout the discussion, until near the end, when communication with him dropped sharply. The group had tried to convince the deviant to agree with them; when it appeared that wouldn't work, they ignored him. In addition, they punished the deviant. After the discussion, they were asked to fill out questionnaires that supposedly pertained to future discussion meetings of their group. The participants were asked to nominate one group member who should be eliminated from further discussions if the size had to be reduced. They nominated the deviant. They were also asked to assign group members to various tasks in future discussions. They assigned the unimportant or boring jobs, such as taking notes, to the deviant. Social groups are well versed in how to bring a nonconformist into line. No wonder we respond as often as we do to normative pressures! You can find out what it's like to resist normative social influence in the Try It! exercise on page 299.

> "Success or failure lies in conformity to the times.
> —Machiavelli

Unveiling Normative Social Influence by Breaking the Rules

Every day, you talk to a lot of people—friends, professors, co-workers, and strangers too. When you have a conversation (whether long or short), you follow certain interaction "rules" that operate in American culture. These rules for conversation include nonverbal forms of behavior that Americans consider "normal" as well as "polite." You can find out how powerful these norms are by breaking them and noting how people respond to you; their response is normative social influence in action.

For example, in conversation, we stand a certain distance from each other—not too far and not too close. Two to three feet is typical in this culture. In addition, we maintain a good amount of eye contact when we are listening to the other person; in comparison, when we're talking, we look away from the person more often.

What happens if you break these normative rules? For example, have a conversation with a friend and stand either too close or too far away (e.g, one foot or seven feet). Have a typical, normal conversation with your friend, changing only the spacing from what you normally use

with this person. Note how he or she responds. If you're too close, your friend will probably back away; if you continue to keep the distance small, he or she may act uncomfortable and even terminate your conversation sooner than usual. If you're too far away, your friend will probably come closer; if you back up, he or she may think you are in a strange mood. In either case, your friend's response will probably include the following: looking at you a lot; having a puzzled look on his or her face; acting uncomfortable or confused; talking less than normal or ending the conversation, and so on.

You have acted in a nonnormative way, and your conversational partner is first, trying to figure out what is going on, and second, responding in such a way so that you will stop acting oddly. From this one brief exercise, you will get the idea of what would happen if you behaved "oddly" all the time—people would try to get you to change, and then they would probably start avoiding or ignoring you.

When you're done, please "debrief" your friend, telling him or her about the exercise, so that your behavior is understood. Let your friend see what it's like to alter interpersonal distance by talking to you too close or too far away.

A recent example of how a deviant is treated by the group is the case of Shannon Faulkner and her experiences as an entering cadet at the Citadel, a military college in Charleston, South Carolina. A federal court order allowed Faulkner to enroll in the 153-year-old, all-male institution; because the Citadel is a public institution supported by South Carolina taxpayers, the court ruled that all residents of the state, regardless of sex, should have the right to apply for admission.

The students and faculty of the Citadel were not pleased that a young woman was entering their ranks. Despite Faulkner's attempt to conform to all the rules and behaviors of the Citadel during the first week, her gender made her a deviant and she was punished. When she arrived the first day, for what the school calls "Hell Week," signs saying "Shannon go home" greeted her and she was heckled. "You should have heard the way they were talking to me, calling me names," Faulkner said. "I never looked in their direction. I did what the other guys were doing. I got in line and did what I was supposed to do" (Rogers, Dampier, & Sieder, 1995, p. 78). However, the stress of being different, of having no support, soon made her sick. After a few days in the school infirmary, Faulkner left permanently. As a male junior cadet said, "You just don't make it here on your own. You have to rely on each other [but] she had no one. No one spoke to her, and that wasn't going to change" (Rogers et al., 1995, p. 80). When news spread that Faulkner had left the campus, the cadets rejoiced boisterously and enthusiastically.

> **I** was . . . silenced solely because cadets did not want Blacks at West Point. Their only purpose was to freeze me out. What they did not realize was that I was stubborn enough to put up with their treatment to reach the goal I had come to attain.
>
> —Benjamin Davis, Jr.

■ One of the reasons we conform to a group's normative social influence is so that we won't be rejected by the group. Shannon Faulkner, the first female cadet at the Citadel, did all she could to conform to the Citadel's rules. But she couldn't conform in terms of her gender. The group harassed, punished, and rejected her until she left the college. Here, the cadets celebrate as they hear she has dropped out of the school.

Normative Social Influence in Everyday Life

Normative social influence operates on many levels in our daily lives. The clothes we wear are but one example. While few of us are slaves of fashion, we nonetheless tend to wear what is considered appropriate and stylish at a given time. Men wore ties that were wide in the 1970s; then they wore ties that were narrow in the 1980s; and undoubtedly they'll be wearing wide ties again. Similarly, women's hemlines have gone up and down over the past century. Normative social influence is at work whenever you notice a "look" shared by people in a certain group. The "bobby-soxer" young women and the "zoot-suiter" young men of the 1940s had such a look. No doubt 20 years from now current fashions will look dated and silly and none of us will conform to them.

Another fairly frivolous example of normative social influence is fads. Certain activities or objects can suddenly become popular and sweep the country. College students in the 1930s ate goldfish; in the 1950s, crammed as many people as possible into telephone booths; and in the 1970s, "streaked" at official gatherings.

Hula-Hoops were the toy you had to have in the 1950s or risk social ostracism. One of us, Robin Akert, remembers a Saturday afternoon with the family in 1958:

> We drove from store to store, trying to find Hula-Hoops. Everywhere we went, they were all sold out. My sister and I sat in the backseat, sobbing with disappointment. Much to our parents' chagrin, we were praying in little, high-pitched voices for help in finding Hula-Hoops before nightfall!

A more sinister form of normative social influence involves women's attempts to conform to cultural definitions of an attractive body. While many, if not most, world societies consider plumpness in females attractive, Western culture and particularly American culture currently value thinness in the female form (Anderson et al., 1992; Furnham, Hester, & Weir, 1990; Ford & Beach, 1952; Garner et al., 1980; Jackson, 1992; Lamb et al., 1993; Rudofsky, 1972; Singh, 1993; Stice & Shaw, 1994).

■ On the left, the "zoot suiter" look in 1942. The jacket had six inches of shoulder pads, and the balloon trousers were hitched chest-high. On the right, the current fashion trend for teenagers—baggy jeans and oversized shirts and sweaters are the "in" look in some regions of the country.

For example, Judith Anderson and colleagues (1992) analyzed what people in 54 cultures considered to be the ideal female body: a heavy body, a body of moderate weight, or a slender body. The researchers also analyzed how reliable the food supply was in each culture. They hypothesized that in societies where food was frequently scarce, a heavy body would be considered the most beautiful—for these would be women who had enough to eat and therefore were healthy and fertile. As you can see in Figure 8.4, their hypothesis was supported. Heavy women were preferred over slender or moderate ones in cultures with un-

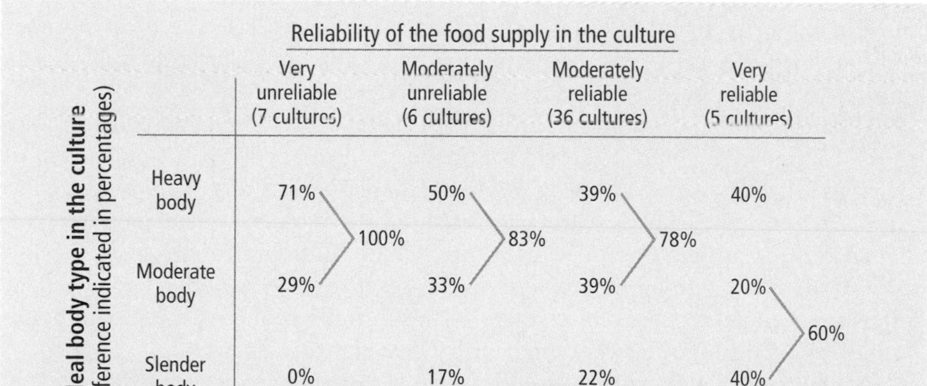

	Reliability of the food supply in the culture			
	Very unreliable (7 cultures)	Moderately unreliable (6 cultures)	Moderately reliable (36 cultures)	Very reliable (5 cultures)
Heavy body	71%	50%	39%	40%
Moderate body	29%	33%	39%	20%
Slender body	0%	17%	22%	40%

Ideal body type in the culture (Preference indicated in percentages)

(diagonal bracket annotations: 100%, 83%, 78% spanning heavy-to-moderate; 60% spanning moderate-to-slender)

■ **FIGURE 8.4   What is the "ideal" female body across cultures?**   Researchers divided 54 cultures into groups, depending on the reliability of their food supply. They then determined what was considered the "ideal" female body in each culture. Heavy female bodies were considered the most beautiful in cultures with unreliable food supplies. Furthermore, the moderate-to-heavy body range was preferred by the majority in all cultures but those with very reliable food supplies. Only in those cultures where food was readily available was the slender body valued, and only in this type of culture did the majority prefer a body in the slender-to-moderate range. (Adapted from Anderson, Crawford, Nadeau, & Lindberg, 1992)

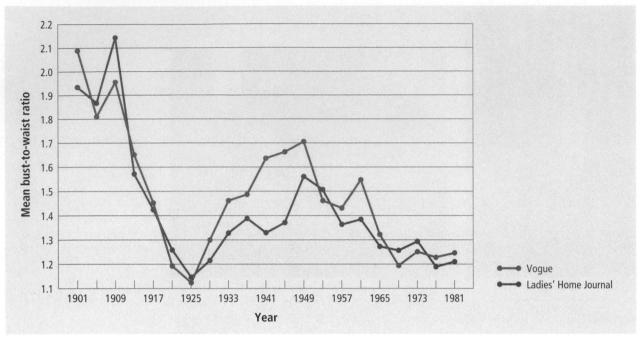

■ **FIGURE 8.5** **The mean bust-to-waist ratios of models in *Vogue* and *Ladies' Home Journal* during this century.** What has been considered an attractive female body has changed dramatically over the past 100 years: from heavy women at the beginning of the century, to rail-thin women during the 1920s, to somewhat heavier, curvaceous women during the 1940s and 1950s, to a return to overly thin women in the 1960s and continuing. (Adapted from Silverstein, Perdue, Peterson, & Kelly, 1986)

reliable food supplies. Furthermore, heavy-to-moderate bodies were preferred by the vast majority in all cultures except those with very reliable food supplies. Only in cultures with very reliable food supplies (like the United States) did the majority prefer moderate-to-slender female bodies.

What is the American standard for the female body? Has it changed over time? To find out, Brett Silverstein and her colleagues (1986) analyzed photographs of women appearing in *Ladies' Home Journal* and *Vogue* magazines from 1901 to 1981. The researchers measured the women's busts and waists in centimeters, creating a bust-to-waist ratio. A high score indicates a heavier, more voluptuous body, while a lower score indicates a thin, lean body type. Their results show a startling series of changes in the cultural definition of female bodily attractiveness during the twentieth century (see Figure 8.5).

At the turn of the century, an attractive woman was voluptuous and heavy; by the "flapper" period of the 1920s, the correct look for women was rail-thin and flat-chested. The normative body changed again in the 1940s, when World War II "pinup girls" like Betty Grable exemplified a heavier standard. The curvaceous, heavier female body remained popular during the 1950s; witness, for example, Marilyn Monroe. However, the "swinging 1960s" fashion look, exemplified by the reed-thin British model Twiggy, introduced a very thin silhouette again. As Brett Silverstein and her colleagues (1986) point out, the average bust-to-waist ratio has been very low since 1963. This is the longest period of time in this century that women have been exposed to an extremely thin standard of feminine physical attractiveness.

■ Cultural standards for women's bodies change rapidly. While today most female models and movie stars are very lean and muscled, the female icons of the 1940s and 1950s, like Marilyn Monroe, were curvaceous, heavier, and less muscle-toned.

Whereas informational social influence is the mechanism by which women learn what kind of body is considered attractive at a given time in their culture, normative social influence helps to explain their attempts to create that body through dieting and, more disturbingly, through eating disorders like anorexia nervosa and bulimia (Gimlin, 1994; Jackson, 1993). As early as 1966, researchers found that 70 percent of the high school girls surveyed were unhappy with their bodies and wanted to lose weight (Heunemann et al., 1966; Hill, Oliver, & Rogers, 1992). In 1991, Elissa Koff and Jill Rierdan found that, when asked if they'd "ever felt overweight" in their lives, 72 percent of the 11- and 12-year-old girls surveyed answered yes (*Boston Globe*, 1992). The sociocultural pressure for thinness that is currently operating on women (and not to the same extent on men; see Silverstein et al., 1986) is a potentially fatal form of normative social influence. The last time that a very thin standard of bodily attractiveness for women existed—the mid-1920s—an epidemic of eating disorders appeared (Herzog et al., 1992; Pliner, Chaiken, & Flett, 1990; Silverstein, Peterson, & Perdue, 1986).

Christian Crandall (1988) has conducted research on conformity pressures and eating disorders—in this case, bulimia, an eating pattern characterized by periodic episodes of uncontrolled "binge" eating, followed by periods of "purging" food through fasting, vomiting, or using laxatives. Crandall's research participants were women members of two college sororities. He found, first, that each sorority had its own social norm for binge eating. In one sorority, the group norm was that the more one binged, the more popular one was in the group. In the other sorority, popularity was associated with binging the right amount—the most popular women binged not too often and not too infrequently, compared to the others.

Did binge eating operate as a form of normative social influence? Yes, it did. Crandall tested the women throughout the school year and found that new members had conformed to the eating patterns of their friends. Probably, the initial conforming behavior was informational, as a new pledge learned from the group how to manage her weight. However, normative conformity processes would then take over, as the woman matched her binging behavior to the sorority's standard and that of her friends. To not engage in the behavior or to do it differently from how the others did could easily have resulted in a loss of popularity and even ostracism.

> You cannot make a man by standing a sheep on its hind-legs. But by standing a flock of sheep in that position you can make a crowd of men.
> —Sir Max Beerbohm

When Will People Conform to Normative Social Influence?

People don't always cave in to peer pressure. Although conformity is commonplace, we are not lemmings who always do what everyone else is doing. And we certainly do not agree on all issues, like abortion or affirmative action. (One need only tune in to a radio talk show to appreciate how much people disagree on topics such as these.) Exactly when are people most likely to conform to normative pressures?

Social Impact Theory
the theory that conforming to social influence depends on the strength, immediacy, and number of other people in a group

The answer to this question is provided by Bibb Latané's (1981) **social impact theory.** According to this theory, the likelihood that you will respond to social influence from other people depends on three variables: (a) *strength*, referring to how important the group of people is to you; (b) *immediacy*, referring to how close the group is to you in space and time during the influence attempt; and (c) *number*, referring to how many people are in the group.

Social impact theory predicts that conformity will increase as strength and immediacy increase. Clearly, the more important a group is to us and the more we are in its presence, the more likely we will be to conform to its normative pressures. For example, the sorority sisters that Crandall (1988) studied experienced a high level of strength and immediacy in their groups, with tragic consequences.

Number, however, operates in a different manner. As the size of the group increases, each additional person has less of an influencing effect—going from 3 to 4 people makes more of a difference than going from 53 to 54 people. It is like the law of diminishing returns in economics, where increasing one's total wealth by $1 seems much greater if we have only $1 to start with than if we already have $1,000. Similarly, if we feel pressure from a group to conform, adding another person to the majority makes much more of a difference if the group consists of 3 rather than 15 people. Latané (1981) constructed a mathematical model that captures these hypothesized effects of strength, immediacy, and number and has applied this formula to the results of many conformity studies. It has done a good job of predicting the actual amount of conformity that occurred (Latané, 1981; Latané & L'Herrou, 1996; Latané, Nowak, & Liu, 1994; Nowak & Latané, 1994).

For example, gay men who lived in communities that were highly involved in AIDS-awareness activities (where strength, immediacy, and number would all be high) reported feeling more social pressure to avoid risky sexual behavior and stronger intentions to do so than did men who lived in less involved communities (Fischbein et al., 1993). Similarly, a sample of heterosexual college students reported that what governed the likelihood of their engaging in risky, AIDS-related sexual behavior was the norms for sexual behavior that operated in their group of friends (Winslow, Franzini, & Hwang, 1992).

Social impact theory covers conformity to all kinds of social influence. For present purposes, let's see in more detail what it says about the conditions under which people will conform to normative social pressures.

When the Group Size Is Three or More

As we just saw, conformity increases as the number of people in the group increases—up to a point. Imagine you are a participant in Solomon Asch's study, where you judged the length of lines. If there are only you and 1 other participant and the latter gives a blatantly wrong answer about the length of the lines, will you be less likely to cave in and conform to the other participant's response than if there were 5 other participants all giving the wrong answer? What if there were 15 people in the majority? Asch (1955) studied this question, and as we can see in

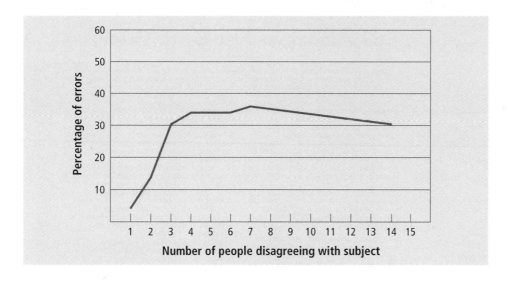

■ **FIGURE 8.6   Effects of group size on conformity.** Asch varied the size of the unanimous majority and found that once the majority numbered four people, adding more people had little influence on conformity. (Adapted from Asch, 1955)

Figure 8.6, conformity increased as the number of people in the group increased, but only up to a point.

Asch's (1955) initial research and that of later researchers has established that in this kind of group situation, conformity does not increase much after the group size reaches 4 or 5 other people (Campbell & Fairey, 1989; Gerard, Wilhelmy, & Conolley, 1968; McGuire, 1968; Rosenberg, 1961)—just as social impact theory suggests. In short, it does not take an extremely large group to create normative social influence. As Mark Twain wrote in *The Adventures of Huckleberry Finn,* "Hain't we got all the fools in town on our side? And ain't that a big enough majority in any town?"

When the Group Is Important

Another tenet of social impact theory is that the strength of the group—defined as how important the group is to us—makes a difference. Normative pressures are much stronger when they come from people whose friendship, love, and respect we cherish, because there is a large cost to losing this love and respect. Thus, groups to which we are highly attracted and with which we strongly identify will exert more normative influence on us than groups for which we have little or no attachment (Abrams et al., 1990; Clark & Maass, 1988; Hogg, 1992; Lott & Lott, 1961; Nowak, Szamrej, & Latané, 1990; Sakurai, 1975; Wolf, 1985). One consequence of this fact is that it can be dangerous to have policy decisions made by highly cohesive groups, because they care more about pleasing each other and avoiding conflict than arriving at the soundest, most logical decision. In Chapter 9, on group processes, we will see several examples of this phenomenon.

When the Group Is Unanimous

Normative social influence is most powerfully felt when everyone in the group says or believes the same thing—for example, when your group of friends all believe that *101 Dalmatians* was the greatest movie ever made. Resisting such unanimous social influence is difficult or even impossible—unless you have an ally. If another person disagrees with the group—say, by nominating *Citizen Kane* as the best movie ever—this behavior will help you to buck the tide as well.

Still a Hoax to Flat-Earth Group

Most people have come to accept the idea that the sun, the earth and the moon are all spheres, and that eclipses occur because of the rotation of the earth around the sun and of the moon around the earth. But one group of people, the International Flat Earth Research Society, contends that such an explanation is merely part of a gigantic hoax.

The president of the Flat Earth Society, Charles K. Johnson of Lancaster, Calif., believes that photographs taken from space, accounts of space travel and virtually everything else connected with modern science are all part of the hoax.

"Ever since Copernicus, the new religion — science, they call it — has been trying to fool the people with this notion that the earth is a ball," Mr. Johnson said in an interview.

"Starting around 1600, the facts were cast away by the priests of the new religion," he said, "and the vast, global con game began. They got most people to accept their hoax, but not us."

Nicolaus Copernicus was a Polish astronomer whose 1543 publication describing the motion of planets around the sun

revolutionized astronomy. Formerly, the views of Ptolemy had prevailed, that the earth was the center of the universe around which everything else circled.

Mr. Johnson said that the society he heads, which was founded in 1888, now has about 1,600 formal members in the United States, in addition to some 2,000 believing outsiders. Members pay a $10 annual fee, for which they receive copies of the society's quarterly magazine, Flat Earth News.

The society president said he planned to "call President Carter's attention to the fact" that in 1959 a movie was made by the Three Stooges about a comic rocket trip to the planet Venus. "Purported photographs taken since then about space travel should be considered in the same category, as entertainment, rather than fact," he said.

"Only 10 or 20 percent of the people in the United States believe the hoax that men have traveled to the moon," Mr. Johnson said.

Asked how he would explain the eclipse of the sun, Mr. Johnson said, "We don't really go into all that. The Bible tells us that the heavens are a mystery."

■ If you can get a few allies to agree with you, it's easier to buck the majority and believe some rather strange things. (*New York Times*, February 26, 1979)

To illustrate the importance of having an ally, Asch (1955) conducted another version of his conformity experiment. In this variation, he had six of the seven confederates give the wrong answer, whereas one confederate gave the right answer on every trial. Now the subject was not alone. While he or she still disagreed with the majority of the group, having one ally helped him or her to resist normative pressures. People conformed on an average of only 6 percent of the trials in this study, compared to 32 percent in the version where all of the confederates gave the wrong answer. Several other studies have found that observing another person resist normative social influence emboldens the individual to do the same (Allen & Levine, 1969; Morris & Miller, 1975; Nemeth & Chiles, 1988).

This effect of allies produces some interesting anomalies in everyday life—people who hold unpopular beliefs are able to maintain them in the face of group pressure if they can convince at least a few others to agree with them. In Chapter 6, we saw the members of a small cult persevere in their belief that the world was going to end (even when it didn't). Clearly, the fact that the other cult members continued to believe helped every individual in the group to ignore the ridicule with which outsiders viewed them (Walsh et al., 1995). Similarly, a man in Lancaster, California believes that the earth is flat—despite proof from scientific experiments over a few centuries that it is not (see the newspaper article above). It is difficult to hold such an unpopular (and wrongheaded!) view; not surprisingly, this man has actively recruited followers and attempts to convince others of his views through his *Flat Earth Newsletter*.

When the Group Is Affected by Culture

"In America, the squeaky wheel gets the grease. In Japan, the nail that stands out gets pounded down" (Markus & Kitayama, 1991; p. 224). Is it the case, as this quote suggests, that the society in which one is raised affects the frequency of normative social influence? Perhaps not surprisingly, the answer is yes. Stanley Milgram (1961, 1977) replicated the Asch studies in Norway and France and

Try It!

Fashion: Normative Social Influence In Action

You can observe social impact theory in action by focusing on fashion—specifically, the clothes and accessories that you and your group of friends wear as well as the "look" of other groups on campus. You can also observe what happens when you break those normative rules for fashion, for example, by dressing in a way that deviates from your group.

When you are with a group of friends and acquaintances, note carefully how everyone is dressed. Pretend you are from another culture and not acquainted with the norms of this group; this will help you notice details that you might otherwise overlook. For example, what kinds of pants, shoes, shirts, jewelry, and so on is worn by this group? Are there similarities in their haircuts? Can you discover their fashion "rules"?

Next, spend some time on campus "people-watching," specifically, observe what other groups of people are wearing. Can you discern different sub-groups on your campus, defined by their style of dress? If so, there are different types of normative conformity operating on your campus: groups of friends are dressing according to the rules of their sub-group and not according to the rules of the campus as a whole.

Finally, if you are brave, break the fashion rules of your normative group. You can do this subtly or you can be very obvious! (But do be sensible; don't get yourself arrested!). For example, if you're male, you could wear a skirt around campus. That would definitely attract attention; you will be not conforming to normative influence in a very major way! If you're female, you'll have to get more creative to break the normative rules (since women's fashion includes pants, blazers and other male-type clothing). You could wear a large, green garbage bag (with holes cut out for your head and arms) over your clothing. In either case, just walk around campus like normal—as if you don't notice you are wearing anything strange at all. The interesting part will be how people react to you. What will your friends say? Will strangers stare at you?

Your group of friends (as well as the students at your school in general) may well have the qualities that social impact theory discusses: the group is important to you; the group size is more than three; and the group is unanimous (which is the case if your group of friends or your college has definite fashion norms). If you stop conforming to this normative social influence, the other group members will exert some kind of pressure on you, trying to get you to return to conformity.

found that the Norwegian participants conformed to a greater degree than the French participants did. Milgram (1961, p. 51) describes Norwegian society as "highly cohesive . . . [with] a deep feeling of group identification," while French society, in comparison, "show[s] far less consensus in both social and political life." In another cross-cultural study of normative social influence, James Whittaker and Robert Meade (1967) found that people in Lebanon, Hong Kong, and Brazil conformed to a similar extent (both to each other and to the American sample), while participants from the Bantu tribe of Zimbabwe conformed to a much greater degree. As the researchers point out, conformity has a very high social value in Bantu culture. While Japanese culture is more highly conforming than our own in many areas, an Asch-type study found that when the group unanimously gave the incorrect answer, Japanese students were less conformist in general than North Americans (Frager, 1970). In Japan, cooperation and loyalty are directed to the groups to which one belongs; there is little expectation that one should conform to the behavior of complete strangers, especially in such an artificial setting as a psychology experiment. Similarly, German research participants have shown less conformity in the Asch experiment than North Americans (Timaeus, 1968); in Germany, conformity to strangers is less valued than conformity to a few well-defined groups (Moghaddam, Taylor, & Sright, 1993).

Recently, Rod Bond and Peter Smith (1996) conducted a meta-analysis of 133 Asch line judgment studies conducted in 17 countries: the United States, Canada, Great Britain, France, Holland, Belgium, Germany, Portugal, Japan, Hong Kong, Fiji, Zimbabwe, Zaire, Ghana, Brazil, Kuwait, and Lebanon. They found that cultural values affected normative social influence. Participants in collectivistic cultures showed higher rates of conformity on the line task than did participants in individualistic cultures. In collectivistic cultures, conformity is a valued trait, not a negative one as in the United States. Because the emphasis is on the group and not the individual, people in collectivistic cultures value normative social influence because it promotes harmony and supportive relationships in the group (Guisinger & Blatt, 1994; Kim et al., 1994; Markus, Kitayama, & Heiman, 1996).

J. W. Berry (1967; Kim & Berry, 1993) explored the issue of conformity as a cultural value by comparing two cultures that had very different strategies for accumulating food. He hypothesized that societies that relied on hunting or fishing would value independence, assertiveness, and adventurousness in their members—traits that were needed to find and bring home food—whereas societies that were primarily agricultural would value cooperativeness, conformity, and acquiescence—traits that made close-living and interdependent farming more successful. Berry compared the Eskimo of Baffin Island in Canada, a hunting and fishing society, to the Temne of Sierra Leone in Africa, a farming society, on an Asch-type conformity task. The Temne showed a significant tendency to accept the suggestions of the group, while the Eskimo almost completely disregarded them. As one Temne put it, "When the Temne people choose a thing, we must all agree with the decision—this is what we call cooperation" (p. 417); in contrast, the few times the Eskimo did conform to the group's wrong answer, they did so with "a quiet, knowing smile" (p. 417).

Finally, there is intriguing evidence that the level of conformity is changing in the United States. For example, replications of the Asch study conducted 25 to 40 years after the original, in western countries like the United States and Great Britain, have found that percentages of conformity are decreasing (Bond & Smith, 1996; Larson, 1990; Lalancette & Standing, 1990; Nicholson, Cole, & Rocklin, 1985; Perrin & Spencer, 1981).

When People Are a Certain Type

Whereas the prior conditions under which normative conformity occurs involve the group, this last condition involves aspects of the individual. Is a certain sort of person more likely to conform to normative pressures than another? Research in this area has focused on two aspects of the individual: personality and gender. It seems reasonable to propose that some people are just conforming types, while others' personalities make them highly resistant to normative pressures. Solomon Asch (1956) suggested that people who have low self-esteem may be particularly conforming because they fear rejection or punishment by the group. In the first study examining personality traits and conformity, Richard Crutchfield (1955) found evidence for this relationship between self-esteem and normative conformity; similarly, Mark Snyder and William Ickes (1985) found that people who perceived themselves as having a strong need for approval from others were more likely to demonstrate normative conformity.

Unfortunately, the relationship between personality traits and conforming behavior is not always so clear-cut. Some studies have found the relationship to be weak or nonexistent (Marlowe & Gergen, 1970). The reason is that, quite often, people are not very consistent in how they respond in different social situations (McGuire, 1968; Mischel, 1968). In other words, they don't always conform, across time and in different situations, the way they would if their personalities alone were affecting their behavior. Instead, the situation affects their behavior as well, so that in some situations they conform, and in other situations they don't, regardless of what type of person they are. You may recall from Chapter 1 that this is a fundamental principle of social psychology: Often the social situation is more important in understanding how someone behaves than his or her personality is.

The second person variable that has been studied is gender. Is it the case that women and men differ in how readily they conform to social pressures? For many years, the prevailing wisdom has been to answer this question in the affirmative: Women are more conforming than men (Crutchfield, 1955). When all three of your authors studied social psychology in college, this finding was presented as a fact. Recent reviews of the literature, however, have shown that matters are not so simple. In the past few years, researchers have taken an objective look at this question by conducting *meta-analyses*. A meta-analysis is a statistical technique that allows you to combine results across a large number of studies and come up with a meaningful statistical summary. Alice Eagly and Linda Carli (1981), for example, performed a meta-analysis of 145 studies of influenceability that included more than 21,000 participants. Consistent with previous reviews of this literature, they found that, on average, men are less influenceable than women. But they found the size of the difference to be very small. A difference in influenceability shows up when one averages across thousands of participants, but that does not mean that every man you encounter will be less influenceable than every woman. In fact, Eagly and Carli (1981) found that only 56 percent of men are less influenceable than the average woman—which means, of course, that 44 percent of men are more influenceable than the average woman.

Not only are sex differences in influenceability small, but they depend on the type of conformity pressures impinging on people. Gender differences are especially likely to be found in group-pressure situations, where an audience can directly observe how much you conform (e.g., the Asch study, where everyone can tell whether you give the same answer as the other participants). When faced with this kind of social pressure, women are more likely to conform than men are. In other situations, we are the only ones who know whether we conform, such as when we listen to someone give a speech against our views and then decide, privately, how much we agree with the speech. In this kind of situation, sex differences in influenceability virtually disappear (Becker, 1986; Eagly, 1987). Alice Eagly (1987) suggests that this pattern of results stems from the social roles men and women are taught in our society. Women are taught to be more agreeable and supportive, whereas men are taught to be more independent in the face of direct social pressures. And, Eagly suggests, both women and men are more likely to exhibit such gender-consistent behaviors in public situations, where everyone can see how they respond (e.g., the Asch-type conformity study). But remember, the size of these differences is small.

One other finding in this area is surprising and controversial. Eagly and Carli (1981) took note of the gender of the researchers who conducted conformity studies and found that male researchers were more likely than female researchers to find that men were less influenceable. Though the reason for this finding is not yet clear, Eagly and Carli (1981) suggest one possibility: Researchers may be more likely to use experimental materials and situations that are familiar to their gender. Male researchers, for example, may be more likely than female researchers to study how people conform to persuasive messages about sports. As we saw earlier, people are more likely to conform when confronted with an unfamiliar, ambiguous situation; thus, women may be more likely to conform in the unfamiliar situations designed by male experimenters.

To summarize, there appears to be a small tendency for women to be more influenceable, especially in group-pressure situations. Further, the already small magnitude of this difference may be exaggerated in studies conducted by male researchers, who are more likely than female researchers to find that women are more influenceable than men.

Resisting Normative Social Influence

Whereas normative social influence is often useful and appropriate, there are times when it is not. What can we do to resist inappropriate normative social influence? The best way to prevent ourselves from following the wrong social norm is to become more aware of what we are doing. If we stop and think carefully about whether the norm that seems to be operating is really the right one to follow, we will be more likely to recognize those times when it is not.

> *People create social conditions and people can change them.*
> —Tess Onwueme

If becoming aware of normative influence is the first step to resistance, taking action is the second. Why do we fail to take action? Because of the possible ridicule, embarrassment, or rejection we may experience. However, we know that having an ally helps us resist normative pressures. Thus, if you are in a situation where you don't want to go along with the crowd but you fear the repercussions if you don't, try to find another person (or better yet, a group) who thinks like you do.

Idiosyncrasy Credits
the credits a person earns, over time, by conforming to group norms; if enough idiosyncrasy credits are earned, the person can, on occasion, behave deviantly without retribution from the group

In addition, the very act of conforming to normative influence most of the time earns you the right to deviate occasionally without serious consequences. This interesting observation was made by Edwin Hollander (1958, 1960), who stated that conforming to a group over time earns you **idiosyncrasy credits,** much like putting money in the bank. Thus, your past conformity allows you, at some point in the future, to deviate from the group (or act idiosyncratically) without getting into too much trouble. If you refuse to lend your car, for example, your friends may not become upset with you if you have followed their friendship norms in other areas in the past, for you've earned the right to be different, to deviate from their normative rules in this area. Thus, resisting normative influence may not be as difficult (or scary) as you might think, if you have earned idiosyncrasy credits with the group.

Minority Influence: When the Few Influence the Many

We shouldn't leave our discussion of normative social influence with the impression that the individual never has an effect on the group. As Serge Moscovici (1985, 1994) says, if groups really did succeed in silencing nonconformists, rejecting deviants, and persuading everyone to go along with the majority point of view, then how could change ever be introduced into the system? We would all be like little robots, marching along with everyone else in monotonous synchrony, never able to adapt to changing reality.

Minority Influence
the case where a minority of group members influence the behavior or beliefs of the majority

Instead, Moscovici (1985, 1994) argues, the individual, or the minority of group members, can influence the behavior or beliefs of the majority. This is called **minority influence.** The key is consistency: People with minority views must express the same view over time, and different members of the minority must agree with each other. If a person in the minority wavers between two different viewpoints or if two individuals express different minority views, then the majority will dismiss them as people who have peculiar and groundless opinions. If, however, the minority expresses a consistent, unwavering view, the majority is likely to take notice and may even adopt the minority view (Moscovici & Nemeth, 1974).

In a recent meta analysis of nearly 100 studies, Wendy Wood and her colleagues describe how minority influence operates (Wood, Lundgren, Ouellette, Busceme, & Blackstone, 1994). People in the majority can cause other group members to conform through normative influence. As in the Asch experiments, the conformity that occurs may be a case of public compliance without private acceptance. People in the minority can rarely influence others through normative means—the majority has little concern for how the minority views them. In fact, majority group members may be loath to agree publicly with the minority; they don't want anyone to think that they agree with those unusual, strange views of the minority. Thus, minorities exert their influence on the group via the other principal method—informational social influence. The minority introduces new, unexpected information to the group and causes the group to examine the issues more carefully. Such careful examination may cause the majority to realize that the minority view has merit, leading the group to adopt all or part of the minority's view (Alvaro & Crano, 1997; Baker & Petty, 1994; Clark, 1994; Levine & Moreland, 1998; Levine & Russo, 1987; Maass & Clark, 1984; Moscovici, Mucchi-Faina, & Maass, 1994; Nemeth et al., 1990; Peterson & Nemeth, 1996; Smith, Tindale, & Dugoni, 1996; Trost, Maass, & Kenrick, 1993; Van Dyne & Saavedra, 1996; Wood et al., 1996). In short, majorities often cause public compliance because of normative social influence, whereas minorities often cause private acceptance because of informational social influence.

> "Never let anyone keep you contained and never let anyone keep your voice silent.
> —Adam Clayton Powell

Compliance: Requests to Change Your Behavior

We have discussed two main reasons why people conform: because other people serve as a useful source of information (informational social influence) and because of pressures to follow social norms (normative social influence). In the remainder of this chapter, we will see how these reasons for conformity apply to some familiar situations in which you might be asked to do something you really do not want to do. Some of these situations are quite common, such as a salesperson pressuring you into subscribing to some magazines or a charity trying to get you to donate money to their cause. Others are less common but more frightening, such as an authority figure asking you to do something that is against your morals. When and why will people conform in these situations?

We will begin with the case of **compliance**—that is, a change in behavior due to a direct request from another person. We can hardly make it through a day without someone asking us to do something we would rather not do, be it a letter from a charity asking for money, a telephone call (invariably during dinner) from someone selling vacation property, or a friend wanting to borrow $25. Social psychologists have studied when and why people are likely to comply with these kinds of requests (Cialdini, 1993).

Compliance
a change in behavior due to a direct request from another person

Mindless Conformity: Operating on Automatic Pilot

We have a friend who recently drove to the center of a large city to attend a concert. He parked his car in an outdoor, commercial lot near the concert hall. As he got out of his car, a woman handed him a ticket to put on his dashboard and said that the parking fee was $5. Our friend gave the woman the money and went on his way, only to be stopped by the real parking attendant. It turned out that the woman did not work for the parking company at all but was a con artist who had found a way to make a quick buck: She made it look like she was the real parking attendant and quickly disappeared with people's money.

It is easy to shake our heads at such stories and think that we would never be so naive as to fall for such a scam. Few of us, however, stop and think carefully about every single social interaction we have; it is much more efficient to follow social norms quickly and automatically. There are many well-learned norms that we follow without thinking much about it, such as ones that say "Wear socks that are the same color," "Greet people by shaking their hands and not patting their heads," and "Give money to legitimate-looking parking attendants." When people follow such norms automatically, we say they have engaged in **mindless conformity,** defined as obeying internalized social norms without deliberating about their actions—as if they were operating on automatic pilot.

There is a great advantage to mindless conformity. If we had to stop and think about how to respond in every single social situation, it would be difficult to make it through the day. In most cases, the social norms we follow automatically lead to appropriate behavior. Most people who give us a ticket in a parking lot really are parking attendants, and most people would rather have us shake their hands than pat their heads. Imagine that every time you parked your car you had to ask the attendant for identification, or that every time you met someone new you had to figure out whether he or she preferred a handshake or a head pat. Not a very efficient way to live our lives.

As we discussed in Chapter 3, however, behaving and thinking automatically come with a cost: By putting ourselves on automatic pilot, without carefully monitoring what we are doing, we sometimes end up following the wrong social norm and behave inappropriately (Cialdini, 1993; Langer, 1989; Santos, Leve, & Pratkanis, 1994). For example, the atomic scientist Robert Oppenheimer is said to have been so engrossed in his newspaper at breakfast one morning that he put a tip down on the table when he got up, forgetting that he was eating at home and not at a restaurant. (Needless to say, his wife was not amused.)

Ellen Langer and her colleagues have studied the conditions under which people engage in mindless conformity. To 40 secretaries at a New York university, they sent a memo that said, "This paper is to be returned immediately to Room 238 through interoffice mail." Like almost all other memos at this university, this one was unsigned. Note that this is a pretty silly request; if the person who sent the memo wanted it, why did he or she send it in the first place? Langer and her colleagues hypothesized that secretaries would go ahead and return the memo because they would mindlessly follow the norm that says "Do what memos tell you to do." They were right; 90 percent of the secretaries dutifully returned the memo to room 238.

When do people go off automatic pilot, realizing that they are following an inappropriate norm? Langer and her colleagues reasoned that anything that would make people stop and think about what they were doing would make them behave less mindlessly. One way of accomplishing this, they figured, was to

Mindless Conformity
obeying internalized social norms without deliberating about one's actions

make the memo look different from the hundreds of ones the secretaries normally received. They sent other secretaries the exact same memo except that it was signed, "Sincerely, John Lewis"—an aspect that was highly unusual at this university. Signing the memo in this way caused at least some of the secretaries to turn off their automatic pilot and think about what they were doing, thereby realizing that it was a silly request: In this condition, only 60 percent of the secretaries returned the memo.

The moral is, if you want people to do what you tell them, find a situation in which they normally comply with requests and do not give them much time to think about what they are doing—as in the case of the con artist in the parking lot. We turn now to another such situation that, though not illegal, is no less effective.

The Door-in-the-Face Technique

Suppose you have agreed to go door-to-door and ask people to donate money to the American Heart Association. Here is a good way to get people to give: First, ask people to donate a large amount of money, with the full expectation that they will refuse. When someone answers the door, you might say, "Hello, I'm asking for donations to the American Heart Association. Do you think you could donate $500?" Once people refuse, you immediately retreat to a more reasonable request: "Well, OK, but do you think you could donate $5?" This approach is called the **door-in-the-face technique,** because the first request is purposefully so large that people will want to slam the door shut. Several studies show that it works well in getting people to agree to the second, more reasonable request (Cialdini & Trost, 1998; Patch, Hoang, & Stahelski, 1997; Reeves et al., 1991; Wang, Brownstein, & Katzer, 1989).

For example, Robert Cialdini and his colleagues (1975) decided to see if they could get students to volunteer to chaperon problem adolescents on a two-hour trip to the zoo. When they approached students on a college campus, only 17 percent agreed to this request. In another condition, before asking people to go on the zoo trip the experimenter made a very large request. "We're currently recruiting university students to work as volunteer, nonpaid counselors at the County Juvenile Detention Center," the experimenter said. "The position would require two hours of your time per week for a minimum of two years. Would you be interested in being considered for one of these positions?" (Cialdini et al., 1975, p. 208). Not surprisingly, no one agreed to such a large time commitment. When students refused, the experimenter said, "Well, we also have another program you might be interested in," and went on to ask if they would chaperon the zoo trip. These students were three times more likely to agree to go on the zoo trip than people asked this smaller request alone (see Figure 8.7).

Why does the door-in-the-face technique work? The answer lies in the **reciprocity norm,** which says that if people do something nice for us, we should reciprocate by doing something nice for them (Cialdini & Trost, 1998; Cialdini, Green, & Rusch, 1992; Uehara, 1995). Salespeople and charities often capitalize on this tendency for people to follow the reciprocity norm mindlessly. They give us a small gift, such as greeting cards, personalized address labels, or free food to taste in the grocery store. Their plan is to make us feel obligated to reciprocate by buying their product or giving money to their cause (Church, 1993; James & Bolstein, 1992). To illustrate how strong the reciprocity norm is—and how mindlessly people follow it—one researcher chose some names at random out of the telephone book and sent each person a Christmas card, signed with his name

Door-in-the-Face Technique
a technique to get people to comply with a request, whereby people are presented first with a large request, which they are expected to refuse, and then with a smaller, more reasonable request, to which it is hoped they will acquiesce

Reciprocity Norm
a social norm stating that receiving anything positive from another person requires you to reciprocate (or behave similarly) in response

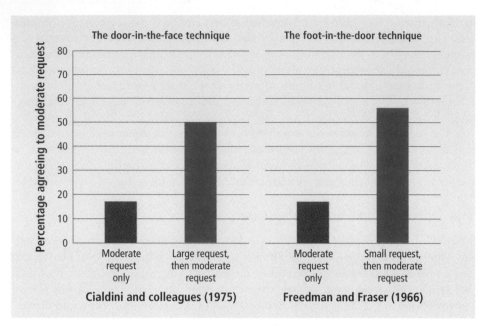

■ **FIGURE 8.7 Two ways to increase compliance with a request.** Both the door-in-the-face technique and the foot-in-the-door technique increase compliance to a moderate request. But which technique is likely to lead to the most *long-term* compliance, whereby people agree to repeated moderate requests? See the text for the answer. (Adapted from Cialdini et al., 1975; Freedman & Fraser, 1966)

(Kunz & Woolcott, 1976). Most people sent a card back to him, even though he was a complete stranger!

In the case of the door-in-the-face technique, the reciprocity norm is invoked when the person backs down from an extreme request to a moderate one. This puts pressure on us to reciprocate by moderating our position too—from an outright "No" to a "Well, OK, I guess so." We feel as if the requester is doing us a favor by changing his or her position, trying to meet us halfway; because of the reciprocity norm, we then feel obligated to return the favor and appear reasonable too.

One disadvantage of the door-in-the-face technique is that it is likely to be short-lived. Once people have agreed to the smaller request, they have met their obligation by meeting the requester halfway; therefore, they will not be more likely to agree to subsequent requests. Suppose, for example, that your goal is to get people to donate money to the American Heart Association on a regular basis. Once you have retreated from your request for $500 to a more reasonable request for $5 and your neighbor has met you halfway by agreeing, his or her obligation is over. If you ask for another $5 next month, he or she may well feel

■ Calvin tries the door-in-the-face-technique.

exploited, thinking, "This person sure is pushy. You'd think I'd get a break after being so reasonable last time." So what should you do if you want long-term compliance?

The Foot-in-the-Door Technique

For long-term compliance, you should use a different technique, called the **foot-in-the-door technique.** With this compliance technique, people are presented first with a small request, to which they are expected to acquiesce, followed by a larger request, to which it is hoped they will also acquiesce. The expression *foot-in-the-door* comes from salespeople who discovered that they were more likely to make a sale if they could get the customer to agree to an initial, smaller request, such as letting them into the house to display their products. This technique is thus the opposite of the door-in-the-face method. Does this technique work? To find out, Jonathan Freedman and Scott Fraser (1966) tested whether homeowners would agree to put up a large, obtrusive sign in their front yards that said "Drive Carefully." When someone came to their door and asked the homeowners to do this, only 17 percent agreed. But what if they had agreed earlier to a smaller request? The researchers first asked a different group of homeowners to sign a petition indicating that they were in favor of safe driving. Just about everyone agreed to this innocuous request. Two weeks later, a different individual approached these homeowners and asked them to put the sign in their front yard. Though the sign was just as big and obtrusive to these people as to those in the control group, who had not been contacted earlier, they were more than three times more likely to agree to put it in their front yard (see Figure 8.7).

The foot-in-the-door technique works for a very different reason than the door-in-the-face technique. Instead of invoking a reciprocity norm, it triggers a kind of informational social influence, whereby people gain information by complying with the first request. In this case, the information people gain is about themselves: By agreeing to the small request, people come to view themselves as the kind of person who helps out on important community issues. Once this self-image is in place, it makes people more likely to agree to the second, larger request, even when it comes later. Thus, if you want to get long-term compliance, it is better to instill the relevant self-image in people with the foot-in-the-door technique. If you are collecting money for the American Heart Association and want your neighbors to donate on a long-term basis, first ask them for a small amount, such as 50 cents or $1. If they agree, they will come to view themselves as the kind of people who give to this worthy cause, increasing the likelihood that future donations will be forthcoming (Burger, 1986; Cialdini, 1993; Cialdini, Trost, & Newsom, 1995; DeJong, 1979; Dillard, 1991; Dillard, Hunter, & Burgoon, 1984; Dolin & Booth-Butterfield, 1995; Gorassini & Olson, 1995).

Foot-in-the-Door Technique
a technique to get people to comply with a request, whereby people are presented first with a small request, to which they are expected to acquiesce, followed by a larger request, to which it is hoped they also acquiesce

Obedience to Authority

The kinds of compliance we have just discussed can be annoying; a skillful salesperson, for example, can make us buy something we don't really need. Rarely, however, do such instances of everyday compliance have life-or-death consequences. Yet unfortunately, another kind of conformity can be extremely serious and even tragic—obeying the orders of an authority figure to hurt or kill a fellow human being. Consider again the My Lai massacre. Why did the soldiers obey

■ Victims of the Holocaust, Nordhausen, April 1945. According to social psychologists, most of the German guards and citizens who participated in the Holocaust were not madmen but ordinary people exposed to extraordinary social influences.

Lieutenant Calley's order to kill the innocent villagers? We suspect that all of the reasons that people conform combined to produce this atrocity: The behavior of the other soldiers made the killing seem like the right thing to do (informational influence); the soldiers wanted to avoid rejection and ridicule from their peers (normative influence); and the soldiers followed the obedience to authority social norm too readily, without questioning or taking personal responsibility for what they were doing (mindless conformity). It was the power of these conformity pressures that led to the tragedy, not personality defects in the American soldiers. This makes the incident all the more frightening, because it implies that similar incidents can occur with any group of soldiers if similar conformity pressures are present.

The twentieth century has been marked by repeated atrocities and genocides—in Germany, Armenia, the Ukraine, Rwanda, Cambodia, Bosnia—and the list goes on. Thus, one of the most important questions facing the world's inhabitants is, where does obedience end and personal responsibility begin? The philosopher Hannah Arendt (1965) argues that most participants in the Holocaust were not sadists or psychopaths who enjoyed the mass murder of innocent people but ordinary citizens subjected to complex and powerful social pressures. She covered the trial of Adolf Eichmann, the Nazi official responsible for the transportation of Jews to the death camps, and concluded that he was not the monster that many people made him out to be but a commonplace bureaucrat like any other bureaucrat, who did what he was told without questioning his orders (Miller, 1995).

Our point is not that Eichmann or the soldiers at My Lai should be excused for the crimes they committed. The point is that it is too easy to explain their behavior as the acts of madmen. It is more fruitful—and indeed more frightening— to view their behavior as the acts of ordinary people exposed to extraordinary social influence. But how do we know whether this interpretation of the Holocaust and My Lai is correct? How can we be sure that it was social influence and not the work of evil people that produced these atrocities? The way to find out is to study social pressure in the laboratory under controlled conditions. We could take a sample of ordinary citizens, subject them to various kinds of social influence, and see to what extent they will conform and obey. Can an experimenter influence ordinary people to commit immoral acts, such as inflicting severe pain on an innocent bystander? Stanley Milgram (1963, 1974, 1976) decided to find out, in what has become the most famous series of studies in social psychology.

Imagine that you were a participant in one of Milgram's studies. You answer an ad in the paper asking for participants in a study on memory and learning. When you arrive at the laboratory, you meet another participant, a 47-year-old, somewhat overweight, pleasant-looking fellow. The experimenter explains that one of you will play the role of a teacher and the other a learner. You draw a slip of paper out of a hat and discover that you will be the teacher. It turns out that your job is to teach the other participant a list of word pairs (e.g., *blue-box, nice-day*) and then test him on the list. The experimenter instructs you to deliver an electric shock to the learner whenever he makes a mistake, because the purpose of the study is to examine the effects of punishment on learning.

You watch as the other participant—the learner—is strapped into a chair in an adjacent room and electrodes are attached to his arm. You are seated in front of a shock generator whose 30 switches deliver varying levels of shock in 15-volt increments, from 15 to 450 volts. There are labels accompanying these switches, from "Slight Shock," to "Danger: Severe Shock," to an ominous "XXX" next to the highest levels (see the photos on this page). The experimenter tells you that the first time the learner makes a mistake, you should give him a shock of 15 volts—the smallest amount—and then increase the amount by 15 volts for each subsequent mistake he makes. So that you will know what the shocks are like, the experimenter gives you a sample shock of 45 volts, which is rather painful.

You read the list of word pairs to the learner and then begin the testing phase. After announcing the first word of a pair, you give four possible answers; the learner responds by pressing one of four switches, which illuminates a light on the answer box in front of you. Everything begins smoothly, as the learner gets the first few right. Then he gets some wrong, and as instructed, you deliver the shocks. At this point, you are probably getting concerned about the number and severity of the shocks you will have to give. When you get to the 75-volt level, the learner, whom you can hear over an intercom, emits a painful "Ugh!" Perhaps you pause and ask the experimenter what you should do. "Please continue," he

■ Left: The shock generator used in the Milgram experiments. Right: The learner (an accomplice of the experimenter) is strapped into the chair, and electrodes are attached to his arm. (Adapted from Milgram, 1974)

TRANSCRIPT OF LEARNER'S PROTESTS IN MILGRAM'S OBEDIENCE EXPERIMENT

75 volts Ugh!

90 volts Ugh!

105 volts Ugh! (louder)

120 volts Ugh! Hey this really hurts.

135 volts Ugh!!

150 volts Ugh!!! Experimenter! That's all. Get me out of here. I told you I had heart trouble. My heart's starting to bother me now. Get me out of here, please. My heart's starting to bother me. I refuse to go on. Let me out.

165 volts Ugh! Let me out! (shouting)

180 volts Ugh! I can't stand the pain. Let me out of here! (shouting)

195 volts Ugh! Let me out of here. Let me out of here. My heart's bothering me. Let me out of here! You have no right to keep me here! Let me out! Let me out of here! Let me out! My heart's bothering me. Let me out! Let me out!

210 volts Ugh!! Experimenter! Get me out of here. I've had enough. I won't be in the experiment any more.

225 volts Ugh!

240 volts Ugh!

255 volts Ugh! Get me out of here.

270 volts (Agonized scream) Let me out of here. Let me out of here. Let me out of here. Let me out. Do you hear? Let me out of here.

285 volts (Agonized scream)

300 volts (Agonized scream) I absolutely refuse to answer any more. Get me out of here. You can't hold me here. Get me out. Get me out of here.

315 volts (Intensely agonized scream) I told you I refuse to answer. I'm no longer part of this experiment.

330 volts (Intense and prolonged agonized scream) Let me out of here. Let me out of here. My heart's bothering me. Let me out, I tell you. (Hysterically) Let me out of here. Let me out of here. You have no right to hold me here. Let me out! Let me out! Let me out of here! Let me out!

Instructions Used by Experimenter to Achieve Obedience

Prod 1: Please continue. *or* Please go on.

Prod 2: The experiment requires that you continue.

Prod 3: It is absolutely essential that you continue.

Prod 4: You have no other choice; you must go on.

The prods were always made in sequence: Only if prod 1 had been unsuccessful could prod 2 be used. If the subject refused to obey the experimenter after prod 4, the experiment was terminated. The experimenter's tone of voice was at all times firm, but not impolite. The sequence was begun anew on each occasion that the subject balked or showed reluctance to follow orders.

Special prods. If the subject asked whether the learner was likely to suffer permanent physical injury, the experimenter said:

Although the shocks may be painful, there is no permanent tissue damage, so please go on. [Followed by prods 2, 3, and 4 if necessary.]

If the subject said that the learner did not want to go on, the experimenter replied: Whether the learner likes it or not, you must go on until he has learned all the word pairs correctly. So please go on. [Followed by prods 2, 3, and 4 if necessary.]

■ **FIGURE 8.8** Transcript of the learner's protests in Milgram's obedience study (left). Transcript of the prods used by the experimenter to get people to continue giving shocks (right). (Adapted from Milgram, 1963, 1974)

responds. As the learner continues to make mistakes, you deliver a few more shocks. The learner protests, shouting, "Ugh! Experimenter! That's all! Get me out of here!" You look at the experimenter with grave concern. He tells you, "It is absolutely essential that you continue." (See Figure 8.8.)

What would you do? How many people do you think would continue to obey the experimenter and increase the levels of shock until they had delivered the maximum amount—450 volts?

When this question was posed to psychology majors at Yale University, they estimated that only about 1 percent of the population would go to this extreme. A sample of middle-class adults and a panel of psychiatrists made similar predictions. However, from our discussion of conformity thus far, you are probably not so optimistic. Whereas no one would have believed that such travesties as the Holocaust or My Lai could have occurred, they did. Like the soldiers at My Lai, most of Milgram's participants succumbed to the pressure of an authority figure. The average maximum amount of shock delivered was 360 volts, and 62.5 percent of the participants delivered the 450-volt shock—the maximum amount. A full 80 percent of the participants continued giving the shocks even after the learner, who earlier had mentioned that he had a heart condition, screamed, "Let me out of here! Let me out of here! My heart's bothering me. Let me out of here! . . . Get me out of here! I've had enough. I won't be in the experiment any more" (Milgram, 1974, p. 56).

It is important to note that the learner was actually an accomplice of the experimenter and playacted his role; he did not receive any actual shocks. It is equally important to note that the study was very convincingly done, so that people believed they really were shocking the learner. Here is Milgram's description of one participant's response to the teacher role:

> I observed a mature and initially poised businessman enter the laboratory smiling and confident. Within 20 minutes he was reduced to a twitching, stuttering wreck, who was rapidly approaching a point of nervous collapse. He constantly pulled on his earlobe, and twisted his hands. At one point he pushed his fist into his forehead and muttered, "Oh God, let's stop it." And yet he continued to respond to every word of the experimenter, and obeyed to the end. (Milgram, 1963, p. 377)

Why did so many research participants (who ranged in age from the twenties to the fifties and included blue-collar, white-collar, and professional workers) conform to the wishes of the experimenter, to the point where they (at least in their own minds) were inflicting great pain on another human being? Why were the college students, middle-class adults, and psychiatrists so wrong in their predictions about what people would do? Each of the reasons that explain why people conform combined in a dangerous way, causing Milgram's participants to obey—just as the soldiers did at My Lai. Let's take a close look at how this worked in the Milgram experiments.

The Role of Normative Social Influence

First, it is clear that normative pressures made it difficult for people to refuse to continue. As we have seen, if someone really wants us to do something, it can be difficult to say no. This is particularly true when the person is in a position of authority over us. Milgram's participants probably believed that if they refused to continue, the experimenter would be disappointed, hurt, or maybe even angry— all of which put pressure on them to continue. It is important to note that this study, unlike the Asch study, was set up so that the experimenter actively attempted to get people to conform, giving such stern commands as "It is absolutely essential that you continue." When an authority figure is so insistent that we obey, it is difficult to say no (Blass, 1991, 1993, 1996; Hamilton, Sanders, & McKearney, 1995; Meeus & Raaijmakers, 1995; Miller, 1986).

The fact that normative pressures were present in the Milgram experiments is clear from a variation of the study that he conducted. This time, there were three

■ **FIGURE 8.9   The results of different versions of the Milgram experiment.** Obedience is highest in the standard version, where the participant is ordered to deliver increasing levels of shock to another person (left panel). Obedience drops when other participants model disobedience or when the authority figure is not present (two middle panels). Finally, when no orders are given to increase the shocks, almost no participants do so (right panel). The contrast in behavior between the far-left and -right panels indicates just how powerful the social norm of obedience is. (Adapted from Milgram, 1974)

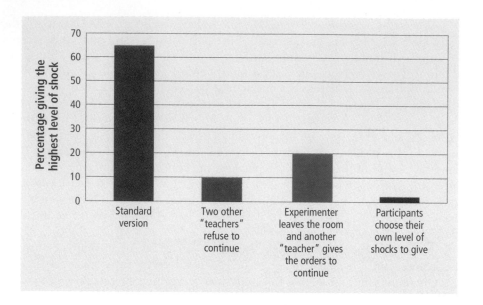

teachers, two of whom were confederates of the experimenter. One confederate was instructed to read the list of word pairs; the other, to tell the learner whether his response was correct. The (real) participant's job was to deliver the shocks, increasing their severity with each error, as in the original experiment. At 150 volts, when the learner gave his first vehement protest, the first confederate refused to continue, despite the experimenter's command that he do so. At 210 volts, the second confederate refused to continue. The result? Seeing their peers disobey made it much easier for the actual participant to disobey too. Only 10 percent of the participants gave the maximum level of shock in this experiment (see Figure 8.9). This result is similar to Asch's finding that people did not conform nearly so much when one accomplice bucked the majority and consistently gave the correct answer.

The Role of Informational Social Influence

Despite the power of the normative pressures in Milgram's original study, they are not the sole reason people complied. The experimenter was authoritative and insistent, but he was not pointing a gun at participants and telling them to "conform or else." The participants were free to get up and leave anytime they wanted to. Why didn't they, especially when the experimenter was a stranger they had never met before and probably would never see again?

As we saw earlier, when people are in a confusing situation and unsure of what they should do, they use other people to reach a definition of the situation. Informational social influence is especially powerful when the situation is ambiguous, when it is a crisis, and when the other people in the situation have some expertise. The situation faced by Milgram's participants was clearly confusing, unfamiliar, and upsetting. It all seemed straightforward enough when the experimenter explained it to them, but then it turned into something else altogether. The learner cried out in pain, but the experimenter told the participant that, while the shocks were painful, they did not cause any permanent tissue damage. The participant didn't want to hurt anyone, but he or she had agreed to be in the study and to follow the directions. When in such a state of conflict, it was only natural for the participants to use an expert—the experimenter—to help them decide what was the right thing to do (Darley, 1995; Hamilton, Sanders, & McKearney, 1995; Krakow & Blass, 1995; Meeus & Raaijmakers, 1995; Miller, 1986; Miller, Collins, & Brief, 1995).

Another version of the experiment that Milgram performed supports the idea that informational influence was operative. This version was identical to the original one except for three critical changes: First, the experimenter never said which shock levels were to be given, leaving this decision up to the teacher (the real participant). Second, before the study began the experimenter received a telephone call and had to leave the room. He told the participant to continue without him. Third, there was a confederate playing the role of an additional teacher, whose job was to record how long it took the learner to respond. When the experimenter left, this other teacher said that he had just thought of a good system: How about if they increased the level of shock each time the learner made a mistake? He insisted that the real participant follow this procedure.

Note that in this situation, the expertise of the person giving the commands has been removed: He was just a regular person, no more knowledgeable than the participants themselves. Because he lacked expertise, people were much less likely to use him as a source of information about how they should respond. As seen in Figure 8.9, in this version compliance dropped from 65 percent giving the maximum amount of shock to only 20 percent. (The fact that 20 percent still complied suggests that some people were so uncertain about what to do that they used even a nonexpert as a guide.)

An additional variation conducted by Milgram underscores the importance of authority-figures-as-experts in eliciting such conformity and obedience. In this variation, two experimenters gave the real participants their orders. At 150 volts, when the learner first cried out that he wanted to stop, the two experimenters began to disagree about whether they should continue the study. At this point, 100 percent of the participant-teachers stopped responding. Note that nothing the victim ever did caused all the participants to stop obeying; however, when the authorities' definition of the situation became unclear, the participants broke out of their conforming role.

Other Causes of Obedience

Both normative and informational social influences were very strong in Milgram's experiments. However, these reasons for complying still fall short of fully explaining why people acted so inhumanely. They seem to account for why people initially complied, but after it became increasingly obvious to people what they were doing to the learner, why didn't they realize that what they were doing was terribly wrong and stop? Just as the soldiers at My Lai persisted in killing the villagers long after it was obvious that they were unarmed and defenseless civilians, many of Milgram's participants pulled the shock levers time after time after time, despite the cries of anguish from a fellow human being.

To understand this continued compliance, we need to consider additional aspects of the situation. First, as we saw earlier, people sometimes follow the wrong social norm, such as the secretaries in Ellen Langer's study who followed the "do what memos tell you to do" norm, even when it was pretty pointless. Sometimes we are on automatic pilot and don't realize that the social norm we are following is inappropriate or nonapplicable to the situation we are in.

We don't mean to imply that Milgram's participants were completely mindless, or unaware of what they were doing. All were terribly concerned about the plight of the victim. The problem was that they were caught in a web of conflicting norms, and it was difficult to determine which one to follow. At the beginning of the experiment, it was perfectly reasonable to obey the norm that says, "Obey expert, legitimate authority figures." The experimenter was confident and knowledgeable, and the study seemed like it was a reasonable test of an interesting hypothesis. So why not cooperate and do as you are told?

But gradually the rules of the game changed, and this "obey authority" norm was no longer appropriate. The experimenter, who seemed so reasonable before, was now asking people to inflict great pain on their fellow participant. But once people are following one norm, it can be difficult to switch midstream, realizing that this norm is no longer appropriate and that another norm, "Do not inflict needless harm on a fellow human being," should be followed. For example, suppose the experimenter had explained, at the outset, that he would like people to deliver possibly fatal shocks to the other participant. How many people would have agreed? Very few, we suspect, because it would have been clear that this violated an important social and personal norm about inflicting harm on others. Instead, the experimenter pulled a kind of "bait-and-switch" routine, whereby he first made it look like an "obey authority" norm was appropriate and then gradually violated this norm (Collins & Brief, 1995).

It was particularly difficult for people to abandon the "obey authority" norm in the Milgram experiments, because of two key aspects of the situation. First, the experiment was fast-paced, preventing the participants from reflecting about what they were doing. They were busy recording the learner's responses, keeping track of which word pairs to test him on next, and determining whether his responses were right or wrong. Given that they had to attend carefully to these details and move along at a fast pace, it was difficult for them to realize that the norm that was guiding their behavior—cooperating with the authority figure—was, after a while, no longer appropriate. We suspect that if halfway through the experiment, Milgram's participants had been told to take a 15-minute break and go sit in a room by themselves, many more would have successfully redefined the situation and refused to continue.

Second, it is important to remember that the experimenter asked people to increase the shocks in very small increments. The participants did not go from giving a small shock to giving a potentially lethal one. Instead, at any given point they were faced with the decision about whether to increase the amount of shock they had just given by 15 volts. As we saw in Chapter 6, every time a person makes an important or difficult decision, dissonance is produced, with resultant pressures to reduce it. An effective way of reducing dissonance produced by a difficult decision is to decide that the decision was fully justified. But because reducing dissonance provides a justification for the preceding action, in some situations it makes a person vulnerable to pressures leading to an escalation of the chosen activity.

Thus, in the Milgram study, once the participants agreed to administer the first shock, it created pressure on them to continue to obey. As the participants administered each successive level of shock, they had to justify it in their own minds. Once a particular shock level was justified, it became very difficult for them to find a place where they could draw the line and stop. How could they say, in effect, "OK, I gave him 200 volts, but not 215—never 215!"? Each succeeding justification laid the groundwork for the next shock and would have been dissonant with quitting; 215 volts is not that different from 200, and 230 is not

> When you think of the long and gloomy history of man, you will find more hideous crimes have been committed in the name of obedience than in the name of rebellion.
>
> —C. P. Snow

■ These individuals are protesting the mayor of New York's proposed budget cuts to AIDS programs. The signs and masks silently reprimand bureaucrats for losing their sense of personal responsibility and hiding behind excuses of conformity and obedience.

that different from 215. Those who did break off the series did so against enormous internal pressure to continue (Darley, 1992; Gilbert, 1981; Meeus & Raaijmakers, 1995; Miller, Collins, & Brief, 1995; Modigliani & Rochat, 1995).

Mika Haritos-Fatouros (1988; Staub, 1989) reports that this incremental approach was used by the Greek military dictatorship of the late 1960s to train torturers. In his interviews with former torturers, Haritos-Fatouros learned that their first contact with political prisoners was to bring them food and "occasionally" give them some blows. Next, they were put on guard while others conducted torture sessions. Next, they would take part in a few group floggings or beatings. The last step, being in charge of a torture session, "was announced suddenly to the [man] by the commander-in-chief without leaving him any time for reflection" (1988, p. 1117).

Before leaving our discussion of the Milgram studies, we should mention one other possible interpretation of his results: Did the participants act so inhumanely because there is an evil side to human nature, lurking just below the surface, ready to be expressed with the flimsiest excuse? After all, it was socially acceptable to inflict harm on another person in the Milgram experiment; in fact, subjects were ordered to do so. Perhaps this factor allowed the expression of a universal aggressive urge. To test this hypothesis, Milgram conducted another version of his study. Everything was the same except that the experimenter told the participants that they could choose any level of shock they wished to give the learner when he made a mistake. Milgram gave people permission to use the highest levels, telling them that there was a lot to be learned from all levels of shock. This instruction should have allowed any aggressive urges to be expressed unchecked. Instead, the participants chose to give very mild shocks (see Figure 8.9). Only 2.5 percent of the participants gave the maximum amount of shock. Thus, the Milgram studies do not show that people have an evil streak that shines through when the surface is scratched. Instead, these studies demonstrate that social pressures can combine in insidious ways to make humane people act in an inhumane manner. Let us conclude this chapter with the words of Stanley Milgram:

Even Eichmann was sickened when he toured the concentration camps, but, in order to participate in mass murder he had only to sit at a desk and shuffle papers. At the same time the man in the camp who actually dropped Cyclon-B into the gas chambers is able to justify his behavior on the grounds that he is only following orders from above. Thus there is fragmentation of the total human act; no one man decides to carry out the evil act and is confronted with its consequences. The person who assumes full responsibility for the act has evaporated. Perhaps this is the most common characteristic of socially organized evil in modern society. (1976, pp. 183–184)

Summary

In this chapter, we focused on **conformity,** or how people change their behavior due to the real (or imagined) influence of others. We found that there are two main reasons people conform: because of informational and normative social influences.

Informational social influence occurs when people do not know what is the correct (or best) thing to do or say. This reaction typically occurs in new, confusing, or crisis situations, where the definition of the situation is unclear. People look to the behavior of others as an important source of information and use it to choose appropriate courses of action for themselves. Informational social influence usually results in **private acceptance,** wherein people genuinely believe in what other people are doing or saying.

People are most likely to use others as a source of information when the situation (and thus what they should do) is *ambiguous;* here a person is open to the influence of others. *Experts* are powerful sources of influence, since they typically have the most information about appropriate responses. A special type of ambiguous situation is a *crisis;* fear, confusion, and panic increase our reliance on others to help us decide what to do.

Using others as a source of information can backfire, however, as when people panic because others are doing so. **Contagion** occurs when emotions and behaviors spread rapidly throughout a group; one example is research on **mass psychogenic illness.** You can best resist the inappropriate use of others as a source of information by checking the information you are getting against your common sense and internal moral compass.

Normative social influence occurs for a different reason: We change our behavior to match that of others not because they seem to know better what is going on but because we want to remain a member of

the group, continue to gain the advantages of group membership, and avoid the pain of ridicule and rejection. We conform to the group's **social norms,** implicit or explicit rules for acceptable behaviors, values and attitudes. Normative social influence can occur even in unambiguous situations; people will conform to others for normative reasons even if they know that what they are doing is wrong. Normative social influence usually results in **public compliance** but not **private acceptance** of other people's ideas and behaviors.

Social impact theory specifies when normative social influence is most likely to occur, by referring to the *strength, immediacy,* and *number* of the group members. We are more likely to conform when the group is one we care about, when the group members are unanimous in their thoughts or behaviors, and when the group size is three or more. Failure to respond to normative social influence can be painful.

Normative social influence operates on many levels in social life: It influences our eating habits, hobbies, fashion, body image, and so on, and it promotes correct (polite) behavior in society.

We can resist inappropriate normative pressures by gathering **idiosyncrasy credits** over time, from a group whose membership we value. Further, **minority influence,** whereby a minority of group members influence the beliefs and behavior of the majority, can occur under certain conditions.

The reasons people conform can be applied to two kinds of everyday behavior: **compliance** and **obedience.** Sometimes people comply with inappropriate requests because of **mindless conformity,** whereby they operate as if on automatic pilot, never questioning or thinking about the social norms they are following.

Another compliance technique is the **door-in-the-face technique,** where a requester starts out with a big request in order to get people to agree to a second, smaller request. This technique works because of the **reciprocity norm;** when the requester retreats from the larger to the smaller request, it puts pressure on people to reciprocate by agreeing to the smaller request. The **foot-in-the-door technique** is also effective; here the requester starts out with a very small request to get people to agree to a larger request.

In the most famous series of studies in social psychology, Stanley Milgram examined the limits of **obedience to authority figures.** Informational and normative pressures combined to cause chilling levels of obedience, to the point where a majority of participants administered what they thought were near-lethal shocks to a fellow human being. In addition, the participants were caught in a web of conflicting social norms, and were asked to increase the level of shocks in small increments. After justifying to themselves that they had delivered one level of shock, it was very difficult for people to decide that a slightly higher level of shock was wrong.

Unfortunately, the conditions that produced such extreme antisocial behavior in Milgram's laboratory have been present in real-life tragedies, such as the Holocaust and the mass murders at My Lai in Vietnam.

If You Are Interested

Anderson, J. L., Crawford, C. B., Nadeau, J., & Lindberg, T. (1992). Was the Duchess of Windsor right? A cross-cultural review of the socioecology of ideals of female body shape. *Ethology and Sociobiology, 13,* 197–227.

Cialdini, R. B. (1993). *Influence: Science and practice* (3rd ed.). New York: HarperCollins. An extremely readable and entertaining account of research on conformity, with applications to everyday life.

Conroy, Pat. *The Lords of Discipline.* A story of conformity and disobedience set in a military academy (similar to the author's alma mater, The Citadel). The main character ultimately defies social norms, and puts his life on the line, to protect the lone African American cadet from the white students' violence.

Keneally, Thomas. *Schindler's List.* The compelling, true story of how one man protected and saved a thousand Polish Jews from certain death in Hitler's concentration camps. In particular, it traces his metamorphosis from a self-centered, opportunistic businessman to a compassionate humanitarian who bravely disobeys the Third Reich. The film based on this work won the Academy Award for Best Picture.

Milgram, S. (1974). *Obedience to authority: An experimental view.* New York: Harper & Row. A detailed description of the most famous studies in social psychology: those in which people were induced to deliver what they believed were lethal shocks to a fellow human being. Nearly 20 years after it was published, Milgram's book remains a poignant and insightful account of obedience to authority.

Priscilla, Queen of the Desert. A hilarious and heartwarming tale of three male transvestite entertainers who take their show on the road in the Australian outback. Needless to say, the townspeople have never seen such nonconformity. Remade in the United States as *To Wong Foo, with love, Julie Newmar,* starring Patrick Swayze and Wesley Snipes.

Salinger, J. D. *The Catcher in the Rye.* The classic "coming of age" novel, still a delight no matter how old you are. Follow teenager Holden Caulfield for a few days as he discourses on "the phonies" and other less than attractive aspects of adult conformity.

Sherif, M. (1936). *The psychology of social norms.* New York: Harper. An entertaining account of Sherif's study of informational social influence, wherein people judged how much a light was moving. It is still worth reading today.

The Age of Innocence. The tale of two star-crossed lovers (Daniel Day-Lewis and Michelle Pfeiffer), caught up in the constricting and unforgiving social norms of upperclass New York in the 1870s. Based on a novel by Edith Wharton.

Turner, J. C. (1991). *Social influence.* Pacific Grove, CA: Brooks/Cole. An in-depth account of social psychological research on social influence and conformity.

Twelve Angry Men. A gripping account of jury deliberations, this 1957 film stars Henry Fonda as the lone dissenter on the jury, desperately trying to convince his peers that their judgment of guilty in a murder case is wrong.

Wharton, Edith. *House of Mirth.* A huge bestseller upon its publication in 1905, this novel chronicles the elaborate and suffocating conformity of late nineteenth-century New York society, and how one young woman is destroyed by it.

CHAPTER 9

GROUP PROCESSES: INFLUENCE IN SOCIAL GROUPS

On a cold January day in 1961, John F. Kennedy was inaugurated as the thirty-fifth president of the United States. The author of a romance novel could not have written a better script: Kennedy was young, bright, and handsome; he came from a wealthy, well-connected family; he was a war hero. He had an intelligent, beautiful wife and two adorable children. In his election victory over Richard Nixon, Kennedy proved to be a master political strategist whose dashing good looks, wit, and charm were perfect for the new medium of television. He surrounded himself with advisers and cabinet members who were so talented that one writer dubbed them "the best and the brightest" (Halberstam, 1972).

As Kennedy took the helm in these heady times, he was immediately faced with a major foreign policy decision. Should he go ahead with a plan, initiated by the Eisenhower administration, to invade Cuba? It might seem odd, from our current 1990s perspective, that a small island off the coast of Florida was considered a major threat to U.S. security. This was in the midst of the cold war, however, and Fidel Castro, who had recently led a Communist revolution in Cuba (with the support of the Soviet Union), was definitely seen as a threat. The Eisenhower plan was to land a

■ J.F.K. and his advisers in 1961. When faced with an important policy decision, is it better for presidents to make up their minds on their own or to have a group of advisers make the decision?

small force of CIA-trained Cuban exiles on the Cuban coast, who would then instigate and lead a mass uprising against Castro.

Kennedy assembled his advisers to examine the pros and cons of such a plan. The group became a tightly knit, cohesive unit that brought a great deal of expertise to the topic. After a lengthy deliberation, they decided to go ahead, and on April 17, 1961, a force of 1,400 exiles invaded an area of Cuba known as the Bay of Pigs. The result was a complete disaster. Castro's forces captured or killed nearly all the invaders. Friendly Latin American countries were outraged that the United States had invaded one of their neighbors. Ironically, Cuba became even more closely allied with the Soviet Union as a result of the botched invasion. President Kennedy was later to ask, "How could we have been so stupid?" (Sorenson, 1966).

What went wrong? How could such a remarkably talented group of people, who met at great length to analyze the options, come up with such a disastrous plan? Most of us assume that groups make better decisions than individuals. However, in this case a committee of experts made an astonishing number of errors. Would President Kennedy have been better off making the decision by himself, without consulting his advisers?

Though you might think so, consider Kennedy's next foreign policy crisis, which also involved Cuba. The following October, the CIA discovered that the

Soviet Union had placed nuclear missiles in Cuba, a scant 90 miles from the coast of Florida. The missiles were aimed toward U.S. cities, and the resulting crisis brought us the closest we have ever come to World War III (Rhodes, 1995). Kennedy and his advisers deftly avoided war with a brilliant strategy of threats, naval blockades, and conciliatory gestures that succeeded in getting Khrushchev, the leader of the Soviet Union, to back down and remove the missiles. What did Kennedy and his advisers do differently this time? Did they simply stumble onto a good strategy, or had they learned from their earlier mistakes at the Bay of Pigs? In this chapter, we will focus on how people interact in groups, which is one of the oldest topics in social psychology (Cartwright & Zander, 1968; Davis, 1992, 1996; Levine & Moreland, 1990, 1998; Levine, Resnick, & Higgins, 1993; Steiner, 1974; Witte, 1996; Zander, 1979). ☐

Definitions: What Is a Group?

In its most basic form, a group can be defined as people who are in the same place at the same time. According to this broad definition, people do not have to be interacting with each other to be considered a group; they simply need to be in each other's presence. Examples include students taking a test together, passengers on an airplane, and fans at a baseball game. In the first section of this chapter, we will consider how being in such **nonsocial groups**—where two or more people are in the same place at the same time but are not interacting with each other—influences an individual's behavior. This is the most fundamental question concerning groups: What are the effects of the mere presence of other people?

> **Nonsocial Groups**
> groups in which two or more people are in the same place at the same time but are not interacting with each other (e.g., fans at a baseball game)

Though the effects of nonsocial groups are interesting, most social psychologists, when defining groups, mean something more than a bunch of people who happen to be occupying the same space. We think of people who have assembled for some common purpose, such as Kennedy's advisers working together to reach a foreign policy decision, citizens meeting to solve a community problem, or people who have gathered to blow off steam at a party. **Social groups** are defined as a collection of two or more people who interact with each other and are interdependent, in the sense that their needs and goals cause them to rely on each other (Cartwright & Zander, 1968; Lewin, 1948). By this definition, Kennedy and his advisers were a social group, whereas a group of strangers waiting for a bus together are a nonsocial group. In the latter part of this chapter we will discuss the structure and composition of social groups, how they make decisions, and how they deal with conflict.

> **Social Groups**
> groups in which two or more people are interacting with each other and are interdependent, in the sense that their needs and goals cause them to rely on each other

Nonsocial Groups: The Effects of the Mere Presence of Others

Do you act differently when other people are around? Simply being in the presence of other people can have a variety of interesting effects on our behavior. Let's begin by looking at how a group affects your performance on something with which you are very familiar—taking a test in a class.

Social Facilitation: When the Presence of Others Energizes Us

It is time for the final exam in your psychology class. You have spent countless hours studying the material, and you feel ready. When you arrive, you see that the exam is scheduled in a tiny, packed room. You squeeze into an empty desk, elbow to elbow with your classmates. The professor arrives and says that if any students are bothered by the close quarters, they can take the test by themselves in one of several smaller rooms down the hall. What should you do?

The question is whether the mere presence of others will affect your performance (Geen, 1989; Guerin, 1993; Kent, 1994; Sanna, 1992). The mere presence of other people can mean one of two things: (a) performing a task with co-workers who are doing the same thing you are or (b) performing a task in front of an audience who is not doing anything except observing you. The point is that in either case, you are not interacting with these other people—they're just present in the same room, constituting a nonsocial group. Does their presence make a difference? If you take your exam in the crowded room, will you feel nervous and have trouble recalling the material? Or will the presence of classmates motivate you to do even better than if you took the test alone?

To answer this question, we need to talk about insects—cockroaches, in fact. Believe it or not, a classic study using cockroaches as research participants suggests an answer to the question of how you should take your psychology test. Robert Zajonc and his colleagues (1969) built a contraption to see how cockroaches' behavior was influenced by the presence of their peers. The researchers placed a bright light (which cockroaches dislike) at the end of a runway and timed how long it took a roach to escape the light by running to the other end, where it could scurry into a darkened box (see the left-hand side of Figure 9.1). The question was, did roaches perform this simple feat faster when they were by themselves or when they were in the presence of other cockroaches?

You might be wondering how the researchers managed to persuade other cockroaches to be spectators. They did so by placing extra roaches in clear plas-

> "Mere social contact begets . . . a stimulation of the animal spirit that heightens the efficiency of each individual workman.
> —Karl Marx (1818–1883)

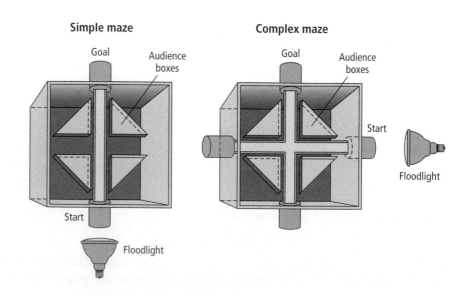

■ **FIGURE 9.1 Cockroaches and social facilitation.** In the maze on the left, cockroaches had a simple task: to go from the starting point down the runway to the darkened box. They performed this feat faster when other roaches were watching than when they were alone. In the maze on the right, the cockroaches had a more difficult task. It took them longer to solve this maze when other roaches were watching than when they were alone. (Adapted from Zajonc, Heingartner, & Herman, 1969)

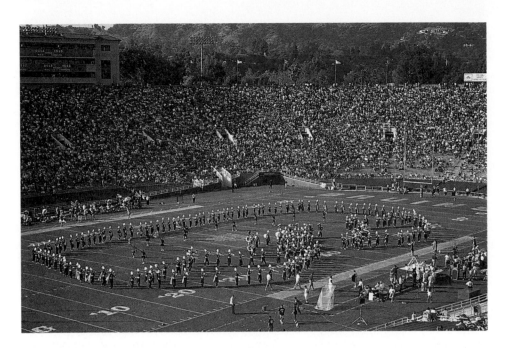

■ Research on social facilitation finds that people do better on a well-learned task when in the presence of others than when they are alone.

tic boxes next to the runway. These roaches were in the bleachers, so to speak, observing the solitary cockroach do its thing (see Figure 9.1). As it happened, the individual cockroaches performed the task faster when they were in the presence of other roaches than when they were by themselves.

Now, we would not give advice, based on one study that used cockroaches, on how you should take your psychology test. But the story does not end here. There have been dozens of studies on the effects of the mere presence of other people, involving human beings as well as other species, such as ants and birds (e.g., Bond & Titus, 1983; Guerin, 1986; Rajecki, Kidd, & Ivins, 1976; Zajonc & Sales, 1966). There is a remarkable consistency to the findings of these studies. As long as the task is a relatively simple, well-learned one—as escaping a light is for cockroaches—the mere presence of others improves performance. For example, in one of the first social psychology experiments ever done, Norman Triplett (1898) asked children to wind up fishing line on a reel, either by themselves or in the presence of other children. They did so faster when in the presence of other children than when by themselves.

Simple versus Difficult Tasks

Before concluding that you should stay in the crowded classroom to take your exam, we need to consider a different set of findings. Remember that we said the presence of others enhances performance on simple, well-learned tasks. Escaping a light is old hat for a cockroach, and winding fishing line on a reel is not difficult, even for a child. What happens when we give people a more difficult task to do and place them in the presence of others? To find out, Zajonc and his colleagues (1969) included another condition in the cockroach experiment. This time, the cockroaches had to solve a maze that had several runways, only one of which led to the darkened box (see the right-hand side of Figure 9.1). When working on this more difficult task, the opposite pattern of results occurred: The roaches took longer to solve it when other roaches were present than when they were alone.

Many other studies have also found that people and animals do worse in the presence of others when the task is difficult (e.g., Bond & Titus, 1983; Geen, 1989).

Arousal and the Dominant Response

In an influential article published in 1965, Robert Zajonc offered an elegant theoretical explanation for why the presence of others facilitates a well-learned or dominant response but inhibits a less practiced or new response. His argument has two steps: First, the presence of others increases physiological arousal (i.e., our bodies become more energized), and second, when such arousal exists, it is easier to do something that is simple (called the *dominant response*) but harder to do something complex or learn something new. Consider, for example, something that is second nature to you, such as riding a bicycle or writing your name. Arousal, caused by the presence of other people watching you, should make it even easier to perform these well-learned behaviors. But let's say you have to do something more complex, such as learning a new sport or working on a difficult math problem. Now arousal will lead you to feel flustered and do less well than if you were alone (Schmitt, Gilovich, Goore, & Joseph, 1986). This phenomenon became known as **social facilitation**, which is the tendency for people to do better on simple tasks and worse on complex tasks, when they are in the presence of others and their individual performance can be evaluated.

> **Social Facilitation**
> the tendency for people to do better on simple tasks and worse on complex tasks, when they are in the presence of others and their individual performance can be evaluated

Suppose, for example, that you decide to stop at a local pool hall and shoot a few racks. Will you perform better or worse if people are watching you wield your pool cue? As we have seen, it should depend on whether shooting pool is a simple or complex task for you. This is what James Michaels and his colleagues (1982) found in a field study conducted in the pool hall of a college student union. A team of four college students observed several different players from a distance, until they found ones who were experienced players (defined as those who made at least two-thirds of their shots) or novices (defined as those who made no more than one-third of their shots). The researchers then casually walked up to the table and watched people play. Imagine that you were one of the players. There you are, shooting a little pool, when suddenly you notice four strangers standing around watching you. What will happen to your performance? The prediction made by social facilitation theory is clear: If you have played so much pool that you would feel comfortable challenging Minnesota Fats, then the arousal caused by the presence of others should improve your game. If you are a novice and feel as if you have four thumbs, then the arousal caused by the presence of others should make your game go to pieces. This is exactly what Michaels and his colleagues (1982) found, as you can see in Figure 9.2. The experts made significantly more of their shots when they were observed, whereas the novices made significantly fewer shots.

Why the Presence of Others Causes Arousal

Why does the presence of others lead to arousal? Researchers have developed three theories to explain the role of arousal in social facilitation: Other people cause us to become particularly alert and vigilant; they make us apprehensive about how we're being evaluated; and they distract us from the task at hand.

The first explanation suggests that the presence of other people makes us more alert. When we are by ourselves reading a book, we don't have to pay attention to anything but the book; we don't have to worry that the lamp will ask

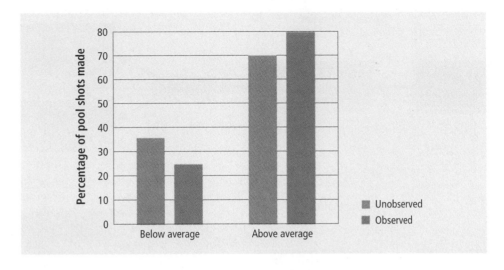

■ **FIGURE 9.2   Social facilitation in a pool hall.** When four observers watched novice players shoot pool, the players made fewer shots (left-hand bars). When the observers watched experienced players shoot pool, the players made more shots (right-hand bars). (Adapted from Michaels et al., 1982)

us a question. When someone else is in the room, however, we have to be alert to the possibility that he or she will do something that requires us to respond. Because other people are less predictable than lamps, we are in a state of greater alertness in their presence. This alertness, or vigilance, causes mild arousal. The beauty of this explanation (which is the one preferred by Robert Zajonc, 1980) is that it explains both the animal and the human studies. A solitary cockroach need not worry about what the cockroach in the next room is doing. However, it needs to be alert when in the presence of another member of its species—and the same goes for human beings.

The second explanation focuses on the fact that people are not cockroaches and often have other concerns about the presence of others. One concern involves what other people think of us. "Evaluation apprehension" refers to feeling worried and nervous (i.e., aroused) because you know that someone is making a judgment about how well you are doing. According to this explanation, what causes arousal is not the mere presence of others but the presence of others who are evaluating us (Bond, Atoum, & VanLeeuwen, 1996; Cottrell, 1968).

The third explanation centers on how distracting other people can be (Baron, 1986; Sanders, 1983). It is similar to Robert Zajonc's (1980) notion that we need to be alert when in the presence of others, except that it focuses on the idea that any source of distraction—be it the presence of other people or noise from the party going on in the apartment upstairs—will put us in a state of conflict, because it is difficult to concentrate on what we are doing. Trying to pay attention to two things at once produces arousal, as anyone knows who has ever tried to read the newspaper while his or her 2-year-old clamors for attention. Consistent with this interpretation, Robert Baron (1986) found that nonsocial sources of distraction, such as a flashing light, cause the same kinds of social facilitation effects as the presence of other people.

We have summarized research on social facilitation in the top half of Figure 9.3 (we will discuss the bottom half in a moment). This figure illustrates that there is more than one reason that the presence of other people is arousing. The consequences of this arousal, however, are the same: When people are around other people, they do better on tasks that are simple and well learned, but they do worse on tasks that are complex and require them to learn something new.

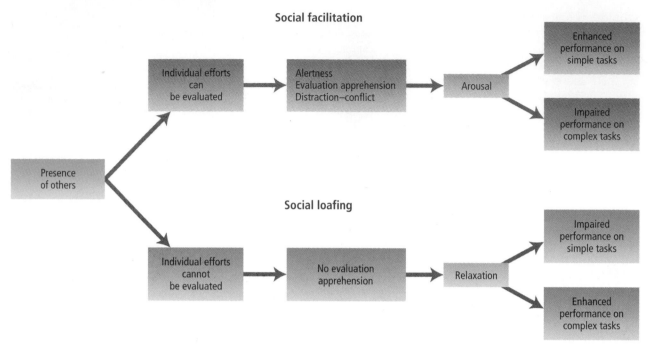

■ **FIGURE 9.3 Social facilitation and social loafing.**   The presence of others can lead to social facilitation or social loafing. The important variables that distinguish the two are evaluation, arousal, and the complexity of the tasks. (Adapted from Cottrell et al., 1968)

We can now conclude that you should take your psychology exam in the presence of your classmates, assuming you know the material well, so that it is relatively simple for you to recall it. The arousal produced by being elbow to elbow with your classmates should improve your performance. We can also conclude, however, that when you study for an exam—that is, when you learn new material—you should do so by yourself, and not in the presence of others. In this situation, the arousal caused by others will make it more difficult to concentrate on the new material.

Social Loafing: When the Presence of Others Relaxes Us

When you take your psychology exam, your individual efforts will be evaluated (you will be graded on the test). This is typical of the research on social facilitation we have reviewed: People are working on something (either alone or in the presence of others), and their individual efforts are easily observed and evaluated. Often when you are in the presence of others, however, your efforts cannot be distinguished from those of the people around you. Such is the case when you clap after a concert (no one can tell how loudly you are clapping) or when you play an instrument in a marching band (your instrument blends in with all of the others).

These situations are just the opposite of the kinds of social facilitation settings we have just considered. In social facilitation, the presence of others puts the spotlight on you, making you aroused. But if being with other people means we can merge into a group, becoming less noticeable than when we are alone, then we should become relaxed. Because no one can tell how well we are doing, we should feel less evaluation apprehension and thus be less willing to try our hardest. What happens then? Will this relaxation produced by becoming lost in the crowd lead to better or worse performance? Once again, the answer depends on whether we are working on a simple or a complex task.

Let's first consider simple tasks, such as trying to pull as hard as we can on a rope. The question of how working with others would influence performance on such a task was first studied in the 1880s by a French agricultural engineer, Max Ringelmann (1913). He found that when a group of men pulled on a rope, each individual exerted less effort than when he did it alone. A hundred years later, social psychologists Bibb Latané, Kipling Williams, and Stephen Harkins (1979) called this **social loafing,** which is the tendency for people to do worse on simple tasks but better on complex tasks, when they are in the presence of others and their individual performance cannot be evaluated. "Many hands make light work," as the proverb says, and social loafing in groups has since been found for a variety of simple tasks, such as clapping your hands, cheering loudly, and thinking of as many uses for an object as you can (Ingham, Levinger, Graves, & Peckham, 1974; Karau & Williams, 1993, 1995; Shepperd, 1993, 1995; Williams, Harkins, & Latané, 1981; Williams, Karau, & Bourgeois, 1993).

Pulling on a rope or cheering loudly are pretty simple tasks. What happens on complex tasks when our performance is lost in the crowd? Recall that when our performance in a group cannot be identified, we become more relaxed. Recall also this chapter's earlier discussion of the effects of arousal on performance: Arousal enhances performance on simple tasks but impairs performance on complex tasks. By the same reasoning, becoming relaxed should impair performance on simple tasks—as we have just seen—but improve performance on complex tasks. The idea is that when people are not worried about being evaluated, they are more relaxed and should thus be less likely to "clam up" on a difficult task and do it better as a result.

To test this idea, Jeffrey Jackson and Kipling Williams (1985) asked participants to work on mazes that appeared on a computer screen. The mazes were either simple or complex. Another participant worked on identical mazes on another computer in the same room. The researchers either said that they would evaluate each person's individual performance (causing evaluation apprehension)

Social Loafing
the tendency for people to do worse on simple tasks but better on complex tasks, when they are in the presence of others and their individual performance cannot be evaluated

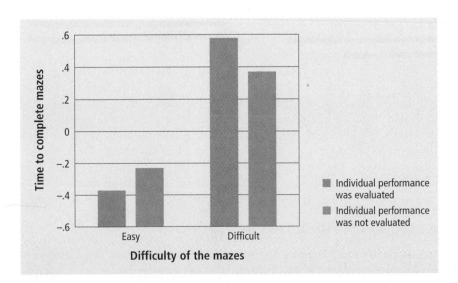

■ **FIGURE 9.4 Social loafing.** When students worked on easy mazes, those who thought their individual performance would not be evaluated did worse (they took more time to complete them, as seen on the left-hand side of the graph). When students worked on difficult mazes, those who thought their individual performance would not be evaluated did better (they took less time to complete them, as seen on the right-hand side of the graph). (Adapted from Jackson & Williams, 1985)

or stated that a computer would average the two participants' scores and no one would ever know how well any one person performed (reducing evaluation apprehension). The results were just as predicted. When people thought their score was being averaged with another person's they were more relaxed, and this relaxation led to better performance (i.e., less time) on the difficult mazes (see the right-hand side of Figure 9.4) but worse performance (i.e., more time) on the easy mazes (see the left-hand side of Figure 9.4).

Gender and Cultural Differences in Social Loafing: Who Slacks Off the Most?

Jane and John are working with several classmates on a class project, and no one can assess their individual contributions. Who is more likely to slack off and let the others do most of the work—John or Jane? If you said John, you are probably right. Steven Karau and Kipling Williams (1993) reviewed more than 150 studies of social loafing and found that the tendency to loaf is stronger in men than women. Why? Women tend to focus on the collective, caring more about the welfare of others in groups. Men, however, tend to be individualistic, focusing more on their own performance and less on the group (Cross & Madson, 1997; Eagly, 1987; Wood, 1987). This different emphasis on collectivism versus individualism, as you may recall from Chapter 5, also exists across cultures. Many Asian societies stress collectivism, whereas many Western societies stress individualism. Consequently, there are also cultural differences in social loafing: Karau and Williams (1993) found that the tendency to loaf is stronger in Western cultures than Asian cultures. It is important not to exaggerate these differences; there is evidence that women and men and members of Asian and Western cultures engage in social loafing when in groups (e.g., Chang & Chen, 1995). Nonetheless, social loafing is stronger in men and members of Western cultures.

> Which of us . . . is to do the hard and dirty work for the rest—and for what pay?
>
> –John Ruskin

To summarize, you need to know two things to predict whether the presence of others will help or hinder your performance—whether your individual efforts can be evaluated and whether the task is simple or complex. If your performance can be evaluated, the presence of others will make you alert and aroused. This will lead to social facilitation effects, where people do better on simple tasks but worse on complex tasks (see top of Figure 9.3). If your efforts cannot be evaluated (i.e., you are one cog in a machine), you are likely to become more relaxed. This leads to social loafing effects, where people do worse on simple tasks but better on complex tasks (see bottom of Figure 9.3).

These findings have numerous implications for the way in which groups should be organized. If you are a manager who wants your employees to work on a relatively simple problem, a little evaluation apprehension is not such a bad thing—it should improve performance. You shouldn't place your employees in groups where their individual performance cannot be observed, because social loafing (lowered performance on simple tasks) is likely to result. On the other hand, if you want your employees to work on a difficult, complex task, then lowering their evaluation apprehension—by placing them in groups in which their individual performance cannot be observed—is likely to result in better performance.

Deindividuation: Getting Lost in the Crowd

If you are going to make people more anonymous, you should be aware of other consequences of being a nameless face in the crowd. So far, we have discussed the ways in which a group affects how hard people work and how successfully they learn new things. Being in a group can also cause **deindividuation,** which is the loosening of normal constraints on behavior when people are in a crowd, leading to an increase in impulsive and deviant acts. In other words, getting lost in a crowd can lead to an unleashing of behaviors that we would never dream of doing by ourselves.

Throughout history, there have been many examples of groups of people committing horrendous acts that no individual would do on his or her own. In Chapter 8, we discussed the My Lai incident in the Vietnam War, where a group of soldiers systematically murdered hundreds of defenseless women, children, and elderly men. In Europe, mobs of soccer fans sometimes attack and bludgeon each other. In the United States, hysterical fans at rock concerts have trampled each other to death. And the United States has a shameful history of whites—often cloaked in the anonymity of white robes—lynching African Americans.

Brian Mullen (1986) content-analyzed newspaper accounts of 60 lynchings committed in the United States between 1899 and 1946 and discovered an interesting fact: The more people there were in the mob, the greater the savagery and viciousness with which they killed their victims. Similarly, Robert Watson (1973) studied 24 cultures and found that warriors who hid their identities before going into battle—for example, by using face and body paint—were significantly more likely to kill, torture, or mutilate captive prisoners than were warriors who did not hide their identities.

Fortunately, lynch mobs and wars are relatively uncommon. It is not so uncommon, however, to be asked to wear uniforms that make us look like everyone else in the vicinity, an arrangement that might also make us feel less accountable for our actions and hence more aggressive. Does wearing a uniform, such as on a sports team, increase aggressiveness? A study by Jurgen Rehm, Michael

Deindividuation
the loosening of normal constraints on behavior when people are in a crowd, leading to an increase in impulsive and deviant acts

■ The robes and hoods of the Ku Klux Klan cloak its members in anonymity; their violent and murderous behavior is consistent with research on deindividuation.

■ Exactly where, when, and by whom this photograph was taken is not known. It is a moving testament to the extraordinary evil of the deindividuated lynch mob.

Steinleitner, and Waldemar Lilli (1987) indicates that it does. They randomly assigned fifth-graders in German schools to various five-person teams and then watched the teams play handball against each other. In every game, all the members of one team wore orange shirts and all the members of the other team wore their normal street clothes. The children who wore the orange shirts (and were thus harder to tell apart) played the game significantly more aggressively than did the children who wore their everyday clothing (and were thus easier to identify).

Exactly what is it about deindividuation that leads to impulsive (and often violent) acts? Research by Steven Prentice-Dunn and Ronald Rogers (1989) and Ed Diener (1980) points to two factors: First, the presence of others (or the wearing of uniforms and disguises) makes people feel less accountable for their actions, because it reduces the likelihood that any individual will be singled out and blamed (Zimbardo, 1970). Second, the presence of others lowers self-awareness, thereby shifting people's attention away from their moral standards. As discussed in Chapter 5, it is difficult to focus inward on ourselves and outward on the world around us at the same time; thus, at any given point we vary in how self-aware we are (Carver & Scheier, 1981; Duval & Wicklund, 1975). One consequence of focusing on ourselves is that we are reminded of our moral standards, making us less likely to behave in some deviant or antisocial manner (e.g., "I believe that hurting other people is wrong; I'm not going to hit this guy"). If we are focusing on our environment, self-awareness will be low and we will be more likely to forget our moral standards and act impulsively.

Imagine that you are at a raucous college party at which everyone is dancing wildly to very loud music. How self-aware do you think you would be? The more stimulation there is in the environment to capture our attention, the lower our self-awareness, possibly leading to more deindividuation. Our attention is focused outward; we are paying less attention to our moral standards which can cause us to act in more impulsive ways (Harkins & Szymanski, 1987; Mullen & Baumeister, 1987; Prentice-Dunn & Rogers, 1989).

This example illustrates that not all impulsive acts are negative or violent. Although deindividuation often leads to an increase in aggression or violence, it can also lead to increases in other impulsive acts, such as dancing wildly at a

66 If you can keep your head when all about you are losing theirs . . .
—Rudyard Kipling

party or eating too much. But what determines whether deindividuation will lead to positive or negative behaviors? Being a good social psychologist, you can probably guess the answer: It depends on whether the context or situation encourages positive or negative behavior (Gergen, Gergen, & Barton, 1973; Johnson & Downing, 1979). If we feel angry toward someone, then being deindividuated will lower our inhibitions, making us more likely to act aggressively. If we are hungry and are at a party where there is lots of good food, then being deindividuated will increase the likelihood that we will eat the entire bowl of clam dip.

Social Groups: Joining, Leading, Working, and Competing

So far, we have considered how the mere presence of others can influence an individual's behavior. When we are in a group, however, we are usually more than passive observers of each other—we socialize, mingle, hobnob, and argue. In short, we interact with each other. We have already discussed many of the consequences of social interaction, such as attitude change (e.g., other people persuading us to change our attitudes—see Chapter 7) and conformity (e.g., other people pressuring us to change our behavior—see Chapter 8). We turn now to the situation in which people interact with and are interdependent on each other. Stop for a moment and think of the number of groups to which you belong. Don't forget to include your family, campus groups (such as fraternities, sororities, or political organizations), community groups (such as churches or synagogues), sports teams, and more temporary groups (such as your classmates in a small seminar). All of these count as social groups, because you interact with the other members and you are interdependent on them, in the sense that you influence them and they influence you.

Why do people join social groups? Forming relationships with other people fulfills a number of basic human needs. So basic, in fact, that there may be an innate need to belong to social groups. Roy Baumeister and Mark Leary (1995) argue that in our evolutionary past, there was a substantial survival advantage to establishing bonds with other people. People who bonded together were better able to hunt for and grow food, find mates, and care for children. Consequently, argue Baumeister and Leary, the need to belong has become innate and is present in all societies. Consistent with this view, people in all cultures are motivated to form relationships with other people and to resist the dissolution of these relationships.

Social groups have a number of other benefits. As we saw in Chapter 8, other people can be an important source of information, helping us to resolve ambiguity about the nature of the social world. Groups become an important part of our identity, helping us to define who we are—witness the number of times people wear shirts with the name of one of their groups (e.g., a fraternity or sorority) emblazoned on it. Groups also help establish social norms, which are explicit or implicit rules defining what is acceptable behavior. Given these significant functions, it is important to consider the nature of social groups and the ways in which they influence our behavior.

The Composition and Structure of Social Groups

What do the groups to which you belong have in common? They probably vary in size from two or three members to several dozen members. Most social groups, however, range in size from two to six members (Desportes & Lemaine, 1998; Levine & Moreland, 1998; McPherson, 1983). This is due in part to our definition of social groups as involving interaction between members. If groups become too large, you cannot interact with all the members; for example, the college or university that you attend is not a social group, because you are unlikely to meet and interact with every other student at that college or university.

Another important feature of social groups is that the members tend to be alike in age, sex, beliefs, and opinions (George, 1990; Levine & Moreland, 1998; Magaro & Ashbrook, 1985). There are two causes of homogeneity in groups. First, many groups tend to attract people who are already similar before they join (Feld, 1982). As we will see in Chapter 10, people are attracted to those who share their attitudes and thus are likely to recruit fellow group members who are similar to them. Second, groups tend to operate in ways that encourage similarity in the members (Moreland, 1987). This can happen in a number of important ways, some of which we discussed in Chapter 8, on conformity.

For example, as we saw in Chapter 8, a powerful determinant of our behavior is social norms. All societies have norms about which behaviors are acceptable, some of which are shared by all members of the society (e.g., formal laws against stealing) and some of which vary from group to group (e.g., rules about what to wear). If you belong to a fraternity or sorority, you can probably think of social norms present in your group, such as whether alcoholic beverages are consumed and how you are supposed to feel about rival fraternities or sororities. It is unlikely that these norms are shared by other groups to which you belong, such as your church or synagogue. Social norms are powerful determinants of our behavior, as shown by what happens if people violate them too often: They are shunned by other group members and, in extreme cases, pressured to leave the group (Schachter, 1951; see Chapter 8).

Roles

shared expectations in a group about how particular people are supposed to behave

Most groups also have well-defined **roles,** which are shared expectations in a group about how particular people are supposed to behave. Whereas norms specify how all group members should behave, roles specify how people who occupy certain positions in the group should behave. A boss and an employee in a business occupy different roles and are expected to act in different ways in that setting. Like social norms, roles can be very helpful, because people know what to expect from each other. When members of a group follow a set of clearly defined roles, they tend to be satisfied and perform well (Bastien & Hostager, 1988; Barley & Bechky, 1994).

There are, however, two potential costs to social roles. First, people can get so "into" a role that their personal identities and personalities get lost. Suppose, for example, that you agreed to take part in a two-week psychology experiment in which you were randomly assigned to play the role of a prison guard or a prisoner in a simulated prison. You might think that the role you were assigned to play would not be very important; after all, everyone knows that it is only an experiment and that people are just pretending to be guards or prisoners. Philip Zimbardo and his colleagues, however, had a different hypothesis. They believed that social roles can be so powerful that they "take over" our personal identities and we become the role we are playing. To see if this is true, Zimbardo and colleagues conducted an unusual study. They built a mock prison in the basement of the psychology department at Stanford University and paid students to play the role of guard or prisoner (Haney, Banks, & Zimbardo, 1973). The role students played was determined by the flip of a coin. The guards were outfitted with a uniform of khaki shirts and pants, a whistle, a police nightstick, and reflecting sun-

■ Philip Zimbardo and his colleagues randomly assigned students to play the role of prisoner or guard in a mock prison. The students assumed these roles all too well. Those playing the role of guard became quite aggressive, whereas those playing the role of prisoner became passive, helpless, and withdrawn. People got "into" their roles so much that their personal identities and sense of decency somehow got lost.

glasses, and the prisoners were outfitted with a loose-fitting smock with an identification number stamped on it, rubber sandals, a cap made from a nylon stocking, and a locked chain attached to one ankle.

The researchers planned to observe the students for two weeks, to see whether they began to act like real prison guards and prisoners. As it turned out, the students quickly assumed these roles—so much so that the researchers had to end the experiment after only six days. Many of the guards became quite abusive, thinking of creative ways of verbally harassing and humiliating the "prisoners." The prisoners became passive, helpless, and withdrawn. Some prisoners, in fact, became so anxious and depressed that they had to be released from the study earlier than the others. Remember, everyone knew that they were in a psychology experiment and that the "prison" was only make-believe. The roles of guard and prisoner were so compelling and powerful, however, that this simple truth was often overlooked. People got "into" their roles so much that their personal identities and sense of decency somehow got lost.

If social roles are so powerful in make-believe prisons, imagine how powerful they are in real prisons and in other institutions with well-defined roles. The roles we assume can shape our behavior in powerful and unexpected ways. Parents of young children, for example, can often be heard exclaiming, "I swore I would never yell at my child in the way my parents yelled at me, and yet I just did!"

The second drawback of social roles is that there is a cost to acting inconsistently with the expectations associated with them. Try telling your boss, the next time you report to your job, that you would just as soon sit back and tell him or her what to do that day. Role expectations are especially problematic when they are arbitrary or unfair, such as societal expectations based on people's gender. All societies have expectations about how people who occupy the roles of women and men should behave. As we discuss in Chapter 13, these role expectations can constrain the way in which people behave and result in negative attitudes toward "uppity" people who decide to act inconsistently with how they are expected to behave. Try It! on page 342 describes a way you can experience this for yourself.

Try It!

Role Violation

Pick a behavior that is part of gender roles in your culture and deliberately violate it. For example, if you are male in the United States you might decide to put on make-up or carry a purse to your next class. If you are female, you might decide to dress like a male to a formal occasion, by wearing a jacket and tie.

Keep a journal describing how others react to you. More than likely, you will encounter a good deal of social disapproval, such as people staring at you or questioning your behavior. For this reason, you want to avoid role violations that are too extreme—consider what happened to Larry Goodwin after wearing women's clothing (see the picture below).

The social pressure that is brought to bear on people who do not conform to their roles explains why it can be so difficult to break out of the roles to which we are assigned, even when they are arbitrary. Of course, there is safety in numbers; when enough people violate role expectations, others do not act nearly so negatively and the roles begin to change. For example, it is now much more acceptable for men to wear earrings than it was 20 years ago. To illustrate this safety in numbers, enlist the help of several same-sex friends and violate the same role expectation together. Again, note carefully how people react to you. Did you encounter more or less social disapproval in the group than you did as an individual?

In many cultures, for example, women are expected to assume the role of wife and mother and have limited opportunities to pursue other careers. In the United States and other countries, these expectations are changing and women have more opportunities than ever before. Conflict can result, however, when expectations change for some roles but not for others occupied by the same person. In India, for instance, women traditionally were permitted to occupy only the

■ People are often punished for violating the expectations associated with their roles, even when these expectations are arbitrary. A man who wears women's clothing, for example, is likely to encounter a good deal of criticism. The man in this picture, Larry Goodwin, is a 51-year-old, heterosexual man who has been married for 29 years and has two children. The only part of the traditional male role that he violates is that he loves to wear women's clothing. He has paid dearly for this role violation—his house has been vandalized, he has been arrested, and he nearly lost his job (Grove, 1997).

roles of wife, mother, agricultural laborer, and domestic worker. In recent years, the rights of women have improved and women have more opportunities in other professions. Many men, however, still expect their wives to assume the traditional role of child rearer and household manager, even if their wives have other careers. Conflict results, because many women are expected to "do it all"—maintain a career, raise the children, clean the house, and attend to their husband's needs (Brislin, 1993). Such conflicts are not limited to India; we suspect that many American readers will find this kind of role conflict all too familiar.

Gender roles are not something we choose or are assigned by others; our gender is determined at conception. Most other roles in social groups are not so predetermined: They are positions that we choose or work for and earn. You choose to occupy the role of student in your social psychology class, for example, and with hard work you might someday occupy the role of teacher or lawyer or president of your own corporation. Perhaps the most important role in any social group is that of the leader. The performance of a group, and sometimes even its very survival, often depends on the abilities of the leader of the group. It is no surprise, then, that a considerable amount of research has been devoted to the topic of who makes the best leader.

Leadership

The question of what makes a great leader has intrigued psychologists, historians, and political scientists for some time (Bass, 1990, 1997; Billsberry, 1996; Burns, 1978; Chemers & Ayman, 1993; Fiedler, 1967; Hollander, 1985; Klenke, 1996; Simonton, 1987). One of the best-known answers to this question is the great person theory, which maintains that certain key personality traits make a person a good leader, regardless of the nature of the situation facing the leader.

If the great person theory is true, then we ought to be able to isolate the key aspects of personality that make someone a great leader. Is it a combination of intelligence, charisma, and courage? Is it better to be introverted or extraverted? Should we add a dollop of ruthlessness to the mix as well, as Niccoló Machiavelli suggested in 1513, in his famous treatise on leadership, *The Prince*? Or do highly moral people make the best leaders?

The relationships between specific personal characteristics and leadership are summarized in the text accompanying the photos on the next page. Some modest relationships have been found; for example, leaders tend to be slightly more intelligent than nonleaders, more driven by the desire for power, more charismatic, more socially skilled, more adaptive and flexible (Albright & Forziati, 1995; Kenny & Zaccaro, 1983; House, Spangler, & Woycke, 1991; Lord, DeVader, & Alliger, 1986; Whitney, Sagrestano, & Maslach, 1994; Zaccaro, Foti, & Kenny, 1991). What is most telling from the summary, however, is the absence of strong relationships. Surprisingly few personality characteristics correlate with leadership effectiveness, and the relationships that have been found tend to be modest. For example, Simonton (1987, 1992) gathered information about 100 personal attributes of all U.S. presidents, such as their family backgrounds, educational experiences, occupations, and personalities. Only three of these variables—height, family size, and the number of books a president published before taking office—correlated with how effective the presidents were in office (as rated by historians). The other 97 characteristics, including personality traits, were not related to leadership effectiveness at all.

Great Person Theory
the theory that certain key personality traits make a person a good leader, regardless of the nature of the situation facing the leader

There is properly no history, only biography.
–Ralph Waldo Emerson (1929)

Intelligence	U.S. Supreme Court Justice Ruth Bader Ginsburg	There is a modest but positive relationship between intelligence and leadership effectiveness (Simonton, 1985; Stogdill, 1974). Judge Ginsburg finished tied for first in her class at Columbia Law School and has had a very distinguished career as a lawyer and judge. She was appointed to the Supreme Court in 1993 by President Clinton.
Morality	Queen Victoria of Great Britain	An examination of historical records showed that in a sample of 600 monarchs, the ones who became the most eminent were those who were either highly moral or highly immoral (Simonton, 1984). This suggests that there are two roads to eminence: having great moral virtue or having Machiavellian deviousness. Queen Victoria of England stood for moral propriety and good manners, to the point where her name came to stand for restraint, politeness, and decorum.
Motivation	Colonel Mu'ammar al-Qaddafi of Libya	Leaders who have a strong power motive (self-direction, a concern for prestige, abundant energy) are somewhat more likely to be effective (McClelland, 1975; Sorrentino & Field, 1986; Winter, 1987). Colonel Qaddafi is generally considered to be a leader with a great need for power. He has managed to remain leader of Libya for a number of years; though whether he is an effective leader is quite another matter.
Family Size	Franklin Delano Roosevelt, thirty-second U.S. president	U.S. presidents who came from small families are more likely to have become great leaders, as rated by historians (Simonton, 1987). President Franklin Roosevelt, generally considered to be one of the finest U. S. presidents, was an only child.
Height	Abraham Lincoln, sixteenth U. S. president	There is a modest correlation between a man's height and the likelihood that he will become the leader of a group (Stogdill, 1974). In the United States, the taller candidate has won every presidential election but two: Richard Nixon versus George McGovern in 1972 and Jimmy Carter versus Gerald Ford in 1976. In 1992, Bill Clinton had a quarter-inch height advantage over George Bush. In 1996, he had a one-half inch advantage over Robert Dole. Once in office, tall presidents, such as Abraham Lincoln, are more likely to be great leaders, as rated by historians (Simonton, 1987; 1992).
Personality Traits	Malcolm X, minister of the Nation of Islam	The great charisma of Malcolm X seems to have contributed to his rise to leadership in the Nation of Islam. However, there is surprisingly little evidence that traits such as charisma, dominance, and self-confidence will predict who will become leaders.

■ **Leadership and Personality Traits.** Some modest relationships between characteristics and leadership performance have been found, but in general, it is difficult to predict how good a leader will be from his or her personal attributes alone.

As you undoubtedly know by now, one of the most important tenets of social psychology is that to understand social behavior, it is not enough to consider personality traits alone—we must take the social situation into account as well. The inadequacy of the great person theory does not mean that personal characteristics are irrelevant to good leadership. Instead, being good social psychologists, we should consider both the nature of the leader and the situation in which he or she is leading. This view of leadership states that it is not enough to be a great person; you have to be the right person at the right time in the right situation.

A business leader, for example, can be highly successful in some situations but not in others. Consider Steve Jobs, who, at age 21, founded the Apple Computer company with Stephen Wozniak. Jobs was anything but an "MBA" type of corporate leader. A product of the 1960s counterculture, he turned to computers only after sampling LSD, traveling to India, and living on a communal fruit farm. In the days when there were no personal computers, Jobs's offbeat style was well suited to starting a new industry. Within five years, he was the leader of a billion-dollar company. Jobs's unorthodox style was ill-suited, however, to the fine points of managing a large corporation in a competitive market. Apple began to suffer in competition with other companies, and in 1985 Jobs was forced to leave Apple by John Sculley, a man who Jobs himself had hired to run the company (Patton, 1989). Interestingly, the Apple company now faces some of the same technological challenges it did at its inception, having to revamp the operating system for its Macintosh computers and regain market share. Who have they hired to advise them in this new challenge? Steve Jobs, of course (Markoff, 1996).

Several theories of leadership focus on characteristics of the leader, his or her followers, and the situation (e.g., Dansereau, Graen, & Haga, 1975; Dienesch & Liden, 1986; Hollander, 1958; House, 1971; Vroom & Yetton, 1973). The best-known theory of this type is Fred Fiedler's (1967, 1978) contingency theory of leadership, which argues that leadership effectiveness depends both on how task-oriented or relationship-oriented the leader is and on the amount of control and influence the leader has over the group. Fiedler's first assumption is that there are two kinds of leaders, those who are task-oriented and those who are relationship-oriented. The task-oriented leader is concerned more with getting the job done than with the feelings of and relationships between the workers. The relationship-oriented leader is concerned primarily with the feelings of and relationships between the workers.

The crux of Fiedler's contingency theory is that neither type of leader is always more effective than the other; it depends on the nature of the situation—specifically, on the amount of control and influence a leader has over the group. In "high-control" work situations, the leader has excellent interpersonal relationships with subordinates, his or her position in the company is clearly perceived as powerful, and the work needing to be done by the group is structured and well defined. In "low-control" work situations, the opposite holds—the leader has poor relationships with subordinates and the work needing to be done is not clearly defined. As seen in Figure 9.5, task-oriented leaders are most effective in situations that are either very high or very low in control. When situational control is very high, people are happy, everything is running smoothly, and there is no need to worry about people's feelings and relationships. The leader who pays attention only to the task will get the most accomplished. When situational control is very low, the task-oriented leader is best at taking charge, imposing some order on a confusing, ill-defined work environment. Relationship-oriented leaders, however, are most effective in situations that are moderate in control. Under

Contingency Theory of Leadership
the theory that leadership effectiveness depends both on how task-oriented or relationship-oriented the leader is and on the amount of control and influence the leader has over the group

Task-Oriented Leader
a leader who is concerned more with getting the job done than with the feelings of and relationships between the workers

Relationship-Oriented Leader
a leader who is concerned primarily with the feelings of and relationships between the workers

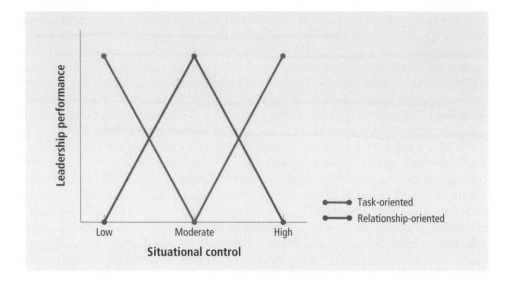

■ **FIGURE 9.5 Fiedler's contingency theory of leadership.**   According to Fiedler, task-oriented leaders perform best when situational control is high or low, whereas relationship-oriented leaders perform best when situational control is moderate.

> ❝Leadership cannot really be taught, it can only be learned.
> –Harold Geneen, 1984

these conditions, the wheels are turning fairly smoothly but some attention to the squeakiness caused by poor relationships and hurt feelings is needed. The leader who can soothe such feelings will be most successful.

Fiedler's contingency theory has been tested with numerous groups of leaders, including business managers, college administrators, military commanders, and postmasters. These studies have generally been supportive, conforming well to the pattern shown in Figure 9.5 (Chemes, 1987; Chemers, Hays, Rhodewalt, & Wysocki, 1985; Peters, Hartke, & Pohlmann, 1985; Schriesheim, Tepper, & Tetrault, 1994; Strube & Garcia, 1981).

Gender and Leadership

When we described the task-oriented and relationship-oriented types of leaders, did they remind you of anyone? Be honest: Did it seem like men are more likely to be task-oriented, whereas women are more likely to be relationship-oriented? If so, you have plenty of company: Stereotypes about the leadership styles of women and men abound. Women are thought to care more about the feelings of their co-workers, to be more interpersonally skilled than men, and thus to be more relationship-oriented. Men are often characterized as controlling, Machiavellian leaders who don't even notice what their co-workers are feeling, much less care about those feelings (Deaux & LaFrance, 1998; Klenke, 1996). Is there any truth to these stereotypes?

To find out, Alice Eagly and her colleagues examined hundreds of studies to answer questions about the leadership styles of women versus men (Eagly & Johnson, 1990; Eagly & Karau, 1991; Eagly, Karau, & Makhijani, 1995; Eagly, Makhijani, & Klonsky, 1992). She has found that, consistent with the stereotype, women do tend to lead more democratically than men, possibly because women tend to have better interpersonal skills, allowing them to seek input from group members when making a decision and to gracefully disregard this input when necessary (Eagly & Johnson, 1990).

Does this mean that women make better leaders than men? As we would expect from the contingency theory of leadership, it depends on the nature of the situation. Alice Eagly, Steven Karau, and Mona Makhijani (1995) found that ~~women tend to be better leaders~~ (as measured by both objective measures of performance and by ratings of co-workers) ~~in jobs that require interpersonal skills, such as jobs in educational settings. Men tend to be better leaders in jobs that require the ability to direct and control people, such as jobs in the military.~~

Before we make too much of this finding, however, we must add some cautionary notes. First, the differences are not that large. Plenty of women are able to adopt the "masculine" leadership style, especially when the job requires it (Eagly & Johnson, 1990). And plenty of men have good interpersonal skills. Further, all studies of leadership effectiveness are plagued by the following problem: Do the findings reflect actual differences in ability, or people's stereotypes about the leader? If a woman is viewed as a less effective leader than a man, for example, is it because she really is a worse leader, or because her co-workers are using a different yardstick to measure her performance?

An old adage says that, because of sex discrimination, a woman has to be "twice as good as a man" in order to advance. Unfortunately, there do seem to be differences in the ways female and male leaders are evaluated. If a woman's style of leadership is stereotypically "masculine," in that she is autocratic, "bossy," and task-oriented, she is evaluated more negatively than men who have the same style are (Eagly et al., 1992). This is especially true if it is men who are doing the evaluating. For example, Doré Butler and Florence Geis (1990) instructed male and female accomplices to assume leadership roles in groups of students attempting to solve a business problem. Both the male and the female leaders were assertive but cordial, taking charge of the group discussion. How did the other members of the group react to these assertive leaders? The results were discouraging. When a man took charge of the group and acted assertively, the group members reacted favorably. When a woman acted in the same fashion, the group members reacted much more negatively—especially the males. It appears that many men are uncomfortable with women who use the same leadership techniques that men typically use.

> "Old-fashioned ways which no longer apply to changed conditions are a snare in which the feet of women become entangled.
> —Jane Addams, 1907

Group Decisions: Are Two (or More) Heads Better Than One?

One of the main functions of groups is to solve problems and make decisions. In the American judicial system, many verdicts are determined by groups of individuals (juries), not single individuals (for a discussion of jury decision making, see "Social Psychology in Action 3: Social Psychology and the Law"). The Supreme Court is made up of nine justices, not a single, sage member of the judiciary. Similarly, governmental and corporate decisions are often made by groups of people who meet to discuss the issues, and all U.S. presidents have a cabinet and the National Security Council to advise them.

© 1995 SALLY FORTH. Greg Howard. Reprinted with special permission of King Features Syndicate.

■ Would you say that Sally's boss is a task-oriented or relationship-oriented leader?

> "Nor is the people's judgement always true: The most may err as grossly as the few.
>
> —John Dryden

Is it true that two (or more) heads are better than one? Most of us assume the answer is yes. A lone individual may be subject to all sorts of whims and biases, whereas several people together can exchange ideas and reach better decisions. Many common assumptions about the value of group decision making, however, turn out not to be true. Sometimes, two heads are not better than one, or at least no better than two heads working alone (Castellan, 1993; Hackman & Morris, 1978; Littlepage, 1991; McGrath, 1984; Tindale, 1993). At the beginning of this chapter, for example, we saw that President Kennedy and his advisers, after deliberating at length, made a foolhardy decision to invade Cuba. Under what conditions will groups make good versus bad decisions?

Whether a group will outperform individuals depends on the type of task with which it is faced. One important question is whether a group is working on a **divisible versus a unitary task** (Steiner, 1972). Divisible tasks are those that can be broken down into different subtasks and assigned to individual members of a group, such as building a house: A carpenter builds the frame and walls, a plumber does the plumbing, and an electrician does the wiring. Obviously, the quality of the group decisions will depend on how well individuals are assigned to the subtasks. If the electrician is assigned to do the plumbing and the plumber is assigned to do the wiring, problems will result.

Unitary tasks are those in which no division of labor is feasible, such as a group working together to push a car out of a ditch or deciding whether to invade Cuba. The key to problem solving on unitary tasks is how each member's outputs are combined to achieve the group's goal. How individual outputs are combined depends on a further distinction between types of unitary tasks: An **additive task** is one in which all group members perform basically the same job and the final product is a sum of all their contributions, such as the total amount of noise made by a group of cheerleaders. As we have seen, social loafing is likely to occur in this type of situation. Thus, a group of four people performing an additive task can be less successful than four individuals working alone, if some members of the group engage in social loafing (see Figure 9.6 on pages 350 and 351).

On a **conjunctive task,** group performance is defined by the skills of the least capable member of the group, or "the weak link in the chain." A mountain-climbing team can climb only as fast as its slowest member, a chamber music group can produce a sound only as good as the least gifted musician, and a doubles tennis team can play only as well as the least proficient member of the pair. Individuals can usually outperform groups working on conjunctive tasks, because the weakest member of the group brings the performance of the group down to his or her level (Steiner & Rajaratnam, 1961; see Figure 9.6, on pages 350 and 351). A more common type of group task is a **disjunctive task, in which group** performance is defined by how well the best member of the group does. Consider a group trying to solve a difficult math problem. If there is one mathematician in the group who knows how to solve the problem, he or she can provide the others with the answer; thus, one gifted individual can dominate the group, raising the performance of average and below-average individuals to his or her level.

In general, groups will do better if they work on a disjunctive task and rely on the person with the most expertise (Davis & Harless, 1996). Clearly, this would be a better strategy than relying on people with little knowledge about how to solve the problem. As straightforward as this sounds, however, it is not always easy to accomplish. A group working on a disjunctive task will perform well only if the most talented member can convince the others that he or she is right—which is not always easy, given that many of us bear a strong resemblance

---

Divisible versus a Unitary Task
divisible tasks are those that can be broken down into different subtasks performed by individual members, whereas unitary tasks are those in which no division of labor is feasible

Additive Task
a task in which all group members perform the same job and the final product is a sum of all their contributions, such as the total amount of noise made by a group of cheerleaders

Conjunctive Task
a group task in which performance depends on how well the least talented member does

Disjunctive Task
a group task in which performance depends on how well the most talented member does

■ In conjunctive tasks, group performance is defined by the skills of the least talented member of the group. A team of mountain climbers, for example, can go only as fast as its least proficient member.

■ Additive tasks are those in which group members' contributions are each added together to create the group product.

to mules when it comes to admitting we are wrong (Henry, 1995; Laughlin, 1980; Maier & Solem, 1952). Several factors, as we will see, can make groups actually do worse than individuals on disjunctive tasks.

Process Loss

You undoubtedly know what it's like to try to convince a group to follow your idea, be faced with opposition and disbelief, and then have to sit there and watch the group make the wrong decision. Ivan Steiner (1972) called this phenomenon **process loss**, defined as any aspect of group interaction that inhibits good problem solving. Process loss can occur because groups do not try hard enough to find out who the most competent member is, because the most competent member has low status and nobody really takes his or her ideas seriously, or because the most competent member finds it difficult to break free from normative conformity pressures that discourage disagreement with the whole group (see our discussion of normative social pressures in Chapter 8). Other causes of process loss involve communication problems within the group—in some groups, people don't listen to each other (see Figure 9.6); in others, one person is allowed to dominate the discussion while the others tune out.

Process Loss
any aspect of group interaction that inhibits good problem solving

Failure to Share Unique Information

Another reason groups can fail to outperform individuals is that group members sometimes fail to share unique information (that only they know) with each other. Frequently, no one member of a group is an expert on all aspects of the problem. Kennedy's advisers, for example, had different areas of expertise relevant to Cuba, the feasibility of an armed invasion, and the political repercussions of such an act. To reach the best decision, the group must pool their resources, so that each member shares his or her particular expertise with the rest of the group.

① <u>Additive Tasks:</u>

Group performance depends on the sum of each members contribution. If <u>social loafing</u> occurs the group performance may not be better than that of an individual working alone.

No Social Loafing

Social Loafing

② <u>Conjunctive Tasks:</u>

Group performance depends on that of the weakest or least talented group member. Groups usually do less well than individuals, since the weak member's performance brings down that of the group.

CHAMBER MUSIC GROUP

3 Disjunctive Tasks:

Group performance depends on how well the best or most talented member does. Groups can outperform individuals if the group has a highly talented member, if that member can convince the others that he or she is right, and if that member (and others) presents to the group unique information only he or she knows.

■ **FIGURE 9.6** (Opposite and above) Will groups perform better than lone individuals? It depends on the type of task.

Interestingly, groups often fail to accomplish this rudimentary condition of good decision making. Garold Stasser and his colleagues have found that groups tend to discuss information that is shared by all the group members, instead of focusing on unique or unshared information (see Figure 9.7). In one study, for example, participants met in groups of four to discuss which candidate for student body president was the most qualified (Stasser & Titus, 1985). In the shared information condition, each participant was given the same packet of information to read, data indicating that candidate A was the best choice for office. As seen at the top of Figure 9.7, all participants in this condition knew that candidate A had eight positive qualities and four negative qualities, making him superior to the other candidates. Not surprisingly, when this group met to discuss the candidates, almost all of the members chose candidate A.

In the unshared information condition, each participant received a different packet of information. As seen at the bottom of Figure 9.7, each person knew that candidate A had two positive qualities and four negative qualities. However, the two positive qualities cited in each person's packet were unique—different from those listed in other participants' packets. Everyone learned that candidate A had the same four negative qualities; thus, if the participants shared with each other the information that was in their packets, they would learn that candidate A had a total of eight positive qualities and four negative qualities—just as people in the shared information condition knew.

■ **FIGURE 9.7   When people are in groups, do they share information that only they know?**   Participants in a study met to discuss candidates for an election. In the shared information condition (top half of figure), each person was given the same positive and negative facts about the candidates. Candidate A was clearly the superior candidate, and most groups preferred him. In the unshared information condition (bottom half of figure), each person was given the same four negative facts about candidate A as well as two unique positive facts. In discussion, these people focused on the information they all shared and failed to mention their unique information; these groups no longer saw candidate A as superior. (Adapted from Stasser & Titus, 1985)

Most of the groups in the unshared information condition never realized that candidate A had more good than bad qualities, because they focused on the information they shared, rather than on the information they did not share. As a result, few of these groups chose candidate A. Thus, even on disjunctive tasks groups often do not outperform the most expert individual, because of process loss and the tendency to focus on information that everyone shares (Gigone & Hastie, 1993; Kim, 1997; Larson, Foster-Fishman, & Keys, 1994; Stasser, Taylor, & Hanna, 1989; Wittenbaum & Stasser, 1996).

One way around the failure to share information is to make sure people know that different members of the group are responsible for different kinds of information (Stasser, Stewart, & Wittenbaum, 1995). Daniel Wegner and his colleagues, for example, have found that married couples use this technique to remember things better; one member of a couple might be responsible for remembering the times of social engagements, whereas the other might be responsible for remembering when to pay the bills (Wegner, Erber, & Raymond, 1991). Similarly, Diane Liang, Richard Moreland, and Linda Argote (1995; Moreland, Argote, & Krishnan, 1996) found that if people know in advance that other group members know things they do not, they are more likely to focus on this unshared information. Liang and colleagues trained people alone or in groups of three to assemble transistor radios. A week later, everyone came back and tried to assemble a radio in groups of three: People who had been trained in groups took part with their same group members, whereas people who had been trained alone took part with two others who had also been trained alone. The people who had been trained in groups remembered significantly more about the task and made fewer errors than the people who had been trained alone. The reason for this superior performance was that the people trained in groups had learned who was best at remembering which details and had developed a system whereby different people were responsible for remembering different parts of the task; at the second session, these group members relied on each other to remember things they had forgotten. Thus, if groups know in advance who is responsible for remembering what, they are more likely to focus on unshared information.

Groupthink: Many Heads, One Mind

A possible limitation of research on group problem solving is that most studies use people who have never met before and give people tasks that are unfamiliar and sometimes trivial. Would groups do better if their members were used to working with each other and if they were dealing with important, real-world problems? Our opening example of President Kennedy and his advisers deciding to invade Cuba at the Bay of Pigs suggests not. Let's see why.

Using real-world events, Irving Janis (1972, 1982) developed an influential theory of group decision making that he called **groupthink**, defined as a kind of thinking in which maintaining group cohesiveness and solidarity is more important than considering the facts in a realistic manner. According to Janis's theory, groupthink is most likely to occur when certain preconditions are met, such as when the group is highly cohesive, isolated from contrary opinions, and ruled by a directive leader who makes his or her wishes known. Kennedy and his advisers were riding high on their close victory in the 1960 election and were a tight-knit, homogenous group. Since they had not yet made any major policy decisions, they lacked well-developed methods for discussing the issues. Moreover, Kennedy made it clear that he favored the invasion, and he asked the group to consider only details of how it should be executed, instead of questioning whether it should proceed at all.

When these preconditions of groupthink are met, several symptoms appear; these are outlined in Figure 9.8. The group begins to feel that it is invulnerable and can do no wrong. People do not voice contrary views (self-censorship), because they are afraid of ruining the high morale, or esprit de corps, of the group or because they are afraid of being criticized by the others. For example, Arthur Schlesinger, one of Kennedy's advisers, reported that he had severe doubts about the Bay of Pigs invasion but did not bring up any of these concerns during the discussions, out of a fear that "others would regard it as presumptuous of him, a college professor, to take issue with august heads of major government institutions" (Janis, 1982, p. 32). If anyone does voice a contrary viewpoint, the rest of the group is quick to criticize that person, pressuring him or her to conform to the majority view. Schlesinger did voice some of his doubts to Dean Rusk, the secretary of state. When Robert Kennedy (the attorney general and the president's brother) got wind of this, he took Schlesinger aside at a party and told him that the president had made up his mind to go ahead with the invasion and that his friends should support him. This kind of behavior creates an illusion of unanimity, where it looks as if everyone agrees. On the day the group voted on whether to invade, President Kennedy asked all those present for their opinion except one: Arthur Schlesinger.

The perilous state of groupthink causes people to implement an inferior decision-making process (see Figure 9.8). The group does not consider the full range of alternatives, does not develop contingency plans, and does not adequately consider the risks of its preferred choice. Can you think of other governmental decisions that were plagued by groupthink? Janis (1972, 1982) discusses several, such as the failure of the U.S. military commanders in Pearl Harbor to anticipate the

> The only sin which we never forgive in each other is difference of opinion.
> —Ralph Waldo Emerson, *Society and Solitude*

Groupthink
a kind of thinking in which maintaining group cohesiveness and solidarity is more important than considering the facts in a realistic manner

Groupthink

Antecedents of groupthink	Symptoms of groupthink	Defective decision-making
The group is highly cohesive: The group is valued and attractive, and people very much want to be members. **Group isolation:** The group is isolated, protected from hearing alternative viewpoints. **A directive leader:** The leader controls the discussion and makes his or her wishes known. **High stress:** The members perceive threats to the group. **Poor decision-making procedures:** No standard methods to consider alternative viewpoints.	**Illusion of invulnerability:** The group feels it is invincible and can do no wrong. **Belief in the moral correctness of the group:** "God is on our side." **Stereotyped views of out-group:** Opposing sides are viewed in a simplistic, stereotyped manner. **Self-censorship:** People decide themselves not to voice contrary opinions, in order to not "rock the boat." **Direct pressure on dissenters to conform:** If people do voice contrary opinions they are pressured by others to conform to the majority. **Illusion of unanimity:** An illusion is created that everyone agrees, by, for example, not calling on people known to disagree. **Mindguards:** Group members protect the leader from contrary viewpoints.	**Incomplete survey of alternatives** **Failure to examine risks of the favored alternative** **Poor information search** **Failure to develop contingency plans**

■ **FIGURE 9.8 Groupthink: Antecedents, symptoms, and consequences.** Under some conditions, maintaining group cohesiveness and solidarity is more important to a group than considering the facts in a realistic manner (see antecedents). When this happens, certain symptoms of groupthink occur, such as the illusion of invulnerability (see symptoms). These symptoms lead to defective decision making. (Adapted from Janis, 1982)

Japanese attack in 1941; President Truman's decision to invade North Korea in 1950, despite explicit warnings from the Chinese that they would attack with massive force; President Johnson's decision to escalate the Vietnam War in the mid-1960s; and the Watergate cover-up by President Nixon and his advisers. Another, more recent example was the fateful decision by NASA to go ahead with the launching of the space shuttle *Challenger,* despite the objections of engineers who said that the freezing temperatures presented a severe danger to the rubber O-ring seals (the ones that eventually failed during the launch, causing the rocket to explode and killing all aboard). All these decisions were plagued by many of the symptoms and consequences of groupthink, outlined in Figure 9.8 (Esser & Lindoerfer, 1989).

Since Janis proposed his theory, it has been put to the test by a number of other researchers. Some of these studies have been disappointing, in that group cohesiveness did not seem to be as related to groupthink as Janis had assumed (Aldag & Fuller, 1993; Mohamed & Wiebe, 1996; Tetlock, Peterson, McGuire, Chang, & Field, 1992). Janis's theory, however, suggests that group cohesiveness will increase groupthink only if other conditions are met, such as the presence of a directive leader and high stress (see Figure 9.8). And indeed, the experimental evidence is consistent with this idea: Group cohesiveness does not increase groupthink by itself, only when it is accompanied by other risk factors (Mullen, Anthony, Salas, & Driskell, 1994; Turner, Pratkanis, Probasco, & Leve, 1992). Thus, support for the groupthink model has been found both in systematic analyses of historical events and in well-controlled laboratory experiments (Schafer & Crichlow, 1996).

■ The decision to launch the space shuttle *Challenger*, which tragically exploded due to defective O-ring seals, appears to have been the result of groupthink on the part of NASA officials, who disregarded engineers' concerns about the quality of the seals.

How can groupthink be avoided? A wise leader can take several steps to ensure that his or her group is immune to this style of decision making. The leader should not take a directive role but remain impartial. He or she should invite outside opinions from people who are not members of the group and who are thus less concerned with maintaining group cohesiveness. He or she should divide the group into subgroups that first meet separately and then meet together to discuss their different recommendations. The leader might also take a secret ballot or ask group members to write down their opinions anonymously; doing so would ensure that people give their true opinions, uncensored by a fear of recrimination from the group (Flowers, 1977; McCauley, 1989; Zimbardo & Andersen, 1993).

Fortunately, President Kennedy learned from his mistakes with the Bay of Pigs decision and, when faced with his next major foreign policy decision, the Cuban missile crisis, took many of these steps to avoid groupthink. When his advisers met to decide what to do about the discovery of Soviet missiles in Cuba, Kennedy often absented himself from the group, so as not to inhibit their discussion. He also brought in outside experts (e.g., Adlai Stevenson) who were not members of the in-group. That Kennedy successfully negotiated the removal of the Soviet missiles was almost certainly due to the improved methods of group decision making he adopted.

Group Polarization: Going to Extremes

Maybe you are willing to grant that groups sometimes make poor decisions. Surely, though, groups will usually make less *risky* decisions than a lone individual will—one individual might be willing to bet the ranch on a risky proposition, but if others help make the decision, they will interject reason and moderation. Or will they? The question of whether groups or individuals make more risky decisions has been examined in numerous studies. Participants are typically given the Choice Dilemmas Questionnaire (CDQ), a series of stories that present a dilemma for the main character and ask the reader to choose how much probability of success there would have to be before the reader would recommend the risky alternative (Kogan & Wallach, 1964). An example of a CDQ item about a chess player appears in the Try It! exercise below. People choose their answers alone and then meet in a group to discuss the options, arriving at a unanimous group decision for each dilemma.

Many of the initial studies found, surprisingly, that groups make riskier decisions than individuals do. For example, when deciding alone, people said that the chess player should make the risky gambit only if there was at least a 30 percent chance of success. But after discussing the problem with others in a group, people said that the chess player should go for it even if there was only a 10 percent chance of success (Wallach, Kogan, & Bem, 1962). Findings such as these became known as the *risky shift*. Yet with increased research, it became clear that such shifts were not the full story. It turns out that groups tend to make decisions that

Try It!

Choice Dilemmas Questionnaire

You will need four or five friends to complete this exercise. First, copy the questionnaire in the table below and give it to each of your friends to complete by themselves, without talking to each other. Do not tell your friends that they will be discussing the questionnaire with the others. Then bring everyone together and ask them to discuss the dilemma and arrive at a *unanimous decision.* They should try to reach consensus such that every member of the group agrees at least partially with the final decision. Finally, compare people's initial decisions (made alone) with the group decision. Who made the riskier decisions on average: People deciding by themselves, or the group?

As discussed in the text, groups tend to make riskier decisions than individuals on problems such as these. In one study, for example, individuals recommended that the chess player make the risky move only if there was at least a 30 percent chance of success, but after discussing the problem with others in a group, they recommended that the chess player make the move even if there was only a 10 percent chance of success. Did you find the same thing? Why or why not? If the group did make a riskier decision, was it due more to the persuasive arguments interpretation discussed in the text, the social comparison interpretation, or both? (Adapted from Wallach, Kogan, & Bem, 1962)

The Choice Dilemmas Questionnaire

A low-ranked participant in a national chess tournament, playing an early match against a highly favored opponent, has the choice of attempting or not a deceptive but risky maneuver that might lead to quick victory if it is successful or almost certain defeat if it fails. Please indicate the lowest probability of success that you would accept before recommending that the chess player play the risky move.

_____   1 chance in 10 of succeeding

_____   3 chances in 10 of succeeding

_____   5 chances in 10 of succeeding

_____   7 chances in 10 of succeeding

_____   9 chances in 10 of succeeding

_____   I would not recommend taking the chance.

are more extreme in the same direction as the individual's initial predispositions, which happened to be risky in the case of the chess problem. What would happen if people were initially inclined to be conservative? In cases such as these, groups tend to make even more conservative decisions than individuals do.

Consider this problem: Roger, a young married man with two children, has a secure but low-paying job and no savings. Someone gives him a tip about a stock that will triple in value if the company's new product is successful but that will plummet if the new product fails. Should Roger sell his life insurance policy and invest in the company? Most people recommend a safe course of action here: Roger should buy the stock only if the new product is very certain to succeed. When they talk it over in a group, they become even more conservative, deciding that the new product would have to have a nearly 100 percent chance of success before they would recommend that Roger buy stock in the company.

The finding that groups make more extreme decisions, in the direction of people's initial inclinations, has become known as **group polarization,** defined as the tendency for groups to make decisions that are more extreme than the initial inclination of its members—toward greater risk if people's initial tendency is to be risky and toward greater caution if people's initial tendency is to be cautious (Brown, 1965; Myers & Arenson, 1972; Teger & Pruitt, 1967). Group polarization occurs for two main reasons. According to the persuasive arguments interpretation, all individuals bring to the group a set of arguments, some of which other individuals have not considered, supporting their initial recommendation. For example, one person might stress that cashing in the life insurance policy is an unfair risk to Roger's children, should he die prematurely. Another person might not have considered this possibility; thus, he or she becomes more conservative as well. A series of studies by Eugene Burnstein and Amiram Vinokur (1977) supports this interpretation of group polarization, whereby each member presents arguments that other members had not considered (Burnstein & Sentis, 1981).

According to the social comparison interpretation, when people discuss an issue in a group they first check out how everyone else feels. What does the group value—being risky or being cautious? In order to be liked, many people then take a position that is similar to everyone else's but a little more extreme. In this way, the individual supports the group's values and also presents him- or herself in a positive light—a person in the vanguard, an impressive thinker. Both the persuasive arguments and the social comparison interpretations of group polarization have received support (Blaskovich, Ginsburg, & Veach, 1975; Brown, 1986; Isenberg, 1986; Zuber, Crott, & Werner, 1992).

Group Polarization
the tendency for groups to make decisions that are more extreme than the initial inclinations of its members

The Culture-Value Theory

Whereas group polarization can go either way, Roger Brown (1965) has proposed that, relatively speaking, Americans value risk more than caution. In his culture-value theory, Brown discusses how American culture, based on the economic system of capitalism, requires a willingness to take risks and try new approaches. In comparison, other cultures operate under a dominant cultural value of caution— a relatively high level of wariness and conservatism. Hence, the hypothesis derived from culture-value theory is that some cultures should be more likely to evince risky shifts, while others should be more likely to evince cautious shifts.

In support of Brown's theory, research has indicated that Americans perceive people who take risks more positively than those who make cautious decisions (Madaras & Bem, 1968), find the riskier alternatives more admirable than the cautious ones (Lamm, Schaude, & Trommsdorff, 1971), and believe high-risk takers are more competent than those who choose cautious alternatives (Jellison & Riskind, 1970). Thus, it appears that risk does have value in the United States. In comparison, two cross-cultural studies have found evidence for a general cultural value of caution in African countries. In both Uganda and Liberia, groups made choices on the CDQ that were typically more cautious than those made by the individual members alone and that were more cautious than those made by Western research participants (Carlson & Davis, 1971; Gologor, 1977). Thus, when group discussion occurs, it reinforces whichever cultural value predominates in that society—for example, group polarization toward caution occurs when individuals learn they are not as cautious as others in the group and caution is valued in their culture.

Conflict and Cooperation

We have just examined how people work together to make decisions; in these situations, group members have a common goal. Often, however, people have incompatible goals, placing them in conflict with each other. This can be true of two individuals, such as romantic partners who disagree about who should clean the kitchen, or two groups, such as a labor union and company management who disagree over wages and working conditions. It can also be true of two nations, such as the long-standing conflict between Israel and its Arab neighbors or between the Serbians, Croatians, and Muslims in the former Yugoslavia. The opportunity for interpersonal conflict exists whenever two or more people interact. Freud (1930) went so far as to argue that conflict is an inevitable byproduct of civilization. The goals and needs of individuals often clash with the goals and needs of their fellow human beings. The nature of conflict, and how it can be resolved, has been the topic of a great deal of social psychological research (Allison, Beggan, & Midgley, 1996; Deutsch, 1973; Levine & Thompson, 1996; Pruitt, 1998; Thibaut & Kelley, 1959).

Many conflicts are resolved peacefully, with little rancor. Couples can find a way to resolve their differences in a mutually acceptable manner, and labor disputes are sometimes settled with a friendly handshake. All too often, however, conflict erupts into open hostilities. The divorce rate in the United States is distressingly high. People sometimes resort to violence to resolve their differences, as shown by the high rate of murders in the United States, "the murder capital of the civilized world" (*Newsweek*, July 16, 1990). Warfare between nations remains an all-too-common solution to international disputes. In fact, when wars over the past five centuries are examined, the twentieth century ranks first in the severity of wars (defined as the number of deaths per war) and second in their frequency (Levy & Morgan, 1984). It is therefore of great importance to find ways of resolving conflicts peacefully.

Social Dilemmas

The interesting thing about many conflicts is that what is best for individuals is not best for the group as a whole. Consider a fund raising appeal by a group you really care about, such as your local public broadcasting television station. You really like watching *Austin City Limits* and *The Newshour with Jim Lehrer* and feel like you should make a contribution. On the other hand you don't have much money and there are other charities you like to support. This is a classic

■ Intergroup conflict is clearly one of the most important problems confronting us today. Centuries-old conflicts persist in many parts of the world, such as the Middle East, Ireland, and Eastern Europe. In this photograph, refugees at a Bosnian checkpoint are seen hiding in a ditch during the shelling.

social dilemma, which is a conflict in which the most beneficial action for an individual will, if chosen by most people, have harmful effects on everyone. You might think, "Things are really tight this month; I'd better not contribute anything to PBS." If everyone adopted this strategy, however, everyone would suffer, because PBS could not exist without private contributions.

There are many perspectives on how people respond to social dilemmas, including sociological studies of social movements and historical, economic, and political analyses of international relations. The social-psychological approach is unique in its attempt to study these conflicts experimentally, testing both their causes and resolutions in the laboratory. A number of different kinds of social dilemmas have been studied in this way.

One of the most common social dilemmas involves a conflict called the Prisoner's Dilemma. To illustrate this game, imagine that two men, Billy and Jesse, have been arrested for armed robbery but the police have only enough

Social Dilemma
a conflict in which the most beneficial action for an individual will, if chosen by most people, have harmful effects on everyone.

■ Conflict often escalates so that neither side can win.

evidence to convict them of the lesser crime of breaking and entering. The police take the defendants to separate interrogation rooms and offer each of them a deal: If they agree to testify against their partner, they will be released with no jail time. What should they do? Should they confess or remain silent? Figure 9.9 illustrates the consequences of each course of action. If both defendants remain silent, they will be convicted of breaking and entering and will each receive a sentence of 3 years. Here both defendants are relatively well-off. If Billy confesses but Jesse remains silent, then Billy is released and Jesse gets a 30-year sentence. If both defendants confess, however, then there is no reason for the police to use one as a witness against the other, and both will receive sentences of 10 years.

This is a classic social dilemma, because it pits people's desire to look out for their own interests against their desire to look out for their partner as well. To find out how people resolve this conflict, social psychologists have asked participants to play this and similar games in hundreds of studies (Blumberg, 1994; Kelley & Thibaut, 1978; Pruitt, 1998; Pruitt & Kimmel, 1977; Rapoport & Chammah, 1965). Instead of using prison sentences, researchers typically use money or points on an exam as payoffs and ask participants to play the game for several trials. Consider, for example, the payoff matrix shown in the Try It! exercise on page 361. Imagine that the numbers in this matrix represent money that you can win or lose and that you are playing against a good friend. You have to choose option X or option Y, without knowing which option your friend will choose. Just as in the Prisoner's Dilemma, your payoff—the amount of money you earn or lose—depends on the choices of both you and your friend. What would you do if you were playing?

If you are like most people, you will start out by choosing option Y. At worst you will lose a dollar, and at best you will win the highest possible number—six dollars. Choosing option X raises the possibility that both sides will win some money, but this is also a very risky choice. If your partner chooses Y while you choose X, you stand to lose a great deal. Because people often do not know how much they can trust their partners, option Y frequently seems like the safest

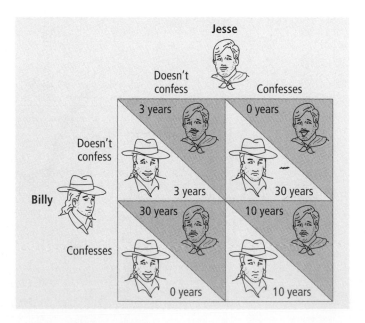

■ **FIGURE 9.9   The Prisoner's Dilemma**   The sentence each defendant receives depends both on whether he confesses and on whether the other person confesses. For example, if Billy confesses but Jesse does not, Billy is released and Jesse receives a 30-year sentence. (Adapted from Rapoport & Chammah, 1965)

choice (Rapoport & Chammah, 1965). The rub is that both players will probably think this way, ensuring that both sides lose (see the lower right-hand corner of the figure in the exercise).

People's actions in these games seem to mirror many conflicts in everyday life. To find a solution desirable to both parties, people must trust each other. Often they do not, and this lack of trust leads to an escalating series of competitive moves, so that in the end no one wins. Two countries locked in an arms race may feel they cannot afford to disarm, out of fear that the other side will take advantage of their weakened position. The result is that both sides add furiously to their stockpile of weapons, neither gaining superiority over the other and both spending money they could use to solve domestic problems (Deustch, 1973). Such an escalation of conflict is also seen all too often among couples who are divorcing. Sometimes the goal seems more to hurt the other person than to further one's own needs (or the children's). In the end, both suffer, because metaphorically speaking, they both choose option Y too often.

Such escalating conflict, though common, is not inevitable. Many studies have found that when people play a Prisoner's Dilemma game they will, under certain conditions, adopt the more cooperative response (option X), ensuring that both sides end up with a positive outcome. Not surprisingly, if people are playing the game with a friend or if they expect to interact with their partner in the future, they are more likely to adopt a cooperative strategy that maximizes

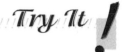

The Prisoner's Dilemma

Your Friend's Options	Your Options	
	Option X	Option Y
Option X	You Win $3 / Your Friend Wins $3	You Win $6 / Your Friend Loses $6
Option Y	You Lose $6 / Your Friend Wins $6	You Lose $1 / Your Friend Loses $1

Instructions: Play this version of a Prisoner's Dilemma game with a friend. First, show the table above to the friend and explain how the game works: On each trial of the game, you and your friend can choose Option X or Option Y, without knowing what the other will choose. You should each write your choice on folded pieces of paper that are opened at the same time. The numbers in the table represent imaginary money that you and your friend win or lose on each trial. For example, if you choose Option X on the first trial and your friend chooses Option Y, then you lose an imaginary $6 and your friend wins an imaginary $6. If both of you choose Option Y, then you both lose an imaginary $1. Play the game for 10 trials and keep track of how much each of you wins or loses. Did you and your friend choose the cooperative option (Option X) or the competitive option (Option Y) more often? Why? Did a pattern of trust or mistrust develop over the course of the game?

Tit-for-Tat Strategy
a means of encouraging cooperation by at first acting cooperatively but then always responding the way your opponent did (cooperatively or competitively) on the previous trial

Public Goods Dilemma
a social dilemma in which individuals must contribute to a common pool in order to maintain the public good

Commons Dilemma
a social dilemma in which everyone takes from a common pool of goods that will replenish itself if used in moderation, but which will disappear if overused

both their and their partner's profits (Pruitt & Kimmel, 1977). In addition, growing up in some societies, such as Asian cultures, seems to foster a more cooperative orientation than growing up in the West does (Bonta, 1997; Leung, 1987; Markus & Kitayama, 1991).

To increase cooperation, you can also try to communicate that you can be trusted not to exploit your opponent. You might do so by choosing option X and sticking with it as the game goes on, thereby showing your partner that you are not trying to exploit him or her. The problem is that you become an easy mark, and your partner knows he or she can nail you at any time by choosing option Y. A better approach is known as the **tit-for-tat strategy,** which is a way of encouraging cooperation by at first acting cooperatively but then always responding the way your opponent did (cooperatively or competitively) on the previous trial. This strategy communicates a willingness to cooperate and an unwillingness to sit back and be exploited if the partner does not cooperate. The tit-for-tat strategy is usually successful in getting the other person to respond with the cooperative, trusting response (Axelrod, 1984; Komorita, Parks, & Hulbert, 1992; McClintock & Liebrand, 1988; Messick & Liebrand, 1995; Pruitt, 1998). The analogy to the arms race would be to match not only any military buildup made by an unfriendly nation but also any conciliatory gesture, such as a ban on nuclear testing.

A number of other kinds of social dilemmas have been studied as well. A **public goods dilemma** is the case in which individuals must contribute to a common pool in order to maintain the public good. Our earlier example of contributions to public television stations was one example; others include maintaining the blood supply in hospitals and paying taxes for public schools. It is to each individual's advantage to pay as little as possible, but if everyone adopts this strategy, everyone suffers. Another is called the **commons dilemma,** defined as a situation in which everyone takes from a common pool of goods that will replenish itself if used in moderation, but which will disappear if overused. This dilemma got its name from Garrett Hardin (1968), who described the case in which there is a common grassy area in the middle of a town. All residents are permitted to let their sheep graze in this common area. This is a classic social dilemma because it is to each individual farmer's benefit to let his or her sheep graze as much as possible, but if all farmers do this, the commons will be overgrazed and the grass will disappear. Modern examples include the use of limited resources such as water and energy. Individuals benefit by using as much as they need, but if everyone does so, shortages often result. We discuss commons dilemmas in "Social Psychology in Action 2: Social Psychology and the Environment," in the context of how to get people to avoid environmentally damaging behaviors.

Using Threats to Resolve Conflict

When caught in a conflict, many of us are tempted to use threats to get the other party to cave in to our wishes, believing that we should "walk quietly and carry a big stick." Parents commonly use threats to get their children to behave, and teachers often threaten their students with demerits or a visit to the principal. More alarming is the increasing number of youths in the United States who carry guns and use them to resolve conflicts that used to be settled with a playground scuffle. Threats are commonly used on an international scale as well, to further the interests of one nation over another.

A classic series of studies by Morton Deutsch and Robert Krauss (1960, 1962) indicates that threats are not an effective means of reducing conflict. These

The Deutsch and Krauss trucking game

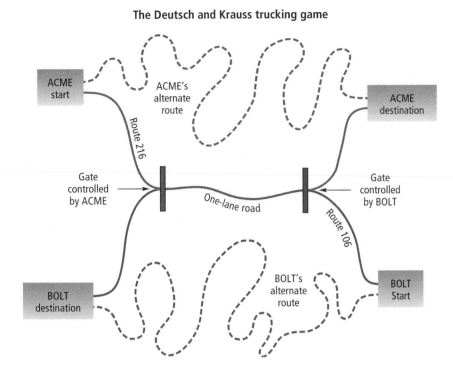

■ **FIGURE 9.10   The trucking game.** Participants play the role of the head of either Acme or Bolt Trucking Company. In order to earn money, they have to drive their truck from the starting point to their destination as quickly as possible. The quickest route is the one-lane road, but both trucks cannot travel on this road at the same time. In some versions of the studies, participants were given gates they used to block the other's progress on the one-lane road. (Adapted from Deutsch & Krauss, 1960)

researchers developed a game in which two participants imagined they were in charge of trucking companies named Acme and Bolt. The goal of each company was to transport merchandise as quickly as possible to a destination. The participants were paid 60 cents for each "trip," but had 1 cent subtracted for every second it took them to make the trip. The most direct route for each company was over a one-lane road on which only one truck could travel at a time. This placed the two companies in direct conflict, as seen in Figure 9.10. If Acme and Bolt both tried to take the one-lane road, then neither truck could pass and both would lose money. Each company could take an alternate route, but this was much longer, guaranteeing they would lose at least 10 cents on each trial. The game lasted until each side had made 20 trips.

How did the participants respond to this dilemma? After a while, most of them worked out a solution that allowed both trucks to make a modest amount of money. They took turns waiting until the other person crossed the one-lane road; then they would take that route as well. In another version of the study, the researchers gave Acme a gate that could be lowered over the one-lane road, thereby blocking Bolt from using that route. You might think that using force—the gate—would increase Acme's profits, because all Acme had to do was to threaten Bolt, telling him or her to stay off the one-lane road or else. In fact, quite the opposite happened. When one side had the gate, both participants lost more than when neither side had the gate—as seen in the left-hand panel of Figure 9.11, on the next page. This figure shows the total amount earned or lost by both sides. (Acme won slightly more than Bolt when it had the gate but won substantially more when neither side had a gate.) Bolt did not like to be threatened and often retaliated by parking its truck on the one-lane road, blocking the other truck's progress. Meanwhile, the seconds ticked away and both sides lost money.

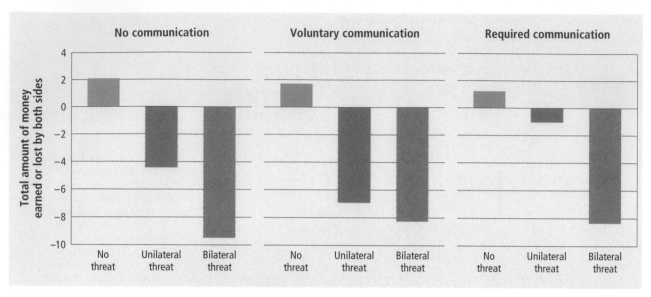

■ **FIGURE 9.11 Results of the trucking game studies.** The left-hand panel shows the amount of money the participants made (summed over Acme and Bolt) when they could not communicate. When threats were introduced by giving one or both sides a gate, both sides lost more money. The middle panel shows the amount of money the participants made when they could communicate as little or as much as they wanted. Once again, giving them gates reduced the amount of money they won. The right-hand panel shows the amount of money the participants made when they were required to communicate on every trial. Once again, giving them gates reduced their winnings. (Adapted from Deutsch & Krauss, 1962)

> "My own belief is that Russian and Chinese behavior is as much influenced by suspicion of our intentions as ours is by suspicion of theirs. This would mean that we have great influence over their behavior—that, by treating them as hostile, we assure their hostility."
>
> —J. William Fulbright

What would happen if the situation were more equitable, with both sides having gates? Surely they would learn to cooperate very quickly, recognizing the stalemate that would ensue if both of them used their gates—right? To the contrary (as you can see in the left-hand panel of Figure 9.11), both sides lost more money in the bilateral threat condition than in any of the others. The owners of the trucking companies both threatened to use their gates and did so with great frequency. Once Acme used the gate to block Bolt, Bolt retaliated and blocked Acme the next time its truck came down the road—producing a stalemate that was in neither of their interests. Sound familiar? For the past few decades, the United States and the former Soviet Union were locked in an escalating nuclear arms race, each threatening the other with destruction.

Effects of Communication

There is a way in which the Deutsch and Krauss (1960, 1962) trucking game does not approximate real life: The two sides could use threats (closing their gates) but were not allowed to communicate with each other. Would the two adversaries work out their differences if they could talk them over? To find out, Deutsch and Krauss ran a version of their study in which the participants could communicate over an intercom. In one condition, the participants were allowed to speak as often or as little as they liked. As seen in the middle of Figure 9.11, this communication had very little effect (compare the middle panel with the left-hand panel in the figure). Interestingly, people chose not to say much to each other in this condition, communicating on only about 5 of the 20 trials.

In another condition, the researchers decided to require the participants to communicate on every trial. Surely if people were forced to talk to each other they would cooperate more. As seen in the right-hand panel of Figure 9.11, however, no dramatic increase in profits occurred in the "required communication" condition. Making people communicate reduced losses somewhat when Acme alone had the gate (the unilateral threat condition), but failed to increase cooperation in either of the two other conditions (no threat; bilateral threat). Overall, requiring people to communicate did not raise profits dramatically. Why not?

The problem with the communication in the trucking studies is that it did not foster trust. To the contrary, people used the intercom to convey threats. Other studies have found that communication is helpful if people learn to use it in such a way as to establish trust (Kerr & Kaufman-Gilliland, 1994). Krauss and Deutsch demonstrated this fact in a later version of their trucking study, in which they specifically instructed people in how to communicate, telling them to work out a solution that was fair to both parties and that they would be willing to accept if they were in the other person's shoes. Under these conditions, verbal communication increased the amount of money both sides won, because it fostered trust, instead of adding fuel to the competitive fires (Deutsch, 1973, 1990; Krauss & Deutsch, 1966; Pruitt, 1998; Voissem & Sistrunk, 1971).

Negotiation and Bargaining

In the laboratory games we have discussed so far, people's options are limited. They have to choose option X or Y in the Prisoner's Dilemma, and they have only a couple of ways of getting their truck to its destination in the trucking game. In everyday life, people often have a wide array of options. Consider two people haggling over the price of a car. Both the buyer and the seller can give in to all of the other's demands, to some of them, or to none of them. Either party can walk away from the deal at any time. Given that there is considerable latitude in how people can resolve the conflict, communication between the parties is all the more important. By talking, bargaining, and negotiating, people can arrive at a satisfactory settlement. **Negotiation** is defined as a form of communication between opposing sides in a conflict, in which offers and counteroffers are made and a solution occurs only when both parties agree (Bazerman & Neale, 1992; Fry, 1985; Pruitt, 1998; Pruitt & Carnevale, 1993; Rubin & Brown, 1975; Thompson, 1997). How successful are people at negotiating mutually beneficial solutions?

One limit to successful negotiation is that people often assume they are locked in a conflict in which only one party can come out ahead. They don't realize that, as in the conflicts we have reviewed, solutions favorable to both parties are available. Consider a labor union and a company who are negotiating a new contract. The company has proposed a 2 percent salary increase and no additional days of annual vacation, whereas the union has proposed a 6 percent salary increase and six additional days of annual vacation. After protracted negotiations, the two sides decide to compromise on both issues, agreeing to a 4 percent salary increase and three additional days of annual vacation. Sounds fair,

Negotiation
a form of communication between opposing sides in a conflict in which offers and counteroffers are made and a solution occurs only when both parties agree

doesn't it? The problem with such compromises is that they assume both issues (in this case, the salary increase and additional vacation days) are equally important to both parties, and often that is not true. Suppose that the labor union cared much more about increasing salaries than getting additional vacation days, whereas the company cared much more about minimizing vacation days than keeping salaries in check. In this case, a better solution for both sides would be to trade off issues, such that the union got the 6 percent salary increase (which it cared about the most) in return for no increase in vacation days (which the company cared about the most). This type of compromise is called an **integrative solution,** defined as a solution to a conflict whereby the parties make trade-offs on issues according to their different interests; each side concedes the most on issues that are unimportant to it but important to the other side.

It might seem like such integrative solutions would be relatively easy to achieve. After all, the two parties simply have to sit down and figure out which issues are the most important to each other. Leigh Thompson and her colleagues have found, however, that there are a number of barriers to identifying integrative solutions (Thompson, 1990, 1991, 1997; Thompson & Hrebec, 1996). For instance, the more people have at stake in a negotiation, the more biased their perceptions of their opponent. They will tend to distrust proposals made by the other side and to overlook interests they have in common (O'Connor & Carnevale, 1997; Ross & Ward, 1995, 1996).

To illustrate this distrust, Thompson (1995) asked students to take sides in a hypothetical conflict between an employee and an employer. As in our example above, the employee had somewhat different interests than the employer; for example, obtaining a high salary was more important to the employee than the employer, whereas keeping medical benefits down was more important to the employer than the employee. Neither party knew the importance of the issues to their opponent; the point was to see how well each side figured this out as they negotiated a solution.

It turned out that people were not very good at discovering their opponents' true interests. And, those who were directly involved in the negotiations were even worse at this task than those who were not. Other students watched videotapes of the negotiations and were simply asked to estimate how important each issue was to each side. These uninvolved observers of the negotiations made more accurate judgments than the people actually involved in the negotiations. When negotiators are in the heat of the battle and care deeply about the outcome, they tend to distrust the other side, making it more difficult to realize that there is common ground beneficial to both parties. This is one reason people often use neutral mediators to solve labor disputes, legal battles, and divorce proceedings: Mediators are often in a better position to recognize that there are mutually agreeable solutions to a conflict (Carnevale, 1986; Emery & Wyer, 1987; Kressel & Pruitt, 1989).

The bottom line? When you are negotiating with someone, it is important to keep in mind that integrative solutions are often available. Try to gain the other side's trust, and communicate your own interests in an open manner. Remember that the way you construe the situation is not necessarily the same as the way the other party construes the situation. You may well discover that the other side communicates its interests more freely as a result, increasing the likelihood that you will find a solution beneficial to both parties.

Integrative Solution
a solution to a conflict whereby the parties make trade-offs on issues according to their different interests; each side concedes the most on issues that are unimportant to it but important to the other side

Yet, there remains another wall. This wall constitutes a psychological barrier between us . . . [a] barrier of distorted and eroded interpretation of every event and statement. . . . I ask why don't we stretch our hands with faith and sincerity so that together we might destroy this barrier?
—Former Egyptian president Anwar al-Sadat, November 29, 1977, in a speech before the Israeli Knesset

■ If the right strategies are used, negotiation can lead to successful resolutions of conflicts. Here Israeli prime minister Yitzhak Rabin and Palestinian Liberation Organization leader Yasser Arafat meet at the White House to sign a Middle East peace accord. Tragically, Rabin was assassinated in November of 1995, two years after this agreement was reached.

Summary

We began this chapter by examining the effects of being in a **nonsocial group,** in which there is no interaction between you and the people around you. We saw that when your individual efforts can be evaluated, the mere presence of others leads to **social facilitation:** Your performance is enhanced on simple tasks but impaired on complex tasks. When your individual efforts cannot be evaluated, the mere presence of others leads to **social loafing:** Your performance is impaired on simple tasks but enhanced on complex tasks. Finally, the mere presence of others can lead to **deindividuation,** which is the loosening of normal constraints on behavior when people are in crowds, leading to an increase in impulsive and deviant acts.

When other people are around, we often join them in **social groups,** which have a number of interesting properties. People often assume **roles** in groups and these roles can shape their behavior in powerful ways. Perhaps the most important role in a group is that of leader. Who makes the most effective leader? There is little support for the **great person theory,** which argues that good leadership is purely a matter of having the right personality traits. Leadership effectiveness is a function of both the kind of person a leader is and the nature of the work situation. Research on Fiedler's **contingency theory of leadership** has found that leadership performance depends both on whether a group has a **task-oriented leader** or a **relationship-oriented leader** and on whether the work environment is high or low in situational control. Women tend to lead more democratically than men, although women are able to adopt a "masculine" leadership style when the job requires it.

Are social groups better or worse than individuals at making decisions? The answer to this question depends on the type of task groups are working on, such as whether it is a **divisible versus a unitary task** (whether the task can be broken down into different subtasks). On unitary tasks, groups often do worse if people's outputs are combined in an **additive** or **conjunctive** manner. Groups will also do worse on a **disjunctive** task if **process loss** occurs—that is, if the most expert individual is unable to sway the rest of the group—and if groups fail to share unique information.

Tightly knit, cohesive groups are also prone to **groupthink,** a phenomenon in which maintaining group cohesiveness and solidarity is more important than considering the facts in a realistic manner. **Group polarization** indicates that groups are also prone to make more extreme decisions in the direction toward which its members were initially leaning; these group decisions can be more risky or more cautious, depending on which attitude is valued in the group.

Conflict often exists when there is tension between two or more individuals. A particularly interesting kind of conflict is a **social dilemma,** in which the most beneficial action for an individual will, if chosen by most people, have harmful effects on everyone. A commonly studied social dilemma is the Prisoner's Dilemma, in which two people must de-

cide whether to look out for only their own interests or for their partner's interests as well. The **tit-for-tat strategy** is a useful way of dealing with conflict, allowing one to respond cooperatively or competitively, given the other person's response. Creating trust is crucial in solving this kind of conflict. Other kinds of social dilemmas are the **public goods dilemma,** in which individuals must contribute to a common pool in order to maintain the public good, and the **commons dilemma,** in which everyone takes from a public pool of goods that will replenish itself if used in moderation, but which will disappear if overused. Finally, we examined the conditions under which hostilities are likely to increase or decrease, including how the use of threats and the inability to communicate can exacerbate a conflict. In **negotiation,** it is important to look for an **integrative solution,** whereby each side concedes the most on issues that are unimportant to it but very important to its adversary.

If You Are Interested

Golding, William (1962). *Lord of the Flies.* After their plane crashes on a deserted island, a group of middle-class English boys must fend for themselves. The society they establish—with its norms, rules, and rejections of deviates—is thought-provoking and frightening.

Janis, I. (1982). *Groupthink: Psychological studies of policy decisions and fiascoes* (2nd ed.). Boston: Houghton Mifflin. Janis argues persuasively that many important policy decisions, from the Bay of Pigs fiasco to the escalation of the Vietnam War, were flawed by groupthink, wherein maintaining group cohesiveness and solidarity was more important than considering the facts in a realistic manner.

Levine, J. M., & Moreland, R. L. (1998). Small groups. In D. Gilbert, S. Fiske, & G. Lindzey (Eds.), *Handbook of social psychology* (4th ed., Vol. 2, pp. 415–469). New York: McGraw-Hill. An up-to-date review of research on small groups by two of the best-known experts in the field.

Malcolm X, & Haley, Alex (1965). *The Autobiography of Malcolm X.* The autobiographical account of the life of

Malcolm X, from his early days in Detroit to his electric leadership role in the Nation of Islam. Malcolm X's life raises many fascinating questions about the origins and causes of leadership. Made into a movie in 1992, directed by Spike Lee.

Pruitt, D. G. (1998). Social conflict. In D. Gilbert, S. Fiske, & G. Lindzey (Eds.), *Handbook of social psychology* (4th ed., Vol. 2, pp. 470–503). New York: McGraw-Hill. A state-of-the art review of research on conflict, including such topics as social dilemmas, negotiation, broader conflict, and conflict resolution.

The Big Chill (1984). Seven college housemates meet again at the funeral of a close friend who has committed suicide. A poignant and often funny look at group dynamics.

Witte, E., & David, J. H. (1996). *Understanding group behavior* (Volumes 1 and 2). Mahwah, NJ: Erlbaum. A collection of chapters on small groups by experts in the field.

CHAPTER 10

INTERPERSONAL ATTRACTION: FROM FIRST IMPRESSIONS TO CLOSE RELATIONSHIPS

Bessie and I have been together since time began, or so it seems. Bessie is my little sister, only she's not so little. She is 101 years old and I am 103. . . . Neither of us ever married and we've lived together most all of our lives, and probably know each other better than any two human beings on this Earth. After so long, we are in some ways like one person" (Delany, Delany, & Hearth, 1993).

So begins the extraordinary story of Bessie and Sadie Delany—sisters, best friends, and lifelong companions for over 100 years. Sadie was born in 1889, Bessie in 1891, the oldest daughters in a family of ten. Their father was born a slave on a plantation in Georgia; he received his freedom at the age of 7 when the Civil War ended. Their mother was of mixed racial heritage and had been born free. Both their parents received college degrees at St. Augustine College; their father became the first black person to be elected a Bishop in the Episcopal Church. All the Delany children went to college; Bessie and Sadie graduated

■ Bessie and Sadie Delany

from Columbia University early in the century. Sadie received her Master's degree in 1925 in education and became the first black home economics teacher in the New York City school system. Bessie received her D.D.S. degree in 1923 and became the second black woman dentist in New York.

The Delany sisters' lives are extraordinary for many reasons. As African American women, they lived through a century of societal change. They experienced both racism and sexism, and they triumphed. At a time when few women were college educated, let alone had a career, they were trailblazers in their professions. And finally, they have shared a relationship that is truly unique. Very few people will ever have a close relationship that lasts for 100 years.

Bessie and Sadie had many suitors as young women; they were attractive, vivacious, and intelligent. However they were also independent and set on having careers. In the 1920s and '30s, having a career and a family was next to impossible for a woman. So Sadie and Bessie remained single and followed their dreams.

While they never married, the sisters had a core, defining personal relationship—their friendship with each other. For 104 years, they lived together, sharing their triumphs and tragedies. Their relationship was broken only by death. In 1995, Bessie died at the age of 104. For the first time, Sadie was alone. In the year after her sister's death, Sadie wrote about what her relationship with her sister had meant to her. There is no more moving description of an intimate relationship than Sadie's words (Delany & Hearth, 1997):

"Losing your sister after living together for more than a hundred years, well it's a pretty terrible thing. It's like you opened the front door of your house and stepped inside, only there was no house, just a hole in the ground and you keep falling and falling" (p. 199).

"This being alone is *hard*. For the first time in my life, I don't have you by my side. I'm 107 years old now and it's like I'm just learning how to walk" (pp. 26–27).

"Your passing has made it harder to be this old, Bessie. When you were here to share things, it wasn't so hard being over one hundred years old. There was someone who remembered the same things" (p. 152).

"You were a part of my life since I was two years old. I don't remember life without you. I can see your face in every memory from my own childhood; playing with our dolls, picking cotton to make a little money, learning how to ride Papa's horse, making candy outdoors at Eastertime. You, you were always there" (pp. 74–75).

"Remember how, after dinner, we used to sit at the dining room table and talk? I surely do miss that! You had *good* sense. You were smart and decisive, and I relied on your good judgment" (p. 141).

"Those lovely days, so many of them throughout our lives, when nothing exceptional happened, but we passed the day pleasantly. . . . I'm so grateful for each and every day of your life, Bessie. You used your time well" (p. 107).

Sadie Delany is now 108 years old. She still grieves the loss of her sister, but she endures. As she puts it, "Bessie, I think I'm going to be all right. . . . Don't worry about me, Sister Bessie. Child, I have *plans*" (pp. 210, 218).

Major Antecedents of Attraction

When Ellen Berscheid asked people of various ages what made them happy, at or near the top of their lists were making and maintaining friendships and having positive, warm relationships (Berscheid, 1985; Berscheid & Peplau, 1983; Berscheid & Reis, 1998). The feelings of loneliness that come from the absence of meaningful relationships with other people make people feel worthless, hopeless, helpless, powerless, and alienated (Baumeister & Leary, 1995; Dykstra, 1995; Gerstein & Tesser, 1987; Hartup & Stevens, 1997; Myers & Diener, 1995; Peplau & Perlman, 1982; Stroebe & Stroebe, 1996; Weiss, 1973).

As Ellen Berscheid (1985; Berscheid & Reis, 1998) has noted, we human beings, being the most social of social animals, have survived as a species largely because of our ability to know whether another creature or human being was good or bad for us. "Matters of interpersonal attraction," she argues, "are, quite literally, of life and death importance, not just to the individual but to all of humankind" (Berscheid, 1985, p. 414). In this chapter, we will discuss the antecedents of attraction, from the initial liking of two people meeting for the first time, to the love that develops in close relationships.

■ Close friendships are often made in college, in part because of prolonged propinquity.

The Person Next Door: The Propinquity Effect

There are approximately 5 billion people in the world. In your lifetime, you have the opportunity to meet and interact with only a minuscule percentage of the people on this planet. Thus, it will not surprise you to learn that one of the simplest determinants of interpersonal attraction is proximity—sometimes called "propinquity." The people who, by chance, are the ones you see and interact with the most often are the most likely to become your friends and lovers (Berscheid & Reis, 1998; Moreland & Beach, 1992; Newcomb, 1961; Priest & Sawyer, 1967; Rawlins, 1994; Segal, 1974).

Now, this might seem obvious. But the striking thing about proximity and attraction, or the **propinquity effect,** as social psychologists call it, is that it works on a very micro level. For example, consider a classic study conducted in a housing complex for married students at MIT. Leon Festinger, Stanley Schachter, and Kurt Back (1950) tracked friendship formation among the couples in the various apartment buildings. For example, one section of the complex, Westgate West, was composed of 17 two-story buildings, each having ten apartments. The residents had been assigned to their apartments at random, as a vacancy opened up, and nearly all of them were strangers when they moved in. The researchers asked

Propinquity Effect
the finding that the more we see and interact with people, the more likely they are to become our friends

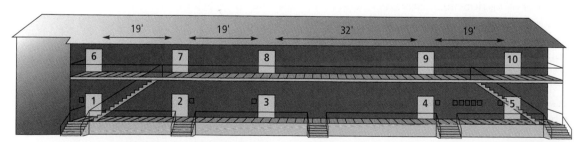

■ **FIGURE 10.1** **The floor plan of a Westgate West building.** All the buildings in the housing complex had the same floor plan. (Adapted from Festinger, Schachter, & Back, 1950)

Mapping the Effect of Propinquity in Your Life

In this exercise you will be examining the relationship between who your friends and acquaintances are and the place(s) where you spend time regularly. Does propinquity explain who your friends are?

First, pick a physical space to focus on. You could choose your dormitory, apartment building, or the building where you work. (We'll use a dormitory as an example.) Draw a rough floor plan of your dormitory floor. Include the location of all the dorm room doors, the stairs or elevator, the restroom, livingroom, and so on. Mark your room with a large *X*. (You can decide whether you need to draw just your floor or more of the building.)

Second, think about who your close friends are on the floor. Mark their dorm rooms with a number *1*. Next, think about who your friends are; mark their rooms with a *2*. Finally, think about your acquaintances—people you say hello to or chat with briefly now and then. Mark their rooms with a number *3*.

Now, examine the pattern of friendships on your map. Are your friends clustered near your room in physical space? Are the dorm rooms with the numbers *1* and *2* among the closest to your room in physical space? Are they physically closer to your room than the ones with number *3*? And what about the dorm rooms that didn't get a number (meaning that you don't really know these people or interact with them)—are these rooms the farthest from yours?

Finally, examine your propinquity map for the presence of *functional distance* as well. Do aspects of the architectural design of your dorm make you more likely to cross paths with some dorm members more than others? For example, the location of the restroom, kitchen, livingroom, stairs or elevator, and mailboxes can play an important role in propinquity and friendship formation. These are all places that you go to frequently; when walking to and from them, you pass some people's dorm rooms and not others. Are the people who live along your path the ones you know the best? If so, propinquity has played an important role in determining the people with whom you have formed relationships!

---

the residents to name their three closest friends in the entire housing project. Just as the propinquity effect would predict, 65 percent of the friends mentioned lived in the same building, even though the other buildings were not far away. Even more striking was the pattern of friendships within a building. Each Westgate West building was designed like the drawing in Figure 10.1; 19 feet separated the majority of the front doors, while the greatest distance between apartment doors was only 89 feet. The researchers found that 41 percent of the next-door neighbors indicated they were close friends, 22 percent of those who lived two doors apart did so, and only 10 percent of those who lived on opposite ends of the hall indicated they were close friends.

Festinger and his colleagues (1950) demonstrated that attraction and propinquity rely not only on actual physical distance but also on the more psychological, functional distance as well. Functional distance is defined as certain aspects of architectural design that make it more likely that some people will come into contact with each other more often than with others. For example, consider the friendship choices of the residents of apartments 1 and 5 (see Figure 10.1). Living at the foot of the stairs and in one case near the mailboxes meant that these couples saw a great deal of upstairs residents. Sure enough, apartment dwellers in apartments 1 and 5 throughout the complex had more friends upstairs than dwellers in the other first-floor apartments did. (You can map out propinquity effects in your life with the Try It! exercise above.)

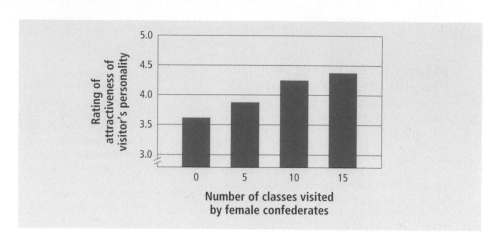

■ **FIGURE 10.2** The effects that mere exposure in the classroom has on attraction. The more often students saw a female confederate in their classroom, the more positively they rated her personality, even though they had never interacted with her. (Adapted from Moreland & Beach, 1992)

Mere Exposure Effect
the finding that the more exposure we have to a stimulus, the more apt we are to like it

Contrary to popular belief, I do not believe that friends are necessarily the people you like best, they are merely the people who got there first.

–Sir Peter Ustinov, 1977

The propinquity effect works because of familiarity, or the **mere exposure effect:** the more exposure we have to a stimulus, the more apt we are to like it. We see certain people a lot, and the more familiar they become, the more friendship blooms. Of course, if the person in question is an obnoxious jerk, then, not surprisingly, the more exposure you have to him or her, the greater your dislike (Swap, 1977). But in the absence of such negative qualities, familiarity breeds attraction and liking (Bornstein, 1989; Bornstein & D'Agostino, 1992; Bornstein, Leone, & Galley, 1987; Griffin & Sparks, 1990; Moreland & Zajonc, 1982; Wilmot & Stevens, 1994; Zajonc, 1968). Familiarity can occur in a new way today—we can get to know each other through electronic mail and computer chat rooms. Computer-mediated communication offers a new twist on the propinquity effect; the fact that someone is thousands of miles away no longer means you can't meet him or her. Are computer-based relationships the same as ones formed in everyday life? Do computer relationships survive when they move from the computer screen to face-to-face interactions? Current research is beginning to explore these questions (Fehr, 1996; Lea & Spears, 1995; McLeod, 1992; Walther, Anderson, & Park, 1994).

A good example of the propinquity and mere exposure effects is your college classroom. All semester long, you see the same people. Does this increase your liking for them? Richard Moreland and Scott Beach (1992) tested this hypothesis by planting female research confederates in a large college classroom. The women did not interact with the professor or the other students; they just walked in and sat quietly in the first row, where everyone could see them. The confederates differed in how many classes they attended, from 15 meetings down to the control condition of none. At the end of the semester, the students in the class were shown slides of the women, whom they rated on several measures of liking and attractiveness. As you can see in Figure 10.2, mere exposure had a definite effect on liking. Even though they had never interacted, the students liked the women more the more often they had seen them in class.

Similarity

While propinquity does affect friendship choices, it is also the case that we don't become good friends with everyone who is near us in physical space. What about the match between our interests, attitudes, values, background, and personality and those of the other person? Are we more attracted to people who are like us (the concept of *similarity*), or are we more attracted to people who are our opposites (the concept of *complementarity*)? Folk wisdom may suggest that "opposites attract," but research evidence proves that it is similarity, not complementarity, that draws people together (Berscheid & Reis, 1998).

For example, dozens of tightly controlled experiments have shown that if all you know about a person (whom you've never met) are his or her opinions on several issues, the more similar those opinions are to yours, the more you will like him or her (e.g., Byrne & Nelson, 1965). And what happens when you do meet? In a classic study, Theodore Newcomb (1961) randomly assigned male college students at the University of Michigan to be roommates in a particular dormitory at the start of the school year. Would similarity predict friendship formation? The answer was yes: Men became friends with those who were demographically similar (e.g., shared a rural background), as well as with those who were similar in attitudes and values (e.g., were also engineering majors or also held liberal political views). Finally, similarity in personality characteristics also promotes liking and attraction. For example, Tom Boyden and his colleagues (1984) found strong support for similarity in personality in gay men's relationships. Gay men who scored high on a test of stereotypical male traits desired a partner who was most of all logical—a stereotypical masculine trait. Gay men who scored high on a test of stereotypical female traits desired a partner who was most of all expressive—a stereotypical feminine trait. The importance of similarity in personality characteristics has also been found for heterosexual couples and for friends (Aube & Koestner, 1995; Caspi & Harbener, 1990; Martin & Anderson, 1995).

Why is similarity so important in attraction? There are at least two possibilities. First, people who are similar provide us with important social validation for our characteristics and beliefs—that is, they provide us with the feeling that we are right (Byrne & Clore, 1970). Second, we make negative inferences about someone who disagrees with us on important issues. We suspect the individual's opinion is indicative of the kind of person we have found in the past to be

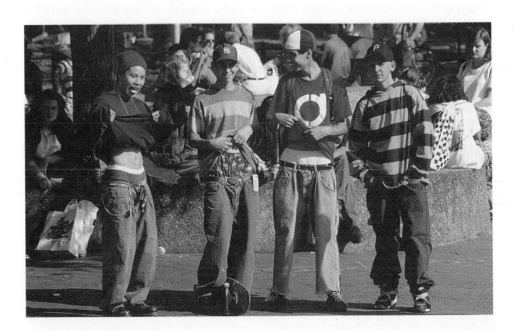

■ Similarity is one of the major determinants of attraction.

■ Despite folklore about how "opposites attract," people are almost always more attracted to those who are similar to them.

unpleasant, immoral, weak, or thoughtless. In short, disagreement on important attitudes leads to repulsion (Rosenbaum, 1986). Thus, the desire to be validated and the conclusions we draw about character both play a role in boosting the attractiveness of a like-minded person and diminishing the attractiveness of someone who is dissimilar (Byrne, Clore, & Smeaton, 1986; Cate & Lloyd, 1992; Condon & Crano, 1988; Dryer & Horowitz, 1997; Fehr, 1996; Felmlee, 1995; Griffitt & Veitch, 1974; Holtz, 1997; Houts, Robins, & Huston, 1996; Tan & Singh, 1995).

Reciprocal Liking

We all like to be liked. This is one of the prime determinants of interpersonal attraction. Liking is so powerful that it can even make up for the absence of similarity. For example, in one experiment, when a young woman expressed interest in male research participants simply by maintaining eye contact, leaning toward them, and listening attentively, the men expressed great liking for her despite the fact that they knew she disagreed with them on important issues (Gold, Ryckman, & Mosley, 1984). Whether the clues are nonverbal or verbal, perhaps the most crucial determinant of whether we will like person A is the extent to which we believe person A likes us (Berscheid & Walster, 1978; Condon & Crano, 1988; Hays, 1984; Kenny, 1994; Kenny & La Voie, 1982; Kenny & Nasby, 1980; Secord & Backman, 1964).

Reciprocal liking can come about because of a self-fulfilling prophecy. Rebecca Curtis and Kim Miller (1986) illustrated this process by conducting the following experiment. College students took part in the study in pairs; they had not known each other prior to meeting at the study. One member of each pair was randomly chosen to receive special information. The researchers led some college students to believe that the other student liked them, and others to believe that the other student disliked them. The pairs of students were then allowed to meet and talk to each other again. Just as predicted, those individuals who thought they were liked behaved in more likable ways with their partner; they disclosed more about themselves, disagreed less about the topic under discussion, and generally behaved in a warmer, more pleasant manner than those individuals who thought they were disliked. Moreover, those who believed they were liked came to be liked by the other student to a far greater extent than those who be-

> **L**ife is to be fortified by many friendships. To love, and to be loved, is the greatest happiness of existence.
>
> —Sydney Smith, 1855

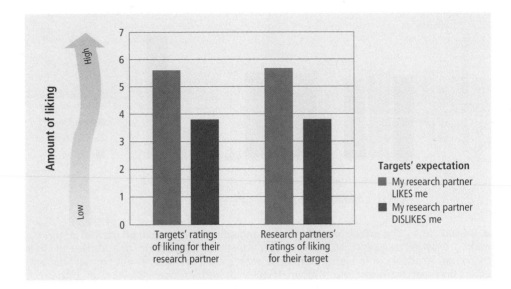

■ **FIGURE 10.3 Liking and being liked** Research participants were given false feedback that their research partner either did or did not like them. They liked their partner more if they had been told beforehand that their partner liked them (see left-hand side of figure), and their partners responded in kind (see right-hand side of figure). Beliefs did indeed create reality. (Adapted from Curtis & Miller, 1986)

lieved they were disliked. In short, the partner tended to mirror the behaviors of the person with whom he or she was paired (see Figure 10.3).

The Role of Self-Esteem in Reciprocal Liking

Most of the time, being liked by a person is a powerful determinant of our liking for them. But William Swann, Jr., has found that the amount of self-esteem a person has affects this process (Swann, 1992; Swann, Stein-Seroussi, & McNulty, 1992). People with a positive or moderate self-concept respond to other's liking with reciprocal liking, as we've discussed above. But people with a negative self-concept respond quite differently—in an experimental setting, such people indicate that they'd prefer to meet and talk to a person they know has criticized them earlier than meet and talk to a person they know has praised them earlier (Swann et al., 1992). If you think of yourself as not being worth very much or even as unlikable, other people's friendly behavior toward you will seem unwarranted and you may not respond.

Does self-esteem affect reciprocal liking in important, close relationships such as marriage? William Swann, Jr., and his colleagues (1992) have startling evidence that it does. They asked married couples to rate themselves and their partners on a series of traits and qualities. They also asked the spouses to rate several questions about how committed they were to their marriages. The researchers then compared the people's level of self-esteem, their commitment to their spouses, and their partner's appraisal of them. As you can see in Figure 10.4, there was little difference between participants when the spouse's appraisal of them was unfavorable or moderate. However, when the spouse's view of them was favorable, only those people whose self-concept was also positive or moderately so responded with reciprocal liking—they indicated a high level of commitment to the spouse. In comparison, people with a negative self-concept whose partner viewed them favorably were significantly less likely to respond in kind—they indicated the lowest level of commitment to their spouse.

What if your partner views you more than favorably; what if he or she thinks you're fabulous? Again, self-esteem plays a role in the extent to which reciprocal

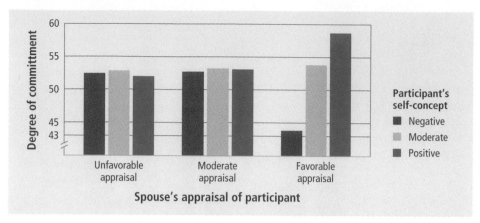

■ **FIGURE 10.4   The effects of self-concept and spouse's appraisal on marital commitment.**   Married couples rated themselves, their spouses, and their commitment to their marriage. As shown in the left and middle panels, the participants' self-concept had no effect on their commitment to their marriages when their spouse's appraisal of them was unfavorable or moderate. However, when their spouse's appraisal was favorable (see right panel), those with a negative self-concept indicated a significantly lower level of commitment than those with more positive self-concepts. (Adapted from Swann, Hixon, & De La Ronde, 1992)

> Love to faults is always blind,
> Always is to joy inclin'd.
> –William Blake, *Poems*

liking occurs. Sandra Murray, John Holmes, and Dale Griffin (1996) studied heterosexual dating couples over the course of one year. They found that satisfying, stable, and secure relationships depended on the partners seeing the best in each other. Furthermore, the higher people's self-esteem, the more they "idealized" their partners—by overlooking their partners' faults and exaggerating or embellishing their partners' virtues. These couples were more happy and confident about their relationships over the year, were less likely to be upset by arguments and conflict, and were less likely to break up than those who did not engage in idealization. Most importantly, being "idealized" by their dating partners actually led men and women to change their self-concepts positively, in the direction of their partners' illusions. A self-fulfilling prophesy occurred: When people's partners thought they were wonderful (e.g., kind and affectionate; understanding; patient), they came to believe that they had those wonderful qualities too.

The Effects of Physical Attractiveness on Liking

Propinquity, similarity, and reciprocal liking are not the only determinants of who we will come to like. How important is physical appearance to our first impressions of people? In field experiments investigating people's actual behavior (rather than what they say they will do), people overwhelmingly go for physical attractiveness. For example, in a classic study Elaine Hatfield (Walster) and her colleagues (1966) randomly matched 752 incoming students at the University of Minnesota for a blind date at a dance during freshman orientation week. While the students had previously taken a battery of personality and aptitude tests, the researchers paired them up at random. On the night of the dance, the couples spent a few hours together dancing and chatting. They then evaluated their date and indicated the strength of their desire to date that person again. Of the many possible characteristics that could have determined whether they liked each other—such as their partner's intelligence, independence, sensitivity, or sincerity—the overriding determinant was physical attractiveness.

What's more, there was no great difference between men and women on this score. This is an interesting point, for while several studies have found that men and women pay equal attention to the physical attractiveness of others (Andersen & Bem, 1981; Crouse & Mehrabian, 1977; Duck, 1994; Stretch & Figley, 1980; Lynn & Shurgot, 1984; Speed & Gangestad, 1997; Woll, 1986), other studies have reported that men value attractiveness more than women do (Buss, 1989; Buss & Barnes, 1986; Howard, Blumstein, & Schwartz, 1987). In a recent meta-analysis of many studies, Alan Feingold (1990) reports that while both sexes value attractiveness, men do value it somewhat more than women do. In particular, Feingold (1990) found that this gender difference was much larger when men's and women's attitudes were being measured than when their actual behavior was being measured. Thus, it may be the case that men are more likely than women to say that physical attractiveness is important to them in a potential friend, date, or mate, but when it comes to actual behavior, the sexes are more similar in their response to the physical attractiveness of others.

The powerful role that physical appearance plays in attraction is not limited to heterosexual relationships. Paul Sergios and James Cody (1985) conducted a replication of the "blind date" study described above, with gay men as the research participants. The gay men responded just as the heterosexual men and women had in the earlier study: The physical attractiveness of their dates was the strongest predictor of their liking for them.

It is only shallow people who do not judge by appearances.
—Oscar Wilde, 1891

Cultural Standards of Beauty

Is physical attractiveness in "the eye of the beholder," or do we all share some of the same notions of what is beautiful and handsome? From early childhood on, the media tell us what is beautiful and they tell us that this specific definition of beauty is associated with goodness. For example, illustrators of most traditional children's books, as well as the people who draw the characters in Disney movies, have taught us that the heroines—as well as the princes who woo and win them—all look alike. They all have regular features; small, pert noses, big eyes, shapely lips, blemish-free complexions; and slim, athletic bodies—pretty much like Barbie and Ken dolls.

Bombarded as we are with media depictions of attractiveness, it is not surprising to learn that we share a set of criteria for defining beauty (Tseëlon, 1995). Look at the photographs on page 382 of models and actors who are considered very attractive in Western culture. Can you describe the facial characteristics that have earned them this label? Michael Cunningham (1986) designed a creative study to determine these standards of beauty. He asked college men to rate the attractiveness of 50 photographs of women, taken from a college yearbook and from an international beauty pageant program. Cunningham then carefully measured the relative size of the facial features in each photograph. He found that high attractiveness ratings were associated with faces with large eyes, a small nose, a small chin, prominent cheekbones and narrow cheeks, high eyebrows, large pupils, and a big smile. Next, Michael Cunningham, Anita Barbee, and Carolyn Pike examined women's ratings of male beauty in the same manner. They found that higher attractiveness ratings were associated with men's faces with large eyes, prominent cheekbones, a large chin, and a big smile (Cunningham, Barbee, & Pike, 1995).

There is some overlap in the men's and women's ratings. Both sexes admire large eyes in the opposite sex, and these are considered a "babyface" feature, for newborn mammals have very large eyes for the size of their faces. Babyface features

Beauty is a greater recommendation than any letter of introduction.
—Aristotle, fourth century B.C.

■ Research has found that we share some standards of beauty. In females, large eyes, prominent cheekbones and narrow cheeks, high eyebrows, and a small chin were associated with beauty; in males, large eyes, prominent cheekbones, and a large chin were rated as most beautiful. Today's popular models and film stars, such as Brad Pitt, Michelle Pfeiffer, Naomi Campbell, and Denzel Washington, fit these criteria.

are thought to be attractive because they elicit feelings of warmth and nurturance in perceivers—for example, our response to babies, kittens, and puppies (e.g., Berry, 1995; McArthur & Berry, 1987; Zebrowitz, 1997; Zebrowitz & Montepare, 1992). Both sexes also admire prominent cheekbones in the opposite sex, an adult feature that is found only in the faces of those who are sexually mature. Note that the female face that is considered beautiful has more baby-face features (small nose, small chin) than the handsome male face, suggesting that beauty in the female is associated more with childlike qualities than male beauty is.

Are people's perceptions of what is beautiful or handsome similar across cultures? The answer is a surprising yes (Cunningham et al., 1995; Jones & Hill, 1993; Langlois & Roggman, 1990; McArthur & Berry, 1987; Perrett, May, & Yoshikawa, 1994). While racial and ethnic groups do vary in specific facial features, people from disparate cultures agree with each other on what is physically attractive in the human face. Researchers in this area asked participants from various countries, ethnicities, and racial groups to rate the physical attractiveness of photographed faces of people who also represent various countries, ethnicities, and racial groups. The participants' ratings agree to a remarkable extent. For example, one review of the literature found that the correlations between partici-

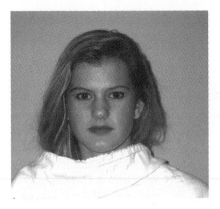  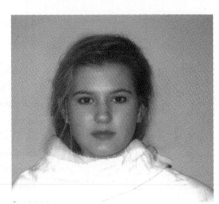

■ **Physical attractiveness of composite faces.** Langlois & Roggman (1990) created composites of faces using a computer. Pictured here is the first step in the process: The two women's photos on the left are merged to create the "composite person" on the right. This composite person has facial features that are the mathematical average of the facial features of the two original women. The final step of the process occurs when 32 individuals' faces have been merged to create one face, the average of all of the prior 32 faces. Perceivers rated the 32-photograph composite face as more physically attractive than any of the individual faces that had created it. (From Langlois, Roggman, & Musselman, 1994)

pants' ratings ranged from .66 to .93 (Langlois & Roggman, 1990), which you will recall from Chapter 2 are very strong correlations. While there *is* variation in people's judgments, across large groups a general consensus emerges: Perceivers think some faces are just better looking than others, regardless of cultural background (Berscheid & Reis, 1998).

The results showing cross-cultural agreement on physical attractiveness led Judith Langlois and Lori Roggman (1990; Langlois, Roggman, & Musselman, 1994) to hypothesize that there are universal dimensions of faces that are attractive to the species, perhaps due to evolutionary mechanisms. They further hypothesized that attractive faces for both sexes are those whose features are the arithmetic mean—or average—for the species and not the extremes.

To test these hypotheses, Langlois and her colleagues (1990, 1994) designed an elegant and original study. They took photographs of many college students (mostly Caucasians, with some Hispanics and Asians) and digitalized each photograph by scanning it into a computer. They then took two people's photographs (men or women) and, using the computer, merged the two photographs into one. The resulting single photograph—or composite—was the exact mathematical average of the facial features of the two original people's photographs. The photographs on this page show the result of this merging; the composite photograph, or average, is a blend of the two original women.

Langlois and Roggman (1990) continued adding new photographs until they created a single photograph composite based on 16 different faces (as well as a composite based on 32 faces), with the composite being created by averaging in the facial features of each added photograph. Next, they asked research participants to rate the physical attractiveness of the composite photograph and the individual photographs that made up the composite. Would the composite photograph—or the arithmetic average of all the faces—be judged more attractive than all the separate faces that helped create that composite? The answer was yes, for both male and female photographs, and across many different sets of photographs. The 16 or 32 face composites produced what the researchers called a typical or "familiar" face. Individual variation in facial features melted away in the composite; what was left was a good-looking human being, whose face had a familiar and highly pleasing aspect to it.

Ellen Berscheid and Harry Reis (1998) conjecture that *familiarity* in its many forms may be the crucial variable that explains interpersonal attraction. As we have just seen, "averaging" many faces together produces one face that looks typical, familiar, and physically attractive. Familiarity also underlies the other concepts we have discussed thus far: propinquity (people we see frequently become familiar through mere exposure); similarity (people who are similar to us will also seem familiar to us); and reciprocal liking (people who like each other get to know and become familiar with each other). As Berscheid and Reis (1998) note, all of these attraction variables "appear to be specific manifestations of an underlying preference for the familiar and safe over the unfamiliar and potentially dangerous" (p. 210).

Assumptions about Attractive People

Most people assume that physical attractiveness is highly correlated with other desirable traits. The results of many studies indicate that beauty constitutes a powerful stereotype—what Karen Dion, Ellen Berscheid, and Elaine Walster (1972) have called the "what is beautiful is good" stereotype (Ashmore & Longo, 1995; Ashmore, Solomon, & Longo, 1996; Brigham, 1980; Calvert, 1988; Dion et al., 1972; Hassebrauck, 1988; Hatfield & Sprecher, 1986; Moore, Graziano, & Millar, 1987).

Luckily for those of us who do not look like supermodels, the stereotype is relatively narrow, affecting people's judgments about an individual only in specific areas. Meta-analyses conducted by Alice Eagly and her colleagues (1991) and by Alan Feingold (1992a) revealed that physical attractiveness has the largest effect on both men's and women's attributions when they are making judgments about social competence: The beautiful are thought to be more sociable, extraverted, and popular than the less attractive. They are also seen as more sexual, more happy, and more assertive.

Does the "what is beautiful is good" stereotype operate across cultures? The answer appears to be yes. Ladd Wheeler and Youngmee Kim (1997) asked college students in Seoul, South Korea to rate a number of yearbook photographs that varied in physical attractiveness. They found that the Korean male and female participants thought the more physically attractive people would also be more socially skilled, friendly, and well-adjusted—the same group of traits that North American participants thought went with physical attractiveness (see Table 10.1). However, Korean and North American students differed in some of the other traits they assigned to the beautiful; these differences highlight what is considered important and valuable in each culture (Markus, Kitayama, & Heiman, 1996; Triandis, 1995). For the American and Canadian students, who live in "individualistic" cultures that value independence, individuality, and self-reliance, the "beautiful" stereotype included traits of personal strength (see Table 10.1). These traits were not part of the Korean "beautiful" stereotype. Instead, for the Korean students, who live in a "collectivistic" culture that values harmonious group relations, the "beautiful" stereotype included traits of integrity and concern for others, traits that were not part of the North American stereotype (see Table 10.1).

Table 10.1

How culture affects the "what is beautiful is good" stereotype

The "what is beautiful is good" stereotype has been explored in two types of cultures: an "individualistic" culture (North America) and a "collectivistic" culture (Asia). Male and female research participants in the United States and Canada and in South Korea rated photographs of people with varying degrees of physical attractiveness. Their responses indicated that some of the traits that make up the stereotype are the same across cultures, while other traits that are associated with the stereotype are different in the two types of culture:

Traits that are shared in the Korean, American, and Canadian stereotype of "what is beautiful is good"

sociable	extraverted
likeable	happy
popular	well-adjusted
friendly	mature
poised	sexually warm and responsive

Additional traits that are present in the American and Canadian stereotype

strong
dominant
assertive

Additional traits that are present in the Korean stereotype

sensitive	empathic
generous	honest
trustworthy	

The basic elements of the "what is beautiful is good" stereotype are shared across cultures; these traits involve social skills and competence. However, individualistic and collectivistic cultures add other elements to the stereotype, reflecting what is valued in each. The United States and Canada are "individualistic" cultures, where independence and self-reliance are valued; the "beautiful" stereotype incorporates these traits of personal strength. Korea is a collectivistic culture where harmony in group relations is valued; the "beautiful" stereotype in that culture reflects traits involving integrity and concern for others. Thus, in both cultures, the physically attractive are seen as having more of the characteristics that are valued in that culture than are the less physically attractive.

Adapted from Eagly, Ashmore, Makhijani, & Longo (1991); Feingold, 1992a; Wheeler & Kim, 1997

Interestingly, the stereotype that the beautiful are particularly gifted in the area of social competence has some research support; highly attractive people do develop good social interaction skills and report having more satisfying interactions with others than the less attractive do (Berscheid & Reis, 1998; Feingold, 1992a; Garcia et al., 1991; Reis, Nezlek, & Wheeler, 1980; Reis et al., 1982). Undoubtedly, this "kernel of truth" in the stereotype occurs because the beautiful, from a young age, receive a great deal of social attention that in turn helps them develop good social skills. You probably recognize the *self-fulfilling prophecy* at work here, a concept we discussed in Chapter 3: The way we treat people affects how they behave and, ultimately, how they perceive themselves. Can a "regular" person be made to act like a "beautiful" one through the self-fulfilling prophecy? Mark Snyder, Elizabeth Decker Tanke, and Ellen Berscheid (1977) decided to find out. They gave college men a packet of information about another research participant, including her photograph. The photograph was rigged; it was either of an attractive woman or of an unattractive woman. The men were told that they would have a telephone conversation with this woman (in this experimental condition, only verbal communication—no gestures or facial expressions—were used). The experimental purpose of the photograph was to invoke the men's stereotype that "what is beautiful is good"—that the woman would be more warm, likable, poised, and fun to talk to if she was physically attractive than if she was unattractive. In fact, the photograph the men were given was not a photo of the woman with whom they spoke. Did the men's beliefs create reality?

Yes: The men who thought they were talking to an attractive woman responded to her in a warmer, more sociable manner than the men who thought they were talking to an unattractive woman did. Not only that, but the men's behavior influenced how the women themselves responded. When independent observers listened to a tape recording of only the woman's half of the conversation (without looking at the photograph), they rated the women whose male partners thought they were physically attractive as more attractive, confident, animated, and warm than the women whose male partners thought they were unattractive. In short, because the male partner thought he was talking to an attractive woman, he spoke to her in a way that brought out her best and most sparkling qualities.

This study was later replicated with the roles switched: Susan Andersen and Sandra Bem (1981) showed women participants a photograph of an attractive or an unattractive man; the women then had a phone conversation with him. The men on the other end of the line were unaware of the women's belief about them. Just as in the Snyder, Tanke, and Berscheid (1977) study, the women acted on their "prophecy" and the unknowing men responded accordingly.

Recollections of Initial Attraction

We've now discussed several predictors of initial attraction and liking: propinquity, similarity, reciprocal liking, and physical attractiveness. At the beginning of the chapter, we asked you to think about why you were first attracted to your friends and romantic partners. Arthur Aron, Donald Dutton, Elaine Aron, and Adrienne Iverson (1989) conducted a similar study, asking both college students and older adults to give accounts of how they fell into love or into friendship with specific people in their lives. The researchers then coded these accounts for the presence of the classic social psychological variables we have discussed. Do people spontaneously report such factors as the cause for their initial feelings of attraction?

Yes, they do. First, for the falling-in-love accounts, Aron and his colleagues found that reciprocal liking and attractiveness (involving both physical and personality qualities) were mentioned spontaneously with very high frequency. The power of these two variables together led the researchers to conclude, "Reading

*O*h, what vileness human beauty is, corroding, corrupting everything it touches.
—Orestes, 408 B.C.

the actual accounts leads to the impression that people are just waiting for an attractive person to do something they can interpret as liking them" (1989, p. 251). Mentioned with moderate frequency were variables such as being ready for or looking for a romantic relationship, and being unhappy in a current relationship. Finally, similarity and propinquity were mentioned with low to moderate frequency. The researchers suggest that these two variables may be underreported because people do not remember or notice experiencing them, or because they are seen as too mundane to explain something so exciting as falling in love. Aron and his colleagues also note that similarity and propinquity may play an important role before one falls in love, by narrowing the field to only those people who are "eligible." This basic pattern of results for falling in love has been found cross-culturally as well, for Chinese American and Mexican American students in the United States (Aron & Rodriguez, 1992) and for students in Japan and Russia (Sprecher et al., 1994).

Second, for the falling-into-friendship accounts, the researchers again found that reciprocal liking and attractiveness were the most frequently mentioned reasons, though they were mentioned less often than in the falling-in-love accounts. For friendship attraction, similarity and propinquity were mentioned very frequently, and more so than in the falling-in-love accounts. Thus, the attraction variables of attractiveness, reciprocal liking, similarity, and propinquity not only predict people's behavior in laboratory experiments but also are present in people's spontaneous recollections of their real-life experiences with attraction (Aron & Aron, 1996).

Steve Duck (1994) also wondered if the classic attraction variables operated when people were getting acquainted in real-life settings. He randomly paired college men and women and sent them off on a "get-acquainted date." When they returned, they filled out several questionnaires for him; specifically, they rated their date on physical attractiveness, on how similar he or she was to themselves, and on the quality of their conversation—a new variable that Duck hypothesized would be a powerful predictor of attraction. Duck found that for both men and women, the strongest predictor of romantic (dating) attraction was the perceived physical attractiveness of the other person. For both men and women, the second strongest predictor of romantic attraction was similarity. Quality of communication did not predict romantic attraction for men or women; it appears that after one date, what he or she looks like and how similar he or she is to you have far more of an effect than anything he or she says!

In comparison, the pattern for opposite-sex friendship attraction was very different for men versus women (Duck, 1994). For men, perceived similarity was the strongest predictor of friendship attraction, followed by physical attractiveness. For women, the strongest predictor of friendship attraction was the quality of communication, followed by similarity. When experiencing friendship attraction, women appear to value conversation and respond positively to quality conversation to a greater extent than men do (Duck, 1994), a finding echoed by other researchers (Bendtschneider & Duck, 1993; Fehr, 1996; Johnson & Aries, 1983; Reisman, 1990).

Theories of Interpersonal Attraction: Social Exchange and Equity

The determinants of attraction we have discussed so far concern aspects of the situation (propinquity, repeated exposure), the individual's attributes (physical

> "Don't threaten me with love, baby. Let's go walking in the rain.
> —Billie Holliday

> **L**ove is often nothing but a favorable exchange between two people who get the most of what they can expect, considering their value on the personality market.
>
> —Erich Fromm, 1955

attractiveness, similarity, self-esteem), and the individual's behavior (conveying liking). We turn now to theories of interpersonal attraction that link these different phenomena together.

Social Exchange Theory

Many of the variables we have discussed can be thought of as examples of social rewards. It is pleasing to have our attitudes validated; thus, the more similar a person's attitudes are to ours, the more rewarded we feel. Likewise, it is rewarding to be around someone who likes us and is physically attractive. One way of summarizing much of our discussion so far is to say that the more social rewards a person provides us with (and the fewer costs), the more we will like him or her. The flip side of this equation is that if a relationship costs (e.g., in terms of emotional turmoil) far more than it gives (e.g., in terms of validation or praise), chances are that it will not last very long.

This simple notion that relationships operate on an economic model of costs and benefits, much like the marketplace, has been expanded by psychologists and sociologists into complex theories of social exchange (Blau, 1964; Homans, 1961; Kelly & Thibaut, 1978; Thibaut & Kelley, 1959). **Social exchange theory** states that how people feel (positively or negatively) about their relationships will depend on their perception of the rewards they receive from the relationship and their perception of the costs they incur, as well as their perception of what kind of relationship they deserve and the probability that they could have a better relationship with someone else. In other words, we buy the best relationship we can get, one that gives us the most value for our emotional dollar. The basic concepts of social exchange theory are reward, cost, outcome, and comparison level (Secord & Backman, 1964).

Rewards are the positive, gratifying aspects of the relationship that make it worthwhile and reinforcing. They include the kinds of personal characteristics and behaviors of our relationship partner that we have already discussed and our ability to acquire external resources by virtue of knowing this person (e.g., gaining access to money, status, activities, or other interesting people; Lott & Lott, 1974). For example, in Brazil friendship is openly used as an exchange value. As Monica Rector and Eduardo Neiva (1996) explain, Brazilians will readily admit that they need a *pistolão* (literally, a big, powerful handgun), meaning they need a person who will use his or her personal connections to help them get what they want. *Costs* are, obviously, the other side of the coin, and all friendships and romantic relationships have some costs attached to them (e.g., putting up with those annoying habits and characteristics of the other person). The outcome of the relationship is a direct comparison of its rewards and costs; you can think of it as a mathematical formula where outcome equals rewards minus costs. (If you come up with a negative number, your relationship is not in good shape.)

How satisfied you are with your relationship depends on another variable—your **comparison level,** or what you expect the outcome of your relationship to be in terms of costs and rewards (Kelley & Thibaut, 1978; Thibaut & Kelley, 1959). Over time, you have amassed a long history of relationships with other people, and this history has led you to have certain expectations as to what your current and future relationships should be like. Some people have a high comparison level, expecting to receive lots of rewards and few costs in their relationships. If a given relationship doesn't match this expected comparison level, they will be un-

Social Exchange Theory the theory holding that how people feel about a relationship depends on their perceptions of the rewards and costs of the relationship, the kind of relationship they deserve, and their chances for having a better relationship with someone else

Comparison Level people's expectations about the level of rewards and punishments they are likely to receive in a particular relationship

happy and unsatisfied. In contrast, people who have a low comparison level would be happy in the same relationship, because they expect relationships to be difficult and costly.

Finally, your satisfaction with a relationship also depends on your perception of the likelihood that you could replace it with a better one—or your **comparison level for alternatives**. There are a lot of people out there—could a relationship with a different person give you a better outcome, or greater rewards for fewer costs, than your current one? People who have a high comparison level for alternatives, either because they believe the world is full of fabulous people dying to meet them or because they know of a fabulous person dying to meet them, are more likely to get into circulation and make a new friend or find a new lover. People with a low comparison level for alternatives will be more likely to stay in a costly relationship, because to them, what they have is not great but is better than their expectation of what they could find elsewhere (Simpson, 1987).

Social exchange theory has received a great deal of empirical support; friends and romantic couples do pay attention to the costs and rewards in their relationships, and these affect how positively people feel about the status of the relationship (Attridge & Berscheid, 1994; Bui, Peplau, & Hill, 1996; Jacobson, Waldron, & Moore, 1980; Rusbult, 1983; Rusbult & Martz, 1995; Rusbult & Van Lange, 1996; South & Lloyd, 1995; Wills, Weiss, & Patterson, 1974).

Comparison Level for Alternatives
people's expectations about the level of rewards and punishments they would receive in an alternative relationship

> **F**riendship is a scheme for the mutual exchange of personal advantages and favors.
> —Francois La Rochefoucauld

Equity Theory

Some researchers have criticized social exchange theory for ignoring an essential variable in relationships—the notion of fairness, or equity. Those propounding **equity theory,** such as Elaine Walster, Ellen Berscheid, and George Homans, argue that people are not just out to get the most rewards for the least cost; they are also concerned about equity in their relationships, wherein the rewards and costs they experience and the contributions they make to the relationship are roughly equal to the rewards, costs, and contributions of the other person (Homans, 1961; Walster, Walster, & Berscheid, 1978). These theorists describe equitable relationships as the most happy and stable type. In comparison, inequitable relationships result in one person feeling overbenefited (getting a lot of rewards, incurring few costs, having to devote little time or energy to the relationship) or underbenefited (getting few rewards, incurring a lot of costs, having to devote a lot of time and energy to the relationship).

According to equity theory, both underbenefited and overbenefited partners should feel uneasy about this state of affairs, and both should be motivated to restore equity to the relationship. This makes sense for the underbenefited person (who wants to continue feeling miserable?), but why should the overbenefited individual want to give up what social exchange theory indicates is a cushy deal—lots of rewards for little cost and little work? Elaine Hatfield (Walster) and her colleagues argue that equity is a powerful social norm—people will eventually feel uncomfortable or even guilty if they get more than they deserve in a relationship. However, let's face facts—being overbenefited just doesn't seem as bad as being underbenefited, and research has borne out that inequity is perceived as more of a problem by the underbenefited individual (Buunk & Van Yperen, 1991; Clark & Chrisman, 1994; Hatfield, Greenberger, Traupmann, & Lambert, 1982; Hegtvedt, Thompson, & Cook, 1993; Sprecher & Schwartz, 1994; Traupmann, Petersen, Utne, & Hatfield, 1981; Van Yperen & Buunk, 1994).

Equity Theory
the theory holding that people are happiest with relationships in which the rewards and costs a person experiences and the contributions he or she makes to the relationship are roughly equal to the rewards, costs, and contributions of the other person

© Sydney Harris

"THIS IS GOODBYE, GENTLEMEN. I HAVE MET ANOTHER BOARD OF DIRECTORS, AND WE HAVE FALLEN IN LOVE."

■ This man has obviously checked his "comparison level for alternatives" and decided his new Board of Directors offers greater rewards for fewer costs than this one.

Close Relationships

After getting to this point in the chapter, you should be in a pretty good position to make a favorable first impression the next time you meet someone. Suppose you want Claudia to like you. You should hang around her so that you become familiar, act in ways that are rewarding to her, emphasize your similarity to her, and let her know you enjoy her company. But what if you want to do more than make a good impression? What if you want to have a close friendship or a romantic relationship?

Until recently, social psychologists had little to say in answer to this question; research on interpersonal attraction focused almost exclusively on first impressions. Why? Primarily because long-term, close relationships are much more difficult to study scientifically than first impressions. As we saw in Chapter 2, random assignment to different conditions is the hallmark of an experiment. When studying first impressions, a researcher can randomly assign you to a get-acquainted session with someone who is similar or dissimilar to you. But a researcher can't randomly assign you to the similar or dissimilar "lover" condition and make you have a relationship! In addition, the feelings and intimacy associated with close relationships can be difficult to measure. Psychologists face a daunting task when trying to measure such inchoate feelings as love and passion.

> Love is something so divine,
> Description would but make it less;
> 'Tis what I feel, but can't define,
> 'Tis what I know, but can't express.
> —Beilby Porteus

Defining Love

Though the difficulties in studying close relationships are severe, they are not insurmountable. In the past decade, social psychologists have made significant strides in studying the nature of love, how it develops, and how it flourishes.

Let's begin with perhaps the most difficult of these questions: What exactly is love?

If you have ever been in love, think back to how you felt about your sweetheart when you first got to know him or her. You probably felt a combination of giddiness, longing, joy, and anxiety. The ancient Greeks considered this strange, bewildering set of feelings to be a form of madness, causing all sorts of irrational and obsessional acts. Though times have changed, we are all familiar with the torment—and exhilaration—that comes with falling in love.

A number of psychologists have developed measures of love (Aron, Aron, & Smollan, 1990; Berscheid, 1988; Berscheid, Snyder, & Omoto, 1989; Henrick & Henrick, 1986; Kelley, 1983; Lee, 1977, 1988; Rubin, 1970, 1973; Shaver, Schwartz, Kirson, & O'Connor, 1987). Initial attempts distinguished between liking and loving, showing that, as you might expect, love is something different from "lots of liking," and it isn't just sexual desire either (Rubin, 1970). Later attempts dived deeper into the phenomenon by addressing what we all know intuitively is true: There seem to be different kinds of love. Let's examine three of these conceptualizations of love.

> **T**ry to reason about love and you will lose your reason.
> –French proverb

Compassionate versus Passionate Love

Consider the love between Sadie and Bessie Delany, a love that lasted over 100 years. They experienced deep feelings of devotion and intimacy. Consider as well the love between Romeo and Juliet, Shakespeare's passionate, turbulent, love-struck teenagers. Then again, there's your grandparents, who probably exemplify a calmer, more tranquil kind of love. We use the word love to describe all these relationships, though each seems to be of a different kind (Berscheid & Meyers, 1996, 1997; Fehr & Russell, 1991).

Social psychologists have recognized that a good definition of love must encompass its myriad forms, including passionate, giddy feelings as well as deep, long-term devotion. One well-known distinction is between companionate love and passionate love (Hatfield, 1988; Hatfield & Walster, 1978). **Companionate love** is defined as the feelings of intimacy and affection we feel toward someone that are not accompanied by passion or physiological arousal. People can experience companionate love in nonsexual relationships, such as close friendships, or in sexual relationships, where they experience great feelings of intimacy (companionate love) but not a great deal of the heat and passion they may once have felt.

Passionate love involves an intense longing for another person. When things are going well—the other person loves us too—we feel great fulfillment and ecstasy. When things are not going well—our love is unrequited—we feel great sadness and despair. This kind of love is characterized by the experience of physiological arousal, wherein we actually feel shortness of breath and a thumping heart in our loved one's presence. Cross-cultural research comparing an individualistic culture (the United States) and a collectivistic culture (China) indicates that American couples tend to value passionate love more than Chinese couples do, and Chinese couples tend to value companionate love more than American couples do (Gao, 1993; Jankowiak, 1995; Toomey & Chung, 1996). In comparison, the Taita of Kenya, East Africa value both equally; they conceptualize romantic love as a combination of companionate love and passionate love. The Taita consider this the best kind of love and achieving it is a primary goal in the society (Bell, 1995).

Companionate Love
the feelings of intimacy and affection we feel for another person when we care deeply for the person but do not necessarily experience passion or arousal in his or her presence

Passionate Love
the feelings of intense longing, accompanied by physiological arousal, we feel for another person; when our love is reciprocated, we feel great fulfillment and ecstasy, but when it is not, we feel sadness and despair

Elaine Hatfield and Susan Sprecher (1986) developed a questionnaire to measure passionate love. Passionate love, as measured by this scale, consists of strong, uncontrollable thoughts; intense feelings; and overt acts toward the target of one's affection. Find out if you are experiencing (or have experienced) passionate love, by filling out the questionnaire in the Try It! exercise, below.

Try It!

The Passionate Love Scale

These items ask you to describe how you feel when you are passionately in love. Please think of the person whom you love most passionately right now. If you are not in love right now, please think of the last person you loved passionately. If you have never been in love, think of the person whom you came closest to caring for in that way. Choose your answer remembering how you felt at the time when your feelings were the most intense.

For each of the 15 items, chose the number between 1 and 9 that most accurately describes your feelings. The answer scale ranges from 1, "not at all true" to 9 "definitely true." Write the number you choose next to each item.

1	2	3	4	5	6	7	8	9
Not at all true				Moderately true			Definitely true	

1. I would feel deep despair if _____ left me.

2. Sometimes I feel I can't control my thoughts; they are obsessively on _____].

3. I feel happy when I am doing something to make _____ happy.

4. I would rather be with _____ than anyone else.

5. I'd get jealous if I thought _____ were falling in love with someone else.

6. I yearn to know all about _____.

7. I want _____ —physically, emotionally, mentally.

8. I have an endless appetite for affection from _____.

9. For me, _____ is the perfect romantic partner.

10. I sense my body responding when _____ touches me.

11. _____ always seems to be on my mind.

12. I want _____ to know me—my thoughts, my fears, and my hopes.

13. I eagerly look for signs indicating _____'s desire for me.

14. I possess a powerful attraction for _____.

15. I get extremely depressed when things don't go right in my relationship with _____.

Scoring: Add up your scores for the 15 items. The total score can range from a minimum of 15 to a maximum of 135. The higher your score, the more your feelings for the person reflect passionate love; the items to which you gave a particularly high score reflect those components of passionate love that you experience most strongly.

(Adapted from Hatfield & Sprecher, 1986)

Triangular Theory of Love

Other researchers are not satisfied with a simple dichotomy of two kinds of love. Robert Sternberg (1986, 1988, 1997; Sternberg & Beall, 1991), for example, presents a **triangular theory of love,** which depicts love as consisting of three basic ingredients: intimacy, passion, and commitment. Intimacy refers to feelings of being close to and bonded with a partner. Passion refers to the "hot" parts of a relationship—namely, the arousal you experience toward your partner, including sexual attraction. Commitment consists of two decisions—the short-term one that you love your partner, and the long-term one to maintain that love and stay with your partner. Sternberg (1988) developed a scale to measure the three components of love, including such questions as "I have a relationship of mutual understanding with _____" (intimacy), "I find myself thinking about _____ frequently during the day" (passion), and "I expect my love for _____ to last for the rest of my life" (commitment).

These three ingredients—intimacy, passion, and commitment—can be combined in varying degrees to form any of the different kinds of love (see Figure 10.5). Love can consist of one component alone or of any combination of these three parts. For example, a person may feel a great deal of passion or physical attraction for another (infatuation love) but not know the person well enough to experience intimacy and not be ready to make any kind of commitment. As the relationship develops, it might blossom into romantic love, characterized by passion and intimacy, and maybe even consummate love—the blending of all three components. Sternberg uses the term *companionate love* in the same way we depicted earlier, to describe love characterized by intimacy and commitment but not passion (Aron & Westbay, 1996; Hassebrauck & Buhl, 1996).

Love Styles

A third approach to defining love has focused on **love styles,** or the basic theories people have about love that guide their behavior in relationships (Hendrick &

Triangular Theory of Love
the idea that different kinds of love consist of varying degrees of three components: intimacy, passion, and commitment

Love Styles
the basic theories people have about love that guide their behavior in relationships; six styles have been identified: eros, ludus, storge, pragma, mania, and agape

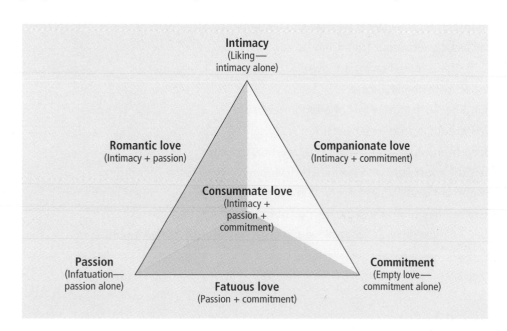

■ **FIGURE 10.5   The triangle of love.** According to the triangular theory of love, there are seven different forms of love, each made up of varying degrees of intimacy, passion, and commitment. (Adapted from Sternberg, 1988)

Try It **!**

The Love Attitudes Scale

Listed below are several statements that reflect different attitudes about love. For each statement, choose the number between 1 and 5 that indicates how much you agree or disagree with that statement. Write the number next to each item. The items refer to a specific love relationship. Whenever possible, answer the questions with your current partner in mind. If you are not currently dating anyone, answer the questions with your most recent partner in mind. If you have never been in love, answer in terms of what you think your responses would most likely be.

> For each statement: 1 = Strongly disagree with the statement
>   2 = Moderately disagree with the statement
>   3 = Neutral—neither agree nor disagree
>   4 = Moderately agree with the statement
>   5 = Strongly agree with the statement

1. My partner and I were attracted to each other immediately after we first met.

2. My partner and I have the right physical "chemistry" between us.

3. Our lovemaking is very intense and satisfying.

4. I feel that my partner and I were meant for each other.

5. My partner and I become emotionally involved rather quickly.

6. My partner and I really understand each other.

7. My partner fits my ideal standards of physical beauty/handsomeness.

8. I try to keep my partner a little uncertain about my commitment to him/her.

9. I believe that what my partner doesn't know about me won't hurt him/her.

10. I have sometimes had to keep my partner from finding out about other partners.

11. I could get over my affair with my partner pretty easily and quickly.

12. My partner would get upset if he/she knew of some of the things I've done with other people.

13. When my partner gets too dependent on me, I want to back off a little.

14. I enjoy playing the "game of love" with my partner and a number of other partners.

15. It is hard for me to say exactly when our friendship turned into love.

16. To be genuine, our love first required *caring* for awhile.

17. I expect to always be friends with my partner.

18. Our love is the best kind because it grew out of a long friendship.

19. Our friendship merged gradually into love over time.

20. Our love is really a deep friendship, not a mysterious, mystical emotion.

21. Our love relationship is the most satisfying because it developed from a good friendship.

22. I considered what my partner was going to become in life before I committed myself to him/her.

23. I tried to plan my life carefully before choosing my partner.

24. In choosing my partner, I believed it was best to love someone with a similar background.

25. A main consideration in choosing my partner was how he/she would reflect on my family.

26. An important factor in choosing my partner was whether or not he/she would be a good parent.

(continued on next page)

The Love Attitudes Scale, *continued*

27. An important factor in choosing my partner was how he/she would reflect on my career.

28. Before getting very involved with my partner, I tried to figure out how compatible his/her hereditary background would be with mine in case we ever had children.

29. When things aren't right with my partner and me, my stomach gets upset.

30. If my partner and I break up, I would get so depressed that I would even think of suicide.

31. Sometimes I get so excited about being in love with my partner that I can't sleep.

32. When my partner doesn't pay attention to me, I feel sick all over.

33. Since I've been in love with my partner, I've had trouble concentrating on anything else.

34. I cannot relax if I suspect that my partner is with someone else.

35. If my partner ignores me for a while, I sometimes do stupid things to try to get his/her attention.

36. I try to always help my partner through difficult times.

37. I would rather suffer myself than let my partner suffer.

38. I cannot be happy unless I place my partner's happiness before my own.

39. I am usually willing to sacrifice my own wishes to let my partner achieve his/hers.

40. Whatever I own is my partner's to use as he/she chooses.

41. When my partner gets angry with me, I still love him/her fully and unconditionally.

42. I would endure all things for the sake of my partner.

Scoring Key: The 42 items are grouped under the six Love Styles as follows. For each Love Style, add up your total number of points for those items. *Eros:* items # 1, 2, 3, 4, 5, 6, and 7. *Ludus:* items # 8, 9, 10, 11, 12, 13, and 14. *Storge:* items # 15, 16, 17, 18, 19, 20, and 21. *Pragma:* items # 22, 23, 24, 25, 26, 27, and 28. *Mania:* items # 29, 30, 31, 32, 33, 34, and 35. *Agape:* items # 36, 37, 38, 39, 40, 41, and 42.

Examine your six totals, one for each Love Style. The totals can run from a minimum of 7 to a maximum of 35. The Style(s) with the highest scores are the ones you endorsed the most strongly, as reflecting your attitude about your relationship. The Style(s) with the lowest scores are ones you felt did not reflect your attitude about your relationship.

(Adapted from Hendrick & Hendrick, 1992).

Hendrick, 1986, 1992; Lee, 1973, 1988). Clyde Hendrick and Susan Hendrick (1986; 1992) have identified six love styles. (You can discover what your love style is by filling out the Love Attitudes Questionnaire in the Try It! exercise above.)

Eros is a passionate, physical love, where the partner's physical appearance is highly important. The Eros lover gets involved very quickly.

Ludus is love played as a game, never taken too seriously. Very playful in their approach to love, ludic lovers don't mean to cause harm but they often do, sometimes with multiple partners at once.

Storge is a slow-growing love, evolving out of affection and friendship. Similarity between partners is extremely important.

Pragma is pragmatic love—commonsensical, realistic, feet on the ground. Pragmic lovers know what they're looking for in a relationship and have "conditions" that must be met.

> "Love is or it ain't. Thin love ain't love at all.
> —Toni Morrison

■ If you organize your love life around "fiscal years," you definitely have a pragmic love style!

"Your wonderful daughter and I would like to become engaged in F.Y. '97, married in F.Y. '98, and if the numbers look good, start a family in F.Y. '99."

Mania is the highly emotional, roller-coaster ride of love. Manic lovers obsess about their partners, vascillate between elation and despair, and generally fit our culture's stereotype of "romantic love."

Agape is a selfless, giving, and altruistic love. Agapic lovers think not of themselves but of their partners and what they can do for them. Their love style is more spiritual than physical.

Clyde Hendrick and Susan Hendrick have found both similarities and differences between the sexes in their love styles. For Eros and Agape, men and women did not differ. However, men were more ludic, and women were more storgic and pragmatic (Hendrick & Hendrick, 1986; Dion & Dion, 1993b). The researchers have also found that real-life couples show considerable similarity in their love styles. In addition, couples whose romantic relationships lasted were more likely than those who broke up to be high on Eros, or passionate love and low on Ludus, or game-playing love (Hendrick, Hendrick, & Adler, 1988).

The Role of Culture in Defining Love

Our discussion thus far has focused on how love is defined in American society. While love is certainly a human emotion experienced everywhere on the planet, culture does play a role in how people label their experiences and in what they expect (and tolerate) in close relationships. For example, the Japanese describe *amae* as an extremely positive emotional state in which one is a totally passive love object, indulged and taken care of by one's romantic partner, much like a mother-infant relationship. There is no equivalent word for *amae* in English or any other Western language; the closest in meaning is the word dependency, an emotional state that is considered by Western cultures to be unhealthy in adult relationships (Dion & Dion, 1993a; Doi, 1988).

The Chinese have an important relationship concept, *gan qing*, which differs from the Western view of romantic love. *Gan qing* is achieved by helping and working for another person; for example, a "romantic" act would be fixing

■ While people all over the world experience love, how "love" is defined varies across cultures.

someone's bicycle or helping them learn new material (Gao, 1996). Another way of conceptualizing love is expressed by the Korean concept of *jung*. Much more than "love," *jung* is what ties two people together. While couples in new relationships feel strong love for each other, they have not yet developed strong *jung*—that takes time and many mutual experiences. Interestingly, *jung* can develop in negative relationships too, for example, between business rivals who dislike each other. *Jung* may unknowingly grow between them over time, with the result that they will feel that a strange connection exists between them (Lim & Choi, 1996).

As you can see from these examples, the definition of love varies across cultures. In addition, Western and Eastern cultures vary in important ways in how the needs of the individual and the collective (or group) are defined. Western societies are individualistic, emphasizing that the individual is autonomous, self-sufficient, and defined by his or her personal qualities. Eastern cultures are collectivistic, emphasizing the individual's loyalty to the group and defining him or her through membership in the group (Hofstede, 1984; Hui & Triandis, 1986; Markus, Kitayama, & Heiman, 1996; Triandis, 1995).

Karen Dion and Kenneth Dion (1988, 1993a) have hypothesized that romantic love is an important, even crucial, basis for marriage in individualistic societies, while it has less value in collectivistic ones. In individualistic societies, romantic love is a heady, highly personal experience; one immerses oneself in the new partner and, if anything, virtually ignores friends and family for a while. The decision as to who to become involved with or marry is for the most part a personal one. In comparison, in collectivistic cultures the individual in love must take into account the wishes of family and other group members; in fact, marriages are often by arrangement, with the respective families matching up the bride and groom (Levine, Sato, Hashimoto, & Verna, 1995). As Francis Hsu (1981) puts it, when in love, "an American asks, 'How does my heart feel?' A Chinese asks, 'What will other people say?'" (p. 50).

Karen Dion and Kenneth Dion (1993b) tested this hypothesis by giving the Love Attitudes Scale, which measures the love styles we discussed above, to a heterogeneous sample of Canadian college students. Their research participants fell into three groups by ethnocultural background: Asian (Chinese, Korean, Vietnamese, Indian, and Pakistani), Anglo-Celtic (English, Irish, and Scottish), and European (Scandinavian, Spanish, German, and Polish). The researchers found that the Asian respondents were significantly more likely to endorse the storgic love style than either of the two other groups. Thus, in comparison to their peers, the Asian students were more likely to identify with a companionable, friendship-based romantic love, a "style of love that would not disrupt a complex network of existing family relationships" (p. 465).

Additional cross-cultural research has supported this interpretation. For example, Carolyn Simmons, Alexander Vom Kolke, and Hideko Shimizu (1986) examined attitudes toward romantic love among single college students in West Germany, Japan, and the United States. They found that the West German sample had the most passionately romantic views of love, and the Japanese sample the least. The American sample's endorsement of romantic love fell between that of the other two cultures. Similarly, Robert Levine and his colleagues (1995) surveyed college students in 11 countries around the world, asking them, "If a man (woman) had all the qualities you desired, would you marry this person if you were not in love with him (her)?" These researchers found that marrying for love was most important to participants in Western and Westernized countries (e.g., the United States, Brazil, England, and Australia) and of least importance to participants in underdeveloped Eastern countries (i.e., India, Pakistan, and Thailand).

The results of these studies indicate that the concept of romantic love is to some extent culturally specific (Beall & Sternberg, 1995; Dion & Dion, 1996; Gao, 1993; Gao & Gudykunst, 1995; Hatfield & Rapson, 1996; Hatfield & Sprecher, 1995; Sprecher et al., 1994). Love can vary in definition and behavior in different societies. We all love, but we do not necessarily all love in the same way—or at least, we don't describe it in the same way. The anthropologist William Jankowiak (1995; Jankowiak & Fischer, 1992) found evidence of romantic (passionate) love in 148 of the 166 cultures he sampled; it was present even in societies "that do not accept (romantic love) or embrace it as a positive ideal" (1995; p. 4). Thus, it may be the case that romantic love is nearly universal in the human species, but cultural rules alter how that emotional state is experienced, expressed, and remembered.

*T*he Causes of Love

Now that scales have been developed to measure love, social psychologists have begun addressing the more important question of how love develops and how it is maintained. Are the causes of love similar to the causes of initial attraction? As you might imagine, some of the same principles apply, but additional variables come into play when one is developing and maintaining a close relationship. We will begin by reviewing some of the factors we discussed in the beginning of the chapter as determinants of first impressions, to see how they play out in intimate relationships.

Social Exchange in Long-Term Relationships

We have seen that, in general, everyone likes rewarding relationships. And according to the rule of social exchange, if we want other people to like us, we must dole out social rewards to them as well (Blau, 1964; Homans, 1961). Research has shown ample support for social exchange theory in intimate relationships (Rusbult 1993; Rusbult & Van Lange, 1996; Rusbult, Yovetich, & Verette, 1996, Rusbult et al., 1991; Yovetich & Rusbult, 1994). For example, Caryl Rusbult

> *W*hat, after all, is our life but a great dance in which we are all trying to fix the best going rate of exchange?
>
> —Malcolm Bradbury, 1992

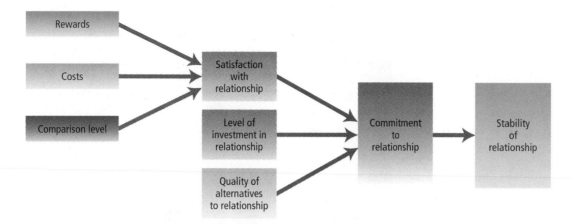

■ **FIGURE 10.6   The investment model of commitment.**   People's commitment to a relationship depends on several variables. First, their *satisfaction* with the relationship is based on their comparing their *rewards* to their *costs* and determining if the outcome exceeds their general expectation of what they should get in a relationship (or *comparison level*). Next, their *commitment* to the relationship depends on three variables: how *satisfied* they are; how much they feel they have *invested* in the relationship; and whether they have good *alternatives* to this relationship. These commitment variables in turn predict how *stable* the relationship will be. For example, a woman who feels her relationship has more costs and less rewards than she considers acceptable would have a "low satisfaction." If she also felt she had little invested in the relationship, and a very attractive person had just asked her for a date—she would have a "low level of commitment." The end result is "low stability;" most likely, she will break up with her current partner. (Adapted from Rusbult, 1983)

(1983) found that college-age dating couples focused much more on rewards during the first three months of their relationships. If the relationships were perceived as offering a lot of rewards, the people reported feeling happy and satisfied. The perception of rewards continued to be important over time. At seven months, couples who were still together, as compared to those who'd broken up, believed their rewards had increased over time. The perception and importance of costs came into play a few months into the relationships; this is when the glow created by all those rewards begins to be dimmed by the realization that costs too are involved. Not surprisingly, Rusbult found that satisfaction with the relationship decreased markedly over time for those who reported that costs were increasing in their relationships. Thus, rewards are always important to the outcome; costs become increasingly important over time.

Of course, we know that many people do not leave their partners, even when they are dissatisfied and their other alternatives look bright. Caryl Rusbult and her colleagues would agree; they say we need to consider at least one additional factor to understand close relationships—a person's level of investment in the relationship (Kelley, 1983; Rusbult, 1980, 1983, 1991). In her **investment model** of close relationships, Rusbult defines investments as anything people have put into a relationship that will be lost if they leave it. Examples include tangible things, such as financial resources and possessions (e.g., a house), as well as intangible things, such as the emotional welfare of one's children, the time and emotional energy spent building the relationship, and the sense of personal integrity that will be lost if one gets divorced. As seen in Figure 10.6, the greater the investment individuals have in a relationship, the less likely they are to leave, even if satisfaction is low and other alternatives look promising. In short, to predict whether

Investment Model
the theory holding that people's commitment to a relationship depends on their satisfaction with the relationship in terms of rewards, costs, and comparison level; their comparison level for alternatives; and how much they have invested in the relationship that would be lost by leaving it

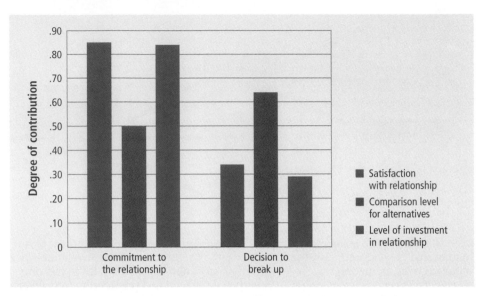

■ **FIGURE 10.7   A test of the investment model.**   This study examined the extent to which college students' satisfaction with a relationship, their comparison level for alternatives, and their investment in the relationship predicted their commitment to the relationship and their decision about whether to break up with their partner. The higher the number, the more each variable predicted commitment and breakup, independently of the two other variables. All three variables were good predictors of how committed people were and whether or not they broke up. (Adapted from Rusbult, 1983)

people will stay in an intimate relationship, we need to know (a) how satisfied they are with the relationship, (b) what they think of the alternatives, and (c) how great their investment in the relationship is.

To test this model, Rusbult (1983) asked college students involved in heterosexual dating relationships to fill out questionnaires for seven months. Every three weeks or so, people answered questions about each of the components of the model shown in Figure 10.6. Rusbult also kept track of whether the students stayed in the relationships or broke up with their partner. As you can see in Figure 10.7, people's satisfaction, alternatives, and investments all predicted how committed they were to the relationship and whether it lasted. (The higher the number on the scale, the more each factor predicted the commitment to and length of the relationship.) Subsequent studies have found results similar to those shown in Figure 10.7 for married couples of diverse ages, for lesbian and gay couples, for close (nonsexual) friendships, and for residents of both the United States and Taiwan (Kurdek, 1992; Lin & Rusbult, 1995; Rusbult, 1991; Rusbult & Buunk, 1993). In a further test of the model, Paul Van Lange and colleagues (1997) focused on couples' willingness to make personal sacrifices for their partner or for the sake of the relationship. Van Lange and colleagues (1997) found that couples willing to make sacrifices for each other had a strong sense of commitment to their relationship. Their high level of commitment was the result of a high degree of satisfaction with the relationship, a high level of investment in the relationship, and the low quality of alternatives to the relationship (see Figure 10.6).

Recently, Rusbult has applied her investment model to the study of destructive relationships. She and John Martz (1995) interviewed women who had sought refuge at a shelter for battered women, asking them about their abusive romantic relationships and marriages. Why had these women stayed in these relationships, even to the point that some of them returned to the abusive male partner when they left the shelter? As the theory would predict, the researchers found that feelings of commitment to the abusive relationship were greater among women who had poorer economic alternatives to the relationship, were more heavily invested in the relationship (e.g., were married; had children), and were less dissatisfied with the relationship (i.e., reported receiving less severe forms of abuse). Thus, when it comes to long-term relationships, commitment is based on more than just the amount of rewards and punishments people dole out; it also depends on people's perceptions of their investments in, satisfaction with, and alternatives to the relationship.

Equity in Long-Term Relationships

Does equity theory operate in long-term relationships the same way it does in new or less intimate relationships? Not exactly: The more we get to know someone, the more reluctant we are to believe that we are simply exchanging favors, and the less inclined we are to expect immediate compensation for a favor done. Elaine Hatfield and Richard Rapson (1993) note that in casual relationships we trade "in kind"—you loan someone your class notes, he buys you a beer. But in intimate relationships, we trade very different resources and it can be difficult to determine if equity has been achieved. As Hatfield and Rapson (1993) put it, does "dinner at an expensive restaurant on Monday balance out three nights of neglect due to a heavy work load"? (p. 130). In other words, long-term, intimate relationships seem to be governed by a looser, give-and-take notion of equity, rather than a rigid, tit-for-tat strategy (Kollack, Blumstein, & Schwartz, 1994).

According to Margaret Clark and Judson Mills, interactions between new acquaintances are governed by equity concerns and are called **exchange relationships**. In exchange relationships, people keep track of who is contributing what and feel taken advantage of when they feel they are putting more into the relationship than they are getting out of it. Interactions between close friends, family

> The friendships which last are those wherein each friend respects the other's dignity to the point of not really wanting anything from him.
>
> —Cyril Connolly

Exchange Relationships relationships governed by the need for equity (i.e., for an equal ratio of rewards and costs)

■ Close relationships can have either exchange or communal properties. Family relationships are typically communal; friendships are typically based on exchange though they can become communal over time.

Communal Relationships
relationships in which people's primary concern is being responsive to the other person's needs

members, and romantic partners are governed less by an equity norm and more by a desire to help each other in times of need (Clark, 1984, 1986; Clark & Mills, 1979, 1993; Clark & Pataki, 1995; Mills & Clark, 1982, 1994). In these **communal relationships,** people give in response to the other's needs, regardless of whether they are paid back. A good example of a communal relationship is parenting. As a friend of ours recently put it, "You spend years catering to your child's every need—changing diapers, sitting up with her in the middle of the night when she is throwing up, coaching her soccer team—knowing full well that sooner or later, she will reach an age when she will prefer to spend her time with anyone but you!"

In a series of experiments, Margaret Clark and her colleagues varied whether people desired an exchange or a communal relationship with another person, and then observed the extent to which they were concerned with equity in the relationship. In such experiments, participants interacted with an interesting person and were told either that this person was new to the area and wanted to make new friends (thereby increasing their interest in establishing a communal relationship with the person), or that the other person was married and visiting the area for only a brief time (thereby making them more inclined to favor an exchange relationship with the person). As predicted, people in the exchange condition operated according to the equity norm, as summarized in Figure 10.8. People in the communal condition, thinking there was a chance for a long-term relationship, were relatively unconcerned with a tit-for-tat accounting of who was contributing what (Clark, 1984; Clark & Mills, 1979; Clark & Waddell, 1985; Williamson & Clark, 1989, 1992). These results are not limited to exchange and

■ **FIGURE 10.8 Exchange versus communal relationships.**

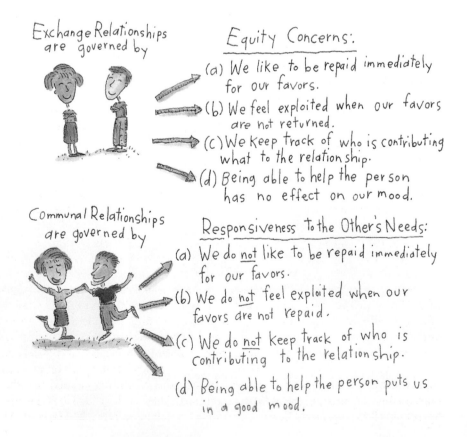

Exchange Relationships are governed by

Equity Concerns:

(a) We like to be repaid immediately for our favors.

(b) We feel exploited when our favors are not returned.

(c) We keep track of who is contributing what to the relationship.

(d) Being able to help the person has no effect on our mood.

Communal Relationships are governed by

Responsiveness to the Other's Needs:

(a) We do <u>not</u> like to be repaid immediately for our favors.

(b) We do <u>not</u> feel exploited when our favors are not repaid.

(c) We do <u>not</u> keep track of who is contributing to the relationship.

(d) Being able to help the person puts us in a good mood.

communal relationships created in the laboratory. Other studies show that ongoing friendships are more communal than relationships between strangers are (Clark, Mills, & Corcoran, 1989).

Are people in communal relationships completely unconcerned with equity? No; as we saw earlier, people do feel distressed if they believe their intimate relationships are inequitable (Walster et al., 1978). However, equity takes on a somewhat different form in communal relationships than it does in less intimate ones. In communal relationships, the partners are more relaxed about what constitutes equity at any given time; they believe that things will eventually balance out and a rough kind of equity will be achieved over time.

Evolutionary Explanations of Love

When asked the question, "Why do I love thee? Let me count the ways," evolutionary theorists will give some rather startling answers. The basic tenet of evolutionary biology is that an animal's "fitness" is measured by its reproductive success—that is, its ability to pass on its genes to the next generation. Reproductive success is not just part of the game; it is the game. Has human behavior evolved in specific ways to maximize reproductive success? Evolutionary psychologists say yes; they argue that males and females have very different agendas due to their differing roles in producing offspring.

For females, reproduction is costly in terms of time, energy, and effort, and this means they must consider carefully when and with whom to reproduce. In comparison, reproduction has few costs for males. The **evolutionary approach to love** concludes that reproductive success for the two sexes translates into two very different behavior patterns: Male animals would do best to pursue frequent pairings with many females, and female animals would do best to pair infrequently and only with a carefully chosen male (Berkow, 1989; Symons, 1979).

Now, what does this have to do with falling in love? David Buss and his colleagues state that this evolutionary approach explains the different strategies of men and women in romantic relationships (1985, 1988a, 1996; Buss & Schmitt, 1993). Buss (1988b) explains that finding (and keeping) a mate requires one to display one's resources—the aspects of oneself that will appear attractive to potential mates. This approach argues that across millennia, human beings have been selected through evolution to respond to certain external cues in the opposite sex. Females, facing high reproductive costs, will look for a male who can supply the resources and support she needs to bear a child. Males will look for a female who appears capable of reproducing successfully. More specifically, men will respond to the physical appearance of women, since age and health denote reproductive fitness, and women will respond to the economic and career achievements of men, since these variables represent resources they and their offspring will need (Buss, 1986b).

Several recent studies have tested these predictions and found support for them. For example, Buss and his colleagues (1989, 1990) asked more than 9,000 adults in 37 countries (representing 6 continents and 5 islands) how important and desirable various characteristics were in choosing a marriage partner. In general, the women participants valued ambition, industriousness, and good earning capacity in a potential mate more than the men did. The men valued physical attractiveness in a mate more than the women did, a finding echoed in other research (Buss & Barnes, 1986; Buss & Schmitt, 1993; Feingold, 1990; Hatfield & Sprecher, 1995; Regan & Berscheid, 1997; Sprecher, Sulivan, & Hatfield, 1994).

Evolutionary Approach to Love
an approach derived from evolutionary biology, which states that men and women are attracted to different characteristics in each other (men are attracted by women's appearance; women are attracted by men's resources) because this maximizes their reproductive success

As we discussed earlier, men are more likely than women to say that physical attractiveness is important to them in a potential date (Feingold, 1990). Other survey studies have indicated that men prefer spouses who are younger than they are (youth indicating greater reproductive fitness), while women prefer spouses around their own age (Buss, 1989; Kenrick & Keefe, 1992). When college students were asked to imagine that their romantic partner had been sexually unfaithful or emotionally unfaithful, the men were more upset by the sexual infidelity scenario than the women were, while the women were relatively more upset by the emotional infidelity story (Buss, Larsen, Westen, & Semmelroth, 1992).

An elaboration of the evolutionary approach to love and mate selection has been offered by Steven Gangestad and David Buss (1993). If physical attractiveness in women is preferred by men because it signals reproductive fitness, then female physical attractiveness should be particularly valued in regions of the world where disease is very common—the idea being that the physically attractive are both healthy and possibly resistant to local diseases. Gangestad and Buss (1993) found that in areas of the world where disease-transmitting parasites are prevalent, people did indicate a stronger preference for physically attractive mates than in areas with a low prevalence of parasites. However, this preference for the physically attractive mate was just as strong among women as it was among men. Thus, this study offers support for the fundamental points of the evolutionary approach but calls into question the proposed gender difference between men and women regarding attractiveness in mate selection.

The evolutionary approach to love has attracted its share of criticism. Some social psychologists argue that the theory is untestable: Because it is so flexible, it can be used to explain anything (Sternberg & Beall, 1991). Others suggest that it is an oversimplification of extremely complex human behavior (Travis & Yeager, 1991). It has been argued that men may value physical attractiveness in a partner simply because they have been taught to value it; they have been conditioned by decades of advertising and media images to value beauty in women and to have a recreational approach to sex (Hatfield & Rapson, 1993). In fact there are some studies that have found women to be just as interested in physical attractiveness in the opposite sex as men (Regan & Berscheid, 1995; Speed & Gangestad, 1997). Furthermore, as Alan Feingold (1990) and Susan Sprecher (1989) found in their research, the women participants were somewhat less likely than the men to *say* that physical appearance was important to them, but in terms of actual behavior, the women indicated that attractiveness was just as important to them as it was to the men (Gangestad & Buss, 1993). Other studies have found that women value physical attractiveness as much as men when they are considering a potential sexual partner (as opposed to a potential marriage partner) (Regan & Berscheid, 1997; Simpson & Gangestad, 1992). Research results are also mixed as to whether women are attracted to potential mates because of the men's ability to provide economic resources. Some researchers have found support for this statement (Buss, 1990; Feingold, 1992b; Hatfield & Sprecher, 1995), and some have not (Jensen-Campbell, Graziano, & West, 1995; Regan & Berscheid, 1995, 1997; Speed & Gangestad, 1997).

Finally, some researchers note that the preference for different qualities in a male or female can be explained without evolutionary psychology: Around the world, women have less power, status, wealth, and other resources than men do. If women need to rely on men to achieve economic security, they must consider this characteristic when choosing a mate. In comparison, men are free to choose

> "Men seek to propagate widely, whereas women seek to propagate wisely.
> —Robert Hinde

> "She's beautiful and therefore to be woo'd.
> —William Shakespeare

a woman using more frivolous criteria like good looks. Thus, in the framework of equity theory, female youth and beauty are considered a fair exchange for male career and economic success. Steven Gangestad (1993) tested this hypothesis by correlating the extent to which women in several countries had access to financial resources and the extent to which women reported male physical attractiveness as an important variable in a mate. (In this study, parasite prevalence was controlled, so it was not a factor in the results.) Gangestad (1993) found an association between the two: The more economic power women had in a given culture, the more women were interested in a physically attractive man. The evolutionary approach is an interesting, exciting, and controversial theory; further theorizing and research will determine the extent to which human love follows a biological imperative.

Attachment Styles and Intimate Relationships

Most of the determinants of love and intimacy we have discussed so far have been in the here-and-now of a relationship: the attractiveness and similarity of the partners, how they treat each other, and so on. The evolutionary approach takes the long view—how people act today is based on behavior patterns that evolved from our species' hominid past. Another recent theory of love takes the middle ground, stating that our behavior in adult relationships is based on our experiences as a young infant with our parents or caregivers. This approach focuses on attachment styles and draws on the ground-breaking work of John Bowlby (1969, 1973, 1980) and Mary Ainsworth (Ainsworth, Blehar, Waters, & Wall, 1978) on how infants form bonds to their primary caregivers (e.g., their mothers or fathers). The theory of **attachment styles** states that the kinds of bonds we form early in life influence the kinds of relationships we form as adults.

Mary Ainsworth and her colleagues (1978) identified three types of relationships between infants and their mothers. Infants with a **secure attachment style** typically have caregivers who are responsive to their needs and who show positive emotions when interacting with them. These infants trust their caregivers, are not worried about being abandoned, and come to view themselves as worthy and well liked. Infants with an **avoidant attachment style** typically have caregivers who are aloof and distant, rebuffing the infant's attempts to establish intimacy. These infants desire to be close to their caregiver but learn to suppress this need, as if they know that attempts to be intimate will be rejected. People with this style find it difficult to develop intimate relationships. Infants with an **anxious/ambivalent attachment style** typically have caregivers who are inconsistent and overbearing in their affection. These infants are unusually anxious, because they can never predict when and how their caregivers will respond to their needs.

The key assumption of attachment theory is that the particular attachment style we learn as infants and young children typically stays with us throughout life and generalizes to all of our relationships with other people: The securely attached person is able to develop mature, lasting relationships; people who have avoidant attachment styles are less able to trust others and find it difficult to develop close, intimate relationships; and people who have anxious/ambivalent attachment styles want to become close to their partners but worry that their partners will not return their affections.

Attachment theory does not imply that if people had unhappy relationships with their parents, they are doomed to repeat this same kind of unhappy relationship with everyone they ever meet. People can and do change; their

Attachment Styles
the expectations people develop about relationships with others, based on the relationship they had with their primary caregiver when they were infants

Secure Attachment Style
an attachment style characterized by trust, a lack of concern with being abandoned, and the view that one is worthy and well liked

Avoidant Attachment Style
an attachment style characterized by a suppression of attachment needs, because attempts to be intimate have been rebuffed; people with this style find it difficult to develop intimate relationships

Anxious/Ambivalent Attachment Style
an attachment style characterized by a concern that others will not reciprocate one's desire for intimacy, resulting in higher-than-average levels of anxiety

experiences in relationships can help them learn new and more healthy ways of relating to others than that which they experienced as young children (Kirkpatrick & Hazan, 1994; Kojetin, 1993). However, people who had avoidant or anxious/ambivalent relationships with their parents are more likely to have these same kinds of relationships with romantic partners, as well as with their own children (Feeney & Noller, 1990; Hazan & Shaver, 1987; Main, Kaplan, & Cassidy, 1985; Reis & Patrick, 1996; Shaver, Collins, & Clark, 1996). This has been shown in several studies that measure adults' attachment styles with questionnaires or interviews and then correlate these styles with the quality of their romantic relationships.

For example, Cindy Hazan and Philip Shaver (1987) asked adults to choose one of the three statements shown in Table 10.2, according to how they typically felt in romantic relationships. Each of these statements was designed to capture the three kinds of attachment styles we described above. The researchers also asked people questions about their current relationships. The results of this study—and several others like it—were consistent with an attachment theory perspective. Securely attached adults report that they easily become close to other people, readily trust others, and have satisfying romantic relationships. People with an avoidant style report that they are uncomfortable becoming close to others, find it hard to trust others, and have less satisfying romantic relationships. And people with an anxious/ambivalent style tend to have less satisfying relationships but of a different type: They are likely to be obsessive and preoccupied with their relationships, fearing that their partners do not want to be as intimate or close as they desire them to be (Collins & Read, 1990; Feeney & Noller, 1990; Hazan & Shaver, 1994a, 1994b; Kirkpatrick & Davis, 1994; Kobak & Hazan, 1991; Mikulincer & Florian, 1995; Shaver, Hazan, & Bradshaw, 1988; Simpson, 1990; Simpson, Rholes, & Nelligan, 1991; Simpson & Rholes, 1994; Simpson, Rholes, & Phillips, 1996; Steele & Steele, 1994).

Judith Feeney and Patricia Noller (1990) reported similar findings: Securely attached individuals had the most enduring, long-term romantic relationships in the sample; anxious/ambivalently attached individuals had the most short-lived romantic relationships; and avoidant individuals were the most likely to report never having been in love or to having the least intense romantic relationships in the sample. Nancy Collins and Stephen Read (1990) found that for heterosexual, college-age dating couples, childhood attachment styles are correlated with the type of romantic partner chosen as well as the outcome of the relationship. In particular, the participants' descriptions of their attachment history with their opposite-sex parent was related to their current choice of romantic partner. For example, men who felt their mothers were cold or inconsistent were more likely to be dating women who were anxious. Women who felt their fathers were warm and responsive were most likely to be dating men who were able to express intimacy.

Finally, attachment styles have also been found to affect couples' behavior in an experimental setting. Jeffry Simpson, William Rholes, and Julia Nelligan (1992) brought heterosexual dating couples into the lab and measured their attachment styles by questionnaire. They then told the woman of each pair that, next, she would be taking part in an experimental procedure that aroused considerable anxiety and distress in most people but they couldn't tell her any more about it then. Each woman was asked to wait a few minutes before "the procedure" began, and did so with her boyfriend. Their interactions were recorded by the experimenters and later analyzed. Securely attached women turned to their

> "In my very own self, I am part of my family.
> —David Herbert Lawrence

■ Attachment theory predicts that the attachment style we learn as infants and young children stays with us throughout life, and generalizes to all of our relationships with other people.

Table 10.2

Measuring attachment styles.		
Secure style	56%	I find it relatively easy to get close to others and am comfortable depending on them and having them depend on me. I don't often worry about being abandoned or about someone getting too close.
Avoidant style	25%	I am somewhat uncomfortable being close; I find it difficult to trust them completely, difficult to allow myself to depend on them. I am nervous when anyone gets close, and often, love partners want me to be more intimate than I feel comfortable being.
Anxious style	19%	I find that others are reluctant to get as close as I would like. I often worry that my partner doesn't really love me or won't stay with me, I want to merge completely with another person, and this desire sometimes scares people away.

NOTE: As part of a survey of attitudes toward love published in a newspaper, people were asked to choose the statement that best described their romantic relationships. The attachment style each statement was designed to measure and the percentage of people who chose each alternative are listed after each statement. (Adapted from Hazan & Shaver, 1987)

boyfriends for support and comfort during the anxious waiting period, while avoidant women did not; they withdrew from their boyfriends. And what about the men? When the girlfriends of securely attached men began to signal their distress, the men responded with more comfort and reassurance. On the other hand, when the girlfriends of avoidant men began indicating they were upset, the men responded with less comfort and support.

As interesting as the results are on attachment theory and adult relationships, you should remember that they are often correlational rather than experimental. As we saw in Chapter 2, it is risky to infer causation from correlational data. Moreover, these studies rely in part on adults' memories of their childhood and how their parents behaved toward them—and these early childhood memories can be inaccurate.

Taken as a whole, however, these studies are highly suggestive and do lend some support to the contention that the kind of relationship we had with our parents is likely to influence our relationships with others in adulthood. When you find yourself having problems in your close relationships, think about these research findings in attachment theory and see if they help you understand your behavior and that of your partner.

Relationships as an Interpersonal Process

What is the best visual metaphor for a close relationship? Are relationships like snapshots in a photo album—one photo per relationship? Or are they like home movies—showing the course of a relationship over time? A new approach to the study of intimate relationships takes the latter view, conceptualizing relationships as an interpersonal "process" and not a static, fixed entity (Duck, 1982, 1991; Duck & Sants, 1983). Relationships are always in a state of flux, continually

> Love, like electricity or revolution or becoming, is a process (not a thing).
> —Al Young

Relational Dialectics
a theory which states that close relationships are always in a state of change, due to opposing forces of autonomy/connection, novelty/predictability, and openness/closedness

Autonomy/Connection
the tension between our desire to maintain our independence and autonomy and our desire to feel emotionally connected to the other person

Novelty/Predictability
the tension between our desire for excitement and newness in the relationship and our desire for what is safe and predictable

Openness/Closedness
the tension between our desire to be open and revealing to the other person and our desire to be private and discrete

going through stages of change and maintenance, growth and retreat (Acitelli & Duck, 1987; Baxter, 1988; Cate & Lloyd, 1988; Dindia & Canary, 1993; Duck, 1995; Montgomery, 1988). People engage in this process through communication—as they define and redefine their relationships, they share their understanding of the relationship with their partners. This ongoing communication about one's feelings and needs creates the sense of a mutually shared relationship (Acitelli, 1992; Duck, 1994; Fletcher & Fincham, 1991; Genero, Miller, Surrey, & Baldwin, 1992). According to this view, many of the attraction variables we have discussed, like similarity and physical appearance, are not only "magnets" that pull us into relationships but characteristics that shape how we behave and think once we are in relationships (Duck, 1991).

This approach is called **relational dialectics**. Close relationships are characterized by tension between opposite but interrelated forces: autonomy/connection, novelty/predictability, and openness/closedness. Leslie Baxter (1988, 1993, 1994) and Barbara Montgomery (1993) state that constant change results from the tension between these forces. For example, the tension within **autonomy/connection** means that as we become emotionally closer to our friend or partner, we feel the need to move away and regain our autonomy; as we become too emotionally distant, we feel the need to move back closer again. **Novelty/predictability** describes our desire for excitement and newness in the relationship, opposed by our desire for what is safe, secure, and understood. **Openness/closedness** refers to the tension partners experience when deciding what information they can share with each other and what information they cannot share—the tension between being revealing and being discrete. Any one or combination of these three forces can be operating in a relationship at any given time. Thus, because of these dialectical forces, relationships are constantly being "tweaked"—changed, modified, and redefined.

Current research on this new approach to relationships offers support for the model and its emphasis on change and negotiation between partners (Braithwaite & Baxter, 1995; Canary & Stafford, 1994; Rawlins, 1992; Sabourin & Stamp,

■ Current research on close relationships stresses that they are continually changing, as partners respond to shifting needs and demands. According to this approach, communication plays an integral role in defining and maintaining the relationship.

1995; Wilmot, 1994; Wilmot & Stevens, 1994). For example, a study of friends, dating partners, and spouses indicated that openness/closedness was a recurrent issue, with one or both members of the relationship periodically moving between the two states (VanLear, 1991). Relational dialectics has been found to predict what issues will be most intense at various developmental stages of a relationship (Baxter, 1990). In the initial stages, issues of openness/closedness are at the forefront. How much should you reveal to your new friend or romantic partner, and when? Is he or she revealing the same amount? Once the relationship is established, issues of autonomy/connection and novelty/predictability become important. How close can you get to this person without losing your identity and independence? Is he or she becoming too distant? Is the relationship becoming boring, or is it too changeable and unpredictable (Baxter, 1990)? Finally, an inability to deal with autonomy/connection pressures can spell the end for some romantic relationships. In people's accounts of why their relationships ended, themes of feeling trapped or suffocated are found, as are themes of too little commitment and sharing (Baxter, 1986).

Terminating Intimate Relationships

Sometimes, romantic relationships end. The current American divorce rate is holding at nearly 50 percent of the current marriage rate; some demographers estimate that two-thirds of all current first marriages will eventually end in separation or divorce (Berscheid & Reis, 1988). In addition, many romantic relationships involving heterosexuals, lesbians, and gays are terminated every day. After several years of studying what love is and how it blooms, social psychologists are now beginning to explore the end of the story—how it dies.

The Process of Breaking Up

Ending a romantic relationship is one of life's more painful experiences. During the past decade, researchers began to examine what makes people end their relationships and the disengagement strategies they use (Baxter, 1986; Felmlee, Sprecher, & Bassin, 1990; Frazier & Cook, 1993; Helgeson, 1994; Rusbult & Zembrodt, 1983; Simpson, 1987). For example, when asked to describe in detail how they had ended a romantic relationship, research participants' accounts revealed five basic categories (Cody, 1982):

positive tone (e.g., telling the partner you care about him or her, but . . .)

verbal de-escalation (e.g., telling the partner you no longer feel in love)

behavioral de-escalation (e.g., avoiding contact with the partner)

negative identity management (e.g., telling the partner you should both start dating other people)

justification (e.g., telling the partner that the relationship isn't meeting your needs)

At the same time, Steve Duck (1982) reminds us that relationship dissolution is not a single event but a process with many steps (see Figure 10.9). Duck theorizes that four stages of dissolution exist, ranging from the intrapersonal (the individual thinks a lot about how he or she is dissatisfied with the relationship), to the dyadic (the individual discusses the breakup with the partner), to the social (the breakup is announced to other people), and back to the intrapersonal (the individual recovers from the breakup and forms an account, or version, of how and

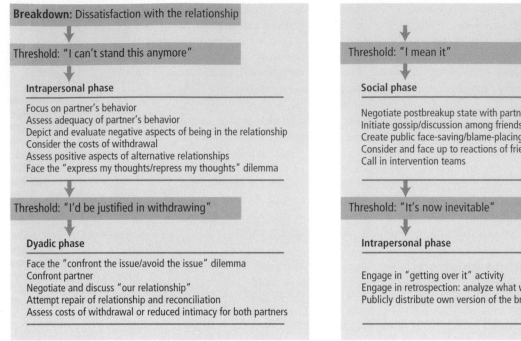

Breakdown: Dissatisfaction with the relationship

↓

Threshold: "I can't stand this anymore"

↓

Intrapersonal phase

Focus on partner's behavior
Assess adequacy of partner's behavior
Depict and evaluate negative aspects of being in the relationship
Consider the costs of withdrawal
Assess positive aspects of alternative relationships
Face the "express my thoughts/repress my thoughts" dilemma

↓

Threshold: "I'd be justified in withdrawing"

↓

Dyadic phase

Face the "confront the issue/avoid the issue" dilemma
Confront partner
Negotiate and discuss "our relationship"
Attempt repair of relationship and reconciliation
Assess costs of withdrawal or reduced intimacy for both partners

↓

Threshold: "I mean it"

↓

Social phase

Negotiate postbreakup state with partner
Initiate gossip/discussion among friends, family, and others
Create public face-saving/blame-placing stories and accounts
Consider and face up to reactions of friends, family, and others
Call in intervention teams

↓

Threshold: "It's now inevitable"

↓

Intrapersonal phase

Engage in "getting over it" activity
Engage in retrospection: analyze what went wrong
Publicly distribute own version of the breakup story

■ **FIGURE 10.9   Steps in dissolving close relationships.** (Adapted from Duck, 1982)

why it happened). In terms of the last stage in the process, John Harvey and his colleagues (1986, 1992) have found that the version of "why the relationship ended" that we present to close friends can be very different from the official (i.e., cleaned-up) version that we present to co-workers or neighbors. Take a moment to examine the stages outlined in Figure 10.9; see if they mirror your experience.

Why relationships end has been studied from several angles. A particularly profitable approach has used the investment model, which we discussed earlier (Bui, Peplau, & Hill, 1996; Drigotas & Rusbult, 1992). Caryl Rusbult and colleagues have elaborated on social exchange theory to create a typology of four types of behavior that occur in troubled relationships (Rusbult, 1987; Rusbult & Zembrodt, 1983). These four types are:

exit: actively harming or terminating the relationship (e.g., abusing the partner; threatening to break up; actually leaving)

voice: actively and constructively attempting to improve conditions (e.g., discussing problems; trying to change; going to a therapist)

loyalty: passively but optimistically waiting for conditions to improve (e.g., hoping things will improve; praying; being supportive instead of fighting)

neglect: passively allowing conditions to deteriorate (e.g., refusing to deal with problems; ignoring partner or spending less time together; putting no energy into relationship)

These four types of behavior differ along two dimensions: how destructive or constructive they are, and how active or passive they are (see Figure 10.10). Rusbult and colleagues have found that destructive behaviors (exit or neglect)

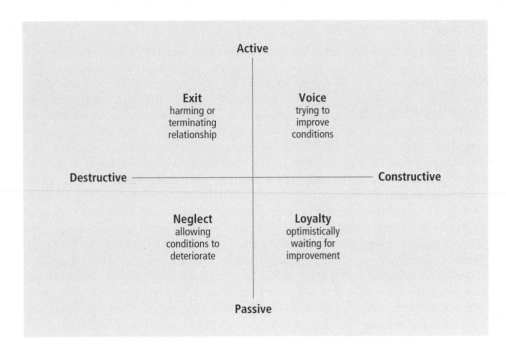

Active

Exit
harming or
terminating
relationship

Voice
trying to
improve
conditions

Destructive ———————————————— **Constructive**

Neglect
allowing
conditions to
deteriorate

Loyalty
optimistically
waiting for
improvement

Passive

■ **FIGURE 10.10   The Exit-Voice-Loyalty-Neglect Typology.** When romantic relationships are troubled or in the process of breaking up, the behavior of the two partners can be described as falling along an active/passive continuum and a destructive/constructive continuum. This results in four possible behavior patterns: exit, voice, neglect, and loyalty. (Adapted from Rusbult, Yovetich & Verette, 1996)

harm a relationship a lot more than constructive behaviors (voice and loyalty) help it. Furthermore, when one partner acts destructively (exit or neglect), the other partner tends to accommodate this behavior by responding constructively (voice or loyalty) in order to save the relationship; when both partners act destructively, the relationship typically ends (Rusbult, Johnson, & Morrow, 1986; Rusbult, Yovetich, & Verette, 1996).

Another approach to studying why relationships end centers on relational dialectics. For example, Diane Felmlee (1995) asked 300 college men and women to focus on a romantic relationship that had ended and to list the qualities that first attracted them to the person and the characteristics they ended up disliking the most about the person. Felmlee found that 30 percent of these breakups were examples of "fatal attractions." The very qualities that were initially so attractive (e.g., "He's so unusual and different," "She's so exciting and unpredictable") became the very reasons why the relationship ended ("He and I have nothing in common," "I can never count on her"). According to relational dialectics, the tension between, for example, novelty and predictability suggests that relationships that begin with a heavy dose of novelty will soon need to be balanced by some predictability. If the partner can't supply it, the relationship is in big trouble. Note too that Felmlee's findings offer strong support for similarity, instead of complementarity, as a characteristic that promotes successful relationships.

If a romantic relationship is in bad shape, can we predict who will end it? Much has been made about the tendency in heterosexual relationships for one sex to end the relationship more than the other, for example, that women end relationships more often than men (Rubin, Hill, & Peplau, 1981). Recent research has found, however, that one sex does not end romantic relationships any more frequently than the other (Akert, 1998; Hagestad & Smyer, 1982; Rusbult, Johnson, & Morrow, 1986).

> Love is like war; easy to begin but very hard to stop.
>
> –H. L. Mencken

The Experience of Breaking Up

Can we predict the different ways people will feel when their relationship ends? One key is the role people play in the decision to end the relationship (Akert, 1998; Helgeson, 1994; Lloyd & Cate, 1985). For example, Robin Akert asked 344 college-age men and women to focus on their most important romantic relationship that had ended and to respond to a questionnaire focusing on their experiences during the breakup. One question asked to what extent they, as compared to their partner, had been responsible for the decision to break up. Participants who indicated a high level of responsibility for the decision were labeled breakers; those who reported a low level of responsibility, breakees; and those who shared the decision making with their partners about equally, mutuals.

Akert found that the role people played in the decision to end the relationship was the single most powerful predictor of their breakup experiences. Not surprisingly, breakees were miserable—they reported high levels of loneliness, depression, unhappiness, and anger, and virtually all reported experiencing physical disorders in the weeks after the breakup as well. Breakers found the end of the relationship the least upsetting, the least painful, and the least stressful of the three. Although breakers did report feeling guilty and unhappy, they had the fewest negative physical symptoms (39 percent), such as head- and stomachaches, and eating and sleeping irregularities.

The mutual role, which carries with it a component of shared decision making, helped individuals evade some of the more negative emotional and physical reactions to breaking up. Mutuals were not as upset or hurt as breakees, but they were not as unaffected as breakers. Some 60 percent of the mutuals reported physical symptoms, indicating that a mutual conclusion to a romantic relationship is a more stressful experience than simply deciding to end it on one's own. Finally, gender played a role as well in the emotional and physical responses of the respondents, with women reporting somewhat more negative reactions to breaking up than men.

■ **FIGURE 10.11**
Importance of remaining friends after the breakup. After ending a romantic relationship, do people want to remain friends with their ex-partner? It depends on both the role they played in the decision to break up and on their gender. Women are more interested than men in staying friends when they are in the breakee or breaker role; men and women are equally interested in staying friends when the relationship ends by mutual decision.

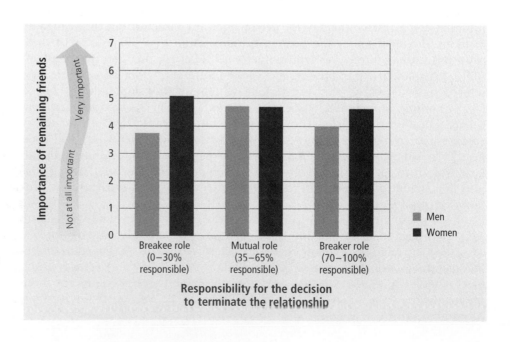

Do people want to stay friends when they break up? It depends on the role one plays in the breakup, as well as one's gender. Akert (1998) found that men are not very interested in remaining friends with their ex-girlfriends when they are in either the breaker or the breakee role, while women are more interested in remaining friends, especially when they are breakees (see Figure 10.11). Interestingly, the mutual role is the one where men's and women's interest in future friendship matches the most. These data suggest that when men experience either great control (breaker) or little control (breakee) over the ending of the relationship, they tend to want to "cut their losses" and move on, severing ties with their ex-partner. In comparison, women tend to want to continue feeling connected to their ex-partner, hoping to reshape the intimate relationship into a platonic friendship. The mutual breakup is the one in which each partner effectively plays the breaker and breakee roles simultaneously. This equality in roles appears to be important in producing an equivalent interest in future friendship for men and women (see Figure 10.11).

The breakup moral? If you find yourself in a romantic relationship and your partner seems inclined to break it off, try to end it mutually. Your experience will be less traumatic because you will share some control over the process (even if you don't want it to happen). Unfortunately for your partner, if you are about to be in the role of breaker, you will experience less pain and suffering if you continue to play that role; however, changing your role from the breaker to the mutual would be an act of kindness toward your soon-to-be ex-loved one.

Summary

In the first part of this chapter, we discussed the variables that cause initial attraction between two people. One such variable is physical proximity, or the **propinquity effect**: People who, by chance, you come into contact with the most are the most likely to become your friends and lovers. This occurs because of the **mere exposure effect**; in general, exposure to any stimulus produces liking for it. **Similarity** between people, whether in attitudes, values, personality traits, or demographic characteristics, is also a powerful cause of attraction and liking. Similarity is a more powerful predictor of attraction than complementarity—the idea that opposites attract. How people behave toward us is also of obvious importance. **Reciprocal liking** states that, in general, we like others who behave as if they like us. Though most people are reluctant to admit it, **physical attractiveness** also plays an important role in liking. Physical attractiveness of the face has a cross-cultural component; people from different cultures rate photographs quite similarly. The "what is beautiful is good" stereotype indicates that people assume physical attractiveness is associated with other desirable traits. Exactly which desirable traits are linked to attractiveness depends on what is valued in one's culture.

Many of these determinants of attractiveness can be explained by **social exchange theory**, which argues that how people feel about their relationships depends on their perception of the *rewards* they receive from the relationship and the *costs* they incur. In addition, in order to determine whether people will stay in a relationship, we also need to know their **comparison level**—their expectations about the outcomes of their relationship—and their **comparison level for alternatives**—their expectations about how happy they would be in other relationships.

There are, however, exceptions to the rule of social exchange. Under some conditions, people do not prefer the person who is most rewarding. For example, some theorists argue that the most important determinant of satisfaction is the amount of equity in the relationship. **Equity theory** states that we are happiest when the ratio of rewards and costs we experience is roughly equal to the ratio of rewards and costs the other person experiences.

In the second part of this chapter, we examined the causes of attraction in long-term, intimate relationships. Social psychologists have offered several definitions of love. One important distinction is between **companionate love**—feelings of intimacy that are not accompanied by intense longing and arousal—and **passionate love**—feelings of intimacy that are accompanied by intense longing and arousal. The **triangular theory of love** distinguishes among three components of love: intimacy, passion, and commitment. A third conceptualization of love focuses on six **love styles**: Eros, ludus, storge, pragma, mania, and agape. While love is universal, *cultural variation* in the definition of love does occur.

Social exchange theories of close relationships, such as the **investment model**, say that to predict whether a couple will stay together, we need to know each person's level of *investment* in and *satisfaction* with the relationship, as well as each person's comparison level and comparison level for alternatives. The notion of equity of rewards and costs is different in long-term versus short-term relationships. Short-term ones are usually **exchange relationships**, in which people are concerned about a fair distribution of rewards and costs. Long-term, intimate relationships are usually **communal relationships**, in which people are less concerned with an immediate accounting of who is contributing what and are more concerned with helping their partner when he or she is in need.

The **evolutionary approach** to love states that men and women are attracted to different character-istics in each other because this maximizes their reproductive success. This view maintains that when choosing a marriage partner, women care more about men's resources and men care more about women's appearance.

The theory of **attachment styles** points to people's past relationships with their parents as a significant determinant of the quality of their close relationships as adults. Infants can be classified as having one of three types of attachment relationships with their primary caregiver: **secure, avoidant,** and **anxious/ambivalent.** There is evidence that people who were securely attached as infants have the most intimate and satisfying romantic relationships of the three types.

Relational dialectics states that close relationships are always in a state of change, due to opposing forces of **autonomy/connection, novelty/predictability,** and **openness/closedness** that the two partners experience and respond to. Relationships are perceived as an ever-changing *process*, not a fixed entity.

Unfortunately, intimate relationships end; the *breaking up process* is composed of stages, not a single event. Strategies for responding to problems in a romantic relationship include the behaviors associated with *exit, voice, loyalty,* and *neglect.* While the experience of breaking up is never pleasant, a powerful variable that predicts how a person will weather the breakup is the *role* he or she plays in the decision to terminate the relationship.

If You Are Interested

Annie Hall. Woody Allen's witty, wacky, and perceptive take on falling in love in New York City, with Diane Keaton. Winner of the 1977 Academy Award for best picture.

Brehm, S. S. (1992). *Intimate relationships* (2nd ed.). New York: McGraw-Hill. A comprehensive overview of the entire field of interpersonal attraction, from first impressions to intimate relationships.

Casablanca. "Play it again, Sam"—the all-time classic film, awarded the Oscar for best picture in 1943. Rick, Elsa, and Victor Laslo: the story of a love triangle set amid pre–World War II intrigue and treachery. It doesn't get any better than this.

Duck, S. (1991). *Understanding relationships*. New York: Guilford. An overview of the field of close relationships by an eminent researcher in this area.

Fried Green Tomatoes. A touching story of the meaning and power of friendship in three women's lives.

Hatfield, E., & Rapson, R. L. (1993). *Love, sex, and intimacy: Their psychology, biology, and history.* New York: HarperCollins. A fascinating look at love and intimacy, including both current scientific studies and historical comparisons between concepts of love in other eras and cultures.

Hendrick, C. (Ed.). (1989). *Close relationships: Review of personality and social psychology* (Vol. 10). Newbury Park, CA: Sage. Chapters on close relationships by the leading researchers in the field, including many whose work we discussed in this chapter.

Márquez, Gabriel García. *Love in the Time of Cholera.* A magical tale of a man's unrequited but intrepid love, which, after 51 years of waiting, is richly rewarded.

McCauley, Stephen. *The Object of My Affection.* A romantic comedy about friends and lovers: a gay man, whose lover has dumped him, and his best friend, a single woman who's pregnant and wants him to be the surrogate dad.

Sternberg, R. J., & Barnes, M. L. (Eds.). (1988). *The psychology of love.* New Haven, CT: Yale University Press. Chapters on love by the leading researchers in the field, including many whose work we discussed in this chapter.

Tyler, Anne. *The Accidental Tourist.* A compassionate, compelling, and extremely funny tale of two apparently mismatched people who fall in love.

PROSOCIAL BEHAVIOR: WHY DO PEOPLE HELP?

n January 1982, Air Florida Flight 90 crashed while attempting to take off from National Airport outside of Washington, D.C. The plane lifted off the runway during an icy, swirling snowstorm but was unable to gain altitude. It clipped a bridge spanning the Potomac River and slammed though the ice into the dark water, making a swishing sound as it sank. Most of the passengers and crew were killed by the impact, but a few survivors clung desperately to the tail section of the plane in the frigid waters of the Potomac. A helicopter from the National Park Service flew quickly to the scene. Every second counted, because no one could survive for long in the 30-degree water. The helicopter crew dropped a rescue line, hoping to tow the survivors to rescue workers waiting on the shore. But most of the survivors were in shock and failed to grab the line as it swung back and forth in the gale-force winds. One passenger, a balding man in his fifties, was more alert than the others and managed to catch the rope. Imagine how strong his desire must have been to be saved from this terrible ordeal. But instead of letting the helicopter pull him to safety, he

■ Lenny Skutnik saves Priscilla Triado after she drops the rescue line.

passed the line to another passenger. Each time the helicopter returned, he grabbed the line and handed it to someone else.

One survivor, Priscilla Triado, lost her grip as the helicopter towed her to shore. She dropped, semiconscious, into the icy water. Lenny Skutnik, a clerk at the Congressional Budget Office, was watching from the banks of the Potomac. Without hesitation, he tore off his coat and boots and dove into the freezing river, dragging Triado to waiting rescue workers. Doctors later found that Triado's body temperature was 81 degrees Fahrenheit and estimated that she was moments away from death when Skutnik reached her. Meanwhile, the helicopter continued to tow the other survivors to the shore. When it returned at last for the selfless man who had been passing the rope to the other passengers, he was nowhere to be found. He had succumbed to the freezing temperatures, slipping wordlessly beneath the black surface of the river.

The horror of the crash of Flight 90 was tempered by these extraordinary acts of self-sacrifice. Lenny Skutnik easily could have died in the freezing temperatures while trying to rescue Priscilla Triado. Instead, he thought, "Somebody had to go into the water," and decided without hesitation that that somebody would be him (*Time*, January 25, 1982). The entire country applauded his courageous, selfless act, as well as that of the unknown passenger who passed the rope to others, paying for his generosity with his life. The fact that he could not be identified added to his mystique. He seemed to represent the capacity in us all to act in selfless, altruistic, even heroic ways.

Basic Motives Underlying Prosocial Behavior: Why Do People Help?

Why is it that sometimes people perform acts of great self-sacrifice and heroism, whereas at other times they act in uncaring, heartless ways, ignoring the desperate pleas of those in need? In this chapter, we will consider the major determinants of **prosocial behavior,** which we define as any act performed with the goal of benefiting another person. We will be particularly concerned with prosocial behavior that is motivated by **altruism,** which is the desire to help another person even if it involves a cost to the helper. Someone might act in a prosocial manner out of self-interest—he or she hopes to get something in return. Altruism is helping purely out of the desire to benefit someone else, with no benefit (and often a cost) to oneself. Lenny Skutnik, for example, dove into the river to save Priscilla Triado, even though he put himself in grave danger.

We will begin by considering the basic origins of prosocial behavior and altruism: Why do people help others? Few questions have intrigued observers of the human condition as much as this one. Is the willingness to help a basic impulse with genetic roots? Is it something that must be taught and nurtured in childhood? Is there a pure motive for helping, such that people are willing to aid their fellow human beings even when they have nothing to gain? Or are people willing to help only when there is something in it for them? Let's see how psychologists have addressed these centuries-old questions.

Prosocial Behavior
any act performed with the goal of benefiting another person

Altruism
the desire to help another person even if involves a cost to the helper

Evolutionary Psychology: Instincts and Genes

According to Charles Darwin's (1859) theory of evolution, natural selection favors genes that promote the survival of the individual. Any gene that furthers our survival and increases the probability that we will produce offspring is likely to be passed on from generation to generation. Genes that lower our chances of survival, such as those causing life-threatening diseases, reduce the chances that we will produce offspring and thus are less likely to be passed on. Evolutionary biologists like E. O. Wilson (1975) and Richard Dawkins (1976) have used these principles of evolutionary theory to explain such social behaviors as aggression and altruism. Several psychologists have pursued these ideas, spawning the field of **evolutionary psychology,** which is the attempt to explain social behavior in terms of genetic factors that evolved over time according to the principles of natural selection (Barkow, Cosmides, & Tooby, 1992; Buss, 1994, 1996; Buss & Kenrick, 1998; Simpson & Kenrick, 1997; Wright, 1994).

Darwin realized early on that a potential problem exists with evolutionary theory: How can it explain altruism? If people's overriding goal is to ensure their own survival, why would they ever help others at a cost to themselves? It would seem that, over the centuries, altruistic behavior would disappear, because people who acted that way would, by putting themselves at risk, produce fewer offspring than people who acted selfishly. Genes promoting selfish behavior should be more likely to be passed on—or should they?

Evolutionary Psychology
the attempt to explain social behavior in terms of genetic factors that evolved over time according to the principles of natural selection

Kin Selection

One way that evolutionary psychologists attempt to resolve this dilemma is with the notion of **kin selection,** the idea that behaviors that help a genetic relative are

Kin Selection
the idea that behaviors that help a genetic relative are favored by natural selection

■ According to evolutionary psychology, prosocial behavior occurs in part because of kin selection, such as this young woman helping her little brother.

favored by natural selection (Hamilton, 1964). People can increase the chances that their genes will be passed along not only by having their own children, but also by ensuring that their genetic relatives have children. Because a person's blood relatives share some of his or her genes, the more that person ensures their survival, the greater the chance that his or her genes will flourish in future generations. Thus, natural selection should favor altruistic acts directed toward genetic relatives. There is support for this notion in the animal kingdom, particularly among social insects. Les Greenberg (1979), for example, released bees near a nest protected by guard bees and observed which ones the guards admitted to the nest and which ones they rebuffed. He had bred the intruders to be of varying genetic similarity to the guards. Some were siblings, some were cousins, and some were more distant relatives. (The guards could tell how related they were to the bees by their odors.) Consistent with the idea of kin selection, the guard bees were much more likely to admit bees that were close relatives, essentially telling their distant relatives that there was no more room at the inn.

There is some evidence that kin selection operates in human beings as well. According to Gene Burnstein, Chris Crandall, and Shinobu Kitayama (1994), people's choice of whom to help is influenced by the "biological importance" of the outcome: People are especially likely to help others who are most related to them when this help increases the likelihood that that person will have children. In one study, for example, people reported that they would be more likely to help genetic relatives than non-relatives in life-and-death situations, such as a house fire. People did not report that they would be more likely to help genetic relatives when the situation was non-life threatening, which is consistent with the idea that people are most likely to help in ways that ensure the survival of their own genes. Interestingly, both males and females, as well as American and Japanese participants, followed this rule of kin selection in life-threatening situations.

Of course, in this study people only reported what they would do; this doesn't prove that in a real fire they would indeed be more likely to save their sibling than their cousin. There is some anecdotal evidence from real emergencies, however, that is consistent with these results. Sime (1983) interviewed survivors of a fire at a vacation complex in 1973 and found that when people became aware there was a fire, they were much more likely to search for family members before exiting the building than they were to search for friends.

Evolutionary psychologists do not mean to imply that people consciously weigh the biological importance of their behavior before deciding whether to help. It is not as if people crassly compute the likelihood that their genes will be passed on before deciding whether to help someone push her or his car out of a ditch. According to evolutionary theory, however, the genes of people who follow this "biological importance" rule are more likely to survive than the genes of people who do not. Thus, over the millennia, kin selection became ingrained in human behavior.

J. Philippe Rushton (1989) goes so far as to suggest that conflict between different ethnic groups may have a genetic basis, stemming in part from evolutionary pressures to help only those who can pass along our genes. One problem with this explanation of prosocial behavior, however, is that it has difficulty explaining why complete strangers sometimes help each other, even when there is no reason for them to assume they share some of the same genes. For example, it seems absurd to say that the unknown hero of Air Florida Flight 90, who passed the rope to other passengers until he drowned, somehow calculated how genetically similar the other passengers were to him before deciding to save their lives.

> "Altruism based on kin selection is the enemy of civilization. If human beings are to a large extent guided to favor their own relatives and tribe, only a limited amount of global harmony is possible.
> —E.O. Wilson, 1978

The Reciprocity Norm

To explain altruism, evolutionary psychologists also point to the **norm of reciprocity,** which is the expectation that helping others will increase the likelihood that they will help us in the future. The idea is that as human beings were evolving, a group of completely selfish individuals, each living in his or her own cave, would have found it more difficult to survive than a group who had learned to cooperate with each other. Of course, if people cooperated too readily, they might have been exploited by an adversary who never helped in return. Those who were most likely to survive, the argument goes, were people who developed an understanding with their neighbors about reciprocity: "I will help you now, with the agreement that when I need help, you will return the favor." Because of its survival value, such a norm of reciprocity may have become genetically based (J. Baron, 1997; Cosmides & Tooby, 1992; de Waal, 1996; Shackelford & Buss, 1996; Trivers, 1971). Try It! on page 422 describes a way you can use the reciprocity norm to collect money for charity.

Norm of Reciprocity
the expectation that helping others will increase the likelihood that they will help us in the future

Learning Social Norms

A third way in which evolutionary theory can explain altruism has been offered by Nobel laureate Herbert Simon (1990). He argues that it is highly adaptive for individuals to learn social norms from other members of a society. People who are the best learners of the norms and customs of a society have a survival advantage, Simon argues, because many of these norms and customs are beneficial. Over the centuries, a culture learns such things as which foods are poisonous and how best to cooperate with each other, and the person who learns these rules is more likely to survive than the person who does not. Consequently, through natural selection the ability to learn social norms has become part of our genetic makeup. One norm that people learn is the value of helping others; this is considered to be a valuable norm in virtually all societies. In short, people are genetically programmed to learn social norms, and one of these norms is altruism (Hoffman, 1981).

Try It!

The Reciprocity Norm

As noted in this chapter and in Chapter 8, the reciprocity norm is very powerful. If you help people in some way they will probably feel obligated to help you in the future. This exercise is designed to take advantage of the reciprocity norm to help you collect money for a good cause. Follow the procedures and see if it works for you.

1. Choose a charity or cause for which you would like to collect money.

2. Make a list of 10 to 15 friends and acquaintances that you are willing to ask to give money to this charity.

3. Go down the list and flip a coin for each name. If the coin comes up tails, assign them to the "favor" condition. If it comes up heads, assign them to the "no favor" condition.

4. Find a way to do a small favor for each person in the favor condition. For example, if you're going to the soda machine, offer to buy a soda for your friend. If you have a car, give him or her a ride somewhere. The exact favor doesn't matter and doesn't have to be the same for each person in your favor condition. The key is that it be a little out of the ordinary, so that your friend feels obligated to you.

5. A day later, ask everyone on your list if they can make a donation to your charity. Keep track of how much each person gives. Chances are, people in your favor condition will give more, on average, than people in your no favor condition.

A Word of Warning: This technique can backfire if your friends perceive your favor as an attempt to manipulate them. That is why it is important to allow a day or so pass between the time you help them and the time you ask them for a donation; if you ask them right after the favor, they are likely to feel that you helped only to get them to give money—and to resent this intrusion. Also, when you ask them for a donation, do not say anything about your earlier favor. After you are done this exercise, you may well want to discuss it with your friends and explain why you did what you did.

In sum, evolutionary psychologists believe that people help others because of three factors that have become ingrained in our genes: kin selection, the norm of reciprocity, and the ability to learn and follow social norms. Evolutionary psychology is a challenging and creative approach to understanding prosocial behavior, though it is important to note that not all psychologists accept its claims. Many are skeptical of the idea that all social behaviors can be traced back to our ancestral roots, becoming instilled in our genes because of their survival value (Batson, 1998; Economos, 1969; Gangestad, 1989; Gould, 1997). For example, just because people are more likely to save family members than strangers from a fire does not necessarily mean that they are genetically programmed to help genetic relatives. It may simply be that they cannot bear the thought of losing a loved one and so go to greater lengths to save the ones they love over people they have never met. We turn now to other possible motives behind prosocial behavior that do not necessarily originate in people's genes.

Social Exchange: The Costs and Rewards of Helping

Though some social psychologists disagree with evolutionary approaches to prosocial behavior, they share the view that altruistic behavior can be based on self-interest. In fact, a theory in social psychology, *social exchange theory,* argues that much of what we do stems from the desire to maximize our rewards and minimize our costs (Homans, 1961; Thibaut & Kelley, 1959). The difference from evolutionary approaches is that there is neither an attempt to trace this desire back to our evolutionary roots nor an assumption that the desire is genetically based. We reviewed this theory in some depth in Chapter 10, on interpersonal attraction, and thus will only summarize it here. Social exchange theorists assume that just as people in an economic marketplace try to maximize the ratio of their monetary profits to their monetary losses, so too do people in their relationships with others try to maximize the ratio of social rewards to social costs.

This does not mean that we keep a little notebook handy, entering a plus every time our friends are nice to us and a minus every time our friends are mean to us. Social exchange theory does argue, however, that we keep track, at a more implicit level, of the rewards and costs in social relationships. Helping can be rewarding in a number of ways. As we saw with the norm of reciprocity, it can increase the likelihood that someone will help us in return. Helping someone is an investment in the future, the social exchange being that someday, someone will help you when you need it. If this sounds a bit far-fetched or even naive, think about how deeply this idea permeates our society on both a secular and a religious level. Being a good person and treating others with compassion (and receiving such treatment in return) are the hallmark of a civilized society, part of what early philosophers called the social contract. Few of us would want to live in a "dog-eat-dog" world; we need to believe that kindness will be reciprocated, at least some of the time.

Helping can be rewarding in a number of other ways, such as relieving the personal distress of the bystander. Considerable evidence indicates that people

> *Let him who neglects to raise the fallen, fear lest, when he falls, no one will stretch out his hand to lift him up.*
> —Saadi (1184–1291)

■ Helping behavior is common in virtually all species of animals. Sometimes, helping behavior even crosses species lines. In August of 1996, a 3-year-old boy fell into a pit containing seven gorillas at the Brookfield, Illinois zoo. Binti, a 7-year-old gorilla, immediately picked up the boy. After cradling him in her arms she placed the boy near a door where zookeepers could get to him. Why did she help? Evolutionary psychologists would argue that prosocial behavior is selected for and thus becomes part of the genetic makeup of the members of many species. Social exchange theorists would argue that Binti had been rewarded for helping in the past. In fact, because she had been rejected by her mother, she had received training in parenting skills from zookeepers, in which she was rewarded for caring for a doll. (Bils & Singer, 1996)

are aroused and disturbed when they see another person suffer and that they help at least in part to relieve their distress (Dovidio, 1984; Dovidio, Piliavin, Gaertner, Schroeder, & Clark, 1991; Eisenberg & Fabes, 1991). By helping others, we can also gain such rewards as social approval from others and increased feelings of self-worth.

The other side of the coin, of course, is that helping can be costly. Helping decreases when the costs are high, as when it would put us in physical danger, result in pain or embarrassment, or simply take too much time (Dovidio, Piliavin, Gaertner, Schroeder, & Clark, 1991; Piliavin, Dovidio, Gaertner, & Clark, 1982; Piliavin, Piliavin, & Rodin, 1975). The basic assumption of social exchange theory is that people help only when the benefits outweigh the costs. Perhaps for Lenny Skutnik, the rewards of helping Priscilla Triado (e.g., relieving his distress at seeing her drown) were greater than the costs (placing himself in direct physical danger). Basically, social exchange theory argues that true altruism, in which people help even when doing so is costly to themselves, does not exist. People help when it is in their interests to do so, but not when the costs outweigh the benefits.

If you are like many of our students, you may be experiencing discomfort over this view of helping behavior, finding it to be a rather cynical portrayal of human nature. Is true altruism, motivated only by the desire to help someone else, really such a mythical act? Must we trace all prosocial behavior back to the self-interest of the helper? Such a view seems to demean prosocial behavior. When someone behaves generously, as by saving another person's life or donating a huge sum to charity, should we view it as a mere act of self-interest undeserving of our esteem?

Well, a social exchange theorist might reply, there are many ways in which people can obtain gratification and we should be thankful that one way is by helping others. After all, wealthy people could decide to get their pleasure only from lavish vacations, expensive cars, and gourmet meals at fancy restaurants. We should applaud their decision to give money to the disadvantaged, even if, ultimately, it is just another way for them to obtain gratification. Prosocial acts are doubly rewarding, in that they help both the giver and the recipient of the aid. Thus, it is to everyone's advantage to promote and praise such acts. Still, many people are dissatisfied with the argument that all helping stems from self-interest. How can it explain why people give up their lives for others, as in the passing of the rope by the unknown hero of Air Florida Flight 90? According to some social psychologists, people do have hearts of gold and sometimes help only for the sake of helping—as we will see now.

Empathy and Altruism: The Pure Motive for Helping

Daniel Batson (1991) is the strongest proponent of the idea that people often help purely out of the goodness of their hearts. Batson acknowledges that people sometimes help others for selfish reasons, such as to relieve their own distress at seeing another person suffer. But he also argues that people's motives are sometimes purely altruistic, in that their only goal is to help the other person, even if doing so involves some cost to themselves. Pure altruism is likely to come into play, he maintains, when we feel **empathy** for the person in need of help, defined as the ability to put ourselves in the shoes of another person, experiencing events and emotions the way that person experiences them. Suppose, for example, that you are at the grocery store and see a man holding a baby and a bag full of diapers, toys, and rattles. As the man reaches for a box of Wheaties, he loses his grip

> "I once saw a man out of courtesy help a lame dog over a stile, and [the dog] for requital bit his fingers.
> —William Chillingworth

> "What seems to be generosity is often no more than disguised ambition.
> —La Rochefoucauld, 1678

Empathy
the ability to put oneself in the shoes of another person—to experience events and emotions (e.g., joy and sadness) the way that person experiences them

on the bag and all of its contents spill on the floor. Will you stop and help him pick up his things? According to Batson, it depends first on whether you feel empathy for him. If you do—if you can "feel his pain," in Bill Clinton's words—you will help, regardless of what you have to gain. Your goal will be to relieve the other person's distress, not to gain something for yourself. This is the crux of Batson's **empathy-altruism hypothesis:** When we feel empathy for another person, we will attempt to help him or her purely for altruistic reasons, regardless of what we have to gain.

What if you do not feel empathy? If, for whatever reason, you do not share the man's distress, then, Batson says, social exchange concerns come into play. What's in it for you? If there is something to be gained, such as obtaining approval from the man or from onlookers, then you will help the man pick up his things. If you will not profit from helping, you will go on your way without stopping. Batson's empathy-altruism hypothesis is summarized in Figure 11.1.

Batson and his colleagues would be the first to acknowledge that it can be very difficult to isolate the exact causes of complex social behaviors. If you saw Sue help the man pick up his possessions, how could you tell whether she was acting out of empathic concern or to gain some sort of social reward? Consider a

Empathy-Altruism Hypothesis
the idea that when we feel empathy for a person, we will attempt to help him or her purely for altruistic reasons, regardless of what we have to gain

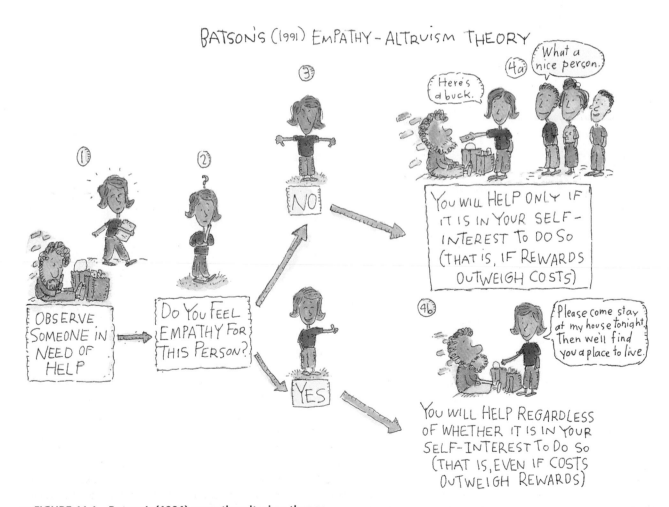

■ **FIGURE 11.1   Batson's (1991) empathy-altruism theory.**

Calvin and Hobbes   by Bill Watterson

■ Calvin seems to be an advocate of social exchange theory.

> ❝It is one of the beautiful compensations of this life that no one can sincerely try to help another without helping himself.❞
>
> –Charles Dudley Warner

famous story about Abraham Lincoln. One day, while riding in a coach, Lincoln and a fellow passenger were debating the very question we are considering: Is helping ever truly altruistic? Lincoln argued that helping always stems from self-interest, whereas the other passenger took the view that true altruism exists. Suddenly the men were interrupted by the screeching whine of a sow, who was trying to save her piglets from drowning in a creek. Lincoln promptly called out, "Driver, can't you stop for just a moment?" He jumped out of the coach, ran down to the creek, and lifted the piglets to the safety of the bank. When he returned, his companion said, "Now, Abe, where does selfishness come in on this little episode?" "Why, bless your soul, Ed," Lincoln replied. "That was the very essence of selfishness. I should have had no peace of mind all day had I gone on and left that suffering old sow worrying over those pigs. I did it to get peace of mind, don't you see?" (Sharp, 1928, p. 75).

As this example shows, an act that seems truly altruistic is sometimes motivated by self-interest. How, then, can we tell which is which? Batson and his colleagues have devised a series of clever experiments to unravel people's motives (e.g., Batson, Duncan, Ackerman, Buckley, & Birch, 1981; Batson & Shaw, 1991; Batson et al., 1996; Batson & Weeks, 1996; Toi & Batson, 1982). Imagine you were one of the participants (who were introductory psychology students) in a study by Miho Toi and Daniel Batson (1982). You are asked to evaluate some tapes of new programs for the university radio station, one of which is called *News from the Personal Side*. There are lots of different pilot tapes for this program, and you are told that only one person will be listening to each tape. The one you hear is an interview with a student named Carol Marcy. She describes a bad automobile accident in which both of her legs were broken and talks about how hard it has been to keep up with her class work as a result of the accident, especially because she is still in a wheelchair. Carol says she is especially concerned about how far she has fallen behind in her introductory psychology class and mentions that she will have to drop the class unless she can find another student to tell her what she has missed.

After you listen to the tape, the experimenter hands you an envelope marked "To the student listening to the Carol Marcy pilot tape." The experimenter says she doesn't know what's in the envelope but was asked by the professor supervising the research to hand it out. You open the envelope and find a note from the professor, saying that he was wondering if the student who listened to Carol's tape would be willing to help her out with her psychology class. Carol was reluctant to ask for help, he says, but because she is way behind in the class, she agreed to write a note to the person listening to her tape. The note asks if you could meet with her and share your introductory psychology lecture notes.

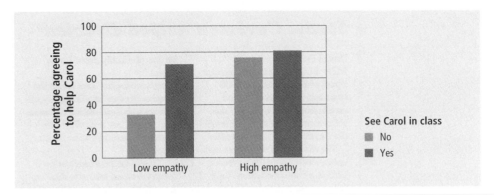

■ **FIGURE 11.2   Altruism versus Self-Interest.**   Under what conditions did people agree to help Carol with the work she missed in her introductory psychology class? When empathy was high, people helped regardless of the costs and rewards (i.e., regardless of whether they would encounter her in their psychology class). When empathy was low, people were more concerned with the rewards and costs for them—they helped only if they would encounter Carol in their psychology class and thus feel guilty about not helping. (Adapted from Toi & Batson, 1982)

As you have no doubt gathered, the point of the study was to look at the conditions under which people agreed to help Carol. Toi and Batson (1982) pitted two motives against each other—self-interest and empathy. First, they varied how much empathy people felt toward Carol by telling different participants to adopt different perspectives when listening to the tape. In the high-empathy condition, people were told to try to imagine how Carol felt about what happened to her and how it changed her life. In the low-empathy condition, people were told to try to be objective and to not be concerned with how Carol felt. These instructions had the expected effect on people's feelings—those in the high-empathy condition reported feeling more sympathy with Carol than people in the low-empathy condition did.

Second, Toi and Batson varied how costly it would be not to help Carol. In one condition, participants learned that Carol would start coming back to class the following week and happened to be in the same psychology section as they were; thus, they would see her every time they went to class and would be reminded of her need for help. This was the high-cost condition, because it would be unpleasant to refuse to help Carol and then run into her every week in class. In the low-cost condition, people learned that Carol would be studying at home and would not be coming to class; thus, they would never have to face her in her wheelchair and feel guilty about not helping her out.

When deciding whether to help Carol, did people take into account the costs involved? According to the empathy-altruism hypothesis, people should have been be motivated by genuine altruistic concern, and helped regardless of the costs—if empathy was high (see Figure 11.1). As you can see in the right-hand side of Figure 11.2, this prediction was confirmed: In the high-empathy condition, about as many people agreed to help when they thought they would see Carol in class as when they thought they would not see her in class. This suggests that people had Carol's interests in mind, and not their own. In the low-empathy condition, however, many more people agreed to help when they thought they would see Carol in class than when they thought they would not see her in class (see the left-hand side of Figure 11.2). This suggests that when empathy was low,

Study: Cavemen helped disabled

United Press International
NEW YORK—The skeleton of a dwarf who died about 12,000 years ago indicates that cave people cared for physically disabled members of their communities, a researcher said yesterday.

The skeleton of the 3-foot-high youth was initially discovered in 1963 in a cave in southern Italy but was lost to anthropologists until American researcher David W. Frayer reexamined the remains and reported his findings in the British journal Nature.

Frayer, a professor of anthropology at the University of Kansas at Lawrence, said in a telephone interview that the youth "couldn't have taken part in normal hunting of food or gathering activities so

he was obviously cared for by others."

Archaeologists have found the remains of other handicapped individuals who lived during the same time period, but their disabilities occurred when they were adults, Frayer said.

"This is the first time we've found someone who was disabled since birth . . . .", Frayer said. He said there was no indication that the dwarf, who was about 17 at the time of his death, had suffered from malnutrition or neglect.

He was one of six individuals buried in the floor of a cave and was found in a dual grave in the arms of a woman, about 40 years old.

■ This touching story of early hominid prosocial behavior is intriguing to think about in terms of different theories of prosocial behavior. Evolutionary psychologists might argue that the caregivers helped the dwarf because he was a relative and that people are programmed to help those who share their genes (kin selection). Social exchange theory would maintain that the dwarf's caregivers received sufficient rewards from their actions so as to outweigh the costs of caring for him. The empathy-altruism hypothesis would hold that the caregivers helped out of strong feelings of empathy and compassion for him—an interpretation supported by the article's final paragraph.

social exchange concerns came into play, in that people based their decision to help on the costs and benefits to themselves. They helped when it was in their interests to do so (i.e., when they would see Carol in her wheelchair and feel guilty for not helping) but not otherwise (i.e., when they thought they would never see her again).

The Toi and Batson (1982) study suggests that true altruism exists when people experience empathy toward the suffering of another. But as illustrated by our example of Abraham Lincoln and the pigs, it can be very difficult to unravel people's exact motives when they help someone, and a lively debate over the empathy-altruism hypothesis has arisen (e.g., Cialdini, 1991; Hornstein, 1991; Martz, 1991; Smith, Keating, & Stotland, 1989; Sorrentino, 1991). Some researchers question whether people who experience empathy help purely out of concern for the person in need or, like Abe Lincoln, help in order to lower their own distress at seeing someone they care about suffer. The empathy-altruism hypothesis has withstood these challenges, however, and appears to have a good deal of validity (Batson, 1998; Piliavin & Charng, 1990). When we feel empathy for another person our motives do seem to be pure, causing us to help even when we have nothing to gain by doing so.

In summary, we have discussed three basic motives underlying prosocial behavior: the idea that helping is an instinctive reaction to promote the welfare of those genetically similar to us (evolutionary psychology); that the rewards of helping often outweigh the costs, making it in people's self-interest to help (social exchange theory); and that under some conditions, powerful feelings of empathy and compassion for the victim prompt selfless giving (the empathy-altruism hypothesis). Each of these approaches has vocal proponents and vociferous critics

Personal Determinants of Prosocial Behavior: Why Do Some People Help More Than Others?

Whatever the nature of people's basic motives, these motives are not the sole determinants of whether people help, for many personal and situational factors can suppress or trigger these motives. If basic human motives were all there was to it, how could we explain the fact that some people are much more helpful than others? Clearly, we need to consider the personal determinants of prosocial behavior that distinguish the helpful person from the selfish one.

Individual Differences: The Altruistic Personality

When you read the example at the beginning of this chapter, did you think about the different personalities of the people involved? It is natural to assume that Lenny Skutnik and the man who passed the rope to his fellow passengers were cut from a different cloth—selfless, caring people who would never dream of ignoring someone's pleas for help. Had they heard Kitty Genovese's screams, she might be alive today. (Genovese is the woman we discussed in Chapter 2 who was murdered in the early 1960s, within earshot of 38 of her neighbors—none of whom called the police or helped her in any way.) Had Kitty Genovese's neighbors been standing on the shore of the Potomac watching the flight attendant lose hold of the rescue line, perhaps they would have stood there and done nothing, allowing Priscilla Triado to perish. Similarly, there are Mother Teresas who devote their lives to others and Saddam Husseins who are bent on destruction and mayhem. And, of course, there are lots of people between these extremes of sainthood and wickedness. Psychologists are very interested in how prosocial behavior develops, as well as the extent to which individual differences in altruism determine prosocial behavior.

Instilling Helpfulness with Rewards and Models

Developmental psychologists have discovered that prosocial behavior occurs early in life. Even children as young as 18 months frequently help others, such as assisting a parent with household tasks or trying to make a crying infant feel better (Rheingold, 1982; Zahn-Waxler, Radke-Yarrow, & King, 1979). One powerful way to encourage prosocial behavior is for parents and others to reward such acts with praise, smiles, and hugs. Several studies suggest that these kinds of rewards increase prosocial behavior in children (Fischer, 1963; Grusec, 1991). Rewards should not, however, be emphasized too much. If children decide to help others only to obtain praise from their parents, they will not come to view themselves as helpful, altruistic people; instead, they will believe it is valuable to help others only when they get rewarded for it. The same is true for adults—believing we are helping someone in order to get a reward diminishes our view of ourselves as altruistic, selfless people (Batson, Coke, Jasnoski, & Hanson, 1978; Uranowitz, 1975).

This undermining effect of rewards is identical to the overjustification effect we discussed in Chapter 5: Rewarding people too strongly for performing a behavior can lower their intrinsic interest in it, because they come to believe they are doing it only to get the reward. The trick is to encourage children to act prosocially but not to be too heavy-handed with rewards. One way of accomplishing

> "On reflecting at dinner that he had done nothing to help anybody all day, he uttered these memorable and praiseworthy words: "Friends, I have lost a day."
> —Suetonius

■ Adult approval serves as a powerful reward for children when they behave prosocially.

> If an accident happens on the highway, everyone hastens to help the sufferer. If some great and sudden calamity befalls a family, the purses of a thousand strangers are at once willingly opened and small but numerous donations pour in to relieve their distress.
>
> –Alexis de Tocqueville, *Democracy in America* (1835)

this is to tell children, after they have helped, that they did so because they are kind and helpful people. Such comments encourage children to perceive themselves as altruistic people, so that they will help in future situations even when no rewards are forthcoming (Grusec, Kuczynski, Rushton, & Simutis, 1979).

Another way for parents to increase prosocial behavior in their children is to behave prosocially themselves. Children often model behaviors they observe in others, including prosocial behaviors (Batson, 1998; Dodge, 1984; Mussen & Eisenberg-Berg, 1977). Children who observe their parents helping others (e.g., volunteering to help the homeless) learn that helping others is a valued act. Interviews with people who have gone to great lengths to help others—such as Christians who helped Jews escape from Nazi Germany during World War II and civil rights activists in this country—indicate that their parents too were dedicated helpers (London, 1970; Rosenhan, 1970).

Children imitate other adults, besides their parents. Teachers, relatives, and even television characters can serve as models for children. J. Philippe Rushton (1975) demonstrated this fact in an interesting study of elementary school children. The children played a bowling game in which they won tokens, which could be exchanged for prizes or donated to a needy child named Bobby as part of a "Save the Children" fund. Before playing the game, the children watched an adult—who was said to be a future teacher at their school—play the game. In one condition, the adult kept all the tokens, refusing to donate any to Bobby. In another condition, the adult put half of her tokens in a jar for Bobby. All the children then played the game by themselves, and the researchers kept track of how many tokens the kids donated to Bobby.

The children who watched the generous adult were much more likely to follow suit, donating some of their tokens. It is not clear, however, whether they did so because they had learned to be more altruistic, or whether they simply felt pressure to give away some of their tokens. It's like when someone passes the hat at the office to buy a birthday present for a colleague. Sometimes we throw in a few dollars because everyone else is, not because we are feeling particularly altru-

■ Children are good imitators and learn prosocial behavior from observing other people (e.g., their parents) behaving prosocially.

istic. Similarly, it is unclear whether the children in Rushton's study had become more altruistic or were trying to avoid looking selfish in the eyes of the adult.

Rushton (1975) conducted a second phase of his experiment to address this question. Two months after the first session, a different experimenter took the children to a room and left them to play the bowling game again. This time, they could choose to donate some of their tokens to a different charity—namely, a fund for starving Asian children. They did not observe any adults giving or not giving to this fund, nor were there any adults present to observe what they did. Nonetheless, the kids who had seen the adult give tokens to Bobby two months earlier donated more tokens to this new charity than did kids who had seen the adult keep all the tokens. The children who had seen the generous adult seem to have become genuinely altruistic, causing them to donate more tokens several weeks later in a new situation, in which no models were present.

The lesson for parents is clear: If you want your children to be altruistic, act in altruistic ways yourself. Is this kind of modeling limited to prosocial behavior? You may be wondering if children also imitate people they see acting aggressively and violently, such as their favorite characters on television. We will see in the next chapter, on aggression, that such antisocial modeling can occur as well.

Is Personality the Whole Story?

As we have just seen, parents and other adults can influence how altruistic a child becomes. We should be careful, however, about the kinds of conclusions we draw from this fact. True, some people have learned to be more altruistic than others (Oliner & Oliner, 1988; Penner, Fritzsche, Craiger, & Freifeld, 1995). We can all think of people who are consistently helpful, such as our saintly Aunt Sarah, who always puts other people's needs ahead of her own, or our cousin Tom, who has just joined the Peace Corps. But this does not mean that when we want to predict how helpful someone will be, all we need to know is how much of an altruistic personality he or she has. If this were all there is to it, then we should be able to divide the world into different types of people: helpers, who regularly come to the aid of their fellow human beings, regardless of the situation, and selfish people, who consistently sit on their duffs when others need help.

As we saw in Chapter 1, however, people's personalities are not the sole determinant of how they behave. According to social psychologists, to understand human behavior—such as how helpful people will behave in a given situation—we need to consider the situational pressures impinging on them as well as their personalities (Carlo, Eisenberg, Troyer, Switzer, & Speer, 1991). Predicting how helpful people will be is no exception to the rule. Consider, for example, a classic study by Hugh Hartshorne and Mark May (1929). They observed how helpful 10,000 elementary and high school students were in a variety of situations, including the students' willingness to find stories and pictures to give to hospitalized children, donate money to charity, and give small gifts to needy children. The researchers assumed that they were measuring the extent to which people had an **altruistic personality**, which are those aspects of a person's makeup that cause him or her to help others in a wide variety of situations. If Nicole is one of those people with an altruistic personality, then she should be more likely than the others to be altruistic in all the situations. If Philip tends to be self-centered, then he should be less willing than the others to do any of the prosocial acts. Makes sense, doesn't it?

Surprisingly, the extent to which the children were prosocial in one situation (e.g., finding many stories and pictures for the hospitalized children) was not highly related to how prosocial they were in another. The average correlation between helping in one situation and helping in another was only .23. This means that if you knew how helpful a child was in one situation, you could not predict with much confidence how helpful he or she would be in another. Moreover, researchers who have studied both children and adults have not found much evidence that people with high scores on personality tests of altruism are more likely to help than those with lower scores (Piliavin & Charng, 1990). Magoo and Khanna (1991), for example, found that students at Indian universities who scored high on a measure of altruism were no more likely to volunteer to give blood than students who scored low on a measure of altruism. Clearly, people's personality is not the only determinant of whether they will help, at least in many situations (Batson, 1998).

Does this mean that any two people—be they like Mother Teresa or Saddam Hussein—are equally likely to help the survivors of a plane crash or a neighbor who is seriously ill? Of course not. It's just that individual differences in personality are not all we need to know when trying to predict how helpful someone will act. We need to take into account several other critical factors, such as what mood the person is in and what kinds of situational pressures are impinging on the person. Even Mother Teresa was probably more likely to help in some situations than in others. And surely Saddam Hussein is not always evil—perhaps some situations are more likely to bring out his diabolic nature than others.

In short, to predict how helpful someone will be, it is most useful to know a lot about his or her personality and the nature of the situation he or she is in. Several studies have demonstrated that certain kinds of people are more likely to help in one situation, whereas other kinds of people are more likely to help in different situations (e.g., Batson, Bolen, Cross, & Neuringer-Benefiel, 1986; Clark, Ouellette, Powell, & Milberg, 1987; Deutsch & Lamberti, 1986). Consider, for example, how helpful you think people would be in these two situations: (a) People are

---

Altruistic Personality those aspects of a person's makeup that cause him or her to help others in a wide variety of situations

standing on the shores of the Potomac, watching the rescue of Flight 90, and see Priscilla Triado lose hold of the rescue line, and (b) a retarded boy befriends a neighbor and asks the neighbor to take him to the movies. Who is most likely to help in the first situation, and who is most likely to help in the second situation?

Gender Differences in Prosocial Behavior

According to a review by Alice Eagly and Maureen Crowley (1986; Eagly, 1987), who focused on differences in helping between males and females, the answer is males in the first situation and females in the second situation. In virtually all cultures, there are different norms for males and females, so that men and women learn to value different traits and behaviors. In Western cultures, part of the male sex role is to be chivalrous and heroic, whereas part of the female sex role is to be nurturant and caring, valuing close, long-term relationships. As a result, we might expect men to help more in situations that call for brief chivalrous and heroic acts, such as Lenny Skutnik's decision to dive into the Potomac and save Priscilla Triado, and women to help more in long-term relationships that involve less danger but more commitment, such as volunteering at a nursing home.

In a review of more than 170 studies on helping behavior, Eagly and Crowley (1986) found that men are indeed more likely to help in chivalrous, heroic ways. For example, of the 7,000 people who received medals from the Carnegie Hero Fund Commission, for risking their lives to save a stranger, 91 percent of them have been men. What about helping that involves more nurturance and commitment? Not nearly as many studies have addressed this issue, because social psychologists have focused primarily on helping of the chivalrous, heroic kind. The few studies that have examined gender differences in long-term, nurturant relationships are consistent with Eagly and Crowley's (1986) speculations: Women help more on these tasks than men do (Belansky & Boggiano, 1994; Otten et al., 1988; Smith, Wheeler, & Diener, 1975). For example, when Anne McGuire

> "Both men and women belie their nature when they are not kind.
> —Gamaliel Bailey (1807–59)

■ Whereas men are more likely to perform chivalrous and heroic acts, women are more likely to be helpful in long-term relationships that involve greater commitment.

(1994) asked students to describe times they had helped friends versus strangers, men reported helping strangers more than women did, but women reported helping friends more than men did.

Cultural Differences in Prosocial Behavior

In previous chapters, we have noted that people who grow up in Western cultures tend to be individualistic and have an *independent view of the self,* whereas people who grow up in many non-Western cultures tend to be collectivist and have an *interdependent view of the self* (see Chapter 5). Because people with an interdependent view of the self are more likely to define themselves in terms of their social relationships and have more of a sense of "connectedness" to others, it might seem as if they would be more likely to help a person in need.

It is important to note, however, that in all cultures, people are more likely to help someone they define as a member of their **in group,** which is the group with which an individual identifies and feels he or she is a member. People everywhere are less likely to help someone they perceive to be a member of an **out group,** a group with which the individual does not identify (Brewer & Brown, 1998; see Chapter 13). Cultural factors come into play in determining how strongly people draw the line between in groups and out groups. In many interdependent cultures, greater importance is attached to the needs of the in group. Consequently, members of these cultures are more likely to help in group members than members of individualistic cultures are (Leung & Bond, 1984; Miller, Bersoff, & Harwood, 1990; Moghaddam, Taylor, & Wright, 1993). However, because the line between "us" and "them" is more firmly drawn in interdependent cultures, people in these cultures are *less* likely to help members of out groups than people in individualistic cultures are (L'Armand and Pepitone, 1975; Leung & Bond, 1984; Triandis, 1994). Thus, to be helped by other people it is always important that they view you as a member of their in group and this is especially true in interdependent cultures.

The Effects of Mood on Prosocial Behavior

We noted earlier that personality alone is an insufficient predictor of people's helping behavior. One reason for this is that helping depends on a person's current mood. Sometimes we feel up and sometimes we feel down, and these transitory emotional states are another key determinant of prosocial behavior. For example, imagine you are at your local shopping mall. As you walk from one store to another, a fellow in front of you suddenly drops a manila folder, and papers go fluttering in all directions. He looks around in dismay, then bends down and starts picking up the papers. Would you stop and help him? What do you think the average shopper would do? One way to answer this question is to think about how many altruistic people there are in the world (or at least in shopping malls). But as we have just seen, it is not enough to consider only differences in personality. The mood people happen to be in at the time can strongly affect their behavior—in this case, whether or not they will offer help.

Effects of Positive Moods: Feel Good, Do Good

Alice Isen and Paul Levin (1972) explored the effect of good moods on prosocial behavior in shopping malls in San Francisco and Philadelphia. They boosted the mood of shoppers in a simple way—namely, by leaving dimes in the coin-return

In Group
the group with which an individual identifies and feels he or she is a member

Out Group
a group with which the individual does not identify

Mood and Helping Behavior

Do people's moods influence how willing they are to help others? Try the experiment described below to find out.

Robert Baron (1997) predicted that people would be in better moods when they are around pleasant fragrances, and that this improved mood would make them more helpful. Consistent with his prediction, shoppers were more likely to help a stranger (by giving change for a dollar) when they were approached in locations with pleasant smells than when they were approached in locations with neutral smells. See if you can replicate this effect at a shopping mall in your area. Pick locations in the mall that have pleasant aromas or neutral aromas. For his pleasant aroma conditions, Baron (1997) used locations near a cookie store, a bakery, and a gourmet coffee cafe. The areas with neutral smells should be as identical as possible in all other respects; for example, Baron (1997) picked locations that were similar in the volume of

pedestrians, lighting, and proximity to mall exits, such as areas outside of clothing stores.

At each location, approach an individual who is by him- or herself. Take out a $1 bill and ask the passerby for change for a dollar. If the person stops and gives you change, count it as helping. If he or she ignores you or says he or she does not have any change, count it as not helping. Did you replicate Baron's (1997) results? He found that 57 percent of people helped in the locations with pleasant aromas, whereas only 19 percent of people helped in the locations with neutral aromas.

Note: Before conducting this study you might want to seek the permission of the manager of the mall. The manager of the mall in which Baron (1997) conducted his study requested that the researchers only approach persons of the same gender as themselves, because of a concern that cross-gender requests for change would be perceived as "pick-up" attempts. You might want to follow this procedure as well.

---

slot of a pay telephone at the mall and waiting for someone to find them. (Remember the year this study was done; it would be like finding a quarter or 35 cents today.) As the lucky shoppers left the phone with their newly found dime, an assistant of Isen and Levine played the role of the man with the manila folder. He purposefully dropped the folder a few feet in front of the shopper, to see whether he or she would stop and help him pick up his papers. It turned out that finding the dime had a dramatic effect on helping. Only 4 percent of the people who did not find a dime helped the man pick up his papers. In comparison, 84 percent of the people who found a dime helped.

Researchers have found this "feel good, do good" effect in diverse situations and have shown that it is not limited to the little boost we get when we find some money. People are more likely to help others when they are in a good mood for a number of reasons, including doing well on a test, receiving a gift, thinking happy thoughts, and listening to pleasant music. And when people are in a good mood, they are more helpful in many ways, including contributing money to charity, helping someone find a lost contact lens, tutoring another student, donating blood, and helping co-workers on the job (Carlson, Charlin, & Miller, 1988; George & Brief, 1992; Salovey, Mayer, & Rosenhan, 1991). See the Try It! exercise above for a way of doing your own test of the "feel good, do good" hypothesis.

What is it about being in a good mood that makes people more altruistic? It turns out that good moods can increase helping for three reasons. First, good moods make us look on the bright side of life. If you saw the man drop his manila folder full of papers, you could view this incident in at least two ways. "What a klutz," you might think. "This guy is really clumsy. Let him clean up his own mess." Or you might have more sympathy for him, thinking, "Oh, that's too bad. I bet he's really in a hurry—the poor guy, he probably feels really frustrated." When we are in a good mood, we tend to see the good side of other people, giving them the benefit of the doubt. A victim who might normally seem clumsy or annoying will, when we are feeling cheerful, seem like a decent, needy person who is worthy of our help (Carlson, Charlin, & Miller, 1988; Forgas & Bower, 1987).

Second, "feel good, do good" occurs because it is an excellent way of prolonging our good mood. If we see someone in need of help, then being a Good Samaritan will spawn even more good feelings, and we can walk away continuing to feel like a million bucks. In comparison, not helping when we know we should is a surefire "downer," deflating our good mood (Clark & Isen, 1982; Isen, 1987; Williamson & Clark, 1989).

Finally, good moods increase self-attention. As we noted in Chapters 5 and 9, at any given time people vary in how much attention they pay to their feelings and values versus the world around them. Sometimes we are particularly attuned to our internal worlds, and sometimes we are not. Good moods increase the amount of attention we pay to ourselves, and this factor in turn makes us more likely to behave according to our values and ideals. Because most of us value altruism and because good moods increase our attention to this value, good moods increase helping behavior (Berkowitz, 1987; Carlson, Charlin, & Miller, 1988; Salovey & Rodin, 1985).

Negative-State Relief: Feel Bad, Do Good

What about when we are in a bad mood? Suppose that when you saw the fellow in the mall drop his folder, you were feeling down in the dumps—would this influence the likelihood that you would help the man pick up his papers? One kind of bad mood clearly leads to an increase in helping—feeling guilty (Baumeister, Stillwell, & Heatherton, 1994). People often act on the idea that good deeds cancel out bad deeds. When they have done something that has made them feel guilty, helping another person balances things out, reducing their guilty feelings. For example, Mary Harris and her colleagues found that churchgoers were more likely to donate money to charities before attending confession than afterward, presumably because confessing to a priest reduced their guilt (Harris, Benson, & Hall, 1975). Thus, if you just realized you had forgotten your best friend's birthday and you felt guilty about it, you would be more likely to help the fellow in the mall, to repair your guilty feelings.

But suppose you just had a fight with a friend or just found out you did poorly on a test and you were feeling sad and blue. Given that feeling happy leads to greater helping, it might seem that feeling sad will decrease helping. Surprisingly, however, sadness can also lead to an increase in helping, at least under certain conditions (Carlson & Miller, 1987; Salovey et al., 1991). When people are sad, they are motivated to engage in activities that make them feel better (Wegener & Petty, 1994). To the extent that helping is rewarding, it can lift us out of the doldrums.

The idea that people help in order to alleviate their own sadness and distress is called the **negative-state relief hypothesis** by Robert Cialdini (Cialdini, Darby, & Vincent, 1973; Cialdini & Fultz, 1990; Cialdini, Schaller, Houlihan, Arps, Fultz, & Beaman, 1987). It is an example of the social exchange theory approach to helping that we discussed earlier. People help someone else with the goal of helping themselves—namely, to relieve their own sadness and distress. This is

Negative-State Relief Hypothesis
the idea that people help in order to alleviate their own sadness and distress

pretty obvious if we help in a way that deals with the cause of our sadness. If our best friend is depressed, we might feel a little depressed as well. As a result, we might bake our friend a batch of cookies. If this cheers up our friend, we have alleviated the cause of our own sadness. Cialdini argues, however, that when we feel blue we are also more likely to help in some totally unrelated way. If we are feeling down because our best friend is unhappy, we are more likely to donate money to a charity. The warm glow of helping the charity reduces our gloom, even though the charity and our friend's unhappiness are unrelated (Cialdini, Darby, & Vincent, 1973).

> If you want others to be happy, practice compassion. If you want to be happy, practice compassion.
> —The Dalai Lama

Situational Determinants of Prosocial Behavior: When Will People Help?

In the previous section, we considered three personal determinants of prosocial behavior: personality differences, gender differences, and people's moods. People differ in how altruistic they are and the way in which they are altruistic, depending on their upbringing, their gender, and their mood. This does not mean, however, that to predict how altruistically people will act, all you need to know is their standing on these three variables. While each contributes a piece to the puzzle of why people help others, they do not complete the picture. To understand more fully why people help, we need to consider the social situation in which they find themselves.

Rural versus Urban Environments

Suppose you are riding your bike one day and, as you turn a corner, your front wheel suddenly drops into a pothole, sending you tumbling over the handlebars. You sit there stunned for a moment, then notice a sharp pain in your shin. Sure enough, you have broken your leg and there is no way you can get up and get help by yourself. You look around, hoping to see someone who will help you out. Now consider this question: Where would you rather have this accident—on the main street of a small, rural town, or in the downtown area of a large city? In which place would passersby be more likely to offer you help?

> Do not wait for extraordinary circumstances to do good actions; try to use ordinary situations.
> —John Paul Richter
> (1763–1826)

If you said the small town, you are right. Several researchers have compared the likelihood that people will help in rural versus urban areas and have consistently found that people in rural areas help more (Korte, 1980; Steblay, 1987). Paul Amato (1983), for example, staged an incident where a man limped down the street and then suddenly fell down with a cry of pain. The man lifted the leg of his pants, revealing a heavily bandaged shin that was bleeding profusely (with theatrical blood that looked real). In small towns, about half the pedestrians who witnessed this incident stopped and offered the man help. In large cities, however, only 15 percent of pedestrians stopped and helped. People in small towns have been found to help more in a multitude of ways, including helping a stranger who has had an accident, helping a lost child, giving directions, participating in a survey, and returning a lost letter. The same relationship between size of town and helping has been found in several countries, including the United States, Canada, Israel, Australia, Turkey, Great Britain, and the Sudan (Hedge & Yousif, 1992; Steblay, 1987).

■ People are less helpful in big cities than in small towns, not because of a difference in values but because the stress of urban life causes them to keep to themselves.

Urban-Overload Hypothesis
the theory that people living in cities are constantly being bombarded with stimulation and that they keep to themselves in order to avoid being overloaded by it

Why are our chances of being helped greater in small towns? One possibility is that the experience of growing up in a small town enhances the altruistic personality, whereas growing up in a big city diminishes the altruistic personality. According to this view, you would be more likely to be helped by someone who grew up in a small town, even if that person were visiting a big city. It is the values the small-town resident has internalized that is the key, not his or her immediate surroundings. Alternatively, it might be people's immediate surroundings that are the key, not their personalities. Stanley Milgram (1970), for example, proposed an **urban-overload hypothesis,** which holds that people living in cities are constantly being bombarded with stimulation and that they keep to themselves in order to avoid being overloaded by it. According to this argument, if you put urban dwellers in a calmer, less stimulating environment, they would be as likely as anyone else to reach out to others.

Interestingly, the evidence supports the urban-overload hypothesis more than the idea that living in cities makes people less altruistic by nature. If the lack of helping in big cities is due to a change in people's personalities, then the key to whether or not people will help should be their birthplace, not the location of the incident providing an opportunity for helping. However, Nancy Steblay (1987), in a review of dozens of studies, found that this explanation did not hold up. When an opportunity for helping arises, it matters more whether the incident occurs in a rural or urban area than which kind of person happens to be there. Further, Robert Levine and his colleagues found, in field studies conducted in 36 cities in the United States, that population density (the number of people per square mile) was more related to helping than population size was (Levine, Martinez, Brase, & Sorenson, 1994). The greater the density of people, the less likely people were to help. This makes sense, according to the urban overload hypothesis: There should be more stimulation in a small area packed with a lot of people than in a large area where the same number of people are spread out. In short, it would be better to have a city slicker witness your bicycle accident in a small town than to have a small-town person witness it in a big city packed with people. The hustle and bustle in cities can be so overwhelming that even caring, altruistic people turn inward, responding less to the people around them.

The Number of Bystanders: The Bystander Effect

Remember Kitty Genovese? We have just seen one reason that her neighbors turned a deaf ear to her cries for help: The murder took place in New York City, one of the most populated areas in the world. Perhaps her neighbors were so overloaded with urban stimulation that they dismissed Genovese's cries as one small addition to the surrounding din. While it is true that people help less in urban environments, this explanation is not the only reason Genovese's neighbors failed to help. Her desperate cries surely must have risen above the everyday noises of garbage trucks and car horns. And there have been cases where people ignored the pleas of their neighbors in small towns. Recently in Fredericksburg, Virginia a convenience store clerk was beaten in front of customers who did nothing to help, even after the assailant had fled and the clerk lay bleeding on the floor (Hsu, 1995). Fredericksburg has only 20,000 residents.

Bibb Latané and John Darley (1970) are two social psychologists who taught at universities in New York at the time of the Genovese murder. As we discussed in Chapter 2, they too were unconvinced that the only reason her neighbors failed to help was the stresses and stimulation of urban life. They focused on the fact that so many people heard her cries. Paradoxically, they thought, it might be that the greater the number of bystanders who observe an emergency, the less likely

■ Kitty Genovese and the alley in which she was murdered. Ironically, she would probably be alive today had fewer people heard her desperate cries for help.

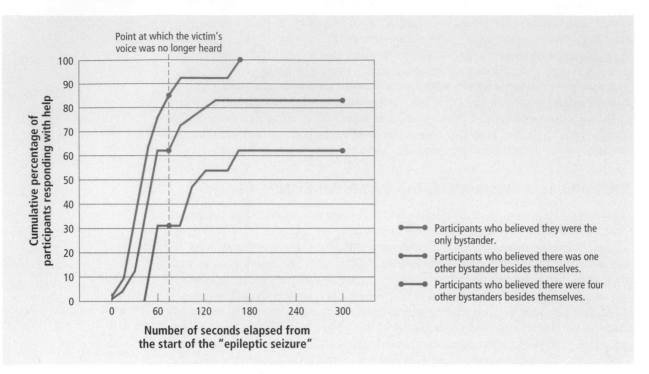

Point at which the victim's voice was no longer heard

Cumulative percentage of participants responding with help

Number of seconds elapsed from the start of the "epileptic seizure"

● Participants who believed they were the only bystander.

● Participants who believed there was one other bystander besides themselves.

● Participants who believed there were four other bystanders besides themselves.

■ **FIGURE 11.3   Bystander intervention: The presence of bystanders reduces helping.** When people believed they were the only one witnessing a student having a seizure— when they were the lone bystander—most of them helped him immediately, and all did within a few minutes. When they believed someone else was listening as well—that there were two bystanders—they were less likely to help and did so more slowly. And when they believed four others were listening—that there were five bystanders—they were even less likely to help. (Adapted from Darley & Latané, 1968)

any one of them is to help. As Bibb Latané put it, "We came up with the insight that perhaps what made the Genovese case so fascinating was itself what made it happen—namely, that not just one or two, but thirty-eight people had watched and done nothing" (1987, p. 78).

How can this be? Surely, the more people who witness an emergency—such as your hypothetical bicycle accident—the greater one's chance of receiving help. In a series of now classic experiments, Latané and Darley (1970) found that just the opposite was true: In terms of receiving help, there is no safety in numbers. Think back to the seizure experiment we discussed in Chapter 2. In this study, people sat in individual cubicles, participating in a group discussion of college life (over an intercom system) with students in other cubicles. One of the other students suddenly had a seizure, crying out, "I could really—er—use some help so if somebody would—er—give me a little h—help—uh—er—er—er—c—could somebody—er—er—help—er—uh—uh—uh (choking sounds) . . . I'm gonna die—er—er—I'm . . . gonna die—er—help—er—er—seizure—er (chokes, then quiet)" (Darley & Latané, 1968, p. 379). There was actually only one real participant in the study. The other "participants," including the one who had the seizure, were prerecorded voices. The point of the study was to see whether the real participant tried to help the seizure victim, by trying to find him or by summoning the experimenter, or whether, like Kitty Genovese's neighbors, he or she simply sat there and did nothing.

As Latané and Darley anticipated, the answer depended on how many people the participant thought witnessed the emergency. When people believed they were the only ones listening to the student have the seizure, most of them (85 percent) helped within 60 seconds. By two and a half minutes, 100 percent of the people who thought they were the only bystander had offered assistance (see Figure 11.3). In comparison, when the research participants believed there was one other student listening, fewer people helped—only 62 percent within 60 seconds. As you can see in Figure 11.3, helping occurred more slowly when there were two bystanders and never reached 100 percent, even after six minutes, when the experiment was terminated. Finally, when the participants believed there were four other students listening in addition to themselves, the percentage of people who helped dropped even more dramatically. Only 31 percent helped in the first 60 seconds, and after six minutes only 62 percent had offered help. Dozens of other studies, conducted in the laboratory and in the field, have found the same thing: The greater the number of bystanders who witness an emergency, the less likely any one of them is to help the victim—a phenomenon called the **bystander effect**.

Why is it that people are less likely to help when other bystanders are present? Latané and Darley (1970) developed a step-by-step description of how people decide whether to intervene in an emergency (see Figure 11.4). Part of this description, as we will see, is an explanation of how the number of bystanders can make a difference. But let's begin with the first step—whether people notice that someone needs help.

Bystander Effect
the finding that the greater the number of bystanders who witness an emergency, the less likely any one of them is to help

Noticing an Event

Sometimes it is clear that an emergency has occurred, as in the seizure experiment, where it was obvious that the other student was in danger. Other times, however, it is not so clear. If you are late for an appointment and are hurrying down a crowded street, you might not notice that someone has collapsed in the doorway of a nearby building. Obviously, if people don't notice that an emergency has occurred, they will not intervene and offer to help.

What determines whether people notice an emergency? John Darley and Daniel Batson (1973) demonstrated that something as seemingly trivial as how much of a hurry people are in can make more of a difference than what kind of person they are. These researchers conducted a study that mirrored the parable of the Good Samaritan, wherein many passersby failed to stop to help a man lying unconscious on the side of the road. The research participants were people we might think would be extremely altruistic—seminary students preparing to devote their lives to the ministry. The students were asked to walk to another building, where the researchers would record them making a brief speech. Some were told that they were late and should hurry to keep their appointment. Others were told that there was no rush, because the assistant in the other building was a few minutes behind schedule. As they walked to the other building, each of the students passed a man who was slumped in a doorway. The man (an accomplice of the experimenters) coughed and groaned as the students each walked by. Did the seminary students stop and offer to help him? If they were not in a hurry, most of them (63 percent) did. If they were hurrying to keep their appointment, however, very few of them (10 percent) did. Many of the students who were in a hurry did not even notice the man.

It is perhaps unsurprising that when people are in a rush, they pay less attention to what's going on around them, making them less likely to help someone in

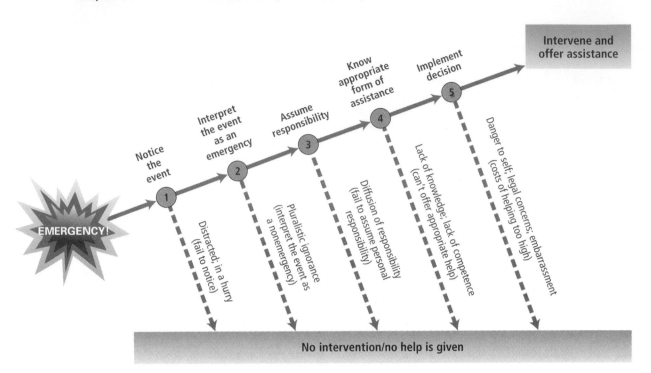

■ **FIGURE 11.4   Bystander intervention decision tree: Five steps to helping in an emergency.** Latané and Darley (1970) showed that people go through five decision-making steps before they help someone in an emergency. If bystanders fail to take any one of the five steps, they will not help. Each step, as well as the possible reasons for why people decide not to intervene, is outlined above. (Adapted from Latané & Darley, 1970)

need. What is surprising is that such a seemingly trivial matter as how much of a hurry we are in can overpower the kind of people we are. Darley and Batson (1973) tested the seminary students on a variety of personality measures that assessed how religious they were and found that people who scored high on these measures were no more likely to help than those who scored low. The researchers also varied the topic of the speech they asked the students to give. Whereas some students were asked to discuss the kinds of jobs seminary students would like to have, others were asked to discuss the parable of the Good Samaritan. It might seem that seminary students who were thinking about the parable of the Good Samaritan would be especially likely to stop and help a man slumped in a doorway, given the similarity of this incident to the parable. However, the topic of the speech made little difference in whether they helped. If the students were in a hurry, they were unlikely to help, even if they were very religious individuals about to give a speech about the Good Samaritan.

Interpreting the Event as an Emergency

Just because people notice someone slumped in a doorway does not mean they will help him or her. The next determinant of helping is whether the bystander interprets the event as an emergency—in other words, as a situation where help is needed (see Figure 11.4). Is the person in the doorway drunk, or seriously ill? If we see white smoke coming out of a vent, is it something innocuous, such as mist from an air conditioner, or a sign that the building is on fire? Is that couple having a particularly loud argument, or is one partner about to beat up the other? If people assume nothing is wrong when an emergency is taking place, obviously they will not help.

Interestingly, when other bystanders are present, people are more likely to assume an emergency is something innocuous. To understand why, think back to our discussion of informational social influence in Chapter 8. This type of social influence occurs when we use other people to help us define reality. When we are uncertain about what's going on, such as whether the smoke we see is a sign of a fire, one of the first things we do is look around to see how other people are responding. If other people look up, shrug, and go about their business, we are likely to assume there is nothing to worry about. If other people look panic-stricken and yell "Fire!" we immediately assume the building is indeed on fire. As we saw in Chapter 8, it's often a good strategy to use other people as a source of information when we are uncertain about what's going on. The danger in doing so, however, is that sometimes no one is sure what is happening. Since an emergency is often a sudden and confusing event, bystanders tend to freeze, watching and listening with blank expressions as they try to figure out what's going on. When they glance at each other, they see an apparent lack of concern on the part of everyone else. This results in a state of **pluralistic ignorance,** which is the phenomenon whereby bystanders assume that nothing is wrong in an emergency, because no one else looks concerned.

Pluralistic ignorance was demonstrated in another classic experiment by Latané and Darley (1970). Imagine that you have agreed to take part in a study of people's attitudes toward the problems of urban life, and you arrive at the appointed time. A sign instructs you to fill out a questionnaire while you are waiting for the study to begin. You take a copy of the questionnaire, sit down, and work on it for a few minutes. Then something odd happens: White smoke starts coming into the room through a small vent in the wall. Before long, the room is so filled with smoke that you can barely see the questionnaire. What will you do?

In fact, there was no real danger—the experimenters were pumping smoke into the room to see how people would respond to this potential emergency. Not surprisingly, when people were by themselves, most of them took action. Within two minutes, 50 percent of the participants left the room and found the experimenter down the hall, reporting that there was a potential fire in the building; by six minutes, 75 percent of the participants left the room to alert the experimenter. But what would happen if people were not alone? Given that 75 percent of the participants who were by themselves reported the smoke, it would seem that the larger the group, the greater the likelihood that someone would report the smoke. In fact, this can be figured mathematically: If there is a 75 percent chance that any one person will report the smoke, then there is a 98 percent chance that at least one person in a three-person group will do so.

To find out if there really is safety in numbers, Latané and Darley (1970) included a condition in which three participants took part at the same time. Everything was identical except that three people sat in the room as the smoke began to seep in. Surprisingly, in only 12 percent of the three-person groups did someone report the smoke within two minutes, and in only 38 percent of the groups did someone report the smoke within six minutes. In the remaining groups, the participants sat there filling out questionnaires even when they had to wave away the smoke with their hands to see what they were writing. What went wrong?

Because it was not clear that the smoke constituted an emergency, the participants used each other as a source of information. If the people next to you glance

Pluralistic Ignorance
the phenomenon whereby bystanders assume that nothing is wrong in an emergency, because no one else looks concerned

■ Emergency situations can be confusing. Does this man need help? Have the bystanders failed to notice him, or has the behavior of the others led each of them to interpret the situation as a nonemergency—an example of pluralistic ignorance?

at the smoke and then go on filling out their questionnaires, you will feel reassured that nothing is wrong; otherwise, why would they be acting so unconcerned? The problem is that they are probably looking at you out of the corner of their eyes, and seeing that you appear to be not overly concerned, they too are reassured that everything is OK. Group members gain false reassurance from each other whenever each person assumes the others know more about what's going on than he or she does. This is particularly likely to happen when the event is ambiguous. If an event is clearly an emergency, as in the case of Kitty Genovese's cries for help, then we do not need to rely on other people to interpret it for us; however, the more ambiguous an event is, the more likely people are to look to each other to define what's going on. As a result, it is in ambiguous situations—such as seeing smoke coming from a vent—that people in groups will be in a state of pluralistic ignorance, convincing each other that nothing is wrong (Clark & Word, 1972; Solomon, Solomon, & Stone, 1978).

Assuming Responsibility

Let's say that as a potential help-giver, you have successfully navigated the first two steps in the decision tree (see Figure 11.4): You have noticed something odd, and you have correctly interpreted it as an emergency where help is needed. What's next? Now you must decide that you will help. After hearing Kitty Genovese cry out, "Oh my God, he stabbed me! Please help me! Please help me!" (Rosenthal, 1964, p. 33), Genovese's neighbors must have believed that something terrible was happening and that she was desperately in need of assistance. That they did nothing indicates that even if we interpret an event as an emergency, we have to decide that it is our responsibility—not someone else's—to do something about it. When dealing with issues of personal responsibility, the number of bystanders is again a crucial variable, but for different reasons. Consider the condition in the Latané and Darley (1968) seizure experiment where participants believed they were the only one listening to the student while he had a seizure. The responsibility was totally on their shoulders. If they didn't help, no one would, and the student might die. As a result, in this condition most people helped almost immediately, and all helped within a few minutes.

But what happens when there are many witnesses? A **diffusion of responsibility** occurs, which is the phenomenon whereby each bystander's sense of responsibility

Diffusion of Responsibility
the phenomenon whereby each bystander's sense of responsibility to help decreases as the number of witnesses increases

to help decreases as the number of witnesses increases. Because other people are present, no individual bystander feels a strong sense that it is his or her personal responsibility to take action. Recall from our earlier discussion that helping often entails costs—we can place ourselves in danger and we can look foolish by over-reacting or doing the wrong thing. Why should we risk these costs when many other people who can help are present? The problem is that everyone is likely to feel this way, making all the bystanders less likely to help. This is particularly true if people cannot tell whether someone else has already intervened. When participants in the seizure experiment believed that other students were witnesses as well, they couldn't tell whether another student had already helped, because the intercom system allowed only the voice of the student having the seizure to be transmitted. Each student probably assumed he or she did not have to help, because surely someone else had already done so. Similarly, Kitty Genovese's neighbors had no way of knowing whether someone else had called the police. Most likely, they assumed there was no need to do so, because someone else had already made the call. Tragically, everyone assumed it was somebody else's responsibility to take action, thereby leaving Kitty Genovese to fight her assailant alone. The sad irony of Kitty Genovese's murder is that she probably would be alive today had fewer people heard her cries for help.

Knowing How to Help

Even if a person has made it this far in the helping sequence—noticing an event has occurred, interpreting it as an emergency, and taking responsibility—an additional condition must still be met: The person must decide what form of help is appropriate. Suppose, for example, that on a hot, summer day you see a woman collapse in the street and decide she is gravely ill. No one else seems to be helping, and so you decide it is up to you. But what should you do? Has the woman had a heart attack? Or is she suffering from heat stroke? Should you call an ambulance, administer CPR, or try to get her out of the sun? If people don't know what form of assistance to give, obviously they will be unable to help.

Deciding to Implement the Help

Finally, even if you know exactly what kind of help is appropriate, there are reasons why you might decide not to intervene. For one thing, you might not be qualified to deliver the right kind of help. It may be clear, for instance, that the woman has had a heart attack and is in desperate need of CPR, but if you don't know how to administer CPR, you'll be unable to help her. Or you might be afraid of making a fool of yourself, of doing the wrong thing and making matters worse, or even of placing yourself in danger by trying to help. Consider, for example, the fate of three CBS technicians who, in 1982, encountered a man beating a woman in a parking lot on the west side of Manhattan, tried to intervene, and were shot and killed by the assailant. Even when we know what kind of intervention is needed, we have to weigh the costs of trying to help.

In sum, five steps have to be taken before people will intervene in an emergency: They have to notice the event, interpret it as an emergency, decide it is their responsibility to help, know how to help, and decide to act. If people fail to take any one of these steps, they will not intervene. Given how difficult it can be to take all five steps, it is not surprising that incidents like the Kitty Genovese murder are all too common.

■ In communal relationships, such as those between parents and their children, people are concerned less with who gets what and more with how much help the other person needs.

The Nature of the Relationship: Communal versus Exchange Relationships

A great deal of research on prosocial behavior has looked at helping between strangers, such as Latané and Darley's research on bystander intervention. Although this research is very important, most helping in everyday life occurs between people who know each other well: family members, lovers, close friends. What determines whether people help in these kinds of relationships?

As we saw earlier, the negative-relief state hypothesis holds that people will help only if there are immediate, short-term benefits for doing so. It is important to point out, however, that when people know each other well, they are often more concerned with the long-term benefits of helping than with the immediate effects (Salovey et al., 1991). Consider the mother of a 4-year-old. One Saturday morning, she sits down with a cup of coffee to read the newspaper. She wants nothing more than a moment's peace while she catches up on the news. Her daughter, however, has other ideas: She asks her mother to read her *The Berenstain Bears Visit the Dentist* for the fiftieth time. Reading to the child has few short-term benefits in this situation. The coffee gets cold, the newspaper goes unread, and the moment's peace disappears. Even when there are no short-term benefits, however, helping can reap large long-term rewards. Parents who sit around sipping coffee and reading the newspaper while ignoring their children are less likely to obtain the long-term satisfaction of having a good relationship with their kids and seeing their kids flourish. Thus, parents might read to their children with this long-term goal in mind, enduring the short-term annoyance of being interrupted and having to read about Brother and Sister Bear's cavities yet again.

Even more fundamentally, in some types of relationships people may not be concerned at all with the rewards they receive. In Chapter 10, we distinguished between communal and exchange relationships. *Communal relationships* are those in which people's primary concern is with the welfare of the other person (e.g., a child), whereas *exchange relationships* are those that are governed by concerns about equity—that what you put into the relationship equals what you get out of it. Most of the research we have reviewed so far has looked at helping in exchange relationships—namely, ones in which people do not know each other well and in which people who help expect to be helped in return. What about helping in communal relationships, such as our example of the parent whose child is clamoring for attention?

One possibility is that the rewards for helping are as important in communal as exchange relationships—it's just that the nature of the rewards differ (Batson, 1993). In exchange relationships, we expect our favors to be repaid pretty quickly. If we invite our new friend Sam to a party, we expect that he will invite us to his next party. If we help a co-worker learn how to use the Internet on Monday, we expect that the co-worker will help us learn how to use the new Xerox machine next week. Maybe people in communal relationships also expect an equal exchange of benefits, but the benefits are different from those in exchange relationships. When parents are deciding whether to help their children, for example, they seldom think, "Well, what have they done for me lately?" Nonetheless, they might help with the expectation that they will eventually be rewarded for their help. In our example of the mother and her 4-year-old, perhaps the mother was motivated by the rewards of seeing her daughter become a healthy, well-adjusted adult. Maybe this relationship involves an exchange of long-term instead of short-term benefits.

Margaret Clark and Judson Mills (1993), however, argue that communal relationships are fundamentally different from exchange relationships: It's not just that different kinds of rewards govern the relationship; people in communal relationships are less concerned with the benefits they will receive by helping, and more with simply satisfying the needs of the other person. In support of this argument, Clark and her colleagues have found that people in communal relationships pay less attention to who is getting what than people in exchange relationships do (Clark, 1984; Clark, Mills, & Corcoran, 1989). Consider a study in which the researchers measured how often people in different relationships looked at some lights, which meant different things in different conditions. In one condition, people thought that the lights would change when their partner in another room needed help on a task. Participants were not in a position to help their partner on the task, but the idea was that the more concerned they were with their partner's needs, the more they would look at the lights. In another condition, people thought that the lights would change whenever their partner in the other room did especially well on a task they were both working on and would be rewarded for. The idea here was that people who were concerned about exchange and equity should be especially likely to look at these lights, to keep track of what they "owed" their partner for helping them to get the reward.

As seen in Figure 11.5, the number of times people looked at the lights in each condition depended on whether they were in a communal relationship (their partner was a friend) or an exchange relationship (their partner was a stranger). In communal relationships, people were much more concerned with the needs of their partner (whether this person needed help on the task) than with whether they "owed" their partner (whether this person did well on the task). Keep in mind that people did not think they could go help their partner; they simply seemed concerned with whether the person was in need. In exchange relationships, people were relatively unconcerned with whether their partner needed

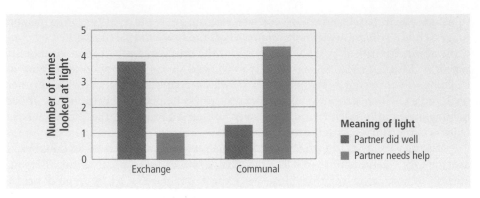

■ **FIGURE 11.5   Keeping track in relationships.**   In communal relationships, people looked at the light the most when it signified how much help their partner needed. In exchange relationships, people looked at the light the most when it signified how well their partner did on a joint task, presumably to keep track of what they "owed" their partner in return. (Adapted from Clark et al., 1989)

help. Instead, they were concerned with how well their partner was doing on the task, presumably to keep track of what they owed their partner in return.

In short, helping in exchange relationships appears to be governed by rules and norms that differ from those governing helping in communal relationships. In exchange relationships, people are concerned more with who is getting what, and they get upset if the scales are tipped too far toward one person ("It seems like I'm always doing favors for Bob, but he never helps me in return"). In communal relationships, people are concerned less with who gets what and more with how much help the other person needs ("My daughter really needs my help right now").

Does this mean that people are more helpful toward friends than strangers? Yes—at least under most circumstances. We are more likely to have communal relationships with friends and thus are more likely to help even when there is nothing in it for us. In fact, we like to help a partner in a communal relationship more than a partner in an exchange relationship (Williamson, Clark, Pegalis, & Behan, 1996). There is, however, an interesting exception to this rule. Research by Abraham Tesser (1988) on self-esteem maintenance (see Chapter 6) shows that when a task is of little relevance to us, we do indeed help friends more than strangers. But suppose that the most important thing in the world for you is to be a doctor, that you are struggling to pass a difficult premed physics course, and that two other people in the class—your best friend and a complete stranger—ask you to lend them your notes from a class they missed. According to Tesser's research, you will be more inclined to help the stranger than your friend (Tesser, 1991; Tesser & Smith, 1980). Why? Because it hurts to see a close friend do better than we do in an area of great importance to our self-esteem. Consequently, we are less likely to help a friend in these important areas than in those areas we don't care as much about.

How Can Helping Be Increased?

Most religions stress some version of the Golden Rule, urging us to do unto others as we would have others do unto us. There are many saintly people in the world who succeed in following this rule, devoting their lives to the welfare of others. We would all be better off, however, if prosocial behavior was more common than it is. How can we get people, when faced with an emergency, to act more like Lenny Skutnik and less like Kitty Genovese's neighbors?

Before addressing this question, we should point out that people do not always want to be helped. Imagine that you are sitting at a computer terminal at the library and are struggling to learn a new E-mail system. You can't figure out how to send and receive mail and are becoming increasingly frustrated as the computer responds with messages like "Command not understood." A confident-looking guy strides into the room and looks over your shoulder for a few minutes. "Boy," he says. "You sure have a lot to learn. Let me show you how this baby works." How would you react? You might feel some gratitude at receiving this guy's help; after all, you will now learn how to send E-mail. More than likely, however, you will also feel some resentment. His offer of help comes with a message: "You are too stupid to figure this out for yourself." Receiving help can make us feel inadequate and dependent. As a result, people do not always react positively when someone offers them aid. People do not want to appear incompetent, and so they often decide to suffer in silence—even if doing so lowers their chances of successfully completing a task (DePaulo, 1983; Nadler, 1991; Nadler & Fisher, 1986; Schneider, Major, Luhtanen, & Crocker, 1996).

Nonetheless, it seems clear that the world would be a better place if more people would help their fellow human beings. How can we increase everyday acts of kindness, such as looking out for an elderly neighbor or volunteering to read to kids at the local school? The answer to this question lies in our discussion of the causes of prosocial behavior. For example, we saw that several personal characteristics of potential helpers are important, and promoting those factors can increase the likelihood that these people will help (Clary, Snyder, Ridge, Miene, & Haugen, 1994; Snyder, 1993). Personal factors, however, are not the sole cause of prosocial behavior. Even kind, altruistic people will fail to help if certain situational constraints are present, such as being in an urban environment or witness-

> When death, the great reconciler, has come, it is never our tenderness that we repent of, but our severity.
>
> –George Eliot
> (Marian Evans Cross)

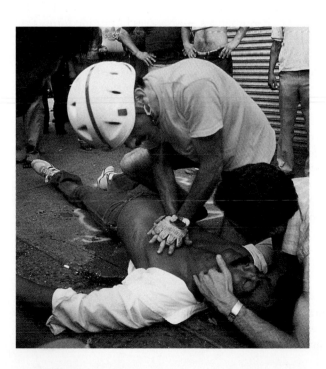

■ Becoming aware of the barriers to helping can actually make people more likely to overcome those barriers. People who learned about Latané and Darley's (1970) research on bystander intervention, for example, were more likely to help in an emergency.

The Lost Letter Technique

Here is a way you can test many of the hypotheses about helping behavior you have read about in this chapter—as well as hypotheses of your own.

An interesting way to study prosocial behavior is to leave some stamped letters lying on the ground and seeing whether people pick them up and mail them. This procedure, called the lost letter technique, was invented by Stanley Milgram (1969). He found that people were more likely to mail letters addressed to organizations they supported; for example, 72 percent of letters addressed to "Medical Research Associates" were mailed, whereas only 25 percent of letters addressed to "Friends of the Nazi Party" were mailed (all were addressed to the same post office box, so that Milgram could count how many were returned).

Use the lost letter technique to test some of the hypotheses about helping behavior we have discussed in this chapter, or hypotheses that you come up with on your own. Put your address on the letters so that you can count how many are returned, but vary where you put the letters or to whom they are addressed. For example, drop some letters in a small town and in an urban area to see whether people in small towns are more likely to mail them (be sure to mark the envelopes in some way that will let you know where they were dropped; e.g., put a little pencil mark on the back of the ones dropped in small towns). Studies by Bridges and Coady (1996) and Hansson and Slade (1977) found that people living in small towns are more likely to mail the letters. Or, you might vary the ethnicity of the name of the person on the address, to see if people are more likely to help members of some ethnic groups more than others. Be creative!

After deciding what you want to vary (e.g., the ethnicity or gender of the addressee), be careful to place envelopes of both types (e.g., those addressed to males and females) in similar locations. It is best to use a fairly large number of letters (e.g., a minimum of 15 to 20 in each condition) to get reliable results. Obviously, you should not leave more than one letter in the same location. You might want to team up with some classmates on this project, so that you can split the cost of the stamps.

ing an emergency in the presence of numerous bystanders. Another important factor is the nature of the relationship between the helper and the person in need.

There is evidence that simply being aware of the barriers to helping can increase people's chances of overcoming those barriers. This was demonstrated in a striking experiment by Arthur Beaman and his colleagues (1978), who randomly assigned students to listen to a lecture on Latané and Darley's (1970) bystander intervention research or a lecture on an unrelated topic. Two weeks later, all the students participated in what they thought was a completely unrelated sociology study, during which they encountered a student lying on the floor. Was he in need of help? Had he fallen and injured himself, or was he simply a student who had fallen asleep after pulling an all-nighter? As we have seen, when in an ambiguous situation such as this, people look and see how other people are reacting. Because an accomplice of the experimenter (posing as another participant) purposefully acted unconcerned, the natural thing to do was to assume nothing was wrong. This is exactly what most of Beaman's participants did, if they had not heard the lecture about bystander intervention research; in this condition, only 25 percent of them stopped to help the student. However, if the participants had heard the lecture about bystander intervention, 43 percent stopped to help the student. Thus, knowing how we can be unwittingly influenced by others can by itself help us overcome this type of social influence. We can only hope that knowing about other barriers to prosocial behavior will make them easier to overcome as well.

We conclude with the reminder that we should not impose help on everyone we meet, whether the person wants it or not. Research on reactions to help indicates that under certain conditions, receiving help can have damaging effects on a person's self-esteem. The goal is to make the help supportive, highlighting your concern for the recipient, rather than using the helping encounter to communicate your superior knowledge and skill. If you would like to learn more about the conditions under which people help others, in an experiment of your own design, see the Try It! exercise on page 450.

Summary

For centuries people have debated the determinants of **prosocial behavior**—that is, acts performed with the goal of benefiting another person. People have been particularly intrigued with the causes of **altruism**, which is the desire to help another person even if it involves cost to the helper. One approach is **evolutionary psychology**, which is the attempt to explain social behavior in terms of genetic factors that evolved over time according to the principles of natural selection. According to this approach, prosocial behavior has genetic roots because it has been selected for in three ways: People further the survival of their genes by helping genetic relatives (**kin selection**); there is a survival advantage to following the **norm of reciprocity**, whereby people help strangers in the hope that they will receive help when they need it; and there is a survival advantage to the ability to learn and follow social norms of all kinds, including altruism. Social exchange theory views helping behavior as a weighing of rewards and costs; helping occurs due to self-interest—that is, in situations where the rewards for helping are greater than the costs. Rewards include recognition, praise, and the relief of personal distress. Neither of these theories sees helping behavior as a form of altruism; self-gain is always involved. In comparison, the **empathy-altruism hypothesis** sees prosocial behavior as motivated only by **empathy** and compassion for those in need.

Prosocial behavior is multidetermined, and both personal and situational factors can override or facilitate basic motives to help. Personal determinants of helping include the **altruistic personality**, the idea that some people are more helpful than others. Children can develop this personality trait by being rewarded for helping by their parents and by modeling people they observe helping. Rewards must be used carefully, however, or they will undermine the child's intrinsic interest in helping—causing an overjustification effect. Gender is another personal factor that comes into play. Though one sex is not more altruistic than the other, the ways in which men and women help often differs, with men more likely to help in heroic, chivalrous ways and women more likely to help in ways that involve a long-term commitment. People's cultural background also matters. Compared to members of individualisitic cultures, members of interdependent cultures are more likely to help people they view as members of their **in group** but are less likely to help people they view as members of an **out group.**

Mood also affects helping. Interestingly, being in either a good or a bad mood—compared to being in a neutral mood—can increase helping. Good moods increase helping for several reasons, including the fact that they make us see the good side of other people, making us more willing to help them. Bad moods increase helping because of the **negative-state relief hypothesis**, which maintains that helping someone makes us feel good, lifting us out of the doldrums.

Social determinants of prosocial behavior include rural versus urban environments, with helping behavior more likely to occur in rural settings. One reason for this is the **urban-overload hypothesis**, which says that cities bombard people with so much stimulation that they keep to themselves to avoid being overloaded. The **bystander effect** points out the impact of the number of bystanders on whether help is given—the fewer the bystanders, the better. The bystander decision tree indicates that a potential helper must make five decisions before providing help: notice the event, interpret the event as an emergency (here **pluralistic ignorance** can occur, whereby everyone assumes nothing is wrong, because no one else looks concerned; pluralistic ignorance is an example of informational social influence), assume personal responsibility (here a **diffusion of responsibility** created by several bystanders may lead us to think it's not our responsibility to act), know how to help, and implement the help. In addition, the nature of the relationship between the helper and the person in need is important. In exchange relationships, people are concerned with equity and keep track of who is contributing what to the relationship. In communal relationships, people are concerned less with who gets what and more with how much help the other person needs.

How can helping be increased? Research has indicated that teaching people about the determinants of prosocial behavior makes them more aware of why they sometimes don't help, with the happy result that they help more in the future.

If You Are Interested

Batson, C. D. (1998). Altruism and prosocial behavior. In D. Gilbert, S. Fiske, & G. Lindzey (Eds.), *The handbook of social psychology* (4th ed., Vol. 2, pp. 282–316). New York: McGraw-Hill. A thorough, up-to-date review of all aspects of prosocial behavior.

Clark, M. S. (1991). *Prosocial behavior: Review of personality and social psychology* (Vol. 12). Newbury Park, CA: Sage. A resource containing chapters by top researchers in the field of prosocial behavior, many of whom were cited in this chapter. Topics include the development of altruism, the debate about whether people are ever truly altruistic or are always concerned with their self-interest, the effects of mood on helping, and the consequences of helping.

DePaulo, B. M., Nadler, A., & Fisher, J. D. (1983). *New directions in helping: Help seeking* (Vol. 2). New York: Academic Press. Chapters address the conditions under which people are likely to seek out help from others and the consequences of receiving help.

DeWaal, F. (1996). *Good natured: The origins of right and wrong in humans and other animals.* Cambridge, MA: Harvard University Press. A fascinating look at morality and prosocial behavior among animals. One does not have to be human, DeWaal argues, in order to be humane.

Gandhi (1982). An award-winning film about the life of Mahatma Gandhi, the Indian leader who captured the minds and hearts of the world by leading a persistent, peaceful revolt against the British Empire. He became an international symbol of selflessness and nonviolence. His life raises many interesting questions about the causes of altruism.

Latané, B., & Darley, J. M. (1970). *The unresponsive bystander: Why doesn't he help?* Englewood Cliffs, NJ: Prentice Hall. A classic look at why bystanders often fail to help victims in emergencies, including an indepth discussion of the "seizure" and "smoke" studies described in this chapter.

Schindler's List (1994, Stephen Spielberg). The true story of how a German profiteer saved the lives of hundreds of Jews during World War II. Whereas Oscar Schindler's original motivation stemmed from a capitalistic need for cheap labor, his actions went far beyond his original intentions—raising intriguing questions about the origins of altruism.

Spacapan, S., & Oskamp, S. (1992). *Helping and being helped: Naturalistic studies.* Newbury Park, CA: Sage. This book contains chapters by researchers investigating helping in everyday life, including self-help groups, spousal caregiving, organ donation, and AIDS volunteerism.

Wolpert, Stanley (1962). *Nine Hours to Rama.* A fictionalized account of the life of Mahatma Gandhi.

CHAPTER 12

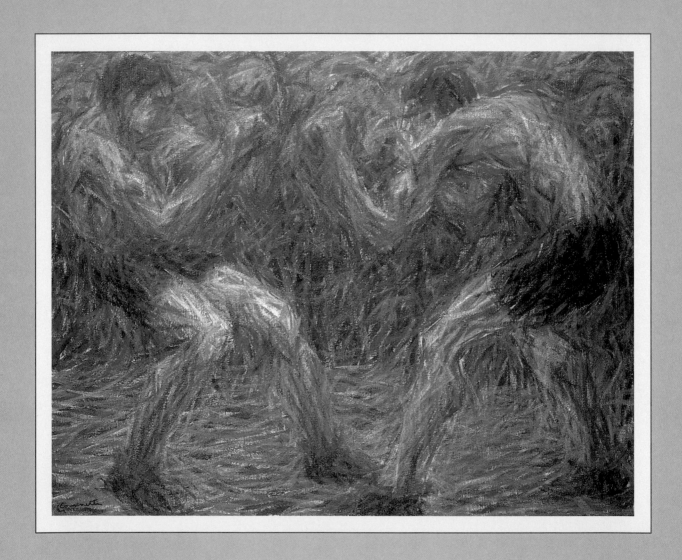

AGGRESSION: WHY WE HURT OTHER PEOPLE

In the spring of 1992, following the acquittal of several members of the Los Angeles Police Department on charges of savagely beating an African American motorist named Rodney King, hundreds of people in the inner city went on a rampage of rioting, arson, and looting. When the smoke cleared, 55 people had been killed, some 2,000 were seriously injured, and entire city blocks in South Central Los Angeles were in flames, resulting in more than a billion dollars in property damage.

On April 19, 1995 a young man named Timothy McVeigh, furious at the federal government's alleged heavy-handedness, loaded a large truck with a volatile mixture of chemical fertilizer and fuel oil, parked it in front of the Alfred P. Murrah federal office building in downtown Oklahoma City, and detonated it. The resulting explosion caused the structure to collapse on itself, killing 168 innocent people—including a roomful of young children at play in a day-care center housed on the second floor of the building. It was the most destructive case of domestic terrorism in our history.

In the aftermath of each of these tragic events, there was no shortage of explanations. Some members of Congress attributed the Rodney King rioting to simple lawlessness.

Others blamed it on grinding poverty. Former Vice-President Dan Quayle blamed it on a breakdown in "family values." Another prominent member of the Republican administration laid the blame on frustration caused by the failure of the antipoverty programs initiated during a Democratic presidency some 25 years earlier. Democrats attributed the rioting to twelve years of the neglect of inner cities and their residents by the Reagan and Bush administrations. Following the Oklahoma City bombing, several commentators, including President Clinton, felt that part of the blame should be laid at the doorstep of certain talk-radio hosts who seemed to feed the anger and frustration of many citizens and direct it at a faceless government. Indeed, shortly before the tragedy in Oklahoma City, one popular talk-radio host, G. Gordon Liddy, had actually provided his listeners with detailed instructions for shooting federal employees.

What is aggression? What causes it? Are human beings instinctively aggressive? Can normal people be inspired to commit violence by the exhortations of a talk-radio host or by the example of violent characters on TV or in films? Can aggression be prevented or reduced? These are social psychological questions of the utmost importance. Needless to say, we don't have all the answers. By the time you get to the end of this chapter, however, we hope you will have gained some insight into those issues. But first, let's be sure we know what we mean by the term.

What Is Aggression?

Social psychologists define **aggressive action** as intentional behavior aimed at causing either physical or psychological pain. It is not to be confused with assertiveness—even though most people often loosely refer to others as "aggressive" if they stand up for their rights, write letters to the editor complaining about real or imagined injustices, work extra hard, display a great deal of ambition, or are real "go-getters." Similarly, in a sexist society a woman who simply speaks her mind or picks up the phone and makes the first move by inviting a male acquaintance to dinner might be called aggressive by some. Our definition is clear: Aggression is an intentional action aimed at doing harm or causing pain. The action might be physical or verbal; it might succeed in its goal or not. It is still aggression. Thus, if someone throws a beer bottle at your head and you duck, so that the bottle misses your head, it is still an aggressive act. The important thing is the intention. By the same token, if a drunk driver unintentionally runs you down while you're attempting to cross the street, that is not an act of aggression, even though the damage would be far greater than that caused by the beer bottle that missed.

It is also useful to distinguish between **hostile aggression** and **instrumental aggression** (Berkowitz, 1993). Hostile aggression is an act of aggression stemming from feelings of anger and aimed at inflicting pain or injury. In instrumental aggression, there is an intention to hurt the other person but the hurting takes place as a means to some goal other than causing pain. For example, in a professional football game, a defensive lineman will usually do whatever it takes to thwart his opponent (the blocker) and tackle the ball carrier. This typically includes intentionally inflicting pain on his opponent if doing so is useful in helping him get the blocker out of the way so that he can get to the ball carrier. This is instrumental aggression. On the other hand, if he believes his opponent has been playing dirty, he might become angry and go out of his way to hurt his opponent, even if doing so does not increase his opportunity to tackle the ball carrier. This is hostile aggression.

Aggressive Action
intentional behavior aimed at causing either physical or psychological pain

Hostile Aggression
an act of aggression stemming from feelings of anger and aimed at inflicting pain

Instrumental Aggression
aggression as a means to some goal other than causing pain

Is Aggression Inborn, or Is It Learned?

Scientists, philosophers, and other serious thinkers are not in complete agreement with one another about whether aggression is an inborn, instinctive phenomenon or whether such behavior must be learned (Baron & Richardson, 1994; Berkowitz, 1993; Geen, 1998). This controversy is not new; it has been raging for centuries. For example, Thomas Hobbes, in his classic work *Leviathan* (first published in 1651), took the view that we human beings, in our natural state, are brutes and that only by enforcing the law and order of society could we curb what to Hobbes was a natural instinct toward aggression. On the other hand, Jean-Jacques Rousseau's concept of the noble savage (a theory he developed in 1762) suggested that we human beings, in our natural state, are gentle creatures and that it is a restrictive society that forces us to become hostile and aggressive.

Hobbes's more pessimistic view was elaborated in the twentieth century by Sigmund Freud (1930), who theorized that human beings are born with an instinct toward life, which he called **Eros,** and an equally powerful death instinct, **Thanatos,** an instinctual drive toward death, leading to aggressive actions. About the death instinct, Freud wrote: "It is at work in every living being and is striving

Eros
the instinct toward life, posited by Freud

Thanatos
according to Freud, an instinctual drive toward death, leading to aggressive actions

Hydraulic Theory
the theory that unexpressed emotions build up pressure and must be expressed to relieve that pressure

to bring it to ruin and to reduce life to its original condition of inanimate matter" (p. 67). Freud believed that aggressive energy must come out somehow, lest it continue to build up and produce illness. Freud's notion can best be characterized as a **hydraulic theory**—that is, the analogy is one of water pressure building up in a container: Unless aggression is allowed to drain off, it will produce some sort of explosion. According to Freud, society performs an essential function in regulating this instinct and in helping people to sublimate it—that is, to turn the destructive energy into acceptable or useful behavior.

Breeding Organisms for Aggression

Much of the evidence on whether or not aggression is instinctive in human beings is based on the observation of and experimentation with species other than the human race. The idea behind this research is that if one can succeed in demonstrating that certain so-called instinctive aggressive behaviors in the lower animals are not rigidly preprogrammed, then surely aggression is not rigidly preprogrammed in human beings. For example, consider the prevalent belief about cats and rats. Among the general public, it is considered obvious that cats will instinctively stalk and kill rats. After all, don't all cats go after rats? Biologist Zing Yang Kuo (1961) attempted to demonstrate that this was a myth. So he performed a simple little experiment: He raised a kitten in the same cage with a rat. What did he find? Not only did the cat refrain from attacking the rat, but the two became close companions. Moreover, when given the opportunity the cat refused either to chase or to kill other rats; thus, the benign behavior was not confined to his buddy, but generalized to rats the cat had never met before.

While this experiment is charming, it fails to prove that aggressive behavior is not instinctive; it merely demonstrates that the aggressive instinct can be inhibited by early experience. What if an organism grows up without any experience with other organisms? Will it or won't it show normal aggressive tendencies?

> "Man's inhumanity to man / Makes countless thousands mourn.
> —Robert Burns,
> *Man Was Made to Mourn*

■ We are all curious about the causes of aggression.

"What are you, anyway—an only child?"

Irenaus Eibl-Eibesfeldt (1963) showed that rats raised in isolation (i.e., without any experience in fighting other rats) will attack a fellow rat when one is introduced into the cage; moreover, the isolated rat uses the same pattern of threat and attack that experienced rats use. Thus, although aggressive behavior can be modified by experience (as shown by Kuo's experiment), Eibl-Eibesfeldt showed that aggression apparently does not need to be learned. On the other hand, one should not conclude from this study that aggression is necessarily instinctive, for, as John Paul Scott (1958) pointed out, in order to draw this conclusion there must be physiological evidence of a spontaneous stimulation for fighting that arises from within the body alone. The stimulus in Eibl-Eibesfeldt's experiment came from the outside—that is, the sight of a new rat stimulated the isolated rat to fight. Scott concluded from his analysis of the evidence that there is no inborn need for fighting: If an organism can arrange its life so there is no outside stimulation to fight, then it will experience no physiological or mental damage as a result of not expressing aggression.

The argument continues to go back and forth. Scott's conclusion was called into question by the Nobel Prize–winning ethologist Konrad Lorenz (1966), who observed the behavior of cichlids—highly aggressive tropical fish. Male cichlids will attack other males of the same species to establish and defend their territory. In its natural environment, the male cichlid does not attack female cichlids; nor does it attack males of a different species—it attacks only males of its own species. What happens if all other male cichlids are removed from an aquarium, leaving only one male alone with no appropriate target? The cichlid will attack males of other species—males it previously ignored. Moreover, if all other males are removed, the male cichlid will eventually attack and kill females.

More recently, Richard Lore and Lori Schultz (1993) report that the universality of aggression among vertebrates strongly suggests that aggressiveness has evolved and has been maintained because it has survival value. At the same time, these researchers underscore the point that nearly all organisms also seem to have evolved strong inhibitory mechanisms that enable them to suppress aggression when it is in their best interests to do so. Thus, even in the most violence-prone species, aggression is an optional strategy—whether or not it is expressed—and is determined by the animal's previous social experiences as well as by the specific social context in which the animal finds itself.

Aggressiveness across Cultures

Social psychologists are in general agreement with the interpretation of the animal research offered by Lore and Schultz. Moreover, where humans are concerned, because of the complexity and importance of our social interactions, the social situation takes on even greater importance than it does among the lower organisms. (Bandura, 1973; Lysak, Rule, & Dobbs, 1989; Berkowitz, 1968, 1993). As Berkowitz (1993) has suggested, we human beings seem to have an inborn tendency to respond to certain provocative stimuli by striking out against the perpetrator. Whether or not the aggressive action is actually expressed is a function of a complex interplay between these innate propensities, a variety of learned inhibitory responses, and the precise nature of the social situation. For example, although it is true that many animals, from insects to apes, will usually attack another animal that invades their territory, it is a gross oversimplification to imply, as some popular writers have, that human beings are likewise programmed to protect their territory and behave aggressively in response to highly

specific stimuli. Rather, much evidence supports the contention held by most social psychologists that, for humankind, innate patterns of behavior are infinitely
modifiable and flexible. This is illustrated by the fact that human cultures vary
widely in their degree of aggressiveness. European history, when condensed, consists of one major war after another; in contrast, certain "primitive" tribes, such
as the Lepchas of Sikkim, the Pygmies of Central Africa, and the Arapesh of New
Guinea live in apparent peace and harmony—with acts of aggression being extremely rare (Baron & Richardson, 1994).

Aggression Among the Iroquois

Within a given culture, changing social conditions frequently lead to striking
changes in aggressive behavior. For example, for hundreds of years the Iroquois
Indians lived in benign peacefulness as a hunting nation; they simply did not engage in aggressive behavior against other tribes. But in the seventeenth century,
barter with the newly arrived Europeans brought the Iroquois into direct competition with the neighboring Hurons over furs, which dramatically increased in
value, because they could now be traded for manufactured goods. A series of
skirmishes with the Hurons ensued, and within a short time the Iroquois developed into ferocious warriors. It would be hard to argue that they were spectacu-
lar warriors because of uncontrollable aggressive instincts; rather, their aggressiveness almost certainly came about because a social change produced increases
in competition (Hunt, 1940).

Aggression in the Deep South

In our own society, there are some striking regional differences in aggressive behavior and in the kinds of events that trigger violence. For example, Richard Nisbett
has shown that homicide rates for white southern males are substantially higher
than those for white northern males, especially in rural areas (Nisbett, 1993). But
this is true only for "argument-related" homicides. Nisbett's research shows that
southerners do not endorse violence more than northerners when survey questions
are expressed in general terms, but that southerners are more inclined to endorse violence for protection and in response to insults. This pattern suggests that the "culture of honor" may be characteristic of particular economic and occupational circumstances, including the herding society of the early South where protection of
the herd was vital. In a follow-up study, Nisbett and his colleagues (Cohen, Nisbett,
Bowdle, & Schwarz, 1996) conducted a series of experiments in which they
demonstrated that these norms characteristic of a "culture of honor" manifest
themselves in the cognitions, emotions, behaviors, and physiological reactions of
contemporary southern white males enrolled at the University of Michigan. In
these experiments, each participant was "accidentally" bumped into by the experimenter's confederate who then insulted him by calling him a denigrating
name. Compared with northern white males (who tended to simply shrug off the
insult) southerners were more likely to think their masculine reputation was
threatened, became more upset (as shown by a rise in cortisol levels in their
bloodstream), were more physiologically primed for aggression (as shown by a
rise in testosterone levels in their bloodstream), became more cognitively primed
for aggression, and, ultimately, were more likely to engage in aggressive and dominant behavior following the incident. (See Try It! p. 461.)

   Taking these findings into account, we would conclude that, although an instinctual component of aggression is almost certainly present in human beings,

■ In a "culture of honor," a real or imagined insult frequently resulted in bloodshed.

aggression is not caused entirely by instinct. There are clear examples of situational and social events that can produce aggressive behavior. Even more importantly we know that, in human beings, such behavior can be modified by situational and social factors. In short, aggressive behavior can be changed.

Try It !

Situational Aggression

Let's take another look at the southern students in Nisbett's experiment. Consider the following hypothesis: Attending college at the University of Michigan would have an effect on a person's tendency to retaliate following a minor insult. How would you go about testing your hypothesis? Hint: Do you think southern students in their freshman year at the University of Michigan would be more prone to retaliate than southern students in their senior year? If so, perhaps this is due to simple maturity. How would you find out?

Situational Causes of Aggression

Neural and Chemical Causes of Aggression

Some of the so-called situational causes of aggression result from situations inside the body (Stoff & Cairns, 1996). For example, an area in the core of the brain called the **amygdala** is associated with aggressive behaviors in human beings as well as in the lower animals. When that area is stimulated, docile organisms become violent; similarly, when neural activity in that area is blocked, violent organisms become docile (Moyer, 1976). But it should be noted that there is flexibility here also: The impact of neural mechanisms can be modified by social factors, even in subhumans. For example, if a male monkey is in the presence of

Amygdala
an area in the core of the brain that is associated with aggressive behaviors

other, less dominant monkeys he will indeed attack the other monkeys when the amygdala is stimulated. But if the amygdala is stimulated while the monkey is in the presence of more dominant monkeys, then he will not attack but will run away instead.

Testosterone

Testosterone
a hormone associated with aggression

Certain chemicals have been shown to influence aggression. For example, the injection of **testosterone,** a male sex hormone, will increase aggression in animals (Moyer, 1983). Among human beings, there is a parallel finding: James Dabbs and his colleagues found that naturally occurring testosterone levels are significantly higher among prisoners convicted of violent crimes than among those convicted of nonviolent crimes. Also, once incarcerated, prisoners with higher testosterone levels violated more prison rules—especially those involving overt confrontation (Dabbs et al., 1988; Dabbs et al., 1995). Dabbs and his colleagues also found that juvenile delinquents have higher testosterone levels than college students (Banks & Dabbs, 1996). Comparing fraternities within a given college, those generally considered most rambunctious, less socially responsible, and "cruder," were found to have the highest average testosterone levels (Dabbs, Hargrove, & Heusel, 1996).

If testosterone level affects aggressiveness, does that mean men are more aggressive than women? Apparently so; in their exhaustive survey of research on children, Eleanor Maccoby and Carol Jacklin (1974) demonstrate convincingly—in dozens of laboratory experiments and field observations and in several cultures and across social classes—that boys are consistently more aggressive than girls. For example, in one study the investigators closely observed children at play in a variety of different cultures, including the United States, Switzerland, and Ethiopia. Among boys, there was far more "nonplayful" pushing, shoving, and hitting than among girls (Deaux & LaFrance, 1998).

Similarly, among adults worldwide, the great majority of persons arrested for criminal offenses of all kinds are men. Further, when women are arrested it is usually for property crimes (forgery, fraud, larceny), rather than for violent crimes (murder, aggravated assault). Are these differences due to biological differences or to social learning differences? We cannot be sure, but there is some evidence of a biological difference. Specifically, in our own country the enormous social changes affecting women during the past 35 years have not produced increases in the incidence of violent crimes committed by women relative to those committed by men. When one looks at the comparative data between men and women involving nonviolent crimes, women have shown a far greater increase relative to that shown by men (Wilson & Herrnstein, 1985).

Needless to say, this should not be construed to mean that aggressiveness among women is unknown or even that it is rare, but aggressiveness does appear to be less common among women than among men (Eagly & Steffen, 1986). Eagly and Steffen also found that when women do commit acts of aggression, they tend to feel more guilt or anxiety about such acts than men do. These investigators suggest that the actual differences between men and women, while consistent, are not great in an absolute sense. Nevertheless, it is the clarity and consistency of these gender differences that stand out—and should not be underestimated. As Eagly has pointed out, in a great many situations small differences can be extremely important (Eagly, 1995, 1996).

The near universality of gender differences is bolstered by the results of a cross-cultural study by Dane Archer and Patricia McDaniel (1995) who asked teenagers from 11 countries to read stories involving conflict among people. The stories were interrupted prior to their resolution, and the teenagers were instructed to complete the story on their own. Archer and McDaniel found that, within each of the 11 countries, young men showed a greater tendency toward violent solutions to conflict than young women did. It is reasonably clear that biochemical differences between men and women are involved in these findings; it is also apparent that these findings are not due *solely* to biochemical differences. Archer and McDaniel found that, although within a given culture men showed evidence of consistently higher levels of aggression than women, culture also played a major role. For example, women from Australia and New Zealand showed greater evidence of aggressiveness than men from Sweden and Korea did.

Alcohol

As most socially active college students know, alcohol tends to lower our inhibitions against committing behaviors frowned on by society, including acts of aggression (Desmond, 1987; Taylor & Leonard, 1983). The linkage between the consumption of alcoholic beverages and aggressive behavior is a common observation (White, 1997; Yudko et al., 1997). For example, we are well aware of the fact that fistfights frequently break out in bars and nightclubs and that family violence is often associated with the abuse of alcohol. A wealth of hard data support these casual observations. For example, crime statistics reveal that 75 percent of those individuals arrested for murder, assault, and other crimes of violence were legally drunk at the time of their arrest (Shupe, 1954). In addition, controlled laboratory experiments demonstrate that when individuals ingest enough alcohol to make them legally drunk, they tend to respond more violently to provocations than those who have ingested little or no alcohol (Taylor & Leonard, 1983).

This does not mean that alcohol automatically increases aggression; people who have ingested alcohol are not necessarily driven to go around picking fights. Rather, the results of well-controlled laboratory and field experiments indicate that alcohol serves as a disinhibitor—that is, our social inhibitions are reduced,

"Oh, that wasn't me talking. It was the alcohol talking."

making us less cautious than we usually are (McDonald, Zanna, & Fong, 1996). Accordingly, under the influence of alcohol, a person's primary tendencies are often evoked, so that people prone to affection will become more affectionate and people prone to violence will become more aggressive. By the same token, after ingesting alcohol people who are subjected to social pressure to aggress or who are frustrated or provoked will experience fewer restraints or inhibitions against committing violent acts (Galanter, 1997; Jeavons & Taylor, 1985; Steele & Josephs, 1990; Steele & Southwick, 1985; Taylor & Sears, 1988).

Pain and Discomfort as a Cause of Aggression

If an animal experiences pain and cannot flee the scene, it will almost invariably attack; this is true of rats, mice, hamsters, foxes, monkeys, crayfish, snakes, raccoons, alligators, and a host of others (Azrin, 1967; Hutchinson, 1983). Such animals will attack members of their own species, members of different species, or anything else in sight, including stuffed dolls and tennis balls. Do you think this is true of human beings as well? A moment's reflection might help you guess that it may very well be. Most of us have experienced becoming irritable when subjected to a sharp, unexpected pain (e.g., when we stub our toe) and hence being prone to lash out at the nearest available target. In a series of experiments, Leonard Berkowitz (1983, 1988) showed that students who underwent the pain of having their hand immersed in very cold water showed a sharp increase in their likelihood to aggress against other students.

By the same token, it has long been speculated that other forms of bodily discomfort, such as heat, humidity, air pollution, and offensive odors, might act to lower the threshold for aggressive behavior (Stoff & Cairns, 1997). During the

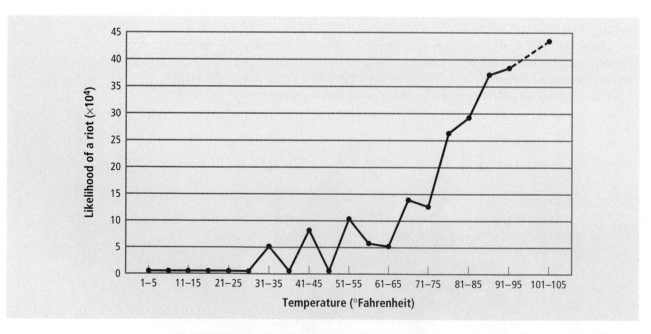

■ **FIGURE 12.1   The long, hot summer.**   Warm temperatures increase the likelihood that violent riots and other aggressive acts will occur. (Adapted from Carlsmith & Anderson, 1979)

late 1960s and early 1970s, when a great deal of tension existed in the United States concerning issues of national policy involving the war in Vietnam, racial injustice, and the like, national leaders worried a lot about a phenomenon they referred to as "the long, hot summer"—that is, the assumed tendency for riots and other forms of civic unrest to occur with greater frequency in the heat of summer than in the fall, winter, or spring. Was this actually true, or mere speculation? It turns out to be true. In a systematic analysis of disturbances occurring in 79 cities between 1967 and 1971, J. Merrill Carlsmith and Craig Anderson (1979) found that riots were far more likely to occur during hot days than during cold days. This is nicely illustrated in Figure 12.1. Similarly, in major American cities, from Houston, Texas, to Des Moines, Iowa, the hotter it is on a given day, the greater the likelihood that violent crimes will occur (Anderson & Anderson, 1984; Cotton, 1981, 1986; Harries & Stadler, 1988; Rotton & Frey, 1985).

As the reader knows by this time, one has to be cautious about interpreting events that take place in natural settings. For example, the scientist in you might be tempted to ask whether increases in aggression are due to the temperature itself or merely to the fact that more people are apt to be outside (getting in one another's way!) on hot days than on cool or rainy days. So how might we determine that it's the heat itself that caused the aggression, and not merely the greater opportunity for contact? We can bring the phenomenon into the laboratory. This is remarkably easy to do. For example, in one such experiment William Griffitt and Roberta Veitch (1971) simply administered a test to students, some of whom took it in a room with normal temperature, while others took it in a room where the temperature was allowed to soar to 90 degrees. The students in the hot room not only reported feeling more aggressive but also expressed more hostility to a stranger whom they were asked to describe and rate. Similar results have been reported by a number of investigators (Anderson, Anderson, & Deuser, 1996; Bell, 1980; Rule et al., 1987). Additional evidence from the natural world helps bolster our belief in the cause of this phenomenon. For example, it has been shown that in major league baseball games, significantly more batters are hit by pitched balls when the temperature is above 90 than when it is below 90 (Reifman, Larrick, & Fein, 1988). And in the desert city of Phoenix, Arizona, drivers without air-conditioned cars are more likely to honk their horns in traffic jams than drivers with air-conditioned cars are (Kenrick & MacFarlane, 1986). See Try It! below.

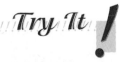

Heat, Humidity, and Aggression

The next time you find yourself caught in a traffic jam, try doing a simple, naturalistic replication of the Kenrick & MacFarlane experiment. Consider the following hypothesis: The greater the heat and humidity, the greater the aggression.

- Take notes on how much aggression you notice (in the form of horn-honking).

- Note down the heat and humidity that day.

- The next two or three times you get caught in a traffic jam, do the same thing.

Can you discern a relationship between heat/humidity and horn-honking?

Social Situations Leading to Aggression

Imagine that your friend Sam is driving you to the airport so that you can take a plane home for the Christmas holidays. Sam is starting out a bit later than you feel comfortable with, but when you mention it, he accuses you of being overly anxious and assures you that he knows the route well and that you will arrive there with a good 30 minutes to spare. Halfway to your destination, Sam's car grinds to a halt in bumper-to-bumper traffic. You glance at your watch. Once again, Sam assures you that there is plenty of time—but this time you detect less confidence in his tone. After a few minutes, you notice that your palms are sweating and you are beginning to wring your hands. A few minutes later, you open the car door and survey the road ahead: There is nothing but gridlock as far as the eye can see. You get back in the car, slam the door, and glare at your friend. Sam smiles lamely and says, "How was I supposed to know there would be so much traffic?" Should he be prepared to duck?

Frustration as a Cause of Aggression

As the above scenario suggests, frustration is a major cause of aggression. Frustration occurs when a person is thwarted on the way to an expected goal or gratification. All of us have experienced some degree of frustration from time to time; indeed, it's unlikely we can get through a week without experiencing it. Research has shown that the experience of frustration can increase the probability of an aggressive response. This tendency is referred to as **frustration-aggression theory,** which holds that people's perception that they are being prevented from obtaining a goal will increase the probability of an aggressive response. As we shall see in a moment, this is not meant to imply that frustration always leads to aggression—but it frequently does, especially when the frustration is a decidedly unpleasant experience. In a classic experiment by Roger Barker, Tamara Dembo, and Kurt Lewin (1941), young children were shown a roomful of attractive toys that were kept out of their reach. The children stood outside a wire screen looking at the toys—fully expecting to play with them—but were unable to reach them. After a painfully long wait, the children were finally allowed to play with the toys. In a control condition, a different group of children were allowed to play with the toys directly, without first being frustrated. This second group of children played joyfully with the toys. But the frustrated group, when finally given access to the toys, were extremely destructive: They tended to smash the toys, throw them against the wall, step on them, and so forth.

Several factors can increase frustration and, accordingly, will increase the probability that some form of aggression will occur. One such factor involves your closeness to the goal or the object of your desire. The closer the goal, the greater the expectation of pleasure that is thwarted; the greater the expectation, the more likely the aggression. This was demonstrated in a field experiment by Mary Harris (1974), who instructed her confederate to cut in line in front of people who were waiting in a variety of places—for movie tickets, outside crowded restaurants, or at the checkout counter of a supermarket. On some occasions, the confederates were instructed to cut in front of the second person in line; on other occasions, they cut in front of the twelfth person in line. The results were clear: The responses of the people standing behind the intruder were much more aggressive when the confederate cut into the second place in line.

Aggression also increases when the frustration is unexpected. James Kulik and Roger Brown (1979) hired students to telephone strangers and ask for dona-

Frustration-Aggression Theory
the theory that frustration—the perception that you are being prevented from obtaining a goal—will increase the probability of an aggressive response

■ Feelings of frustration can occur when we are blocked or delayed as we strive to reach a goal. For example, being stuck in a bad traffic jam can elicit aggressive responses, ranging from honking pointlessly to precipitating fistfights or even shootings.

tions to a charity. The students were hired on a commission basis—that is, they received a small fraction of each dollar pledged. Some of the students were led to expect a high rate of contributions; others, to expect far less success. The experiment was rigged so that none of the potential donors agreed to make a contribution. The experimenters found that the callers with high expectations directed more verbal aggression toward the nondonors, speaking more harshly and slamming down the phone with more force than the callers with low expectations.

Other Factors Affecting the Frustration/Aggression Link

As mentioned above, frustration does not always produce aggression. Rather, it seems to produce anger or annoyance and a readiness to aggress if other things about the situation are conducive to aggressive behavior (Berkowitz, 1978, 1988, 1989, 1993; Gustafson, 1989). What are those other things? Well, one obvious other thing would be the size and strength of the person responsible for your frustration—as well as that person's ability to retaliate. It is undoubtedly easier to slam the phone down on a reluctant donor who is miles away and has no idea who you are than to take out your anger against your frustrator if he turned out to be the middle linebacker of the Green Bay Packers and was staring you right in the face. Similarly, if the frustration is understandable, legitimate, and unintentional, the tendency to aggress will be reduced. For example, in an experiment by Eugene Burnstein and Philip Worchel (1962), when a confederate "unwittingly" sabotaged the problem solving of his groupmates because his hearing aid stopped working, the resulting frustration did not lead to a measurable degree of aggression.

This doesn't mean that aggression is always rational or sensible. Jody Dill and Craig Anderson (1995) recently performed an experiment in which college students were either (a) allowed to attain their desired goal without impediment or (b) prevented from attaining their goal in a way that was justified, or (c) prevented from attaining their goal in a way that was totally unjustified. As one would imagine, when they were prevented from attaining their goal in an unjustified manner, this produced the greatest amount of hostile aggression. But, even when the frustration was fully justified, significantly more hostile aggression occurred than when there was no frustration at all. Thus, although mitigating circumstances can reduce the aggression caused by frustration (as in the Burnstein and Worchel experiment), frustration—even when justified—is painful and therefore can produce aggression—albeit less than when unjustified.

We should also point out that frustration is not the same as deprivation. Children who simply don't have toys do not aggress more than children who do have toys. In the experiment by Barker and his colleagues discussed above, frustration and aggression occurred because the children had every reason to expect to play with the toys, and their reasonable expectation was thwarted; this thwarting was what caused the children to behave destructively. In accord with this distinction, the Reverend Jesse Jackson (1981), with great insight, pointed out that the race riots of 1967 and 1968 occurred "in the middle of rising expectations and the increased, though inadequate, social spending." In short, Jackson was suggesting that thwarted expectations were largely responsible for the frustration and aggression. This is consistent with the earlier observations of psychiatrist Jerome Frank (1978), who pointed out that the most serious riots in that era occurred not in the geographic areas of greatest poverty but in Watts and Detroit, where things were not nearly so bad for African Americans as they were in some other sections of the country. The point is that things were bad, relative to their perception of how white people were doing and relative to the positive changes many African Americans had a right to expect. Thus, what causes aggression is not deprivation but **relative deprivation**: the perception that you (or your group) have less than you deserve, less than what you have been led to expect, or less than what people similar to you have.

A similar phenomenon occurred in Eastern Europe in 1991, when serious rebellion against the Soviet monolith took place only after the chains had been loosened somewhat. In the same vein, Primo Levi (1985), a survivor of Auschwitz, contends that even in concentration camps the few instances of rebellion were performed not by the inmates at the very bottom of the camp totem pole—the suffering victims of unrelenting horror—but "by prisoners who were privileged in some way"(p. 203).

Direct Provocation and Reciprocation

There you are, at your part-time job behind the counter, flipping hamburgers in a crowded fast-food restaurant. You are working harder than usual, because the other short-order cook went home ill, and the customers are lining up at the counter, clamoring for their burgers. In your eagerness to speed up the process, you spin around too fast and knock over a large jar of pickles, which smashes on the floor just as the boss enters the workplace. "Boy, are you clumsy!" he screams. "I'm gonna dock your pay $10 for that one; grab a broom and clean up, you moron! I'll take over here!" You glare at him. If looks could kill! You feel like telling him what he can do with this lousy job!

One obvious cause of aggression stems from the need to reciprocate after being provoked by aggressive behavior from another person. While the Christian plea to "turn the other cheek" is wonderful advice, it is not an accurate description of the ordinary behavior of most human beings. This has been illustrated in countless experiments in and out of the laboratory. Typical of this line of research is an experiment by Robert Baron (1988) in which subjects prepared an advertisement for a new product; their ad was then evaluated and criticized by an accomplice of the experimenter. In one condition, the criticism, while strong, was done in a gentle and considerate manner ("I think there's a lot of room for im-

Relative Deprivation
the perception that you (or your group) have less than you deserve, less than you have been led to expect, or less than people similar to you have

provement"); in the other condition, the criticism was given in an insulting manner ("I don't think you could be original if you tried"). When provided with an opportunity to retaliate, subjects who were treated harshly were far more likely to do so than those in the "gentle" condition.

As you might imagine, when provoked, people do not always reciprocate. One determinant of reciprocation is the intentionality of the provocation; if we are convinced it was unintentional, most of us will not reciprocate (Kremer & Stephens, 1983). Similarly, if there are mitigating circumstances, counteraggression will not occur. But in order to be effective at curtailing an aggressive response, these mitigating circumstances must be known at the time of the provocation. This was demonstrated in an experiment by Johnson and Rule (1986). Students were insulted by the experimenters' assistant, but half of them were first told that the assistant was upset after receiving an unfair low grade on a chemistry exam, whereas the other students were given this information only after the insult was delivered. All subjects later had an opportunity to retaliate by choosing the level of unpleasant noise with which to zap the assistant. Those students who knew about the mitigating circumstances before being insulted delivered less intense bursts of noise. How can we account for this difference? Apparently, at the time of the insult, the informed students simply did not take it personally and therefore had no strong need to retaliate. This interpretation is bolstered by evidence of their physiological arousal: At the time of the insult, the heartbeat of the insulted students did not increase as rapidly if they knew about the assistant's unhappy state of mind beforehand. (See Try It! below.)

> "Nothing is more costly, nothing is more sterile, than revenge.
> —Winston Churchill
> (1874–1965)

Aggressive Objects as a Cause of Aggressive Behavior

Certain stimuli seem to impel us to action. Is it conceivable that the mere presence of an **aggressive stimulus**—an object that is associated with aggressive responses (e.g., a gun) might increase the probability of aggression? In a classic experiment by Leonard Berkowitz and Anthony LePage (1967), college students were made angry. Some of them were made angry in a room in which a gun was left lying around (ostensibly from a previous experiment), and others were made angry in a room in which a neutral object (a badminton racket) was substituted for the gun. Subjects were then given the opportunity to administer some electric shocks to a fellow college student. Those individuals who had been made angry in the presence of the gun administered more intense electric shocks than those made angry in the presence of the badminton racket. The results are illustrated in Figure 12.2. The basic findings have been replicated a great many times in the United States and Europe (Frodi, 1975; Turner & Leyens, 1992; Turner & Simmons, 1974; Turner et al., 1977). These findings are provocative and point to a conclusion

Aggressive Stimulus
an object that is associated with aggressive responses (e.g., a gun) and whose mere presence can increase the probability of aggression

Try It!

Insults and Aggression
Think about the last time you were insulted.

- Who did it to you?

- What were the circumstances?

- Did you take it personally or not?

- How did you respond?

How does your behavior relate to the material you have just finished reading?

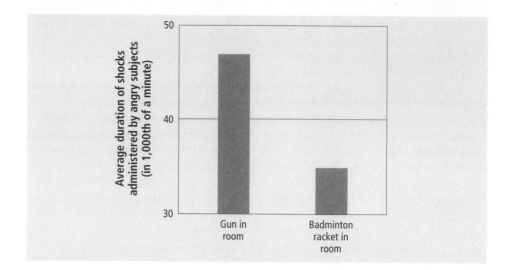

■ **FIGURE 12.2 The trigger can pull the finger.** Aggressive cues, such as weapons, tend to increase levels of aggression. (Adapted from Berkowitz & LePage, 1967)

opposite to a familiar slogan often used by opponents of gun control "Guns don't kill; people do." Guns do kill. As Leonard Berkowitz (1981, p. 12) puts it, "An angry person can pull the trigger of his gun if he wants to commit violence; but the trigger can also pull the finger or otherwise elicit aggressive reactions from him, if he is ready to aggress and does not have strong inhibitions against such behavior."

Consider Seattle, Washington, and Vancouver, British Columbia. They are virtually twin cities in a lot of ways; they have very similar climates, populations, economies, general crime rates, and rates of physical assault. They differ in two respects: (a) Vancouver severely restricts handgun ownership, while Seattle does not, and (b) the murder rate in Seattle is more than twice as high as that in Vancouver (Sloan et al., 1988). Is the one the cause of the other? We cannot be sure. But the laboratory experiments discussed above strongly suggest that the

■ Does the finger pull the trigger, or does the trigger pull the finger?

"There's a burglar prowling in the Blue Room, sir. Would you care to have a crack at him before I notify the police?"

ubiquitous presence of that aggressive stimulus in the United States might be a factor. This speculation receives additional support from Dane Archer and Rosemary Gartner (1984), who, in a cross-national study of violence, found that the homicide rate in countries all over the world is highly correlated with the availability of handguns. Britain, for example, where handguns are banned, has one-fourth the population of the United States and one-sixteenth as many homicides.

In a large-scale follow-up study, Archer and his colleagues (Archer, 1994; Archer & McDaniel, 1995) asked teenagers from the United States and ten other countries to read stories involving conflict among people and to supply their own guess as to the outcome of the conflict. The data show that American teenagers were more likely to anticipate a violent conclusion to the conflict than teenagers from other countries were. Moreover, the violent conclusions drawn by American teenagers were far more likely to be "lethal, gun-laden and merciless" than those by teenagers in any of the other countries were (Archer, 1994, p. 19). The conclusions are undeniable: Lethal violence, especially involving guns, is simply a major part of American society—and therefore plays a major role in the expectations and fantasies of American youngsters.

> "Children have never been very good at listening to their elders, but they have never failed to imitate them.
> —James Baldwin, *Nobody Knows My Name*, 1961

Imitation and Aggression

A major cause of aggression has its roots in social learning. Children frequently learn to solve conflicts aggressively by imitating adults and their peers, especially when they see that the aggression is rewarded. For example, in most high-contact sports (e.g., football and hockey) it is frequently the case that the more aggressive players achieve the greatest fame (and the highest salaries) and the more aggressive teams win more games. In these sports, it usually doesn't pay to be a gentle soul—or, as famed baseball manager Leo Durocher once said, "Nice guys finish last!" The data bear him out. For instance, in one study it was found that among hockey players, those most frequently sent to the penalty box for overly aggressive play tended to be the ones who scored the most goals (McCarthy & Kelley, 1978). To the extent that athletes serve as role models for children and adolescents, what is being modeled might be that fame and fortune go hand in hand with excessive aggressiveness.

It is also the case that a large percentage of physically abusive parents were themselves abused by their own parents when they were kids (Silver, Dublin, & Lourie, 1969; Strauss & Gelles, 1980). The speculation is that when children experience aggressive treatment at the hands of their parents, they learn that violence is the proper way to socialize their own kids. But, of course, that is not the only conclusion one might draw from these family data. As mentioned earlier, aggressiveness may have a strong genetic component; if so, perhaps aggressive parents simply breed aggressive children. How can one determine whether or not imitation might be operating here? As you might guess, the clearest strategy would be to investigate the phenomenon in the laboratory. In a classic series of experiments, Albert Bandura and his associates (1961, 1963) demonstrated the power of **social learning theory**—the theory holds that we learn social behavior (e.g. aggression) by observing others and imitating them. The basic procedure in the Bandura experiments was to have an adult knock around a plastic, air-filled "Bobo" doll (the kind that bounces back after it's been knocked down). The adult would smack the doll around with the palm of his or her hand, strike it with a mallet, kick it, and yell aggressive things at it. The kids were then allowed to play with the doll. In these experiments, the children imitated the aggressive models and treated the doll in an abusive manner. Children in a control

Social Learning Theory
the theory that we learn social behavior (e.g., aggression) by observing others and imitating them

■ It is clear from the studies of Bandura and colleagues (1961, 1963) that children learn aggressive behavior through imitation and modeling.

condition, who did not see the aggressive adult in action, almost never unleashed any aggression against the hapless doll. Moreover, the children who watched the aggressive adult used identical actions and identical aggressive words as the adult. In addition, many went beyond mere imitation—they also engaged in novel forms of aggressive behavior.

The Effects of Watching Violence in the Media

The classic experiments by Albert Bandura and his colleagues make it clear that observing other people behaving aggressively can increase the aggressive behavior of the viewer. This raises the obvious question: Does watching violence on TV make people more violent? Let's take a close look at the data.

Effects on Children

There is no doubt that television plays an important role in the the socialization of children (Huston & Wright, 1996). There is also no doubt that TV remains steeped in violence. According to a recent study (see Seppa, 1997) , 58 percent of all TV programs contain violence—and, of those, 78 percent had no remorse, criticism, or penalty for that violence. Indeed, some 40 percent of the violent incidents seen on TV during the past year were initiated by characters portrayed as heroes or other attractive role models for children (Cantor, 1994; Kunkel et al., 1995).

Exactly what do children learn from watching violence on TV? A number of long-term studies indicate that the more violence individuals watch on TV as children, the more violence they exhibit years later as teenagers and young adults (Eron, 1982, 1987; Eron et al., 1996; Huesmann, 1982; Huesman & Miller, 1994; Turner et al., 1986). In a typical study of this kind teenagers are asked to recall which shows they watched on TV when they were kids and how frequently they watched them; the shows are independently rated by judges as to how violent they are; then, the general aggressiveness of the teenagers is independently rated by their teachers and classmates. Not only is there a high correlation be-

Television has brought back murder into the home—where it belongs.
–Alfred Hitchcock, *Observer*, December 19, 1965

tween the amount of violent TV watched and the viewer's subsequent aggressiveness, but the impact also accumulates over time—that is, the strength of the correlation increases with age. While these are fairly powerful data, they do not definitively prove that watching a lot of violence on TV causes children to become violent teenagers. After all, it is at least conceivable that the aggressive kids were born with a tendency to enjoy violence and that this enjoyment manifests itself in both their aggressive behavior and their liking for watching violence on TV. Once again, we see the value of the controlled experiment in helping us to understand what causes what. In order to demonstrate conclusively that watching violence on TV actually causes violent behavior, the relationship must be shown experimentally.

Because this is an issue of great importance to society, it has been well researched. While not all of the research is consistent, the overwhelming thrust of the experimental evidence demonstrates that watching violence does indeed increase the frequency of aggressive behavior in children (for reviews of the literature, see Donnerstein, Slaby, & Eron, 1994; Eron et al., 1996; Geen, 1994, 1998; Huesmann & Miller, 1994; Hughes & Hasbrouck, 1996). For example, in an early experiment on this issue, Robert Liebert and Robert Baron (1972) exposed a group of children to an extremely violent TV episode of a police drama. In a control condition, a similar group of children were exposed to an exciting but nonviolent TV sporting event for the same length of time. Each child was then allowed to play in another room with a group of other children. Those who had watched the violent police drama showed far more aggression against their playmates than those who had watched the sporting event. The results of this experiment are depicted in Figure 12.3.

A subsequent experiment by Wendy Josephson (1987) showed, as one might expect, that watching TV violence has the greatest impact on youngsters who are somewhat prone to violence to begin with. In this experiment, youngsters were exposed to either a film depicting a great deal of police violence or an exciting, nonviolent film about bike racing. The youngsters then played a game of floor hockey. Watching the violent film had the effect of increasing the number of aggressive acts committed during the hockey game—primarily by those youngsters

■ Does watching violence on TV promote violence and aggression in children? What about in adults?

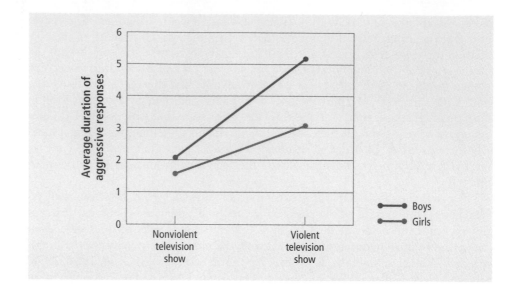

■ **FIGURE 12.3   TV violence and aggression.** Being exposed to violence on TV increases aggressive behavior in children. (Adapted from Liebert & Baron, 1972)

who had previously been rated as highly aggressive by their teachers. These kids hit others with their sticks, threw elbows, and yelled aggressive things at their opponents to a much greater extent than either the kids rated as nonaggressive who had also watched the violent film or the kids rated as aggressive who had watched the nonviolent film. Thus, it may be that watching media violence in effect serves to give aggressive kids permission to express their aggression. Josephson's experiment suggests that youngsters who do not have aggressive tendencies to begin with do not necessarily act aggressively—at least, not on the basis of seeing only one violent film.

That last phrase is an important one, because it may be that even youngsters who are not prone toward aggression will become more aggressive if exposed to a steady diet of violent films over a long period. That is exactly what was found in a set of field experiments performed in Belgium by Phillippe Leyens and his colleagues (Leyens et al., 1975; Parke et al., 1977). In these experiments, different groups of children were exposed to differing amounts of media violence over a longer period than typically happens in the "one-shot" laboratory experiments described above. In these field experiments, the great majority of the kids (even those without strong aggressive tendencies) who were exposed to a high degree of media violence over a long period were more aggressive than those who watched more benign shows.

We might mention, in passing, that at a recent congressional hearing on TV violence, it was estimated that the average 12-year-old has witnessed more than 100,000 acts of violence on television (Signorielli, Gerbner, & Morgan, 1995). We mention this because we believe that one of the crucial factors involved in the above findings (in addition to social learning and imitation) is the simple phenomenon of priming. That is, just as exposing children to rifles and other weapons left lying around the house or the laboratory has a tendency to increase the probability of an aggressive response when children subsequently experience pain or frustration, so too might exposing children to an endless supply of violence in films and on TV have a similar tendency to prime an aggressive response.

What about Adults?

Thus far, in discussing the effects of media violence we have focused much of our attention on children—and for good reason. Youngsters are by definition much more malleable than adults—that is, it is generally assumed that their attitudes and behaviors can be more deeply influenced by the things they view. But the effect of media violence on violent behavior may not be limited to children. On numerous occasions, adult violence seems to be a case of life imitating art. For example, a few years ago a man drove his truck through the window of a crowded cafeteria in Killeen, Texas, emerged from the cab, and began shooting people at random. By the time the police arrived, he had killed 22 people, making this the most destructive shooting spree in American history. He then turned the gun on himself. In his pocket, police found a ticket stub to *Fisher King*, a film depicting a deranged man firing a shotgun into a crowded bar, killing several people.

Did seeing the film cause the violent act? We cannot be sure. But we do know that violence in the media can and does have a profound impact on the behavior of adults. Several years ago, David Phillips (1983, 1986) scrutinized the daily homicide rates in the United States and found that they almost always increased during the week following a heavyweight boxing match. Moreover, the more publicity surrounding the fight, the greater the subsequent increase in homicides. Still more striking, the race of prizefight losers was related to the race of victims of murders after the fights: After white boxers lost fights, there was a corresponding increase in murders of white men but not of black men; after black boxers lost fights, there was a corresponding increase in murders of black men but not of white men. Phillips's results are convincing; they are far too consistent to be dismissed as merely a fluke. Again, this should not be construed as indicating that all people or even a sizable percentage of people are motivated to commit violence through watching media violence. But the fact that some people are influenced—and that the results can be tragic—cannot be denied.

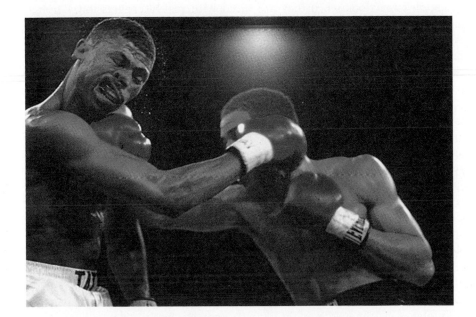

■ Do violent sports events increase homicide rates?

The Numbing Effect of TV Violence

It seems to be the case that repeated exposure to difficult or unpleasant events tends to have a numbing effect on our sensitivity to those events. One of the authors of this book, Elliot Aronson, offers the following personal example:

> Several years ago, I moved to Manhattan for a few months. Soon after my arrival, I was walking down Fifth Avenue with a friend who is a native New Yorker. I was struck and touched by the great number of obviously homeless people, living in cardboard boxes, carrying their meager possessions in paper bags or wheeling them around in broken-down supermarket shopping carts. I was both deeply moved and appalled. All during our walk, I kept reaching into my pockets and dropping coins into the hands of those unfortunate souls. My friend was appalled at my behavior. "You'll have to learn to ignore these people," my friend said. "Never," I replied, indignantly and self-righteously. Yet sure enough, within a few weeks I found myself walking down the streets of Manhattan staring straight ahead and keeping my hands out of my pockets. Amazingly, I had gotten so accustomed to the sight that, for all intents and purposes, I had become virtually indifferent to it.

Is it possible that, by a similar process, being constantly exposed to violence on TV tends to make people more tolerant of real violence? There is good evidence that this is so. In one experiment, Victor Cline and his associates (1973) measured the physiological responses of several young men while they were watching a rather brutal and bloody boxing match. Those who watched a lot of TV in their daily lives seemed relatively indifferent to the mayhem in the ring—that is, they showed little physiological evidence of excitement, anxiety, or the like. They treated the violence in a lackadaisical manner. On the other hand, those who typically watched relatively little TV underwent major physiological arousal. The violence really got to them. In a related vein, Margaret Hanratty Thomas and her colleagues (1977) demonstrated that viewing television violence can subsequently numb people's reactions when they are faced with real-life aggression. Thomas had her subjects watch either a violent police drama or an exciting but nonviolent volleyball game. After a short break, they were allowed to observe a verbally and physically aggressive interaction between two preschoolers. Those who had watched the police show responded less emotionally than those who had watched the volleyball game. It seems that viewing the initial violence served to desensitize them to further acts of violence—they were not upset by an incident that by all rights should have upset them. While such a reaction may psychologically protect us from upset, it may also have the unintended effect of increasing our indifference to victims of violence and perhaps render us more accepting of violence as a necessary aspect of life in the modern era. In a follow-up experiment, Thomas (1982) took this reasoning a step further. She demonstrated that college students, exposed to a great deal of TV violence not only showed physiological evidence of greater acceptance of violence but, in addition, when subsequently given the opportunity to administer electric shocks to a fellow student, administered more powerful electric shocks than those in the control condition.

Why Does Media Violence Affect Viewers' Aggression?

As suggested throughout this section, there are four distinct reasons that exposure to violence via the media might increase aggression:

> "Death has been tidied up, cleansed of harmful ingredients, and repackaged in prime-time segments that pander to baser appetites but leave no unpleasant aftertaste. The Caesars of network television permit no mess on the living room floor.
> –Donald Goddard, *New York Times*, February 27, 1977

1. **"If they can do it, so can I."** When people watch characters on TV expressing violence, it might simply weaken their previously learned inhibitions against violent behavior.
2. **"Oh, so that's how you do it!"** When people watch characters on TV expressing violence, it might trigger imitation, providing them with ideas as to how they might go about it.
3. **"I think it must be aggressive feelings that I'm experiencing."** There is a sense in which watching violence makes feelings of anger more easily available and makes an aggressive response more likely simply through priming. Thus, an individual might erroneously construe his or her own feelings of mild irritation as anger—and might be more likely to lash out.
4. **"Ho-hum, another brutal beating; what's on the other channel?"** Watching a lot of mayhem seems to reduce both our sense of horror about violence and our sympathy for the victims, thereby making it easier for us to live with violence and perhaps easier for us to act aggressively.

Violent Pornography and Violence against Women

A particularly troubling aspect of aggression in this country involves violence expressed by some men against women in the form of rape. According to national surveys, during the past 25 years, almost half of all rapes or attempted rapes do not involve assaults by a stranger but are attributed to so called "date rape," in which the victim is acquainted with the assailant. Many date rapes take place because the male refuses to take the word no at face value, in part because of some confusion around the "sexual scripts" adolescents learn as they are coming into sexual maturity. **Scripts** are ways of behaving socially that we learn implicitly from the culture. The sexual scripts adolescents are exposed to suggest that the traditional female role is to resist the male's sexual advances and the male's role is to be persistent (Check & Malamuth, 1983; White, Donat, & Humphrey, 1995). Thus, in one survey of high school students, although 95 percent of the males and 97 percent of the females agreed that the man should stop his sexual advances as soon as the woman says no, nearly half of those same students also believed that when a woman says no she doesn't always mean it (*Cox News Service,* 1992). This confusion has prompted several colleges to suggest that dating couples negotiate an explicit contract about their sexual conduct and limitations at the very beginning of the date. Given the problems associated with sexual scripts and the unpleasant (and occasionally tragic) consequences of misunderstandings, it is understandable that college administrators would resort to these extreme precautions. At the same time, it should be noted that more than a few social critics have deplored these measures on the grounds that they encourage fear and paranoia, destroy the spontaneity of romance, and reduce the excitement of dating to the point where it resembles a field trip to a lawyer's office (e.g., Roiphe, 1994).

Coincidental with the increase in date rape has been an increase in the availability of magazines, films, and videocassettes depicting vivid, explicit sexual behavior. For better or worse, in recent years our society has become increasingly freer and more tolerant of pornography. If viewing aggression in films and on television contributes to aggressiveness, doesn't it follow that viewing pornographic material could increase the incidence of rape? Although this possibility has been presented as an undeniable fact by some of our nation's self-appointed guardians of morality, careful scientific research indicates that it is incorrect. Because pornography is a hot-button political issue in this country, research

Scripts
ways of behaving socially that we learn implicitly from our culture

findings often get ignored in the heat of rhetoric. In 1970, after carefully studying all the evidence, the Presidential Commission on Obscenity and Pornography concluded that explicit sexual material, in and of itself, does not contribute to sexual crimes, violence against women, or other antisocial acts. But as you will recall, in Chapter 2 we discussed the fact that in 1985, Edwin Meese, while serving as Ronald Reagan's attorney general, convened a commission that disagreed with the findings of the earlier report and concluded that pornography does indeed contribute to violent crimes against women. Which commission was right? Or were both right—that is, was new evidence uncovered during the intervening 15 years that led the Meese Commission to a different conclusion?

After carefully analyzing the available evidence, we can find no foundation for the conclusions drawn by the Meese Commission. Instead, those conclusions appear to have been politically and ideologically motivated, rather than the result of dispassionate scientific inquiry. This is not to say that the issue is simple, for it is not. Indeed, the reader should note that the key phrase in our description of the findings of the 1970 report is "in and of itself." That is, now as in 1970, we would conclude that viewing explicit sexual material, in and of itself, is harmless. But we would also conclude that there are clearly undesirable effects caused by viewing materials that combine sex with violence. During the past two decades, Neil Malamuth, Edward Donnerstein, and their colleagues have conducted careful studies, both in naturalistic and laboratory settings, to determine the effects of violent pornography. Taken as a whole, these studies indicate that exposure to violent pornography promotes greater acceptance of sexual violence toward women and is almost certainly a factor associated with actual aggressive behavior toward women (Donnerstein, 1980; Donnerstein & Berkowitz, 1981; Donnerstein & Linz, 1994; Malamuth, 1981, 1986; Malamuth & Briere, 1986; Malamuth et al., 1995; Dean & Malamuth, 1997). In one experiment (Donnerstein & Berkowitz, 1981), male subjects were angered by a female accomplice. They were then shown one of three films—an aggressive-erotic one involving rape, a purely erotic one without violence, or a film depicting nonerotic violence against women. After viewing one of these films, the men took part in a supposedly unrelated experiment that involved teaching the female accomplice by

■ In the United States, we try to protect children from erotic films. But research shows that violent films are much more harmful.

"AT LAST, A MOVIE WITHOUT ALL THOSE FILTHY SEX SCENES!"

means of administering electric shocks to her whenever she gave incorrect answers. They were also allowed to choose whatever level of shock they wished to use. (Needless to say, as with other experiments using this procedure, no shocks were actually received.) Those men who had earlier seen the violent pornographic film subsequently administered the most intense shocks; those who had seen the pornographic but nonviolent film administered the lowest level of shocks. There is also evidence showing that, under these conditions, subjects who view violent pornographic films will administer more intense shocks to a female confederate than to a male confederate (Donnerstein, 1980).

Similarly, Neil Malamuth (1981) conducted an experiment in which male college students viewed one of two erotic films. One version portrayed two mutually consenting adults engaged in lovemaking; the other version portrayed a rape incident. After viewing the film, the men were asked to engage in sexual fantasy. Those men who had watched the rape version of the film created more violent sexual fantasies than those who had watched the mutual consent version. Further, just as we saw with violence, prolonged exposure to depictions of sexual violence against women (so-called slasher films) makes viewers more accepting of this kind of violence and less sympathetic toward the victim (Linz, Donnerstein, & Penrod, 1984, 1988; Zillmann & Bryant, 1984). Interestingly, this applies to female viewers as well as male viewers. Again, it should be underscored that these experiments do not support the conclusion of the Meese Commission. That is, there is no evidence indicating that scenes depicting sexual behavior between consenting adults cause any harm. These experiments make it clear that it is only the films depicting explicit sexual violence against women that produce measurable harmful effects.

How to Reduce Aggression

Throughout history, beleaguered parents have attempted to curb the aggressive behavior of their children. One of the prime techniques is punishment. After all, as the old folk saying goes, "Spare the rod and spoil the child." How well does punishment work? Let's take a close look at the data.

Does Punishing Aggression Reduce Aggressive Behavior?

Punishment is a complex event, especially as it relates to aggression. On the one hand, one might guess that punishing any behavior, including aggression, might reduce its frequency. On the other hand, since severe punishment itself usually takes the form of an aggressive act, then the punishers are actually modeling aggressive behavior for the person whose aggressive behavior they are trying to stamp out and might induce that person to imitate the action. This seems to be true—for children. As we have seen earlier in this chapter, children who grow up with punitive, aggressive parents tend to be prone toward violence when they grow up (Vissing et al., 1991).

Moreover, as we saw in Chapter 6, several experiments with preschoolers have demonstrated that the threat of relatively severe punishment for committing a transgression has little impact on diminishing the attractiveness of the transgression. On the other hand, the threat of mild punishment—of a degree just powerful enough to get the child to cease the undesired activity temporarily— serves to induce the child to try to justify his or her restraint and, as a result, can produce a diminution in the attractiveness of the action (Aronson & Carlsmith,

> All punishment is mischief; all punishment itself is evil.
> —Jeremy Bentham, *Principles of Morals and Legislation*

■ If a parent wants to curb the aggression of his or her child, threats of severe punishment will have only a temporary effect.

1963; Freedman, 1965). These findings were confirmed by Dan Olweus over 25 years later (Olweus, 1991, 1994, 1995, 1996, 1997). Working directly with the Norwegian and Swedish school systems, Olweus was able to reduce the occurrence of bullying behavior among fourth- through seventh-graders by as much as 50 percent by training teachers and administrators to be vigilant to the problem and to make moderate and swift interventions. The intervention strategy was effective both immediately and over the long haul. This research indicates that children, who have not yet formed their values, are more apt to develop a distaste for aggression if the punishment for aggressive actions is swift and not severe enough to make it unnecessary for the children to justify their restraint.

But what about adults, especially those who already manifest a tendency to commit aggressive acts? Here a slightly different picture emerges. On a societal level, the criminal justice system of most cultures administers harsh punishments as a means of deterring violent crimes. Does the implicit threat of harsh punishments for crimes like murder, manslaughter, and rape diminish the occurrence of such crimes? Do people who are about to commit such crimes say to themselves, "I'd better think twice about this, because if I get caught, I'll be severely punished"? Here the scientific evidence is mixed. Under ideal conditions, laboratory experiments indicate that punishment can act as a deterrent (Bower & Hilgard, 1981). By "ideal conditions," we mean that the punishment must be both prompt and certain; that is, it must come close on the heels of the commission of the violent act, and the chances of escaping punishment must be virtually non-existent. Needless to say, these ideal conditions are almost never met in the real world, especially in a complex society with a high crime rate like our own. In most American cities, the probability of a person committing a violent crime and being apprehended, charged, tried, and convicted is not high. Moreover, given the clogged calendars that exist in our courts, as well as the necessary care and caution with which the criminal justice system must operate, promptness is rarely possible—punishment is typically delayed by months or even years. Consequently, in the real world of the criminal justice system, severe punishment is unlikely to have the kind of deterrent effect that it does in the laboratory.

Given these realities, you will not be surprised to learn that severe punishment does not seem to deter violent crimes. Countries that invoke the death penalty for murder do not have fewer murders per capita than those that do not invoke the death penalty. Similarly, within our own country, states that have abolished the death penalty have not experienced the increase in capital crimes

> Something of vengeance I had tasted for the first time; an aromatic wine it seemed, on swallowing, warm and racy; its after-flavour, metallic and corroding, gave me a sensation as if I had been poisoned.
> —Charlotte Brontë, *Jane Eyre*, 1847

that some experts predicted (Archer & Gartner, 1984; Nathanson, 1987). In the same vein, Ruth Peterson and William Bailey (1988) examined a period in our nation just after a national hiatus on the death penalty, resulting from a Supreme Court ruling that found it to constitute cruel and unusual punishment; when the Court reversed itself in 1976, there was no indication that the return to capital punishment produced a decrease in homicides. Some representative homicide data, comparing the United States with other countries, are shown in Figure 12.4.

Similarly, a recent study by the National Academy of Sciences (see Berkowitz, 1993) demonstrates that consistency and certainty of punishment are far more effective deterrents of violent behavior than severe punishment and do have a deterrent effect on violent crime. In the realm of domestic violence, or, more specifically, wife-battering, mild punishment, consistently meted out, has been effective, at least in the short term. Domestic violence has been a thorny problem for the police, who traditionally have been reluctant to intervene in family disputes. In the past, when the police have intervened in a wife-battering situation, they would almost never arrest the husband but instead would either give him on-the-spot counseling or ask him to leave the scene for a few hours until he cooled off.

How effective is this kind of intervention? Would arresting the violent husband be more effective? To find out, the Minneapolis Police Department conducted a simple but powerful field experiment (Sherman & Berk, 1984; Cohen, 1987). In this experiment, police officers were randomly assigned to one of three conditions: In the first condition, they performed brief, on-the-spot counseling; in the second condition, they asked the perpetrator to leave the scene for eight hours; and in the third condition, they placed the perpetrator under arrest. Police reports were then carefully monitored over the next six months. The results indicated that, during those months, 19 percent of the perpetrators given counseling and 24 percent of those asked to leave the premises repeated their aggressive actions, whereas only 10 percent of those placed under arrest (and made to spend a

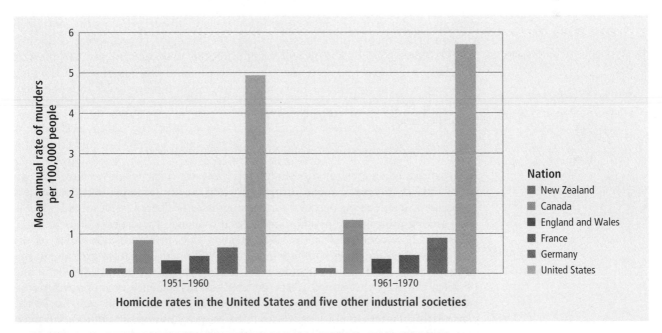

FIGURE 12.4   America leads the way. The homicide rate in the United States far outstrips that of other industrial countries. (Adapted from Archer & Gartner, 1984)

night or two in jail) repeated their actions. These data show that when law en-forcement officers demonstrate they are taking the offense seriously by hauling the perpetrator off to jail, domestic violence is diminished. The findings led the Minneapolis Police Department to revamp its policies regarding the arrest of per-petrators of domestic violence and have attracted national attention. Unfortunately, subsequent research reported by Langer (1986) and Sherman (1992) suggests that the deterrent effects of this procedure tend to diminish over time. More detailed research is needed to determine the ideal conditions for long-term results (Berk, Fenstermaker, & Newton, 1988; Berk, Campbell, & Clark, 1992).

Catharsis and Aggression

It is generally believed that one way for an individual to reduce his or her feelings of aggression is to do something aggressive. "Get it out of your system" has been a common piece of advice for a great many years. So if you are feeling angry (the belief goes), don't try to ignore it, but instead yell, scream, curse, throw some crockery at the wall—and then you'll be rid of it and it won't fester and grow into something truly uncontrollable. This common belief is based on an oversimplifi-cation of the psychoanalytic notion of **catharsis** (see Freud, 1933; Dollard, 1939) that has filtered down to the popular culture. As we mentioned earlier in this chapter, Freud held a "hydraulic" idea of aggressive impulses; he believed that unless people were allowed to express their aggression in relatively harmless ways, the aggressive energy would be dammed up, pressure would build, and the energy would seek an outlet, either exploding into acts of extreme violence or manifesting itself as symptoms of mental illness. There is some evidence suggest-ing that stifled feelings can produce illness (Pennebaker, 1990; Pennebaker & Francis, 1996).

However, this does not necessarily mean that venting those feelings indis-criminately is either healthy or useful. Freud was a brilliant and complex thinker who invariably stopped short of giving simplistic advice. Alas, as the simplified version of his theory of catharsis got into the hands of famed advice columnist Ann Landers (1969), she translated it into the pronouncement: "Youngsters should be taught to vent their anger." The idea behind this advice is that blowing off steam will not only make angry people feel better but also serve to make them less likely to engage in subsequent acts of destructive violence. Does this square with the data?

The Effects of Aggressive Acts on Subsequent Aggression

Many of us, when frustrated or angry, have felt less tense when we have "blown off steam" by yelling, cursing, or perhaps even hitting someone. But does an act of aggression reduce the need for further aggression? There is widespread belief—even among professional psychologists—that this might be the case. For example, William Menninger (1948), the distinguished therapist and co-founder of the justly famous Menninger Clinic, tells us that "competitive games provide an un-usually satisfactory outlet for the instinctive aggressive drive" (p. 344). It would be great if it were that simple. Alas, we can find no evidence to support this con-tention (Johnson, 1970; Patterson, 1974). Actually, the reverse seems to be the case. Arthur Patterson (1974) measured the hostility of high school football play-ers, rating them both one week before and one week after the football season. If it were true that the intense competitiveness and aggressive behavior that are part

Catharsis
the notion that "blowing off steam"—by performing an aggressive act, watching others engage in aggressive behaviors, or engaging in a fantasy of aggression—relieves built-up aggressive energies and hence reduces the likelihood of further aggressive behavior

■ Fans watching aggressive sports do not become less aggressive.

of playing football serve to reduce the tension caused by pent-up aggression, then the players would be expected to exhibit a decline in hostility over the course of the season. Instead, the results showed a significant increase in feelings of hostility. This is not to say that people do not get pleasure out of these games; they do. But engaging in these games does not decrease participants' aggressive feelings—if anything, it increases them.

Even though engaging in competitive and aggressive games does not result in less aggression, perhaps watching these kinds of games does. Gordon Russell (1983), a Canadian sports psychologist, tested this proposition by measuring the hostility of spectators at an especially violent hockey game. As the game progressed, the spectators became increasingly belligerent; toward the end of the final period, their level of hostility was enormous and did not return to the pregame level until several hours after the game was over. Similar results have been found among spectators at football games and wrestling matches (Arms, Russell, & Sandilands, 1979; Goldstein & Arms, 1971; Branscombe & Wann, 1992). Thus, as with participating in an aggressive sport, watching one serves to increase aggressive behavior.

What about acts of direct aggression against the source of your anger? Do such actions reduce the need for further aggression? The overwhelming majority of experiments on the topic have failed to find such effects (Geen & Quanty, 1977; Geen, 1998). In fact, by far the most common finding resembles the research on watching violence, as cited above—namely, when people commit acts of aggression, such acts increase the tendency toward future aggression. For example, in an experiment by Russell Geen and his associates (1975), each of the subjects in their experiment (male college students) was paired with another student, who was actually a confederate of the experimenters. First, the subject was angered by the confederate; during this phase, which involved the exchanging of opinions on various issues, the subject was given electric shocks when his partner disagreed with his opinion. Next, during a bogus study of "the effects of punishment on learning," the subject acted as a teacher, while the confederate served as learner. On the first learning task, some of the subjects were required to deliver electric shocks to the confederate each time he made a mistake; other subjects merely recorded his errors. On the next task, all the subjects were given the opportunity to deliver shocks. If a cathartic effect were operating, we would expect the subjects who had previously given shocks to the confederate to administer fewer and less intense shocks the second time. This didn't happen; in fact, the subjects who had previously delivered shocks to the confederate expressed even greater aggression when given the subsequent opportunity to attack him. This phenomenon is not limited to the laboratory; the same tendency has also been systematically observed in naturally occurring events in the real world, where verbal acts of aggression served to facilitate further attacks. In one such "natural experiment," several technicians who had recently been laid off were given a chance to verbalize their hostility against their ex-bosses; later, when asked to describe that person, these technicians were much more punitive in their descriptions than those technicians who had not previously voiced their feelings (Ebbesen, Duncan, & Konecni, 1975). In summary, the weight of the evidence does not support the catharsis hypothesis.

Blaming the Victim of Our Aggression

On the surface, catharsis appears to be a reasonable idea, in a limited way. That is, when somebody angers us, venting our hostility against that person does indeed seem to relieve tension and make us feel better. But "feeling better" should not be confused with a reduction in our hostility. With human beings, aggression is dependent not merely on tensions—what a person feels—but also on what a person thinks. Put yourself in the place of a subject in the previous experiments: After once administering shocks to another person or expressing hostility against your ex-boss, it becomes easier to do so a second time. Aggressing the first time can reduce your inhibitions against committing other such actions; in a sense, the aggression is legitimized, making it easier to carry out such assaults. Further, and more importantly, the main thrust of the research on this issue indicates that committing an overt act of aggression against a person changes one's feelings about that person, increasing one's negative feelings toward the target and therefore increasing the probability of future aggression against that person.

Does this material begin to sound familiar? It should. As we have seen in Chapter 6, when one person does harm to another person, it sets in motion cognitive processes aimed at justifying the act of cruelty. Specifically, when you hurt another person, you experience cognitive dissonance. The cognition "I have hurt Charlie" is dissonant with the cognition "I am a decent, reasonable person." A good way for you to reduce dissonance is somehow to convince yourself that hurting Charlie was not an indecent, unreasonable, bad thing to do. You can accomplish this by blinding yourself to Charlie's virtues and emphasizing his faults, by convincing yourself that Charlie is a terrible human being who deserved to be hurt. This would especially hold if the target was an innocent victim of your aggression. Thus, as discussed in Chapter 6, in experiments by David Glass (1964) and by Keith Davis and Edward E. Jones (1960) the subjects inflicted either psychological or physical harm on an innocent person who had done them no prior harm. The subjects then proceeded to derogate their victims, convincing themselves they were not nice people and therefore deserved what they got. This reduces dissonance, all right—and it also sets the stage for further aggression, for once a person has succeeded in derogating someone, it makes it easier for him or her to do further harm to the victim in the future.

> In war, the state is sanctioning murder. Even when the war is over, this moral corruption is bound to linger for many years.
>
> —Erasmus, 1514

What happens if the victim isn't totally innocent? That is, imagine the victim has done something that hurts or disturbs you and is therefore deserving of your retaliation. Here the situation becomes more complex and more interesting. One of several experiments to test this idea was performed several years ago by Michael Kahn (1966). In Kahn's experiment, a young man posing as a medical technician, taking some physiological measurements from college students, made derogatory remarks about the students. In one experimental condition, the subjects were allowed to vent their hostility by expressing their feelings about the technician to his employer—an action that looked as though it would get the technician into serious trouble, perhaps even cost him his job. In another condition, the subjects were not given the opportunity to express any aggression against the person who had aroused their anger. Those who were allowed to express their aggression subsequently felt greater dislike and hostility for the technician than those who were inhibited from expressing their aggression did. In other words, expressing aggression did not inhibit the tendency to aggress; rather, it tended to increase it—even when the target was not simply an innocent victim.

These results suggest that when people are made angry, they frequently engage in overkill. In this case, costing the technician his job is much more devastating than the minor insult delivered by the technician. The overkill produces dissonance in much the same way hurting an innocent person produces dissonance. That is, if there is a major discrepancy between what the person did to you and the force of your retaliation, you must justify that discrepancy by derogating the object of your wrath.

If our reasoning is correct, it might help to explain why it is that when two nations are at war, a relatively small percentage of the members of the victorious nation feel much sympathy for the innocent victims of the nation's actions. For example, near the end of World War II, American planes dropped atom bombs on Hiroshima and Nagasaki. More than 100,000 civilians—including a great many children—were killed, and countless thousands suffered severe injuries. Shortly thereafter, a poll taken of the American people indicated that less than 5 percent

■ During World War II, we derogated the Japanese by depicting them as less than human. This helped to justify our own destructiveness—as in the bombing of Nagasaki.

felt we should not have used those weapons, whereas 23 percent felt we should have used many more of them before giving Japan the opportunity to surrender. Why would so many Americans favor the wanton death and destruction of innocent victims? Our guess is that, in the course of the war, a sizable proportion of Americans gradually adopted increasingly derogatory attitudes toward the Japanese that made it increasingly easy to accept the fact that we were causing them a great deal of misery. The more misery we inflicted on them, the more these Americans derogated them—leading to an endless spiral of aggression and the justification of aggression, even to the point of favoring a delay in the ending of the war so that still more destruction might be inflicted.

Does this sound like ancient history? We hasten to remind you that, in this decade, our nation won a swift and stunning victory over Iraq in a lopsided war in which American casualties were few but tens of thousands of Iraqis—including numerous civilians—lost their lives. The vast majority of U.S. citizens were elated by the outcome of the war; there were celebrations, parades, and a huge—if temporary—increase in the popularity of then President George Bush. Please note that we are not raising the question of whether or not the war was just or necessary. The only question we are raising is this: What percentage of the American population do you suppose paused for a few moments to feel sadness or regret about the Iraqi civilians who were killed in that war? The polls indicate little sympathy for the innocent victims. How come? Are we a particularly callous, unsympathetic nation? We don't believe so. You now have the tools to begin to understand the mechanics of how that phenomenon comes about.

Interestingly, when a nation is at war the impact of that situation extends even beyond feelings of hostility toward the enemy. Specifically, being at war makes the population—even the noncombatants—more prone to commit aggressive actions against one another. Dane Archer and Rosemary Gartner (1976, 1984) compared the crime rates for 110 countries since 1900 (see Figure 12.5). They found that, compared with similar nations that remained at peace, countries that fought wars exhibited substantial postwar increases in their homicide rates. This should not be surprising; it is consistent with everything we have been saying about the social causes of aggression. In a sense, when a nation is at war it's like one big, violent TV drama. Thus, just as with overexposure to TV vio-

> **T**o jaw-jaw is better than to war-war.
> —Winston Churchill, 1954

■ **FIGURE 12.5 The effects of war on combatants versus noncombatants.** Immediately after a war, combatant countries are more likely to show an increase in violent crimes than countries not involved in a war. How would you explain this? (Adapted from Archer & Gartner, 1976)

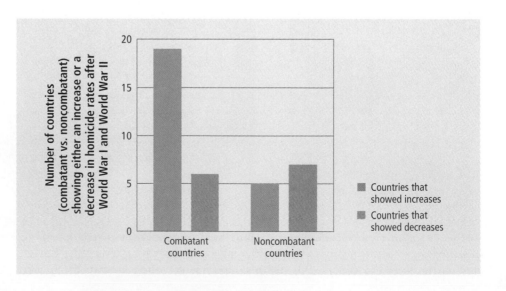

lence, the fact that a nation is at war (a) weakens the population's inhibitions against aggression, (b) leads to imitation of aggression, (c) makes aggressive responses more available, and (d) numbs our senses to the horror of cruelty and destruction, making us less sympathetic toward the victims. In addition, being at war serves to legitimize to the population the use of violent solutions to address difficult problems.

What Are We Supposed to Do with Our Anger?

If violence leads to self-justification, which in turn breeds more violence, then if we are feeling angry at someone, what are we to do with our angry feelings—stifle them? Surely, Sigmund Freud and Ann Landers were not totally wrong when they indicated that stifled anger might be harmful to the individual. Indeed, as mentioned earlier, recent research suggests that stifling powerful emotions can lead to physical illness (Pennebaker, 1990). But if it is harmful to keep our feelings bottled up and harmful to express them, what are we supposed to do with them? This dilemma isn't as difficult as it might seem.

Venting versus Self-Awareness

We would suggest that there is an important difference between being angry and expressing that anger in a violent and destructive manner. To experience anger in appropriate circumstances is normal and usually harmless. It is certainly possible to express that anger in a nonviolent manner—for example, by making a clear and simple statement indicating that you are feeling angry and why. Indeed, such a statement in itself is a vehicle for self-assertion and probably serves to relieve tension and to make the angered person feel better. At the same time, because no actual harm befalls the target of your anger, such a response does not set in motion the cognitive processes that would lead you to justify your behavior by ridiculing or derogating the target person. Moreover, when such feelings are expressed among friends or acquaintances in a clear, open, non-punitive manner, greater mutual understanding and a strengthening of the friendship can result. It almost seems too simple. Yet we have found such behavior to be a reasonable option that will have more beneficial effects than shouting, name-calling, and throwing crockery, on the one hand, or suffering in silence as you grin and bear it, on the other (Aronson, 1995).

> I was angry with my friend; I told my wrath, my wrath did end.
> —William Blake
> (1757–1827)

While it is probably best to reveal your anger to the friend who caused it, you may also derive some benefit from sharing your anger with a third party. Although he did not work specifically with anger, the research of James Pennebaker (1990) indicates that when we are experiencing emotional stress, it is helpful to reveal that emotion to another person. In Pennebaker's experiments with people undergoing a wide range of traumatic events, those who were induced to reveal the details of the event, as well as their feelings at the time they were experiencing the event, felt healthier and suffered fewer physical illnesses six months later than either people who were allowed to suffer in silence or those who were induced to talk about the details of the events but not the underlying feelings.

Pennebaker suggests that the beneficial effects of "opening up" are due not simply to the venting of feeling, but primarily to the insights and self-awareness that usually accompany such self-disclosure. Some independent corroboration of this suggestion comes from a rather different experiment by Leonard Berkowitz and Bartholmeu Troccoli (1990). In this experiment, young women listened to another woman talk about herself as part of a job interview. Half of the listeners did so while extending their nondominant arm, unsupported (causing discomfort and mild pain), while the others listened with their arms resting comfortably on the table. In each condition, half of the subjects were asked to rate their feelings while they were listening to the job interview; according to the researchers, this procedure provided those subjects with a vehicle for understanding their discomfort and a way to gain insight into it. The results were striking: Those subjects who experienced pain and discomfort during the interview, but were not given the opportunity to process it, experienced the most negative feelings toward the interviewee—and the more unpleasant the experience was for them, the more negative they felt toward the interviewee. On the other hand, those subjects who were given the opportunity to process their pain were able to avoid being unfairly harsh to the interviewee.

Defusing Anger through Apology

An effective way to reduce aggression in another person is to take some action aimed at diminishing the anger and annoyance that caused it. For example, earlier in this chapter we learned that when people had been frustrated by someone and then learned that he or she simply couldn't do any better, that frustration was less likely to bubble over into anger or aggression. This suggests that one way to reduce aggression is for the individual who caused the frustration to take responsibility for the action, apologize for it, and indicate that it is unlikely to happen again. Suppose you are scheduled to be at your friend's house at 7:30 P.M. in order to drive her to a concert scheduled to start at 8:00. The concert is an exciting one for her—it involves one of her favorite soloists—and she has been looking forward to it for several weeks. You rush out of your house with just barely enough time to get there, but after driving for a few minutes, you discover that you have a flat tire. By the time you change the tire and get to her house, you are already twenty minutes late for the concert. Imagine her response if you (a) casually walk in, grin at her, and say, "Oh well, it probably wouldn't have been an interesting concert anyway. Lighten up; it's not such a big deal. Where's your sense of humor?" or (b) run in with a sad and anguished look on your face, show her your greasy and dirty hands, tell her you left your house in time to make it but unaccountably got this flat, apologize sincerely and profusely, and vow to find a way to make it up to her.

Our guess is that your friend would be prone toward aggression in the first instance but not in the second. This guess is supported by the results of several experiments (Baron, 1988, 1990; Ohbuchi & Sato, 1994; Weiner, Amirkhan, Folkes, & Verette, 1987). Typical of these experiments is one by Ohbuchi, Kameda, and Agarie (1989), in which college students performed poorly on a complex task because of errors made by the experimenter's assistant while presenting the materials. In three conditions, the assistant either apologized publicly, apologized privately, or did not apologize at all. In a fourth condition, the senior experimenter removed the harm by indicating that he surmised there was an administrative blunder and therefore did not hold the students responsible for their poor performance. The results were clear: The students liked the assistant better and showed far less tendency to aggress against him if he apologized than if he didn't apologize, even if the harm was subsequently removed by the experimenter. Moreover, whether the apology was public or private made little difference; any apology—sincerely given, and in which the perpetrator took full responsibility—proved to be an effective way to reduce aggression.

With this in mind, one of the authors of this book (Elliot Aronson) has occasionally speculated about the great advantages that might be gained by equipping automobiles with "apology" signals. Picture the scene: You stop at a stop sign and then proceed, but too late you realize you have taken the right of way that wasn't really yours. What happens? In most urban centers, the offended driver will honk his or her horn angrily at you, or open the window and give you that near-universal symbol of anger and contempt that consists of the middle finger pointed skyward. Because nobody likes to be the recipient of such abuse, you might be tempted to honk back—and the escalating anger and aggression could be unpleasant. Such escalation might be avoided, though, if in addition to the horn (which throughout the world is most often used as an instrument of aggression), every car were equipped with an apology signal—perhaps at the push of a button, a little flag could pop up, saying, "Whoops! Sorry!" In the foregoing scenario, had you pushed such a button as soon as you became aware of your transgression, doing so might well have defused the cycle of anger and retaliation that is all too frequently a part of the driving experience.

The Modeling of Nonaggressive Behavior

We have seen that children will be more aggressive (toward dolls as well as other children) if they witness examples of aggressive behavior in similar situations. What if we were to turn that inside out and expose children to nonaggressive models—to people who, when provoked, expressed themselves in a restrained, rational, pleasant manner? This has been tested in several experiments (Baron, 1972; Donnerstein & Donnerstein, 1976; Vidyasagar & Mishra, 1993) and found to work. In those experiments, children were first allowed to witness the behavior of youngsters who behaved nonaggressively when provoked; when the children were subsequently placed in a situation in which they themselves were provoked, they showed a much lower frequency of aggressive responses than children who were not exposed to the nonaggressive models.

> "Man must evolve for all human conflict a method which rejects revenge, aggression and retaliation.
> —Martin Luther King, Jr.,
> *Nobel Prize Acceptance Speech*,
> December 11, 1964

Training in Communication and Problem-Solving Skills

It is impossible to go through life—or, in some circumstances, to get through the day—without experiencing frustration, annoyance, anger, or conflict. As we have

■ Martin Luther King, Jr., was effective in reducing and preventing violence by using and modeling nonviolence. Being nonviolent in the face of violence is difficult but effective.

indicated earlier, there is nothing wrong with anger—it is part of being human. What causes the problem is the expression of anger in violent ways. Yet we are not born with the knowledge of how to express anger or annoyance in constructive, nonviolent, nondisruptive ways. Indeed, as we have seen, it seems almost natural to lash out when we are angry. As Hans Toch (1980) has indicated, in most societies it is precisely the people who lack proper social skills who are most prone to violent solutions to interpersonal problems. Thus, one way to reduce violence is to teach people how to communicate anger or criticism in constructive ways, how to negotiate and compromise when conflicts arise, how to be more sensitive to the needs and desires of others, and so on. There is some evidence that such formal training can be an effective means of reducing aggression (see Aronson, 1995; Studer, 1996). For example, in an experiment by Joel Davitz (1952), children were allowed to play in groups of four. Some of these groups were taught constructive ways to relate to one another and were rewarded for such behavior; others were not so instructed but were rewarded for aggressive or competitive behavior. Next, the youngsters were deliberately frustrated. This was accomplished by building up the expectation that they would be shown a series of entertaining movies and be allowed to have fun. The experimenter began to show a movie and to hand out candy bars, but then he abruptly terminated the movie at the point of highest interest and took the candy bars away. Now the children were allowed to play freely. As you have learned, this was a setup for the occurrence of aggressive behavior. But those children who had been trained for constructive behavior displayed far more constructive activity and far less aggressive behavior than those in the other group. A great many elementary and secondary schools are now specifically training students to employ these non-aggressive strategies for resolving conflict (Eargle, Guerra, & Tolan, 1994; Ester, 1995).

Building Empathy

Let's look at horn-blowing again. Picture the following scene: A long line of cars is stopped at a traffic light at a busy intersection; the light turns green; the lead car hesitates for ten seconds. What happens? Almost inevitably, there will be an eruption of horn-honking. We're talking not about one little jab of the horn (which might be a way of informing the lead car that the light has changed) but about loud and persistent honking. In a controlled experiment, Robert Baron (1976) found that when the lead car failed to move after the light turned green, almost 90 percent of the drivers of the second car honked their horn in a relentless, aggressive manner. As part of the same experiment, a pedestrian crossed the street between the first and the second car while the light was still red and was out of the intersection by the time the light turned green. As you might imagine, this did not have an effect on the behavior of the drivers of the next car in line—almost 90 percent honked their horn when the light turned green. But in another condition, the pedestrian was on crutches. Even though he was on crutches, he was able to hobble across the street before the light turned green. Interestingly, however, in this condition only 57 percent of the drivers honked their horn. How come? Apparently, seeing a person on crutches evoked feelings of **empathy**—the ability to put oneself in the shoes of another person and vicariously experience some of the same feelings that person is experiencing. In this instance, once evoked, the feeling of empathy infused the consciousness of the potential horn-honkers and decreased their urge to be aggressive. The results of this experiment are shown in Figure 12.6.

Empathy
the ability to put oneself in the shoes of another person—to experience events and emotions (e.g., joy and sadness) the way that person experiences them

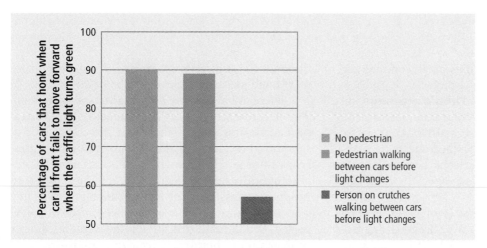

■ **FIGURE 12.6   The effect of empathy on aggression.**   When we are feeling empathy, in this case brought on by seeing a person on crutches, we are less likely to behave aggressively. (Adapted from Baron, 1976)

Empathy is an important human phenomenon. As Seymour and Norma Feshbach (1969, 1971, 1978) have observed, most people find it difficult to inflict pain on another human being unless they can find some way of dehumanizing their victim. Thus, when our nation was fighting wars against Asians (Japanese in the 1940s, Koreans in the 1950s, Vietnamese in the 1960s), our military personnel frequently referred to them as "gooks." We see this as a dehumanizing rationalization for acts of cruelty; it's easier to commit violent acts against a gook than against a fellow human being. But as you know, this kind of rationalization not only makes it possible for us to aggress against another person but also guarantees we will continue to aggress against him or her. Once we succeed in convincing ourselves that our enemy is not really a human being at all but just a gook, it lowers our inhibitions for committing all kinds of atrocities. The photos on page 485 illustrate this point.

An understanding of the process of dehumanization is the first step toward reversing it. Specifically, if it is true that most individuals must dehumanize their victims in order to commit an extreme act of aggression, then by building empathy among people, aggressive acts will become more difficult to commit. The research data lend strong support to this contention. In their ground-breaking research, Feshbach and Feshbach (1969) found a negative correlation between empathy and aggression in children: The more empathy a child has, the less he or she resorts to aggressive actions. More recently, Deborah Richardson and her colleagues (1994) have demonstrated a direct causal link between empathy and aggression, showing that specifically training students to take the perspective of the other person directly inhibited their aggressive behavior toward that person. In a similar vein, Ken-ichi Obuchi and his colleagues (Obuchi, 1988; Obuchi, Ohno, & Mukai, 1993) worked with Japanese students. In Obuchi's study, students were instructed to deliver electric shocks to another student as part of a learning experiment. In one condition, the victims first disclosed something personal about themselves, in the other condition, they were not afforded this opportunity. Subjects administered less severe shocks when the victim disclosed information about herself.

Summary

We define an **aggressive action** as an intentional act aimed at doing harm or causing physical or psychological pain to another person. **Hostile aggression** involves having the goal of inflicting pain; **instrumental aggression** involves inflicting pain on the way to some other goal. Aggression has become an increasingly serious concern to Americans because of the rapid increase in violent crimes, especially in major urban centers.

Over the centuries, there has been a great deal of disagreement among scholars over whether aggressiveness is primarily instinctive or learned. Sigmund Freud theorized that human beings are born with an instinct toward life, called **Eros,** and a death instinct, **Thanatos.** The death instinct, when turned inward, manifests itself as suicide and, when turned outward, as hostility, destructiveness, and murder. Freud's **hydraulic theory** states that aggressive energy must be released to avoid buildup resulting in an explosion.

Because aggressiveness has had survival value, most contemporary social psychologists accept the proposition that it is part of our evolutionary heritage. At the same time, we know that human beings have developed exquisite mechanisms for controlling their aggressive impulses and that human behavior is flexible and adaptable to changes in the environment. Thus, whether or not aggression is actually expressed depends on a complex interplay between our biological propensities, our innate and learned inhibitory responses, and the precise nature of the social situation.

There are many situational causes of aggression, ranging from the neurological and chemical to the social. The area in the core of the brain called the **amygdala** is thought to control aggression. It is reasonably clear that the hormone **testosterone** is correlated with aggressive behavior—for example, prisoners convicted of violent crimes tend to have higher levels of testosterone than those convicted of nonviolent crimes. This is consistent with the more general finding that men are more aggressive than women. At least one other chemical, alcohol, is associated with increases in aggression, due to the fact that alcohol acts as a general disinhibitor, lowering a person's inhibitions against violent behavior, as well as a variety of other behaviors frowned on by society. It has also been shown that pain and other physical discomforts (e.g., the proverbial "long, hot summer") will increase aggressive behavior.

There are also many social causes of aggression. Among these, frustration is prominent. The **frustration-aggression theory** states that the experience of frustration can increase the probability of an aggressive response. However, frustration alone does not automatically lead to aggression; it is more likely to produce aggression if one is thwarted on the way to a goal in a manner that is either illegitimate or unexpected. In addition, frustration is the result not simply of deprivation, but of **relative deprivation**—the feeling that comes from knowing that you have less than what you deserve, less than what you have been led to expect, or less than what people similar to you have.

Aggression can also be produced by social provocation or the mere presence of an **aggressive stimulus,** or an object associated with aggressive responses, such as a gun. **Social learning theory** states that aggression can also be produced through the imitation of aggressive models, either in face-to-face situations or by viewing violence in films or on TV. The possible effects of viewing violence in the media are of particular interest to social psychologists in our country because of the pervasiveness of violent programming. Violence in the media has been shown not only to lead to greater aggressiveness in the viewer but also to create a numbing effect, making us more accepting of violence in society. The viewing of pornographic material appears to be relatively harmless; however, if the pornographic material is of a violent nature, it promotes greater acceptance of sexual violence toward women and is almost certainly a factor associated with actual aggressive behavior toward women.

Aggression can be reduced in a number of ways. These include discussing the reasons for anger and hostility, modeling non-aggressive behavior, training people in the use of nonviolent solutions to conflict and in communication and negotiation skills, and building people's **empathy** toward others. Building empathy is particularly useful as a means of thwarting the human tendency to dehumanize one's victim.

Punishing aggressive behavior in order to reduce it is tricky; punishment can be effective if it is not too severe and if it follows closely on the heels of the aggressive act. But severe or delayed punishment is not an effective way to reduce aggression. Similarly, there is no evidence to support the notion of **catharsis**—the idea that committing an aggressive action or watching others behave aggressively is a good way to get the impulse toward aggression out of one's system. On the contrary, careful research has shown that committing an act of aggression can trigger the tendency to justify that action and might thus eventually produce an increase in aggressive behavior.

If You Are Interested

Baron, R. A. & Richardson, D. R. (1994). *Human aggression*. New York: Plenum. A penetrating analysis of the social psychology of aggression.

Berkowitz, L. (1993). *Aggression: Its causes, consequences, and control.* New York: McGraw-Hill. One of the greatest living experts on aggression summarizes his thinking in this up-to-date revision of his classic work.

Eron, L. D., Gentry, J. H., & Schlegel, P. (Eds.) (1994). *Reason to hope: A psychosocial perspective on violence and youth.* Washington DC: American Psychological Association.

Geen, R. Aggression. (1998). In D. Gilbert, S. Fiske, & G. Lindzey (Eds.), *The handbook of social psychology* (4th. ed., Vol. 1). New York: McGraw-Hill.

Tavris, C. (1989). *Anger: The misunderstood emotion.* New York: Touchstone/Simon & Schuster. An interesting and well-written analysis of anger.

CHAPTER 13

PREJUDICE: CAUSES AND CURES

In the 1930s when Thurgood Marshall was a young lawyer working for the NAACP, he was sent to a small town in the South to defend a black man who was accused of a serious crime. When he arrived, he was shocked and dismayed to learn that the defendant was already dead—lynched by an angry white mob. With a heavy heart, Mr. Marshall returned to the railroad station to wait for a train back to New York. Not having eaten for several hours, he realized that he was very hungry; luckily, there was a small food stand on the platform. As he walked toward the stand, he debated with himself whether to go right up to the front and order a sandwich (as was his legal right) or to go around to the back of the stand (as was the common practice for African Americans in the South at that time). But, before he reached the stand, he was approached by a large, bulky man who looked at him suspiciously. Mr. Marshall took him to be a lawman of some sort because he walked with an air of authority and had a bulge in his pants pocket that could only have been made by a handgun.

> "Hey, boy," the man shouted at Marshall, "What are you doing here?" "I'm just waiting for a train," Marshall replied. The man scowled, took a few steps closer, glared at him menacingly, and said, "I didn't hear you. What did you say, boy?"

495

■ Thurgood Marshall, NAACP chief counsel, in front of the Supreme Court in 1954.

Marshall realized that his initial reply had not been sufficiently obsequious. "I beg your pardon, sir, but I'm waiting for a train." There was a long silence, during which the man slowly looked Marshall up and down, and then said, "And you'd better catch that train, boy—and soon, because in this town, the sun has never set on a live nigger."

As Marshall later recalled, at that point his internal debate about *how* to get the sandwich proved academic. He decided not to get a sandwich at all but to catch the very next train out—no matter where it was headed. Besides, somehow he didn't feel hungry anymore.

Thurgood Marshall went on to become chief counsel for the NAACP; in 1954 he argued the Supreme Court case of *Brown v. Board of Education* that put an end to legalized racial segregation in public schools. Subsequently, Marshall was appointed to the Supreme Court where he served with distinction until his retirement in 1991. We are not sure what became of the man with the bulge in his pocket.

Of all the social behaviors we discuss in this book, prejudice is perhaps the most widespread and certainly among the most dangerous. Prejudice touches nearly everyone's life. We are all victims or potential victims of stereotyping and discrimination, for no other reason than our membership in an identifiable group—whether it be ethnic, religious, gender, national origin, sexual preference, obesity, disability, or what have you.

A great many years have passed since the incident involving Justice Marshall. No one can deny that the civil rights movement has made enormous progress during his lifetime—and ours. But, even though most manifestations of prejudice tend to be both less frequent and less flagrant than they used to be, prejudice continues to exact a heavy toll on its victims. There are still hate crimes, church burnings, and countless miscellaneous acts of prejudice-induced violence—as well as "lesser" outrages—like the futility of trying to get a cab to stop for you late at night in an American metropolis if you happen to be a black man (Fountain, 1997).

Moreover, on a wide variety of important social issues, there is a huge racial divide in this country in terms of attitude and experience. While sophisticated observers have long been aware of this divide, it was brought home with stunning force in the mid-1990s during the trial of O. J. Simpson for the murders of Nicole Brown Simpson and Ronald Goldman. The trial was powerful, dramatic, and, alas, entertaining—capturing the rapt attention of millions of Americans. From the outset, it seemed as if white Americans and black Americans were watching two different trials. The overwhelming majority of whites firmly believed that Simpson was guilty of murder; the overwhelming majority of blacks believed that the evidence was unconvincing, at best.

Social critics will be pondering this particular example of the "racial divide" for many years to come. Among other things, they will try to decide whether this huge difference was due to differences among the racial groups in their respective experiences with the criminal justice system, or differences in the degree to which they found the defendant to be attractive and sympathetic (Gates, 1995; Toobin, 1995). In order to understand this phenomenon and others like it, we must take a long look at prejudice as a social psychological phenomenon.

*P*rejudice: The Ubiquitous Social Phenomenon

The above paragraphs contain the unintended implication that only minority groups are the targets of prejudice at the hands of the dominant majority. Needless to say, this aspect of prejudice is extremely powerful and poignant. But the truth is that prejudice is ubiquitous; in one form or another, it affects all of us. For one thing, prejudice is a two-way street; it frequently flows from the minority group to the majority group as well as from the majority to the minority. In addition, any group can be a target of prejudice for someone. Let us take one of the most superordinate groups to which you belong—your nationality. As you well know, Americans are not universally loved, respected, and admired; at one time or another, we Americans have been the target of prejudice in just about every corner of the world. To take some recent examples, in the 1960s and 1970s, North Vietnamese Communists referred to Americans as the "running dogs of capitalist imperialism." In the 1980s, the Iranian regime under the Ayatollah Khomeini depicted America as a ruthless, power-hungry, amoral nation—

referring to us as "the great Satan." In many parts of our own hemisphere, many of our neighbors to the south look upon Americans (or, strictly speaking, North Americans) as over-fed economic and military bullies.

On a more subtle level, even our political allies see us as stereotypically American. For example, in research on stereotyping it turns out that British citizens tend to label Americans as intrusive, forward, and pushy (Campbell, 1967). Needless to say, stereotyping cuts both ways: Americans tend to label the British as cold, unemotional, and detached—a stereotype, incidentally, that was thoroughly belied by the voluminous outpouring of public grief following the death of Princess Diana (Lane, 1997).

Your nationality is only one of a number of aspects of your identity that can cause you to be labeled and discriminated against. Racial and ethnic identity is a major focal point for prejudiced attitudes. As you know, all Americans of mixed heritage and nationality (e.g., African Americans, Asian Americans, Hispanic Americans, or Native Americans) are targets of prejudice. So are some groups of Anglo or white Americans: Note the long-standing popularity of Polish jokes, or the negative stereotypes used throughout this century to describe Italian Americans and Irish Americans. Other aspects of your identity also leave you vulnerable to prejudice—for example, your gender, your sexual preference, and your religion. Your appearance or physical state can arouse prejudice as well; obesity, disabilities, and diseases like AIDS, for instance, cause people to be treated unfairly by others. In recent years, a new type of joke has been sweeping the country—"dumb blond" jokes. The old stereotype that blondes are ditzy bimbos has been given a new life. Finally, even your profession or hobbies can lead to your being stereotyped. We all know the "dumb jock" and the "computer nerd" stereotypes. Some people have negative attitudes about blue-collar workers; others, about Fortune 500 CEOs. The point is that none of us emerges completely unscathed from the effects of prejudice; it is a problem of and for all humankind.

In addition to being widespread, prejudice is dangerous. Simple dislike of a group can be relentless and can lead to extreme hatred, to thinking of its members as less than human, and to torture, murder, and even genocide. But even when murder or genocide is not the culmination of prejudiced beliefs, the targets of prejudice will suffer in less dramatic ways. One nearly inevitable consequence of being the target of relentless prejudice is a diminution of one's self-esteem. As we discussed in Chapter 6, self-esteem is a vital aspect of a person's life. Who we think we are is a key determinant of how we behave and who we become. A person with low self-esteem will, by definition, conclude that he or she is unworthy of a good education, a decent job, an exciting romantic partner, and so on. Thus, a person with low self-esteem is more likely to be unhappy and unsuccessful than a person with high self-esteem. In a democracy, such a person is also less likely to take advantage of available opportunities.

For those who are the targets of relentless prejudice, the seeds of low self-esteem are sown early in life. In a classic experiment conducted in the late 1940s, social psychologists Kenneth Clark and Mamie Clark (1947) demonstrated that African American children—some of them only 3 years old—were already convinced that it was not particularly desirable to be black. In this experiment, the children were offered a choice between playing with a white or a black doll. The great majority of them rejected the black doll, feeling that the white doll was prettier and generally superior.

In his argument before the Supreme Court in 1954, Thurgood Marshall cited this experiment as evidence that, psychologically, segregation did irreparable

> A little black girl yearns for the blue eyes of a little white girl, and the horror at the heart of her yearning is exceeded only by the evil of fulfillment.
>
> —Toni Morrison, *The Bluest Eye*, 1970

THE BOSTON GLOBE   THURSDAY, OCTOBER 18, 1988

In Japan, an ancient bias endures

By Tom Ashbrook
Globe Staff

TOKYO — THEY WERE Japanese | Japanese minorities includ 600,000 — Koreans 4 '

THE NEW ... INTERNATIONAL NEWS   WEDNESDAY, NOVEMBER 18, 1987

Gypsies Not Welcome! Romans Say

By ROBERTO SURO

ROME, Nov. 17 — In the suburbs where this city becomes an impoverished and ramshackle metropolis, old women blocked railroad tracks this week and young men set tires aflame at a highway toll station. "I hear ...

Roadblocks and banners carry a message of hate.

'That's the way it is — we're white and we're proud.'

Across the Generations, 1915 Haunts Armenians

THE NEW YORK TIMES   National News   TUESDAY, JANUARY 27, 1987

The Sound of Hate Reverberates in North Georgia

■ Anyone can be the target of prejudice.

harm to the self-esteem of African American children. Taking this evidence into consideration, the Court ruled that separating black children from white children on the basis of race alone "generates a feeling of inferiority as to their status in the community that may affect their hearts and minds in a way unlikely ever to be undone.... [S]eparate educational facilities are therefore inherently unequal" (Justice Earl Warren, speaking for the majority in the case of *Brown v. Board of Education*, 1954, quoted in Stephan, 1978).

The diminution of self-esteem has affected other oppressed groups as well. For example, Philip Goldberg (1968) demonstrated that, like African Americans, women in this culture have learned to consider themselves intellectually inferior to men. In his experiment, Goldberg asked female college students to read scholarly articles and to evaluate them in terms of their competence and writing style. For some students, specific articles were signed by male authors (e.g., "John T. McKay"), while for others, the same articles were signed by female authors (e.g., "Joan T. McKay"). The female students rated the articles much higher if they were attributed to a male author than if the same articles were attributed to a female author. In other words, these women had learned their place; they regarded the output of other women as necessarily inferior to that of men, just as the African American youngsters learned to regard black dolls as inferior to white dolls. This is the legacy of a prejudiced society.

Clark and Clark's experiment was conducted over 50 years ago; Goldberg's was conducted over 30 years ago. As we have indicated, significant changes have taken place in American society since then. For example, the number of blatant acts of overt prejudice and discrimination has decreased sharply, legislation on

■ If an African American girl believes that white dolls are more desirable than black dolls, should we be concerned about her self esteem?

affirmative action has opened the door to greater opportunities for women and minorities, and the media have increased our exposure to women and minorities doing important work in positions of power and influence. As one might expect, these changes are reflected in the gradual increase in self-esteem of people in these groups, an increase underscored by the fact that most recent research has failed to replicate the results of those earlier experiments. African American children have gradually become more content with black dolls than they were in 1947 (Porter, 1971; Porter & Washington, 1979, 1989; Gopaul-McNicol, 1987), and people no longer discriminate against a piece of writing simply because it is attributed to a woman (Swim et al., 1989, 1994). Similarly, recent research suggests that there might not be any major differences in global self-esteem between blacks and whites or between men and women (Crocker & Major, 1989; Steele, 1992, 1997; J. Aronson, Quinn, & Spencer, 1998). While this progress is real, it would be a mistake to conclude that prejudice has ceased to be a serious problem in our country. As mentioned earlier, prejudice exists in countless subtle and not-so-subtle ways. For the most part, here in America at the close of the twentieth century, prejudice has gone underground and become less overt (Pettigrew, 1985, 1989). During the past half-century, social psychologists have contributed greatly to our understanding of the psychological processes underlying prejudice and have begun to identify and demonstrate some possible solutions. What is prejudice? How does it come about? How can it be reduced?

Prejudice, Stereotyping, and Discrimination Defined

Prejudice is an attitude. As we discussed in Chapter 8, attitudes are made up of three components: an affective or emotional component, representing both the type of emotion linked with the attitude (e.g., anger, warmth) and the extremity of the attitude (e.g., mild uneasiness, outright hostility); a cognitive component, involving the beliefs or thoughts (cognitions) that make up the attitude; and a behavioral component, relating to one's actions—people don't simply hold attitudes; they usually act on them as well.

"It's a cat calendar, so it may not be all that accurate."

■ Prejudice is ubiquitous!

Prejudice: The Affective Component

The term *prejudice* refers to the general attitude structure and its affective (emotional) component. Technically, there are positive and negative prejudices. For example, you could be prejudiced against Texans or prejudiced in favor of Texans. In one case, your emotional reaction is negative; when a person is introduced to you as "This is Bob from Texas," you will expect him to act in particular ways that you associate with "those obnoxious Texans." Conversely, if your emotional reaction is positive, you will be delighted to meet another one of "those wonderful, uninhibited Texans," and you'll expect Bob to demonstrate many positive qualities, such as warmth and friendliness. While prejudice can involve either positive or negative affect, social psychologists (and people in general) reserve the word prejudice for use only when it refers to negative attitudes about others. Specifically, **prejudice** is defined as a hostile or negative attitude toward people in a distinguishable group, based solely on their membership in that group. For example, when we say an individual is prejudiced against blacks, we mean that he or she is primed to behave coolly or with hostility toward blacks and that he or she feels that all blacks are pretty much the same. Thus, the characteristics this individual assigns to blacks are negative and zealously applied to the group as a whole—the individual traits or behaviors of the target of prejudice will either go unnoticed or be dismissed.

Prejudice
a hostile or negative attitude toward a distinguishable group of people, based solely on their membership in that group

Stereotypes: The Cognitive Component

Close your eyes for a moment and imagine the looks and characteristics of the following people: a high school cheerleader, a New York cab driver, a Jewish doctor, a black musician. Our guess is that this task was not difficult. We all walk around with images of various "types" of people in our heads. The distinguished journalist Walter Lippmann (1922), who was the first to introduce the term stereotype, described the distinction between the world out there and stereotypes—"the little pictures we carry around inside our heads." Within a given culture, these pictures tend to be remarkably similar. For example, we would be surprised if your image of the high school cheerleader was anything but bouncy, full of pep, pretty, nonintellectual, and (of course!) female. We would also be surprised if the Jewish doctor or the New York cab driver in your head was female—or if the black musician was playing classical music.

It goes without saying that there are male cheerleaders, female doctors, and black classical musicians. Deep down, we know that New York cab drivers come in every size, shape, race, and gender. But we tend to categorize according to what we regard as normative. And within a given culture, what people regard as normative is very similar, in part because these images are perpetuated and broadcast widely by the media of that culture. Stereotyping, however, goes a step beyond simple categorization. A **stereotype** is a generalization about a group of people in which identical characteristics are assigned to virtually all members of the group, regardless of actual variation among the members. Once formed, stereotypes are resistant to change on the basis of new information.

It is important to point out that stereotyping is not necessarily emotional and does not necessarily lead to intentional acts of abuse. Frequently, stereotyping is merely a way we have of simplifying how we look at the world—and we all do it to some extent. For example, Gordon Allport (1954) described stereotyping as "the law of least effort." According to Allport, the world is just too complicated for us to have a highly differentiated attitude about everything. Instead, we maximize our cognitive time and energy by developing elegant, accurate attitudes about some topics, while relying on simple, sketchy beliefs for others. (This should remind you of the many facets of social cognition that we discussed in Chapter 4.) Given our limited information-processing capacity, it is reasonable for human beings to behave like "cognitive misers"—to take shortcuts and adopt certain rules of thumb in our attempt to understand other people (Fiske, 1989; Fiske & Depret, 1996; Jones, 1990; Taylor, 1981; Taylor & Falcone, 1982). To the extent that the resulting stereotype is based on experience and is at all accurate, it can be an adaptive, shorthand way of dealing with complex events. On the other hand, if the stereotype blinds us to individual differences within a class of people, it is maladaptive, unfair, and potentially abusive. See Try It! box on page 503.

Sports, Race, and Attribution

The potential abuse engendered by stereotyping can be blatant and obvious—as when one ethnic group is considered lazy or another ethnic group is considered greedy. But the potential abuse can be more subtle—and it might even involve a stereotype about a positive attribute. For example, in 1992, Twentieth Century Fox produced an amusing film about two-on-two street basketball (starring Wesley Snipes, Woody Harrelson, and Rosie Perez) called *White Men Can't Jump*. What are we to make of the title? The implication is that African American men are better at basketball than white men. Well, it turns out that in the National Basketball Association 75 to 80 percent of the players are African American (Hoose, 1989; Gladwell, 1997). This is far greater than one would expect from comparative population statistics (approximately 13 percent of the U.S. population is African American).

Stereotype
a generalization about a group of people in which identical characteristics are assigned to virtually all members of the group, regardless of actual variation among the members

/// *Try It* !

Stereotype and Aggression

Close your eyes. Conjure up in your mind the following image: a very aggressive construction worker. Okay, take a couple of minutes: How is this person dressed, where is this person located and, specifically, what is this person doing to express aggression? Write it down. Be as specific as you can possibly be about the actions of the person.

Now conjure up in your mind the following image: A very aggressive lawyer. How is this person dressed, where is this person located, and, specifically, what is this person doing to express aggression? Write it down. Be as specific as you can possibly be about the actions of this person.

This is actually the basic procedure in a recent experiment (Kunda, Sinclair, & Griffin, 1997). If you are anything like their subjects, your stereotype of the construction worker and of the lawyer would have influenced the way you construed the term aggression: Most of their subjects had the construction worker using physical aggression and the lawyer using verbal aggression.

///

There are several possible situational causes for this disparity. For example, it may be that basketball is a natural sport for the inner city simply because the game requires very little space and is, therefore, easy and inexpensive for municipalities to hang a basket on a small patch of asphalt and call it a basketball court. Because a high percentage of African Americans grow up in the inner cities, they might tend to play more basketball than suburban kids. It is also possible that a great many African Americans simply work harder at perfecting their basketball skills—for socio-economic reasons: For a young black male, basketball may be perceived as one of the few available tickets out of dead-end jobs and grinding poverty and, as such, it may inspire hope for an athletic college scholarship and dreams of a lucrative professional career (Jones & Hochner, 1973).

But, in this case, what is abusive to the minority? What's wrong with the implication that black men *can* jump? The abuse enters when we ignore the overlap in the distributions—i.e., when we ignore the fact that a great many African American kids are not adept at basketball and a great many white kids are. Thus, if we meet a young African American man and are astonished at his ineptitude on the basketball court, we are, in a very real sense, denying him his individuality. And there is ample evidence that this kind of potentially abusive stereotyping occurs (Brinson & Robinson, 1991; Edwards, 1973). In a recent experiment, Jeff Stone, Zachary Perry, and John Darley, (1997) exposed college students to a 20-minute audio tape recording of a college basketball game. They were asked to focus on one of the players, Mark Flick, and were allowed to peruse a folder containing information about Mr. Flick. Included in the folder was a photograph—allegedly of Flick. For half of the participants, the photo was of an African American male; for the others, the photo was of a white male. After listening to the game, the students rated Mr. Flick's performance. Their ratings reflected the prevailing stereotypes: Those students who believed Flick was African American rated him as having more athletic ability and as having played a better game than did those who thought he was white. Those who thought he was white rated him as having greater hustle and greater basketball sense.

Stereotypes, Attribution, and Gender

A particularly interesting manifestation of stereotyping takes place in the perception of gender differences. It is almost universal for women to be seen as more nurturant and less assertive than men (Deaux & Lewis, 1984). It is possible that this perception may be entirely role-related—that is, traditionally women have been assigned the role of homemaker and thus, may be seen as more nurturant (see Deaux & LaFrance, 1998). At the other end of the continuum, evolutionary social psychologists (Buss, 1995, 1996; Buss & Kenrick, 1998; Buss & Schmitt, 1993) suggest that female behavior and male behavior differ in precisely those domains in which the sexes have faced different adaptive problems. From a Darwinian perspective, there are powerful biological reasons why women might have evolved as more nurturant than men. Specifically, among our ancient ancestors, for anatomical reasons, women were always the early caregivers of infants; those women who were not nurturant did not have many babies who survived. Therefore, their non-nurturing genes were less likely to be passed on.

Although there is no clear way of determining whether or not caregiving is more likely to be part of a woman's genetic nature than a man's, it does turn out that the cultural stereotype is not far from reality. As Alice Eagly, Wendy Wood, and Janet Swim have shown, compared to men, women do tend to manifest behaviors that can best be described as more socially sensitive, friendlier, and more concerned with the welfare of others—while men tend to behave in ways that are more dominant, controlling, and independent (Eagly, 1993; Eagly & Wood, 1991; Swim, 1994). Indeed, if anything, Swim's (1994) data indicate that the stereotype tends to *underestimate* the actual gender differences obtained. Again, as with our basketball example, we should emphasize the fact that there is a great deal of overlap between men and women on these characteristics. Nonetheless, as Eagly (1995, 1996) has argued, the differences are too consistent to be dismissed as unimportant.

■ In this cartoon, while the teacher may not intend to be hurtful, his obvious sexism is offensive.

© 1992 Gary Hallgren.

Needless to say, the phenomenon of gender stereotyping often *does* depart from reality and can cut deeply. In one experiment, for example, when confronted with a highly successful female physician, male undergraduates perceived her as being less competent and having had an easier path toward success than a successful male physician (Feldman-Summers & Kiesler, 1974). Female undergraduates saw things differently: Although they saw the male physician and the female physician as being equally competent, they saw the male as having had an easier time of it. Both males and females attributed higher motivation to the female physician. It should be noted that attributing a high degree of motivation to a woman can be one way of implying that she has less skill than her male counterpart (i.e., "She's not very smart, but she tries hard"). This possibility comes into clear focus when we examine a similar study by Kay Deaux and Tim Emsweiler (1974), in which they found that if the sexual stereotype is strong enough, even members of the stereotyped group tend to buy it. Specifically, male and female students were shown a highly successful performance on a complex task by a fellow student and were asked how it came about. When it was a man who succeeded, both male and female students attributed his achievement almost entirely to his ability; when it was a woman who succeeded, students of both genders thought the achievement was largely a matter of luck.

But this research was done a quarter of a century ago. American society has undergone a great many changes since then. Have these changes impacted the stereotypes held of women? Not so you'd notice. In an analysis of contemporary research on the issue, Janet Swim and Lawrence Sanna (1996) carefully studied some 58 separate experiments done over the past 20 years and found that the results are remarkably consistent with the earlier experiments. Swim and Sanna found that if a man was successful on a given task, observers attributed his success to ability; if a woman was successful at that same task, observers attributed her success to hard work. If a man failed on a given task, observers attributed his failure either to bad luck or to lower effort; if a woman failed, observers felt the task was simply too hard for her ability level.

Research has also shown that young girls have a tendency to downplay their own ability. In one experiment, while fourth-grade boys attributed their own successful outcomes on a difficult intellectual task to their ability, girls tended to derogate their own successful performance. Moreover, this experiment also showed that while boys had learned to protect their egos by attributing their own failures to bad luck, girls took more of the blame for failures on themselves (Nichols, 1975). In a subsequent study, Deborah Stipek and Heidi Gralinski (1991) showed that the tendency girls have to downplay their own ability may be most prevalent in traditionally male domains—like math. Specifically Stipek and Galinski found that junior high school girls attributed their success on a math exam to luck, while boys attributed their success to ability. Girls also showed less feelings of pride than boys following success on a math exam.

Needless to say, these self-defeating beliefs do not develop in a vacuum. They can be influenced by the attitudes of our society in general, and most powerfully, by the most important people in the young girl's life—her parents. In this regard, Janis Jacobs and Jacquelynne Eccles (1992) explored the influence of mothers' gender stereotypic beliefs on the way these same mothers perceived the abilities of their 11 and 12-year-old sons and daughters. Jacobs and Eccles then tested to see what impact this might have on the children's perceptions of their own abilities. As one might expect, those mothers who held the strongest stereotypic gender beliefs also believed that their own daughters had relatively low math ability and that their sons had relatively high math ability. Those mothers who did not hold generally stereotypic beliefs did not see their daughters as less able in math than their sons. These beliefs had an impact on the beliefs of the children involved. The daughters of women with strong gender stereotypes believed that they did not have much math ability. The daughters of women who did not hold strong gender stereotypes showed no such self-defeating belief. This is an interesting variation on the self-fulfilling prophecy discussed in chapters 3 and 4: Here, if your *mother* doesn't expect you to do well, chances are you will not do as well as you might have.

Discrimination: The Behavioral Component

Discrimination
unjustified negative or harmful action toward a member of a group, simply because of his or her membership in that group

This brings us to the final component of prejudice—the action component. Stereotypic beliefs often result in unfair treatment. We call this **discrimination**, defined as unjustified negative or harmful action toward the members of a group, simply because of their membership in that group.

If you are a fourth-grade math teacher and you have the stereotypic belief that little girls are hopeless at math, you might be less likely to spend as much time in the classroom coaching a girl than a boy. If you are a police officer and you have the stereotypic belief that African Americans are more violent than whites, this might affect your behavior toward a specific black man you are trying to arrest.

In one study, Charles Bond and his colleagues (1988), compared the treatment of patients in a psychiatric hospital run by an all-white professional staff. The results of the study are illustrated in Figure 13.1. The researchers examined the two most common methods used by staff members to handle patients' violent behavior: (a) secluding the individual in a time-out room and (b) restraining the individual in a straitjacket and administering tranquilizing drugs. An examination of hospital records over 85 days revealed that the harsher method—physical and chemical restraint—was used against black patients nearly four times as often as against white patients. This was the case despite the virtual lack of differences in the number of violent incidents committed by the black and the white patients. Moreover, this discriminatory treatment occurred even though the black

■ **FIGURE 13.1   Use of extreme measures against black mental patients.** During the first 30 days of confinement, there appeared to be an assumption that blacks would be more violent than whites. (Adapted from Bond et al., 1988)

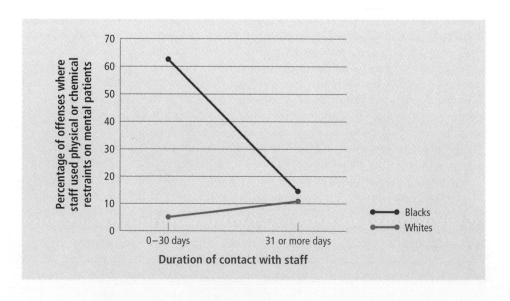

patients, on being admitted to the hospital, had been diagnosed as slightly less violent than the white patients.

This study did uncover an important positive finding: After several weeks, reality managed to overcome the effects of the existing stereotype. The staff eventually noticed that the black and the white patients did not differ in their degree of violent behavior, and they began to treat black and white patients equally. While this is encouraging, the overall meaning of the study is both clear and disconcerting: The existing stereotype resulted in undeserved, harsher initial treatment of black patients by trained professionals. At the same time, the fact that reality overcame the stereotype is a tribute to the professionalism of the staff, because, as we shall see, in most cases deeply rooted prejudice, stereotypes, and discrimination are not easy to change.

> Prejudices are the props of civilization.
> —André Gide, 1939

What Causes Prejudice?

What makes people prejudiced? Is it "natural" or "unnatural"? As we noted in Chapter 11, evolutionary psychologists have suggested that animals have a strong tendency to feel more favorably toward genetically similar others and to express fear and loathing toward genetically dissimilar organisms, even if the latter have never done them any harm (Buss & Kenrick, 1998; Rushton, 1989; Trivers, 1985). Thus, prejudice might be built in—an essential part of our biological survival mechanism inducing us to favor our own family, tribe, or race, and to express hostility toward outsiders. On the other hand, it is conceivable that, as humans, we are different from the lower animals; perhaps our natural inclination is to be friendly, open, and cooperative. If this were the case, then prejudice would not come naturally. Rather, the culture (parents, the community, the media) might, intentionally or unintentionally, instruct us to assign negative qualities and attributes to people who are different from us.

The bottom line is that although we human beings might have inherited biological tendencies that predispose us toward prejudicial behavior, no one knows for sure whether or not prejudice is a vital and necessary part of our biological makeup. In any case, most social psychologists would agree that the specifics of prejudice must be learned. How easy is it to learn prejudice? It may be that young children pick up the prejudices espoused by their parents, but they do not necessarily retain those prejudices in adulthood. In a recent study, Meg Rohan and Mark Zanna (1996) took a close look at the folk wisdom that "the apple never falls far from the tree," by examining attitude and value similarity between parents and their adult children. They found that the folk wisdom was most applicable when parents held egalitarian attitudes and values. That is, similarity was significantly stronger between children and parents when parents held egalitarian attitudes and values than between children and parents when parents held prejudice-related attitudes and values. Our guess is that this discrepancy takes place because the culture as a whole is more egalitarian than the bigoted parents. Thus, when children of bigoted parents leave home (e.g., to go off to college) they are more likely to be exposed to competing views.

At the same time, it is reasonably clear that children can be taught prejudice. Several years ago, Jane Elliot (1977), a third-grade teacher in Riceville, Iowa, was concerned that her young students were leading too sheltered a life. The children all lived in rural Iowa, they were all white, and they were all Christian. Elliot felt it was important for their development to give them some direct experience about what stereotyping and discrimination felt like from both sides. To achieve this end, Elliot divided her class by eye color. She told her students that blue-eyed people were superior to brown-eyed people—smarter, nicer, more trustworthy, and so on. The brown-eyed youngsters were required to wear special cloth collars around their necks so that they would be instantly recognizable as a member of the inferior group. She gave special privileges to the blue-eyed youngsters; they got to play longer at recess, could have second helpings at the cafeteria, were praised in the classroom, and so on. How did the children respond?

In a matter of hours, Elliot succeeded in creating a microcosm of a prejudiced society in her classroom. Just a few hours before the experiment began, the children had been a cooperative, cohesive group; once the seeds of divisiveness were planted, there was trouble. The "superior" blue-eyed kids made fun of the brown-eyed kids, refused to play with them, tattled on them to the teacher, thought up new restrictions and punishments for them, and even started a fist fight in the school yard. The "inferior" brown-eyed kids became self conscious, depressed and demoralized. They performed poorly on classroom tests that day.

The next day, Ms. Elliot switched the stereotypes about eye color. She said she'd made a dreadful mistake—that brown-eyed people were really the superior ones. She told the brown-eyed kids to put their collars on the blue-eyed kids. They gleefully did so. The tables had turned—and the brown-eyed kids exacted their revenge.

On the morning of the third day, Ms. Elliot explained to her students that they had been learning about prejudice and discrimination and how it feels to be a person of color in this society. The children discussed the two-day experience and clearly understood its message. In a follow-up, Elliot met with these students at a class reunion, when they were in their mid twenties. Their memories of the exercise were startlingly clear—they reported that the experience had a powerful and lasting impact on their lives. They felt that they were less prejudiced and more aware of discrimination against others because of this childhood experience.

> The world is full of
> pots jeering at kettles.
> —La Rochefoucauld, 1678

The Way We Think: Social Cognition

Our first explanation for what causes prejudice is that it is the inevitable byproduct of the way we process and organize information—in other words, it is the dark side of human social cognition (as discussed in Chapter 4). Our tendency to categorize and group information together, to form schemas and to use these to interpret new or unusual information, to rely on potentially inaccurate heuristics (shortcuts in mental reasoning), and to depend on what are often faulty memory processes—all of these aspects of social cognition can lead us to form negative stereotypes and to apply them in a discriminatory fashion. Let's examine this dark side of social cognition more closely.

Social Categorization: Us versus Them

The first step in prejudice is the creation of groups—that is, the categorization of some people into one group based on certain characteristics and of others into another group based on their different characteristics. The underlying theme of human social cognition is such categorization—grouping stimuli according to their similarities and contrasting stimuli according to their disparities (Brewer & Brown, 1998; Rosch & Lloyd, 1978; Taylor, 1981; Wilder, 1986). For example, we make sense out of the physical world by grouping animals and plants into taxonomies; we make sense out of our social world by grouping people by gender, nationality, ethnicity, and so on. We do not react to each stimulus we encounter as new and completely unknown. Instead, we rely on our perceptions of what similar stimuli have been like in the past to help us determine how to react to this particular stimulus (Andersen & Klatzky, 1987). Thus, social categorization is both useful and necessary; however, this simple cognitive process has profound implications.

For example, in Jane Elliot's third-grade classroom, children grouped according to eye color began to act differently based on that social categorization. Blue-eyed children, the superior group, stuck together and actively promoted and used their higher status and power in the classroom. They formed an *in-group,* defined as the group with which an individual identifies and of which he or she feels a member. The blue-eyed kids saw the brown-eyed ones as outsiders—different and inferior. To the blue-eyed children, the brown-eyed kids were the *out-group,* defined as the group with which the individual does not identify.

Kurt Vonnegut captures this concept beautifully in his novel *Cat's Cradle*. A woman discovers that a person she has just met, casually, on a plane, is from Indiana. Immediately, a bond is formed between them:

"My God," she said, "are you a Hoosier?"

I admitted I was.

"I'm a Hoosier too," she crowed. "Nobody has to be ashamed of being a Hoosier."

"I'm not," I said. "I never knew anybody who was."

What is the mechanism that produces this *in-group bias*—that is, positive feelings and special treatment for people we have defined as being part of our in-group, and negative feelings and unfair treatment for others simply because we have defined them as being in the out-group? The British social psychologist Henri Tajfel (1982) discovered that the major underlying motive is self-esteem: Individuals seek to enhance their self-esteem by identifying with specific social groups. Yet self-esteem will be enhanced only if the individual sees these groups as superior to other groups. Thus, for members of the Ku Klux Klan it is not enough to believe the races should be kept separate; they must convince themselves of the supremacy of the white race in order to feel good about themselves.

To get at the pure, unvarnished mechanisms behind this phenomenon, Tajfel and his colleagues have created entities that they refer to as minimal groups (Tajfel, 1982; Tajfel & Billig, 1974; Tajfel & Turner, 1979). In these experiments, complete strangers are formed into groups using the most trivial criteria imaginable. For example, in one experiment participants watched a coin toss that randomly assigned them to either group X or group W. In another experiment, participants were first asked to express their opinions about artists they had never heard of and were then randomly assigned to a group that appreciated either the "Klee style" or the "Kandinsky style," ostensibly due to their picture preferences. The striking thing about the Tajfel research is that despite the fact that the participants were strangers prior to the experiment and didn't interact with one another during it, they behaved as if those who shared the same meaningless label were their dear friends or close kin. They liked the members of their own group better; they rated the members of their in-group as more likely to have pleasant personalities and to have done better work than out-group members. Most striking, the participants allocated more money and other rewards to those who shared their label and did so in a rather hostile, cutthroat manner—that is, when

■ Wearing our school colors is a way of demonstrating that we are a member of the in-group.

given a clear choice, they preferred to give themselves only $2, if it meant giving the out-group person $1, over giving themselves $3, if that meant the out-group member received $4 (Brewer, 1979; Hogg & Abrams, 1988; Oakes & Turner, 1980; Wilder, 1981; Mullen, Brown, & Smith, 1992).

In short, even when the reasons for differentiation are minimal, being in the in-group makes you want to win against members of the out-group and leads you to treat the latter unfairly, because such tactics serve to build your self-esteem. And when your group does win, it strengthens your feelings of pride and identification with that group. For example, our casual observation suggests that there was much more flag-waving and many more parades and patriotic speeches by politicians following the victorious Desert Storm war against Iraq than there was following the less than victorious war in Vietnam. In a more systematic observation, Robert Cialdini and his colleagues (1976, 1993) simply counted the number of college insignia T-shirts and sweatshirts worn to classes on the Monday following a football game at seven different universities. The results? You guessed it: Students were more likely to wear their university's insignia after victory than after defeat.

Besides the in-group bias, there is another consequence of social categorization: the perception of **out-group homogeneity** (Linville, Fischer, & Salovey, 1989; Quattrone, 1986). This is the belief that "they" are all alike. In-group members tend to perceive those in the out-group as being more similar to each other (homogeneous) than they really are, as well as more homogeneous than the in-group members are. Does your college have a traditional rival, whether in athletics or academics? If so, as an in-group member, you probably value your institution more highly than this rival (thereby raising and protecting your self-esteem) and you probably perceive students at this rival school to be more similar to each other (e.g., as a given type) than you perceive students at your own institution to be. George Quattrone and Edward E. Jones (1980) studied this phenomenon using rival universities: Princeton and Rutgers. The rivalry between these colleges is based on athletics, academics, and even class-consciousness, with Princeton being private and Rutgers public. Male research participants at the two schools watched videotaped scenes in which three different young men were asked to make a decision—for example, in one videotape an experimenter asked a man whether he wanted to listen to rock music or classical music while he par-

Out-Group Homogeneity
the perception that those in the out-group are more similar (homogeneous) to each other than they really are, as well as more similar than the members of the in-group are

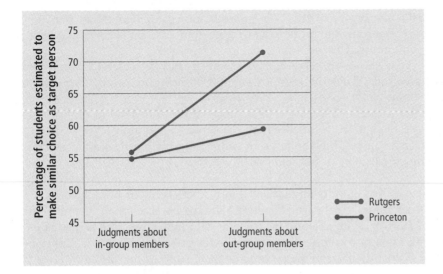

■ **FIGURE 13.2   Judgments about in-group and out-group members.**
After watching the target person make a choice between two alternatives, participants were asked to estimate what percentage of students at their school (in-group) and their rival school (out-group) would make the same choice. An out-group homogeneity bias was found: Students' estimates for out-group members were higher (greater similarity) than for in-group members. (Adapted from Quattrone & Jones, 1980)

ticipated in an experiment on auditory perception. The participants were told that the man was either a Princeton or a Rutgers student; thus, for some of them the student in the videotape was an in-group member, and for others, an out-group member. The participants' job was to predict what the man in the videotape would choose. After they saw the man make his choice (e.g., rock or classical music), they were asked to predict what percentage of male students at that institution would make the same choice. Did the predictions vary due to the in- or out-group status of the target men? As you can see in Figure 13.2, the results support the out-group homogeneity hypothesis: When the target person was an out-group member, the participants believed his choice was more predictive of what his peers would choose than when he was an in-group member (a student at their own school). In other words, if you know something about one out-group member, you are more likely to feel you know something about all of them. Similar results have been found in a wide variety of experiments in the United States, Europe, and Australia (Duck, Hogg, & Terry, 1995; Judd & Park, 1988; Park & Rothbart, 1982; Hartstone & Augoustinos, 1995; Ostrom & Sedikides, 1992).

The Failure of Logic

Anyone who has ever tried to argue with people who hold a deep-seated prejudice against some group knows it is difficult to get them to change their minds. Even people who are usually sensible and reasonable about most topics become relatively immune to rational, logical arguments when it comes to the topic of their prejudice. Why is this so? There are two reasons, involving the affective and cognitive aspects of an attitude. First, it is primarily the emotional aspect of attitudes that makes a prejudiced person so hard to argue with; as you well know, logical arguments are not effective in countering emotions. The difficulty of using reason to change prejudiced attitudes is beautifully illustrated by Gordon Allport in his landmark book *The Nature of Prejudice* (1954). Allport reports a dialogue between Mr. X and Mr. Y:

- Mr. X: The trouble with the Jews is that they only take care of their own group.

> Our minds thus grow in spots; and like grease spots, the spots spread. But we let them spread as little as possible; we keep unaltered as much of our old knowledge, as many of our old prejudices and beliefs, as we can.
>
> —William James, 1907

- Mr. Y: But the record of the Community Chest campaign shows that they gave more generously, in proportion to their numbers, to the general charities of the community than did non-Jews.
- Mr. X: That shows they are always trying to buy favor and intrude into Christian affairs. They think of nothing but money; that is why there are so many Jewish bankers.
- Mr. Y: But a recent study shows that the percentage of Jews in the banking business is negligible, far smaller than the percentage of non-Jews.
- Mr. X: That's just it; they don't go in for respectable business; they are only in the movie business or run night clubs. (Allport, 1954, pp. 13–14)

> The mind of a bigot is like the pupil of the eye; the more light you pour upon it the more it will contract.
> —Oliver Wendell Holmes, Jr., 1901

Because Mr. X is emotionally involved in his beliefs about Jews, he does not feel particularly bound by the usual confines of a logical discussion. In effect, the prejudiced Mr. X is saying, "Don't trouble me with facts; my mind is made up." He makes no attempt to refute the powerful data presented by Mr. Y. Either he proceeds to distort the facts in order to make them support his hatred of Jews or he ignores them and simply initiates a new area of attack. The prejudiced attitude remains intact, despite the fact that the specific arguments Mr. X began with are now lying in tatters at his feet.

Second, the cognitive component of a prejudiced attitude, in and of itself, presents difficulties for the person trying to reduce a friend's prejudice because, as we discussed in earlier chapters, an attitude tends to organize the way we process relevant information about the targets of that attitude. None of us is a 100 percent reliable accountant when it comes to processing social information we care about; the way the human mind works, we simply do not tally events objectively. Accordingly, individuals who hold specific opinions (or schemas) about certain groups will process information about those groups differently from the way they process information about other groups. Specifically, information consistent with their notions about these target groups will be given more attention, will be rehearsed (or recalled) more often, and therefore will be remembered better than information that is not consistent with these notions (Bodenhausen, 1988; Bodenhausen & Lichtenstein, 1987; Dovidio, Evans, & Tyler, 1986; O'Sullivan & Durso, 1984; Wyer, 1988). These are the familiar effects of schematic processing that we discussed in Chapter 4. Applying these effects to the topic of prejudice, we can see that whenever a member of a group behaves as we expect him or her to, the behavior confirms and even strengthens our stereotype. Thus, stereotypes become relatively impervious to change; after all, proof that they are accurate is always out there—that is, when our beliefs guide us to see it.

The Activation of Stereotypes

Stereotypes reflect cultural beliefs—that is, within a given society, they are easily recognized descriptions of members of a particular group. For example, we all know the stereotype of the woman driver or the overemotional female. Even if we don't believe these stereotypes, we can easily recognize them as common beliefs held by others. For instance, in a series of studies conducted at Princeton University over 36 years, students were asked to assign traits to members of various ethnic and national groups (Gilbert, 1951; Karlins, Coffman, & Walters, 1969; Katz & Braly, 1933). The participants could do so easily, and to a large extent they agreed with each other. They knew the stereotypes, even for groups about whom they had little real knowledge, such as Turks. Table 13.1 shows some of the results of these studies, which were conducted in 1933, 1951, and 1969. Note how negative the early stereotypes were in 1933 and how they became somewhat less negative over time. What is particularly interesting about these studies is that participants in 1951 began to voice discomfort with the task (such discomfort, by the way, didn't exist in 1933). By 1969, many participants not only felt discomfort but they also were reluctant to label the various groups, because they did not believe the stereotypes (Karlins et al., 1969). In an experiment performed a quarter of a century later, Patricia Devine and Andrew Elliot (1995) made it clear that the stereotypes were not really fading at all; they demonstrated that virtually all the participants were fully aware of the negative stereotypes of African Americans—it's just that the less prejudiced people were reluctant to state them openly.

This brings us to an intriguing social cognition puzzle: If you know a stereotype, will it affect your cognitive processing about a target person, even if you neither believe the stereotype nor consider yourself prejudiced against this group? Imagine this scenario: You are a member of a group, judging another person's performance. Someone in your group makes an ugly, stereotypical comment about the individual. Will the comment affect your judgment of his or her

Table 13.1

Some common stereotypes held by Princeton students over the years.

GROUP	1933	1951	1969
Americans	industrious intelligent materialistic ambitious progressive	materialistic intelligent industrious pleasure-loving individualistic	materialistic ambitious pleasure-loving industrious conventional
Japanese	intelligent industrious progressive shrewd sly	imitative sly extremely nationalistic treacherous	industrious ambitious efficient intelligent progressive
Jews	shrewd mercenary industrious grasping intelligent	shrewd intelligent industrious mercenary ambitious	ambitious materialistic intelligent industrious shrewd
Negroes (African Americans)	superstitious lazy happy-go-lucky ignorant musical	superstitious musical lazy ignorant pleasure-loving	musical happy-go-lucky lazy pleasure-loving ostentatious

SOURCE: Adapted from Gilbert, 1951; Karlins, Coffman, & Walters, 1969; Katz & Braly, 1933.

NOTE: The general stability as well as changes in these stereotypes.

performance? "No," you are probably thinking; "I'd disregard it completely." But would you be able to do so? Is it possible that the comment would trigger in your mind all the other negative stereotypes and beliefs about people in that group and affect your judgment about this particular individual?

Jeff Greenberg and Tom Pyszczynski (1985) decided to find out. They had two confederates, one African American and one white, stage a debate about nuclear energy for groups of research participants. For half the groups, the African American debater presented far better arguments and clearly won the debate; for the other half, the white debater performed far better and won the debate. The participants were asked to rate both debaters' skill. However, just before the critical experimental manipulation occurred. A confederate planted in the group did one of three things: (a) He made a highly racist remark about the African American debater—"There's no way that nigger won the debate"; (b) he made a nonracist remark about the African American debater—"There's no way the pro [or con] debater won the debate"; or (c) he made no comment at all.

The researchers reasoned that if those participants who heard the racist comment were able to disregard it completely, they would not rate the African American debater any differently from the way participants in the other conditions, who had not heard such a comment, rated him. Was that the case? The data presented in Figure 13.3 clearly show that the answer is no. The data compared the ratings of skill given to the African American and white debaters when they were each in the losing role. As you can see, the participants rated the African American and white debaters as being equally skillful when no comment was made; similarly, when a nonracist, nonstereotypical comment was made about the African American debater, he was rated as being just as skillful as the white debater. However, after the racial stereotype was activated in participants' minds by the racist comment, they rated the African American debater significantly lower than participants in the other groups did. In other words, this derogatory comment activated other negative, stereotypical beliefs about African Americans, so that the participants who heard it rated the same performance by the debater as less skilled than those who had not heard the racist remark.

Similar results were obtained by Eaaron Henderson-King and Richard Nisbett (1997) who showed that all it took was one negative action by one African American (actually a confederate of the experimenters) to activate the negative stereotypes against blacks and to discourage the participants from wanting to interact with a different African American. These findings suggest stereotypes exist in most of us and lurk just beneath the surface. It doesn't require much to activate the stereotype and, once activated, it can have dire consequences for how a particular member of that out-group is perceived and treated.

How does this activation process work? Patricia Devine and her colleagues (Devine, 1989; Zuwerink et al., 1996) have done some fascinating research on how stereotypical and prejudiced beliefs affect cognitive processing. Devine differentiates between automatic processing of information and controlled processing of information. An automatic process is one over which we have no control. For example, even if you score very low on a prejudice scale, you are certainly familiar with certain stereotypes that exist in the culture, such as "African Americans are hostile," "Jews are materialistic," or "Homosexual men are effeminate." These stereotypes are automatically triggered under certain conditions—they just pop into one's mind. Since the process is automatic, you can't control it or stop it from occurring. You know the stereotypes, and thus they come to mind—say, when you are meeting someone or rating a person's perfor-

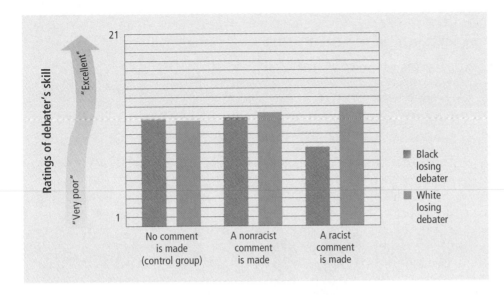

■ **FIGURE 13.3 The activation of a stereotypical belief.** When a derogatory comment was made about the black debater, it activated the latent stereotype held by the observers, causing them to lower their rating of his performance. (Adapted from Greenberg & Pyszczynski, 1985)

mance. However, for people who are not deeply prejudiced, their controlled processes can suppress or override these stereotypes. For example, such a person can say to him- or herself, "Hey, that stereotype isn't fair and it isn't right—African Americans are no more hostile than whites. Ignore the stereotype about this person's ethnicity."

What Devine's theory suggests, therefore, is a two-step model of cognitive processing: The automatic processing brings up information—in this case, stereotypes—but the controlled (or conscious) processing can refute or ignore it. But what happens if you are busy, overwhelmed, distracted, or not paying much attention? You may not initiate that controlled level of processing, meaning that the information supplied by the automatic process—the stereotype—is still present in your mind and unrefuted. Devine (1989) set out to study exactly this process: that a stereotype is automatically activated when a member of an out-group is encountered, and the stereotype can be ignored through conscious processing—for example, by people who are not prejudiced (see Figure 13.4).

First, Devine administered a test of prejudice to a large number of students and, according to their scores, divided them into high-prejudice and low-prejudice groups. Next, she demonstrated that, regardless of prejudice, both groups possessed equal knowledge of racial stereotypes. Next came the test of automatic and conscious processing: She flashed stereotyped words (e.g., *black, hostile, lazy, welfare*) and neutral words (e.g., *however, what, said*) on a screen so quickly that the words were just below the participants' perceptual (conscious) awareness. They saw something, but they weren't sure what—that is, their conscious processing couldn't identify the words. However, their automatic processing could recognize the words. How could Devine be sure?

After flashing the words, she asked the participants to read a story about "Donald" (his ethnicity was not mentioned) and to rate their impressions of him. Donald was described somewhat ambiguously; he did some things in the story that could be interpreted either positively or negatively. The participants who had seen the words reflecting the stereotype of black Americans interpreted Donald significantly more negatively than those who had seen the neutral words did. Thus, for one group the negative stereotype had been primed

■ **FIGURE 13.4   A two-step model of the cognitive processing of stereotypes.**

(activated unconsciously through automatic processing); without their aware-ness, the participants were affected by these hostile and negative words, as indi-cated in their ratings of the Donald character. Because these stereotypes were op-erating outside their conscious cognitive control, white students who were low in prejudice were just as influenced by the cultural stereotype (e.g., that blacks are hostile) as the prejudiced students.

In her final experiment, Devine gave the students a task that involved their conscious processing: She asked them to list all the words they could think of that are used to describe black Americans. The high-prejudice students listed signifi-cantly more negative words than the low-prejudice students did. In other words, the less prejudiced participants used their conscious processing to edit out the negative stereotype and therefore were able to respond in a manner that was free of its influence.

While Devine's work is of great interest, recent research has suggested some important correctives—primarily, that the phenomenon is not as universal as she believed. Let us explain: According to Devine, pretty much everyone in American society has learned the negative stereotype of African Americans; thus, this negative stereotype is activated automatically in everyone. Accordingly, to be nonprejudiced we must learn to suppress or overcome this automatic response. But Russell Fazio and his colleagues have shown that considerable variability exists in people's automatic processing of negative stereotypes (Fazio, Jackson, Dunton, & Williams, 1995).

The Fazio team developed a clever way of measuring people's automatic processing of stereotypes. They presented people with words on a computer screen and asked them to judge whether the meaning of the words was good or bad. For example, when people saw the word attractive they pressed a key to indicate that this word has a good meaning, and when they saw the word disgusting they pressed a key to indicate that this word has a bad meaning.

On some trials, the words were preceded by a quick flash of a picture of a human face. People were told to look at the faces but to respond only to the meaning of the word that subsequently appeared on the screen. Thus, if you were a participant you would have seen a quick flash of a face, then a word such as attractive, and pressed a key to indicate that this was a "good" word. Now here's the interesting part: It just so happened that some of the faces were of African Americans and some were of whites. Remember, these faces were flashed very quickly (for about a third of a second). This was long enough for people to see the faces and have an automatic emotional reaction to them but too brief for people to control or suppress this reaction. As soon as they had a positive or negative reaction to the face, the word appeared on the screen and they had to decide whether the word was good or bad.

The point of the study was to see whether or not the presentation of the faces influenced how long it took people to respond to positive and negative words. Think about how this would work: If a participant is prejudiced against African Americans and this prejudice is ingrained and automatic, then negative feelings will be triggered automatically when the person sees a picture of an African American. This negative reaction should make it easier to respond "bad" to a negative word such as disgusting, because negative feelings are already present when the word appears. A negative reaction should make it harder to respond "good" to a positive word such as attractive, because this feeling is opposite to the meaning of the word.

The researchers constructed an index of automatic prejudice by computing the extent to which faces of African Americans slowed down responses to positive words and sped up responses to negative words. Fazio and his colleagues found considerable variability in people's level of automatic prejudice. Some people appeared to have automatic negative reactions to African Americans, whereas others did not. Further, this amount of automatic prejudice was found to predict people's behavior. At the end of the study, all participants were debriefed by an experimenter who "happened" to be an African American woman. This experimenter rated how friendly the participants treated her. Those who had shown the highest level of automatic prejudice on the word judgment task tended to act in a cold and disinterested manner toward the experimenter, whereas those who had shown the lowest amount of prejudice were far more likely to act in a warm and friendly manner.

Fazio and his colleagues suggest that, regarding attitudes toward African Americans, there are three kinds of people: (a) those who do not have an automatic negative reaction to African Americans, (b) those who do have an automatic negative reaction but have no qualms about expressing these feelings (i.e., are willing to be prejudiced), and (c) those who have an automatic negative reaction but want to suppress this reaction.

John Bargh has taken the idea of automatic prejudice a step further, showing that it can be triggered when certain ideas about the target group come to mind. Bargh and his colleagues examined negative reactions of men toward women (Bargh, Raymond, Pryor, & Strack, 1995). As you know, some men are more prone than most toward using sexual violence against women. Bargh and his colleagues investigated the possibility that in these men's minds there may be an automatic link between power and sex, such that thinking about power automatically triggers sexual attraction, without the men even recognizing this link. Just as some people have negative feelings toward African Americans that are expressed quickly and automatically, so too may some men have aggressive, sexual reactions to women that are expressed automatically, especially when power is on their minds.

To illustrate this idea, Bargh and his colleagues gave men a questionnaire that measured how prone they were toward sexual aggression (e.g., how much of a "turn-on" they found rape fantasies to be). The men also participated in a laboratory study in which the concept of power was primed in some men but not in others. (Recall that priming is a technique designed to activate a concept and make it salient.)

In the experiment, the men participated in the company of a young woman who they believed was another participant but who was really a confederate of the experimenter. After the priming procedure, the men were asked to rate how attractive they thought this woman was. Did priming the concept of power increase their attraction to the woman? The answer was yes for men who scored high on the sexual aggression questionnaire but no for the men who scored low on that questionnaire. In other words, for some men (but not for others) there is an automatic link in their minds between power and sexual attractiveness; priming or activating the concept of power increases the extent to which they find women attractive. The disturbing implication of this research is that these men are not aware of the link between power and sex in their minds and thus may not know that their attraction to women is influenced by feelings of power. They may simply "not get it," due to the fact that these feelings are triggered automatically, with no conscious awareness of where they came from (Bargh & Raymond, 1995; Bargh & Barndollar, 1996; Chartand & Bargh, 1996).

The Illusory Correlation

Illusory Correlation
the tendency to see relationships, or correlations, between events that are actually unrelated

Another way that our cognitive processing perpetuates stereotypical thinking is through the phenomenon of **illusory correlation** (Chapman, 1967; Garcia-Marques & Hamilton, 1996; Haslam, McGarty, & Brown, 1996). When we expect two things to be related, we fool ourselves into believing that they are—even when they are actually unrelated. Many illusory correlations exist in our society. For example, there is a common belief that couples who haven't been able to have children will conceive a child after they adopt a child—apparently because after the adoption, they feel less anxious and stressed. Guess what? This correlation is entirely illusory. Occasionally, an apparently infertile couple does conceive after adopting a child, but this occurs with no greater frequency than for apparently infertile couples who do not adopt. The former event, because it is so charmingly vivid, simply makes more of an impression on us when it happens, creating the illusory correlation (Gilovich, 1991).

What does all this have to do with prejudice and stereotypes? Illusory correlations are most likely to occur when the events or people are distinctive or con-

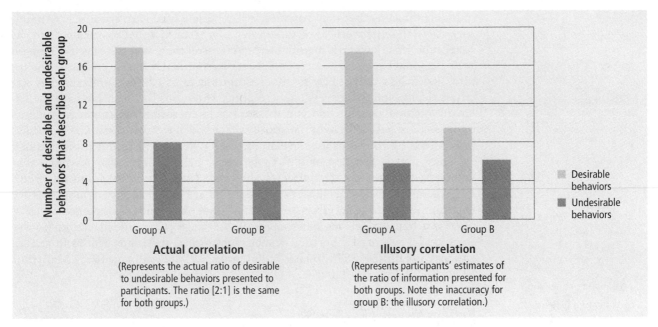

■ **FIGURE 13.5   The illusory correlation.**   The less information you have about a group, the more likely it is that you will fall victim to the illusory correlation. (Adapted from Hamilton & Gifford, 1976)

spicuous—that is, when they are different from the run-of-the-mill, typical social scene we are accustomed to (Hamilton, 1981; Hamilton et al., 1993). Minority group members—for example, as defined by race—are, by definition, distinctive, since fewer of them are present in the society. Other groups, who are not distinctive in terms of numbers—such as women, who make up 50 percent of the species—may nonetheless become distinctive or conspicuous because of a non-stereotypical profession or talent—for example, a woman member of the U.S. Senate. David Hamilton and Robert Gifford (1976) have shown that such distinctiveness leads to the creation of and belief in an illusory correlation—that is, a relationship between the distinctive target person and the behavior he or she displays. This illusory correlation is then applied to all members of the target group. Hamilton and Gifford presented information to research participants about two hypothetical groups of people: the A's and the B's. Of the information presented, two-thirds was positive about both groups, and one-third was negative about both groups. However, more information in general was presented about group A than about group B. Thus, while the ratio of desirable to undesirable information was the same for both groups, more than twice as much information of both types was given about the A's than about the B's. When asked to estimate how much information of both types was presented about each group, the participants overestimated the number of times the two most distinctive (less frequent) variables were paired—group B and undesirable behavior. Figure 13.5 depicts this finding. B's were more distinctive because there were fewer of them; undesirable behavior was more distinctive because there was less of it; and—voilà!—an illusory correlation was perceived between the two.

How does this work in everyday life? Let's say you don't know many Jews, so that for you, interacting with a Jew is a distinctive event and for you, Jews in general are distinctive people. Let's say you meet a Jewish individual who is an investment banker. Let's say you meet a second Jew who is an economist. An illusory correlation between Jews and money is created. If you also are aware of the stereotype that Jews are materialistic, the correlation you perceived based on your personal experiences seems all the more sound. The result is that, in the future, you will be more likely to notice situations in which Jews are behaving materialistically; you will be less likely to notice situations in which Jews are not behaving materialistically; and you will be less likely to notice situations in which non-Jews are behaving materialistically. You will have processed new information guided by your illusory correlation, seeing what you expect to see. You will also have strengthened your illusory correlation, confirming in your mind that your stereotype is right (Hamilton & Sherman, 1989; Mullen & Johnson, 1988).

We should note that illusory correlations are created in a far more passive fashion too. It is not necessary to have personal experience with people in a distinctive group—television, newspapers, and other forms of media create illusory correlations when they portray women, minorities, and other groups in stereotypical roles (Busby, 1975; Deaux & LaFrance, 1998; Friedman, 1977; McArthur & Resko, 1975).

Revising Stereotypical Beliefs

Our discussion of the perils of information processing may have left you feeling a bit depressed. How do you get people to change their stereotypical beliefs? Is it possible to override these social cognition processes? What sort of information would refute a stereotype? Let's say our next-door neighbor harbors two pet stereotypes that we find particularly annoying: He thinks that professors are lazy and that African Americans and Asian Americans are unpatriotic. What would happen if we provided him with evidence that his stereotypes are incorrect? For example, what if we showed him data demonstrating that professors at the local university work a 50-hour week? What if we pointed out that General Colin Powell, former chairman of the Joint Chiefs of Staff and one of the most universally admired people in the country, happens to be African American? What if we told him that the most highly decorated combat unit in World War II was composed solely of Asian Americans? Would this information affect our neighbor's stereotypes?

Not necessarily. In a recent experiment, Ziva Kunda and Kathryn Oleson (1997), found that when people are presented with examples that strongly challenge their existing stereotype, they tend to dismiss the disconfirming example as "the exception that proves the rule," and some actually strengthen their stereotypic belief.

Needless to say, there are some situations in which disconfirming evidence can be used to change a stereotype. Renée Webber and Jennifer Crocker (1983) show that a great deal depends on how the disconfirming information is presented. Webber and Crocker proposed three possible models for revising stereotypical beliefs: (a) the **bookkeeping model**, wherein each piece of disconfirming information modifies the stereotype; (b) the **conversion model**, wherein the stereotype radically changes in response to a powerful, salient piece of information; and (c) the **subtyping model**, wherein new subtype or subcategory stereotypes are created to accommodate the disconfirming information.

Webber and Crocker then conducted several experiments to see which model(s) might be right. They presented participants with information that disconfirmed their stereotypes about two occupational groups: librarians and corpo-

---

A fanatic is one who can't change his mind and won't change the subject.
—Winston Churchill, 1944

Bookkeeping Model information inconsistent with a stereotype that leads to a modification of the stereotype

Conversion Model information inconsistent with a stereotype that leads to a radical change in the stereotype

Subtyping Model information inconsistent with a stereotype that leads to the creation of a new substereotype to accommodate the information without changing the initial stereotype

■ General Colin Powell is a popular hero and the first African American to have received serious consideration for the presidency. Might a bigoted person vote for him? Perhaps if the bigot characterized General Powell as "the exception that proves the rule."

rate lawyers. In one condition, the participants received information in the book-keeping style, one disconfirming fact after another. In another condition, the participants received conversion information, a fact that strongly disconfirmed their stereotype. In the final condition, the participants received information that could lead them to create a subtype of their stereotype. Did these three styles of disconfirming information change people's minds about their stereotypes?

Webber and Crocker found that the bookkeeping information and the subtyping information did weaken the participants' stereotypes but that the conversion information did not. Why? Here is what occurred. When the information inconsistent with the stereotype was dispersed, with many members of the categorized group exhibiting the disconfirming traits, participants employed a bookkeeping strategy and gradually modified their beliefs. In other words, if our neighbor found out, on many occasions, that numerous professors worked a 50-hour week, this would slowly but eventually lead him to abandon the notion that professors are lazy. In contrast, when the disconfirming traits were concentrated among only a few individuals of the group, participants used a subtyping model. In other words, if our neighbor was confronted with the undeniable patriotism of General Powell, this would lead to the persistence of the old stereotype about African Americans, plus the creation of a new substereotype to the effect that "There may be a few exceptions, like Colin Powell"; thus, as in the Kunda and Oleson experiment discussed above, General Powell becomes the exception that proves the rule, leaving the original stereotype intact. Finally, the conversion approach just didn't work: One fact about an out-group that is evidence against the stereotype was just not powerful enough to change people's minds—which shouldn't surprise you, given our discussion of social cognition processes.

Two points need to be emphasized: (a) We all stereotype others to some extent—it is part of being a cognitive miser—and (b) emotional attitudes are harder to change than nonemotional ones. Thus, a strongly prejudiced person engages in stereotyping in a deeper, more thorough manner than the rest of us. Through this process, prejudiced attitudes become like a fortress—a closed circuit of cognitions, if you will—and this fortress drastically reduces the effectiveness of logical argument or disconfirming information.

The Way We Assign Meaning: Attributional Biases

As we discussed in Chapter 5, the people and situations we encounter in our social world are not labeled with neon signs telling us everything we need to know about them. Instead, we must rely on one aspect of social cognition—attributional processes—to determine why people behave as they do. Just as we form attributions to make sense out of one person's behavior, so too do we make attributions about whole groups of people. As you shall see, the attributional biases we discussed in Chapter 5 come back to haunt us now in a far more damaging and dangerous form: prejudice and discrimination.

Dispositional versus Situational Explanations

One reason stereotypes are so insidious and persistent is the human tendency to make dispositional attributions—that is, to leap to the conclusion that a person's behavior is due to some aspect of his or her personality rather than to some aspect of the situation. This is the familiar fundamental attribution error we discussed in Chapter 5. Although attributing people's behavior to their dispositions is often accurate, human behavior is also shaped by situational forces. Thus, an over reliance on dispositional attributions frequently leads us to make attributional mistakes. Given that this process operates on an individual level, you can only imagine the problems and complications that arise when we overzealously act out the fundamental attribution error for a whole group of people—an out-group.

Stereotypes are dispositional attributions—negative ones. Thomas Pettigrew (1979) has called our tendency to make dispositional attributions about an entire group of people the **ultimate attribution error**. For example, some of the stereotypes that characterize anti-Semitism are the result of Christians committing the fundamental attribution error when interpreting the behavior of Jews. These stereotypes have a long history, extending over several centuries. When the Jews were first forced to flee their homeland during the third Diaspora, some 2,500 years ago, they were not allowed to own land or become artisans in the new regions in which they settled. Needing a livelihood, some took to lending money—one of the few professions to which they were allowed easy access. Although this choice of occupation was an accidental byproduct of restrictive laws, it led to a dispositional attribution about Jews: that they were interested only in dealing with money and not in honest labor, like farming. As this attribution became an ultimate attribution error, Jews were labeled conniving, vicious parasites of the kind dramatized and immortalized by Shakespeare in the character of Shylock in *The Merchant of Venice* or of Fagin in Dickens's *Oliver Twist*. This dispositional stereotype contributed greatly to the barbarous consequences of anti-Semitism in Europe during the 1930s and 1940s and has persisted even in the face of clear, disconfirming evidence—such as that produced by the birth of the State of Israel, where Jews tilled the soil and made the desert bloom.

Similarly, many Americans have a stereotype about African American and Hispanic men that involves aggression and the potential for violence—a very powerful dispositional attribution. Galen Bodenhausen (1988) found that college students, playing the role of jurors in a mock trail, were more likely to find a defendant guilty of a given crime simply if his name was Carlos Ramirez rather than Robert Johnson. Thus, any situational information or extenuating circumstances that might have explained the defendant's actions were ignored when the powerful dispositional attribution was stereotypically triggered—in this case, by the Hispanic name.

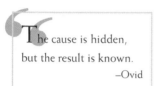

The cause is hidden, but the result is known.
—Ovid

Ultimate Attribution Error our tendency to make dispositional attributions about an entire group of people

In a further study, Galen Bodenhausen and Robert Wyer (1985) set up another dispositional versus situational possibility, wherein college students read fictionalized files on prisoners who were being considered for parole, and used the information contained in the files to make a parole decision. Sometimes the crime matched the common stereotype of the offender—for example, when a Hispanic male, Carlos Ramirez, committed assault and battery, or when an upper-class Anglo American, Ashley Chamberlaine, committed embezzlement. In other instances, the crimes were inconsistent with the stereotypes. When the prisoners' crimes were consistent with participants' stereotypes, the students were harsher in their recommendations for parole. In addition, they tended to ignore other information that was relevant to a parole decision but was inconsistent with the stereotype, such as evidence of good behavior in prison. Thus, when people behave in a way that conforms to our stereotype, we tend to blind ourselves to information that would provide clues about why they might have behaved as they did. Instead, we assume that something about their character or disposition, and not their situation or life circumstances, caused their behavior. In other words, when the fundamental attribution error raises its ugly head, we make dispositional attributions (based on our stereotypical beliefs about an ethnic or racial group) and not situational ones.

The Bell Curve Revisited

During the past several years we have witnessed the re-emergence of an angry and vituperative debate that has raged in our society for almost two centuries. The most recent flare-up occurred when a scholarly book, *The Bell Curve* (Herrnstein & Murray, 1995), suggested that the statistically significant difference in academic performance between African Americans and Anglo Americans might have a genetic component.

Let us look at the facts. There *is* a statistical difference in academic test performance among various cultural groups in this country. In general, although there is considerable overlap, as a group Asian Americans perform slightly better than Anglo Americans, who in turn perform better than African Americans. This difference is undeniably real. The key question is, why does it occur? Is the reason for the difference dispositional or situational? In a striking series of experiments, Claude Steele and Joshua Aronson (Steele, 1997; Steele & Aronson, 1995a, 1995b; Aronson, Quinn, & Spencer, 1998) demonstrated that at least one major contributing factor is clearly situational and is based on a phenomenon they call stereotype threat. Specifically, when African American students find themselves in highly evaluative educational situations, most tend to experience apprehension about confirming the existing negative cultural stereotype of "intellectual inferiority." In effect, they are saying, "If I perform poorly on this test, it will reflect poorly on me and on my race." This extra burden of apprehension in turn interferes with their ability to perform well in these situations. For example, in one of their experiments Steele and Aronson administered a difficult verbal test, the GRE, individually to African American and white students at Stanford University. Half the students of each race were led to believe that the investigator was interested in measuring their intellectual ability; the other half were led to believe that the investigator was merely trying to develop the test itself—and, because the test was not yet valid or reliable, they were assured that their performance would mean nothing in terms of their actual ability.

Stereotype Threat
the apprehension experienced by members of a minority group that they might behave in a manner that confirms an existing cultural stereotype

■ Shortly before his untimely death, tennis star Arthur Ashe asserted that part of the burden of being black in American society involved constantly being evaluated as a representative of his race. This constant race-based scrutiny underlies what Steele & Aronson refer to as "stereotype threat."

The results confirmed the researchers' speculations. White students performed equally well regardless of whether or not they believed the test was being used as a diagnostic tool. Those African American students who believed the test was nondiagnostic of their abilities performed as well as white students; in contrast, those African American students who were led to believe that the test was measuring their abilities performed less well than white students. In subsequent experiments in the same series, Steele and Aronson also found that, if race is made more salient, the decrement in performance among African Americans is even more pronounced.

The phenomenon of stereotype threat is not limited to race but applies to gender as well. Thus, a similar pattern of results was found for women (compared to men) when taking math tests (Spencer & Steele, 1996). That is, as you know, a common stereotype of women: that compared to men, they are not very good at math. In this experiment, when women were led to believe that a particular test was gender-relevant, they did not perform as well as men; however, in another condition, when women were led to believe that the same test was not gender-relevant, they performed as well as men.

Expectations and Distortions

As we noted above, when a member of an out-group behaves as we expected him or her to behave, it confirms and even strengthens our stereotype. But what happens when an out-group member behaves in an unexpected, nonstereotypical fashion? Attribution theory provides the answer: We can simply engage in some attributional fancy footwork and emerge with our dispositional stereotype intact. Principally, we can make situational attributions about the exception—for example, that the person really is like that but it just isn't apparent in this situation.

This phenomenon was beautifully captured in the laboratory by William Ickes and his colleagues (1982). Here college men were scheduled, in pairs, to participate in the experiment. In one condition, the experimenter casually informed one participant that his partner was extremely unfriendly; in the other condition, the experimenter told one participant that his partner was extremely

Alain © 1951 The New Yorker: 25th Annual Album, Harper & Bros.

■ This cartoon depicts a common stereotype of the Mexican as lazy. Note how your eye focuses on the one sleeping person but tends to ignore the ten hardworking persons. Without intending to, the cartoonist is showing us how powerfully distorting a stereotype can be.

friendly. In both conditions, the participants went out of their way to be nice to their partner, and their partner returned their friendliness—that is, he behaved warmly and smiled a lot, as college men tend to do when they are treated nicely. The difference was that those participants who expected their partner to be unfriendly interpreted his friendly behavior as phony—as a temporary, fake response to their own nice behavior. They were convinced that underneath it all, he really was an unfriendly person. Accordingly, when the observed behavior—friendliness—was unexpected and contrary to their dispositional attribution, participants attributed it to the situation: "He's just pretending to be friendly." The dispositional attribution emerged unscathed.

The cartoon above demonstrates this ability to explain away disconfirming situational evidence and maintain a dispositional stereotype. This cartoon, from 1951, capitalizes on the stereotype of Mexicans as lazy. While ten Mexicans are seen in the background working hard, the cartoon focuses on the stereotypical image in the foreground. The cartoon's message is that the lazy individual is the true exemplar of his ethnic group. No matter how many others refute the stereotype, the cartoon is implying, it is still true. (Note that some half a century ago, not only was this message considered acceptable, but this cartoon was chosen as one of the best of the year.)

Blaming the Victim

Try as they might, it is not always easy for people who have rarely been discriminated against to fully understand what it's like to be a target of prejudice. Well-intentioned members of the dominant majority will sympathize with the plight of African Americans, Hispanic Americans, Asian Americans, Jews, women, homosexuals, and other groups who are oppressed in our society, but true empathy does not come easily to those who are accustomed to being judged on the basis of

> ❝I will look at any additional evidence to confirm the opinion to which I have already come.
>
> –Lord Molson,
> British politician

Blaming the Victim
our tendency to blame individuals (make dispositional attributions) for their victimization, typically motivated by a desire to see the world as a fair place

their own merit and not their racial, ethnic, religious, or other group membership. And when empathy is absent, it is sometimes hard to avoid falling into the trap of **blaming the victim** for his or her plight. This may take the form of the "well-deserved reputation." It goes something like this: "If the Jews have been victimized throughout their history, they must have been doing something to deserve it," or "That woman who got herself raped should have been more suspicious of her date." Such suggestions constitute a demand that members of the out-group conform to more stringent standards of behavior than those set for the majority.

Ironically, as we discussed in Chapter 5, this tendency to blame victims for their victimization—attributing their predicaments to deficits in their abilities and character—is typically motivated by an understandable desire to see the world as a fair and just place, one where people get what they deserve and deserve what they get. As Melvin Lerner and his colleagues have shown (1980, 1991; Lerner & Grant, 1990), most people, when confronted with evidence of an inequitable outcome that is otherwise difficult to explain, find a way to blame the victim. For example, in one experiment Lerner and his colleagues found that if two people worked equally hard on the same task and, by the flip of a coin, one received a sizable reward and the other received nothing, observers—after the fact—tended to reconstruct what happened and convince themselves that the unlucky person must have worked less hard. Similarly, negative attitudes toward the poor and the homeless—including blaming them for their own plight—are more prevalent among individuals who display a strong belief in a just world (Furnham & Gunter, 1984).

How does the belief in a just world lead to derogation of a victim? When something bad happens to another person (e.g., the person is mugged or raped), we will undoubtedly feel sorry for him or her but at the same time will also feel relieved that this horrible thing didn't happen to us. In addition, we will also feel scared that such a thing might happen to us in the future. How can we cope with these fears and worries? The best way to protect ourselves from the fear we feel when we hear about someone else's tragedy is to convince ourselves that the person must have done something to bring it on him- or herself. Therefore, in our own minds we are safe, because we would have behaved more cautiously (Jones & Aronson, 1973).

Most of us are quite adept at reconstructing situations after the fact, in order to support our belief in a just world. It simply requires making a dispositional attribution—to the victim—and not a situational one—to the scary, random events that can happen to anyone at any time. In a fascinating experiment by Ronnie Janoff-Bulman and her colleagues (1985), college students who were provided with a description of a young woman's friendly behavior toward a man judged that behavior as completely appropriate. Yet in another condition of the experiment, students were given the same description, plus the information that the encounter ended with the young woman being raped by the man. In this condition, the students rated her behavior as inappropriate, as her having brought the rape on herself. Such findings are not limited to American college students reading hypothetical cases. For example, in a survey conducted in England, a striking 33 percent of the population were found to believe that victims of rape are almost always to blame for it (Wagstaff, 1982). How can we account for such harsh attributions? Most of us find it frightening to think that we live in a world where people, through no fault of their own, can be raped, discriminated against, deprived of equal pay for equal work, or denied the basic necessities of life. By the same token, if 6 million Jews are exterminated for no apparent reason, it is, in some strange way, comforting to believe they must have done something to bring those events on themselves. The irony is overwhelming: Such thinking makes the world seem safer to us.

Self-Fulfilling Prophecies

All other things being equal, if you believe that Amy is stupid and treat her accordingly, chances are that she will not say a lot of clever things in your presence. This is the well-known **self-fulfilling prophecy,** discussed in Chapter 4. How does this come about? If you believe Amy is stupid, you probably will not ask her interesting questions and you will not listen intently while she is talking; indeed, you might even look out the window or yawn. You behave this way because of a simple expectation: Why waste energy paying attention to Amy if she is unlikely to say anything smart or interesting? This is bound to have an important impact on Amy's behavior, for if the people she is talking to aren't paying much attention, she will feel uneasy and will probably clam up and not come out with all the poetry and wisdom within her. This serves to confirm the belief you had about her in the first place. The circle is closed; the self-fulfilling prophecy is complete.

Self-Fulfilling Prophecy the case whereby people (a) have an expectation about what another person is like, which (b) influences how they act toward that person, which (c) causes that person to behave in a way consistent with people's original expectations

The relevance of this phenomenon to stereotyping and discrimination was elegantly demonstrated in an experiment by Carl Word, Mark Zanna, and Joel Cooper (1974). They asked white college undergraduates to interview several job applicants; some of the applicants were white, and others were African American. Unwittingly, the college students displayed discomfort and lack of interest when interviewing African American applicants. For example, they sat farther away, they tended to stammer when talking, and they terminated the interview far sooner than was the case when they were interviewing white applicants. Can you guess how this behavior might have affected the African American applicants? To find out, the researchers, in a second experiment, systematically varied the behavior of the interviewers (actually confederates) so that it coincided with the way the real interviewers had treated the African American or white interviewees in the first experiment. But in the second experiment, all of the interviewees were white. The researchers videotaped the proceedings and had the applicants rated by independent judges. They found that those applicants who were interviewed the way African Americans had been interviewed in the first experiment were judged to be far more nervous and far less effective than those who were interviewed the way whites had been interviewed in the first experiment. In sum, these experiments demonstrate clearly that when African Americans are interviewed by whites, they are unintentionally placed at a disadvantage and are likely to perform less well than their white counterparts (see Figure 13.6).

On a societal level, the insidiousness of the self-fulfilling prophecy goes even further. Suppose there is a general belief that a particular group is irredeemably stupid, uneducable, and fit only for menial jobs. Why waste educational resources on them? Hence, they are given inadequate schooling. Thirty years later, what do you find? An entire group that, with few exceptions, is fit only for menial jobs. "See? I was right all the time," says the bigot. "How fortunate that we didn't waste our precious educational resources on such people!" The self-fulfilling prophecy strikes again.

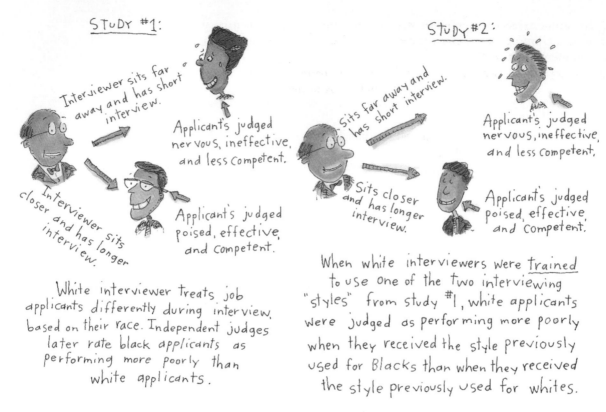

STUDY #1:

Interviewer sits far away and has short interview.

Applicant's judged nervous, ineffective, and less competent.

Interviewer sits closer and has longer interview.

Applicant's judged poised, effective, and competent.

White interviewer treats job applicants differently during interview, based on their race. Independent judges later rate black applicants as performing more poorly than white applicants.

STUDY #2:

Sits far away and has short interview.

Applicant's judged nervous, ineffective, and less competent.

Sits closer and has longer interview.

Applicant's judged poised, effective, and competent.

When white interviewers were trained to use one of the two interviewing "styles" from study #1, white applicants were judged as performing more poorly when they received the style previously used for Blacks than when they received the style previously used for whites.

■ **FIGURE 13.6 An experiment demonstrating self-fulfilling prophecies.**

The Way We Allocate Resources: Realistic Conflict Theory

One of the most obvious sources of conflict and prejudice is competition—for scarce resources, for political power, and for social status. Indeed, it can be said that whatever problems result from the simple in-group versus out-group phenomenon, they will be magnified by real economic, political, or status competition. **Realistic conflict theory** holds that limited resources lead to conflict among groups and result in prejudice and discrimination (Jackson, 1993; Levine & Campbell, 1972; Olzak & Nagel, 1986; Sherif, 1966; White, 1977). Thus, prejudiced attitudes tend to increase when times are tense and conflict exists over mutually exclusive goals. For example, prejudice has existed between Anglos and Mexican American migrant workers over a limited number of jobs, between Arabs and Israelis over disputed territory, and between northerners and southerners over the abolition of slavery. At the present time, such realistic conflict in Germany is erupting in violence against residents of Turkish origin at the hands of the German neo-Nazis.

Economic and Political Competition

In his classic study of prejudice in a small industrial town, John Dollard (1938) was among the first to document the relationship between discrimination and economic competition. While initially there was no discernible prejudice against the new German immigrants to this American town, prejudice flourished as jobs grew scarce:

Realistic Conflict Theory
the theory that limited resources lead to conflict between groups and result in increased prejudice and discrimination

Local whites largely drawn from the surrounding farms manifested considerable direct aggression toward the newcomers. Scornful and derogatory opinions were expressed about these Germans, and the native whites had a satisfying sense of superiority toward them. . . . The chief element in the permission to be aggressive against the Germans was rivalry for jobs and status in the local woodenware plants. The native whites felt definitely crowded for their jobs by the entering German groups and in case of bad times had a chance to blame the Germans, who by their presence provided more competitors for the scarcer jobs. There seemed to be no traditional pattern of prejudice against Germans unless the skeletal suspicion against all out-groupers (always present) can be invoked in its place. (Dollard, 1938)

In a similar fashion, the prejudice, violence, and negative stereotyping directed against Chinese immigrants in the United States fluctuated wildly throughout the nineteenth century, as a result of changes in economic competition. For example, when the Chinese joined the gold rush in California, in direct competition with miners of Anglo-Saxon origin, they were described as "depraved and vicious . . . gross gluttons, . . . bloodthirsty and inhuman" (Jacobs & Landau, 1971, p. 71). However, only a few years later, when they were willing to accept backbreaking work as laborers on the transcontinental railroad—work few white Americans were willing to do—they were regarded as sober, industrious, and law-abiding. They were so highly regarded, in fact, that Charles Crocker, one of the great tycoons financing the railroad, wrote, "They are equal to the best white men. . . . They are very trusty, very intelligent and they live up to their contracts" (Jacobs & Landau, 1971, p. 81). With the end of the Civil War came an influx of former soldiers into an already tight job market. This was immediately followed by a dramatic increase in negative attitudes toward the Chinese: The stereotype changed to criminal, conniving, crafty, and stupid (Jacobs & Landau, 1971).

These changes suggest that when times are tough and resources are scarce, members of the in-group will feel more threatened by members of the out-group and will therefore show more of an inclination toward prejudice, discrimination, and violence toward the latter. How might the hypothesis be tested? We might look for increases in violent acts directed at minority group members during times of economic hardship. Carl Hovland and Robert Sears (1940) did just that, by correlating two sets of very different data: (a) the price of cotton in the southern states from 1882 to 1930 and (b) the number of lynchings of southern African Americans during that same period. During this period, cotton was by far the most important crop in the South; as cotton went, so went the economy. Hovland and Sears (1940) found that a significant correlation existed between the two variables, $r = -.72$. As you'll recall from Chapter 2, this is both a large correlation, meaning that the two variables are highly related, and a negative correlation, meaning that increases in one variable are related to decreases in the other variable. In other words, as the price of cotton dropped, the number of lynchings increased (see Figure 13.7). In short, as members of the in-group experienced the hardships of an economic depression, they became more hostile toward out-group members, whom they almost certainly perceived as a threat to their livelihood. This hostility led to an increase in the number of violent acts. (Although these data were gathered almost 60 years ago, we hasten to add that they are extremely reliable; modern investigators, using more sophisticated statistical techniques, have confirmed the accuracy of the original research (Hepworth & West, 1988). Similarly, in a survey conducted in the 1970s, most antiblack prejudice

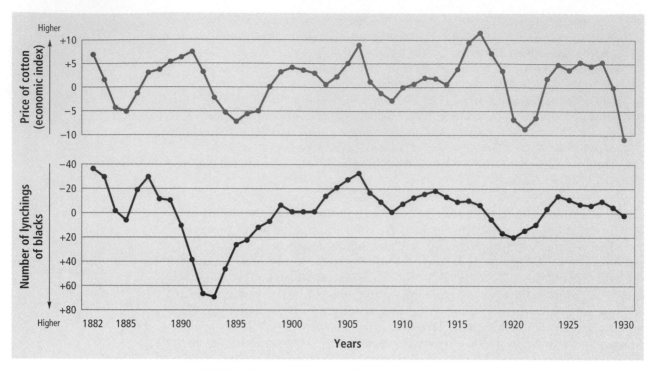

■ **FIGURE 13.7   Relation of total lynchings to the price of cotton.** Note that the lynching scale shows greatest frequency at the bottom of the graph. (Adapted from Hovland & Sears, 1940)

was found among people who were just one rung above the African Americans socioeconomically. And as we might expect, prejudice was most pronounced when whites and African Americans were in close competition for jobs (Simpson & Yinger, 1985; Vanneman & Pettigrew, 1972). We should note, however, that this research is correlational; as we discussed in Chapter 2, experimental research designs allow us to make cause-and-effect statements with far more confidence than we can on the basis of correlational research. How might we study the relationship between competition and prejudice experimentally?

In a classic experiment, Muzafer Sherif and his colleagues (1961) tested group conflict theory using the natural environment of a Boy Scout camp. The participants in the camp were normal, well-adjusted 12-year-old boys who were randomly assigned to one of two groups, the Eagles or the Rattlers. Each group stayed in its own cabin; the cabins were located quite a distance apart in order to reduce contact between the two groups. The youngsters were placed in situations designed to increase the cohesiveness of their own group. This was done by arranging enjoyable activities like hiking and swimming and by having the campers work with their group on various building projects, preparing group meals, and so on.

After feelings of cohesiveness developed within each group, the researchers set up a series of competitive activities in which the two groups were pitted against each other—for example, in games like football, baseball, and tug-of-war, where prizes were awarded to the winning team. These competitive games aroused feelings of conflict and tension between the two groups. In addition, the investigators created other situations to further intensify the conflict. For example, a camp party was arranged, but each group was told it started at a different time, thereby ensuring that the Eagles would arrive well before the Rattlers. The refreshments at the party consisted of two different kinds of food: Half the food was fresh, appealing, and appetizing, while the other half was squashed, ugly, and unappetizing. As one might expect, the early arriving Eagles grabbed most of the appealing refreshments, leaving only the less interesting, less appetizing, squashed, and damaged food for their adversaries. When the Rattlers finally arrived and saw what had happened, they became angry—so angry, in fact, they began to call the exploitive group rather uncomplimentary names. Because the Eagles believed they deserved what they got (first come, first served), they resented the name-calling and responded in kind. Name-calling escalated into food-throwing, and within a short time, punches were thrown and a full-scale riot ensued.

Following this incident, the investigators tried to reverse the hostility they had promoted. Competitive games were eliminated, and a great deal of nonconflictual social contact was initiated. Once hostility had been aroused, however, simply eliminating the competition did not eliminate the hostility. Indeed, hostility continued to escalate, even when the two groups were engaged in such benign activities as watching movies together. Eventually, the investigators did manage to reduce the hostility between the two groups; exactly how this was accomplished will be discussed at the end of this chapter.

The Role of the Scapegoat

A special case of the conflict-competition theory is the scapegoat theory (Allport, 1954; Berkowitz & Green, 1962; Blanchard, Adelman, & Cook, 1975; Gemmill, 1989; Miller & Bugelski, 1948). As indicated above, if times are tough and things are going poorly, individuals have a tendency to lash out at members of an out-group with whom they are in direct competition for scarce resources. But there are situations in which a logical competitor does not exist. For example, in Germany following World War I, inflation was out of control and people were extremely poor, demoralized, and frustrated. When the Nazis gained power in the 1930s, they managed to focus the frustration of the German population on the Jews, an easily identifiable, powerless out-group. The Jews were not the reason the German economy was in such bad shape, but who was? It's hard to fight back against world events, or one's government—particularly when one's government is evading responsibility by blaming someone else. Thus, the Nazis created the illusion that if the Jews could be punished, deprived of their civil rights, and ultimately eliminated, all of the problems then plaguing Germany would disappear. The Jews served as a convenient scapegoat because they were easily identifiable and were not in a position to defend themselves or strike back (Berkowitz, 1962).

It is not always easy to separate prejudice due entirely and directly to economic competition from prejudice due to general scapegoating. For example, the correlation we discussed between the price of cotton and the number of lynchings in the South probably had elements of both. Another example of the combination of these two elements is the tragic case of a young Asian American who was beaten to death by several white Americans in Detroit several years ago. The murderers were unemployed autoworkers, angry at the Japanese auto industry because they felt that competition from this industry was the main reason for their unemployment. And so in their frustration, their irrational hostility toward all people of Japanese origin erupted, and they took it out on this unfortunate young man (who, ironically, was Chinese American).

Does scapegoating occur whenever people are feeling frustrated and angry, even in the absence of direct competition or conflict? In an experiment by Ronald

Rogers and Steven Prentice-Dunn (1981), white students at the University of Alabama were instructed to administer a series of electric shocks to another student as part of a learning experiment. The students were free to adjust the level of intensity of the shocks. In actuality, the learner was a confederate who was not really connected to the shock apparatus. There was no conflict or competition involved in this study; however, for some participants, feelings of frustration and anger were aroused. The confederate was trained to be either friendly or insulting to the participant. In addition, the confederate was either black or white. Would angry white students respond more aggressively toward a black peer than a white one? The answer is yes. When the confederate insulted them, the students administered far more intense shocks to the black student than to the white student; when the confederate was friendly, the students administered slightly less intense shocks to the black student. The results of this experiment are shown in Figure 13.8.

This experiment produced findings almost identical with those of an earlier experiment performed by Donald Weatherly (1961). In Weatherly's experiment, college students were subjected to a great deal of frustration. Some of these students were highly anti-Semitic; others were not. The subjects were then asked to write stories based on pictures they were shown. For some subjects, the characters in these pictures were assigned Jewish names; for others, they were not. Two major findings emerged: (a) After being frustrated, anti-Semitic subjects wrote stories that directed more aggression toward the Jewish characters than people who were not anti-Semitic did, and (b) no difference between the anti-Semitic students and the others was found when the characters they were writing about were not identified as Jewish. In a conceptually similar experiment performed in Canada, English-speaking Canadians, after undergoing a frustrating failure experience, rated members of the out-group (French-speaking Canadians) more negatively than those who had not undergone the frustrating experience (Meindl & Lerner, 1985).

Once again, the laboratory experiments help to clarify the dynamics that underlie real-world events. What all three of the above experiments have in common is **scapegoating**. The general picture emerges that individuals, when frustrated or unhappy, tend to displace aggression onto groups that are disliked, are

Scapegoating
the tendency for individuals, when frustrated or unhappy, to displace aggression onto groups that are disliked, visible, and relatively powerless

■ **FIGURE 13.8**
Scapegoating. When insulted, people are more prone to aggress against minorities. (Adapted from Rogers & Prentice-Dunn, 1981)

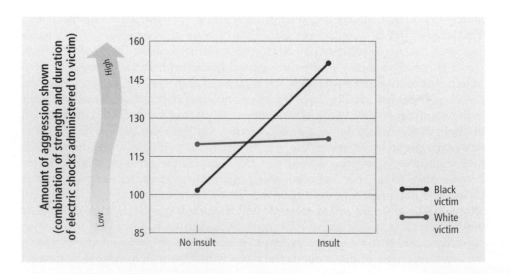

visible, and are relatively powerless. Moreover, the form the aggression takes depends on what is allowed or approved by the in-group in question. In the past 50 years, lynchings of African Americans and pogroms against Jews have diminished dramatically, because these are now deemed illegal by the dominant subculture. But not all progress is linear. In the past several years, we have seen the former Soviet Union lose its grip on several Eastern European countries. Although we are cheered by the new freedom that exists in this region, that freedom has been accompanied by increased feelings of nationalism ("us versus them") that in turn have produced intensified feelings of rancor and prejudice against out-groups. Thus, in the Baltics and Balkans the rise in nationalistic feelings has been accompanied by eruptions of hostility (and war) among Serbs, Muslims, and Croats, between Azerbaijanis and Armenians, and so on. And, of course, over the past several years we have also seen increases in the inevitable hostility toward the world's favorite scapegoat, with anti-Semitism on the rise throughout Eastern Europe (Singer, 1990).

The Way We Conform: Normative Rules

As we have seen, prejudice is created and maintained by many forces in the social world. Some we can observe operating within the individual, such as the ways we process information and assign meaning to observed events. Some we can observe operating on whole groups of people, such as the effects of competition, conflict, and frustration. Our final explanation for what causes prejudice is also observed on the group level—conformity to normative standards or rules in the society. As we discussed in Chapter 7, conformity is a frequent part of social life, whether we conform to gain information (informational conformity) or to fit in and be accepted (normative conformity). Again, a relatively innocuous social behavior—in this case, conformity—becomes particularly dangerous and debilitating when we enter the realm of prejudice.

Social Learning Theory

Norms are beliefs held by a society as to what is correct, acceptable, and permissible. Obviously, norms vary widely across cultures. Important regional differences in norms also occur within the same country. For example, until recently, the racial segregation of hotels, eating places, motion picture theaters, drinking fountains, and toilet facilities was normative in the American South but not in the North. Indeed, it can be said that, prior to 1954, segregation controlled most aspects of social life in the South.

These norms do not have to be taught directly. But, even when not taught directly, if an entire culture or subculture subscribes to nonegalitarian norms and values, chances are children will imbibe them and, unless they move into a situation where they encounter different norms, will continue to maintain them. In other words, simply by living in a society where stereotypical information abounds and where discriminatory behavior is the norm, the vast majority of us will unwittingly develop prejudiced attitudes and discriminatory behavior to some extent. We refer to this as institutional discrimination, or, more specifically, as **institutionalized racism** and **institutionalized sexism.** For example, if you grow up in a society where minority and female professors, business executives, or physicians are few but where most people in these groups tend to hold menial jobs, then simply living in that society will increase your likelihood of developing certain (negative) attitudes about the native abilities of minorities and women.

Institutionalized Racism
racist attitudes that are held by the vast majority of us because we are living in a society where stereotypes and discrimination are the norm

Institutionalized Sexism
sexist attitudes that are held by the vast majority of us because we are living in a society where stereotypes and discrimination are the norm

This state of affairs can come about without anyone actively teaching you that minorities and women are inferior and without any law or decree banning minorities and women from college faculties, boardrooms, or medical schools. Instead, societal barriers have created a lack of opportunity for these groups that makes their success extremely unlikely.

Normative Conformity
the tendency to go along with the group in order to fulfill their expectations and gain acceptance

How does normative prejudice work? As you'll recall from our discussion of **normative conformity** in Chapter 7, there is a strong tendency to go along with the group in order to fulfill their expectations and gain exceptance. Being a nonconformist can be painful. Thus, as Thomas Pettigrew (1958, 1985, 1991) has noted, many people hold prejudiced attitudes and engage in discriminatory behaviors in order to conform to, or fit in with, the prevailing majority view of their culture. It's as if people say, "Hey, everybody else thinks X's are inferior; if I behave cordially toward X's, people will think I'm crazy. They won't like me. They'll say bad things about me. I don't need the hassle. I'll just go along with everybody else." Pettigrew argues convincingly that while economic competition, frustration, and social cognition processes do account for some prejudice, by far the greatest determinant of prejudice is slavish conformity to social norms.

For example, Ernest Campbell and Thomas Pettigrew (1959) studied the ministers of Little Rock, Arkansas after the 1954 Supreme Court decision ushered in desegregation. As religious people, most ministers favored integration and equality for all American citizens. However, they kept these views to themselves. They were afraid to support desegregation from their pulpits, because they knew that their white congregations were violently opposed to it. Going against the prevailing norm would have meant losing church members and contributions, and under such normative pressure, even ministers found it difficult to do the right thing.

Another way to determine the role of normative conformity is to track changes in prejudice and discrimination over time. As social norms change, so too should the strength of prejudiced attitudes and the amount of discriminatory behavior. For example, what happens when people move from one part of the country to another? If conformity is a factor in prejudice, we would expect individuals to show dramatic increases in their prejudice when they move to an area in which the norm is more prejudicial and to show dramatic decreases when they move to an area in which the norm is less prejudicial. And that is just what happens. In one study, Jeanne Watson (1950) found that people who had recently moved to New York City and had come into direct contact with an anti-Semitic norm became more anti-Semitic themselves. In another study, Pettigrew (1958) found that when southerners entered the army and came into contact with a less prejudiced set of social norms, their prejudice against African Americans gradually decreased. A somewhat different example of shifting norms was found by researchers in a small mining town in West Virginia: African American miners and white miners developed a pattern of living that consisted of total integration while they were under the ground and total segregation while they were above the ground (Minard, 1952; Reitzes, 1952).

Moreover, surveys conducted over the past six decades make it clear that what is going on inside the minds of Americans has changed a great deal. For example, in 1942 the overwhelming majority of white Americans believed that it was a good idea to have separate sections for African American and white people on buses. Two out of every three white Americans surveyed believed that schools should be segregated. In the South, the numbers were even more striking: In 1942, fully 98 percent of the white population was opposed to desegregating

■ What a difference a decade makes! On the left, in 1963, Governor George Wallace defies a federal order by physically blocking the entrance of the first black student to the University of Alabama. On the right, ten years later, Governor Wallace happily congratulates the University of Alabama homecoming queen.

schools (Hyman & Sheatsley, 1956). In contrast, by 1988 only 3 percent of white Americans said they wouldn't want their child to attend school with black children. That is a dramatic change indeed!

Shifting cultural norms are well illustrated by the two photographs on this page, each depicting Governor George Wallace of Alabama. In one, the governor, along with his state militia, is attempting to block the doors of the University of Alabama as the first African American students seek to register for college. Only the presence of federal troops and telephone intervention by President John Kennedy caused Governor Wallace to back down. And yet just a decade later, the normative climate of Alabama had changed to the extent that Governor Wallace could be seen—as in the second photograph—congratulating the young African American woman whom the University of Alabama student body had chosen to be homecoming queen (Knopke, Norrell, & Rogers, 1991).

Modern Racism

While normative changes in our own country have led to decreases in discrimination, prejudice is in no way eradicated. Instead, it has become more subtle. As the norm changes to become one of tolerance for out-groups, many people simply become more careful—outwardly acting unprejudiced, yet inwardly maintaining their stereotyped views. This phenomenon is called **modern racism**. Here people's prejudice is typically revealed in subtle, indirect ways, because they have learned to hide prejudice in order to avoid being labeled as racist. When the situation becomes safe, however, their prejudice will be revealed (Dovidio & Gaertner, 1996; Gaertner & Dovidio, 1986; Kinder & Sears, 1981; McConahay, 1986).

For example, while it is true that few Americans say they are generally opposed to school desegregation, it is interesting that most white parents oppose busing their own children to achieve racial balance. When questioned, these parents insist that their opposition has nothing to do with prejudice; they simply don't want their kids to waste a lot of time on a bus. But as John McConahay

Modern Racism
prejudice revealed in subtle, indirect ways because people have learned to hide prejudiced attitudes in order to avoid being labeled as racist

(1982) has shown, most white parents are quite tranquil about busing when their kids simply are being bused from one white school to another—most show vigorous opposition only when the busing is interracial in nature.

Given the properties of modern prejudice, racism and sexism can best be studied with subtle or unobtrusive measures (Crosby, Bromley, & Saxe, 1980). For example, Edward E. Jones and Harold Sigall (1971) created an ingenious contraption, the bogus pipeline, to get at the real attitudes—not simply the socially desirable ones—of their research participants. The bogus pipeline is an impressive-looking machine that is described to research participants as a kind of lie detector. In fact, it is just a pile of electronic hardware whose dials the experimenter can secretly manipulate. Here's how researchers use the pipeline: Participants are randomly assigned to one of two conditions, in which they indicate their attitudes either on a paper-and-pencil questionnaire (where it is easy to give socially correct responses) or by using the bogus pipeline (where they believe the machine will reveal their true attitudes if they lie). Sigall and Richard Page (1971) found that more racial prejudice was present in students' responses when the bogus pipeline was used. In a similar experiment, college men and women expressed almost identical positive attitudes about women's rights and women's roles in society on a paper-and-pencil measure. However, when the bogus pipeline was used, most of the men displayed far less sympathy to women's issues than the women did (Tourangeau, Smith, & Rasinski, 1997).

We can also find examples of racism and sexism in overt behavior. For example, Ian Ayers and his colleagues (1991) visited 90 automobile dealerships in the Chicago area and, using a carefully rehearsed, uniform strategy to negotiate the lowest possible price on a new car (one that cost the dealer approximately $11,000), found that white males were given a final price that averaged $11,362; white females, $11,504; African American males, $11,783; and African American females, $12,237. Thus, all other things being equal, when it comes to buying a new car, being African American or female puts a person at a disadvantage.

Subtle and Blatant Prejudice in Western Europe

Although this chapter has dealt primarily with prejudice and stereotyping in the United States, it goes without saying that prejudice exists throughout the world. Examples of blatant prejudice abound in daily newspaper headlines: ethnic cleansing in Bosnia, violent conflict between Arabs and Jews in the Middle East, mass murder between warring tribes in Rwanda. This prejudice exists in "modern" forms as well. For example, in a transnational study, Thomas Pettigrew and R. W. Meertens (1995) demonstrated the existence of blatant as well as more "modern," subtle racism in three major Western European countries: France, the Netherlands, and Great Britain. These researchers showed that the difference between blatant and subtle racism is important and has interesting consequences. One of their major findings is that, while the targets of prejudice differ in the three countries, the behavior of the native population toward recent immigrants can be predicted from a knowledge of how the natives score on both blatant and subtle measures of prejudice. For example, in all three countries those people who score high on the blatant prejudice scale want to send immigrants back to their home country and wish to restrict their meager rights even further. In contrast, those who score low on both scales want to improve the rights of immigrants, are prepared to take action to help them remain in the country, and are willing to act forcefully to improve the relations between immigrants and natives.

> We all decry prejudice, yet all are prejudiced.
> –Herbert Spencer, 1873

Those who score high on the subtle racism scale but low on the blatant scale tend to reject immigrants in ways that are more covert and socially acceptable. Specifically, while they will not take action to send immigrants back to their home country, they are willing neither to do anything to help improve their relations with the immigrant population nor to go along with any attempt to increase that population's civil rights.

How Can Prejudice Be Reduced?

Sometimes subtle, sometimes brutally overt—prejudice is indeed ubiquitous. Does this mean that prejudice is an essential aspect of human social interaction and will therefore always be with us? We social psychologists do not take such a pessimistic view. We tend to agree with Thoreau (see his statement in the margin). People can change. But how? What can we do to eliminate or at least reduce this noxious aspect of human social behavior?

> It is never too late to give up our prejudices.
> —Henry David Thoreau, 1854

Because stereotypes and prejudice are based on erroneous information, for many years social observers believed that all one needed to do was educate people—expose them to accurate information—and their prejudice would disappear. But this has proved to be a naive hope (Lazarsfeld, 1940). After reading this chapter thus far, you can see why this might be the case. Because of the underlying emotional aspects of prejudice, as well as some of the cognitive ruts we get into (e.g., attributional biases, biased expectations, and illusory correlations), stereotypes based on misinformation are difficult to modify simply by providing people with correct information. On the other hand, there is hope. As you have perhaps experienced in your own life, repeated contact with members of an outgroup can have a positive effect on stereotypes and prejudice. But as we shall see, mere contact is not enough; it must be a special kind of contact. Let's take a long look at what we mean by "a special kind of contact."

The Contact Hypothesis

In 1954, when the U.S. Supreme Court ordered an end to segregated schools, there was widespread excitement among social psychologists. Because segregation lowered the self-esteem of minority children, most social psychologists believed that desegregating the schools would lead to increases in these youngsters' self-esteem. In addition, social psychologists hoped that the desegregation of schools would be the beginning of the end of prejudice. The idea was that by bringing children of different races and ethnicities together, this contact would eventually erode prejudice.

There was good reason for this optimism, for not only did it make sense theoretically, but empirical evidence supported the power of contact among races. For example, as early as 1951 Morton Deutsch and Mary Ellen Collins examined the attitudes of Caucasians toward African Americans in two public housing projects that differed in their degree of racial integration. Specifically, in one housing situation, African American and Caucasian families had been randomly assigned to buildings in a segregated manner—that is, they were assigned to separate buildings in the same project. In another situation, their assignment was to integrated buildings—African American and Caucasian families were placed in the same building. After several months, residents in the integrated project reported a greater positive change in their attitudes toward blacks than residents of the segregated project did, even though the former had not chosen to live in an integrated building initially.

But the desegregation of schools did not work as smoothly as most knowledgeable people had expected. Indeed, far from producing the hoped-for harmony, school desegregation frequently led to tension and turmoil within the classroom. In his careful analysis of the research examining the impact of desegregation, Walter Stephan (1978, 1985) was unable to find a single study demonstrating a significant increase in self-esteem among African American children, whereas 25 percent of the studies showed a significant *decrease* in the self-esteem of African American children following desegregation. In addition, prejudice was not reduced. Stephan (1978) found that in 53 percent of the studies, prejudice actually *increased*; in 34 percent of the studies, no change in prejudice occurred. And if one had taken an aerial photograph of the school yards of most desegregated schools, one would have found that there was very little true integration: White kids tended to cluster with white kids, African American kids tended to cluster with African American kids, Hispanic kids tended to cluster with Hispanic kids, and so on (Aronson, 1978; Aronson & Gonzalez, 1988; Aronson & Thibodeau, 1992; Schofield, 1986). Clearly, mere contact did not work.

What went wrong? Why did desegregated housing work better than desegregated schools? Let's take a closer look at the contact hypothesis. A moment's reflection will make it obvious that not all kinds of contact will reduce prejudice and raise self-esteem. For example, in the South, African Americans and whites have had a great deal of contact, dating back to the time when African Americans first arrived on slave ships; however, prejudice flourished nonetheless. Obviously, the kind of contact they were having was not the kind that would lead to pleasant outcomes. In his strikingly prescient masterwork *The Nature of Prejudice*, Gordon Allport (1954) stated the contact hypothesis this way:

> Prejudice may be reduced by equal status contact between majority and minority groups in the pursuit of common goals. The effect is greatly enhanced if this contact is sanctioned by institutional supports (i.e., by law, custom or local atmosphere), and provided it is of a sort that leads to the perception of common interests and common humanity between members of the two groups. (1954, p. 281)

In other words, Allport is not talking about mere contact; he is clear that contact must be between people who are of equal status and in pursuit of common goals. Note that implicit in the Deutsch and Collins (1951) housing study was the fact that the two groups were of equal status within the project and that no obvious issues of conflict existed between them. Four decades of research have substantiated Allport's early claim that these conditions must be met before contact will lead to a decrease in prejudice between groups (Cook, 1985). Let's now turn to a discussion of these conditions.

When Contact Reduces Prejudice: Six Conditions

Remember Muzafer Sherif's (1961) study at the boys' camp—the "Eagles" and the "Rattlers"? Stereotyping and prejudice were created by instigating conflict and competition between the boys. As part of the study, Sherif and his colleagues also staged several events to reduce the prejudice they had created. Their findings at the boys' camp tell us a great deal about what contact can and cannot do.

"I WISH WE COULD HAVE MET
UNDER DIFFERENT CIRCUMSTANCES . . ."

■ This caption is amusing, but in actuality, a cooperative effort enhances liking; thus, the circumstances are ideal.

First, the researchers found that once hostility and distrust were established, harmony between the boys could not be restored simply by removing the conflict and the competition. As a matter of fact, all attempts to bring the two groups together in neutral situations served only to increase the hostility and distrust. For example, the children in these groups had trouble with each other even when they were simply watching a movie together.

How did Sherif succeed in reducing their hostility? By placing the two groups of boys in situations where they experienced **mutual interdependence**—a situation where two or more groups need each other and must depend on each other in order to accomplish a goal that is important to each of them. For example, the investigators set up an emergency situation by damaging the water supply system. The only way the system could be repaired was if all the Rattlers and Eagles cooperated immediately. On another occasion, the camp truck broke down while the boys were on a camping trip. In order to get the truck going again, it was necessary to pull it up a rather steep hill. This could be accomplished only if all the youngsters pulled together, regardless of whether they were Eagles or Rattlers. Eventually, these sorts of situations brought about a diminution of hostile feelings and negative stereotyping among the campers. In fact, after these cooperative situations were introduced, the number of boys who said their closest friend was in the other group increased dramatically (see Figure 13.9). Thus, two of the key factors in the success of contact are mutual interdependence and a common goal—a situation where two or more groups need each other and must depend on each other in order to accomplish a goal that is important to each of them (Amir, 1969, 1976).

The third condition is equal status. At the boys' camp (Sherif et al., 1961) and in the public housing project (Deutsch & Collins, 1951), the group members were very much the same in terms of status and power. For example, no one was the boss, and no one was the less powerful employee. When status is unequal, interactions can easily follow stereotypical patterns. The whole point of contact is to allow people to learn that their stereotypes are inaccurate; contact and interaction should lead to disconfirmation of negative, stereotyped beliefs. However, if status is unequal between the groups, their interactions will be shaped by that status difference—the bosses will act like stereotypical bosses, the employees like stereotypical subordinates—and no one will learn new, disconfirming information about the other group (Pettigrew, 1969; Wilder, 1984).

Fourth, contact must occur in a friendly, informal setting, where in-group members can interact with out-group members on a one-to-one basis (Brewer & Miller, 1984; Cook, 1984; Wilder, 1986). Simply placing two groups in contact in

Mutual Interdependence a situation where two or more groups need each other and must depend on each other in order to accomplish a goal that is important to each of them

We must recognize that beneath the superficial classification of sex and race the same potentialities exist, recurring generation after generation only to perish because society has no place for them.
    —Margaret Mead,
    Male and Female, 1943

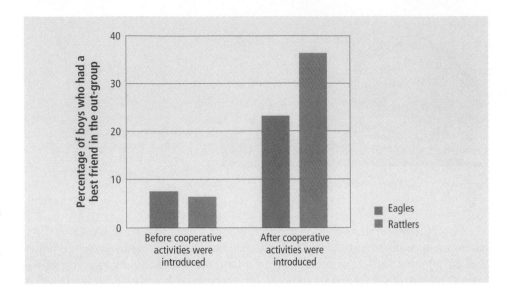

■ FIGURE 13.9   Intergroup relations. Intergroup tensions were eased only after members engaged in cooperative activities. (Adapted from Sherif et al., 1961)

a room where they can remain segregated will do little to promote their understanding or knowledge of each other.

Fifth, through friendly, informal interactions with multiple members of the out-group, an individual will learn that his or her beliefs about the out-group are wrong. It is crucial for the individual to believe that the out-group members he or she comes to know are typical of their group; otherwise, the stereotype can be maintained by labeling one out-group member as the exception (Wilder, 1984). For example, a study of male police officers assigned female partners in Washington, D.C. found that although the men were satisfied with their female partner's performance, they still felt strongly that more women should not be hired as police officers. They perceived their partner as an exception; their stereotypes about women's ability to do police work remained unchanged and in fact were identical with those of male officers with male partners (Milton, 1972).

Sixth and last, contact is most likely to lead to reduced prejudice when social norms that promote and support equality among groups are operating in the situation (Amir, 1969; Wilder, 1984). We know the power of social norms; here they can be harnessed to motivate people to reach out to members of the out-group. For example, if the boss in a work setting or the professor in a classroom creates and reinforces a norm of acceptance and tolerance, group members will modify their own behavior to fit the norm.

To conclude, when these six conditions of contact—mutual interdependence; a common goal; equal status; informal, interpersonal contact; multiple contacts; and social norms of equality—are met, suspicious or even hostile groups will reduce their stereotyping, prejudice, and discriminatory behavior (Aronson & Bridgeman, 1979; Cook, 1984; Riordan, 1978).

Cooperation and Interdependence: The Jigsaw Classroom

Now that we know what conditions must exist for contact to work, we can better understand the problems that occurred when schools were first desegregated. Let's paint a typical scenario. Imagine a sixth-grader of Mexican American origin, whom we will call Carlos. Carlos has been attending schools in an underprivileged neighborhood for his entire life. Because the schools in his neighbor-hood were not well equipped or well staffed, his first five years of education were somewhat deficient. Suddenly, without much warning or preparation, he is bused to a school in a predominantly white middle-class neighborhood.

As you know from experience, the traditional classroom is a highly competi-tive environment. The typical scene involves the teacher asking a question; imme-diately, several hands go into the air as the children strive to show the teacher that they know the answer. When a teacher calls on one child, several others groan, because they've missed an opportunity to show the teacher how smart they are. If the child who is called on hesitates or comes up with the wrong answer, there is a renewed and intensified flurry of hands in the air, perhaps even accompanied by whispered, derisive comments directed at the student who failed. Thus, Carlos finds he must compete against white middle-class students who have had better preparation than he and who have been reared to hold white middle-class values, which include working hard in pursuit of good grades, raising one's hand enthu-siastically whenever the teacher asks a question, and so on. In effect, Carlos has been thrust into a highly competitive situation for which he is unprepared and in which payoffs are made for abilities he has not yet developed. He is virtually guaranteed to lose. After a few failures, Carlos, feeling defeated, humiliated, and dispirited, stops raising his hand and can hardly wait for the bell to ring to signal the end of the school day.

In the typical desegregated classroom, to use Allport's (1954) terms, the stu-dents were not of equal status and were not pursuing common goals. Indeed, one might say that they were in a tug-of-war on an uneven playing field. When one examines the situation closely, it is easy to see why Stephan (1978) found a gen-eral decrease in the self-esteem of minority youngsters following desegregation. Moreover, given the competitive atmosphere of the classroom, it is likely that the situation would have exacerbated whatever stereotypes were present in the youngsters' minds prior to desegregation. Specifically, given that the minority kids were ill-prepared for the competitiveness of the classroom, it is not surpris-ing that some of the white kids quickly concluded that the minority kids were stu-pid, unmotivated, and sullen—just as they had suspected (Wilder & Shapiro, 1989). Moreover, it is likely that the minority kids might conclude that the white kids were arrogant show-offs. This is an example of the self-fulfilling prophecy we discussed earlier.

How could we change the atmosphere of the classroom so that it comes closer to Gordon Allport's prescription for the effectiveness of contact? Specifically, how could we get white students and minority students to be of equal status, mutually dependent, and in pursuit of common goals? One of the authors of this textbook got to find out. In 1971, the school system of Austin, Texas was desegregated. Within a few weeks, the schools were in turmoil. African American, white, and Mexican American children were in open conflict; fist fights broke out between the various racial groups in the corridors and school yards. The school superintendent invited Elliot Aronson, who was then a profes-sor at the University of Texas, to enter the system with the mandate to do any-thing within reason to create a more harmonious environment. After spending a few days observing the dynamics of several classrooms, Aronson and his gradu-ate students were strongly reminded of the situation that existed in the Sherif (1961) camp experiment. With the findings of that study in mind, they developed a technique that created an interdependent classroom atmosphere, designed to place the students of various racial and ethnic groups in pursuit of common

■ When the classroom is structured so that students of various ethnic groups work together cooperatively, prejudice decreases and self esteem increases.

Jigsaw Classroom
a classroom setting designed to reduce prejudice and raise the self-esteem of children by placing them in small, desegregated groups and making each child dependent on the other children in his or her group to learn the course material and do well in the class

goals. They called it the **jigsaw classroom,** because it resembled the assembling of a jigsaw puzzle (Aronson, 1992; Aronson & Bridgeman, 1979; Aronson & Gonzalez, 1988; Aronson, Stephan, Sikes, Blaney, & Snapp, 1978; Aronson & Patnoe, 1997; Brown & Campione, 1994; Wolfe & Spencer, 1996).

Here is how the jigsaw classroom works: Students are placed in diverse six-person learning groups. The day's lesson is divided into six paragraphs, so that each student has one segment of the written material. For example, if the students are to learn the life of Eleanor Roosevelt, her biography is arranged in six parts. Each student has possession of a unique and vital part of the information, which, like the pieces of a jigsaw puzzle, must be put together before anyone can learn the whole picture. The individual must learn his or her own section and teach it to the other members of the group—who do not have any other access to that material. Thus, if Debbie wants to do well on the ensuing exam about the life of Eleanor Roosevelt, she must pay close attention to Carlos (who is reciting on Roosevelt's girlhood years), to Natalie (who is reciting on Roosevelt's years in the White House), and so on.

Unlike the traditional classroom, where students are competing against each other, the jigsaw classroom has students depending on each other. In the traditional classroom, if Carlos, because of anxiety and discomfort, is having difficulty reciting, the other students can easily ignore him (or even put him down) in their zeal to show the teacher how smart they are. But in the jigsaw classroom, if Carlos is having difficulty reciting, it is now in the best interests of the other students to be patient, make encouraging comments, and even ask friendly, probing questions to make it easier for Carlos to bring forth the knowledge within him.

Through the jigsaw process, the children begin to pay more attention to each other and to show respect for each other. As you might expect, a child like Carlos would respond to this treatment by simultaneously becoming more relaxed and more engaged; this would inevitably produce an improvement in his ability to communicate. In fact, after a couple of weeks the other students were struck by their realization that Carlos was a lot smarter than they had thought he was. They began to like him. Carlos began to enjoy school more and began to see the Anglo students in his group not as tormentors but as helpful and responsible

Try It!

Jigsaw-type Group Study

The next time a quiz is coming up in one of your courses, try to organize a handful of your classmates into a jigsaw-type group for purposes of studying for the quiz.

Assign each person a segment of the reading. That person is responsible for becoming the world's greatest expert on their material. That person will organize the material into a report which she or he will give to the rest of the group. The rest of the group will feel free to ask questions in order to make sure they fully understand the material. At the end of the session, ask the group members the following questions:

1. Compared to studying alone, was this more or less enjoyable?

2. Compared to studying alone, was this more or less efficient?

3. How are you feeling about each of the people in the group—compared to how you felt about them prior to the session?

4. Would you like to do this again?

You should realize that this situation is probably a lot less powerful than the jigsaw groups described in this book. Why?

---

teammates. Moreover, as he began to feel increasingly comfortable in class and started to gain more confidence in himself, Carlos's academic performance began to improve. As his academic performance improved, so did his self-esteem. The vicious circle had been broken; the elements that had been causing a downward spiral were changed—the spiral moved dramatically upward.

The formal data that Aronson and his colleagues gathered from the jigsaw experiments were clear and striking. Compared to students in traditional classrooms, students in jigsaw groups showed a decrease in prejudice and stereotyping, as well as an increase in their liking for their groupmates, both within and across ethnic boundaries. In addition, children in the jigsaw classrooms performed better on objective exams and showed a significantly greater increase in self-esteem than children in traditional classrooms. Children in the jigsaw classrooms also showed far greater liking for school than those in traditional classrooms. Moreover, children in schools where the jigsaw technique was practiced showed substantial evidence of true integration—that is, in the school yard there was far more intermingling among the various races and ethnic groups than in the yards of schools using more traditional classroom techniques. Finally, children in the jigsaw classrooms developed a greater ability to empathize with others and to see the world through the perspective of others than children in traditional classrooms did (Aronson & Bridgeman, 1979). See the Try It! box above.

According to Samuel Gaertner and his colleagues (1990), one reason for its effectiveness is that simply participating in a cooperative group succeeds in breaking down in-group versus out-group perceptions and allows the individual to develop the cognitive category of "one group." Another reason for the effectiveness of the cooperative strategy is that it places people in a "favor-doing" situation. You will recall that, in Chapter 6, we discussed an experiment by Mike Leippe and Donna Eisenstadt (1994, 1998) who demonstrated that people who acted in a way that benefited others subsequently came to feel more favorably toward the people they helped.

The jigsaw approach was first tested in 1971; since then, several similar cooperative techniques have been developed (Cook, 1985; Johnson & Johnson, 1987, 1989; Meier, 1995; Sharan, 1980; Slavin, 1980, 1996). The striking results

> "Two are better than one because they have a good reward for their toil. For if they fail, one will lift up his fellow, but woe to him who is alone when he falls and has not another to lift him up. Again, if two lie together, they are warm; but how can one be warm alone?
> —Ecclesiastes 4:9–12

described above have been successfully replicated in thousands of classrooms in all regions of the country and abroad. What began as a simple experiment in one school system has spread dramatically and has been adopted by a great many schools in the United States and abroad. Cooperative learning has become a major force within the field of public education and is generally accepted as one of the most effective ways of improving race relations and instruction in desegregated schools (McConahay, 1981; Deutsch, 1997; Slavin, 1996).

Summary

Prejudice is a widespread phenomenon, present in all societies of the world. Social psychologists define **prejudice** as a hostile or negative attitude toward a distinguishable group of people based solely on their group membership. A **stereotype** is the cognitive component of the prejudiced attitude; it is defined as a generalization about a group whereby identical characteristics are assigned to virtually all members, regardless of actual variation among the members. **Discrimination**, the behavioral component of the prejudiced attitude, is defined as unjustified negative or harmful action toward members of a group based on their membership in that group.

As a broad-based and powerful attitude, prejudice has many causes. We discussed four aspects of social life that bring about prejudice: the way we think, the way we assign meaning or make attributions, the way we allocate resources, and the way we conform to social rules.

Social cognition processes are an important element in the creation and maintenance of stereotypes and prejudice. Categorization of people into groups leads to the formation of in-groups and out-groups. The in-group bias means that we will treat members of our own group more positively than members of the out-group, as demonstrated by the research on minimal groups. The perception of **out-group homogeneity** is another consequence of categorization: In-group members perceive out-group members as being more similar to each other than the in-group members are. Stereotypes are widely known in a culture; even if you do not believe in them, they can affect your cognitive processing of information about an out-group member. For example, recent research has shown that stereotypes are activated by automatic processing; they must be ignored or suppressed by conscious, controlled processing. The **illusory correlation** is another way that cognitive

processing perpetuates stereotypical thinking; we tend to see correlations where they don't exist, particularly if the events or people are distinctive. Social cognition research has indicated that stereotypes can be revised; the **bookkeeping model** and the **subtyping model** (but not the **conversion model**) describe processes through which stereotypes change.

The fundamental attribution error applies to prejudice—we tend to overestimate the role of dispositional forces when making sense out of others' behavior. Stereotypes can be described as the **ultimate attribution error**—making negative dispositional attributions about an entire out-group. When out-group members act nonstereotypically, we tend to make situational attributions about them, thereby maintaining our stereotypes. For their part, members of an out-group experience **stereotype threat**—a fear they might behave in a manner that confirms an existing stereotype about their group. Our belief in a just world leads us to derogate victims as well as members of out-groups—we see them as causing their fate and circumstances, a phenomenon known as **blaming the victim.** Finally, **self-fulfilling prophecies** are an attributional process by which we find confirmation and proof for our stereotypes by unknowingly creating stereotypical behavior in out-group members through our treatment of them.

Realistic conflict theory states that prejudice is the inevitable byproduct of real conflict between groups for limited resources—whether involving economics, power, or status. Competition for resources leads to derogation of and discrimination against the competing out-group. **Scapegoating** is a process whereby frustrated and angry people tend to displace their aggression from its real source to a convenient target—an out-group that is disliked, visible, and relatively powerless. Social learning theory states that we learn the appropriate norms of our culture—including stereotypes and prejudiced attitudes—from adults, peers, the media, and so on.

Institutionalized racism and institutionalized sexism are norms operating throughout the society's structure. Normative conformity, or the desire to be accepted and "fit in," leads us to go along with stereotyped beliefs and not challenge them. Modern racism is an example of a shift in normative rules about prejudice: Nowadays, many people reveal their prejudice in subtle, indirect ways, for they have learned to hide their prejudice in situations where it would lead them to be labeled as racist. Given the more hidden nature of prejudice today, techniques like the bogus pipeline are used to study people's real attitudes about out-groups.

How can prejudice be reduced? The most important way to reduce prejudice is through contact—bringing in- and out-group members together. However, mere contact, as occurred when public schools were first desegregated, is not enough and can even exacerbate the existing negative attitudes. Instead, contact situations must include the following conditions: mutual interdependence; a common goal; equal status; informal, interpersonal contact; multiple contacts; and social norms of equality. The jigsaw classroom, a learning atmosphere in which children must depend on each other and work together to learn and to reach a common goal, has been found to be a powerful way to reduce stereotyping and prejudice among children of different ethnicities.

If You Are Interested

Allport, G. (1954). *The nature of prejudice.* Reading, MA: Addison-Wesley. Written the same year as the landmark Supreme Court decision on desegregation, this classic work remains an exciting and penetrating analysis of the social psychology of prejudice.

Aronson, E. & Patnoe, S. (1997). *Cooperation in the classroom: The jigsaw method.* New York: Longman. An updated account of the story of the classroom experiment that helped make school desegregation work—and that contributed to the launching of the trend toward cooperative education.

Brewer, M. & Brown, R. (1998). Intergroup relations. In D. Gilbert, S. Fiske, & G. Lindzey (Eds.), *The handbook of social psychology* (4th ed., Vol. 1). New York: McGraw-Hill. A brief, scholarly introduction to the areas of prejudice and prejudice reduction.

Fiske, S. (1998). Prejudice, stereotyping and discrimination. In D. Gilbert, S. Fiske, & G. Lindzey (Eds.), *The handbook of social psychology* (4th ed., Vol. 1). New York: McGraw-Hill. A thorough treatment of stereotyping, its causes, and consequences.

PBS has produced a series of videos called *Discovering Psychology,* written and narrated by Professor Philip Zimbardo. Video #20, *Constructing Social Reality,* contains a segment on Jane Elliot's blue-eyed/brown-eyed experiment as well as a depiction of the jigsaw classroom in action.

Pettigrew, T. F. & Meertens, R. W. (1995). Subtle and blatant prejudice in Western Europe. *European Journal of Social Psychology, 25,* 57–75. An excellent analysis of the distinctive difference between blatant and subtle forms of prejudice and how they affect behavior in different ways.

SOCIAL PSYCHOLOGY
IN ACTION 1

SOCIAL PSYCHOLOGY AND HEALTH

*L*et us introduce you to Beatrice Cole, a vivacious, energetic woman in her nineties who greets each day "as a gift that I unwrap with anticipation, and live each day as if it were the last" (Cole, 1991, p. 20). She keeps a busy schedule, rising early every morning to take her dog, Pierre, for a long walk. After returning to her Manhattan apartment, she eats a large breakfast, reads the newspaper, and does some housecleaning; when the mood strikes her she ties Pierre to a shopping cart and goes to the market. She spends one day a week doing volunteer work at a local synagogue, and another in the public relations department of a museum. Every night she prepares a four-course dinner, serving herself as if she were a guest. She entertains regularly, treating her friends to a fancy dinner and a game of Scrabble.

Ms. Cole's life is not free of misfortune. A few years ago, after finding herself asking people to repeat what they had said, she realized that her hearing was failing. When she was 88, she kept turning her ankle and falling, due to nerve damage in her spine. Characteristically, however, she treats these hardships as minor inconveniences. "Deafness is not a bad handicap," she says. "At night when I remove my hearing aids . . . the silence is delicious" (p. 21). She obtained a brace for her leg and now, with the help of a cane, is as

■ Beatrice Cole relaxes with her dog, Pierre.

mobile as ever. She regularly takes buses around Manhattan, and she frequently travels outside the city to visit friends and family. Her personal philosophy is that you should always look on the bright side and never brood about anything for more than 20 minutes.

Ms. Cole last wrote about her life when she was 90, nearly 10 years ago. We recently called her up to see how she was doing. She was quite cheerful when we reached her, saying that she still takes Pierre for a walk every day and continues to do volunteer work at two New York museums—not bad for someone who will soon celebrate her 100th birthday.

How does Ms. Cole feel about the fact that her life is drawing to a close? Far from feeling depressed or apprehensive, she approaches her impending death with characteristic optimism:

> There is still one adventure ahead of me that is the greatest experience of all—the only perfect happenstance in life, with no strings attached, no loose ends. Absolute perfection. That is death. I think of it as the perfect end to a long, happy life. (p. 21)

Why has Beatrice Cole lived such a long and satisfying life? Is it a coincidence that her life seems to be remarkably free of stress, or is this related to her good health? What about her positive outlook on life—is this related to her longevity, or is she simply blessed with good genes and good luck? It is impossible, of course, to answer these questions definitively about any one person.

Fortunately, with careful research, it is possible to find some answers on a broader scale. Looking at people in general, what are the effects of stress on the human body? Do people's outlooks on life influence their physical health? Questions such as these about the relation between the mind and the body have intrigued human beings for centuries, and recent research suggests some fascinating answers. As we will see, it may be more than a coincidence that Ms. Cole is so upbeat and in control of her life and in such good health in her nineties.

This chapter is concerned with the application of social psychology to physical and mental health, which is a flourishing area of research (Cohen & Herbert, 1996; Pennebaker, 1982; Salovey, Rothman, & Rodin, 1998; Taylor, 1995; Taylor, Repetti, & Seeman, 1997). We will focus on topics that are on the interface of social psychology and health: how people cope with stress in their lives, the relationship between their coping styles and their physical and mental health, and how we can get people to behave in healthier ways.

Stress and Human Health

A great deal of anecdotal evidence indicates that stress can affect the body in dramatic ways. Consider these examples, reported by the psychologist W. B. Cannon (1942):

- After eating some fruit, a New Zealand woman learns that it came from a forbidden supply reserved for the chief. Horrified, her health deteriorates, and the next day she dies—even though it was a perfectly fine piece of fruit.
- A man in Africa has breakfast with a friend, eats heartily, and goes on his way. A year later, he learns that his friend made the breakfast from a wild hen, a food strictly forbidden in his culture. The man immediately begins to tremble and is dead within 24 hours.
- An Australian man's health deteriorates after a witch doctor casts a spell on him. He recovers only when the witch doctor removes the spell.

These examples probably sound pretty bizarre, like something you would read in the "Ripley's Believe It or Not" column in the Sunday paper. But let's fast-forward to the end of the twentieth century in the United States, where many similar cases of sudden death occur following a psychological trauma. When people undergo a major upheaval in their lives, such as losing a spouse, declaring bankruptcy, or being forced to resettle in a new culture, their chance of dying increases (Morse, Martin, & Moshonov, 1991). There are many cases of sudden, unexplained deaths of people who are experiencing major life changes, such as among refugees who escaped Southeast Asia and resettled in the United States (Kirschner, Eckner, & Baron, 1986). Or consider the plight of an older person who is institutionalized in a long-term health care facility in the United States. In many such institutions, the residents have little responsibility for or control over their own lives. They cannot choose what to eat, what to wear, or even when to go to the bathroom. Residents in such institutions often become passive and withdrawn and fade into death as if they have simply given up. Quite a contrast to the zest shown by Beatrice Cole in her tenth decade of life! These examples suggest that there is more to our physical health than germs and disease—we also need to consider the amount of stress in our lives and how we deal with that stress (Inglehart, 1991).

Effects of Negative Life Events

Among the pioneers in research on stress was Hans Selye (1956, 1976), who defined stress as the body's physiological response to threatening events. He focused on how the human body adapts to threats from the environment, regardless of the source of a threat—be it a psychological or physiological trauma. Later researchers have examined what it is about a life event that makes it threatening. Holmes and Rahe (1967), for example, suggested that stress is the degree to which people have to change and readjust their lives in response to an external event. The more change that is required, the more stress that occurs. For example, if a spouse or partner dies, just about every aspect of a person's life is disrupted, leading to a great deal of stress. This definition of stress applies to happy events in one's life as well, if the event causes a person to change his or her daily routine. Graduating from college is a happy occasion, but it can be stressful because of the major changes it creates in one's life.

To assess such life changes, Holmes and Rahe (1967) developed a measure called the Social Readjustment Rating Scale (see Table SPA1.1). Some events, such as the death of a spouse or partner, have many "life change units," because they involve the most change in people's daily routines. Other events, such as getting a traffic ticket, have relatively few life change units. Here's how the scale works: Participants check all the events that have occurred to them in the preceding year and then get a score for the total number of life change units caused by those events. The scores are then correlated with the frequency with which the participants become sick or have physical complaints. Several studies have found that the more life changes people report, the more anxiety they feel and the more likely they are to have been sick (Elliot & Eisdorfer, 1982; Seta, Seta, & Wang, 1990).

These findings probably don't come as much of a surprise; it seems pretty obvious that people who are experiencing a lot of change and upheaval in their lives are more likely to feel anxious and get sick. A closer look, however, reveals that these findings aren't all that straightforward. One problem, as you may have recognized, is that most studies in this area use correlational designs, not experimental designs. Just because life changes are correlated with health problems does not mean that the life changes caused the health problems (see our discussion in Chapter 2 of correlation and causality). Some researchers have argued persuasively for the role of "third variables," whereby certain kinds of people are more likely to be experiencing difficult life changes and to report that they are ill (Schroeder & Costa, 1984; Watson & Pennebaker, 1989). According to these researchers, it is not life changes that cause health problems. Instead, people with certain personality traits, such as the tendency to experience negative moods, are more likely to experience life difficulties and to have health problems.

Another problem with inventories such as Holmes and Rahe's is that it focuses on stressors experienced by the middle class and underrepresents stressors experienced by the poor and members of minority groups. As pointed out by

Table SPA1.1

The Social Readjustment Scale

Rank	Life Event	Life Change Units
1	Death of spouse	100
2	Divorce	73
3	Marital separation	65
4	Jail term	63
5	Death of a close family member	63
6	Personal injury or illness	53
7	Marriage	50
8	Fired at work	47
9	Marital reconciliation	45
10	Retirement	45
11	Change in health of a family member	44
12	Pregnancy	40
13	Sex difficulties	39
14	Gain of new family member	39
15	Business readjustment	39
16	Change in financial state	38
17	Death of close friend	37
18	Change to different line of work	36
19	Change in number of arguments with spouse	35
20	Mortgage over $10,000	31
21	Foreclosure of mortgage or loan	30
22	Change in responsibilities at work	29
23	Son or daughter leaving home	29
24	Trouble with in-laws	29
25	Outstanding personal achievement	28
26	Spouse begins or stops work	26
27	Begin or end school	26
28	Change in living conditions	25
29	Revision of personal habits	24
30	Trouble with boss	23
31	Change in work hours or conditions	20
32	Change in residence	20
33	Change in schools	20
34	Change in recreation	19
35	Change in church activities	19
36	Change in social activities	18
37	Mortgage or loan less than $10,000	17
38	Change in sleeping habits	16
39	Change in number of family get-togethers	15
40	Change in eating habits	15
41	Vacation	13
42	Christmas	12
43	Minor violations of the law	11

NOTE: According to Holmes and Rahe (1967), the greater the number of "life change units" you are experiencing right now, the greater the likelihood that you will become physically ill. (Adapted from Holmes & Rahe, 1967)

■ Some of these events are happy, yet they cause stress. Which of these situations might make you experience stress?

James Jackson and Marita Inglehart (1995), variables such as poverty and racism are potent causes of stress. Moreover, the way in which these variables influence health is not always so obvious. It will probably come as no surprise that the more racism and financial strain experienced by members of minority groups, the worse their health. It might be more surprising that the more racism expressed by majority groups, such as white Americans, the worse their health (Jackson & Inglehart, 1995). Racism is often associated with hostility and aggression, and as we will see later in this chapter, there is evidence that hostility is related to health problems such as coronary heart disease. Clearly, then, to understand the relationship between stress and health, we need to understand better such community- and cultural-level variables as poverty and racism.

Perceived Stress and Health

A further limitation of simply counting the number of negative life events that people experience—such as whether people have gotten married or lost their job—is that it violates a basic principle of social psychology: Subjective situations have more of an impact on people than objective situations do (Griffin & Ross, 1991). Now, we certainly acknowledge that some situations are objectively bad for one's health, regardless of how one interprets them. (Jackson & Inglehart,

1995; Taylor, Repetti, & Seeman, 1997). Children growing up in smog-infested areas such as Los Angeles, for example, have been found to have 10 to 15 percent less efficiency in their lungs than children who grow up in less polluted areas (see "Social Psychology in Action 2: Social Psychology and the Environment"). Still, there are environmental events that are open to interpretation, and seem to have negative effects only on people who construe these events in certain ways. Some people view getting a traffic ticket as a major hassle, whereas others view it as a minor inconvenience. Some people view a major life change such as getting divorced as a liberating escape from an abusive relationship, whereas others view it as a devastating personal failure. As recognized by Richard Lazarus (1966, 1993) in his pioneering work on stress, it is subjective, not objective, stress that causes problems. An event is stressful for people only if they interpret it as stressful; thus, we can define **stress** as the negative feelings and beliefs that occur whenever people feel unable to cope with demands from their environment (Lazarus & Folkman, 1984).

Consider, for instance, our opening example of Beatrice Cole. If she were filling out the Social Readjustment Rating Scale, she would check "personal injury or illness," given that she was experiencing a number of health problems. She would thus receive a large number of life change units. According to the theory, she should be at high risk for further physical problems, due to the stress caused by her hearing loss and problems with her spine. But as we saw, Ms. Cole is not particularly bothered by these problems. With her characteristic optimism, she looks on the bright side, welcoming the fact that her deafness blocks out annoying sounds at night. Because she finds these events relatively easy to cope with, they do not fit our definition of stress.

In a series of classic studies, Richard Lazarus (1966) showed that it is people's interpretation of an event that influences how stressful they find it. In one study, for example, he asked people to watch a film of gory industrial accidents, such as a scene in which a worker operating a power saw accidentally cuts off his finger. How upsetting was this film? It depended on how people interpreted it. Lazarus instructed some participants to adopt an intellectual stance while watching the film, concentrating less on the accident and more on the relationships between the workers. Compared to people who were given no special instructions, this group was relatively unaffected by the film. Just as a physician reacts to blood and gore differently from how most other people do, these participants succeeded in adopting a detached, clinical view of the accidents, turning a stressful experience into a relatively neutral one.

Studies using this subjective definition of stress confirm the idea that negative life experiences are bad for our health. In fact, stress caused by negative interpretations of events can directly affect our immune systems, making us more susceptible to disease. Consider, for example, the common cold. When people are exposed to the virus that causes a cold, only 20 to 60 percent of them become sick. Is it possible that stress is one determinant of who this 20 to 60 percent will be? To find out, Sheldon Cohen, David Tyrrell, and Andrew Smith (1991, 1993) asked volunteers to spend a week at a research institute in southern England. As a measure of stress the participants listed recent events that had had a negative impact on their lives. That is, consistent with our definition of stress, the participants listed only those events they perceived to be negative.

The researchers then gave participants nasal drops that contained either the virus that causes the common cold or saline (salt water). The participants were

Stress
the negative feelings and beliefs that occur whenever people feel unable to cope with demands from their environment

> The greatest griefs are those we cause ourselves
> —Sophocles
> (c. 496–406 B.C.)

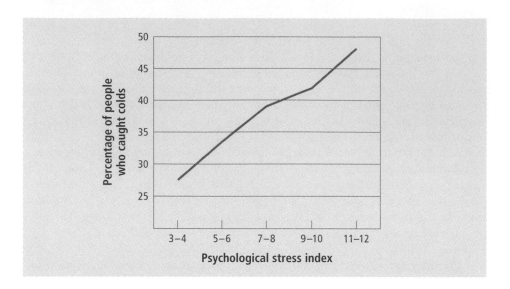

■ **FIGURE SPA1.1 Stress and the likelihood of catching a cold.** People were first exposed to the virus that causes the common cold and then isolated. The greater the amount of stress they were experiencing, the greater the likelihood that they caught a cold from this virus. (Adapted from Cohen et al., 1991)

subsequently quarantined for several days, so that they had no contact with other people. As you can see in Figure SPA1.1, the people who were experiencing a great deal of stress in their lives were more likely to catch a cold from the virus. Among people who reported the least amount of stress, about 27 percent came down with a cold. This rate increased steadily the more stress people reported, topping out at a rate of nearly 50 percent in the group that was experiencing the most stress. This effect of stress was found even when several other factors that influence catching a cold were taken into account, such as the time of year people participated and the participants' age, weight, and gender. This study, along with others like it, shows that the more stress people experience, the lower their immunity to disease (Cohen, 1996; Cohen et al., in press; Cohen & Herbert, 1996; Cohen & Williamson, 1991; Herbert & Cohen, 1993; Krantz, Grunberg, & Baum, 1985; O'Leary, 1990; Stone et al., 1993).

The careful reader will have noted that the Cohen and colleagues study used a correlational design and that this must make us cautious about its interpretation. The amount of stress people were experiencing was measured and correlated with the likelihood that people caught a cold. It is possible that stress itself did not lower people's immunity, but rather that some variable correlated with stress did. It would have been ethically impermissable, of course, to conduct an experimental study in which people were randomly assigned to a condition in which they experienced a great deal of prolonged stress. Who would want to participate in a study in which you were tormented by the researchers for a long period of time, to see if you caught all sorts of diseases? There are studies, however, in which people's immune responses are measured before and after undergoing mildly stressful tasks in the laboratory, such as solving mental arithmetic problems continuously for six minutes, or giving speeches on short notice. John Cacioppo and his colleagues have found that even relatively mild stressors such as these can lead to a suppression of the immune system (Cacioppo, in press; Cacioppo et al., in press).

The finding that stress has negative effects on people's health raises an important question: What exactly is it that makes people perceive a situation as stressful? One important determinant, as we will now see, is the amount of control they believe they have over the event.

Feeling in Charge: The Importance of Perceived Control

Compared to many other people in their nineties, Beatrice Cole has a great deal of control over her life: She lives alone and can decide what to do with each day; she is responsible for taking care of her dog, Pierre; and she decides when to entertain guests and when to take out-of-town trips to visit friends and family. Is it possible that the control she has over her life is related to her good health?

Studies with the chronically ill suggest that it is. Shelley Taylor and her colleagues (1984), for example, interviewed women with breast cancer and found that many of them believed they could control whether their cancer returned. Here is how one man described his wife: "She got books, she got pamphlets, she studied, she talked to cancer patients. She found out everything that was happening to her and she fought it. She went to war with it. She calls it 'taking in her covered wagons and surrounding it'" (quoted in Taylor, 1989, p. 178). The researchers found that women who believed their cancer was controllable were better adjusted psychologically. And there is some evidence that people who try to control their cancer and its treatment live slightly longer than those who do not (Taylor, 1989).

It is important to note that the beliefs of at least some of the women about their control over their cancer were probably incorrect. One woman, who worked in a dress shop, said that for years she carried dresses from the racks to the fitting room over her left arm, so that the hangers banged against her left breast. When she developed a tumor in her left breast, she assumed these repeated blows had caused it. From that point on, she put the dresses on a rack and rolled them to the fitting room. According to the experts, blows to the breast are not a cause of cancer. Nonetheless, this woman gained a sense of control by believing she knew the cause of her tumor and by doing something she believed helped. This suggests that **perceived control,** defined as the belief that we can influence our environment in ways that determine whether we experience positive or negative outcomes, is as important as real control (Averill, 1973; Burger, 1992; Skinner, 1995, 1996).

Again, we should note that studies of perceived control in the chronically ill by necessity use correlational rather than experimental designs. Researchers measure the amount of control people are experiencing and correlate this with their psychological and physical adjustment to the disease. These studies cannot prove that feelings of control cause one's health to improve; for example, it is possible that improving health causes one to feel more in control. To address the question of whether feelings of control have beneficial causal effects, we need to conduct experimental studies in which people are randomly assigned to conditions of "high" versus "low" perceived control. Fortunately, a number of such experimental studies have been conducted (Heckhausen & Schulz, 1995; Rodin, 1986).

Some of the most dramatic effects of perceived control have been found in studies of older people in nursing homes. Many people who end up in nursing homes and hospitals feel they have lost control of their lives (Raps, Peterson, Jonas, & Seligman, 1982). People are often placed in long-term care facilities against their wishes and, once there, have little say in what they do, whom they see, or what they eat. Ellen Langer and Judith Rodin (1976) believed that it would be beneficial to these residents to boost their feelings of control. To do so, they asked the director of a nursing home in Connecticut to convey to the residents that, contrary to what they might think, they had a lot of responsibility for their own lives. Here is an excerpt of his speech:

> The knowledge that one has a remedy within reach is often as effectual as the remedy itself.
> —F. Anstey, 1900

Perceived Control
the belief that we can influence our environment in ways that determine whether we experience positive or negative outcomes

Take a minute to think of the decisions you can and should be making. For example, you have the responsibility of caring for yourselves, of deciding whether or not you want to make this a home you can be proud of and happy in. You should be deciding how you want your rooms to be arranged—whether you want it to be as it is or whether you want the staff to help you rearrange the furniture. You should be deciding how you want to spend your time. . . . If you are unsatisfied with anything here, you have the influence to change it. . . . These are just a few of the things you could and should be deciding and thinking about now and from time to time every day. (Langer & Rodin, 1976, pp. 194–195)

The director went on to say that a movie would be shown on two nights the next week and that the residents should decide which night they wanted to attend. Finally, he gave each resident a gift of a house plant, emphasizing that it was up to him or her to take care of it.

The director also gave a speech to residents assigned to a comparison group. This speech was different in one crucial way—all references to making decisions and being responsible for oneself were deleted. The director emphasized that he wanted the residents to be happy, but he did not say anything about the control they had over their lives. He said that a movie would be shown on two nights the next week but that the residents would be assigned to see it on one night or the other. He gave plants to these residents as well but said that the nurses would take care of the plants.

The director's speech might not seem like a major change in the lives of the residents. The people in the induced control group heard one speech about the responsibility they had for their lives and were given one plant to water. That doesn't seem like very strong stuff, does it? The important point to keep in mind is that to an institutionalized person, who feels helpless and constrained, even a small boost in control can have a dramatic effect. Langer and Rodin (1976) found that the residents in the induced control group became happier and more active than residents in the comparison group. Most dramatically of all, the induced control intervention affected the residents' health and mortality (Rodin &

■ Giving senior citizens a sense of control over their lives has been found to have positive benefits, both physically and psychologically.

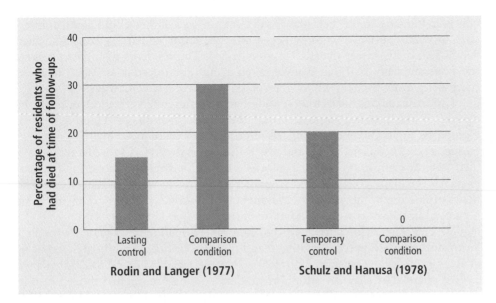

Percentage of residents who had died at time of follow-ups

Rodin and Langer (1977)
- Lasting control
- Comparison condition

Schulz and Hanusa (1978)
- Temporary control
- Comparison condition: 0

■ **FIGURE SPA1.2   Perceived control and mortality.**   In two studies, elderly residents in nursing homes were made to feel more in control of their lives. In one (Rodin & Langer, 1977), the intervention endured over time, so that people continued to feel in control. As seen in the left-hand side of the figure, this intervention had positive effects on mortality rates. Those who received it were more likely to be alive 18 months later than those who did not. In the other study (Schulz & Hanusa, 1978), the intervention was temporary. Being given control and then having it taken away had negative effects on mortality rates, as seen in the right-hand side of the figure. (Adapted from Rodin & Langer, 1977, and Schulz & Hanusa, 1978)

Langer, 1977). Eighteen months after the director's speech, 15 percent of the residents in the induced control group had died, compared to 30 percent in the comparison condition (see the left-hand side of Figure SPA1.2).

Richard Schulz (1976) increased feelings of control in residents of nursing homes in a different way. Schulz started a program in a North Carolina nursing home wherein undergraduates visited the residents once a week for two months. In the induced control condition, the residents decided when the visits would occur and how long they would last. In a randomly assigned comparison condition, it was the students, not the residents, who decided when the visits would occur and how long they would last. Thus, the residents received visits in both conditions, but in only one could they control the visits' frequency and duration. This may seem like a minor difference, but again, giving the residents some semblance of control over their lives had dramatic effects. After two months, those in the induced control condition were happier, healthier, more active, and were taking fewer medications than those in the comparison group.

Schulz returned to the nursing home several months later to assess the long-term effects of his intervention, including its effect on mortality rates. Based on the results of the Langer and Rodin (1976) study, we might expect that those residents who could control the students' visits would be healthier and more likely to still be alive than those residents who could not. But there is a crucial difference between the two studies that should affect how long-lasting the interventions were: The residents in the Langer and Rodin study were given an enduring sense of control, whereas the residents in the Schulz study were not. Langer and Rodin's participants could continue to choose which days to participate in different activities,

> To be discouraged is to yield to misfortune.
>
> —Daniel Defoe,
> *Moll Flanders*, 1722

continue to take care of their plant, and continue to feel they could make a difference in what happened to them—even after the study ended. By contrast, when Schulz's study was over the student visits ended. The residents who could control the visits suddenly had that control taken away. The question is, What happens when people are given a sense of control, only to have it taken away?

Unfortunately, Schulz's intervention had an unintended effect: Over time, the people in the induced control group did worse (Schulz & Hanusa, 1978). Compared to people in the comparison group, they were more likely to have experienced deteriorating health and zest for life, and they were more likely to have died (see the right-hand side of Figure SPA1.2). This study has sobering implications for the many college-based volunteer programs in which students visit residents of nursing homes, prisons, and mental hospitals. These programs might be beneficial in the short run but do more harm than good after they end.

We end this section with a word of caution. Though there is evidence for a relationship between perceived control and physical health, it can be dangerous to exaggerate that relationship. As noted by Susan Sontag (1978, 1988), when a society is plagued by a deadly but poorly understood disease, such as tuberculosis in the nineteenth century and AIDS today, the illness is often blamed on some kind of human frailty, such as a lack of faith, a moral weakness, or a broken heart. As a result, people sometimes blame themselves for their illnesses, even to the point where they do not seek out effective treatment. Thus, whereas it is beneficial for people to feel that they are in control of their illnesses, the downside of this strategy is that if a person does not get better, he or she may feel a sense of self-blame and failure. Tragically, diseases such as cancer can be fatal no matter how much control a person feels. It only adds to the tragedy if people with serious diseases feel a sense of moral failure, blaming themselves for a disease that was unavoidable.

Fortunately, there are ways to maintain a sense of control even when one's health fails. Suzanne Thompson and her colleagues studied people with serious illnesses such as cancer and AIDS and found that even if they felt no control over the disease, many of them believed they could control the consequences of the disease (e.g., their emotional reactions and the nature of the physical symptoms related to the disease). These perceptions of control over the consequences were highly related to people's psychological adjustment. The more people felt they could control the consequences, the better adjusted they were, even if they knew they could not control the course of the disease. In short, it is important to feel in control of something—even if it is not the disease itself (Heckhausen & Schulz, 1995; Thompson, Nanni, & Levine, 1994; Thompson, Sobolew-Shubin, Galbraith, Schwankovsky, & Cruzen, 1993).

Knowing You Can Do It: Self-Efficacy

Believing we have control over our lives is one thing. According to Albert Bandura (1986, 1997), we also have to believe that we can actually execute the specific behaviors that will get us what we want. Sam might have a general sense that he is in control of his life, but will this mean that he will find it easy to stop smoking? According to Bandura, we have to examine his **self-efficacy** in this domain, which is the belief in one's ability to carry out specific actions that produce desired outcomes. If Sam believes that he is able to perform the behaviors that will enable him to quit smoking—throwing away his cigarettes, avoiding situations in which he is most tempted to smoke, distracting himself when he craves a

Self-Efficacy
the belief in one's ability to carry out specific actions that produce desired outcomes

cigarette—then chances are, he will succeed. If he has low self-efficacy in this domain—he believes that he can't perform the behaviors necessary to quit—then he is likely to fail (Brod & Hall, 1984; Holden, 1991; Carey & Carey, 1993).

People's level of self-efficacy has been found to predict a number of important health behaviors, such as the likelihood that they will quit smoking, lose weight, lower their cholesterol, and exercise regularly (Bandura, 1997; Salovey et al., 1998). Again, it is not a general sense of control that predicts these behaviors, but the confidence that one can perform the specific behaviors in question. A person might have high self-efficacy in one domain, such as high confidence that she can lose weight, but low self-efficacy in another domain, such as low confidence that she can quit smoking.

Self-efficacy increases the likelihood that people will engage in healthier behaviors in two ways. First, it influences people's persistence and effort at a task. People with low self-efficacy tend to give up easily, whereas people high in self-efficacy set higher goals, try harder, and persist more in the face of failure—thereby increasing the likelihood that they will succeed (Cervone & Peake, 1986; Litt, 1988). Second, self-efficacy influences the way our bodies react while we are working toward our goals. For example, people with high self-efficacy experience less anxiety while working on a difficult task and their immune system functions more optimally (Widenfield et al., 1990; Bandura, Cioffi, Taylor, & Broillard, 1988). In short, self-efficacy operates as a kind of self-fulfilling prophecy. The more you believe that you can accomplish something, such as quitting smoking, the greater the likelihood that you will.

How can self-efficacy be increased? A study by Mordechai Blittner, Joel Goldberg, and Michael Merbaum (1978) on smoking cessation suggests one way. The participants were adult smokers who answered an advertisement for a treatment program to quit smoking. After filling out some initial questionnaires, they were randomly assigned to one of three groups. In the self-efficacy condition, people were told that they had been chosen for the study because they "showed that they had strong willpower and great potential to control and conquer their desires and behavior" and that "it was quite certain that during the course of the treatment they would completely stop smoking" (Blittner et al., 1978, p. 555). These participants then underwent a 14 week program that taught them how to quit, by, for example, starting with the situations in which they found it easiest not to smoke and gradually working up to the situations in which they found it the hardest not to smoke.

Participants in the treatment alone condition underwent the same 14-week program as people in the self-efficacy condition, with one important difference: Instead of being told that they had been selected because of their high potential for quitting, they were told that they had been chosen at random for the treatment program. Finally, participants in the no treatment control condition did not receive self-efficacy instructions or take part in the treatment program. They were told that they would be contacted for the study at a later time.

As seen in Figure SPA1.3, the self-efficacy instructions were quite effective. By the end of the treatment period, 67 percent of people in the self-efficacy condition had quit smoking, compared to only 28 percent in the treatment-alone group and 6 percent in the no-treatment control group. Remember, the only way in which the self-efficacy and treatment-only conditions differed was that the former participants believed that they had high potential for quitting. Believing that we can do something is a powerful determinant of whether we succeed.

■ **FIGURE SPA1.3   The role of self-efficacy in smoking cessation.**   Adult smokers were randomly assigned to one of three conditions. In the self-efficacy condition, people were told that they were selected for the study because they had great potential to quit. They then underwent a 14 week smoking cessation program. People in the treatment alone condition participated in the same program, but were told that they had been randomly selected for it. People in the no treatment condition did not take part in the program. At the end of the 14 week period substantially more people in the self-efficacy condition had quit smoking. Believing that one has the ability to carry out beneficial behaviors—having high self-efficacy—is an important determinant of whether people succeed. (Adapted from Blittner et al., 1978)

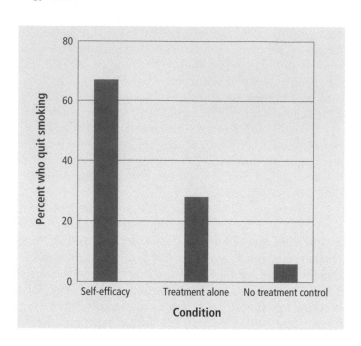

Explaining Negative Events: Learned Helplessness

What happens when we experience a setback? Despite our beliefs in ourselves, maybe we failed to quit smoking or did poorly on a midterm. Another important determinant of our physical and mental health is how we explain to ourselves why a negative event occurred. For example, consider two college students who both got poor grades on their first calculus test. Student 1 says to herself, "I bet the professor deliberately made the test difficult, to motivate us to do better. I'll just have to study harder. If I really buckle down for the next test, I'll do better." Student 2 says to himself, "Wow—I guess I can't really cut it here at State U. I was worried that I wasn't smart enough to make it in college, and boy, was I ever right." Which student do you think will do better on the next test? Clearly the first one, because she has explained her poor performance in a way that is more flattering to herself and makes her feel more in control. In contrast, the second student is likely to settle into a state of **learned helplessness,** defined as the state of pessimism that results from explaining a negative event as due to stable, internal, and global factors (Abramson, Seligman, & Teasdale, 1978).

Explaining a negative event as due to a stable cause—that is, making a **stable attribution**—is the belief that the cause of the event is due to factors that will not change over time (e.g., your intelligence), as opposed to unstable factors that can change over time (e.g., the amount of effort you put into a task). Explaining a negative event as due to an internal cause—that is, making an **internal attribution**—is the belief that the cause of the event is due to things about you (e.g., your own ability or effort), as opposed to factors that are external to you (e.g., the difficulty of a test). Finally, explaining an event as due to a global cause—that is, making a **global attribution**—is the belief that the cause of an event is due to factors that apply in a large number of situations (e.g., your intelligence, which will influence your performance in many areas), as opposed to the belief that the cause is specific and applies in only a limited number of situations (e.g., your music ability, which will affect your performance in music courses but not in other courses). According

Learned Helplessness
the state of pessimism that results from explaining a negative event as due to stable, internal, and global factors

Stable Attribution
the belief that the cause of an event is due to factors that will not change over time (e.g., your intelligence), as opposed to unstable factors that will change over time (e.g., the amount of effort you put into a task)

Internal Attribution
the belief that the cause of an event is due to things about you (e.g., your own ability or effort), as opposed to factors that are external to you (e.g., the difficulty of a test)

to learned helplessness theory, making stable, internal, and global attributions for negative events leads to hopelessness, depression, reduced effort, and difficulty in learning (see Figure SPA1.4).

Student 2, for example, believes that the cause of his poor grade is stable (being unintelligent will last forever), internal (something about him is to blame), and global (being unintelligent will affect him in many situations other than calculus classes). This kind of explanation will lead to learned helplessness, thereby producing depression, reduced effort, and the inability to learn new things. Student 1, on the other hand, believes that the cause of her poor grade is unstable (the professor will make the tests easier, and she can study harder next time), external (the professor purposefully made the test hard), and specific (the things that caused her poor calculus grade are unlikely to affect anything else, e.g., her grade in English). People who explain bad events in this more optimistic way are less likely to be depressed and more likely to do better on a broad range of tasks (Joiner & Wagner, 1995; Peterson & Seligman, 1984; Sweeney, Anderson, & Bailey, 1986).

Learned helplessness theory is intimately related to attribution theory, which we discuss in Chapter 4. Attribution theorists assume that your attitudes and behaviors depend on how you interpret the causes of events, an assumption that

Global Attribution
the belief that the cause of an event is due to factors that apply in a large number of situations (e.g., your intelligence, which will influence your performance in many areas), as opposed to the belief that the cause is specific and applies in only a limited number of situations (e.g., your music ability, which will affect your performance in music courses but not in other courses)

■ **FIGURE SPA1.4   The theory of learned helplessness.**   Explaining a negative event in a pessimistic manner leads to learned helplessness (depression, lowered effort, poor learning).

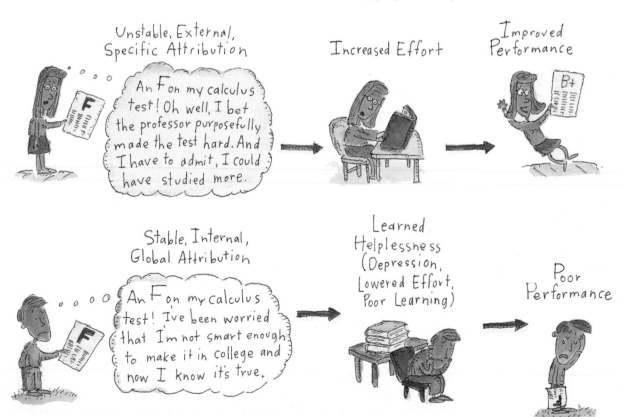

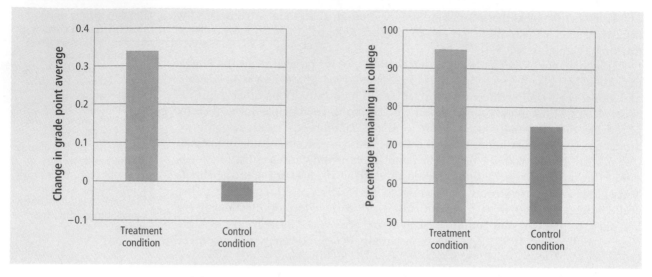

■ **FIGURE SPA1.5   Combating learned helplessness in first-year college students.**   In the treatment condition, first-year college students learned that the causes of poor academic performance in the first year can be temporary. This knowledge led to improvements in their grade point average and made them less likely to drop out of college. (Adapted from Wilson & Linville, 1982)

> If the human mind will busy itself to make the worst of every disagreeable occurrence, it will never want a woe.
> –Samuel Richardson, 1747

learned helplessness shares. Note that we do not know the real reason our hypothetical students did poorly on their calculus test. Instead, learned helplessness theory states that it is more important to consider people's perceptions of these causes. The real causes, of course, are not irrelevant. If the students lack ability in calculus, they are likely to do poorly on future calculus tests. However, often in life what actually causes our behavior is not so clear-cut or so fixed. In such situations, people's attributions about the causes of their problems can be very important.

To explore this link between learned helplessness and academic performance, Tim Wilson and Patricia Linville (1982, 1985) conducted a study with first-year college students. They assumed that many first-year students experience academic difficulties because of a damaging pattern of attributions. Due to the difficulty of adjusting to a new academic and social environment, the first year of college has its rough spots for nearly everyone. The problem is, many first-year students do not realize how common such adjustment problems are and assume that their problems are due to personal predicaments that are unlikely to change—just the kind of attribution that leads to learned helplessness.

Wilson and Linville tried to combat this pessimism by convincing students that the causes of poor performance are often temporary. At Duke University, first-year students who were concerned about their academic performance took part in what they thought was a survey of college experiences. In the treatment condition the students watched videotaped interviews of four upper-class students, each of whom, during the interviews, mentioned that his or her grades were poor or mediocre during the first year but had improved significantly since then. The students were also given statistics indicating that academic performance is often poor in the first year of college but improves thereafter. The researchers hypothesized that this simple message would help prevent learned helplessness, increasing the students' motivation to try harder and removing needless worries about their abilities. Judging by the students' future performance, this is just what happened. Compared to students in a control group who participated in the study but did not watch the videotaped interviews or see the statistics, students in the treatment condition improved their grades more in the following year and were less likely to drop out of college (see Figure SPA1.5). Similar results have been found in studies in other countries, such as Canada and Belgium (Menec et al., 1994; Van Overwalle & De Metsenaere, 1990).

Because people's attributions were not directly measured in the Wilson and Linville (1982) study, we can only infer that the students improved their academic performance because of a beneficial change in their attributions. However, several other studies have directly measured people's attributions and found that people who explain bad events in optimistic ways are less depressed, in better health, and do better in school and in their careers (Burhans & Dweck, 1995; Nolen-Hoeksema, Girgus, & Seligman, 1986; Peterson, Seligman, & Vaillant, 1988; Seligman & Schulman, 1986; Snyder, Irving, & Anderson, 1991).

What determines whether people will explain their setbacks in a pessimistic or optimistic manner? Interestingly, the culture in which we grow up can be very powerful in providing such explanations. Cultural wisdom about why people do what they do abounds, some of it inaccurate and damaging. For example, in the United States there is a cultural stereotype that African Americans are less intelligent than whites. What effect might this stereotype have on attributions for one's own performance? Suppose an African American and a white college student are taking the same test and are having difficulty solving the same problem. Both students are likely to be worried about their performance, but the African American has a worry the white student does not—the fear of confirming the cultural stereotype that African Americans are unintelligent. If the white student does poorly, it reflects badly only on him- or herself. If the African American does poorly, it not only reflects badly on him- or herself but also confirms the negative stereotype about African Americans.

Claude Steele and Joshua Aronson (1995) called this worry *stereotype threat*—that is, apprehension about confirming a negative stereotype of one's group (Steele, 1997). As we saw in Chapter 13, Steele and Aronson (1995) reasoned that preventing such negative explanations might improve academic performance, by short-circuiting the worry and apprehension associated with stereotype threat. They administered a difficult verbal test to African American and

> Twixt the optimist and
> the pessimist the
> difference is droll:
> The optimist see the
> doughnut
> But the pessimist sees
> the hole.
> —McLandburgh Wilson,
> 1915

■ People can experience learned helplessness in a variety of settings, including at work. Fortunately, most bosses do not encourage learned helplessness as much as Dilbert's does.

DILBERT reprinted by permission of United Feature Syndicate, Inc.

white students at Stanford University. Half of the students of each race were led to believe that the investigator was measuring their intellectual ability—which was likely to raise concerns about stereotype threat among the African Americans. The other half were led to believe that the investigator was merely trying to develop a new test and that, because the test was not yet valid or reliable, their performance would mean nothing in terms of their actual ability. The results were striking: White students performed equally well regardless of whether they believed the test was a measure of their intelligence. African American students who believed they were taking a test of intellectual ability performed less well than the whites; in contrast, African Americans who believed the test was not measuring their ability performed as well as whites.

Similar results were found by Steven Spencer, Claude Steele, and Diane Quinn (1997) in a study of women's and men's performance on difficult math tests. Women performed as well as men when they were told that there were no gender differences on the test. When told that men and women tended to do differently on the test, however, women did significantly worse—presumably because of their anxiety over confirming the cultural stereotype that men are better at math than women are (see Figure SPA1.6). These studies, along with Wilson and Linville's (1982), show that the way in which people explain their academic performance can have considerable effects on how well they do. Finding ways of preventing negative, unflattering explanations can be quite beneficial, by preventing the anxiety and worry such explanations trigger.

In summary, we have seen that people's feelings of control and self-efficacy, and the kinds of attributions they make for their performance, are important determinants of their psychological and physical adjustment. People who feel a lack of control and self-efficacy, or explain events in pessimistic terms (i.e., who experience learned helplessness or stereotype threat) are more likely to be in poor health and experience academic and professional problems. The power of our minds over our bodies is, of course, limited. But research shows that perceived control, self-efficacy, and optimistic attributions are beneficial, making it easier for us to cope with the hardships life deals us.

■ **FIGURE SPA1.6   Stereotype threat and performance on math tests.**   When female college students believed there were gender differences on the difficult math test they were taking, they did worse than male college students. When they took the same test but believed there were no gender differences, they did as well as men. (Adapted from Spencer, Steele, & Quinn, 1997)

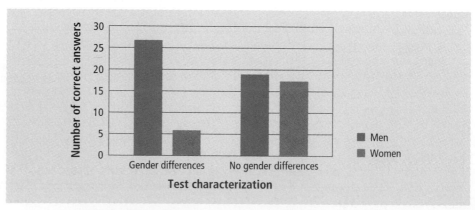

■ Stereotype threat occurs when people are apprehensive about confirming a negative stereotype concerning their group. African Americans taking academic tests, for example, might worry that a bad performance will confirm the negative cultural stereotype that African Americans are unintelligent. This worry can, paradoxically, make it more difficult to do well. Studies have shown that when African American college students think a test is a measure of intelligence, they do less well than whites. When they think the same test is not a measure of intelligence—thereby removing concerns about stereotype confirmation—they do as well as whites. (Steele & Aronson, 1996)

Coping with Stress

Now that we know what the causes of perceived stress are, it is important to consider how people deal with stress. There has been a great deal of research on **coping styles,** defined as the ways in which people react to stressful events (e.g., Aspinwall & Taylor, 1997; Lazarus & Folkman, 1984; Lehman, Davis, DeLongis, & Wortman, 1993; Moos & Schaefer, 1993; Pennebaker & Harber, 1993; Salovey et al., 1998; Taylor & Aspinwall, 1993). What are these styles and how successful are they? We will examine a few coping styles here, beginning with research on personality traits that are related to coping.

Coping Styles
the ways in which people react to stressful events

Personality and Coping Styles

What is it about some people that seems to make them more resistant to stress? A number of personality variables have been studied, such as optimism. As we have just seen, explaining events in an optimistic fashion has some definite advantages. Michael Scheier and Charles Carver (1987, 1992) have looked at this from the vantage point of personality: It seems that some people are by nature optimistic, generally expecting the best out of life, whereas others are sourpusses who always see the dark underside of life. Consistent with research on learned helplessness, there is evidence that optimistic people react better to stress and are healthier than their pessimistic counterparts (Armor & Taylor, in press; Carver & Scheier, in press; Scheier & Carver, 1987; Scheier et al., 1990; Scheier, Weintraub, & Carver, 1986). To get an idea of how optimistic you tend to be, complete the Try It! exercise on page 566.

Try It!

The Life Orientation Test

Please indicate the extent of your agreement with each of the following 10 statements, using the scale below. Please be as accurate and honest as you can on all items, and try not to let your answer to one question influence your answer to other questions. There are no right or wrong answers.

0	1	2	3	4
strongly disagree	disagree	neutral	agree	strongly agree

1. In uncertain times, I usually expect the best.   _____

2. It's easy for me to relax.   _____

3. If something can go wrong for me, it will.   _____

4. I'm always optimistic about my future.   _____

5. I enjoy my friends a lot.   _____

6. It's important for me to keep busy.   _____

7. I hardly ever expect things to go my way.   _____

8. I don't get upset too easily.   _____

9. I rarely count on good things happening to me.   _____

10. Overall, I expect more good things to happen to me than bad.   _____

Scoring: First, reverse your answers to questions 3, 7, and 9. That is, for these questions, change a *0* to a *4*, a *1* to a *3*, a *3* to a *1*, and a *4* to a *0*. Then, sum these reversed scores and the scores you gave to questions 1, 4, and 10. (Ignore questions 2, 5, 6, and 8, because they were filler items.)

This is a measure of dispositional optimism created by Scheier, Carver, and Bridges (1994). According to these researchers, the higher your score, the more optimistic is your approach to life. The average score for college students in their study was 14.3, with no significant differences between women and men. Several studies have found that optimistic people cope better with stress and are healthier than their pessimistic counterparts.

The good news is that most people have been found to have optimistic outlooks on life. In fact, there is evidence that most people are *unrealistically* optimistic about their lives (Armor & Taylor, in press; Taylor & Brown, 1988, 1994). Neil Weinstein (1980), for example, asked college students to estimate how likely a variety of events were to happen to them, compared to how likely these events were to happen to their peers. The events included both positive things, such as liking your postgraduation job and living past 80, and negative things, such as getting divorced and contracting lung cancer. People were overly optimistic, in that nearly everyone thought that the good events were more likely to happen to them than their peers, and that the negative events were less likely to happen to them than their peers (we know that people were wrong, on average, because not everyone could be more likely than others to experience the good things and avoid the bad things).

This kind of unrealistic optimism would be a problem if it caused people to make serious mistakes about their prospects in life. Obviously it would not be a good idea to convince ourselves that we will never get lung cancer and therefore

■ It is important to try to adopt an optimistic approach to life, because optimists have been found to be healthier and to react better to stress.

smoke three packs of cigarettes a day. David Armor and Shelley Taylor (in press), however, suggest that most people have a healthy balance of optimism and reality-monitoring. We manage to put a positive spin on many aspects of our lives, which leads to increased feelings of control and self-efficacy—which, as we have seen, is a good thing. At the same time, Armor and Taylor (in press) found that most people are able to keep their optimistic biases in check when they are faced with a real threat and to take steps to deal with that threat.

Another personality variable that has received a great deal of attention is the **Type A versus B personality,** which is a personality typology based on how people typically confront challenges in their lives (Rosenman, 1993). The Type A individual is typically competitive, impatient, hostile, aggressive, and control-oriented, whereas the Type B person is typically patient, relaxed, and noncompetitive. We are all familiar with the Type A pattern; this is the person who honks and yells at other drivers when they don't drive to his or her satisfaction. People with this personality trait appear to deal with stress efficiently and aggressively. Their hard-driving, competitive approach to life pays off in some respects; Type A individuals tend to get good grades in college and to be successful in their careers (Kliewer, Lepore, & Evans, 1990; Ovcharchyn, Johnson, & Petzel, 1981). However, this success comes with some costs. Type A individuals spend relatively little time on nonwork activities and have more trouble in balancing their work and family lives (Burke & Greenglass, 1990; Greenglass, 1991). Further, numerous studies show that Type A individuals are more prone to getting coronary heart disease, as compared to Type B people (Matthews, 1988). Subsequent studies have tried to narrow down what it is about the Type A personality that is most related to heart disease. The most likely culprit is hostility (Matthews, 1988; Salovey et al., 1998; Miller, Smith, Turner, Guijarro, & Jallet, 1996; Williams, 1987). Competitiveness and a fast-paced life might not be so bad by themselves, but if a person is chronically hostile, they are more at risk for coronary disease.

What determines whether people have Type A or Type B personalities? A number of factors have been found to be related to which type you are. You are more likely to be a Type A if you are male, your parents are Type A, and you live in an urban rather than a rural area (Rosenman, 1993). The culture in which you grow up may also play a role. It is well known that a higher incidence of coronary disease exists in many Western cultures than in many Asian cultures, such as Japan. Triandis (1995) suggests that one reason for this disparity is the emphasis

Type A versus B Personality
a personality typology based on how people typically confront challenges in their lives; the Type A person is typically competitive, impatient, hostile, and control-oriented, whereas the Type B person is typically patient, relaxed, and noncompetitive

■ People with a Type A personality—those who are impatient, competitive, and hostile—are more likely to get coronary disease than people with a Type B personality—those who are relaxed, patient, and nonhostile. Recent research suggests that it is hostility in particular that is most related to coronary disease.

on independence and individualism in Western cultures and on interdependence and collectivism in Asian cultures. He points to two ways in which these emphases might be related to heart disease: First, cultures that stress individualism emphasize competitiveness more and thus might encourage personality types more like Type A. Second, people who live in cultures that stress collectivism might have more support from other people when they experience stress, and as we will see shortly, such social support is a valuable way of making stress more manageable.

Investigations such as these are in the domain of personality psychology, in that they focus on traits that set people apart: What is it about one person that makes her or him more resistant to health problems than another person? The social psychologist takes a different tack: Can we identify ways of coping with stress that everyone can adopt to make it easier to deal with the blows life deals us?

"Opening Up": Confiding to Others

When something traumatic happens to you, is it best to try to bury it as deep as you can and never talk about it, or to open up and discuss your problems with others? Although folk wisdom has long held that it is best to open up, only recently has this assumption been put to the test. James Pennebaker (1990, 1997) and his colleagues have conducted a number of interesting experiments on the value of confiding in others. Pennebaker and Beale (1986), for example, asked college students to write, for 15 minutes on each of four consecutive nights, about a traumatic event that had happened to them. Students in a control condition wrote for the same amount of time about a trivial event. The traumas that people chose to write about were highly personal and in many cases quite tragic, including such events as rape and the death of a sibling. Writing about these events was upsetting in the short run: People who wrote about traumatic events reported more negative moods and showed greater increases in blood pressure. However, there were long-term benefits: The people who wrote about traumatic events were less likely to visit the student health center during the next six months and they reported having fewer illnesses. Similarly, Pennebaker and his colleagues found that first-year college students who wrote about the problems of entering

■ Research by Pennebaker (1990) on "opening up" shows that there are long-term health benefits to writing or talking about one's personal traumas.

college improved their health over the next several months (Pennebaker, Colder, & Sharp, 1990) and that survivors of the Holocaust who disclosed the most about their World War II experiences showed the largest improvements in health over the next several months (Pennebaker, Barger, & Tiebout, 1989).

What is it about "opening up" that leads to better health? Pennebaker argues that actively trying to inhibit or not think about a traumatic event takes a lot of mental and physical energy and is thus itself stressful. Having to constantly fight back thoughts about a trauma exerts a toll on our bodies that might lead to health problems. Further, trying to suppress negative thoughts can lead to an obsession with those very thoughts, such that people think about them more and more (Wegner, 1994). Writing about or confiding in others about a traumatic event may help people to gain a better understanding of the event, helping to put it behind them. It might also elicit emotional support from others—which, as we will now see, can be an important part of the coping process.

Social Support: Getting Help from Others

A final coping strategy is to feel that there are other people available to help us. A number of studies find that **social support,** defined as the perception that others are responsive and receptive to one's needs, is an important aid in dealing with stress (Cohen & Wills, 1985; Dunkel-Schetter, Sagrestano, Feldman, & Killingsworth, 1996; Helgeson, 1993; Helgeson & Cohen, 1996; Hobfoll & Vaux, 1993; Sarason, Sarason, & Pierce, 1990; Stroebe & Stroebe, 1996; Uchino, Cacioppo, & Keicolt-Glaser, 1996). For example, Fran Norris and Krzysztof Kaniasty (1996) studied the survivors of two hurricanes, Hurricane Hugo that struck North and South Carolina in 1989 and Hurricane Andrew that struck southern Florida in 1992. Both storms caused wide devastation, killing dozens of people and destroying the homes and property of thousands of others. Norris and Kaniasty (1996) found that the people who coped with these disasters the best were those who felt that they had the most social support, such as having others

Social Support
the perception that others are responsive and receptive to one's needs

to talk to and to help solve problems. Clearly, when we believe that we have someone to lean on, we can deal better with life's problems.

Evidence for the role of social support also comes from cross-cultural studies. People who live in cultures that stress interdependence and collectivism suffer less from stress-related diseases, possibly because it is easier for people in these cultures to obtain social support. People who live in cultures that stress individualism are expected more to "go it alone" (Bond, 1991; Brislin, 1993). The problem is, going it alone can take its toll on our health. James House and his colleagues (1982) assessed the level of social support in a large sample of men and women in the years 1967–1969. They found that men with a low level of social support were two to three times more likely to die over the next 12 years than men with a high level of social support were. Women with a low level of social support were 1.5 to 2 times more likely to die than women with a high level of social support were (Berkman & Syme, 1979; Schwarzer & Leppin, 1991; Stroebe & Stroebe, 1996).

One of the most dramatic studies of social support was conducted by David Spiegel and his colleagues (Spiegel, Bloom, Kraemer, & Gottheil, 1989), who randomly assigned women with advanced breast cancer to a social support condition or a control condition. People in the social support condition met weekly with other patients and doctors to discuss their problems and fears, whereas people in the control group did not have access to this support system. Not only did the social support improve women's moods and reduce their fears; it lengthened their lives by an average of 18 months.

Does this mean that you should always seek out comfort and advice from others? Not necessarily. According to the **buffering hypothesis,** we need social support only when we are under stress (Cohen & Wills, 1985). When things are going great and we feel in control of our lives, we can go it alone. When times are tough—we've just broken up with our girlfriend or boyfriend, or our parents have gone off the deep end again—social support helps in two ways. First, it can help us interpret an event as less stressful than we otherwise would. Suppose you've just found out that you have midterms in your psychology and calculus classes on the same day. If you have several friends in these classes who can commiserate with you and help you study, you are likely to find the tests as less of a big deal than if you had to deal with them on your own. Second, even if we do interpret an event as stressful, social support can help us cope. Say you've just done poorly on a midterm and feel badly about it. It's best to have close friends nearby to help you deal with this and figure out how to do better on the next test (Stroebe & Stroebe, 1996). The moral? The countless pop songs you've heard are right: In times of stress, find a friend to lean on. To get an idea of the amount of social support you feel is available in your life, complete the Try It! exercise on page 571.

Buffering Hypothesis
the hypothesis that we need social support only when we are under stress, because it protects us against the detrimental effects of this stress

Prevention: Improving Health Habits

In addition to helping people reduce stress, it would be beneficial to get people to change their health habits more directly—to stop smoking, lose weight, eat a healthier diet, and stop abusing alcohol or other drugs. This is an area in which social psychology can be especially helpful.

Americans are doing a pretty good job of improving some of their health habits. A 1993 Harris poll found that only 24 percent of adults smoked cigarettes, the lowest smoking rate ever recorded (*USA Today*, March 12, 1993). People are more likely today to avoid high-cholesterol and fatty foods than they

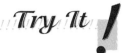

//

Social Support

This scale is made up of a list of statements each of which may or may not be true about you. For each statement we would like you to circle *probably* TRUE (T) if the statement is true about you or *probably* FALSE (F) if the statement is not true about you.

You may find that many of the statements are neither clearly true nor clearly false. In these cases, try to decide *quickly* whether probably TRUE (T) or probably FALSE (F) is most descriptive of you. Although some questions will be difficult to answer, it is important that you pick one alternative or the other. Remember to circle only one of the alternatives for each statement.

Please read each item quickly but carefully before responding. Remember that this is not a test and there are no right or wrong answers.

1. There is at least one person I know whose advice I really trust.	T	F
2. There is really no one I can trust to give me good financial advice.	T	F
3. There is really no one who can give me objective feedback about how I'm handling my problems.	T	F
4. When I need suggestions for how to deal with a personal problem I know there is someone I can turn to.	T	F
5. There is someone who I feel comfortable going to for advice about sexual problems.	T	F
6. There is someone I can turn to for advice about handling hassles over household responsibilities.	T	F
7. I feel that there is no one with whom I can share my most private worries and fears.	T	F
8. If a family crisis arose few of my friends would be able to give me good advice about how to handle it.	T	F
9. There are very few people I trust to help solve my problems.	T	F
10. There is someone I could turn to for advice about changing my job or finding a new one.	T	F

Scoring: You get one point each time you answered TRUE to questions 1, 4, 5, 6, and 10 and one point for each time you answered FALSE to questions 2, 3, 7, 8, and 9.

This is a scale that Cohen et al. (1985) developed to measure what they call appraisal social support, or "the perceived availability of someone to talk to about one's problems" (pp. 75–76). One of their findings was that when people were not under stress, those low in social support had no more physical symptoms than people high in social support did. However, when people were under stress, those low in social support had more physical symptoms than people high in social support did. This is support for the buffering hypothesis talked about in the text: we need social support the most when times are tough. Another finding was that women scored reliably higher on the social support scale than men did. (Adapted from Cohen et al., 1985)

//

were a few years ago and more women are getting Pap smears to detect cancer. There is definitely room for improvement, however. A more recent Harris poll found that 71 percent of Americans are overweight—more than ever before. As seen in Figure SPA1.7, Americans are among the heaviest people in the world. Other polls have found that people drink more alcohol, exercise less, and get fewer hours of sleep than they did five years earlier (*Washington Post Health*, January 9, 1996). Also, binge drinking on college campuses is occurring at an alarmingly high rate. One study found that 50% of college men and 39% of

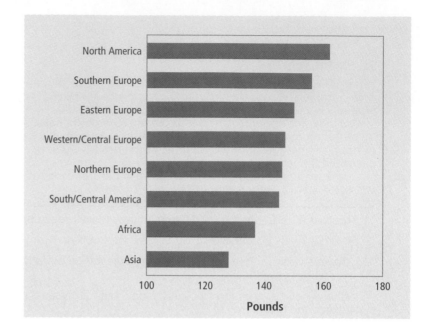

■ **FIGURE SPA1.7   Average weight of 5-foot-4 men and women.**   The percentage of Americans who are overweight has increased substantially over the past several years. In addition, as seen from this graph, Americans tend to weigh more than people in any other part of the world. Source: Fumento, M. (1997, Sept. 12–14). Why we need a new war on weight. *USA Weekend* (p. 4).

college women engage in binge drinking (Wechsler, Dowdall, Davenport, & Castillo, 1995). Although most binge drinkers believe that it will be easy to stop after leaving college, many will find it very hard to do so and will develop serious drinking problems. Finally, people who are at risk for getting AIDS are not taking as many precautions as they should. In a recent poll, only 58 percent of single, sexually active Americans reported that they use condoms (Clements & Hales, 1997). How can we persuade people to change their health habits?

Message Framing: Stressing Gains versus Losses

One approach, as we discussed in Chapter 7 on attitude change, is to present people with persuasive communications urging them to act in healthier ways. For example, we could show people vivid pictures of someone dying of skin cancer, sending the message that if they don't protect themselves from the sun by using sunscreen lotions, this could happen to them. Many public service advertisements take this approach, trying to scare people into applying sunscreen, using condoms, and wearing seatbelts.

It is always best to scare people, emphasizing what they have to lose by acting in unhealthy ways? Suppose, for example, that you were devising a public service ad to lower fatalities from skin cancer. Your goal is to get people to examine their skin regularly for cancer and to use sunscreen lotions when they are exposed to the sun. You could frame your message in terms of what people have to lose by not performing these behaviors; for example, you might emphasize that most skin cancers are fatal if not detected at an early stage. Or, you could frame your message in a more positive way by emphasizing what people have to gain; for example, you could say that skin cancers are curable if detected early and that people can decrease their chances of getting skin cancer by using sunscreen.

It might seem as if these different messages would have the same effect; after all, they convey the same information—it is a good idea to examine your skin regularly and use sunscreen lotions. Alex Rothman and Peter Salovey (1997), though, found that framing messages in terms of losses versus gains can make a big difference. When trying to get people to *detect* the presence of a disease, it is best to use a loss frame, emphasizing what they have to lose by avoiding this behavior (e.g., the costs of not examining one's skin for cancer; Meyerowitz & Chaiken, 1987; Rothman, Salovey, Antone, Keough, & Martin, 1993; Wilson, Purdon, & Wallston, 1988). When trying to get people to engage in behaviors that will *prevent* disease, it is best to use a gain frame, emphasizing what they have to gain by engaging in these behaviors (e.g., using sunscreen; Christophersen & Gyulay, 1981; Linville, Fischer, & Fischhoff, 1993; Rothman et al., 1993). Alex Rothman (1993) and his colleagues, for example, found that framing a message in terms of losses increased college women's intentions to examine their skin for cancer (a detection behavior), whereas framing a message in terms of gains increased college women's intentions to use sunscreen (a prevention behavior; see Figure SPA1.8).

Why does the way in which a message is framed make a difference? Rothman and Salovey (1997) suggest that it changes the way in which people think about their health. A loss frame focuses people's attention on the possibility that they might have a problem that can be dealt with by performing detection behaviors (e.g., examining their skin for cancer or performing breast self-exams). A gain frame focuses people's attention on the fact that they are in a good state of health and that to stay that way, it is best to perform preventative behaviors (e.g., using

■ **FIGURE SPA1.8   Framing health messages in terms of gains or losses.**   Rothman et al. (1993) presented women with information trying to get them to avoid skin cancer. Some participants received a message framed in terms of gains that focused on the positive benefits of being concerned about skin cancer, e.g., "If they are detected early, most of these cancers are curable." Other participants received a message framed in terms of losses that focused on the negative consequences of not being concerned about skin cancer, e.g., "unless they are detected and treated early, most of these cancers are not curable." As seen in the left hand side of the figure, the loss frame message worked best on detection behaviors (people's intention to perform exams of their skin). As seen in the right hand side of the figure, the gain frame message worked best with a prevention behavior (requesting a sample of sunscreen). (Adapted from Rothman et al., 1993)

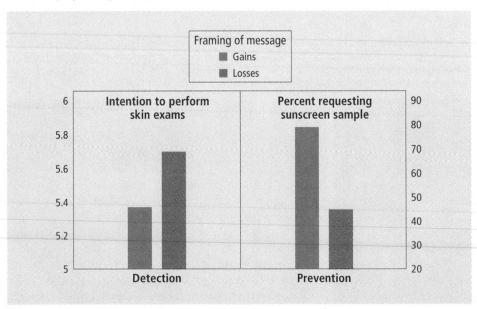

sunscreen when exposed to the sun and condoms when having sex). So, before designing your public health ad, decide which kind of behavior you are going to target—a prevention or detection behavior—and design your ad accordingly.

Changing Health-Relevant Behaviors Using Dissonance Theory

Unfortunately, when it comes to changing some intractable, ingrained health habits, public service ads may be of limited success. The problem is that with many health problems, there are overwhelming barriers to change. Consider the use of condoms. Most people are aware that AIDS is a serious problem and that using condoms provides some protection against AIDS. Still, a surprisingly small percentage of people use condoms. One reason is that many people find condoms to be inconvenient and unromantic, as well as a reminder of disease—something they don't want to be reminded of when they are having sex. Where sexual behavior is involved, there is a strong tendency to go into denial—in this case, to decide that whereas AIDS is a problem, we are not at risk. What can be done to change this potentially fatal attitude?

One of the most important messages of social psychology is that to change people's behavior, you need to challenge their self-esteem in such a way that it becomes to their advantage—psychologically—to change their behavior. By doing so, they feel good about themselves, maintaining their self-esteem. Sound familiar? This is a basic tenet of dissonance theory. As we discussed in Chapter 6, Elliot Aronson and his colleagues have recently shown that the principles of dissonance theory can be used to get people to behave in healthier ways, including using condoms more often. To review briefly, Aronson, Fried, and Stone (1991; Stone, Aronson, Crain, Winslow, & Fried, 1994) asked college students to compose a speech describing the dangers of AIDS and advocating the use of condoms "every single time you have sex." The students gave their speech in front of a video camera, after being informed that the resulting videotape would be played to an audience of high school students. Was giving this speech sufficient to change their own behavior, making the students more likely to use condoms themselves?

■ Americans are making progress in improving some areas of health; for example, more and more people are quitting smoking. Americans are not doing very well in other areas. Many people find it difficult to lose weight and maintain a regular exercise program. How can social psychology help people act in healthier ways?

Changing Your Health Habits

Pick a health habit of yours and try to improve it, using the principles we have discussed in this chapter. For example, you might try to lose a few pounds, exercise more, or cut down on your smoking. We should mention right away that this is not easy. If it were, we would all be svelte, physically fit, nonsmokers! We suggest that you start small with a limited goal; try to lose 5 pounds, for example, or increase your exercise by one or two hours a week.

Here are some specific suggestions as to how to change your behavior:

- Increase your feelings of control over your behavior, particularly your self-efficacy in this domain. One way to do this is to start small. If you are trying to lose weight, for example, begin slowly with some easy-to-control behaviors. You might start by eliminating one food or beverage from your diet that you do not like all that much but which is pretty fattening. Suppose, for example, that you drink a 200-calorie fruit juice five times a week. Replacing the juice with water will save 52,000 calories a year, which is equivalent to 13 pounds! The idea is to gain mastery over your behavior slowly, improving your feelings of self-efficacy. When you've mastered one behavior, try another. You can do it!

- If you experience a setback, such as eating two pieces of cake at a birthday party when you really didn't mean to, avoid a damaging pattern of attributions. Do not assume that the setback was due to internal, stable, global causes—this will cause learned helplessness. Remember, almost everyone fails the first time they try to diet or quit smoking. It often takes people several attempts, thus, a setback or two are not due to something unchangeable about you. Keep trying.

- Try your own little dissonance experiment, such as the one we discussed by Elliot Aronson and colleagues on safer sex. There are two steps: First, make a speech to others urging them to adopt the behaviors you are trying to change. For example, tell all your friends about the dangers of obesity (e.g., the World Health Organization estimates that each year, 300,000 Americans die prematurely because they are overweight; Fumento, 1997). The more involved and detailed you make your speech and the wider your audience, the better. Second, make a detailed list of times when you did not practice what you preached (e.g., when you gained weight). You might find it easier to quit once you have put yourself through this "hypocrisy" procedure.

- It can be stressful to change a well-ingrained habit and it is at times of stress that social support is most important. Talk with your friends and family about your attempts to change your behavior. Seek their advice and support. Even better, convince several friends to try these techniques with you. Make it a group project, in which you and your friends support each others' efforts to alter your behavior.

The answer is, only when the students were also made mindful of their own failures to use condoms by making a list of the circumstances in their own lives when they found it particularly difficult, awkward, or "impossible" to use condoms. These students were most aware of their own hypocrisy—namely, that they were preaching behavior to high school students that they themselves were not practicing. Because no one likes to feel like a hypocrite, these participants needed to take steps to fix their damaged self-esteem. A clear way of doing this would be to start practicing what they were preaching. This is exactly what Aronson and his colleagues found: Students in the hypocrisy condition showed the greatest willingness to use condoms in the future and, when given the opportunity, purchased significantly more condoms for their own use than students in the nonhypocrisy conditions did.

The Aronson and colleagues (1991) condom study is yet another illustration of a familiar point: Sometimes the best way to change people's behavior is to change their interpretation of themselves and the social situation. No attempt was made to modify the research participants' behavior (their use of condoms) directly. They were not rewarded for using condoms; nor were they given any information about what would happen if they didn't. Instead, the researchers altered the way in which the participants interpreted their failure to use condoms. In the hypocrisy condition, the failure to use condoms took on a new meaning. Before the study, the students probably viewed failing to use a condom as no big deal; after all, surely they would never contract AIDS. After creating a speech for high school students and thinking about their own past actions, not using a condom took on a very different meaning: It became an unprincipled, hypocritical act, and—presto!—the students now wanted to use condoms more. We cannot overemphasize this important social psychological message: One of the best ways to solve applied problems is often to change people's interpretation of the situation.

Now that you have read about several of the factors that influence health behaviors, see if you can improve your habits by completing the Try It! exercise on page 575.

Summary

We examined the effects of stress on human health, the causes of stress, how people cope with stress, and how to encourage people to change their health habits. Stress has been found to have a number of negative effects, such as an impairment of the immune system. **Stress** is best defined as the negative feelings that occur when people feel they cannot cope with the environment and is thus related to the way in which people perceive the objective world. One key determinant of stress is how much **perceived control** people have over their environment. The less control people believe they have, the more likely it is that the event will cause them physical and psychological problems. For example, the loss of control experienced by many older people in nursing homes can have negative effects on their health. It is also important for people to have high **self-efficacy** in a particular domain, which is the belief in one's ability to carry out specific actions that produce desired outcomes. In addition, the way in which people explain the causes of negative events is critical to how stressful those events will be. When bad things happen, **learned helplessness** results if people make **stable, internal,** and **global attributions** for those events. Learned helplessness leads to depression, reduced effort, and difficulty in learning new material. Sometimes our culture encourages a damaging pattern of attributions. For example, because there is a cultural stereotype that women are worse at math

than men, women may experience stereotype threat when taking a math test, which is apprehension about confirming a negative stereotype of one's group. Removing stereotype threat, by telling women that there are no gender differences on a particular math test, has been found to improve women's performance.

People's **coping styles** refer to the ways in which they react to stressful events. Research on personality traits, such as optimism and the **Type A versus B personality,** focuses on how people typically deal with stress and how these styles are related to their physical health. Optimistic people tend to react better to stress and to be healthier. Type A individuals—particularly those with high levels of hostility—are more at risk for coronary disease. Other researchers focus on ways of coping with stress that everyone can adopt. Several studies show that "opening up," which involves writing or talking about one's problems, has long-term health benefits. **Social support**—the perception that other people are responsive to one's needs—is also beneficial. According to the **buffering hypothesis,** social support is especially helpful in times of stress, by making people less likely to interpret an event as stressful and by helping them cope with stressful events.

It is also important to explore ways of getting people to act in healthier ways. One way is to present people with persuasive communications urging them to adopt better health habits. To be successful, it is important to tailor these messages to the kinds of behaviors you want people to adopt. To get people to perform detection behaviors, such as examining their skin for cancer, it is best to use messages framed in terms of losses (the negative consequences of failing to act). To get people to perform preventa-tive behaviors, such as using sunscreen, it is best to use messages framed in terms of gains (the positive consequences of performing the behaviors). Even more powerful are techniques that arouse dissonance that is reduced by changing one's health habits, such as making people feel hypocritical about their failure to use condoms.

If You Are Interested

Burke, R. J., & Greenglass, E. R. (1990). Type A behavior and non-work activities. *Personality and Individual Differences, 11,* 945–952.

Goldberger, L., & Breznitz, S. (Eds.) (1993). *Handbook of stress: Theoretical and clinical aspects* (2nd ed.). New York: Free Press. A large collection of chapters on all aspects of stress, written by experts in the field. The topics include basic psychological and biological aspects of stress, the measurement of stress and coping, sociocultural and developmental sources of stress, and treatment for stress.

Greenglass, E. R. (1991). Type A behavior, career aspirations, and role conflict in professional women. In M. J. Strube (ed.), *Type A behavior* (pp. 277–292). Newbury Park, CA: Sage.

Kleiwer, W., Lepore, S. J., & Evans, G. W. (1990). The costs of Type B behavior: Females at risk in achievement situations. *Journal of Applied Social Psychology, 20,* 1369–1382.

Pennebaker, J. W. (1990). *Opening up: The healing powers of confiding in others*. New York: William Morrow. An insightful, accessible presentation of research on the value of discussing one's problems with other people.

Salovey, P., Rothman, A. J., & Rodin, J. (1998). Social psychology and health behavior. In D. Gilbert, S. Fiske, & G. Lindzey (Eds.), *The handbook of social psychology* (4th ed., Vol. 2, pp. 633–683). New York: McGraw-Hill. A broad, insightful review of the emerging field of health psychology.

Seligman, M. E. P. (1990). *Learned optimism*. New York: Springer-Verlag. An interesting book on optimism and learned helplessness theory, by one of its originators.

Taylor, S. E. (1989). *Positive illusions: Creative self-deception and the healthy mind*. New York: Basic Books. A readable book that examines the relationship between people's illusions about themselves and the social world and their physical and mental health. Includes an in-depth discussion of many of the issues covered in this module, including perceived control and learned helplessness.

The Doctor (1991). A surgeon discovers what it is like to be on the other side of the health system when he develops throat cancer. The surgeon develops a close relationship with a terminally ill patient as he struggles with his own mortality. An interesting look at issues of learned helplessness and perceived control and health.

Wechsler, H., Dowdall, G., Davenport, A., & Castillo, S. (1995). Correlates of college student binge drinking. *American Journal of Public Health, 85,* 921–926.

SOCIAL PSYCHOLOGY
IN ACTION 2

SOCIAL PSYCHOLOGY AND THE ENVIRONMENT

Michael and Jeanne Schatzki wanted to escape the hustle and bustle of urban life. After a long search, they finally found what seemed like an idyllic spot—a house at the end of a cul-de-sac in a peaceful, secluded neighborhood in Far Hills, New Jersey. "Then spring came," reports Mr. Schatzki, "and we were sitting on the porch out back. And I said to Jeannie, 'You know, there are an awful lot of airplanes overhead.' And I looked up, and it was one after another" ("Jet Noise," 1991, p. 31). It turned out that the Federal Aviation Administration (FAA) had just changed the landing patterns at Newark Airport, 35 miles from Far Hills. Whereas the planes landing and taking off at Newark Airport used to fly some distance from Far Hills, as many as 300 jets a day now roared directly over the Schatzkis' house.

Christopher Marzec and his wife moved to an apartment in Englewood, New Jersey specifically to escape the noise they had encountered in their old neighborhood in Hoboken. They enjoyed the peace and quiet of Englewood for a couple of years until the FAA revised the landing patterns again, routing hundreds of planes directly over the

■ As the human population increases, the physical world is becoming an increasingly important source of stress. Noise from airplanes and traffic, for example, is an increasingly common feature of urban life.

Marzec's apartment. One day, Mr. Marzec came home and found his wife in tears. "We've pretty much arranged now to be gone during the bulk of the hours when the jets are passing over," Mr. Marzec said. "Psychologically, we don't live here anymore. It's not like living under a bridge, but there's a sense of homelessness" ("Jet Noise," 1991, p. 32).

As we human beings continue to populate the earth at an alarming rate, our physical world is becoming an increasingly important source of stress. It is getting more difficult to escape the noise caused by such things as jetliners and heavy traffic. The presence of other people can be quite aggravating, such as the overcrowding in many urban areas. How do people deal with stress from their physical environments?

Just as our environments exert stress on us, so do we exert stress on our environments. Few problems are as pressing as the damage we are doing to the environment, including toxic waste, overflowing landfills, pollution, global warming, and the destruction of rain forests. In this unit we will consider both of these questions: To what extent and under what conditions is the environment a source of stress? And, how can social influence techniques be used to get people to behave in more environmentally sound ways?

The Environment as a Source of Stress

Have you ever been stuck in rush-hour traffic, venting your anger and frustration by leaning on your car horn? Ever been bothered by the noise we humans generate from cars, planes, and loud parties? If so, you have found your environment to be a source of stress. But what makes our environments stressful? Why is it that the identical event—such as loud music—can be enjoyable on some occasions but highly stressful on others? The answer has to do with a basic assumption of social psychology: It is not objective but subjective situations that influence people. The same stimulus, such as loud music, is interpreted as a source of pleasure on some occasions and as an annoying interruption on others. To understand when our environment will be stressful, then, we need to understand how and why people construe that environment as a threat to their well-being.

In one sense, the environment has always been a source of stress to human beings. We sometimes forget, as we sit in our comfortable, well-heated homes, eating food we purchased at the grocery store, how tenuous our existence has been throughout most of our history. Starvation was no stranger to our ancestors, no further away than one bad harvest or unlucky hunting season. Severe winters claimed many victims, as did diseases that spread unchecked due to contaminated drinking water, poor sanitation, and close living quarters.

As we approach the twenty-first century, we have learned to master most of the harsh environmental hazards that plagued our ancestors (though tragically, in many areas of the world starvation and preventable diseases are still a major cause of death). The irony is that, as human beings have learned how to master the environment, we have created new environmental stressors that our ancestors did not have to face.

Consider, for example, the lives of a group of people called the Mabaan, who live in the Republic of Sudan in Africa, near the equator. When studied by Samuel Rosen and his colleagues in 1962, this culture was relatively untouched by modern civilization. The Mabaan lived in bamboo huts, wore little clothing, and

> The earth we abuse and the living things we kill, in the end, take their revenge; for in exploiting their presences we are diminishing our future.
> –Marys Mannes, 1958

■ Just as our environment can exert stress on us, so too can we exert stress on our environment.

thrived on a diet of grains, fish, and small game. Their environment was quiet and uncrowded, free of many of the stressors associated with modern urban life. There were no sleep-jarring noises from sirens and trucks, no traffic jams to endure at the end of the day, and little fear of crime. Rosen and his colleagues found that, compared to adults in the United States, the Mabaan had less hypertension (high blood pressure), less obesity, and superior hearing.

We cannot be sure, of course, that the absence of modern environmental stressors, such as the problems with urban life, was responsible for the excellent health of the Mabaan. Even if it was, we might not want to conclude that living in modern, urban areas is always stressful, inevitably causing health problems. As we mentioned, the same objective event, such as loud noise, is experienced as stressful under some conditions and pleasurable under others. When will modern environmental conditions like noise and crowding be stressful? Social psychologists have conducted numerous studies to find out.

Noise as a Source of Stress

It is well known that repeated exposure to loud noises eventually causes hearing loss. Samuel Rosen and his colleagues (1962), for example, attributed the superior hearing of the Mabaan in part to the fact that the environment in which they lived was, compared to modern, urban areas, extremely quiet. Are loud noises always psychologically stressful? As you probably know by now, it depends on how people interpret the noise and how much control they feel they have over it. Many people voluntarily go to rock concerts where the music is extremely loud, louder than the sounds of jets flying overhead. Many people thrive on the hustle, bustle, and noise of urban life, as long as they can escape to a quiet corner of their apartment when they choose to do so. In contrast, Michael and Jeanne Schatzki did not choose to hear the jets screaming over their house and could not escape this noise.

As compelling as our examples may be, we cannot be sure that perceived control eliminates the stressful effects of noise without conducting well-controlled experiments. Fortunately, David Glass and Jerome Singer (1972) have performed just such a series of studies. A typical experiment went like this: Participants were given several problems to solve, such as complex addition problems and a proofreading task. While they worked on these problems, they heard very loud bursts of noise. The noise was of such things as a mimeograph machine, a typewriter, and two people speaking in Spanish. The noise was played at 108 decibels, about what you would hear if you were operating a riveting machine or were standing near the runway when a large commercial jet took off.

In one condition, the bursts of noise occurred at unpredictable lengths and at unpredictable intervals over the course of the 25-minute session. In a second condition, people heard the same sequence of noises but were given a sense of control over them. The experimenter told participants that they could stop the noise at any point by pressing a button. "Whether or not you press the button is up to you," explained the experimenter. "We'd prefer that you do not, but that's entirely up to you" (Glass & Singer, 1972, p. 64). A key fact to remember is that no one actually pressed the button. Thus, people in this condition heard the same amount of noise as people in the uncontrollable noise condition; the only difference was that they believed they could stop the noise whenever they wanted. Finally, a third condition was included wherein people worked on the problem in

> **N**oise, *n*. A stench in the ear. . . . The chief product and authenticating sign of civilization.
>
> —Ambrose Bierce, *Devil's Dictionary,* 1911

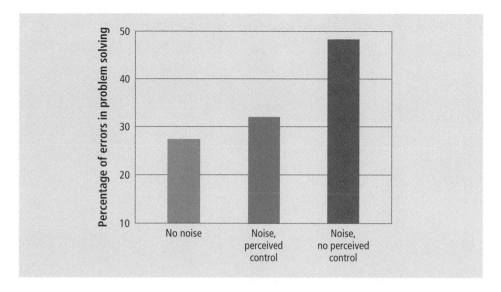

■ **FIGURE SPA2.1 Noise and perceived control.** People who believed they could control the noxious noise did about as well on a subsequent task as people who heard no noise at all. (Adapted from Glass & Singer, 1972)

peace and quiet. After the 25-minute session was over, people in all conditions worked on new problems without any noise being played.

Interestingly, the noise had little effect on people during the initial 25-minute session. As long as a task was not too complex, people could bear down and ignore unpleasant noises, doing just as well on the problems as people who worked on them in quiet surroundings. A different picture emerged, however, when people worked on problems in the next session, in which everyone could work in peace and quiet. As you can see in Figure SPA2.1, those who had endured the uncontrollable noises made significantly more errors during this session than did people who had not heard noises during the first session. And what about the people who heard the noises but believed they could control them? As Figure SPA2.1 shows, these people did almost as well on the subsequent problems as the people who heard no noise at all. When people knew they could turn off the noise at any point, the noise was much easier to tolerate and did not impair later performance—even though people never actually turned it off.

Why did noise lower performance after it ended, and why did this occur only in the condition where the noise couldn't be controlled? When people are initially exposed to uncontrollable, negative events, they often attempt to overcome them as best they can. Many of the people who lived under the new landing pattern at Newark Airport initially fought back, repeatedly contacting officials at the FAA to protest the din of the jets. As long as they felt progress was being made, the noise was probably bearable. Similarly, in Glass and Singer's (1972) study, people initially were able to overcome the noxious effects of the noise by bearing down and concentrating as best they could.

However, if negative, uncontrollable events continue despite our best efforts to overcome them, learned helplessness sets in (Abramson et al., 1978; Wortman & Brehm, 1975). As discussed in the chapter on health, learned helplessness occurs when people explain a negative event in a pessimistic way, by, for example, assuming that the event is caused by things that can't be changed. One consequence of learned helplessness is reduced effort and difficulty in learning new material. Thus, those participants who could not control the noise in the Glass and Singer (1972) experiment were able to deal with it and do well on the problems

■ Frequent, unpredictable noises are an unavoidable fact of urban life. Studies have shown that children who are exposed to constant noises have higher blood pressure, are more easily distracted, and are more likely to give up when working on difficult puzzles than other children are.

initially, but the lack of control they experienced eventually took its toll, causing them to do poorly on the second task. In contrast, those participants who believed they could control the noise never experienced learned helplessness and thus were able to do well on the second set of problems.

Unfortunately, in modern, urban life loud noises are often not controllable, and they last a lot longer than the 25-minute sessions in the Glass and Singer (1972) study. Sheldon Cohen and his colleagues have shown that people who are exposed to such real-life noises respond like the participants in the uncontrollable noise condition of Glass and Singer's (1972) studies. For example, these researchers studied children living in a New York City high-rise apartment building located right next to a busy highway (Cohen, Glass, & Singer, 1973). The children who lived on the lower floors and thus were subjected to the most traffic noise did poorer on reading tests than children living on the upper floors did.

In a later study, Cohen and his colleagues (1980, 1981) studied children who attended schools in the air corridor of Los Angeles Airport. More than 300 jets roared over these schools every day, causing an extremely high level of noise. Compared to children who attended quiet schools (matched on the basis of their race, ethnic group, economic background, and social class), the children at the noisy schools had higher blood pressure, were more easily distracted, and were more likely to give up when working on difficult puzzles. These deficits are classic signs of learned helplessness. Many of these problems were still there when the researchers tested the kids again a year later, suggesting that long-term exposure to loud, uncontrollable noise can cause serious problems in children. More recent studies have also found detrimental effects of noise (Evans, in press; Evans, Hygge, & Bullinger, 1995; Nivison & Endresen, 1993; Staples, 1996; Topf, 1992). Due in part to studies such as these, attempts have recently been made to reduce the amount of noise to which people are subjected—for example, by adding soundproofing materials to schools and devices to jet engines that make them less noisy.

Crowding as a Source of Stress

As we write, more than 5.7 billion human beings inhabit the earth—more people than the total number of all human beings who have ever lived before. The world's population is increasing at the rate of 250,000 people every day. At our current rate of growth, the world population will double by the year 2025 and double again at increasingly shorter intervals. Two hundred years ago, the English clergyman Thomas Malthus warned that the human population was expanding so rapidly that soon there would not be enough food to feed everyone. He was wrong about when such a calamity would occur, largely because of technological advances in agriculture that have vastly improved grain yields. The food supply is dwindling, however, and the number of malnourished people in the world is increasing (Sadik, 1991). Malthus's timing may have been a little off, but many scientists fear his predictions are becoming truer every day.

Even when there is enough food for everyone, overcrowding can be a source of considerable stress to both animals and human beings. When animals are crowded together, in either their natural environments or the laboratory, they reproduce more slowly, take inadequate care of their young, and become more susceptible to disease (Calhoun, 1973; Christian, 1963). Studies of crowding in human beings show similar negative effects. As crowding increases in prisons, for example, disciplinary problems, suicides, and overall death rates also increase (Paulus et al., 1981). Studies at universities find that students living in crowded dorms (e.g., ones that have long corridors with common bathroom and lounge facilities) are more withdrawn socially and are more likely to show signs of learned helplessness than students living in less crowded dorms (e.g., ones with smaller suites that have their own bathrooms; Baum & Valins, 1977, 1979; Evans, Lepore, & Schroeder, 1996).

What is it about crowding that is so aversive? To answer this question, we must first recognize that the presence of other people is not always unpleasant. Many people love living in large cities. When Saturday night arrives, many of us are ready to join our friends for an evening of fun, feeling that the more people we round up, the merrier. This fact has led researchers to distinguish between two

■ As the human population explodes, our planet is becoming more and more crowded. Under what conditions will crowding be stressful?

Density
the number of people who occupy a given space

Crowding
the subjective feeling of unpleasantness due to the presence of other people

> *The thing which in the subway is called congestion is highly esteemed in the night spots as intimacy.*
> —Simeon Strunsky, 1954

> *[Describing London] crowds without company and dissipation without pleasure.*
> —Edward Gibbon, *Memoirs*, 1796

terms: **Density** is a neutral term that refers to the number of people who occupy a given space. A classroom with 20 students has a lower density of people than the same classroom with 50 students. **Crowding** is the subjective feeling of unpleasantness due to the presence of other people; it is the stress we feel when density becomes unpleasant. Under some circumstances, the class with 20 students might feel more crowded than the class with 50 students.

Crowding and Perceived Control

When will density turn into crowding? One factor, as you might expect, pertains to how people interpret the presence of others, including how much control they feel they have over the crowded conditions (Baron & Rodin, 1978; Schmidt & Keating, 1979; Sherrod & Cohen, 1979). If the presence of others lowers our feelings of control—for example, making us feel it is harder to move around as freely as we would like, or harder to avoid running into people we would just as soon avoid—then we are likely to experience a crowd as stressful. If we feel we have control over the situation—for example, if we know we can leave the crowd at any point and find solace in a quiet spot—then we are unlikely to experience it as stressful.

To test this hypothesis, Drury Sherrod (1974) performed a study that was very much like the one Glass and Singer (1972) conducted on the effects of noise. He asked high school students to work on some problems in a room that was jam-packed with other people. In one condition, he told the students that they were free to leave at any point. "In the past, some people who have been in the experiment have chosen to leave," he said. "Others have not. We would prefer that you do not, but that's entirely up to you" (Sherrod, 1974, p. 176). Students in a second condition worked under identical crowded conditions but were not given the choice to leave at any point. Finally, students in a third condition worked in uncrowded conditions. After working on the initial set of problems, the participants were moved to uncrowded quarters, where they worked on a series of difficult puzzles.

The results mirrored those of Glass and Singer (1972). First, students who were crowded—regardless of whether or not they had a sense of control—solved as many problems as students who were not crowded. Initially, they were able to

■ **FIGURE SPA2.2   Crowding and perceived control.**   People who believed they had control over the crowded conditions tried almost as hard on a subsequent task as people who were not crowded at all. (Adapted from Sherrod, 1974)

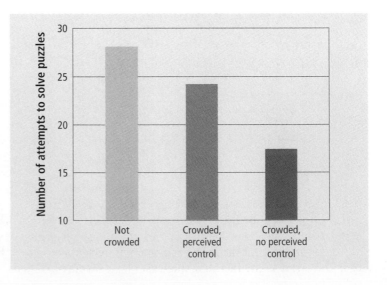

concentrate, ignoring the fact that they were shoulder to shoulder with other people. However, in the condition where the students thought they could not escape, the lack of control eventually took its toll. As seen in Figure SPA2.2, those students who had no control over the crowded conditions in the first session tried to solve significantly fewer puzzles in the second session, as compared to students in the other conditions. The students who had a sense of perceived control over the crowded conditions worked on almost as many difficult puzzles as the students who had not been crowded at all.

Thus, the effects of noise and crowding appear to be similar. If we feel we have control over these environmental conditions, they do not bother us very much. If we feel we do not have control over them, we can, in the short run, concentrate on our tasks and ignore the unpleasant effects of these stressors. Eventually, however, they take their toll, impairing our ability to cope.

Consequently, it is important for people to feel they can control how crowded and noisy their environments are. It might seem like this is much easier in some parts of the world than others. If you live in a high-rise in New York City, for example, it would seem to be more difficult to avoid crowded conditions than if you live on a farm in Iowa. Similarly, homes and apartments are much smaller in Japan than in the United States, and to Americans, at least, it might seem that it is more difficult to escape crowded conditions in Japan than in the United States. Yet even in areas where the density of people is quite high, norms develop to protect people's privacy and to allow an escape from feeling overcrowded. Richard Brislin (1993) notes, for instance, that in both Japan and the slums of Mexico, both of which have a very high density of people, norms about visiting people in their homes are different from those in the United States. In Mexico, people's homes are respected as a sacrosanct place where people can be by themselves and escape the stress of crowded conditions; it is virtually unheard of for people to "drop in" at someone else's house (Pandey, 1990). Similarly, the Japanese entertain in their homes much less than Americans do; they are more likely to invite guests for a meal in a restaurant. The way in which people in different cultures gain control over crowding differs, then, but the need for control appears to be universal (Fuller, Edwards, Vorakitphokatorn, & Sermsri, 1996).

Crowding and Attribution

In addition to perceived control, other factors determine how aversive people will find crowded conditions. It is well known, for example, that the presence of others makes people physiologically aroused (Zajonc, 1965). As we have seen elsewhere (see Chapter 5), arousal can have intriguing consequences. It can lead to quite different emotions, depending on the attributions people make about the source of their arousal (Schachter & Singer, 1962). Thus, as we might expect, an important determinant of how aversive crowding will be is the nature of the attributions people make for the arousal caused by crowding. If people attribute their arousal to the presence of the other people, they will interpret it as a sign that the setting is too crowded and will feel uncomfortable, cramped, and irritated. If they attribute the arousal to another source, they will not feel crowded (Aiello, Thompson, & Brodzinsky, 1983; Schmidt & Keating, 1979). For example, if a student in a class of 300 people attributes her arousal to the stimulating and fascinating lecture she is hearing, she will feel less crowded than if she attributes her arousal to the fact that she feels like a sardine in a can.

■ Pollution and waste hurt many other species besides humans.

"Help!"

Crowding and Sensory Overload

Sensory Overload
the situation in which we receive more stimulation from the environment than we can pay attention to or process

Finally, crowding will be aversive if it leads to **sensory overload** (Cohen, 1978; Milgram, 1970), which occurs when we receive more stimulation from the environment than we can pay attention to or process. Since other people are a key source of stimulation, one instance in which sensory overload can occur is when so many people are around that we cannot pay attention to everyone. For example, if you were being interviewed for a job by a committee of ten persons, you'd feel that you had to pay close attention to everything each interviewer said and did. The result? A severe demand placed on your attentional system—and most likely negative consequences for you. To examine density and crowding in your life, see the Try It! exercise on page 589.

In sum, as humans have evolved, we have learned to master many environmental hazards but in the process have produced new ones, such as noise and crowding. We turn now to another consequence of having become a crowded and technologically advanced society: People are harming the physical environment in multiple ways. Changes in attitudes and behaviors are urgently needed in order to avoid environmental catastrophe. Social psychologists have studied a number of techniques involving social influence and social interaction that encourage people to behave in more environmentally sound ways (Oskamp, 1995; Sundstrom, Bell, Busby, & Asmus, 1996).

Using Social Psychology to Change Environmentally Damaging Behaviors

Human beings have been treating the planet as a humongous garbage can, rapidly filling up the ground, water, and atmosphere with all sorts of pollutants. When human beings lived in small groups of hunters and gatherers, they could get away with discarding their trash wherever they pleased; now that there are

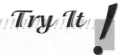

///

When Do People Feel Crowded?

Over a period of a few days observe people in a variety of situations in which crowding might occur, such as a fraternity party, a busy bus stop, a line to enter a movie theater or dining hall, or a rock concert. In each situation, make the following ratings:

1. What is the density of people in this setting? That is, how many people are there per square yard? Obviously this will be hard to measure exactly, but come up with a rough estimate.

2. How much control do people have in this situation? Specifically, how easily could they leave and find a less crowded setting, if they so desired? Make your rating based on this scale:

   In this situation, people seem to feel:

        1   2   3   4   5   6   7   8   9

   very little control   *complete control*

3. How crowded do people appear to be? Specifically, how negative an experience is it to be in this setting? Make your ratings based on this scale:

   People seem to find this setting:

        1   2   3   4   5   6   7   8   9

   very unpleasant   *very pleasant*

After sampling several situations, see which predicts your answers to number 3 the best: The density of people (question 1) or how much control people feel (question 2). If you have had a course in statistics, you can compute the correlation coefficient between your answers to questions 1 and 3 and between your answers to questions 2 and 3, to see which one is bigger. If you haven't, no big deal—just examine the pattern of answers and see whether your answers to question 3 seem to follow your answers to question 1 or question 2 more. Based on the research discussed in the text, it is likely that your answers to question 3 depended more on the amount of control people felt (question 2) than the objective density of people in the situation (question 1).

///

more than 5.7 billion of us (and counting), and we have developed toxic wastes that will remain poisonous for centuries, we have to change our ways (Gilbert, 1990). Pollution in the Los Angeles area is so bad that children who grow up there have lungs that function 10 to 15 percent less efficiently than the lungs of children who grow up in less polluted areas (Basu, 1989). In the fall of 1997, several thousand fish mysteriously died in the waterways of Maryland and Virginia, with strange lesions on their skin. Scientists discovered that they had been killed by a toxic microbe named pfiesteria, which seems to thrive in water contaminated by agricultural run-off from farms. There is growing suspicion that pfiesteria has harmful effects on humans as well, causing nerve damage, memory loss, and confusion. One scientist who worked with pfiesteria lost all feeling in his legs and had to crawl out of his laboratory (Warrick & Brown, 1997).

Clearly, it is important to find ways of convincing people to treat the environment better to avoid problems such as these. Naturally, you will recognize this as a classic social psychological question, in that it concerns how we can change people's attitudes and behaviors. Let's see what solutions social psychologists have come up with for the planet's pressing environmental problems.

Resolving Social Dilemmas

The first step is to realize that we are dealing with a classic *social dilemma*. As we discussed in Chapter 9, a social dilemma is a conflict in which the most beneficial action for an individual will, if chosen by most people, have harmful effects on everyone. Of particular relevance to the environment is a variant called the *commons dilemma*, defined as a situation in which everyone takes from a common pool of goods that will replenish itself if used in moderation, but which will disappear if overused. Examples include the use of limited resources such as water and energy. Individuals benefit by using as much as they need, but if everyone does so, shortages often result. The outbreak of pfiesteria in Maryland appears to be due to a classic commons dilemma. Farmers in that state are urged to follow a voluntary nutrient management plan, whereby they monitor the amounts of nutrients in their soil and apply only as much fertilizer as is necessary for plants to thrive. An individual farmer might become lax, however, because it is difficult and expensive to follow the plan. If only a few farmers failed to comply, then the common resource of water would remain unpolluted. As with many social dilemmas, however, so many individuals act in their self-interest that everyone suffers (Dawes, 1980; Hardin, 1968; Komorita & Parks, 1995; Levine & Moreland, 1998; Liebrand, Messick, & Wilke, 1992; Pruitt, 1998). How can we resolve social dilemmas, convincing people to act for the greater good of everyone, rather than purely out of self-interest?

"God gave Noah
the rainbow sign,
No more water,
the fire next time.
–"Home in the Rock,"
Negro spiritual

Social psychologists have devised some fascinating laboratory games to try to answer this question. For example, imagine you were a participant in a game developed by John Orbell, Alphons van de Kragt, and Robin Dawes (1988). You arrive for the study and discover that there are six other participants you have never met before. The experimenter gives you and the other participants $6 and says each of you can keep the money. There is, however, another option. Each person can donate his or her money to the rest of the group, to be divided equally among the six other members. If anyone does so, the experimenter will double the contribution. For example, if you donate your money, it will be doubled to $12 and divided evenly among the six other participants. If other group members donate their money to the pot, it will be doubled and you will get a share.

Think about the dilemma with which you are faced. If everyone (including you) cooperates by donating his or her money to the group, once it is doubled and divided up, your share will be $12—double what you started with. Donating your money is risky, however; if you are the only one who does so, you will end up with nothing, while having increased everyone else's winnings (see Table SPA2.1). Clearly, the most selfish (and safest) course of action is to keep your money, hoping everyone else donates theirs. That way, you would make up to $18—your $6, plus your share of the money everyone else threw into the pot. Of course, if everyone thinks this way, you'll make only $6, because no one will donate any money to the group. Note that this dilemma is similar to the one faced by Maryland farmers over land management: Individuals gain by not following the expensive land management procedures, but if everyone adopts this course of action, everyone suffers.

What would you do if you were in the Orbell and colleagues (1988) study? If you are like most of the actual participants, you would keep your six bucks. After all, as you can see in Table SPA2.1, you will always earn more money by keeping your $6 than by giving it away (i.e., the winnings in the top row of Table SPA2.1 are always higher than the winnings in the bottom row). The only problem with

Table SPA2.1

	Other People's Decision						
Your Decision	**6 Keep 0 Give**	**5 Keep 1 Give**	**4 Keep 2 Give**	**3 Keep 3 Give**	**2 Keep 4 Give**	**1 Keep 5 Give**	**0 Keep 6 Give**
Keep Your $6	$6	$8	$10	$12	$14	$16	$18
Give Your $6	$0	$2	$4	$6	$8	$10	$12

NOTE: Amount of money you stand to win in the Orbell, van de Kragt, and Dawes experiment. You can either keep your $6 or donate it to the six other group members. If you donate it, the money will be doubled, so that each group member will receive $2. Most people who play this game want to keep their money, to maximize their own gains. The more people who keep their money, however, the more everyone loses. (Adapted from Orbell et al., 1988)

this strategy is that because most people adopted it, everyone suffered. That is, the total pool of money to be divided remained low, because few people allowed the experimenter to double the money by donating it to the group. As with many social dilemmas, most people looked out for themselves, and as a result, everyone lost.

How can people be convinced to trust their fellow group members, cooperating in such a way that everyone benefits? It is notoriously difficult to resolve social dilemmas, as indicated by the difficulty of getting people to conserve water when there are droughts, recycle their waste goods, and clean up a common area in a dormitory or apartment. In another condition of their experiment, however, John Orbell and his colleagues (1988) found an intriguing result: Simply allowing the group to talk with each other for ten minutes dramatically increased the number of people who donated money to the group, from 38 to 79 percent. The increase in the number of donators led to a larger pool of money to be divided, from an average of $32 to $66. Communication works because it allows each person to find out whether the others are planning to act cooperatively or competitively, as well as to persuade others to act for the common good, e.g., "I'll donate my money if you donate yours" (Bouas & Komorita, 1996; Kerr & Kaufman-Gilliland, 1994).

This finding is encouraging, but it may be limited to small groups that are able to communicate face to face. What happens when an entire community is caught in a social dilemma? It would be impossible for all the farmers in Maryland to gather together and talk about land management practices. When large groups are involved, alternative approaches are needed. One approach is to make people's behavior as public as possible. If people can take the selfish route privately, undiscovered by their peers, they will often do so. But if their actions are public, then the kinds of normative pressures we discussed in Chapter 8 come into play, making people's behavior more consistent with group norms. For example, some Maryland farmers might be tempted to allow runoff of fertilizers from their land if no one will find out about it, but if they believe they will become the object of derision and scorn from their neighbors, they will most likely refrain from doing so.

Another proven technique is to change the way in which people perceive themselves and their social behavior. In the unit on health, we saw that Aronson, Fried, and Stone (1991) succeeded in getting people to behave in healthier and more socially responsible ways—purchasing (and presumably using) more condoms—by making them see their own past actions as hypocritical. Could similar techniques be used to convince people to behave in more environmentally sound ways, such as conserving water?

Conserving Water

> In an age where man has forgotten his origins and is blind even to his most essential needs for survival, water along with other resources has become the victim of his indifference.
>
> –Rachel Carson,
> *The Silent Spring*, 1962

Several years ago, when California was experiencing severe water shortages, the administrators at one campus of the University of California realized that an enormous amount of water was being wasted by students utilizing the university athletic facilities. The administrators posted signs in the shower rooms of the gymnasiums, exhorting students to conserve water by taking briefer, more efficient showers. The signs appealed to the students' conscience by urging them to take brief showers and to turn off the water while soaping up. The administrators were confident the signs would be effective because the vast majority of students at this campus were ecology-minded and believed in preserving natural resources. However, systematic observation revealed that less than 15 percent of the students complied with the conservation message on the posted signs.

The administrators were puzzled—perhaps the majority of the students hadn't paid attention to the sign? After all, a sign on the wall is easy to ignore. So administrators made each sign more obtrusive, putting it on a tripod at the entrance to the showers so that the students needed to walk around the sign in order to get into the shower room. While this increased compliance slightly (19 percent turned off the shower while soaping up), it apparently made a great many students angry—the sign was continually being knocked over and kicked around, and a large percentage of students took inordinately long showers, apparently as a reaction against being told what to do. The sign was doing more harm than good, puzzling the administrators even more. Time to call in the social psychologists.

Elliot Aronson and his students (Dickerson, Thibodeau, Aronson, & Miller, 1992) decided to apply the hypocrisy technique they had used in the condom study to this new situation. The procedure involved intercepting female students who were on their way from the swimming pool to the women's shower room, introducing the experimental manipulations, then having a research assistant casually follow them into the shower room, where she unobtrusively timed their showers. Research participants in one condition were asked to respond to a brief questionnaire about their water use, a task designed to make them mindful of how they sometimes wasted water while showering. In another condition, research participants made a public commitment, exhorting others to take steps to conserve water. Specifically, these participants were asked to sign their names to a public poster that read, "Take Shorter Showers. Turn Shower Off While Soaping Up. If I Can Do It, So Can YOU!" In the crucial condition—the "hypocrisy" condition—the participants did both; that is, they were made mindful of their own wasteful behavior and they indicated publicly (on the poster) that they were practicing water conservation. In short, they were made aware that they were preaching behavior they themselves were not practicing. Just as in the condom study described earlier, those participants who were made to feel like hypocrites changed their behavior so that they could feel good about themselves. In this case, they

took very brief showers. Indeed, the procedure was so effective that the average time students in this condition spent showering was reduced to three and a half minutes. The hypocrisy procedure has been found to increase other environmentally sound practices as well, such as recycling (Fried & Aronson, 1995).

Conserving Energy

It may be possible to draw on other social psychological techniques to increase environmentally sound behaviors. Consider the case of energy conservation. As a nation, the United States consumes far more energy, per capita, than any other nation on earth. Historically, we have felt perfectly content using as much energy as we needed, assuming that the planet had an infinite supply of oil, natural gas, and electric power. But this is not true. We have already depleted many of our national oil reserves, and we must import much of our oil from other countries.

Let's take private homes as an example. By taking such simple measures as increasing ceiling, wall, and floor insulation, plugging air leaks, using more efficient light bulbs, and maintaining furnaces properly, the typical American energy consumer could reduce the amount of energy used to heat, light, and cool his or her home by 50 to 75 percent (Williams & Ross, 1980). The technology needed to increase energy efficiency currently exists and is well within the financial means of most homeowners. Not only would this technology save energy, but it would also save the individual homeowner a great deal of money. Yet despite the fact that the societal and financial advantages of conservation have been well publicized, the vast majority of homeowners have not taken action. How come? Why have Americans been slow to act in a manner that is in their economic self-interest? This lack of compliance has puzzled economists and policymakers, because they have failed to see that the issue is partly a social psychological one.

In Chapter 5, we noted that people's attention is typically directed to the aspects of their environment that are conspicuous and vivid. Elliot Aronson and his colleagues (Aronson, 1990; Aronson & Yates, 1985; Coltrane, Archer, & Aronson, 1986; Stern & Aronson, 1984) reasoned that energy conservation in the home is not a particularly vivid problem and so people do not spend much time thinking about it. The bill for natural gas and electricity comes only once a month and is spread out over dozens of appliances; thus, the homeowner has no clear idea which of the many appliances is using the most energy. It is as if you were buying food in a supermarket where the prices of individual items were unmarked and you were billed only at the end of the month. How would you know what to do to save money on your purchases? Perhaps if the sources of home energy consumption were made more vivid, people would take action.

To test this hypothesis, Elliot Aronson and his colleagues (Aronson & Gonzales, 1990; Gonzales, Aronson, & Costanzo, 1988) worked with several energy auditors in California. As in many states, California utility companies offer a free service wherein an auditor will come to people's homes and give them a customized assessment of what needs to be done to make their homes more energy efficient. What a deal! The problem was that less than 20 percent of the individuals requesting audits were actually following the auditors' recommendations.

To increase compliance, the Aronson research team trained the auditors to present their findings in a more vivid manner. For example, let's consider weather stripping: For most people, a small crack under the door didn't seem like a huge drain of energy, so when an auditor told them they should put in some weather stripping, they thought, "Yeah, big deal." Aronson and his colleagues told the auditors to make this statement more vivid:

> If you were to add up all the cracks around and under the doors of your home, you'd have the equivalent of a hole the size of a football in your living room wall. Think for a moment about all the heat that would escape from a hole that size. That's precisely why I'm recommending that you install weather stripping. (Gonzales et al., 1988, p. 1052)

Similar attempts were made to make other problems more vivid—for example, referring to an attic that lacks insulation as a "naked attic" that is like "facing winter not just without an overcoat, but without any clothing at all." (Gonzales et al., 1988, p. 1052)

The results were striking. The percentage of homeowners who followed the vivid recommendations jumped to 61 percent. This study demonstrates that people will act in a manner that is sensible in terms of national goals and their own economic self-interest, but if old habits are involved, the communication must be one that is vivid enough to break through those established habits.

Frans Siero and his colleagues have recently demonstrated a simple but powerful way to get people to conserve energy in the workplace (Siero, Bakker, Dekker, & Van Den Burg, 1996). At one unit of a factory in the Netherlands, the employees were urged to engage in energy-saving behaviors. For example, announcements were placed in the company magazine asking people to close windows during cold weather and to turn off lights when leaving a room. In addition, the employees got weekly feedback on their behavior; graphs were posted that showed how much they had improved their energy-saving behaviors, such as how often they had turned off the lights. This intervention resulted in modest improvement. By the end of the program, for example, the percentage of times people left the lights on decreased by 27 percent.

Another unit of the factory took part in an identical program, with one difference. In addition to receiving weekly feedback on their own energy-saving actions, they received feedback about how the other unit was doing. Siero et al.

> "And willful wastes, depend upon't, brings, almost always, woeful want!
> —Ann Taylor (1782–1866)

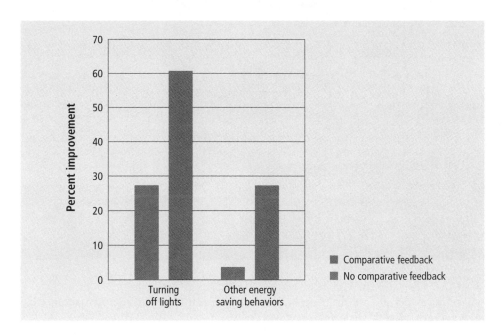

■ **FIGURE SPA2.3 Effects of comparative feedback on energy-saving behaviors.** Two units of a factory were urged to conserve energy and received feedback about how their unit was doing. Only one of the units, however, received comparative feedback about how they were doing relative to the other unit. As seen in the graph, this second unit improved their behavior the most, especially by turning off lights more. (Adapted from Siero et al., 1996)

(1996) hypothesized that this social comparison information would motivate people to do better than their colleagues in the other unit. As seen in Figure SPA2.3, they were right. By the end of the program, the percentage of times people left lights on had decreased by 61 percent. Engaging people's competitive spirit can have a large impact on their behavior.

Reducing Litter

Compared to other environmental problems, littering may not seem to be all that serious a matter. Although billboards implore us to "Keep America Beautiful," most people seem to think it isn't a big deal to leave their paper cup at the side of the road instead of in a trash barrel. Unfortunately, those paper cups add up. In California, for example, littering has increased steadily over the past 15 years, to the point where $100 million of tax money is spent cleaning it up—every year (Cialdini, Kallgren, & Reno, 1991). The stuff we discard is polluting our water systems, endangering wildlife, and costing us millions of dollars.

Littering is another classic social dilemma. Sometimes it's a pain to find a trash can, and from an individual's point of view, big deal—what's one more paper cup added to the side of the road? As with all social dilemmas, the problem is that if everyone thinks this way, everyone suffers. How can we get people to act less selfishly when they have that empty paper cup in hand?

According to Robert Cialdini, Raymond Reno, and Carl Kallgren, the answer is to remind people of the social norms against littering (Cialdini, Kallgren, & Reno, 1991; Cialdini, Reno, & Kallgren, 1990; Reno, Cialdini, & Kallgren, 1993). The phrase "social norm," which has a long history in social psychology and sociology, actually has several meanings. Cialdini and his colleagues (1991) suggest that two of these meanings are critical to understanding when people will litter. First, there are **injunctive norms**, which are socially sanctioned behaviors— that is, people's perceptions of what behaviors are approved by others, regardless of what other people really are doing. For example, we may be in an environment

Injunctive Norms
socially sanctioned behaviors—that is, people's perceptions of what behaviors are approved of by others

■ Besides being unsightly, litter can cost millions of dollars to clean up. Social psychologists have found that emphasizing different kinds of social norms against littering is an effective way to prevent it.

Descriptive Norms
people's perceptions of how other people are actually behaving in a given situation, regardless of what behaviors are socially sanctioned

"We live in an environment whose principal product is garbage.
  —Russell Baker, 1968

where many people are littering but know there is an injunctive norm against littering—most people disapprove of it.

Second, there are **descriptive norms,** which are people's perceptions of how people are actually behaving in a given situation, regardless of what behaviors are socially sanctioned. Even if there were no injunctive norms against littering, people might be reluctant to litter if they saw that no one else was doing so. As we saw in Chapter 8, we often use observations of other people's behavior to decide on the proper course of action in a particular situation.

Focusing people's attention on either of these norms reduces littering. For example, Raymond Reno and his colleagues (1993) conducted a field experiment to investigate the power of injunctive norms. As people left a local library and approached their cars in the parking lot, an accomplice walked by them, picked up a fast-food bag that had been discarded on the ground, and put the bag in the trash. In a control condition, no bag was on the ground, and the accomplice simply walked by the library patrons. When the patrons got to their car, they found a handbill on their windshield. The question was, How many of these people would litter by throwing the handbill on the ground? Reno and colleagues hypothesized that seeing the accomplice pick up the fast-food bag would be a vivid reminder of the injunctive norm—littering is bad, and other people disapprove of it—and hence would lower their own inclination to litter. They were right: In this condition, only 7 percent of the people tossed the handbill on the ground, compared to 37 percent in the control condition. If you would like to try to replicate this effect in an experiment of your own, see the Try It! exercise on page 597.

What is the best way to communicate descriptive norms against littering? The most straightforward way, it would seem, would be to clean up all the litter in an environment, to illustrate that "no one litters here." In general, this is true: The less litter there is in an environment, the less likely people are to litter (Huffman, Grossnickle, Cope, & Huffman, 1995; Krauss, Freedman, & Whitcup, 1978; Reiter & Samuel, 1980). There is, however, an interesting exception to this finding. Cialdini and colleagues (1990) figured that seeing one conspicuous piece of litter on the ground, spoiling an otherwise clean environment, would be a better reminder of descriptive norms than seeing a completely clean environment. The single piece of trash sticks out like a sore thumb, reminding people that no one has littered here—except one thoughtless person. In compari-

Reducing Littering with Injunctive Norms

See if you can get people to pick up litter by invoking injunctive norms, using the techniques discovered by Raymond Reno and his colleagues (Reno, Cialdini, and Kallgren, 1993). This exercise is easiest to do in pairs with a friend. Here's how it works:

Find an environment in which people are likely to litter. For example, at one of our universities the student newspaper often comes with an advertising insert. When people pick up a copy of the newspaper in the psychology building, they often discard the insert onto the floor. This exercise is best done with a friend who can observe people unobtrusively to see if they litter.

Next, plant a conspicuous piece of litter in this environment. Reno et al. (1993) used a fast food bag stuffed with trash. Place it in a location that people are sure to see, such as near a doorway.

In one condition, wait until an individual enters the environment and is in full view of the piece of trash you planted. Then, pick up the trash, throw it away, and go on your way. It is critical that the person realize that it wasn't your bag but that you decided to pick it up and throw it away anyway. In a second condition, walk by the trash, glance at it, and continue on your way without picking it up. Make sure to randomly assign passersby to one of these two conditions.

The observer should watch to see whether people litter; for example, whether they throw the advertising insert on the floor or put it in a trash can. As discussed in the text, Reno et al. (1993) found that when people saw someone pick up another person's litter, they were much less likely to litter themselves. Did you replicate this effect? Why or why not, do you think?

son, if there is no litter on the ground, people might not even think about what the descriptive norm is. Ironically, then, littering may be more likely to occur in a totally clean environment than in one containing a single piece of litter.

To test this hypothesis, the researchers stuffed students' mailboxes with handbills and then observed, from a hidden vantage point, how many of the students dropped the handbills on the floor (Cialdini et al., 1990). In the first condition, the researchers cleaned up the mailroom so that there were no other pieces of litter to be seen. In the second condition, they placed one very noticeable piece of litter on the floor—a hollowed-out piece of watermelon. In the third condition, they not only put the watermelon rind on the floor but also spread out dozens of discarded handbills. As predicted, the lowest rate of littering occurred in the condition where there was a single piece of trash on the floor (see Figure SPA2.4). The single violation of a descriptive norm highlighted the fact that no one had littered but the one dufus who had dropped the watermelon rind on the floor. Now that people's attention was focused on the descriptive norm against littering, virtually none of the students littered. The highest percentage of littering occurred when the floor was littered with lots of handbills; here it was clear that there was a descriptive norm in favor of littering, and many of the students followed suit.

Thus, drawing people's attention to both injunctive and descriptive norms can reduce littering. Of the two kinds of norms, Robert Cialdini and his colleagues suggest that injunctive norms work better. Descriptive norms work only if everyone cooperates—for example, by keeping an environment relatively free of litter. This method is not perfect, however; if trash starts accumulating, then the descriptive norm becomes "See, lots of people litter here!" and littering will increase. In contrast, Raymond Reno and his colleagues (1993) found that reminding people of the injunctive norm works in a wide variety of situations, regardless

■ **FIGURE SPA2.4   Descriptive norms and littering.** Who littered the least—people who saw that no one else had littered, people who saw one piece of litter on the floor, or people who saw several pieces of litter? As shown in the figure, it was people who saw one piece of litter. Seeing the single piece of litter was most likely to draw people's attention to the fact that most people had not littered, making people less likely themselves to litter. (Adapted from Cialdini et al., 1990)

of how clean the environment is. Once we are reminded that "people disapprove of littering," we are less likely to litter in virtually all circumstances.

Getting People to Recycle

Suppose we succeeded in getting people to stop littering. That would be wonderful, because roadsides would look pretty and we wouldn't have to spend millions of dollars in tax money to clean up people's litter. But, the problem of what to do with our trash, once it is collected and thrown away, would remain. Consider the barge full of trash that nobody wanted. In 1987, a load of garbage from New York City was rejected by a landfill in Islip, New York because the landfill was already overflowing. The company hauling the trash hired some entrepreneurs to take it somewhere else. These unlucky transporters filled a barge called the Mobro 4000 with the trash and departed for a dump in Morehead City, North Carolina. Their idea was to sell it to a gas conversion project there, profiting from the methane gas that would be released as the trash decayed. This plan was quickly rejected by North Carolina authorities, who would not even allow the barge to dock. You see, these days trash is not simply trash. Many of the things we throw away contain toxic chemicals and dangerous metals, and the North Carolinians did not want their backyard poisoned with the decay from New York's toxic waste.

Thus began the lonely, meandering, 6,000-mile voyage of the Mobro 4000. For six months, the barge owners searched for someone to take the trash, making ports of call in Florida, Alabama, Mississippi, Louisiana, Mexico, Belize, and the Bahamas. But there were no takers. Finally, the barge returned home. After considerable wrangling by local and state officials, the trash was incinerated and buried in—you guessed it—the landfill in Islip, New York.

To reduce the amount of trash that ends up in landfills, many cities are encouraging their residents to recycle materials such as glass, paper, and aluminum. But as you know, it can be inconvenient to do so; in some areas you have to load your car with boxes of cans and bottles and drop them off at a recycling center, which might be several miles from your house. Other cities have curbside recycling, whereby a truck picks up recycling materials that you put out on the curb on a designated day. Even here, though, you have to remember to separate your cans and bottles from the rest of the trash and find a place to store them until the pickup day. We thus have another social dilemma—a behavior that, while good for us all (recycling), is effortful and unpleasant for individuals. As you might imagine, several social psychologists have turned their attention to ways of getting people to recycle more.

There have been two general approaches to this problem. First, some psychologists have focused on ways of changing people's attitudes and values in a pro-environment direction, with the assumption that their behavior will follow suit. This assumption is consistent with social psychological research on attitudes, which has found that under many conditions, people's attitudes are good predictors of their behavior (see Chapter 7). Several studies have found that people's attitudes toward recycling, are, in fact, good predictors of their recycling behaviors, suggesting that a mass media campaign that targets people's attitudes is a good way to go (Thøgersen, 1996).

Sometimes, though, we might fail to act consistently with our attitudes, despite our best intentions. Perhaps the recycling center is too far away or we just can't find the time to sort our trash, even though we know we should. Kurt Lewin (1947), one of the founders of social psychology, made the observation that big social changes can sometimes occur by removing small barriers from people's environments (Ross & Nisbett, 1991). In the context of recycling, it might be better to simply remove some of the hassles involved, such as instituting curbside recycling, than to try to change people's attitudes toward the environment. A number of studies have found this to be true. Increasing the number of recycling bins in a community, instituting curbside recycling, and allowing residents to mix materials, instead of having to sort them, have all been found to increase people's recycling behaviors (Porter, Leeming, & O'Dwyer, 1995; Schultz, Oskamp, & Mainieri, 1995).

Consider a natural experiment by Gregory Guagnano, Paul Stern, and Thomas Dietz (1995), conducted in Fairfax County, Virginia. Curbside recycling had begun in Fairfax and the county was in the process of giving residents plastic bins in which to put their recyclable materials. At the time of the study, only about a quarter of the residents had received the bins; the others had to find their own containers in which to put their bottles and cans. Now, it might seem like this would not be much of an impediment to recycling; if people really care about the environment, they should be able to find their own box. As Lewin argued,

■ More and more communities are encouraging people to recycle materials such as bottles, cans, and newspapers. Social psychologists have identified several ways of increasing the likelihood that people will recycle.

Changing Environmentally Damaging Behaviors

Use the techniques discussed in this chapter to change people's behavior in ways that help the environment. Here's how to proceed:

• *Choose the behavior you want to change.* You might try to increase the amount that you and your roommates recycle, reduce the amount of energy wasted in your dorm, or increase water conservation.

• *Choose the technique you will use to change the behavior.* For example, you might use the comparative feedback technique used by Frans Siero and colleagues to increase energy conservation. Encourage two areas of your dormitory to reduce energy usage or to recycle, and give each feedback about how they are doing relative to the other area. (To do this you will have to have an easy, objective way of measuring people's behavior, such as the number of times lights are left on at night or the number of cans that are recycled.) Or, you might try the hypocrisy technique used by Elliot Aronson and colleagues

to increase water conservation, whereby you ask people to sign a public poster that encourages recycling and have them fill out a questionnaire that makes them mindful of times they have failed to recycle. Be creative and feel free to use more than one technique.

• *Measure the success of your intervention.* Find an easy way to measure people's behavior, such as the amount that they recycle. Assess their behavior before and after your intervention. Best of all, include a control group of people who do not receive your intervention (randomly assigned, of course). In the absence of such a control group it will be difficult to gauge the success of your intervention; for example, if people's behavior changes over time, you won't be able to tell if it is because of your intervention or some other factor (e.g., an article on recycling that happened to appear in the newspaper). By comparing the changes in behavior in your target group to the control group, you will have a better estimate of the success of your intervention.

---

however, sometimes little barriers have big effects, and indeed, the people who had the bins were much more likely to recycle. Guagnano and his colleagues also measured people's attitudes toward recycling, to see if those with positive attitudes were more likely to recycle than those who were not. Interestingly, people's attitudes only predicted behavior when they did *not* possess a recycling bin. When there was a barrier preventing easy compliance—people had to search through the garage to find a suitable box—only those with positive attitudes exerted the energy to circumvent the barrier. When there was no barrier—people had a convenient container provided by the county—then attitudes did not matter as much. People were likely to conform even if they did not have strong, proenvironmental attitudes.

The moral? There are two ways to get people to act in more environmentally sound ways. First, you can try to change people's attitudes in a pro-environmental direction; this will motivate them to act in environmentally friendly ways, even if there are barriers that make it hard to do so (such as having to find a box for your bottles and cans and taking it to a recycling center). It is often easier, however, simply to remove the barriers (such as instituting curbside recycling and giving people containers). When it is easy to comply many people will do so, even if they do not have strong, pro-environmental attitudes. Now that you have read about several ways of changing people's behavior in ways that help the environment, you are in a position to try them out yourself. See the Try It! exercise above for suggestions on how to do this.

Summary

We discussed the environment as a source of stress on people. As we human beings continue to populate the earth at an alarming rate, our physical world is becoming a crowded and noisy place to live. Social psychologists have focused on how people interpret and explain crowded conditions and noise. One key interpretation is how much perceived control people have over the event. The less control people believe they have, the more likely it is that the event will cause them physical and psychological problems. For example, if people in high **density** settings feel they have a low level of control (i.e., they believe it is difficult to escape to a less dense setting), they will experience **crowding,** the subjective feeling of unpleasantness due to the presence of other people. Crowding can also be aversive if it leads to **sensory overload,** which occurs when other people place a severe demand on our attentional system. In addition, the way in which people explain the causes of negative events is critical to how an event is interpreted and thus to how stressful it will be.

We also discussed the effects people are having on the environment and the ways in which social influence techniques can be used to get people to behave in more environmentally sound ways. This is not easy because many environmental problems are classic social dilemmas, wherein actions that are beneficial for individuals are, if performed by most people, harmful to everyone. Using proven techniques to change people's attitudes and behaviors, however, social psychologists have had some success in getting people to act in more environmentally sound ways. One technique is to arouse dissonance in people by making them feel that they are not practicing what they are preaching—for example, that even though they believe in water conservation, they are taking long showers. Another is to remind people of both **injunctive** and **descriptive** norms against environmentally damaging acts, such as littering. Focusing people's attention on injunctive norms against littering—the idea that throwing trash on the ground is not a socially accepted behavior—was found to be especially effective. Finally, removing barriers that make pro-environmental behaviors difficult, such as instituting curbside recycling and providing people with recycling bins, has been shown to be effective.

If You Are Interested

Cohen, S., Evans, G. W., Stokols, D. S., & Krantz, D. S. (1986). *Behavior, health, and environmental stress.* New York: Plenum. An in-depth discussion of stress and human health, with a focus on studies the authors conducted on the effects of aircraft noise on children.

Gore, Al (1992). *Earth in the balance: Ecology and the human spirit.* New York: Houghton Mifflin. A sobering look at the relationship between human beings and the environment.

Komorita, S. S., & Parks, C. D. (1994). *Social dilemmas.* Dubuque, IA: Brown & Benchmark. A readable introduction to research on social dilemmas. Several examples relevant to environmental issues are used.

Liebrand, W. B. G., Messick, D. M., & Wilke, H. A. M. (1992). *Social dilemmas: Theoretical issues and research findings.* Oxford, England: Pergamon Press. A collection of state-of-the-art chapters by researchers investigating the causes and cures of social dilemmas.

Winter, D. D. H. (1996). *Ecological psychology: Healing the split between planet and self.* New York: Addison Wesley. Deborah Du Hann Winter argues that because environmental problems have been caused by human behaviors, beliefs, and values, they are directly related to psychology and it is in psychology that the solutions will be found.

Woodstock (1970). A documentary about the definitive rock festival; in addition to vintage rock-and-roll, the movie shows some interesting crowd scenes. An interesting application of research on crowding: When is a dense crowd of people pleasing and when is it stressful?

SOCIAL PSYCHOLOGY IN ACTION 3

SOCIAL PSYCHOLOGY AND THE LAW

ou be the jury and decide how you would vote, after hearing the following testimony, taken from an actual case in Texas:

In November of 1976, on a cold, dark night, police officer Robert Wood and his partner spotted a car driving with its headlights off. Wood signaled the car to pull over, got out, and walked up to the driver's side. He intended only to tell the driver to turn on his lights, but he never got the chance. Before Wood could even speak, the driver pointed a handgun at Wood and shot him, killing him instantly. Wood's partner emptied her revolver at the car as it sped away, but the killer escaped.

A month later, the police picked up a suspect, 16-year-old David Harris. Harris admitted that he had stolen a neighbor's car and revolver the day before the murder, that this was the car Officer Wood had pulled over that night, and that he was in the car when the murder occurred. Harris denied, however, that he was the one who shot Wood. He said he had picked up a hitchhiker by the name of Randall Adams and had let Adams drive. It was Adams, he claimed, who reached under the seat, grabbed the revolver, and shot the officer.

When the police questioned Randall Adams, he admitted he had gotten a ride from David Harris but said Harris had dropped him off at his motel three hours before the murder occurred. It was Harris, he claimed, who was the murderer. Who was telling the truth? It was Harris's word against Adams's—until the police found three eyewitnesses who corroborated Harris's story. Emily and Robert Miller testified that they were driving by just before Officer Wood was shot. Though it was very dark, they said they got a good look at the driver of the car, and both identified him as Randall Adams. "When he rolled down the window that's what made his face stand out," said Robert Miller. "He had a beard, mustache, kind of dishwater blond hair" (Morris, 1988). David Harris was clean-shaven, and at the time of the murder, Randall Adams did indeed fit Miller's description, as seen in the photo on the next page. Michael Randell, a salesman, also happened to be driving by right before the murder and claimed to have seen two people in the car. He too said the driver had long hair and a mustache.

Who do you think committed the murder? The real jury believed the eyewitnesses and convicted Adams, sentencing him to death. However, as Adams languished in jail, waiting for the courts to hear his appeals, several experts began to doubt he was guilty. New evidence came to light (largely because of a film made about the case, Errol Morris's *The Thin Blue Line*), and it is now almost certain that David Harris was the murderer. Harris was later convicted of another murder and, while on death row, strongly implied that he, not Randall Adams, had shot Officer Wood. An appeals court finally overturned Adams's conviction. He was a free man—after spending 12 years in prison for a crime he did not commit.

If Adams was innocent, why did the eyewitnesses say that the driver of the car had long hair and a mustache? And why did the jury believe them? How common are such miscarriages of justice? In this chapter, we will discuss the answers to these questions, focusing on the role social psychological processes play in the legal system.

Let's begin with a brief review of the American justice system. When someone commits a crime and the police arrest a suspect, a judge or a grand jury decides whether there is enough evidence to press formal charges. If there is, lawyers for the defense and the prosecution gather evidence and negotiate with each other. As a result of these negotiations, the defendant often pleads guilty to a lesser charge. About a quarter of the cases go to trial, in which a jury or a

■ Randall Adams (left) and David Harris (right). The fact that eyewitnesses said the murderer had long hair and a mustache was the main reason Adams was convicted of murdering Officer Wood.

judge decides the defendant's fate. There are also civil trials, where one party (the plaintiff) brings a complaint against another (the defendant) for violating the former's rights in some way.

All of these steps in the legal process are intensely social psychological. For example, first impressions of the accused and of the witnesses have a powerful effect on police investigators and the jury; attributions about what caused the criminal behavior are made by police, lawyers, jurors, and the judge; prejudiced beliefs and stereotypical ways of thinking affect those attributions; attitude change and persuasion techniques abound in the courtroom, as lawyers for each side argue their case and jurors later debate with one another; and the processes of social cognition affect the jurors' decision making when deciding guilt or innocence. Social psychologists have studied the legal system a great deal in recent years, both because it offers an excellent applied setting in which to study basic psychological processes and because of its immense importance in daily life. If you, through no fault of your own, become the accused in a court trial, what do you need to know to convince the system of your innocence?

We will begin our discussion with eyewitness testimony, the most troubling aspect of the Randall Adams case we just presented. In Chapter 4, we saw that whereas people do form accurate impressions of others, systematic biases can come into play, leading to serious misunderstandings. A closely related question is, How accurate are people at identifying someone who has committed a crime?

Eyewitness Testimony

The American legal system assigns a great deal of significance to eyewitness testimony. If an eyewitness fingers you as the culprit, you are quite likely to be convicted, even if considerable circumstantial evidence indicates you are innocent. Randall Adams was convicted largely because of the eyewitnesses who identified him, even though in other ways the case against him was weak: He had no criminal record, he had just found steady employment, and he had no reason to be concerned about being pulled over by the police—he was only a hitchhiker (if, indeed, he really was in the car at the time of the shooting). In comparison, David Harris had many reasons to fear the police: He had stolen the car and was in possession of a stolen, loaded handgun. Given these facts, why would Randall Adams murder a police officer? Doesn't David Harris seem a more logical suspect? Despite the implausibility of the Adams-as-murderer scenario and despite the lack of physical evidence linking Adams to the scene of the crime, the eyewitness testimony that Adams was driving the car was enough to convict him.

Systematic experiments have confirmed that jurors rely heavily on eyewitness testimony when they are deciding whether someone is guilty. Unfortunately, jurors also tend to overestimate the accuracy of eyewitnesses (Ellsworth & Mauro, 1998; Leippe, Manion, & Romanczyk, 1992; R. Lindsay, 1994; Loftus, 1979; Wells, R. Lindsay, & Ferguson, 1979). Rod Lindsay and his colleagues (1981) conducted a clever experiment that illustrates both of these points. The researchers first staged the theft of a calculator in front of unsuspecting students and then saw how accurately the students could pick out the "thief" from a set of six photographs. In one condition, it was difficult to identify the thief because he had worn a knit cap pulled over his ears and was in the room for only 12 seconds. In the second condition, the thief had worn the knit cap higher on his head, revealing some of his hair, so that it was easier to identify him. In the third condition, the thief had worn no hat and stayed in the room for 20 seconds, making it easiest to identify him.

The first set of results is as we'd expect: The more visual information available about the thief, the higher the percentage of students who correctly identified

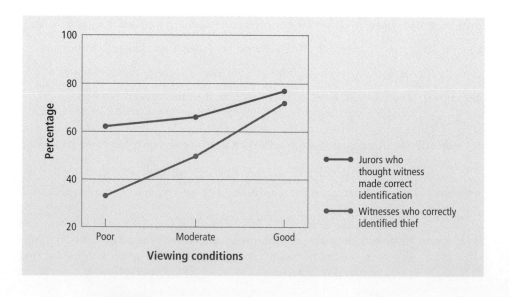

■ **FIGURE SPA3.1 The accuracy of eyewitness identification.** The accuracy of eyewitness identification depends on the viewing conditions at the time the crime was committed. As in this study, however, most jurors believe that witnesses can correctly identify the criminal even when viewing conditions are poor. (Adapted from R. Lindsay et al., 1981)

him in the photo lineup (see the bottom line in Figure SPA3.1). In the next stage of the experiment, a researcher playing the role of lawyer questioned the students about their eyewitness identifications, just as a real lawyer would cross-examine witnesses in a trial. These question-and-answer sessions were videotaped. A new group of participants, playing the role of jurors, watched the videotapes of these cross-examinations and rated the extent to which they believed the witnesses had correctly identified the thief. As seen by the top line in Figure SPA3.1, the jurors overestimated the accuracy of the witnesses, especially in the condition where the thief was difficult to identify.

How accurate are eyewitnesses to real crimes? Although it is impossible to say exactly what percentage of the time eyewitnesses are accurate, there is reason to believe that they often make mistakes. Researchers have documented more than 1,000 cases of wrongful arrests and in a remarkably high proportion of these cases the wrong person was convicted because an eyewitness mistakenly identified him or her as the criminal (Brandon & Davies, 1973; Cutler & Penrod, 1995; Span, 1994; Sporer, Koehnken, & Malpass, 1996; Wells, 1993).

Why Are Eyewitnesses Often Wrong?

The problem is that our minds are not like video cameras that can record an event, store it over time, and play it back later, all with perfect accuracy. Think back to our discussion of social perception in Chapters 3 and 4, where we saw that a number of distortions in social cognition and attribution can occur. Because eyewitness identification is a form of social perception, it is subject to similar problems, particularly ones involving memory. In order for someone to be an accurate eyewitness, he or she must successfully complete three stages of memory processing: acquisition, storage, and retrieval of the events witnessed. **Acquisition** refers to the process whereby people notice and pay attention to information in the environment. Because people cannot perceive everything that is happening around them, they acquire only a subset of the information available in the environment. **Storage** refers to the process by which people store in memory information they have acquired from the environment, whereas **retrieval** refers to the process by which people recall information stored in their memories (see Figure SPA3.2). Eyewitnesses can be inaccurate because of problems at any of these three stages.

Acquisition

No one doubts that people accurately perceive a great deal of information about the world around them. Nonetheless, our ability to take in information is limited, particularly when we observe unexpected, complex events. The psychologist Hugo Münsterberg (1908), for example, described the following event, which occurred at a scientific meeting attended by psychologists, lawyers, and physicians: In the middle of the meeting, a clown burst into the room, followed closely by a man with a revolver. The two men shouted wildly, grabbed each other, then fell to the ground in a fierce struggle. One of them fired a shot; then both men ran out of the room.

All the witnesses were asked to write down an exact account of what they had just seen (which was actually an event staged by two actors). Even though the eyewitness were educated people with (presumably) good memories, their accounts were surprisingly inaccurate. Most of the witnesses omitted or wrote

Acquisition
the process by which people notice and pay attention to information in the environment; because people cannot perceive everything that is happening around them, they acquire only a subset of the information available in the environment

Storage
the process by which people store in memory information they have acquired from the environment

Retrieval
the process by which people recall information stored in their memories

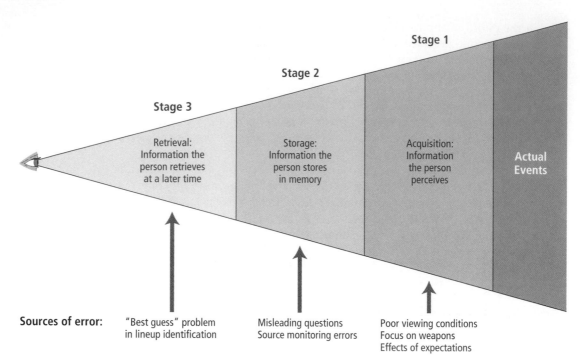

Stage 1

Stage 2

Stage 3

Retrieval:
Information the
person retrieves
at a later time

Storage:
Information the
person stores
in memory

Acquisition:
Information
the person
perceives

Actual
Events

Sources of error: "Best guess" problem
in lineup identification

Misleading questions
Source monitoring errors

Poor viewing conditions
Focus on weapons
Effects of expectations

■ **FIGURE SPA3.2   Acquisition, storage, and retrieval.**   To be an accurate eyewitness, people must complete these three stages of memory processing. There are sources of error at each of the three stages.

mistaken accounts of about half the actions they had observed. Most made errors about how long the incident had occurred—though the two men were in the room for about 20 seconds, the witnesses' estimates ranged from a few seconds to several minutes.

Patricia Tollestrup, John Turtle, and John Yuille (1994) found many similar eyewitness errors in a study of actual criminal cases. They examined police records of robbery and fraud cases in which a suspect was caught and confessed to the crime. They then assessed the accuracy of both victims' and bystanders' descriptions of the criminal, by comparing the witness's initial descriptions of the criminal to the criminal's actual physical characteristics (for example, were witnesses correct that the criminal had blond hair and a mustache?). Eyewitnesses weren't too bad at remembering some details; 100 percent of bystanders correctly remembered whether or not the criminal had facial hair (although crime victims correctly remembered this only 60 percent of the time). Only 48 percent of the bystanders and 38 percent of the victims correctly remembered the suspect's hair color, however. Most importantly, neither bystanders nor victims did a very good job of picking the criminal out of a lineup; overall, they correctly identified the criminal only 48 percent of the time.

A number of factors limit the amount of information about a crime that people take in, such as how much time they have to watch an event and the nature of the viewing conditions. As obvious as this may sound, people sometimes forget how these factors limit eyewitness reports of crimes. Crimes usually occur under the very conditions that make acquisition difficult: quickly, unexpectedly, and under poor viewing conditions, such as at night. These conditions certainly describe the scene of the murder of Officer Wood. Eyewitnesses were driving down a

■ Eyewitness testimony has a far greater effect on jurors than it should, given that it is often inaccurate. Many cases of wrongful arrests and convictions are due to mistaken identifications made by eyewitnesses.

dimly lit road, past a pulled-over car, when the unexpected happened—shots were fired and a policeman crumpled to the ground. How well could they see? How much information could they take in, in the few seconds it took to drive by?

We should also remember that eyewitnesses who are the victims of a crime will be terribly afraid, and this alone can make it difficult to take in everything that is happening. As we saw, Patricia Tollestrup and her colleagues (1994) found that robbery victims tended to make more mistakes than bystanders. Another reason victims of crimes have a poor memory for a suspect is that they focus their attention mostly on any weapon they see and less on the suspect's features (Christianson, 1992; Deffenbacher, 1983; Kramer, Buckhout, & Eugenio, 1990; Loftus, Loftus, & Messo, 1987; Williams, Loftus, & Deffenbacher, 1992). If someone points a gun at you and demands your money, your attention is likely to be more on the gun than on whether the robber has blue or brown eyes.

The information people notice and pay attention to is also influenced by what they expect to see. Consider our friend Alan, a social psychologist who is an expert on social perception. One Sunday, Alan was worried because his neighbor, a frail woman in her eighties, did not appear for church. After knocking on her door repeatedly and receiving no response, Alan jimmied open a window and searched her house. Soon his worst fears were realized: The woman was lying dead on the floor of her bedroom.

Shaken, Alan went back to his house and telephoned the police. After spending a great deal of time in the woman's house, a detective came over and asked Alan increasingly detailed questions, such as whether he had noticed any suspicious activity in the past day or two. Alan was confused by this line of questioning and finally burst out, "Why are you asking me these questions? Isn't it obvious that my neighbor died of old age? Shouldn't we be notifying her family?" Now it was the detective's turn to look puzzled. "Aren't you the one who discovered the body?" he asked. Alan said he was. "Well," said the detective, "didn't you notice that her bedroom had been ransacked, that there was broken glass everywhere, and that there was a belt tied around her neck?"

> When an actual perceptual fact is in conflict with expectation, expectation may prove a stronger determinant of perception and memory than the situation itself.
> —Gordon Allport and Leo Postman, 1947

■ Imagine you are on this street corner and suddenly witness a holdup across the street. A thief robs a man of his wallet and is gone in a matter of seconds. How accurate do you think your description of the thief would be?

It turned out that Alan's neighbor had been strangled by a man who had come to spray her house for insects. There had been a fierce struggle and the fact that the woman was murdered could not have been more obvious. But Alan saw none of the signs. He was worried that his elderly neighbor had passed away. When he discovered that she had in fact died, he was quite upset and the farthest thing from his mind was that she had been murdered. As a result, he saw what he expected and failed to see what he did not expect. When the police later showed him photographs of the crime scene, he felt as though he had never been there. He recognized almost nothing. Alan's experiences are consistent with our discussion in Chapter 3 of how people use theories and schemas. We have many theories about the world and the people in it, and these theories influence what we notice and remember.

Similarly, the information we take in is influenced by how familiar we are with it. Unfamiliar things are more difficult to remember than familiar things. For example, people are better at recognizing faces that are of the same race as they are, a finding which is called the **own-race bias**. Whites are better at recognizing white faces than Black or Asian faces, Blacks are better at recognizing Black than white faces, and Asians are better at recognizing Asian than white faces (Anthony, Cooper, & Mullen, 1992; Bothwell, Brigham, & Malpass, 1989; Ng & R. Lindsay, 1994; Shapiro & Penrod, 1986). Though the reason for this finding has been difficult to nail down, there is some evidence that it is a matter of familiarity. The more contact people have with members of a particular race, the better they are at recognizing members of that race (Chance & Goldstein, 1996; Chiroro & Valentine, 1995).

Own-Race Bias
the finding that people are better at recognizing faces of their own race than those of other races

Storage

We have just seen that several variables limit what people perceive and thus what they are able to store in their memories. Once a piece of information is in memory, it might seem like it stays there, unaltered, until we recall it at a later time.

Many people think memory is like a photograph album. We record a picture of an event, such as the face of a robber, and place it in the memory "album." The picture may not be perfect—after all, few of us have photographic memories. Further, it might fade a bit over time, because memories, like real photographs, fade with age. It seems unlikely, however, that the picture can be altered or re-touched, such that things are added to or subtracted from the image. If the robber we saw was clean-shaven, surely we will not pencil in a mustache at some later time. Thus, the fact that the witnesses who testified at the Randall Adams trial re-membered that the driver of the car had long hair and a mustache seems like pretty incriminating evidence for Randall Adams.

Unfortunately, the way in which our memories actually work is not so sim-ple. People can get mixed up about where they heard or saw something, so that memories in one "album" get confused with memories in another. As a result, people can have quite inaccurate recall about what they saw. This is the conclu-sion reached by Elizabeth Loftus and her colleagues after years of research on **re-constructive memory,** defined as the process whereby memories for an event be-come distorted by information encountered after the event has occurred (Hirt, McDonald, & Erikson, 1995; Loftus, 1979; Loftus & Hoffman, 1989; McDonald & Hirt, 1997; Schacter, 1996; Weingardt, Toland, & Loftus, 1994). According to Loftus, information we obtain after witnessing an event can change our memories of the event.

Reconstructive Memory
the process whereby memories for an event become distorted by information encountered after the event has occurred

In one of her studies, she showed students 30 slides depicting different stages of an automobile accident. The contents of one slide varied; some students saw a car stopped at a stop sign, whereas others saw the same car stopped at a yield sign (see the photos on page 612). After the slide show, the students were asked several questions about the car accident they had "witnessed." The key question varied how the traffic sign was described. In one version, the question asked, "Did another car pass the red Datsun while it was stopped at the stop sign?" In the other version, the question asked, "Did another car pass the red Datsun while it was stopped at the yield sign?" Thus, for half the participants the question de-scribed the traffic sign as they had in fact seen it. But for the other half, the word-ing of the question subtly introduced new information—for example, if they had seen a stop sign, the question described it as a yield sign. Would this small change (akin to what might occur when witnesses are being questioned by police investi-gators or attorneys) have an effect on people's memories of the actual event?

All the students were shown the two pictures reproduced on the next page and asked which one they had originally seen. Most people (75 percent) who were asked about the sign they had actually seen chose the correct picture; that is, if they had seen a stop sign and were asked about a stop sign, most of them cor-rectly identified the stop-sign photograph (note that 25 percent made a crucial mistake on what would seem to be an easy question). However, of those who had received the misleading question, only 41 percent chose the correct photograph (Loftus, Miller, & Burns, 1978).

In subsequent experiments, Loftus and her colleagues have found that mis-leading questions can change people's minds about how fast a car was going, whether broken glass was at the scene of an accident, whether a traffic light was green or red, and—of relevance to the Randall Adams trial—whether a robber had a mustache (Loftus, 1979). Her studies show that the way in which the police and lawyers question witnesses can change the witnesses' reports about what they saw. (There is some suspicion that in the Randall Adams case, the police may have led the witnesses by asking questions that implicated Adams and not Harris.

■ Students saw one of these pictures and then tried to remember whether they had seen a stop sign or a yield sign. Many of those who heard leading questions about the street sign made mistaken reports about which sign they had seen. (From Loftus, Miller, & Burns, 1978)

At the time of the murder, Harris was a juvenile and could not receive the death penalty for killing a police officer; Adams was in his thirties and was eligible for the death penalty. According to this reasoning, Adams was a "better" suspect in the eyes of the police). But, we might ask, do misleading questions alter what is stored in eyewitnesses' memories, or do the questions change only what these people are willing to report, without retouching their memories?

Though some controversy exists over the answer to this question (Belli, 1989; Loftus & Hoffman, 1989; McCloskey & Zaragoza, 1985; Smith & Ellsworth, 1987; Tversky & Tuchin, 1989), most researchers endorse the following position: Misleading questions cause a problem with **source monitoring,** the process by which people try to identify the source of their memories (Crombag, Wagenaar, & Van Koppen, 1996; Johnson, Hashtroudi, & D. Lindsay, 1993; D. Lindsay, 1994; D. Lindsay & Johnson, 1989). People who saw a stop sign but received the misleading question about a yield sign now have two pieces of information in memory, the stop sign and the yield sign. This is all well and good, as long as they remember where these memories came from: the stop sign from the accident they saw earlier, and the yield sign from the question they were asked later. The problem is that people often get mixed up about where they heard or saw something, mistakenly believing that the yield sign looks familiar, because they saw it during the slide show. This process is similar to the misattribution effects we discussed in Chapter 5, wherein people are unsure about what has

Source Monitoring
the process whereby people try to identify the source of their memories

caused their arousal. It's easy to get confused about the source of our memories as well. When information gets stored in memory, it is not always well "tagged" as to where it came from.

The implications for legal testimony are sobering. Eyewitnesses who are asked misleading questions often report seeing things that were not really there. In addition, eyewitnesses might be confused as to why a suspect looks familiar. It is likely, for example, that the eyewitnesses in the Randall Adams trial saw pictures of Adams in the newspaper before they testified about what they saw the night of the murder. When asked to remember what they saw that night, they might have become confused because of a source-monitoring error. They remembered seeing a man with long hair and a mustache, but they may have gotten mixed up about where they had seen his face before.

Another source monitoring error may have occurred in the Oklahoma City bombing incident. On April 19, 1995 a bomb went off in the Federal Building in Oklahoma City, killing 168 people. Timothy McVeigh was later convicted of the crime and sentenced to death. But did he act alone? Tom Kessinger, a mechanic in a truck rental office, said that he saw McVeigh and another man rent a Ryder truck the day before the blast. Kessinger described the second suspect, who became known as "John Doe No. 2," as a large, muscular man wearing a black T-shirt and a baseball hat. A world-wide search for this suspect ensued, but the police were never able to find him, triggering suspicion that one of the bombers was still at large. It later came to light, though, that Kessinger had made a source monitoring error. Feeling pressure to identify McVeigh's companion, Kessinger mixed him up with a man who had been in the office the day before McVeigh, Private Todd Bunting from Fort Riley, Kansas who had nothing to do with the bombing (Thomas, 1997).

> "Give us a dozen healthy memories, well-formed, and . . . we'll guarantee to take any one at random and train it to become any type of memory we might select—hammer, screwdriver, wrench, stop sign, yield sign, Indian chief—regardless of its origin or the brain that holds it.
>
> –Elizabeth Loftus and Hunter Hoffman, 1989

■ Police distributed this sketch of "John Doe No. 2," a suspect in the Oklahoma City bombing in April of 1995. The sketch was based on a description given by a mechanic in a truck rental office, who said that he saw Timothy McVeigh and the man in the sketch rent a truck. The employee later acknowledged, however, that he became confused and actually described a man who had been in the office the day before McVeigh and who had nothing to do with the bombing. This appears to be a classic source monitoring error. The employee had an actual memory of the person he described, but was mistaken about where he had seen this person.

Retrieval

Suppose the police have arrested a suspect and want to see if you, the eyewitness, can identify the person. It is common practice for the police to arrange a lineup at the police station, where you will be asked whether one of several people is the perpetrator. Sometimes you will be asked to look through a one-way mirror at an actual lineup of the suspect and some foils (people known not to have committed the crime). Other times you will be asked to examine videotapes of a lineup or photographs of the suspect and the foils. In each case, if a witness identifies a suspect as the culprit, the suspect is likely to be charged and convicted of the crime. After all, the argument goes, if an eyewitness saw the suspect commit the crime and then picked the suspect out of a lineup later, that's pretty good evidence the suspect is the guilty party.

Just as there are problems with acquisition and storage of information, so too can there be problems with how people retrieve information from their memories (Ellsworth & Mauro, 1998; Koehnken, Malpass, & Wogalter, 1996). A number of things other than the image of a person that is stored in memory can influence whether eyewitnesses will pick someone out of a lineup. Witnesses often choose the person in a lineup who most resembles the criminal, even if the resemblance is not very strong. Suppose, for example, that a 19-year-old woman committed a robbery and the police mistakenly arrest you, a 19-year-old woman, for the crime. They put you in a lineup and ask witnesses to pick out the criminal. Which do you think would be more fair: if the other people in the lineup were a 20-year-old man, a 3-year old child, and an 80-year-old woman, or if the other people were all 19-year-old women? In the former case, the witnesses might pick you only because you are the one who most resembles the actual criminal (Buckhout, 1974). In the latter case, it is much less likely that the witnesses will mistake you for the criminal, because everyone in the lineup is the same age and sex as the culprit (Wells, 1993; Wells & Luus, 1990).

To avoid this "best guess" problem wherein witnesses pick the person who looks most like the suspect, social psychologists recommend that police follow these five steps:

■ Lineups have to be carefully constructed to avoid mistaken identifications.

© 1985 Far Works, Inc. Dist. by Universal Press Syndicate

"That's him! That's the one! ... I'd recognize that silly little hat anywhere!"

1. Make sure everyone in the lineup resembles the witness's description of the suspect. Doing so will minimize the possibility that the witness will simply choose the person who looks most like the culprit (Wells, Seelau, Rydell, & Luus, 1994).

2. Tell the witnesses that the person suspected of the crime may or may not be in the lineup. If witnesses believe the culprit is present, they are much more likely to choose the person who looks most like the culprit, rather than saying that they aren't sure or that the culprit is not present. As a result, false identifications are more likely to occur when people believe the culprit is in the lineup (Gonzalez, Ellsworth, & Pembroke, 1993; Malpass & Devine, 1981; Wells et al., 1994).

3. Do not always include the suspect in an initial lineup. If a witness picks out someone as the culprit from a lineup that includes only foils, then you will know the witness is not reliable (Wells, 1984).

4. Present pictures of people sequentially instead of simultaneously, because doing so makes it more difficult for witnesses to compare all the pictures, choosing the one that most resembles the criminal, even when the criminal is not actually in the lineup (R. Lindsay & Wells, 1985; Sporer, 1994).

5. Present witnesses with both photographs of people and sound recordings of their voices. Witnesses who both see and hear members of a lineup are much more likely to identify the person they saw commit a crime than people who only see the pictures or only hear the voice recordings are (Melara, DeWitt-Rikards, & O'Brien, 1989).

Judging Whether Eyewitnesses Are Mistaken

Suppose you are a police detective or a member of a jury who is listening to a witness describe a suspect. How can you tell whether the witness's memory is accurate or whether he or she is making one of the many mistakes in memory we have just documented? It might seem like the answer to this question is pretty straightforward: Pay careful attention to how confident the witness is. Suppose the witness stands up in the courtroom, points her finger at the defendant, and says, "That's the man I saw commit the crime. There's absolutely no doubt in my mind—I'd recognize him anywhere." Sounds pretty convincing, doesn't it? Compare this testimony to a witness who says, "Well, gee, I'm really not sure, because it all happened so quickly. If I had to guess, I'd say it was the defendant, but I could be wrong." Which witness would you be more likely to believe? The eyewitness who was more confident, of course. The U.S. Supreme Court concurs with this reasoning, ruling that the amount of confidence witnesses express is a good indicator of their accuracy (*Neil v. Biggers*, 1972).

The only problem—and it is a big one—is that numerous studies have shown that a witness's confidence is not strongly related to how accurate he or she is (Bothwell, Deffenbacher, & Brigham, 1987; Luus & Wells, 1994a; Smith, Kassin, & Ellsworth, 1989). We don't mean to say there is no relation between confidence and accuracy; if witnesses pick a suspect out of a lineup, there is a modest relationship between how confident they are and whether their identification is correct (Sporer, Penrod, Read, & Cutler, 1995). Surprisingly, however, this relationship is not very strong, and it is dangerous to assume that because a witness is very confident he or she must be correct. For example, in the Lindsay and colleagues (1981) experiment we discussed earlier, witnesses who saw the crime under poor viewing conditions (in which the thief wore the cap over his ears) had as

Take nothing on its looks; take everything on evidence. There's no better rule.
—Charles Dickens,
Great Expectations, 1861

much confidence in their identifications as witnesses who saw the crime under moderate or good viewing conditions, even though they were considerably less accurate (see Figure SPA3.1).

The reason confidence is not always a sign of accuracy is that the things that influence people's confidence are not necessarily the same things that influence their accuracy. After identifying a suspect, for example, a person's confidence increases if he or she finds out that other witnesses identified the same suspect and decreases if he or she finds out that other witnesses identified a different suspect (Luus & Wells, 1994b; Penrod & Cutler, 1995). This change in confidence cannot influence the accuracy of the identification the person made earlier. Thus, just because a witness is confident does not mean he or she is accurate.

How, then, can we tell whether a witness's testimony is correct? It is by no means easy, but research by David Dunning and Lisa Beth Stern (1994; Stern & Dunning, 1994) suggests some answers. They showed participants a film in which a man stole some money from a woman's wallet, asked participants to pick the man out of a photo lineup, and then asked participants to describe how they had made up their minds. Dunning and Stern found some interesting differences between the reports of people who accurately identified the man and the reports of people who did not. Accurate witnesses tended to say that they didn't really know how they recognized the man, that his face just "popped out" at them. Inaccurate witnesses tended to say that they used a process of elimination whereby they deliberately compared one face to another. Ironically, taking more time and thinking more carefully about the pictures were associated with making more mistakes. We should thus be more willing to believe a witness who says "I knew it was the defendant as soon as I saw him in the lineup" than one who says "I compared everyone in the lineup to each other, thought about it, and decided it was the defendant."

The research by Dunning and Stern, while intriguing, leaves unanswered an important question: Did taking more time on the identification task make people less accurate, or did people who were less accurate to begin with simply take more time? Maybe some people did not pay close attention to the film of the robbery and thus had difficulty recognizing the robber in the lineup. Consequently, they had to spend more time thinking about it and comparing the faces, such that inaccuracy caused a longer decision time. Alternatively, there might have been something about making identifications thoughtfully and deliberately that impaired accuracy. Maybe there was something about making an identification slowly and deliberately that made people less accurate.

Some fascinating studies by Jonathan Schooler and Tonya Engstler-Schooler (1990) support this second possibility and suggest that trying to put an image of a face into words can cause problems. They showed students a film of a bank robbery and asked some of the students to write detailed descriptions of the robber's face (the verbalization condition). The others spent the same amount of time completing an unrelated task (the no verbalization condition). All students then tried to pick out the robber from a photo lineup of eight faces. It might seem that writing a description of the robber would be a good memory aid and make people more accurate. In fact, the reverse was true: Only 38 percent of the people in the verbalization condition correctly identified the robber, compared to 64 percent of the people in the no verbalization condition.

Schooler and Engstler-Schooler (1990) suggest that trying to put a face into words is difficult and impairs memory for that face. Using the word "squinty" to describe a robber's eyes, for example, might be a general description of what his eyes looked like, but probably does not capture the subtle contours of his eyes,

> "No subjective feeling of certainty can be an objective criterion for the desired truth.
>
> —Hugo Münsterberg, 1908

Try It !

//

The Accuracy of Eyewitness Testimony

Try this demonstration with a group of friends who you know will be gathered in one place, such as a dorm room or apartment. The idea is to stage an "incident," in which someone comes into the room suddenly, acts in a strange manner, and then leaves. Your friends will then be asked to recall as much as they can about this person, to see if they are good eyewitnesses. Here are some specific instructions about how you might do this.

1. Take one friend, who we will call the actor, into your confidence before you do this exercise. Ideally, the actor should be a stranger to the people who will be the eyewitnesses. The actor should suddenly rush into the room where you and your other friends are gathered and act in a strange (but nonthreatening) manner. For example, the actor could hand someone a flower and say, "The flower man cometh!" Or, he or she could go up to each person and say something unexpected, like, "Meet me in Moscow at the millennium." Ask the actor to hold something in his or her hand during this episode, such as a pencil, shoelace, or banana. **Important note:** The actor should not act in a violent or threatening way, or make the eyewitnesses uncomfortable. The goal is to act in unexpected and surprising ways, not to frighten people. After a few minutes, the actor should leave the room.

2. Inform your friends that you staged this event as a demonstration of eyewitness testimony and that if they are willing, they should try to remember, in as much detail as possible, what occurred. Ask them to write down answers to these questions:

   a. What did the actor look like? Write down a detailed description.
   b. What did the actor say? Write down his or her words as best as you can remember.
   c. How much time passed between the time the actor entered the room and the time he or she left?
   d. Did the actor touch anyone? If yes, who?
   e. What was the actor holding in his or her hand?

3. After everyone has answered these questions, ask them to read their answers out loud. How much did they agree? How accurate were people's answers? Discuss with your friends why they were correct or incorrect in their descriptions.

Note: This demonstration will work best if you have access to a video camera and can record the actor's actions. That way, you can play the tape to assess the accuracy of the eyewitnesses' descriptions. If you cannot videotape it, keep track of how much time elapsed so that you can judge the accuracy of people's time estimates.

//

eyelids, eyelashes, eyebrows, and upper cheeks. When you see the photo lineup, you look for eyes that are squinty, and doing so interferes with your attention to the finer details of the faces. If you ever witness a crime, then, you should not try to put into words what the criminal looked like. And if you hear someone say she or he wrote down a description of the criminal and then took a long time deciding whether the person was present at a lineup, you might doubt the accuracy of the witness's identification.

By now we have seen several factors that make eyewitness testimony inaccurate, leading to all too many false identifications. Perhaps the legal system in the United States should rely less on eyewitness testimony than it now does. In the legal systems of some countries, a suspect cannot be convicted on the basis of a sole eyewitness; at least two independent witnesses are needed. Adopting this more stringent standard in the United States might mean that some guilty people go free, but it would avoid many false convictions. To see how accurate you and your friends are at eyewitness testimony, and to illustrate some of the pitfalls we have discussed, do the Try It! exercise above.

Judging Whether Eyewitnesses Are Lying

There is yet another reason eyewitness testimony can be inaccurate: Even if witnesses have very accurate memories for what they saw, they might deliberately lie when on the witness stand. After Randall Adams was tried and convicted, evidence came to light suggesting that some of the eyewitnesses who testified against him had lied. One witness may have struck a deal with the police, agreeing to say what they wanted her to say, in return for lenient treatment of her daughter (who had been arrested for armed robbery). If this witness was lying, why couldn't the jurors see through her story that it was Randall Adams at the wheel of the car the night of the murder?

Consider the controversy over the guilt or innocence of O. J. Simpson. Was he lying when he denied murdering Nicole Simpson and Ronald Goldman? What about the testimony of Mark Fuhrman, the police detective who discovered the bloody glove at O. J. Simpson's house? Some people believe that Fuhrman was lying and that he planted the glove at the estate. Others believe that while he may well be a racist, he was telling the truth about finding the glove. How can we tell whether witnesses such as these are lying or telling the truth?

Several studies have tested people's ability to detect deception (DePaulo & Friedman, 1998). When people watch videotapes of actors who are either lying or telling the truth, their ability to tell who is lying is only slightly better than chance guessing (DePaulo, 1994; DePaulo, Stone, & Lassiter, 1985). But surely some people must be very good at detecting deception; after all, some jobs require exactly that skill. For example, law enforcement officials, most of whom have spent years with suspects who concoct stories professing their innocence, may be much more skilled than the average person at seeing through these stories to the underlying truth. Unfortunately, research by Bella DePaulo and Roger Pfeiffer (1986) and Paul Ekman and Maureen O'Sullivan (1991) suggests otherwise. These researchers tested the ability of experienced law enforcement officers—including members of the U.S. Customs Service, the Secret Service, the armed

> **I**f falsehood, like truth, had only one face, we would be in better shape. For we would take as certain the opposite of what the liar said. But the reverse of truth has a hundred thousand shapes.
>
> —Montaigne, *Essays*, 1595

■ **FIGURE SPA3.3** **Does experience in law enforcement improve the ability to detect deception?** Experienced law enforcement officers were no better at telling who was lying than inexperienced law enforcement officers or college students were. People could get 50% correct simply by guessing, thus, none of the participants were very accurate. (Adapted from DePaulo & Pfeiffer, 1986)

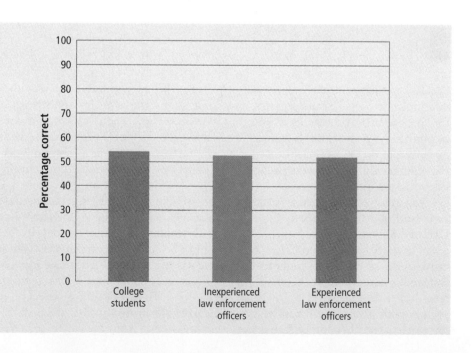

forces, police detectives, and judges—to detect deception. In general, these officials were no better at telling whether someone was lying than untrained college students were (see Figure SPA3.3). The problem is that both untrained people and experts tend to think that there are reliable cues to deception, such as whether a person refuses to look you in the eye (Akehurst, Kohnken, Vrij, & Bull, 1996). Unlike Pinocchio's nose, though, there are no signs that are the same for every person in every situation. If people are lying they often get away with it, regardless of whether they are talking to law enforcement experts, friends, or strangers (DePaulo & Friedman, 1998; Kashy & DePaulo, 1996).

If people are poor lie detectors, perhaps machines can do better. You've probably heard of a **polygraph,** which is a machine that measures people's physiological responses, such as their heart rate and breathing rate; polygraph operators attempt to tell if someone is lying by observing how that person responds physiologically while answering questions. In one version, called the *control question test*, the operator asks people both relevant questions about a crime (e.g., "did you steal money from the cash register of the restaurant?") and control questions that are known to produce truthful responses (e.g., "have you ever stolen anything in your whole life?"). The assumption is that when people lie, they become anxious and this anxiety can be detected by increases in heart rate, breathing rate, and so on. Thus, the operator sees whether you have more of a physiological response to the relevant question than the control question.

Another version is called the *guilty knowledge test*. Here, people answer multiple choice questions about specific aspects of a crime, the answers to which are known only by the police and the culprit. For example, you might be asked, "Was the amount stolen from the cash register $10, $23, $34, $54, or $110?" The idea is that only the criminal would know the correct answer and thus will be anxious when that answer is read. For example, the thief who knows that he stole $23 will probably be more anxious when this amount is read than will an innocent person who does not know how much money was stolen.

A great deal of controversy over the accuracy of polygraph tests exists and the test has both strong supporters (e.g., Raskin, 1986) and steadfast critics (e.g., Lykken, 1984). How well do they work? The first thing to realize is that they are only as good as the person operating and interpreting the test. With several responses being measured it is not always easy to tell whether a person has had more of a physiological response to one question versus another. One disturbing finding is that operators often disagree with one another, suggesting that the test is by no means infallible (Ellsworth & Mauro, 1998).

When the test is administered under optimal conditions by an experienced examiner, it does reveal whether someone is lying or telling the truth at levels better than chance. But even then it is not perfect (Ellsworth & Mauro, 1998; Saxe, 1994; Saxe, Dougherty, & Cross, 1985). The error rates vary somewhat, depending on the technique used to administer the test. Some studies have found that false negatives, in which liars are found to be telling the truth, are the most common kind of error (Honts, 1994). Others have found very high rates of false positives, in which innocent people are found to be lying (Patrick & Iacono, 1989). A review by Paul Ekman (1992), averaging across all the different techniques, estimates that the polygraph typically misidentifies about 15 percent of liars as truth-tellers (false negatives) and about 15 percent of truth-tellers as liars (false positives).

Suppose you are an honest employee working in a convenience store. The owners tell you that someone has been stealing money from the cash register, and

Polygraph
a machine that measures people's physiological responses (e.g., their heart rate); polygraph operators attempt to tell if someone is lying by observing how that person responds physiologically while answering questions

■ Though polygraphs can detect whether someone is lying at levels better than chance, they are by no means infallible.

they want you to take a lie-detector test to prove your innocence. "If you are innocent," they say, "what do you have to fear?" What you have to fear is the 15 percent chance that the machine will say you are guilty when you are not (this chance is even higher if the examiner is inexperienced). Would you be willing to take a 15 percent chance of losing your job and being arrested for a crime you did not commit? Because of this high rate of error, most states do not allow the results of polygraph tests to be used in court. In 1988, Congress passed the Employee Polygraph Protection Act, which bars the use of lie-detector machines by private employers, except under special circumstances (e.g., employees who have direct access to drugs can be tested).

To see how well you and your friends can tell whether someone is lying, do the Try It! exercise on page 621. How did you do? It would be nice if there were a foolproof method of telling whether or not someone is lying. Controversies like the O. J. Simpson case could be easily resolved, and Randall Adams would never have had to endure 12 long years in prison for a crime he did not commit. Many psychologists doubt, though, that such a test will ever be developed; the nuances of human behavior are too rich and complex to allow foolproof tests of honesty.

Can Eyewitness Testimony Be Improved?

We have seen a number of ways in which eyewitness testimony can go wrong. Given how important such testimony is in criminal trials, are there ways to improve it? Two general approaches have been tried but unfortunately, neither has proven to be very successful.

The first involves hypnosis. You may have seen movies in which a witness to a terrible crime has no memory of what occurred—until he or she is put under hypnosis. Then, while in a trance-like state, the person is able to describe the murderer in great detail. Unfortunately, this is a case in which the movies do not reflect real life. There is no hard evidence that people's memory improves when they are hypnotized (Ellsworth & Mauro, 1998; Erdelyi, 1994). There is some evidence that when people are under hypnosis they are more susceptible to suggestion, coming to believe that they saw things that they did not (Sanders & Simmons, 1983; Sheehan & Tilden, 1984). Even worse, people tend to become more confident in their memories after they have been hypnotized, even if they

Lie Detection

The purpose of this exercise, which should be done with a group of friends, is to see how well people can tell if someone is lying. Ask for a volunteer to be the speaker and the others to be the audience. The speaker's job will be to lie about how much he or she likes five high school acquaintances and to tell the truth about how much he or she likes five other high school acquaintances. The audience's job is to try to guess when the speaker is telling the truth and when he or she is lying. Here are some specific instructions:

Instructions for the speaker: Make a list of ten people you knew in high school and think about how much you like each person. Randomly choose five people and put a "T" next to their names. These are the people about whom you will be truthful. Put an "L" next to the other names. These are the people about whom you will lie. Take a few minutes to think about what you will say. When you are ready, describe your feelings toward each person (truthfully or not) to the audience. Give a few sentences about each person.

Instructions for the audience: The speaker will be describing her or his feelings toward ten high school acquaintances. He or she will be telling the truth about half the people and lying about the other half. Listen carefully and try to guess when the speaker is telling the truth and when he or she is lying. You may use any cues you want to make your decision. Make a list from one to ten, and put "truth" or "lie" next to each person the speaker describes.

Scoring: When the speaker is done, he or she should reveal when he or she was telling the truth versus lying. The audience members should tally how often they were right. People should be correct half the time just by guessing; scores that are substantially above 50 percent may indicate that you are good at detecting deception. Trade notes about what kinds of cues you paid attention to in the speaker. What did he or she do that made you think he or she was telling a lie?

Variation: Here is an interesting variation you can try: Have half of the audience sit with their backs to the speaker so they can hear but not see him or her. The other half of the audience should sit facing the speaker. Which group was better at detecting when the speaker was lying? Bella DePaulo, Dan Lassiter, and Julie Stone (1983) found that people who were instructed to pay special attention to a speaker's tone of voice did better at lie detection than did people instructed to pay attention to how the speaker looked. When people can see a speaker, they tend to focus on facial cues that they think are good indications of lying but in fact are not. Thus, the group of people who cannot see the speaker might rely more on his or her tone of voice, and thus may be more accurate.

---

are no more accurate (Spiegel & Spiegel, 1987). This is dangerous, because as we saw earlier, juries often use confidence as a sign of how accurate a witness is, even though confidence is not very related to accuracy.

The second way people have tried to increase eyewitness accuracy is with the use of the **cognitive interview** (Geiselman & Fischer, 1989). With this technique, a trained interviewer tries to improve eyewitnesses' memories by focusing their attention on the details and context of the event. This is done chiefly by asking the person to recall the event several times from different starting points (e.g., from the beginning of the event and from the middle of the event) and by asking the person to create a mental image of the scene. Initial research using this technique looked promising, finding that it improved people's memory by as much as 35 percent (Memon & Stevenage, 1996). Subsequent research, however, has been more sobering, finding that the cognitive interview may increase errors and confabulations of memory, especially when used with children (Memom & Stevenage, 1996; Roberts, 1996). One reason for this is that repeatedly imagining an event has been found to increase source monitoring errors, whereby people

Cognitive Interview
a technique whereby a trained interviewer tries to improve eyewitnesses' memories by focusing their attention on the details and context of the event

■ Sometimes people are hypnotized as a way of improving their memory of a crime. Unfortunately, there is no evidence that hypnosis improves the accuracy of eyewitnesses' memories.

become confused about whether they actually witnessed an event or simply imagined it later (Johnson, Raye, Wang, & Taylor, 1979).

As of yet, then, there is no tried-and-true way to improve eyewitnesses' memories—other than by trying to avoid the pitfalls we have discussed in this chapter.

Juries: Group Processes in Action

Ultimately, it is not a polygraph that decides whether witnesses are telling the truth but a judge or jury. Juries are of particular interest to social psychologists, because the way they reach verdicts is directly relevant to social psychological research on group processes and social interaction. The right to be tried by a jury of one's peers has a long tradition in English and American law. Trial by jury was an established institution in England at the beginning of the seventeenth century, and the people who founded the first permanent English settlement in North America, at Jamestown, Virginia, carried this tradition with them (though this right was not granted to Native Americans or other nonwhites or to a few rebellious English settlers who were summarily hanged). In the United States today, everyone has the right, under most circumstances, to be tried by a jury.

Despite this tradition, the jury system has often come under attack. Millions of television viewers placed themselves in the role of a juror during the O. J. Simpson criminal trial and formed strong opinions about whether he was guilty of murder—sometimes disagreeing with the verdict of the actual jurors (not guilty). In the Randall Adams trial, it is now clear that the jury reached the wrong decision. Harry Kalven, Jr., and Hans Zeisel (1966) found that judges who presided over criminal jury trials disagreed with the verdict rendered by the jury a full 25 percent of the time. More recent observers have also criticized the jury system, questioning the ability of jurors to understand complex evidence and reach a dispassionate verdict. Stephen Adler (1994), for example, suggests that in some cases (e.g., complex civil suits) we dispense with juries altogether. As noted by a former dean of the Harvard Law School, "Why should anyone think that 12 persons brought in from the street, selected in various ways, for their lack of gen-

'Tis with our judgements as our watches, none go just alike, yet each believes his own.

—Alexander Pope
(1688–1744)

eral ability, should have any special capacity for deciding controversies between persons?" (Kalven & Zeisel, 1966, p. 5).

The jury system has its staunch supporters, of course, and few people argue that it should be abolished. The point is that it is not a perfect system and that, based on research in social psychology, there are ways we might expect it to go wrong. Problems can arise at each of three phases of a jury trial: the way in which jurors use information they obtain before the trial begins, the way in which they process information during the trial, and the way in which they deliberate in the jury room, after all the evidence has been presented.

Effects of Pretrial Publicity

Because the murder of Officer Wood in Texas received considerable attention in the media, it is possible that the jury, before the trial began, was biased by what they had read in the newspapers. The press reported that a key eyewitness had picked Randall Adams out of a police lineup, but this information was untrue and was never presented to the jury during the trial. Nonetheless, two jurors mentioned during the deliberations that they believed the eyewitness had picked Adams out of the lineup (*Dallas Morning News*, May 4, 1987). Similarly, the jurors in the O. J. Simpson and Timothy McVeigh murder trials probably had heard a lot about these cases before the trial, given the amount of media attention they received. What are the effects of such pretrial publicity?

Even when the information reported by the media is accurate, it is often stacked against a suspect for a simple reason—the press gets much of its information from the police and the district attorney, who are interested in presenting as strong a case as they can against the suspect (Imrich, Mullin, & Linz, 1995). Thus, it's not surprising that the more people hear about a case in the media, the more they believe the suspect is guilty (Kerr, 1995; Moran & Cutler, 1991; Otto, Penrod, & Dexter, 1994).

> " A court is no better than each . . . of you sitting before me on this jury. A court is only as sound as its jury, and a jury is only as sound as the [people] who make it up.
>
> –Harper Lee, *To Kill a Mockingbird*, 1960

"*Since you have already been convicted by the media, I imagine we can wrap this up pretty quickly.*"

■ Research shows that jurors are swayed by pretrial publicity about a case, even when they are asked to ignore it.

Geoffrey Kramer, Norbert Kerr, and John Carroll (1990) showed that emotional publicity that arouses public passions, such as lurid details about a murder, is particularly biasing. They contacted people who had just finished serving on juries in Michigan and asked them to watch a videotaped trial of a man accused of robbing a supermarket. Before the jurors viewed the trial, the researchers exposed them to emotional publicity (reports that a car matching the one used in the robbery struck and killed a 7-year-old girl after the robbery), factual publicity (a report that the suspect had an extensive prior criminal record), or no publicity. After watching the trial and deliberating in 12-member mock juries, the participants rated whether they would vote to convict the suspect. The emotional publicity biased jurors the most, significantly increasing the percentage of jurors who gave guilty verdicts—even though the jurors knew they were not supposed to be influenced by any information they learned before viewing the trial.

Judges and lawyers have a variety of options to try to remedy this problem. First, lawyers are allowed to question prospective jurors before the trial (a process called *voir dire*). The lawyers ask people whether they have heard anything about the case, and if so, whether they feel they can render an unbiased verdict. One problem with this approach, however, is that people are often unaware they have been biased by pretrial publicity (Ogloff & Vidmar, 1994). In the Kramer and colleagues (1990) study we just reviewed, for example, the researchers put the jurors through a *voir dire* process, removing from the study any jurors who said that because of the pretrial publicity they could not form an unbiased opinion. Nonetheless, the emotional publicity still influenced the verdicts given by the remaining jurors.

Second, judges can instruct jurors to disregard what they have heard in the media. Several studies have shown, however, that these instructions do little to erase the effects of pretrial publicity and may even increase the likelihood that jurors use it (Fein, McCloskey, & Tomlinson, 1997; Kramer et al., 1990; Shaw & Skolnick, 1995). One reason this can happen is that it's very difficult to erase something from our minds once we have heard it. In fact, as mentioned in Chapter 3, the more we try not to think about something, the more that very thing keeps popping into consciousness (Wegner, 1989, 1992, 1994).

Another problem with pretrial publicity is that linking a person's name with incriminating events can cause negative impressions of the person, even if the media explicitly deny any such connection. Daniel Wegner, Richard Wenzlaff, Michael Kerker, and Ann Beattie (1981) found that when research participants read a headline denying any wrongdoing on someone's part—such as "Bob Talbert Not Linked with Mafia"—they had a more negative impression of the person than participants who read an innocuous headline—such as "Bob Talbert Arrives in City." The mere mention of Bob Talbert and the Mafia in the same headline was enough to plant seeds of doubt in readers, despite the headline's explicit denial of a connection. Thus, media reports can have unintended negative effects, and once there, those effects are hard to erase. The best solution is to include in a trial only those jurors who have heard nothing about the case. In highly publicized cases such as the O. J. Simpson trial, finding such jurors can be difficult. Sometimes a trial is moved to a new location where there has been less publicity.

Information Processing During the Trial

How do individual jurors think about the evidence they hear during a trial? As we saw in Chapter 3, people often construct theories and schemas to interpret the world around them, and the same is true of jurors (Hart, 1995; Kuhn, Weinstock, & Flaton, 1994; Smith, 1991). Nancy Pennington and Reid Hastie (1990, 1992, 1993; Hastie & Pennington, 1991, 1995) suggest that jurors decide on one story that best explains all the evidence; they then try to fit this story to the possible verdicts they are allowed to render, and if one of those verdicts fits well with their preferred story, they are likely to vote to convict on that charge.

This explanation has important implications for how lawyers present their cases. Lawyers typically present the evidence in one of two ways. In the first, called the *story order*, they present the evidence in the sequence events occurred, corresponding as closely as possible to the story they want the jurors to believe. In the second, called the *witness order*, they present witnesses in the sequence they think will have the greatest impact, even if this means that events are described out of order. For example, a lawyer might save his or her best witness for last, so that the trial ends on a dramatic, memorable note, even if this witness describes events that occurred early in the alleged crime.

If you were a lawyer, in which order would you present the evidence? You probably can guess which order Pennington and Hastie hypothesized would be the most successful. If jurors are ultimately swayed by the story or schema they think best explains the sequence of events, then the best strategy should be to present the evidence in the story order and not the witness order. To test their hypothesis, Pennington and Hastie (1988) asked mock jurors to listen to a simulated murder trial. The researchers varied the order in which the defense attorney and the prosecuting attorney presented their cases. In one condition, both used the story order, whereas in another condition, both used the witness order. In other conditions, one attorney used the story order, whereas the other used the witness order.

The results provided clear and dramatic support for the story order strategy. As seen in Table SPA3.1, when the prosecutor used the story order and the defense used the witness order, the jurors were most likely to believe the prosecutor—78 percent voted to convict the defendant. When the prosecutor used the witness order and the defense used the story order, the tables were turned—only 31 percent voted to convict. Pennington and Hastie (1990) speculate that one

Table SPA3.1

How should lawyers present their cases?

Percentage of people voting to convict the defendant

	Defense evidence	
	Story order	Witness order
Prosecution evidence		
Story order	59%	78%
Witness order	31%	63%

NOTE: Lawyers can present their cases in a variety of ways. This study found that the story order, in which lawyers present the evidence in the order that corresponds most closely to the "story" they want the jurors to believe, works best. (Adapted from Pennington & Hastie, 1988)

reason the conviction rate in felony trials in America is so high—approximately 80 percent—is that in real trials, prosecutors usually present evidence in the story order, whereas defense attorneys usually use the witness order. To those of our readers who are budding lawyers, remember this when you are preparing for your first trial!

Deliberations in the Jury Room

You may have noticed that our discussion so far has left out a crucial part of the jury process—the part where the jury retires to the jury room and deliberates before deciding on the verdict. Even if most jurors are inclined to vote to convict, there might be a persuasive minority who change their fellow jurors' minds. Sometimes this can be a minority of one, as in the classic movie *Twelve Angry Men*. When this film begins, a jury has just finished listening to the evidence in a murder case and all the jurors except one vote to convict the defendant. But over the course of the next 90 minutes, the lone holdout, played by Henry Fonda, persuades his peers that there is reason to doubt that the young Hispanic defendant is guilty. At first, the other jurors pressure Fonda to change his mind (using techniques of normative and informational conformity, as discussed in Chapter 8), but in the end, reason triumphs and the other jurors come to see that Fonda is right.

As entertaining as this movie is, research indicates that it does not reflect the reality of most jury deliberations (Ellsworth & Mauro, 1998; Kalven & Zeisel, 1966; MacCoun, 1989; Stasser, Stella, Hanna, & Colella, 1984). In the Randall Adams trial, for example, a majority of the 12-person jury (7 men and 5 women) initially voted to convict Adams. After eight hours of deliberations, the majority prevailed: The holdouts changed their minds, and the jury voted unanimously to convict. In the O. J. Simpson trial, 1 juror initially voted guilty, but quickly changed her mind. Harry Kalven, Jr. and Hans Zeisel (1966) interviewed the

■ In the classic movie *Twelve Angry Men,* Henry Fonda convinces all of his fellow jurors to change their minds about a defendant's guilt. In real life, however, such cases of a minority in a jury convincing the majority to change its mind are rare.

members of more than 200 juries in actual criminal trials. In the vast majority of the cases (97 percent), the jury's final decision was the same as the one favored by a majority of the jurors on the initial vote. Thus, just as we saw in Chapter 8 on conformity, majority opinion usually carries the day, bringing dissenting jurors into line.

If jury deliberation is stacked toward the initial, majority opinion, why not just abandon the deliberation process, letting the jury's initial vote determine a defendant's guilt or innocence? For two reasons, this would not be a good idea. First, forcing juries to reach a unanimous verdict makes them consider the evidence more carefully, rather than simply assuming their initial impressions of the case were correct (Hastie, Penrod, & Pennington, 1983). Second, even if minorities seldom succeed in persuading the majority to change their minds about guilt or innocence, minorities often do change people's minds about how guilty a person is. In criminal trials, juries usually have some discretion about the type of guilty verdict they can reach. In a murder trial, for example, they often can decide whether to convict the defendant of first-degree murder, second-degree murder, or manslaughter. Pennington and Hastie (1990) found that people on a jury who have a minority point of view often convince the majority to change their minds about the specific verdict to render. Thus, while a minority are unlikely to convince a majority to change their verdict from first-degree murder to not guilty, they might well convince the majority to change the verdict to second-degree murder.

Jury Size: Are 12 Heads Better Than 6?

Imagine that your worst nightmare has come true: You are falsely accused of murder and have to stand trial. Would you rather be judged by a jury of 12 people or a jury of 6 people? Although juries have traditionally been composed of 12 people, in 1970 the United States Supreme Court decided that there was nothing sacrosanct about this number and allowed smaller juries in some cases. Their decision was criticized by a number of social psychologists and since that time, several experiments have been performed to see how the size of a jury influences its decisions (Davis, Kerr, Atkin, Hold, & Meek, 1975; Nemeth, 1977; Saks, 1977).

One problem with small juries is that they reduce the probability that minority members will be represented. Suppose that 10 percent of the members of a particular community are Hispanic. There is a 72 percent chance that at least one Hispanic will be a member of a 12-person jury, but only a 47 percent chance at least one Hispanic will be a member of a 6-person jury. What about the decision processes of the group? Suppose that there is a small minority of the community that is likely to be sympathetic to your case and that on a 6-person jury, there is one such person, whereas on a 12-person jury, there are two such people. The Supreme Court reasoned that because the proportion of people with the minority viewpoint would be identical on both juries (⅙ versus ²⁄₁₂), the overall size of the jury was unimportant. Ring any bells? Being a good social psychologist, you know this is not true. Recall our discussion of the Asch conformity experiments in Chapter 8, where we saw that it is much more difficult to withstand pressure from a majority if you are a lone dissenter than if you have one other person who agrees with you. A minority of one on a 6-person jury is much more likely to conform than two people on a 12-person jury are.

In 1978, the Supreme Court rejected the use of 5-person juries in Georgia, based in part on the results of social psychological research. However, the court still allowed 6-person juries in some cases (e.g., civil trials). As noted by Phoebe Ellsworth and Robert Mauro (1998), this decision was ironic, because most of the arguments the court used to criticize 5-person juries apply to 6-person juries as well. Most social psychologists who have conducted research in this area believe that all juries should consist of 12 people.

Why Do People Obey the Law?

Ultimately, the success of the legal system depends on keeping people out of it. We should, of course, find ways to improve the accuracy of eyewitness testimony and help juries make better decisions. It is even more important, though, to find ways of preventing people from committing crimes in the first place. We thus close this chapter with a discussion of how to get people to obey the law.

Do Severe Penalties Deter Crime?

In October of 1997 the FBI reported some encouraging news: The murder rate in the United States had dropped for the fifth consecutive year. In fact, in the past few years, violent crimes of all types have been declining in America. Attorney General Janet Reno attributed this promising trend to, among other things, stiffer penalties for crimes ("Juveniles committing fewer violent crimes," 1997). It makes perfect sense that the harsher the penalty for a crime, the less likely people are to commit it. As we have seen many times in this book, however, common sense is not always correct, and in the case of crime and prison sentences, the story is not as straightforward as it might seem. Some analysts have suggested that the drop in violent crime is due not to stiffer penalties, but to the fact that the population of adolescents and young adults, who are mostly responsible for violent crimes, has been declining in the past few years.

How can we tell whether the attorney general or the other experts are correct? Unfortunately it is not easy. Unlike many of the other questions we have posed in this book, this one cannot be answered by randomly assigning people to different experimental conditions. It would be impossible, for example, to take a group of people convicted of drunk driving and randomly assign half of them to get ten-year prison sentences and the other half to get one-year sentences. The next best thing to an experiment, though, is to compare groups of people that have been naturally assigned to one "condition" or the other, such as residents of a state that has a severe penalty for drunk driving and residents of a state that has a milder penalty for drunk driving. Such data are imperfect, of course, because the residents of the two states might differ in other important ways. Nonetheless, such studies can be informative about the relationship between the severity of penalties and crime rates.

Let's begin with a theory that argues that stiff penalties do prevent crimes. **Deterrence theory** argues that people refrain from criminal activity because of the threat of legal punishment, as long as the punishment is perceived as severe, certain, and swift (Gibbs, 1985; Williams & Hawkins, 1986). Undoubtedly this theory is correct under some circumstances. Imagine, for example, that you are driving to an important appointment one day and get ensnarled in a traffic jam on the interstate. At last the traffic clears, but unless you hurry, you will be late. "Maybe I'll speed up just a little," you think, as the speedometer creeps up to 75. Your decision to exceed the speed limit was probably based on a consideration of the

Deterrence Theory
the theory that people refrain from criminal activity because of the threat of legal punishment, as long as the punishment is perceived as relatively severe, certain, and swift

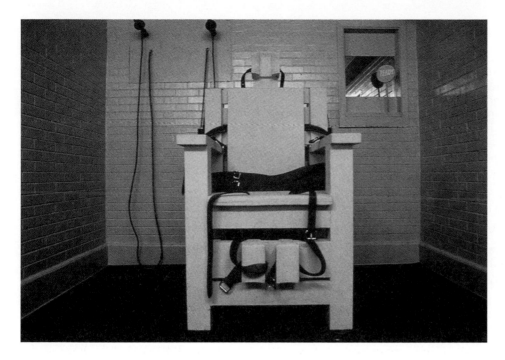

■ Many people are in favor of capital punishment because they believe that it deters other murders. Not only have studies failed to support this claim, some have found that executions are followed by an increase in the murder rate.

facts that (a) you are unlikely to get caught and that (b) if you do, the penalty won't be all that severe. But suppose you knew that the interstate is always patroled by the state police and that the penalty for speeding is a five-year prison sentence. Chances are, you would not dare to let your foot press too hard on the accelerator.

In this example we have made a couple of important assumptions. First, we assumed that you know what the penalties for speeding are. Second, we assumed that you have good control over your behavior and that whether you speed is a rational decision that you make after reflecting about the consequences. For many crimes, these assumptions do not hold. Surveys have found that many people are ignorant of the penalties for different crimes; if they do not know what they are, obviously the penalties cannot act as a deterrent. (To see how well you know the penalties for various federal crimes, complete the Try It! quiz on p. 630.) Further, other types of crimes are not based on a rational decision process. Many murders, for example, are impulsive crimes of passion committed by people in highly emotional states, not by people who carefully weigh the pros and cons. In general, severe penalties will only work when people know what they are, believe they are relatively certain to be caught, and weigh the consequences before deciding whether to commit a crime.

To illustrate these points, let's consider two very different kinds of crimes: Drunk driving and murder. The decision about whether to drink and drive is one that most of us can control; when we go to a party or a bar and know that we will be driving home afterwards, we can decide how much we will drink. Given that this decision is a relatively rational one—at least under most circumstances—we would expect that certain, severe penalties would act as a deterrent. William Evans, Doreen Neville, and John Graham (1991) found some support for this conclusion by comparing states with different drunk driving laws. Increasing the severity of penalties for drunk driving was not related, by itself, to

/// *Try It* !

Are You Aware of the Penalties for Federal Crimes?

Deterrence theory holds that legal penalties will prevent crimes if people perceive them to be severe, certain, and swift. If people are unaware that a crime has a severe penalty, then those penalties cannot act as a deterrent. Are you aware, for example, of which federal crimes are punishable by death? Take the following quiz to find out. The answers are printed upside down below.

Which of the Following Federal Crimes Are Punishable By Death?

Crime	Punishable by Death?	
1. Drug trafficking in large quantities, where no death results	no	yes
2. Attempted killing by a drug kingpin of a public officer	no	yes
3. Attempting to kill a juror or witness in a case involving a continuing criminal enterprise	no	yes
4. Carjacking which results in death	no	yes
5. Kidnaping which results in death	no	yes
6. Train sabotage which results in death	no	yes
7. Smuggling aliens where death results	no	yes
8. Aircraft hijacking which results in death	no	yes
9. Assassination of members of congress	no	yes
10. Assassination of a major vice-presidential candidate	no	yes
11. Assassination of a cabinet officer	no	yes
12. Assassination of Supreme Court justice	no	yes
13. Assassination of the president	no	yes
14. Espionage	no	yes
15. Treason	no	yes

ANSWERS
All of the crimes listed are punishable by death (Bedau, 1997).

///

lower alcohol-related, motor-vehicle fatalities. However, consistent with deterrence theory, increasing the certainty of being caught for drunk driving, by allowing police to perform sobriety checkpoints and breath-alcohol tests, was associated with lower alcohol-related motor vehicle fatalities. These results suggest that severity itself does not act as a deterrent, but that an increase in certainty of being caught does.

Now consider a very different crime and a very different penalty—murder and capital punishment. A majority of Americans support the death penalty for murder, in part because they believe that it acts as a deterrent. There is no more severe penalty than death, of course, and if the death penalty prevents even a few murders, it might be worth it—or so the argument goes. To see if this argument is correct, a number of studies have compared the murder rates in American states that have the death penalty with those that do not, compared the murder rates in American states before and after they adopt the death penalty, and compared the murder rates in other countries before and after they adopt the death penalty. The results are clear: There is no evidence that the death penalty prevents murders (Archer & Gartner, 1984; Bedau, 1997; Ellsworth & Mauro, 1998).

Opponents of the death penalty point out that, as we mentioned, most murders are crimes of passion that are not preceded by a rational consideration of the consequences. Because people are not considering the consequences of their actions, the death penalty does not act as a deterrent. Proponents of the death penalty argue that severity of the crime is not enough—as argued by deterrence theory, severe penalties must be applied with certainty and speed. The last of these conditions is almost never met in the United States. The time between a conviction for murder and the execution of the murderer is often many years, because of the slowness of the judicial system and the many avenues of appeal open to prisoners on death row. Were the process speeded up, this argument goes, the death penalty would act as a deterrent.

Although this is an empirical question, there is reason to doubt that the death penalty would act as a deterrent, even if it were applied swiftly. We refer to a few studies that have found that executions are followed not by a decrease but an *increase* in murders (Archer & Gartner, 1984; Bailey & Peterson, 1997; Bowers & Pierce, 1980). This might seem like a bizarre finding; why would the execution of a convicted murderer increase the likelihood that someone else would commit a murder? If you recall our discussion in Chapter 12, though, on aggression, the finding makes sense. As we saw, observing someone else commit a violent act weakens people's inhibitions against aggression, leads to imitation of aggression, and numbs their sense of horror over violence. Could it be that observing the government put someone to death lowers other people's inhibitions, making them more likely to commit murders? Though the data are not conclusive, this argument makes eminent social psychological sense—and there is some evidence to support it (Bailey & Peterson, 1997).

Procedural Justice: People's Sense of Fairness

We have just seen that one reason people obey the law is because they fear being caught and punished. An even more important reason, however, is because of their moral values about what constitutes good behavior. People will obey a law if they think it is just, even if it is unlikely that they will be caught for breaking it. For example, many people are honest on their tax returns because they think cheating is wrong, not because they fear being caught for cheating.

Thus, if you were a lawmaker, you could try to prevent crime in two ways. You could increase the penalties for breaking the law and the probability that people will be caught, or you could try to convince people that the law is just and fair. As we have seen, the former approach is difficult and sometimes ineffective. If we wanted to prevent people from driving through red lights, we could increase the penalties for doing so and make sure that we stationed a police officer at every intersection. But it would be far simpler to convince people that it is wrong to run red lights, so that they comply with the law even when no police officers are around.

What determines whether people think a law is just? One important factor is their perception of the fairness of legal proceedings. **Procedural justice** is defined as people's judgments about the fairness of the procedures used to determine

"American legislators suffer from a monumental illusion in their belief that long prison sentences will reduce the crime rate.
–Jack Gibbs (1985)

Procedural Justice people's judgments about the fairness of the procedures used to determine outcomes, such as whether they are innocent or guilty of a crime

outcomes, such as whether they are innocent or guilty of a crime (Kelley & Thibaut, 1978; Lind & Tyler, 1988; Miller & Ratner, 1996; Thibaut & Walker, 1975; Tyler, Boeckmann, Smith, & Huo, 1997). People who feel that they have been treated fairly are more likely to comply with the law than people who feel that they have been treated unfairly are (Tyler, 1990). Consider, for example, what happens when the police are called because of a domestic assault. What determines whether the person accused of assault will repeat this crime in the future? Surprisingly, it is not whether suspects are arrested or threatened with punishment; it is whether they feel that they were treated fairly by the police ("Misconceptions about why people obey laws," 1997).

As another example, imagine that you receive a traffic ticket one day for failing to stop at a stop sign. You believe the ticket is unfair because your view of the stop sign was obstructed by branches from a large tree that should have been trimmed by the city. You decide to go to court to protest the ticket. You take photographs of the tree, make careful diagrams of the intersection, and spend hours practicing your testimony before your friends. Finally, your day in court arrives. Now, imagine that one of these two things occurs: In the first scenario, your ticket is dismissed without a hearing because the officer who gave you the ticket could not appear in court that day. In the second scenario you get to present your case. The judge listens carefully, asks you a number of questions, and compliments you on your photographs and diagrams. After carefully considering all the facts, however, she rules against you, arguing that the stop sign, while obstructed, was still visible. Which outcome would you prefer—the first or the second one?

It might seem like people would prefer the first scenario, because here they received a positive outcome—no fine, no points on their driving record, no increase in their insurance rates. Research by Tom Tyler (1990), however, suggests that people prefer the second scenario. Here, even though the outcome was negative, people's sense of procedural justice is high—they had their day in court and were treated with fairness and respect. It is often more important to people to maintain a sense of procedural justice than to receive positive outcomes.

In sum, social psychological research indicates that the American legal system can go wrong in a number of ways: Juries rely heavily on eyewitness testimony, when in fact such testimony is often in error; determining when witnesses are telling the truth is difficult, even with the use of polygraphs; and since juries are groups of people who try to reach consensus by discussing, arguing, and bargaining, the kinds of conformity pressures and group processes we discussed in Chapters 8 and 9 can lead to faulty decisions. By illuminating these problems in their research, however, social psychologists can help to initiate change in the legal system—change that will lead to greater fairness and equity and to a greater sense of procedural justice.

> "Justice should not only be done, but should manifestly and undoubtedly be seen to be done.
> —Viscount Hewart

Summary

Many social psychological principles predict how people will respond in the legal arena. Because of the limitations of people's memory, eyewitness testimony is often inaccurate. A number of factors bias the **acquisition**, **storage**, and **retrieval** of what people observe, sometimes leading to the false identification of criminals. For example, research on the **own-race bias** shows that people find it more difficult to recognize members of other races than members of their own race. Research on **reconstructive memory** indicates that errors in **source monitoring** can occur, whereby people become confused about where they saw or heard something. Jurors often place a great deal of faith in eyewitness testimony, even though jurors are not very good at telling when someone is lying. Because the **polygraph** is also an imperfect measure of lie detection, false testimony by eyewitnesses and others sometimes goes undetected. Because of these problems with eyewitness testimony, researchers have tried to develop ways of improving it. Although techniques such as hypnosis and the **cognitive interview** have been tried, neither is very successful at improving the accuracy of eyewitness testimony.

Juries are of particular interest to social psychologists, because the way they reach verdicts is directly relevant to social psychological research on group processes and social interaction. Jurors are susceptible to the same kinds of biases and social pressures we documented in earlier chapters. They are sometimes biased by pretrial publicity, even when trying to put it out of their minds. During a trial, jurors attempt to make sense out of the testimony and often decide on one story that explains all of the evidence. Juries are thus most swayed by lawyers who present the evidence in a way that tells a consistent story. During deliberations, jurors with minority views are often pressured into conforming to the view of the majority; thus, verdicts usually correspond to the initial feelings of the majority of jurors. What about the size of juries—are 6 jurors as good as 12, as suggested by the Supreme Court? Social psychological research suggests that 12 jurors are better than 6. On larger juries, minorities are more likely to be represented and people with minority viewpoints are less likely to be pressured to conform.

It is also important to examine people's perception of the legal system, because these perceptions have a lot to do with how likely people are to obey the law. For example, **deterrence theory** holds that people refrain from criminal activity if they view penalties as severe, certain, and swift. Deterrence theory may be correct about crimes that are the result of rational thought, but is unlikely to apply to crimes of passion that are not rational, such as many murders. There is no evidence, for example, that the death penalty deters murders, and there is even some evidence that it increases the murder rate. Finally, people are more likely to obey the law if their sense of **procedural justice** is high; that is, if they believe that the procedures used to determine their guilt or innocence are fair.

If You Are Interested

Abramson, J. (1995). *We, the Jury: The Jury System and the Ideal of Democracy*. New York: Basic Books. An analysis of the jury system in the United States, with a discussion of such topics as whether juries should be required to reach unanimous verdicts and when an individual juror will conform to the opinion of the rest of the jury.

Bedau, H. A. (Ed.) (1997). *The death penalty in America: Current controversies*. New York: Oxford University Press. An excellent collection of articles about capital punishment, considering such issues as whether the death penalty acts as a deterrent and whether it is applied equally to people of all races. The book includes chapters by both proponents and opponents of the death penalty.

Ross, D. F., Read, D. J., & Toiglia, M. P. (Eds.) (1994). *Adult eyewitness testimony: Current trends and developments*. New York: Cambridge University Press. A collection of chapters about eyewitness testimony from leading researchers in the field. They cover such topics as what factors influence the accuracy of eyewitness testimony, how to construct unbiased lineups, and how to tell whether an eyewitness is accurate.

Thin Blue Line (1988). Errol Morris's classic film portrays the Randall Adams case discussed in this chapter. It is a fascinating portrayal of the way in which the American justice system can go wrong.

Turow, Scott (1987). *Presumed Innocent*. New York: Farrar, Straus, & Giroux. An engrossing story of a trial in which an innocent man is accused of murder. It is an interesting portrayal of the intricacies of the American justice system.

Twelve Angry Men (1957). A classic film in which a character played by Henry Fonda convinces all of his fellow jurors that a defendant accused of murder is innocent. As discussed in the chapter, the film is an interesting depiction of jury decision making, but is not one that reflects everyday life. In real life, a lone juror seldom succeeds in changing the minds of the other 11 jurors.

Tyler, T. R. (1990). *Why people obey the law*. New Haven: Yale University Press. A very interesting look at why people obey laws, with an emphasis on people's sense of procedural justice.

GLOSSARY

Accessibility   the ease with which different thoughts and ideas can be brought to mind; an idea that is accessible is already on our minds or can easily be brought to mind [4]

Acquisition   the process by which people notice and pay attention to information in the environment; because people cannot perceive everything that is happening around them, they acquire only a subset of the information available in the environment [SPA3]

Actor/Observer Difference   the tendency to see other people's behavior as dispositionally caused, while focusing more on the role of situational factors when explaining one's own behavior [4]

Additive Task   a task in which all group members perform the same job and the final product is a sum of all their contributions, such as the total amount of noise made by a group of cheerleaders [9]

Affect Blends   a facial expression where one part of the face is registering one emotion and another part of the face is registering a different emotion [4]

Affectively Based Attitude   an attitude based more on people's feelings and values than on their beliefs about the nature of an attitude object [7]

Aggressive Action   a behavior aimed at causing either physical or psychological pain [12]

Aggressive Stimulus   an object that is associated with aggressive responses (e.g., a gun) and whose mere presence can increase the probability of aggression [12]

Altruism   the desire to help another person even if it involves cost to the helper [11]

Altruistic Personality   the aspects of a person's makeup that are said to make him or her likely to help others in a wide variety of situations [11]

Amygdala   an area in the core of the brain that is associated with aggressive behaviors [12]

Anchoring and Adjustment Heuristic   a mental shortcut that involves using a number or value as a starting point, and then adjusting one's answer away from this anchor; people often do not adjust their answer sufficiently [3]

Anxious/Ambivalent Attachment Style   an attachment style characterized by a concern that others will not reciprocate one's desire for intimacy, resulting in higher-than-average levels of anxiety [10]

Applied Research   studies designed specifically to solve a particular social problem; building a theory of behavior is usually secondary to solving a specific problem [2]

Archival Analysis   a form of systematic observation whereby the researcher observes social behavior by examining the accumulated documents, or archives, of a culture (e.g., diaries, novels, magazines, and newspapers) [2]

Attachment Styles   the expectations people develop about relationships with others, based on the relationship they had with their primary caregiver when they were infants [10]

Attitude   an enduring evaluation—positive or negative—of people, objects, and ideas [7]

Attitude Accessibility   the strength of the association between an object and a person's evaluation of that object; accessibility is measured by the speed with which people can report how they feel about an issue or object [7]

Attitude Inoculation   the process of making people immune to attempts to change their attitudes by initially exposing them to small doses of the arguments against their position [7]

Attribution Theory   a description of the way in which people explain the causes of their own and other people's behavior [4]

Autobiographical Memories   memories about one's own past thoughts, feelings, and behaviors [5]

Automatic Processing   thinking that is nonconscious, unintentional, involuntary, and effortless [3]

Autonomy/Connection   the tension between our desire to maintain our independence and autonomy and our desire to feel emotionally connected to the other person [10]

Availability Heuristic   a mental rule of thumb whereby people base a judgment on the ease with which they can bring something to mind [3]

Avoidant Attachment Style   an attachment style characterized by a suppression of attachment needs, because attempts to be intimate have been rebuffed; people with this style find it difficult to develop intimate relationships [10]

Base Rate Information   information about the frequency of members of different categories in the population [3]

Basic Research   studies that are designed to find the best answer to the question of why people behave the way they do and that are conducted purely for reasons of intellectual curiosity [2]

Behaviorally Based Attitude   an attitude based on observations of how one behaves toward an attitude object [7]

Behaviorism   a school of psychology maintaining that to understand human behavior, one need only consider the reinforcing properties of the environment—that is, how positive and negative events in the environment are associated with specific behaviors [1]

Belief in a Just World   a form of defensive attribution wherein people assume that bad things happen to bad people and that good things happen to good people [4]

Biased Sampling   making generalizations from samples of information that are known to be biased or atypical [3]

Blaming the Victim   our tendency to blame individuals (make dispositional attributions) for their victimization, typically motivated by a desire to see the world as a fair place [13]

Bookkeeping Model   information inconsistent with a stereotype that leads to a modification of the stereotype [13]

Buffering Hypothesis   the hypothesis that we need social support only when we are under stress, because it protects us against the detrimental effects of stress [SPIA2]

Bystander Effect   the finding that the greater the number of bystanders who witness an emergency, the less likely any one of them is to help [11]

Category-Based Expectancies   expectations about people based on the groups to which they belong, such as expecting someone to love going to parties because he or she belongs to a party-loving fraternity or sorority [4]

Catharsis   the notion that "blowing off steam"—by performing an aggressive act, watching others engage in aggressive behaviors, or engaging in a fantasy of aggression—relieves built-up aggressive energies and hence reduces the likelihood of further aggressive behavior [12]

Causal Theories   theories about the causes of one's own feelings and behaviors; often we learn such theories from our culture (e.g., "absence makes the heart grow fonder") [5]

Central Route to Persuasion   the case whereby people elaborate on a persuasive communication, listening carefully to and thinking about the arguments; this occurs when people have both the ability and the motivation to listen carefully to a communication [7]

Classical Conditioning   the case whereby a stimulus that elicits an emotional response is repeatedly experienced along with a neutral stimulus that does not, until the neutral stimulus takes on the emotional properties of the first stimulus [7]

Cognitions   thoughts, feelings, beliefs, or pieces of knowledge [6]

Cognitive Appraisal Theories of Emotion   theories holding that emotions result from people's interpretations and explanations of events, in the absence of any physiological arousal [5]

Cognitive Dissonance   a drive or feeling of discomfort, originally defined as being caused by holding two or more inconsistent cognitions and subsequently defined as being caused by performing an action that is discrepant from one's customary, typically positive self-conception [6]

Cognitive Interview   A technique whereby a trained interviewer tries to improve eyewitnesses' memories by focusing their attention on the details and context of the event. [SPIA3]

Cognitive Misers   The idea that people are so limited in their ability to think and make inferences that they take mental shortcuts whenever they can [3]

Cognitively Based Attitude   an attitude based primarily on people's beliefs about the properties of an attitude object [7]

Commons Dilemma   a social dilemma in which everyone takes from a common pool of goods that will replenish itself if used in moderation, but which will disappear if overused [9]

Communal Relationships   relationships in which people's primary concern is being responsive to the other person's needs [10]

Companionate Love   the feelings of intimacy and affection we feel for another person when we care deeply for the person but do not necessarily experience passion or arousal in his or her presence [10]

Comparison Level   people's expectations about the level of rewards and punishments they are likely to receive in a particular relationship [10]

Comparison Level for Alternatives   people's expectations about the level of rewards and punishments they would receive in an alternative relationship [10]

Compliance   a change in behavior due to a direct request from another person [8]

Conformity   a change in behavior due to the real or imagined influence of other people [8]

Conjunctive Task   a group task in which performance depends on how well the least talented member does [9]

Consensus Information   information about the extent to which other people behave the same way toward the same stimulus as the actor does [4]

Consistency Information   information about the extent to which the behavior between one actor and one stimulus is the same across time and circumstances [4]

Construal   the way in which people perceive, comprehend, and interpret the social world [1]

Contagion   the rapid spread of emotions or behaviors through a crowd [8]

Contingency Theory of Leadership   the theory that leadership effectiveness depends both on how task-oriented or relationship-oriented the leader is and on the amount of control and influence the leader has over the group [9]

Controllability   information that indicates whether the cause of the success (or failure) is something the individual can control or cannot control [4]

Controlled Processing   thinking that is conscious, intentional, voluntary, and effortful [3]

Conversion Model   information inconsistent with a stereotype that leads to a radical change in the stereotype [13]

Coping Styles   the ways in which people react to stressful events [SPIA1]

Correlation Coefficient   the statistical technique that assesses how well you can predict one variable from another; e.g., how well you can predict people's weight from their height [2]

Correlational Method   the method whereby two or more variables are systematically measured and the relationship between them (i.e., how much one can be predicted from the other) is assessed [2]

Correspondent Inference Theory   the theory that we make internal attributions about a person when there are (a) few noncommon effects of his or her behavior and (b) the behavior is unexpected [4]

Counter-attitudinal Advocacy   the process that occurs when a person states an opinion or attitude that runs counter to his or her private belief or attitude [6]

Counterfactual Thinking   mentally changing some aspect of the past as a way of imagining what might have been [3]

Covariation Model   a theory which states that in order to form an attribution about what caused a person's behavior, we systematically note the pattern between the presence (or absence) of possible causal factors and whether or not the behavior occurs [4]

Cover Story   a description of the purpose of a study, given to participants, that is different from its true purpose; cover stories are used to maintain psychological realism [2]

Crowding   the subjective feeling of unpleasantness due to the presence of other people [SPIA2]

Debriefing   the process of explaining to participants, at the end of the experiment, the purpose of the study and exactly what transpired [2]

Deception   the procedure whereby participants are misled about the true purpose of a study or the events that will actually transpire [2]

Decode   to interpret the meaning of the nonverbal behavior other people express, such as deciding that a pat on the back was an expression of condescension and not kindness [4]

Defensive Attributions   explanations for behavior that avoid feelings of vulnerability and mortality [4]

Dehumanization   the act of seeing victims as nonhumans (e.g., "gooks" instead of fellow human beings); dehumanization lowers inhibitions against aggressive actions and makes continued aggression easier and more likely [12]

Deindividuation   the loosening of normal constraints on behavior when people are in a crowd, leading to an increase in impulsive and deviant acts [9]

Density   the number of people who occupy a given spiace [SPIA2]

Dependent Variable   the variable a researcher measures to see if it is influenced by the independent variable; the researcher hypothesizes that the dependent variable will depend on the level of the independent variable [2]

Descriptive Norms   people's perceptions of how other people are actually behaving in a given situation, regardless of what behaviors are socially sanctioned [SPIA2]

Deterrence Theory   the theory that people refrain from criminal activity because of the threat of legal punishment, as long as the punishment is perceived as relatively severe, certain, and swift [SPIA3]

Diffusion of Responsibility   the phenomenon whereby each bystander's sense of responsibility to help decreases as the number of witnesses increases [11]

Discounting underestimating the effects of one cause of our behavior because another cause is conspicuous [5]

Discrimination unjustified negative or harmful action toward a member of a group, simply because of his or her membership in that group [13]

Disjunctive Task a group task in which performance depends on how well the most talented member does (e.g., a group of people trying to solve a difficult math problem) [9]

Display Rules culturally determined rules about which nonverbal behaviors are appropriate to display [4]

Distinctiveness Information information about the extent to which one particular actor behaves in the same way to different stimuli [4]

Divisible versus a Unitary Task divisible tasks are those that can be broken down into different subtasks performed by individual members, whereas unitary tasks are those in which no division of labor is feasible [9]

Door-in-the-Face Technique a technique to get people to comply with a request, whereby people are presented first with a large request, which they are expected to refuse, and then with a smaller, more reasonable request, to which it is hoped they will acquiesce [8]

Downward Social Comparison the process whereby we compare ourselves to people who are worse than we are on a particular trait or ability [5]

Elaboration Likelihood Model the theory that there are two ways in which persuasive communications can cause attitude change; the central route occurs when people are motivated and have the ability to pay attention to the arguments in the communication, and the peripheral route occurs when people do not pay attention to the arguments but are instead swayed by surface characteristics (e.g., who gave the speech) [7]

Emblems nonverbal gestures that have well-understood definitions within a given culture; they usually have direct verbal translations, such as the "OK" sign [4]

Empathy the ability to put oneself in the shoes of another person—to experience events and emotions (e.g., joy and sadness) the way that person experiences them [11, 12]

Empathy-Altruism Hypothesis the idea that when we feel empathy for a person, we will attempt to help him or her purely for altruistic reasons—that is, regardless of what we have to gain [11]

Encode to express or emit nonverbal behavior, such as smiling or patting someone on the back [4]

Equity Theory the theory holding that people are happiest with relationships in which the rewards and costs a person experiences and the contributions he or she makes to the relationship are roughly equal to the rewards, costs, and contributions of the other person [10]

Eros the instinct toward life, posited by Freud [12]

Evolutionary Approach to Love an approach derived form evolutionary biology, which states that men and women are attracted to different characteristics in each other (men are attracted by women's appearance; women are attracted by men's resources) because this maximizes their reproductive success [10]

Evolutionary Psychology the attempt to explain social behavior in terms of genetic factors that evolved over time according to the principles of natural selection [11]

Exchange Relationships relationships governed by the need for equity (i.e., for an equal ratio of rewards and costs) [10]

Experimental Method the method of choice to study cause-and-effect relationships; the researcher randomly assigns participants to different conditions and ensures that these conditions are identical except for the independent variable (the one thought to have a causal effect on people's responses) [2]

External Attribution the inference that a person is behaving a certain way because of something about the situation he or she is in; the assumption is that most people would respond the same way in that situation [4]

External Justification a person's reason or explanation for his or her dissonant behavior that resides outside the individual (e.g., in order to receive a large reward or avoid a severe punishment) [6]

External Validity the extent to which the results of a study can be generalized to other situations and other people [2]

Extrinsic Motivation the desire to engage in an activity because of external rewards or pressures, not because we enjoy the task or find it interesting [5]

Factorial Design an experimental design in which there is more than one independent variable; each independent variable has more than one version, or level; and all possible combinations of these levels occur in one study [2]

False Memory Syndrome a memory of a past traumatic experience that is objectively false but that people believe occurred [5]

Fear-Arousing Communications persuasive messages that attempt to change people's attitudes by arousing their fears [7]

Field Experiments   experiments conducted in real-life settings, rather than in the laboratory [2]

Foot-in-the-Door Technique   a technique to get people to comply with a request, whereby people are presented with a small request, to which they are expected to acquiesce, followed by a larger request, to which it is hoped they also acquiesce [8]

Frustration-Aggression Theory   the theory that frustration—the perception that you are being prevented from obtaining a goal—will increase the probability of an aggressive response [12]

Fundamental Attribution Error   the tendency to overestimate the extent to which people's behavior is due to internal, dispositional factors, and to underestimate the role of situational factors [1, 4]

Gain-Loss Effect   the finding that we like people the most if we feel we have gained in their estimation of us (i.e., if they initially disliked us but now like us) and that we dislike people the most if we feel we have lost their favor (i.e., if they initially liked us but now dislike us) [10]

Gestalt Psychology   a school of psychology stressing the importance of studying the subjective way in which an object appears in people's minds, rather than the objective, physical attributes of the object [1]

Global Attribution   the belief that the cause of an event is due to factors that apply in a large number of situations (e.g., your intelligence, which will influence your performance in many areas), as opposed to the belief that the cause is specific and applies in only a limited number of situations (e.g., your music ability, which will affect your performance in music courses but not in other courses) [SPIA1]

Great Person Theory   the theory that certain key personality traits make a person a good leader, regardless of the nature of the situation facing the leader [9]

Group Polarization   the tendency for groups to make decisions that are more extreme than the initial inclinations of its members [9]

Groupthink   a kind of thinking in which maintaining group cohesiveness and solidarity is more important than considering the facts in a realistic manner [9]

Heuristic-Systematic Model of Persuasion   the theory that there are two ways in which persuasive communications can cause attitude change; people either systematically process the merits of the arguments or use mental shortcuts (heuristics), such as "Experts are always right" [7]

Hostile Aggression   an act of aggression stemming from feelings of anger and aimed at inflicting pain [12]

Hostile Media Phenomenon   the finding that opposing partisan groups both perceive neutral, balanced media presentations as hostile to their side, because the media have not presented the facts in the one-sided fashion the partisans "know" to be true [3]

Hydraulic Theory   the theory that unexpressed emotions build up pressure and must be expressed to relieve that pressure [12]

Idiosyncrasy Credits   the credits a person earns, over time, by conforming to group norms; if enough idiosyncrasy credits are earned, the person can, on occasion, behave deviantly without retribution from the group [8]

Illusory Correlation   the tendency to see relationships, or correlations, between events that are actually unrelated [13]

Implicit Personality Theory   a type of schema people use to group various kinds of personality traits together; for example, many people believe that if someone is kind, he or she is generous as well [4]

Impression Management   our conscious or unconscious orchestration of a carefully designed presentation of self so as to create a certain impression that fits our goals or needs in a social interaction [5]

In-Group Bias   especially positive feelings and special treatment for people we have defined as being part of our in group, and negative feelings and unfair treatment for others simply because we have defined them as being in the out group [13]

In Group   the group with which an individual identifies and feels he or she is a member [11]

Independent Variable   the variable a researcher changes or varies to see if it has an effect on some other variable [2]

Independent View of the Self   a way of defining oneself in terms of one's own internal thoughts, feelings, and actions, and not in terms of the thoughts, feelings, and actions of other people [5]

Individual Differences   the aspects of people's personalities that make them different from other people [1]

Informational Social Influence   the influence of other people that leads us to conform because we see them as a source of information to guide our behavior; we conform because we believe that others' interpretation of an ambiguous situation is more accurate than ours and will help us choose an appropriate course of action [8]

Informed Consent   the procedure whereby the nature of the experiment is explained to participants before it begins and their consent to participate in the experiment is obtained [2]

Ingratiation   the process whereby people flatter, praise, and generally try to make themselves likable to another, often higher-status person [5]

Injunctive Norms   socially sanctioned behaviors—that is, people's perceptions of what behaviors are approved of by others [SPIA2]

Institutionalized Racism   racist attitudes that are held by the vast majority of us because we are living in a society where stereotypes and discrimination are the norm [13]

Institutionalized Sexism   sexist attitudes that are held by the vast majority of us because we are living in a society where stereotypes and discrimination are the norm [13]

Instrumental Aggression   aggression as a means to some goal other than causing pain [12]

Insufficient Punishment   the dissonance aroused when individuals lack sufficient external justification for having resisted a desired activity or object, usually resulting in individuals devaluing the forbidden activity or object [6]

Integrative Solution   a solution to a conflict whereby the parties make trade-offs on issues according to their different interests; each side concedes the most on issues that are unimportant to it but important to the other side [9]

Interdependent View of the Self   a way of defining oneself in terms of one's relationships to other people; recognizing that one's behavior is often determined by the thoughts, feelings, and actions of others [5]

Interjudge Reliability   the level of agreement between two or more people who independently observe and code a set of data; by showing that two or more judges independently come up with the same observations, researchers ensure that the observations are not the subjective, distorted impressions of one individual [2]

Internal Attribution   the inference that a person is behaving in a certain way because of something about him or her, such as the person's attitudes, character, or personality [4, SPIA1]

Internal Justification   the reduction of dissonance by changing something about oneself (e.g., one's attitude or behavior) [6]

Internal Validity   making sure that nothing else besides the independent variable can affect the dependent variable; this is accomplished by controlling all extraneous variables and by randomly assigning people to different experimental conditions [2]

Intrapersonal Conflict   tension within one individual due to two or more incompatible goals (e.g., a parent's desires to stay home with his or her children and to pursue a career) [9]

Intrinsic Motivation   the desire to engage in an activity because we enjoy it or find it interesting, not because of external rewards or pressures [5]

Introspection   the process whereby people look inward and examine their own thoughts, feelings, and motives [5]

Investment Model   the theory holding that people's commitment to a relationship depends on their satisfaction with the relationship in terms of rewards, costs, and comparison level; their comparison level for alternatives; and how much they have invested in the relationship that would be lost by leaving it [10]

Jigsaw Classroom   a classroom setting designed to reduce prejudice and raise the self-esteem of children by placing them in small, desegregated groups and making each child dependent on the other children in his or her group to learn the course material and do well in the class [13]

Judgmental Heuristics   mental shortcuts people use to make judgments quickly and efficiently [3]

Justification of Effort   the tendency for individuals to increase their liking for something they have worked hard to attain [6]

Kin Selection   the idea that behaviors that help a genetic relative are favored by natural selection [11]

Learned Helplessness   the state of pessimism that results from explaining a negative event as due to stable, internal, and global factors [SPIA1]

Locus   information that indicates whether the cause of the success (or failure) is internal or external [4]

Looking-Glass Self   the idea that we see ourselves through the eyes of other people and incorporate their views into our self-concept [5]

Love Styles   the basic theories people have about love that guide their behavior in relationships; six styles have been identified: Eros, Ludus, storge, pragma, mania, and Agape [10]

Lowballing   an unscrupulous strategy whereby a salesperson induces a customer to agree to purchase a product at a very low cost, subsequently claims it was an error, and then raises the price; frequently the customer will agree to make the purchase at the inflated price [6]

Mass Psychogenic Illness   the occurrence, in a group of people, of similar physical symptoms with no known physical cause [8]

Mere Exposure Effect   the finding that the more exposure we have to a stimulus, the more apt we are to like it [10]

Meta Analysis   a statistical technique that averages the results of two or more studies to see if the effect of an independent variable is variable [2]

Mindless Conformity   obeying internalized social norms without deliberating about one's actions [8]

Minimal Groups   meaningless groups formed by grouping strangers on the basis of trivial criteria; minimal group members still display in-group biases, however [13]

Minority Influence   the case where a minority of group members influence the behavior or beliefs of the majority [8]

Misattribution of Arousal   the process whereby people make mistaken inferences about what is causing them to feel the way they do [5]

Mixed-Motive Conflict   conflict in which both parties can gain by cooperating but in which one side can gain even more by competing against its opponent [9]

Modern Racism   prejudice revealed in subtle, indirect ways because people have learned to hide prejudiced attitudes in order to avoid being labeled as racist [13]

Motivated Tacticians   the idea that people have a large arsenal of mental rules and strategies, and choose wisely among these strategies depending on their particular needs and goals [3]

Mundane Realism   the extent to which an experiment is similar to real-life situations [2]

Mutual Interdependence   a situation where two or more groups need each other and must depend on each other in order to accomplish a goal that is important to each of them [13]

Need for Cognition   a personality variable reflecting the extent to which people engage in and enjoy effortful cognitive activities [7]

Negative Correlation   a relationship between two variables wherein increases in the value of one variable are associated with decreases in the value of the other variable [2]

Negative-State Relief Hypothesis   the idea that people help in order to alleviate their own sadness and distress [11]

Negotiation   a form of communication between opposing sides in a conflict in which offers and counteroffers are made and a solution occurs only when both parties agree [9]

Noncommon Effects   effects produced by a particular course of action that could not be produced by alternative courses of action [4]

Nonsocial Groups   groups in which two or more people are in the same place at the same time but are not interacting with each other (e.g., fans at a baseball game) [9]

Nonverbal Communication   the way in which people communicate, intentionally or unintentionally, without words; nonverbal cues include facial expressions, tone of voice, gestures, body position and movement, the use of touch, and eye gaze [4]

Norm of Reciprocity   the expectation that helping others will increase the likelihood that they will help us in the future [11]

Normative Conformity   the tendency to go along with the group in order to fulfill their expectations and gain acceptance [13]

Normative Social Influence   the influence of other people that leads us to conform in order to be liked and accepted by them; this type of conformity results in public compliance with the group's beliefs and behaviors, but not necessarily with private acceptance of the group's beliefs and behaviors [8]

Novelty/Predictability   the tension between our desire for excitement and newness in the relationship and our desire for what is safe and predictable [10]

Observational Method   the technique whereby a researcher observes people and systematically records measurements of their behavior [2]

Openness/Closedness   the tension between our desire to be open and revealing to the other person and our desire to be private and discrete [10]

Operant Conditioning   the case whereby behaviors that people freely choose to perform increase or decrease in frequency, depending on whether they are followed by positive reinforcement or punishment [7]

Out Group   a group with which an individual does not identify [11]

Out-Group Homogeneity   the perception that those in the out group are more similar (homogeneous) to each other than they really are, as well as more similar than the members of the in group are [13]

Overconfidence Barrier   the finding that people usually have too much confidence in the accuracy of their judgments; people's judgments are usually not as correct as they think they are [3]

Overjustification Effect   the case whereby people view their behavior as caused by compelling extrinsic reasons, making them underestimate the extent to which their behavior was caused by intrinsic reasons [5]

Own-Race Bias the finding that people are better at recognizing faces of their own race than those of other races [SPIA3]

Participant Observation a form of systematic observation whereby the observer interacts with the people being observed, but tries not to alter the situation in any way [2]

Passionate Love the feelings of intense longing, accompanied by physiological arousal, we feel for another person; when our love is reciprocated, we feel great fulfillment and ecstasy, but when it is not, we feel sadness and despiair [10]

Perceived Control the belief that we can influence our environment in ways that determine whether we experience positive or negative outcomes [SPIA1]

Perceptual Salience information that is the focus of people's attention; people tend to overestimate the causal role of perceptually salient information [4]

Performance-Contingent Rewards rewards that are based on how well we perform a task [5]

Peripheral Route to Persuasion the case whereby people do not elaborate on the arguments in a persuasive communication but are instead swayed by peripheral cues [7]

Perseverance Effect the finding that people's beliefs about themselves and the social world persist even after the evidence supporting these beliefs is discredited [3]

Persuasive Communication communication (e.g., a speech or television ad) advocating a particular side of an issue [7]

Pluralistic Ignorance the phenomenon whereby bystanders assume that nothing is wrong in an emergency, because no one else looks concerned [11]

Polygraph a machine that measures people's physiological responses (e.g., their heart rate); polygraph operators attempt to tell if someone is lying by observing how that person responds physiologically while answering questions [SPIA3]

Positive Correlation a relationship between two variables wherein increases in the value of one variable are associated with increases in the value of the other variable [2]

Postdecision Dissonance dissonance that is inevitably aroused after a person makes a decision; in this situation, dissonance is typically reduced by enhancing the attractiveness of the chosen alternative and devaluing the rejected alternatives [6]

Prejudice a hostile or negative attitude toward a distinguishable group of people, based solely on their membership in that group [13]

Primacy Effect the process whereby our first impression of another person causes us to interpret his or her subsequent behavior in a manner consistent with the first impression [3]

Priming the process by which recent experiences increase a trait's accessibility [4]

Private Acceptance conforming to other people's behavior out of a genuine belief that what they are doing or saying is right [8]

Probability Level (*p*-value) a number, calculated with statistical techniques, that tells researchers how likely it is that the results of their experiment occurred by chance and not because of the independent variable(s); the convention in science, including social psychology, is to consider results significant if the probability level is less than 5 in 100 that the results might be due to chance factors and not the independent variable(s) studied [2]

Procedural Justice people's judgments about the fairness of the procedures used to determine outcomes, such as whether they are innocent or guilty of a crime [SPIA3]

Process Loss any aspect of group interaction that inhibits good problem solving [9]

Propinquity Effect the finding that the more we see and interact with people, the more likely they are to become our friends [10]

Prosocial Behavior any act performed with the goal of benefiting another person [11]

Psychological Realism the extent to which the psychological processes triggered in an experiment are similar to psychological processes occurring in everyday life; psychological realism can be high in an experiment, even if mundane realism is low [2]

Public Compliance conforming to other people's behavior publicly, without necessarily believing in what we are doing or saying [8]

Public Goods Dilemma a social dilemma in which individuals must contribute to a common pool in order to maintain the public good [9]

Random Assignment to Condition the process whereby all participants have an equal chance of taking part in any condition of an experiment; through random assignment, researchers can be relatively certain that differences in the participants' personalities or backgrounds are distributed evenly across conditions [2]

Random Selection a way of ensuring that a sample of people is representative of a population, by giving everyone in the population an equal chance of being selected for the sample [2]

Rationalization Trap   the potential for dissonance reduction to produce a succession of self-justifications that ultimately result in a chain of stupid or immoral actions [6]

Reactance Theory   the idea that when people feel their freedom to perform a certain behavior is threatened, an unpleasant state of reactance is aroused; people can reduce this reactance by performing the threatened behavior [7]

Realistic Conflict Theory   the theory that limited resources lead to conflict between groups and result in increased prejudice and discrimination [13]

Reasons-Generated Attitude Change   attitude change resulting from thinking about the reasons for one's attitudes; people assume their attitudes match the reasons that are plausible and easy to verbalize [5]

Reciprocity Norm   a social norm stating that receiving anything positive from another person requires you to reciprocate (or behave similarly) in response [8]

Reconstructive Memory   the process whereby memories for an event become distorted by information encountered after the event has occurred [SPIA3]

Recovered Memories   recollections of a past event, such as sexual abuse, that had been forgotten or repressed; a great deal of controversy surrounds the accuracy of such memories [5]

Relational Dialectics   a theory which states that close relationships are always in a state of change, due to opposing forces of autonomy/connection, novelty/predictability, and openness/closedness [10]

Relationship-Oriented Leader   a leader who is concerned primarily with the feelings of and relationships between the workers [9]

Relative Deprivation   the perception that you (or your group) have less than you deserve, less than you have been led to expect, or less than people similar to you have [12]

Replication   repetition of a study, often with different subject populations or in different settings [2]

Representativeness Heuristic   a mental shortcut whereby people classify something according to how similar it is to a typical case [3]

Retrieval   the process by which people recall information stored in their memories [SPIA3]

Roles   shared expectations in a group about how particular people are supposed to behave [9]

Scapegoating   the tendency for individuals, when frustrated or unhappy, to displace aggression onto groups that are disliked, visible, and relatively powerless [13]

Schemas   mental structures people use to organize their knowledge about the social world by themes or subjects; schemas powerfully affect what information we notice, think about, and remember [3]

Scripts   ways of behaving socially that we learn implicitly from our culture [12]

Secure Attachment Style   an attachment style characterized by trust, a lack of concern with being abandoned, and the view that one is worthy and well liked [10]

Self-Affirmation Theory   a theory suggesting that people will reduce the impact of a dissonance-arousing threat to their self-concept by focusing on and affirming their competence on some dimension unrelated to the threat [6]

Self-Awareness   the act of thinking about ourselves [5]

Self-Awareness Theory   the idea that when people focus their attention on themselves, they evaluate and compare their behavior to their internal standards and values [5]

Self-Concept   the contents of the self; that is, our knowledge about who we are [5, 6]

Self-Efficacy   the belief in one's ability to carry out specific actions that produce desired outcomes [SPIA1]

Self-Esteem   people's evaluations of their own self-worth—that is, the extent to which they view themselves as good, competent, and decent [1]

Self-Evaluation Maintenance Theory   the theory that one's self-concept can be threatened by another individual's behavior and that the level of threat is determined by both the closeness of the other individual and the personal relevance of the behavior [6]

Self-Fulfilling Prophecy   the case whereby people (a) have an expectation about what another person is like, which (b) influences how they act toward that person, which (c) causes that person to behave consistently with people's original expectations [3, 13]

Self-Handicapping   creating obstacles and excuses for ourselves, so that if we do poorly on a task, we have ready-made excuses [5]

Self-Justification   the tendency to justify one's actions in order to maintain one's self-esteem [6]

Self-Perception Theory   the theory that when our attitudes and feelings are uncertain or ambiguous, we infer these states by observing our behavior and the situation in which it occurs [5]

Self-Persuasion   a long-lasting form of attitude change that results from attempts at self-justification [6]

Self-Presentation   the attempt to present who we are, or who we want people to believe we are, through our words, nonverbal behaviors, and actions [5]

Self-Schemas   organized knowledge structures about ourselves, based on our past experiences, that help us understand, explain, and predict our own behavior [5]

Self-Serving Attributions   explanations for one's successes that credit internal, dispositional factors and explanations for one's failures that blame external, situational factors [4]

Self-Verification Theory   a theory suggesting that people have a need to seek confirmation of their self-concept, whether the self-concept is positive or negative; in some circumstances, this tendency can conflict with the desire to uphold a favorable view of oneself [6]

Sensory Overload   the situation in which we receive more stimulation from the environment than we can pay attention to or process [SPIA2]

Social Cognition   how people think about themselves and the social world; more specifically, how people select, interpret, remember, and use social information to make judgments and decisions [1, 3]

Social Comparison Theory   the idea that we learn about our own abilities and attitudes by comparing ourselves to other people [5]

Social Dilemma   a conflict in which the most beneficial action for an individual will, if chosen by most people, have harmful effects on everyone [9]

Social Exchange Theory   the theory holding that how people feel about a relationship depends on their perceptions of the rewards and costs of the relationship, the kind of relationship they deserve, and their chances for having a better relationship with someone else [10]

Social Facilitation   the tendency for people to do better on simple tasks and worse on complex tasks, when they are in the presence of others and their individual performance can be evaluated [9]

Social Groups   groups in which two or more people are interacting with each other and are interdependent, in the sense that to fulfill their needs and goals they must rely on each other [9]

Social Impact Theory   the theory that conforming to social influence depends on the strength, immediacy, and number of other people in a group [8]

Social Learning Theory   the theory that we learn social behavior (e.g., aggression) by observing others and imitating them [12]

Social Loafing   the tendency for people to do worse on simple tasks and better on complex tasks, when they are in the presence of others and their individual performance cannot be evaluated [9]

Social Norms   the implicit or explicit rules a group has for the acceptable behaviors, values, and beliefs of its members [8]

Social Perception   the study of how we form impressions of and make inferences about other people [4]

Social Psychology   the scientific study of the way in which people's thoughts, feelings, and behaviors are influenced by the real or imagined presence of other people. [1]

Social-Role Theory   the theory that sex differences in social behavior are due to society's division of labor between the sexes; this division leads to differences in gender-role expectations and sex-typed skills, both of which are responsible for differences in men's and women's social behavior [4]

Social Support   the perception that others are responsive and receptive to one's needs [SPIA1]

Sociobiology   the application of evolutionary theory to social behavior [11]

Source Monitoring   the process whereby people try to identify the source of their memories [SPIA3]

Split Cable Market Tests   techniques used to test the effectiveness of advertising, whereby advertisers, in conjunction with cable television companies and grocery stores, show a commercial to a randomly selected group of people and then see whether these people are more likely to buy the product than those who did not see the commercial are [7]

Stability   information that indicates whether the cause of the success (or failure) is an enduring characteristic or one that changes or disappears over time [4]

Stable Attribution   the belief that the cause of an event is due to factors that will not change over time (e.g., your intelligence), as opposed to unstable factors that will change over time (e.g., the amount of effort you put into a task) [SPIA1]

Stereotype   a generalization about a group of people in which identical characteristics are assigned to virtually all members of the group, regardless of actual variation among the members [13]

Stereotype Threat   the apprehension experienced by members of a minority group that they might behave in a manner that confirms an existing cultural stereotype [13]

Storage   the process by which people store in memory information they have acquired from the environment [SPIA3]

Stress   the negative feelings and beliefs that occur whenever people feel they cannot cope with demands from their environment [SPIA1]

Subjective Norms   people's beliefs about how those they care about will view the behavior in question [7]

Subliminal Messages   words or pictures that are not consciously perceived but that supposedly influence people's judgments, attitudes, and behaviors [7]

Subtyping Model   information inconsistent with a stereotype that leads to the creation of a new substereotype to accommodate the information without changing the initial stereotype [13]

Systematic Observation   a form of the observational method whereby the observer is a trained social scientist who sets out to answer questions about a particular social phenomenon by observing and coding it according to a prearranged set of criteria [2]

Target-Based Expectancies   expectations about a person based on his or her past actions, such as expecting someone to go to the beach on vacation because he or she has always gone to the beach in the past [4]

Task-Contingent Rewards   rewards that are given for performing a task, regardless of how well we do that task [5]

Task-Oriented Leader   a leader who is concerned more with getting the job done than with the feelings of and relationships between the workers [9]

Taxonomy of Success and Failure Attributions   the types of internal and external attributions we can make about a person's performance, for example, success or failure [4]

Testosterone   a hormone associated with aggression [12]

Thanatos   according to Freud, an instinctual drive toward death, leading to aggressive actions [12]

Theory of Planned Behavior   a theory holding that the best predictors of a person's planned, deliberate behaviors are the person's attitudes toward specific behaviors, subjective norms, and perceived behavior control [7]

Thought Suppression   the attempt to avoid thinking about something we would just as soon forget [3]

Tit-for-Tat Strategy   a means of encouraging cooperation by at first acting cooperatively but then always responding the way your opponent did (cooperatively or competitively) on the previous trial [9]

Triangular Theory of Love   the idea that different kinds of love consist of varying degrees of three components: intimacy, passion, and commitment [10]

Two-Factor Theory of Emotion   the idea that emotional experience is the result of a two-step self-perception process in which people first experience physiological arousal and then seek an appropriate explanation for it [5]

Two-Step Process of Attribution   when people analyze another person's behavior, they typically make an internal attribution automatically (the first step in the process); they may then consciously choose to engage in the effortful, second step in the process, where they think about possible situational reasons for the behavior; after engaging in the second step, they may adjust their original internal attribution to take into account situational factors [4]

Type A versus B Personality   a personality typology based on how people typically confront challenges in their lives; the Type A person is typically competitive, impatient, hostile, and control-oriented, whereas the Type B person is typically patient, relaxed, and noncompetitive [SPIA1]

Ultimate Attribution Error   our tendency to make dispositional attributions about an entire group of people [13]

Unrealistic Optimism   a form of defensive attribution wherein people think that good things are more likely to happen to them than to their peers and that bad things are less likely to happen to them than to their peers [4]

Upward Social Comparison   the process whereby we compare ourselves to people who are better than we are on a particular trait or ability [5]

Urban-Overload Hypothesis   the theory that people living in cities are constantly being bombarded with stimulation and that they keep to themselves in order to avoid being overloaded by it [11]

Yale Attitude Change Approach   the study of the conditions under which people are most likely to change their attitudes in response to persuasive messages; researchers in this tradition focus on "who said what to whom"—that is, on the source of the communication, the nature of the communication, and the nature of the audience [7]

Zero-Sum Conflict   conflict in which one side's gain is always the other side's loss, as in athletic contests [9]

REFERENCES

Aaker, D. A., & Myers, J. G. (1987). *Advertising management.* Englewood Cliffs, NJ: Prentice Hall.

Abelson, R. P. (1976). Script processing in attitude formation and decision making. In J. S. Carroll & J. W. Payne (Eds.), *Cognition and social behavior* (pp. 13–32). Hillsdale, NJ: Erlbaum.

Abelson, R. P., Kinder, D. R., Peters, M. D., & Fiske, S. T. (1982). Affective and semantic components in political person perception. *Journal of Personality and Social Psychology, 42,* 619–630.

Abraham, M. M., & Lodish, L. M. (1990). Getting the most out of advertising and promotion. *Harvard Business Review, 68,* 50–60.

Abrams, D., Wetherell, M., Cochrane, S., Hogg, M.A., & Turner, J. C. (1990). Knowing what to think by knowing who you are: Self-categorization and the nature of norm formation, conformity, and group polarization. *British Journal of Social Psychology, 29,* 97–119.

Abramson, L. Y., Seligman, M. E. P., & Teasdale, J. D. (1978). Learned helplessness in humans: Critique and reformulation. *Journal of Abnormal Psychology, 87,* 49–74.

Acitelli, L. K. (1992). Gender differences in relationship awareness and marital satisfaction among young married couples. *Personality and Social Psychology Bulletin, 18,* 102–110.

Acitelli, L. K., & Duck, S. W. (1987). Intimacy as the proverbial elephant. In D. Perlman and S. W. Duck (Eds.), *Intimate relationships: Development, dynamics, and deterioration* (pp. 297–308). Beverly Hills, CA: Sage.

Adler, J. (1997, Spring/Summer). It's a wise father who knows . . . *Newsweek,* p. 73.

Adler, S. J. (1994). *The jury: Trial and error in the American courtroom.* New York: Times Books.

Adorno, T. W., Frenkel-Brunswick, E., Levinson, D. J., & Sanford, R. N. (1950). *The authoritarian personality.* New York: Harper & Row.

Agnoli, F. (1991). Development of judgmental heuristics and logical reasoning: Training counteracts the representativeness heuristic. *Cognitive development, 6,* 195–217.

Aiello, J. R., Thompson, D. E., & Brodzinsky, D. M. (1983). How funny is crowding anyway? Effects of room size, group size, and the introduction of humor. *Basic and Applied Social Psychology, 4,* 193–207.

Ainsworth, M. D. S., Blehar, M. C., Waters, E., & Wall, S. (1978). *Patterns of attachment: A psychological study of the strange situation.* Hillsdale, NJ: Erlbaum.

Ajzen, I. (1985). From intentions to actions: A theory of planned behavior. In J. Kuhl & J. Beckmann (Eds.), *Action-control: From cognition to behavior* (pp. 11–39). Heidelberg, Germany: Springer.

Ajzen, I. (1996). The directive influence of attitudes on behavior. In P. M. Gollwitzer & J. A. Bargh (Eds.), *The psychology of action: Linking cognition and motivation to behavior* (pp. 385–403). New York: Guilford.

Ajzen, I., & Fishbein, M. (1980). *Understanding attitudes and predicting social behavior.* Englewood Cliffs, NJ: Prentice Hall.

Akehurst, L., Kohnken, G., Vrij, A., & Bull, R. (1996). Lay persons' and police officers' beliefs regarding deceptive behaviour. *Applied Cognitive Psychology, 10,* 461–471.

Akert, R. M. (1993). *The effect of autobiographical memories on the current definition of self.* Unpublished manuscript, Wellesley College.

Akert, R. M. (1998). *Terminating romantic relationships: The role of personal responsibility and gender.* Unpublished manuscript, Wellesley College.

Akert, R. M., Chen, J., & Panter, A. T. (1991). *Facial prominence and stereotypes: The incidence and meaning of faceism in print and television media.* Unpublished manuscript, Wellesley College.

Akert, R. M., & Panter, A. T. (1988). Extraversion and the ability to decode nonverbal communication. *Personality and Individual Differences, 9,* 965–972.

Albright, L., & Forziati, C. (1995). Cross-situational consistency and perceptual accuracy in leadership. *Personality and Social Psychology Bulletin, 21,* 1269–1276.

Albright, L., Malloy, T. E., Dong, Q., Kenny, D. A., Fang, X., Winquist, L., & Yu, D. (1997). Cross-cultural consensus in personality judgments. *Journal of Personality and Social Psychology, 72,* 558–569.

Aldag, R. J., & Fuller, S. R. (1993). Beyond fiasco: A reappraisal of the groupthink phenomenon and a new model of group decision processes. *Psychological Bulletin, 113,* 533–552.

Alford, A. (1995, July 10). Earning a few extra bucks by learning. *Houston Chronicle,* p. A13.

Allen, M. (1991). Meta-analysis comparing the persuasiveness of one-sided and two-sided messages. *Western Journal of Speech Communication, 55,* 390–404.

Allen, M., Hale, J., Mongeau, P., Berkowits-Stafford, S., Stafford, S., Shanahan, W., Agee, P., Dillon, K., Jackson, R., & Ray, C. (1990). Testing a model of message sidedness: Three replications. *Communication Mongraphs, 57,* 274–291.

Allen, V. L. (1965). Situational factors in conformity. In L. Berkowitz (Ed.), *Advances in experimental social psychology* (Vol. 2, pp. 133–175). New York: Academic Press.

Allen, V. L., & Levine, J. M. (1969). Consensus and conformity. *Journal of Personality and Social Psychology, 5,* 389–399.

Allison, P. D. (1992). The cultural evolution of beneficent norms. *Social Forces, 71,* 279–301.

Allison, S. T., & Beggan, J. K. (1994). Estimating popular support for group decision outcomes: An anchoring and adjustment model. *Journal of Social Behavior and Personality, 9,* 617–638.

Allison, S. T., Beggan, J. K., & Midgley, E. H. (1996). The quest for "similar instances" and "simultaneous possibilities": Metaphors in social dilemma research. *Journal of Personality and Social Psychology, 71,* 479–497.

Allison, S. T., Mackie, D. M., Muller, M. M., & Worth, L. T. (1993). Sequential correspondence biases and perceptions of change: The Castro studies revisited. *Personality and Social Psychology Bulletin, 19,* 151–157.

Alloy, L. B., & Abramson, L. Y. (1988). Depressive realism: Four theoretical perspectives. In L. B. Alloy (Ed.), *Cognitive processes in depression* (pp. 223–265). New York: Guilford Press.

Alloy, L. B., Abramson, L. Y., & Viscusi, D. (1981). Induced mood and the illusion of control. *Journal of Personality and Social Psychology, 41,* 1129–1140.

Alloy, L. B., & Tabachnik, N. (1984). Assessment of covariation by humans and animals: The joint influence of prior expectations and current situational information. *Psychological Review, 91,* 112–149.

Allport, G. (1954). *The nature of prejudice.* Reading, MA: Addison-Wesley.

Allport, G. W. (1985). The historical background of social psychology. In G. Lindzey & E. Aronson (Eds.), *The handbook of social psychology* (Vol. 1, pp. 1–46). Reading, MA: Addison-Wesley.

Alvaro, E. M., & Crano, W. D. (1997). Indirect minority influence: Evidence for leniency in source evaluation and counterargumentation. *Journal of Personality and Social Psychology, 72,* 949–964.

Amabile, T. M. (1983). Brilliant but cruel: Perceptions of negative evaluators. *Journal of Experimental Social Psychology, 19,* 146–156.

Amabile, T. M., Hennessey, B. A., & Grossman, B. S. (1986). Social influences on creativity: The effects of contracted-for reward. *Journal of Personality and Social Psychology, 50,* 14–23.

Amato, P. R. (1983). Helping behavior in urban and rural environments: Field studies based on a taxonomic organization of helping episodes. *Journal of Personality and Social Psychology, 45,* 571–586.

Ambady, N., & Rosenthal, R. (1992). Thin slices of expressive behavior as predictors of interpersonal consequences: A meta-analysis. *Psychological Bulletin, 111,* 256–274.

Ambady, N., & Rosenthal, R. (1993). Half a minute: Predicting teacher evaluations from thin slices of nonverbal behavior and physical attractiveness. *Journal of Personality and Social Psychology, 64,* 431–441.

American Psychological Association. (1992). Ethical principles of psychologists and code of conduct. *American Psychologist, 47,* 1597–1611.

Amir, I. (1969). Contact hypothesis in ethnic relations. *Psychological Bulletin, 71,* 319–342.

Amir, Y. (1976). The role of intergroup contact in change of prejudice and ethnic relations. In P. Katz (Ed.), *Towards the elimination of racism.* New York: Pergamon Press.

Andersen, B. L., & Cyranowski, J. M. (1994). Women's sexual self-schema. *Journal of Personality and Social Psychology, 67,* 1079–1100.

Andersen, S. M. (1984). Self-knowledge and social inference: II. The diagnosticity of cognitive/affective and behavioral data. *Journal of Personality and Social Psychology, 46,* 294–307.

Andersen, S. M., & Bem, S. L. (1981). Sex typing and androgyny in dyadic interaction: Individual differences in responsiveness to physical attractiveness. *Journal of Personality and Social Psychology, 41,* 74–86.

Andersen, S. M., & Klatzky, R. L. (1987). Traits and social stereotypes: Levels of categorization in person perception. *Journal of Personality and Social Psychology, 53,* 235–246.

Andersen, S. M., & Ross, L. D. (1984). Self-knowledge and social inference: I. The impact of cognitive/affective and behavioral data. *Journal of Personality and Social Psychology, 46,* 280–293.

Anderson, C., Anderson, B., & Denser, W. (1996). Examining an affective aggression framework: Weapon and temperature effects on aggressive thoughts, affect, and attitudes. *Personality and Social Psychology Bulletin, 22,* 366–376.

Anderson, C. A. (1995). Implicit personality theories and empirical data: Biased assimilation, belief perseverance and change, and covariation detection sensitivity. *Social Cognition, 13,* 25–48.

Anderson, C. A., & Anderson, D. C. (1984). Ambient temperature and violent crime: Tests of the linear and curvilinear hypotheses. *Journal of Personality and Social Psychology, 46,* 91–97.

Anderson, C. A., & Bushman, B. J. (1997). External validity of "trivial" experiments: The case of laboratory aggression. *Review of General Psychology, 1,* 19–41.

Anderson, C. A., Lepper, M. R., & Ross, L. (1980). The perseverance of social theories: The role of explanation in the persistence of discredited information. *Journal of Personality and Social Psychology, 39,* 1037–1049.

Anderson, C. A., & Sechler, E. S. (1986). Effects of explanation and counterexplanation on the development and use of social theories. *Journal of Personality and Social Psychology, 50,* 24–34.

Anderson, C. A., & Sedikides, C. (1990). Thinking about people: Contributions of a typological alternative to associationistic and dimensional models of person perception. *Journal of Personality and Social Psychology, 60,* 203–217.

Anderson, J. L., Crawford, C. B., Nadeau, J., & Lindberg, T. (1992). Was the Duchess of Windsor right? A cross-cultural review of the socioecology of ideals of female body shape. *Ethology and Sociobiology, 13,* 197–227.

Ann Landers, Dear (1991, September 10). *Boston Globe,* p. 52.

Anthony, T., Cooper, C., & Mullen, B. (1992). Cross-racial facial identification: A social cognitive interpretation. *Personality and Social Psychology Bulletin, 18,* 296–301.

Archer, D. (1991). "A World of Gestures: Culture and Nonverbal Communication" (Videotape and manual). Berkeley, CA: University of California Extension Media Center.

Archer, D. (1994). American violence: How high and why? *Law Studies,* Albany: New York State Bar Association, *19ü* 12–20.

Archer, D. (1997a). "A World of Differences: Understanding cross-cultural communication" (Videotape and manual). Berkeley, CA: University of California Extension Center for Media and Independent Learning.

Archer, D. (1997b). Unspoken diversity: Cultural differences in gestures. *Qualitative Sociology, 20,* 79–105.

Archer, D., & Akert, R. M. (1977a, October). How well do you read body language? *Psychology Today,* pp. 68–69, 72, 119–120.

Archer, D., & Akert, R. M. (1977b). Words and everything else: Verbal and nonverbal cues in social interaction. *Journal of Personality and Social Psychology, 35,* 443–449.

Archer, D., & Akert, R. M. (1980). The encoding of meaning: A test of three theories of social interaction. *Sociological Inquiry, 50*(3–4), 393–419.

Archer, D., & Akert, R. M. (1984). Problems of context and criterion in nonverbal communication: A new look at the accuracy issue. In M. Cook (Ed.), *Issues in person perception* (pp. 114–144). London and New York: Methuen.

Archer, D., & Akert, R. M. (in press). *The Interpretation of Behavior: Verbal and Nonverbal Factors in Person Perception.* New York: Cambridge University Press.

Archer, D., & Gartner, R. (1976). Violent acts and violent times: A comparative approach to postwar homicide rates. *American Sociological Review, 41,* 937–963.

Archer, D., & Gartner, R. (1984). *Violence and crime in cross-national perspective.* New Haven, CT: Yale University Press.

Archer, D., Iritani, B., Kimes, D. D., & Barrios, M. (1983). Faceism: Five studies of sex differences in facial prominence. *Journal of Personality and Social Psychology, 45,* 725–735.

Archer, D., & McDaniel, P. (1995). Violence and gender: Differences and similarities across societies. In R. B. Ruback & N. A. Weiner (Eds.), *Interpersonal violent behaviors: social and cultural aspects* (pp. 63–88). New York: Springer Publishing.

Arendt, H. (1965). *Eichmann in Jerusalem: A report on the banality of evil.* New York: Viking.

Argyle, M. (1975). *Bodily communication.* New York: International Universities Press.

Arkes, H. R. (1991). Costs and benefits of judgment errors: Implications for debiasing. *Psychological Bulletin, 110,* 486–498.

Arkin, R. M., & Baumgardner, A. H. (1985). Self-handicapping. In J. H. Harvey & G. Weary (Eds.), *Basic issues in attribution theory and research* (pp. 169–202). New York: Academic Press.

Arkin, R. M., & Maruyama, G. M. (1979). Attribution, affect, and college exam performance. *Journal of Educational Psychology, 71,* 85–93.

Arkin, R. M., & Shepperd, J. A. (1990). Strategic self-presentation: An overview. In M. J. Cody & M. L. McLaughlin (Eds.), *The psychology of tactical communication: Monographs in social psychology of language* (Vol. 2, pp. 175–193). Clevedon, England: Multilingual Matters.

Armor, D. A., & Taylor, S. E. (in press). Situated optimism: Specific outcome expectancies and self-regulation. In M. P. Zanna (Ed.), *Advances in experimental social psychology* (Vol. 30). New York: Academic Press.

Arms, R. L., Russell, G. W., & Sandilands, M. L. (1979). Effects on the hostility of spectators of viewing aggressive sports. *Social Psychology Quarterly, 42,* 275–279.

Arnett, J. (1995). The young and the reckless: Adolescent reckless behavior. *Current Directions in Psychological Science, 4,* (June), 67–71.

Arnold, D. W., & Greenberg, C. J. (1980). Deviate rejection within differentially manned groups. *Social Psychology Quarterly, 43,* 419–424.

Aron, A., & Aron, E. N. (1996). Self and self-expansion in relationships. In G. J. O. Fletcher & J. Fitness (Eds.), *Knowledge Structures in Close Relationships: A Social Psychological Approach* (pp.325–344). Mahwah, NJ: Erlbaum.

Aron, A., Aron, E. N., & Smollan, D. (1990). The Inclusion of Other in the Self (IOS) scale and the structure of interpersonal closeness. *Journal of Personality and Social Psychology, 63,* 596–612.

Aron, A., Dutton, D. G., Aron, E. A., & Iverson, A. (1989). Experiences of falling in love. *Journal of Social and Personal Relationships, 6,* 243–257.

Aron, A., & Rodriguez, G. (1992). Scenarios of falling in love among Mexican, Chinese, and Anglo-Americans. In A. Aron (Chair), *Ethnic and cultural differences in love.* Symposium conducted at the Sixth International Conference on Personal Relationships, Orono, ME.

Aron, A., & Westbay, L. (1996). Dimensions of the prototype of love. *Journal of Personality and Social Psychology, 70,* 535–551.

Aronson, E. (1968). Dissonance theory:Progress and problems. In R. P. Abelson, E. Aronson, W. J. McGuire, T. M. Newcomb, M. J. Rosenberg, and P. H. Tannenbaum (Eds.), *Theories of Cognitive Consistency:A Sourcebook* (pp. 5–27). Chicago:Rand McNally.

Aronson, E. (1969). The theory of cognitive dissonance: A current perspective. In L. Berkowitz (Ed.), *Advances in experimental social psychology* (Vol. 4, pp. 1–34). New York: Academic Press.

Aronson, E. (1978). *The jigsaw classroom.* Beverly Hills, CA:Sage.

Aronson, E. (1990). Applying social psychology to prejudice reduction and energy conservation. *Personality and Social Psychology Bulletin, 16,* 118–132.

Aronson, E. (1992). Stateways can change folkways. In R. Baird & S. Rosenbaum (Eds.), *Bigotry, prejudice and hatred: Definitions, causes and solutions.* Buffalo, NY: Prometheus Books.

Aronson, E. (1992a). *The social animal.* New York: Freeman.

Aronson, E. (1992b). The return of the repressed: Dissonance theory makes a comeback. *Psychological Inquiry, 3,* 303–311.

Aronson, E. (1997). The giving away of psychology—and condoms. *APS Observer, 10,* 17–35.

Aronson, E. (1997). The theory of cognitive dissonance: The evolution and vicissitudes of an idea. In C. McGarty & S. Alexander Haslam (Eds.), *The message of social psychology: Perspectives on mind in society* (pp. 20–35). Oxford, England: Blackwell Publishers, Inc.

Aronson, E. (1998). Dissonance, hypocrisy, and the self-concept. In E. Harmon-Jones & J. S. Mills, *Cognitive dissonance theory: Revival with revisions and controversies.* Washington, DC: American Psychological Association.

Aronson, E., & Bridgeman, D. (1979). Jigsaw groups and the desegregated classroom: In pursuit of common goals. *Personality and Social Psychology Bulletin, 5,* 438–446.

Aronson, E., & Carlsmith, J. M. (1962). Performance expectancy as a determinant of actual performance. *Journal of Abnormal and Social Psychology, 65,* 178–182.

Aronson, E., & Carlsmith, J. M. (1963). Effect of severity of threat in the devaluation of forbidden behavior. *Journal of Abnormal and Social Psychology, 66,* 584–588.

Aronson, E., & Carlsmith, J. M. (1968). Experimentation in social psychology. In G. Lindzey & E. Aronson (Eds.), *The handbook of social psychology* (Vol. 2, pp. 1 79). Reading, MA: Addison-Wesley.

Aronson, E., Chase, T., Helmreich, R., & Ruhnke, R. (1974). A two-factor theory of dissonance reduction: The effect of feeling stupid or feeling awful on opinion change. *International Journal for Research and Communication, 3,* 59–74.

Aronson, E., Ellsworth, P., Carlsmith, J. M., & Gonzales, M. (1989). *Methods of research in social psychology* (2nd ed.) New York: McGraw-Hill.

Aronson, E., Fried, C., & Stone, J. (1991). Overcoming denial and increasing the intention to use condoms through the induction of hypocrisy. *American Journal of Public Health, 81,* 1636–1638.

Aronson, E., & Gonzalez, A. (1988). Desegregation, jigsaw, and the Mexican-American experience. In P. A. Katz & D. Taylor (Eds.), *Towards the elimination of racism: Profiles in controversy.* New York: Plenum.

Aronson, E., & Gonzales, M. (1990). The social psychology of energy conservation. In J. Edwards (Ed.), *Social influence processes and prevention.* New York: Plenum.

Aronson, E., & Linder, D. (1965). Gain and loss of esteem as determinants of interpersonal attractiveness. *Journal of Experimental Social Psychology, 1,* 156–171.

Aronson, E., & Mettee, D. (1968). Dishonest behavior as a function of differential levels of induced self-esteem. *Journal of Personality and Social Psychology, 9,* 121–127.

Aronson, E., & Mills, J. (1959). The effect of severity of initiation on liking for a group. *Journal of Abnormal and Social Psychology, 59,* 177–181.

Aronson, E., & Patnoe, S. (1997). *Cooperation in the classroom: The jigsaw method.* New York: Longman.

Aronson, E., Stephan, C., Sikes, J., Blaney, N., & Snapp, M. (1978). *The jigsaw classroom.* Beverly Hills, CA: Sage.

Aronson, E., & Thibodeau, R. (1992). The jigsaw classroom: A cooperative strategy for reducing prejudice. In J. Lynch, C. Modgil, & S. Modgil (Eds.), *Cultural diversity in the schools.* London: Falmer Press.

Aronson, E., Wilson, T. D., & Brewer, M. (1998). Experimental methods. In D. Gilbert, S. Fiske, & G. Lindzey (Eds.), *The handbook of social psychology* (4th ed., Vol. 1, pp. 99–142). New York: Random House.

Aronson, E., & Worchel, P. (1966). Similarity versus liking as determinants of interpersonal attractiveness. *Psychonomic Science, 5,* 157–158.

Aronson, E., & Yates, S. (1985). Social psychological aspects of energy conservation. In D. Hafemeister, H. Kelly, & B. Levi, (Eds.), *Energy sources: Conservation and renewables* (pp. 81–91). New York: American Institute of Physics Press.

Aronson, J., Blanton, H., & Cooper, J. (1995). From dissonance to disidentification: Selectivity in the self-affirmation process. *Journal of Personality and Social Psychology, 58,* 1062–1072.

Aronson, J., Cohen, J., & Nail, P. (1998). Self-affirmation theory: An update and appraisal. In E. Harmon-Jones & J. S. Mills, *Cognitive dissonance theory: Revival with revisions and controversies.* Washington, DC: American Psychological Association.

Aronson, J., Quinn, D., & Spencer, S. (1997). Stereotype threat and the academic underperformance of women and minorities. In J. Swim & C. Stangor (Eds.), *Stigma: The target's perspective.* New York: Academic Press.

Aronson, J. M., & Jones, E. E., (1992). Inferring abilities after influencing performance. *Journal of Experimental Social Psychology, 28,* 277–299.

Asch, S. E. (1951). Effects of group pressure upon the modification and distortion of judgment. In H. Guetzkow (Ed.), *Groups, leadership, and men.* Pittsburgh, PA: Carnegie Press.

Asch, S. E. (1955). Opinions and social pressure. *Scientific American, 193,* 31–35.

Asch, S. E. (1956). Studies of independence and conformity: A minority of one against a unanimous majority. *Psychological Monographs, 70* (9, Whole No. 416).

Asch, S. E. (1957). An experimental investigation of group influence. In *Symposium on preventive and social psychiatry* (pp. 15–17). Walter Reed Army Institute of Research. Washington, DC: U.S. Government Printing Office.

Asch, S. E. (1959). A perspective on social psychology. In S. Koch (Ed.), *Psychology: A study of science* (Vol. 3, pp. 363–383). New York: McGraw-Hill.

Asendorf, J. (1987). Videotape reconstruction of emotions and cognitions related to shyness. *Journal of Personality and Social Psychology, 53,* 542–549.

Ashmore, R. D., & DelBoca, F. K. (1976). Psychological approaches to understanding intergroup conflict. In P. A. Katz (Ed.), *Towards the elimination of racism.* Elmsford, NY: Pergamon Press.

Ashmore, R. D., & Longo, L. C. (1995). Accuracy of stereotypes: What research on physical attractiveness can teach us. In Y.-T. Lee, L. J. Jussim, & C. R. McCauley (Eds.), *Stereotype accuracy: Toward appreciating group difference* (pp. 63–86). Washington, DC: American Psychological Association.

Ashmore, R. D., Solomon, M. R., & Longo, L. C. (1996). Thinking about fashion models' looks: A multidimensional approach to the structure of perceived physical attractiveness. *Personality and Social Psychology Bulletin, 22,* 1083–1104.

Aspinwall, L. G., & Taylor, S. E. (1993). Effects of social comparison direction, threat, and self-esteem on affect, evaluation, and expected success. *Journal of Personality and Social Psychology, 64,* 708–722.

Aspinwall, L. G., & Taylor, S. E. (1997). A stitch in time: Self-regulation and proactive coping. *Psychological Bulletin, 121,* 417–436.

Attridge, M. & Berscheid, E. (1994). Entitlement in romantic relationships in the United States: A social exchange perspective. In M. J. Lerner & G. Mikula (Eds.), *Entitlement and the affectional bond: justice in close relationships* (pp. 117–148). New York: Plenum.

Aube, J., & Koestner, R. (1995). Gender characteristics and relationship adjustment: Another look at similarity-complementarity hypotheses. *Journal of Personality, 63,* 879–904.

Averill, J. R. (1973). Personal control over aversive stimuli and its relationship to stress. *Psychological Bulletin, 80,* 286–303.

Axelrod, R. (1984). *The evolution of cooperation.* New York: Basic Books.

Axsom, D. (1989). Cognitive dissonance and behavior change in psychotherapy. *Journal of Experimental Social Psychology, 25,* 234–252.

Ayres, I. (1991). Fair driving: Gender and race discrimination in retail car negotiations. *Harvard Law Review, 104,* 817–872.

Azrin, N. H. (1967, May). Pain and aggression. *Psychology Today,* pp. 27–33.

Babad, E. (1993). Pygmalion—25 years after interpersonal expectations in the classroom. In P. D. Blank (Ed.), *Interpersonal expectations: Theory, research, and applications* (pp. 125–153). New York: Cambridge University Press.

Bahrick, H. P., Hall, L. K., & Berger, S. A. (1996). Accuracy and distortion in memory for high school grades. *Psychological Science, 7,* 265–271.

Bailey, W. C., & Peterson, R. D. (1997). Murder, capital punishment, and deterrence: A review of the literature. In H. A. Bedau, *The death penalty in America: Current controversies* (pp. 135–161). New York: Oxford University Press.

Baker, S. M., & Petty, R. E. (1994). Majority and minority influence: Source-position imbalance as a determinant of message scrutiny. *Journal of Personality and Social Psychology, 67,* 5–19.

Baldwin, M. W., Carrell, S. E., & Lopez, D. F. (1990). Priming relationship schemas: My advisor and the pope are watching me from the back of my mind. *Journal of Experimental Social Psychology, 26,* 435–454.

Banaji, M. R., & Prentice, D. A. (1984). The self in social contexts. *Annual Review of Psychology, 45,* 297–332.

Bandura, A. (1973). *Aggression: A social learning analysis.* Englewood Cliffs, NJ: Prentice Hall.

Bandura, A. (1986). *Social foundations of thought and action.* Englewood Cliffs, NJ: Prentice Hall.

Bandura, A. (1997). *Self-efficacy: The exercise of control.* New York: Freeman.

Bandura, A., Cioffi, D., Taylor, C. B., Gauthier, J., & Gossard, D. (1987). Perceived self-efficacy in coping with cognitive stressors and opioid activation. *Journal of Personality and Social Psychology, 55,* 563–571.

Bandura, A., Ross, D., & Ross, S. (1961). Transmission of aggression through imitation of aggressive models. *Journal of Abnormal and Social Psychology, 63,* 575–582.

Bandura, A., Ross, D., & Ross, S. (1963). Imitation of film-mediated aggressive models. *Journal of Abnormal and Social Psychology, 66,* 3–11.

Banks, T., & Dabbs, J. M., Jr. (1996). Salivary testosterone and cortisol in delinquent and violent urban subculture. *Journal of Social Psychology, 136,* 49–56.

Bar-Tal, D., & Saxe, L. (1976). Perceptions of similarly and dissimilarly attractive couples and individuals. *Journal of Personality and Social Psychology, 33,* 772–781.

Bargh, J., & Barndollar, K. (1996). Automaticity in action: The unconscious as repository of chronic goals and motives. In P. M. Gollwitzer & J. A. Bargh (Eds.), *The psychology of action: Linking cognition and motivation to behavior* (pp. 457–481). New York: Guilford.

Bargh, J. A. (1990). Auto-motives: Preconscious determinants of social interaction. In E. T. Higgins & R. M. Sorrentino (Eds.), *Handbook of motivation and cognition* (Vol. 2, pp. 93–130). New York: Guilford.

Bargh, J. A. (1994). The four horseman of automaticity: Awareness, intention, efficiency, and control in social cognition. In R. S. Wyer, Jr., & T. K. Srull (Eds.), *Handbook of Social Cognition* (Vol. 1, pp. 1–40). Hillsdale, NJ: Erlbaum.

Bargh, J. A. (1996). Automaticity in social psychology. In E. T. Higgins & A. W. Kruglanski (Eds.), *Social psychology: Handbook of basic principles* (pp. 169–183). New York: Guilford.

Bargh, J. A., Chaiken, S., Raymond, P., & Hymes, C. (1996). The automatic evaluation effect: Unconditional automatic attitude activation with a pronunciation task. *Journal of Experimental Social Psychology, 32,* 104–128.

Bargh, J. A., & Pietromonaco, P. (1982). Automatic information processing and social perception: The influence of trait information presented outside of conscious awareness on impression formation. *Journal of Personality and Social Psychology, 43,* 437–449.

Bargh, J. A., & Raymond, P. (1995). The naive misuse of power: Nonconscious sources of sexual harassment. *Journal of Social Issues, 51,* 85–96.

Bargh, J. A., Raymond, P., Pryor, J. B., & Strack, F. (1995). Attractiveness of the underling: An automatic power-sex association and its consequences for sexual harassment and aggression. *Journal of Personality and Social Psychology, 68,* 768–781.

Barker, R., Dembo, T., & Lewin, K. (1941). Frustration and aggression: An experiment with young children. *University of Iowa Studies in Child Welfare, 18,* 1–314.

Barkow, L., Cosmides, L., & Tooby, J. (1992). *The adapted mind: Evolutionary psychology and the generation of culture.* New York: Oxford University Press.

Barley, S. R., & Bechky, B. A. (1994). In the backrooms of science: The work of technicians in science labs. *Work and Occupations, 21,* 85–126.

Baron, J. (1997). The illusion of morality as self-interest: A reason to cooperate in social dilemmas. *Psychological Science, 8,* 330–335.

Baron, L., & Straus, M. A. (1984). Sexual stratification, pornography, and rape. In N. M. Malamuth & E. Donnerstein (Eds.), *Pornography and sexual aggression* (pp. 186–209). New York: Academic Press.

Baron, R., & Rodin, J. (1978). Personal control as a mediator of crowding. In A. Baum, J. S. Singer, & S. Valins (Eds.), *Advances in environmental psychology* (Vol. 1, pp. 145–190). Hillsdale, NJ: Erlbaum.

Baron, R. A. (1972). Reducing the influence of an aggressive model: The restraining effects of peer censure. *Journal of Experimental Social Psychology, 8,* 266–275.

Baron, R. A. (1976). The reduction of human aggression: A field study on the influence of incompatible responses. *Journal of Applied Social Psychology, 6,* 95–104.

Baron, R. A. (1988). Negative effects of destructive criticism: Impact on conflict, self-efficacy, and task performance. *Journal of Applied Psychology, 73,* 199–207.

Baron, R. A. (1990). Countering the effects of destructive criticism: The relative efficacy of four interventions. *Journal of Applied Psychology, 75,* 235–245.

Baron, R. A. (1997). The sweet smell of . . . helping: Effects of pleasant ambient fragrance on prosocial behavior in shopping malls. *Personality and Social Psychology Bulletin, 23,* 498–503.

Baron, R. A., & Richardson, D. R. (1994). *Human aggression* (2nd ed.). New York: Plenum.

Baron, R. S. (1986). Distraction/conflict theory: Progress and problems. In L. Berkowitz (Ed.), *Advances in experimental social psychology* (Vol. 19, pp. 1–40). Orlando, FL: Academic Press.

Baron, R. S., Inman, M., Kao, C., & Logan, H. (1992). Emotion and superficial social processing. *Motivation and Emotion, 16,* 323–345.

Baron, R. S., Vandello, J. A., & Brunsman, B. (1996). The forgotten variable in conformity research: Impact of task importance on social influence. *Journal of Personality and Social Psychology, 71,* 915–927.

Bartlett, D. C. (1932). *Remembering.* Cambridge: Cambridge University Press.

Bass, B. M. (1990). *Bass and Stogdill's handbook of leadership: Theory, research, and managerial applications* (3rd ed.). New York: Free Press.

Bass, B. M. (1997). Does the transactional-transformational leadership paradigm transcend organizational and national boundaries? *American Psychologist, 52,* 130–139.

Bass, E., & Davis, L. (1994). *The courage to heal: A guide for women survivors of child sexual abuse* (3rd ed.). New York: HarperCollins.

Bastien, D., & Hostager, T. (1988). Jazz as a process of organizational innovation. *Communication Research, 15,* 582–602.

Basu, J. E. (1989, August). Why no one's safe: Effects of smog on residents in Los Angeles Basin. *American Health,* 64.

Batson, C. D. (1991). *The altruism question: Toward a social-psychological answer.* Hillsdale, NJ: Erlbaum.

Batson, C. D. (1993). Communal and exchange relationships: What's the difference? *Personality and Social Psychology Bulletin, 19,* 677–683.

Batson, C. D. (1998). Altruism and prosocial behavior. In D. Gilbert, S. Fiske, & G. Lindzey (Eds.), *The handbook of social psychology* (4th ed., Vol. 2, pp. 282–316). New York: McGraw-Hill.

Batson, C. D., Batson, J. G., Griffit, C. A., Barrientos, S., Brandt, J. R., Sprengelmeyer, P., & Bayly, M. J. (1989). Negative-state relief and the empathy-altruism hypothesis. *Journal of Personality and Social Psychology, 56,* 922–933.

Batson, C. D., Bolen, M. H., Cross, J. A., & Neuringer-Benefiel, H. E. (1986). Where is the altruism in the altruistic personality? *Journal of Personality and Social Psychology, 50,* 212–220.

Batson, C. D., Coke, J. S., Jasnoski, M. L., & Hanson, M. (1978). Buying kindness: Effect of an extrinsic incentive for helping on perceived altruism. *Personality and Social Psychology Bulletin, 4,* 86–91.

Batson, C. D., Duncan, B. D., Ackerman, P., Buckley, T., & Birch, K. (1981). Is empathic emotion a source of altruistic motivation? *Journal of Personality and Social Psychology, 40,* 290–302.

Batson, C. D., Dyck, J. L., Brandt, J. R., Batson, J. G., Powell, A. L., McMaster, M. R., & Griffit, C. (1988). Five studies testing two new egoistic alternatives to the empathy-altruism hypothesis. *Journal of Personality and Social Psychology, 55,* 52–77.

Batson, C. D., & Shaw, L. L. (1991). Evidence for altruism: Toward a pluralism of prosocial motives. *Psychological Inquiry, 2,* 107–122.

Batson, C. D., & Weeks, J. L. (1996). Mood effects of unsuccessful helping: Another test of the empathy-altruism hypothesis. *Personality and Social Psychology Bulletin, 22,* 148–157.

Batson, C. D., Sympson, S. C., Hindman, J. L., Decruz, P., Todd, R. M., Weeks, J. L., Jennings, G., & Burris, C. T. (1996). "I've been there, too": Effect on empathy of prior experience with need. *Personality and Social Psychology Bulletin, 22,* 474–482.

Battle for your brain. (1991, August). *Consumer Reports,* pp. 520–521.

Baum, A., & Valins, S. (1977). *Architecture and social behavior: Psychological studies of social density.* Hillsdale, NJ: Erlbaum.

Baum, A., & Valins, S. (1979). Architectural mediation of residential density and control: Crowding and the regulation of social contract. In L. Berkowitz (Ed.), *Advances in experimental social psychology* (Vol. 12, pp. 131–175). New York: Academic Press.

Baumeister, R. (1987). How the self became a problem: A psychological review of historical research. *Journal of Personality and Social Psychology, 52,* 163–176.

Baumeister, R. (Ed.) (1993). *Self-esteem: The puzzle of low self-regard.* New York: Plenum.

Baumeister, R. F. (1991). *Escaping the self: Alcoholism, spirituality, masochism, and other flights from the burden of selfhood.* New York: Basic Books.

Baumeister, R. F. (1998). The self. In D. T. Gilbert, S. T. Fiske, & G. Lindzey (Eds.), *The handbook of social psychology* (4th ed., Vol. 1, pp. 680–740). New York: McGraw-Hill.

Baumeister, R. F., & Leary, M. R. (1995). The need to belong: Desire for interpersonal attachment as a fundamental human motivation. *Psychological Bulletin, 117,* 497–529.

Baumeister, R. F., & Sommer, K.L. (1997). What do men want? Gender differences and two spheres of belongingness: Comment on Cross and Madson (1997*). Psychological Bulletin, 122,* 38–44.

Baumeister, R. F., Stillwell, A. M., & Heatherton, T. F. (1994). Guilt: An interpersonal approach. *Psychological Bulletin, 115,* 243–267.

Baumgardner, A. H., Lake, E. A., & Arkin, R. M. (1985). Claiming mood as a self-handicap. *Personality and Social Psychology Bulletin, 11,* 349–357.

Baxter, L. (1986). Gender differences in the heterosexual relationship rules embedded in break-up accounts. *Journal of Social and Personal Relationships, 3,* 289–306.

Baxter, L. (1988). A dialectical perspective on communication strategies in relationship development. In S. W. Duck, D. F. Hay, S. E. Hobfoll, W. Ickes, & B. M. Montgomery (Eds.), *Handbook of personal relationships: Theory, research and interventions* (pp. 257–273). New York: Wiley.

Baxter, L. (1990) Dialectical contradictions in relationship development. *Journal of Social and Personal Relationships, 7,* 69–88.

Baxter, L. A. (1993). The social side of personal relationships: A dialectical perspective. In S. W. Duck (Ed.), *Social contexts of relationships* (Understanding relationship processes series, Vol. 3, pp. 139–165). Newbury Park, CA: Sage.

Baxter, L. A. (1994). A dialogic approach to relationship maintenance. In D. J. Canary & L. Stafford (Eds.), *Communication and Relational Maintenance* (pp. 233–254). New York: Academic Press.

Bazerman, M., & Neale, M. (1992). *Negotiating rationally.* New York: Free Press.

Beach, S., Tesser, A., Mendolia, M., & Anderson, P. (1996). Self-evaluation maintenance in marriage: Toward a performance ecology of the marital relationship. *Journal of Family Psychology, 10,* 379–396.

Beach, S. R. H., & Tesser, A. (1995). Self-esteem and the extended self-evaluation maintenance model. In M. H. Kernis (Ed.), *Efficacy, agency, and self-esteem* (pp. 145–170). New York: Plenum.

Beall, A. E., & Sternberg, R. J. (1995). The social construction of love. *Journal of Social and Personal Relationships, 12,* 417–438.

Beaman, A. L., Barnes, P. J., Klentz, B., & McQuirk, B. (1978). Increasing helping rates through informational dissemination: Teaching pays *Personality and Social Psychology Bulletin, 4,* 406–411.

Beaman, A. L., Klentz, B., Diener, E., & Svanum, S. (1979). Objective self-awareness and transgression in children: A field study. *Journal of Personality and Social Psychology, 37,* 1835–1846.

Beauvois, J., & Joule, R. (1993). Dissonance reduction and causal explanation in a forced compliance situation. *European Journal of Social Psychology, 23,* 103–107.

Beauvois, J., & Joule, R. (1996). *A Radical Dissonance Theory.* London: Taylor & Francis.

Beauvois, J., & Joule, R. (1998). A radical point of view on dissonance theory. In E. Harmon-Jones, & J. S. Mills, *Cognitive dissonance theory: Revival with revisions and controversies.* Washington, DC: American Psychological Association.

Becker, B. J. (1986). Influence again: Another look at studies of gender differences in social influence. In J. S. Hyde & M. C. Linn (Eds.), *The psychology of gender: Advances through meta-analysis* (pp. 178–209). Baltimore, MD: Johns Hopkins University Press.

Becker, M. H., & Josephs, J. G. (1988). AIDS and behavioral change to reduce risk: A review. *American Journal of Public Health, 78,* 394–410.

Bedau, H. A. (Ed.) (1997). *The death penalty in America: Current controversies.* New York: Oxford University Press.

Belansky, E. S., & Boggiano, A. K. (1994). Predicting helping behaviors: The role of gender and instrumental/expressive self-schemata. *Sex Roles, 30,* 647–661.

Bell, J. (1995). Notions of love and romance among the Taita of Kenya. In W. Jankowiak (Ed.), *Romantic Passion: A Universal Experience?* (pp. 152–165). New York: Columbia University Press.

Bell, P. A. (1980). Effects of heat, noise, and provocation on retaliatory evaluative behavior. *Journal of Social Psychology, 110,* 97–100.

Bell, S. T., Kuriloff, P. J., & Lottes, I. (1994). Understanding attributions of blame in stranger rape and date rape situations: An examination of gender, race, identification, and students' social perceptions of rape victims. *Journal of Applied Social Psychology, 24,* 1719–1734.

Belli, R. F. (1989). Influences of misleading postevent information: Misinformation interference and acceptance. *Journal of Experimental Psychology: General, 118,* 72–85.

Bem, D. J. (1967). Self-perception: An alternative interpretation of cognitive dissonance phenomena. *Psychological Review, 74,* 183–200.

Bem, D. J. (1972). Self-perception theory. In L. Berkowitz (Ed.), *Advances in experimental social psychology* (Vol. 6, pp. 1–62). New York: Academic Press.

Bendtschneider, L., & Duck, S. (1993). What's yours is mine and what's mine is yours: Couple friends. In P. Kalbfleisch (Ed.), *Interpersonal Communication: Evolving Interpersonal Relationships,* (pp. 169–186). Hillsdale, NJ: Erlbaum.

Berger, P. L. (1963). *Invitation to sociology: A humanistic perspective.* Garden City, NY: Anchor Books.

Berger, P. L., & Luckmann, T. (1967). *The social construction of reality: A treatise on the sociology of knowledge.* Garden City, NY: Anchor Books.

Berglas, S., & Jones, E. E. (1978). Drug choice as a self-handicapping strategy in response to noncontingent success. *Journal of Personality and Social Psychology, 36,* 405–417.

Berk, R., Campbell, A., Klap, R., & Western, B. (1992). The deterrent effect of arrest in incidents of domestic violence: A Bayesian analysis of four field experiments. *American Sociological Review, 57,* 698–708.

Berk, R., Fenstermaker, S., & Newton, P. (1988). An empirical analysis of police responses to incidents of wife battery. In G. Hotaling, D. Finkelhor, J. Kirkpatrick, & M. Straus (Eds.), *Coping with family violence: Research and policy perspectives,* (pp. 158–168). Newbury Park, CA: Sage.

Berkman, L. F., & Syme, S. L. (1979). Social networks, host resistance, and mortality: A nine-year follow-up study of Alameda County residents. *American Journal of Epidemiology, 109,* 186–204.

Berkow, J. H. (1989). *Darwin, sex, and status: Biological approaches to mind and culture.* Toronto: University of Toronto Press.

Berkowitz, L. (1962). *Aggression: A social psychological analysis.* New York: McGraw-Hill.

Berkowitz, L. (1968, September). Impulse, aggression, and the gun. *Psychology Today,* pp. 18–22.

Berkowitz, L. (1971). *Control of aggression.* Unpublished manuscript, University of Wisconsin.

Berkowitz, L. (1973, September). The case for bottling up rage. *Psychology Today,* pp. 24–31.

Berkowitz, L. (1978). Whatever happened to the frustration-aggression hypothesis? *American Behavioral Scientist, 21,* 691–708.

Berkowitz, L. (1981, June). How guns control us. *Psychology Today,* pp. 11–12.

Berkowitz, L. (1983). Aversively simulated aggression. *American Psychologist, 38,* 1135–1144.

Berkowitz, L. (1987). Mood, self-awareness, and willingness to help. *Journal of Personality and Social Psychology, 52,* 721–729.

Berkowitz, L. (1988). Frustrations, appraisals, and aversively stimulated aggression. *Aggressive Behavior, 14,* 3–11.

Berkowitz, L. (1989). Frustration-aggression hypothesis: Examination and reformulation. *Psychological Bulletin, 106,* 59–73.

Berkowitz, L. (1993). *Aggression.* New York: McGraw-Hill.

Berkowitz, L., & Frodi, A. (1979). Reactions to a child's mistakes as affected by her/his looks and speech. *Social Psychology Quarterly, 42,* 420–425.

Berkowitz, L., & Green, J. A. (1962). The stimulus qualities of the scapegoat. *Journal of Abnormal and Social Psychology, 64,* 293–301.

Berkowitz, L., & LePage, A. (1967). Weapons as aggression-eliciting stimuli. *Journal of Personality and Social Psychology, 7,* 202–207.

Berkowitz, L., & Troccoli, B., (1990). Feelings, direction of attention, and expressed evaluations of others. *Cognition and Emotion, 4,* 305–325.

Berman, J. S., & Kenny, D. A. (1976). Correlational bias in observer ratings. *Journal of Personality and Social Psychology, 34,* 263–273.

Berry, D. S. (1995). Beyond beauty and after affect: An event perception approach to perceiving faces. In R. A. Eder (Ed.), *Craniofacial Anomalies: Psychological Perspectives.* New York: Springer-Verlag.

Berry, D. S., & McArthur, L. Z. (1986). Perceiving character in faces: The impact of age-related craniofacial changes in social perception. *Psychological Bulletin, 100,* 3–18.

Berry, J. W. (1967). Independence and conformity in subsistence-level societies. *Journal of Personality and Social Psychology, 7,* 415–418.

Berscheid, E. (1983). Emotion. In H. H. Kelley, E. Berscheid, A. Christensen, J. H. Harvey, T. L. Huston, G. Levinger, E. McClintock, L. A. Peplau, & D. R. Peterson (Eds.), *Close relationships* (pp. 110–168). New York: Freeman.

Berscheid, E. (1985). Interpersonal attraction. In G. Lindzey & E. Aronson (Eds.), *The handbook of social psychology* (pp. 413–484). New York: McGraw-Hill.

Berscheid, E. (1988). Some comments on love's anatomy: Or, whatever happened to old-fashioned lust? In R. J. Sternberg & M. L. Barnes (Eds.), *The psychology of love* (pp. 359–374). New Haven, CT: Yale University Press.

Berscheid, E. (1994). Interpersonal relationships. *Annual Review of Psychology, 45,* 79–129.

Berscheid, E., Boye, D., & Walster (Hatfield), E. (1968). Retaliation as a means of restoring equity. *Journal of Personality and Social Psychology, 10,* 370–376.

Berscheid, E., & Meyers, S. A. (1996). A social categorical approach to a question about love. *Personal Relationships, 3,* 19–43.

Berscheid, E., & Meyers, S. A. (1997). The language of love: The difference a preposition makes. *Personality and Social Psychology Bulletin, 23,* 347–362.

Berscheid, E., & Peplau, L. A. (1983). The emerging science of relationships. In H. H. Kelley, E. Berscheid, A. Christensen, J. H. Harvey, T. L. Huston, G. Levinger, E. McClintock, L. A. Peplau, & D. R. Peterson (Eds.), *Close relationships* (pp. 1–19). New York: Freeman.

Berscheid, E., & Reis, H. T. (1998). Attraction and close relationships. In D. Gilbert, S. Fiske, & G. Lindzey (Eds.), *The handbook of social psychology* (4th ed., Vol. 2, pp. 193–281). New York: McGraw-Hill.

Berscheid, E., Snyder, M., & Omoto, A. M. (1989). Issues in studying close relationships: Conceptualizing and measuring closeness. In C. Hendrick (Ed.), *Close relationships: Review of personality and social psychology* (Vol. 10, pp. 63–91). Newbury Park, CA: Sage.

Berscheid, E., & Walster (Hatfield), E. (1978). *Interpersonal attraction.* Reading, MA: Addison-Wesley.

Bertenthal, B. I., & Fisher, K. W. (1978). Development of self-recognition in the infant. *Developmental Psychology, 14,* 44–50.

Bickman, L. (1974). The social power of a uniform. *Journal of Applied Social Psychology, 4,* 47–61.

Biehl, M., Matsumoto, D., Ekman, P., Hearn, V., Heider, K., Kudoh, T., & Ton, V. (1997). Matsumoto and Ekman's Japanese and Caucasian facial expressions of emotion (JACFEE): Reliability and cross-national differences. *Journal of Nonverbal Behavior, 21,* 3–21.

Biek, M., Wood, W., Chaiken, S. (1996). Working knowledge, cognitive processing, and attitudes: On the determinants of bias. *Personality and Social Psychology Bulletin, 22,* 547–556.

Billsberry, J. (Ed.) (1996). *The effective manager: Perspectives and illustrations.* London, England: Sage.

Bils, J., & Singer, S. (1996, August 16). Gorilla saves tot in Brookfield ape pit. *Chicago Tribune,* p. 1.

Blanchard, F., Adelman, L., & Cook, S. (1975). Effect of group success and failure upon interpersonal attraction in cooperating interracial groups. *Journal of Personality and Social Psychology, 31,* 1020–1030.

Blank, P. D. (1993). Interpersonal expectations in the courtroom: Studying judges' and juries' behavior. In P. D. Blank (Ed.), *Interpersonal expectations: Theory, research, and applications* (pp. 64–87). New York: Cambridge University Press.

Blank, P. D. (Ed.) (1993). *Interpersonal expectations: Theory, research, and applications.* New York: Cambridge University Press.

Blanton, H., Cooper, J., Skurnik, I., & Aronson, J. (1997). When bad things happen to good feedback: Exacerbating the need for self-justification with self-affirmations. *Personality and Social Psychology Bulletin, 23,* 684–693.

Blaskovich, J., Ginsburg, G. P., & Veach, T. L. (1975). A pluralistic explanation of choice shifts on the risk dimension. *Journal of Personality and Social Psychology, 31,* 422–429.

Blass, T. (1991). Understanding behavior in the Milgram Obedience Experiment. *Journal of Personality and Social Psychology, 60,* 398–413.

Blass, T. (1993). Psychological perspectives on the perpetrators of the Holocaust: The role of situational pressures, personal dispositions, and their interactions. *Holocaust and Genocide Studies, 7,* 30–50.

Blass, T. (1996). Attribution of responsibility and trust in the Milgram obedience experiment. *Journal of Applied Social Psychology, 26,* 1529–1535.

Blau, P. M. (1964). *Exchange and power in social life.* New York: Wiley.

Bless, H., Bohner, G., Schwarz, N., & Strack, F. (1990). Mood and persuasion: A cognitive response analysis. *Personality and Social Psychology Bulletin, 16,* 331–345.

Blittner, M., Goldberg, J., & Merbaum, M. (1978). Cognitive self-control factors in the reduction of smoking behavior. *Behavior Therapy, 9,* 553–561.

Blumberg, H. H. (1994). Bargaining, coalitions, and games. In A. P. Hare, H. H. Blumberg, M. F. Davies, & M. V. Kent (Eds.), *Small group research: A handbook* (pp. 237–257). Norwood, NJ: Ablex.

Bochner, S. (1994). Cross-cultural differences in the self-concept: A test of Hofstede's individualism/collectivism distinction. *Journal of Cross-Cultural Psychology, 25,* 273–283.

Bodenhausen, G. V. (1988). Stereotypic biases in social decision making and memory: Testing process models of stereotype use. *Journal of Personality and Social Psychology, 55,* 726–737.

Bodenhausen, G. V., & Lichenstein, M. (1987). Social stereotypes and information-processing strategies. The impact of task complexity. *Journal of Personality and Social Psychology, 52,* 871–880.

Bodenhausen, G. V., & Wyer, R. (1985). Effects of stereotypes on decision making and information processing strategies. *Journal of Personality and Social Psychology, 48,* 267–282.

Bond, C., DiCandia, C., & McKinnon, J. R. (1988). Response to violence in a psychiatric setting. *Personality and Social Psychology Bulletin, 14,* 448–458.

Bond, C. F., Atoum, A. O., & VanLeeuwen, M. D. (1996). Social impairment of complex learning in the wake of public embarrassment. *Basic and Applied Social Psychology, 18,* 31–44.

Bond, C. F., & Titus, L. J. (1983). Social facilitation: A meta-analysis of 241 studies. *Psychological Bulletin, 94,* 264–292.

Bond, M. (1991). Chinese values and health: A culture-level examination. *Psychology and Health, 5,* 137–152.

Bond, M. H. (Ed.). (1988). *The cross-cultural challenge to social psychology.* Newbury Park, CA: Sage.

Bond, R., & Smith, P. B. (1996). Culture and conformity: A meta-analysis of studies using Asch's (1952b, 1956) Line Judgment task. *Psychological Bulletin, 119,* 111–137.

Bonora, D., & Huteau, M. (1991). L'efficience comparée des garçons et des filles en mathematiques. *Orientation Scolaire et Professionnelle, 20,* 269–290.

Bonta, B. D. (1997). Cooperation and competition in peaceful societies. *Psychological Bulletin, 121,* 299–320.

Borgida, E., & Howard-Pitney, B. (1983). Personal involvement and the robustness of perceptual salience effects. *Journal of Personality and Social Psychology, 45,* 560–570.

Bornstein, R. F. (1989). Exposure and affect: Overview and meta-analysis of research, 1968–1987. *Psychological Bulletin, 106,* 265–289.

Bornstein, R. F., & D'Agostino, P. R. (1992). Stimulus recognition and the mere exposure effect. *Journal of Personality and Social Psychology, 63,* 545–552.

Bornstein, R. F., Leone, D. R., & Galley, D. J. (1987). The generalizability of subliminal mere exposure effects: Influence of stimuli perceived without awareness on social behavior. *Journal of Personality and Social Psychology, 53,* 1070–1079.

Bornstein, R. F., & Pittman, T. S. (Eds.). (1992). *Perception without awareness: Cognitive, clinical, and social perspectives.* New York: Guilford.

Bossard, J. H. S. (1932). Residential propinquity as a factor in marriage selection. *American Journal of Sociology, 38,* 219–224.

Bothwell, R. K., Brigham, J. C., & Malpass, R. S. (1989). Cross-racial identification. *Personality and Social Psychology Bulletin, 15,* 19–26.

Bothwell, R. K., Deffenbacher, K. A., & Brigham, J. C. (1987). Correlation of eyewitness accuracy and confidence: Optimality hypothesis revisited. *Journal of Applied Psychology, 72,* 691–695.

Bouas, K. S., & Komorita, S. S. (1996). Group discussion and cooperation in social dilemmas. *Personality and Social Psychology Bulletin, 22,* 1144–1150.

Bouchard, T. J., Barsaloux, J., & Drauden, G. (1974). Brainstorming procedure, group size, and sex as determinants of the problem-solving effectiveness of groups and individuals. *Journal of Applied Psychology, 59,* 135–138.

Bower, G. H., & Hilgard, E. R. (1981). *Theories of learning* (15th ed.). Englewood Cliffs, NJ: Prentice Hall.

Bowlby, J. (1969). *Attachment and loss: Vol. 1. Attachment.* New York: Basic Books.

Bowlby, J. (1973). *Attachment and loss: Vol. 2. Separation: Anxiety and anger.* New York: Basic Books.

Bowlby, J. (1980). *Attachment and loss: Vol. 3. Loss.* New York: Basic Books.

Boyden, T., Carroll, J. S., & Maier, R. A. (1984). Similarity and attraction in homosexual males: The effects of age and masculinity-femininity. *Sex Roles, 10,* 939–948.

Bragg, R. (1995, August 4). "A killer's only confidant: The man who caught Susan Smith." *New York Times,* p. A10.

Braithwaite, D. O., & Baxter, L. A. (1995). "I do" again: The relational dialectics of renewing marriage vows. *Journal of Social and Personal Relationships, 12,* 177–198.

Brandon, R., & Davies, C. (1973). *Wrongful imprisonment: Mistaken convictions and their consequences.* London: Allen & Unwin.

Brannon, L. A., & Brock, T. C. (1994). The subliminal persuasion controversy. In S. Shavitt & T. C. Brock (Eds.), *Persuasion: Psychological insights and perspectives* (pp. 279–293). Boston: Allyn & Bacon.

Branscombe, N. R., Owen, S., Garstka, T. A., & Coleman, J. (1996). Rape and accident counterfactuals: Who might have done otherwise and would it have changed the outcome? *Journal of Applied Social Psychology, 26,* 1042–1067.

Bransford, J. D., & Johnson, M. K. (1973). Considerations of some problems of comprehension. In W. G. Chase (Ed.), *Visual information processing* (pp. 383–438). New York: Academic Press.

Brattesani, K. A., Weinstein, R. S., & Marshall, H. H. (1984). Student perceptions of differential teacher treatment as moderators of teacher expectation effects. *Journal of Educational Psychology, 76,* 236–247.

Breckler, S. J. (1984). Empirical validation of affect, behavior, and cognition as distinct components of attitude. *Journal of Personality and Social Psychology, 47,* 1191–1205.

Breckler, S. J., & Wiggins, E. C. (1989). On defining attitude and attitude theory: Once more with feeling. In A. R. Pratkanis, S. J. Breckler, & A. G. Greenwald (Eds.), *Attitude structure and function* (pp. 407–427). Hillsdale, NJ: Erlbaum.

Brehm, J. W. (1956). Postdecision changes in the desirability of alternatives. *Journal of Abnormal and Social Psychology, 52,* 384–389.

Brehm, J. W. (1966). *A theory of psychological reactance.* New York: Academic Press.

Brehm, J. W., & Cohen, A. R. (1962). *Explorations in cognitive dissonance*. New York: Wiley.

Brehm, S. S. (1992). *Intimate relationships* (2nd ed.). New York: McGraw-Hill.

Brewer, M. B. (1979). In-group bias in the minimal intergroup situation: A cognitive-motivational analysis. *Psychological Bulletin, 86*, 307–324.

Brewer, M. B., & Brown, R. J. (1998). Intergroup relations. In D. Gilbert, S. Fiske, & G. Lindzey (Eds.), *The handbook of social psychology* (4th ed., Vol. 2, pp. 554–594). New York: McGraw-Hill.

Brewer, M. B., & Miller, N. (1984). Beyond the contact hypothesis: Theoretical perspectives on desegregation. In N. Miller & M. B. Brewer (Eds.), *Groups in contact: The psychology of desegregation* (pp. 281–302). New York: Academic Press.

Brigham, J. C. (1980). Limiting conditions of the "physical attractiveness stereotype": Attributions about divorce. *Journal of Research in Personality, 14*, 365–375.

Bringle, R. G. (1981). Conceptualizing jealousy as a disposition. *Alternative Lifestyles, 4*, 274–290.

Brinson, L., & Robinson, E. (1991). The African-American athlete: A psychological perspective. In L. Diamant (Ed.), *Psychology of sports, exercise, and fitness* (pp. 249–259). New York: Hemisphere.

Brislin, R. (1993). *Understanding culture's influence on behavior*. Fort Worth, TX: Harcourt Brace.

Brock, T. C., Edelman, S., Edwards, S., & Schuck, J. (1965). Seven studies of performance expectancy as a determinant of actual performance. *Journal of Experimental Social Psychology, 1*, 295–310.

Brod, M. I., & Hall, S. M. (1984). Joiners and nonjoiners in smoking treatment: A comparison of psychosocial variables. *Addictive Behaviors, 9*, 217–221.

Brophy, J. E. (1983). Research on the self-fulfilling prophecy and teacher expectations. *Journal of Educational Psychology, 75*, 631–661.

Brothers flush with excitement over restroom advertising. (1997, August 31). *The Daily Progress*, p. B5.

Brown, A., & Campione, J. (1994). Guided discovery in a community of learners. In K. McGilly (Ed.), *Classroom lessons: Integrating cognitive theory and classroom practice* (pp. 229–270). Cambridge: MIT Press.

Brown, J. D. (1990). Evaluating one's abilities: Shortcuts and stumbling blocks on the road to self-knowledge. *Journal of Experimental Social Psychology, 26*, 149–167.

Brown, J. D., & Rogers, R. J. (1991). Self-serving attributions: The role of physiological arousal. *Personality and Social Psychology Bulletin, 17*, 501–506.

Brown, R. (1965). *Social psychology*. New York: Free Press.

Brown, R. (1986). *Social psychology: The second edition*. New York: Free Press.

Browning, D. L. (1983). Aspects of authoritarian attitudes in ego development. *Journal of Personality and Social Psychology, 45*, 137–144.

Bruch, H. (1973). *Eating disorders*. New York: Basic Books.

Bruch, H. (1978). *The golden cage*. Cambridge, MA: Harvard University Press.

Brunstein, J., & Gollwitzer, P. (1996). Effects of failure on subsequent performance: The importance of self-defining goals. *Journal of Personality and Social Psychology, 70*, 395–407.

Buck, R. (1984). *The communication of emotion*. New York: Guilford Press.

Buckhout, R. (1974). Eyewitness testimony. *Scientific American, 231*, 23–31.

Buehler, R., & Griffin, D. (1994). Change-of-meaning effects in conformity and dissent: Observing construal processes over time. *Journal of Personality and Social Psychology, 67*, 984–996.

Bui, K-V. T., Peplau, L. A., & Hill, C. T. (1996). Testing the Rusbult Model of relationship committment and stability in a 15-year study of hetereosexual couples. *Personality and Social Psychology Bulletin, 22*, 1244–1257.

Burger, J. M. (1981). Motivational biases in the attribution of responsibility for an accident: A meta-analysis of the defensive-attribution hypothesis. *Psychological Bulletin, 90*, 496–512.

Burger, J. M. (1986). Increasing compliance by improving the deal: The that's-not-all technique. *Journal of Personality and Social Psychology, 51*, 277–283.

Burger, J. M. (1991). Changes in attributions over time: The ephemeral fundamental attribution error. *Social Cognition, 9*, 182–193.

Burger, J. M. (1992). *Desire for control: Personality, social, and clinical perspectives*. New York: Plenum.

Burgoon, M. (1993). Interpersonal expectations, expectancy violations, and emotional communication. *Journal of Language and Social Psychology, 12*, 30–48.

Burhans, K. K., & Dweck, C. S. (1995). Helplessness in early childhood: The role of contingent worth. *Child Development, 66*, 1719–1738.

Burke, R.J., & Greenglass, E. R. (1990). Type A Behavior and non-work activities. *Personality and Individual Differences, 11*, 945–952.

Burns, J. M. (1978). *Leadership*. New York: Harper Torchbooks.

Burnstein, E., Crandall, C., & Kitayama, S. (1994). Some neo-Darwinian decision rules for altruism: Weighing cues for inclusive fitness as a function of the biological importance of the decision. *Journal of Personality and Social Psychology, 67*, 773–789.

Burnstein, E., & Sentis, K. (1981). Attitude polarization in groups. In R. E. Petty, T. M. Ostrom, & T. C. Brock (Eds.), *Cognitive responses in persuasion* (pp. 197–216). Hillsdale, NJ: Erlbaum

Burnstein, E., & Vinokur, A. (1977). Persuasive argumentation and social comparison as determinants of attitude polarization. *Journal of Experimental Social Psychology, 13*, 315–332.

Burnstein, E., & Worchel, P. (1962). Arbitrariness of frustration and its consequences for aggression in a social situation. *Journal of Personality, 30*, 528–540.

Burr, W. R. (1973). *Theory construction and the sociology of the family*. New York: Wiley.

Burt, M. R. (1980). Cultural myths and supports for rape. *Journal of Personality and Social Psychology, 38*, 217–230.

Busby, L. J. (1975). Defining the sex-role standard in commercial network television programming directed at children. *Journalism Quarterly, 51*, 690–696.

Buss, D. (1994). *The evolution of desire*. New York: Basic Books.

Buss, D. (1995). Evolutionary psychology: A new paradigm for psychological science. *Psychological Inquiry, 1995, 6*, 1–30.

Buss, D. (1996). Sexual conflict: Evolutionary insights into feminism and the "battle of the sexes." In D. Buss & N. Malamuth (Eds.), *Sex, power, conflict: Evolutionary and feminist perspectives* (pp. 296–318). New York: Oxford University Press.

Buss, D. (1996). The evolutionary psychology of human social strategies. In E. T. Higgins & A. W. Kruglanski (Eds.), *Social psychology: Handbook of basic principles* (pp. 3–38). New York: Guilford.

Buss, D. M. (1985). Human mate selection. *American Scientist, 73*, 47–51.

Buss, D. M. (1988a). The evolution of human intrasexual competition. *Journal of Personality and Social Psychology, 54*, 616–628.

Buss, D. M. (1988b). Love acts: The evolutionary biology of love. In R. J. Sternberg & M. L. Barnes (Eds.), *The psychology of love* (pp. 110–118). New Haven, CT: Yale University Press.

Buss, D. M. (1989). Sex differences in human mate preferences: Evolutionary hypotheses tested in 37 cultures. *Behavioral and Brain Sciences, 12,* 1–49.

Buss, D. M., Abbott, M., Angleitner, Aerian, A., Biaggio, A., Blanco-Villasenor, A., Bruchon-Schweitzer, M., Ch'U, H., Czapinski, J., Deraad, B., Ekehammar, B., El Lohamy, N., Fioravanti, M., Georgas, J., Gjerde, P., Guttman, R., Hazan, F., Iwawaki, S., Janakiramaiah, N., Khosroshani, F., Kreitler, S., Lachenicht, L., Lee, M., Liik, K., Little, B., Mika, S., Moadel-Shahid, M., Moane, G., Montero, M., Mundy-Castle, A. C., Niit, T., Nsenduluka, E., Pienkowski, R., Pirttila-Backman, A., Ponce de Leon, J., Rousseau, J., Runco, M., Safir, M. P., Samuels, C., Sanitioso, R., Serpell, R., Smid, N., Spencer, C., Tadinac, M., Todorova, E. N., Troland, K., Van Den Brande, L., Van Heck, G., Van Langenhove, L., & Yang, K. (1990). International preferences in selecting mates: A study of 37 cultures. *Journal of Cross-Cultural Psychology, 21,* 5–47.

Buss, D. M., & Barnes, M. (1986). Preferences in human mate selection. *Journal of Personality and Social Psychology, 50,* 559–570.

Buss, D. M., & Kenrick, D. T. (1998). Evolutionary social psychology. In D. Gilbert, S. Fiske, & G. Lindzey (Eds.), *The handbook of social psychology* (4th ed., Vol. 2, pp. 982–1026). New York: Random House.

Buss, D. M., Larsen, R. J., Westen, D., & Semmelroth, J. (1992). Sex differences in jealousy: Evolution, physiology, and psychology. *Psychological Science, 3,* 251–255.

Buss, D. M., & Schmitt, D. P. (1993). Sexual strategies theory: An evolutionary perspective on human mating. *Psychological Bulletin, 100,* 204–232.

Butler, D., & Geis, F. L. (1990). Nonverbal affect responses to male and female leaders: Implications for leadership evaluations. *Journal of Personality and Social Psychology, 58,* 48–59.

Buunk, B. (1982). Anticipated sexual jealousy: Its relationship to self-esteem, dependency, and reciprocity. *Personality and Social Psychology Bulletin, 8,* 310–316.

Buunk, B., & Hupka, R. B. (1987). Cross-cultural differences in the elicitation of sexual jealousy. *Journal of Sex Research, 23,* 12–22.

Buunk, B. P., & Van Yperen, N. W. (1991). Referential comparisons, relational comparisons, and exchange orientation: Their relation to marital satisfaction. *Personality and Social Psychology Bulletin, 17,* 709–717.

Buzbee, S. S. (1995, March 3). "Earn to Learn" pays children to read. *Cavalier Daily,* p. 4.

Bybee, J., Luthar, S., Zigler, E., & Merisca, R. (1997). The fantasy, ideal, and ought selves: Content, relationship to mental health, and functions. *Social Cognition, 15,* 37–53.

Byrne, D. (1961). Interpersonal attraction and attitude similarity. *Journal of Abnormal and Social Psychology, 62,* 713–715.

Byrne, D. (1971). *The attraction paradigm.* New York: Academic Press.

Byrne, D., & Clore, G. L. (1970). A reinforcement model of evaluative processes. *Personality: An International Journal, 1,* 103–128.

Byrne, D., Clore, G. L., & Smeaton, G. (1986). The attraction hypothesis: Do similar attitudes affect anything? *Journal of Personality and Social Psychology, 51,* 1167–1170.

Byrne, D., & Nelson, D. (1965). Attraction as a linear function of positive reinforcement. *Journal of Personality and Social Psychology, 1,* 659–663.

Cacioppo, J. T. (in press). Somatic responses to psychological stress: The reactivity hypothesis. *Advances in Psychological Science.*

Cacioppo, J. T., Berntson, G. G., Malarkey, W. B., Kiecolt-Glaser, J. K., Sheridan, J. F., Poehlmann, K. M., Burleson, M. H., Ernst, J. M., Hawkley, L. C., & Glaser, R. (in press). Autonomic, neuroendocrine, and immune responses to psychological stress: The reactivity hypothesis. *Annals of the New York Academy of Sciences.*

Cacioppo, J. T., Marshall-Goodell, B. S., Tassinary, L. G., & Petty, R. E. (1992). Rudimentary determinants of attitudes: Classical conditioning is more effective when prior knowledge about the attitude stimulus is low than high. *Journal of Experimental Social Psychology, 28,* 207–233.

Cacioppo, J. T., Petty, R. E., Feinstein, J., & Jarvis, B. (1996). Dispositional differences in cognitive motivation: The life and times of individuals low versus high in need for cognition. *Psychological Bulletin, 119,* 197–253.

Cadinu, M. R., & Rothbart, M. (1996). Self-anchoring and differentiation processes in minimal group setting. *Journal of Personality and Social Psychology, 70,* 661–677.

Calder, B. J., & Staw, B. M. (1975). Self-perception of intrinsic and extrinsic motivation. *Journal of Personality and Social Psychology, 31,* 599–605.

Caldwell, M., & Peplau, L. (1982). Sex differences in same-sex friendship. *Sex Roles, 8,* 721–732.

Calhoun, J. B. (1973). Death squared: The explosive growth and demise of a mouse population. *Proceedings of the Royal Society of Medicine, 66,* 80–88.

Callahan, P. (1996, March 4). Bucks for books. *Denver Post,* p. A1.

Calvert, J. D. (1988). Physical attractiveness: A review and reevaluation of its role in social skill research. *Behavioral Assessment, 10,* 29–42.

Campbell, D. T. (1967). Stereotypes and the perception of group differences. *American Psychologist, 22,* 817–829.

Campbell, D. T., & Stanley, J. C. (1967). *Experimental and quasi-experimental designs for research.* Chicago: Rand McNally.

Campbell, E. Q., & Pettigrew, T. F. (1959). Racial and moral crisis: The role of Little Rock ministers. *American Journal of Sociology, 64,* 509–516.

Campbell, J. (1980). Complementarity and attraction: A reconceptualization in terms of dyadic behavior. *Representative Research in Social Psychology, 11,* 74–95.

Campbell, J. D. (1990). Self-esteem and clarity of the self-concept. *Journal of Personality and Social Psychology, 59,* 941–951.

Campbell, J. D., & Fairey, P. J. (1989). Informational and normative routes to conformity: The effect of faction size as a function of norm extremity and attention to the stimulus. *Journal of Personality and Social Psychology, 57,* 457–468.

Campos, J. J., & Sternberg, C. (1981). Perception, appraisal, and emotion: The onset of social referencing. In M. E. Lamb & L. R. Sherrod (Eds.), *Infant social cognition: Empirical and theoretical considerations* (pp. 273–314). Hillsdale, NJ: Erlbaum.

Canary, D. J., & Stafford, L. (1994). Maintaining relationships through strategic and routine interaction. In D. J. Canary & L. Stafford (Eds.), *Communication and Relational Maintenance* (pp. 3–22). New York: Academic Press.

Cannon, W. B. (1942). "Voodoo" death. *American Anthropologist, 44,* 169–181.

Cantor, J. (1994). Confronting children's fright responses to mass media. In D. Zillmann, J. Bryant, & Aletha C. Huston (Eds.), *Media, children, and the family: Social scientific, psychodynamic, and clinical perspectives* (pp. 139–150). Hillsdale, NJ: Erlbaum.

Cantor, N., & Kihlstrom, J. F. (1987). *Personality and social intelligence.* Englewood Cliffs, NJ: Prentice Hall.

Cantril, H. (1940). *The invasion from Mars: A study in the psychology of panic.* New York: Harper & Row.

Carey, K. B., & Carey, M. P. (1993). Chances in self-efficacy resulting from unaided attempts to quit smoking. *Psychology of Addictive Behaviors, 7,* 219–224.

Carlo, G., Eisenberg, N., Troyer, D., Switzer, G., & Speer, A. L. (1991). The altruistic personality: In what contexts is it apparent? *Journal of Personality and Social Psychology, 61,* 450–458.

Carlsmith, J. M., & Anderson, C. A. (1979). Ambient temperature and the occurrence of collective violence: A new analysis. *Journal of Personality and Social Psychology, 37,* 337–344.

Carlson, J., & Davis, D. M. (1971). Cultural values and the risky shift: A cross-cultural test in Uganda and the United States. *Journal of Personality and Social Psychology, 20,* 392–399.

Carlson, M., Charlin, V., & Miller, N. (1988). Positive mood and helping behavior: A test of six hypotheses. *Journal of Personality and Social Psychology, 55,* 211–229.

Carlson, M., & Miller, N. (1987). Explanation of the relationship between negative mood and helping. *Psychological Bulletin, 102,* 91–108.

Carlston, D. E., & Skowronski, J. J. (1994). Savings in the relearning of trait information as evidence of spontaneous inference generation. *Journal of Personality and Social Psychology, 66,* 840–856.

Carlyle, T. (1841). *On heroes, hero-worship, and the heroic in history: Six lectures.* New York: Appleton.

Carnevale, P. J. (1986). Strategic choice in mediation. *Negotiation Journal, 2,* 41–56.

Carretta, T. R., & Moreland, R. L. (1982). Nixon and Watergate: A field demonstration of belief perseverance. *Personality and Social Psychology Bulletin, 6,* 446–453.

Cartwright, D. (1979). Contemporary social psychology in historical perspective. *Social Psychology Quarterly, 42,* 82–93.

Cartwright, D., & Zander, A. (Eds.). (1968). *Group dynamics: Research and theory* (3rd ed.). New York: Harper & Row.

Carver, C. S. (1975). Physical aggression as a function of objective self-awareness and attitudes toward punishment. *Journal of Experimental Social Psychology, 11,* 510–519.

Carver, C. S., DeGregorio, E., & Gillis, R. (1980). Ego-defensive attribution among two categories of observers. *Personality and Social Psychology Bulletin, 6,* 4–50.

Carver, C. S., & Scheier, M. F. (1981). *Attention and self-regulation: A control-theory approach to human behavior.* New York: Springer-Verlag.

Carver, C. S., & Scheier, M. F. (in press). *On the self-regulation of behavior.* New York: Cambridge.

Cash, T. F., & Derlega, V. J. (1978). The matching hypothesis: Physical attractiveness among same-sex friends. *Personality and Social Psychology Bulletin, 4,* 240–243.

Caspi, A., & Harbener, E. S. (1990). Continuity and change: Assortive marriage and the consistency of personality in adulthood. *Journal of Personality and Social Psychology, 58,* 250–258.

Castellan, N. J., Jr. (Ed.) (1993). *Individual and group decision making.* Hillsdale, NJ: Erlbaum.

Cervone, D., & Peake, P. (1986). Anchoring, efficacy, and action: The influence of judgmental heuristics on self-efficacy judgments and behavior. *Journal of Personality and Social Psychology, 50,* 492–501.

Chaiken, S. (1980). Heuristic versus systematic information processing and the use of source versus message cues in persuasion. *Journal of Personality and Social Psychology, 39,* 752–766.

Chaiken, S. (1987). The heuristic model of persuasion. In M. P. Zanna, J. M. Olson, & C. P. Herman (Eds.), *Social influence: The Ontario Symposium* (Vol. 5, pp. 3–39). Hillsdale, NJ: Erlbaum.

Chaiken, S., & Baldwin, M. W. (1981). Affective-cognitive consistency and the effect of salient behavioral information on the self-perception of attitudes. *Journal of Personality and Social Psychology, 41,* 1–12.

Chaiken, S., Liberman, A., & Eagly, A. H. (1989). Heuristic and systematic information processing within and beyond the persuasion context. In J. S. Uleman & J. A. Bargh (Eds.), *Unintended thought* (pp. 212–252). New York: Guilford Press.

Chaiken, S., Wood, W., & Eagly, A. H. (1996). Principles of persuasion. In E. T. Higgins & A. W. Kruglanski (Eds.), *Social psychology: Handbook of basic principles* (pp. 702–742). New York: Guilford.

Chance, J., & Goldstein, A. G. (1996). The other-race effect and eyewitness identification. In S. L. Sporer, R. S. Malpass, & G. Koehnken (Eds.), *Psychological issues in eyewitness identification* (pp. 153–176). Mahwah, NJ: Erlbaum.

Chang, C., & Chen, J. (1995). Effects of different motivation strategies on reducing social loafing. *Chinese Journal of Psychology, 37,* 71–81.

Chapman, G. B., & Bornstein, B. H. (1996). The more you ask for, the more you get: Anchoring in personal injury verdicts. *Applied Cognitive Psychology, 10,* 519–540.

Chapman, L. J. (1967). Illusory correlation in observational report. *Journal of Verbal Learning and Verbal Behavior, 5,* 151–155.

Chapman, L. J., & Chapman, J. P. (1967). Genesis of popular but erroneous psychodiagnostic observations. *Journal of Abnormal Psychology, 72,* 193–204.

Chartrand, T. L., & Bargh, J. A. (1996). Automatic activation of impression formation and memorization goals: Nonconscious goal priming reproduces effects of explicit task instructions. *Journal of Personality & Social Psychology, 71,* 464–478.

Chassin, L., Presson, C. G., & Sherman, S. J. (1990). Social psychological contributions to the understanding and prevention of adolescent cigarette smoking. *Personality and Social Psychology Bulletin, 16,* 133–151.

Cheek, J. M., & Buss, A. H. (1981). Shyness and sociability. *Journal of Personality and Social Psychology, 41,* 330–339.

Cheek, J. M., & Melchoir, L. A. (1990). Shyness, self-esteem, and self-consciousness. In H. Leitenberg (Ed.), *Handbook of social and evaluation anxiety.* New York: Plenum.

Chemers, M. M. (1987). Leadership processes: Intrapersonal, interpersonal, and societal influences. In C. Hendrick (Ed.), *Review of Personality and Social Psychology* (Vol. 8, pp. 252–277). Newbury Park, CA: Sage.

Chemers, M. M., & Ayman, R. (Eds.). (1993). *Leadership theory and research: Perspectives and directions.* San Diego, CA: Academic Press.

Chemers, M. M., Hays, R. G., Rhodewalt, F., & Wysocki, J. (1985). A person-environment analysis of job stress: A contingency model explanation. *Journal of Personality and Social Psychology, 49,* 628–635.

Cheng, P. W., Holyoak, K. J., Nisbett, R. E., & Oliver, L. M. (1986). Pragmatic versus syntactic approaches to training deductive reasoning. *Cognitive Psychology, 18,* 293–328.

Chipman, S. F. (1996). Still far too sexy a topic. *Behavioral and Brain Sciences, 19,* 248–249.

Chiro, P., & Valentine, T. (1995). An investigation of the contact hypothesis of the own-race bias in face recognition. *Quarterly Journal of Experimental Psychology, 48A,* 879–894.

Christensen, L. (1988). Deception in psychological research: When is its use justified? *Personality and Social Psychology Bulletin, 14,* 664–675.

Christian, J. J. (1963). The pathology of overpopulation. *Military Medicine, 128,* 571–603.

Christianson, S. (1992). Emotional stress and eyewitness memory: A critical review. *Psychological Bulletin, 112,* 284–309.

Christophersen, E. R., & Gyulay, J. E. (1981). Parental compliance with car seat usage: A positive approach with long term follow-up. *Journal of Pediatric Psychology, 6,* 301–312.

Church, A. H. (1993). Estimating the effects of incentives on mail survey response rates: A meta-analysis. *Public Opinion Quarterly, 57,* 62–79.

Cialdini, R. B. (1991). Altruism or egoism? That is (still) the question. *Psychological Inquiry, 2,* 124–126.

Cialdini, R. B. (1993). *Influence: Science and practice.* (3rd ed.). New York: HarperCollins.

Cialdini, R. B., Borden, R. J., Thorne, A., Walker, M. R., Freeman, S., & Sloan, L. R. (1976). Basking in reflected glory: Three (football) field studies. *Journal of Personality and Social Psychology, 34,* 366–375.

Cialdini, R. B., Cacioppo, J., Basset, R., & Miller, J. (1978). Low-ball procedure for producing compliance: Commitment then cost. *Journal of Personality and Social Psychology, 36,* 463–476.

Cialdini, R. B., Darby, B. L., & Vincent, J. E. (1973). Transgression and altruism: A case for hedonism. *Journal of Experimental Social Psychology, 9,* 502–516.

Cialdini, R. B., & Fultz, J. (1990). Interpreting the negative mood-helping literature via "mega"-analysis: A contrary view, *Psychological Bulletin, 107,* 210–214.

Cialdini, R. B., Green, B. L., & Rusch, A. J. (1992). When tactical pronouncements of change become real change: The case of reciprocal persuasion. *Journal of Personality and Social Psychology, 63,* 30–40.

Cialdini, R. B., Kallgren, C. A., & Reno, R. R. (1991). A focus theory of normative conduct: A theoretical refinement and reevaluation of the role of norms in human behavior. In M. P. Zanna (Ed.), *Advances in experimental social psychology* (Vol. 24, pp. 201–234). San Diego, CA: Academic Press.

Cialdini, R. B., Reno, R. R., & Kallgren, C. A. (1990). A focus theory of normative conduct: Recycling the concept of norms to reduce littering in public places. *Journal of Personality and Social Psychology, 58,* 1015–1026.

Cialdini, R. B., Schaller, M., Houlihan, D., Arps, K., Fultz, J., & Beaman, A. L. (1987). Empathy-based helping: Is it selflessly or selfishly motivated? *Journal of Personality and Social Psychology, 52,* 749–758.

Cialdini, R. B., & Trost, M. R. (1998). Social influence: Social norms, conformity, and compliance. In D. Gilbert, S. Fiske, & G. Lindzey (Eds.), *The handbook of Social Psychology* (4th ed., Vol. 2, pp. 151–192). New York: McGraw-Hill.

Cialdini, R. B., Trost, M. R., & Newsom, J. T. (1995). Preference for consistency: The development of a valid measure and the discovery of surprising behavioral implications. *Journal of Personality and Social Psychology, 69,* 318–328.

Cialdini, R. B., Vincent, J. E., Lewis, S. K., Catalan, J., Wheeler, D., & Darby, B. L. (1975). Reciprocal concessions procedure for inducing compliance: The door-in-the-face technique. *Journal of Personality and Social Psychology, 31,* 206–215.

Clark, K., & Clark, M. (1947). Racial identification and preference in Negro children. In T. M. Newcomb & E. L. Hartley (Eds.), *Readings in social psychology* (pp. 169–178). New York: Holt.

Clark, M. S. (1984). Record keeping in two types of relationships. *Journal of Personality and Social Psychology, 47,* 549–577.

Clark, M. S. (1986). Evidence of the effectiveness of manipulations of communal and exchange relationships. *Personality and Social Psychology Bulletin, 12,* 414–425.

Clark, M. S., & Chrisman, K. (1994). Resource allocation in intimate relationships: Trying to make sense of a confusing literature. In M. J. Lerner & G. Mikula (Eds.), *Entitlement and the Affectional Bond: Justice in Close Relationships* (pp. 65–88). New York: Plenum.

Clark, M. S., & Isen, A. M. (1982). Toward understanding the relationship between feeling states and social behavior. In A. H. Hastorf & A. M. Isen (Eds.), *Cognitive social psychology* (pp. 73–108). New York: Elsevier.

Clark, M. S., & Mills, J. (1979). Interpersonal attraction in exchange and communal relationships. *Journal of Personality and Social Psychology, 37,* 12–24.

Clark, M. S., & Mills, J. (1993). The difference between communal and exchange relationships: What it is and is not. *Personality and Social Psychology Bulletin, 19,* 684–691.

Clark, M. S., Mills, J., & Corcoran, D. M. (1989). Keeping track of needs and inputs of friends and strangers. *Personality and Social Psychology Bulletin, 15,* 533–542.

Clark, M. S., Ouellette, R., Powell, M. C., & Milberg, S. (1987). Recipient's mood, relationship type, and helping. *Journal of Personality and Social Psychology, 53,* 94–103.

Clark, M. S., & Pataki, S. P. (1995). Interpersonal processes influencing attraction and relationships. In A. Tesser (Ed.), *Advanced Social Psychology* (pp. 282–331). New York: McGraw-Hill.

Clark, M. S., & Waddell, B. (1985). Perception of exploitation in communal and exchange relationships. *Journal of Social and Personal Relationships, 2,* 403–413.

Clark, R. D., III (1994). The role of censorship in minority influence. *European Journal of Social Psychology, 24,* 331–338.

Clark, R. D., III, & Maass, A. (1988). The role of social categori-zation and perceived source credibility in minority influence. *European Journal of Social Psychology, 18,* 347–364.

Clark, R. D., III, & Word, L. E. (1972). Why don't bystanders help? Because of ambiguity? *Journal of Personality and Social Psychology, 24,* 392–400.

Clarke, A. C. (1952). An examination of the operation of residual propinquity as a factor in mate selection. *American Sociological Review, 27,* 17–22.

Clary, E. G., Snyder, M., Ridge, R. D., Miene, P. K., & Haugen, J. A. (1994). Matching messages to motives in persuasion: A functional approach to promoting volunteerism. *Journal of Applied Social Psychology, 24,* 1129–1149.

Clement, M., & Hales, D. (1997, Sept. 7). How healthy are we? *Parade Magazine,* pp. 4–7.

Cline, V. B., Croft, R. G., & Courrier, S. (1973). Desensitization of children to television violence. *Journal of Personality and Social Psychology, 27,* 360–365.

Cochran, S. D., Mays, V. M., Ciarletta, J., Caruso, C., & Mallon, D. (1992). Efficacy of the theory of reasoned action in predicting AIDS-related sexual risk reduction among gay men. *Journal of Applied Social Psychology, 22,* 1481–1501.

Cody, M. J. (1982). A typology of disengagement strategies and an examination of the role intimacy reactions to inequity and relational problems play in strategy selection. *Communication Monographs, 49,* 148–170.

Cohen, A. R. (1962). An experiment on small rewards for discrepant compliance and attitude change. In J. W. Brehm & A. R. Cohen (Eds.), *Explorations in cognitive dissonance* (pp. 73–78). New York: Wiley.

Cohen, C. E. (1981). Person categories and social perception: Testing some boundary conditions of the processing effects of prior knowledge. *Journal of Personality and Social Psychology, 40,* 441–452.

Cohen, C. E. (1983). Inferring the characteristics of other people: Categories and attribute accessibility. *Journal of Personality and Social Psychology, 44,* 34–44.

Cohen, D. (Ed.). (1977). *Psychologists on psychology.* New York: Taplinger.

Cohen, D., & Nisbett, R. E. (1994). Self-protection and the culture of honor: Explaining Southern violence. *Personality and Social Psychology Bulletin, 20,* 551–567.

Cohen, D., Nisbett, R. E., Bowdle, B. F., & Schwarz, N. (1996). Insult, aggression, and the southern culture of honor: An "experimental ethnography." *Journal of Personality and Social Psychology, 70,* 945–960.

Cohen, D. J., Whitmyer, J. W., & Funk, W. H. (1960). Effect of group cohesiveness and training upon group thinking. *Journal of Applied Psychology, 44,* 319–322.

Cohen, L. J. (1981). Can human rationality be experimentally demonstrated? *The Behavioral and Brain Sciences, 4,* 317–370.

Cohen, R. (1997). AH-lo-ween: An American holiday in Paris? *New York Times,* (Oct. 31), p. A1; A4.

Cohen, S. (1978). Environmental load and the allocation of attention. In A. Baum, J. S. Singer, & S. Valins (Eds.), *Advances in environmental psychology* (Vol. 1, pp. 1–29). Hillsdale, NJ: Erlbaum.

Cohen, S. (1996). Psychological stress, immunity, and upper respiratory infections. *Current Directions in Psychological Science, 5,* 86–90.

Cohen, S., Evans, G. W., Krantz, D. S., & Stokols, D. (1980). Physiological, motivational, and cognitive effects of aircraft noise on children. *American Psychologist, 35,* 231–243.

Cohen, S., Evans, G. W., Krantz, D. S., Stokols, D., & Kelly, S. (1981). Aircraft noise and children: Longitudinal and cross-sectional evidence on adaptation to noise and the effectiveness of noise abatement. *Journal of Personality and Social Psychology, 40,* 331–345.

Cohen, S., Frank, E., Doyle, W. J., Skoner, D. P., Rabin, B. S., & Gwaltney, J. M., Jr. (in press). Type of stressors that increase susceptibility to the common cold. *Health Psychology.*

Cohen, S., Glass, D. C., & Singer, J. E. (1973). Apartment noise, auditory discrimination, and reading ability in children. *Journal of Experimental Social Psychology, 9,* 407–422.

Cohen, S., & Herbert, T. B. (1996). Health psychology: Psychological factors and physical disease from the perspective of human psychoneuroimmunology. *Annual Review of Psychology, 47,* 113–142.

Cohen, S., Tyrrell, D. A. J., & Smith, A. P. (1991). Psychological stress in humans and susceptibility to the common cold. *New England Journal of Medicine, 325,* 606–612.

Cohen, S., Tyrrell, D. A. J., & Smith, A. P. (1993). Negative life events, perceived stress, negative affect, and susceptibility to the common cold. *Journal of Personality and Social Psychology, 64,* 131–140.

Cohen, S., & Williamson, G. M. (1991). Stress and infectious disease in humans. *Psychological Bulletin, 109,* 5–24.

Cohen, S., & Wills, T. A. (1985). Stress, social support, and buffering. *Psychological Bulletin, 98,* 310–357.

Cole, B. L. (1991, September 15). I greet each day as a gift. *Parade Magazine,* pp. 20–21.

Colligan, M. J., & Murphy, L. R. (1979). Mass psychogenic illness in organizations: An overview. *Journal of Occupational Psychology, 52,* 77–90.

Colligan, M. J., Pennebaker, J. W., & Murphy, L. R. (Eds.). (1982). *Mass psychogenic illness: A social psychological analysis.* Hillsdale, NJ: Erlbaum.

Collins, B. E., & Brief, D. E. (1995). Using person-perception vignette methodologies to uncover the symbolic meanings of teacher behaviors in the Milgram paradigm. *Journal of Social Issues, 51,* 89–106.

Collins, N. L., & Read, S. J. (1990). Adult attachment, working models, and relationship quality in dating couples. *Journal of Personality and Social Psychology, 58,* 644–663.

Collins, R. L. (1996). For better or worse: The impact of upward social comparison on self-evaluations. *Psychological Bulletin, 119,* 51–69.

Coltrane, S., Archer, D., & Aronson, E. (1986). The social-psychological foundations of successful energy conservation programs. *Energy Policy, 14,* 133–148.

Condon, J. W., & Crano, W. D. (1988). Inferred evaluation and the relation between attitude similarity and interpersonal attraction. *Journal of Personality and Social Psychology, 54,* 789–797.

Conway, M., & Ross, M. (1984). Getting what you want by revising what you had. *Journal of Personality and Social Psychology, 47,* 738–748.

Cook, S. W. (1984). Cooperative interaction in multiethnic contexts. In N. Miller & M. Brewer (Eds.), *Groups in contact: The psychology of desegregation.* New York: Academic Press.

Cook, S. W. (1985). Experimenting on social issues: The case of school desegregation. *American Psychologist, 40,* 452–460.

Cooley, C. H. (1902). *Human nature and social order.* New York: Scribner's.

Cooper, J. (1980). Reducing fears and increasing assertiveness: The role of dissonance reduction. *Journal of Experimental Social Psychology, 47,* 738–748.

Cooper, J. (1998). Unwanted consequences and the self: In search of the motivation for dissonance reduction. In E. Harmon-Jones & J. S. Mills, *Cognitive dissonance theory: Revival with revisions and controversies.* Washington, DC: American Psychological Association.

Cordova, D. I., & Lepper, M. R. (1996). Intrinsic motivation and the process of learning: Beneficial effects of contextualization, personalization, and choice. *Journal of Educational Psychology, 88,* 715–730.

Cosmides, L., & Tooby, J. (1992). Cognitive adaptations for social exchange. In J. H. Barkow, L. Cosmides, & J. Tooby (Eds.), *The adapted mind: Evolutionary psychology and the generation of culture* (pp. 163–228). New York: Oxford University Press.

Cotton, J. L. (1981). *Ambient temperature and violent crime.* Paper presented at the meeting of the Midwestern Psychological Association, Chicago.

Cotton, J. L. (1986). Ambient temperature and violent crime. *Journal of Applied Social Psychology, 16,* 786–801.

Cottrell, N. B. (1968). Performance in the presence of other human beings: Mere presence, audience, and affiliation effects. In E. C. Simmel, R. A. Hoppe, & G. A. Milton (Eds.), *Social facilitation and imitative behavior* (pp. 91–110). Boston: Allyn & Bacon.

Cottrell, N. B., Wack, K. L., Sekerak, G. J., & Rittle, R. (1968). Social facilitation in dominant responses by the presence of an audience and the mere presence of others. *Journal of Personality and Social Psychology, 9,* 245–250.

Cowan, G., & Campbell, R. R. (1994). Racism and sexism in interracial pornography. *Psychology of Women Quarterly, 18,* 323–338.

Crandall, C. S. (1988). Social contagion of binge eating. *Journal of Personality and Social Psychology, 55,* 588–598.

Crandall, C. S., & Greenfield, B. S. (1986). Understanding the conjunction fallacy: A conjunction of effects? *Social Cognition, 4,* 408–419.

Crites, S. L., Jr., Fabrigar, L. R., & Petty, R. E. (1994). Measuring the affective and cognitive properties of attitudes: Conceptual and methodological issues. *Personality and Social Psychology Bulletin, 20,* 619–634.

Crocker, J. (1981). Judgment of covariation by social perceivers. *Psychological Bulletin, 90,* 272–292.

Crocker, J., Hannah, D. B., & Weber, R. (1983). Personal memory and causal attributions. *Journal of Personality and Social Psychology, 44,* 55–56.

Crocker, J., & Major, B. (1989). Social stigma and self-esteem: The self-protective properties of stigma. *Psychological Review, 96,* 608–630.

Crombag, H. F. M., Wagenaar, W. A., & Van Koppen, P. J. (1996). Crashing memories and the problem of "source monitoring." *Applied Cognitive Psychology, 10,* 95–104.

Crosby, F., Bromley, S., & Saxe, L. (1980). Recent unobtrusive studies of black and white discrimination and prejudice: A literature review. *Psychological Bulletin, 87,* 546–563.

Cross, S. E. (1995). Self-construals, coping, and stress in cross-cultural adaptation. *Journal of Cross-Cultural Psychology, 26,* 673–697.

Cross, S. E., & Madson, L. (1997). Models of the self: Self-construals and gender. *Psychological Bulletin, 122,* 5–37.

Crouse, B. B., & Mehrabian, A. (1977). Affiliation of opposite-sexed strangers. *Journal of Research in Personality, 11,* 38–47.

Crowley, A. E., & Hoyer, W. D. (1994). An integrative framework for understanding two-sided persuasion. *Journal of Consumer Research, 20,* 561–574.

Croyle, R., & Cooper, J. (1983). Dissonance arousal: Physiological evidence. *Journal of Personality and Social Psychology, 45,* 782–791.

Croyle, R. T., & Jemmott, J. B., III. (1990). Psychological reactions to risk factor testing. In J. A. Skelton & R. T. Croyle (Eds.), *The mental representation of health and illness* (pp. 121–157). New York: Springer-Verlag.

Crutchfield, R. A. (1955). Conformity and character. *American Psychologist, 10,* 191–198.

Csikszentmihalyi, M. (1975). *Beyond boredom and anxiety.* San Francisco: Jossey-Bass.

Csikszentmihalyi, M. (1979). The concept of flow. In B. Sutton-Smith (Ed.), *Play and learning.* New York: Gardner Press.

Csikszentmihalyi, M. (1988). The flow experience and its significance for human psychology. In M. Csikszentmihalyi & I. S. Csikszentmihalyi (Eds.), *Optimal experience: Psychological studies of flow in consciousness* (pp. 15–35). New York: Cambridge University Press.

Csikszentmihalyi, M., & Figurski, T. J. (1982). Self-awareness and aversive experience in everyday life. *Journal of Personality, 50,* 15–28.

Cunningham, M. R., Roberts, A. R., Barbee, A. P., Druen, P. B., & Wu, C. (1995). "Their ideas of beauty are, on the whole, the same as ours": Consistency and variability in the cross-cultural perception of female physical attractiveness. *Journal of Personality and Social Psychology, 68,* 261–279.

Curtis, R. C., & Miller, K. (1986). Believing another likes or dislikes you: Behaviors making the beliefs come true. *Journal of Personality and Social Psychology, 51,* 284–290.

Curtiss, S. (1977). *Genie: A psycholinguistic study of a modern-day "wild child."* New York: Academic Press.

Cutler, B. L., & Penrod, S. D. (1995). *Mistaken identification: The eyewitness, psychology, and the law.* New York: Cambridge University Press.

Czaczkes, B., & Ganzach, Y. (1996). The natural selection of prediction heuristics: Anchoring and adjustment versus representativeness. *Journal of Behavioral Decision Making, 9,* 125–139.

Dabbs, J. M., Carr, T. S., Frady, R. L., & Riad, J. K. (1995). Testosterone, crime, and misbehavior among 692 male prison inmates. *Personality and Individual Differences, 18,* 627–633.

Dabbs, J. M., Jr., Hargrove, M. F., & Heusel, C. (1996). Testosterone differences among college fraternities: Well-behaved vs. rambunctious. *Personality and Individual Differences, 20,* 157–161.

Dabbs, J. M., Jr., Ruback, R. B., Frady, R. L., Hopper, C. H., & Sgoutas, D. S. (1988). Saliva testosterone and criminal violence among women. *Personality and Individual Differences, 7,* 269–275.

Dalbert, C., & Yamauchi, L. A. (1994). Belief in a just world and attitudes toward immigrants and foreign workers: A cultural comparison between Hawaii and Germany. *Journal of Applied Social Psychology, 24,* 1612–1626.

Dansereau, F., Graen, G., & Haga, W. J. (1975). A vertical dyad linkage approach to leadership within formal organizations: A longitudinal investigation of the role making process. *Organizational Behavior, 13,* 46–78.

Darley, J. M. (1992). Social organization for the production of evil. *Psychological Inquiry, 3,* 199–218.

Darley, J. M. (1995). Constructive and destructive obedience: A taxonomy of principal-agent relationships. *Journal of Social Issues, 51,* 125–154.

Darley, J. M., & Akert, R. M. (1993). *Biographical interpretation: The influence of later events in life on the meaning of and memory for earlier events.* Unpublished manuscript, Princeton University.

Darley, J. M., & Batson, C. D. (1973). From Jerusalem to Jericho: A study of situational and dispositional variables in helping behavior. *Journal of Personality and Social Psychology, 27,* 100–108.

Darley, J. M., & Fazio, R. H. (1980). Expectancy confirmation processes arising in the social interaction sequence. *American Psychologist, 35,* 867–881.

Darley, J. M., & Gilbert, D. T. (1985). Social psychological aspects of environmental psychology. In G. Lindzey & E. Aronson (Eds.), *Handbook of social psychology* (3rd ed., Vol. 2, pp. 949–991). New York: McGraw-Hill.

Darley, J. M., & Gross, P. H. (1983). A hypothesis-confirming bias in labeling effects. *Journal of Personality and Social Psychology, 44,* 20–33.

Darley, J. M., & Latané, B. (1968). Bystander intervention in emergencies: Diffusion of responsibility. *Journal of Personality and Social Psychology, 8,* 377–383.

Darwin, C. (1872). *The expression of emotions in man and animals.* London: John Murray.

Darwin, C. R. (1859). *The origin of species.* London: John Murray.

Davidson, A. R., & Jaccard, J. J. (1979). Variables that moderate the attitude behavior relation: Results of a longitudinal survey. *Journal of Personality and Social Psychology, 37,* 1364–1376.

Davidson, L., & Duberman, L. (1982). Friendship: Communication and interactional patterns in same-sex dyads. *Sex Roles, 8,* 809–822.

Davies, R. (1988). *The lyre of Orpheus.* New York: Penguin Books.

Davis, C. G., & Lehman, D. R. (1995). Counterfactual thinking and coping with traumatic life events. In N. J. Roese & J. M. Olson (Eds.), *What might have been: The social psychology of counterfactual thinking* (pp. 353–374). Mahwah, NJ: Erlbaum.

Davis, C. G., Lehman, D. R., Wortman, C. B., Silver, R. C., & Thompson, S. C. (1995). The undoing of traumatic life events. *Personality and Social Psychology Bulletin, 21,* 109–124.

Davis, D. D., & Harless, D. W. (1996). Group versus individual performance in a price-searching experiment. *Organizational Behavior and Human Decision Processes, 66,* 215–227.

Davis, J. H. (1992). Some compelling intuitions about group consensus decisions, theoretical and empirical research, and interpersonal aggregation phenomena: Selected examples, 1950–1990. *Organizational Behavior and Human Decision Processes, 52,* 3–38.

Davis, J. H. (1996). Small-group research and the Steiner questions: The once and future thing. In E. H. Witte & J. H. Davis (Eds.), *Understanding group behavior: Consensual action by small groups* (Vol. 1, pp. 3–12). Mahwah, NJ: Erlbaum.

Davis, K. E., & Jones, E. E. (1960). Changes in interpersonal perception as a means of reducing cognitive dissonance. *Journal of Abnormal and Social Psychology, 61,* 402–410.

Davis, J. H., Kerr, N. L., Atkin, R. S., Holt, R., & Meek, D. (1975). The decision processes of 6- and 12-person mock juries assigned unanimous and two-thirds majority rules. *Journal of Personality and Social Psychology, 32,* 1–14.

Davis, K. E., Kirpatrick, L. A., Levy, M. B., & O'Hearn, R. E. (1994). Stalking the elusive love style: Attachment styles, love styles, and relationship development. In R. Erber & R. Gilmour (Eds.), *Theoretical Frameworks for Personal Relationships* (pp. 179–210). Hillsdale, NJ: Erlbaum.

Davis, M. H., & Stephan, W. G. (1980). Attributions for exam performance. *Journal of Applied Social Psychology, 10,* 235–248.

Davitz, J. (1952). The effects of previous training on post-frustration behavior. *Journal of Abnormal and Social Psychology, 47,* 309–315.

Dawes, R. M. (1980). Social dilemmas. *Annual Review of Psychology, 31,* 169–193.

Dawes, R. M. (1998). Behavioral decision making and judgment. In D. Gilbert, S. Fiske, & G. Lindzey (Eds.), *The handbook of social psychology* (4th ed., Vol. 1, pp. 497–548). New York: McGraw Hill.

Dawkins, R. (1976). *The selfish gene.* New York: Oxford University Press.

De Houwer, J., Baeyens, F., Eelen, P. (1994). Verbal evaluative conditioning with undetected US presentations. *Behavioral Research and Therapy, 32,* 629–633.

De Houwer, J., Hermans, D., & Eelen, P. (1996). *Affective and identity priming with episodically associated stimuli.* Unpublished manuscript, University of Leuven, Leuven, Belgium.

Deaux, K. (1993). Reconstructing social identity. *Personality and Social Psychology Bulletin, 19,* 4–12.

Deaux, K., & Emsweiler, T. (1974). Explanations of successful performance of sex-linked tasks: What is skill for male is luck for the female. *Journal of Personality and Social Psychology, 29,* 80–85.

Deaux, K., & LaFrance, M. (1998). Gender. In D. T. Gilbert, S. T. Fiske, & G. Lindzey (Eds.), *The handbook of social psychology* (4th ed., Vol. 1, pp. 788–828). New York: McGraw-Hill.

Deaux, K., & Lewis, L. (1984). Structure of gender stereotypes: Interrelationships among components and gender label. *Journal of Personality and Social Psychology, 46,* 991–1004.

Deaux, K., & Major, B. (1987). Putting gender into context: An interactive model of gender-related behavior. *Psychological Review, 94,* 369–389.

Deaux, K., & Taynor, J. (1973). Evaluation of male and female ability: Bias works two ways. *Psychological Reports, 32,* 261–262.

DeBono, K. G., & Snyder, M. (1995). Acting on one's attitudes: The role of a history of choosing situations. *Personality and Social Psychology Bulletin, 21,* 629–636.

Deci, E. L., Eghrari, H., Patrick, B. C., & Leone, D. R. (1994). Facilitating internalization: The self-determination theory perspective. *Journal of Personality, 62,* 119–142.

Deci, E. L., & Flaste, R. (1995). *Why we do what we do: The dynamics of personal autonomy.* New York: G. P. Putnam's Sons.

Deci, E. L., & Ryan, R. M. (1985). *Intrinsic motivation and self-determination in human behavior.* New York: Plenum.

Deffenbacher, K. (1983). The influence of arousal on reliability of testimony. In S. Lloyd-Bostock & B. Clifford (Eds.), *Evaluating witness testimony* (pp. 235–251). London: Wiley.

DeJong, W. (1979). An examination of self-perception mediation of the foot-in-the-door effect. *Journal of Personality and Social Psychology, 37,* 2221–2239.

DeJong, W., & Winsten, J. A. (1989). *Recommendations for future mass media campaigns to prevent preteen and adolescent substance abuse.* Unpublished manuscript, Center for Health Communication, Harvard School of Public Health.

Delany, S. L., & Delany, A. E., with Hearth, A. H. (1993). *Having Our Say: The Delany Sisters' First 100 Years.* New York: Dell Publishing.

Delany, S. L., with Hearth, A. H. (1997). *On My Own at 107: Reflections on Life Without Bessie.* Thorndike, ME: G. K. Hall and Co.

DeMarco, P. (1994, September 28). "Dear diary," *New York Times,* p. C2.

Dennett, D. C. (1991). *Consciousness explained.* Boston: Little, Brown.

DePaulo, B. M. (1983). Perspectives on help-seeking. In B. M. DePaulo, A. Nadler, & J. D. Fisher (Eds.), *New directions in helping: Help seeking* (Vol. 2, pp. 3–12). New York: Academic Press.

DePaulo, B. M. (1992). Nonverbal behavior and self-presentation. *Psychological Bulletin, 111,* 203–243.

DePaulo, B. M. (1994). Spotting lies: Can humans learn to do better? *Current Directions in Psychological Science, 3,* 83–86.

DePaulo, B. M., Epstein, J. A., & Wyer, M. M. (1993). Sex differences in lying: How women and men deal with the dilemma of deceit. In M. Lewis and C. Saarni (Eds.), *Lying and Deception in Everyday Life* (pp. 126–147). New York: Guilford.

DePaulo, B. M., & Friedman, H. S. (1998). Nonverbal communication. In D. Gilbert, S. Fiske, & G. Lindzey (Eds.), *The handbook of social psychology* (4th ed., Vol. 2, pp. 3–40). New York: McGraw Hill.

DePaulo, B. M., Kenny, D. A., Hoover, C. W., Webb, W., & Oliver, P. (1987). Accuracy of person perception: Do people know what kinds of impressions they convey? *Journal of Personality and Social Psychology, 52,* 303–315.

DePaulo, B. M., Lassiter, G. D., & Stone, J. I. (1983). Attentional determinants of success at detecting deception and truth. *Personality and Social Psychology Bulletin, 8,* 273–279.

DePaulo, B. M., & Pfeiffer, R. L. (1986). On-the-job experience and skill at detecting deception. *Journal of Applied Social Psychology, 16,* 249–267.

DePaulo, B. M., & Rosenthal, R. (1979). Telling lies. *Journal of Personality and Social Psychology, 37,* 1713–1722.

DePaulo, B. M., Stone, J. I., & Lassiter, G. D. (1985). Deceiving and detecting deceit. In B. R. Schlenker (Ed.), *The self and social life* (pp. 323–370). New York: McGraw-Hill.

Deppe, R. K., & Harackiewicz, J. M. (1996). Self-handicapping and intrinsic motivation: Buffering intrinsic motivation from the threat of failure. *Journal of Personality and Social Psychology, 70,* 868–876.

Dermer, M., & Thiel, D. L. (1975). When beauty may fail. *Journal of Personality and Social Psychology, 31,* 1168–1176.

Desmond, E. W. (1987, November 30). Out in the open. *Time,* pp. 80–90.

Desportes, J. P., & Lemaine, J. M. (1988). The sizes of human groups: An analysis of their distributions. In D. Canter, J. C. Jesuino, L. Soczka, & G. M. Stephenson (Eds.), *Environmental social psychology* (pp. 57–65). Dordrecht, Netherlands: Kluwer.

Deutsch, F. M., & Lamberti, D. M. (1986). Does social approval increase helping? *Personality and Social Psychology Bulletin, 12,* 149–157.

Deutsch, M. (1973). *The resolution of conflict: Constructive and destructive processes.* New Haven, CT: Yale University Press.

Deutsch, M. (1990). Cooperation, conflict, and justice. In S. A. Wheelan, E. A. Pepitone, & V. Abt (Eds.), *Advances in field theory* (pp. 149–164). Newbury Park, CA: Sage.

Deutsch, M. (1997). Comments on cooperation and prejudice reduction. At the symposium on: Reflections on 100 Years of Social Psychology, April 1997, Yosemite National Park, CA.

Deutsch, M., & Collins, M. E. (1951). *Interracial housing: A psychological evaluation of a social experiment.* Minneapolis: University of Minnesota Press.

Deutsch, M., & Gerard, H. G. (1955). A study of normative and informational social influence upon individual judgment. *Journal of Abnormal and Social Psychology, 51,* 629–636.

Deutsch, M., & Krauss, R. M. (1960). The effect of threat upon interpersonal bargaining. *Journal of Abnormal and Social Psychology, 61,* 181–189.

Deutsch, M., & Krauss, R. M. (1962). Studies of interpersonal bargaining. *Journal of Conflict Resolution, 6,* 52–76.

Devine, P. (1998). Moving beyond attitude change in the study of dissonance-related processes. In E. Harmon-Jones & J. S. Mills, *Cognitive dissonance theory: Revival with revisions and controversies.* Washington, DC: American Psychological Association.

Devine, P., & Elliot, A. (1995). Are racial stereotypes really fading? The Princeton trilogy revisited. *Personality and Social Psychology Bulletin, 21,* 1139–1150.

Devine, P. G. (1989a). Automatic and controlled processes in prejudice: The roles of stereotypes and personal beliefs. In A. R. Pratkanis, S. J. Breckler, & A. G. Greenwald (Eds.), *Attitude structure and function* (pp. 181–212). Hillsdale, NJ: Erlbaum.

Devine, P. G. (1989b). Stereotypes and prejudice: Their automatic and controlled components. *Journal of Personality and Social Psychology, 56,* 5–18.

DeWaal, F. (1996). *Good natured: The origins of right and wrong in humans and other animals.* Cambridge, MA: Harvard University Press.

Dickerson, C., Thibodeau, R., Aronson, E., & Miller, D. (1992). Using cognitive dissonance to encourage water conservation. *Journal of Applied Social Psychology, 22,* 841–854.

Diddling the subconscious: Subliminal advertising. (1957, October 5). *Nation,* p. 206.

Diehl, M., & Stroebe, W. (1987). Productivity loss in brain-storming groups: Toward the solution of a riddle. *Journal of Personality and Social Psychology, 53,* 497–509.

Diener, E. (1980). Deindividuation: The absence of self-awareness and self-regulation in group members. In P. B. Paulus (Ed.), *Psychology of group influence* (pp. 209–242). Hillsdale, NJ: Erlbaum.

Diener, E., & Wallbom, M. (1976). Effects of self-awareness on antinormative behavior. *Journal of Research in Personality, 10,* 107–111.

Dienesch, R. M., & Liden, R. C. (1986). Leader-member exchange model of leadership: A critique and further development. *Academy of Management Review, 11,* 618–634.

Dietz, P. D., & Evans, B. E. (1982). Pornographic imagery and prevalence of paraphilia. *American Journal of Psychiatry, 139,* 1493–1495.

Dijksterhuis, A., & van Knippenberg, A. (1996). The knife that cuts both ways: Facilitated and inhibited access to traits as a result of stereotype activation. *Journal of Experimental Social Psychology, 32,* 271–288.

Dillard, J. P. (1991). The current status of research on sequential-request compliance techniques. *Personality and Social Psychology Bulletin, 17,* 283–288.

Dillard, J. P., Hunter, J. E., & Burgoon, M. (1984). Sequential-request persuasive strategies: Meta-analysis of foot-in-the-door and door-in-the-face. *Human Communications Research, 10,* 461–488.

Dion, K. (1972). Physical attractiveness and evaluations of children's transgressions. *Journal of Personality and Social Psychology, 24,* 207–213.

Dion, K., Berscheid, E., & Walster (Hatfield), E. (1972). What is beautiful is good. *Journal of Personality and Social Psychology, 24,* 285–290.

Dion, K. K., & Dion, K. L. (1996). Cultural perspectives on romantic love. *Personal Relationships, 3,* 5–17.

Dix, T. (1993). Attributing dispositions to children: An interactional analysis of attribution in socialization. *Personality and Social Psychology Bulletin, 19,* 633–643.

Dodge, M. K. (1984). Learning to care: Developing prosocial behavior among one- and two-year-olds in group settings. *Journal of Research and Development in Education, 17,* 26–30.

Dolin, D. J., & Booth-Butterfield, S. (1995). Foot-in-the-door and cancer prevention. *Health Communication, 7,* 55–66.

Dollard, J. (1938). Hostility and fear in social life. *Social Forces, 17,* 15–26.

Dollard, J., Doob, L., Miller, N., Mowrer, O. H., & Sears, R. R. (1939). *Frustration and aggression.* New Haven, CT: Yale University Press.

Donnerstein, E., & Donnerstein, M. (1976). Research in the control of interracial aggression. In R. G. Green & E. C. O'Neal (Eds.), *Perspectives on aggression* (pp. 133–168). New York: Academic Press.

Donnerstein, E., Linz, D., & Penrod, S. (1987). *The question of pornography: Research findings and policy implications.* New York: Free Press.

Dovidio, J., & Gaertner, S. (1996). Affirmative action, unintentional racial biases, and intergroup relations. *Journal of Social Issues, 52,* 51–75.

Dovidio, J. F. (1984). Helping behavior and altruism: An empirical and conceptual overview. In L. Berkowitz (Ed.), *Advances in experimental social psychology* (Vol. 17, pp. 361–427). New York: Academic Press.

Dovidio, J. F., Evans, N., & Tyler, R. B. (1986). Racial stereotypes: The contents of their cognitive representations. *Journal of Experimental Social Psychology, 22,* 22–37.

Dovidio, J. F., Piliavin, J. A., Gaertner, S. I., Schroeder, D. A., & Clark, R. D. III. (1991). The arousal: cost-reward model and the process of intervention. In M. S. Clark (Ed.), *Review of personality and social psychology* (Vol. 12, pp. 86–118). Newbury Park, CA: Sage.

Dowd, E. T., Hughes, S., Brockbank, L., Halpain, D., Seibel, C., & Seibel, P. (1988). Compliance-based and defiance-based intervention strategies and psychological reactance in the treatment of free and unfree behavior. *Journal of Counseling Psychology, 35,* 363–369.

Dryer, D. C., & Horowitz, L. M. (1997). When do opposites attract? Interpersonal complementarity versus similarity. *Journal of Personality and Social Psychology, 72,* 592–603.

Duck, J., Hogg, M., & Terry, D. (1995). Me, us and them: Political identification and the third-person effect in the 1993 Australian federal election. *European Journal of Social Psychology, 25,* 195–215.

Duck, S. (1982). A typography of relationship disengagement and dissolution. In S. Duck (Ed.), *Personal relationships 4: Dissolving personal relationships* (pp. 1–30). London: Academic Press.

Duke: The ex-Nazi who would be governor. (1991, November 10). *New York Times,* pp. 1, 26.

Dunkel-Schetter, C., Sagrestano, L. M., Feldman, P., & Killingsworth, C. (1996). Social support and pregnancy: A comprehensive review focusing on ethnicity and culture. In G. R. Pierce, B. R. Sarason & I. G. Sarason (Eds.), *Handbook of social support and the family* (pp. 375–412). New York: Plenum.

Dunn, A. (1997, May 14). If *Deep Blue* wrote *Hamlet,* would it change the endgame? *New York Times Cybertimes* (www.nytimes.com).

Dunn, D. S., & Wilson, T. D. (1990). When the stakes are high: A limit to the illusion of control effect. *Social Cognition, 8,* 305–323.

Dunning, D., Griffin, D. W., Milojkovic, J., & Ross, L. (1990). The overconfidence effect in social prediction. *Journal of Personality and Social Psychology, 58,* 568–581.

Dunning, D., & Hayes, A. F. (1996). Evidence of egocentric comparison in social judgment. *Journal of Personality and Social Psychology, 71,* 213–229.

Dunning, D., & Stern, L. B. (1994). Distinguishing accurate from inaccurate eyewitness identifications via inquiries about decision processes. *Journal of Personality and Social Psychology, 67,* 818–835.

Dutton, D. G., & Aron, A. P. (1974). Some evidence for heightened sexual attraction under conditions of high anxiety. *Journal of Personality and Social Psychology, 30,* 510–517.

Duval, S., & Wicklund, R. A. (1972). *A theory of objective self-awareness.* New York: Academic Press.

Dykstra, P. (1995). Loneliness among the never and formerly married: The importance of supportive friendships and a desire for independence. *Journals of Gerontology: Psychological Sciences and Social Sciences, 50B,* S321–S329.

Eagly, A. H. (1987). *Sex differences in social behavior: A social-role interpretation.* Hillsdale, NJ: Erlbaum.

Eagly, A. H. (1991). Explaining sex differences in social behavior: A meta-analytic perspective. Special Issue: Meta-analysis in personality and social psychology. *Personality & Social Psychology Bulletin, 17,* 306–315.

Eagly, A. H. (1995). The science and politics of comparing women and men. *American Psychologist, 50,* 145–158.

Eagly, A. H. (1996). Differences between women and men: Their magnitude, practical importance, and political meaning. *American Psychologist, 51,* 158–159.

Eagly, A. H., Ashmore, R. D., Makhijani, M. G., & Longo, L. C. (1991). What is beautiful is good, but . . . : A meta-analytic review of research on the physical attractiveness stereotype. *Psychological Bulletin, 110,* 109–128.

Eagly, A. H., & Carli, L. L. (1981). Sex of researchers and sex-typed communications as determinants of sex differences in influenceability: A meta-analysis of social influence studies. *Psychological Bulletin, 90,* 1–20.

Eagly, A. H., & Chaiken, S. (1975). An attribution analysis of communicator characteristics on opinion change: The case of communicator attractiveness. *Journal of Personality and Social Psychology, 32,* 136–244.

Eagly, A. H., & Chaiken, S. (1993). *The psychology of attitudes.* Fort Worth, TX: Harcourt Brace Jovanovich.

Eagly, A. H., & Chaiken, S. (1998). Attitude structure and function. In D. T. Gilbert, S. T. Fiske, & G. Lindzey (Eds.), *The handbook of social psychology* (4th ed., Vol. 1, pp. 269–322). New York: McGraw-Hill.

Eagly, A. H., & Crowley, M. (1986). Gender and helping behavior: A meta-analytic review of the social psychological literature. *Psychological Bulletin, 100,* 283–308.

Eagly, A. H., & Johnson, B. T. (1990). Gender and leadership style: A meta-analysis. *Psychological Bulletin, 108,* 233–256.

Eagly, A. H., & Karau, S. J. (1991). Gender and the emergence of leaders: A meta-analysis. *Journal of Personality and Social Psychology, 60,* 685–710.

Eagly, A. H., Karau, S. J., & Makhijani, M. G. (1995). Gender and the effectiveness of leaders: A meta-analysis. *Psychological Bulletin, 117,* 125–145.

Eagly, A. H., Makhijani, M. G., & Klonsky, B. G. (1992). Gender and the evaluation of leaders: A meta-analysis. *Psychological Bulletin, 111,* 3–22.

Eagly, A. H., Mladinic, A., & Otto, S. (1994). Cognitive and affective bases of attitudes toward social groups and social policies. *Journal of Experimental Social Psychology, 30,* 113–137.

Eagly, A. H., & Steffen, V. J. (1984). Gender stereotypes stem from the distribution of women and men into social roles. *Journal of Personality & Social Psychology, 46,* 735–754.

Eagly, A. H., & Steffen, V. J. (1986). Gender and aggressive behavior: A meta-analytic review of the social psychological literature. *Psychological Bulletin, 100,* 309–330.

Eagly, A. H., & Wood, W. (1991). Explaining sex differences in social behavior: A meta-analytic perspective. *Personality and Social Psychology Bulletin, 17,* 306–315.

Eargle, A., Guerra, N., & Tolan, P. (1994). Preventing aggression in inner-city children: Small group training to change cognitions, social skills, and behavior. *Journal of Child and Adolescent Group Therapy, 4,* 229–242.

Ebbesen, E., Duncan, B., & Konecni, V. (1975). Effects of content of verbal aggression: A field experiment. *Journal of Experimental and Social Psychology, 11,* 192–204.

Economos, J. (1989). Altruism, nativism, chauvinism, racism, schism, and jizzum. *Behavioral and Brain Sciences, 12,* 521–523.

Eden, D., & Zuk, Y. (1995). Seasickness as a self-fulfilling prophecy: Raising self-efficacy to boost performance at sea. *Journal of Applied Psychology, 80,* 628–635.

Edwards, H. (1973). The black athletes: 20th century gladiators in white America. *Psychology Today, 7,* 43–52.

Edwards, K. (1990). The interplay of affect and cognition in attitude formation and change. *Journal of Personality and Social Psychology, 59,* 202–216.

Edwards, K., & Smith, E. (1996). A disconfirmation bias in the evaluation of arguments. *Journal of Personality and Social Psychology, 71,* 5–24.

Edwards, K., & von Hippel, W. (1995). Hearts and minds: The priority of affective versus cognitive factors in person perception. *Personality and Social Psychology Bulletin, 21,* 996–1011.

Edwards, W. (1968). Conservatism in human information processing. In B. Kleinmutz (Ed.), *Formal representation of human judgment* (pp. 17–52). New York: Wiley.

Eibl-Eibesfeldt, I. (1963). Aggressive behavior and ritualized fighting in animals. In J. H. Masserman (Ed.), *Science and psychoanalysis: Vol. 6. Violence and war.* New York: Grune & Stratton.

Eisenberg, N., & Fabes, R. A. (1991). Prosocial behavior and empathy: A multimethod developmental perspective. In M. S. Clark (Ed.), *Review of personality and social psychology* (Vol. 12, pp. 34–61). Newbury Park, CA: Sage.

Eisenman, R. (1994). *Political issues and social problems: A social psychological perspective*. Orlando, FL: Harcourt Brace.

Ekman, P. (1965). Communication through nonverbal behavior: A source of information about an interpersonal relationship. In S. S. Tomkins & C. E. (Eds.), *Affect, cognition, and personality* (pp. 390–442). New York: Springer- Verlag.

Ekman, P. (1985). *Telling lies*. New York: Norton.

Ekman, P. (1992). *Telling lies: Clues to deceit in the marketplace, politics, and marriage* (rev. ed.). New York: Norton.

Ekman, P. (1993). Facial expression and emotion. *American Psychologist, 48*, 384–392.

Ekman, P. (1994). Strong evidence for universals in facial expressions: A reply to Russell's mistaken critique. *Psychological Bulletin, 115*, 268–287.

Ekman, P., & Davidson, R. J. (Eds.) (1994). *The Nature of Emotion: Fundamental Questions*. New York: Oxford University Press.

Ekman, P., & Friesen, W. V. (1969). The repertoire of nonverbal behavior: Categories, origins, usage, and coding. *Semiotica, 1*, 49–98.

Ekman, P., & Friesen, W. V. (1971). Constants across cultures in the face and emotion. *Journal of Personality and Social Psychology, 17,* 124–129.

Ekman, P., & Friesen, W. V. (1975). *Unmasking the face*. Englewood Cliffs, NJ: Prentice Hall.

Ekman, P., Friesen, W. V., & Ellsworth, P. (1982a). Does the face provide accurate information? In P. Ekman (Ed.), *Emotion in the human face* (pp. 56–97). Cambridge, England: Cambridge University Press.

Ekman, P., Friesen, W. V., & Ellsworth, P. (1982b). What are the similarities and differences in facial behavior across cultures? In P. Ekman (Ed.), *Emotion in the human face* (pp. 128–143). Cambridge, England: Cambridge University Press.

Ekman, P., Friesen, W. V., O'Sullivan, M., Chan, A., Diacoyanni-Tarlatzis, I., Heider, K., Krause, R., LeCompre, W. A., Pitcairn, T., Ricci-Bitti, P. E., Scherer, K., Tomita, M., & Tzavras, A. (1987). Universals and cultural differences in the judgments of facial expressions of emotions. *Journal of Personality and Social Psychology, 53,* 712–717.

Ekman, P., & O'Sullivan, M. (1991). Who can catch a liar? *American Psychologist, 46*, 913–920.

Ekman, P., O'Sullivan, M., & Matsumoto, D. (1991a). Confusions about content in the judgment of facial expression: A reply to "Contempt and the relativity thesis." *Motivation and Emotion, 15*, 169–176.

Ekman, P., O'Sullivan, M., & Matsumoto, D. (1991b). Contradictions in the study of contempt: What's it all about? Reply to Russell. *Motivation and Emotion, 15*, 293–296.

Elig, T. W., & Frieze, I. H. (1979). Measuring causal attributions for success and failure. *Journal of Personality and Social Psychology, 38,* 270–277.

Elkin, R., & Leippe, M. (1986). Physiological arousal, dissonance, and attitude change: Evidence for a dissonance-arousal link and a "don't remind me" effect. *Journal of Personality and Social Psychology, 51*, 55–65.

Elliot, A. J., & Devine, P. G. (1994). On the motivational nature of cognitive dissonance: Dissonance as psychological discomfort. *Journal of Personality and Social Psychology, 67*, 382–294.

Elliot, G. R., & Eisdorfer, C. (1982). *Stress and human health: Analysis and implications of research*. New York: Springer.

Elliot, J. (1977). The power and pathology of prejudice. In P. Zimbardo & F. Ruch (Eds.), *Psychology and life*, 9th ed., diamond printing. Glenview, IL: Scott Foresman.

Ellsworth, P. C. (1994). William James and emotion: Is a century of fame worth a century of misunderstanding? *Psychological Review, 101*, 222–229.

Ellsworth, P. C., & Mauro, R. (1998). Psychology and law. In D. Gilbert, S. Fiske, & G. Lindzey (Eds.), *The handbook of social psychology* (4th ed., Vol. 2, pp. 684–732). New York: McGraw Hill.

Elms, A. C., & Milgram, S. (1966). Personality characteristics associated with obedience and defiance toward authoritative command. *Journal of Experimental Research in Personality, 1,* 282–289.

Emanuelson, I., & Fischbein, S. (1986). Vive la difference? A study on sex and schooling. *Scandinavian Journal of Educational Research, 30,* 71–84.

Emerson, R. W. (1929). *The complete works of Ralph Waldo Emerson*. New York: Wm. H. Wise.

Emery, R. E., & Wyer, M. M. (1987). Divorce mediation. *American Psychologist, 42,* 472–480.

Eraker, S. A., & Politser, P. (1988). How decisions are reached: Physicians and the patient. In J. Dowie & A. S. Elstein (Eds.), *Professional judgment: A reader in clinical decision making* (pp. 379–394). Cambridge, England: Cambridge University Press.

Erdelyi, M. H. (1984). Hypnotic hypermnesia: The empty set of hypermnesia. *International Journal of Clinical and Experimental Hypnosis, 24,* 379–390.

Eron, L. D. (1982). Parent-child interaction, television violence, and aggression of children. *American Psychologist, 37,* 197–211.

Eron, L. D. (1987). The development of aggressive behavior from the perspective of a developing behaviorism. *American Psychologist, 42,* 425–442.

Eron, L. D., Huesmann, L. R., Lefkowitz, M. M., & Walder, L. O. (1996). Does television violence cause aggression? In: D. F. Greenberg (Ed.), *Criminal careers, 2,* 311–321. The international library of criminology, criminal justice, and penology. Aldershot, England: Dartmouth Publishing Company Limited.

Esser, J. K., & Lindoerfer, J. S. (1989). Groupthink and the space shuttle *Challenger* accident: Toward a quantitative case analysis. *Journal of Behavioral Decision Making, 2,* 167–177.

Evans, G. W. (in press). Environmental stress and health. In A. Baum, T. Revenson, & J. E. Singer (Eds.), *Handbook of health psychology*. Mahwah, NJ: Erlbaum.

Evans, G. W., Hygge, S., & Bullinger, M. (1995). Chronic noise and psychological stress. *Psychological Science, 6,* 333–338.

Evans, G. W., Lepore, S. J., & Schroeder, A. (1996). The role of interior design elements in human responses to crowding. *Journal of Personality and Social Psychology, 70,* 41–46.

Evans, W. N., Neville, D., & Graham, J. D. (1991). General deterrence of drunk driving: Evaluation of American policies. *Risk Analysis, 11,* 279–289.

Ezekiel, R. S. (1995). *The racist mind: Portraits of American neo-nazis and klansmen*. New York: Viking.

Falck, R., & Craig, R. (1988). Classroom-oriented, primary prevention programming for drug abuse. *Journal of Psychoactive Drugs, 20,* 403–408.

Faranda, J. A., Kaminski, J. A., & Giza, B. K. (1979). *An assessment of attitudes toward women with the bogus pipeline*. Paper presented at the meeting of the American Psychological Association.

Fazio, R. H. (1987). Self-perception theory: A current perspective. In M. P. Zanna, J. M. Olson, & C. P. Herman (Eds.), *Social influence: The Ontario Symposium* (Vol. 5, pp. 129–150). Hillsdale, NJ: Erlbaum.

Fazio, R. H. (1989). On the power and functionality of attitudes: The role of attitude accessibility. In A. R. Pratkanis, S. J. Breckler, & A. G. Greenwald (Eds.), *Attitude structure and function* (pp. 153–179). Hillsdale, NJ: Erlbaum.

Fazio, R. H. (1990). Multiple processes by which attitudes guide behavior: The MODE model as an integrative framework. In M. P. Zanna (Ed.), *Advances in experimental social psychology* (Vol. 23, pp. 75–109). San Diego: Academic Press.

Fazio, R. H. (1995). Attitudes as object-evaluation associations: Determinants, consequences, and correlates of attitude accessibility. In R. Petty, & J. Krosnick (Eds.), *Attitude strength: Antecedents and consequences* (pp. 247–282). Hillsdale, NJ: Erlbaum.

Fazio, R. H., Effrein, E. A., & Falender, V. J. (1981). Self-perceptions following social interaction. *Journal of Personality and Social Psychology, 41,* 232–242.

Fazio, R. H., Jackson, J. R., Dunton, B. C., & Williams, C. J. (1995). Variability in automatic activation as an unobtrusive measure of racial attitudes: A bona fide pipeline? *Journal of Personality and Social Psychology, 69,* 1013–1027.

Fazio, R. H., Powell, M. C., & Williams, C. J. (1989). The role of attitude accessibility in the attitude-to-behavior process. *Journal of Consumer Research, 16,* 280–288.

Fazio, R. H., Sanbonmatsu, D. M., Powell, M. C., & Kardes, F. R. (1986). On the automatic activation of attitudes. *Journal of Personality and Social Psychology, 50,* 229–238.

Fazio, R. H., & Zanna, M. P. (1981). Direct experience and attitude-behavior consistency. In L. Berkowitz (Ed.), *Advances in experimental social psychology* (Vol. 14, pp. 162–202). New York: Academic Press.

Fazio, R. H., Zanna, M. P., & Cooper, J. (1977). Dissonance and self-perception: An integrative view of each theory's proper domain of application. *Journal of Experimental Social Psychology, 13,* 464–479.

Feeney, J. A., & Noller, P. (1990). Attachment style as a predictor of adult romantic relationships. *Journal of Personality and Social Psychology, 58,* 281–291.

Fehr, B. (1996). *Friendship processes.* Thousand Oaks, CA: Sage Publications.

Fehr, B., & Russell, J. A. (1991). The concept of love viewed from a prototype perspective. *Journal of Personality and Social Psychology, 60,* 425–438.

Fein, S. (1996). Effects of suspicion on attributional thinking and the correspondence bias. *Journal of Personality and Social Psychology, 70,* 1164–1184.

Fein, S., McCloskey, A. L., & Tomlinson, T. M. (1997). Can the jury disregard that information? The use of suspicion to reduce the prejudicial effects of pretrial publicity and inadmissible testimony. *Personality and Social Psychology Bulletin, 23,* 1215–1226.

Fein, S., & Spencer, S. J. (1997). Prejudice as self-image maintenance: Affirming the self through derogating others. *Journal of Personality and Social Psychology, 73,* 31–44.

Feingold, A. (1990). Gender differences in effects of physical attractiveness on romantic attraction: A comparison across five research paradigms. *Journal of Personality and Social Psychology, 59,* 981–993.

Feingold, A. (1992a). Good-looking people are not what we think. *Psychological Bulletin, 111,* 304–341.

Feingold, A. (1992b). Gender differences in mate selection preferences: A test of the parental investment model. *Psychological Bulletin, 112,* 125–139.

Feingold, A. (1996). On an evolutionary model of sex differences in mathematics: Do the data support the theory? *Behavioral and Brain Sciences, 19,* 252.

Feld, S. L. (1982). Social structural determinants of similarity among associates. *American Sociological Review, 47,* 797–801.

Feldman-Summers, S., & Kiesler, S. B. (1974). Those who are number two try harder: The effect of sex on attributions of causality. *Journal of Personality and Social Psychology, 38,* 846–855.

Ferris, T. (1997, April 14). The wrong stuff. *New Yorker,* p. 32.

Feshbach, N. (1978, March). *Empathy training: A field study in affective education.* Paper presented at the meetings of the American Educational Research Association, Toronto, Ontario, Canada.

Feshbach, N., & Feshbach, S. (1969). The relationship between empathy and aggression in two age groups. *Developmental Psychology, 1,* 102–107.

Feshbach, S. (1971). Dynamics and morality of violence and aggression: Some psychological considerations. *American Psychologist, 26,* 281–292.

Festinger, L. (1954). A theory of social comparison processes. *Human Relations, 7,* 117–140.

Festinger, L. (1957). *A theory of cognitive dissonance.* Stanford, CA: Stanford University Press.

Festinger, L. (1980). Looking backward. In L. Festinger (Ed.), *Restrospections on social psychology* (pp. 236–254). New York: Oxford University Press.

Festinger, L., & Aronson, E. (1960). The arousal and reduction of dissonance in social contexts. In D. Cartwright & A. Zander (Eds.), *Group dynamics* (pp. 214–231). Evanston, IL: Row, Peterson.

Festinger, L., & Carlsmith, J. M. (1959). Cognitive consequences of forced compliance. *Journal of Abnormal and Social Psychology, 58,* 203–211.

Festinger, L., & Maccoby, N. (1964). On resistance to persuasive communications. *Journal of Abnormal and Social Psychology, 68,* 359–366.

Festinger, L., Riecken, H. W., & Schachter, S. (1956). *When prophecy fails.* Minneapolis: University of Minnesota Press.

Festinger, L., Schachter, S., & Back, K. (1950). *Social pressures in informal groups: A study of human factors in housing.* New York: Harper & Bros.

Festinger, L., & Thibaut, J. (1951). Interpersonal communication in small groups. *Journal of Abnormal and Social Psychology, 46,* 92–99.

Fiedler, F. (1967). *A theory of leadership effectiveness.* New York: McGraw-Hill.

Fiedler, F. (1978). The contingency model and the dynamics of the leadership process. In L. Berkowitz (Ed.), *Advances in experimental social psychology* (Vol. 11, pp. 59–112). Orlando, FL: Academic Press.

Fiedler, K., & Semin, G. R. (1992). Attribution and language as a socio-cognitive environment. In G. R. Semin & K. Fiedler (Eds.), *Language, interaction, and social cognition* (pp. 79–101). London: Sage.

Fiedler, K., Semin, G. R., Finkenauer, C., & Berkel, I. Actor-observer bias in close relationships: The role of self-knowledge and self-related language. *Personality and Social Psychology Bulletin, 21,* 525–538.

Fincher, J. (1981, October). Presumed guilty: The ordeal of Robert Dillen. *Reader's Digest,* pp. 104–109.

Finney, P. D. (1987). When consent information refers to risk and deception: Implications for social research. *Journal of Social Behavior and Personality, 2,* 37–48.

Fischer, W. F. (1963). Sharing in preschool children as a function of amount and type of reinforcement. *Genetic Psychology Monographs, 68,* 215–245.

Fischhoff, B. (1975). Hindsight foresight: The effect of outcome knowledge on judgment under uncertainty. *Journal of Experimental Psychology: Human Perception and Performance, 1*, 288–299.

Fishbein, M., & Ajzen, I. (1975). *Belief, attitude, intention, and behavior: An introduction to theory and research.* Reading, MA: Addison-Wesley.

Fishbein, M., Chan, D., O'Reilly, K., Schnell, D., Wood, R., Beeker, C., & Cohn, C. (1993). Factors influencing gay men's attitudes, subjective norms, and intentions with respect to performing sexual behaviors. *Journal of Applied Social Psychology, 23*, 417–438.

Fiske, A. P., Kitayama, S., Markus, H. R., & Nisbett, R. E. (1998). The cultural matrix of social psychology. In D. Gilbert, S. Fiske, & G. Lindzey (Eds.), *The handbook of social psychology* (4th ed., Vol 2, pp. 915–981). New York: McGraw Hill.

Fiske, S. (1998). Prejudice, stereotyping and discrimination. In D. Gilbert, S. Fiske, & G. Lindzey (Eds.), *The handbook of social psychology* (4th ed., Vol. 1, pp. 357–414). New York: McGraw Hill

Fiske, S., & Depret, E. (1996). Control, interdependence, and power: Understanding social cognition in its social context. In W. Stroebe & M. Hewstone (Eds.), *European Review of Social Psychology, 7*, 31–61. New York: Wiley.

Fiske, S. T. (1989a). Examining the role of intent: Toward understanding its role in stereotyping and prejudice. In J. S. Uleman & J. A. Bargh (Eds.), *Unintended thought* (pp. 253–283). New York: Guilford.

Fiske, S. T. (1989b). *Interdependence and stereotyping: From the laboratory to the Supreme Court (and back).* Invited address, American Psychological Association, New Orleans.

Fiske, S. T. (1993). Social cognition and social perception. *Annual Review of Psychology, 44*, 155–194.

Fiske, S. T., & Goodwin, S. A. (1994). Social cognition research and small group research. *Small Group Research, 25*, 47–171.

Fiske, S. T., & Taylor, S. E. (1991). *Social cognition* (2nd ed.). New York: McGraw-Hill.

Fletcher, G. J. O., Reeder, G. D., & Bull, V. (1990). Bias and accuracy in attitude attribution: The role of attributional complexity. *Journal of Experimental Social Psychology, 26*, 275–288.

Fletcher, G. J. O., & Ward, C. (1988). Attribution theory and processes: A cross-cultural perspective. In M. H. Bond (Ed.), *The Cross-Cultural Challenge to Social Psychology.* Newbury Park, CA: Sage.

Flink, C., & Park, B. (1991). Increasing consensus in trait judgments through outcome dependency. *Journal of Experimental Social Psychology, 27*, 453–467.

Flowers, M. L. (1977). A lab test of some implications of Janis' groupthink hypothesis. *Journal of Personality and Social Psychology, 35*, 888–897.

Flynn, L. J. (1997, March 16). Channel One garners new criticism for link to advertiser on web site. *New York Times Cybertimes* (www.nytimes.com).

Fong, G. T., Krantz, D. H., & Nisbett, R. E. (1986). The effects of statistical training on thinking about everyday problems. *Cognitive Psychology, 18*, 253–292.

Ford, C. S., & Beach, F. A. (1952). *Patterns of sexual behavior.* New York: Ace Books.

Forgas, J. P. (1995). Mood and judgment: The affect infusion model (AIM). *Psychological Bulletin, 117*, 39–66.

Forgas, J. P., & Bower, G. H. (1987). Mood effects on person-perception judgments. *Journal of Personality and Social Psychology, 53*, 53–60

Forsterling, F. (1989). Models of covariation and attribution: How do they relate to the analogy of analysis of variance? *Journal of Personality and Social Psychology, 57*, 615–625.

Fountain, J.W. (1997). No fare. *Washington Post*, May 4, F01.

Four year study of girls shows concern over weight. (1992, January 5). *Boston Globe* , West Weekly Section, pp. 1, 4.

Fox, J. (1980). Making decisions under the influence of memory. *Psychological Review, 87*, 190–211.

Frager, R. (1970). Conformity and anticonformity in Japan. *Journal of Personality and Social Psychology, 15*, 203–210.

Frank, J. D. (1978). *Psychotherapy and the human predicament: A psychosocial approach.* Ed. P. E. Dietz, New York: Schocken Books.

Frank, M. G., & Gilovich, T. (1989). Effect of memory perspective on retrospective causal attributions. *Journal of Personality and Social Psychology, 57*, 399–403.

Freedman, D., Pisani, R., Purves, R., & Adhikari, A. (1991). *Statistics* (2nd ed.). New York: Norton.

Freedman, J. (1965). Long-term behavioral effects of cognitive dissonance. *Journal of Experimental and Social Psychology, 1*, 145–155.

Freedman, J. L., & Fraser, S. C. (1966). Compliance without pressure: The foot-in-the-door technique. *Journal of Personality and Social Psychology, 4*, 195–202.

Freud, S. (1930). *Civilization and its discontents* (Joan Riviere, Trans.). London: Hogarth Press.

Freud, S. (1933). *New introductory lectures on psycho-analysis.* New York: Norton.

Fried, C., & Aronson, E. (1995). Hypocrisy, misattribution, and dissonance reduction: A demonstration of dissonance in the absence of aversive consequences. *Personality and Social Psychology Bulletin, 21*, 925–933.

Friedman, H. S. (1993). Interpersonal expectations and the maintenance of health. In P. D. Blank (Ed.), *Interpersonal expectations: Theory, research, and applications* (pp. 179–193). New York: Cambridge University Press.

Friedman, L. (1977). *Sex-role stereotyping in the mass media: An annotated bibliography.* New York: Garland Press.

Friesen, W. V. (1972). *Cultural differences in facial expressions in a social situation: An experimental test of the concept of display rules.* Unpublished dissertation, University of California, San Francisco.

Frijda, N. H. (1986). *The emotions.* Cambridge, England: Cambridge University Press.

Frodi, A. (1975). The effect of exposure to weapons on aggressive behavior from a cross-cultural perspective. *International Journal of Psychology, 10*, 283–292.

Fry, W. R. (1985). The effect of dyad Machiavellianism and visual access on integrative bargaining outcomes. *Personality and Social Psychology Bulletin, 11*, 51–62.

Fuller, T. D., Edwards, J. N., Vorakitphokatorn, S., & Sermsri, S. (1996). Chronic stress and psychological well-being: Evidence from Thailand on household crowding. *Social Science and Medicine, 42*, 265–280.

Fumento, M. (1997, Sept. 12–14). Why we need a new war on weight. *USA Weekend*, pp. 4–6.

Funder, D. C., & Colvin, C. R. (1988). Friends and strangers: Acquaintanceship, agreement, and the accuracy of personality judgment. *Journal of Personality and Social Psychology, 55*, 149–158.

Furnham, A. (1993). Just world beliefs in twelve societies. *Journal of Social Psychology, 133*, 317–329.

Furnham, A., & Gunter, B. (1984). Just world beliefs and attitudes toward the poor. *British Journal of Social Psychology, 23*, 265–269.

Furnham, A., Hester, C., & Weir, C. (1990). Sex differences in the preferences for specific female body shapes. *Sex Roles, 22*, 743–754.

Furnham, A., & Procter, E. (1989). Beliefs in a just world: Review and critique of the individual difference literature. *British Journal of Social Psychology, 28,* 365–384.

Gaertner, S. L., & Dovidio, J. F. (1986). The aversive form of racism. In J. F. Dovidio & S. L. Gaertner (Eds.), *Prejudice, discrimination, and racism: Theory and research* (pp. 61–89). New York: Academic Press.

Gaertner, S. L., Mann, J. A., Dovidio, J. F., & Murrell, A. J. (1990). How does cooperation reduce intergroup bias? *Journal of Personality & Social Psychology, 59,* 692–704.

Gallup, G. G. (1977). Self-recognition in primates: A comparative approach to the bidirectional properties of consciousness. *American Psychologist, 32,* 329–338.

Gallup, G. G. (1993). Mirror, mirror on the wall which is the most heuristic theory of them all? *New Ideas in Psychology, 11,* 327–335.

Gallup, G. G. (1994). Monkeys, mirrors, and minds. *Behavioral and Brain Sciences, 17,* 572–573.

Gallup, G. G., Povinelli, D. J., Suarez, S. D., Anderson, J. R., Lethmate, J., & Menzel, E. W., Jr. (in press). Further reflections on self-recognition in primates. *Animal Behavior.*

Gallup, G. G., & Suarez, S. D. (1986). Self-awareness and the emergence of mind in humans and other primates. In J. Suls & A. G. Greenwald (Eds.), *Psychological perspectives on the self* (Vol. 3, pp. 3–26). Hillsdale, NJ: Erlbaum.

Gangestad, S. W. (1989). Uncompelling theory, uncompelling data. *Behavioral and Brain Sciences, 12,* 525–526.

Gangestad, S. W. (1993). Sexual selection and physical attractiveness: Implications for mating dynamics. *Human Nature, 4,* 205–235.

Gangestad, S. W., & Buss, D. M. (1993). Pathogen prevalence and human mate preferences. *Ethology and Sociobiology, 14,* 89–96.

Ganzach, Y. (1996). Preference reversals in equal-probability gambles: A case for anchoring and adjustment. *Journal of Behavioral Decision Making, 9,* 95–109.

Gao, G. (1993, May). An investigation of love and intimacy in romantic relationships in China and the United States. Paper presented at the annual conference of the International Communication Association, Washington, DC.

Gao, G. (1996). Self and other: A Chinese perspective on interpersonal relationships. In W. B. Gudykunst, S. Ting-Toomey, & T. Nishida (Eds.), *Communication in Personal Relationships Across Cultures* (pp. 81–101). Thousand Oaks, CA: Sage.

Gao, G., & Gudykunst, W. B. (1995). Attributional confidence, perceived similarity, and network involvement in Chinese and European American romantic relationships. *Communication Quarterly, 43,* 431–445.

Garb, H. N. (1996). The representativeness and past-behavior heuristics in clinical judgment. *Professional Psychology: Research and Practice, 27,* 272–277.

Garcia, L. T., & Milano, L. (1990). A content analysis of erotic videos. *Journal of Psychology and Human Sexuality, 3,* 95–103.

Garcia, S., Stinson, L., Ickes, W. Bissonnette, V., & Briggs, S. (1991). Shyness and physical attractiveness in mixed sex dyads. *Journal of Personality and Social Psychology, 61,* 35–49.

Garcia-Marques, L., & Hamilton, D. L. (1996). Resolving the apparent discrepancy between the incongruency effect and the expectancy-based illusory correlation effect: The TRAP model. *Journal of Personality and Social Psychology, 71,* 845–860.

Garfinkle, H. (1967). *Studies in ethnomethodology.* Englewood Cliffs, NJ: Prentice Hall.

Garner, D. M., Garfinkel, P. E., Schwartz, D., & Thompson, M. (1980). Cultural expectations of thinness in women. *Psychological Reports, 47,* 483–491.

Gates, H. L., Jr. (1995, October 23). Thirteen ways of looking at a black man. *New Yorker,* pp. 56–65.

Gavanski, I., & Hoffman, C. (1987). Awareness of influences on one's own judgments: The roles of covariation detection and attention. *Journal of Personality and Social Psychology, 52,* 453–463.

Geary, D. C. (1996). Sexual selection and sex differences in mathematical abilities. *Behavioral and Brain Sciences, 19,* 229–284.

Geen, R. (1994). Television and aggression: Recent developments in research and theory. In D. Zillmann, J. Bryant, A. C. Huston (Eds.), *Media, children, and the family: Social scientific, psychodynamic, and clinical perspectives* (pp. 151–162). Hillsdale, NJ: Erlbaum.

Geen, R. (1998). Aggression and anti-social behavior. In D. Gilbert, S. Fiske, & G. Lindzey (Eds.), *The handbook of social psychology* (4th ed., Vol. 2, pp. 317–356). New York: McGraw Hill.

Geen, R., & Quanty, M. (1977). The catharsis of aggression: An evaluation of an hypothesis. In L. Berkowitz (Ed.), *Advances in experimental social psychology* (Vol. 10, pp. 1–36). New York: Academic Press.

Geen, R., Stonner, D., & Shope, G. (1975). The facilitation of aggression by aggression: A study in response inhibition and disinhibition. *Journal of Personality and Social Psychology, 31,* 721–726.

Geen, R. G. (1989). Alternative conceptions of social facilitation. In P. B. Paulus (Ed.), *Psychology of group influence* (2nd ed., pp. 15–51). Hillsdale, NJ: Erlbaum.

Geiselman, R. E., & Fisher, R. P. (1989). The cognitive interview technique for victims and witnesses of crime. In D. C. Raskin (Ed.), *Psychological methods in criminal investigation and evidence* (pp. 191–215). New York: Springer.

Gemmill, G. (1998). The dynamics of scapegoating in small groups. *Small Group Behavior, 20,* 406–418.

George, J. M. (1990). Personality, affect, and behavior in groups. *Journal of Applied Psychology, 75,* 107–116.

George, J. M., & Brief, A. P. (1992). Feeling good–doing good: A conceptual analysis of the mood at workÑorganizational spontaneity relationship. *Psychological Bulletin, 112,* 310–329.

Gerard, H. B. (1953). The effect of different dimensions of disagreement on the communication process in small groups. *Human Relations, 6,* 249–271.

Gerard, H. B., & Mathewson, G. C. (1966). The effects of severity of initiation on liking for a group: A replication. *Journal of Experimental Social Psychology, 2,* 278–287.

Gerard, H. B., Wilhelmy, R. A., & Conolley, E. S. (1968). Conformity and group size. *Journal of Personality and Social Psychology, 8,* 79–82.

Gerbner, G., Gross, L., Morgan, M., & Signorielli, N. (1980). The "mainstreaming" of America: Violence profile no. 11. *Journal of Communication, 30*(3), 10–29.

Gerdes, E. P. (1979). College students' reactions to social psychological experiments involving deception. *Journal of Social Psychology, 107,* 99–110.

Gergen, K. J. (1971). *The concept of self.* New York: Holt, Rinehart & Winston.

Gergen, K. J., Gergen, M. M., & Barton, W. H. (1973). Deviance in the dark. *Psychology Today, 7,* 129–130.

Gerstein, L. H., & Tesser, A. (1987). Antecedents and responses associated with loneliness. *Journal of Social and Personal Relationships, 4,* 329–363.

Ghiselin, M. T. (1996). Differences in male and female cognitive abilities: Sexual selection or division of labor? *Behavioral and Brain Sciences, 19,* 254–255.

Gibbons, F. X. (1978). Sexual standards and reactions to pornography: Enhancing behavioral consistency through self-focused attention. *Journal of Personality and Social Psychology, 36,* 976–987.

Gibbons, F. X., Eggleston, T. J., Benthin, A. C. (1997). Cognitive reactions to smoking relapse: The reciprocal relation between dissonance and self-esteem. *Journal of Personality and Social Psychology, 72,* 184–195.

Gibbs, J. P. (1985). Deterrence theory and research. *Nebraska Symposium on Motivation, 33,* 87–130.

Giesler, R., Josephs, R., & Swann, W. (1996). Self-verification in clinical depression: The desire for negative evaluation. *Journal of Abnormal Psychology, 105,* 358–368.

Gifford, R. (1991). Mapping nonverbal behavior on the interpersonal circle. *Journal of Personality and Social Psychology, 61,* 279–288.

Gifford, R. (1994). A lens-mapping framework for understanding the endcoding and decoding of interpersonal dispositions in nonverbal behavior. *Journal of Personality and Social Psychology, 66,* 398–412.

Gigerenzer, G. (1993). The bounded rationality of probabilistic mental models. In K. I. Manktelow & D. E. Over (Eds.), *Rationality: Psychological and philosophical perspectives* (pp. 284–313). London: Routledge.

Gigerenzer, G., & Goldstein, D. G. (1996). Reasoning the fast and frugal way: Models of bounded rationality. *Psychological Review, 103,* 650–669.

Gigone, D., & Hastie, R. (1993). The common knowledge effect: Information sharing and group judgment. *Journal of Personality and Social Psychology, 65,* 959–974.

Gilbert, B. (1990, April). Earth Day plus 20, and counting. *Smithsonian,* pp. 47–55.

Gilbert, D. T. (1989). Thinking lightly about others: Automatic components of the social inference process. In J. S. Uleman & J. A. Bargh (Eds.), *Unintended thought* (pp. 189–211). New York: Guilford Press.

Gilbert, D. T. (1991). How mental systems believe. *American Psychologist, 46,* 107–119.

Gilbert, D. T. (1993). The assent of man: Mental representation and the control of belief. In D. M. Wegner & J. W. Pennebaker, (Eds.), *The handbook of mental control* (pp. 57–87). Englewood Cliffs, NJ: Prentice Hall.

Gilbert, D. T. (1998). Ordinary personology. In D. T. Gilbert, S. T. Fiske, & G. Lindzey (Eds.), *The handbook of social psychology* (4th ed., Vol. 2, pp. 89–150). New York: McGraw-Hill.

Gilbert, D. T., Giesler, R. B., & Morris, K. A. (1995). When comparisons arise. *Journal of Personality and Social Psychology, 69,* 227–236.

Gilbert, D. T., & Malone, P. S. (1995). The correspondence bias. *Psychological Bulletin, 117,* 21–38.

Gilbert, D. T., & Osborne, R. E. (1989). Thinking backward: Some curable and incurable consequences of cognitive busyness. *Journal of Personality and Social Psychology, 57,* 940–949.

Gilbert, D. T., Pelham, B. W., & Krull, D. S. (1988). On cognitive busyness: When person perceivers meet persons perceived. *Journal of Personality and Social Psychology, 54,* 733–740.

Gilbert, D. T., Tafarodi, R. W., & Malone, P. S. (1993). You can't not believe everything you read. *Journal of Personality and Social Psychology, 65,* 221–233.

Gilbert, G. M. (1951). Stereotype persistence and change among college students. *Journal of Abnormal and Social Psychology, 46,* 245–254.

Gilbert, S. J. (1981). Another look at the Milgram obedience studies: The role of the gradated series of shocks. *Personality and Social Psychology Bulletin, 4,* 690–695.

Gilovich, T. (1991). *How we know what isn't so: The fallibility of human reasoning in everyday life.* New York: Free Press.

Gilovich, T., & Medvec, V. H. (1995). Some counterfactual determinants of satisfaction and regret. In N. J. Roese & J. M. Olson (Eds.), *What might have been: The social psychology of counterfactual thinking* (pp. 259–282). Mahwah, NJ: Erlbaum.

Gilovich, T., & Medvec, V. H. (1995). The experience of regret: What, when, and why. *Psychological Review, 102,* 379–395.

Gilovich, T., Medvec, V. H., & Chen, S. (1995). Commission, omission, and dissonance reduction: Coping with regret in the "Monty Hall" problem. *Personality and Social Psychology Bulletin, 21,* 182–190.

Gimlin, D. (1994). The anorexic as overconformist: Toward a reinterpretation of eating disorders. In K. A. Callaghan (Ed.), *Ideals of Feminine Beauty: Philosophical, Social, and Cultural Dimensions* (pp. 99–111). Westport, CN: Greenwood.

Giner-Sorolla, R., & Chaiken, S. (1994). The causes of hostile media judgments. *Journal of Experimental Social Psychology, 30,* 165–180.

Gladwell, M. (1997). The Sports Taboo. *New Yorker, 73,* May 19, 50–55.

Glass, D. C. (1964). Changes in liking as a means of reducing cognitive discrepancies between self-esteem and aggression. *Journal of Personality, 32,* 531–549.

Glass, D. C., & Singer, J. E. (1972). *Urban stress: Experiments on noise and social stressors.* New York: Academic Press.

Gleick, E. (1997, April 7). Planet earth about to be recycled. Your only chance to survive—Leave with us. *Time,* pp. 28–36.

Goethals, G. R. (1986). Social comparison theory: Psychology from the lost and found. *Personality and Social Psychology Bulletin, 12,* 261–278.

Goethals, G. R., & Darley, J. M. (1977). Social comparison theory: An attributional approach. In J. M. Suls & R. L. Miller (Eds.), *Social comparison processes: Theoretical and empirical perspectives* (pp. 259–278). Washington, DC: Hemisphere/Halsted.

Goffman, E. (1955). On face-work: An analysis of ritual elements in social interaction. *Psychiatry, 18,* 213–231.

Goffman, E. (1959). *Presentation of self in everyday life.* Garden City, NY: Doubleday Anchor Books.

Goffman, E. (1967). *Interaction ritual.* Garden City, NY: Doubleday.

Goffman, E. (1971). *Relations in public.* New York: Basic Books.

Goffman, E. (1976). *Gender advertisements.* New York: Harper & Row.

Gold, J. A., Ryckman, R. M., & Mosley, N. R. (1984). Romantic mood induction and attraction to a dissimilar other: Is love blind? *Personality and Social Psychology Bulletin, 10,* 358–368.

Goldberg, P. (1968, April). Are women prejudiced against women? *Trans-Action,* pp. 28–30.

Goldstein, J. H., & Arms, R. L. (1971). Effect of observing athletic contests on hostility. *Sociometry, 34,* 83–90.

Goleman, D. (1982, January). Make-or-break resolutions. *Psychology Today,* p. 19.

Gollwitzer, P. M. (1986). *Public vs. private self-symbolizing.* Unpublished manuscript, Max-Planck Institute for Psychological Research, Munich, Germany.

Gollwitzer, P. M., & Wicklund, R. A. (1985). Self-symbolizing and the neglect of others' perspectives. *Journal of Personality and Social Psychology, 48,* 702–715.

Gologor, E. (1977). Group polarization in a non-risk-taking culture. *Journal of Cross-Cultural Psychology, 8,* 331–346.

Gonzales, M. H., Aronson, E., & Costanzo, M. (1988). Using social cognition and persuasion to promote energy conservation: A quasi-experiment. *Journal of Applied Social Psychology, 18,* 1049–1066.

Gonzalez, R., Ellsworth, P. C., & Pembroke, M. (1993). Response biases in lineups and showups. *Journal of Personality and Social Psychology, 64,* 525–537.

Goodman, N. G. (Ed.). (1945). *A Benjamin Franklin reader.* New York: Thomas Y. Crowell.

Gopaul-McNicol, S.-A. A. (1987). A cross-cultural study of the effects of modeling, reinforcement, and color meaning word association on doll color preference of Black preschool children and White preschool children in New York and Trinidad. *Dissertation Abstracts International, 48,* 340–341.

Gorassini, D. R., & Olson, J. M. (1995). Does self-perception change explain the foot-in-the-door effect? *Journal of Personality and Social Psychology, 69,* 91–105.

Gordon, R. A. (1996). Impact of ingratiation on judgments and evaluations: A meta-analytic investigation. *Journal of Personality and Social Psychology, 71,* 54–70.

Gorn, G. J. (1982). The effects of music in advertising on choice behavior: A classical conditioning approach. *Journal of Marketing, 46,* 94–101.

Gould, S. J. (1997, June 26). Evolution: The pleasures of pluralism. *The New York Review,* pp. 47–52.

Granberg, D., & Brown, T. (1989). On affect and cognition in politics. *Social Psychology Quarterly, 52,* 171–182.

Graybar, S. R., Antonuccio, D. O., Boutilier, L. R., & Varble, D. L. (1989). Psychological reactance as a factor affecting patient compliance to physician advice. *Scandinavian Journal of Behaviour Therapy, 18,* 43–51.

Graziano, W. G., Jensen-Campbell, L. A., & Finch, J. F. (1997). The self as a mediator between personality and adjustment. *Journal of Personality and Social Psychology, 73,* 392–404.

Greeley, A., & Sheatsley, P. (1971). The acceptance of desegregation continues to advance. *Scientific American, 225*(6), 13–19.

Greenberg, J. (1983). *Difficult goal choice as a self-handicapping strategy.* Unpublished manuscript, Ohio State University.

Greenberg, J., & Musham, C. (1981). Avoiding and seeking self-focused attention. *Journal of Research in Personality, 15,* 191–200.

Greenberg, J., & Pyszczynski, T. (1985). The effect of an overheard slur on evaluations of the target: How to spread a social disease. *Journal of Experimental Social Psychology, 21,* 61–72.

Greenberg, J., Pyszczynski, T., & Paisley, C. (1984). The role of extrinsic incentives in the use of test anxiety as an anticipatory attributional defense: Playing it cool when the stakes are high. *Journal of Personality and Social Psychology, 47,* 1136–1145.

Greenberg, J., Pyszczynski, T., & Solomon, S. (1982). The self-serving attributional bias: Beyond self-presentation. *Journal of Experimental Social Psychology, 18,* 56–67.

Greenberg, J., Pyszczynski, T., & Solomon, S. (1986). The causes and consequences of the need for self-esteem: A terror management theory. In R. F. Baumeister (Ed.), *Public self and private self* (pp. 189–212). New York: Springer-Verlag.

Greenberg, L. (1979). Genetic component of bee odor in kin recognition. *Science, 206,* 1095–1097.

Greene, D., Sternberg, B., & Lepper, M. R. (1976). Overjustification in a token economy. *Journal of Personality and Social Psychology, 34,* 1219–1234.

Greenglass, E. R. (1991). Type A behavior, career aspirations, and role conflict in professional women. In M. J. Strube (Ed.), *Type A behavior* (pp. 277–292). Newbury Park, CA: Sage.

Greening, L., & Chandler, C. C. (1997). Why it can't happen to me: The base rate matters, but overestimating skill leads to underestimating risk. *Journal of Applied Social Psychologoy, 27,* 760–780.

Greenwald, A. G. (1980). The totalitarian ego: Fabrication and revision of personal history. *American Psychologist, 35,* 603–618.

Greenwald, A. G., & Banaji, M. R. (1989). The self as a memory system: Powerful, but ordinary. *Journal of Personality and Social Psychology, 57,* 41–54.

Greenwald, A. G., & Ronis, D. L. (1978). Twenty years of cognitive dissonance: Case study of the evolution of a theory. *Psychological Review, 85,* 53–57.

Greenwald, A. G., Spangenberg, E. R., Pratkanis, A. R., & Eskenazi, J. (1991). Double-blind tests of subliminal self-help audiotapes. *Psychological Science, 2,* 119–122.

Grice, H. P. (1975). Logic as conversation. In P. Cole & J. L. Morgan (Eds.), *Syntax and semantics: Vol. 3. Speech acts.* (pp. 365–372). New York: Seminar Press.

Griffin, D. W., Dunning, D., & Ross, L. (1990). The role of construal processes in overconfident predictions about the self and others. *Journal of Personality and Social Psychology, 59,* 1128–1139.

Griffin, D. W., & Ross, L. (1991). Subjective construal, social inference, and human misunderstanding. In L. Berkowitz (Ed.), *Advances in experimental social psychology* (Vol. 24, pp. 319–359). San Diego, CA: Academic Press.

Griffin, E., & Sparks, G. G. (1990). Friends forever: A longitudinal exploration of intimacy in same-sex pairs and platonic pairs. *Journal of Social and Personal Relationships, 7,* 29–46.

Griffitt, W., & Veitch, R. (1971). Hot and crowded: Influences of population density and temperature on interpersonal affective behavior. *Journal of Personality and Social Psychology, 17,* 92–98.

Griffitt, W., & Veitch, R. (1974). Preacquaintance attitude similarity and attraction revisited: Ten days in a fall-out shelter. *Sociometry, 37,* 163–173.

Groenland, E. A. G., & Schoormans, J. P. L. (1994). Comparing mood-induction and affective conditioning as mechanisms influencing product evaluation and choice. *Psychology and Marketing, 11,* 183–197.

Grove, L. (1997, August 21). A man named Sissy. *Washington Post,* pp. C1; C4.

Grusec, J. E. (1991). The socialization of altruism. In M. S. Clark (Ed.), *Review of personality and social psychology* (Vol. 12, pp. 9–33). Newbury Park, CA: Sage.

Grusec, J. E., Kuczynski, L., Rushton, J. P., & Simutis, Z. M. (1979). Modeling, direct instruction, and attributions: Effects on altruism. *Developmental Psychology, 14,* 51–57.

Guagnano, G. A., Stern, P. C., & Dietz, T. (1995). Influences on attitude-behavior relationships: A natural experiment with curbside recycling. *Environment and Behavior, 27,* 699–718.

Gudykunst, W. B. (1988). Culture and intergroup processes. In M. H. Bond (Ed.), *The cross-cultural challenge to social psychology* (pp. 165–181). Newbury Park, CA: Sage.

Gudykunst, W. B., Ting-Toomey, S., & Nishida, T. (1996). *Communication in Personal Relationships Across Cultures.* Thousand Oaks, CA: Sage Publications.

Guerin, B. (1986). Mere presence effects in humans: A review. *Journal of Experimental Social Psychology, 22,* 38–77.

Guerin, B. (1993). *Social facilitation.* Cambridge, England: Cambridge University Press.

Guisinger, S., & Blatt, S. J. (1994). Individuality and relatedness: Evolution of a fundamental dialect. *American Psychologist, 49,* 104–111.

Gump, B. B., & Kulik, J. A. (1997). Stress, affiliation, and emotional contagion. *Journal of Personality and Social Psychology, 72,* 305–319.

Gustafson, R. (1989). Frustration and successful vs. unsuccessful aggression: A test of Berkowitz' completion hypothesis. *Aggressive Behavior, 15,* 5–12.

Hackman, J. R., & Morris, C. G. (1978). Group process and group effectiveness: A reappraisal. In L. Berkowitz (Ed.), *Group processes* (pp. 57–66). New York: Academic Press.

Haddock, G., Zanna, M. P., & Esses, V. M. (1993). Assessing the structure of prejudicial attitudes: The case of attitudes toward homosexuals. *Journal of Personality and Social Psychology, 65,* 1105–1118.

Hagestad, G. O., & Smyer, M. A. (1982). Dissolving long-term relationships: Patterns of divorcing in middle age. In S. Duck (Ed.), *Personal relationships 4: Dissolving personal relationships* (pp. 155–188). London: Academic Press.

Haggard, E. A., & Issacs, F. S. (1966). Micromomentary facial expressions as indicators of ego mechanisms in psychotherapy. In L. A. Gottschalk & A. H. Auerback (Eds.), *Methods of research in psychotherapy* (pp. 154–165). New York: Appleton-Century-Crofts.

Halberstadt, J. B., & Levine, G. L. (1997). *Effects of reasons analysis on the accuracy of predicting basketball games.* Unpublished manuscript, Indiana University.

Halberstam, D. (1972). *The best and the brightest.* New York: McGraw-Hill.

Hall, E. T. (1969). *The hidden dimension.* Garden City, NY: Doubleday.

Hall, J. A. (1979). *A cross-national study of gender differences in nonverbal sensitivity.* Unpublished manuscript, Northeastern University.

Hall, J. A. (1984). *Nonverbal sex differences: Communication accuracy and expressive style.* Baltimore, MD: Johns Hopkins University Press.

Hamill, R. C., Wilson, T. D., & Nisbett, R. E. (1980). Ignoring sample bias: Inferences about populations from atypical cases. *Journal of Personality and Social Psychology, 39,* 578–589.

Hamilton, D., Stroessner, S., & Mackie, D. (Eds.) (1993). The influence of affect on stereotyping: The case of illusory correlations. *Affect, cognition, and stereotyping: Interactive processes in group perception,* pp. 39–61. San Diego, CA: Academic Press.

Hamilton, D. L. (1970). The structure of personality judgments: Comments on Kuusinen's paper and further evidence. *Scandinavian Journal of Psychology, 11,* 261–265.

Hamilton, D. L. (1981a). Cognitive representations of persons. In E. T. Higgins, C. P. Herman, & M. P. Zanna (Eds.), *Social cognition: The Ontario Symposium* (Vol. 1, pp. 135–159). Hillsdale, NJ: Erlbaum.

Hamilton, D. L. (1981b). Illusory correlation as a basis for stereotyping. In D. L. Hamilton (Ed.), *Cognitive Processes in Stereotyping and Intergroup Behavior.* Hillsdale, NJ: Erlbaum.

Hamilton, D. L., & Gifford, R. K. (1976). Illusory correlation in interpersonal perception: A cognitive basis of stereotypic judgments: *Journal of Experimental Social Psychology, 12,* 392–407.

Hamilton, D. L., & Sherman, S. J. (1989). Illusory correlations: Implications for stereotype theory and research. In D. Bar-Tal, C. F. Graumann, A. W. Kruglanski, & W. Stroebe (Eds.), *Stereotypes and prejudice: Changing conceptions* (pp. 59–82). New York: Springer-Verlag.

Hamilton, V. L., & Sanders, J. (1995). Crimes of obedience and conformity in the workplace: Surveys of Americans, Russians, and Japanese. *Journal of Social Issues, 51,* 67–88.

Hamilton, V. L., Sanders, J., & McKearney, S. J. (1995). Orientations toward authority in an authoritarian state: Moscow in 1990. *Personality and Social Psychology Bulletin, 21,* 356–365.

Hamilton, W. D. (1964). The genetical evolution of social behavior. *Journal of Theoretical Biology, 7,* 1–52.

Hamm, R. M. (1996). Physicians neglect base rates, and it matters. *Behavioral and Brain Sciences, 19,* 25–26.

Han, S., &Shavitt, S. (1994). Persuasion and culture:Advertising appeals in individualistic and collectivistic societies. *Journal of Experimental Social Psychology, 30,* 326–350.

Haney, C., Banks, C., & Zimbardo, P. (1973). Interpersonal dynamics in a simulated prison. *International Journal of Criminology and Penology, 1,* 69–97.

Hansen, C. H., & Hansen, R. D. (1988). Finding the face in the crowd: An anger superiority effect. *Journal of Personality and Social Psychology, 17,* 917–924.

Hansson, R. O., & Slade, K. M. (1977). Altruism toward a deviant in a city and small town. *Journal of Applied Social Psychology, 7,* 272–279.

Harackiewicz, J. M. (1979). The effects of reward contingency and performance feedback on intrinsic motivation. *Journal of Personality and Social Psychology, 37,* 1352–1363.

Harackiewicz, J. M. (1989). Performance evaluation and intrinsic motivation processes: The effects of achievement orientation and rewards. In D. Buss & N. Cantor (Eds.), *Personality psychology: Recent trends and emerging directions* (pp. 128–137). New York: Springer-Verlag.

Harackiewicz, J. M., & Elliot, A. J. (1993). Achievement goals and intrinsic motivation. *Journal of Personality and Social Psychology, 65,* 904–915.

Harackiewicz, J. M., & Elliot, A. J. (in press). The joint effects of target and purpose goals on intrinsic motivation: A mediational analysis. *Personality and Social Psychology Bulletin.*

Harackiewicz, J. M., Manderlink, G., & Sansone, C. (1984). Rewarding pinball wizardry: Effects of evaluation and cue value on intrinsic interest. *Journal of Personality and Social Psychology, 47,* 287–300.

Harackiewicz, J. M., Manderlink, G., & Sansone, C. (1992). Competence processes and achievement motivation: Implications for intrinsic motivation. In A. K. Boggiano & T. S. Pittman (Eds.), *Achievement and motivation: A social-developmental perspective* (pp. 115–137). New York: Cambridge University Press.

Hardin, G. (1968). The tragedy of the commons. *Science, 162,* 1243–1248.

Haritos-Fatouros, M. (1988). The official torturer: A learning model for obedience to the authority of violence. *Journal of Applied Social Psychology, 18,* 1107–1120.

Harkins, S. G., & Szymanski, K. (1987). Social loafing and social facilitation: Old wine in new bottles. In C. Hendrick (Ed.), *Group processes and intergroup relations* (Vol. 9, pp. 167–188). Newbury Park, CA: Sage.

Harkness, A. R., DeBono, K. G., & Borgida, E. (1985). Personal involvement and strategies for making contingency judgments: A stake in the dating game makes a difference. *Journal of Personality and Social Psychology, 49,* 22–32.

Harmon-Jones, E. (1998). Is feeling personally responsible for the production of aversive consequences necessary to cause dissonance effects? In E. Harmon-Jones & J. S. Mills, *Cognitive dissonance theory: Revival with revisions and controversies.* Washington, DC: American Psychological Association.

Harmon-Jones, E., & Mills, J.S. (1998). *Cognitive dissonance theory: Revival with revisions and controversies.* Washington, DC: American Psychological Association.

Harries, K. D., & Stadler, S. J. (1988). Heat and violence: New findings from Dallas field data, 1980–1981. *Journal of Applied Social Psychology, 18,* 129–138.

Harrigan, J. A., & O'Connell, D. M. (1996). How do you feel when feeling anxious? Facial displays of anxiety. *Personality and Individual Differences, 21,* 205–212.

Harris, B. (1986). Reviewing 50 years of the psychology of social issues. *Journal of Social Issues, 42,* 1–20.

Harris, M. (1974). Mediators between frustration and aggression in a field experiment. *Journal of Experimental and Social Psychology, 10,* 561–571.

Harris, M., & Perkins, R. (1995). Effects of distraction on interpersonal expectancy effects: A social interaction test of the cognitive busyness hypothesis. *Social Cognition, 13,* 163–182.

Harris, M. B., Benson, S. M., & Hall, C. (1975). The effects of confession on altruism. *Journal of Social Psychology, 96,* 187–192.

Harris, P. (1996). Sufficient grounds for optimism? The relationship between perceived controllability and optimistic bias. *Journal of Social and Clinical Psychology, 15,* 9–52.

Harris, R. J. (1994). The impact of sexually explicit material. In J. Bryant & D. Zillmann (Eds.), *Media effects: Advances in theory and research* (pp. 247–272). Hillsdale, NJ: Erlbaum.

Harrison, J. A., & Wells, R. B. (1991). Bystander effects on male helping behavior: Social comparison and diffusion of responsibility. *Representative Research in Social Psychology, 19,* 53–63.

Hart, A. J. (1995). Naturally occurring expectation effects. *Journal of Personality and Social Psychology, 68,* 109–115.

Hart, D., & Damon, W. (1986). Developmental trends in self-understanding. *Social Cognition, 4,* 388–407.

Harter, S. (1993). Causes and consequences of low self-esteem in children and adolescents. In: Baumeister, R., Ed., *Self-esteem: The puzzle of low self-regard.* New York: Plenum, pp. 87–116.

Hartshorne, H., & May, M. A. (1929). *Studies in the nature of character: Studies in service and self-control* (Vol. 2). New York: Macmillan.

Hartstone, M., & Augoustinos, M. (1995). The minimal group paradigm: Categorization into two versus three groups. *European Journal of Social Psychology, 25,* 179–193.

Hartup, W. W., & Stevens, N. (1997). Friendships and adaptation in the life course. *Psychological Bulletin, 121,* 355–370.

Harvey, J. H., Flanary, R., & Morgan, M. (1986). Vivid memories of vivid loves gone by. *Journal of Personal and Social Relationships, 3,* 359–373.

Harvey, J. H., Orbuch, T. L., & Weber, A. L. (1992). The convergence of the attribution and accounts concepts in the study of close relationships. In J. H. Harvey, T. L. Orbuch, & A. L. Weber (Eds.), *Attributions, Accounts and Close Relationships* (pp. 1–18). New York: Springer.

Haslam, S. A, McGarty, C., & Brown, P. (1996). The search for differentiated meaning is a precursor to illusory correlation. *Personality and Social Psychology Bulletin, 22,* 611–619.

Hassebrauck, M. (1988). Beauty is more than "name" deep: The effect of women's first names on ratings of physical attractiveness and personality attributes. *Journal of Applied Social Psychology, 18,* 721–726.

Hassebrauck, M., & Buhl, T. (1996). Three-dimensional love. *Journal of Social Psychology, 136,* 121–122.

Hastie, R. (1980). Memory for behavioral information that confirms or contradicts a personality impression. In R. Hastie, T. M. Ostrom, E. B. Ebbesen, R. S. Wyer, D. L. Hamilton, & D. E. Carlston (Eds.), *Person memory: The cognitive basis of social perception* (pp. 141–172). Hillsdale, NJ: Erlbaum.

Hastie, R., & Pennington, N. (1991). Cognitive and social processes in decision making. In L. B. Resnick, J. M. Levine, & S. D. Teasley (Eds.), *Perspectives on socially shared cognition* (pp. 308–327). Washington, DC: American Psychological Association.

Hastie, R., & Pennington, N. (1995). The big story: Is it a story? In R. S. Wyer, Jr. (Ed.), *Knowledge and memory: The real story. Advances in social cognition* (Vol. 8, pp. 133–138). Hillsdale, NJ: Erlbaum.

Hastie, R., Penrod, S. D., & Pennington, N. (1983). *Inside the jury.* Cambridge MA: Harvard University Press.

Hastorf, A., & Cantril, H. (1954). They saw a game: A case study. *Journal of Abnormal and Social Psychology, 49,* 129–134.

Hatfield, E. (1988). Passionate and companionate love. In R. J. Sternberg & M. L. Barnes (Eds.), *The psychology of love* (pp. 191–217). New Haven, CT: Yale University Press.

Hatfield, E., Cacioppo, J. T., & Rapson, R. L. (1993). *Emotional Contagion.* New York: Cambridge University Press.

Hatfield, E., Greenberger, E., Traupmann, J., & Lambert, P. (1982). Equity and sexual satisfaction in recently married couples. *Journal of Sex Research, 18,* 18–32.

Hatfield, E., & Rapson, R. L. (1996). *Love and Sex: Cross Cultural Perspectives.* Boston: Allyn & Bacon.

Hatfield, E., & Sprecher, S. (1986a). *Mirror, mirror: The importance of looks in everyday life.* Albany: State University of New York Press.

Hatfield, E., & Sprecher, S. (1986b). Measuring passionate love in intimate relationships. *Journal of Adolescence, 9,* 383–410.

Hatfield, E., & Sprecher, S. (1995). Men's and women's preferences in marital partners in the United States, Russia, and Japan. *Journal of Cross-Cultural Psychology, 26,* 728–750.

Hatfield, E., & Walster, G. W. (1978). *A new look at love.* Reading, MA: Addison-Wesley.

Haugtvedt, C. P., & Wegener, D. T. (1994). Message order effects in persuasion: An attitude strength perspective. *Journal of Consumer Research, 21,* 205–218.

Hays, R. B. (1984). The development and maintenance of friendship. *Journal of Social and Personal Relationships, 1,* 75–98.

Hazan, C., & Shaver, P. (1987). Romantic love conceptualized as an attachment process. *Journal of Personality and Social Psychology, 52,* 511–524.

Hazan, C., & Shaver, P. (1994a). Attachment as an organizational framework for research on close relationships. *Psychological Inquiry, 5,* 1–22.

Hazan, C., & Shaver, P. (1994b). Deeper into attachment theory. *Psychological Inquiry, 5,* 68–79.

Hazelwood, J. D., & Olson, J. M. (1986). Covariation information, causal questioning, and interpersonal behavior. *Journal of Experimental Social Psychology, 22,* 276–291.

Hearold, S. (1986). A synthesis of 1043 effects of television on social behavior. In G. Comstock (Ed.), *Public communication and behavior,* (Vol. 1, pp. 65–133). Orlando, FL: Academic Press.

Heckhausen, J., & Schulz, R. (1995). A life-span theory of control. *Psychological Review, 102,* 284–304.

Hedge, A., & Yousif, Y. H. (1992). Effects of urban size, urgency, and cost on helpfulness. *Journal of Cross-Cultural Psychology, 23,* 107–115.

Hedges, L. V., & Nowell, A. (1995). Sex differences in mental test scores, variability, and numbers of high-scoring individuals. *Science, 269,* 41–45.

Hedges, S. J. (April, 1997). Www.masssuicide.com: How an obscure cult mixed computers, UFOs, and New Age theology so its 39 members could take the ultimate journey. *U. S. News and World Report,* pp. 26–30.

Hegtvedt, K. A., Thompson, E. A., & Cook, K. S. (1993). Power and equity: What counts in attributions for exchange outcomes? *Social Psychology Quarterly, 56,* 100–119.

Heider, F. (1958). *The psychology of interpersonal relations.* New York: Wiley.

Heine, S., & Lehman, D. (1997). Culture, dissonance, and self-affirmation. *Personality and Social Psychology Bulletin, 23,* 389–400.

Heine, S. J., & Lehman, D. R. (1995). Cultural variation in unrealistic optimism: Does the West feel more vulnerable than the East? *Journal of Personality and Social Psychology, 68,* 595–607.

Heine, S. J., & Lehman, D. R. (1997). The cultural construction of self-enhancement: An examination of group-serving biases. *Journal of Personality and Social Psychology, 72,* 1268–1283.

Helgeson, V. S. (1993). Two important dimensions in social support: Kind of support and perceived versus received. *Journal of Applied Social Psychology, 23,* 825–845.

Helgeson, V. S., & Cohen, S. (1996). Social support and adjustment to cancer: Reconciling descriptive, correlational, and intervention research. *Health Psychology, 15,* 135–148.

Helgeson, V. S., & Mickelson, K. D. (1995). Motives for social comparison. *Personality and Social Psychology Bulletin, 21,* 1200–1209.

Henderson-King, E., & Nisbett, R. (1996). Anti-Black prejudice as a function of exposure to the negative behavior of a single Black person. *Journal of Personality and Social Psychology, 71,* 654–664.

Hendrick, C., & Hendrick, S. S. (1990). A relationship-specific version of the love attitudes scale. *Journal of Social Behavior and Personality, 5,* 239–254.

Hendrick, S. S., & Hendrick, C. (1986). A theory and method of love. *Journal of Personality and Social Psychology, 50,* 392–402.

Hendrick, S. S., & Hendrick, C. (1992). *Liking, loving and relating* (2nd ed.). Pacific Grove, CA: Brooks/Cole.

Henley, N. M. (1977). *Body politics: Power, sex, and nonverbal communication.* Englewood Cliffs, NJ: Prentice Hall.

Hennessey, B. A., Amabile, T., & Martinage, M. (1989). Immunizing children against the negative effects of reward. *Contemporary Educational Psychology, 14,* 212–227.

Hennessey, B. A., & Zbikowski, S. M. (1993). Immunizing children against the negative effects of reward: A further examination of intrinsic motivation focus sessions. *Creativity Research Journal, 6,* 297–307.

Henry, R. A. (1995). Using relative confidence judgments to evaluate group effectiveness. *Basic and Applied Social Psychology, 16,* 333–350.

Hepworth, J. T., & West, S. G. (1988). Lynchings and the economy: A time-series reanalysis of Hovland and Sears (1940). *Journal of Personality and Social Psychology, 55,* 239–247.

Herbert, T. B., & Cohen, S. (1993). Stress and immunity in humans: A meta-analytic review. *Psychosomatic Medicine, 55,* 364–379.

Hermans, D., De Houwer, J., & Eelen, P. (1994). The affective priming effect: Automatic evaluation of evaluative information in memory. *Cognition and Emotion, 8,* 515–533.

Herrnstein, R. J., &Murray, C. A. (1994). *The bell curve:Intelligence and class structure in American life.* New York:Free Press.

Hersh, S. M. (1970). *My Lai 4: A report on the massacre and its aftermath.* New York: Vintage Books.

Hertwig, R., Gigerenzer, G., & Hoffrage, U. (1997). The reiteration effect in hindsight bias. *Psychological Review, 104,* 194–202.

Herzog, D. B., Newman, K. L., Yeh, C. J., & Warshaw, M. (1992). Body image satisfaction in homosexual and heterosexual women. *International Journal of Eating Disorders, 11,* 391–396.

Herzog, T. A. (1994). Automobile driving as seen by the actor, the active observer, and the passive observer. *Journal of Applied Social Psychology, 24,* 2057–2074.

Heunemann, R. L., Shapiro, L. R., Hampton, M. C., & Mitchell, B. W. (1966). A longitudinal study of gross body composition and body conformation and their association with food and activity in the teenage population. *American Journal of Clinical Nutrition, 18,* 325–338.

Hewstone, M., & Jaspars, J. (1987). Covariation and causal attribution: A logical model of the intuitive analysis of variance. *Journal of Personality and Social Psychology, 53,* 663–672.

Higgins, E. T. (1987). Self-discrepancy: A theory relating self and affect. *Psychological Review, 94,* 319–340.

Higgins, E. T. (1989). Knowledge accessibility and activation: Subjectivity and suffering from unconscious sources. In J. S. Uleman & J. A. Bargh (Eds.), *Unintended thought* (pp. 75–123). New York: Guilford Press.

Higgins, E. T. (1989). Self-discrepancy theory: What patterns of self-beliefs cause people to suffer? In L. Berkowitz (Ed.), *Advances in experimental social psychology* (Vol. 22, pp. 93–136). New York: Academic Press.

Higgins, E. T. (1996). Knowledge application: Accessibility, applicability, and salience. In E. T. Higgins and A. R. Kruglanski (Eds.), *Social psychology: Handbook of basic principles.* New York: Guilford, pp. 133–168.

Higgins, E. T. (1996). The "self-digest": Self-knowledge serving self-regulatory functions. *Journal of Personality and Social Psychology, 71,* 1062–1083.

Higgins, E. T., & Bargh, J. A. (1987). Social cognition and social perception. *Annual Review of Psychology, 38,* 369–425.

Higgins, E. T., Bond, R. N., Klein, R., & Strauman, T. (1986). Self-discrepancies and emotional vulnerability: How magnitude, accessibility, and type of discrepancy influence affect. *Journal of Personality and Social Psychology, 51,* 5–15.

Higgins, E. T., & Brendl, C. M. (1995). Accessibility and applicability: Some "activation rules" influencing judgment. *Journal of Experimental Social Psychology, 31,* 218–243.

Higgins, E. T., Klein, R., & Strauman, T. (1987). Self-discrepancies: Distinguishing among self-states, self-state conflicts, and emotional vulnerabilities. In K. M. Yardley & T. M. Honess (Eds.), *Self and identity: Psychosocial perspectives* (pp. 173–186). New York: Wiley.

Higgins, E. T., Rholes, W. S., & Jones, C. R. (1977). Category accessibility and impression formation. *Journal of Experimental Social Psychology, 13,* 141–154.

Higgins, R. L., & Harris, R. N. (1988). Strategic "alcohol" use: Drinking to self-handicap. *Journal of Social and Clinical Psychology, 6,* 191–202.

Hill, A. J., Oliver, S., & Rogers, P. J. (1992). Eating in the adult world: The rise of dieting in childhood and adolescence. *British Journal of Clinical Psychology, 31,* 95–105.

Hill, C. T., Rubin, Z., & Peplau, L. A. (1976). Breakups before marriage: The end of 103 affairs. *Journal of Social Issues, 32,* 147–168.

Hilton, J. L., & Darley, J. M. (1991). The effects of interaction goals on person perception. In M. P. Zanna (Ed.), *Advances in experimental social psychology* (Vol. 24, pp. 235–267). San Diego, CA: Academic Press.

Hilton, J. L., Fein, S., & Miller, D. T. (1993). Suspicion and dispositional inference. *Journal of Personality and Social Psychology, 19,* 501–512.

Hinds, M. deCourcy. (1993, October 19). Not like the movie: 3 take a dare, and lose. *New York Times*, pp. A1, A22.

Hippler, H. J., Schwarz, N., & Sudman, S. (Eds.). (1987). *Social information processing and survey methodology*. New York: Springer-Verlag.

Hirt, E. R., Deppe, R. K., & Gordon, L. J. (1991). Self-reported versus behavioral self-handicapping: Empirical evidence for a theoretical distinction. *Journal of Personality and Social Psychology*, *61*, 981–991.

Hirt, E. R., McDonald, H. E., & Erikson, G. A. (1995). How do I remember thee? The role of encoding set and delay in reconstructive memory processes. *Journal of Experimental Social Psychology*, *31*, 379–409.

Hirt, E. R., Melton, J. R., McDonald, H. E., & Harackiewicz, J. M. (1996). Processing goals, task interest, and the mood-performance relationship: A mediational analysis. *Journal of Personality and Social Psychology, 71*, 245–261.

Hobbes, T. (1986). *Leviathan*. Harmondsworth, England: Penguin Press. (Original work published 1651)

Hobfoll, S. E., & Vaux, A. (1993). Social support: Social resources and social context. In L. Goldberger & S. Breznitz (Eds.), *Handbook of stress: Theoretical and clinical aspects* (2nd ed., pp. 685–705). New York: Free Press.

Hoffman, C., Lau, I., & Johnson, D. R. (1986). The linguistic relativity of person cognition: An English-Chinese comparison. *Journal of Personality and Social Psychology, 51*, 1097–1105.

Hoffman, M. L. (1981). Is altruism a part of human nature? *Journal of Personality and Social Psychology, 40*, 121–137.

Hofstede, G. (1986). Cultural differences in teaching and learning. *International Journal of Intercultural Relations, 10*, 301–320.

Hoge, W. (1997, September 5). Responding to Britain's sorrow, Queen will address the nation; Hurt by criticism, Royal family mourns openly. *The New York Times*, pp. A1; A6.

Hogg, M. A. (1992). *The Social Psychology of Group Cohesiveness: From Attraction to Social Identity*. London, England: Harvester-Wheatsheaf.

Hogg, M. A., & Abrams, D. (1988). *Social identifications*. London: Routledge. (cf. Chapter 3)

Holden, G. (1991). The relationship of self-efficacy appraisals to subsequent health related outcomes: A meta-analysis. *Social Work in Health Care, 16*, 53–93.

Hollander, E. P. (1958). Conformity, status, and idiosyncrasy credit. *Psychological Review, 65*, 117–127.

Hollander, E. P. (1960). Competence and conformity in the acceptance of influence. *Journal of Abnormal and Social Psychology, 61*, 361–365.

Hollander, E. P. (1985). Leadership and power. In G. Lindzey & E. Aronson (Eds.), *Handbook of social psychology* (3rd ed., Vol. 2, pp. 485–537). New York: McGraw-Hill.

Holmes, T. H., & Rahe, R. H. (1967). The social readjustment rating scale. *Journal of Psychosomatic Research, 11*, 213–218.

Holtz, R. (1997). Length of group membership, assumed similarity, and opinion certainty: The dividend for veteran members. *Journal of Applied Social Psychology, 27*, 539–555.

Homans, G. C. (1961). *Social behavior: Its elementary forms*. New York: Harcourt Brace & World.

Hong, G. W. (1992). Contributions of "culture-absent"cross-cultural psychology. Paper presented at annual meeting of Society for Cross-Cultural Research, Santa Fe, New Mexico.

Honts, C. R. (1994). Psychophysiological detection of deception. *Current Directions in Psychological Science, 3*, 77–82.

Hoose, P. M., (1989). *Necessities: Racial barriers in American sports*. New York: Random House.

Hornstein, H. A. (1991). Empathic distress and altruism: Still inseparable. *Psychological Inquiry, 2*, 133–135.

Hornstein, H. A., LaKind, E., Frankel, G., & Manne, S. (1975). Effects of knowledge about remote social events on prosocial behavior, social conception, and mood. *Journal of Personality and Social Psychology, 32*, 1038–1046.

House, J. S., Robbins, C., & Metzner, H. L. (1982). The association of social relationships and activities with mortality: Prospective evidence from the Tecumseh Community Health Study. *American Journal of Epidemiology, 116*, 123–140.

House, R. J. (1971). A path-goal theory of leadership effectiveness. *Administrative Science Quarterly, 16*, 321–338.

House, R. J., Spangler, W. D., & Woycke, J. (1991). Personality and charisma in the U.S. presidency: A psychological theory of leader effectiveness. *Administrative Science Quarterly. 36*, 364–396.

Houston, D. A., & Fazio, R. H. (1989). Biased processing as a function of attitude accessibility: Making objective judgments subjectively. *Social Cognition, 7*, 51–66.

Houts, R. M., Robins, E., & Huston, T. L. (1996). Compatibility and the development of premarital relationships. *Journal of Marriage and the Family, 58*, 7–20.

Hovland, C. I., Janis, I. L., & Kelley, H. H. (1953). *Communication and persuasion: Psychological studies of opinion change*. New Haven, CT: Yale University Press.

Hovland, C. I., & Sears, R. R. (1940). Minor studies in aggression: 6. Correlation of lynchings with economic indices. *Journal of Psychology, 9*, 301–310.

Hovland, C. I., & Weiss, W. (1951). The influence of source credibility on communication effectiveness. *Public Opinion Quarterly, 15*, 635–650.

Howard, D. J. (1997). Familiar phrases as peripheral persuasion cues. *Journal of Experimental Social Psychology, 33*, 231–243.

Hsu, F. L. K. (1981). The self in cross-cultural perspective. In A. J. Marsella, B. De Vos, & F. L. K. Hsu (Eds.), *Culture and self* (pp. 24–55). London: Tavistock.

Hsu, S. S. (1995, April 8). Fredericksburgh searches its soul after clerk is beaten as 6 watch. *Washington Post*, pp. A1, A13.

Huesmann, L. R. (1982). Television violence and aggressive behavior. In D. Pearly, L. Bouthilet, & J. Lazar (Eds.), *Television and behavior: Vol. 2. Technical reviews* (pp. 220–256). Washington, DC: National Institute of Mental Health.

Huffman, K. T., Grossnickle, W. F., Cope, J. G., & Huffman, K. P. (1995). Litter reduction: A review and integration of the literature. *Environment and Behavior, 27*, 153–183.

Hull, J. G. (1981). A self-awareness model of the causes and effects of alcohol consumption. *Journal of Personality and Social Psychology, 90*, 586–600.

Hull, J. G., & Young, R. D. (1983). Self-consciousness, self-esteem, and success-failure as determinants of alcohol consumption in male social drinkers. *Journal of Personality and Social Psychology, 44*, 1097–1109.

Hull, J. G., Young, R. D., & Jouriles, E. (1986). Applications of the self-awareness model of alcohol consumption: Predicting patterns of use and abuse. *Journal of Personality and Social Psychology, 51*, 790–796.

Hunt, G. T. (1940). *The wars of the Iroquois*. Madison: University of Wisconsin Press.

Hurley, D., & Allen, B. P. (1974). The effect of the number of people present in a nonemergency situation. *Journal of Social Psychology, 92*, 27–29.

Huston, A., & Wright, J. (1996). Television and socialization of young children. In T. M. MacBeth (Ed.), *Tuning in to young viewers: Social science perspectives on television* (pp. 37–60). Thousand Oaks, CA: Sage

Hutchinson, R. R. (1983). The pain-aggression relationship and its expression in naturalistic settings. *Aggressive Behavior, 9*, 229–242.

Hyde, J. S. (1997). Mathematics: Is biology the cause of gender differences in performance? In M. R. Walsh (Ed.), *Women, men, and gender: Ongoing debates* (pp. 271–273). New Haven, CT: Yale University Press.

Hyman, J. J., & Sheatsley, P. B. (1956; 1964). Attitudes toward desegregation. *Scientific American, 195*(6), 35–39, and *211*(1), 16–23.

Ickes, W., & Layden, M. A. (1978). Attributional styles. In J. H. Harvey, W. Ickes, & R. F. Kidd (Eds.), *New directions in attribution research* (Vol. 2, pp. 119–152). Hillsdale, NJ: Erlbaum.

Ickes, W., Patterson, M. L., Rajecki, D. W., & Tanford, S. (1982). Behavioral and cognitive consequences of reciprocal versus compensatory responses to preinteraction expectancies. *Social Cognition, 1*, 160–190.

Ickes, W., Robertson, E., Tooke, W., & Teng, G. (1986). Naturalistic social cognition: Methodology, assessment, and validation. *Journal of Personality and Social Psychology, 51*, 66–82.

Imrich, D. J., Mullin, C., & Linz, D. (1995). Measuring the extent of prejudicial pretrial publicity in major American newspapers: A content analysis. *Journal of Communication, 45*, 94–117.

Ingham, A. G., Levinger, G., Graves, J., & Peckham, V. (1974). The Ringelmann effect: Studies of group size and group performance. *Journal of Experimental Social Psychology, 10*, 371–384.

Inglehart, M. R. (1991). *Reactions to critical life events: A social psychological analysis.* New York: Praeger.

Insko, C. A., Smith, R. H., Alicke, M. D., Wade, J., & Taylor, S. (1985). Conformity and group size: The concern with being right and the concern with being liked. *Personality and Social Psychology Bulletin, 11*, 41–50.

Isen, A. M. (1987). Positive affect, cognitive processes, and social behavior. In L. Berkowitz (Ed.), *Advances in experimental social psychology* (Vol. 20, pp. 203–253). San Diego, CA: Academic Press.

Isen, A. M., & Levin, P. A. (1972). Effect of feeling good on helping: Cookies and kindness. *Journal of Personality and Social Psychology, 21*, 384–388.

Isenberg, D. J. (1986). Group polarization: A critical review and meta-analysis. *Journal of Personality and Social Psychology, 50*, 1141–1151.

Izard, C. (1969). The emotions and emotion constructs in personality and culture research. In R. B. Cattell (Ed.), *Handbook of modern personality theory* (pp. 496–510). Chicago: Aldine.

Izard, C. (1977). *Human emotions.* New York: Plenum.

Izard, C. E. (1994). Innate and universal facial expressions: Evidence from developmental and cross-cultural research. *Psychological Bulletin, 115*, 288–299.

Jackson, J. (1981, July 19). Syndicated newspaper column.

Jackson, J. M., & Williams, K. D. (1985). Social loafing on difficult tasks: Working collectively can improve performance. *Journal of Personality and Social Psychology, 49*, 937–942.

Jackson, J. S., & Inglehart, M. R. (1995). Reverberation theory: Stress and racism in hierarchically structured communities. In S. E. Hobfoll & M. W. de Vries (Eds.), *Extreme stress and communities: Impact and intervention* (pp. 353–373). Dordrecht, Netherlands: Kluwer Academic Publishers.

Jackson, J. W. (1993). Realistic group conflict theory: A review and evaluation of the theoretical and empirical literature. *Psychological Record, 43*, 395–413.

Jackson, L. A. (1992). *Physical Appearance and Gender: Sociobiological and Sociocultural Perspectives.* Albany, NY: State University of New York Press.

Jackson, L. A., Hunter, J. E., & Hodge, C. N. (1995). Physical attractiveness and intellectual competence: A meta-analytic review. *Social Psychology Quarterly, 58*, 108–122.

Jacobs, J., & Eccles, J. (1992). The impact of mothers' gender-role stereotypic beliefs on mothers' and children's ability perceptions. *Journal of Personality and Social Psychology, 63*, 932–944.

Jacobs, P., & Landau, S. (1971). *To serve the devil* (Vol. 2, p. 71). New York: Vintage Books.

Jacobson, M., & Hacker, G. (1985, May 6). The case for curbing alcohol advertising. *Broadcasting*, p. 19.

Jacobson, N. S., Waldron, H., & Moore, D. (1980). Toward a behavioral profile of marital distress. *Journal of Consulting and Clinical Psychology, 48*, 696–703.

Jacoby, L. L., Lindsay, S. D., & Toth, J. P. (1992). Unconscious influences revealed: Attention, awareness, and control. *American Psychologist, 47*, 802–809.

James, J. M., & Bolstein, R. (1992). Large monetary incentives and their effect on mail survey response rates. *Public Opinion Quarterly, 56*, 442–453.

James, W. (1890). *The principles of psychology.* New York: Holt.

James, W. (1910). *The principles of psychology* (Vols. 1–2). London: Macmillan.

"Jammy man" actor's plight. (1988, October 18). *New York Times*, p. A25.

Janis, I. L. (1972). *Victims of groupthink.* Boston: Houghton Mifflin.

Janis, I. L. (1982). *Groupthink* (2nd ed.). Boston: Houghton Mifflin.

Janis, I. L., & Feshbach, S. (1953). Effects of fear-arousing communications. *Journal of Abnormal and Social Psychology, 49*, 78–92.

Jankowiak, W. (1995). Introduction. In W. Jankowiak (Ed.), *Romantic Passion: A Universal Experience?* (pp. 1–19). New York: Columbia University Press.

Jankowiak, W., & Fischer, E. (1992). A cross-cultural perspective on romantic love. *Ethnology, 31*, 149–155.

Janoff-Bulman, R., Timko, C., & Carli, L. L. (1985). Cognitive biases in blaming the victim. *Journal of Experimental Social Psychology, 21*, 161–177.

Jeavons, C. M., & Taylor, S. P. (1985). The control of alcohol related aggression: Redirecting the inebriate's attention to socially appropriate conduct. *Aggressive Behavior, 11*, 93–101.

Jecker, J., & Landy, D. (1969). Liking a person as a function of doing him a favor. *Human Relations, 22*, 371–378.

Jellison, J. M., & Riskind, J. A. (1970). A social comparison of abilities interpretation of risk-taking behavior. *Journal of Personality and Social Psychology, 15*, 375–390.

Jennings, D. J., Amabile, T. M., & Ross, L. (1982). Informal covariation assessment: Data-based versus theory-based judgments. In D. Kahneman, P. Slovic, & A. Tversky (Eds.), *Judgment under uncertainty: Heuristics and biases* (pp. 211–230). New York: Cambridge University Press.

Jensen-Campbell, L. A., Graziano, W. G., & West, S. G. (1995). Dominance, prosocial orientation, and female preference: Do nice guys really finish last? *Journal of Personality and Social Psychology, 68*, 427–440.

Jepson, C., & Chaiken, S. (1990). Chronic issue-specific fear inhibits systematic processing of persuasive communications. *Journal of Social Behavior and Personality, 5*, 61–84.

Jet noise. (1991, Oct. 21). *New Yorker*, pp. 30–32.

Job, R. F. S. (1988). Effective and ineffective use of fear in health promotion campaigns. *American Journal of Public Health, 78,* 163–167.

Johnson, B. T., & Eagly, A. H. (1989). Effects of involvement on persuasion: A meta-analysis. *Psychological Bulletin, 106,* 290–314.

Johnson, B. T., & Eagly, A. H. (1990). Involvement and persuasion: Types, traditions, and evidence. *Psychological Bulletin, 107,* 375–384.

Johnson, D. M. (1945). The phantom anesthetist of Mattoon: A field study of mass hysteria. *Journal of Abnormal and Social Psychology, 40,* 175–186.

Johnson, D. W., & Johnson, R. T. (1987). *Learning together and alone: Cooperative, competitive, and individualistic learning* (2nd ed.). Englewood Cliffs, NJ: Prentice Hall.

Johnson, D. W., & Johnson, R. T. (1989). *A meta-analysis of cooperative, competitive, and individualistic goal structures.* Hillsdale, NJ: Erlbaum.

Johnson, F. L., & Aries, E. J. (1983). Conversational patterns among same-sex pairs of late-adolescent close friends. *Journal of Genetic Psychology, 142,* 225–238.

Johnson, G. (1997, May 9). Conventional wisdom says machines cannot think. *New York Times Cybertimes* (www.nytimes.com).

Johnson, J. T. (1986). The knowledge of what might have been: Affective and attributional consequences of near outcomes. *Personality and Social Psychology Bulletin, 12,* 136–153.

Johnson, J. T., & Boyd, K. R. (1995). Dispositional traits versus the content of experience: Actor/observer differences in judgments of the "authentic self." *Personality and Social Psychology Bulletin, 21,* 375–383.

Johnson, L. B. (1971). *The vantage point: Perspectives of the presidency, 1963–69.* New York: Holt, Rinehart & Winston.

Johnson, M. K., & Raye, C. L. (1981). Reality monitoring. *Psychological Review, 88,* 67–85.

Johnson, M. K., Hashtroudi, S., & Lindsay, D. S. (1993). Source monitoring. *Psychological Bulletin, 114,* 3–28.

Johnson, R. D., & Downing, R. L. (1979). Deindividuation and valence of cues: Effects of prosocial and antisocial behavior. *Journal of Personality and Social Psychology, 37,* 1532–1538.

Johnson, T. E., & Rule, B. G. (1986). Mitigating circumstance information, censure, and aggression. *Journal of Personality and Social Psychology, 50,* 537–542.

Joiner, T. E., Jr., & Wagner, K. D. (1995). Attributional style and depression in children and adolescents: A meta-analytic review. *Clinical Psychology Review, 15,* 777–798.

Jones, C., & Aronson, E. (1973). Attribution of fault to a rape victim as a function of the respectability of the victim. *Journal of Personality and Social Psychology, 26,* 415–419.

Jones, D., & Hill, K. (1993). Criteria of facial attractiveness in five populations. *Human Nature, 4,* 271–296.

Jones, E., & Kohler, R. (1959). The effects of plausibility on the learning of controversial statements. *Journal of Abnormal and Social Psychology, 57,* 315–320.

Jones, E. E. (1964). *Ingratiation: A social psychological analysis.* New York: Appleton-Century-Crofts.

Jones, E. E. (1979). The rocky road from acts to dispositions. *American Scientist, 34,* 107–117.

Jones, E. E. (1990). *Interpersonal perception.* New York: Freeman.

Jones, E. E., & Berglas, S. (1978). Control of attributions about the self through self-handicapping strategies: The appeal of alcohol and the role of underachievement. *Personality and Social Psychology Bulletin, 4,* 200–206.

Jones, E. E., & Davis, K. E. (1965). From acts to dispositions: The attribution process in social psychology. In L. Berkowitz (Ed.), *Advances in experimental social psychology* (Vol. 2, pp. 219–266). New York: Academic Press.

Jones, E. E., Davis, K. E., & Gergen, K. J. (1961). Role playing variations and their informational value for person perception. *Journal of Abnormal and Social Psychology, 63,* 302–310.

Jones, E. E., & Harris, V. A. (1967). The attribution of attitudes. *Journal of Experimental Social Psychology, 3,* 1–24.

Jones, E. E., & McGillis, D. (1976). Correspondent inferences and the attribution cube: A comparative reappraisal. In J. H. Harvey, W. J. Ickes, & R. F. Kidd (Eds.), *New directions in attribution research* (Vol. 1, pp. 389–420). Hillsdale, NJ: Erlbaum.

Jones, E. E., & Nisbett, R. E. (1972). The actor and the observer: Divergent perceptions of the causes of behavior. In E. E. Jones, D. E. Kanouse, H. H. Kelley, R. E. Nisbett, S. Valins, & B. Weiner (Eds.), *Attribution: Perceiving the causes of behavior* (pp. 79–94). Morristown, NJ: General Learning Press.

Jones, E. E., & Pittman, T. S. (1982). Toward a general theory of strategic self-presentation. In J. Suls (Ed.), *Psychological perspectives on the self* (pp. 231–262). Hillsdale, NJ: Erlbaum.

Jones, E. E., Rhodewalt, F., Berglas, S., & Skelton, J. A. (1981). Effects of strategic self-presentation on subsequent self-esteem. *Journal of Personality and Social Psychology, 41,* 407–421.

Jones, E. E., Rock, L., Shaver, K. G., Goethals, G. R., & Ward, L. M. (1968). Pattern of performance and ability attribution: An unexpected primacy effect. *Journal of Personality and Social Psychology, 10,* 317–340.

Jones, E. E., & Sigall, H. (1971). The bogus pipeline: A new paradigm for measuring affect and attitude. *Psychological Bulletin, 76,* 349–364.

Jones, E. E., & Wortman, C. B. (1973). *Ingratiation: An attributional approach.* Morristown, NJ: General Learning Press.

Jones, J., Jones, M., & Hochner, A. (1973). Racial differences in sports activities: A look at the self-paced versus reactive hypothesis. *Journal of Personality and Social Psychology, 27,* 86–95.

Jones, M. B., & Jones, R. D. (1995). Preferred pathways of behavioral contagion. *Journal of Psychiatric Research, 29,* 193–209.

Jordan, M. (1996, January 15). In Japan, bullying children to death. *Washington Post,* pp. A1; A15.

Jordan, M., & Sullivan, K. (1995, September 8). A matter of saving face: Japanese can rent mourners, relatives, friends, even enemies to buff an image. *Washington Post,* pp. A1, A28.

Josephson, W. D. (1987). Television violence and children's aggression: Testing the priming, social script, and disinhibition prediction. *Journal of Personality and Social Psychology, 53,* 882–890.

Judd, C., & McClelland, G. (1998). Measurement. In D. Gilbert, S. Fiske, & G. Lindzey (Eds.), *The handbook of social psychology* (4th ed., Vol. 1, pp. 180–232). New York: Random House.

Judd, C. M., & Park, B. (1988). Out-group homogeneity: Judgments of variability at the individual and group levels. *Journal of Personality and Social Psychology, 54,* 778–788.

Jussim, L. (1986). Self-fulfilling prophecies: A theoretical and integrative review. *Psychological Review, 93,* 429–445.

Jussim, L. (1989). Teacher expectations: Self-fulfilling prophecies, perceptual biases, and accuracy. *Journal of Personality and Social Psychology, 57,* 469–480.

Jussim, L. (1991). Social perception and social reality: A reflection-construction model. *Psychological Review, 98,* 54–73.

Jussim, L., & Eccles, J. S. (1992). Teacher expectations: II: Construction and reflection of student achievement. *Journal of Personality and Social Psychology, 63,* 947–961.

Juveniles committing fewer violent crimes. (1997, Oct. 3). *Charlottesville Daily Progress,* pp. A1; A9.

Kahn, M. (1966). The physiology of catharsis. *Journal of Personality and Social Psychology, 3,* 278–298.

Kahneman, D., & Miller, D. T. (1986). Norm theory: Comparing reality to its alternatives. *Psychological Review, 93,* 136–153.

Kahneman, D., & Tversky, A. (1973). On the psychology of prediction. *Psychological Review, 80,* 237–251.

Kahneman, D., & Tversky, A. (1982). The simulation heuristic. In D. Kahneman, P. Slovic, & A. Tversky (Eds.), *Judgment under uncertainty: Heuristics and biases* (pp. 201–208). New York: Cambridge University Press.

Kahneman, D., & Tversky, A. (1983). Can irrationality be intelligently discussed? *The Behavioral and Brain Sciences, 6,* 509–510.

Kalick, S. M. (1977). *Plastic surgery, physical appearance, and person perception.* Unpublished doctoral dissertation, Harvard University.

Kallgren, C. A., & Wood, W. (1986). Access to attitude-relevant information in memory as a determinant of attitude-behavior consistency. *Journal of Experimental Social Psychology, 22,* 328–338.

Kalven, H., Jr., & Zeisel, H. (1966). *The American jury.* Boston: Little, Brown.

Kappas, A. (1997). The fascination with faces: Are they windows to our soul? *Journal of Nonverbal Behavior, 21,* 157–162.

Karau, S. J., & Williams, K. D. (1993). Social loafing: A meta-analytic review and theoretical integration. *Journal of Personality and Social Psychology, 65,* 681–706.

Karau, S. J., & Williams, K. D. (1995). Social loafing: Research findings, implications, and future directions. *Current Directions in Psychological Science, 5,* 134–140.

Karlins, M., Coffman, T. L., & Walters, G. (1969). On the fading of social stereotypes: Studies in three generations of college students. *Journal of Personality and Social Psychology, 13,* 1–16.

Kashy, D. A., & DePaulo, B. M. (1996). Who lies? *Journal of Personality and Social Psychology, 70,* 1037–1051.

Kassarjian, H., & Cohen, J. (1965). Cognitive dissonance and consumer behavior. *California Management Review, 8,* 55–64.

Katz, A. M., & Hill, R. (1958). Residential propinquity and marital selection: A review of theory, method, and fact. *Marriage and Family Living, 20,* 237–335.

Katz, D. (1960). The functional approach to the study of attitudes. *Public Opinion Quarterly, 24,* 163–204.

Katz, D., & Braly, K. W. (1933). Racial stereotypes of 100 college students. *Journal of Abnormal and Social Psychology, 28,* 280–290.

Kauffman, D. R., & Steiner, I. D. (1968). Conformity as an ingratiation technique. *Journal of Experimental Social Psychology, 4,* 404–414.

Kelley, H. H. (1950). The warm-cold variable in first impressions of persons. *Journal of Personality, 18,* 431–439.

Kelley, H. H. (1955). The two functions of reference groups. In G. E. Swanson, T. M. Newcomb, & E. L. Hartley (Eds.), *Readings in social psychology* (2nd ed., pp. 410–414). New York: Holt.

Kelley, H. H. (1967). Attribution theory in social psychology. In D. Levine (Ed.), *Nebraska Symposium on Motivation* (Vol. 15, pp. 192–238). Lincoln: University of Nebraska Press.

Kelley, H. H. (1972). Attribution in social interaction. In E. E. Jones, D. E. Kanouse, H. H. Kelley, R. E. Nisbett, S. Valins, & B. Weiner (Eds.), *Attribution: Perceiving the causes of behavior* (pp. 1–26). Morristown, NJ: General Learning Press.

Kelley, H. H. (1983). Love and commitment. In H. H. Kelley, E. Berscheid, A. Christensen, J. H. Harvey, T. L. Huston, G. Levinger, E. McClintock, L. A. Peplau, & D. R. Peterson (Eds.), *Close relationships* (pp. 265–314). New York: Freeman.

Kelley, H. H., & Thibaut, J. (1978). *Interpersonal relations: A theory of interdependence.* New York: Wiley.

Kelly, J. G., Ferson, J. E., & Holtzman, W. H. (1958). The measurement of attitudes toward the Negro in the South. *Journal of Social Psychology, 48,* 305–312.

Kelman, H. C. (1997). Group processes in the resolution of international conflicts: Experiences from the Israeli-Palestinian case. *American Psychologist, 52,* 212–220.

Keltner D. (1995). Signs of appeasement: Evidence for the distinct displays of embarrassment, amusement, and shame. *Journal of Personality and Social Psychology, 68,* 441–454.

Keltner, D., & Buswell, B. N. (1996). Evidence for the distinctness of embarrassment, shame, and guilt: A study of recalled antecedents and facial expressions. *Cognition and Emotion, 10,* 155–171.

Kenny, D., Kashy, D., & Bolger, N. (1998). Data analysis in social psychology. In D. Gilbert, S. Fiske, & G. Lindzey (Eds.), *The handbook of social psychology* (4th ed., Vol. 1, pp. 233–268). New York: McGraw-Hill.

Kenny, D. A. (1991). A general model of consensus and accuracy in interpersonal perception. *Psychological Review, 98,* 155–163.

Kenny, D. A. (1994). Using the social relations model to understand relationships. In R. Erber & R. Gilmour (Eds.), *Theoretical Frameworks for Personal Relationships* (pp. 111–127). Hillsdale, NJ: Erlbaum.

Kenny, D. A., Albright, A., Malloy, T. E. & Kashy, D. A. (1994). Consensus in interpersonal perception: Acquaintance and the big five. *Psychological Bulletin, 116,* 245–258.

Kenny, D. A., Horner, C., Kashy, D. A., & Chu, L. (1992). Consensus at zero acquaintance: Replication, behavioral cues, and stability. *Journal of Personality and Social Psychology, 62,* 88–97.

Kenny, D. A., & La Voie, L. (1982). Reciprocity of interpersonal attraction: A confirmed hypothesis. *Social Psychology Quarterly, 45,* 54–58.

Kenny, D. A., & Nasby, W. (1980). Splitting the reciprocity correlation. *Journal of Personality and Social Psychology, 38,* 249–256.

Kenny, D. A., & Zaccaro, S. L. (1983). An estimate of variance due to traits in leadership. *Journal of Applied Psychology, 68,* 678–685.

Kenrick, D. T., & MacFarlane, S. W. (1986). Ambient temperature and horn honking: A field study of the heat/aggression relationship. *Environment and Behavior, 18,* 179–191.

Kent, M. V. (1994). The presence of others. In A. P. Hare, H. H. Blumberg, M. F. Davies, & M. V. Kent (Eds.), *Small group research: A handbook* (pp. 81–105). Norwood, NJ: Ablex.

Kerckhoff, A. C., & Back, K. W. (1968). *The June bug: A study of hysterical contagion.* New York: Appleton-Century-Crofts.

Kerckhoff, A. C., & Davis, K. E. (1962). Value consensus and need complementarity in mate selection. *American Sociological Review, 27,* 295–305.

Kerr, N. L. (1995). Social psychology in court: The case of the prejudicial pretrial publicity. In G. G. Brannigan & M. R. Merrens (Eds.), *The social psychologists: Research adventures* (pp. 247–262). New York: McGraw-Hill.

Kerr, N. L., & Kaufman-Gilliland, C. M. (1994). Communication, commitment, and cooperation in social dilemmas. *Journal of Personality and Social Psychology, 66,* 513–529.

Kerr, N. L., & Stanfel, J. A. (1993). Role schemata and member motivation in task groups. *Personality and Social Psychology Bulletin, 19,* 432–442.

Key, W. B. (1973). *Subliminal seduction.* Englewood Cliffs, NJ: Signet.

Key, W. B. (1989). *Age of manipulation: The con in confidence and the sin in sincere.* New York: Holt.

Kiernan, L. (1995, July 2). Cabrini kids learn how to cash in on a Newt idea. *Chicago Tribune,* p. C1.

Kiesler, C. A., & Kiesler, S. B. (1969). *Conformity.* Reading, MA: Addison-Wesley.

Kihlstrom, J. F. (1987). The cognitive unconscious. *Science, 237,* 1445–1452.

Kihlstrom, J. F. (1996). The trauma-memory argument and recovered memory therapy. In K. Pezdek & W. P. Banks (Eds.), *The recovered memory/false memory debate* (pp. 297–311). San Diego: Academic Press.

Kihlstrom, J. F. (1997). Memory, abuse, and science. *American Psychologist, 52,* 994–995.

Kihlstrom, J. F., & Klein, S. B. (1994). The self as a knowledge structure. In R. S. Wyer & T. K. Srull (Eds.), *Handbook of social cognition. Vol. 1: Basic processes* (pp. 153–206). Hillsdale, NJ: Erlbaum.

Killen, J. D. (1985). Prevention of adolescent tobacco smoking: The social pressure resistance training approach. *Journal of Child Psychology and Psychiatry, 26,* 7–15.

Killian, L. M. (1964). Social movements. In R. E. L. Farris (Ed.), *Handbook of modern sociology* (pp. 426–455). Chicago: Rand McNally.

Kim, M. P., & Rosenberg, S. (1980). Comparison of two structural models of implicit personality theory. *Journal of Personality and Social Psychology, 38,* 375–389.

Kim, P. H. (1997). When what you know *can* hurt you: A study of experiential effects on group discussion and performance. *Organizational Behavior and Human Decision Processes, 69,* 165–177.

Kim, U., & Berry, J. W. (1993). *Indigenous Psychologies: Research and Experience in Cultural Context.* Newbury Park, CA: Sage.

Kim, U., Triandis, H. C., Kagitcibasi, C., Choi, S. C., & Yoon, G. (Eds.) (1994). *Individualism and Collectivism: Theory, Method and Applications.* Thousand Oaks, CA: Sage.

Kimura, D. (1987). Are men's and women's brains really different? *Canadian Psychology, 28,* 133–147.

Kinder, D. R., & Sears, D. O. (1981). Prejudice and politics: Symbolic racism versus racial threats to the good life. *Journal of Personality and Social Psychology, 40,* 414–431.

King, A. S. (1971, September). Self-fulfilling prophecies in training the hard-core: Supervisors' expectations and the under-privileged workers' performance. *Social Science Quarterly,* pp. 369–378.

Kipnis, D. M. (1957). Interaction between members of bomber crews as a determinant of sociometric choice. *Human Relations, 10,* 263–270.

Kirkpatrick, L. A., & Davis, K. E. (1994). Attachment style, gender, and relationship stability: A longitudinal analysis. *Journal of Personality and Social Psychology, 66,* 502–512.

Kirkpatrick, L. A., & Hazan, C. (1994). Attachment styles and close relationships: A four-year prospective study. *Personal Relationships, 1,* 123–142.

Kirschner, R. H., Eckner, F., & Baron, R. C. (1986). The cardiac pathology of sudden unexplained nocturnal death in Southeast Asian refugees. *Journal of the American Medical Association, 256,* 2819–2918.

Kitayama, S., & Karasawa, M. (1997). Implicit self-esteem in Japan: Name letters and birthday numbers. *Personality and Social Psychology Bulletin, 23,* 736–742.

Kitayama, S., & Markus, H. R. (1994). Culture and the self: How cultures influence the way we view ourselves. In D. Matsumoto (Ed.), *People: Psychology from a cultural perspective* (pp. 17–37). Pacific Grove, CA: Brooks/Cole.

Kitayama, S., Markus, H. R., Matsumoto, H., & Norasakkunkit, V. (1997). Individual and collective processes in the construction of the self: Self-enhancement in the United States and self-criticism in Japan. *Journal of Personality and Social Psychology, 72,* 1245–1267.

Klein, W. M. (1996). Maintaining self-serving social comparisons: Attenuating the perceived significance of risk-increasing behaviors. *Journal of Social and Clinical Psychology, 15,* 120–142.

Kleiwer, W., Lepore, S. J., & Evans, G. W. (1990). The costs of Type B behavior: Females at risk in achievement situations. *Journal of Applied Social Psychology, 20,* 1369–1382.

Klenke, K. (1996). *Women and leadership: A Contextual Perspective.* New York: Springer.

Knapp, M. L. (1980). *Essentials of nonverbal communication.* New York: Holt, Rinehart & Winston.

Knapp, M. L., & Comadena, M. E. (1979). Telling it like it isn't: A review of theory and research on deceptive communications. *Human Communication Research, 5,* 270–285.

Knapp, M. L., & Hall, J. A. (1997). *Nonverbal Communication in Human Interaction.* New York: Harcourt Brace College Publishers.

Knopke, H., Norrell, R., & Rogers, R. (1991). *Opening doors: Perspectives on race relations in contemporary America.* Tuscaloosa, AL: The University of Alabama Press.

Knowles, E. S., & Sibicky, M. E. (1990). Continuity and diversity in the stream of selves: Metaphorical resolutions of William James's one-in-many-selves paradox. *Personality and Social Psychology Bulletin, 16,* 676–687.

Knox, R., & Inkster, J. (1968). Postdecision dissonance at post time. *Journal of Personality and Social Psychology, 8,* 319–323.

Kobak, R. R., & Hazan, C. (1991). Attachment in marriage: Effects of security and accuracy of working models. *Journal of Personality and Social Psychology, 60,* 861–869.

Koditz, T. A., & Arkin, R. M. (1982). An impression management interpretation of the self-handicapping strategy. *Journal of Personality and Social Psychology, 43,* 492–502.

Koehler, J. J. (1993). The base rate fallacy myth. *PSYCOLOQUY, 4*(49).

Koehler, J. J. (1996). The base rate fallacy reconsidered: Descriptive, normative, and methodological challenges. *Behavioral and Brain Sciences, 19,* 1–53.

Koehnken, G., Malpass, R. S., & Wogalter, M. S. (1996). Forensic applications of line-up research. In S. L. Sporer, R. S. Malpass, & G. Koehnken (Eds.), *Psychological issues in eyewitness identification* (pp. 205–231). Mahwah, NJ: Erlbaum.

Koestler, A. (1959). The initiates. In R. Crossman (Ed.), *The god that failed.* New York: Bantam.

Kogan, N., & Wallach, M. A. (1964). *Risk-taking: A study in cognition and personality.* New York: Holt.

Kohn, A. (1986). *No contest.* Boston: Houghton Mifflin.

Kohn, A. (1993). *Punished by rewards.* Boston: Houghlin Mifflin.

Kojetin, B. A. (1993). Adult attachment styles with romantic partners, friends, and parents. Unpublished doctoral dissertation, University of Minnesota, Minneapolis.

Kollack, P., Blumstein, P. & Schwartz, P., (1994). The judgment of equity in intimate relationships. *Social Psychology Quarterly, 57,* 340–351.

Komorita, S. S., & Parks, C. D. (1995). Interpersonal relations: Mixed-motive interaction. *Annual Review of Psychology, 46,* 183–207.

Komorita, S. S., Parks, C. D., & Hulbert, L. G. (1992). Reciprocity and the induction of cooperation in social dilemmas. *Journal of Personality and Social Psychology, 62,* 607–617.

Koriat, A., Lichtenstein, S., & Fischhoff, B. (1980). Reasons for confidence. *Journal of Experimental Psychology: Human Learning and Memory, 6,* 107–118.

Korte, C. (1980). Urban-nonurban differences in social behavior and social psychological models of urban impact. *Journal of Social Issues, 36,* 29–51.

Krackow, A., & Blass, T. (1995). When nurses obey or defy inappropriate physician orders: Attributional differences. *Journal of Social Behavior and Personality, 10,* 585–594.

Kramer, G. P., Kerr, N. L., & Carroll, J. S. (1990). Pretrial publicity, judicial remedies, and jury bias. *Law and Human Behavior, 14,* 409–438.

Kramer, T. H., Buckhout, R., & Eugenio, P. (1990). Weapon focus, arousal, and eyewitness memory: Attention must be paid. *Law and Human Behavior, 14,* 167–184.

Krantz, D. S., Grunberg, N. E., & Baum, A. (1985). Health psychology. *Annual Review of Psychology, 36,* 349–383.

Krauss, R. M., & Deutsch, M. (1966). Communication in interpersonal bargaining. *Journal of Personality and Social Psychology, 4,* 572–577.

Krauss, R. M., Freedman, J. L., & Whitcup, M. (1978). Field and laboratory studies of littering. *Journal of Experimental Social Psychology, 14,* 109–122.

Kremer, J. F., & Stephens, L. (1983). Attributions and arousal as mediators of mitigation's effects on retaliation. *Journal of Personality and Social Psychology, 45,* 335–343.

Kressel, K., & Pruitt, D. G. (1989). A research perspective on the mediation of social conflict. In K. Kressel & D. G. Pruitt (Eds.), *Mediation research: The process and effectiveness of third party intervention* (pp. 394–435). San Francisco: Jossey-Bass.

Krosnick, J. A., & Abelson, R. P. (1991). The case for measuring attitude strength in surveys. In J. Tanur (Ed.), *Questions about survey questions* (pp. 177–203). New York: Russell Sage.

Krosnick, J. A., & Alwin, D. F. (1989). Aging and susceptibility to attitude change. *Journal of Personality and Social Psychology, 57,* 416–425.

Kruglanski, A. W. (1989). *Lay epistemics and human knowledge.* New York: Plenum.

Kruglanski, A. W. (1989). The psychology of being "right": The problem of accuracy in social perception and cognition. *Psychological Bulletin, 106,* 395–409.

Kruglanski, A. W., & Mayseless, O. (1990). Classic and current social comparison research: Expanding the perspective. *Psychological Bulletin, 108,* 195–208.

Kruglanski, A. W., & Webster, D. M. (1991). Group members' reactions to opinion deviates and conformists at varying degrees of proximity to decision deadline and of environmental noise. *Journal of Personality and Social Psychology, 61,* 212–225.

Kruglanski, A. W., & Webster, D. M. (1996). Motivated closing of the mind: "Seizing" and "freezing." *Psychological Review, 103,* 263–283.

Krull, D. (1993). Does the grist change the mill? The effect of the perceiver's inferential goal on the process of social inference. *Personality and Social Psychology Bulletin, 19,* 340–340.

Krull, D. S., & Dill, J. C. (1996). On thinking first and responding fast: Flexibility in social inference processes. *Personality and Social Psychology Bulletin, 22,* 949–959.

Kuhn, D., Weinstock, M., & Flaton, R. (1994). How well do jurors reason? Competence dimensions of individual variation in a juror reasoning task. *Psychological Science, 5,* 289–296.

Kulik, J., & Brown, R. (1979). Frustration, attribution of blame, and aggression. *Journal of Experimental Social Psychology, 15,* 183–194.

Kunda, Z. (1990). The case for motivated reasoning. *Psychological Bulletin, 108,* 480–498.

Kunda, Z., Fong, G. T., Sanitioso, R., & Reber, E. (1993). Directional questions about self-conceptions. *Journal of Experimental Social Psychology, 29,* 63–86.

Kunda, Z., & Nisbett, R. E. (1986). The psychometrics of everyday life. *Cognitive Psychology, 18,* 195–224.

Kunda, Z., & Oleson, K. C. (1997). When exceptions prove the rule: How extremity of deviance determines the impact of deviant examples on stereotypes. *Journal of Personality and Social Psychology, 72,* 965–979.

Kunda, Z., Sinclair, L., & Griffin, D. (1997). Equal ratings but separate meanings: Stereotypes and the construal of traits. *Journal of Personality and Social Psychology, 72,* 720–734.

Kunkel, D., Wilson, B., Donnerstein, E., Blumenthal, E., et al. (1995). Measuring television violence: The importance of context. *Journal of Broadcasting and Electronic Media, 39,* 284–291.

Kunz, P. R., & Woolcott, M. (1976). Season's greetings: From my status to yours. *Social Science Research, 5,* 269–278.

Kuo, Z. Y. (1961). Genesis of the cat's response to the rat. In *Instinct* (p. 24). Princeton, NJ: Van Nostrand.

Kuusinen, J. (1969). Factorial invariance of personality ratings. *Scandinavian Journal of Psychology, 10,* 33–44.

Kuykendall, D., & Keating, J. P. (1990). Altering thoughts and judgments through repeated association. *British Journal of Social Psychology, 29,* 79–86.

Kytle, C. (1969). *Gandhi, soldier of nonviolence: His effect on India and the world today.* New York: Grosset & Dunlap.

L'Armand, K., & Pepitone, A. (1975). Helping to reward another person: A cross-cultural analysis. *Journal of Personality and Social Psychology, 31,* 189–198.

Laird, J. D. (1974). Self-attribution of emotion: The effects of expressive behavior on the quality of emotional experience. *Journal of Personality and Social Psychology, 33,* 475–486.

Laird, J. D., & Bressler, C. (1992). The process of emotional experience: A self-perception theory. In M. S. Clark (Ed.), *Review of personality and social psychology* (pp. 213–234). Newbury Park, CA: Sage.

Lalancette, M. F., & Standing, L. (1990). Asch fails again. *Social Behavior and Personality, 18,* 7–12.

Lamb, C. S., Jackson, L. A., Cassiday, P. B., & Priest, D. J. (1993). Body figure preferences of men and women: A comparison of two generations. *Sex Roles, 28,* 345–358.

Lamm, H., Schaude, E., & Trommsdorff, G. (1971). Risky shift as a function of group members' value of risk and need for approval. *Journal of Personality and Social Psychology, 20,* 430–435.

Lammers, H. B., & Becker, L. A. (1980). Distraction: Effects on the perceived extremity of a communication and on cognitive responses. *Personality and Social Psychology Bulletin, 6,* 261–266.

Landman, J. (1993*). Regret: The persistence of the possible.* New York: Oxford University Press.

Lane, A. (1997). Last rites. *New Yorker,* Sept., pp. 4–5.

Langer, E. J. (1975). The illusion of control. *Journal of Personality and Social Psychology, 32,* 311–328.

Langer, E. J. (1989). Minding matters: The consequences of mindlessness-mindfulness. In L. Berkowitz (Ed.), *Advances in experimental social psychology* (Vol. 22, pp. 137–174). San Diego, CA: Academic Press.

Langer, E. J., Blank, A., & Chanowitz, B. (1978). The mindlessness of ostensibly thoughtful action: The role of "placebic" information in interpersonal interaction. *Journal of Personality and Social Psychology, 36*, 635–642.

Langer, E. J., & Rodin, J. (1976). The effects of choice and enhanced personal responsibility for the aged: A field experiment. *Journal of Personality and Social Psychology, 34*, 191–198.

Langer, P. A. (1986). *Preventing domestic violence against women.* Washington, DC: U.S. Department of Justice, U.S. Government Printing Office.

Langlois, J. H., & Roggman, L. A. (1990). Attractive faces are only average. *Psychological Science, 1*, 115–121.

Langlois, J. H., Roggman, L. A., & Musselman, L. (1994). What is average and what is not average about attractive faces? *Psychological Science, 5*, 214–220.

LaPiere, R. T. (1934). Attitudes vs. actions. *Social Forces, 13*, 230–237.

Larsen, K. S. (1990). The Asch conformity experiment: Replication and transhistorical comparisons. *Journal of Social Behavior and Personality, 5*, 163–168.

Larson, J. R., Jr., Foster-Fishman, P. G., & Keys, C. B. (1994). Discussion of shared and unshared information in decision-making groups. *Journal of Personality and Social Psychology, 67*, 446–461.

Latané, B. (Ed.). (1966). Studies in social comparison: Introduction and overview. *Journal of Experimental Social Psychology, Supplement 1*, 1–5.

Latané, B. (1981). The psychology of social impact. *American Psychologist, 36*, 343–356.

Latané, B. (1987). From student to colleague: Retracing a decade. In N. E. Grunberg, R. E. Nisbett, J. Rodin, & J. E. Singer (Eds.), *A distinctive approach to psychological research: The influence of Stanley Schachter* (pp. 66–86). Hillsdale, NJ: Erlbaum.

Latané, B., & Dabbs, J. M. (1975). Sex, group size, and helping in three cities. *Sociometry, 38*, 108–194.

Latané, B., & Darley, J. M. (1968). Group inhibition of bystander intervention. *Journal of Personality and Social Psychology, 10*, 215–221.

Latané, B., & Darley, J. M. (1970). *The unresponsive bystander: Why doesn't he help?* Englewood Cliffs, NJ: Prentice Hall.

Latané, B., & L'Herrou, T. (1996). Spatial clustering in the conformity game: Dynamic social impact in electronic games. *Journal of Personality and Social Psychology, 70*, 1218–1230.

Latané, B., & Nida, S. (1981). Ten years of research on group size and helping. *Psychological Bulletin, 89*, 308–324.

Latané, B., Nowak, A., & Liu, J. (1994). Measuring emergent social phenomena: Dynamism, polarization, and clustering as order parameters of social systems. *Behavioral Science, 39*, 1–24.

Latané, B., Williams, K., & Harkins, S. (1979). Many hands make light work: The causes and consequences of social loafing. *Journal of Personality and Social Psychology, 37*, 822–832.

Latané, B., & Wolf, S. (1981). The social impact of majorities and minorities. *Psychological Review, 88*, 438–453.

Lau, R. R., & Russell, D. (1980). Attributions in the sports pages: A field test of some current hypotheses about attribution research. *Journal of Personality and Social Psychology, 39*, 29–38.

Laughlin, P. R. (1980). Social combination processes of cooperative problem-solving groups as verbal intellective tasks. In M. Fishbein (Ed.), *Progress in social psychology* (Vol. 1, pp. 127–155). Hillsdale, NJ: Erlbaum.

Lazarsfeld, P. (Ed.). *Radio and the printed page.* New York: Duell, Sloan & Pearce.

Lazarus, R. S. (1966). *Psychological stress and the coping process.* New York: McGraw-Hill.

Lazarus, R. S. (1993). Why we should think of stress as a subset of emotion. In L. Goldberger & S. Breznitz (Eds.), *Handbook of stress: Theoretical and clinical aspects* (2nd ed., pp. 21–39). New York: Free Press.

Lazarus, R. S. (1995). Vexing research problems inherent in cognitive-mediational theories of emotion—and some solutions. *Psychological Inquiry, 6*, 183–196.

Lazarus, R. S., & Folkman, S. (1984). *Stress, appraisal, and coping.* New York: Springer-Verlag.

Lea, M., & Spears, R. (1995). Love at first byte: Building personal relationships over computer networks. In J. T. Wood & S. Duck (Eds.), *Understudied Relationships: Off the Beaten Track* (pp. 197–233). Thousand Oaks, CA: Sage.

Leary, M. R. (1995). *Self-presentation: Impression management and interpersonal behavior.* Madison, WI: Brown & Benchmark.

Leathers, D. G. (1997). *Successful Nonverbal Communication: Principles and Applications.* Boston: Allyn & Bacon.

LeBon, G. (1895). *The crowd.* London: F. Unwin.

Lee, D. (1959). *Freedom and culture.* Englewood Cliffs, NJ: Prentice Hall.

Lee, F., Hallahan, M., & Herzog, T. (1996). Explaining real-life events: How culture and domain shape attributions. *Personality and Social Psychology Bulletin, 22*, 732–741.

Lee, J. A. (1973). *The colors of love: An exploration of the ways of loving.* Don Mills, Ontario: New Press.

Lee, J. A. (1977). A typology of styles of loving. *Personality and Social Psychology Bulletin, 3*, 173–182.

Lee, J. A. (1988). Love-styles. In R. J. Sternberg & M. L. Barnes (Eds.), *The psychology of love* (pp. 38–67). New Haven, CT: Yale University Press.

Lehman, D. R., Davis, C. G., DeLongis, A., & Wortman, C. B. (1993). Positive and negative life changes following bereavement and their relations to adjustment. *Journal of Social and Clinical Psychology, 12*, 90–112.

Lehman, D. R., Lempert, R. O., & Nisbett, R. E. (1988). The effects of graduate training on reasoning. *American Psychologist, 43*, 431–442.

Leippe, M., & Eisenstadt, D. (1998). A self-accountability model of dissonance reduction: Multiple modes on a continuum of elaboration. In E. Harmon-Jones & J. S. Mills, *Cognitive dissonance theory: Revival with revisions and controversies.* Washington, DC: American Psychological Association.

Leippe, M. R., & Eisenstadt, D. (1994). Generalization of dissonance reduction: Decreasing prejudice through induced compliance. *Journal of Personality and Social Psychology, 67*, 395–413.

Leippe, M. R., Manion, A. P., & Romanczyk, A. (1992). Eyewitness persuasion: How and how well do fact finders judge the accuracy of adults' and children's memory reports? *Journal of Personality and Social Psychology, 63*, 181–197.

Leishman, K. (1988, February). Heterosexuals and AIDS. *Atlantic Monthly.*

Leo, J. (1991, July 15). Hostility among the ice cubes. *U.S. News and World Report*, p. 18.

Lepper, M. (1995). Theory by numbers? Some concerns about meta-analysis as a theoretical tool. *Applied Cognitive Psychology, 9*, 411–422.

Lepper, M. (1996). Intrinsic motivation and extrinsic rewards: A commentary on Cameron and Pierce's meta-analysis. *Review of Educational Research, 66,* 5–32.

Lepper, M. R., & Greene, D. (1978). *The hidden costs of reward.* Hillsdale, NJ: Erlbaum.

Lepper, M. R., Greene, D., & Nisbett, R. E. (1973). Undermining children's intrinsic interest with extrinsic reward: A test of the overjustification hypothesis. *Journal of Personality and Social Psychology, 28,* 129–137.

Lepper, M. R., Keavney, M., & Drake, M. (1996). Intrinsic motivation and extrinsic rewards: A commentary on Cameron and Pierce's meta analysis. *Review of Educational Research, 66,* 5–32.

Lerner, M. J. (1980). *The belief in a just world: A fundamental decision.* New York: Plenum.

Lerner, M. J. (1991). The belief in a just world and the "heroic motive": Searching for "constants" in the psychology of religious ideology. *International Journal for the Psychology of Religion,1,* 27–32.

Lerner, M. J., Grant, P. R. (1990). The influences of commitment to justice and ethnocentrism on children's allocations of pay. *Social Psychology Quarterly, 53,* 229–238.

Lerner, M. J., & Miller, D. T. (1978). Just world research and the attribution process: Looking back and ahead. *Psychological Bulletin, 85,* 1030–1051.

Lerner, M. J., & Simmons, C. H. (1966). Observers' reaction to the innocent victim: Compassion or rejection? *Journal of Personality and Social Psychology, 4,* 203–210.

Leung, K., & Bond, M. H. (1984). The impact of cultural collectivism on reward allocation. *Journal of Personality and Social Psychology, 47,* 793–804.

Leung, K., & Van De Vijver, F. (1996). Cross-cultural research methodology. In F. T. L. Leong & J. T. Austin (Eds.), *The psychology of research handbook: A guide for graduate students and research assistants* (pp. 351–358). Thousand Oaks, CA: Sage.

Leventhal, H. (1970). Findings and theory in the study of fear communications. In L. Berkowitz (Ed.), *Advances in experimental social psychology* (Vol. 5, pp. 119–186). New York: Academic Press.

Leventhal, H., Watts, J. C., & Pagano, F. (1967). Effects of fear and instructions on how to cope with danger. *Journal of Personality and Social Psychology, 6,* 313–321.

Levi, P. (1986). *"Survival in Auschwitz"; and "The Reawakening: Two memoirs."* New York: Summit Books.

Levine, G. L., Halberstadt, J. B., & Goldstone, R. (1996). Reasoning and the weighting of attributes in attitude judgments. *Journal of Personality and Social Psychology, 70,* 230–240.

Levine, J., Resnick, L., & Higgins, E. T. (1993). Social foundations of cognition. *Annual Review of Psychology, 44,* 585–612.

Levine, J. M. (1980). Reaction to opinion deviance in small groups. In P. Paulus (Ed.), *Psychology of group influence* (pp. 375–427). Hillsdale, NJ: Erlbaum.

Levine, J. M. (1989). Reaction to opinion deviance in small groups. In P. B. Paulus (Ed.), *Psychology of group influence,* (2nd ed., pp. 187–231). Hillsdale, NJ: Erlbaum.

Levine, J. M., & Moreland, R. L. (1990). Progress in small group research. *Annual Review of Psychology, 41,* 585–634.

Levine, J. M., & Moreland, R. L. (1995). Group processes. In A. Tesser (Ed.), *Advanced social psychology* (pp. 419–465). New York: McGraw-Hill.

Levine, J. M., & Moreland, R. L. (1998). Small groups. In D. Gilbert, S. Fiske, & G. Lindzey (Eds.), *The handbook of social psychology* (4th ed., Vol. 2, pp. 415–469). New York: McGraw Hill.

Levine, J. M., & Russo, E. M. (1987). Majority and minority influence. In C. Hendrick (Ed.), *Group processes: Review of personality and social psychology* (Vol. 8, pp. 13–54). Newbury Park, CA: Sage.

Levine, J. M., & Thompson, L. (1996). Conflict in groups. In E. T. Higgins & A. W. Kruglanski (Eds.), *Social psychology: Handbook of basic principles* (pp. 745–776). New York: Guilford.

Levine, R. A., & Campbell, D. T. (1972). *Ethnocentrism: theories of conflict, ethnic attitudes, and group behavior.* New York: Wiley.

Levine, R. V., Martinez, T. S., Brase, G., & Sorenson, K. (1994). Helping in 36 U.S. cities. *Journal of Personality and Social Psychology, 67,* 69–82.

Levinger, G. (1964). Note on need complementarity in marriage. *Psychological Bulletin, 61,* 153–157.

Levinger, G., Senn, D. J., & Jorgensen, B. W. (1970). Progress toward permanence in courtship: A test of the Kerckhoff-Davis hypothesis. *Sociometry, 33,* 427–433.

Levitas, M. (1969). *America in crisis.* New York: Holt, Rinehart & Winston.

Levy, J. S., & Morgan, T. C. (1984). The frequency and seriousness of war: An inverse relationship? *Journal of Conflict Resolution, 28,* 731–749.

Levy, S. (1979). Authoritarianism and information processing. *Bulletin of the Psychonomic Society, 13,* 240–242.

Levy-Leboyer, C. (1988). Success and failure in applying psychology. *American Psychologist, 43,* 779–785.

Lewin, K. (1943). Defining the "field at a given time." *Psychological Review, 50,* 292–310.

Lewin, K. (1947). Frontiers in group dynamics. *Human Relations, 1,* 5–41.

Lewin, K. (1948). *Resolving social conflicts: Selected papers in group dynamics.* New York: Harper.

Lewin, K. (1951). Problems of research in social psychology. In D. Cartwright (Ed.), *Field theory in social science* (pp. 155–169). New York: Harper & Row.

Lewis, C. S. (1952). *Mere Christianity.* New York: Macmillan.

Lewis, M. (1986). Origins of self-knowledge and individual differences in early self-recognition. In J. Suls & A. G. Greenwald (Eds.), *Psychological perspectives on the self* (Vol. 3, pp. 55–78). Hillsdale, NJ: Erlbaum.

Lewis, M., & Brooks, J. (1978). Self-knowledge and emotional development. In M. Lewis & L. Rosenblum (Eds.), *The development of affect* (pp. 205–226). New York: Plenum.

Leyens, J. P., Camino, L., Parke, R. D., & Berkowitz, L. (1975). Effects of movie violence on aggression in a field setting as a function of group dominance and cohesion. *Journal of Personality and Social Psychology, 32,* 346–360.

Leyens, J. P., Cisneros, T., & Hossay, J. F. (1976). Decentration as a means of reducing aggression after exposure to violent stimuli. *European Journal of Social Psychology, 6,* 459–473.

Liang, D. W., Moreland, R., & Argote, L. (1995). Group versus individual training and group performance: The mediating role of transactive memory. *Personality and Social Psychology Bulletin, 21,* 384–393.

Liberman, A., & Chaiken, S. (1992). Defensive processing of personally relevant health messages. *Personality and Social Psychology Bulletin, 18,* 669–679.

Lichtenstein, S., Fischhoff, B., & Phillips, L. D. (1982). Calibration of probabilities: The state of the art to 1980. In D. Kahneman, P. Slovic, & A. Tversky (Eds.), *Judgment under uncertainty: Heuristics and biases* (pp. 306–334). New York: Cambridge University Press.

Liebert, R. M., & Baron, R. A. (1972). Some immediate effects of televised violence on children's behavior. *Developmental Psychology, 6,* 469–475.

Liebert, R. M., & Sprafkin, J. (1988). *The early window* (3rd ed.). New York: Pergamon.

Liebrand, W. B. G., Messick, D. M., & Wilke, H. A. M. (Eds.). (1992). *Social dilemmas: Theoretical issues and research findings*. Oxford, England: Pergamon Press.

Lim, T.-S., & Choi, S.-H. (1996). Interpersonal relationships in Korea. In W. B. Gudykunst, S. Ting-Toomey, & T. Nishida (Eds.), *Communication in Personal Relationships Across Cultures* (pp. 122–136). Thousand Oaks, CA: Sage.

Lind, E. A., & Tyler, T. R. (1988). *The social psychology of procedural justice*. New York: Plenum.

Lindsay, D. S. (1994). Memory source monitoring and eyewitness testimony. In D. F. Ross, J. D. Read, & M. P. Toglia (Eds.), *Adult eyewitness testimony: Current trends and developments* (pp. 27–55). New York: Cambridge University Press.

Lindsay, D. S., & Johnson, M. K. (1989). The eyewitness suggestibility effect and memory for source. *Memory and Cognition, 17*, 349–358.

Lindsay, R. C. L. (1994). Expectations of eyewitness performance: Jurors' verdicts do not follow from their beliefs. In D. F. Ross, J. D. Read, & M. P. Toglia (Eds.), *Adult eyewitness testimony: Current trends and developments* (pp. 362–384). New York: Cambridge University Press.

Lindsay, R. C. L., & Wells, G. L. (1985). Improving eyewitness identifications from lineups: Simultaneous versus sequential lineup presentation. *Journal of Applied Psychology, 70*, 556–564.

Linville, P. W., & Carlston, D. E. (1994). Social cognition and the self. In P. G. Devine, D. L. Hamilton, & T. M. Ostrom (Eds.), *Social cognition: Impact on social psychology* (pp. 144–193). San Diego: Academic Press.

Linville, P. W., Fischer, G. W., & Fischhoff, B. (1993). AIDS risk perceptions and decision biases. In J. B. Pryor & G. D. Reeder (Eds.), *The social psychology of HIV infection* (pp. 5–38). Hillsdale, NJ: Erlbaum.

Linville, P. W., Fischer, G. W., & Salovey, P. (1989). Perceived distributions of characteristics of in-group and out-group members: Empirical evidence and a computer simulation. *Journal of Personality and Social Psychology, 57*, 165–188.

Lipkus, I. M., Dalbert, C., & Siegler, I. C. (1996). The importance of distinguishing the belief in a just world for self versus for others: Implications for psychological well-being. *Personality and Social Psychology Bulletin, 22*, 666–677.

Litt, M. D. (1988). Self-efficacy and perceived control: Cognitive mediators of pain tolerance. *Journal of Personality and Social Psychology, 54*, 149–160.

Littlepage, G. E. (1991). Effects of group size and task characteristics on group performance: A test of Steiner's model. *Personality and Social Psychology Bulletin, 17*, 449–456.

Livesley, W. J., & Bromley, D. B. (1973). *Person perception in childhood and adolescence*. New York: Wiley.

Lloyd Morgan, C. (1961). C. Lloyd Morgan. In C. Murchison (Ed.), *History of psychology in autobiography* (Vol. 2, pp. 237–264). New York: Russell & Russell. (Original work published 1930)

Lloyd, S. A., & Cate, R. M. (1985). The developmental course of conflict in dissolution of premarital relationships. *Journal of Social and Personal Relationships, 2*, 179–194.

Lodish, L. M., Abraham, M., Kalmenson, S., Lievelsberger, J., Lubetkin, B., Richardson, B., & Stevens, M. E. (1995). How T.V. advertising works: A meta-analysis of 389 real world split cable T.V. advertising experiments. *Journal of Marketing Research, 32*, 125–139.

Loftus, E. F. (1979). *Eyewitness testimony*. Cambridge, MA: Harvard University Press.

Loftus, E. F. (1993). The reality of repressed memories. *American Psychologist, 48*, 518–537.

Loftus, E. F., & Hoffman, H. G. (1989). Misinformation and memory: The creation of new memories. *Journal of Experimental Psychology: General, 118*, 100–104.

Loftus, E. F., & Ketcham, K. (1994). *The myth of repressed memory: False memories and allegations of sexual abuse*. New York: St. Martin's Press.

Loftus, E. F., Loftus, G. R., & Messo, J. (1987). Some facts about "weapons focus." *Law and Human Behavior, 11*, 55–62.

Loftus, E. F., Miller, D. G., & Burns, H. J. (1978). Semantic integration of verbal information into a visual memory. *Journal of Experimental Psychology: Human Learning and Memory, 4*, 19–31.

Loftus, E. F., & Palmer, J. C. (1974). Reconstruction of automobile destruction: An example of the interaction between language and memory. *Journal of Verbal Learning and Verbal Behavior, 13*, 585–589.

London, P. (1970). The rescuers: Motivational hypotheses about Christians who saved Jews from the Nazis. In J. R. Macaulay & L. Berkowitz (Eds.), *Altruism and helping behavior* (pp. 241–250). New York: Academic Press.

Lonner, W., & Berry, J. (Eds.). (1986). *Field methods in cross-cultural research*. Beverly Hills, CA: Sage.

Lord, C. G., Lepper, M. R., & Preston, E. (1984). Considering the opposite: A corrective strategy for social judgment. *Journal of Personality and Social Psychology, 47*, 1231–1243.

Lord, C. G., Ross, L., & Lepper, M. (1979). Biased assimilation and attitude polarization: The effects of prior theories on subsequently considered evidence. *Journal of Personality and Social Psychology, 37*, 2098–2109.

Lord, C. G., Scott, K. O., Pugh, M. A., & Desforges, D. M. (1997). Leakage beliefs and the correspondence bias. *Personality and Social Psychology Bulletin, 23*, 824–836.

Lord, R. G., DeVader, C. L., & Alliger, G. M. (1986). A meta-analysis of the relation between personality traits and leadership perceptions: An application of validity generalization procedures. *Journal of Applied Psychology, 71*, 402–410.

Lore, R. K., & Schultz, L. A. (1993). Control of human aggression. *American Psychologist, 48*, 16–25.

Lorenz, K. (1966). *On aggression* (M. Wilson, Trans.). New York: Harcourt, Brace & World.

Losch, M., & Cacioppo, J. (1990). Cognitive dissonance may enhance sympathetic tonus, but attitudes are changed to reduce negative affect. *Journal of Experimental Social Psychology, 26*, 289–304.

Lott, A. J., & Lott, B. E. (1961). Group cohesiveness, communication level, and conformity. *Journal of Abnormal and Social Psychology, 62*, 408–412.

Lott, A. J., & Lott, B. E. (1974). The role of reward in the formation of positive interpersonal attitudes. In T. Huston (Ed.), *Foundations of interpersonal attraction*. New York: Academic Press.

Lowry, D. T., Love, G., & Kirby, M. (1981). Sex on the soap operas: Patterns of intimacy. *Journal of Communication, 31*, 90–96.

Lumsdaine, A. A., & Janis, I. L. (1953). Resistance to "counterpropaganda"; produced by one-sided and two-sided "propaganda" presentations. *Public Opinion Quarterly, 17*, 311–318.

Lupfer, M. B., & Layman, E. (1996). Invoking naturalistic and religious attributions: A case of applying the availability heuristic? The representativeness heuristic? *Social Cognition, 14*, 55–76.

Luus, C. A. E., & Wells, G. L. (1994a). Eyewitness identification confidence. In D. F. Ross, J. D. Read, & M. P. Toglia (Eds.), *Adult eyewitness testimony: Current trends and developments* (pp. 348–361). New York: Cambridge University Press.

Luus, C. A. E., & Wells, G. L. (1994b). The malleability of eye-witness confidence: Co-witness and perserverance effects. *Journal of Applied Psychology, 79,* 714–723.

Lyall, S. (1997, September 5). A ruler who lives firmly by the rules. *The New York Times,* pp. A1; A6.

Lykken, D. T. (1984). Polygraphic interrogation. *Nature, 307,* 681–684.

Lynn, M., & Shurgot, B. A. (1984). Responses to lonely hearts advertisements: Effects of reported physical attractiveness, physique, and coloration. *Personality and Social Psychology Bulletin, 10,* 349–357.

Lysak, H., Rule, B. G., & Dobbs, A. R. (1989). Conceptions of aggression: Prototype or defining features? *Personality and Social Psychology Bulletin, 15,* 233–243.

Lyubomirsky, S., & Nolen-Hoeksema, S. (1993). Self-perpetuating properties of depressive rumination. *Journal of Personality and Social Psychology, 65,* 339–349.

Maass, A., & Clark, R. D., III. (1984). Hidden impact of minorities: Fifteen years of research. *Psychological Bulletin, 95,* 428–450.

Maccoby, E. E. (1990). Gender and relationships: A developmental account. *American Psychologist, 45,* 513–520.

Maccoby, E. E., & Jacklin, C. N. (1974). *The psychology of sex differences.* Stanford, CA: Stanford University Press.

MacCoun, R. J. (1989). Experimental research on jury decision-making. *Science, 244,* 1046–1050.

MacDonald, T., Zanna, M., & Fong, G. (1996). Why common sense goes out the window: Effects of alcohol on intentions to use condoms. *Personality and Social Psychology Bulletin, 22,* 763–775.

Mackie, D. M. (1987). Systematic and nonsystematic processing of majority and minority persuasive communications. *Journal of Personality and Social Psychology, 53,* 41–52.

MacKinnon, C. (1993, July–August). "Turning rape into pornography: Postmodern genocide." *Ms.,* pp. 24–30.

Maclean, N. (1983). *A river runs through it.* Chicago: University of Chicago Press.

Madaras, G. R., & Bem, D. J. (1968) Risk and conservatism in group decision making. *Journal of Experimental Social Psychology, 4,* 350–366.

Madon, S., Jussim, L., & Eccles, J. (1997). In search of the powerful self-fulfilling prophecy. *Journal of Personality and Social Psychology, 72,* 791–809.

Magaro, P. A., & Ashbrook, R. M. (1985). The personality of societal groups. *Journal of Personality and Social Psychology, 48,* 1479–1489.

Magoo, G., & Khanna, R. (1991). Altruism and willingness to donate blood. *Journal of Personality and Clinical Studies, 7,* 21–24.

Maier, N. R. F., & Solem, A. R. (1952). The contribution of a discussion leader to the quality of group thinking: The effective use of minority opinions. *Human Relations, 5,* 277–288.

Main, M., Kaplan, N., & Cassidy, J. (1985). Security in infancy, childhood, and adulthood: A move to the level of representation. In T. Bretherton & E. Waters (Eds.), *Growing points of attachment theory and research. Monographs of the Society for Research on Child Development, 50,* 66–104.

Maio, G. R., & Olson, J. M. (1995). Relations between values, attitudes, and behavioral intentions: The moderating role of attitude function. *Journal of Experimental Social Psychology, 31,* 266–285.

Major, B. (1980). Information acquisition and attribution process. *Journal of Personality and Social Psychology, 39,* 1010–1023.

Major, B., & Schmader, T. (1998). Coping with stigma through psychological disengagement. In J. Swim & C. Stangor (Eds.), *Stigma: The target's perspective.* New York: Academic Press.

Malamuth, N. M., Check, J., & Briere, J. (1986). Sexual arousal in response to aggression: Ideological, aggressive, and sexual correlates. *Journal of Personality and Social Psychology, 50,* 330–350.

Malamuth, N. M., & Donnerstein, E. (1983). The effects of aggressive-pornographic mass media stimuli. In L. Berkowitz (Ed.), *Advances in experimental social psychology* (Vol. 15, pp. 103–136). New York: Academic Press.

Malle, B. F., & Horowitz, L. M. (1995). The puzzle of negative self-views: An exploration using the schema concept. *Journal of Personality and Social Psychology, 68,* 470–484.

Malle, B. F., & Knobe, J. (1997). Which behaviors do people explain? A basic actor-observer asymmetry. *Journal of Personality and Social Psychology, 72,* 288–304.

Malpass, R. S., & Devine, P. G. (1981). Eyewitness identification: Lineup instructions and the absence of the offender. *Journal of Applied Psychology, 66,* 482–489.

Mandler, G. (1975). *Mind and emotion.* New York: Wiley.

Manis, M., Shedler, J., Jonides, J., & Nelson, T. E. (1993). Availability heuristic in judgments of set size and frequency of occurrence. *Journal of Personality and Social Psychology, 65,* 448–457.

Maracek, J., & Mettee, D. R. (1972). Avoidance of continued success as a function of self-esteem, level of esteem certainty, and responsibility for success. *Journal of Personality and Social Psychology, 22,* 90–107.

Marcus, D. K., Wilson, J. R., & Miller, R. S. (1996). Are perceptions of emotion in the eye of the beholder? A social relations analysis of judgments of embarrassment. *Personality and Social Psychology Bulletin, 22,* 1220–1228.

Marion, R. (1995, August). The girl who mewed. *Discover,* pp. 38–40.

Markman, K. D., Gavanski, I., Sherman, S. J., & McMullen, M. N. (1995). The impact of perceived control on the imagination of better and worse possible worlds. *Personality and Social Psychology Bulletin, 21,* 588–595.

Markoff, J. (1996, Dec. 21). Steven Jobs making move back to Apple. *New York Times,* p. 37.

Markus, H. (1977). Self-schemata and processing information about the self. *Journal of Personality and Social Psychology, 35,* 63–78.

Markus, H., & Kitayama, S. (1991). Culture and the self: Implications for cognition, emotion, and motivation. *Psychological Review, 98,* 224–253.

Markus, H. R., & Nurius, P. (1986). Possible selves. *American Psychologist, 41,* 954–969.

Markus, H. R., Kitayama, S., & Heiman, R. J. (1996). Culture and "basic" psychological principles. In E. T. Higgins & A. W. Kruglanski (Eds.), *Social psychology: Handbook of basic principles* (pp. 857–913). New York: Guilford.

Markus, H. R., Smith, J., & Moreland, R. L. (1985). Role of the self-concept in the social perception of others. *Journal of Personality and Social Psychology, 49,* 1494–1512.

Marlowe, D., & Gergen, K. J. (1970). Personality and social behavior. In K. J. Gergen & D. Marlowe (Eds.), *Personality and social behavior* (p. 1–75). Reading, MA: Addison-Wesley.

Marshall, G. D., & Zimbardo, P. G. (1979). Affective consequences of inadequately explained physiological arousal. *Journal of Personality and Social Psychology, 37,* 970–988.

Martin, L. L. (1986). Set/reset: Use and disuse of concepts in impression formation. *Journal of Personality and Social Psychology, 51,* 493–504.

Martin, L. L., Seta, J. J., & Crelia, R. (1990). Assimilation and contrast as a function of people's willingness and ability to expend effort in forming an impression. *Journal of Personality and Social Psychology, 59,* 27–37.

Martin, M. M., & Anderson, C. M. (1995). Roommate similarity: Are roommates who are similar in their communication traits more satisfied? *Communication Research Reports, 12,* 46–52.

Martin, N. G., Eaves, L. J., Heath, A. R., Jardine, R., Feingold, L. M., & Eysenck, H. J. (1986). Transmission of social attitudes. *Proceedings of the National Academy of Science, 83,* 4364–4368.

Martz, J. M. (1991). Giving Batson's strawman a brain . . . and a heart. *American Psychologist, 20,* 162–163.

Maslach, C. (1979). Negative emotional biasing of unexplained arousal. *Journal of Personality and Social Psychology, 37,* 953–969.

Matthews, K. A. (1988). Coronary heart disease and Type A behaviors: Update on and alternative to the Booth-Kewley and Friedman (1987) quantitative review. *Psychological Bulletin, 104,* 373–380.

McAlister, A., Perry, C., Killen, J., Slinkard, L. A., & Maccoby, N. (1980). Pilot study of smoking, alcohol, and drug abuse prevention. *American Journal of Public Health, 70,* 719–721.

McAllister, H. A. (1996). Self-serving bias in the classroom: Who shows it? Who knows it? *Journal of Educational Psychology, 88,* 123–131.

McArthur, L. (1972). The how and what of why: Some determinants and consequences of causal attribution. *Journal of Personality and Social Psychology, 22,* 171–193.

McArthur, L. Z. (1990). *Social perception.* Pacific Grove, CA: Brooks/Cole.

McArthur, L. Z., & Baron, R. M. (1983). Toward an ecological theory of social perception. *Psychological Review, 90,* 215–238.

McArthur, L. Z., & Berry, D. S. (1987). Cross cultural agreement in perceptions of babyfaced adults. *Journal of Cross-Cultural Psychology, 18,* 165–192.

McArthur, L. Z., & Resko, G. B. (1975). The portrayal of men and women in American television commercials. *Journal of Social Psychology, 97,* 209–220.

McAuley, E., & Gross, J. G. (1983). Perceptions of causality in sport: An application of the Causal Dimension Scale. *Journal of Sport Psychology, 5,* 72–76.

McCarthy, J. F., & Kelly, B. R. (1978). Aggressive behavior and its effect on performance over time in ice hockey athletes: An archival study. *International Journal of Sport Psychology, 9,* 90–96.

McCauley, C. (1989). The nature of social influence in groupthink: Compliance and internalization. *Journal of Personality and Social Psychology, 57,* 250–260.

McClelland, D. C. (1975). *Power: The inner experience.* New York: Irvington.

McClintock, C. G., & Liebrand, W. B. G. (1988). Role of interdependence structure, individual value orientation, and another's strategy in social decision making: A transformational analysis. *Journal of Personality and Social Psychology, 55,* 396–409.

McCloskey, M., & Zaragoza, M. (1985). Misleading postevent information and memory for events: Arguments and evidence against memory impairment hypotheses. *Journal of Experimental Psychology: General, 114,* 1–16.

McConahay, J. B. (1981). Reducing racial prejudice in desegregated schools. In W. D. Hawley (Ed.), *Effective school desegregation.* Beverly Hills, CA: Sage.

McConahay, J. B. (1986). Modern racism, ambivalence, and the Modern Racism Scale. In J. F. Dovidio & S. L. Gaertner (Eds.), *Prejudice, discrimination, and racism: Theory and Research* (pp. 91–125). New York: Academic Press.

McDonald, H. E., & Hirt, E. R. (1997). When expectancy meets desire: Motivational effects in reconstructive memory. *Journal of Personality and Social Psychology, 72,* 5–23.

McFarland, C., & Miller, D. T. (1994). The framing of relative performance feedback: Seeing the glass as half empty or half full. *Journal of Personality and Social Psychology, 66,* 1061–1073.

McFarland, C., & Ross, M. (1987). The relation between current impressions and memories of self and dating partners. *Personality and Social Psychology Bulletin, 13,* 228–238.

McGowan, W. (1993, May 7). Class ads. *Scholastic Update,* pp. 14–15.

McGrath, J. E. (1984). *Groups: Interaction and performance.* Englewood Cliffs, NJ: Prentice Hall.

McGuire, A. M. (1994). Helping behaviors in the natural environment: Dimensions and correlates of helping. *Personality and Social Psychology Bulletin, 20,* 45–56.

McGuire, W. J. (1964). Inducing resistance to persuasion. In L. Berkowitz (Ed.), *Advances in experimental social psychology* (Vol. 1, pp. 192–229). New York: Academic Press.

McGuire, W. J. (1968). Personality and susceptibility to social influence. In E. F. Borgatta & W. W. Lambert (Eds.), *Handbook of personality theory and research* (pp. 1130–1187). Chicago: Rand McNally.

McGuire, W. J. (1985). Attitudes and attitude change. In G. Lindzey & E. Aronson (Eds.), *Handbook of social psychology* (3rd ed., Vol. 2, pp. 233–346). New York: McGraw-Hill.

McGuire, W. J., & McGuire, C. V. (1981). The spontaneous self-concept as affected by personal distinctiveness. In M. D. Lynch, A. A. Norem-Hebeisen, & K. J. Gergen (Eds.), *Self-concept: Advances in theory and research* (pp. 147–171). Cambridge, MA: Ballinger.

McGuire, W. J., McGuire, C. V., Child, P., & Fujioka, T. (1978). Salience of ethnicity in the spontaneous self-concept as a function of one's ethnic distinctiveness in the social environment. *Journal of Personality and Social Psychology, 36,* 511–520.

McGuire, W. J., & Padawer-Singer, A. (1976). Trait salience in the spontaneous self-concept. *Journal of Personality and Social Psychology, 33,* 743–754.

McHugo, G. J., & Smith, C. A. (1996). The power of faces: A review of John T. Lanzetta's research on facial expression and emotion. *Motivation and Emotion, 21,* 85–120.

McLeod, P. L. (1992). An assessment of the experimental literature on electronic support of group work: Results of a meta-analysis. *Human Computer Interaction, 7,* 257–280.

McNamara, Robert S. In retrospect:the tragedy and lessons of Vietnam / Robert S. McNamara with Brian VanDeMark. New York:Times Books, 1995.

McPherson, J. M. (1983). The size of voluntary associations. *American Sociological Review, 61,* 1044–1064.

Mead, G. H. (1934). *Mind, self, and society.* Chicago: University of Chicago Press.

Mead, M. (1977). Jealousy: Primitive and socialized. In G. Clanton & L. G. Smith (Eds.), *Jealousy* (pp. 115–127). Englewood Cliffs, NJ: Prentice Hall.

Medalia, N. Z., & Larsen, O. N. (1969). Diffusion and belief in a collective delusion: The Seattle windshield pitting epidemic. In R. Evans (Ed.), *Readings in collective behavior* (pp. 247–258). Chicago: Rand McNally.

Medvec, V. H., Madey, S. F., & Gilovich, T. (1995). When less is more: Counterfactual thinking and satisfaction among Olympic medalists. *Journal of Personality and Social Psychology, 69,* 603–610.

Meeus, W. H. J., & Raaijmakers, Q. A. W. (1995). Obedience in modern society: The Utrecht Studies. *Journal of Social Issues, 51,* 155–175.

Meier, D. (1995). *The power of their ideas.* New York: Beacon.

Meindl, J. R., & Lerner, M. J. (1985). Exacerbation of extreme responses to an out-group. *Journal of Personality and Social Psychology, 47,* 71–84.

Melara, R. D., DeWitt-Rickards, T. S., & O'Brien, T. P. (1989). Enhancing lineup identification accuracy: Two codes are better than one. *Journal of Applied Psychology, 74,* 706–713.

Memon, A., & Stevenage, S. V. (1996). Interviewing witnesses: What works and what doesn't? *Psycholoquy, 7* witness-memory.1.memon.

Menec, V. H., Perry, R. P., Struthers, C. W., Schonwetter, D. J., Hechter, F. J., & Eichholz, B. L. (1994). Assisting at-risk college students with attributional retraining and effective teaching. *Journal of Applied Social Psychology, 24,* 675–701.

Menninger, W. (1948). Recreation and mental health. *Recreation, 42,* 340–346.

Merikle, P. M. (1988). Subliminal auditory messages: An evaluation. *Psychology and Marketing, 5,* 355–372.

Merton, R. K. (1948). The self-fulfilling prophecy. *Antioch Review, 8,* 193–210.

Messick, D., & Liebrand, W. B. G. (1995). Individual heuristics and the dynamics of cooperation in large groups. *Psychological Review, 102,* 131–145.

Mettee, D., & Aronson, E. (1974). Affective reactions to appraisal from others. In T. L. Huston (Ed.), *Foundations of interpersonal attraction.* New York: Academic Press.

Mettee, D., Taylor, S. E., & Friedman, H. (1973). Affect conversion and the gain-loss effect. *Sociometry, 36,* 505–519.

Meyer, J. P. (1980). Causal attributions for success and failure: A multivariate investigation of dimensionality, formation, and consequences. *Journal of Personality and Social Psychology, 38,* 704–715.

Meyer, J. P., & Pepper, S. (1977). Need compatibility and marital adjustment in young married couples. *Journal of Personality and Social Psychology, 35,* 331–342.

Meyerowitz, B. E., & Chaiken, S. (1987). The effect of message framing on breast self-examination attitudes, intentions, and behavior. *Journal of Personality and Social Psychology, 52,* 500–510.

Michaels, J. W., Blommel, J. M., Brocato, R. M., Linkous, R. A., & Rowe, J. S. (1982). Social facilitation and inhibition in a natural setting. *Replications in Social Psychology, 2,* 21–24.

Middleton, W., Harris, P., & Surman, M. (1996). Give 'em enough rope: Perception of health and safety risks in bungee jumpers. *Journal of Social and Clinical Psychology, 15,* 68–79.

Mikulincer, M., & Florian, V. (1995). Appraisal of and coping with a real-life stressful situation: The contribution of attachment styles. *Personality and Social Psychology Bulletin, 21,* 406–414.

Milgram, S. (1961). Nationality and conformity. *Scientific American, 205,* 45–51.

Milgram, S. (1963). Behavioral study of obedience. *Journal of Abnormal and Social Psychology, 67,* 371–378.

Milgram, S. (1969). The lost letter technique. *Psychology Today, 3,* pp. 30–33, 67–68.

Milgram, S. (1970). The experience of living in cities. *Science, 167,* 1461–1468.

Milgram, S. (1974). *Obedience to authority: An experimental view.* New York: Harper & Row.

Milgram, S. (1976). Obedience to criminal orders: The compulsion to do evil. In T. Blass (Ed.), *Contemporary social psychology: Representative readings* (pp. 175–184). Itasca, IL: F. E. Peacock.

Milgram, S. (1977). *The individual in a social world.* Reading, MA: Addison-Wesley.

Milgram, S., & Sabini, J. (1978). On maintaining urban norms: A field experiment in the subway. In A. Baum, J. E. Singer, & S. Valins (Eds.), *Advances in environmental psychology* (Vol. 1, pp. 9–40). Hillsdale, NJ: Erlbaum.

Mill, J. S. (1974). *A system of logic ratiocinative and inductive.* Toronto: University of Toronto Press. (Original work published 1843)

Millar, M. G., & Tesser, A. (1986). Effects of affective and cognitive focus on the attitude-behavior relationship. *Journal of Personality and Social Psychology, 51,* 270–276.

Miller, A. F. (1995). Constructions of the obedience experiments: A focus upon domains of relevance. *Journal of Social Issues, 51,* 33–53.

Miller, A. G. (1986). *The Obedience Experiments: A Case Study of Controversy in Social Science.* New York: Praeger.

Miller, A. G., Ashton, W., & Mishal, M. (1990). Beliefs concerning the features of constrained behavior: A basis for the fundamental attribution error. *Journal of Personality and Social Psychology, 59,* 635–650.

Miller, A. G., Collins, B. E., & Brief, D. E. (1995). Perspectives on obedience to authority: The legacy of the Milgram experiments. *Journal of Social Issues, 51,* 1–19.

Miller, C. (1972). *Women in policing.* Washington, DC: Police Foundation.

Miller, C. E., & Anderson, P. D. (1979). Group decision rules and the rejection of deviates. *Social Psychology Quarterly, 42,* 354–363.

Miller, C. T. (1982). The role of performance-related similarity in social comparison of abilities: A test of the related attributes hypothesis. *Journal of Experimental Social Psychology, 18,* 513–523.

Miller, D. T., & Prentice, D. A. (1996). The construction of social norms and standards. In E. T. Higgins & A. W. Kruglanski (Eds.), *Social Psychology: Handbook of Basic Principles* (pp. 799–829). New York: Guilford.

Miller, D. T., & Ratner, R. K. (1996). The power of the myth of self-interest. In L. Montada & M. Lerner (Eds.), *Current societal concerns about justice* (pp. 25–48). New York: Plenum.

Miller, D. T., & Ross, M. (1975). Self-serving biases in the attribution of causality: Fact or fiction? *Psychological Bulletin, 82,* 213–225.

Miller, D. T., Turnbull, W., & McFarland, C. (1990). Counterfactual thinking and social perception: Thinking about what might have been. In M. P. Zanna (Ed.), *Advances in experimental social psychology* (Vol. 23, pp. 305–331). San Diego, CA: Academic Press.

Miller, J. G. (1984). Culture and the development of everyday social explanation. *Journal of Personality and Social Psychology, 46,* 961–978.

Miller, J. G., Bersoff, D. M., & Harwood, R. L. (1990). Perceptions of social responsibilities in India and the United States: Moral imperatives or personal decisions? *Journal of Personality and Social Psychology, 58,* 33–47.

Miller, N., & Bugelski, R. (1948). Minor studies in aggression: The influence of frustrations imposed by the in-group on attitudes expressed by the out-group. *Journal of Psychology, 25,* 437–442.

Miller, N., & Campbell, D. T. (1959). Recency and primacy in persuasion as a function of the timing of speeches and measurements. *Journal of Abnormal and Social Psychology, 59,* 1–9.

Miller, R. S., & Marcus, D. K. (1996). A social relations analysis of perceptions of embarrassment and anxiety during class presentations. In D. K. Marcus (Chair), *Interpersonal*

Perception and the Social Relations Model. Symposium conducted at the Meeting of the Southwestern Psychological Association, Houston, TX.

Miller, T. Q., Smith, T. W., Turner, C. W., Guijarro, M. L., & Hallet, A. J. (1996). A meta-analytic review of research on hostility and health. *Psychological Bulletin, 119,* 322– 348.

Mills, J. (1958). Changes in moral attitudes following temptation. *Journal of Personality, 26,* 517–531.

Mills, J., & Clark, M. S. (1982). Communal and exchange relationships. In L. Wheeler (Ed.), *Review of personality and social psychology* (Vol. 2, pp. 121–144). Beverly Hills, CA: Sage.

Mills, J., & Clark, M. S. (1994). Communal and exchange relationships: Controversies and research. In R. Erber & R. Gilmour (Eds.), *Theoretical Frameworks for Personal Relationships* (pp. 29–42). Hillsdale, NJ: Erlbaum.

Minard, R. D. (1952). Race relations in the Pocohontas coal field. *Journal of Social Issues, 8,* 29–44.

Mischel, W. (1968). *Personality and assessment.* New York: Wiley.

Mischel, W., Cantor, N., & Feldman, S. (1996). Principles of self-regulation: The nature of willpower and self-control. In E. T. Higgins & A. W. Kruglanski (Eds.), *Social psychology: Handbook of basic principles* (pp. 329–360). New York: Guilford.

Misconceptions about why people obey laws and accept judicial decisions. (1997, Sept.). *American Psychological Society Observer, 5,* 12–13, 46.

Mita, T. H., Dermer, M., & Knight, J. (1977). Reversed facial images and the mere-exposure hypothesis. *Journal of Personality and Social Psychology, 35,* 597–601.

Modigliani, A., & Rochat, F. (1995). The role of interaction sequences and the timing of resistance in shaping obedience and defiance to authority. *Journal of Social Issues, 51,* 107–123.

Moghaddam, F. M., Taylor, D. M., & Wright, S. C. (1993). *Social psychology in cross-cultural perspective.* New York: Freeman.

Mohamed, A. A., & Wiebe, F. A. (1996). Toward a process theory of groupthink. *Small Group Research, 27,* 416–430.

Montemayor, R., & Eisen, M. (1977). The development of self-conceptions from childhood to adolescence. *Developmental Psychology, 13,* 314–319.

Montgomery, B. M. (1993). Relationship maintenance versus relationship change: A dialectical dilemma. *Journal of Social and Personal Relationships, 10,* 205–224.

Moore, J. S., Graziano, W. G., & Millar, M. C. (1987). Physical attractiveness, sex role orientation, and the evaluation of adults and children. *Personality and Social Psychology Bulletin, 13,* 95–102.

Moore, S. R., Smith, R. E., & Gonzalez, R. (1997). Personality and judgment heuristics: Contextual and individual difference interactions in social judgment. *Personality and Social Psychology Bulletin, 23,* 76–83.

Moore, T. E. (1982). Subliminal advertising: What you see is what you get. *Journal of Marketing, 46,* 38–47.

Moore, T. E. (1992). Subliminal perception: Facts and fallacies. *Skeptical Inquirer, 16,* 273–281.

Moore, T. E. (1995). Subliminal self-help tapes: An empirical test of perceptual consequences. *Canadian Journal of Behavioural Science, 27,* 9–20.

Moos, R. H., & Schaefer, J. A. (1993). Coping resources and processes: Current concepts and measures. In L. Goldberger & S. Breznitz (Eds.), *Handbook of stress: Theoretical and clinical aspects* (2nd ed., pp. 234–257). New York: Free Press.

Moran, G., & Cutler, B. L. (1991). The prejudicial impact of pretrial publicity. *Journal of Applied Social Psychology, 21,* 345–367.

Moreland, R. L. (1987). The formation of small groups. In C. Hendrick (Ed.), *Review of personality and social psychology* (Vol. 8, pp. 80–110). Newbury Park, CA: Sage.

Moreland, R. L., Argote, L., & Krishnan, R. (1996). Socially shared cognition at work: Transactive memory and group performance. In J. L. Nye & A. M. Brower (Eds.), *What's social about social cognition?* (pp. 57–84). Thousand Oaks, CA: Sage.

Moreland, R. L., & Beach, R. (1992). Exposure effects in the classroom: The development of affinity among students. *Journal of Experimental Social Psychology, 28,* 255–276.

Moreland, R. L., & Zajonc, R. B. (1982). Exposure effects in person perception: Familiarity, similarity, and attraction. *Journal of Experimental Social Psychology, 18,* 395–415.

Morris, E. (Director). (1988). *Thin blue line* [Film]. New York: HBO Videos.

Morris, M. W., & Peng, K. (1994). Culture and cause: American and Chinese attributions for social and physical events. *Journal of Personality and Social Psychology, 67,* 949–971.

Morris, W. N., & Miller, R. S. (1975). The effects of consensus-breaking and consensus-preempting partners on reduction of conformity. *Journal of Experimental Social Psychology, 11,* 215–223.

Morsbach, H. (1973). Aspects of nonverbal communication in Japan. *Journal of Nervous and Mental Disease, 157,* 262–277.

Morse, D. R., Martin, J., & Moshonov, J. (1991). Psychosomatically induced death: Relative to stress, hypnosis, mind control, and voodoo: Review and possible mechanisms. *Stress Medicine, 7,* 213–232.

Moscovici, S. (1980). Toward a theory of conversion behavior. In L. Berkowitz (Ed.), *Advances in experimental social psychology* (Vol. 13, pp. 209–239). Orlando, FL: Academic Press.

Moscovici, S. (1985). Social influence and conformity. In G. Lindzey & E. Aronson (Eds.), *Handbook of social psychology* (Vol. 2, pp. 347–412). New York: McGraw-Hill.

Moscovici, S. (1994). Three concepts: Minority, conflict, and behavioral style. In S. Moscovici, A. Mucchi-Faina, & A. Maass (Eds.), *Minority Influence* (pp. 233–251). Chicago: Nelson-Hall.

Moscovici, S., & Nemeth, C. (1974). Minority influence. In C. Nemeth (Ed.), *Social psychology: Classic and contemporary integrations* (pp. 217–249). Chicago: Rand McNally.

Moscovici, S., Mucchi-Faina, A., & Maass, A. (Eds.) (1994). *Minority Influence.* Chicago: Nelson-Hall.

Moyer, K. E. (1976). *The psychobiology of aggression.* New York: Harper & Row.

Moyer, K. E. (1983). The physiology of motivation: Aggression as a model. In C. J. Scheier & A. M. Rogers (Eds.), *G. Stanley Hall Lecture Series* (Vol. 3). Washington, DC: American Psychological Association.

Mullen, B. (1986). Atrocity as a function of lynch mob composition: A self-attention perspective. *Personality and Social Psychology Bulletin, 12,* 187–197.

Mullen, B. (1991). Group composition, salience, and cognitive representations: The phenomenology of being in a group. *Journal of Experimental Social Psychology, 27,* 297–323.

Mullen, B., Anthony, T., Salas, E., & Driskell, J. E. (1994). Group cohesiveness and quality of decision making: An integration of tests of the groupthink hypothesis. *Small Group Research, 25,* 189–204.

Mullen, B., & Baumeister, R. F. (1987). Group effects on self-attention and performance: Social loafing, social facilitation, and social impairment. In C. Hendrick (Ed.), *Group processes and intergroup relations* (Vol. 9, pp. 189–206). Newbury Park, CA: Sage.

Mullen, B., Brown, R., & Smith, C. (1992). Ingroup bias as a function of salience, relevance, and status: An integration. *European Journal of Social Psychology, 22,* 103–122.

Mullen, B., & Johnson, C. (1988). *Distinctiveness-based illusory correlation and stereotyping: A meta-analytic integration.* Unpublished manuscript, Syracuse University.

Mullen, B., Johnson, C., & Salas, E. (1991). Productivity loss in brainstorming groups. *Basic and Applied Social Psychology, 12,* 3–24.

Münsterberg, H. (1908). *On the witness stand: Essays on psychology and crime.* New York: Doubleday, Page.

Murphy, S. T., & Zajonc, R. B. (1993). Affect, cognition, and awareness: Affective priming with optimal and suboptimal stimulus exposures. *Journal of Personality and Social Psychology, 64,* 723–739.

Murray, S. L., Holmes, J. G., & Griffin, D. W. (1996). The self-fulfilling nature of positive illusions in romantic relationships: Love is not blind, but prescient. *Journal of Personality and Social Psychology, 71,* 1155–1180.

Mussen, P., & Eisenberg-Berg, N. (1977). *Roots of caring, sharing, and helping: The development of prosocial behavior in children.* San Francisco: Freeman.

My Lai: An American tragedy. (1969, December 5). *Time,* pp. 26–32.

Myers, D. G., & Arenson, S. J. (1972). Enhancement of dominant risk tendencies in group discussion. *Psychological Reports, 30,* 615–623.

Myers, D. G., & Diener, E. (1995). Who is happy? *Psychological Science, 6,* 10–19.

Nadler, A. (1991). Help-seeking behavior: Psychological costs and instrumental benefits. In M. S. Clark (Ed.), *Prosocial behavior: Review of personality and social psychology* (Vol. 12, pp. 290–311). Newbury Park, CA: Sage.

Nadler, A., & Fisher, J. D. (1986). The role of threat to self-esteem and perceived control in recipient reactions to help: Theory development and empirical validation. In L. Berkowitz (Ed.), *Advances in experimental social psychology* (Vol. 19, pp. 81–123). New York: Academic Press.

Nahemow, L., & Lawton, M. P. (1975). Similarity and propinquity in friendship formation. *Journal of Personality and Social Psychology, 32,* 205–213.

Nail, P. R. (1986). Toward an integration of some models and theories of social response. *Psychological Bulletin, 100,* 190–206.

Nail, P. R., Van Leeuwen, M. D., & Powell, A. B. (1996). The effectance versus the self-presentational view of reactance: Are importance ratings influenced by anticipated surveillance? *Journal of Social Behavior and Personality, 11,* 573–584.

Nario, M. R., & Branscombe, N. R. (1995). Comparison processes in hindsight and causal attribution. *Personality and Social Psychology Bulletin, 21,* 1244–1255.

Nathanson, S. (1987). *An eye for an eye? The morality of punishing by death.* Totowa, NJ: Roman & Littlefield.

Neil v. Biggers, 409 U.S. 188 (1972).

Neisser, U. (1976). *Cognition and reality: Principles and implications of cognitive psychology.* San Francisco: Freeman.

Nel, E., Helmreich, R., & Aronson, E. (1969). Opinion change in the advocate as a function of the persuasibility of his audience: A clarification of the meaning of dissonance. *Journal of Personality and Social Psychology, 12,* 117–124.

Nemeth, C. (1977). Interactions between jurors as a function of majority vs. unanimity decision rules. *Journal of Applied Social Psychology, 7,* 38–56.

Nemeth, C. J. (1986). Differential contributions of majority and minority influence. *Psychological Review, 93,* 23–32.

Nemeth, C. J., & Chiles, C. (1988). Modeling courage: The role of dissent in fostering independence. *European Journal of Social Psychology, 18,* 275–280.

Nemeth, C. J., Mayseless, O., Sherman, J., & Brown, Y. (1990). Exposure to dissent and recall of information. *Journal of Personality and Social Psychology, 58,* 429–437.

Neuberg, S. L. (1988). Behavioral implications of information presented outside of awareness: The effect of subliminal presentation of trait information on behavior in the Prisoner's Dilemma game. *Social Cognition, 6,* 207–230.

Neuberg, S. L. (1989). The goal of forming accurate impressions during social interactions: Attenuating the impact of negative expectancies. *Journal of Personality and Social Psychology, 56,* 374–386.

Neuberg, S. L. (in press). Expectancy-confirmation processes in stereotype-tinged social encounters: The moderating role of social goals. In M. P. Zanna & J. M. Olson (Eds.), *Psychology of prejudice: The seventh annual Ontario Symposium on Personality and Social Psychology.* Hillsdale, NJ: Erlbaum.

New Yorker (1957, September 21), p. 33.

New Yorker (1991, November 4), p. 106.

Newcomb, T. M. (1947). Autistic hostility and social reality. *Human Relations, 1,* 69–86.

Newcomb, T. M. (1961). *The acquaintance process.* New York: Holt, Rinehart & Winston.

Newcomb, T. M. (1963). Persistence and regression of changed attitudes: Long-range studies. *Journal of Social Issues, 19,* 3–14.

Newman, L. S. (1991). Why are traits inferred spontaneously? A developmental approach. *Social Cognition, 9,* 221–253.

Newman, L. S. (1996). Trait impressions as heuristics for predicting future behavior. *Personality and Social Psychology Bulletin, 22,* 395–411.

Newman, L. S., & Uleman, J. S. (1993). When are you what you did? Behavior identification and dispositional inference in person memory, attribution, and social judgment. *Personality and Social Psychology Bulletin, 19,* 513–525.

Newtson, D. (1974). Dispositional inferences from effects of actions: Effects chosen and effects forgone. *Journal of Experimental Social Psychology, 10,* 489–496.

Newtson, D. (1990). Alternatives to representation or alternative representations: Comments on the ecological approach. *Contemporary Social Psychology, 14,* 163–174.

Ng, W., & Lindsay, R. C. L. (1994). Cross-racial facial recognition: Failure of the contact hypothesis. *Journal of Cross-Cultural Psychology, 25,* 217–232.

Nichols, J. G. (1975). Casual attributions and other achievement-related cognitions: Effects of task outcome, attainment value, and sex. *Journal of Personality and Social Psychology, 31,* 379–389.

Nicholson, N., Cole, S. G., & Rocklin, T. (1985). Conformity in the Asch situation: A comparison between contemporary British and U.S. university students. *British Journal of Social Psychology, 24,* 59–63.

Niedenthal, P. M., & Beike, D. R. (1997). Interrelated and isolated self-concepts. *Personality and Social Psychology Review, 1,* 106–128.

Niedenthal, P. M., & Kitayama, S. (1994). (Eds.). *The heart's eye: Emotional influences in perception and attention.* San Diego, CA: Academic Press.

Niedenthal, P. M., Tangney, J. P., & Gavanski, I. (1994). "If only I weren't" versus "If only I hadn't": Distinguishing shame and guilt in counterfactual thinking. *Journal of Personality and Social Psychology, 67,* 585–595.

Nietzsche, F. W. (1918). *The genealogy of morals*. New York: Modern Library.

Nisbett, R. E. (1993). Violence and U.S. regional culture. *American Psychologist, 48,* 441–449.

Nisbett, R. E., Caputo, C., Legant, P., & Marecek, J. (1973). Behavior as seen by the actor and by the observer. *Journal of Personality and Social Psychology, 27,* 154–164.

Nisbett, R. E., & Cohen, D. (1996). *Culture of honor: The psychology of violence in the South.* Boulder, CO: Westview Press.

Nisbett, R. E., Fong, G. T., Lehman, D. R., & Cheng, P. W. (1987). Teaching reasoning. *Science, 238,* 625–631.

Nisbett, R. E., Krantz, D. H., Jepson, C., & Kunda, Z. (1983). The use of statistical heuristics in everyday inductive reasoning. *Psychological Review, 90,* 339–363.

Nisbett, R. E., & Ross, L. (1980). *Human inference: Strategies and shortcomings of human judgment.* Englewood Cliffs, NJ: Prentice Hall.

Nisbett, R. E., & Valins, S. (1972). Perceiving the causes of one's own behavior. In E. E. Jones, D. E. Kanouse, H. H. Kelley, R. E. Nisbett, S. Valins, & B. Weiner (Eds.), *Attribution: Perceiving the causes of behavior* (pp. 63–78). Morristown, NJ: General Learning Press.

Nisbett, R. E., & Wilson, T. D. (1977a). Telling more than we can know: Verbal reports on mental processes. *Psychological Review, 84,* 231–259.

Nisbett, R. E., & Wilson, T. D. (1977b). The halo effect: Evidence for unconscious alteration of judgments. *Journal of Personality and Social Psychology, 35,* 250–256.

Nivison, M. E., & Endresen, I. M. (1993). An analysis of relationships among environmental noise, annoyance and sensitivity to noise, and the consequences for health and sleep. *Journal of Behavioral Medicine, 16,* 257–276.

Nixon, R. M., (1990). *In the arena: a memoir of victory, defeat, and renewal.* New York: Simon & Schuster.

Nolen-Hoeksema, S. (1990). *Sex differences in depression.* Stanford, CA: Stanford University Press.

Nolen-Hoeksema, S., Girgus, J. S., & Seligman, M. E. P. (1986). Learned helplessness in children: A longitudinal study of depression, achievement, and explanatory style. *Journal of Personality and Social Psychology, 51,* 435–442.

Norris, F. H., & Kaniasty, K. (1996). Received and perceived social support in times of stress: A test of the social support deterioration model. *Journal of Personality and Social Psychology, 71,* 498–511.

Nowak, A. & Latané, B. (1994). Simulating the emergence of social order from individual behavior. In N. Gilbert & J. Doran (Eds.), *Simulating societies: The computer simulation of social processes* (pp. 63–84). Chicago: University of Chicago Press.

Nowak, A., Szamrej, J., & Latané, B. (1990). From private attitude to public opinion: A dynamic theory of social impact. *Psychological Review, 97,* 362–376.

O'Connor, K. M., & Carnevale, P. J. (1997). A nasty but effective negotiation strategy: Misrepresentation of a common-value issue. *Personality and Social Psychology Bulletin, 23,* 504–515.

O'Leary, A. (1990). Stress, emotion, and human immune function. *Psychological Bulletin, 108,* 363–382.

O'Sullivan, C. S., & Durso, F. T. (1984). Effects of schema-incongruent information on memory for stereotypical attributes. *Journal of Personality and Social Psychology, 47,* 55–70.

Oakes, P. J., & Turner, J. C. (1980). Social categorization and intergroup behavior: Does minimal intergroup discrimination make social identity more positive? *European Journal of Social Psychology, 10,* 295–301.

Ofshe, R., & Watters, E. (1994). *Making monsters: False memories, psychotherapy, and sexual hysteria.* New York: Charles Scribner's Sons.

Ogloff, J. R., & Vidmar, N. (1994). The impact of pretrial publicity on jurors: A study to compare the relative effects of television and print media in a child sex abuse case. *Law and Human Behavior, 18,* 507–525.

Ohbuchi, K., Chiba, S., & Fukushima, O. (1996). Mitigation of interpersonal conflicts: Politeness and time pressure. *Personality and Social Psychology Bulletin, 22,* 1035–1042.

Ohbuchi, K., Kamdea, M., & Agarie, N. (1989). Apology as aggression control: Its role in mediating appraisal of and response to harm. *Journal of Personality and Social Psychology, 56,* 219–227.

Ohbuchi, K., Ohno, T., & Mukai, H. (1993). Empathy and aggression: Effects of self-disclosure and fearful appeal. *Journal of Social Psychology 133,* 243–253.

Ohbuchi, K., & Sato, K. (1994). Children's reactions to mitigating accounts: Apologies, excuses, and intentionality of harm. *Journal of Social Psychology, 134,* 5–17.

Oliner, S. P., & Oliner, P. M. (1988). *The altruistic personality: Rescuers of Jews in Nazi Europe.* New York: The Free Press.

Olson, J. M. (1990). Self-perception of humor: Evidence for discounting and augmentation effects. *Journal of Personality and Social Psychology, 62,* 369–377.

Olson, J. M., Roese, N. J., & Zanna, M. P. (1996). Expectancies. In E. T. Higgins & A. W. Kruglanski (Eds.), *Social psychology: Handbook of basic principles* (pp. 211–238). New York: Guilford.

Olson, J. M., & Zanna, M. P. (1993). Attitudes and attitude change. *Annual Review of Psychology, 44,* 117–154.

Olweus, D. (1991). Bully/victim problems among schoolchildren: Basic facts and effects of a school-based intervention program. In D. Pepler & K. Rubin (Eds.), *The development and treatment of childhood aggression* (pp. 411–448). Hillsdale, NJ: Erlbaum.

Olweus, D. (1995). Annotation: Bullying at school: Basic facts and effects of a school based intervention program. *Journal of Child Psychology and Psychiatry, 35,* 1171–1190.

Olweus, D. (1995). Bullying or peer abuse at school: Facts and interventions. *Current Directions in Psychological Science, 4,* 196–200.

Olweus, D. (1995). Bullying or peer abuse in school: Intervention and prevention. In G. Davies, S. Lloyd-Bostock, M. McMurran, & C. Wilson (Eds.), *Psychology, law, and criminal justice: International developments in research and practice* (pp. 248–263). Berlin, Germany: Walter de Gruyter.

Olweus, D. (1996). Bullying at school: Knowledge base and an effective intervention program. In C. Ferris & T. Grisso (Eds.), *Understanding aggressive behavior in children.* New York Academy of Sciences, Annals of the New York Academy of Sciences, Vol. 794 (pp. 265–276). New York: Academy of Sciences.

Olweus, D. (1997). Tackling peer victimization with a school-based intervention program. In D. Fry & K. Bjorkqvist (Eds.), *Cultural variation in conflict resolution: Alternatives to violence* (pp. 215–231). Mahwah, NJ: Erlbaum.

Olzak, S., & Nagel, J. (1986). *Competitive ethnic relations.* New York: Academic Press.

Omdahl, B. L. (1995). *Cognitive appraisal, emotion, and empathy.* Mahwah, NJ: Erlbaum.

Opp, K. D. (1982). The evolutionary emergence of norms. *British Journal of Social Psychology, 21,* 139–149.

Orbell, J. M., van de Kragt, A. J. C., & Dawes, R. M. (1988). Explaining discussion-induced comparison. *Journal of Personality and Social Psychology, 54,* 811–819.

Ortony, A., Clore, G., & Collins, A. (1988). *The cognitive structure of emotions*. Cambridge, England: Cambridge University Press.

Osborn, A. F. (1957). *Applied imagination*. New York: Scribner.

Osherow, N. (1988). Making sense of the nonsensical: An analysis of Jonestown. In E. Aronson (Ed.), *Readings about the social animal* (pp. 68–86). New York: Freeman.

Oskamp, S. (1995). Applying social psychology to avoid ecological disaster. *Journal of Social Issues, 51*, 217–238.

Ostrom, T., & Sedikides, C. (1992). Out-group homogeneity effects in natural and minimal groups. *Psychological Bulletin, 112*, 536–552.

Otten, C. A., Penner, L. A., & Waugh, G. (1988). That's what friends are for: The determinants of psychological helping. *Journal of Social and Clinical Psychology, 7*, 34–41.

Otto, A. L., Penrod, S. D., & Dexter, H. R. (1994). The biasing impact of pretrial publicity on juror judgments. *Law and Human Behavior, 18*, 453–469.

Ovcharchyn, C. A., Johnson, H. H., & Petzel, T. P. (1981). Type A behavior, academic aspirations, and academic success. *Journal of Personality, 49*, 248–256.

Packard, V. (1957). *The hidden persuaders*. New York: D. McKay.

Palazzoli, M. P. (1974). *Anorexia nervosa*. London: Chaucer.

Pallak, M. S., & Pittman, T. S. (1972). General motivation effects of dissonance arousal. *Journal of Personality and Social Psychology, 21*, 349–358.

Pandey, J. (1990). The environment, culture, and behavior. In R. Brislin (Ed.), *Applied cross-cultural psychology* (pp. 254–277). Thousand Oaks, CA: Sage.

Park, B., & Rothbart, M. (1982). Perception of out-group homogeneity and levels of social categorization: Memory for the subordinate attributes of in-group and out-group members. *Journal of Personality and Social Psychology, 42*, 1051–1068.

Parke, R. D., Berkowitz, L., Leyens, J. P., West, S. G., & Sebastian, R. J. (1977). Some effects of violent and nonviolent movies on the behavior of juvenile delinquents. In L. Berkowitz (Ed.), *Advances in experimental social psychology* (Vol. 10, pp. 135–172). New York: Academic Press.

Parsons, J. E., Kaczala, C. M., & Meece, J. L. (1982). Socialization of achievement attitudes and beliefs: Classroom influences. *Child Development, 53*, 322–339.

Patch, M. E. (1986). The role of source legitimacy in sequential request strategies of compliance. *Personality and Social Psychology Bulletin, 12*, 199–205.

Patch, M. E., Hoang, V. R., & Stahelski, A. J. (1997). The use of metacommunication in compliance: Door-in-the-face and single-request strategies. *Journal of Social Psychology, 137*, 88–94.

Patrick, C. J., & Iacono, W. G. (1989). Psychopathy, threat, and polygraph test accuracy. *Journal of Applied Psychology, 74*, 347–355.

Patterson, A. (1974, September). *Hostility catharsis: A naturalistic quasi-experiment*. Paper presented at the meeting of the American Psychological Association, New Orleans.

Patton, P. (1989, August 6). Steve Jobs out for revenge. *New York Times Magazine*, pp. 23, 52, 56, 58.

Paulus, P. B., Dzindolet, M. T., Poletes, G., & Camacho, L. M. (1993). Perception of performance in group brainstorming: The illusion of group productivity. *Personality and Social Psychology Bulletin, 19*, 78–89.

Paulus, P. B., McCain, G., & Cox, V. (1981). Prison standards: Some pertinent data on crowding. *Federal Probation, 15*, 48–54.

Pedersen, D. M. (1965). The measurement of individual differences in perceived personality-trait relationships and their relation to certain determinants. *Journal of Social Psychology, 65*, 233–258.

Pelham, B. W. (1991). On confidence and consequence: The certainty and importance of self-knowledge. *Journal of Personality and Social Psychology, 60*, 518–530.

Pelham, B. W., & Neter, E. (1995). The effect of motivation on judgment depends on the difficulty of the judgment. *Journal of Personality and Social Psychology, 68*, 581–594.

Pennebaker, J., & Francis, M. (1996). Cognitive, emotional, and language processes in disclosure. *Cognition and Emotion, 10*, 601–626.

Pennebaker, J. W. (1982). *The psychology of physical symptoms*. New York: Springer-Verlag.

Pennebaker, J. W. (1990). *Opening up: The healing powers of confiding in others*. New York: William Morrow.

Pennebaker, J. W. (1997). Writing about emotional experiences as a therapeutic process. *Psychological Science, 8*, 162–166.

Pennebaker, J. W., Barger, S. D., & Tiebout, J. (1989). Disclosure of traumas and health among Holocaust survivors. *Psychosomatic Medicine, 51*, 577–589.

Pennebaker, J. W., & Beale, S. K. (1986). Confronting a traumatic event: Toward an understanding of inhibition and disease. *Journal of Abnormal Psychology, 95*, 274–281.

Pennebaker, J. W., Colder, M., & Sharp, L. K. (1990). Accelerating the coping process. *Journal of Personality and Social Psychology, 58*, 528–537.

Pennebaker, J. W., & Harber, K. D. (1993). A social stage model of collective coping: The Loma Prieta earthquake and the Persian Gulf War. *Journal of Social Issues, 49*, 125–145.

Pennebaker, J. W., & Sanders, D. Y. (1976). American graffiti: Effects of authority and reactance arousal. *Personality and Social Psychology Bulletin, 2*, 264–267.

Penner, L. A., Fritzsche, B. A., Craiger, J. P., & Freifeld, T. S. (1995). Measuring the prosocial personality. In J. Butcher & C. Spielberger (Eds.), *Advances in personality assessment* (Vol. 10, pp. 147–163). Hillsdale, NJ: Erlbaum.

Pennington, N., & Hastie, R. (1988). Explanation-based decision making: Effects of memory structure on judgment. *Journal of Experimental Psychology: Learning, Memory, and Cognition, 14*, 521–533.

Pennington, N., & Hastie, R. (1990). Practical implications of psychological research on juror and jury decision making. *Personality and Social Psychology Bulletin, 16*, 90–105.

Pennington, N., & Hastie, R. (1992). Explaining the evidence: Tests of the story model for juror decision making. *Journal of Personality and Social Psychology, 62*, 189–206.

Pennington, N., & Hastie, R. (1993). Reasoning in explanation-based decision making. *Cognition, 49*, 123–163.

Penrod, S., & Cutler, B. (1995). Witness confidence and witness accuracy: Assessing their forensic relation. *Psychology, Public Policy, and Law, 1*, 817–845.

Peplau, L. A., & Perlman, D. (1982). Perspectives on loneliness. In L. A. Peplau & D. Perlman (Eds.), *Loneliness: A sourcebook of current theory, research, and therapy*. New York: Wiley.

Perrett, D. I., May, K. A., & Yoshikawa, S. (1994). Facial shape and judgments of female attractivenesss. *Nature, 368*, 239–242.

Perrin, S., & Spencer, C. (1981). Independence or conformity in the Asch experiment as a reflection of cultural or situational factors. *British Journal of Social Psychology, 20*, 205–209.

Pertman, A. (1995, February 3). "Gestures aren't body of evidence," Ito warns. *Boston Globe*, p. 3.

Peters, L. H., Hartke, D. D., & Pohlmann, J. T. (1985). Fiedler's contingency theory of leadership: An application of the meta-analysis procedures of Schmidt and Hunter. *Psychological Bulletin, 97*, 274–285.

Peters, W. (1987). A Class Divided: Then and Now. New Haven: Yale University Press.

Peterson, C., & Seligman, M. E. P. (1984). Causal explanations as a risk factor for depression: Theory and evidence. *Psychological Review, 91,* 347–374.

Peterson, C., Seligman, M. E. P., & Vaillant, G. E. (1988). Pessimistic explanatory style is a risk factor for physical illness: A thirty-five-year longitudinal study. *Journal of Personality and Social Psychology, 55,* 23–27.

Peterson, R. D., & Bailey, W. C. (1988). Murder and capital punishment in the evolving context of the post-Furman era. *Social Forces, 66,* 774–807.

Peterson, R. S., & Nemeth, C. J. (1996). Focus versus flexibility: Majority and minority influence can both improve performance. *Personality and Social Psychology Bulletin, 22,* 14–23.

Pettigrew, T. F. (1958). Personality and sociocultural factors and intergroup attitudes: A cross-national comparison. *Journal of Conflict Resolution, 2,* 29–42.

Pettigrew, T. F. (1969). Racially separate or together? *Journal of Social Issues, 25,* 43–69.

Pettigrew, T. F. (1979). The ultimate attribution error: Extending Allport's cognitive analysis of prejudice. *Personality and Social Psychology Bulletin, 5,* 461–476.

Pettigrew, T. F. (1981). Extending the stereotype concept. In D. L. Hamilton (Ed.), *Cognitive processes in stereotyping and intergroup behavior.* Hillsdale, NJ: Erlbaum.

Pettigrew, T. F. (1985). New black-white patterns: How best to conceptualize them? *Annual Review of Sociology, 11,* 329–346.

Pettigrew, T. F. (1991). Normative theory in intergroup relations: Explaining both harmony and conflict. Special Issue: Conflict and harmony in pluralistic societies. *Psychology and Developing Societies, 3,* 3–16.

Pettigrew, T. F., & Meertens, R. W. (1995). Subtle and blatant prejudice in western Europe. *European Journal of Social Psychology, 25,* 57–75.

Petty, R. E. (1995). Attitude change. In A. Tesser (Ed.), *Advanced social psychology* (pp. 195–255). New York: McGraw-Hill.

Petty, R. E., & Brock, T. C. (1981). Thought disruption and persuasion: Assessing the validity of attitude change experiments. In R. E. Petty, T. M. Ostrom, & T. C. Brock (Eds.), *Cognitive responses in persuasion* (pp. 55–79). Hillsdale, NJ: Erlbaum.

Petty, R. E., & Cacioppo, J. T. (1981). *Attitudes and persuasion: Classic and contemporary approaches.* Dubuque, IA: William C. Brown.

Petty, R. E., & Cacioppo, J. T. (1986). *Communication and persuasion: Central and peripheral routes to attitude change.* New York: Springer-Verlag.

Petty, R. E., Cacioppo, J. T., & Goldman, R. (1981). Personal involvement as a determinant of argument-based persuasion. *Journal of Personality and Social Psychology, 41,* 847–855.

Petty, R. E., Haugtvedt, C. P., & Smith, S. M. (1995). Elaboration as a determinant of attitude strength. In R. E. Petty & J. A. Krosnick (Eds.), *Attitude strength: Antecedents and consequences* (pp. 93–130). Mahway, NJ: Erlbaum.

Petty, R. E., & Krosnick, J. A. (1995). *Attitude strength: Antecedents and consequences.* Hillsdale, NJ: Erlbaum.

Petty, R. E., & Wegener, D. T. (1998). Attitude change: Multiple roles for persuasion variables. In D. T. Gilbert, S. T. Fiske, & G. Lindzey (Eds.), *The handbook of social psychology* (4th ed., Vol. 1, pp. 323–390). New York: McGraw-Hill.

Petty, R. E., & Wegener, D. T. (in press). The elaboration likelihood model: Current status and controversies. In S. Chaiken & Y. Trope (Eds.), *Dual process theories in social psychology.* New York: Guilford.

Petty, R. E., Wegener, D. T., & Fabrigar, L. R. (1997). Attitudes and attitude change. *Annual Review of Psychology, 48,* 609–647.

Petty, R. E., Wells, G. L., & Brock, T. C. (1976). Distraction can enhance or reduce yielding to propaganda: Thought disruption versus effort justification. *Journal of Personality and Social Psychology, 34,* 874–884.

Pezdek, K., & Banks, W. P. (Ed.) (1996). *The recovered memory/false memory debate.* San Diego, CA: Academic Press.

Phillips, D. P. (1983). The impact of mass media violence on U.S. homicides. *American Sociological Review, 48,* 560–568.

Phillips, D. P. (1986). Natural experiments on the effects of mass media violence on fatal aggression: Strengths and weaknesses of a new approach. In L. Berkowitz (Ed.), *Advances in experimental social psychology* (Vol. 19, pp. 207–250). Orlando, FL: Academic Press.

Piliavin, I. M., Piliavin, J. A., & Rodin, J. (1975). Costs, diffusion, and the stigmatized victim. *Journal of Personality and Social Psychology, 32,* 429–438.

Piliavin, I. M., Rodin, J., & Piliavin, J. (1969). Good Samaritanism: An underground phenomenon? *Journal of Personality and Social Psychology, 13,* 289–299.

Piliavin, J. A., & Charng, H. (1990). Altruism: A review of recent theory and research. *Annual Review of Sociology, 16,* 27–65.

Piliavin, J. A., Dovidio, J. F., Gaertner, S., & Clark, R. D. III. (1981). *Emergency intervention.* New York: Academic Press.

Piliavin, J. A., & Piliavin, I. M. (1972). The effect of blood on reactions to a victim. *Journal of Personality and Social Psychology, 23,* 253–261.

Pines, A., & Aronson, E. (1983). Antecedents, correlates, and consequences of romantic jealousy. *Journal of Personality, 51,* 108–136.

Pinker, S. (1994). *The language instinct.* New York: William Morrow.

Pittman, T. S., & D'Agostino, P. R. (1985). Motivation and attribution: The effects of control deprivation on subsequent information processing. In J. Harvey & G. Weary (Eds.), *Attribution: Basic Issues and Applications.* New York: Academic Press.

Pittman, T. S., & Heller, J. F. (1987). Social motivation. *Annual Review of Psychology, 38,* 461–489.

Pleban, R., & Tesser, A. (1981). The effects of relevance and quality of another's performance on interpersonal closeness. *Social Psychology Quarterly, 44,* 278–285.

Pliner, P., Chaiken, S., & Flett, G. L. (1990). Gender differences in concern with body weight and physical appearance over the life span. *Personality and Social Psychology Bulletin, 16,* 263–273.

Plous, S. (1993). *The psychology of judgment and decision making.* New York: McGraw-Hill.

Plous, S. (1995). A comparison of strategies for reducing interval overconfidence in group judgments. *Journal of Applied Psychology, 80,* 443–454.

Pomerantz, E. M., Chaiken, S., & Tordesillas, R. S. (1995). Attitude strength and resistance processes. *Journal of Personality and Social Psychology 69,* 408–419.

Pope, K. S. (1996). Memory, abuse, and science: Questioning claims about the false memory syndrome epidemic. *American Psychologist, 51,* 957–974.

Porter, B. E., Leeming, F. C., & Dwyer, W. O. (1995). Solid waste recovery: A review of behavioral programs to increase recycling. *Environment and Behavior, 27,* 122–152.

Porter, J. R. (1971). *Black child, white child: The development of racial attitudes.* Cambridge, MA: Harvard University Press.

Porter, J. R., & Washington, R. E. (1979). Black identity and self-esteem, 1968–1978. *Annual Review of Sociology.* Stanford, CA: Annual Reviews.

Porter, J. R., & Washington, R. E. (1989). Developments in research on Black identity and self-esteem: 1979–1988. *Revue Internationale de Psychologie Sociale, 2,* 339–353.

Povinelli, D. J. (1993). Reconstructing the evolution of mind. *American Psychologist, 48,* 493–509.

Povinelli, D. J. (1994). A theory of mind is in the head, not the heart. *Behavioral and Brain Sciences, 17,* 573–574.

Povinelli, D. J., Landau, K. R., & Perilloux, H. K. (1996). Self-recognition in young children using delayed versus live feedback: Evidence of a developmental asynchrony. *Child Development, 67,* 1540–1554.

Powledge, F. (1991). *Free at last? The civil rights movement and the people who made it.* Boston: Little, Brown.

Pratkanis, A. R. (1992). The cargo-cult science of subliminal persuasion. *Skeptical Inquirer, 16,* 260–272.

Pratkanis, A. R., & Aronson, E. (1991). *Age of propaganda: The everyday use and abuse of persuasion.* New York: Freeman.

Pratkanis, A. R., Eskenazi, J., & Greenwald, A. G. (1994). What you expect is what you believe (but not necessarily what you get): A test of the effectiveness of subliminal self-help tapes. *Basic and Applied Social Psychology, 15,* 251–276.

Prentice-Dunn, S., & Rogers, R. W. (1989). Deindividuation and the self-regulation of behavior. In P. B. Paulus (Ed.), *Psychology of group influence* (2nd ed., pp. 87–109). Hillsdale, NJ: Erlbaum.

Priest, R. F., & Sawyer, J. (1967). Proximity and peership: Bases of balance in interpersonal attraction. *American Journal of Sociology, 72,* 633–649.

Proust, M. (1934). *Remembrance of things past* (C. K. Scott-Moncrieff, Trans.). New York: McGraw-Hill.

Pruitt, D. G. (1998). Social conflict. In D. Gilbert, S. Fiske, & G. Lindzey (Eds.), *The handbook of social psychology* (4th ed., Vol. 2, pp. 470–503). New York: McGraw Hill.

Pruitt, D. G., & Carnevale, P. J. (1993). *Negotiation in social conflict.* Buckingham, England: Open University Press.

Pruitt, D. G., & Kimmel, M. J. (1977). Twenty years of experimental gaming: Critique, synthesis, and suggestions for the future. *Annual Review of Psychology, 28,* 363–392.

Pryor, J. B. (1980). Self-reports and behavior. In D. M. Wegner & R. R. Vallacher (Eds.), *The self in social psychology* (pp. 206–228). New York: Oxford University Press.

Purdum, T. S. (1997, March 28). Tapes Left by Cult Suggest Comet Was the Sign to Die. *New York Times.*

Pyszczynski, T., Solomon, S., Greenberg, J., & Stewart-Fouts, M. (1995). The liberating and constraining aspects of self: Why the freed bird finds a new cage. In A. Oosterwegel, R. A. Wicklund (Eds.), *The self in European and North American culture: Development and processes* (pp. 357–373). NATO advanced science institutes series. Dordrecht, Netherlands: Kluwer Academic Publishers.

Pyszczynski, T. A., & Greenberg, J. (1987). Toward an integration of cognitive and motivational perspectives on social inference: A biased hypothesis-testing model. In L. Berkowitz (Ed.), *Advances in experimental social psychology* (Vol. 20, pp. 297–340). San Diego, CA: Academic Press.

Pyszczynski, T. A., Greenberg, J., & LaPrelle, J. (1985). Social comparison after success and failure: Biased search for information consistent with a self-serving conclusion. *Journal of Experimental Social Psychology, 21,* 195–211.

Quattrone, G. A. (1982). Behavioral consequences of attributional bias. *Social Cognition, 1,* 358–378.

Quattrone, G. A. (1986). On the perception of a group's variability. In S. Worchel & W. G. Austin (Eds.), *Psychology of intergroup relations* (2nd ed.). Chicago: Nelson-Hall.

Quattrone, G. A., & Jones, E. E. (1980). The perception of variability within ingroups and outgroups: Implications for the law of small numbers. *Journal of Personality and Social Psychology, 38,* 141–152.

Quattrone, G. A., Lawrence, C. P., Finkel, S. E., & Andrus, D. C. (1984). *Explorations in anchoring: The effects of prior range, anchor extremity, and suggestive hints.* Unpublished manuscript, Stanford University.

Rajecki, D. W., Kidd, R. F., & Ivins, B. (1976). Social facilitation in chickens: A different level of analysis. *Journal of Experimental Social Psychology, 12,* 233–246.

Ramsey, S. J. (1981). The kinesics of femininity in Japanese women. *Language Sciences, 3,* 104–123.

Rapoport, A., & Chammah, A. M. (1965). *Prisoner's Dilemma: A study in conflict and cooperation.* Ann Arbor: University of Michigan Press.

Raps, C. S., Peterson, C., Jonas, M., & Seligman, M. E. P. (1982). Patient behavior in hospitals: Helplessness, reactance, or both? *Journal of Personality and Social Psychology, 42,* 1036–1041.

Raskin, D. C. (1986). The polygraph in 1986: Scientific, professional, and legal issues surrounding applications and acceptance of polygraph evidence. *Utah Law Review,* 29–74.

Rawlins, W. K. (1992). *Friendship matters.* Hawthorne, NY: Aldine de Gruyter.

Rawlins, W. K. (1994). Being there and growing apart: Sustaining friendships through adulthood. In D. J. Canary & L. Stafford (Eds.), *Communication and Relational Maintenance* (pp. 275–294). New York: Academic Press.

Reagan, R. (1990). *An American life.* New York: Simon & Schuster.

Rector, M., & Neiva, E. (1996). Communication and personal relations in Brazil. In W. B. Gudykunst, S. Ting-Toomey, & T. Nishida, *Communication in Personal Relationships Across Cultures* (pp. 156–173). Thousand Oaks, CA: Sage.

Reeves, R. A., Baker, G. A., Boyd, J. G., & Cialdini, R. B. (1991). The door-in-the-face technique: Reciprocal concessions vs. self-presentational explanations. *Journal of Social Behavior and Personality, 6,* 545–558.

Regan, P. C., & Berscheid, E. (1995). Gender differences in beliefs about the causes of male and female sexual desire. *Personal Relationships, 2,* 345–358.

Regan, P. C., & Berscheid, E. (1997). Gender differences in characteristics desired in a potential sexual and marriage partner. *Journal of Psychology and Human Sexuality, 9,* 25–37.

Regan, P. C., Snyder, M., & Kassin, S. M. (1995). Unrealistic optimism: Self-enhancement or person positivity? *Personality and Social Psychology Bulletin, 21,* 1073–1082.

Rehm, J., Steinleitner, M., & Lilli, W. (1987). Wearing uniforms and aggression: A field experiment. *European Journal of Social Psychology, 17,* 357–360.

Reifman, A., Larrick, R. P., Crandall, C. S., & Fein, S. (1996). *Predicting sporting events: Accuracy as a function of reasons analysis, expertise, and task difficulty.* Unpublished manuscript, Research Institute on Addictions, Buffalo, NY.

Reifman, A. S., Larrick, R., & Fein, S. (1988). *The heat-aggression relationship in major-league baseball.* Paper presented at the meeting of the American Psychological Association, San Francisco.

Reinecke, J., Schmidt, P., & Ajzen, I. (1996). Application of the theory of planned behavior to adolescents' condom use: A panel study. *Journal of Applied Social Psychology, 26,* 749–772.

Reis, H. T., Nezlek, J., & Wheeler, L. (1980). Physical attractiveness in social interaction. *Journal of Personality and Social Psychology, 38,* 604–617.

Reis, H. T., & Patrick, B. C. (1996). Attachment and intimacy: Component processes. In E. T. Higgins & A. W. Kruglanski (Eds.), *Social Psychology: Handbook of Basic Principles* (pp. 523–563). New York: Guilford.

Reis, H. T., Wheeler, L., Speigel, N., Kernis, M. H., Nezlek, J., & Perri, M. (1982). Physical attractiveness in social interaction 2: Why does appearance affect social experience? *Journal of Personality and Social Psychology, 43,* 979–996.

Reis, T. J., Gerrard, M., & Gibbons, F. X. (1993). Social comparison and the pill: Reactions to upward and downward comparison of contraceptive behavior. *Personality and Social Psychology Bulletin, 19,* 13–20.

Reisman, J. M. (1990). Intimacy in same-sex friendships. *Sex Roles, 23,* 65–82.

Reiter, S. M., & Samuel, W. (1980). Littering as a function of prior litter and the presence or absence of prohibitive signs. *Journal of Applied Social Psychology, 10,* 45–55.

Reitzes, D. C. (1952). The role of organizational structures: Union versus neighborhood in a tension situation. *Journal of Social Issues, 9,* 37–44.

Reno, R., Cialdini, R., & Kallgren, C. A. (1993). The trans-situational influence of social norms. *Journal of Personality and Social Psychology, 64,* 104–112.

Reno, R. R., Cialdini, R. B., & Kallgren, C. A. (1993). The transituational influence of social norms. *Journal of Personality and Social Psychology, 64,* 104–112.

Rheingold, H. L. (1982). Little children's participation in the work of adults: A nascent prosocial behavior. *Child Development, 53,* 114–125.

Rhodes, N., & Wood, W. (1992). Self-esteem and intelligence affect influenceability: The mediating role of message reception. *Psychological Bulletin, 111,* 156–171.

Rhodes, R. (1995, June 19). The general and World War III. *New Yorker,* pp. 47–59.

Rhodewalt, F., & Davison, J. (1984). *Self-handicapping and subsequent performance: The role of outcome valence and attitudinal certainty.* Unpublished manuscript, University of Utah.

Rhodewalt, F., Sanbonmatsu, D. M., Tschanz, B., Feick, D. L., & Waller, A. (1995). Self-handicapping and interpersonal trade-offs: The effects of claimed self-handicaps on observers' performance evaluations and feedback. *Personality and Social Psychology Bulletin, 21,* 1042–1050.

Rholes, W. S., Newman, L. S., & Ruble, D. N. (1990). Understanding self and other: Developmental and motivational aspects of perceiving persons in terms of invariant dispositions. In E. T. Higgins & R. M. Sorrentino (Eds.), *Handbook of Motivation and Cognition: Foundations of Social Behavior,* (Vol. 2). New York: Guilford.

Richardson, D., Hammock, G., Smith, S., & Gardner, W. (1994). Empathy as a cognitive inhibitor of interpersonal aggression. *Aggressive Behavior, 20,* 275–289.

Richmond, V. P., & McCroskey, J. C. (1995). *Nonverbal Behavior in Interpersonal Relations.* Boston: Allyn & Bacon.

Richmond, V. P., McCroskey, J. C., & Payne, S. K. (1991). *Nonverbal behavior in interpersonal relations.* Englewood Cliffs, NJ: Prentice Hall.

Rigby, K. (1988). Sexist attitudes and authoritarian personality characteristics among Australian adolescents. *Journal of Research in Personality, 22,* 465–473.

Ringelmann, M. (1913). Recherches sur les moteurs animés: Travail de l'homme. Annales de l'Institut National Argonomique, 2e srie, tom 12, 1–40.

Riordan, C. A. (1978). Equal-status interracial contact: A review and revision of a concept. *International Journal of Intercultural Relations, 2,* 161–185.

Roberts, K. P. (1996). How research on source monitoring can inform cognitive interview techniques. *Psycholoquy, 7* witness-memory.15.roberts.

Robins, R. W., Spranca, M. D., & Mendelson, G. A. (1996). The actor-observer effect revisited: Effects of individual differences and repeated social interactions on actor and observer attributions. *Journal of Personality and Social Psychology, 71,* 375–389.

Rodin, J. (1985). The application of social psychology. In G. Lindzey & E. Aronson (Eds.), *Handbook of social psychology* (3rd. ed., Vol. 2, pp. 805–881). New York: McGraw-Hill.

Rodin, J. (1986). Aging and health: Effects of the sense of control. *Science, 233,* 1271–1276.

Rodin, J., & Langer, E. J. (1977). Long-term effects of a control-relevant intervention with the institutional aged. *Journal of Personality and Social Psychology, 35,* 897–902.

Roesch, S. C., & Amirkhan, J. H. (1997). Boundary conditions for self-serving attributions: Another look at the sports pages. *Journal of Applied Social Psychology, 27,* 245–261.

Roese, N. J. (1997). Counterfactual thinking. *Psychological Bulletin, 121,* 133–148.

Roese, N. J., & Olson, J. M. (1996). Counterfactuals, causal attributions, and the hindsight bias: A conceptual integration. *Journal of Experimental Social Psychology, 32,* 197–227.

Roese, N. J., & Olson, J. M. (1997). Counterfactual thinking: The intersection of affect and function. In M. Zanna (Ed.), *Advances in experimental social psychology* (Vol. 29). San Diego, CA: Academic Press.

Rogers, R. (1983). Cognitive and physiological processes in fear appeals and attitude change: A revised theory of protection motivation. In J. T. Cacioppo & R. E. Petty (Eds.), *Social psychophysiology: A sourcebook* (pp. 153–176). New York: Guilford Press.

Rogers, R., & Prentice-Dunn, S. (1981). Deindividuation and anger-mediated interracial aggression: Unmasking regressive racism. *Journal of Personality and Social Psychology, 41,* 63–73.

Rohan, M., & Zanna, M. (1996). Value transmission in families. In C. Seligman, J. Olson, & M. Zanna (Eds.), *The psychology of values: The Ontario symposium on personality and social psychology, Vol. 8,* pp. 253–276. Mahwah, NJ: Erlbaum.

Rohrer, J. H., Baron, S. H., Hoffman, E. L., & Swander, D. V. (1954). The stability of autokinetic judgments. *Journal of Abnormal and Social Psychology, 49,* 595–597.

Roiphe, K. (1994). *The Morning After: Sex, Fear, and Feminism.* New York: Little Brown.

Rosch, E., & Lloyd, B. (1978). (Eds.) *Cognition and categorization.* Hillsdale, NJ: Erlbaum.

Roseman, I. J., Antoniou, A. A., & Jose, P. E. (1996). Appraisal determinants of emotion: Constructing a more accurate and comprehensive theory. *Cognition and Emotion, 10,* 241–277.

Rosen, S., Bergman, M., Plester, D., El-Mofty, A., & Satti, M. (1962). Prebycusis study of a relatively noise-free population in the Sudan. *Annals of Otology, Rhinology, and Laryngology, 71,* 727–743.

Rosenbaum, M. E. (1986). The repulsion hypothesis: On the nondevelopment of relationships. *Journal of Personality and Social Psychology, 51,* 1156–1166.

Rosenberg, L. A. (1961). Group size, prior experience, and conformity. *Journal of Abnormal and Social Psychology, 63,* 436–437.

Rosenberg, M. J., Davidson, A. J., Chen, J., Judson, F. N., & Douglas, J. M. (1992). Barrier contraceptives and sexually transmitted diseases in women: A comparison of female-dependent methods and condoms. *American Journal of Public Health, 82,* 669–674.

Rosenberg, S., Nelson, S., & Vivekananthan, P. S. (1968). A multidimensional approach to the structure of personality impressions. *Journal of Personality and Social Psychology, 9,* 283–294.

Rosenhan, D. L. (1970). The natural socialization of altruistic autonomy. In J. R. Macaulay & L. Berkowitz (Eds.), *Altruism and helping behavior* (pp. 251–268). New York: Academic Press.

Rosenhan, D. L. (1973). On being sane in insane places. *Science, 179,* 250–258.

Rosenman, R. H. (1993). Relationship of the Type A behavior pattern with coronary heart disease. In L. Goldberger & S. Breznitz (Eds.), *Handbook of stress: Theoretical and clinical aspects* (2nd ed., pp. 449–476). New York: Free Press.

Rosenthal, A. M. (1964). *Thirty-eight witnesses.* New York: McGraw-Hill.

Rosenthal, R. (1994). Interpersonal expectancy effects: A 30-year perspective. *Current Directions in Psychological Science, 3,* 176–179.

Rosenthal, R. (1995). Critiquing Pygmalion: A 25-year perspective. *Current Directions in Psychological Science, 4,* 171–172.

Rosenthal, R., & DePaulo, B. M. (1979). Sex differences in accommodation in nonverbal communication. In R. Rosenthal (Ed.), *Skill in nonverbal communication: Individual differences* (pp. 68–103). Cambridge, MA: Oelgeschlager, Gunn & Hain.

Rosenthal, R., Hall, J. A., DiMatteo, M. R., Rogers, P. L., & Archer, D. (1979). *Sensitivity to nonverbal communication: The PONS test.* Baltimore, MD: Johns Hopkins University Press.

Rosenthal, R., & Jacobson, L. (1968). *Pygmalion in the classroom: Teacher expectation and student intellectual development.* New York: Holt, Rinehart & Winston.

Ross, L. (1977). The intuitive psychologist and his shortcomings: Distortions in the attribution process. In L. Berkowitz (Ed.), *Advances in experimental social psychology* (Vol. 10, pp. 173–220). Orlando, FL: Academic Press.

Ross, L., Amabile, T. M., & Steinmetz, J. L. (1977). Social roles, social control, and biases in social perception. *Journal of Personality and Social Psychology, 35,* 485–494.

Ross, L., Lepper, M. R., & Hubbard, M. (1975). Perseverance in self perception and social perception: Biased attributional processes in the debriefing paradigm. *Journal of Personality and Social Psychology, 32,* 880–892.

Ross, L., & Nisbett, R. E. (1991). *The person and the situation: Perspectives of social psychology.* New York: McGraw-Hill.

Ross, L., & Samuels, S. M. (1993). *The predictive power of personal reputation versus labels and construal in the Prisoner's Dilemma game.* Unpublished manuscript, Stanford University.

Ross, L., & Ward, A. (1995). Psychological barriers to dispute resolution. In M. P. Zanna (Ed.), *Advances in experimental social psychology* (Vol. 27, pp. 255–304). San Diego, CA: Academic Press.

Ross, L., & Ward, A. (1996). Naive realism: Implications for social conflict and misunderstanding. In T. Brown, E. Reed, & E. Turiel (Eds.), *Values and knowledge.* Hillsdale, NJ: Erlbaum.

Ross, M. (1989). Relation of implicit theories to the construction of personal histories. *Psychological Review, 96,* 341–357.

Ross, M., & Conway, M. (1985). Remembering one's own past: The construction of personal histories. In R. Sorrentino & E. T. Higgins (Eds.), *Handbook of motivation and cognition* (pp. 122–144). New York: Guilford Press.

Ross, M., & McFarland, C. (1988). Constructing the past: Biases in personal memories. In D. Bar-Tel & A. Kruglanski (Eds.), *The social psychology of knowledge* (pp. 299–314). New York: Cambridge University Press.

Ross, M., & Olson, J. M. (1981). An expectancy-attribution model of the effects of placebos. *Psychological Review, 88,* 408–437.

Rosselli, F., Skelly, J. J., & Mackie, D. M. (1995). Processing rational and emotional messages: The cognitive and affective mediation of persuasion. *Journal of Experimental Social Psychology, 31,* 163–190.

Rothbart, M., & John, O. P. (1985). Social categorization and behavioral episodes: A cognitive analysis of the effects of intergroup contact. *Journal of Social Issues, 41*(3), 81–104.

Rothbart, M., & Park, B. (1986). On the confirmability and disconfirmability of trait concepts. *Journal of Personality and Social Psychology, 50,* 131–142.

Rothman, A. J., & Hardin, C. D. (1997). Differential use of the availability heuristic in social judgment. *Personality and Social Psychology Bulletin, 23,* 123–138.

Rothman, A. J., & Salovey, P. (1997). Shaping perceptions to motivate healthy behavior: The role of message framing. *Psychological Bulletin, 121,* 3–19.

Rothman, A. J., Salovey, P., Antone, C., Keough, K., & Martin, C. D. (1993). The influence of message framing on intentions to perform health behaviors. *Journal of Experimental Social Psychology, 29,* 408–432.

Rotton, J., & Frey, J. (1985). Air pollution, weather, and violent crimes: Concomitant time-series analysis of archival date. *Journal of Personality and Social Psychology, 49,* 1207–1220.

Rousseau, J. J. (1930). *The social contract and discourses.* New York: Dutton.

Rubin, J., & Brown, B. (1975). *The social psychology of bargaining and negotiation.* New York: Academic Press.

Rubin, Z. (1970). Measurement of romantic love. *Journal of Personality and Social Psychology, 16,* 265–273.

Rubin, Z. (1973). *Liking and loving: An invitation to social psychology.* New York: Holt, Rinehart & Winston.

Rubin, Z., Peplau, L. A., & Hill, C. T. (1981). Loving and leaving: Sex differences in romantic attachments. *Sex Roles, 7,* 821–835.

Ruble, D. N., & Feldman, N. S. (1976). Order of consistency, distinctiveness, and consistency information and causal attribution. *Journal of Personality and Social Psychology, 31,* 930–937.

Rudman, L. A., & Borgida, E. (1995). The afterglow of construct accessibility: The behavioral consequences of priming men to view women as sexual objects. *Journal of Experimental Social Psychology, 31,* 493–517.

Rudolfsky, M. P. (1972). *The unfashionable human body.* New York: Doubleday.

Rule, B. G., Taylor, B. R., & Dobbs, A. R. (1987). Priming affects of heat on aggressive thoughts. *Social Cognition, 5,* 131–143.

Rusbult, C. E. (1980). Commitment and satisfaction in romantic associations: A test of the investment model. *Journal of Experimental Social Psychology, 16,* 172–186.

Rusbult, C. E. (1983). A longitudinal test of the investment model: The development (and deterioration) of satisfaction and commitment in heterosexual involvements. *Journal of Personality and Social Psychology, 45,* 101–117.

Rusbult, C. E. (1987). Responses to dissatisfaction in close relationships: The exit-voice-loyalty-neglect model. In D. Perlman & S. Duck (Eds.), *Intimate Relationships: Development, Dynamics, and Deterioration* (pp. 209–237). Newbury Park, CA: Sage.

Rusbult, C. E. (1991). *Commitment processes in close relationships: The investment model.* Paper presented at the meeting of the American Psychological Association, San Francisco.

Rusbult, C. E. (1993). Understanding responses to dissatisfaction in close relationships: The exit-voice-loyalty-neglect model. In S. Worchel & J. A. Simpson (Eds.), *Conflict Between People and Groups: Causes, Processes, and Resolutions* (pp. 30–59). Chicago: Nelson-Hall.

Rusbult, C. E., & Buunk, A. P. (1993). Commitment processes in close relationships: An interdependence analysis. *Journal of Social and Personal Relationships, 10,* 175–204.

Rusbult, C. E., Johnson, D. J., & Morrow, G. D. (1986). Impact of couple patterns of problem solving on distress and nondistress in dating relationships. *Journal of Personal and Social Psychology, 50,* 744–753.

Rusbult, C. E., & Martz, J. M. (1995). Remaining in an abusive relationship: An investment model analysis of nonvoluntary dependence. *Personality and Social Psychology Bulletin, 21,* 558–571.

Rusbult, C. E., Morrow, G. D., & Johnson, D. J. (1987). Impact of couple patterns of problem solving on distress and nondistress in dating relationships. *Journal of Personality and Social Psychology, 50,* 744–753.

Rusbult, C. E., & Van Lange, P. A. M. (1996). Interdependence processes. In E. T. Higgins & A. W. Kruglanski (Eds.), *Social Psychology: Handbook of Basic Principles* (pp. 564–596). New York: Guilford.

Rusbult, C. E., Verette, J., Whitney, G. A., Slovik, L. F., & Lipkus, I. (1991). Accommodation processes in close relationship: Theory and preliminary empirical evidence. *Journal of Personality and Social Psychology, 60,* 53–78.

Rusbult, C. E., Yovetich, N. A., & Verette, J. (1996). An interdependence analysis of accommodation processes. In G. J. O. Fletcher & J. Fitness (Eds.), *Knowledge Structures in Close Relationships: A Social Psychological Approach* (pp. 63–90). Mahwah, NJ: Erlbaum.

Rusbult, C. E., & Zembrodt, I. M. (1983). Responses to dissatisfaction in romantic involvements: A multidimensional scaling analysis. *Journal of Experimental Social Psychology, 19,* 274–293.

Rushton, J. P. (1975). Generosity in children: Immediate and long-term effects of modeling, preaching, and moral judgment. *Journal of Personality and Social Psychology, 31,* 459–466.

Rushton, J. P. (1989). Genetic similarity, human altruism, and group selection. *Behavioral and Brain Sciences, 12,* 503–559.

Russell, B., & Branch, T. (1979). *Second wind: The memoirs of an opinionated man.* New York: Ballantine Books.

Russell, D. (1982). The Causal Dimension Scale: A measure of how individuals perceive causes. *Journal of Personality and Social Psychology, 42,* 1137–1145.

Russell, D. E. H. (1997). Pornography causes harm to women. In Walsh, M. R. (Ed.), *Women, men, and gender: Ongoing debates* (pp. 158–169). New Haven, CT: Yale University Press.

Russell, G. W. (1983). Psychological issues in sports aggression. In J. H. Goldstein (Ed.), *Sports violence.* New York: Springer-Verlag.

Russell, J. A. (1994). Is there universal recognition of emotion from facial expression? A review of the cross-cultural studies. *Psychological Bulletin, 115,* 102–141.

Russell, J. A., Ward, L. M., & Pratt, G. (1981). Affective quality attributed to environments: A factor analytic study. *Environment and Behavior, 13,* 259–288.

Ryan, B., Jr. (1991). *It works! How investment spending in advertising pays off.* New York: American Association of Advertising Agencies.

Ryan, R. M., & Deci, E. L. (1996). When paradigms clash: Comments on Cameron and Pierce's claim that rewards do not undermine intrinsic motivation. *Review of Educational Research, 66,* 33–38.

Ryle, G. (1949). *The concept of mind.* London: Hutchinson.

Sabourin, T. C., & Stamp, G. H. (1995). Communication and the experience of dialectical tensions in family life: An examination of abusive and nonabusive families. *Communication Monographs, 62,* 213–242.

Sacks, O. (1987). *The man who mistook his wife for a hat and other clinical tales.* New York: Harper & Row.

Sadik, N. (1991). World population continues to rise. *Futurist, 25,* 9–14.

Sadker, M., & Sadker, D. (1985, March). Sexism in the schoolroom of the '80s. *Psychology Today,* pp. 54–57.

Sadker, M., & Sadker, D. (1994). *Failing at fairness: How America's schools cheat girls.* New York: Charles Scribner's Sons.

Saks, M. J. (1977). *Jury verdicts.* Lexington, MA: Heath.

Sakurai, M. M. (1975). Small group cohesiveness and detrimental conformity. *Sociometry, 38,* 340–357.

Salovey, P., Mayer, J. D., & Rosenhan, D. L. (1991). Mood and helping: Mood as a motivator of helping and helping as a regulator of mood. In M. S. Clark (Ed.), *Prosocial behavior: Review of personality and social psychology* (Vol. 12, pp. 215–237). Newbury Park, CA: Sage.

Salovey, P., & Rodin, J. (1985). Cognitions about the self: Connecting feeling states and social behavior. In P. Shaver (Ed.), *Self, situations, and social behavior: Review of personality and social psychology* (Vol. 6, pp. 143–166). Beverly Hills, CA: Sage.

Salovey, P., & Rodin, J. (1989). Envy and jealousy in close relationships. In C. Hendrick (Ed.), *Close relationships: Review of personality and social psychology* (pp. 221–246). Newbury Park, CA: Sage.

Salovey, P., & Rodin, J. (1991). Provoking jealousy and envy: Domain relevance and self-esteem threat. *Journal of Social and Clinical Psychology, 10,* 395–413.

Salovey, P., Rothman, A. J., & Rodin, J. (1998). Social psychology and health behavior. In D. Gilbert, S. Fiske, & G. Lindzey (Eds.), *The handbook of social psychology* (4th ed., Vol. 2, pp. 633–683). New York: McGraw-Hill.

Sanders, G. S. (1983). An attentional process model of social facilitation. In A. Hare, H. Bumberg, V. Kent, & M. Davies (Eds.), *Small groups.* London: Wiley.

Sanders, G. S., & Simmons, W. L. (1983). Use of hypnosis to enhance eyewitness memory: Does it work? *Journal of Applied Psychology, 68,* 70–77.

Sanger, D. E. (1993, May 30). The career and the kimono. *New York Times Magazine,* pp. 18–19.

Sanna, L. J. (1992). Self-efficacy theory: Implications for social facilitation and social loafing. *Journal of Personality and Social Psychology, 62,* 774–786.

Sanna, L. J., & Turley, K. J. (1996). Antecedents to spontaneous counterfactual thinking: Effects of expectancy, violation and outcome valence. *Personality and Social Psychology Bulletin, 22,* 906–919.

Sansone, C., & Harackiewicz, J. M. (1996). "I don't feel like it": The function of interest in self-regulation. In L. L. Martin & A. Tesser (Eds.), *Striving and feeling: Interactions among goals, affect, and self-regulation* (pp. 203–228). Mahwah, NJ: Erlbaum.

Sansone, C., & Harackiewicz, J. M. (1997). *"Reality" is complicated: Comment on Eisenberger and Cameron.* Unpublished manuscript, University of Utah.

Santos, M. D., Leve, C., & Pratkanis, A. R. (1994). Hey buddy, can you spare seventeen cents? Mindful persuasion and the pique technique. *Journal of Applied Social Psychology, 24,* 755–764.

Sarason, I. G., Sarason, B. R., & Pierce, G. R. (1990). (Eds.). *Social support: An interactional view.* New York: Wiley.

Saxe, L. (1994). Detection of deception: Polygraph and integrity tests. *Current Directions in Psychological Science, 3,* 69–73.

Saxe, L., Dougherty, D., & Cross, T. (1985). The validity of polygraph testing: Scientific analysis and public controversy. *American Psychologist, 40,* 355–366.

Schacter, D. L. (1995, April). Memory wars. *Scientific American,* pp. 135–139.

Schacter, D. L. (1996). *Searching for memory: The brain, the mind, and the past.* New York: Basic Books.

Schachter, S. (1951). Deviation, rejection, and communication. *Journal of Abnormal and Social Psychology, 46,* 190–207.

Schachter, S. (1959). *The psychology of affiliation.* Stanford, CA: Stanford University Press.

Schachter, S. (1964). The interaction of cognitive and physiological determinants of emotional state. In L. Berkowitz (Ed.), *Advances in experimental social psychology* (Vol. 1, pp. 49–80). New York: Academic Press.

Schachter, S. (1977). Nicotine regulation in heavy and light smokers. *Journal of Experimental Psychology: General, 106,* 5–12.

Schachter, S., & Singer, J. E. (1962). Cognitive, social, and physiological determinants of emotional states. *Psychological Review, 69,* 379–399.

Schachter, S., & Singer, J. E. (1979). Comments on the Maslach and Marshall-Zimbardo experiments. *Journal of Personality and Social Psychology, 37,* 989–995.

Schafer, M., & Crichlow, S. (1996). Antecedents of groupthink: A quantitative study. *Journal of Conflict Resolution, 40,* 415–435.

Schafer, R. B., & Keith, P. M. (1980). Equity and depression among married couples. *Social Psychology Quarterly, 43,* 430–435.

Schaller, M., Asp, C. H., & Heim, S. J. (1996). Training in statistical reasoning inhibits formation of erroneous group stereotypes. *Personality and Social Psychology Bulletin, 22,* 829–844.

Schaufeli, W. B. (1988). Perceiving the causes of unemployment: An evaluation of the Causal Dimension Scale in a real-life situation. *Journal of Personality and Social Psychology, 54,* 347–356.

Scheier, M. F., & Carver, C. S. (1987). Dispositional optimism and physical well-being: The influence of generalized outcome expectancies on health. *Journal of Personality, 55,* 169–210.

Scheier, M. F., & Carver, C. S. (1992). Effects of optimism on psychological and physical well being: Theoretical overview and empirical update. *Cognitive Therapy and Research, 16,* 201–228.

Scheier, M. F., Carver, C. S., & Bridges, M. W. (1992). Distinguishing optimism from neuroticism (and trait anxiety, self-mastery, and self-esteem): A revision of the Life Orientation Test. *Journal of Personality and Social Psychology, 67,* 1063–1078.

Scheier, M. F., Matthews, K. A., Owens, J., Magovern, G. J., Lefebvre, R. C., Abbott, R. A., & Carver, C. S. (1990). Dispositional optimism and recovery from coronary artery bypass surgery: The beneficial effects of physical and psychological well-being. *Journal of Personality and Social Psychology, 57,* 1024–1040.

Scheier, M. F., Weintraub, J. K., & Carver, C. (1986). Coping with stress: Divergent strategies of optimists and pessimists. *Journal of Personality and Social Psychology, 51,* 1257–1264.

Scherer, K. R. (1988). Cognitive antecedents of emotion. In V. Hamilton, G. H. Bower, & N. H. Frijda (Eds.), *Cognitive perspectives on emotion and motivation* (pp. 89–126). Dordrecht, the Netherlands: Kluwer.

Schiffmann, A., Cohen, S., Nowik, R., & Selinger, D. (1978). Initial diagnostic hypotheses: Factors which distort physicians' judgment. *Organizational Behavior and Human Performance, 21,* 305–315.

Schlenker, B. R. (1980). *Impression management: The self-concept, social identity, and interpersonal relations.* Monterey, CA: Brooks/Cole.

Schlenker, B. R., Britt, T. W., & Pennington, J. (1996). Impression regulation and management: Highlights of a theory of self-identification. In R. M. Sorrentino & E. T. Higgins (Eds.), *Handbook of motivation and cognition* (Vol. 2, pp. 118–147). New York: Guilford.

Schlenker, B. R., Dlugolecki, D. W., & Doherty, K. (1994). The impact of self-presentations on self-appraisals and behavior: The power of public commitment. *Personality and Social Psychology Bulletin, 20,* 20–33.

Schlenker, B. R., & Weigold, M. F. (1992). Interpersonal processes involving impression regulation and management. *Annual Review of Psychology, 43,* 133–168.

Schmidt, D. E., & Keating, J. P. (1979). Human crowding and personal control: An integration of the research. *Psychological Bulletin, 86,* 680–700.

Schmitt, B. H., Gilovich, T., Goore, N., & Joseph, L. (1986). Mere presence and social facilitation: One more time. *Journal of Experimental Social Psychology, 22,* 228–241.

Schmitt, D. P., & Buss, D. M. (1996). Strategic self-promotion and competitor derogation: Sex and context effects on the perceived effectiveness of mate attraction tactics. *Journal of Personality and Social Psychology, 70,* 1185–1204.

Schneider, D. J. (1973). Implicit personality theory: A review. *Psychological Bulletin, 79,* 294–309.

Schneider, D. J., Hastorf, A. H., & Ellsworth, P. C. (1979). *Person perception* (2nd ed.). Reading, MA: Addison-Wesley.

Schneider, M. E., Major, B., Luhtanen, R., & Crocker, J. (1996). Social stigma and the potential costs of assumptive help. *Personality and Social Psychology Bulletin, 22,* 201–209.

Schoeneman, T. J., & Rubanowitz, D. E. (1985). Attributions in the advice columns: Actors and observers, causes and reasons. *Personality and Social Psychology Bulletin, 11,* 315–325.

Schofield, J. W. (1986). Causes and consequences of the color-blind perspective. In J. F. Dovidio & S. L. Gaertner (Eds.), *Prejudice, discrimination, and racism* (pp. 231–253). Orlando, FL: Academic Press.

Schooler, J. W., & Engstler-Schooler, T. Y. (1990). Verbal overshadowing of visual memories: Some things are better left unsaid. *Cognitive Psychology, 22,* 36–71.

Schriesheim, C. A., Tepper, B. J., & Tetrault, L. A. (1994). Least preferred co-worker score, situational control, and leadership effectiveness: A meta-analysis of contingency model performance predictions. *Journal of Applied Psychology, 79,* 561–573.

Schroeder, D. A., Dovidio, J. F., Sibicky, M. E., Matthews, L. L., & Allen, J. L. (1988). Empathy concern and helping behavior: Egoism or altruism? *Journal of Experimental Social Psychology, 24,* 333–353.

Schroeder, D. H., & Costa, P. T., Jr. (1984). Influence of life event stress on physical illness: Substantive effects or methodological flaws? *Journal of Personality and Social Psychology, 46,* 853–863.

Schuler, E. A., & Parenton, V. J. (1943). A recent epidemic of hysteria in a Louisiana high school. *Journal of Social Psychology, 17,* 221–235.

Schultz, P. W., Oskamp, S., & Mainieri, T. (1995). Who recycles and when? A review of personal and situational factors. *Journal of Environmental Psychology, 15,* 105–121.

Schulz, R. (1976). Effects of control and predictability on the physical and psychological well-being of the institutionalized aged. *Journal of Personality and Social Psychology, 33,* 563–573.

Schulz, R., & Hanusa, B. H. (1978). Long-term effects of control and predictability-enhancing interventions: Findings and ethical issues. *Journal of Personality and Social Psychology, 36,* 1202–1212.

Schuman, H., & Kalton, G. (1985). Survey methods. In G. Lindzey & E. Aronson (Eds.), *Handbook of social psychology* (3rd ed., Vol. 1, pp. 635–697). New York: McGraw-Hill.

Schwarz, N., & Bless, H. (1992). Constructing reality and its alternative: An inclusion/exclusion model of assimilation and contrast effects in social judgment. In L. L. Martin & A. Tesser (Eds.), *The construction of social judgment* (pp. 217–245). Hillsdale, NJ: Erlbaum.

Schwarz, N., Bless, H., Strack, F., Klumpp, G., Rittenauer-Schatka, H., & Simmons, A. (1991). Ease of retrieval as information: Another look at the availability heuristic. *Journal of Personality and Social Psychology, 61,* 195–202.

Schwarz, N., & Clore, G. I. (1988). How do I feel about it? Informative functions of affective states. In K. Fiedler & J. Forgas (Eds.), *Affect, cognition, and social behavior* (pp. 44–62). Toronto: Hogrefe.

Schwarz, N., Groves, R. M., & Schuman, H. (1998). Survey methods. In D. Gilbert, S. Fiske, & G. Lindzey (Eds.), *The handbook of social psychology* (4th ed., Vol. 1, pp. 143–179). New York: Random House.

Schwartz, S. H. (1992). Universals in the content and structure of values: Theoretical advances and empirical tests in 20 countries. In M. P. Zanna (Ed.), *Advances in experimental social psychology* (Vol. 25, pp. 1–65). San Diego, CA: Academic Press.

Schwartz, S. H., & Gottlieb, A. (1976). Bystander reactions to a violent theft: Crime in Jerusalem. *Journal of Personality and Social Psychology, 34,* 1188–1199.

Schwarzer, R., & Leppin, A. (1992). Social support and health: A theoretical and empirical overview. *Health Psychology, 8,* 99–127.

Scott, J. E., & Cuvelier, S. J. (1993). Violence and sexual violence in pornography: Is it increasing? *Archives of Sexual Behavior, 22,* 357–371.

Scott, J. P. (1958). *Aggression.* Chicago: University of Chicago Press.

Sears, D. O. (1981). Life stage effects on attitude change, especially among the elderly. In S. B. Kiesler, J. N. Morgan, & V. K. Oppenheimer (Eds.), *Aging: Social change* (pp. 183–204). New York: Academic Press.

Secord, P. F., & Backman, C. W. (1964). *Social psychology.* New York: McGraw-Hill.

Sedikides, C., & Anderson, C. A. (1994). Causal perceptions of intertrait relations: The glue that holds person types together. *Personality and Social Psychology Bulletin, 21,* 294–302.

Sedikides, C., & Skowronski, J. J. (1997). The symbolic self in evolutionary context. *Personality and Social Psychology Review, 1,* 80–102.

Sedikides, C., & Strube, M. J. (1997). Self-evaluation: To thine own self be good, to thine own self be sure, to thine own self be true, and to thine own self be better. In M. Zanna (Ed.), *Advances in experimental social psychology* (Vol. 29, pp. 209–269). San Diego: Academic Press.

Segal, M. W (1974). Alphabet and attraction: An unobtrusive measure of the effect of propinquity in a field setting. *Journal of Personality and Social Psychology, 30,* 654–657.

Seligman, M. E. P., & Schulman, P. (1986). Explanatory style as a predictor of productivity and quitting among life insurance agents. *Journal of Personality and Social Psychology, 50,* 832–838.

Selye, H. (1956). *The stress of life.* New York: McGraw-Hill.

Selye, H. (1976). *Stress in health and disease.* Woburn, MA: Butterworth.

Semin, G. R., & Fiedler, K. (1989). Relocating attributional phenomena within a language-cognition interface: The case of actors' and observers' perspectives. *European Journal of Social Psychology, 19,* 491–508.

Semin, G. R., & Fiedler, K. (1991). The linguistic category model, its bases, applications, and range. In W. Stroege & M. Hewstone (Eds.), *European review of social psychology* (Vol. 1, pp. 1–30). Chichester, England: Wiley.

Seppa, N. (1997). Children's TV remains steeped in violence. *APA Monitor, 28,* p. 36.

Sergios, P. A., & Cody, J. (1985). Physical attractiveness and social assertiveness skills in male homosexual dating behavior and partner selection. *Journal of Social Psychology, 125,* 505–514.

Seta, J. J., Seta, C. E., & Wang, M. A. (1990). Feelings of negativity and stress: An averaging-summation analysis of impressions of negative life experiences. *Personality and Social Psychology Bulletin, 17,* 376–384.

Shackelford, T. K., & Buss, D. M. (1996). Betrayal in mateships, friendships, and coalitions. *Personality and Social Psychology Bulletin, 22,* 1151–1164.

Shaffer, D. R. (1986). Is mood-induced altruism a form of hedonism? *Humboldt Journal of Social Relations, 13,* 195–216.

Shapiro, P. N., & Penrod, S. D. (1986). Meta-analysis of facial identification studies. *Psychological Bulletin, 100,* 139–156.

Sharan, S. (1980). Cooperative learning in small groups. *Review of Educational Research, 50,* 241–271.

Sharp, F. C. (1928). *Ethics.* New York: Century.

Shaver, K. (1970). Defensive attribution: Effects of severity and relevance on the responsibility assigned for an accident. *Journal of Personality and Social Psychology, 14,* 101–113.

Shaver, P. R., Collins, N., & Clark, C. L. (1996). Attachment styles and internal working models of self and relationship partners. In G. J. O. Fletcher & J. Fitness (Eds.), *Knowledge Structures in Close Relationships: A Social Psychological Approach* (pp. 25–62). Mahwah, NJ: Erlbaum.

Shaver, P. R., Hazan, C., & Bradshaw, D. (1988). Love as attachment: The integration of three behavioral systems. In R. J. Sternberg & M. L. Barnes (Eds.), *The psychology of love* (pp. 68–99). New Haven, CT: Yale University Press.

Shaver, P. R., Schwartz, J., Kirson, D., & O'Connor, C. (1987). Emotion knowledge: Further exploration of a prototype approach. *Journal of Personality and Social Psychology, 52,* 1061–1086.

Shavitt, S. (1989). Operationalizing functional theories of attitude. In A. R. Pratkanis, S. J. Breckler, & A. G. Greenwald (Eds.), *Attitude structure and function* (pp. 311–337). Hillsdale, NJ: Erlbaum.

Shavitt, S. (1990). The role of attitude objects in attitude function. *Journal of Experimental Social Psychology, 26,* 124–148.

Shaw, J. I., & Skolnick, P. (1995). Effects of prohibitive and informative judicial instructions on jury decision making. *Social Behavior and Personality, 23,* 319–325.

Shaw, M. E. (1971). *Group dynamics: The psychology of small group behavior.* New York: McGraw-Hill.

Sheehan, P. W., & Tilden, J. (1984). Real and simulated occurrences of memory distortion in hypnosis. *Journal of Abnormal Psychology, 93,* 259–265.

Sheehan, S. (1975). Profiles: A welfare mother in Brooklyn. *New Yorker*, pp. 42–46.

Sheehan, S. (1982). *Is there no place on earth for me?* Boston: Houghton Mifflin.

Sheppard, B. H., Hartwick, J., & Warshaw, P. R. (1988). The theory of reasoned action: A meta-analysis of past research with recommendations for modifications and future research. *Journal of Consumer Research, 15*, 325–343.

Shepperd, J. A. (1993). Productivity loss in performance groups: A motivation analysis. *Psychological Bulletin, 113*, 67–81.

Shepperd, J. A. (1995). Remedying motivation and productivity loss in collective settings. *Current Directions in Psychological Science, 4*, 131–134.

Sherif, M. (1966). *In common predicament:Social psychology of intergroup conflict and cooperation.* Boston: Houghton Mifflin.

Sherif, M., Harvey, O. J., White, J., Hood, W., & Sherif, C. (1961). Intergroup conflict and cooperation: The robber's cave experiment. Norman: University of Oklahoma, Institute of Intergroup Relations.

Sherif, M., & Sherif, C. W. (1969). *Social psychology.* New York: Harper & Row.

Sherman, I. W., & Berk, R. A. (1984). The specific deterrent effects or arrest for domestic assault. *American Sociological Review, 49*, 261–272.

Sherman, J. W., & Klein, S. B. (1994). Development and representation of personality impressions. *Journal of Personality and Social Psychology, 67*, 972–983.

Sherman, L. W. (1992). The influence of criminology on criminal law: Evaluating arrests for misdemeanor domestic violence. *Journal of Criminal Law and Criminology, 83*, 1–45.

Sherman, S. J., & McConnell, A. R. (1995). Dysfunctional implications of counterfactual thinking: When alternatives to reality fail us. In N. J. Roese & J. M. Olson (Eds.), *What might have been: The social psychology of counterfactual thinking* (pp. 199–232). Mahwah, NJ: Erlbaum.

Sherrod, D. R. (1974). Crowding, perceived control, and behavioral aftereffects. *Journal of Applied Social Psychology, 4*, 171–186.

Sherrod, D. R., & Cohen, S. (1979). Density, personal control, and design. In A. Baum & J. R. Aiello (Eds.), *Residential crowding and design* (pp. 217–227). New York: Plenum.

Shettel-Neuber, J., Bryson, J. B., & Young, L. E. (1978). Physical attractiveness of the "other person" and jealousy. *Personality and Social Psychology Bulletin, 4*, 612–615.

Shotland, R. L., & Straw, M. K. (1976). Bystander response to an assault: When a man attacks a woman. *Journal of Personality and Social Psychology, 34*, 990–999.

Shupe, L. M. (1954). Alcohol and crimes: A study of the urine alcohol concentration found in 882 persons arrested during or immediately after the commission of a felony. *Journal of Criminal Law and Criminology, 33*, 661–665.

Sigall, H., & Aronson, E. (1969). Liking for an evaluator as a function of her physical attractiveness and nature of the evaluations. *Journal of Experimental Social Psychology, 5*, 96–100.

Sigall, H., & Page, R. (1971). Current stereotypes: A little fading, a little faking. *Journal of Personality and Social Psychology, 18*, 247–255.

Sigall, H., & Ostrove, N. (1975). Beautiful but dangerous: Effects of offender attractiveness and nature of the crime on juridic judgment. *Journal of Personality and Social Psychology, 31*, 410–414.

Silver, L. B., Dublin, C. C., & Lourie, R. S. (1969). Does violence breed violence? Contributions from a study of the child abuse syndrome. *American Journal of Psychiatry, 126*, 404–407.

Silverstein, B., Perdue, L., Peterson, B., & Kelly, E. (1986). The role of the mass media in promoting a thin standard of bodily attractiveness for women. *Sex Roles, 14*, 519–532.

Silverstein, B., Peterson, B., & Perdue, L. (1986). Some correlates of the thin standard of bodily attractiveness for women. *International Journal of Eating Disorders, 5*, 895–906.

Sime, J. D. (1983). Affiliative behavior during escape to building exits. *Journal of Environmental Psychology, 3*, 21–41.

Simmons, C. H., Vom Kolke, A., & Shimizu, H. (1986). Attitudes toward romantic love among American, German, and Japanese students. *Journal of Social Psychology, 126*, 327–336.

Simon, H. A. (1990). A mechanism for social selection and successful altruism. *Science, 250*, 1665–1668

Simonton, D. K. (1984). *Genius, creativity, and leadership: Historiometric inquiries.* Cambridge, MA: Harvard University Press.

Simonton, D. K. (1985). Intelligence and personal influence in groups: Four nonlinear models. *Psychological Review, 92*, 532–547.

Simonton, D. K. (1987). *Why presidents succeed: A political psychology of leadership.* New Haven, CT: Yale University Press.

Simonton, D. K. (1992). Presidential greatness and personality: A response to McCann (1992). *Journal of Personality and Social Psychology, 63*, 676–679.

Simonton, D. K. (in press). Historiometric methods in social psychology. *European Review of Social Psychology.*

Simpson, G., & Yinger, J. M., (1885). *Racial and cultural minorities.* New York: Harper.

Simpson, J. A. (1987). The dissolution of romantic relationships: Factors involved in relationship stability and emotional distress. *Journal of Personality and Social Psychology, 53*, 683–692.

Simpson, J. A. (1990). Influence of attachment styles on romantic relationships. *Journal of Personality and Social Psychology, 59*, 971–980.

Simpson, J. A., & Gangestad, S. W. (1992). Sociosexuality and romantic partner choice. *Journal of Personality, 60*, 31–51.

Simpson, J. A., & Kenrick, D. T. (Eds.) (1997). *Evolutionary social psychology.* Mahwah, NJ: Erlbaum.

Simpson, J. A., & Rholes, W. S. (1994). Stress and secure base relationships in adulthood. In K. Bartholomew & D. Perlman (Eds.), *Advances in Personal Relationships. Vol. 5: Attachment Processes in Adulthood* (pp. 181–204). Bristol, PA: Jessica Kingsley.

Simpson, J. A., Rholes, W. S., & Nelligan, J. S. (1992). Support seeking and support giving within couples in an anxiety-provoking situation: The role of attachment styles. *Journal of Personality and Social Psychology, 62*, 434–446.

Simpson, J. A., Rholes, W. S., & Philips, D. (1996). Conflict in close relationships: An attachment perspective. *Journal of Personality and Social Psychology, 71*, 899–914.

Sinclair, R. C., Hoffman, C., Mark, M. M., Martin, L. L., & Pickering, T. L. (1994). Construct accessibility and the misattribution of arousal: Schachter and Singer revisited. *Psychological Science, 5*, 15–19.

Sinclair, R. C., Mark, M. M., & Clore, G. L. (1994). Mood-related persuasion depends on (mis)attributions. *Social Cognition, 12*, 309–326.

Singelis, T. M. (1994). The measurement of independent and interdependent self-construals. *Personality and Social Psychology Bulletin, 20*, 580–591.

Singer, J. E., Baum, C. S., Baum, A., & Thew, B. D. (1982). Mass psychogenic illness: The case for social comparison. In M. J. Colligan, J. W. Pennebaker, & L. R. Murphy (Eds.), *Mass psychogenic illness: A social psychological analysis* (pp. 155–169). Hillsdale, NJ: Erlbaum.

Singer, M. (1990, January 29). Talk of the town. *New Yorker,* pp. 25–26.

Singh, D. (1993). Adaptive significance of female physical attractiveness: Role of waist to hip ratio. *Journal of Personality and Social Psychology, 65,* 293–307.

Sirois, F. (1982). Perspectives on epidemic hysteria. In M. J. Colligan, J. W. Pennebaker, & L. R. Murphy (Eds.), *Mass psychogenic illness: A social psychological analysis* (pp. 217–236). Hillsdale, NJ: Erlbaum.

Skinner, B. F. (1938). *The behavior of organisms.* New York: Appleton-Century-Crofts.

Skinner, E. A. (1995). *Perceived control, motivation, and coping.* Thousand Oaks, CA: Sage.

Skinner, E. A. (1996). A guide to constructs of control. *Journal of Personality and Social Psychology, 71,* 549–570.

Slavin, R. (1996). Cooperative learning in middle and secondary schools. (Special section: Young adolescents at risk) *Clearing House 69,* 200–205.

Slavin, R. E. (1980). Cooperative learning and desegregation. Paper presented at the meeting of the American Psychological Association.

Sloan, J. H., Kellerman, A. L., Reay, D. T., Ferris, J. A., Koepsell, T., Rivara, F. P., Rice, C., Gray, L., & LoGerfo, J. (1988). Handgun regulations, crime, assaults, and homicide: A tale of two cities. *New England Journal of Medicine, 319,* 1256–1261.

Slovic, P., Fischhoff, B., & Lichtenstein, S. (1976). Cognitive processes and societal risk taking. In J. S. Carroll & J. W. Payne (Eds.), *Cognition and social behavior* (pp. 165–184). Hillsdale, NJ: Erlbaum.

Slovic, P., & Lichtenstein, S. (1971). Comparison of Bayesian and regression approaches to the study of information processing in judgment. *Organizational Behavior and Human Performance, 6,* 649–744.

Slusher, M. P., & Anderson, C. A. (1989). Belief perseverance and self-defeating behavior. In R. Curtis (Ed.), *Self-defeating behaviors: Experimental research, clinical impressions, and practical implications* (pp. 11–40). New York: Plenum.

Smith, C. M., Tindale, R. S., & Dugoni, B. L. (1996). Minority and majority influence in freely interacting groups: Qualitative versus quantitative differences. *British Journal of Social Psychology, 35,* 137–149.

Smith, D. D. (1976). The social content of pornography. *Journal of Communication, 26,* 16–24.

Smith, K. D., Keating, J. P., & Stotland, E. (1989). Altruism reconsidered: The effect of denying feedback on a victim's status to empathic witnesses. *Journal of Personality and Social Psychology, 57,* 641–650.

Smith, M. B., Bruner, J., & White, R. W. (1956). *Opinions and personality.* New York: Wiley.

Smith, R. E., Wheeler, G., & Diener, E. (1975). Faith without works: Jesus people, resistance to temptation, and altruism. *Journal of Applied Psychology, 5,* 320–330.

Smith, S. S., & Richardson, D. (1983). Amelioration of deception and harm in psychological research: The important role of debriefing. *Journal of Personality and Social Psychology, 44,* 1075–1082.

Smith, V. L. (1991). Prototypes in the courtroom: Lay representation of legal concepts. *Journal of Personality and Social Psychology, 61,* 857–872.

Smith, V. L., & Ellsworth, P. C. (1987). The social psychology of eyewitness accuracy: Misleading questions and communicator expertise. *Journal of Applied Psychology, 72,* 294–300.

Smith, V. L., Kassin, S. M., & Ellsworth, P. C. (1989). Eyewitness accuracy and confidence: Within- versus between-subjects correlations. *Journal of Applied Psychology, 74,* 356–359.

Snyder, C. R., & Higgins, R. L. (1988). Excuses: Their effective role in the negotiation of reality. *Psychological Bulletin, 104,* 23–35.

Snyder, C. R., Irving, L. M., & Anderson, J. R. (1991). Hope and health. In C. R. Snyder & D. R. Forsyth (Eds.), *Handbook of clinical and social psychology* (pp. 285–305). New York: Pergamon.

Snyder, C. R., Smith, T. W., Augelli, R. W., & Ingram, R. E. (1985). On the self-serving function of social anxiety: Shyness as a self-handicapping strategy. *Journal of Personality and Social Psychology, 48,* 970–980.

Snyder, M. (1984). When belief creates reality. In L. Berkowitz (Ed.), *Advances in experimental social psychology* (Vol. 18, pp. 247–305). Orlando, FL: Academic Press.

Snyder, M. (1993). Basic research and practical problems: The promise of a "functional" personality and social psychology. *Personality and Social Psychology Bulletin, 19,* 251–264.

Snyder, M., & DeBono, K. G. (1989). Understanding the functions of attitudes: Lessons for personality and social behavior. In A. R. Pratkanis, S. J. Breckler, & A. G. Greenwald (Eds.), *Attitude structure and function* (pp. 339–359). Hillsdale, NJ: Erlbaum.

Snyder, M., & Ickes, W. (1985). Personality and social behavior. In G. Lindzey & E. Aronson (Eds.), *Handbook of social psychology* (3rd ed., pp. 883–947). New York: Random House.

Snyder, M., & Swann, W. B., Jr. (1978). Hypothesis-testing procedures in social interaction. *Journal of Personality and Social Psychology, 36,* 1202–1212.

Snyder, M., Tanke, E. D., & Berscheid, E. (1977). Social perception and interpersonal behavior: On the self-fulfilling nature of social stereotypes. *Journal of Personality and Social Psychology, 35,* 656–666.

Soames, R. F. (1988). Effective and ineffective use of fear in health promotion campaigns. *American Journal of Public Health, 78,* 163–167.

Solomon, L. Z., Solomon, H., & Stone, R. (1978). Helping as a function of number of bystanders and ambiguity of emergency. *Personality and Social Psychology Bulletin, 4,* 318–321.

Sontag, S. (1978). *Illness as metaphor.* New York: Farrar, Straus & Giroux.

Sontag, S. (1988). *AIDS and its metaphors.* New York: Farrar, Straus & Giroux.

Sorenson, T. C. (1966). *Kennedy.* New York: Bantam.

Sorrels, J. P., & Kelley, J. (1984). Conformity by omission. *Personality and Social Psychology Bulletin, 10,* 302–304.

Sorrentino, R. M. (1991). Evidence for altruism: The lady is still in waiting. *Psychological Inquiry, 2,* 147–150.

Sorrentino, R. M., & Field, N. (1986). Emergent leadership over time: The functional value of positive motivation. *Journal of Personality and Social Psychology, 50,* 1091–1099.

South, S. J., & Lloyd, K. M. (1995). Spousal alternatives and marital dissolution. *American Sociological Review, 60,* 21–35.

Span, P. (1994, December 14). The gene team: Innocence project fights injustice with DNA testing. *Washington Post,* pp. C1, C14.

Speed, A., & Gangestad, S. W. (1997). Romantic popularity and mate preferences: A peer-nomination study. *Personality and Social Psychology Bulletin, 23,* 928–935.

Spencer, S., Steele, C. M., & Quinn, D. (1997). *Under suspicion of inability: Stereotype threat and women's math performance.* Unpublished manuscript, Stanford University.

Spencer, S. J., Josephs, R. A., & Steele, C. M. (in press). Low self-esteem: The uphill battle for self-integrity. In R. F. Baumeister (Ed.), *Self-esteem and the puzzle of low self-regard* (pp. 21–36). New York: Wiley.

Spiegel, D., Bloom, J. R., Krawmer, H. C., & Gottheil, E. (1989). Psychological support for cancer patients. *Lancet, 2,* 1447.

Spiegel, H., & Spiegel, D. (1987). *Trance and treatment: Clinical uses of hypnosis.* Washington, DC: American Psychiatric Press. (Original work published in 1978.)

Sporer, S. L. (1994). Decision times and eyewitness identification accuracy in simultaneous and sequential lineups. In D. F. Ross, J. D. Read, M. P. Toglia (Eds.), *Adult eyewitness testimony: Current trends and developments* (pp. 300–327). New York: Cambridge University Press.

Sporer, S. L., Koehnken, G., & Malpass, R. S. (1996). Introduction: 200 years of mistaken identification. In S. L. Sporer, R. S. Malpass, & G. Koehnken (Eds.), *Psychological issues in eyewitness identification* (pp. 1–6). Mahwah, NJ: Erlbaum.

Sporer, S. L., Penrod, S., Read, D., & Cutler, B. (1995). Choosing, confidence, and accuracy: A meta-analysis of the confidence-accuracy relation in eyewitness identification studies. *Psychological Bulletin, 118,* 315–327.

Sprecher, S. (1989). The importance to males and females of physical attractiveness, earning potential and expressiveness in initial attraction. *Sex Roles, 21,* 591–607.

Sprecher, S., Aron, A., Hatfield, E., Cortese, A. Potapova, E., & Levitskaya, A. (1994). Love: American style, Russian style, and Japanese style. *Personal Relationships, 1,* 349–369.

Sprecher, S., & Schwartz, P. (1994). Equity and balance in the exchange of contributions in close relationships. In M. J. Lerner & G. Mikula (Eds.), *Entitlement and the Affectional Bond: Justice in Close Relationships* (pp. 11–42). New York: Plenum.

Sprecher, S., Sullivan, Q., & Hatfield, E. (1994). Mate selection preference: Gender differences examined in a national sample. *Journal of Personality and Social Psychology, 66,* 1074–1080.

Stahyl, S. M., & Lebedun, M. (1974). Mystery gas: An analysis of mass hysteria. *Journal of Health and Social Behavior, 15,* 44–50.

Stangor, C., & McMillan, D. (1992). Memory for expectancy-congruent and expectancy-incongruent information: A review of the social and social developmental literatures. *Psychological Bulletin, 111,* 42–61.

Staples, S. L. (1996). Human response to environmental noise: Psychological research and public policy. *American Psychologist, 51,* 143–150.

Stasser, G., Stella, N., Hanna, C., & Colella, A. (1984). The majority effect in jury deliberations: Number of supporters versus number of supporting arguments. *Law and Psychology Review, 8,* 115–127.

Stasser, G., & Titus, W. (1985). Pooling of unshared information in group decision making: Biased information sampling during discussion. *Journal of Personality and Social Psychology, 48,* 1467–1478.

Stasser, G., Stewart, D. D., & Wittenbaum, G. M. (1995). Expert roles and information exchange during discussion: The importance of knowing who knows what. *Journal of Experimental and Social Psychology, 31,* 244–265.

Stasser, G., Taylor, L. A., & Hanna, C. (1989). Information sampling in structured and unstructured discussions in three- and six-person groups. *Journal of Personality and Social Psychology, 57,* 67–78.

Stasson, M., & Fishbein, M. (1990). The relation between perceived and preventive action: A within-subject analysis of perceived driving risk and intentions to wear seatbelts. *Journal of Applied Social Psychology, 20,* 1541–1557.

Staub, E. (1974). Helping a distressed person: Social, personality, and stimulus determinants. In L. Berkowitz (Ed.), *Advances in experimental social psychology* (Vol. 7, pp. 293–341). New York: Academic Press.

Staub, E. (1989). *The Roots of Evil: The Origins of Genocide and Other Group Violence.* Cambridge, England: Cambridge University Press.

Steblay, N. M. (1987). Helping behavior in rural and urban environments: A meta-analysis. *Psychological Bulletin, 102,* 346–356.

Steele, C. (1992). Race and the schooling of Black Americans. *The Atlantic Monthly,* April.

Steele, C. (1997). A threat in the air: How stereotypes shape intellectual identity and performance. *American Psychologist, 52,* 613–629.

Steele, C., & Aronson, J. (1995). Stereotype vulnerability and intellectual performance. In E. Aronson, (Ed.), *Readings about the social animal (7th ed.).* New York: Freeman.

Steele, C. M. (1988). The psychology of self-affirmation: Sustaining the integrity of the self. In L. Berkowitz (Ed.), *Advances in experimental social psychology* (Vol. 21, pp. 261–302). New York: Academic Press.

Steele, C. M. (1992, April). Race and the schooling of black Americans. *Atlantic Monthly,* pp. 68–78.

Steele, C. M. (1997). A threat in the air: How stereotypes shape intellectual ability and performance. *American Psychologist, 52,* 613–629.

Steele, C. M., & Aronson, J. (1995). Stereotype-threat and the intellectual test performance of African-Americans. *Journal of Personality and Social Psychology, 69,* 797–811.

Steele, C. M., Hoppe, H., & Gonzales, J. (1986). *Dissonance and the lab coat: Self-affirmation and the free choice paradigm.* Unpublished manuscript, University of Washington.

Steele, C. M., & Josephs, R. A. (1990). Alcohol myopia: Its prized and dangerous effects. *American Psychologist, 45,* 921–933.

Steele, C. M., & Liu, T. J. (1981). Making the dissonance act unreflective of the self: Dissonance avoidance and the expectancy of a value affirming response. *Personality and Social Psychology Bulletin, 7,* 383–387.

Steele, C. M., & Liu, T. J. (1983). Dissonance processes as self affirmation. *Journal of Personality and Social Psychology, 45,* 5–19.

Steele, C. M., & Southwick, L. (1985). Alcohol and social behavior I: The psychology of drunken excess. *Journal of Personality and Social Psychology, 48,* 18–34.

Steele, C. M., Spencer, S. J., & Josephs, R. (1992). *Seeking self-relevant information: The effects of self-esteem and stability of the information.* Unpublished manuscript, University of Michigan.

Steele, C. M., Spencer, S. J., & Lynch, M. (1993). Self-image resilience and dissonance: The role of affirmational resources. *Journal of Personality and Social Psychology, 64,* 885–896.

Steele, C. M., Spencer, S. J., & Lynch, M. (in press). Dissonance and self-affirmation resources: Resilience against self-image threats. *Journal of Personality and Social Psychology.*

Steele, H., & Steele, M. (1994). Intergenerational patterns of attachment. In K. Bartholomew & D. Perlman (Eds.), *Advances in Personal Relationships Vol. 5: Attachment Processes in Adulthood* (pp. 93–120). Bristol, PA: Jessica Kingsley.

Steffen, V. J. (1990). Men's motivation to perform the testicle self-exam: Effects of prior knowledge and an educational brochure. *Journal of Applied Social Psychology, 20,* 681–702.

Steinbeck, J. (1988/1961). *Travels with Charley: In search of America*. New York: Penguin Books.

Steiner, I. D. (1972). *Group process and productivity*. New York: Academic Press.

Steiner, I. D. (1974). Whatever happened to the group in social psychology? *Journal of Experimental Social Psychology, 10*, 94–108.

Steiner, I. D., & Rajaratnam, N. A. (1961). A model for the comparison of individual and group performance scores. *Behavioral Science, 11*, 273–283.

Stephan, W. G. (1978). School desegregation: An evaluation of predictions made in Brown vs. Board of Education. *Psychological Bulletin, 85*, 217–238.

Stephan, W. G. (1985). Intergroup relations. In G. Lindzey & E. Aronson (Eds.), *The handbook of social psychology* (Vol. 2, pp. 599–658). New York:. Random House.

Stern, L. B., & Dunning, D. (1994). Distinguishing accurate from inaccurate eyewitness identifications: A reality monitoring approach. In D. F. Ross, J. D. Read, & M. P. Toglia (Eds.), *Adult eyewitness testimony: Current trends and developments* (pp. 273–299). New York: Cambridge University Press.

Stern, M., & Hildebrandt, K. A. (1986). Prematurity stereotyping: Effects on mother-infant interaction. *Child Development, 57*, 308–315.

Stern, P. C., & Aronson, E. (1984). *Energy use: The human dimension*. New York: Freeman.

Sternberg, R. J. (1986). A triangular theory of love. *Psycho- logical Review, 93*, 119–135.

Sternberg, R. J. (1988). *The triangle of love*. New York: Basic Books.

Sternberg, R. J. (1997). Construct validation of a triangular love scale. *European Journal of Social Psychology, 27*, 313–335.

Sternberg, R. J., & Grajek, S. (1984). The nature of love. *Journal of Personality and Social Psychology, 47*, 312–329.

Stewart, D. D., & Stasser, G. (in press). Expert role assignment and information sampling during collective recall and decision making. *Journal of Personality and Social Psychology*.

Stice, E., & Shaw, H. E. (1994). Adverse effects of the media portrayed thin-ideal on women and linkages to bulimic symptomology. *Journal of Social and Clinical Psychology, 13*, 288–308.

Stich, S. (1990). *The fragmentation of reason: Preface to a pragmatic theory of cognitive evaluation*. Cambridge, MA: MIT Press.

Stiff, J. B. (1994). *Persuasive Communication*. New York: Guilford.

Stipek, D. & Gralinski, J. H. (1991). Gender differences in children's achievement-related beliefs and emotional responses to success and failure in mathematics. *Journal of Educational Psychology, 83*, 361–371.

Stoff, D. M., & Cairns, R. B. (Eds.) (1996). Aggression and violence: Genetic, neurobiological, and biosocial perspectives. Mahwah, NJ: Erlbaum.

Stogdill, R. M. (1974). *Handbook of leadership*. New York: Free Press.

Stokols, D., & Altman, I. (1987). *Handbook of environmental psychology*. New York: Wiley.

Stone, A. A., Bovbjerg, D. H., Neale, J. M., Napoli, A., Valdimarsdottir, H., Cox, D., Hayden, F. G., & Gwaltney, J. M. (1993). Development of common cold symptoms following experimental rhinovirus infection is related to prior stressful life events. *Behavioral Medicine, 8*, 115–120.

Stone, J. (1998). The Self Concept in Dissonance Theory. In E. Harmon-Jones & J. S. Mills, Eds. (in press). Cognitive Dissonance Theory: Revival with Revisions and Controversies. Washington, DC: American Psychological Association Books.

Stone, J., Aronson, E., Crain, A. L., Winslow, M. P., & Fried, C. (1994). Inducing hypocrisy as a means of encouraging young adults to use condoms. *Personality and Social Psychology Bulletin, 20*, 116–128.

Stone, J., Perry, Z., & Darley, J. (1997). "White men can't jump": Evidence for perceptual confirmation of racial stereotypes following a basketball game. *Basic and Applied Social Psychology, 19*, 291–306.

Stone, J., Wiegand, A., Cooper, J., & Aronson, E. (1997). When exemplification fails: Hypocrisy and the motive for self-integrity. *Journal of Personality and Social Psychology, 72*, 54–65.

Stormo, K. J., Lang, A. R., & Stritzke, W. G. K. (1997). Attributions about acquaintance rape: The role of alcohol and individual differences. *Journal of Applied Social Psychology, 27*, 279–305.

Storms, M. (1973). Videotape and the attribution process: Reversing actors' and observers' points of view. *Journal of Personality and Social Psychology, 27*, 165–175.

Storms, M. D., & McCaul, K. D. (1976). Attribution processes and emotional exacerbation of dysfunctional behavior. In J. H. Harvey, W. J. Ickes, & R. F. Kidd (Eds.), *New directions in attribution research* (Vol. 1, pp. 143–164). Hillsdale, NJ: Erlbaum.

Storms, M. D., & Nisbett, R. E. (1970). Insomnia and the attribution process. *Journal of Personality and Social Psychology, 16*, 319–328.

Stouffer, S. A., Suchman, E. A., DeVinney, L. C., Star, S. A., & Williams, R. M., Jr. (1949). *The American soldier: Adjustment during army life* (Vol. 1). Princeton, NJ: Princeton University Press.

Strack, F., & Hannover, B. (1996). Awareness of influence as a precondition for implementing correctional goals. In P. M. Gollwitzer & J. A. Bargh (Eds.), *The psychology of action: Linking cognition and motivation to behavior* (pp. 579–596). New York: Guilford.

Strack, F., Martin, L. L., & Stepper, S. (1988). Inhibiting and facilitating conditions of the human smile: A nonobtrusive test of the facial feedback hypothesis. *Journal of Personality and Social Psychology, 54*, 768–777.

Strack, F., & Mussweiler, T. (in press). The enigmatic anchoring effect: A pervasive phenomenon in search of a viable explanation. *Journal of Personality and Social Psychology*.

Strauman, T. J., & Higgins, E. T. (1987). Automatic activation of self-discrepancies and emotional syndromes: When cognitive structures influence affect. *Journal of Personality and Social Psychology, 53*, 1004–1014.

Strauss, M. A., & Gelles, R. J. (1980). *Behind closed doors: Violence in the American family*. New York: Anchor/Doubleday.

Stretch, R. H., & Figley, C. R. (1980). Beauty and the boast: Predictors of interpersonal attraction in a dating experiment. *Psychology, A Quarterly Journal of Human Behavior, 17*, 34–43.

Stroebe, W., & Diehl, M. (1994). Why groups are less effective than their members: On productivity losses in idea-generating groups. *European Review of Social Psychology, 5*, 271–303.

Stroebe, W., & Stroebe, M. (1996). The social psychology of social support. In E. T. Higgins & A. W. Kruglanski (Eds.), *Social psychology: Handbook of basic principles* (pp. 597–621). New York: Guilford.

Strossen, N. (1997). Why censoring pornography would not reduce discrimination or violence against women. In Walsh, M. R. (Ed.), *Women, men, and gender: Ongoing debates* (pp. 170–179). New Haven, CT: Yale University Press.

Strough, J., Berg, C. A., & Sansone, C. (1996). Goals for solving everyday problems across the life span: Age and gender differences in the salience of interpersonal concerns. *Developmental Psychology, 32,* 1106–1115.

Strube, M., & Garcia, J. (1981). A meta-analysis investigation of Fiedler's contingency model of leadership effectiveness. *Psychological Bulletin, 90,* 307–321.

Stuart, E. W., Shimp, T. A., & Engle, R. W. (1987). Classical conditioning of consumer attitudes: Four experiments in an advertising context. *Journal of Consumer Research, 14,* 334–349.

Studer, J. (1996). Understanding and preventing aggressive responses in youth. *Elementary School Guidance and Counseling, 30,* 194–203.

Suls, J., & Fletcher, B. (1983). Social comparison in the social and physical sciences: An archival study. *Journal of Personality and Social Psychology, 44,* 575–580.

Suls, J., & Wills, T. A. (1991). (Eds.). *Social comparison: Contemporary theory and research.* Hillsdale, NJ: Erlbaum.

Suls, J. M., & Miller, R. L. (Eds.). (1977). *Social comparison processes: Theoretical and empirical perspectives.* Washington, DC: Hemisphere/Halstead.

Summers, G., & Feldman, N. S. (1984). Blaming the victim versus blaming the perpetrator: An attributional analysis of spouse abuse. *Journal of Social and Clinical Psychology, 2,* 339–347.

Sundstrom, E., Bell, P. A., Busby, P. L., & Asmus, C. (1996). Environmental psychology. *Annual Review of Psychology, 47,* 485–512.

Swann, W. (1996). *Self-traps: The elusive quest for higher self-esteem.* New York: W. H. Freeman & Co.

Swann, W. B., Jr. (1984). Quest for accuracy in person perception: A matter of pragmatics. *Psychological Review, 91,* 457–477.

Swann, W. B., Jr. (1990). To be adored or to be known? The interplay of self-enhancement and self-verification. In R. M. Sorrentino & E. T. Higgins (Eds.), *Motivation and cognition* (pp. 404–448). New York: Guilford Press.

Swann, W. B., Jr., & Ely, R. J. (1984). A battle of the wills: Self-verification versus behavioral confirmation. *Journal of Personality and Social Psychology, 46,* 1287–1302.

Swann, W. B., Jr., & Hill, C. A. (1982). When our identities are mistaken: Reaffirming self-conceptions through social interaction. *Journal of Personality and Social Psychology, 43,* 59–66.

Swann, W. B., Jr., Hixon, G., & De La Ronde, C. (1992). Embracing the bitter "truth": Negative self-concepts and marital commitment. *Psychological Science, 3,* 118–121.

Swann, W. B., Jr., & Pelham, B. W. (1988). *The social construction of identity: Self-verification through friend and intimate selection.* Unpublished manuscript, University of Texas-Austin.

Swann, W. B., Jr., & Schroeder, D. B. (1995). The search for beauty and truth: A framework for understanding reactions to evaluations. *Personality and Social Psychology Bulletin, 21,* 1307–1318.

Swap, W. C. (1977). Interpersonal attraction and repeated exposure to rewarders and punishers. *Personality and Social Psychology Bulletin, 3,* 248–251.

Sweeney, P. D., Anderson, K., & Bailey, S. (1986). Attributional style in depression: A meta-analytic review. *Journal of Personality and Social Psychology, 50,* 974–991.

Swim, J., Borgida, E., Maruyama, G., & Myers, D. G. (1989). Joan McKay vs. John McKay: Do gender stereotypes bias evaluations? *Psychological Bulletin, 105,* 409–429.

Swim, J., & Sanna, L. (1996). He's skilled, she's lucky: A meta-analysis of observers' attributions for women's and men's successes and failures. *Personality and Social Psychology Bulletin, 22,* 507–519.

Symons, C. S., & Johnson, B. T. (1997). The self-reference effect in memory: A meta-analysis. *Psychological Bulletin, 121,* 371–394.

Tafarodi, R. W., & Swann, W. B. (1996). Individualism-collectivism and global self-esteem: Evidence for a cultural trade-off. *Journal of Cross-Cultural Psychology, 27,* 651–672.

Tajfel, H. (1982a). *Social identity and intergroup relations.* Cambridge, England: Cambridge University Press.

Tajfel, H. (1982b). Social psychology of intergroup relations. *Annual Review of Psychology, 33,* 1–39.

Tajfel, H., & Billig, M. (1974). Familiarity and categorization in intergroup behavior. *Journal of Experimental Social Psychology, 10,* 159–170.

Tajfel, H., & Turner, J. C. (1979). An integrative theory of social contact. In W. Austin & S. Worchel (Eds.), *The social psychology of intergroup relations.* Monterey, CA: Brooks/Cole.

Tan, D. T. Y., & Singh, R. (1995). Attitudes and attraction: A developmental study of the similarity-attraction and dissimilarity-repulsion hypotheses. *Personality and Social Psychology Bulletin, 21,* 975–986.

Tanford, S., & Penrod, S. (1984). Social influence model: A formal integration of research on majority and minority influence processes. *Psychological Bulletin, 95,* 189–225.

Tang, S., & Hall, V. C. (1995). The overjustification effect: A meta-analysis. *Applied Cognitive Psychology, 9,* 365–404.

Tata, J., Anthony, T., Lin, H., Newman, B., Tang, S., Milson, M., & Sivakumar, K. (1996). Proportionate group size and rejection of the deviate: A meta-analytic integration. *Journal of Social Behavior and Personality, 11,* 739–752.

Tavris, C. (1989). *Anger: The misunderstood emotion.* New York: Touchstone/Simon & Schuster.

Taylor, S. (1989). *Positive illusions: Creative self-deception and the healthy mind.* New York: Basic Books.

Taylor, S., & Armor, D. (1996). Positive illusions and coping with adversity. *Journal of Personality, 64,* 873–898.

Taylor, S., & Gollwitzer, P. (1995). Effects of mindset on positive illusions. *Journal of Personality and Social Psychology, 69,* 213–226.

Taylor, S. E. (1981). A categorization approach to stereotyping. In D. L. Hamilton (Ed.), *Cognitive processes in stereotyping and intergroup relations* (pp. 418–429). Hillsdale, NJ: Erlbaum.

Taylor, S. E. (1981). The interface of cognitive and social psychology. In J. Harvey (Ed.), *Cognition, social behavior, and the environment* (pp. 189–211). Hillsdale, NJ: Erlbaum.

Taylor, S. E. (1989). *Positive illusions: Creative self-deception and the healthy mind.* New York: Basic Books.

Taylor, S. E. (1995). *Health psychology* (3rd ed.). New York: McGraw-Hill.

Taylor, S. E., & Aspinwall, L. G. (1993). Coping with chronic illness. In L. Goldberger & S. Breznitz (Eds.), *Handbook of stress: Theoretical and clinical aspects* (2nd ed., pp. 511-531). New York: Free Press.

Taylor, S. E., & Brown, J. (1988). Illusion and well-being: A social psychological perspective on mental health. *Psychological Bulletin, 103,* 193–210.

Taylor, S. E., & Brown, J. D. (1994). Positive illusions and well-being revisited: Separating fact from fiction. *Psychological Bulletin, 116,* 21–27.

Taylor, S. E., & Crocker, J. (1981) Schematic bases of social information processing. In E. T. Higgins, C. P. Herman, & M. P. Zanna (Eds.), *Social cognition: The Ontario Symposium* (Vol. 1, pp. 89–134). Hillsdale, NJ: Erlbaum.

Taylor, S. E., & Fiske, S. T. (1975). Point of view and perceptions of causality. *Journal of Personality and Social Psychology, 32,* 439–445.

Taylor, S. E., Lichtman, R. R., & Wood, J. V. (1984). Attributions, beliefs about control, and adjustment to breast cancer. *Journal of Personality and Social Psychology, 46,* 489–502.

Taylor, S. E., Repetti, R. L., & Seeman, T. (1997). Health psychology: What is an unhealthy environment and how does it get under the skin? *Annual Review of Psychology, 48,* 411–447.

Taylor, S. P., & Leonard, K. E. (1983). Alcohol and human physical aggression. In R. Geen & E. Donnerstein (Eds.), *Aggression: Theoretical and empirical reviews.* New York: Academic Press.

Taylor, S. P., & Sears, J. D. (1988). The effects of alcohol and persuasive social pressure on human physical aggression. *Aggressive Behavior, 14,* 237–243.

Tedeschi, J. T. (Ed.). (1981). *Impression management theory and social psychological research.* New York: Academic Press.

Teger, A. L., & Pruitt, D. G. (1967). Components of group risk taking. *Journal of Experimental Social Psychology, 3,* 189–205.

Tesser, A. (1980). Self esteem maintenance in family dynamics. *Journal of Personality and Social Psychology, 39,* 77–91.

Tesser, A. (1988). Toward a self-evaluation maintenance model of social behavior. In L. Berkowitz (Ed.), *Advances in experimental social psychology* (Vol. 21, pp. 181–227). Orlando, FL: Academic Press.

Tesser, A. (1991). Emotion in social comparison and reflection processes. In J. Suls & T. A. Wills (Eds.), *Social comparison: Contemporary theory and research* (pp. 117–148). Hillsdale, NJ: Erlbaum.

Tesser, A. (1993). The importance of heritability in psychological research: The case of attitudes. *Psychological Review, 100,* 129–142.

Tesser, A., & Brodie, M. (1971). A note on the evaluation of a computer date. *Psychonomic Science, 23,* 300.

Tesser, A., Campbell, J., & Mickler, S. (1983). The role of social pressure, attention to the stimulus, and self-doubt in conformity. *European Journal of Social Psychology, 13,* 217–233.

Tesser, A., & Cornell, D. P. (1991). On the confluence of self processes. *Journal of Experimental Social Psychology, 27,* 501–526.

Tesser, A., & Martin, L. (1996). The psychology of evaluation. In E. T. Higgins & A. W. Kruglanski (Eds.), *Social psychology: Handbook of basic principles* (pp. 400–432). New York: Guilford.

Tesser, A., Martin, L., & Mendolia, M. (1995). The impact of thought on attitude extremity and attitude-behavior consistency. In R. Petty & J. Krosnick, (Eds.) *Attitude strength: Antecedents and consequences* (pp. 73–92). Ohio State University series on attitudes and persuasion, Vol. 4. Mahwah, NJ: Lawrence Erlbaum Associates, Inc.

Tesser, A., & Paulus, D. (1983). The definition of self: Private and public self-evaluation management strategies. *Journal of Personality and Social Psychology, 44,* 672–682.

Tesser, A., & Smith, J. (1980). Some effects of friendship and task relevance on helping: You don't always help the one you like. *Journal of Experimental Social Psychology, 16,* 582–590.

Tetlock, P. E. (1981). The influence of self-presentational goals on attributional reports. *Social Psychology Quarterly, 44,* 300–311.

Tetlock, P. E. (1992). The impact of accountability on judgment and choice: Toward a social contingency model. In M. P. Zanna (Ed.), *Advances in experimental social psychology* (Vol. 25, pp. 331–376). San Diego, CA: Academic Press.

Tetlock, P. E., Peterson, R. S., McGuire, C., Chang, S., & Field, P. (1992). Assessing political group dynamics: A test of the groupthink model. *Journal of Personality and Social Psychology, 63,* 403–425.

Theus, K. T. (1994). Subliminal advertising and the psychology of processing unconscious stimuli: A review. *Psychology and Marketing, 11,* 271–290.

Thibaut, J. W., & Kelley, H. H. (1959). *The social psychology of groups.* New York: Wiley.

Thibaut, J., & Walker, L. (1975). *Procedural justice: A psychological analysis.* Hillsdale, NJ: Erlbaum.

Thibodeau, R., & Aronson, E. (1992). Taking a closer look: Reasserting the role of the self-concept in dissonance theory. *Personality and Social Psychology Bulletin, 18,* 591–602.

Thøgersen, J. (1996). Recycling and morality: A critical review of the literature. *Environment and Behavior, 28,* 536–538.

Thomas, J. (1997, Jan. 30). Suspect's sketch in Oklahoma case called an error. *New York Times,* pp. 1–2.

Thomas, M. (1982). Physiological arousal, exposure to a relatively lengthy aggressive film, and aggressive behavior. *Journal of Research in Personality, 16,* 72–81.

Thomas, M. H., Horton, R., Lippincott, E., & Drabman, R. (1977). Desensitization to portrayals of real-life aggression as a function of exposure to television violence. *Journal of Personality and Social Psychology, 35,* 450–458.

Thomas, W. I. (1928). *The child in America.* New York: Alfred A. Knopf.

Thompson, C. P., Skowronski, J. J., Larsen, S. F., & Betz, A. (1996). *Autobiographical memory: Remembering what and remembering when.* Mahwah, NJ: Erlbaum.

Thompson, L. (1990). Negotiation behavior and outcomes: Empirical evidence and theoretical issues. *Psychological Bulletin, 108,* 515–532.

Thompson, L. (1991). Information exchange in negotiation. *Journal of Experimental Social Psychology, 27,* 161–179.

Thompson, L. (1995). They saw a negotiation: Partisanship and involvement. *Journal of Personality and Social Psychology, 68,* 839–853.

Thompson, L. (1997). *The mind and heart of the negotiator.* Englewood Cliffs, NJ: Prentice-Hall.

Thompson, L., & Hrebec, D. (1996). Lose-lose agreements in interdependent decision making. *Psychological Bulletin, 120,* 396–409.

Thompson, L., Peterson, E., & Brodt, S. (1996). Team negotiation: An examination of integrative and distributive bargaining. *Journal of Personality and Social Psychology, 70,* 66–78.

Thompson, S. C. (1981). Will it hurt less if I can control it? A complex answer to a simple question. *Psychological Bulletin, 90,* 89–101.

Thompson, S. C., Nanni, C., & Levine, A. (1994). Primary versus secondary and central versus consequence-related control in HIV-positive men. *Journal of Personality and Social Psychology, 67,* 540–547.

Thompson, S. C., Sobolew-Shubin, A., Galbraith, M. E., Schwankovsky, L., & Cruzen, D. (1993). Maintaining perceptions of control: Finding perceived control in low-control circumstances. *Journal of Personality and Social Psychology, 64,* 293–304.

Thomsen, C. T., & Borgida, E. (1996). Throwing out the baby with the bathwater? Let's not overstate the overselling of the base rate fallacy. *Behavioral and Brain Sciences, 19,* 39–40.

Thornton, D., & Arrowood, A. J. (1966). Self-evaluation, self-enhancement, and the locus of social comparison. *Journal of Experimental Social Psychology*, (Suppl. 1), 40–48.

Thornton, W. (1984). Defensive attribution of responsibility: Evidence for an arousal-based motivational bias. *Journal of Personality and Social Psychology, 46*, 721–734.

Tice, D. (1993). The social motivations of people with low self-esteem. In: Baumeister, R. *Self-esteem: The puzzle of low self-regard*. New York: Plenum Press, pp. 37–53.

Tice, D. M., & Baumeister, R. F. (1990). Self-esteem, self-handicapping, and self-presentation: The strategy of inadequate practice. *Journal of Personality, 58*, 443–464.

Timaeus, E. (1968). Untersuchungen zum sogenannten konformen Verhatten. *Zeitschrift fur Experimentelle und Angewandte Psychologie, 15*, 176–194.

Tindale, R. S. (1993). Decision errors made by individuals and groups. In N. J. Castellan, Jr. (Ed.), *Individual and group decision making* (pp. 109–124). Hillsdale, NJ: Erlbaum.

Ting-Toomey, S. & Chung, L. (1996). Cross-cultural interpersonal communication: Theoretical trends and research directions. In W. B. Gudykunst, S. Ting-Toomey, & Nishida, T. (Eds.), *Communication in Personal Relationships Across Cultures* (pp. 237–261). Thousand Oaks, CA: Sage.

Toch, H. (1965). *The social psychology of social movements*. Indianapolis: Bobbs-Merrill.

Toch, H. (1980). *Violent men* (rev. ed.). Cambridge, MA: Schenkman.

Toch, T. (1992, November 9). Homeroom sweepstakes. *U.S. News & World Report*, pp. 86–89.

Toi, M., & Batson, C. D. (1982). More evidence that empathy is a source of altruistic motivation. *Journal of Personality and Social Psychology, 43*, 281–292.

Tollestrup, P. A., Turtle, J. W., & Yuille, J. C. (1994). Expectations of eyewitness performance: Jurors' verdicts do not follow from their beliefs. In D. F. Ross, J. D. Read, & M. P. Toglia (Eds.), *Adult eyewitness testimony: Current trends and developments* (pp. 144–162). New York: Cambridge University Press.

Toobin, J. (1995, October 23). A horrible human event. *New Yorker*, pp. 40–49.

Topf, M. (1992). Stress effects of personal control over hospital noise. *Behavioral Medicine, 18*, 84–94.

Tourangeau, R., Smith, T., & Rasinski, K. (1997). Motivation to report sensitive behaviors on surveys: Evidence from a bogus pipeline experiment. *Journal of Applied Social Psychology, 27*, 209–222.

Trafimow, D. (1996). The importance of attitudes in the prediction of college students' intentions to drink. *Journal of Applied Social Psychology, 26*, 2167–2188.

Trafimow, D., & Finlay, K. A. (1996). The importance of subjective norms for a minority of people: Between-subjects and within-subjects analyses. *Personality and Social Psychology Bulletin, 22*, 820–828.

Trafimow, D., & Schneider, D. J. (1994). The effects of behavioral, situational, and person information on different attribution judgments. *Journal of Experimental Social Psychology, 30*, 351–369.

Trafimow, D., Triandis, H. C., & Goto, G. (1991). Some tests of the distinction between the private self and the collective self. *Journal of Personality and Social Psychology, 60*, 649–655.

Trafimow, D., & Wyer, R. S. (1993). Cognitive representation of mundane social events. *Journal of Personality and Social Psychology, 64*, 365–376.

Trappey, C. (1996). A meta-analysis of consumer choice and subliminal advertising. *Psychology and Marketing, 13*, 517–530.

Traupmann, J., Petersen, R., Utne, M., & Hatfield, E. (1981). Measuring equity in intimate relations. *Applied Psychology Measurement, 5*, 467–480.

Travis, C. B., Phillippi, R. H., & Tonn, B. E. (1989). Judgment heuristics and medical decisions. *Patient Education and Counseling, 13*, 211–220.

Triandis, H. C. (1989). The self and social behavior in differing cultural contexts. *Psychological Review, 96*, 506–520.

Triandis, H. C. (1990). Cross-cultural studies of individualism and collectivism. In J. J. Berman (Ed.), *Nebraska Symposium on Motivation, 1989* (pp. 41–133). Lincoln: University of Nebraska Press.

Triandis, H. C. (1994). *Culture and social behavior*. New York: McGraw-Hill.

Triandis, H. C. (1995). *Individualism and Collectivism*. Boulder, CO: Westview Press.

Triplett, N. (1898). The dynamogenic factors in pace making and competition. *American Journal of Psychology, 9*, 507–533.

Trivers, R. (1985). *Social evolution*. Menlo Park, CA: Benjamin-Cummings.

Trivers, R. L. (1971). The evolution of reciprocal altruism. *Quarterly Review of Biology, 46*, 35–57.

Trolier, T. K., & Hamilton, D. L. (1986). Variables influencing judgments of correlational relations. *Journal of Personality and Social Psychology, 50*, 879–888.

Trope, Y., & Lieberman, A. (1996). Social hypothesis testing: Cognitive and motivational mechanisms. In E. T. Higgins & A. W. Kruglanski (Eds.), *Social psychology: Handbook of basic principles* (pp. 239–270). New York: Guilford.

Trost, M. R., Maass, A., & Kenrick, D. T. (1992). Minority influence: Personal relevance biases cognitive processes and reverses private acceptance. *Journal of Experimental Social Psychology, 28*, 234–254.

Tseëlon, E. (1995). *The Presentation of Woman in Everyday Life*. Thousand Oaks, CA: Sage.

Turner, C., & Leyens, J. (1992). The weapons effect revisited: The effects of firearms on aggressive behavior. In P. Suedfeld & P. Tetlock (Eds.), *Psychology and social policy* (pp. 201–221). New York: Hemispheres.

Turner, C., & Simons, L. (1974). Effects of subject sophistication and evaluation apprehension on aggressive responses to weapons. *Journal of Personality and Social Psychology, 30*, 341–348.

Turner, C., Simons, L., Berkowitz, L., & Frodi, A. (1977). The stimulating and inhibiting effects of weapons on aggressive behavior. *Aggressive Behavior, 3*, 355–378.

Turner, C. W., Hesse, B. W., & Peterson-Lewis, S. (1986). Naturalistic studies of the long-term effects of television violence. *Journal of Social Issues, 42*(3), 51–74.

Turner, F. J. (1932). *The significance of sections in American history*. New York: H. Holt.

Turner, M. E., Pratkanis, A. R., Probasco, P., & Leve, C. (1992). Threat, cohesion, and group effectiveness: Testing a social identity maintenance perspective on groupthink. *Journal of Personality and Social Psychology, 63*, 781–796.

Tversky, A., & Kahneman, D. (1973). Availability: A heuristic for judging frequency and probability. *Cognitive Psychology, 5*, 207–232.

Tversky, A., & Kahneman, D. (1974). Judgment under uncertainty: Heuristics and biases. *Science, 185*, 1124–1131.

Tversky, A., & Kahneman, D. (1983). Extensional versus intuitive reasoning: The conjunction fallacy in probability judgment. *Psychological Review, 90*, 293–315.

Tversky, B., & Tuchin, M. (1989). A reconciliation of the evidence on eyewitness testimony: Comments on McCloskey and Zaragoza. *Journal of Experimental Psychology: General, 118*, 86–91.

Tyler, T. R. (1990). *Why people obey the law*. New Haven: Yale University Press.

Tyler, T. R., Boeckmann, R. J., Smith, H. J., & Huo, Y. J. (1997). *Social justice in a diverse society*. Boulder, CO: Westview Press.

Uchino, B. N., Cacioppo, J. T., & Keicolt-Glaser, J. K. (1996). The relationship between social support and physiological processes: A review with emphasis on underlying mechanisms and implications for health. *Psychological Bulletin, 119,* 488–531.

Uehara, E. S. (1995). Reciprocity reconsidered: Gouldner's "moral norm of reciprocity" and social support. *Journal of Social and Personal Relationships, 12,* 483–502.

Uleman, J. S., & Moskowitz, G. B. (1994). Unintended effects of goals on unintended inferences. *Journal of Personality and Social Psychology, 66,* 490–501.

Uranowitz, S. W. (1975). Helping and self-attributions: A field experiment. *Journal of Personality and Social Psychology, 32,* 852–854.

Valacich, J. S., Dennis, A. R., & Connolly, T. (1994). Idea generation in computer-based groups: A new ending to an old story. *Organizational Behavior and Human Decision Processes, 57,* 448–467.

Valins, S. (1966). Cognitive effects of false heart-rate feedback. *Journal of Personality and Social Psychology, 4,* 400–408.

Vallerand, R. J., & Richer, F. (1988). On the use of the Causal Dimension Scale in a field setting: A test with confirmatory factor analysis in success and failure situations. *Journal of Personality and Social Psychology, 54,* 704–712.

Vallone, R. P., Griffin, D. W., Lin, S., & Ross, L. (1990). The overconfident prediction of future actions and outcomes by self and others. *Journal of Personality and Social Psychology, 58,* 582–592.

Vallone, R. P., Ross, L., & Lepper, M. R. (1985). The hostile media phenomenon: Biased perception and perceptions of media bias in coverage of the Beirut massacre. *Journal of Personality and Social Psychology, 49,* 577–585.

Van Dyne, L., & Saavedra, R. (1996). A naturalistic minority influence experiment: Effects of divergent thinking, conflict and originality in work-groups. *British Journal of Social Psychology, 35,* 151–167.

Van Lange, P. A. M., Rusbult, C. E., Drigotas, S. M., Arriaga, X. B., Witcher, B. S., & Cox, C. L. (1997). Willingness to sacrifice in close relationships. *Journal of Personality and Social Psychology, 72,* 1373–1395.

Van Overwalle, F., & De Metsenaere, M. (1990). The effects of attribution-based intervention and study strategy training on academic achievement in college freshmen. *British Journal of Educational Psychology, 60,* 299–311.

Van Yperen, N. W., & Buunk, B. P. (1994). Social comparison and social exchange in marital relationships. In M. J. Lerner & G. Mikula (Eds.), *Entitlement and the affectional bond: Justice in close relationships* (pp. 89–116). New York: Plenum.

Vance, C. S. (1986, August 2–9). The Meese Commission on the road. *Nation,* pp. 65, 76.

Vanneman, R. D., & Pettigrew, T. (1972). Race and relative deprivation in the urban United States. *Race, 13,* 461–486.

Video news releases. (1995, July). *Public Relations Tactics,* p. 15.

Vissing, Y., Straus, M., Gelles, R., & Harrop, J. (1991).Verbal aggression by parents and psychosocial problems of children. *Child Abuse and Neglect, 15,* 223–238.

Voissem, N. H., & Sistrunk, F. (1971). Communication schedules and cooperative game behavior. *Journal of Personality and Social Psychology, 19,* 160–167.

Vokey, J. R., & Read, J. D. (1985). Subliminal messages: Between the devil and the media. *American Psychologist, 40,* 1231–1239.

Von Hippel, W., Jonides, J., Hilton, J. L., & Narayan, S. (1993). Inhibitory effect of schematic processing on perceptual encoding. *Journal of Personality and Social Psychology, 64,* 921–935.

Vonk, R. (1995). Effects of inconsistent behaviors on person perception: A multidimensional study. *Personality and Social Psychology Bulletin, 21,* 674–685.

Vonnegut, K. (1963). *Cat's Cradle.* New York: Delacorte Press.

Vroom, V. H., & Yetton, P. W. (1973). *Leadership and decision-making.* Pittsburgh, PA: University of Pittsburgh Press.

Wagner, R. C. (1975). Complementary needs, role expectations, interpersonal attraction, and the stability of work relationships. *Journal of Personality and Social Psychology, 32,* 116–124.

Wagstaff, G. (1982). Attitudes to rape: The "just world" strikes again? *Bulletin of the British Psychological Society, 35,* 277–279.

Wallach, M. A., Kogan, N., & Bem, D. J. (1962). Group influences on individual risk taking. *Journal of Abnormal and Social Psychology, 65,* 75–86.

Walsh, Y., Russell, R. J. H., Wells, P. A. (1995). The personality of ex-cult members. *Personality and Individual Differences, 19,* 339–344.

Walster, E. (1966). Assignment of responsibility for an accident. *Journal of Personality and Social Psychology, 3,* 73–79.

Walster, E., Aronson, V., Abrahams, D., & Rottman, L. (1966). Importance of physical attractiveness in dating behavior. *Journal of Personality and Social Psychology, 5,* 508–516.

Walster, E., & Festinger, L. (1962). The effectiveness of "overheard" persuasive communication. *Journal of Abnormal and Social Psychology, 65,* 395–402.

Walster, E., Walster, G. W., & Berscheid, E. (1978). *Equity: Theory and research.* Boston: Allyn & Bacon.

Walster, E., Walster, G. W., & Traupmann, J. (1978). Equity and premarital sex. *Journal of Personality, 36,* 82–92.

Walster, E., Walster, G. W., Piliavin, J., & Schmidt, L. (1973). "Playing hard to get": Understanding an elusive phenomenon. *Journal of Personality and Social Psychology, 26,* 113–121.

Walther, J., Anderson, J. F., & Park, D. W. (1994). Interpersonal effects in computer mediated interaction: A meta-analysis of social and antisocial communication. *Communication Research, 21,* 460–487.

Wang, T., Brownstein, R., & Katzev, R. (1989). Promoting charitable behavior with compliance techniques. *Applied Psychology: An International Review, 38,* 165–184.

Wänke, M., Schwarz, N., Bless, H. (1995). The availability heuristic revisited: Experienced ease of retrieval in mundane frequency estimates. *Acta Psychologica, 89,* 83–90.

Warren, B. L. (1966). A multiple variable approach to the assortive mating phenomenon. *Eugenics Quarterly, 13,* 285–298.

Warrick, J., & Brown, D. (1997, Sept. 18). One scary, mysterious microbe. *Washington Post,* p. A1.

Washburn, S., & Hamburg, D. (1965). The implications of primate research In I. DeVore (Ed.), *Primate behavior: Field studies of monkeys and apes* (pp. 607–622). New York: Holt, Rinehart & Winston.

Watson, D. (1982). The actor and the observer: How are their perceptions of causality divergent? *Psychological Bulletin, 92,* 682–700.

Watson, D., & Pennebaker, J. W. (1989). Health complaints, stress, and distress: Exploring the central role of negative affectivity. *Psychological Review, 96,* 234–254.

Watson, J. (1924). *Behaviorism.* Chicago: University of Chicago Press.

Watson, J. (1950). Some social and psychological situations related to change in attitude. *Human Relations, 3,* 15–56.

Watson, R. I. (1973). Investigation into deindividuation using a cross-cultural survey technique. *Journal of Personality and Social Psychology, 25,* 342–345.

Wattenberg, M. P. (1987). The hollow realignment: Partisan change in a candidate-centered era. *Public Opinion Quarterly, 51,* 58–74.

Weary, G., & Arkin, R. C. (1981). Attributional self-presentation. In J. H. Harvey, W. Ickes, & R. F. Kidd (Eds.), *New directions in attribution research* (Vol. 3, pp. 223–246). New York: Erlbaum.

Weatherly, D. (1961). Anti-Semitism and the expression of fantasy aggression. *Journal of Abnormal and Social Psychology, 62,* 454–457.

Webber, R., & Crocker, J. (1983). Cognitive processes in the revision of stereotypic beliefs. *Journal of Personality and Social Psychology, 45,* 961–977.

Weber, E. U., Bockenholt, U., Hilton, D. J., & Wallace, B. (1993). Determinants of diagnostic hypothesis generation: Effects of information, base rates, and experience. *Journal of Experimental Psychology: Learning, Memory, and Cognition, 19,* 1151–1164.

Webster, D. M. (1993). Motivated augmentation and reduction of the overattributional bias. *Journal of Personality and Social Psychology, 65,* 261–271.

Wechsler, H., Dowdall, G., Davenport, A., Castillo, S. (1995). Correlates of college student binge drinking. *American Journal of Public Health, 85,* 921–926.

Wegener, D. T., & Petty, R. E. (1994). Mood management across affective states: The hedonic contingency hypothesis. *Journal of Personality and Social Psychology, 66,* 1034–1048.

Wegener, D. T., & Petty, R. E. (1995). Flexible correction processes in social judgment: The role of naive theories in corrections for perceived bias. *Journal of Personality and Social Psychology, 68,* 36–51.

Wegener, D. T., & Petty, R. E. (1996). Effects of mood on persuasion processes: Enhancing, reducing, and biasing scrutiny of attitude-relevant information. In L. L. Martin & A. Tesser (Eds.), *Striving and feeling: Interactions between goals and affect* (pp. 329–362). Mahwah, NJ: Erlbaum.

Wegener, D. T., & Petty, R. E. (1997). The flexible correction model: The role of naive theories of bias in bias correction. In M. Zanna (Ed.), *Advances in experimental social psychology* (Vol. 29, pp. 141–208). San Diego: Academic Press.

Wegener, D. T., Petty, R. E., & Smith, S. M. (1995). Positive mood can increase or decrease message scrutiny: The hedonic contingency view of mood and message processing. *Journal of Personality and Social Psychology, 69,* 5–15.

Wegner, D. M. (1986). Transactive memory: A contemporary analysis of the group mind. In B. Mullen & G. R. Goethals (Eds.), *Theories of group behavior* (pp. 185–208). New York: Springer-Verlag.

Wegner, D. M. (1989). *White bears and other unwanted thoughts: Suppression, obsession, and the psychology of mental control.* New York: Viking.

Wegner, D. M. (1992). You can't always think what you want: Problems in the suppression of unwanted thoughts. In M. P. Zanna (Ed.), *Advances in experimental social psychology* (pp. 193–225). San Diego, CA: Academic Press.

Wegner, D. M. (1994). Ironic processes of mental control. *Psychological Review, 101,* 34–52.

Wegner, D. M., Ansfield, M., & Pilloff, D. (in press). The putt and the pendulum: Ironic effects of the mental control of action. *Psychological Science.*

Wegner, D. M., & Bargh, J. A. (1998). Control and automaticity in social life. In D. Gilbert, S. Fiske, & G. Lindzey (Eds.), *The handbook of social psychology* (4th ed., Vol. 1, pp. 446–498). New York: McGraw Hill.

Wegner, D. M., Bowman, R. E., & Erber, R. (1995). *Sexism and mental control: When thought and speech betray egalitarian beliefs.* Unpublished manuscript, University of Virginia.

Wegner, D. M., Erber, R., & Raymond, P. (1991). Transactive memory in close relationships. *Journal of Personality and Social Psychology, 61,* 923–929.

Wegner, D. M., Quillan, F., & Houston, C. (in press). Memories out of order: Thought suppression and the disassembly of remembered experience. *Journal of Personality and Social Psychology.*

Wegner, D. M., Wenzlaff, R., Kerker, M., & Beattie, A. E. (1981). Incrimination through innuendo: Can media questions become public answers? *Journal of Personality and Social Psychology, 40,* 822–832.

Weinberg, R. S., Richardson, P. A., & Jackson, A. (1983). Effect of situation criticality on tennis performance of males and females. *Newsletter of the Society of the Advancement of Social Psychology, 9,* 8–9.

Weiner, B. (Ed.). (1974). *Achievement motivation and attribution theory.* Morristown, NJ: General Learning Press.

Weiner, B. (1985). "Spontaneous" causal thinking. *Psychological Bulletin, 97,* 74–84.

Weiner, B. (1986). *An attributional theory of emotion and motivation.* New York: Springer-Verlag.

Weiner, B., Amirkhan, J., Folkes, V. S., & Verette, J. A. (1987). An attributional analysis of excuse giving: Studies of a naive theory of emotion. *Journal of Personality and Social Psychology, 52,* 316–324.

Weiner, B., Frieze, L., Kukla, A., Reed, L., Rest, S. & Rosenbaum, R. M. (1972). Perceiving the causes of success and failure. In E. E. Jones, H. H. Kelley, R. E. Nisbett, S. Valins, & B. Weiner (Eds.), *Attribution: Perceiving the causes of behavior.* Morristown, NJ: General Learning Press.

Weiner, B., Nierenberg, R., & Goldstein, M. (1976). Social learning (locus of control) versus attributional (causal stability) interpretations of expectancy for success. *Journal of Personality, 44,* 52–68.

Weingardt, K. R., Toland, H. K., & Loftus, E. F. (1994). Reports of suggested memories: Do people truly believe them? In D. F. Ross, J. D. Read, & M. P. Toglia (Eds.), *Adult eyewitness testimony: Current trends and developments* (pp. 3–26). New York: Cambridge University Press.

Weinstein, N. D. (1980). Unrealistic optimism about future life events. *Journal of Personality and Social Psychology, 39,* 806–820.

Weinstein, N. D., & Klein, W. M. (1996). Unrealistic optimism: Present and future. *Journal of Social and Clinical Psychology, 15,* 1–8.

Weir, W. (1984, October 15). Another look at subliminal "facts." *Advertising Age,* p. 46.

Weiss, R. S. (1973). *Loneliness: The experience of emotional and social isolation.* Cambridge, MA: MIT Press.

Weisz, C., & Jones, E. E. (1993). Expectancy disconfirmation and dispositional inference: Latent strength of target-based and category-based expectancies. *Personality and Social Psychology Bulletin, 19,* 563–573.

Wells, G. L. (1984). The psychology of lineup identifications. *Journal of Applied Social Psychology, 14,* 89–103.

Wells, G. L. (1993). What do we know about eyewitness identification? *American Psychologist, 48,* 553–571.

Wells, G. L., Lindsay, R. C. L., & Ferguson, T. J. (1979). Accuracy, confidence, and juror perceptions in eyewitness identification. *Journal of Applied Psychology, 64,* 440–448.

Wells, G. L., & Luus, C. A. E. (1990). Police lineups as experiments: Social methodology as a framework for properly conducted lineups. *Personality and Social Psychology Bulletin, 16,* 106–117.

Wells, G. L., Seelau, E. P., Rydell, S. M., & Luus, S. M. (1994). Recommendations for properly conducted lineup identification tasks. In D. F. Ross, J. D. Read, & M. P. Toglia (Eds.), *Adult eyewitness testimony: Current trends and developments* (pp. 223–244). New York: Cambridge University Press.

Wells, W. D. (Ed.), (1997). *Measuring advertising effectiveness.* Mahwah, NJ: Erlbaum.

West, S. G., Gunn, S. P., & Chernicky, P. (1975). Ubiquitous Watergate: An attributional analysis. *Journal of Personality and Social Psychology, 32,* 55–62.

Wheeler, L., & Kim, Y. (1997). What is beautiful is culturally good: The physical attractiveness stereotype has different content in collectivistic cultures. *Personality and Social Psychology Bulletin, 23,* 795–800.

Wheeler, L., Koestner, R., & Driver, R. (1982). Related attributes in the choice of comparison others: It's there, but it isn't all there is. *Journal of Experimental Social Psychology, 18,* 489–500.

Wheeler, L., & Kunitate, M. (1992). Social comparison in everyday life. *Journal of Personality and Social Psychology, 62,* 760–773.

Wheeler, L., Martin, R., & Suls, J. (1997). The proxy model of social comparison for self-assessment of ability. *Personality and Social Psychology Review, 1,* 54–61.

White, G. L. (1980). Physical attractiveness and courtship progress. *Journal of Personality and Social Psychology, 39,* 660–668.

White, G. L. (1981a). A model of romantic jealousy. *Motivation and Emotion, 5,* 295–310.

White, G. L. (1981b). Some correlates of romantic jealousy. *Journal of Personality, 49,* 129–147.

White, H. (1997). Longitudinal perspective on alcohol and aggression during adolescence. In M. Galanter (Ed.), *Recent developments in alcoholism, Vol. 13: Alcohol and violence: Epidemiology, neurobiology, psychology, family issues* (pp. 81–103). New York: Plenum.

White, R. K. (1977). Misperception in the Arab-Israeli conflict. *Journal of Social Issues, 33,* 190–221.

Whitly, B. E., & Frieze, I. H. (1985) Children's causal attributions for success and failure in achievement settings: A meta-analysis. *Journal of Educational Psychology, 77,* 608–616.

Whitney, K., Sagrestano, L., & Maslach, C. (1994). Establishing the social impact of individuation. *Journal of Personality and Social Psychology, 66,* 1140–1153.

Whittaker, J. O., & Meade, R. D. (1967). Social pressure in the modification and distortion of judgment: A cross-cultural study. *International Journal of Psychology, 2,* 109–113.

Whorf, B. L. (1956). *Language, thought, and reality.* New York: Wiley.

Wicker, A. W. (1969). Attitudes versus actions: The relationship between verbal and overt behavioral responses to attitude objects. *Journal of Social Issues, 25,* 41–78.

Wicklund, R., & Brehm, J. (1998). Resistance to change: The cornerstone of cognitive dissonance theory. In E. Harmon-Jones & J. S. Mills, *Cognitive dissonance theory: Revival with revisions and controversies.* Washington, DC: American Psychological Association.

Wicklund, R. A. (1975). Objective self-awareness. In L. Berkowitz (Ed.), *Advances in experimental social psychology* (Vol. 8, pp. 233–275). New York: Academic Press.

Wicklund, R. A., & Frey, D. (1980). Self-awareness theory: When the self makes a difference. In D. Wegner & R. Vallacher (Eds.), *The self in social psychology* (pp. 31–54). New York: Oxford University Press.

Wicklund, R. A., & Gollwitzer, P. M. (1982). *Symbolic self-completion.* Hillsdale, NJ: Erlbaum.

Wiedenfeld, S. A., O'Leary, A., Bandura, A., Brown, S., Levine, S., & Raska, K. (1990). Impact of perceived self-efficacy in coping with stressors on components of the immune system. *Journal of Personality and Social Psychology, 59,* 1082–1094.

Wilder, D. A. (1981). Perceiving persons as a group: Categorization and intergroup relations. In D. L. Hamilton (Ed.), *Cognitive processes in stereotyping and intergroup behavior.* Hillsdale, NJ: Erlbaum.

Wilder, D. A. (1984). Intergroup contact: The typical member and the exception to the rule. *Journal of Experimental Psychology, 20,* 177–194.

Wilder, D. A. (1986). Social categorization: Implications for creation and reduction of intergroup bias. In L. Berkowitz (Ed.), *Advances in experimental social psychology* (Vol. 19, pp. 291–355). New York: Academic Press.

Wilder, D. A., & Shapiro, P. N. (1989). Role of competition-induced anxiety in limiting the beneficial impact of positive behavior by an out-group member. *Journal of Personality and Social Psychology, 56,* 60–69.

Williams, K., Harkins, S., & Latané, B. (1981). Identifiability as a deterrent to social loafing: Two cheering experiments. *Journal of Personality and Social Psychology, 40,* 303–311.

Williams, K., Karau, S., & Bourgeois, M. (1993). Working on collective tasks: Social loafing and social compensation. In M. A. Hogg & D. Abrams (Eds.), *Group motivation: Social psychological perspectives* (pp. 130–148). New York: Harvester Wheatsheaf.

Williams, K. D., Loftus, E. F., & Deffenbacher, K. A. (1992). Eyewitness evidence and testimony. In D. K. Kagehiro & W. S. Laufer (Eds.), *Handbook of psychology and law* (pp. 141–166). New York: Springer-Verlag.

Williams, K. R., & Hawkins, R. (1986). Perceptual research on general deterrence: A critical review. *Law and Society Review, 20,* 545–572.

Williams, R. B., Jr. (1987). Refining the Type A hypothesis: Emergence of the hostility complex. *American Journal of Cardiology, 60,* 27J–32J.

Williams, R. H., & Ross, M. H. (1980, March–April). Drilling for oil and gas in our houses. *Technology Review,* pp. 24–36.

Williams, R. L. (1983, December). For the all-too-common cold, we are perfect, if unwilling, hosts. *Smithsonian,* pp. 47–55.

Williamson, G. M., & Clark, M. S. (1989). Providing help and desired relationship type as determinants of changes in moods and self-evaluations. *Journal of Personality and Social Psychology, 56,* 722–734.

Williamson, G. M., & Clark, M. S. (1992). Impact of desired relationship type on affective reactions to choosing and being required to help. *Personality and Social Psychology Bulletin, 18,* 10–18.

Williamson, G. M., Clark, M. S., Pegalis, L. J., & Behan, A. (1996). Affective consequences of refusing to help in communal and exchange relationships. *Personality and Social Psychology Bulletin, 22,* 34–47.

Wills, T. A., Weiss, R. L., & Patterson, G. R. (1974). A behavioral analysis of the determinants of marital satisfaction. *Journal of Consulting and Clinical Psychology, 42,* 802–811.

Wilmot, W. W. (1994). Relationship rejuvenation. In D. J. Canary & L. Stafford (Eds.), *Communication and Relational Maintenance* (pp. 255–273). New York: Academic Press.

Wilmot, W. W., & Stevens, D. C. (1994). Relationship rejuvenation: Arresting decline in personal relationships. In D. Conville (Ed.), *Uses of Structure in Communication Studies* (pp. 103–124). Westport, CT: Praeger.

Wilson, D. K., Purdon, S. E., & Wallston, K. A. (1988). Com-pli-ance in health recommendations: A theoretical overview of message framing. *Health Education Research, 3,* 161–171.

Wilson, E. O. (1975). *Sociobiology: The new synthesis.* Cambridge, MA: Belknap Press of Harvard University Press.

Wilson, E. O. (1978). *On human nature.* Cambridge, MA: Harvard University Press.

Wilson, J. Q., & Hernstein, R. J. (1985). *Crime and human nature.* New York: Simon & Schuster.

Wilson, T. D. (1985). Strangers to ourselves: The origins and accuracy of beliefs about one's own mental states. In J. H. Harvey & G. Weary (Eds.), *Attribution in contemporary psychology* (pp. 9–36). New York: Academic Press.

Wilson, T. D. (1990). Self-persuasion via self-reflection. In J. Olson & M. Zanna (Eds.), *Self-inference: The Ontario Symposium* (Vol. 6, pp. 43–67). Hillsdale, NJ: Erlbaum.

Wilson, T. D. (1994). The proper protocol: Validity and completeness of verbal reports. *Psychological Science, 5,* 249–252.

Wilson, T. D., & Brekke, N. C. (1994). Mental contamination and mental correction: Unwanted influences on judgments and evaluations. *Psychological Bulletin, 116,* 117–142.

Wilson, T. D., Dunn, D. S., Bybee, J. A., Hyman, D. B., & Rotondo, J. A. (1984). Effects of analyzing reasons on atti-tude-behavior consistency. *Journal of Personality and Social Psychology, 47,* 5–16.

Wilson, T. D., Dunn, D. S., Kraft, D., & Lisle, D. J. (1989). Introspection, attitude change, and attitude-behavior con-sistency: The disruptive effects of explaining why we feel the way we do. In L. Berkowitz (Ed.), *Advances in experi-mental social psychology* (Vol. 19, pp. 123–205). Orlando, FL: Academic Press.

Wilson, T. D., Gilbert, D. T., & Wheatley, T. (in press). Protecting our minds: The role of lay beliefs. To appear in V. Yzerbyt, G. Lories, & B. Dardenne (Eds.), *Metacognition: Cognitive and social dimensions.* New York: Sage.

Wilson, T. D., & Hodges, S. D. (1992). Attitudes as temporary constructions. In A. Tesser & L. Martin (Eds.), *The con-struction of social judgment* (pp. 37–65). Hillsdale, NJ: Erlbaum.

Wilson, T. D., Hodges, S. D., & LaFleur, S. J. (1995). Effects of introspecting about reasons: Inferring attitudes from acces-sible thoughts. *Journal of Personality and Social Psychology, 69,* 16–28.

Wilson, T. D., Houston, C. E., & Meyers, J. M. (in press). Choose your poison: Effects of lay beliefs about mental processes on attitude change. *Social Cognition.*

Wilson, T. D., Houston, C. E., Etling, K. M., & Brekke, N. (1996). A new look at anchoring effects: Basic anchoring and its antecedents. *Journal of Experimental Psychology: General, 125,* 387–402.

Wilson, T. D., & Kraft, D. (1993). Why do I love thee? Effects of repeated introspections about a dating relationship on at-titudes toward the relationship. *Personality and Social Psychology Bulletin, 19,* 409–418.

Wilson, T. D., & LaFleur, S. J. (1995). Knowing what you'll do: Effects of analyzing reasons on self-prediction. *Journal of Personality and Social Psychology, 68,* 21–35.

Wilson, T. D., LaFleur, S. J., & Lindsey, S. (in press). Knowledge and the effects of introspection on attitude change. To ap-pear in R. E. Nisbett, & J. Caverni (Eds.), *The psychology of expertise.* Elsevier.

Wilson, T. D., Laser, P. S., & Stone, J. I. (1982). Judging the pre-dictors of one's own mood: Accuracy and the use of shared theories. *Journal of Experimental Social Psychology, 18,* 537–556.

Wilson, T. D., & Linville, P. W. (1982). Improving the academic performance of college freshmen: Attribution therapy revis-ited. *Journal of Personality and Social Psychology, 42,* 367–376.

Wilson, T. D., & Linville, P. W. (1985). Improving the perfor-mance of college freshmen using attributional techniques. *Journal of Personality and Social Psychology, 49,* 287–293.

Wilson, T. D., Lisle, D., Schooler, J., Hodges, S. D., Klaaren, K. J., & LaFleur, S. J. (1993). Introspecting about reasons can reduce post-choice satisfaction. *Personality and Social Psychology Bulletin, 19,* 331–339.

Wilson, T. D., & Stone, J. I. (1985). Limitations of self-knowl-edge: More on telling more than we can know. In P. Shaver (Ed.), *Review of personality and social psychology* (Vol. 6, pp. 167–183). Beverly Hills, CA: Sage.

Winch, R. (1958). *Mate selection: A study of complementary needs.* New York: Harper & Row.

Winslow, R. W., Franzini, L. R., & Hwang, J. (1992). Perceived peer norms, casual sex, and AIDS risk prevention. *Journal of Applied Social Psychology, 22,* 1809–1827.

Winter, D. G. (1987). Leader appeal, leader performance, and the motive profiles of leaders and followers: A study of American presidents and elections. *Journal of Personality and Social Psychology, 52,* 196–202.

Wiseman, F. (Director). (1967). *Titicut follies* [Film]. Cambridge, MA: Zipporah Films.

Witelson, S. F. (1992). Cognitive neuroanatomy: A new era. *Neurology, 42,* 709–713.

Witte, E. H. (1996). Small-group research and the crisis of social psychology: An introduction. In E. H. Witte & J. H. Davis (Eds.), *Understanding group behavior: Small group processes and interpersonal relations* (Vol. 2, pp. 1–8). Mahwah, NJ: Erlbaum.

Wittenbaum, G. M., & Stasser, G. (1996). Management of infor-mation in small groups. In J. L. Nye & A. M. Brower (Eds.), *What's social about social cognition? Social cognition re-search in small groups* (pp. 3–28). Newbury Park, CA: Sage.

Wolf, S. (1985). Manifest and latent influence of majorities and minorities. *Journal of Personality and Social Psychology, 48,* 899–908.

Wolfe, C., & Spencer, S. (1996). Stereotypes and prejudice: Their overt and subtle influence in the classroom. *American Behavioral Scientist, 40,* 176–185.

Woll, S. (1986). So many to choose from: Decision strategies in videodating. *Journal of Social and Personal Relationships, 3,* 43–52.

Wood, J. V. (1989). Theory and research concerning social com-parisons of personal attributes. *Psychological Bulletin, 106,* 231–248.

Wood, J. V. (1996). What is social comparison and how should we study it? *Personality and Social Psychology Bulletin, 22,* 520–537.

Wood, J. V., Taylor, S. E., & Lichtman, R. R. (1985). Social comparison in adjustment to breast cancer. *Journal of Personality and Social Psychology, 49,* 1169–1183.

Wood, W. (1982). Retrieval of attitude-relevant information from memory: Effects on susceptibility to persuasion and on intrinsic motivation. *Journal of Personality and Social Psychology, 42,* 798–810.

Wood, W. (1987). Meta-analytic review of sex differences in group performance. *Psychological Bulletin, 102,* 53–71.

Wood, W., Pool, G. J., Leck, K., & Purvis, D. (1996). Self-definition, defensive processing, and influence: The normative impact of majority and minority groups. *Journal of Personality and Social Psychology, 71,* 1181–1193.

Wood, W., Rhodes, N., & Biek, M. (1995). Working knowledge and attitude strength: An information-processing analysis. In R. E. Petty & J. A. Krosnick (Eds.), *Attitude strength: Antecedents and consequences* (pp. 283–313). Mahwah, NJ: Erlbaum.

Word, C. O., Zanna, M. P., & Cooper, J. (1974). The nonverbal mediation of self-fulfilling prophecies in interracial interaction. *Journal of Experimental Social Psychology, 10,* 109–120.

Worth, L. T., & Mackie, D. M. (1987). Cognitive mediation of positive affect in persuasion. *Social Cognition, 5,* 76–94.

Wortman, C. B., & Brehm, J. W. (1975). Response to uncontrollable outcomes: An integration of reactance theory and the learned helplessness model. In L. Berkowitz (Ed.), *Advances in experimental social psychology* (Vol. 8, pp. 277–336). New York: Academic Press.

Wright, E. F., Luus, C. A. E., & Christie, S. D. (1990). Does group discussion facilitate the use of consensus information in making causal attributions? *Journal of Personality and Social Psychology, 59,* 261–269.

Wright, J. C., & Murphy, G. L. (1984). The utility of theories in intuitive statistics: The robustness of theory-based judgments. *Journal of Experimental Psychology: General, 113,* 301–322.

Wright, L. (1994). *Remembering Satan.* New York: Knopf.

Wright, R. (1994). *The moral animal: Why we are the way we are: The new science of evolutionary psychology.* New York: Random House.

Wrightsman, L. S. (1987). *Psychology and the legal system.* Pacific Grove, CA: Brooks/Cole.

Wuthnow, R. (1991). *Acts of compassion: Caring for others and helping ourselves.* Princeton, NJ: Princeton University Press.

Wyer, R. S., & Srull, T. K. (1989). *Memory and cognition in its social context.* Hillsdale, NJ: Erlbaum.

Wyer, R. S., Jr. (1988). Social memory and social judgment. In P. R. Solomon, G. R. Goethals, C. M. Kelley, & B. R. Stephens (Eds.), *Perspectives on memory research.* New York: Springer-Verlag.

Yamaguchi, K., & Kandel, D. B. (1984). Patterns of drug use from adolescence to young adulthood: III. Predictors of progression. *American Journal of Public Health, 74,* 673–681.

Yee, D., & Eccles, J. S. (1988). Parent perceptions and attributions for children's math achievement. *Sex Roles, 19,* 317–333.

Yovetich, N. A., & Rusbult, C. E. (1994). Accommodative behavior in close relationships: Exploring transformation of motivation. *Journal of Experimental Social Psychology, 30,* 138–164.

Yudko, E., Blanchard, D., Henne, J., & Blanchard, R. (1997). Emerging themes in preclinical research on alcohol and aggression. In M. Galanter (Ed.), *Recent developments in alcoholism, Vol. 13: Alcohol and violence: Epidemiology, neurobiology, psychology, family issues* (pp. 123–138). New York: Plenum.

Yuille, J. C., & Cutshall, J. L. (1986). A case study of eyewitness memory of a crime. *Journal of Applied Psychology, 71,* 291–301.

Zaccaro, S. J., Foti, R. J., & Kenny, D. A. (1991). Self-monitoring and trait-based variance in leadership: An investigation of leader flexibility across multiple group situations. *Journal of Applied Psychology, 76,* 308–315.

Zahn-Waxler, C., Radke-Yarrow, M., & King, R. A. (1979). Child rearing and children's prosocial initiations toward victims of distress. *Child Development, 50,* 319–330.

Zajonc, R. B. (1965). Social facilitation. *Science, 149,* 269–274.

Zajonc, R. B. (1968). Attitudinal effects of mere exposure. *Journal of Personality and Social Psychology, 9,* Monograph Suppl. No. 2, Pt. 2.

Zajonc, R. B. (1980). Compresence. In P. B. Paulus (Ed.), *Psychology of group influence* (pp. 35–60). Hillsdale, NJ: Erlbaum.

Zajonc, R. B., Heingartner, A., & Herman, E. M. (1969). Social enhancement and impairment of performance in the cockroach. *Journal of Personality and Social Psychology, 13,* 83–92.

Zajonc, R. B., & Sales, S. M. (1966). Social facilitation of dominant and subordinate responses. *Journal of Experimental Social Psychology, 2,* 160–168.

Zander, A. (1979). The psychology of group processes. *Annual Review of Psychology, 30,* 417–451.

Zanna, M., & Cooper, J. (1974). Dissonance and the pill: An attribution approach to studying the arousal properties of dissonance. *Journal of Personality and Social Psychology, 29,* 703–709.

Zanna, M., & Cooper, J. (1976). Dissonance and the attribution process. In J. H. Harvey, W. Ickes, & R. F. Kidd (Eds.), *New directions in attribution research* (Vol. 1, pp. 199–217). New York: Erlbaum.

Zanna, M. P., & Fazio, R. H. (1982). The attitude-behavior relation: Moving toward a third generation of research. In M. P. Zanna, E. T. Higgins, & C. P. Herman (Eds.), *Consistency in social behavior: The Ontario Symposium* (Vol. 2, pp. 283–301). Hillsdale, NJ: Erlbaum.

Zanna, M., Goethals, G. R., & Hill, J. (1975). Evaluating a sex-related ability: Social comparison with similar others and standard setters. *Journal of Experimental Social Psychology, 11,* 86–93.

Zanna, M., & Rempel, J. K. (1988). Attitudes: A new look at an old concept. In D. Bar-Tal & A. W. Kruglanski (Eds.), *The social psychology of attitudes* (pp. 315–334). New York: Cambridge University Press.

Zanot, E. J., Pincus, J. D., & Lamp, E. J. (1983). Public perceptions of subliminal advertising. *Journal of Advertising, 12,* 39–45.

Zebrowitz, L. A. (1997). *Reading Faces: Window to the Soul?* Boulder, CO: Westview Press.

Zebrowitz, L. A., & Montepare, J. M. (1992). Impressions of babyfaced individuals across the life-span. *Developmental Psychology, 28,* 1143–1152.

Zebrowitz-McArthur, L. (1988). Person perception in cross-cultural perspective. In M. H. Bond (Ed.), *The cross-cultural challenge to social psychology* (pp. 245–265). Newbury Park, CA: Sage.

Zillmann, D. (1978). Attribution and misattribution of excitatory reactions. In J. H. Harvey, W. J. Ickes, & R. F. Kidd (Eds.), *New directions in attribution research* (Vol. 2, pp. 335–370). Hillsdale, NJ: Erlbaum.

Zillmann, D. (1994). Erotica and family values. In J. Bryant, D. Zillmann, & A. C. Huston (Eds.), *Media, children, and the family: Social scientific, psychodynamic, and clinical perspectives* (pp. 199–213). Hillsdale, NJ: Erlbaum.

Zimbardo, P., & Andersen, S. (1993). Understanding mind control: Exotic and mundane mental manipulations. In M. D. Langone (Ed.), *Recovery from cults* (pp. 104–125). New York: Norton.

Zimbardo, P. G. (1970). The human choice: Individuation, reason, and order versus deindividuation, impulse, and chaos. In W. J. Arnold & D. Levine (Eds.), *Nebraska Symposium on Motivation: 1969* (Vol. 17, pp. 237–307). Lincoln: University of Nebraska Press.

Zimbardo, P. G., Weisenberg, M., Firestone, I., & Levy, B. (1965). Communicator effectiveness in producing public conformity and private attitude change. *Journal of Personality, 33,* 233–255.

Zubek, J. P. (Ed.). (1969). *Sensory deprivation: Fifteen years of research.* New York: Appleton-Century-Crofts.

Zuber, J. A., Crott, H. W., & Werner, J. (1992). Choice shift and group polarization: An analysis of the status of arguments and social decision schemes. *Journal of Personality and Social Psychology, 62,* 50–61.

Zuckerman, M. (1978). Actions and occurrences in Kelley's cube. *Journal of Personality and Social Psychology, 36,* 647–656.

Zuckerman, M., DePaulo, B. M., & Rosenthal, R. (1981). Verbal and nonverbal communication of deception. In L. Berkowitz (Ed.), *Advances in experimental social psychology* (Vol. 14, pp. 1–59). New York: Academic Press.

Zuwerink, J., Monteith, M., Devine, P., & Cook, D. (1996). Prejudice toward Blacks: With and without compunction? *Basic and Applied Social Psychology, 18,* 131–150.

CREDITS

Harper Collins Publisher's Inc. **p. 168:** Figure 5.3 adapted from Greene, et al., "Overjustification in a token economy," *Journal of Personality and Social Psychology*, 34. © 1976 by the American Psychological Association. Adapted by permission. **p. 169:** from B. Russell and T. Branch, *Second wind: The memoirs of an opinioned man.* © 1979. Reprinted by permission of Ballantine Books. **p. 170:** Figure 5.4 from Hennessey, et al., "Immunizing children against the negative effect of reward: A further examination of intrinsic motivation focus sessions," *Creativity Research Journal*, 6, pp. 297-307. © 1993. Reprinted by permission of Albex Publishing Corp. **p. 175:** Figure 5.6 adapted from Dutton, et al., "Some evidence for heightened sexual attraction under conditions of high anxiety," *Journal of Personality and Social Psychology*, 30. © 1974 by the American Psychological Association. Adapted by permission. **p. 180:** Figure 5.7 adapted from Gallup, "Self-recognition in primates: A comparative approach to the bidi-rectional properties of conscious," *American Psychologist,* 32. © 1977 by the American Psychological Association. Adapted by permission.
Photos and Cartoons: Page 148: © Private Collection/Daniel Nevins/SuperStock; **150:** © David M. Grossman; **152:** © Harper Collins Archives; **153:** © AP/Wide World Photos; **161:** Frascino © 1977 The New Yorker Collection. All rights reserved. **163:** © Kagan/Monkmeyer Press; **166:** © 1991 North America Syndicate; **168:** © 1995 United Feature Syndicate, Inc.; **169:** © Focus on Sports; **174:** © Ted Kerasote/Photo Researchers; **178:** © Steve Bloom; **182:** Hamilton from The New Yorker Collection. All rights reserved. **184L:** © Smith/Sygma; **184R:** © F. Lee Cockran/Sygma

CHAPTER 6

Text and Art: p. 194: Figure 6.2 adapted from Jones and Kohler, "The effects of plausibility on the learning of controversial statements," *Journal of Abnormal and Social Psychology*, 57, pp. 315-320, 1959. **p. 201:** Figure 6.3 adapted from Aronson and Mills, "The effect of severity of ini-tiation on liking for a group," *Journal of Abnormal and Social Psychology*, 1959. **p. 206:** Figure 6.4 adapted from Stone, Aronson, Crain, Winslow, and Fried, "Inducing hypocrisy as a means of encouraging young adults to use condoms," Personality and Social Psychology Bulletin. © 1993 Sage Publications. Reprinted by permission. **p. 210:** Figure 6.5 adapted from Freedman, "Long term behavioral effects of cognitive disso-nance," *Journal of Experimental Social Psychology*, 1, pp. 145-155. © 1963, 1965 by the American Psychological Association. Reprinted by permission. **p. 213:** Figure 6.6 adapted from Jecker and Landy, "Liking a person as a function of doing him a favor." *Human relations*, 22, pp. 371-378. © 1969. Reprinted by permission of Plenum Publishing Company. **p. 217:** Figure 6.7 adapted from Zanna, et al., "Dissonance and the pill: An attribution approach to studying the arousal properties of disso-nance," *Journal of Experimental Social Psychology*, 29. © 1974 by the American Psychological Association. Adapted by permission. **p 224:** Figure 6.9 adapted from Tesser & Smith, 1980. **p. 226:** Figure 6.10 from C.M. Steele, "Dissonance and the lab coat: Self-affirmation and the free choice of paradigm." © 1986. Reprinted by permission of the author.
Photos and Cartoons: Page 188: © Superstock; **191:** © Peanuts reprinted by permission of United Feature Syndicate, Inc.; **196:** © D & I MacDonald/The Picture Cube; **197:** © Antman/The Image Works; **200:** © Jim Daniels/The Picture Cube; **204:** © Robert Trippett/Sipa Press; **208:** © Lawrence Migdale/Stock Boston; **212:** © The Historical Society of Penns[y]lvania; **214:** © AP/Wide World; **216:** © AP/Wide World

CHAPTER 7

Text and Art: p. 239: Reprinted with permission (Smokey Robinson lyrics). **p. 250:** Figure 7.4 adapted from Petty, et al., *Communication and persuasion*. © 1981. Reprinted by permission of Springer-Verlag. **p. 251:** (Try It!) Cacioppo et al., 1996. **p. 254:** Figure 7.5 adapted from Bless, Bohner, Schwarz, & Strack, 1990. **p. 255:** Figure 7.6 from Leventhal, et al., "Effects of fear and instructions on how to cope with danger*,*" *Journal of Personality and Social Psychology*, 6. © 1967 by the American Psychological Association. Adapted with permission. **p. 258:** Figure 7.7 adapted from Shavitt, "The role of attitude objects in attitude function," *Journal of Social Psychology*, 26, pp. 124-148. © 1990. Reprinted by per-mission. **p. 264:** Figure 7.8 adapted from Ajzen/Fishbein, *Understanding*

and predicting social behavior. © 1985. Adapted by permission of Prentice Hall, Inc., Upper Saddle River, NJ. **p.272:** Figure 7.9 adapted from Murphy & Zajonc, 1993.
Photos and Cartoons: Page 234: © Christie's Images/SuperStock; **240:** © Paul Conklin/Photo Edit; **243:** © Goldberg/Monkmeyer Press; **245:** Reprinted with permission from NIKE, Inc.; **253:** © David Wells/The Image Works; **256:** © Partnership for a Drug Free America; **258:** © 1997 The Rockport Company, Inc. All Rights Reserved. ROCKPORT is a reg-istered trademark and UNCOMPROMISE is a trademark of The Rockport Company, Inc.; **260:** © M. Siluk/The Image Works; **263:** © LeDuc/Monkmeyer Press; **267:** © Miele; **270:** © American Association of Advertising Agencies; **269:** Hamilton © 1984 The New Yorker Collection. All rights reserved.

CHAPTER 8

Text and Art: p. 285: Figure 8.1 adapted from Sherif, *The psychology of social norms.* © 1936 by HarperCollins Publishers. Reprinted by permis-sion. **p. 289:** From Johnson, "The phantom anesthetist of Mattoon: A field study of mass hysteria," *Journal of Abnormal and Social Psychology*, 40, 1945. **p. 295:** Figure 8.2 from Asch, "Studies of independence and conformity: A minority of one against a unanimous majority," *Psychological Monographs*, 70 (9, Whole No. 416). **p. 297:** Figure 8.3 adapted from Asch, "Symposium on preventive and social psychiatry." **p. 305:** Figure 8.6 adapted from Sherif, *The psychology of social norms.* © 1936 by HarperCollins Publishers. Reprinted by permission. **p. 314:** Figure 8.7 adapted from Cialdini et al., 1975; Freedman & Fraser, 1966. **p. 318:** Figure 8.8 adapted from S. Milgram, from *Obedience to authority.* © 1974. Reprinted by permission of HarperCollins Publishers, Inc. **p. 320:** Figure 8.9 adapted from S. Milgram, *From Obedience to authority.* © 1974. Reprinted by permission of HarperCollins Publishers, Inc.
Photos and Cartoons: Page 278: © Russian State Museum, St. Petersburg, Russia/SuperStock; **280:** © AP/Wide World Photos; **281:** © AP/Wide World Photos; **282:** © 1995, Washington Post Writers Group; **283:** Ron Haeberle/Life Magazine: © 1969 Time-Warner, Inc.; **287:** *The New York Times,* Oct. 31, 1938, © 1938 The New York Times Company; **289:** © G. Erikson, *Herald-American,* September 9, 1944; **290:** © Reuters/PJean-Christophe Kahn/Archive Photos; **293:** Robert Mankoff © 1997 The New Yorker Collection. All Rights Reserved.; **296:** © William Vandivert; **300:** © Mic Smith/Sygma; **301L:** © Marie Hansen/Life Magazine © Time-Warner, Inc.; **301R:** © Nancy Richmond/The Image Works; **303:** © Bernard of Hollywood/Sygma; **306:** *The New York Times,* February 26, 1979. ©1979 The New York Times; **314:** © Universal Press Syndicate; **316:** Johnny Florea/Life Magazine: © Time-Warner, Inc.; **317L:** © 1965 by Stanely Milgram. from *Obedience* (film), distributed by the Pennsylvania State University PCR, Courtesy of Alexandra Milgram; **317R:** © 1965 by Stanely Milgram. from *Obedience* (film), distributed by the Pennsylvania State University PCR, Courtesy; **323:** © John Sotomayor/NYT Pictures

CHAPTER 9

Text and Art: p. 330: Figure 9.1 adapted from Zajonc, et al., "Social enhancement and impairment of performance in the cockroach," *Journal of Personality and Social Psy*chology, 13. © 1969 by the American Psychological Association. Adapted by permission. **p. 333:** Figure 9.2 adapted from Michaels, et al., "Social facilitation and inhibition in a nat-ural setting," *Replications in Social Psychology*, 2, pp. 21-24. Reprinted by permission. **p. 334:** Figure 9.3 adapted from Cotrell, et al., "Social facilitation in dominant responses by the presence of an audience and the mere presence of others," *Journal of Personality and Social Psychology*, 9. © 1968 by the American Psychological Association. Adapted by permis-sion. **p. 335:** Figure 9.4 adapted from Jackson, et al., "Social loafing on difficult tasks," *Journal of Personality and Social Psychology*, 49. © 1985 by the American Psychological Association. Adapted by permission. **p. 346:** Figure 9.5 adapted from Jackson, "Deindividuation and valence of cues," *Journal of Personality and Social Psychology*, 49. © 1985 by the American Psychological Association. Adapted by permission. **p. 352:** Figure 9.7 adapted from Stasser, et al., "Pooling of unshared information in group decision making: Biased information and sampling during discussion," *Journal of Personality and Social Psychology*, 48. **p. 354:** Figure 9.8 adapted from Janis, *Victims of groupthink.* © 1982 by Houghton Mifflin and Company. Reprinted by permission. **p. 356:** (Try It!) adapted from Wallach, et al., An example of an item from the choice Dilemmas Questionnaire, *Journal of Abnormal and Social Psychology*, 65. **p. 360:** Figure 9.9 adapted from Rappaport et al., *Prisoner's dilemas: A study in conflict and cooperation.* © 1965. Reprinted by permission. **p. 363:** Figure 9.10 adapted from Deutsch and Krauss, "The effect of threat upon interpersonal bargaining," *Journal of Abnormal and Social Psychology*, 1960, pp. 181-189. **p. 364:** Figure 9.11 adapted from Deutsch & Krauss, "Studies of interpersonal bargaining," *Journal of Conflict Resolution*, 6, pp. 52-76. © 1962. Reprinted by permission of Sage Publications. **Photos and Cartoons:** Page 326: © Diana Ong/SuperStock; 328: © UPI/Corbis-Bettmann; 331: © David Young-Wolff/Photo Edit; 337: ©Bob Daemmrich; 338: © UPI/Bettmann; 341: © Dr. Phillip G. Zimbardo; 342: © 1997, The Washington Post. Reprinted with permission.; 344-1: © P. Price/The Picture Cube; 344-2: © Topham/The Image Works; 344-3: © Alain Nogues/Sygma; 344-4: © Photo Trends/Globe Photos, Inc.; 344-5: © The Bettmann Archive; 344-6: © John Launois/Black Star; 347: © 1995 SALLY FORTH. Greg Howard. Reprinted with special permission of King Features Syndicate.; 349L: © Phillipe Royer/Photo Researchers; 349R: Daemmrich/Stock Boston; 355: © NASA; 359T: © David Brauchli/Sygma; 359B: © 1986 Watterson/Distributed by Universal Press Syndicate. All rights reserved.; 367: © Paul Conklin/Photo Edit

CHAPTER 10

Text and Art: **p. 374:** Figure 10.1 adapted from *Social pressures in informal groups* by Leon Festinger, Stanley Schachter, and Kurt Back with the permission of the publishers, Stanford University Press. © 1950 by Leon Festinger, Stanley Schachter, and Kurt Back. **p. 376:** Figure 10.2 adapted from R.L. Moreland and R. Beach, "Exposure effects in the classroom: The development of affinity among students," *Journal of Experimental and Social Psychology*, 28, pp. 255-276. © 1992. Reprinted by permission. **p. 379:** Figure 10.3 adapted from Curtis, et al., "Amount of liking," *Journal of Personality and Social Psychology*, 51. © 1986 by the American Psychological Association. Adapted by permission. **p. 380:** Figure 10.4 adapted from Hixon & De La Ronde, 1992. **p. 392** (Try It!) adapted from Hatfield & Sprecher, 1986. **p. 393:** Figure 10.5 adapted from Sternberg, *The triangle of love.* © 1988. Reprinted by permission of HarperCollins Publishers, Inc. **p. 399:** Figure 10.6 adapted from Rusbult, "A longitudinal test of the investment model," *Journal of Personality and Social Psychology*, 45. © 1983 by the Amerian Psychological Association. Adapted by permission. **p. 400:** Figure 10.7 adapted from Rusbult, 1983. **p. 407:** Table 10.2 adapted from Hazan and Shaver, 1987. **p. 410:** Figure 10.9 adapted from S.W. Duck (ed.), *Personal relationships 4: Dissolving personal relationships.* © 1982. Reprinted by permission. **p. 412:** Figure 10.11 adapted from Robin M. Akert, "Terminating romantic relationships." © 1992. Reprinted by permission. **Photos and Cartoons:** Page 370: © Diana Ong/SuperStock; 372: © Jacques M. Chenet/Gamma Liaison; 374: © McGlynn/The Image Works; 377: © Renato Rotolo/Gamma Liaison; 378: Edward Koren © 1992 from The New Yorker Collection. All Rights Reserved.; 382TL: © Evan Agostini/Gamma Liaison; 382TR: © Popperfoto/Archive Photos; 382BR: © S. Shapiro/Gamma Liaison; 382BL: © Tina Paul/Archive Newsphotos; 383L Judith H. Langlios/Dept. of Psychology/University of Texas, Austin; 383M: Judith H. Langlios/Dept. of Psychology/University of Texas, Austin; 383R: Judith H. Langlios/Dept. of Psychology/University of Texas, Austin; 390: © Sidney Harris; 396: Edward Koren © 1997 from The New Yorker Collection. All rights reserved.; 397: © Bob Daemmrich/Stock Boston; 401L: © UPI/Bettmann; 401R: ©Wojnarowicz/The Image Works; 406: © Elizabeth Crews/The Image Works; 408: © M. Antman/The Image Works

CHAPTER 11

Text and Art: **p. 418:** From *Time*, January 25, 1982. **p. 425:** Figure 11.1 adapted from Batson, *The altrusim question: Toward a social psychological answer.* 1991 Lawrence Erlbaum Associates. **p. 427:** Figure 11.2

adapted from M. Toi and C. D. Batson, "More evidence that empathy is a source of altruistic motivation," *Journal of Personality and Social Psychology*, 43, pp. 281-292. © 1982. Reprinted by permission. **p. 440:** Figure 11.3 adapted from Darley, et al., "Bystander intervention in emergencies: Diffusion and responsibility," *Journal of Personality and Social Psychology*, 8. © 1968 by the American Psychological Association. Adapted by permission. **p. 442:** Figure 11.4 adapted from Latane & Darley, *The unresponsive bystander: Why doesn't he help?* © 1970. Reprinted by permission of Simon & Schuster. **p. 448:** Figure 11.5 from Clark et al., 1989. **Photos and Cartoons:** Page 416: © Private Collection/Fratelli Alinari/SuperStock; 418: © AP/Wide World Photos; 420: © Rhoda Sidney/The Image Works; 423: © B. Lambert/Sygma; 426: © 1995 Watterson/Distributed by Universal Press Syndicate.; 427: © United Press International, Inc.; 430: © Jim Pickerell/Stock Boston; 431: © Michael Newman/Photo Edit; 433: © Elena Rooraid/PhotoEdit; 438L: © Frank Siteman/Photo Edit; 438R: © Kindra Clineff/The Picture Cube; 439: ©New York Times Pictures; 439inset: ©New York Times Pictures; 444: ©Steve McCurry/Magnum Photos; 446: ©Charles Gupton/Stock Boston; 449: © Jan Halaska/Photo Researchers

CHAPTER 12

Text and Art: **p. 464:** Figure 12.1 adapted from Carlsmith, et al., "Ambient temperature and the occurrence of collective violence," *Journal of Personality and Social Psychology*, 37. © 1979 by the American Psychological Association. Adapted by permission. **p. 470:** Figure 12.2 adapted from Berkowitz, et al., "Weapons as aggression eliciting stimuli," *Journal of Personality and Social Psychology*, 7. © 1967 by the American Psychological Association. Adapted by permission. **p. 474:** Figure 12.3 adapted from Liebert, et al., "Some immediate effects of televised violence on children's behavior," *Developmental Psychology*, 6. © 1972 by the American Psychological Association. Adapted by permission. **p. 476:** From Donald Goddard, *The New York Times*, February 27, 1977. Figure 12.4 from Archer, et al., *Violence and Crime in Cross National Perspective.* © 1984. Reprinted by permission of Yale University Press. **p. 481:** Figure 12.4 adapted from Archer & Gartner, 1984. **p. 486:** Figure 12.5 adapted from Archer and Gartner, "Violent acts and violent times: A comparative approach to postwar incident rates," *American Sociological Review*, 41. © 1976. Reprinted by permission. **p. 491:** Figure 12.6 adapted from Baron, "The reduction of human aggression: A field study on the influence of incompatible responses," *Journal of Applied Social Psychology*, 6. © 1976. Reprinted by permission. **Photos and Cartoons:** Page 454: © Lucia Gallery, New York City/TF Chen/SuperStock; 456: © Les Stone/Sygma; 458: © D. Reilly © 1994 from the New Yorker Collection. All rights reserved.; 461: © Phototest; 463: Dana Fradon © 1985 from the New Yorker Collection. All rights reserved.; 467: © Jonathan Nourok/Photo Edit; 470: Peter Amo © 1940 from the New Yorker Collection. All rights reserved.; 472: © Albert Bandura/Stanford University ; 473: © Eric Liebowitz/ABC; 475: © John Coletti/Stock Boston; 478: © 1973 Universal Press Syndicate; 480: © Catherine Ursillo/Photo Researchers; 483: © Photo Researchers; 485L: U.S. Army Photo; 485R: From " Faces of the Enemy" by Sam Keen/Harper & Row: © 1986; 489: © Charles Moore/Black Star

CHAPTER 13

Text and Art: **p. 506:** Figure 13.1 adapted from Bond, et al., "Response to violence in a psychiatric setting," *Personality and Social Psychology Bulletin*, 14, pp. 448-458. © 1988. Reprinted by permission of Sage publications. **p. 511:** Figure 13.2 adapted from Quattrone, et al., "The perception of variability within ingroups and outgroups: Implications for the law of small numbers," *Journal of Personality and Social Psychology*, 38. © 1980 by the American Psychological Association. Adapted by permission. **p. 512:** Excerpts from G. Allport, *The nature of prejudice.* © 1979 by Addison-Wesley Publishing Co., Inc. Reprinted by permission of Addison-Wesley Publishing Co., Inc. **p. 513:** Table 13.1 adapted from Gilbert, 1951; Karlins, Coffman, & Walters, 1969; Katz & Braly, 1933. **p. 515:** Figure 13.3 adapted from Rogers, et al., "Deindividuation and anger-mediated interracial aggression," *Journal of Personality and Social*

Name Index

SUBJECT INDEX

prejudice in Western Europe and, 536–37
Randell, Michael, 604
Random assignment to condition, 51, 58
Random selection, 43
Rape
    blaming victim of, 141, 526
    pornography and, 46–47, 477
Rational behavior, rationalizing vs., 193–94
Rationalizing behavior, 193–94
    postdecision, 199
    rationalization trap and, 229, 230
Reactance theory, 261–62
Reagan, Ronald, 43
Realism
    mundane, 53
    psychological, 53
Realistic conflict theory, 528–33
Reasoning. *See* Inferences; Social cognition
Reasoning skills, teaching, 99–101
Reasons-generated attitude change, 164–65
Recency effects, 74
Reciprocal liking, 378–80
Reciprocation, aggression and, 468–69
Reciprocity, norm of, 313–14, 421, 422
Reconstructive memory, 68–69, 611
Record album experiment, on cognitive
    dissonance, 225
Recovered memories, 177–79
Recycling, encouraging, 598–600
Reduced accountability, deindividuation and,
    338
Reduced self-awareness, deindividuation and,
    338–39
Reinforcement, 17
Relational dialectics, 408–9
    breakup of romantic relationship and, 411
Relationship-oriented leader, 345–46
Relationships. *See also* Dating relationship;
    Friendship; Love and long-term
    relationships
    close, 390–98
    as interpersonal process, 407–9
    self-evaluation maintenance theory and,
    223–24
Relative deprivation, 468
Relevance, personal, 248–49, 250
Reliability, interjudge, 38
Reno, Janet, 9, 628
Replication, 54–56
Representativeness heuristic, 86–87, 90
Research. *See also* Cross-cultural research
    applied, 59–60
    basic, 59–60
Research methods. *See* Methodology
Resistance to attitude change, 259–62
Responsibility
    diffusion of, 36, 444–45
    Milgram on evil acts and, 323–24
Retrieval (information), 607, 608, 614–15
Rewards, use of, 150–51
    instilling helpfulness by, 420–31
    overjustification effect and, 166–69
    social exchange theory and, 388
Rio de Janeiro, Brazil, "surfing" game of
    teenagers in, 293–94
Riot
    expectations and, 468
    in Los Angeles, 455
        Reginald Denny and, 298
    temperature and, 465
Risky shift, 356–57
Role expectations, 342–43
Roles, social, 340–43
Romantic relationships. *See* Dating relationship;
    Love and long-term relationships
Roosevelt, Franklin Delano, 43, 44, 344

Rural environment, prosocial behavior and,
    437–39
Rusk, Dean, 353
Russell, Bill, 169
Ryan, Leo, 5, 279

Sadness, helping behavior and, 436
Salespeople, lowballing technique of, 197–98
Salience, perceptual, 129–31, 135–37
Sampling, biased, 88–89
    in 1936 *Literary Digest* poll, 43, 44
Sarcasm, communicating, 107
Saving face, 183–84
Scapegoats, 531–33
Schatzki, Michael and Jeanne, 579
Schema(s), 68–80, 89
    automatic processing and, 92–93
    causal theory, 162
    cultural determinants of, 71–72
    defined, 68
    function of, 69–71
    implicit personality and, 116
    inaccuracy from, 143
    judgmental heuristics and, 89
    persistence after discredited, 75–76
    problem with, 72–75
    self-concept as, 153
    self-fulfilling prophecy and, 76–80
    self-schemas, 176–79
    stereotypes and, 512
Schlesinger, Arthur, 353
Scholastic Aptitude Test (SAT), 76–77
School desegregation, 534–38
    jigsaw classroom and, 540–44
Scripts, 477
Sculley, John, 345
Secure attachment style, 405, 406–7
Segregation, in U.S. South, 533, 534–35. *See
    also* Prejudice
    cognitive-dissonance experiment and, 193–94
Seizure experiment, 48–55, 57, 62
Self, 151–56. *See also* Self-concept
    actual, 153, 218, 219
    cultural differences in definition of, 153–55
    function of, 152–53, 156
    gender differences in definition of, 155–56
    ideal, 153, 218, 219
    independent view of, 154, 434
    interdependent view of, 154, 434
    looking-glass, 180
    ought, 153, 218, 219
Self-affirmation, 230
Self-affirmation theory, 224–26
Self-awareness
    anger and, 487–88
    defined, 151
    deindividuation and, 338–39
    venting vs., 487–88
Self-awareness theory, 157–60
Self-beliefs, role of negative, 226–29
Self-blame, control of illness and, 558
Self-completion theory, 220–21
Self-concept, 151–52, 153. *See also* Self-
    knowledge
    changes in, through age, 152
    cross-cultural definitions of, 153–55
    gender differences in, 155–56
    introspection as basis of, 156–65
Self-definition, self-esteem and, 222–23
Self-discrepancy theory, 218–20
Self-efficacy, 558–60
Self-enhancement needs, 227–28
Self-esteem, 21–23, 193. *See also* Self-
    justification
    asking for help and, 448
    behavior change and, 575

denial and, 28
desegregation of schools and, 537
in-group bias and, 509
normative conformity and, 308
prejudice and, 498–500
reciprocal liking and, 379–80
self-affirmation theory and, 224–26
self-completion theory and, 220–21
self-discrepancy theory and, 218–20
self-evaluation maintenance theory and,
    221–24
self-handicapping and, 185
self-serving attributions and, 137–41
threat to, 198
Self-evaluation maintenance theory, 221–24
Self-fulfilling prophecy, 25, 76–80, 144
    attraction and, 378, 380
    automatic processing and, 93
    desegregation of schools and, 541
    faulty reasoning processes and, 99
    gender stereotypes and, 506
    physical attractiveness and, 386
    prejudice and, 527–28
    self-efficacy as kind of, 559
Self-handicapping, 185
Self-help tapes, test of effectiveness of, 270
Self-justification, 21–23, 189–233
    need to justify our actions, 190–217
        aftermath of good and bad deeds, 211–16
        cognitive dissonance and, 191–93
        insufficient justification and, 201–11
        justification of effort, 199–201, 202
        motivational arousal, evidence for,
        216–17
        postdecision dissonance and, 195–99, 225
        rational behavior vs. rationalizing
        behavior, 193–94
    new directions in research on, 217–26
        self-affirmation theory, 224–26
        self-completion theory, 220–21
        self-discrepancy theory, 218–20
        self-evaluation maintenance theory,
        221–24
    self-maintenance vs., 226–30
    self-verification theory and, 228
    suffering and, 21–23
Self-knowledge, 149–87
    through introspection, 156–65
    through observation of behavior, 165–76
    through self-schemas, 176–79
    through social interaction, 179–83
Self-perception theory, 165–66, 241
    emotion and, 171–73
    overjustification effect and, 166–69
Self-persuasion, 208–9
Self-presentation, 183–85
Self-recognition, 152
Self-schemas, 176–79
Self-serving attributions, 137–41
Self-symbolizing activities, 220
Self-verification theory, 227–28
Sensory overload, 588
Sexism and sex discrimination. *See also* Women
    in behavior, 536
    institutionalized sexism, 533–34
Sex-role stereotyping, 41, 274
    leadership and, 346–47
Sexual abuse, recovered memories of, 178–79
Sexual aggression, priming concept of power
    and, 518
Sexual behavior, AIDS and, 572
Sexually transmitted diseases (STDs),
    contraception methods and, 45–46. *See
    also* AIDS epidemic
Similarity, attraction and, 376–78, 384, 387
Simpson, Nicole Brown, 497, 618